DUN & BRADSTREET/ GALE GROUP

Industry Handbook

1521-6640

DUN & BRADSTREET/ GALE GROUP

Industry Handbook

Computers &
Software
and
Broadcasting &
Telecommunications

Jennifer Zielinski, Editor

GALE GROUP

Detroit
San Francisco
London
Boston
Woodbridge, CT

Jennifer Zielinski and Mary Alampi, *Editors*
Erin E. Braun, *Managing Editor*

Wendy Blurton, *Buyer*
Dorothy Maki, *Manufacturing Manager*

Cynthia Baldwin, *Product Design Manager*
Michelle DiMercurio, *Senior Art Director*

ISBN 0-7876-3617-7
ISBN 0-7876-4909-0 (5 volume set)

Printed in the United States of America

CONTENTS

INTRODUCTION

This section presents a general introduction to the contents of *Dun & Bradstreet/Gale Industry Handbook: Computers & Software and Broadcasting & Telecommunications*. In addition to presenting information on the book's contents, sources, organization, indices, and appendix, special explanations are provided for (1) the statistical tables and the projections used for some years of data and (2) the industry norms and ratios used in the Dun & Bradstreet, Inc. data. Information for contacting the editors completes the introduction.

Dun & Bradstreet/Gale Industry Handbook: Computers & Software and Broadcasting & Telecommunications is a timely compilation of information on companies, associations, consultants, trade publications, and trade shows participating in or supporting these two industries. Recent statistics from corporate and government sources highlight financial, employment, and other trends. Descriptive materials are included on major industry issues (Foreword), industry history and trends (Industry Overview) and on recent mergers and acquisitions (Mergers & Acquisitions). Overall, *Computers & Software and Broadcasting & Telecommunications* provides an up-to-date and comprehensive guide to these industries for all—the analyst, investor, planner, marketeer, benchmarker, student, or interested member of the public.

CONTENTS AND SOURCES

Computers & Software and Broadcasting & Telecommunications is divided into two parts, with Part I featuring *Computers & Software* and Part II featuring *Broadcasting & Telecommunications*. Each part has the same structure but different content.

Part I - Computers & Software covers 24 industries and *Part II - Broadcasting & Telecommunications* covers 12 industries as defined in the Standard Industrial Classification (SIC) system. The SIC system is presently undergoing a major revision, with SIC codes in the process of being replaced by North American Industry Classification System (NAICS) codes. This book is still organized by SIC code because most data providers still use the "old" system. However, an SIC to NAICS and a NAICS to SIC conversion table is provided in the appendix. Data provided in *Computers & Software and Broadcasting & Telecommunications*, shown here in chapter order, include the following categories—

Description and Context. The Foreword presents an expert view of each industry at the beginning of each part. In each part, Chapter 1 features an overview of the industry, including its history, important participants, current trends, and future directions.

Statistics. Chapter 2 presents federal government statistics and projections from 1987 to 1998. These data include establishments, employment, compensation, revenues, and ratios. Data in this chapter are drawn from the most recent edition of *Manufacturing USA*.

Company Information. Chapter 3 shows financial norms and ratios for 1996, 1997 and 1998. A full discussion of norms and ratios is presented, below, under the heading **Industry Norms and Ratios**. Chapter 4 presents company capsules for leading participants in each industry in directory format, including company name, parent, address, telephone, sales, employment, company type, SIC classification, description, and name and title of the leading company officer. Chapter 5 shows companies in rank order, first by sales volume and then by employment. The data in Chapters 3-5 in each part were prepared by and are shown by special arrangement with Dun & Bradstreet, Inc. Chapter 6 presents a summary of recent merger and acquisition activity in each industry.

Association Data. Chapter 7 presents a listing of domestic and international associations directly involved in each industry or in support of their activities. Information provided includes name of the organization, electronic access (url and/or e-mail), address, contact person, telephone and fax number, and a full description of the organization's activities, including such categories as founding date, membership, staff. Data shown are adapted from Gale's *Encyclopedia of Associations*.

Consultants. Information on industry consultants is shown in Chapter 8, adapted from Gale's *Consultants and Consulting Organizations Directory*. Categories shown include the name of the organization, e-mail and/or url for electronic access, address, leading officer, telephone and fax numbers, and a full description, including founding date and staff.

Trade Information Sources. Chapter 9 features publications offering trade information for each of the industries covered. The entries are adapted from Gale's *Encyclopedia of Business Information Sources* and include name of the book, periodical, or database, publisher, electronic contact (e-mail, url), complete address, telephone and fax numbers, and a description.

Trade Show Information. Chapter 10 presents information needed by all those planning to visit or to participate in trade shows for the computers, software, broadcasting, or telecommunications sectors. Data are drawn from Gale's *Trade Shows Worldwide*. Entries include the name of the show, sponsoring organization, electronic access (e-mail, url), address, telephone and fax numbers, and a description including such categories as frequency of the event, audience, and principal exhibits.

ORGANIZATION

Computers & Software and Broadcasting & Telecommunications is divided into two parts and organized by chapter. A common Master Index, Geographical Index, and an SIC Index follow Part II. The Appendix presents an SIC to NAICS and a NAICS to SIC lookup guide. Each chapter in each part begins with a brief description of contents and formats (if required). Additional explanatory materials are provided in this Introduction to *Chapter 2, Industry Statistics & Performance Indicators* (see **Statistics and Projections**, below) and *Chapter 3, Financial Norms and Ratios* (see **Industry Norms and Ratios**, below). The formats of these chapters are the same in both parts.

Chapter 1   Industry Overview
Chapter 2   Industry Statistics & Performance Indicators
Chapter 3   Financial Norms and Ratios
Chapter 4   Company Directory
Chapter 5   Rankings and Companies
Chapter 6   Mergers & Acquisitions
Chapter 7   Associations
Chapter 8   Consultants
Chapter 9   Trade Information Sources
Chapter 10   Trade Shows

INDEXES AND APPENDIX

Computers & Software and Broadcasting & Telecommunications features three indexes. Each index provides combined coverage of Parts I and II. The **Master Index** shows company, organization, topical terms, and personal names in alphabetical order, with page references. Also included, in alphabetical order, are industry names followed by SIC codes in parentheses. The **Geographical Company Index** shows companies arranged by state and then in alphabetical order, with page references to each part's Chapter 4. The **Company Index by SIC** presents the Chapter 4 company information arranged numerically by SIC codes.

The Appendix, **SIC/NAICS Conversion Guide**, is a two part look-up facility featuring SIC to NAICS conversions in the first part and NAICS to SIC conversions in the second part. The first part is organized by SIC codes in ascending order; the second part is sorted by NAICS codes in ascending order.

STATISTICS AND PROJECTIONS

The tables presented in each part's Chapter 2 are drawn from federal government sources. Federal surveys are comprehensive and accurate, but they are published at some significant delay from the time of data collection. For this reason, projections were used to show data for more recent or future years in the tables in Chapter 2. In this section, terminology used in government data sources is briefly explained and the methods used in making the projections are outlined.

Terminology. Federal data make use of two terms subject to some misunderstanding. These are *establishments* and *value of shipments*.

- **Establishments** are physical locations where economic activity takes place. The establishment count for an industry is rarely the same as a census of the number of *companies* participating. There are typically more establishments than companies in an industry: many companies have multiple locations.

- **Value of Shipments** includes all products shipped from a plant, including primary and secondary products, transfers of goods to another plant, miscellaneous receipts (including contact work and work not related to the SIC at all), sales of scrap, and sales of purchased and resold products. Value of shipments, therefore, includes more than is normally associated with the concept of industry *sales*. The government makes a distinction between value of shipments and value of *product* shipments. In some SICs, the two values are very close (with value of shipments typically slightly higher). In others, there is a significant spread between the two.

Projections. The projections shown in the tables of Chapter 2 are footnoted to indicate that values are estimates. Projections are based on a curve-fitting algorithm using the least-squares method. In essence, the algorithm calculates a trend line for the data using existing data points (survey data). The trend line is the best "straight" line that can be laid over the existing points. Once the trend line has been established, it can be extended into the future. Estimated values, therefore, are points on the extended trend line indicated by past information.

INDUSTRY NORMS AND RATIOS

For each industry, as denoted by SIC, two tables are presented in each part's Chapter 3. The first, entitled **D&B Industry Norms**, presents financial norms for that industry. The second, entitled **D&B Key Business Ratios**, presents ratios. In what follows, each type of table is explained in some detail.

INDUSTRY NORMS

This table shows data for the years 1996-1998. Each table is entitled *D&B Industry Norms* followed by the SIC code and industry name of the industry featured. Next to each year, in parenthesis, is shown the number of companies in the sample used. The "typical" balance-sheet figures are in the first column and the "common-size" balance-sheet figures (in percent) are in the second.

The Common-Size Financial Statement. The common-size balance-sheet and income statement present each item of the financial statement (e.g., *Cash*) as a percentage of its respective aggregate total (e.g., *Total Assets*). Common-size percentages are computed for all statement items for each company in the industry sample. An average for each item is then calculated and presented as the industry norm. This enables the analyst to examine the current composition of assets, liabilities and sales of a particular industry.

The Typical Financial Statement. The typical balance-sheet figures are the result of translating the common-size percentages into dollar figures. They permit, for example, a quick check of the relative size of assets

and liabilities between one's own company and that company's own line of business.

Typical values are computed as follows: after the common-size percentages have been calculated for the sample, the actual financial statements are sorted by both total assets and total sales, with the median, or mid-point figure in both of these groups serving as the "typical" amount. Next, the typical balance-sheet and income statement dollar figures are computed by multiplying the item totals by the common-size percentages.

For example, if the median *Total Assets* for an SIC category is $669,599 and the common-size figure for *Cash* is 9.2 percent, then multiplying the two produces a cash figure of $61,603 for the typical balance sheet (669,559 x 0.092).

KEY BUSINESS RATIOS

This table shows data for the years 1996-1998. For each year, data are provided for the upper quartile, median, and lower quartile of the sample, providing the analyst with an even more refined set of figures. These ratios cover critical areas of business performance with indicators of solvency, efficiency and profitability.

The data serve as the basis for a profound and well-documented insight into all aspects of performance for anyone interested in the financial workings of business—executives and managers, credit executives, bankers, lenders, investors, academicians and students. An explanation of the ratios follows.

In the ratio tables shown, the figures are broken down into the median, upper, and lower quartiles. The *median* is the midpoint of all companies in the sample. The *upper* quartile shows the midpoint of the upper half, the *lower* quartile the midpoint of the lower half of the total sample.

Upper quartile figures are not always the highest numerical value, nor are lower quartile figures always the lowest numerical value. The quartile listings reflect *judgmental ranking*, thus the upper quartile represents the best condition for any given ratio and is not necessarily the highest numerical value. For example, a low numerical value is *better* for such ratios as Total Liabilities-to-Net Worth or Collection Period, indicating low liabilities and rapid collection of receivables.

Each of the 14 ratios is calculated individually for every company in the sample. These individual figures are then sorted for each ratio according to condition (best to worst). The value that falls in the middle of this series becomes the median (or mid-point) for that ratio in that line of business. The figure halfway between the median and the best condition of the series becomes the upper quartile; and the number halfway between the median and the least favorable condition of the series is the lower quartile.

In a statistical sense, each median is considered the *typical* ratio figure for a concern in a given category.

SOLVENCY RATIOS

Quick Ratio

$$\frac{Cash + Accounts\ Receivable}{Current\ Liabilities}$$

The Quick Ratio is computed by dividing cash plus accounts receivable by total current liabilities. Current liabilities are all the liabilities that fall due within one year. This ratio reveals the protection afforded short-term creditors in cash or near-cash assets. It shows the number of dollars of liquid assets available to cover each dollar of current debt. Any time this ratio is as much as 1 to 1 (1.0) the business is said to be in a liquid condition. The larger the ratio the greater the liquidity.

Current Ratio

$$\frac{Current\ Assets}{Current\ Liabilities}$$

Total current assets are divided by total current liabilities. Current assets include cash, accounts and notes receivable (less reserves for bad debts), advances on inventories, merchandise inventories and marketable securities. This ratio measures the degree to which current assets cover current liabilities. The higher the ratio the more assurance exists that the retirement of current liabilities can be made. The current ratio measures the margin of safety available to cover any possible shrinkage in the value of current assets. Normally a ratio of 2 to 1 (2.0) or better is considered good.

Current Liabilities to Net Worth

$$\frac{Current\ Liabilities}{Net\ Worth}$$

Current Liabilities to Net Worth is derived by dividing current liabilities by net worth. This contrasts the funds that creditors are risking temporarily with the funds permanently invested by the owners. The smaller the net worth and the larger the liabilities, the less security is afforded the creditors. Care should be exercised when selling any firm with current liabilities exceeding two-thirds (66.6 percent) of net worth.

Current Liabilities to Inventory

$$\frac{Current\ Liabilities}{Inventory}$$

Dividing current liabilities by inventory yields another indication of the extent to which the business relies on funds from disposal of unsold inventories to meet its debts. This ratio combines with Net Sales to Inventory to indicate how management controls inventory. It is possible to have decreasing liquidity while maintaining consistent sales-to-inventory ratios. Large increases in sales with corresponding increases in inventory levels can cause an inappropriate rise in current liabilities if growth isn't managed wisely.

Total Liabilities to Net Worth

Total Liabilities

Net Worth

This ratio is obtained by dividing total current plus long-term and deferred liabilities by net worth. The effect of long-term (funded) debt on a business can be determined by comparing this ratio with Current Liabilities to Net Worth. The difference will pinpoint the relative size of long-term debt, which, if sizable, can burden a firm with substantial interest charges. In general, total liabilities should not exceed net worth (100 percent) since in such cases creditors have more at stake than owners.

Fixed Assets to Net Worth

Fixed Assets

Net Worth

Fixed assets are divided by net worth. The proportion of net worth that consists of fixed assets will vary greatly from industry to industry, but generally a smaller proportion is desirable. A high ratio is unfavorable because heavy investment in fixed assets indicates that either the concern has a low net working capital and is overtrading or has utilized large funded debt to supplement working capital. Also, the larger the fixed assets, the bigger the annual depreciation charge that must be deducted from the income statement. Normally, fixed assets above 75 percent of net worth indicate possible over-investment and should be examined with care.

EFFICIENCY RATIOS

Collection Period

Accounts Receivable

Sales x 365

Accounts receivable are divided by sales and then multiplied by 365 days to obtain this figure. The quality of the receivables of a company can be determined by this relationship when compared with selling terms and industry norms. In some industries where credit sales are not the normal way of doing business, the percentage of cash sales should be taken into consideration. Generally, where most sales are for credit, any collection period more than one-third over normal selling terms (40.0 for 30-day terms) is indicative of some slow-turning receivables. When comparing the collection period of one concern with that of another, allowances should be made for possible variations in selling terms.

Sales to Inventory

Sales

Inventory

Obtained by dividing annual net sales by inventory. Inventory control is a prime management objective since poor controls allow inventories to become costly to store, obsolete, or insufficient to meet demands. The sales-to-inventory relationship is a guide to the rapidity at which merchandise is being moved and the effect on the flow of funds into the business. This ratio varies widely between lines of business, and a company's figure is only meaningful when compared with industry norms. Individual figures that are outside either the upper or lower quartiles for a given industry should be examined with care. Although low figures are usually the biggest problem, as they indicate excessively high inventories, extremely high turnovers might reflect insufficient merchandise to meet customer demand and result in lost sales.

Asset to Sales

Total Assets

———————

Net Sales

Assets to sales are calculated by dividing total assets by annual net sales. This ratio ties in sales and the total investment that is used to generate those sales. While figures vary greatly from industry to industry, by comparing a company's ratio with industry norms it can be determined whether a firm is overtrading (handling an excessive volume of sales in relation to investment) or undertrading (not generating sufficient sales to warrant the assets invested). Abnormally low percentages (above the upper quartile) can indicate overtrading which may lead to financial difficulties if not corrected. Extremely high percentages (below the lower quartile) can be the result of overly conservative or poor sales management, indicating a more aggressive sales policy may need to be followed.

Sales to Net Working Capital

Sales

———

Net Working Capital

Net sales are divided by net working capital (net working capital is current assets minus current liabilities). This relationship indicates whether a company is overtrading or conversely carrying more liquid assets than needed for its volume. Each industry can vary substantially and it is necessary to compare a company with its peers to see if it is either overtrading on its available funds or being overly conservative. Companies with substantial sales gains often reach a level where their working capital becomes strained. Even if they maintain an adequate total investment for the volume being generated (Assets to Sales), that investment may be so centered in fixed assets or other noncurrent items that it will be difficult to continue meeting all current obligations without additional investment or reducing sales.

Accounts Payable to Sales

Accounts Payable

———————

Annual Net Sales

Computed by dividing accounts payable by annual net sales. This ratio measures how the company is paying its suppliers in relation to the volume being transacted. An increasing percentage, or one larger than the industry norm, indicates the firm may be using suppliers to help finance operations. This ratio is especially important to short-term creditors since a high percentage could indicate potential problems in paying vendors.

PROFITABILITY RATIOS

Return on Sales (Profit Margin)

Net Profit After Taxes

———————

Annual Net Sales

Obtained by dividing net profit after taxes by annual net sales. This reveals the profits earned per dollar of sales and therefore measures the efficiency of the operation. Return must be adequate for the firm to be able to achieve satisfactory profits for its owners. This ratio is an indicator of the firm's ability to withstand adverse conditions such as falling prices, rising costs and declining sales.

Return on Assets

Net Profit After Taxes

———————

Total Assets

Net profit after taxes divided by total assets. This ratio is the key indicator of profitability for a firm. It matches operating profits with the assets available to earn a return. Companies efficiently using their assets will have a relatively high return while less well-run businesses will be relatively low.

Return on Net Worth (Return on Equity)

Net Profit After Taxes
_____

Net Worth

Obtained by dividing net profit after tax by net worth. This ratio is used to analyze the ability of the firm's management to realize an adequate return on the capital invested by the owners of the firm. Tendency is to look increasingly to this ratio as a final criterion of profitability. Generally, a relationship of at least 10 percent is regarded as a desirable objective for providing dividends plus funds for future growth.

USING INDUSTRY NORMS FOR FINANCIAL ANALYSIS

The principal purpose of financial analysis is to identify irregularities that require explanations to completely understand an industry's or company's current status and future potential. Comparing the industry norms with the figures of specific companies (comparative analysis) can identify these irregularities. D&B's Industry Norms are specifically formatted to accommodate this analysis.

Relative Position

Common-size and typical balance sheets provide an excellent picture of the makeup of the industry's assets and liabilities. Are assets concentrated in inventories or accounts receivable? Are payables to the trade or bank loans more important as a method for financing operations? The answers to these and other important questions are clearly shown by the Industry Norms, its common-size balance sheet approach and is then further crystallized by the typical balance sheets.

Financial Ratio Trends

Key Business Ratio changes indicate trends in the important relationships between key financial items, such as the relationship between Net Profits and Net Sales (a common indicator of profitability). Ratios that reflect short and long-term liquidity, efficiency in managing assets and controlling debt, and different measures of profitability are all included in the Key Business Ratios sections of the Industry Norms.

Comparative Analysis

Comparing a company with its peers is a reliable method for evaluating financial status. The key to this technique is the composition of the peer group and the timeliness of the data. The D&B Industry Norms are unique in scope for sample size and in level of detail.

Sample Size

The number of firms in the sample must be representative or they will be unduly influenced by irregular figures from relatively few companies. The more than one million companies used as a basis for the Industry Norms allow for more than adequate sample sizes in most cases.

Key Business Ratios Analysis

Valuable insights into an industry's performance can be obtained by equating two related statement items in the form of a financial ratio. For really effective ratio analysis, the items compared must be meaningful and the comparison should reflect the combined effort of two potentially diverse trends. While dozens of different ratios can be computed from financial statements, the fourteen included in the Industry Norms and Key Business Ratio books are those most commonly used and were rated as the most significant as shown in a survey of financial analysts. Many of the other ratios in existence are variations on these fourteen.

The 14 Key Business Ratios are categorized into three major groups:

Solvency, or liquidity, measurements are significant in evaluating a company's ability to meet short and long-term obligations. These figures are of prime interest to credit managers of commercial companies and financial institutions.

Efficiency ratios indicate how effectively a company uses and controls its assets. This is critical information for evaluating how a company is managed. Studying these ratios is useful for credit, marketing and investment purposes.

Profitability ratios show how successfully a business is earning a return to its owners. Those interested in mergers and acquisitions consider this key data for selecting candidates.

Recent research efforts have revealed that the use of financial analysis (via Industry Norms) is very useful in several functional areas. To follow are only a few of the more widely used applications of this unique data.

Credit

Industry Norm data has proven to be an invaluable tool in determining minimum acceptable standards for risk. The credit worthiness of an existing or potential account is immediately visible by ranking its solvency status and comparing its solvency trends to that of the industry. Short term solvency gauges, such as the quick and current ratios, are ideal indicators when evaluating an account. Balance sheet comparisons supplement this qualification by allowing a comparison of the make-up of current assets and liability items. Moreover, leverage ratios such as current liability to net worth and total liability to net worth provide valuable benchmarks to spot potential problem accounts while profitability and collection period figures provide cash flow comparisons for an overall evaluation of accounts.

In addition to evaluating individual accounts against industry standards, internal credit policies also benefit from Industry Norm data. Are receivables growing at an excessive rate as compared to the industry? If so, how does your firm's collections stack up to the industry?

Finance

Here exists a unique opportunity for financial executives to rank their firm, or their firm's subsidiaries and divisions, against its peers. Determine the efficiency of management via ratio quartile breakdowns which provides you the opportunity to pinpoint your firm's profitability position versus the industry. For example, are returns on sales and gross profit margins comparatively low thereby indicating that pricing per unit may be too low or that the cost of goods is unnecessarily high?

In much the same way, matching the firm's growth and efficiency trends to that of the industry reveals conditions which prove to be vital in projecting budgets. If asset expansion exceeds the industry standard while asset utilization (as indicated by the asset to sales ratio) is sub par, should growth be slowed?

Investment executives have also utilized this diverse information when identifying optimal investment opportunities. By uncovering which industries exhibit the strongest sales growth while maintaining adequate returns, risk is minimized.

Corporate Planning

Corporate plans, competitive strategies and merger & acquisition decisions dictate a comprehensive analysis of the industry in question. Industry Norm data provides invaluable information in scrutinizing the performance of today's highly competitive, and sometimes unstable, markets. Does the liquidity of an industry provide a sufficient cushion to endure the recent record-high interest levels or is it too volatile to risk an entry? Are the profitability and equity conditions of an acquisition candidate among the best in the industry thereby qualifying it as an ideal acquisition target?

Industry Norm data provide these all-important benchmarks for setting strategic goals and measuring overall corporate performance.

Marketing and Sales

Attaining an in-depth knowledge of a potential or existing customer base is a key factor when developing successful marketing strategies and sales projections. Industry Norm data provide a competitive edge when determining market potential and market candidates. Identify those industries that meet or exceed your qualifications and take it one step further by focusing in on the specific region or size category that exhibits the greatest potential. For example, isolate the industries which have experienced the strongest growth trends in sales and inventory turnover and then fine tune marketing and sales strategies by identifying the particular segment which is the most attractive (such as firms with assets of $1 million or more).

This information can also be used in a different context by examining the industries of existing accounts. If an account's industry shows signs of faltering profitability and stagnating sales, should precautionary measures be taken? Will the next sale be profitable for your company or will it be written-off? Industry Norm data assist in answering these and many other important questions.

COMMENTS AND SUGGESTIONS

Comments on or suggestions for improvement of the usefulness, format, and coverage of *Dun & Bradstreet/ Gale Industry Handbook* are always welcome. Although every effort is made to maintain accuracy, errors may occasionally occur; the editors will be grateful if these are called to their attention. Please contact—

Editors
Dun & Bradstreet/Gale Industry Handbook
27500 Drake Rd.
Farmington Hills, MI 48331-3535
248-699-GALE

PART I
COMPUTERS & SOFTWARE

THE COMPUTING INDUSTRY:
CURRENT PRACTICES AND FUTURE DIRECTIONS

Bruce R. Maxim
Computer and Information Science
University of Michigan-Dearborn

Writing an overview for a multi-faceted enterprise like the modern computing industry is a risky affair. Computing knowledge and technologies become obsolete in as little as eighteen months. This makes it is easy to overlook an important emerging technology. Likewise it is easy to champion a computing technology that has a very short useful commercial life span. Companies form and dissolve strategic alliances almost as quickly. The computing industry is not immune from the effects of corporate politics or government decisions. With this in mind, there are several developments in the computing industry that may have significant impact on its future directions.

GLOBAL COMPETITION

New economic opportunities are being made possible by advances in computing technology and reductions in its cost. Competition in the marketplace has become a global affair in many industries and the computing industry is no exception. The United States computing industry cannot assume that the global dominance it has enjoyed in the past will ensure its continued dominance in the future. Chip manufacturing costs are significantly less outside the United States, as are software development costs.

There seems to be a widespread shortage of skilled programmers and software engineers. In many parts of the country, graduates of good university computing programs receive multiple job offers several months before graduation. This is happening, despite the fact that many newly graduated computing professionals will not become fully productive until they have been on the job for 12 months or longer. Many graduate programs in computing and information technologies are losing students to industry several months before they complete their degrees. Students from foreign countries are filling these vacant seats in many United States computing and technology degree programs.

YEAR 2000 PROBLEM

The year 2000 problem has had a significant impact on the computing industry as businesses and government agencies struggle to make their computing applications Y2K compliant. The very existence of the Y2K problem underscores the short sightedness of software designers who never dreamed that their software would be used for 20 years or more. Finding programmers

who are willing to spend two or more years working on legacy systems has not been easy. Newly graduated programmers are unfamiliar with the older programming tools and development environments. Experienced professionals fear being left behind by advancing technology while working on these old systems. Companies are being forced to pay premium wages to employees willing join their Y2K task forces.

According to a 1997 survey conducted by the Deloitte & Touche Consulting Group, the cost of correcting Y2K problems is staggering. Like all maintenance programming tasks, writing code to correct a Y2K bug is only part of the task. Any time a programmer makes a change to a program module in an existing system, regression testing must take place to ensure that correcting a problem in one program module has not created new problems in the other sections of the program that interact with the altered module. Translating existing data files to allow for changes from two-digit date fields to four-digit fields requires programmers to write many error free programs that may only be used one time each. As data files containing many records are rewritten to include larger date fields the new file sizes may exceed the capacities of the data storage devices used by the original files. Maintaining backup copies of these edited files further adds to the cost of this process. According to Ed Yourdon, a renowned expert in the software engineering field, most Internet routers and switches are not currently Y2K compliant and will need to be replaced or reprogrammed. Even systems written using new languages, like Java, are not guaranteed to be free of Y2K logic problems.

INFORMATION TECHNOLOGY COST

Cost containment is part of every commercial enterprise these days. Computing hardware costs have been declining every quarter for the past several years. The product lifetimes of both hardware and software have become shorter, often 18 months or less. Consequently, the cost of keeping up with current computing technology is taking a significant portion of many corporate budgets. There is an old saying that "computing shows up everywhere but in the company productivity figures." This seems to be especially true today.

Many employers seem to have the perception that every office worker needs a computer, and is capable of using it correctly to satisfy all his or her information processing needs. Widespread computerization of business processes often has significant hidden training costs as employees adjust to using new computer-based systems. In-house development of computing applications that match a company's needs exactly is both time-consuming and expensive. Customizing off the shelf software to match local company requirements can also be quite costly. New business software is appearing at such a rapid pace that it is hard to find specialists capable of customizing these new applications packages.

OUTSOURCING INFORMATION TECHNOLOGY

There seems to be an attitude among some corporate managers that software development and deployment is an intensive, but short-term endeavor. There are several large companies that have already made plans to out-source all their information technology work and hire software engineers as new projects arise. Several years ago, *Fortune* magazine published an article that predicted the end of the job by the year 2000. The article suggested that professionals in many fields might expect to become journeyman entrepreneurs. Whether this comes to pass or not, the explosive growth of large consulting companies (Andersen Consulting, Compuware, Electronic Data Systems) and the expansion of the contract services divisions in other large companies (International Business Machines, Unisys) suggests that the practice of hiring contract programmers is likely to continue. One danger inherent in this practice is that the program author is not always available when software maintenance tasks need to be performed. Another problem is expecting that analysts from outside the company will understand the local problems and constraints as well as a long-term employee.

Enterprise Resource Planning (ERP) software is the modern term for computing applications that manage all the activities of a company's production cycle. These computing applications support distribution (order entry, inventory, shipping), manufacturing (scheduling, planning, purchasing), human resources (payroll, benefits, skills, recruiting), accounting, and other necessary business functions. Several products (SAP R/3, Oracle Apps, Peoplesoft, Bann, etc.) have come into the marketplace which allow companies to purchase all these functions in a single package, rather

than have in-houses analysts define the necessary system requirements from scratch. These ERP products typically include embedded knowledge of business rules, best business practices, and integrated workflows. There is a large demand for skilled technicians who can implement and customize these systems. In some cases, companies may attempt to contain costs by modifying their business practices to match ERP software. Forcing users to adapt to the computer's way of doing things is rarely a wise business decision. The principles of good software engineering suggest that software is only cost effective when it supports the user's primary tasks without requiring extensive retraining.

INTELLECTUAL PROPERTY RIGHTS

The high costs of software development have sensitized the computing industry to several intellectual property issues. Using today's computing technology it is very easy to duplicate and distribute multi-media products. Software piracy is rampant in some sectors of society. Some industry analysts estimate that for many pieces of software there is one illegal copy in circulation for each legal copy purchased. In some cases vendors (Microsoft, Borland) have dropped their prices and liberalized their single end user agreements, hoping to make up for lost income though volume sales. There are signs though, that the licensing agreements for networked copies of some popular commercial software may return to being based on the total number of workstations capable of network access, rather than the maximum number of concurrent users who will actually be using the product simultaneously.

Software products developed for one vendor's hardware platform or operating system are being reverse-engineered for another platform without compensation to the original authors. There have been several lawsuits, as software designers have tried to standardize the "look and feel" of the user interfaces of similar or related software products. Opinion on "look and feel" lawsuits seems to be divided between software designers and senior level managers. As a group, user interface designers argue that using a common screen display for all computing applications makes them easier for the typical user to learn and easier to use effectively. Managers are likely to argue that having a product family with a unique user interface makes it more likely that customers will buy future products from their company exclusively, and they tend to guard their screen displays carefully. The courts have sent mixed messages about which user interface components are protected and which are not.

INTERNET POPULARITY

Evidence of increased use of the Internet by the general public is everywhere. Low cost Internet providers are appearing in every major market and price wars over monthly access charges abound. The decision to bundle a free web-browsing tool with Microsoft Windows '98 has been extremely controversial. Microsoft and Netscape are battling for browser market share, after eliminating most of their competitors by giving their browsers to home users free of charge. Industry analysts are predicting that the next product war will be among e-mail software vendors.

Even modest-sized businesses include the URLs of their web sites in their advertising materials. The availability of visual web authoring tools has allowed virtually every web user to become a web content provider. The lack of editorial control over web content has made searching for information on the World Wide Web a time consuming process. The information resulting from a web search is often highly redundant and is sometimes of questionable quality.

Web technology makes it very easy to provide remote access to distributed databases. The ease of with which databases can be accessed has also heightened people's concerns about unauthorized access to personal and corporate information. Privacy concerns regarding the safety of using the Internet to conduct business have surfaced. The ability of web applications to collect and report information stored on a user's hard disk is at times disturbing. Network packet sniffers allow their users to read unencrypted information with ease as it passes through the Internet. Demand for network and database security consultants is growing rapidly in the computing industry. Internet security is becoming a specialization in its own right.

SOCIAL ACCOUNTABILITY

As computing technologies become more pervasive in society, the public is demanding greater accountability from computing professionals. Systems designers are expected to ensure that their systems are reliable and

safe. The major accrediting agencies for university computing programs (the Accreditation Board for Engineering & Technology, and the Computer Science Accreditation Board) mandate coursework on computing ethics and the social impact of technology. This work on ethics and social impact is supposed to be integrated as thread running throughout the students' curricula, not just appear as a single course during their senior year. Social impact statements are being included as part the design documents for new computing systems. Social impact statements describe the stakeholders, benefits, concerns, potential barriers, risks, and costs associated with undertaking new projects. Whether social impact concerns become as pervasive in business as environmental impact concerns are today is not yet known.

Computer systems are viewed as tools of user empowerment. As the prerequisite knowledge required to make use of computing applications becomes less, the pressure to provide access to computing by all persons in society has become greater. As more personal services go on-line (e.g. banking and personal record management) the question of who pays for computing access on behalf of those who cannot afford to pay for it themselves, becomes a real concern. If all personal business transactions become paperless, not having computing access is as serious as not having access to a telephone. Hardware and software manufacturers have given minimal amounts of attention to designing systems that support the needs of persons with physical disabilities.

There are some people (like those from EDUCOM) who are concerned that, if we are not careful, we may be in danger of creating a new disadvantaged class in our society—the "information poor." If there are persons who do not have access to meaningful computing resources. Many parents feel that computing skills are essential to gaining good jobs. Most people would argue that reasonable home or public (e.g. library) access to computing is necessary to obtain good computing skills. Simply using a computer is not enough. For example, some studies have shown that disadvantaged urban school districts spend the same kind of money on computing hardware and software as suburban districts. However, in the city, students are more likely to use the computer to run drill and practice software, whereas suburban students are more likely to use computers as problem solving tools in several classes. This is most likely an administrative choice that may reflect the need for more computer literate teachers in the urban schools, rather than an indication that there are differences between the needs of urban and suburban students.

VIRTUAL ORGANIZATIONS

Using web technology to create virtual organizations is emerging as a popular notion. Many catalog sales operations have already entered the world of e-commerce. Several other types of businesses (e.g., used car sales, service providers, banking) are testing the waters. Many organizations have shifted their customer support activities to on-line services (e.g., e-mail, web sites, bulletin boards). It is cheaper to publish on-line users' manuals as web pages than to print them and give them away. Distributing bug fixes using FTP is less expensive than using surface mail services. Software vendors make use of on-line product registration procedures to build e-mail lists of potential buyers for product upgrades.

The Internet has also allowed companies to create extended supply chains. It is entirely possible for two companies like Chrysler and Daimler to merge and leverage their combined buying power to reduce costs. In this day and age, it may be cheaper to find a product somewhere on the Internet and ship it to Germany than it is to buy the product locally in Germany.

Many students are finding that the travel demands of their jobs are making it hard to attend class. Universities and other educational organizations are beginning to explore distance learning alternatives. One model for distance learning involves using the Internet to provide access to instructional materials by students from home or on the job. Desktop video conferencing technology can be used to allow students to participate in classroom activities from remote sites. This may cause some profound changes in how education is perceived by students. Students may have to settle for mass-produced training rather than personalized education. Professors may have to settle for reduced personal contact with their students. Students may have greater difficulties interacting with classmates on group projects. Educational organizations have to decide whether any level of participation by students from remote sites is better than no participation at all (from a fee standpoint).

Virtual museums and digital libraries are beginning to provide after hours access to portions of their holdings. Electronic publishing offers the promise of faster dissemination of research results. There are concerns from the academic world that the review process for electronic publications will not be as thorough as that used now for print materials. There are some concerns that web content providers may be violating intellectual property rights when they post web-based training materials. There are additional concerns about the reliable collection of fees from users of web these materials.

While opportunities to create web-based virtual organizations are many, there are some pitfalls that cannot be ignored. Collecting fees over the Internet requires careful protection of customer credit card information. There are signs that the Internet is already nearing its maximum capacity. Many Internet service providers experience regular failure of their e-mail systems and web server crashes. Protecting customers from receiving spam type e-mail and virus infections of their local hard drives are two other problems that come with doing business on the web.

INFORMATION QUALITY

Obtaining information from the World Wide Web is not risk free. Since virtually anyone can be a content provider, information on the web varies greatly in terms of its accuracy and quality. Many copies of the same information appear on many different web pages, making version control hard to guarantee. The question of who is to blame when information obtained from the web causes a user to experience some loss has yet to be answered. This may be a special concern for organizations like health care information services that are hosted on the web. Will it be the domain expert, the web content provider, the Internet service provider, or server manufacturer who is held accountable? Based on similar concerns regarding the use of advice obtained from expert systems, it is not clear who is responsible for misuse of web information.

Managing information on the Internet is not easy, since few web-based management tools have been developed. The high volatility of web information makes it hard to ensure that all web page links point to active information sources. It is hard to determine whether or not web page content has changed, without physically accessing the page itself. It is also hard to determine where the original source for a piece of information lies.

KNOWLEDGE MANAGEMENT

There has been shift in thinking from corporate data management to enterprise wide knowledge management. Many people seem to regard control of information as a source of personal power. Managers are beginning to discover that one of the key issues in knowledge management is getting people to share their information with one another. Another problem is getting people to reuse information maintained by other people, rather than maintaining their own copy of the same information. Information officers must also weigh concerns regarding information security against ease of access to the information by users. Data concerning customer-buying habits, corporate productivity, and decision support tools are being guarded as proprietary information.

Widely distributed, heterogeneous databases are being linked together to form data warehouses. Web browsers are being used to provide cost effective access to data warehouses. Knowledge discovery technologies are being defined as artificial intelligence techniques are used to uncover new relations among the elements stored in data warehouses. Work on more robust search engines is being undertaken to allow complex searches of both text and graphical information to be specified. Feature extraction techniques seem to be promising solutions to the problems encountered while searching image or sound libraries. Designers are struggling with the task of trying to avoid overwhelming the user with information. Visual techniques are being explored as means of guiding data warehouse searches and displaying the search results more effectively.

REUSABLE SOFTWARE

Twenty years ago about 80% of the budget for developing a new computing system was taken up by the cost of the hardware required. Today, 80% of the budget for a new computing system is likely to be cost of developing the software. Cost containment efforts have influenced a majority of software development activity in recent years. Another important influence on software development in recent years has been public concern for software reliability. The existence of several well-publicized software bugs, and the increasing reliance on software control of mission critical processes in the commercial world have made product managers question the wisdom of developing each component of a new software application in-house. The "not invented here" syndrome has been hard to remove from the programmer's mindset.

In engineering disciplines other than software engineering, there is a strong tradition of building new systems and artifacts out of existing components whose function and reliability are well known. One way to improve the reliability of a new system is to build the system using existing components that have already been tested and proven to be reliable. In theory this should also reduce the cost of building software systems too. There are at least two problems with taking this approach to software construction. In software engineering, there is no agreed upon set of standard software components and there are few standards for software component interface specifications. Designers in other engineering disciplines have widely agreed upon design processes to use in building a system or artifact. Software engineering is a young discipline and widely accepted design practices are still emerging. Designing reusable software components has been a major concern of software developers during the past 10 years.

It is estimated that there are over 1,000,000 C++ programmers in the world today and that a majority of all hardware, software, and operating-system developers use C++. Java's growing popularity as an Internet development tool may be related to the similarities between Java source code and C++ source code. Both Java and C++ support the creation of user-defined objects and allow programs to make use to external component libraries. The popularity of C++ and Java as commercial development languages may be an indication that programmers are seeking better ways to make use of existing code libraries in the implementation of their own software designs. As programmers become more proficient in using objects in their computing applications they become more aware that using object-oriented programming by itself is not the complete answer to building reusable code. Fundamental changes need to be made in the methods used by developers to formulate their software designs.

Many software developers (i.e., Oracle, Hughes Information Technology, Coopers and Lybrand Consulting, American Airlines, Chrysler-Daimler, Federal Express) have begun using object-oriented design methods in their new software projects. In object-oriented design, the behavior of the entire computing application is defined in terms of interacting components or objects. Describing a component as producing information for other components to use and indicating which components produce the information a component needs to consume is the heart of object-oriented design. Object-oriented design methods provide a means of creating code that is more readily reusable in future applications. Object-oriented applications frameworks have begun to appear in several program development environments. Most of these applications frameworks (Visual Basic, Visual C++, Java Beans, X-windows, etc.) contain user interface development tools and not much else. However, one advantage of using these frameworks is that they may encourage designers to develop the habit of incorporating standard software components in their own designs.

Platform independent development environments (e.g., Java) have provided some motivation for both code reuse and the development of design standards. Their use has also rekindled the debate over which is better: using interpreters to allow flexibility of writing machine independent code or using native code compilers to increase program run-time performance. Java applets run very slowly when compared to comparable C++ code. However it is hard to distribute compiled object libraries for languages like C++ to programmers without their source code. To distribute compiled object libraries, the developer needs to have access to compilers for every possible user's target machine and maintain object code versions for each machine (a version control nightmare).

There are still large numbers of computing applications that are not implemented using object-oriented programming languages. Software reuse efforts in these applications have focused on component-based design techniques. Typically software component libraries are designed for use within the company that built them. In-house developers are expected to make use of these components in any future designs calling for the functions implemented by these components. This provides limited standardization within a family

of software products and may benefit licensed OEM applications developers.

Another popular design strategy is to purchase an existing application package and then customize the application to meet the needs of its intended users. This strategy has the advantage of reduced cost over developing an application from scratch, assuming the vendor is willing to provide development support to the programmers. Many designers have expressed concerns over the risks incurred by using another vendor's software without verifying the correctness and reliability of this software in the new application environment.

SOFTWARE ENGINEERING PROCESSES

The long development time inherent in the traditional waterfall model of software development makes it likely that the client's needs may change between the date the system requirements are defined and the date the first executable code is delivered. To reduce this risk many software designers have switched to using iterative software development techniques like rapid prototyping. In the rapid prototyping model, the client is given many opportunities to review the evolving application as the software design team adds new functionality to the product. Processes found in object-oriented analysis and object-oriented design are very similar to those of found in the rapid prototyping model.

The availability of the Internet has made distributed software development possible. A number of computer-based information systems have been implemented on the World Wide Web. The use of web programming tools makes local development and integration of distributed software components highly feasible. Collaborative applications sharing tools (e.g. Lotus Notes, MS NetMeeting) allow several developers to work on the same standalone application concurrently. Interest in life cycle CASE tools and GroupWare is extremely keen in many software development organizations. Adding knowledge to web applications may allow businesses to operate 24 hours a day, 7 days a week by removing some of the productivity barriers imposed by the 40-hour workweek used by humans.

The capability maturity model developed by the Software Engineering Institute has attracted much attention in recent years. Software engineers are beginning to focus on developing reusable software design patterns as a means of reducing the costs of developing new products. This is possible only when organizations become experienced in developing a class of similar computing applications. At least one company (Motorola) has set a corporate goal of having all corporate processes at the capability maturity model level 4 (managed processes) by the year 2000. Companies operating at the managed process level use detailed quantitative measures to understand and control both their software products and processes. This is a very ambitious goal since is has been hypothesized that most other companies are even not operating at the capability maturity model level 2 (repeatable processes) right now. Companies operating at the repeatable process level are able to use historical data to complete projects similar to those undertaken in the past, in an efficient manner. Designers must be committed to the concept of using standard design methodologies before the use of design patterns makes any sense. The notion of creating standard design methodologies has not come easily in the software industry.

KNOWLEDGE-BASED SOFTWARE

One side effect of the migration to distributed desktop computing is that many users are now in control of their own mission critical software applications. Knowledge-based computing applications are being introduced into several commercial environments as software designers try to make complex computing tasks more accessible to non-programmers. Many software applications suites come with wizards designed to lead users through the process of installing or creating routine applications. Application integration middleware allows users to pass information among several software packages without any programming knowledge. Toolkits allowing the integration of expert systems and neural networks with conventional programming applications are beginning to appear in the marketplace. Some industry critics warn of the dangers of de-skilling the workforce, by providing an over-abundance of knowledge-based systems to users.

On-line document storage systems are gaining popularity as cost effective alternatives to paper document storage. Optical character recognition is becoming an affordable technology for converting paper documents to machine-readable formats that allow both browsing and indexing of documents to take place automatically. Voice synthesis and voice recognition technologies are becoming more affordable and are appearing in many applications packages. Seamless integration of these and other multimedia technologies into enterprise-wide business applications will be a major challenge to future software designers.

User interfaces are beginning to receive more attention from software designers. The perceived quality of a user interface often determines the commercial success or failure of a software product in the consumer market. The early popularity of the Macintosh family of computers made some software designers rethink their priorities in developing new products. There are signs that vendors are beginning to focus on usability in many new software applications. Part of the reason for this, is the perception that many smaller business users are expected to service their own software applications after they are deployed. Embedded trouble shooting wizards are being included in numerous software packages to assist the user with the diagnosis of systems problems and suggest error corrections.

COMPUTING HARDWARE

The useful lifetime of many varieties of computing hardware has declined to 18 months or less. Computing hardware has been decreasing in cost and increasing in computing power. Processor speeds seem to be increasing every quarter. The costs of memory and secondary storage are decreasing every quarter. Computer displays are increasing in both their size and resolution, while decreasing in their cost. Indeed most home computer systems are capable of performance that exceeds that of the computers used by NASA to land a man on the moon. The major weakness of many PC architectures is slow data bus speeds relative to their processor clock speeds. As computer systems get smaller and faster this weakness is becomes a larger concern.

In many businesses, distributed networks of PCs and workstations have replaced central mainframes as the production environment for all computing applications. Highly redundant arrays of networked disk drives are replacing the need for large disk drives. Client-server computing has become the dominant paradigm for accessing corporate information resources. Businesses are inclined to buy hardware capable of running a specific application package and then try to make the information produced by the application available to other applications using some type of server technology. Computing clients have become globally distributed as many companies try to make use of the Internet to connect proprietary intranets and isolated workstations. This has created the need to integrate disparate hardware together in a seamless way. Sales of computing hardware based on open systems standards have been great. Vendors selling hardware based on proprietary standards have often disappeared from the marketplace.

Highly parallel computing has not become the dominant computing architecture predicted 10 years ago. While many PCs and Unix workstations are sold with three or four processors, very few computers are sold with hundreds or thousands of processors. Support for instruction level parallel processing (e.g. Pentium MMX technology) is beginning to appear in desktop computing architectures. Compilers have been slow to take advantage of true parallel processing capabilities. Implementing parallel algorithms is a very time consuming task for programmers to undertake. Most parallel algorithms do not scale well and have to be mapped by hand to the specific parallel machine used for production runs. Programmers seem to have better understanding of distributed computing architectures than parallel architectures.

FUTURE HARDWARE TRENDS

The most likely change in the future of computing hardware is a move to 64-bit architectures. Hardware/software co-design is emerging as the common paradigm for developing new semi-conductor products. Processor functions are migrating from hardware to software, to allow easier customization for new applications. Software simulation of virtual chip designs is becoming popular. Some recent bugs in new chip designs have turned out to be software problems (not manufacturing defects). These bugs are expensive to fix after a chip is fabricated, if the only remedy possible involves modifying the chip design and then fabricating a new chip prototype. Indeed a recent bug in the Pentium II chip was fixed by simply inserting new code into the computer's bootstrap program.

Moore's law suggests that chip densities will double at a fairly rapid rate (unless we encounter some limitation imposed by science or economics). This means that we may not be too far away from the time when complete computing systems will be implemented as a single chip. Indeed the capabilities of many information appliances (e.g. fax machines, palmtop computers) are beginning to approach those of PCs produced a few years ago. Many household appliances will have embedded processors added to them. Smart wall plugs may enable the wiring in our houses to handle voice, data, and power simultaneously. This technology will allow for practical computer control of home and office environments. Some people are predicting the development of web servers on a chip. This may pave way for Internet enabled cars in the next 5 years.

Providing computing support to disconnected, nomadic users is a challenge for the computing industry. It is estimated that 40% of all computer sales today are notebooks. Many employees spend as much as half their workweek on the road or telecommuting from home. Improving flat panel display technology is an important part of this support. Developing good wireless network technologies is another part. Wireless network technologies are being explored as one way of reducing the weight of the wiring harness in vehicles like cars and planes.

Optical computing networks may become common place in the near future. The communication speeds of optical networks and their ability to be dynamically reconfigured by software make them very attractive to support high speed computing networks and as replacements for conventional data buses. Technology for storing holographic images is also emerging. A nationwide parallel-computing network may come into being as a means of tapping unused clock cycles in widely distributed computers.

POWER POLITICS

Power politics in the computing industry may be as important to its future direction as new technology developments are. What has happened to industry leaders like WordPerfect, Novell, and Borland? How did they go from dominance in the market to near oblivion? How did Netscape and Yahoo come from no where to attract so much money? Why did Microsoft decide to invest heavily in rival Apple? Why did Oracle's CEO consider purchasing Apple after dropping all Oracle database development support for the Macintosh? How did the United States allow Europe to grab the cell phone standards to the detriment of our own Motorola?

The computer industry is beginning to show signs of some highly predatory pricing practices. Some vendors are allowing students to purchase complete software products for very low prices in attempts to create a large base of future users when they graduate and become computing professionals. Some vendors are giving their products away to home users in hopes that this will inspire enough sales of their products in the commercial sector to corner their market niche.

Changing technology seems to create new opportunities for control and profit in the industry. Many industry decisions seem to be made more for political reasons than for technological reasons. Microsoft may have supported Java in an attempt to make Windows NT an attractive alternative to Unix as the standard commercial operating system. Apple's resistance to jumping on the open systems bandwagon may have been an attempt to maintain its market share longer than it so deserved. Many industry insiders feel that it is not possible to understand the computing industry without considering impact of computing industry politics.

COMPUTERS AND SOFTWARE

It is extremely difficult to keep up with a diverse and rapidly changing field like computing. The value of a reference book like this one is that it provides extensive coverage of the computer and software industry, and the related broadcasting and communications field, in a single volume. This allows students and experienced industry professionals the opportunities to explore the field of computing and to discover information on emerging trends. The combination of Gale's extensive data collection and key financial information from Dun and Bradstreet gives readers accessibility to timely information on computing and software industry resources. This information will allow readers to assess the impact of several important computing industry trends and to draw their own conclusions.

INDUSTRY OVERVIEW

This chapter presents a comprehensive overview of the Computers & Software industry. Major topics covered include an Industry Snapshot, Organization and Structure, Background and Development, Pioneers in the Industry, Current Conditions and Future Projections, Industry Leaders, Work Force, North America and the World, and Research and Technology. A suggested list for further reading, including web sites to visit, completes the chapter. Additional company information is presented in Chapter 6 - Mergers & Acquisitions.

Industry Snapshot

If there is any doubt as to the extent that computers have affected us, consider these figures: 43% of U.S. households contain at least one personal computer, 55 million people surf the Internet, more than 400,000 businesses have Web sites, cybertransactions in 1998 are expected to be worth over five billion dollars, and IBM, the world's top-selling computer manufacturer, has annual sales of $78 billion.

These statistics, while impressive enough, do not reflect the countless ways that computers are utilized: by governments, to assign social security numbers, cut welfare checks, compute taxes, control nuclear power plants, navigate space shuttles; by hospitals, to conduct medical examinations and to maintain patient records; by retail establishments, to scan the price of purchases, bill credit cards, conduct inventories; by banks, to compute interest, record transactions, generate statements, operate ATMs; by automobile manufacturers, to operate robotic assemble workers and to design and test prototypes; and so on and so on. Suffice it to say, computers are an integral part of everyday American life.

The computer industry is so large that it encompasses every aspect of the computer, from the manufacture of the microchip up through that of the computer game software, as well as the wide array of services related to the computer, from data entry to consulting services. In fact, the industry is comprised of 24 SICs. Hardware categories include **3571: Electronic Computers**, the hardware, which includes the processor, the operating system, and the memory; **3572: Computer Storage Devices**, such as disk drives; **3575: Computer Terminals**; **3577: Computer Peripheral Equipment, Not Elsewhere Classified**, such as keyboards, printers, and scanners; **3578: Calculating and Accounting Machines**; **3672 Printed Circuit Boards**; **3674: Semiconductors and related devices**; **3675-3679: Electronic components** such as capacitors, resistors, coils and transformers, and connectors; **3694: Engine Electrical Systems**; **3695: Magnetic and Optical Recording Media**, such as diskettes; and **3699: Electrical Equipment and Supplies, Not Elsewhere Classified**.

The industry also includes software and services. SIC categories are **7371: Computer Programming Servi-** ces; **7372: Prepackaged Software**, which are the programs that communicate instructions to the computer; **7373: Computer Integrated Systems Design**, development, modification, and integration of software to serve networks; **7374: Computer Processing and Data Preparation and Processing Services**, off-site data entry, processing, and verification services; **7375: Information Retrieval Services**, online service providers; **7376: Computer Facilities Management Services**, onsite management of computer and data processing facilities; **7377: Computer Rental and Leasing**, renting or leasing computer and related equipment for use at the customer's facility; **7378: Computer Maintenance and Repair**; and **7379: Computer Related Services, Not Elsewhere Classified**, such as consulting.

Organization and Structure

Not long ago, the manufacture of computer hardware was based on a proprietary, or closed, system, whereby all components were designed and produced by the computer manufacturer. Outsourcing the production of most of these components, a method popularized by IBM in the early 1980s, has the benefit of providing access to the best and cheapest technology available, as smaller, more focused companies usually have the ability to develop advancements sooner than larger, broad-based businesses. Components are typically obtained through third-party suppliers. They are standardized and available from a variety of vendors, thereby creating a competitive market.

Two components are exceptions to the flexible supplier market: the motherboard (containing the circuitry, memory chips, and microprocessor) and the CPU, or central processing unit (the component that interprets and executes program instructions). These two critical pieces are entrusted to only a handful of vendors who can be relied upon to produce the delicate and complex components accurately. Currently Intel Corporation produces 85% of the CPU processors used in PCs worldwide, and it is producing a growing number of motherboards.

The consumer and corporation can purchase a computer through a variety of avenues. The traditional channel is the computer dealer or the value-added reseller. Retail stores, however, have encroached upon that turf, as more consumers feel comfortable in the familiar retail system. A third approach, embraced by Gateway 2000 and Dell Computer, is the direct-sales method. This strategy benefits the consumer by eliminating the middleman and the cost mark-ups associated with it. The manufacturer operates on a build-to-order basis, allowing it to maintain low inventory levels and avoid the necessity of producing enough units in advance in order to keep retailers well-stocked with its products.

In addition to the computer hardware, four industries serve the consumer directly—storage devices, terminals, peripheral equipment, and prepackaged software. As with the hardware, these items are readily available to consumers at retail outlets. Some stores, such as CompUsa, Corporate Software, and Egghead Discount Software, specialize in software products.

Information retrieval services provide consumers online access to one or more databases. They do not typically produce the database, they merely link customers to them by connections through telephone or telecommunications networks. The customer pays for such access either on a contract or fee basis.

With innovations in the computer industry occurring at an ever-accelerating pace, companies are frequently reluctant to invest in new systems. So, to stay abreast of the latest technology, more and more are turning to the rental/lease option, gaining the flexibility to upgrade without losing substantial investments. A variety of lease options are available, such as the operating lease, in which the lessor owns the equipment and assumes responsibility for its depreciation; the sale-lease-back, where a company sells its equipment to the lessor and then leases it back; and the dollar-out lease, wherein equipment is purchased by the company at the end of the lease term for one dollar.

Two types of companies handle the maintenance and repair of computers and their peripheral equipment. Third-party maintenance (TPM) companies service the equipment of a variety of manufacturers, while original equipment manufacturers (OEMs) service only the computers that they have also manufactured. The market for TPMs is growing as OEMs are increasingly hiring TPMs to handle this task for them.

Computer programming services, including integrated systems design and facilities management, are virtual necessities for most large companies. These services may include the programming of custom software, debugging existing programs, and integrating new software into an existing system. Since these are valuable services and the need for them may arise unexpectedly, many firms maintain in-house programming departments, hiring facilities management servers to manage the computer facilities as well as the data processing responsibilities. Other companies outsource their programming tasks to outside companies, often in foreign countries where the rates are lower.

Both computer consulting and computer processing services operate on an as-need, temporary basis. A company hires the consultant when input is required for such issues as purchasing a new computer system, designing a database, or recommending a data processing outfit. Data processors, in turn, can be either onsite or offsite. Onsite units are known as facilities managers, and are discussed above. Offsite services rent their own facilities and resources for temporary data processing and tabulating tasks.

A Web developer's customers are the companies that commission the creation of a Web site. The final product's ownership is either the developer or the client, depending upon the contractual terms. Since the cost of purchasing a site, ranging between $300,000 and $3.5 million, can be prohibitive, especially for relatively small companies, two other options are available: renting the site from the developer, or making an initial payment plus commission on sales generated by the site.

Background and Development

Although it may not seem obvious at first glance, the history of computing extends back to the year 3000 B. C. The abacus did then what computers of today were first designed to do—calculate. More recently, however, the computer can be traced back to Blaise Pascal, who invented a mechanical adding machine in the 17th century; to Herman Hollerith's punch-card tabulator used in the 1890 U.S. census; and to Dr. John V. Atanasoff's 1942 creation—an electronic machine devised to perform complex physics calculations by utilizing memory and logic circuits with a binary numbering system.

The electronic computer, however, the more direct forerunner of modern computers, was developed in 1944 by a program sponsored by International Business Machines (IBM). The result of this program was the Automatic Sequence Controlled Calculator, also known as Mark I. It was the first electromechanical computer, spanning a length of 51 feet and a height of eight feet, and weighing in at nearly five tons.

By the end of World War II, in 1946, the first fully-operational electric computer was completed. The mission of the Electronic Numerical Integrator and Computer (ENAIC) was in part to improve the U.S. Army's trajectory accuracy.

The year 1951 is known as the beginning of the First Generation of Computers, which is distinguished by vacuum tube technology. During this year, the Remington-Rand Corporation introduced the first commercial digital computer, the UNIVAC I. Following its release, IBM realized the market potential for commercial computers, and released the IBM 701 in 1952. In 1959, Rear Admiral Grace Hopper developed the COBOL programming language and coined the term "debug" when she removed a moth from inside a computer.

The short-lived Second Generation of Computers, marked by the use of the transistor, began in 1959 with the introduction of the Honeywell 400. Four years later, Digital Equipment Corporation released the PDP-8, the first minicomputer, which, priced at $18,000, made computer technology more accessible to smaller companies than the previous machines, which frequently cost upwards of one million dollars.

The System/360, introduced by IBM in 1964, heralded the beginning of the Third Generation, characterized by the use of integrated circuits. This machine introduced the concept of differentiation between hardware, software, and peripheral equipment thereby allowing users to upgrade obsolete components of the system instead of purchasing an entirely new system. This year also marked the introduction of the BASIC programming language by professors at Dartmouth College who wanted to create a language that would be easily understood by beginning programmers.

The potential for computers as communication tools, rather than just as calculating devices, was first recog-

nized in 1969. The U.S. Department of Defense's Advanced Research Project Agency (ARPA) created AR-PANET, the forerunner of the Internet, to allow scientists to share information with geographically dispersed colleagues.

The Fourth Generation began in 1971 with the introduction of large-scale integrated circuits, which are integrated circuits that have begun to undergo miniaturization, thereby allowing more to fit in a given space. The first personal computer, the Altair 8800, was released in 1975 by Micro Instrumentation and Telemetry Systems. Priced below $400, it brought individuals into the computer market. It also redirected manufacturing by introducing mass-production and an open systems architecture, giving users flexibility in selecting and integrating peripheral equipment.

IBM's personal computer, the IBM PC, was released in 1981, incorporating MS-DOS, or Microsoft Disk Operating System. Its popularity prompted software companies to produce products compatible with this system, which in turn spurred IBM competitors to create replicas of the IBM PC.

In 1984, Apple Computer released the Macintosh. This machine popularized the graphical user interface (GUI), utilizing pictures, or icons, to make computing more user-friendly. Similarly, Microsoft Corp. introduced the Windows operating system the following year.

By 1990, ARPANET officially retired, having long-since been penetrated by businesses and individuals as a communication tool, notably by the appeal of electronic mail, or e-mail. This year also marks Tim Berners-Lee's introduction of the World Wide Web, allowing multimedia document exchange over the Internet. Internet services were first offered by Delphi Internet Services in 1993. America Online, CompuServe, and Prodigy soon followed suit, introducing their own complete services two years later.

In 1997, the U.S. Supreme Court confirmed the unconstitutionality of the Communications Decency Act of 1996, upholding the right of online services to set their own internal standards of decency, defamation, and discussions of illegal activities.

June of 1998 saw the largest acquisition in the history of the computer industry, as Compaq Computers Corp. acquires Digital Equipment Corp. for $9 billion, thereby creating a company with revenues of $37.5 billion, and displacing IBM as the world's largest hardware manufacturer.

Pioneers and Newsmakers in the Industry

Tim Berners-Lee

Unlike other revolutionary inventions in the computer industry—the PC, the integrated circuit, the Internet—the World Wide Web began not by a team, but by a single man. That man is Tim Berners-Lee.

Prior to the Web, data could be transmitted and received over the Internet in only one of two ways: as generic text within the body of a message, or as attached binary files requiring offline viewing. Berners-Lee changed that.

After graduating from Oxford University in 1976, he held a variety of computer-related jobs, and in 1984 he began a fellowship at the European Particle Physics Laboratory (CERN) in Geneva, Switzerland. In March 1989, Berners-Lee proposed an internal computer system utilizing hyperlinks, buttons within a document that allow the user to jump to related documents. In November of 1990, he introduced the first Web software on the NeXT computer system. It was released on all central CERN computers in May 1991, and that August it was launched on the Internet.

In 1993, the Mosaic browser, which brought graphics to the Web, was introduced by the National Center for Supercomputing Applications. Usage of the Web skyrocketed: in January 1993, there were approximately 50 http servers; by November 1994, that number was estimated to be 150,000.

Having grown overwhelmed by the project, in September 1994 the CERN turned it over to Berners-Lee's newly-formed World Wide Web Consortium (W3C), a non-profit organization serving as an open forum for standardization and development issues concerning the Web.

In 1998, the Web boasted 55 million users, and Berners-Lee served as director of W3C and as a principal research scientist at the Massachusetts Institute of Technology (MIT). How does the father of the Web feel about his success of his brainchild? As he told *Forbes ASAP*, "It's very gratifying to see an idea take off like that. Although sometime I wish I hadn't put the double slash in the URL address because it is a bit unwieldy."

Bill Gates

Computers...Microsoft...Bill Gates. The three terms are virtually synonymous to most computer users. And for good reason—over 90% of the PCs sold in mid-1998 utilize Microsoft's Windows operating system.

William H. Gates III has been a computer enthusiast since his youth. Born in 1955 in Seattle, Washington, he began programming in BASIC at the age of fourteen. He and his friend Paul Allen worked on-and-off as computer consultants throughout high school. The duo separated when Allen attended Washington State University while Gates pursued a legal career at Harvard University.

The introduction of the Altair 8800 in January 1975 reunited the friends, who approached Altair's manufacturer, Micro Instrumentation and Telemetry Systems, with the proposal of creating a BASIC interpreter for the system. The offer was met with enthusiasm, and six weeks later the newly-formed Microsoft firm delivered. Having had the foresight to retain the rights to their program, they soon began customizing it for other computers, such as those produced by Apple Computer and Commodore. Gates designed the operating system—MS-DOS (short for Microsoft Disk Operating System)— for the 1981 breakthrough, the IBM PC.

Microsoft's Windows operating system, introduced in 1985, revolutionized computers by making them more user-friendly by way of a graphical user interface, just as the Macintosh had done for Apple's customers the prior year. Microsoft improved upon itself with the 1990 launch of Windows 3.0, which, he boasted, was "a better DOS than DOS." In 1987, after Microsoft went public, Gates officially became a billionaire. Before the company's initial public offering, Gates' worth was impossible to calculate since most of his holdings were in Microsoft stock. The following year, Microsoft became the largest PC software company in the U.S.

The company spent $200 million on publicity for the release of Windows 95. This product created an industry-wide upgrade cycle, a sudden surge in hardware sales to meet the requirements of a more powerful operating system. The U.S. Department of Justice (DOJ), however, was ready to pounce. It accused Microsoft of forcing licensees of Windows 95, the computer manufacturers, to include Microsoft's Internet Explorer, thereby giving the company an unfair trade advantage over other Internet browsers. Shortly thereafter, a consent decree prohibited Microsoft from requiring manufacturers to license other Microsoft products as part of the Windows package, while permitting Microsoft to continue producing integrated products. These two words, "integrated products," are the crux of the December 1997 anti-trust suit, with DOJ and Microsoft at odds over the exact meaning of the term. The aim of the suit is to force Microsoft either to "unbundle" its browser from its operating system or to offer other browsers inclusion in Windows.

These suits have not slowed Gates nor Microsoft—*Windows 98* was released in June of that year, and on June 23, 1998, the U.S. Court of Appeals overturned the 1997 injunction against Microsoft.

Ted Hoff

Marcian Edward "Ted" Hoff, Jr., was born in 1937 in Rochester, New York. He earned a Bachelor's, a Master's, and in 1962, a Ph.D. in electrical engineering. In 1968, Hoff was hired as the twelfth employee of the newly formed Intel Corp.

In 1969, Intel was hired by Japan-based Busicom to push the limits of available technology by creating a single chip to control all of the functions of a calculator, a promising new invention. In theory, this idea was not new, as industry experts forecast its development in the years ahead, but no one had successfully designed it, much less built it. Hoff's first project at Intel was the Busicom challenge. He immediately realized that the company's 12-chip specification would be complex, costly, and limited to calculators. Although

calculators were, at present, the only practical application of such a chip, Hoff tried to convince Busicom to allow him to pursue a general purpose chip. Rejected, he later received permission from his bosses at Intel to pursue his idea, and soon defined a four-chip architecture consisting of a four-bit chip, read-only and random-access memories, and a shift register for connections.

While the design worked on paper, Hoff needed someone to translate it into a working chip. That person would prove to be Federico Faggin, who joined Intel in 1970. Within three months, Faggin had successfully built Intel's "4000 Family," a four-chip set containing the important 4004 chip, the first microprocessor. This tiny gadget had a computing ability comparable to the room-sized Eniac computer. In early 1971, the set was shipped to Busicom, but by now, the company was entrenched in calculator price wars and was no longer interested in it. It consequently sold the rights to it back to Intel for $60,000 and a manufacturing price reduction. In November 1971, Intel launched the market release of the microprocessor.

Hoff remained at Intel for the next decade, and was awarded the company's highest technical position, that of Intel Fellow, in 1980. He later worked at Atari, and Teklicon, Inc.

Grace Hopper

Grace Brewster Murray Hopper was born on December 9, 1906, in New York City. Her natural curiosity for things mechanical was encouraged by her parents, who refused to allow conventional norms to deny her an advanced mathematics education simply because of her gender. After earning a Bachelor's degree from Vassar College in 1928, she began teaching mathematics there in 1931. Within three years, she acquired Master's and Doctoral degrees in mathematics.

Hopper joined the U.S. Naval Reserve in 1943 and was assigned to work on the Mark I computer. While working on that project, she coined the term "computer bug" when a moth entered the computer's circuitry. Remaining a Naval reservist, in 1949 Hopper joined the Eckert-Mauchly Computer Corp. in its development of the Univac I, the first commercial electronic computer.

During the 1950s, she invented COBOL (common business-oriented language), the first user-friendly business software program. In 1952, she invented the Flow-Matic, the first English language compiler, which stored in memory repetitive code common to all computer programs, thereby reducing programming time.

Commander Hopper retired in 1966, but was called back to active service the following year to standardize the Navy's computer languages. The first woman to achieve the rank of Rear Admiral, she again retired in 1986. Several weeks later, at the age of 79, Hopper began working as a speaker for Digital Equipment Corp. She died on New Year's Day, 1992, and is buried at Arlington National Cemetery.

Among her numerous achievements and awards, including 37 honorary doctorates, "The Grandmother of COBOL" earned the 1969 Data Processing Management Association's Computer Sciences "Man of the Year" award and the 1990 National Medal of Technology.

Current Conditions, Future Projections

PC Market

Personal computers constitute the greatest portion of the hardware market, growing 15.8% in 1997. Multi-user systems, such as mainframes, server networks, and supercomputers, account for the next highest share, 35%. Workstations trail last, generating approximately six percent of total worldwide spending on computer hardware.

While the PC market is the most competitive, the fastest growing segment is the client/server system. These systems aim to replace mainframe systems, in which a single, powerful computer supports a number of smaller units. In the client/server model, the mainframe is replaced with a team of smaller computers, the servers, that provides processing or other services for a host of client units. The advantages of this system are two-fold: the servers, very often PCs, are faster and cheaper than mainframes; and because of their multiple access points, several programmers can execute applications simultaneously. Disadvantages include a lack of both security and the power to support exceptionally large applications.

The introduction of PCs costing under $1,000, known as segment-zero PCs, has rocked the computer industry: in 1997, segment-zero PCs comprised 30% of all U.S. PC sales; by mid-1998, segment-zeros accounted for 50% of such sales. In an industry where the speed of microprocessors doubles every 18 months, manufacturers were previously able to count on frequent upgrade sales. A new computer capable of running the latest software used to cost between three and four thousand dollars. Now, the sub-$1,000 PC is already as fast as most of the public requires for running software and accessing the Internet, since for Internet users, the speed of the microprocessor is less important than the speed of the modem. In response to this trend, Intel introduced its first microprocessor designed for this market, the Celeron, in April 1998. Experts predict that while sales of these PCs will increase, revenues will not increase proportionally. In 1998, forecasts indicate that the number of units sold will increase over 13%, but revenues will climb only 4.5%.

The sale of laptop computers is growing at a faster rate than that of desktops. In early 1998, laptops accounted for 35% of total sales, and by the year 2000 they are expected to make up half of all sales. The reasons for the boom include an increase in available features on the laptops, such as CD-ROM drives, color screens, decent keyboards, and larger hard drives. Improvements in remote access appeal to business users who need to stay in touch with the office. These features do not come cheaply—capital and operational expenses are typically 50% higher than for desktops—but many individuals and companies are willing to pay for the convenience, citing increased telecommuting and business travel as the main reasons. Companies are beginning to take cost-cutting measures to offset the higher total cost of ownership. By leasing the laptops, costs are spread out on a monthly basis and upgrading to state-of-the-art technology is relatively easy. To reduce the cost of supporting remote users, remote systems management software is becoming more readily available.

Software Sales

Business applications were the best-selling segment of PC software sales in 1997. Of the $3.3 billion in total PC software sold, business products accounted for $1.44 billion, a 15.4% increase over the previous year's $1.25 billion. The most successful product was Microsoft's Windows 95 CD Upgrade, which sold 659,000 units. In terms of revenue generated, another Microsoft product, Office 97, generated the highest sales—$78.7 million.

Consumer software sales reached $908 million, an increase of 21.7% over 1996. The top-selling game in 1997 was Riven: The Sequel to Myst, by Red Orb Entertainment. Released on October 28, it generated $28 million in sales of 640,000 units before the end of the year. Riven is the successor to Myst, a unique four-year old game that remains one of the top-five yearly bestsellers.

Y2K

The clock is ticking...literally. If not corrected before January 1, 2000, computer systems around the world will either malfunction or fail altogether. The problem lies in the way in which software programs were written prior to the 1990s. In the interest of saving valuable memory, years were programmed with a two-character rather than a four-character representation. So the year 1987 was simply 87. However, as the millennium turns, computers will misinterpret its 00 representation as 1900. This error will impact calculations, severely crippling such industries as banking and insurance, while doing damage to all businesses that rely on computers to calculate dates of billing, order, or expiration. Governments, too, will be hit by the problem, as they rely on computers for such purposes as power generation, military requirements, social security and welfare payments, and income tax computation. This is the Year 2000 problem, also known as the Y2K, or Millennium, bug.

Y2K is dire news for the world's economy in general, and may even lead to a recession. The computer systems of many companies will crash, leaving businesses virtually inoperable. Other firms will have partial operation if the bug affects only certain segments of their system. Inflation will rise as these companies, and even the companies that foresaw the problem far enough in advance to complete corrections, must divert both financial and programming resources into correcting it, leaving less time and money to carry on business as usual. As a result, experts predict, U.S. companies will lose $119 billion in economic output through the year 2001. Moreover, the growth rate of businesses will drop.

The scramble to beat the clock has had a positive effect on segments of the computer industry, however. With an estimated 85% of software programs impacted by Y2K, software manufacturers have created programs that, while not miracle cures, can help to hunt out and identify the troublesome codes programmed in systems. Computer consultants and programmers are in great demand as problem-solvers, and sales are boosted by companies that opt to replace existing equipment with new software and hardware rather than fix the problem.

E-commerce

The Internet has changed the way that we communicate and conduct research; increasingly, it is also altering the way that we do business. More than 400,000 businesses have web sites through which they reach customers. Consumers in the U.S. and Europe are expected to spend some $5 billion in 1998 through such cybertransactions.

In addition to providing access to end-consumers, the Internet is an ideal environment for businesses to transact with each other. Business-to-business transactions constitute the largest market for e-commerce, expected to account for 78% of all cybertransactions in 1998. In the U.S., this segment's revenues totaled $8 billion in 1997, and are projected to reach $183 billion in 2002.

For direct monetary transactions, the Internet is used for purchasing wholesale products, placing orders with contract manufacturers, connecting with distributors, and delegating unsold merchandise to online brokerages. To keep the business running smoothly, companies also use the Internet to order office supplies; exchange sales contracts and product designs; contact support services like advertising agencies, accountants, and lawyers; and send invoices via email.

Initially, consumer e-commerce transactions primarily consisted of computer hardware and software sales, the two areas of most interest to pioneers of cyberspace. Computers are still the largest segment of online sales. The top e-seller is Dell Computers, which had 1997 sales of more than three million dollars each day for an annual total of $11 billion. But flat-rate pricing for Internet connection has facilitated the market to expand into such areas as tourism, finance, retail products, and unique products from small, remote vendors. Consumer e-commerce generated revenues of $2.4 billion in 1997, as 27 million people used the Internet to research and "shop around," while 10 million actually made online purchases.

The industry that is expected to experience the greatest increase in cybertransactions is the travel industry. In 1997, tourism sales over the Internet reached $654 million, and this figure has been projected to skyrocket to $7.4 billion in 2001. Consumers can easily research destinations, compare fares, and purchase tickets via the Internet without the assistance of a travel agent. While this is good new for the consumer, it is bad news for the displaced agent. Although e-commerce is squeezing out these industry-specific middlemen, it is creating a market for others to handle the management of transaction processing and the design of web sites and online catalogs.

In just a short time, e-commerce has evolved from simply a browsing area for online catalogs and advertisements to a comprehensive means of conducting business through the use of encryption, digital cash, and authentication. It has changed the very nature of conducting business-companies are now expected to reveal business details as well as product information, and the direct contact with consumers has intensified the importance of customer relations.

New services are springing up to make e-shopping more convenient and less worrisome for consumers wary of online credit card transactions. Western Union Financial Services International's QuickPay service allows customers to pay for their online purchases at any Western Union location. Internet checks, offered by InfoDial, permit customers to complete online banking forms, which are later printed out as checks by the merchant. And on behalf of online consumers, the Better Business Bureau's BBBOnline web site monitors online businesses.

A shift away from all-inclusive Internet malls toward large or specialty retailers is apparent: IBM's World Avenue mall shut down in June 1997 after less than one year of operation; the Industry.Net marketplace went bankrupt in the summer of 1997; MCI Communications' music retailing site closed in 1996; and by the end of 1997, the Amazon.com book retailer has yet to show a profit despite sales surpassing $30 million.

In short, e-commerce serves to: offer consumers more choices and buying power, lower costs and improve company productivity, and increase the speed of product development by improving the flow of information about purchasing trends.

Java

Java, a computer programming language released by Sun Microsystems Inc. in 1996, allows software to be interpreted by any computer, regardless of its architecture and operating system. Java-written programs called "applets" are small applications run directly from an Internet browser. The language works by translating programs into a generic "bytecode" format, which is then interpreted by a platform-specific operating system, such as Microsoft's Windows. Java's slogan, "write once, run anywhere," implies that a single software package or Internet site can be read by any computer, whether it is a Macintosh or an IBM, for example, and some experts believe that Java may reduce the industry's dependence on Microsoft's operating systems.

CASE

A recent breakthrough in systems development is the CASE, or computer-aided software engineering, tool. Formerly manual processes, such as database creation and information flow documentation, are now automated by CASE commercially available software. An array of CASE products are being created to meet a variety of specific applications, but most CASE kits include tools for design, information repository, and program development. Just as operating systems have developed into user-friendly devices requiring less reliance on computer professionals, CASE products are expected to evolve similarly.

Telecommuting

In many ways, we are becoming a mobile society. Cellular telephones and portable PCs allow us to stay in touch while on the go. On the other hand, computers have also allowed us to remain more stationary-by allowing us to telecommute to work. In 1997, the number of employees who worked at home surpassed 40 million, and this figure is likely to rise in upcoming years. Both employee and employer cite advantages: the employee enjoys greater flexibility, increased production, and avoidance of commutes; while the employer reports reduced absenteeism and improved employee morale.

Industry Leaders

IBM

The world's largest computer manufacturer was formed in June 1911 as the Computing-Tabulating-Recording Company, which manufactured a wide range of products in addition to the tabulators, punch card devices, and time recording equipment on which its name was based. In time it established itself in foreign markets, and changed its name to International Business Machines Corporation (IBM) in 1924. By 1939, sales of $50 million made it the largest office machine manufacturer in the U.S.

Its 1944 project, the Automatic Sequence Controlled Calculator (also known as Mark I), was the world's first electromechanical computer. This accomplishment was followed up by the 1952 release of its first vacuum tube-based computer, the IBM 701. That same year, the U.S. government filed an anti-trust suit against IBM, and four years later, the company entered into a decree that forced it to reorganize into several autonomous division (IBM would have to adhere to these restrictions until the government lifted them four decades later, in May 1997). The IBM 305 Random Access Method of Accounting and Control (RAMAC), released in April 1964, incorporated the first computer disk storage system. In January 1969, the federal government filed another antitrust suit against IBM; this suit is ultimately dragged out until its dismissal in 1982.

The company entered the personal computer market in 1981 with the release of the IBM PC. Incorporating

MS-DOS, or Microsoft Disk Operating System, its popularity prompted software companies to produce compatible products, and hardware companies to produce clones. By 1986, such clones were outselling the IBM originals. The company began to lose ground due to economic depression and an industry redirection toward smaller and more powerful compact computers—IBM's strength had been on the larger mainframe systems.

Down but not out, the firm released a laptop in 1992, and in 1995 it acquired Lotus Development Corporation to establish itself in the software industry. It also began to focus on becoming a supplier of components to other manufacturers rather than a manufacturer of hardware itself.

IBM gained worldwide recognition in May 1997 when its Deep Blue computer beat the World Chess Champion Garry Kasparov—the first time a machine had ever defeated a human champion in tournament play. That year, revenues totaled $78 billion, net earnings were $6 million, and employees totaled 270,000.

Intel Corp.

Robert Noyce and Gordon Moore incorporated NM Electronics in July 1968 to produce LSI semiconductor memories. The firm's name soon changed to Intel, borrowing the first syllables of "integrated electronics." In 1971, Intel released its first microprocessor, the 4004; that year it also developed erasable programmable read-only memory, EPROM. The 8080 microprocessor was used in the 1975 Altair, the industry's first personal computer. Its 8088 microprocessor was used in the IBM PC of 1978; this computer's success landed Intel a spot on *Fortune* magazine's Fortune 500 list. The 286, released in 1982, was the first processor capable of running software built for older processors. By 1990, Intel was the world's third-largest independent semiconductor producer.

The Pentium processor, released in 1993, allowed computers to incorporate graphics and audio input. This product, whose name was splashed across hardware boxes, soon became a household word. The next year, however, the discovery that the Pentium was prone to calculation errors cost Intel millions of dollars in chip replacement charges and an indeterminable amount in consumer confidence. In 1995, the Pentium

Pro processor was introduced for engineering and scientific applications. The Pentium II, released in 1997, was designed for more efficient integration of video, audio, and graphics data. In February 1998, it ventured into computer networking by introducing a line of networking tools. Four months later, the U.S. government filed an antitrust complaint against Intel, alleging that the company threatened to cut off the supply of processors to manufacturers who have developed competing products.

Intel's 1997 revenues increased 20% to $21.5 billion, while net income rose to $6.9 billion. Intel's challenge in upcoming months will be the development of products to meet expectations of sub-$1,000 PCs. The company has already begun to do so, having introduced its first microprocessor designed for this market, the Celeron, in April 1998.

Oracle Corp.

Ranked second in software sales only to Microsoft Corporation, Oracle Corporation is the world's leader in information management software. This Redwood Shores, California, company was founded in 1977 by two computer programmers, Lawrence J. Ellison and Robert N. Miner. At this time, IBM was working on the creation of Structured Query Language (SQL), a relational database that would allow computers to retrieve data in any form. Confident that the IBM program would become an industry standard, Oracle began the development of an SQL-compatible relational database management system (RDBMS), and in 1979 it became the first company to introduce a commercially available RDBMS. Four years later, it released the next generation, a portable RDBMS capable of serving mainframes, minicomputers, workstations, and PCs.

Oracle's strategy of marketing to multinational companies served to boost 1986 sales to $55.4 million, prompting analysts to dub it the world's fastest-growing software manufacturer. It justified this title the next year, when its record sales of $100 million pushed it into the industry's number-one position.

In 1988, Oracle debuted its first computer-aided software engineering (CASE) application development tools, which partially automate the programming tasks of creating databases and documenting information

flow. Ten years later, Oracle is an established leader in CASE technology, and sales reached seven billion dollars, up from three billion in 1995.

Sun Microsystems, Inc.

One of the top-ten computer hardware manufacturers, Sun Microsystems, Inc. has been particularly newsworthy in recent years. In 1996, the company released Java, a programming language that is expected to break the bounds between platform-specific operating systems.

Sun was founded in 1982 by four Stanford University graduates—Andreas Bechtolsheim, Bill Joy, Vinod Khosla, and Scott McNealy. The partners entered the business of selling licenses for Bechtolsheim's invention, the Sun-1 computer, and the firm became profitable in its first year. In 1984 Sun began licensing its NFS software, which allowed data to be shared throughout a computer network regardless of processor type. By the next year, its hardware product offerings for workstations totaled 300. In 1988 it made over $1 billion in revenue—the first company ever to achieve this mark so quickly. A decade later, Sun reported a 21% increase in revenues to $8.6 billion, while net income skyrocketed 60% to $762 million. As further evidence that the Palo Alto, California-based Sun is on the fast-track to growth, employee count jumped 24% in 1998 to 21,500.

America Online, Inc.

Quantum Computer Services, Inc. was founded in 1985 by Stephen M. Case to offer an online service, Q-Link, for Apple's Commodore computers. Two years later, it began extending services to other manufacturers' computers. In 1989 it introduced American Online (AOL), a nationwide online network. The success of this venture spurred the company to change its name to America Online, Inc. in 1991.

In 1994 its subscriber base surpassed one million; by the end of the next year that total had tripled. In December 1996, after changing its pricing platform from a usage-based to a flat-rate plan, subscribers numbered eight million. This increase in traffic flooded the system, and brought about legal threats from angry customers who were unable to get online. AOL responded by instituting a $350 million infrastructure expansion and cutting back on marketing.

In 1997, AOL purchased CompuServe Corporation, the first consumer online service, keeping the two services separate. By mid-1998, AOL and CompuServe had subscriber bases of 12 million and two million, respectively.

NEC Corporation

NEC Corporation was established in 1899 as the Nippon Electric Company, Ltd. This company, based in Tokyo, Japan, was the result of the first Japanese joint venture with participants from outside the country, and began operations as an importer of telephone equipment from Western Electric Company and General Electric Company

For fifty years, NEC's activities centered on telecommunications and consumer electronics. In 1954, it initiated research and development activities in the field of computers, and five years later it debuted its transistor-based computer, the NEAC-2201. After several years of continued advancements in computers, the company released Japan's first microprocessor in 1974. Having changed its name to NEC Corporation in 1983, the company became the world's leading independent producer of semiconductors in 1985. With the next year's introduction of the industry's first 4-megabit dynamic random access memory (DRAM) chip, NEC surpassed IBM to become Japan's second-ranked computer manufacturer. It followed this innovation with successive improvements, which culminated in the 1995 release of the first 1-gigabit DRAM. Marking the first time that the U.S. government purchases a Japanese supercomputer, in 1996 the National Center for Atmospheric Research contracted NEC to build a weather forecasting machine.

Revenues for fiscal 1998 reached $4.9 trillion yen, or approximately $36.9 billion, while net income was recorded at $41.3 billion yen.

Dell Computer Corporation

Dell Computer Corporation, the most successful direct-sales computer manufacturer, was founded in May 1984 in the dorm room of Michael Dell, a computer

components salesman in his spare time. By the end of 1985, Dell had introduced its first computers, and revenues reached $34 million. Business continued briskly, and by September 1987, the company received incoming telephone calls totaling 1,700 per day (in 1998, this daily count surpassed 200,000).

Dell broke new ground in 1991 when its computers featured pre-installed software at no additional cost to the buyer; this service is known as DellPlus by 1998. Company milestones occurred on nearly a yearly basis: its first notebook PC, in 1991; the award-winning line of inexpensive Dimension PCs, in 1992; its first integrated multimedia systems, in 1993; the industry's first notebook with coast-to-coast battery life, the Dell Latitude, in 1994; and the low-priced Dell Precision workstation, in 1997.

Fiscal 1998 net income leapt 82% to $944 million, while revenues increased 59% to $12.3 billion. Of the total revenues, sales of desktops accounted for 71%, portables for 20%, and enterprise systems contributed nine percent.

Comdisco Incorporated

Illinois-based Comdisco Incorporated, one of the world's leading computer lessors, was formed as Computer Discount Corporation by Ken Pontikes in 1969. The leasing of used IBM computer equipment proved lucrative, as first-year revenues reached one million dollars. Two years later, its name was shortened to Comdisco Incorporated. In 1972 it became the nation's largest lessor of used IBM products, fueled by the industry's rapid technological advancements and corresponding cost increases.

Experiencing steady growth over the next decade, it reached one billion dollars in annual lease financing in 1983. That same year, Comdisco expanded into the leasing and remarketing of non-IBM products. During the 1980s and 1990s, the company diversified into such arenas as asset management, business continuity (disaster recovery), and network services while continuing to provide equipment leasing and remarketing services. Revenues increased 16% to $2.8 billion in 1997, while pre-tax net earnings grew to $211 million and its worldwide employee count reached 2,400.

Work Force

The demand for qualified computer professionals far outweighs the supply—it is an employee's market. As a result, turnover within the industry is high, and employers aim to protect their investment by offering increased wages and other perks as incentives for continued employment. The Office of Computers and Business Equipment (OCBE), a division of the U.S. Department of Commerce's International Trade Administration, reports that the hourly wage for computer programmers in 1996 was $21.53. The Bureau of Labor Statistic's *Occupational Outlook Handbook* forecasts that computer scientists, computer engineers, and systems analysts will be the three fastest growing occupations through the year 2006.

Demand for computer professionals is so high that companies are increasingly hiring freshly graduated applicants, offering to pay for their training on top of an appealing incentives package. Because there are a limited number of such graduates, and because competition among suitors is fierce, some companies have begun infiltrating the undergraduate pool. College students are lured by computer businesses to quit school and join the workforce. These new recruits cite the advantages of an immediate paycheck and the elimination of college expenses, while their new employers cite the new hires' boundless energy and enthusiasm as benefits for the business. Detractors of this trend, however, warn that the short-term benefits will be shadowed by long-term disadvantages. Not only is the ex-student robbing himself of a well-rounded education and the achievement of a college degree, but this trend will also create an even larger chasm between supply and demand. If most computer-proficient people join the ranks as employees, they ask, who will remain to educate and train the upcoming generations of computer professionals?

Despite these warnings, jobs are being filled at an ever-increasing rate. The OCBE reports that in 1997, U.S. employment in the software industry alone reached 306,400, while that for the hardware industry was estimated at 230,000, reflecting an annual growth rate of 12.7% and 4%, respectively. The combined employment of computer scientists, computer engineers, and systems analysts reached 933,000 in 1996.

Certification, while usually not a job requirement, may allow a potential employee to negotiate higher wages. Certification programs are offered through training centers, companies like Novell and Microsoft, and organizations such as the Institute for Certification of Computer Professionals (ICCP) and the Quality Assurance Institute (QAI).

Temporary and contract employment of computer professionals is on the rise as companies hire such specialists on an as-need basis rather than for the long term. When a company looks to obtain a new computer system, it may hire consultants to advise on the purchase of the system, others to program and install the system, and still others to train employees in its use. With so many diverse, specialized aspects to the computer industry, best results can be obtained from a variety of specialists rather than a single type of professional.

North America and the World

United States

The U.S. dominates the computer industry, in terms of both production and consumption. In software, U.S. consumers account for 40% of the worldwide market, and the software industry has been ranked as the nation's third-largest manufacturing business, behind automobiles and electronics. Japan is the second-largest software consumer, claiming 11% of the 1996 world market, while Western Europe as a whole accounts for 32%.

In 1997, the U.S. reported its seventh consecutive annual trade deficit for computer equipment (including hardware, parts, and peripherals). This deficit increased 19.3% to $27 billion, and is expected to rise to $35.2 billion in 1998, according to the U.S. Office of Computers and Business Equipment. Exports of computer equipment in 1997 totaled $41.4 billion. Europe accounted for the largest share, purchasing 38%, or $15.6 billion worth; Asia was the second-largest market, with a 30% share valued at $12.4 billion; and the Latin American market continued its meteoric rise, jumping 25% to $6.5 billion, or 16% of total U.S. exports. Domestic imports rose 13.5% to $68.4 billion in 1997. Asia as a whole accounted for 80%, or $54.4 billion worth, with the most successful individual Asian countries ranked as Japan, Singapore, Taiwan, and

Malaysia. The only non-Asian country in the top-five was Mexico, which, with $4.4 billion in sales to the U.S., ranked as the fourth-largest vendor.

Japan

After years of steady growth, Japan's computer industry underwent a decline in 1997. According to the Japan Electronic Industry Development Association, Japanese manufacturers experienced an overall drop of one percent in total sales volume, while gaining a 4.5% in value. Unit sales in Japan rose three percent with an increase in value of one percent. Overseas sales dropped 22% in volume, although value increased 17%.

Causes for the sales decline include: a consumption tax increase from three to five percent; a lack of consumer confidence in the economy in light of the Asian currency and Japanese bank loan crises; a drop in demand from smaller companies; a delay in the release of Microsoft's Windows 98 program; a lack in demand for home PCs, since the Japanese public has yet to recognize the recreational uses for the Internet; and a rise in domestic PC prices, which, while increasing the value of sales, made many consumers less inclined to make a purchase. In response to these factors, manufacturers are lowering prices; copying Dell Computer Corporation's direct sales strategy; and offering training, support, and software upgrade programs before and after computer purchases.

Encryption

Tight restrictions on the export of U.S. encryption software—technology that encodes computer data for security purposes—have been imposed, not by foreign countries, but by the U.S. government. In its battle to curtail international crime and terrorism, the federal government has instituted stringent controls on U.S. companies. In September 1997, it introduced a measure disallowing U.S. companies from designing or selling encryption products, even domestically, without supplying law enforcement agencies access to their decoding "key" and a back door into the system. The most secure encryption available, 128-bit, was excluded from export without the acquisition of a waiver, often a costly and time-consuming process. Opposition criticized the measures, pointing out that: criminals and terrorists can easily obtain 128-bit en-

cryption from non-U.S. companies, American firms operating internationally are forced to purchase foreign-made encryption for their overseas offices and subsidiaries, and foreign manufacturers will quickly step up to fill the market gap created by America's withdrawal from it. As reported in *Computerworld*, the Economic Strategy Institute predicts that over the next five years, domestic software companies whose products incorporate encryption could lose between $1.2 billion and $3.3 billion in sales, while U.S. encryption vendors could lose nearly $9 billion. The restrictions were loosened somewhat in early July 1998 to allow the export of encryption software of any bit-length without a license—but only to banks, securities firms, brokers, and credit card companies in the 45 nations that have acceptable anti-money-laundering laws.

Research and Technology

Technological innovation during the past few decades has progressed at a breathtaking pace, a pace that is expected to increase in the foreseeable future. To succeed in this swiftly changing industry, start-ups must quickly establish themselves by penetrating or creating a niche market. Industry leaders have more resources to invest in research and development (R&D), and even they must spend more and more to remain profitable. Microsoft's 1998 R&D budget was $2.6 billion, and chairman Bill Gates anticipates that this amount is likely to be doubled in upcoming years. In 1998, Intel suddenly found itself priced out of the growing sub-$1,000 PC market, and plans to earmark nearly one-quarter of its $8 billion R&D budget to its development in this area.

To assist companies with the ever-growing demand for increased R&D financing, the federal government has begun to collaborate with manufacturers and academic institutions in a mutually beneficial arrangement. The U.S. Department of Energy has established the Accelerated Strategic Computing Initiative to achieve a four-fold improvement in computer system performance by the year 2005. The government benefits by having an outlet for its technology in the post-Cold War era; universities benefit from the relatively enormous commercial R&D budgets; and the manufacturers benefit by gaining access to the industry's leading minds in an arrangement that can be less expensive than the funding for their own R&D departments.

The scope of computers is virtually boundless. Companies are hurriedly improving on existing technologies, striving to increase the speed of microprocessors, shrink chips and hardware, and improve the capabilities of applications and storage. Meanwhile, discoveries for new uses and capabilities boggle the imagination. Voice-activated systems, self-driving cars, and telemedicine are examples of innovations that are currently under development. In the summer of 1998, researchers at Stanford University and at the Massachusetts Institute of Technology revealed success in the development of computers capable of sensing the frustration level of its user and responding by rewording error messages and initiating dialogues. Scientists and other visionaries are proving that computers have the power to turn the imagined into reality.

Further Reading

1998-99 Occupational Outlook Handbook. Bureau of Labor Statistics: January 15, 1998. Available from http://www.bls.gov/ocohome.htm.

About Comdisco, July 1998. Available from http://www.comdisco.com/about/.

AOL Profile, July 1998. Available from http://www.aol.com/corp/profile/.

Berners-Lee, Tim. "The Founder's Message." *Forbes ASAP.* December 1, 1997.

Buckler, Grant. "Notebooks Moving Steadily into Desktop Space." *Computing Canada.* June 15, 1998.

Burrows, Peter, with Gary McWilliams, and Robert D. Hof. "Cheap PCs." *Business Week.* March 23, 1998.

Choy, Jon. "Japan's Personal Computer Market in Flux." *JEI Report.* February 20, 1998.

"Electronic Marketplace Sales Will Total $102.04 Billion in 2002, According to Simba." *Electronic Advertising & Marketplace Report.* 9 June 1998.

"Financial Highlights." *IBM 1997 Annual Report.* July 1998. Available from http://www.ibm.com/cgi-bin/ar/go.cgi.

"Financial Highlights." *Sun Microsystems 1997 Annual Report.* July 1998. Available from http://www.seast2.usec.sun.com/corporateoverview/ InvestorRelations/AnnualReport/1997/fihi.html.

Gates, Bill, with Nathan Myhrvold, and Peter Rinearson. *The Road Ahead.* New York: Penguin Books, 1996.

"Gates Says Microsoft R&D Spending Will Double Soon." *Computergram International.* March 18, 1998.

Green, Heather, and Linda Himelstein, with Paul C. Judge. "Portal Combat Comes to the Net." *Business Week.* March 2, 1998.

Hafner, Katie, and Matthew Lyon. *Where Wizards Stay up Late: The Origins of the Internet.* New York: Simon & Schuster, 1996.

Hof, Robert D., with Gary McWilliams, and Gabrielle Saveri. "The 'Click Here' Economy." *Business Week.* June 22, 1998.

Holstein, William J. "Just Because He's Paranoid." *U.S. News and World Report.* April 6, 1998.

Hunt, Kimberly N., and AnnaMarie L. Sheldon, eds. *Notable Corporate Chronologies.* 2nd ed. Detroit: Gale Research, 1999.

"Intel Revenue Hits $25B." *Computerworld.* January 19, 1998.

Long, Larry, and Nancy Long. *Computers.* 5th ed. Upper Saddle River, NJ: Prentice-Hall, 1998.

Mandel, Michael J., with Peter Coy, and Paul C. Judge. "Zap! How the Year 2000 Bug Will Hurt the Economy." *Business Week.* March 2, 1998.

Manes, Stephen, and Paul Andrews. *Gates: How Microsoft's Mogul Reinvented an Industry—and Made Himself the Richest Man in America.* New York: Doubleday, 1993.

McHugh, Josh. "Annual Report on American Industry." *Forbes.* January 12, 1998.

Mitchell, Russ, with Marianne Lavelle, William J. Cook, and Susan Gregory Thomas. "Don't Cry for Me, Janet Reno." *U.S. News and World Report.* June 1, 1998.

"NEC Financial Results for Fiscal 1998—Year to March 31, 1998." *EDGE: Work-Group Computing Report.* June 1, 1998.

Oracle at a Glance, July 1998. Available from http://www.oracle.com/corporate/pressroom/html/textci.html.

"The PC Squeeze: Falling Prices Are Shaking up the Computer Industry." *Maclean's.* May 11, 1998.

Radding, Alan. "Encryption and You." *Computerworld.* June 29, 1998.

Reinhardt, Andy. "Log on, Link up, Save Big." *Business Week.* June 22, 1998.

Scally, Robert. "PC, Video Game Software Sales Hit Record High in 1997." *Discount Store News.* March 9, 1998.

Shein, Esther. "Laptops Force Trade-offs; Increased Travel and Remote Access Change TCO Formula." *PC Week.* March 30, 1998.

Spencer, Donald D. *Great Men and Women of Computing.* Ormand Beach, FL: Camelot Publishing, 1996.

Standard & Poor's Industry Surveys. New York: Standard & Poor's, 1998.

Story of IBM, July 1998. Available from http://www.ibm.com/IBM/history/story/.

U.S. Industry Trends and Reports, The Office of Computers and Business Equipment. July 1998. Available from http://infoserv2.ita.doc.gov/ocbe/USIndust.nsf/.

Watson, Thomas J., Jr., and Peter Petre. *Father, Son, and Co.: My Life at IBM and Beyond.* New York: Bantam Books, 1990.

Weinberg, Neil. "Does Not Compute." *Forbes.* March 9, 1998.

—Deborah J. Untener

INDUSTRY STATISTICS & PERFORMANCE INDICATORS

This chapter presents statistical information on the Computers & Software industry. This view of the industry is through the lens of federal statistics. All the data shown are drawn from government sources, including the 100 percent surveys of the Economic Census and the partial surveys of manufacturing and other industries conducted annually by the U.S. Department of Commerce. Tables include general statistics, indices of change, and selected ratios.

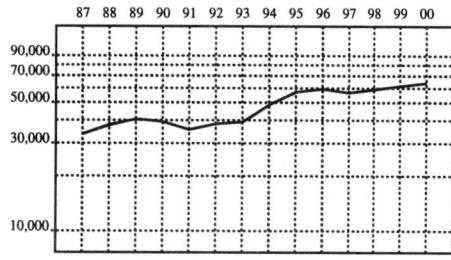

Revenues ($ millions)

SIC 3571 ELECTRONIC COMPUTERS: GENERAL STATISTICS

Year	Estab-lish-ments	Employment Total (000)	Production Workers (000)	Hours (mil.)	Compensation Payroll ($ mil.)	Wages ($/hr)	Production ($ mil.) Cost of Materials	Value of Shipments	Capital Inves.
1987	974	151.9	54.7	105.8	4,953.0	10.64	15,222.9	33,626.5	1,223.3
1988	983	150.6	54.7	109.2	5,513.9	11.09	18,090.6	37,683.3	1,304.0
1989	829	143.7	49.7	100.3	5,454.8	12.05	20,307.8	40,550.7	1,304.5
1990	783	126.0	44.0	90.0	5,264.5	12.45	19,355.7	39,293.6	1,222.3
1991	766	126.0	38.1	78.7	5,343.7	12.80	19,078.4	35,572.9	1,153.5
1992	834	110.8	31.2	65.5	4,855.9	12.51	21,388.9	38,205.9	1,242.4
1993	747	99.5	28.8	60.2	4,514.7	13.49	23,498.6	39,176.8	1,042.9
1994	657	109.4	30.4	62.7	5,073.9	13.54	27,046.1	48,546.9	932.7
1995	539	108.7	35.1	71.3	4,846.4	13.12	35,684.2	57,054.0	907.2
1996	554[1]	101.8	31.0	62.9	4,499.6	12.68	35,086.3	59,413.6	845.9
1997	507[1]	89.2[1]	23.1[1]	49.3[1]	4,585.5[1]	13.87[1]	33,411.3[1]	56,577.2[1]	835.1[1]
1998	460[1]	83.0[1]	20.1[1]	43.6[1]	4,504.4[1]	14.13[1]	34,878.5[1]	59,061.7[1]	783.7[1]
1999	413[1]	76.9[1]	17.1[1]	37.8[1]	4,423.2[1]	14.38[1]	36,345.7[1]	61,546.2[1]	732.3[1]
2000	366[1]	70.8[1]	14.0[1]	32.1[1]	4,342.0[1]	14.64[1]	37,812.9[1]	64,030.7[1]	680.9[1]

Source: 1987 and 1992 Economic Census; *Annual Survey of Manufactures*, 88-91, 93-96. Establishment counts for non-Census years are from *County Business Patterns*. Extracted from *Manufacturing USA*, 6th Edition, Gale, 1998. Note: 1. Projections by the editors.

SIC 3571 ELECTRONIC COMPUTERS: INDICES OF CHANGE

Year	Estab-lish-ments	Employment Total (000)	Production Workers (000)	Hours (mil.)	Compensation Payroll ($ mil.)	Wages ($/hr)	Production ($ mil.) Cost of Materials	Value of Shipments	Capital Inves.
1987	117	137	175	162	102	85	71	88	98
1988	118	136	175	167	114	89	85	99	105
1989	99	130	159	153	112	96	95	106	105
1990	94	114	141	137	108	100	90	103	98
1991	92	114	122	120	110	102	89	93	93
1992	100	100	100	100	100	100	100	100	100
1993	90	90	92	92	93	108	110	103	84
1994	79	99	97	96	104	108	126	127	75
1995	65	98	112	109	100	105	167	149	73
1996	66[1]	92	99	96	93	101	164	156	68
1997	61[1]	80[1]	74[1]	75[1]	94[1]	111[1]	156[1]	148[1]	67[1]
1998	55[1]	75[1]	64[1]	66[1]	93[1]	113[1]	163[1]	155[1]	63[1]
1999	49[1]	69[1]	55[1]	58[1]	91[1]	115[1]	170[1]	161[1]	59[1]
2000	44[1]	64[1]	45[1]	49[1]	89[1]	117[1]	177[1]	168[1]	55[1]

Source: Same as General Statistics. Values reflect change from the base year, 1992. Values above 100 mean greater than 1992, values below 100 mean less than 1992, and a value of 100 in the 1982-91 or 1993-2000 period means same as 1992. Note: 1. Projections by the editors.

SIC 3571 ELECTRONIC COMPUTERS: SELECTED RATIOS

| For
1996 | Average of All
Manufacturing | Analyzed
Industry | Index |
|---|---|---|---|
| Employees per Establishment | 49 | 184 | 377 |
| Payroll per Establishment | 1,574,035 | 8,117,544 | 516 |
| Payroll per Employee | 32,350 | 44,200 | 137 |
| Production Workers per Establishment | 34 | 56 | 164 |
| Wages per Establishment | 890,687 | 1,438,867 | 162 |
| Wages per Production Worker | 26,064 | 25,728 | 99 |
| Hours per Production Worker | 2,055 | 2,029 | 99 |
| Wages per Hour | 12.68 | 12.68 | 100 |
| Value Added per Establishment | 4,932,584 | 41,769,020 | 847 |
| Value Added per Employee | 101,376 | 227,434 | 224 |
| Value Added per Production Worker | 144,340 | 746,865 | 517 |
| Cost per Establishment | 5,569,059 | 63,297,760 | 1,137 |
| Cost per Employee | 114,457 | 344,659 | 301 |
| Cost per Production Worker | 162,965 | 1,131,816 | 695 |
| Shipments per Establishment | 10,422,474 | 107,185,648 | 1,028 |
| Shipments per Employee | 214,207 | 583,631 | 272 |
| Shipments per Production Worker | 304,989 | 1,916,568 | 628 |
| Investment per Establishment | 394,953 | 1,526,054 | 386 |
| Investment per Employee | 8,117 | 8,309 | 102 |
| Investment per Production Worker | 11,557 | 27,287 | 236 |

Source: Same as General Statistics. The 'Average of All Manufacturing' column represents the average of all manufacturing industries reported for the most recent complete year available. The Index shows the relationship between the Average and the Analyzed Industry. For example, 100 means that they are equal; 500 that the Analyzed Industry is five times the average; 50 means that the Analyzed Industry is half the national average. The abbreviation 'na' is used to show that data are 'not available'.

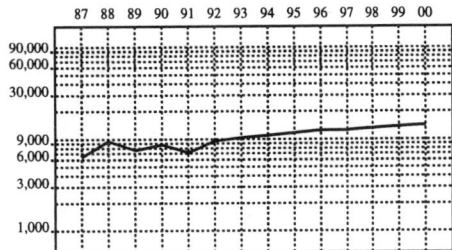

Revenues ($ millions)

SIC 3572 COMPUTER STORAGE DEVICES: GENERAL STATISTICS

Year	Estab-lish-ments	Employment Total (000)	Production Workers (000)	Hours (mil.)	Compensation Payroll ($ mil.)	Wages ($/hr)	Production ($ mil.) Cost of Materials	Value of Shipments	Capital Inves.
1987	106	43.3	15.0	31.0	1,442.6	10.58	3,252.8	6,394.8	347.0
1988	125	56.1	20.2	42.6	1,975.9	10.44	5,470.7	9,543.9	404.4
1989	114	44.7	16.6	34.7	1,684.3	11.31	4,087.8	7,612.5	432.4
1990	118	41.7	15.4	32.1	1,490.1	11.12	4,368.9	8,751.1	426.5
1991	126	36.0	12.2	27.1	1,444.1	13.01	3,674.2	7,188.6	392.8
1992	179	40.8	15.2	31.3	1,795.4	13.64	4,991.7	9,544.3	455.6
1993	178	43.8	17.6	34.9	1,796.0	13.72	6,110.0	10,395.3	557.7
1994	164	39.8	19.7	44.0	1,650.5	14.83	6,759.4	11,004.5	521.9
1995	175	37.5	17.0	38.3	1,779.4	16.05	7,110.3	11,725.6	614.4
1996	191[1]	38.6	17.2	37.7	1,871.6	15.72	7,349.0	12,511.1	956.3
1997	201[1]	36.0[1]	17.4[1]	38.3[1]	1,812.5[1]	16.76[1]	7,412.6[1]	12,619.4[1]	772.8[1]
1998	211[1]	34.9[1]	17.5[1]	38.9[1]	1,834.2[1]	17.44[1]	7,749.3[1]	13,192.5[1]	820.4[1]
1999	220[1]	33.8[1]	17.6[1]	39.4[1]	1,856.0[1]	18.11[1]	8,085.9[1]	13,765.7[1]	868.1[1]
2000	230[1]	32.7[1]	17.8[1]	40.0[1]	1,877.7[1]	18.79[1]	8,422.6[1]	14,338.8[1]	915.7[1]

Source: 1987 and 1992 Economic Census; *Annual Survey of Manufactures,* 88-91, 93-96. Establishment counts for non-Census years are from *County Business Patterns.* Extracted from *Manufacturing USA*, 6th Edition, Gale, 1998. Note: 1. Projections by the editors.

SIC 3572 COMPUTER STORAGE DEVICES: INDICES OF CHANGE

Year	Estab-lish-ments	Employment Total (000)	Production Workers (000)	Hours (mil.)	Compensation Payroll ($ mil.)	Wages ($/hr)	Production ($ mil.) Cost of Materials	Value of Shipments	Capital Inves.
1987	59	106	99	99	80	78	65	67	76
1988	70	138	133	136	110	77	110	100	89
1989	64	110	109	111	94	83	82	80	95
1990	66	102	101	103	83	82	88	92	94
1991	70	88	80	87	80	95	74	75	86
1992	100	100	100	100	100	100	100	100	100
1993	99	107	116	112	100	101	122	109	122
1994	92	98	130	141	92	109	135	115	115
1995	98	92	112	122	99	118	142	123	135
1996	107[1]	95	113	120	104	115	147	131	210
1997	112[1]	88[1]	114[1]	123[1]	101[1]	123[1]	148[1]	132[1]	170[1]
1998	118[1]	86[1]	115[1]	124[1]	102[1]	128[1]	155[1]	138[1]	180[1]
1999	123[1]	83[1]	116[1]	126[1]	103[1]	133[1]	162[1]	144[1]	191[1]
2000	129[1]	80[1]	117[1]	128[1]	105[1]	138[1]	169[1]	150[1]	201[1]

Source: Same as General Statistics. Values reflect change from the base year, 1992. Values above 100 mean greater than 1992, values below 100 mean less than 1992, and a value of 100 in the 1982-91 or 1993-2000 period means same as 1992. Note: 1. Projections by the editors.

SIC 3572 COMPUTER STORAGE DEVICES: SELECTED RATIOS

For 1996	Average of All Manufacturing	Analyzed Industry	Index
Employees per Establishment	49	202	415
Payroll per Establishment	1,574,035	9,784,723	622
Payroll per Employee	32,350	48,487	150
Production Workers per Establishment	34	90	263
Wages per Establishment	890,687	3,098,342	348
Wages per Production Worker	26,064	34,456	132
Hours per Production Worker	2,055	2,192	107
Wages per Hour	12.68	15.72	124
Value Added per Establishment	4,932,584	26,326,634	534
Value Added per Employee	101,376	130,459	129
Value Added per Production Worker	144,340	292,773	203
Cost per Establishment	5,569,059	38,420,563	690
Cost per Employee	114,457	190,389	166
Cost per Production Worker	162,965	427,267	262
Shipments per Establishment	10,422,474	65,408,016	628
Shipments per Employee	214,207	324,122	151
Shipments per Production Worker	304,989	727,390	238
Investment per Establishment	394,953	4,999,535	1,266
Investment per Employee	8,117	24,775	305
Investment per Production Worker	11,557	55,599	481

Source: Same as General Statistics. The 'Average of All Manufacturing' column represents the average of all manufacturing industries reported for the most recent complete year available. The Index shows the relationship between the Average and the Analyzed Industry. For example, 100 means that they are equal; 500 that the Analyzed Industry is five times the average; 50 means that the Analyzed Industry is half the national average. The abbreviation 'na' is used to show that data are 'not available'.

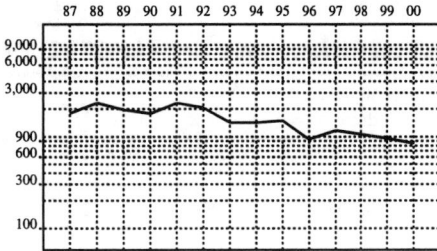

Revenues ($ millions)

SIC 3575 COMPUTER TERMINALS: GENERAL STATISTICS

Year	Estab-lish-ments	Employment Total (000)	Production Workers (000)	Production Hours (mil.)	Compensation Payroll ($ mil.)	Compensation Wages ($/hr)	Production ($ mil.) Cost of Materials	Production ($ mil.) Value of Shipments	Production ($ mil.) Capital Inves.
1987	121	15.0	5.5	10.7	441.7	11.60	742.0	1,799.0	58.0
1988	129	15.8	5.9	11.2	451.5	10.96	1,159.2	2,332.6	42.7
1989	141	15.8	6.3	12.9	450.5	11.47	1,219.1	1,969.2	69.3
1990	138	13.5	4.8	9.8	412.9	11.96	1,035.5	1,790.0	45.4
1991	154	11.7	5.2	10.3	386.1	11.99	1,429.5	2,326.5	42.4
1992	190	9.3	4.2	8.0	344.1	12.84	1,288.2	2,070.7	44.4
1993	177	7.9	3.5	6.8	307.2	12.25	807.8	1,435.0	29.3
1994	169	6.6	2.7	5.2	260.4	12.85	894.7	1,427.5	41.7
1995	157	7.3	3.2	6.0	284.4	13.43	1,001.5	1,498.7	54.0
1996	185[1]	5.8	2.7	5.5	221.4	12.51	590.8	938.6	26.0
1997	192[1]	4.0[1]	2.2[1]	4.2[1]	207.3[1]	13.32[1]	737.6[1]	1,171.8[1]	32.2[1]
1998	198[1]	2.7[1]	1.8[1]	3.4[1]	180.2[1]	13.53[1]	670.4[1]	1,065.0[1]	29.8[1]
1999	205[1]	1.4[1]	1.4[1]	2.6[1]	153.2[1]	13.74[1]	603.2[1]	958.3[1]	27.4[1]
2000	211[1]	0.2[1]	0.9[1]	1.8[1]	126.2[1]	13.94[1]	536.0[1]	851.6[1]	25.1[1]

Source: 1987 and 1992 Economic Census; *Annual Survey of Manufactures,* 88-91, 93-96. Establishment counts for non-Census years are from *County Business Patterns.* Extracted from *Manufacturing USA,* 6th Edition, Gale, 1998. Note: 1. Projections by the editors.

SIC 3575 COMPUTER TERMINALS: INDICES OF CHANGE

Year	Estab-lish-ments	Employment Total (000)	Production Workers (000)	Production Hours (mil.)	Compensation Payroll ($ mil.)	Compensation Wages ($/hr)	Production ($ mil.) Cost of Materials	Production ($ mil.) Value of Shipments	Production ($ mil.) Capital Inves.
1987	64	161	131	134	128	90	58	87	131
1988	68	170	140	140	131	85	90	113	96
1989	74	170	150	161	131	89	95	95	156
1990	73	145	114	123	120	93	80	86	102
1991	81	126	124	129	112	93	111	112	95
1992	100	100	100	100	100	100	100	100	100
1993	93	85	83	85	89	95	63	69	66
1994	89	71	64	65	76	100	69	69	94
1995	83	78	76	75	83	105	78	72	122
1996	97[1]	62	64	69	64	97	46	45	59
1997	101[1]	43[1]	52[1]	53[1]	60[1]	104[1]	57[1]	57[1]	73[1]
1998	104[1]	29[1]	42[1]	43[1]	52[1]	105[1]	52[1]	51[1]	67[1]
1999	108[1]	15[1]	32[1]	32[1]	45[1]	107[1]	47[1]	46[1]	62[1]
2000	111[1]	2[1]	23[1]	22[1]	37[1]	109[1]	42[1]	41[1]	56[1]

Source: Same as General Statistics. Values reflect change from the base year, 1992. Values above 100 mean greater than 1992, values below 100 mean less than 1992, and a value of 100 in the 1982-91 or 1993-2000 period means same as 1992. Note: 1. Projections by the editors.

SIC 3575 COMPUTER TERMINALS: SELECTED RATIOS

For 1996	Average of All Manufacturing	Analyzed Industry	Index
Employees per Establishment	49	31	64
Payroll per Establishment	1,574,035	1,195,321	76
Payroll per Employee	32,350	38,172	118
Production Workers per Establishment	34	15	43
Wages per Establishment	890,687	371,473	42
Wages per Production Worker	26,064	25,483	98
Hours per Production Worker	2,055	2,037	99
Wages per Hour	12.68	12.51	99
Value Added per Establishment	4,932,584	1,902,579	39
Value Added per Employee	101,376	60,759	60
Value Added per Production Worker	144,340	130,519	90
Cost per Establishment	5,569,059	3,189,682	57
Cost per Employee	114,457	101,862	89
Cost per Production Worker	162,965	218,815	134
Shipments per Establishment	10,422,474	5,067,427	49
Shipments per Employee	214,207	161,828	76
Shipments per Production Worker	304,989	347,630	114
Investment per Establishment	394,953	140,372	36
Investment per Employee	8,117	4,483	55
Investment per Production Worker	11,557	9,630	83

Source: Same as General Statistics. The 'Average of All Manufacturing' column represents the average of all manufacturing industries reported for the most recent complete year available. The Index shows the relationship between the Average and the Analyzed Industry. For example, 100 means that they are equal; 500 that the Analyzed Industry is five times the average; 50 means that the Analyzed Industry is half the national average. The abbreviation 'na' is used to show that data are 'not available'.

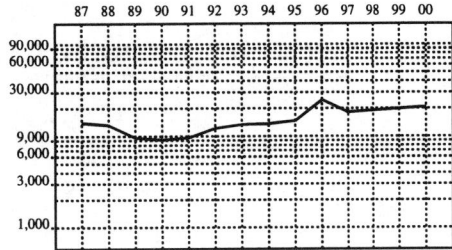

Revenues ($ millions)

SIC 3577 COMPUTER PERIPHERAL EQUIPMENT, NEC: GENERAL STATISTICS

Year	Estab-lish-ments	Employment			Compensation		Production ($ mil.)		
		Total (000)	Production		Payroll ($ mil.)	Wages ($/hr)	Cost of Materials	Value of Shipments	Capital Inves.
			Workers (000)	Hours (mil.)					
1987	549	76.2	26.2	58.7	2,625.4	9.87	7,107.3	13,965.5	391.2
1988	663	67.8	24.0	46.8	2,330.6	11.00	7,761.3	13,213.3	461.5
1989	616	77.2	24.2	46.8	1,992.2	11.22	4,909.0	9,625.2	341.6
1990	597	78.1	25.4	49.9	1,857.5	10.75	5,239.3	9,146.3	299.1
1991	651	53.5	20.7	42.3	1,963.9		5,779.9	9,614.7	223.8
1992	772	59.3	23.5	48.4	2,175.7	11.00	7,166.4	12,156.5	393.0
1993	786	59.3	24.0	49.5	2,260.4	11.31	8,184.2	13,366.6	415.1
1994	787	57.6	23.1	48.4	2,383.8	12.91	8,293.2	13,665.9	410.8
1995	789	60.3	24.6	50.7	2,494.7	12.32	9,141.0	14,718.5	360.2
1996	844[1]	75.0	32.5	65.3	3,511.5	16.60	15,242.1	24,729.1	855.5
1997	875[1]	59.4[1]	26.6[1]	54.0[1]	2,776.3[1]		11,205.9[1]	18,180.7[1]	559.6[1]
1998	905[1]	58.1[1]	26.9[1]	54.6[1]	2,852.1[1]		11,739.4[1]	19,046.2[1]	585.9[1]
1999	936[1]	56.8[1]	27.3[1]	55.2[1]	2,927.8[1]		12,272.9[1]	19,911.8[1]	612.1[1]
2000	967[1]	55.5[1]	27.6[1]	55.8[1]	3,003.6[1]		12,806.4[1]	20,777.3[1]	638.4[1]

Source: 1987 and 1992 Economic Census; *Annual Survey of Manufactures*, 88-91, 93-96. Establishment counts for non-Census years are from *County Business Patterns*. Extracted from *Manufacturing USA*, 6th Edition, Gale, 1998. Note: 1. Projections by the editors.

SIC 3577 COMPUTER PERIPHERAL EQUIPMENT, NEC: INDICES OF CHANGE

Year	Estab-lish-ments	Employment			Compensation		Production ($ mil.)		
		Total (000)	Production		Payroll ($ mil.)	Wages ($/hr)	Cost of Materials	Value of Shipments	Capital Inves.
			Workers (000)	Hours (mil.)					
1987	71	128	111	121	121	90	99	115	100
1988	86	114	102	97	107	100	108	109	117
1989	80	130	103	97	92	102	69	79	87
1990	77	132	108	103	85	98	73	75	76
1991	84	90	88	87	90		81	79	57
1992	100	100	100	100	100	100	100	100	100
1993	102	100	102	102	104	103	114	110	106
1994	102	97	98	100	110	117	116	112	105
1995	102	102	105	105	115	112	128	121	92
1996	109[1]	126	138	135	161	151	213	203	218
1997	113[1]	100[1]	113[1]	112[1]	128[1]		156[1]	150[1]	142[1]
1998	117[1]	98[1]	115[1]	113[1]	131[1]		164[1]	157[1]	149[1]
1999	121[1]	96[1]	116[1]	114[1]	135[1]		171[1]	164[1]	156[1]
2000	125[1]	94[1]	117[1]	115[1]	138[1]		179[1]	171[1]	162[1]

Source: Same as General Statistics. Values reflect change from the base year, 1992. Values above 100 mean greater than 1992, values below 100 mean less than 1992, and a value of 100 in the 1982-91 or 1993-2000 period means same as 1992. Note: 1. Projections by the editors.

SIC 3577 COMPUTER PERIPHERAL EQUIPMENT, NEC: SELECTED RATIOS

For 1996	Average of All Manufacturing	Analyzed Industry	Index
Employees per Establishment	49	89	183
Payroll per Establishment	1,574,035	4,160,956	264
Payroll per Employee	32,350	46,820	145
Production Workers per Establishment	34	39	113
Wages per Establishment	890,687	1,284,463	144
Wages per Production Worker	26,064	33,353	128
Hours per Production Worker	2,055	2,009	98
Wages per Hour	12.68	16.60	131
Value Added per Establishment	4,932,584	11,182,739	227
Value Added per Employee	101,376	125,831	124
Value Added per Production Worker	144,340	290,378	201
Cost per Establishment	5,569,059	18,061,143	324
Cost per Employee	114,457	203,228	178
Cost per Production Worker	162,965	468,988	288
Shipments per Establishment	10,422,474	29,302,775	281
Shipments per Employee	214,207	329,721	154
Shipments per Production Worker	304,989	760,895	249
Investment per Establishment	394,953	1,013,726	257
Investment per Employee	8,117	11,407	141
Investment per Production Worker	11,557	26,323	228

Source: Same as General Statistics. The 'Average of All Manufacturing' column represents the average of all manufacturing industries reported for the most recent complete year available. The Index shows the relationship between the Average and the Analyzed Industry. For example, 100 means that they are equal; 500 that the Analyzed Industry is five times the average; 50 means that the Analyzed Industry is half the national average. The abbreviation 'na' is used to show that data are 'not available'.

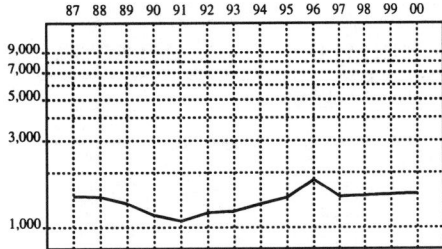

Revenues ($ millions)

SIC 3578 CALCULATING AND ACCOUNTING MACHINES: GENERAL STATISTICS

Year	Estab-lish-ments	Employment			Compensation		Production ($ mil.)		
		Total (000)	Production		Payroll ($ mil.)	Wages ($/hr)	Cost of Materials	Value of Shipments	Capital Inves.
			Workers (000)	Hours (mil.)					
1987	98	12.8	6.0	12.4	380.7	11.51	560.6	1,486.8	40.2
1988	94	12.3	5.2	10.4	348.4	9.25	568.5	1,469.1	50.7
1989	87	11.8	3.8	7.7	332.3	9.99	535.6	1,352.1	46.0
1990	84	9.4	4.0	8.1	214.1	10.44	544.7	1,170.2	101.3
1991	84	7.6	3.6	7.3	211.9	9.44	482.4	1,086.6	15.7
1992	95	6.5	2.7	5.3	191.2	10.66	443.6	1,206.5	25.5
1993	100	6.6	3.1	6.0	198.4	11.80	458.7	1,229.4	29.9
1994	95	6.6	2.9	6.3	226.5	10.52	592.8	1,346.8	34.8
1995	97	7.8	3.9	8.2	294.9	9.72	649.8	1,462.5	67.1
1996	96[1]	8.1	3.9	8.3	300.4	10.16	945.7	1,835.2	113.8
1997	96[1]	5.3[1]	2.7[1]	5.7[1]	213.4[1]	10.32[1]	760.9[1]	1,476.5[1]	69.7[1]
1998	97[1]	4.6[1]	2.5[1]	5.3[1]	203.1[1]	10.31[1]	771.4[1]	1,496.9[1]	72.9[1]
1999	97[1]	4.0[1]	2.3[1]	4.9[1]	192.9[1]	10.31[1]	781.9[1]	1,517.3[1]	76.0[1]
2000	98[1]	3.3[1]	2.1[1]	4.5[1]	182.6[1]	10.30[1]	792.4[1]	1,537.6[1]	79.1[1]

Source: 1987 and 1992 Economic Census; *Annual Survey of Manufactures*, 88-91, 93-96. Establishment counts for non-Census years are from *County Business Patterns*. Extracted from *Manufacturing USA*, 6th Edition, Gale, 1998. Note: 1. Projections by the editors.

SIC 3578 CALCULATING AND ACCOUNTING MACHINES: INDICES OF CHANGE

Year	Estab-lish-ments	Employment			Compensation		Production ($ mil.)		
		Total (000)	Production		Payroll ($ mil.)	Wages ($/hr)	Cost of Materials	Value of Shipments	Capital Inves.
			Workers (000)	Hours (mil.)					
1987	103	197	222	234	199	108	126	123	158
1988	99	189	193	196	182	87	128	122	199
1989	92	182	141	145	174	94	121	112	180
1990	88	145	148	153	112	98	123	97	397
1991	88	117	133	138	111	89	109	90	62
1992	100	100	100	100	100	100	100	100	100
1993	105	102	115	113	104	111	103	102	117
1994	100	102	107	119	118	99	134	112	136
1995	102	120	144	155	154	91	146	121	263
1996	101[1]	125	144	157	157	95	213	152	446
1997	101[1]	82[1]	100[1]	108[1]	112[1]	97[1]	172[1]	122[1]	273[1]
1998	102[1]	71[1]	92[1]	101[1]	106[1]	97[1]	174[1]	124[1]	286[1]
1999	103[1]	61[1]	84[1]	93[1]	101[1]	97[1]	176[1]	126[1]	298[1]
2000	103[1]	51[1]	76[1]	85[1]	96[1]	97[1]	179[1]	127[1]	310[1]

Source: Same as General Statistics. Values reflect change from the base year, 1992. Values above 100 mean greater than 1992, values below 100 mean less than 1992, and a value of 100 in the 1982-91 or 1993-2000 period means same as 1992. Note: 1. Projections by the editors.

SIC 3578 CALCULATING AND ACCOUNTING MACHINES: SELECTED RATIOS

For 1996	Average of All Manufacturing	Analyzed Industry	Index
Employees per Establishment	49	85	174
Payroll per Establishment	1,574,035	3,140,070	199
Payroll per Employee	32,350	37,086	115
Production Workers per Establishment	34	41	119
Wages per Establishment	890,687	881,477	99
Wages per Production Worker	26,064	21,623	83
Hours per Production Worker	2,055	2,128	104
Wages per Hour	12.68	10.16	80
Value Added per Establishment	4,932,584	9,869,686	200
Value Added per Employee	101,376	116,568	115
Value Added per Production Worker	144,340	242,103	168
Cost per Establishment	5,569,059	9,885,366	178
Cost per Employee	114,457	116,753	102
Cost per Production Worker	162,965	242,487	149
Shipments per Establishment	10,422,474	19,183,275	184
Shipments per Employee	214,207	226,568	106
Shipments per Production Worker	304,989	470,564	154
Investment per Establishment	394,953	1,189,547	301
Investment per Employee	8,117	14,049	173
Investment per Production Worker	11,557	29,179	252

Source: Same as General Statistics. The 'Average of All Manufacturing' column represents the average of all manufacturing industries reported for the most recent complete year available. The Index shows the relationship between the Average and the Analyzed Industry. For example, 100 means that they are equal; 500 that the Analyzed Industry is five times the average; 50 means that the Analyzed Industry is half the national average. The abbreviation 'na' is used to show that data are 'not available'.

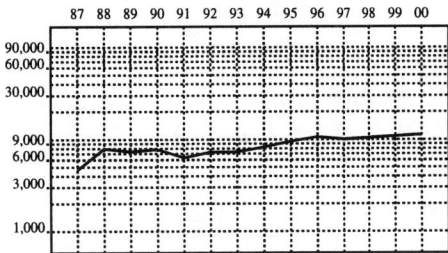

Revenues ($ millions)

SIC 3672 PRINTED CIRCUIT BOARDS: GENERAL STATISTICS

Year	Estab-lish-ments	Employment			Compensation		Production ($ mil.)		
		Total (000)	Production		Payroll ($ mil.)	Wages ($/hr)	Cost of Materials	Value of Shipments	Capital Inves.
			Workers (000)	Hours (mil.)					
1987	1,009	66.6	48.6	100.0	1,378.5	8.36	2,023.8	4,672.6	239.3
1988	871	80.9	53.9	112.1	1,957.1	9.12	3,041.9	7,960.6	336.8
1989	982	72.0	52.4	107.9	2,006.4	9.44	2,776.2	7,354.4	372.8
1990	1,060	69.4	51.0	109.1	2,104.4	9.68	2,886.7	7,844.1	405.1
1991	1,187	69.9	47.1	99.4	1,920.7	9.92	2,678.0	6,352.9	311.1
1992	1,324	75.8	50.8	104.8	2,110.6	10.17	2,972.8	7,311.8	316.8
1993	1,346	73.6	50.5	105.0	2,129.4	10.58	3,151.2	7,377.6	282.8
1994	1,396	75.7	53.1	112.6	2,162.6	10.49	3,376.9	8,262.4	365.9
1995	1,409	82.8	59.6	126.9	2,384.1	10.32	3,944.4	9,577.9	455.3
1996	1,523[1]	88.3	63.9	135.0	2,531.4	10.75	4,231.0	10,701.6	585.4
1997	1,593[1]	83.7[1]	59.2[1]	125.8[1]	2,548.9[1]	11.15[1]	3,979.0[1]	10,064.3[1]	485.4[1]
1998	1,662[1]	85.2[1]	60.3[1]	128.4[1]	2,636.2[1]	11.38[1]	4,146.0[1]	10,486.6[1]	506.9[1]
1999	1,732[1]	86.7[1]	61.4[1]	131.1[1]	2,723.6[1]	11.62[1]	4,313.0[1]	10,908.9[1]	528.4[1]
2000	1,801[1]	88.2[1]	62.5[1]	133.7[1]	2,810.9[1]	11.85[1]	4,479.9[1]	11,331.2[1]	549.9[1]

Source: 1987 and 1992 Economic Census; _Annual Survey of Manufactures_, 88-91, 93-96. Establishment counts for non-Census years are from _County Business Patterns_. Extracted from _Manufacturing USA_, 6th Edition, Gale, 1998. Note: 1. Projections by the editors.

SIC 3672 PRINTED CIRCUIT BOARDS: INDICES OF CHANGE

Year	Estab-lish-ments	Employment			Compensation		Production ($ mil.)		
		Total (000)	Production		Payroll ($ mil.)	Wages ($/hr)	Cost of Materials	Value of Shipments	Capital Inves.
			Workers (000)	Hours (mil.)					
1987	76	88	96	95	65	82	68	64	76
1988	66	107	106	107	93	90	102	109	106
1989	74	95	103	103	95	93	93	101	118
1990	80	92	100	104	100	95	97	107	128
1991	90	92	93	95	91	98	90	87	98
1992	100	100	100	100	100	100	100	100	100
1993	102	97	99	100	101	104	106	101	89
1994	105	100	105	107	102	103	114	113	115
1995	106	109	117	121	113	101	133	131	144
1996	115[1]	116	126	129	120	106	142	146	185
1997	120[1]	110[1]	117[1]	120[1]	121[1]	110[1]	134[1]	138[1]	153[1]
1998	126[1]	112[1]	119[1]	123[1]	125[1]	112[1]	139[1]	143[1]	160[1]
1999	131[1]	114[1]	121[1]	125[1]	129[1]	114[1]	145[1]	149[1]	167[1]
2000	136[1]	116[1]	123[1]	128[1]	133[1]	116[1]	151[1]	155[1]	174[1]

Source: Same as General Statistics. Values reflect change from the base year, 1992. Values above 100 mean greater than 1992, values below 100 mean less than 1992, and a value of 100 in the 1982-91 or 1993-2000 period means same as 1992. Note: 1. Projections by the editors.

SIC 3672 PRINTED CIRCUIT BOARDS: SELECTED RATIOS

For 1996	Average of All Manufacturing	Analyzed Industry	Index
Employees per Establishment	49	58	119
Payroll per Establishment	1,574,035	1,661,841	106
Payroll per Employee	32,350	28,668	89
Production Workers per Establishment	34	42	123
Wages per Establishment	890,687	952,733	107
Wages per Production Worker	26,064	22,711	87
Hours per Production Worker	2,055	2,113	103
Wages per Hour	12.68	10.75	85
Value Added per Establishment	4,932,584	4,309,010	87
Value Added per Employee	101,376	74,334	73
Value Added per Production Worker	144,340	102,718	71
Cost per Establishment	5,569,059	2,777,614	50
Cost per Employee	114,457	47,916	42
Cost per Production Worker	162,965	66,213	41
Shipments per Establishment	10,422,474	7,025,505	67
Shipments per Employee	214,207	121,196	57
Shipments per Production Worker	304,989	167,474	55
Investment per Establishment	394,953	384,310	97
Investment per Employee	8,117	6,630	82
Investment per Production Worker	11,557	9,161	79

Source: Same as General Statistics. The 'Average of All Manufacturing' column represents the average of all manufacturing industries reported for the most recent complete year available. The Index shows the relationship between the Average and the Analyzed Industry. For example, 100 means that they are equal; 500 that the Analyzed Industry is five times the average; 50 means that the Analyzed Industry is half the national average. The abbreviation 'na' is used to show that data are 'not available'.

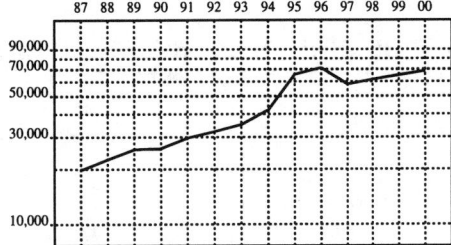

Revenues ($ millions)

SIC 3674 SEMICONDUCTORS AND RELATED DEVICES: GENERAL STATISTICS

Year	Estab-lish-ments	Employment			Compensation		Production ($ mil.)		
		Total (000)	Production		Payroll ($ mil.)	Wages ($/hr)	Cost of Materials	Value of Shipments	Capital Inves.
			Workers (000)	Hours (mil.)					
1987	853	184.6	87.4	175.4	5,494.8	10.57	6,462.5	19,794.9	1,920.8
1988	831	179.4	86.5	170.7	5,899.4	11.38	7,248.8	22,596.6	
1989	837	188.8	90.5	176.0	6,314.1	12.02	7,956.3	25,707.7	3,132.0
1990	858	181.3	87.7	174.9	6,532.4	12.58	8,197.3	25,977.3	3,439.3
1991	901	175.0	86.2	177.4	6,490.8	12.69	9,197.7	29,668.1	2,945.0
1992	921	171.9	84.7	172.2	6,879.8	13.55	9,823.3	32,157.0	3,118.0
1993	930	162.5	82.2	167.2	6,770.4	14.08	8,937.5	35,151.5	3,838.5
1994	940	173.6	89.1	177.5	7,464.2	14.48	10,388.9	42,252.1	5,697.8
1995	938	193.4	99.0	200.6	8,803.1	14.86	14,895.4	65,622.9	9,181.7
1996	964[1]	189.6	96.2	195.7	9,042.2	15.29	15,399.9	71,413.4	11,991.4
1997	979[1]	181.7[1]	92.0[1]	189.0[1]	8,783.7[1]	15.83[1]	12,505.0[1]	57,989.0[1]	
1998	994[1]	182.0[1]	92.5[1]	190.8[1]	9,107.0[1]	16.31[1]	13,262.1[1]	61,500.0[1]	
1999	1,009[1]	182.3[1]	93.0[1]	192.5[1]	9,430.3[1]	16.79[1]	14,019.2[1]	65,010.9[1]	
2000	1,024[1]	182.6[1]	93.5[1]	194.3[1]	9,753.5[1]	17.27[1]	14,776.4[1]	68,521.9[1]	

Source: 1987 and 1992 Economic Census; *Annual Survey of Manufactures,* 88-91, 93-96. Establishment counts for non-Census years are from *County Business Patterns.* Extracted from *Manufacturing USA,* 6th Edition, Gale, 1998. Note: 1. Projections by the editors.

SIC 3674 SEMICONDUCTORS AND RELATED DEVICES: INDICES OF CHANGE

Year	Estab-lish-ments	Employment			Compensation		Production ($ mil.)		
		Total (000)	Production		Payroll ($ mil.)	Wages ($/hr)	Cost of Materials	Value of Shipments	Capital Inves.
			Workers (000)	Hours (mil.)					
1987	93	107	103	102	80	78	66	62	62
1988	90	104	102	99	86	84	74	70	
1989	91	110	107	102	92	89	81	80	100
1990	93	105	104	102	95	93	83	81	110
1991	98	102	102	103	94	94	94	92	94
1992	100	100	100	100	100	100	100	100	100
1993	101	95	97	97	98	104	91	109	123
1994	102	101	105	103	108	107	106	131	183
1995	102	113	117	116	128	110	152	204	294
1996	105[1]	110	114	114	131	113	157	222	385
1997	106[1]	106[1]	109[1]	110[1]	128[1]	117[1]	127[1]	180[1]	
1998	108[1]	106[1]	109[1]	111[1]	132[1]	120[1]	135[1]	191[1]	
1999	110[1]	106[1]	110[1]	112[1]	137[1]	124[1]	143[1]	202[1]	
2000	111[1]	106[1]	110[1]	113[1]	142[1]	127[1]	150[1]	213[1]	

Source: Same as General Statistics. Values reflect change from the base year, 1992. Values above 100 mean greater than 1992, values below 100 mean less than 1992, and a value of 100 in the 1982-91 or 1993-2000 period means same as 1992. Note: 1. Projections by the editors.

SIC 3674 SEMICONDUCTORS AND RELATED DEVICES: SELECTED RATIOS

For 1996	Average of All Manufacturing	Analyzed Industry	Index
Employees per Establishment	49	197	404
Payroll per Establishment	1,574,035	9,378,806	596
Payroll per Employee	32,350	47,691	147
Production Workers per Establishment	34	100	292
Wages per Establishment	890,687	3,103,643	348
Wages per Production Worker	26,064	31,105	119
Hours per Production Worker	2,055	2,034	99
Wages per Hour	12.68	15.29	121
Value Added per Establishment	4,932,584	58,407,554	1,184
Value Added per Employee	101,376	297,001	293
Value Added per Production Worker	144,340	585,357	406
Cost per Establishment	5,569,059	15,973,179	287
Cost per Employee	114,457	81,223	71
Cost per Production Worker	162,965	160,082	98
Shipments per Establishment	10,422,474	74,071,847	711
Shipments per Employee	214,207	376,653	176
Shipments per Production Worker	304,989	742,343	243
Investment per Establishment	394,953	12,437,794	3,149
Investment per Employee	8,117	63,246	779
Investment per Production Worker	11,557	124,651	1,079

Source: Same as General Statistics. The 'Average of All Manufacturing' column represents the average of all manufacturing industries reported for the most recent complete year available. The Index shows the relationship between the Average and the Analyzed Industry. For example, 100 means that they are equal; 500 that the Analyzed Industry is five times the average; 50 means that the Analyzed Industry is half the national average. The abbreviation 'na' is used to show that data are 'not available'.

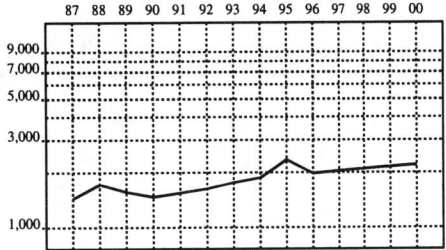

Revenues ($ millions)

SIC 3675 ELECTRONIC CAPACITORS: GENERAL STATISTICS

Year	Estab-lish-ments	Employment			Compensation		Production ($ mil.)		
		Total (000)	Production		Payroll ($ mil.)	Wages ($/hr)	Cost of Materials	Value of Shipments	Capital Inves.
			Workers (000)	Hours (mil.)					
1987	148	21.7	16.4	31.7	392.8	7.86	551.3	1,440.1	78.2
1988	138	24.0	18.1	36.3	465.0	8.17	663.3	1,723.9	95.3
1989	135	24.8	15.7	30.6	408.1	8.10	614.9	1,563.2	55.6
1990	130	22.1	14.4	28.2	398.4	8.37	609.8	1,471.6	52.1
1991	125	18.5	13.5	27.2	417.8	8.82	618.6	1,546.1	57.1
1992	117	17.9	13.4	26.3	415.7	9.43	703.0	1,630.1	64.0
1993	115	18.7	13.7	27.9	438.7	9.37	788.2	1,762.8	63.9
1994	115	18.8	14.2	29.4	474.2	9.99	879.8	1,871.9	78.5
1995	117	21.2	16.8	34.7	514.3	9.38	1,047.6	2,346.0	156.6
1996	117[1]	18.4	14.2	28.3	472.1	9.57	984.6	1,977.9	212.3
1997	116[1]	16.3[1]	11.9[1]	24.8[1]	469.4[1]	10.33[1]	1,016.7[1]	2,042.4[1]	119.1[1]
1998	115[1]	15.4[1]	11.3[1]	23.7[1]	474.1[1]	10.59[1]	1,043.4[1]	2,096.0[1]	122.5[1]
1999	114[1]	14.6[1]	10.7[1]	22.7[1]	478.7[1]	10.86[1]	1,070.0[1]	2,149.5[1]	126.0[1]
2000	112[1]	13.8[1]	10.0[1]	21.6[1]	483.3[1]	11.12[1]	1,096.7[1]	2,203.1[1]	129.5[1]

Source: 1987 and 1992 Economic Census; *Annual Survey of Manufactures*, 88-91, 93-96. Establishment counts for non-Census years are from *County Business Patterns*. Extracted from *Manufacturing USA*, 6th Edition, Gale, 1998. Note: 1. Projections by the editors.

SIC 3675 ELECTRONIC CAPACITORS: INDICES OF CHANGE

Year	Estab-lish-ments	Employment			Compensation		Production ($ mil.)		
		Total (000)	Production		Payroll ($ mil.)	Wages ($/hr)	Cost of Materials	Value of Shipments	Capital Inves.
			Workers (000)	Hours (mil.)					
1987	126	121	122	121	94	83	78	88	122
1988	118	134	135	138	112	87	94	106	149
1989	115	139	117	116	98	86	87	96	87
1990	111	123	107	107	96	89	87	90	81
1991	107	103	101	103	101	94	88	95	89
1992	100	100	100	100	100	100	100	100	100
1993	98	104	102	106	106	99	112	108	100
1994	98	105	106	112	114	106	125	115	123
1995	100	118	125	132	124	99	149	144	245
1996	100[1]	103	106	108	114	101	140	121	332
1997	99[1]	91[1]	89[1]	94[1]	113[1]	110[1]	145[1]	125[1]	186[1]
1998	98[1]	86[1]	84[1]	90[1]	114[1]	112[1]	148[1]	129[1]	191[1]
1999	97[1]	82[1]	80[1]	86[1]	115[1]	115[1]	152[1]	132[1]	197[1]
2000	96[1]	77[1]	75[1]	82[1]	116[1]	118[1]	156[1]	135[1]	202[1]

Source: Same as General Statistics. Values reflect change from the base year, 1992. Values above 100 mean greater than 1992, values below 100 mean less than 1992, and a value of 100 in the 1982-91 or 1993-2000 period means same as 1992. Note: 1. Projections by the editors.

SIC 3675 ELECTRONIC CAPACITORS: SELECTED RATIOS

For 1996	Average of All Manufacturing	Analyzed Industry	Index
Employees per Establishment	49	157	322
Payroll per Establishment	1,574,035	4,021,445	255
Payroll per Employee	32,350	25,658	79
Production Workers per Establishment	34	121	354
Wages per Establishment	890,687	2,306,994	259
Wages per Production Worker	26,064	19,073	73
Hours per Production Worker	2,055	1,993	97
Wages per Hour	12.68	9.57	75
Value Added per Establishment	4,932,584	8,559,094	174
Value Added per Employee	101,376	54,609	54
Value Added per Production Worker	144,340	70,761	49
Cost per Establishment	5,569,059	8,387,026	151
Cost per Employee	114,457	53,511	47
Cost per Production Worker	162,965	69,338	43
Shipments per Establishment	10,422,474	16,848,161	162
Shipments per Employee	214,207	107,495	50
Shipments per Production Worker	304,989	139,289	46
Investment per Establishment	394,953	1,808,415	458
Investment per Employee	8,117	11,538	142
Investment per Production Worker	11,557	14,951	129

Source: Same as General Statistics. The 'Average of All Manufacturing' column represents the average of all manufacturing industries reported for the most recent complete year available. The Index shows the relationship between the Average and the Analyzed Industry. For example, 100 means that they are equal; 500 that the Analyzed Industry is five times the average; 50 means that the Analyzed Industry is half the national average. The abbreviation 'na' is used to show that data are 'not available'.

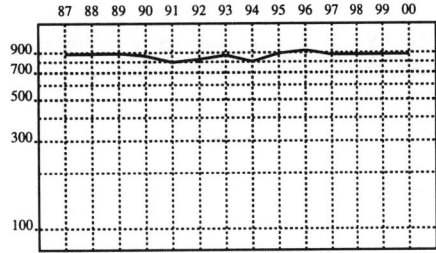

Revenues ($ millions)

SIC 3676 ELECTRONIC RESISTORS: GENERAL STATISTICS

Year	Estab-lish-ments	Employment			Compensation		Production ($ mil.)		
		Total (000)	Production		Payroll ($ mil.)	Wages ($/hr)	Cost of Materials	Value of Shipments	Capital Inves.
			Workers (000)	Hours (mil.)					
1987	118	15.7	10.9	21.4	293.4	7.02	281.3	882.7	43.5
1988	106	16.1	10.7	19.6	291.2	7.58	283.5	888.3	48.9
1989	101	15.9	11.7	21.0	285.4	7.21	323.9	890.3	56.3
1990	102	14.4	10.1	19.6	273.0	7.13	328.5	862.7	53.3
1991	99	12.9	8.6	16.2	244.4	7.16	277.7	797.1	33.6
1992	105	11.7	8.3	16.1	258.7	8.34	258.3	827.2	21.3
1993	102	10.8	7.9	16.1	249.9	8.76	277.8	870.5	25.7
1994	101	9.7	6.9	14.3	237.2	9.26	258.7	806.0	53.0
1995	96	9.9	7.0	13.8	244.6	9.41	303.1	890.7	40.6
1996	100[1]	9.5	6.7	13.7	241.8	9.73	295.5	927.0	42.1
1997	100[1]	8.8[1]	6.3[1]	12.6[1]	243.7[1]	9.70[1]	279.4[1]	876.6[1]	
1998	99[1]	8.1[1]	5.9[1]	11.8[1]	240.7[1]	9.97[1]	279.9[1]	878.0[1]	
1999	99[1]	7.4[1]	5.4[1]	11.0[1]	237.7[1]	10.24[1]	280.3[1]	879.4[1]	
2000	98[1]	6.8[1]	5.0[1]	10.1[1]	234.7[1]	10.51[1]	280.8[1]	880.8[1]	

Source: 1987 and 1992 Economic Census; _Annual Survey of Manufactures,_ 88-91, 93-96. Establishment counts for non-Census years are from _County Business Patterns._ Extracted from _Manufacturing USA_, 6th Edition, Gale, 1998. Note: 1. Projections by the editors.

SIC 3676 ELECTRONIC RESISTORS: INDICES OF CHANGE

Year	Estab-lish-ments	Employment			Compensation		Production ($ mil.)		
		Total (000)	Production		Payroll ($ mil.)	Wages ($/hr)	Cost of Materials	Value of Shipments	Capital Inves.
			Workers (000)	Hours (mil.)					
1987	112	134	131	133	113	84	109	107	204
1988	101	138	129	122	113	91	110	107	230
1989	96	136	141	130	110	86	125	108	264
1990	97	123	122	122	106	85	127	104	250
1991	94	110	104	101	94	86	108	96	158
1992	100	100	100	100	100	100	100	100	100
1993	97	92	95	100	97	105	108	105	121
1994	96	83	83	89	92	111	100	97	249
1995	91	85	84	86	95	113	117	108	191
1996	95[1]	81	81	85	93	117	114	112	198
1997	95[1]	75[1]	76[1]	78[1]	94[1]	116[1]	108[1]	106[1]	
1998	95[1]	69[1]	71[1]	73[1]	93[1]	120[1]	108[1]	106[1]	
1999	94[1]	64[1]	65[1]	68[1]	92[1]	123[1]	109[1]	106[1]	
2000	94[1]	58[1]	60[1]	63[1]	91[1]	126[1]	109[1]	106[1]	

Source: Same as General Statistics. Values reflect change from the base year, 1992. Values above 100 mean greater than 1992, values below 100 mean less than 1992, and a value of 100 in the 1982-91 or 1993-2000 period means same as 1992. Note: 1. Projections by the editors.

SIC 3676 ELECTRONIC RESISTORS: SELECTED RATIOS

For 1996	Average of All Manufacturing	Analyzed Industry	Index
Employees per Establishment	49	95	195
Payroll per Establishment	1,574,035	2,414,551	153
Payroll per Employee	32,350	25,453	79
Production Workers per Establishment	34	67	196
Wages per Establishment	890,687	1,331,108	149
Wages per Production Worker	26,064	19,896	76
Hours per Production Worker	2,055	2,045	99
Wages per Hour	12.68	9.73	77
Value Added per Establishment	4,932,584	6,326,961	128
Value Added per Employee	101,376	66,695	66
Value Added per Production Worker	144,340	94,567	66
Cost per Establishment	5,569,059	2,950,785	53
Cost per Employee	114,457	31,105	27
Cost per Production Worker	162,965	44,104	27
Shipments per Establishment	10,422,474	9,256,776	89
Shipments per Employee	214,207	97,579	46
Shipments per Production Worker	304,989	138,358	45
Investment per Establishment	394,953	420,399	106
Investment per Employee	8,117	4,432	55
Investment per Production Worker	11,557	6,284	54

Source: Same as General Statistics. The 'Average of All Manufacturing' column represents the average of all manufacturing industries reported for the most recent complete year available. The Index shows the relationship between the Average and the Analyzed Industry. For example, 100 means that they are equal; 500 that the Analyzed Industry is five times the average; 50 means that the Analyzed Industry is half the national average. The abbreviation 'na' is used to show that data are 'not available'.

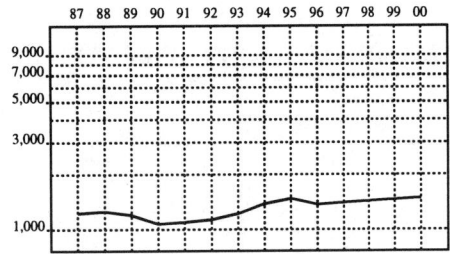

Revenues ($ millions)

SIC 3677 ELECTRONIC COILS AND TRANSFORMERS: GENERAL STATISTICS

Year	Estab-lish-ments	Employment			Compensation		Production ($ mil.)		
		Total (000)	Production		Payroll ($ mil.)	Wages ($/hr)	Cost of Materials	Value of Shipments	Capital Inves.
			Workers (000)	Hours (mil.)					
1987	416	23.9	18.3	34.8	396.3	6.84	476.1	1,228.4	29.1
1988	399	24.9	19.1	37.3	413.2	6.74	502.7	1,254.7	17.5
1989	394	24.3	18.7	33.5	382.4	6.96	502.2	1,199.3	28.8
1990	392	22.5	17.4	30.4	365.8	7.27	470.1	1,074.6	25.3
1991	391	21.8	16.6	29.6	355.4	6.97	458.5	1,098.8	21.1
1992	423	19.2	14.1	27.2	374.0	7.66	452.3	1,133.8	20.1
1993	431	19.7	15.2	28.9	388.5	7.78	476.8	1,222.9	21.9
1994	407	20.8	16.5	31.6	410.1	7.57	538.5	1,380.3	31.8
1995	404	21.3	17.0	32.1	425.1	7.89	549.9	1,471.7	28.9
1996	418[1]	20.0	15.7	31.3	431.7	7.93	521.7	1,364.8	21.8
1997	421[1]	19.5[1]	14.9[1]	28.2[1]	430.5[1]	8.40[1]	534.3[1]	1,397.9[1]	
1998	424[1]	19.1[1]	14.5[1]	27.5[1]	438.0[1]	8.60[1]	545.4[1]	1,426.8[1]	
1999	427[1]	18.7[1]	14.2[1]	26.9[1]	445.5[1]	8.80[1]	556.5[1]	1,455.8[1]	
2000	429[1]	18.3[1]	13.8[1]	26.2[1]	453.0[1]	9.00[1]	567.6[1]	1,484.8[1]	

Source: 1987 and 1992 Economic Census; *Annual Survey of Manufactures*, 88-91, 93-96. Establishment counts for non-Census years are from *County Business Patterns*. Extracted from *Manufacturing USA*, 6th Edition, Gale, 1998. Note: 1. Projections by the editors.

SIC 3677 ELECTRONIC COILS AND TRANSFORMERS: INDICES OF CHANGE

Year	Estab-lish-ments	Employment			Compensation		Production ($ mil.)		
		Total (000)	Production		Payroll ($ mil.)	Wages ($/hr)	Cost of Materials	Value of Shipments	Capital Inves.
			Workers (000)	Hours (mil.)					
1987	98	124	130	128	106	89	105	108	145
1988	94	130	135	137	110	88	111	111	87
1989	93	127	133	123	102	91	111	106	143
1990	93	117	123	112	98	95	104	95	126
1991	92	114	118	109	95	91	101	97	105
1992	100	100	100	100	100	100	100	100	100
1993	102	103	108	106	104	102	105	108	109
1994	96	108	117	116	110	99	119	122	158
1995	96	111	121	118	114	103	122	130	144
1996	99[1]	104	111	115	115	104	115	120	108
1997	100[1]	102[1]	106[1]	104[1]	115[1]	110[1]	118[1]	123[1]	
1998	100[1]	100[1]	103[1]	101[1]	117[1]	112[1]	121[1]	126[1]	
1999	101[1]	98[1]	101[1]	99[1]	119[1]	115[1]	123[1]	128[1]	
2000	102[1]	96[1]	98[1]	96[1]	121[1]	117[1]	125[1]	131[1]	

Source: Same as General Statistics. Values reflect change from the base year, 1992. Values above 100 mean greater than 1992, values below 100 mean less than 1992, and a value of 100 in the 1982-91 or 1993-2000 period means same as 1992. Note: 1. Projections by the editors.

SIC 3677 ELECTRONIC COILS AND TRANSFORMERS: SELECTED RATIOS

For 1996	Average of All Manufacturing	Analyzed Industry	Index
Employees per Establishment	49	48	98
Payroll per Establishment	1,574,035	1,032,449	66
Payroll per Employee	32,350	21,585	67
Production Workers per Establishment	34	38	110
Wages per Establishment	890,687	593,614	67
Wages per Production Worker	26,064	15,809	61
Hours per Production Worker	2,055	1,994	97
Wages per Hour	12.68	7.93	63
Value Added per Establishment	4,932,584	2,005,827	41
Value Added per Employee	101,376	41,935	41
Value Added per Production Worker	144,340	53,420	37
Cost per Establishment	5,569,059	1,247,693	22
Cost per Employee	114,457	26,085	23
Cost per Production Worker	162,965	33,229	20
Shipments per Establishment	10,422,474	3,264,042	31
Shipments per Employee	214,207	68,240	32
Shipments per Production Worker	304,989	86,930	29
Investment per Establishment	394,953	52,137	13
Investment per Employee	8,117	1,090	13
Investment per Production Worker	11,557	1,389	12

Source: Same as General Statistics. The 'Average of All Manufacturing' column represents the average of all manufacturing industries reported for the most recent complete year available. The Index shows the relationship between the Average and the Analyzed Industry. For example, 100 means that they are equal; 500 that the Analyzed Industry is five times the average; 50 means that the Analyzed Industry is half the national average. The abbreviation 'na' is used to show that data are 'not available'.

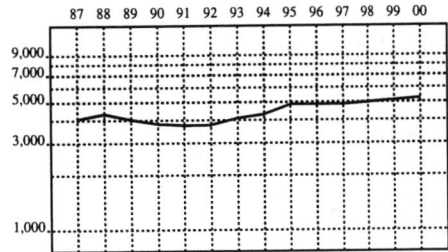

87 88 89 90 91 92 93 94 95 96 97 98 99 00

Revenues ($ millions)

SIC 3678 ELECTRONIC CONNECTORS: GENERAL STATISTICS

Year	Estab-lish-ments	Employment			Compensation		Production ($ mil.)		
		Total (000)	Production		Payroll ($ mil.)	Wages ($/hr)	Cost of Materials	Value of Shipments	Capital Inves.
			Workers (000)	Hours (mil.)					
1987	271	43.8	30.4	61.5	1,013.2	9.56	1,516.9	4,065.0	153.2
1988	275	41.5	28.9	57.4	996.0	10.22	1,704.0	4,333.2	132.5
1989	255	39.7	26.4	55.0	938.0	10.18	1,482.4	4,037.2	146.1
1990	249	38.1	26.2	54.1	958.0	10.32	1,427.5	3,820.9	173.5
1991	251	33.6	23.7	48.3	887.5	10.94	1,321.3	3,751.2	142.2
1992	285	30.7	21.1	42.4	909.2	11.92	1,390.2	3,773.5	144.3
1993	283	30.7	20.9	42.2	916.3	12.22	1,514.5	4,112.3	210.7
1994	281	30.8	21.7	45.8	954.3	12.29	1,686.2	4,304.3	200.4
1995	280	32.9	23.8	51.3	1,090.1	12.36	1,871.5	4,860.2	207.1
1996	301[1]	33.1	24.3	51.8	1,118.0	12.89	1,899.5	4,863.2	228.1
1997	309[1]	31.1[1]	21.6[1]	46.6[1]	1,089.8[1]	13.30[1]	1,896.6[1]	4,855.9[1]	198.4[1]
1998	316[1]	30.4[1]	21.1[1]	45.9[1]	1,111.9[1]	13.66[1]	1,947.6[1]	4,986.3[1]	201.8[1]
1999	323[1]	29.7[1]	20.6[1]	45.2[1]	1,134.1[1]	14.01[1]	1,998.5[1]	5,116.7[1]	205.2[1]
2000	331[1]	29.0[1]	20.1[1]	44.5[1]	1,156.3[1]	14.37[1]	2,049.5[1]	5,247.2[1]	208.5[1]

Source: 1987 and 1992 Economic Census; *Annual Survey of Manufactures*, 88-91, 93-96. Establishment counts for non-Census years are from *County Business Patterns.* Extracted from *Manufacturing USA*, 6th Edition, Gale, 1998. Note: 1. Projections by the editors.

SIC 3678 ELECTRONIC CONNECTORS: INDICES OF CHANGE

Year	Estab-lish-ments	Employment			Compensation		Production ($ mil.)		
		Total (000)	Production		Payroll ($ mil.)	Wages ($/hr)	Cost of Materials	Value of Shipments	Capital Inves.
			Workers (000)	Hours (mil.)					
1987	95	143	144	145	111	80	109	108	106
1988	96	135	137	135	110	86	123	115	92
1989	89	129	125	130	103	85	107	107	101
1990	87	124	124	128	105	87	103	101	120
1991	88	109	112	114	98	92	95	99	99
1992	100	100	100	100	100	100	100	100	100
1993	99	100	99	100	101	103	109	109	146
1994	99	100	103	108	105	103	121	114	139
1995	98	107	113	121	120	104	135	129	144
1996	106[1]	108	115	122	123	108	137	129	158
1997	108[1]	101[1]	103[1]	110[1]	120[1]	112[1]	136[1]	129[1]	138[1]
1998	111[1]	99[1]	100[1]	108[1]	122[1]	115[1]	140[1]	132[1]	140[1]
1999	113[1]	97[1]	98[1]	107[1]	125[1]	118[1]	144[1]	136[1]	142[1]
2000	116[1]	94[1]	95[1]	105[1]	127[1]	121[1]	147[1]	139[1]	145[1]

Source: Same as General Statistics. Values reflect change from the base year, 1992. Values above 100 mean greater than 1992, values below 100 mean less than 1992, and a value of 100 in the 1982-91 or 1993-2000 period means same as 1992. Note: 1. Projections by the editors.

SIC 3678 ELECTRONIC CONNECTORS: SELECTED RATIOS

For 1996	Average of All Manufacturing	Analyzed Industry	Index
Employees per Establishment	49	110	226
Payroll per Establishment	1,574,035	3,711,305	236
Payroll per Employee	32,350	33,776	104
Production Workers per Establishment	34	81	236
Wages per Establishment	890,687	2,216,499	249
Wages per Production Worker	26,064	27,477	105
Hours per Production Worker	2,055	2,132	104
Wages per Hour	12.68	12.89	102
Value Added per Establishment	4,932,584	9,828,983	199
Value Added per Employee	101,376	89,453	88
Value Added per Production Worker	144,340	121,848	84
Cost per Establishment	5,569,059	6,305,567	113
Cost per Employee	114,457	57,387	50
Cost per Production Worker	162,965	78,169	48
Shipments per Establishment	10,422,474	16,143,844	155
Shipments per Employee	214,207	146,924	69
Shipments per Production Worker	304,989	200,132	66
Investment per Establishment	394,953	757,199	192
Investment per Employee	8,117	6,891	85
Investment per Production Worker	11,557	9,387	81

Source: Same as General Statistics. The 'Average of All Manufacturing' column represents the average of all manufacturing industries reported for the most recent complete year available. The Index shows the relationship between the Average and the Analyzed Industry. For example, 100 means that they are equal; 500 that the Analyzed Industry is five times the average; 50 means that the Analyzed Industry is half the national average. The abbreviation 'na' is used to show that data are 'not available'.

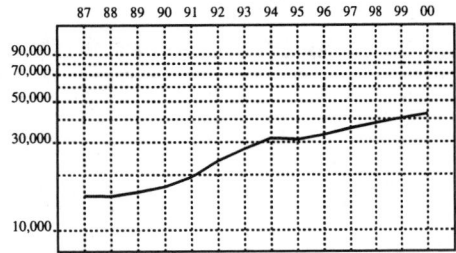

Revenues ($ millions)

SIC 3679 ELECTRONIC COMPONENTS, NEC: GENERAL STATISTICS

| Year | Estab-lish-ments | Employment | | | Compensation | | Production ($ mil.) | | |
| | | Total (000) | Production | | Payroll ($ mil.) | Wages ($/hr) | Cost of Materials | Value of Shipments | Capital Inves. |
			Workers (000)	Hours (mil.)					
1987	2,900	162.6	97.3	187.9	3,890.7	8.93	7,285.2	15,438.5	533.3
1988	2,846	157.6	99.9	196.9	3,738.1	8.98	7,139.2	15,299.4	448.1
1989	2,499	166.8	103.3	202.9	4,013.8	8.94	8,403.6	16,122.5	539.4
1990	2,441	161.0	101.1	203.2	4,107.6	9.06	8,380.0	17,222.4	485.0
1991	2,503	165.4	101.6	219.5	4,530.5	8.99	9,875.8	19,450.3	540.3
1992	3,295	182.4	109.2	238.8	5,180.5	9.32	11,842.4	23,869.9	740.8
1993	2,995	195.2	115.5	257.2	5,857.6	9.27	16,051.6	27,687.1	991.9
1994	3,024	196.5	118.9	261.6	5,964.7	9.33	16,872.5	31,609.5	990.6
1995	3,006	204.3	126.4	267.5	6,171.6	9.66	18,452.2	31,070.6	992.3
1996	3,068[1]	205.8	129.2	277.4	6,265.0	9.99	18,960.4	32,969.0	1,082.4
1997	3,115[1]	212.6[1]	130.3[1]	290.4[1]	6,773.9[1]	9.82[1]	20,581.6[1]	35,788.0[1]	1,158.7[1]
1998	3,161[1]	218.5[1]	133.9[1]	301.2[1]	7,101.6[1]	9.92[1]	21,911.0[1]	38,099.6[1]	1,235.8[1]
1999	3,208[1]	224.5[1]	137.6[1]	311.9[1]	7,429.2[1]	10.03[1]	23,240.4[1]	40,411.3[1]	1,313.0[1]
2000	3,255[1]	230.4[1]	141.2[1]	322.7[1]	7,756.8[1]	10.13[1]	24,569.9[1]	42,722.9[1]	1,390.1[1]

Source: 1987 and 1992 Economic Census; *Annual Survey of Manufactures*, 88-91, 93-96. Establishment counts for non-Census years are from *County Business Patterns*. Extracted from *Manufacturing USA*, 6th Edition, Gale, 1998. Note: 1. Projections by the editors.

SIC 3679 ELECTRONIC COMPONENTS, NEC: INDICES OF CHANGE

| Year | Estab-lish-ments | Employment | | | Compensation | | Production ($ mil.) | | |
| | | Total (000) | Production | | Payroll ($ mil.) | Wages ($/hr) | Cost of Materials | Value of Shipments | Capital Inves. |
			Workers (000)	Hours (mil.)					
1987	88	89	89	79	75	96	62	65	72
1988	86	86	91	82	72	96	60	64	60
1989	76	91	95	85	77	96	71	68	73
1990	74	88	93	85	79	97	71	72	65
1991	76	91	93	92	87	96	83	81	73
1992	100	100	100	100	100	100	100	100	100
1993	91	107	106	108	113	99	136	116	134
1994	92	108	109	110	115	100	142	132	134
1995	91	112	116	112	119	104	156	130	134
1996	93[1]	113	118	116	121	107	160	138	146
1997	95[1]	117[1]	119[1]	122[1]	131[1]	105[1]	174[1]	150[1]	156[1]
1998	96[1]	120[1]	123[1]	126[1]	137[1]	106[1]	185[1]	160[1]	167[1]
1999	97[1]	123[1]	126[1]	131[1]	143[1]	108[1]	196[1]	169[1]	177[1]
2000	99[1]	126[1]	129[1]	135[1]	150[1]	109[1]	207[1]	179[1]	188[1]

Source: Same as General Statistics. Values reflect change from the base year, 1992. Values above 100 mean greater than 1992, values below 100 mean less than 1992, and a value of 100 in the 1982-91 or 1993-2000 period means same as 1992. Note: 1. Projections by the editors.

SIC 3679 ELECTRONIC COMPONENTS, NEC: SELECTED RATIOS

For 1996	Average of All Manufacturing	Analyzed Industry	Index
Employees per Establishment	49	67	138
Payroll per Establishment	1,574,035	2,042,047	130
Payroll per Employee	32,350	30,442	94
Production Workers per Establishment	34	42	123
Wages per Establishment	890,687	903,268	101
Wages per Production Worker	26,064	21,449	82
Hours per Production Worker	2,055	2,147	104
Wages per Hour	12.68	9.99	79
Value Added per Establishment	4,932,584	4,604,074	93
Value Added per Employee	101,376	68,636	68
Value Added per Production Worker	144,340	109,329	76
Cost per Establishment	5,569,059	6,180,052	111
Cost per Employee	114,457	92,130	80
Cost per Production Worker	162,965	146,752	90
Shipments per Establishment	10,422,474	10,746,089	103
Shipments per Employee	214,207	160,199	75
Shipments per Production Worker	304,989	255,178	84
Investment per Establishment	394,953	352,803	89
Investment per Employee	8,117	5,259	65
Investment per Production Worker	11,557	8,378	72

Source: Same as General Statistics. The 'Average of All Manufacturing' column represents the average of all manufacturing industries reported for the most recent complete year available. The Index shows the relationship between the Average and the Analyzed Industry. For example, 100 means that they are equal; 500 that the Analyzed Industry is five times the average; 50 means that the Analyzed Industry is half the national average. The abbreviation 'na' is used to show that data are 'not available'.

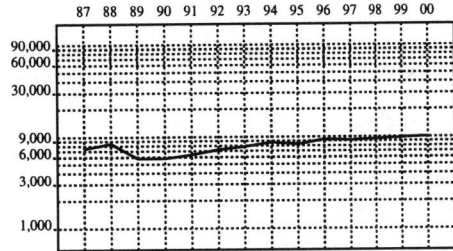

Revenues ($ millions)

SIC 3694 ENGINE ELECTRICAL EQUIPMENT: GENERAL STATISTICS

Year	Estab-lish-ments	Employment			Compensation		Production ($ mil.)		
		Total (000)	Production		Payroll ($ mil.)	Wages ($/hr)	Cost of Materials	Value of Shipments	Capital Inves.
			Workers (000)	Hours (mil.)					
1987	486	67.1	51.8	102.5	1,713.2	11.56	4,040.3	7,472.6	237.7
1988	476	66.6	52.0	104.0	1,775.2	11.94	4,840.3	8,490.6	172.2
1989	450	64.3	45.6	91.4	1,704.0	12.54	4,601.3	5,817.0	271.0
1990	456	61.7	36.2	72.7	1,258.3	11.75	2,975.7	5,810.5	197.2
1991	461	44.9	34.7	69.2	1,312.9	12.97	3,177.9	6,407.8	158.6
1992	522	50.0	39.4	77.2	1,407.7	12.87	3,441.4	7,238.7	167.1
1993	512	52.8	41.8	84.4	1,481.7	12.59	3,918.5	7,832.7	201.8
1994	497	53.8	42.8	86.7	1,612.8	13.22	4,383.5	8,683.2	209.2
1995	506	52.1	40.8	81.9	1,505.2	12.48	4,249.6	8,290.9	224.1
1996	516[1]	53.5	42.6	85.8	1,600.3	13.46	4,814.5	9,369.8	240.0
1997	523[1]	55.7[1]	42.7[1]	87.1[1]	1,704.0[1]	14.04[1]	4,719.8[1]	9,185.5[1]	239.4[1]
1998	529[1]	55.8[1]	42.9[1]	87.7[1]	1,743.6[1]	14.33[1]	4,877.1[1]	9,491.6[1]	245.7[1]
1999	536[1]	56.0[1]	43.1[1]	88.3[1]	1,783.2[1]	14.63[1]	5,034.3[1]	9,797.6[1]	251.9[1]
2000	542[1]	56.1[1]	43.2[1]	89.0[1]	1,822.8[1]	14.92[1]	5,191.6[1]	10,103.7[1]	258.1[1]

Source: 1987 and 1992 Economic Census; *Annual Survey of Manufactures*, 88-91, 93-96. Establishment counts for non-Census years are from *County Business Patterns*. Extracted from *Manufacturing USA*, 6th Edition, Gale, 1998. Note: 1. Projections by the editors.

SIC 3694 ENGINE ELECTRICAL EQUIPMENT: INDICES OF CHANGE

Year	Estab-lish-ments	Employment			Compensation		Production ($ mil.)		
		Total (000)	Production		Payroll ($ mil.)	Wages ($/hr)	Cost of Materials	Value of Shipments	Capital Inves.
			Workers (000)	Hours (mil.)					
1987	93	134	131	133	122	90	117	103	142
1988	91	133	132	135	126	93	141	117	103
1989	86	129	116	118	121	97	134	80	162
1990	87	123	92	94	89	91	86	80	118
1991	88	90	88	90	93	101	92	89	95
1992	100	100	100	100	100	100	100	100	100
1993	98	106	106	109	105	98	114	108	121
1994	95	108	109	112	115	103	127	120	125
1995	97	104	104	106	107	97	123	115	134
1996	99[1]	107	108	111	114	105	140	129	144
1997	100[1]	111[1]	108[1]	113[1]	121[1]	109[1]	137[1]	127[1]	143[1]
1998	101[1]	112[1]	109[1]	114[1]	124[1]	111[1]	142[1]	131[1]	147[1]
1999	103[1]	112[1]	109[1]	114[1]	127[1]	114[1]	146[1]	135[1]	151[1]
2000	104[1]	112[1]	110[1]	115[1]	129[1]	116[1]	151[1]	140[1]	154[1]

Source: Same as General Statistics. Values reflect change from the base year, 1992. Values above 100 mean greater than 1992, values below 100 mean less than 1992, and a value of 100 in the 1982-91 or 1993-2000 period means same as 1992. Note: 1. Projections by the editors.

SIC 3694 ENGINE ELECTRICAL EQUIPMENT: SELECTED RATIOS

For 1996	Average of All Manufacturing	Analyzed Industry	Index
Employees per Establishment	49	104	213
Payroll per Establishment	1,574,035	3,101,092	197
Payroll per Employee	32,350	29,912	92
Production Workers per Establishment	34	83	242
Wages per Establishment	890,687	2,237,926	251
Wages per Production Worker	26,064	27,110	104
Hours per Production Worker	2,055	2,014	98
Wages per Hour	12.68	13.46	106
Value Added per Establishment	4,932,584	8,923,658	181
Value Added per Employee	101,376	86,075	85
Value Added per Production Worker	144,340	108,099	75
Cost per Establishment	5,569,059	9,329,632	168
Cost per Employee	114,457	89,991	79
Cost per Production Worker	162,965	113,016	69
Shipments per Establishment	10,422,474	18,156,980	174
Shipments per Employee	214,207	175,136	82
Shipments per Production Worker	304,989	219,948	72
Investment per Establishment	394,953	465,077	118
Investment per Employee	8,117	4,486	55
Investment per Production Worker	11,557	5,634	49

Source: Same as General Statistics. The 'Average of All Manufacturing' column represents the average of all manufacturing industries reported for the most recent complete year available. The Index shows the relationship between the Average and the Analyzed Industry. For example, 100 means that they are equal; 500 that the Analyzed Industry is five times the average; 50 means that the Analyzed Industry is half the national average. The abbreviation 'na' is used to show that data are 'not available'.

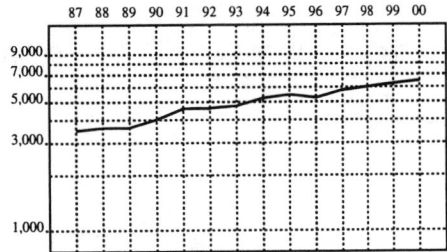

Revenues ($ millions)

SIC 3695 MAGNETIC AND OPTICAL RECORDING MEDIA: GENERAL STATISTICS

Year	Estab-lish-ments	Employment			Compensation		Production ($ mil.)		
		Total (000)	Production		Payroll ($ mil.)	Wages ($/hr)	Cost of Materials	Value of Shipments	Capital Inves.
			Workers (000)	Hours (mil.)					
1987	200	25.6	16.3	33.0	638.6	9.82	1,836.6	3,504.0	225.6
1988	191	25.1	16.2	32.6	662.1	10.32	2,067.0	3,630.7	269.1
1989	214	25.5	16.9	32.6	651.1	10.78	2,080.0	3,644.2	219.8
1990	215	25.5	16.1	31.4	651.9	11.29	2,365.9	4,032.1	286.8
1991	243	25.4	16.1	33.2	734.7	11.24	2,734.8	4,615.9	305.2
1992	261	22.6	15.1	32.2	695.0	11.30	2,513.6	4,641.3	394.2
1993	261	22.2	15.0	31.2	689.6	12.18	2,406.1	4,765.5	337.9
1994	262	23.7	15.5	30.3	778.5	14.16	2,637.5	5,256.3	325.7
1995	263	24.7	17.2	32.5	816.2	13.97	2,711.2	5,481.5	388.9
1996	285[1]	23.7	16.7	31.3	844.6	14.81	2,827.6	5,271.5	522.5
1997	295[1]	23.0[1]	16.1[1]	31.1[1]	837.7[1]	14.99[1]	3,105.3[1]	5,789.3[1]	470.3[1]
1998	305[1]	22.8[1]	16.1[1]	30.9[1]	859.7[1]	15.54[1]	3,232.6[1]	6,026.5[1]	496.3[1]
1999	315[1]	22.5[1]	16.1[1]	30.7[1]	881.8[1]	16.08[1]	3,359.9[1]	6,263.8[1]	522.2[1]
2000	325[1]	22.3[1]	16.1[1]	30.5[1]	903.9[1]	16.63[1]	3,487.1[1]	6,501.1[1]	548.2[1]

Source: 1987 and 1992 Economic Census; *Annual Survey of Manufactures*, 88-91, 93-96. Establishment counts for non-Census years are from *County Business Patterns*. Extracted from *Manufacturing USA*, 6th Edition, Gale, 1998. Note: 1. Projections by the editors.

SIC 3695 MAGNETIC AND OPTICAL RECORDING MEDIA: INDICES OF CHANGE

Year	Estab-lish-ments	Employment			Compensation		Production ($ mil.)		
		Total (000)	Production		Payroll ($ mil.)	Wages ($/hr)	Cost of Materials	Value of Shipments	Capital Inves.
			Workers (000)	Hours (mil.)					
1987	77	113	108	102	92	87	73	75	57
1988	73	111	107	101	95	91	82	78	68
1989	82	113	112	101	94	95	83	79	56
1990	82	113	107	98	94	100	94	87	73
1991	93	112	107	103	106	99	109	99	77
1992	100	100	100	100	100	100	100	100	100
1993	100	98	99	97	99	108	96	103	86
1994	100	105	103	94	112	125	105	113	83
1995	101	109	114	101	117	124	108	118	99
1996	109[1]	105	111	97	122	131	112	114	133
1997	113[1]	102[1]	107[1]	96[1]	121[1]	133[1]	124[1]	125[1]	119[1]
1998	117[1]	101[1]	107[1]	96[1]	124[1]	137[1]	129[1]	130[1]	126[1]
1999	121[1]	100[1]	106[1]	95[1]	127[1]	142[1]	134[1]	135[1]	132[1]
2000	125[1]	98[1]	106[1]	95[1]	130[1]	147[1]	139[1]	140[1]	139[1]

Source: Same as General Statistics. Values reflect change from the base year, 1992. Values above 100 mean greater than 1992, values below 100 mean less than 1992, and a value of 100 in the 1982-91 or 1993-2000 period means same as 1992. Note: 1. Projections by the editors.

SIC 3695 MAGNETIC AND OPTICAL RECORDING MEDIA: SELECTED RATIOS

For 1996	Average of All Manufacturing	Analyzed Industry	Index
Employees per Establishment	49	83	171
Payroll per Establishment	1,574,035	2,964,954	188
Payroll per Employee	32,350	35,637	110
Production Workers per Establishment	34	59	172
Wages per Establishment	890,687	1,627,295	183
Wages per Production Worker	26,064	27,758	106
Hours per Production Worker	2,055	1,874	91
Wages per Hour	12.68	14.81	117
Value Added per Establishment	4,932,584	8,618,235	175
Value Added per Employee	101,376	103,586	102
Value Added per Production Worker	144,340	147,006	102
Cost per Establishment	5,569,059	9,926,241	178
Cost per Employee	114,457	119,308	104
Cost per Production Worker	162,965	169,317	104
Shipments per Establishment	10,422,474	18,505,510	178
Shipments per Employee	214,207	222,426	104
Shipments per Production Worker	304,989	315,659	103
Investment per Establishment	394,953	1,834,227	464
Investment per Employee	8,117	22,046	272
Investment per Production Worker	11,557	31,287	271

Source: Same as General Statistics. The 'Average of All Manufacturing' column represents the average of all manufacturing industries reported for the most recent complete year available. The Index shows the relationship between the Average and the Analyzed Industry. For example, 100 means that they are equal; 500 that the Analyzed Industry is five times the average; 50 means that the Analyzed Industry is half the national average. The abbreviation 'na' is used to show that data are 'not available'.

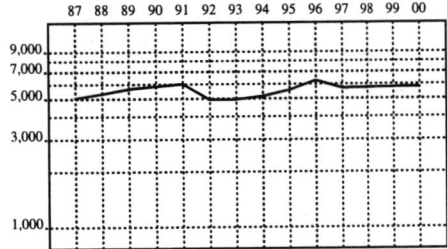

Revenues ($ millions)

SIC 3699 ELECTRICAL EQUIPMENT & SUPPLIES, NEC: GENERAL STATISTICS

| Year | Estab-lish-ments | Employment | | | Compensation | | Production ($ mil.) | | |
| | | Total (000) | Production | | Payroll ($ mil.) | Wages ($/hr) | Cost of Materials | Value of Shipments | Capital Inves. |
			Workers (000)	Hours (mil.)					
1987	1,379	60.3	32.4	63.0	1,466.4	8.70	2,198.7	5,056.1	180.6
1988	1,342	60.6	31.9	60.7	1,557.7	9.36	2,227.0	5,328.2	166.6
1989	1,249	66.4	29.0	56.4	1,633.1	10.50	2,259.4	5,666.5	170.5
1990	1,185	63.4	28.6	54.9	1,683.4	10.11	2,558.9	5,848.3	178.4
1991	1,192	52.7	25.9	51.2	1,622.5	10.98	2,468.7	6,015.7	196.8
1992	892	43.4	20.9	39.9	1,375.6	10.42	2,035.2	4,934.0	118.7
1993	912	40.9	19.7	37.8	1,287.5	10.26	2,198.5	4,963.0	112.0
1994	863	40.6	20.3	39.3	1,350.9	10.37	2,278.5	5,148.1	126.8
1995	861	42.1	22.2	43.1	1,486.8	11.05	2,386.5	5,576.6	169.0
1996	724[1]	45.8	23.4	44.6	1,680.3	11.18	2,708.9	6,278.9	211.7
1997	650[1]	36.1[1]	18.0[1]	34.5[1]	1,467.0[1]	11.41[1]	2,457.1[1]	5,695.4[1]	156.5[1]
1998	575[1]	33.3[1]	16.6[1]	31.9[1]	1,458.4[1]	11.61[1]	2,473.9[1]	5,734.2[1]	155.3[1]
1999	500[1]	30.4[1]	15.2[1]	29.2[1]	1,449.8[1]	11.81[1]	2,490.7[1]	5,773.1[1]	154.1[1]
2000	426[1]	27.6[1]	13.9[1]	26.6[1]	1,441.2[1]	12.01[1]	2,507.5[1]	5,812.0[1]	152.9[1]

Source: 1987 and 1992 Economic Census; *Annual Survey of Manufactures*, 88-91, 93-96. Establishment counts for non-Census years are from *County Business Patterns*. Extracted from *Manufacturing USA*, 6th Edition, Gale, 1998. Note: 1. Projections by the editors.

SIC 3699 ELECTRICAL EQUIPMENT & SUPPLIES, NEC: INDICES OF CHANGE

| Year | Estab-lish-ments | Employment | | | Compensation | | Production ($ mil.) | | |
| | | Total (000) | Production | | Payroll ($ mil.) | Wages ($/hr) | Cost of Materials | Value of Shipments | Capital Inves. |
			Workers (000)	Hours (mil.)					
1987	155	139	155	158	107	83	108	102	152
1988	150	140	153	152	113	90	109	108	140
1989	140	153	139	141	119	101	111	115	144
1990	133	146	137	138	122	97	126	119	150
1991	134	121	124	128	118	105	121	122	166
1992	100	100	100	100	100	100	100	100	100
1993	102	94	94	95	94	98	108	101	94
1994	97	94	97	98	98	100	112	104	107
1995	97	97	106	108	108	106	117	113	142
1996	81[1]	106	112	112	122	107	133	127	178
1997	73[1]	83[1]	86[1]	87[1]	107[1]	109[1]	121[1]	115[1]	132[1]
1998	64[1]	77[1]	79[1]	80[1]	106[1]	111[1]	122[1]	116[1]	131[1]
1999	56[1]	70[1]	73[1]	73[1]	105[1]	113[1]	122[1]	117[1]	130[1]
2000	48[1]	64[1]	66[1]	67[1]	105[1]	115[1]	123[1]	118[1]	129[1]

Source: Same as General Statistics. Values reflect change from the base year, 1992. Values above 100 mean greater than 1992, values below 100 mean less than 1992, and a value of 100 in the 1982-91 or 1993-2000 period means same as 1992. Note: 1. Projections by the editors.

SIC 3699 ELECTRICAL EQUIPMENT & SUPPLIES, NEC: SELECTED RATIOS

For 1996	Average of All Manufacturing	Analyzed Industry	Index
Employees per Establishment	49	63	130
Payroll per Establishment	1,574,035	2,320,144	147
Payroll per Employee	32,350	36,688	113
Production Workers per Establishment	34	32	95
Wages per Establishment	890,687	688,501	77
Wages per Production Worker	26,064	21,309	82
Hours per Production Worker	2,055	1,906	93
Wages per Hour	12.68	11.18	88
Value Added per Establishment	4,932,584	5,058,944	103
Value Added per Employee	101,376	79,996	79
Value Added per Production Worker	144,340	156,573	108
Cost per Establishment	5,569,059	3,740,427	67
Cost per Employee	114,457	59,146	52
Cost per Production Worker	162,965	115,765	71
Shipments per Establishment	10,422,474	8,669,853	83
Shipments per Employee	214,207	137,094	64
Shipments per Production Worker	304,989	268,329	88
Investment per Establishment	394,953	292,314	74
Investment per Employee	8,117	4,622	57
Investment per Production Worker	11,557	9,047	78

Source: Same as General Statistics. The 'Average of All Manufacturing' column represents the average of all manufacturing industries reported for the most recent complete year available. The Index shows the relationship between the Average and the Analyzed Industry. For example, 100 means that they are equal; 500 that the Analyzed Industry is five times the average; 50 means that the Analyzed Industry is half the national average. The abbreviation 'na' is used to show that data are 'not available'.

SIC 7371 - COMPUTER PROGRAMMING SERVICES: GENERAL STATISTICS

Year	Estab- lish- ments	Employ- ment (000)	Payroll ($ mil.)	Revenues ($ mil.)		Ownership	
				SAS	Census	Sole Prop.	Partner- ships
1987	14,687	184.2	6,286.6		14,170.2	1,293	287
1988	13,182	202.5	7,781.4				
1989	12,057	208.4	8,086.3				
1990	12,443	217.2	8,906.8	21,318.0			
1991	13,225	220.5	9,483.8	23,376.0			
1992	23,265	242.7	10,890.2	24,973.0	23,548.1	1,537	348
1993	23,225	262.1	12,067.5	27,352.0			
1994	23,957[1]	272.4[1]	13,416.8[1]	31,069.0[1]			
1995	25,519[1]	310.9[1]	16,291.1[1]	35,053.0[1]			
1996	27,019[1]	306.4[1]	15,929.2[1]	42,163.0[1]			
1997	28,832[1]	320.6[1]	17,043.7[1]	42,469.9[1]			
1998	30,646[1]	334.7[1]	18,158.2[1]	45,755.0[1]			

Source: Data for 1987 and 1992 are from Census of Service Industries, Bureau of the Census, U.S. Department of Commerce. Data labeled SAS are from the *Service Annual Survey* for 1996, which also presented revisions for ealier years. Data for 1988-1991 and 1993-1995, when shown, are derived from *County Business Patterns* for those years from the Bureau of the Census. Extracted from *Service Industries USA*, 4th edition, Gale, 1998. Note: 1. Projections made by the editor.

SIC 7371 - COMPUTER PROGRAMMING SERVICES: INDICES OF CHANGE

Year	Estab- lish- ments	Employ- ment (000)	Payroll ($ mil.)	Revenues ($ mil.)		Ownership	
				SAS	Census	Sole Prop.	Partner- ships
1987	63	76	58		60	84	82
1988	57	83	71				
1989	52	86	74				
1990	53	90	82	85			
1991	57	91	87	94			
1992	100	100	100	100	100	100	100
1993	100	108	111	110			
1994	103[1]	112[1]	123[1]	124[1]			
1995	110[1]	128[1]	150[1]	140[1]			
1996	116[1]	126[1]	146[1]	169[1]			
1997	124[1]	132[1]	157[1]	170[1]			
1998	132[1]	138[1]	167[1]	183[1]			

Source: Same as General Statistics. The values shown reflect change from the base year, 1992, which is always 100. Data points earlier or later than 1992 are less than 1992 if less than 100 and greater than 1992 if greater than 100. Note: 1. Index based on a projected value.

SIC 7371 - COMPUTER PROGRAMMING SERVICES: SELECTED RATIOS

For 1992	Average of All Services	Analyzed Industry	Index
Employees per establishment	13	10	77
Revenues per establishment	810,117	1,012,169	125
Payroll per establishment	314,133	468,094	149
Payroll per employee	23,335	44,870	192
Revenue per employee	60,179	97,023	161
Sole proprietors as % of establishments	30.1	6.6	22
Partnerships as % of establishments	5.7	1.5	26

Source: Same as General Statistics. The 'Average of all Services' column represents the average of all service industries of which this SIC is a part. The Index shows the relationship between the Average and the Analyzed Industry. For example, 100 means that they are equal; 500 that the Analyzed Industry is five times the average; 50 means that the Analyzed Industry is half the national average.

SIC 7372 - PREPACKAGED SOFTWARE: GENERAL STATISTICS

Year	Estab-lish-ments	Employ-ment (000)	Payroll ($ mil.)	Revenues ($ mil.)		Ownership	
				SAS	Census	Sole Prop.	Partner-ships
1987	3,392	55.7	2,052.4		5,894.2	209	92
1988	3,156	58.3	2,473.1				
1989	3,643	68.0	2,882.8				
1990	3,755	76.3	3,516.8	16,523.0			
1991	3,786	87.2	4,083.0	18,306.0			
1992	7,108	131.0	6,614.3	21,236.0	20,802.4	438	114
1993	6,970	142.4	7,373.2	25,188.0			
1994	6,853[1]	149.9[1]	8,345.0[1]	28,864.0[1]			
1995	6,991[1]	162.2[1]	10,076.3[1]	33,249.0[1]			
1996	8,030[1]	178.8[1]	10,417.7[1]	39,325.0[1]			
1997	8,622[1]	193.9[1]	11,447.5[1]	41,230.1[1]			
1998	9,214[1]	209.0[1]	12,477.4[1]	45,013.0[1]			

Source: Data for 1987 and 1992 are from Census of Service Industries, Bureau of the Census, U.S. Department of Commerce. Data labeled SAS are from the *Service Annual Survey* for 1996, which also presented revisions for ealier years. Data for 1988-1991 and 1993-1995, when shown, are derived from *County Business Patterns* for those years from the Bureau of the Census. Extracted from *Service Industries USA*, 4th edition, Gale, 1998. Note: 1. Projections made by the editor.

SIC 7372 - PREPACKAGED SOFTWARE: INDICES OF CHANGE

Year	Estab-lish-ments	Employ-ment (000)	Payroll ($ mil.)	Revenues ($ mil.)		Ownership	
				SAS	Census	Sole Prop.	Partner-ships
1987	48	43	31		28	48	81
1988	44	45	37				
1989	51	52	44				
1990	53	58	53	78			
1991	53	67	62	86			
1992	100	100	100	100	100	100	100
1993	98	109	111	119			
1994	96[1]	114[1]	126[1]	136[1]			
1995	98[1]	124[1]	152[1]	157[1]			
1996	113[1]	136[1]	158[1]	185[1]			
1997	121[1]	148[1]	173[1]	194[1]			
1998	130[1]	160[1]	189[1]	212[1]			

Source: Same as General Statistics. The values shown reflect change from the base year, 1992, which is always 100. Data points earlier or later than 1992 are less than 1992 if less than 100 and greater than 1992 if greater than 100. Note: 1. Index based on a projected value.

SIC 7372 - PREPACKAGED SOFTWARE: SELECTED RATIOS

For 1992	Average of All Services	Analyzed Industry	Index
Employees per establishment	13	18	137
Revenues per establishment	810,117	2,926,621	361
Payroll per establishment	314,133	930,549	296
Payroll per employee	23,335	50,483	216
Revenue per employee	60,179	158,773	264
Sole proprietors as % of establishments	30.1	6.2	20
Partnerships as % of establishments	5.7	1.6	28

Source: Same as General Statistics. The 'Average of all Services' column represents the average of all service industries of which this SIC is a part. The Index shows the relationship between the Average and the Analyzed Industry. For example, 100 means that they are equal; 500 that the Analyzed Industry is five times the average; 50 means that the Analyzed Industry is half the national average.

SIC 7373 - COMPUTER INTEGRATED SYSTEMS DESIGN: GENERAL STATISTICS

| Year | Estab-lish-ments | Employ-ment (000) | Payroll ($ mil.) | Revenues ($ mil.) | | Ownership | |
				SAS	Census	Sole Prop.	Partner-ships
1987	3,515	66.3	2,199.8		7,089.9	233	102
1988	3,495	64.4	2,482.7				
1989	3,191	72.2	2,945.5				
1990	3,273	81.6	3,506.5	12,916.0			
1991	3,510	85.5	3,715.0	13,751.0			
1992	5,011	97.6	4,150.8	15,177.0	14,804.9	301	123
1993	5,179	115.2	5,090.5	16,212.0			
1994	5,402[1]	103.4[1]	4,557.0[1]	17,037.0[1]			
1995	5,781[1]	110.9[1]	5,259.9[1]	17,485.0[1]			
1996	5,970[1]	121.7[1]	5,717.3[1]	20,202.0[1]			
1997	6,312[1]	128.3[1]	6,107.3[1]	20,566.6[1]			
1998	6,653[1]	134.9[1]	6,497.2[1]	21,680.4[1]			

Source: Data for 1987 and 1992 are from Census of Service Industries, Bureau of the Census, U.S. Department of Commerce. Data labeled SAS are from the *Service Annual Survey* for 1996, which also presented revisions for earlier years. Data for 1988-1991 and 1993-1995, when shown, are derived from *County Business Patterns* for those years from the Bureau of the Census. Extracted from *Service Industries USA*, 4th edition, Gale, 1998. Note: 1. Projections made by the editor.

SIC 7373 - COMPUTER INTEGRATED SYSTEMS DESIGN: INDICES OF CHANGE

| Year | Estab-lish-ments | Employ-ment (000) | Payroll ($ mil.) | Revenues ($ mil.) | | Ownership | |
				SAS	Census	Sole Prop.	Partner-ships
1987	70	68	53		48	77	83
1988	70	66	60				
1989	64	74	71				
1990	65	84	84	85			
1991	70	88	90	91			
1992	100	100	100	100	100	100	100
1993	103	118	123	107			
1994	108[1]	106[1]	110[1]	112[1]			
1995	115[1]	114[1]	127[1]	115[1]			
1996	119[1]	125[1]	138[1]	133[1]			
1997	126[1]	131[1]	147[1]	136[1]			
1998	133[1]	138[1]	157[1]	143[1]			

Source: Same as General Statistics. The values shown reflect change from the base year, 1992, which is always 100. Data points earlier or later than 1992 are less than 1992 if less than 100 and greater than 1992 if greater than 100. Note: 1. Index based on a projected value.

SIC 7373 - COMPUTER INTEGRATED SYSTEMS DESIGN: SELECTED RATIOS

For 1992	Average of All Services	Analyzed Industry	Index
Employees per establishment	13	19	145
Revenues per establishment	810,117	2,954,483	365
Payroll per establishment	314,133	828,335	264
Payroll per employee	23,335	42,528	182
Revenue per employee	60,179	151,687	252
Sole proprietors as % of establishments	30.1	6.0	20
Partnerships as % of establishments	5.7	2.5	43

Source: Same as General Statistics. The 'Average of all Services' column represents the average of all service industries of which this SIC is a part. The Index shows the relationship between the Average and the Analyzed Industry. For example, 100 means that they are equal; 500 that the Analyzed Industry is five times the average; 50 means that the Analyzed Industry is half the national average.

SIC 7374 - DATA PROCESSING SERVICES: GENERAL STATISTICS

Year	Estab-lish-ments	Employ-ment (000)	Payroll ($ mil.)	Revenues ($ mil.)		Ownership	
				SAS	Census	Sole Prop.	Partner-ships
1987	7,332	202.7	4,580.0		14,068.4	604	322
1988	6,811	217.9	5,445.6				
1989	6,776	222.7	5,817.9				
1990	6,773	228.9	6,442.7	17,820.0			
1991	6,821	225.2	6,682.2	18,824.0			
1992	7,286	230.3	6,795.9	20,477.0	20,199.5		
1993	7,093	235.7	7,567.5	23,716.0			
1994	7,093[1]	236.8[1]	7,818.9[1]	29,177.0[1]			
1995	7,914[1]	270.1[1]	9,509.4[1]	35,607.0[1]			
1996	7,460[1]	259.5[1]	9,297.5[1]	41,036.0[1]			
1997	7,532[1]	265.4[1]	9,809.0[1]	34,478.4[1]			
1998	7,604[1]	271.3[1]	10,320.5[1]	36,254.0[1]			

Source: Data for 1987 and 1992 are from Census of Service Industries, Bureau of the Census, U.S. Department of Commerce. Data labeled SAS are from the *Service Annual Survey* for 1996, which also presented revisions for ealier years. Data for 1988-1991 and 1993-1995, when shown, are derived from *County Business Patterns* for those years from the Bureau of the Census. Extracted from *Service Industries USA*, 4th edition, Gale, 1998. Note: 1. Projections made by the editor.

SIC 7374 - DATA PROCESSING SERVICES: INDICES OF CHANGE

Year	Estab-lish-ments	Employ-ment (000)	Payroll ($ mil.)	Revenues ($ mil.)	
				SAS	Census
1987	101	88	67		70
1988	93	95	80		
1989	93	97	86		
1990	93	99	95	87	
1991	94	98	98	92	
1992	100	100	100	100	100
1993	97	102	111	116	
1994	97[1]	103[1]	115[1]	142[1]	
1995	109[1]	117[1]	140[1]	174[1]	
1996	102[1]	113[1]	137[1]	200[1]	
1997	103[1]	115[1]	144[1]	168[1]	
1998	104[1]	118[1]	152[1]	177[1]	

Source: Same as General Statistics. The values shown reflect change from the base year, 1992, which is always 100. Data points earlier or later than 1992 are less than 1992 if less than 100 and greater than 1992 if greater than 100. Note: 1. Index based on a projected value.

SIC 7374 - DATA PROCESSING SERVICES: SELECTED RATIOS

For 1992	Average of All Services	Analyzed Industry	Index
Employees per establishment	13	32	235
Revenues per establishment	810,117	2,772,374	342
Payroll per establishment	314,133	932,734	297
Payroll per employee	23,335	29,503	126
Revenue per employee	60,179	87,692	146
Sole proprietors as % of establishments	30.1	na	na
Partnerships as % of establishments	5.7	na	na

Source: Same as General Statistics. The 'Average of all Services' column represents the average of all service industries of which this SIC is a part. The Index shows the relationship between the Average and the Analyzed Industry. For example, 100 means that they are equal; 500 that the Analyzed Industry is five times the average; 50 means that the Analyzed Industry is half the national average.

SIC 7375 - INFORMATION RETRIEVAL SERVICES: GENERAL STATISTICS

Year	Estab-lish-ments	Employ-ment (000)	Payroll ($ mil.)	Revenues ($ mil.)		Ownership	
				SAS	Census	Sole Prop.	Partner-ships
1987	463	13.1	354.6		1,175.9	22	13
1988	494	13.9	396.0				
1989	446	14.5	435.7				
1990	508	16.7	515.7	3,547.0			
1991	690	20.2	629.9	3,691.0			
1992	1,090	31.9	1,097.6	3,931.0	3,900.0		
1993	1,128	31.2	1,107.4	4,277.0			
1994	1,245[1]	36.5[1]	1,387.9[1]	4,559.0[1]			
1995	1,694[1]	39.2[1]	1,659.7[1]	5,343.0[1]			
1996	1,622[1]	42.5[1]	1,686.2[1]	6,916.0[1]			
1997	1,774[1]	46.2[1]	1,854.8[1]	6,614.7[1]			
1998	1,926[1]	49.9[1]	2,023.5[1]	7,116.1[1]			

Source: Data for 1987 and 1992 are from Census of Service Industries, Bureau of the Census, U.S. Department of Commerce. Data labeled SAS are from the *Service Annual Survey* for 1996, which also presented revisions for ealier years. Data for 1988-1991 and 1993-1995, when shown, are derived from *County Business Patterns* for those years from the Bureau of the Census. Extracted from *Service Industries USA*, 4th edition, Gale, 1998. Note: 1. Projections made by the editor.

SIC 7375 - INFORMATION RETRIEVAL SERVICES: INDICES OF CHANGE

Year	Estab-lish-ments	Employ-ment (000)	Payroll ($ mil.)	Revenues ($ mil.)	
				SAS	Census
1987	42	41	32		30
1988	45	44	36		
1989	41	45	40		
1990	47	52	47	90	
1991	63	63	57	94	
1992	100	100	100	100	100
1993	103	98	101	109	
1994	114[1]	115[1]	126[1]	116[1]	
1995	155[1]	123[1]	151[1]	136[1]	
1996	149[1]	133[1]	154[1]	176[1]	
1997	163[1]	145[1]	169[1]	168[1]	
1998	177[1]	157[1]	184[1]	181[1]	

Source: Same as General Statistics. The values shown reflect change from the base year, 1992, which is always 100. Data points earlier or later than 1992 are less than 1992 if less than 100 and greater than 1992 if greater than 100. Note: 1. Index based on a projected value.

SIC 7375 - INFORMATION RETRIEVAL SERVICES: SELECTED RATIOS

For 1992	Average of All Services	Analyzed Industry	Index
Employees per establishment	13	29	217
Revenues per establishment	810,117	3,577,982	442
Payroll per establishment	314,133	1,006,939	321
Payroll per employee	23,335	34,440	148
Revenue per employee	60,179	122,376	203
Sole proprietors as % of establishments	30.1	na	na
Partnerships as % of establishments	5.7	na	na

Source: Same as General Statistics. The 'Average of all Services' column represents the average of all service industries of which this SIC is a part. The Index shows the relationship between the Average and the Analyzed Industry. For example, 100 means that they are equal; 500 that the Analyzed Industry is five times the average; 50 means that the Analyzed Industry is half the national average.

SIC 7376 - COMPUTER FACILITIES MANAGEMENT: GENERAL STATISTICS

Year	Estab-lish-ments	Employ-ment (000)	Payroll ($ mil.)	Revenues ($ mil.)		Ownership	
				SAS	Census	Sole Prop.	Partner-ships
1987	738	18.5	505.2		1,198.2	46	15
1988	731	22.2	605.5				
1989	640	22.7	645.2				
1990	639	24.3	753.3	1,994.0			
1991	627	24.9	796.8	2,206.0			
1992	675	23.4	934.4	2,608.0	2,576.8	30	19
1993	697	31.1	1,169.1	2,557.0			
1994	728[1]	29.8[1]	1,170.8[1]	2,652.0[1]			
1995	792[1]	30.9[1]	1,301.2[1]	2,856.0[1]			
1996	726[1]	32.6[1]	1,384.8[1]	2,911.0[1]			
1997	732[1]	34.1[1]	1,486.6[1]	3,125.6[1]			
1998	738[1]	35.6[1]	1,588.5[1]	3,271.8[1]			

Source: Data for 1987 and 1992 are from Census of Service Industries, Bureau of the Census, U.S. Department of Commerce. Data labeled SAS are from the *Service Annual Survey* for 1996, which also presented revisions for ealier years. Data for 1988-1991 and 1993-1995, when shown, are derived from *County Business Patterns* for those years from the Bureau of the Census. Extracted from *Service Industries USA*, 4th edition, Gale, 1998. Note: 1. Projections made by the editor.

SIC 7376 - COMPUTER FACILITIES MANAGEMENT: INDICES OF CHANGE

Year	Estab-lish-ments	Employ-ment (000)	Payroll ($ mil.)	Revenues ($ mil.)		Ownership	
				SAS	Census	Sole Prop.	Partner-ships
1987	109	79	54		46	153	79
1988	108	95	65				
1989	95	97	69				
1990	95	104	81	76			
1991	93	106	85	85			
1992	100	100	100	100	100	100	100
1993	103	133	125	98			
1994	108[1]	128[1]	125[1]	102[1]			
1995	117[1]	132[1]	139[1]	110[1]			
1996	108[1]	140[1]	148[1]	112[1]			
1997	108[1]	146[1]	159[1]	120[1]			
1998	109[1]	152[1]	170[1]	125[1]			

Source: Same as General Statistics. The values shown reflect change from the base year, 1992, which is always 100. Data points earlier or later than 1992 are less than 1992 if less than 100 and greater than 1992 if greater than 100. Note: 1. Index based on a projected value.

SIC 7376 - COMPUTER FACILITIES MANAGEMENT: SELECTED RATIOS

For 1992	Average of All Services	Analyzed Industry	Index
Employees per establishment	13	35	257
Revenues per establishment	810,117	3,817,462	471
Payroll per establishment	314,133	1,384,341	441
Payroll per employee	23,335	40,008	171
Revenue per employee	60,179	110,327	183
Sole proprietors as % of establishments	30.1	4.4	15
Partnerships as % of establishments	5.7	2.8	49

Source: Same as General Statistics. The 'Average of all Services' column represents the average of all service industries of which this SIC is a part. The Index shows the relationship between the Average and the Analyzed Industry. For example, 100 means that they are equal; 500 that the Analyzed Industry is five times the average; 50 means that the Analyzed Industry is half the national average.

SIC 7377 - COMPUTER RENTAL & LEASING: GENERAL STATISTICS

Year	Estab-lish-ments	Employ-ment (000)	Payroll ($ mil.)	Revenues ($ mil.)		Ownership	
				SAS	Census	Sole Prop.	Partner-ships
1987	1,061	8.7	319.6		2,165.5	86	64
1988	954	8.8	378.3				
1989	865	11.5	476.1				
1990	808	15.2	645.9	2,644.0			
1991	875	13.1	581.4	2,396.0			
1992	854	8.1	348.5	2,385.0	2,212.1	53	30
1993	766	7.8	300.4	2,482.0			
1994	812[1]	7.8[1]	334.3[1]	2,658.0[1]			
1995	821[1]	10.2[1]	569.8[1]	2,937.0[1]			
1996	740[1]	9.2[1]	457.7[1]	3,295.0[1]			
1997	715[1]	9.0[1]	461.4[1]	3,157.9[1]			
1998	689[1]	8.8[1]	465.0[1]	3,276.0[1]			

Source: Data for 1987 and 1992 are from Census of Service Industries, Bureau of the Census, U.S. Department of Commerce. Data labeled SAS are from the *Service Annual Survey* for 1996, which also presented revisions for ealier years. Data for 1988-1991 and 1993-1995, when shown, are derived from *County Business Patterns* for those years from the Bureau of the Census. Extracted from *Service Industries USA*, 4th edition, Gale, 1998. Note: 1. Projections made by the editor.

SIC 7377 - COMPUTER RENTAL & LEASING: INDICES OF CHANGE

Year	Estab-lish-ments	Employ-ment (000)	Payroll ($ mil.)	Revenues ($ mil.)		Ownership	
				SAS	Census	Sole Prop.	Partner-ships
1987	124	107	92		98	162	213
1988	112	109	109				
1989	101	142	137				
1990	95	188	185	111			
1991	102	163	167	100			
1992	100	100	100	100	100	100	100
1993	90	96	86	104			
1994	95[1]	96[1]	96[1]	111[1]			
1995	96[1]	126[1]	163[1]	123[1]			
1996	87[1]	113[1]	131[1]	138[1]			
1997	84[1]	111[1]	132[1]	132[1]			
1998	81[1]	108[1]	133[1]	137[1]			

Source: Same as General Statistics. The values shown reflect change from the base year, 1992, which is always 100. Data points earlier or later than 1992 are less than 1992 if less than 100 and greater than 1992 if greater than 100. Note: 1. Index based on a projected value.

SIC 7377 - COMPUTER RENTAL & LEASING: SELECTED RATIOS

For 1992	Average of All Services	Analyzed Industry	Index
Employees per establishment	13	9	70
Revenues per establishment	810,117	2,590,340	320
Payroll per establishment	314,133	408,137	130
Payroll per employee	23,335	43,100	185
Revenue per employee	60,179	273,544	455
Sole proprietors as % of establishments	30.1	6.2	21
Partnerships as % of establishments	5.7	3.5	61

Source: Same as General Statistics. The 'Average of all Services' column represents the average of all service industries of which this SIC is a part. The Index shows the relationship between the Average and the Analyzed Industry. For example, 100 means that they are equal; 500 that the Analyzed Industry is five times the average; 50 means that the Analyzed Industry is half the national average.

SIC 7378 - COMPUTER MAINTENANCE & REPAIR: GENERAL STATISTICS

| Year | Estab-lish-ments | Employ-ment (000) | Payroll ($ mil.) | Revenues ($ mil.) | | Ownership | |
				SAS	Census	Sole Prop.	Partner-ships
1987	3,693	53.3	1,717.1		5,749.1	352	74
1988	3,644	50.1	1,658.3				
1989	3,261	51.2	1,817.7				
1990	3,294	53.2	1,874.6	7,000.0			
1991	3,611	54.0	1,982.9	6,919.0			
1992	5,041	63.1	2,299.9	7,660.0	7,352.7	460	125
1993	4,876	62.5	2,448.7	8,291.0			
1994	4,846[1]	56.4[1]	2,117.6[1]	9,277.0[1]			
1995	4,887[1]	63.3[1]	2,569.9[1]	10,678.0[1]			
1996	5,241[1]	63.9[1]	2,593.8[1]	12,040.0[1]			
1997	5,464[1]	65.5[1]	2,701.7[1]	12,302.9[1]			
1998	5,687[1]	67.0[1]	2,809.7[1]	13,169.1[1]			

Source: Data for 1987 and 1992 are from Census of Service Industries, Bureau of the Census, U.S. Department of Commerce. Data labeled SAS are from the *Service Annual Survey* for 1996, which also presented revisions for ealier years. Data for 1988-1991 and 1993-1995, when shown, are derived from *County Business Patterns* for those years from the Bureau of the Census. Extracted from *Service Industries USA*, 4th edition, Gale, 1998. Note: 1. Projections made by the editor.

SIC 7378 - COMPUTER MAINTENANCE & REPAIR: INDICES OF CHANGE

| Year | Estab-lish-ments | Employ-ment (000) | Payroll ($ mil.) | Revenues ($ mil.) | | Ownership | |
				SAS	Census	Sole Prop.	Partner-ships
1987	73	84	75		78	77	59
1988	72	79	72				
1989	65	81	79				
1990	65	84	82	91			
1991	72	86	86	90			
1992	100	100	100	100	100	100	100
1993	97	99	106	108			
1994	96[1]	89[1]	92[1]	121[1]			
1995	97[1]	100[1]	112[1]	139[1]			
1996	104[1]	101[1]	113[1]	157[1]			
1997	108[1]	104[1]	117[1]	161[1]			
1998	113[1]	106[1]	122[1]	172[1]			

Source: Same as General Statistics. The values shown reflect change from the base year, 1992, which is always 100. Data points earlier or later than 1992 are less than 1992 if less than 100 and greater than 1992 if greater than 100. Note: 1. Index based on a projected value.

SIC 7378 - COMPUTER MAINTENANCE & REPAIR: SELECTED RATIOS

For 1992	Average of All Services	Analyzed Industry	Index
Employees per establishment	13	13	93
Revenues per establishment	810,117	1,458,584	180
Payroll per establishment	314,133	456,238	145
Payroll per employee	23,335	36,469	156
Revenue per employee	60,179	116,591	194
Sole proprietors as % of establishments	30.1	9.1	30
Partnerships as % of establishments	5.7	2.5	43

Source: Same as General Statistics. The 'Average of all Services' column represents the average of all service industries of which this SIC is a part. The Index shows the relationship between the Average and the Analyzed Industry. For example, 100 means that they are equal; 500 that the Analyzed Industry is five times the average; 50 means that the Analyzed Industry is half the national average.

SIC 7379 - COMPUTER RELATED SERVICES, NEC: GENERAL STATISTICS

Year	Estab- lish- ments	Employ- ment (000)	Payroll ($ mil.)	Revenues ($ mil.)		Ownership	
				SAS	Census	Sole Prop.	Partner- ships
1987	4,820	34.9	1,126.7		2,587.8	396	117
1988	4,674	39.5	1,414.8				
1989	5,348	46.4	1,769.0				
1990	6,823	51.2	2,017.4	4,537.0			
1991	8,133	59.0	2,382.7	4,894.0			
1992	8,722	57.7	2,466.2	6,234.0	5,676.8	740	164
1993	11,174	76.4	3,304.5	7,845.0			
1994	13,820[1]	87.7[1]	4,119.3[1]	10,285.0[1]			
1995	17,688[1]	115.0[1]	5,732.3[1]	13,176.0[1]			
1996	16,728[1]	107.4[1]	5,208.3[1]	16,504.0[1]			
1997	18,269[1]	116.3[1]	5,709.2[1]	11,341.1[1]			
1998	19,810[1]	125.1[1]	6,210.2[1]	11,732.6[1]			

Source: Data for 1987 and 1992 are from Census of Service Industries, Bureau of the Census, U.S. Department of Commerce. Data labeled SAS are from the *Service Annual Survey* for 1996, which also presented revisions for ealier years. Data for 1988-1991 and 1993-1995, when shown, are derived from *County Business Patterns* for those years from the Bureau of the Census. Extracted from *Service Industries USA*, 4th edition, Gale, 1998. Note: 1. Projections made by the editor.

SIC 7379 - COMPUTER RELATED SERVICES, NEC: INDICES OF CHANGE

Year	Estab- lish- ments	Employ- ment (000)	Payroll ($ mil.)	Revenues ($ mil.)		Ownership	
				SAS	Census	Sole Prop.	Partner- ships
1987	55	60	46		46	54	71
1988	54	68	57				
1989	61	80	72				
1990	78	89	82	73			
1991	93	102	97	79			
1992	100	100	100	100	100	100	100
1993	128	132	134	126			
1994	158[1]	152[1]	167[1]	165[1]			
1995	203[1]	199[1]	232[1]	211[1]			
1996	192[1]	186[1]	211[1]	265[1]			
1997	209[1]	201[1]	232[1]	182[1]			
1998	227[1]	217[1]	252[1]	188[1]			

Source: Same as General Statistics. The values shown reflect change from the base year, 1992, which is always 100. Data points earlier or later than 1992 are less than 1992 if less than 100 and greater than 1992 if greater than 100. Note: 1. Index based on a projected value.

SIC 7379 - COMPUTER RELATED SERVICES, NEC: SELECTED RATIOS

For 1992	Average of All Services	Analyzed Industry	Index
Employees per establishment	13	7	49
Revenues per establishment	810,117	650,865	80
Payroll per establishment	314,133	282,754	90
Payroll per employee	23,335	42,712	183
Revenue per employee	60,179	98,317	163
Sole proprietors as % of establishments	30.1	8.5	28
Partnerships as % of establishments	5.7	1.9	33

Source: Same as General Statistics. The 'Average of all Services' column represents the average of all service industries of which this SIC is a part. The Index shows the relationship between the Average and the Analyzed Industry. For example, 100 means that they are equal; 500 that the Analyzed Industry is five times the average; 50 means that the Analyzed Industry is half the national average.

FINANCIAL NORMS AND RATIOS

Industry-specific financial norms and ratios are shown in this chapter for twenty-three industries in the Computers & Software sector. For each industry in the sector, balance sheets are presented for the years 1996 through 1998, with the most recent year shown first. As part of each balance sheet, additional financial averages for net sales, gross profits, net profits after tax, and working capital are shown. The number of establishments used to calculate the averages are shown for each year.

The second table in each display shows D&B Key Business Ratios for the SIC-denominated industry. These data, again, are for the years 1996 through 1998. Ratios measuring solvency (e.g., Quick ratio), efficiency (e.g., Collection period, in days), and profitability (e.g. % return on sales) are shown. A total of 14 ratios are featured. Ratios are shown for the upper quartile, median, and lowest quartile of the D&B sample.

This product includes proprietary data of Dun & Bradstreet Inc.

D&B INDUSTRY NORMS: SIC 3571 - ELECTRONIC COMPUTERS

	1998 (142) Estab.		1997 (183) Estab.		1996 (152) Estab.	
	$	%	$	%	$	%
Cash	1,120,614	15.9	327,211	15.2	324,064	15.8
Accounts Receivable	2,396,282	34.0	774,972	36.0	742,476	36.2
Notes Receivable	28,192	.4	4,305	.2	8,204	.4
Inventory	1,677,397	23.8	510,190	23.7	477,892	23.3
Other Current Assets	620,214	8.8	124,857	5.8	127,164	6.2
Total Current Assets	5,842,699	82.9	1,741,535	80.9	1,679,800	81.9
Fixed Assets	768,220	10.9	277,698	12.9	264,584	12.9
Other Non-current Assets	436,969	6.2	133,467	6.2	106,654	5.2
Total Assets	7,047,888	100.0	2,152,700	100.0	2,051,038	100.0
Accounts Payable	1,571,679	22.3	454,220	21.1	393,799	19.2
Bank Loans	28,192	.4	2,153	.1	-	-
Notes Payable	204,389	2.9	81,803	3.8	90,246	4.4
Other Current Liabilities	1,437,769	20.4	406,860	18.9	391,748	19.1
Total Current Liabilities	3,242,029	46.0	945,036	43.9	875,793	42.7
Other Long Term	577,927	8.2	221,728	10.3	207,155	10.1
Deferred Credits	7,048	.1	2,153	.1	4,102	.2
Net Worth	3,220,885	45.7	983,784	45.7	963,988	47.0
Total Liabilities & Net Worth	7,047,889	100.0	2,152,701	100.0	2,051,038	100.0
Net Sales	7,756,000	100.0	6,000,000	100.0	5,136,439	100.0
Gross Profits	2,381,092	30.7	1,776,000	29.6	1,576,887	30.7
Net Profit After Tax	-23,268	-	156,000	2.6	169,502	3.3
Working Capital	2,600,671	-	796,499	-	804,007	-

Source: Dun & Bradstreet. Data in this table are copyright (c) 1999 of Dun & Bradstreet. Reprinted by special arrangement with D&B. *Notes:* Values in parentheses above columns indicate the number of establishments in the sample. Data shown are for all companies.

D&B KEY BUSINESS RATIOS: SIC 3571

	1998			1997			1996		
	UQ	MED	LQ	UQ	MED	LQ	UQ	MED	LQ
Solvency									
Quick ratio	1.8	1.1	.7	1.9	1.2	.8	2.2	1.1	.8
Current ratio	3.0	1.9	1.3	3.2	1.8	1.4	3.4	2.0	1.3
Current liabilities/Net worth (%)	38.8	90.4	180.8	39.2	85.8	174.9	27.9	65.9	139.2
Current liabilities/Inventory (%)	123.3	188.7	330.6	119.2	185.3	305.0	107.0	178.1	236.1
Total liabilities/Net worth (%)	44.5	106.9	243.7	46.8	101.8	212.8	39.8	91.5	205.8
Fixed assets/Net worth (%)	12.0	23.0	40.2	10.2	26.6	49.8	9.3	23.9	43.8
Efficiency									
Collection period (days)	33.3	54.0	90.9	30.9	49.7	74.7	28.9	45.8	82.8
Sales to Inventory	20.7	10.5	6.1	23.0	12.5	8.1	18.3	10.3	6.8
Assets/Sales (%)	28.2	58.0	96.4	22.3	38.1	64.0	22.0	37.5	75.5
Sales/Net Working Capital	12.8	5.3	2.5	16.8	7.7	4.0	15.8	6.5	4.0
Accounts payable/Sales (%)	5.0	8.0	13.1	3.7	6.3	9.9	2.6	6.2	10.0
Profitability									
Return - Sales (%)	5.4	1.2	-1.0	7.0	2.3	.3	6.1	2.5	.3
Return - Assets (%)	10.1	4.6	.4	14.4	6.8	.7	13.0	5.8	1.4
Return - Net Worth (%)	28.4	11.7	.4	46.4	18.4	3.7	30.9	17.1	3.6

Source: Dun & Bradstreet. Data in this table are copyright (c) 1999 of Dun & Bradstreet. Reprinted by special arrangement with D&B. *Note:* UQ stands for "Upper Quartile" and represents the top 25 percent of sample; MED stands for "Median"; and LQ stands for "Lower Quartile" and represents the lowest 25 percent.

D&B INDUSTRY NORMS: SIC 3572 - COMPUTER STORAGE DEVICES

	1998 (55) Estab.		1997 (50) Estab.		1996 (55) Estab.	
	$	%	$	%	$	%
Cash	998,879	14.1	649,860	16.4	638,989	16.9
Accounts Receivable	2,337,802	33.0	1,264,058	31.9	1,209,920	32.0
Notes Receivable	42,505	.6	3,963	.1	30,248	.8
Inventory	1,551,451	21.9	1,061,967	26.8	918,783	24.3
Other Current Assets	552,571	7.8	190,203	4.8	173,926	4.6
Total Current Assets	5,483,208	77.4	3,170,051	80.0	2,971,866	78.6
Fixed Assets	1,076,806	15.2	530,983	13.4	574,712	15.2
Other Non-current Assets	524,234	7.4	261,529	6.6	234,422	6.2
Total Assets	7,084,248	100.0	3,962,563	100.0	3,781,000	100.0
Accounts Payable	1,282,249	18.1	816,288	20.6	733,514	19.4
Bank Loans	42,505	.6	-	-	-	-
Notes Payable	283,370	4.0	166,428	4.2	162,583	4.3
Other Current Liabilities	1,381,429	19.5	590,422	14.9	597,398	15.8
Total Current Liabilities	2,989,553	42.2	1,573,138	39.7	1,493,495	39.5
Other Long Term	722,593	10.2	400,219	10.1	438,596	11.6
Deferred Credits	-	-	7,925	.2	-	-
Net Worth	3,372,103	47.6	1,981,282	50.0	1,848,909	48.9
Total Liabilities & Net Worth	7,084,249	100.0	3,962,564	100.0	3,781,000	100.0
Net Sales	15,091,914	100.0	6,306,171	100.0	6,605,000	100.0
Gross Profits	4,769,045	31.6	2,213,466	35.1	2,252,305	34.1
Net Profit After Tax	120,735	.8	-94,593	-	125,495	1.9
Working Capital	2,493,656	-	1,596,912	-	1,478,371	-

Source: Dun & Bradstreet. Data in this table are copyright (c) 1999 of Dun & Bradstreet. Reprinted by special arrangement with D&B. *Notes:* Values in parentheses above columns indicate the number of establishments in the sample. Data shown are for all companies.

D&B KEY BUSINESS RATIOS: SIC 3572

	1998			1997			1996		
	UQ	MED	LQ	UQ	MED	LQ	UQ	MED	LQ
Solvency									
Quick ratio	2.4	1.3	.8	2.3	1.2	.7	2.1	1.2	.8
Current ratio	4.1	2.1	1.4	3.8	2.3	1.5	3.3	2.3	1.5
Current liabilities/Net worth (%)	26.0	49.0	149.1	26.1	59.6	190.2	31.1	57.1	114.3
Current liabilities/Inventory (%)	121.9	163.3	239.3	97.0	150.8	218.1	109.3	171.2	233.3
Total liabilities/Net worth (%)	30.4	74.0	172.7	31.7	76.1	197.7	40.4	81.4	120.4
Fixed assets/Net worth (%)	9.1	21.9	55.9	9.1	23.4	47.4	10.1	19.0	35.4
Efficiency									
Collection period (days)	38.0	58.4	79.3	33.6	45.1	65.6	38.3	52.6	64.6
Sales to Inventory	16.1	10.5	5.9	17.1	8.0	5.8	21.6	8.8	6.1
Assets/Sales (%)	34.5	48.4	82.9	27.1	42.0	71.4	33.8	52.9	66.7
Sales/Net Working Capital	11.3	4.3	2.8	7.8	6.2	2.9	7.2	5.3	3.2
Accounts payable/Sales (%)	5.2	8.2	14.5	4.3	7.8	11.3	4.8	7.2	12.5
Profitability									
Return - Sales (%)	8.4	2.5	-5.3	6.6	2.8	-.1	8.3	3.0	-3.0
Return - Assets (%)	15.5	4.3	-12.1	13.7	7.7	-.3	16.2	8.0	-4.7
Return - Net Worth (%)	26.0	12.4	-13.1	33.7	15.3	-.3	31.7	19.1	5.6

Source: Dun & Bradstreet. Data in this table are copyright (c) 1999 of Dun & Bradstreet. Reprinted by special arrangement with D&B. *Note:* UQ stands for "Upper Quartile" and represents the top 25 percent of sample; MED stands for "Median"; and LQ stands for "Lower Quartile" and represents the lowest 25 percent.

D&B INDUSTRY NORMS: SIC 3575 - COMPUTER TERMINALS

	1998 (53) Estab.		1997 (49) Estab.		1996 (38) Estab.	
	$	%	$	%	$	%
Cash	385,656	13.9	514,586	15.2	326,340	14.9
Accounts Receivable	885,068	31.9	958,078	28.3	700,865	32.0
Notes Receivable	8,324	.3	40,625	1.2	-	-
Inventory	624,264	22.5	815,890	24.1	508,127	23.2
Other Current Assets	144,274	5.2	162,501	4.8	67,896	3.1
Total Current Assets	2,047,586	73.8	2,491,680	73.6	1,603,228	73.2
Fixed Assets	568,774	20.5	639,847	18.9	363,574	16.6
Other Non-current Assets	158,147	5.7	253,908	7.5	223,401	10.2
Total Assets	2,774,507	100.0	3,385,435	100.0	2,190,203	100.0
Accounts Payable	460,568	16.6	585,680	17.3	359,193	16.4
Bank Loans	5,549	.2	-	-	-	-
Notes Payable	110,980	4.0	77,865	2.3	81,038	3.7
Other Current Liabilities	402,304	14.5	501,044	14.8	295,677	13.5
Total Current Liabilities	979,401	35.3	1,164,589	34.4	735,908	33.6
Other Long Term	371,784	13.4	365,627	10.8	243,113	11.1
Deferred Credits	5,549	.2	3,385	.1	17,522	.8
Net Worth	1,417,773	51.1	1,851,833	54.7	1,193,661	54.5
Total Liabilities & Net Worth	2,774,507	100.0	3,385,434	100.0	2,190,204	100.0
Net Sales	15,318,934	100.0	9,940,868	100.0	15,487,573	100.0
Gross Profits	3,845,052	25.1	2,743,680	27.6	4,042,257	26.1
Net Profit After Tax	168,508	1.1	318,108	3.2	201,338	1.3
Working Capital	1,068,185	-	1,327,090	-	867,321	-

Source: Dun & Bradstreet. Data in this table are copyright (c) 1999 of Dun & Bradstreet. Reprinted by special arrangement with D&B. *Notes:* Values in parentheses above columns indicate the number of establishments in the sample. Data shown are for all companies.

D&B KEY BUSINESS RATIOS: SIC 3575

	1998			1997			1996		
	UQ	MED	LQ	UQ	MED	LQ	UQ	MED	LQ
Solvency									
Quick ratio	2.5	1.1	.9	2.6	1.5	.8	2.5	1.6	.9
Current ratio	3.9	2.2	1.4	4.5	2.7	1.4	3.8	2.5	1.6
Current liabilities/Net worth (%)	20.5	44.2	97.0	23.2	46.8	91.8	24.4	41.2	156.7
Current liabilities/Inventory (%)	71.0	126.6	224.1	66.0	119.0	213.3	76.7	132.5	228.6
Total liabilities/Net worth (%)	25.6	82.8	139.6	25.8	54.8	137.0	35.5	67.4	170.2
Fixed assets/Net worth (%)	8.4	20.4	62.4	12.2	18.5	64.3	13.9	26.0	45.5
Efficiency									
Collection period (days)	38.6	49.6	75.2	29.2	46.0	57.5	34.3	56.2	73.2
Sales to Inventory	19.1	8.4	6.0	15.1	9.4	5.1	15.8	9.2	4.9
Assets/Sales (%)	26.6	55.5	81.3	33.8	52.3	69.3	26.8	57.8	78.8
Sales/Net Working Capital	15.1	5.3	3.4	10.9	4.8	2.3	7.1	4.2	2.6
Accounts payable/Sales (%)	6.3	8.7	11.9	3.1	6.3	9.4	3.8	6.6	9.8
Profitability									
Return - Sales (%)	3.6	1.2	-.9	7.2	3.4	.7	5.8	1.7	-1.9
Return - Assets (%)	8.9	2.9	-1.2	19.8	8.9	1.6	16.3	2.4	-2.8
Return - Net Worth (%)	30.1	9.9	-1.4	35.4	13.9	2.6	23.0	4.3	-6.0

Source: Dun & Bradstreet. Data in this table are copyright (c) 1999 of Dun & Bradstreet. Reprinted by special arrangement with D&B. *Note:* UQ stands for "Upper Quartile" and represents the top 25 percent of sample; MED stands for "Median"; and LQ stands for "Lower Quartile" and represents the lowest 25 percent.

D&B INDUSTRY NORMS: SIC 3577 - COMPUTER PERIPHERAL EQUIPMENT, NEC

	1998 (278) Estab.		1997 (295) Estab.		1996 (258) Estab.	
	$	%	$	%	$	%
Cash	1,307,237	17.9	352,690	15.6	303,023	16.3
Accounts Receivable	2,176,294	29.8	687,294	30.4	540,979	29.1
Notes Receivable	7,303	.1	6,783	.3	3,718	.2
Inventory	1,679,690	23.0	576,513	25.5	496,362	26.7
Other Current Assets	664,573	9.1	144,693	6.4	117,119	6.3
Total Current Assets	5,835,097	79.9	1,767,973	78.2	1,461,201	78.6
Fixed Assets	934,784	12.8	345,908	15.3	275,137	14.8
Other Non-current Assets	533,119	7.3	146,954	6.5	122,696	6.6
Total Assets	7,303,000	100.0	2,260,835	100.0	1,859,034	100.0
Accounts Payable	1,007,814	13.8	377,559	16.7	314,177	16.9
Bank Loans	7,303	.1	2,261	.1	1,859	.1
Notes Payable	204,484	2.8	65,564	2.9	66,925	3.6
Other Current Liabilities	1,153,874	15.8	368,516	16.3	308,600	16.6
Total Current Liabilities	2,373,475	32.5	813,900	36.0	691,561	37.2
Other Long Term	635,361	8.7	228,344	10.1	189,622	10.2
Deferred Credits	7,303	.1	13,565	.6	5,577	.3
Net Worth	4,286,861	58.7	1,205,025	53.3	972,275	52.3
Total Liabilities & Net Worth	7,303,000	100.0	2,260,834	100.0	1,859,035	100.0
Net Sales	12,987,150	100.0	5,257,562	100.0	5,157,832	100.0
Gross Profits	4,805,246	37.0	2,076,737	39.5	2,037,344	39.5
Net Profit After Tax	77,923	.6	205,045	3.9	103,157	2.0
Working Capital	3,461,622	-	954,072	-	769,641	-

Source: Dun & Bradstreet. Data in this table are copyright (c) 1999 of Dun & Bradstreet. Reprinted by special arrangement with D&B. *Notes:* Values in parentheses above columns indicate the number of establishments in the sample. Data shown are for all companies.

D&B KEY BUSINESS RATIOS: SIC 3577

	1998			1997			1996		
	UQ	MED	LQ	UQ	MED	LQ	UQ	MED	LQ
Solvency									
Quick ratio	2.8	1.7	.9	2.8	1.4	.8	2.2	1.3	.8
Current ratio	5.0	2.8	1.6	4.8	2.2	1.5	4.3	2.2	1.5
Current liabilities/Net worth (%)	19.8	38.9	106.7	21.4	55.4	141.7	23.5	65.6	145.8
Current liabilities/Inventory (%)	75.7	132.5	203.3	74.1	138.9	211.9	72.2	149.5	226.8
Total liabilities/Net worth (%)	23.7	52.3	137.9	26.3	82.1	173.9	28.2	90.5	179.0
Fixed assets/Net worth (%)	10.0	17.9	34.2	8.8	20.2	41.5	8.4	19.8	41.7
Efficiency									
Collection period (days)	40.5	59.5	81.4	34.9	50.0	68.0	36.1	52.6	71.2
Sales to Inventory	13.9	7.2	4.6	16.0	8.1	5.2	15.3	7.8	4.9
Assets/Sales (%)	34.3	60.6	103.3	29.6	47.8	74.6	31.6	49.7	75.7
Sales/Net Working Capital	8.5	3.3	1.9	10.8	5.1	2.7	9.8	5.1	2.7
Accounts payable/Sales (%)	4.4	7.3	11.9	4.5	6.6	10.5	3.5	6.6	10.8
Profitability									
Return - Sales (%)	8.9	2.7	-4.4	8.3	3.0	.6	7.9	2.4	-.2
Return - Assets (%)	17.2	6.2	-6.8	16.0	7.4	1.3	16.7	5.8	-1.9
Return - Net Worth (%)	29.8	12.8	-5.9	30.5	13.3	3.5	31.7	13.1	-2.8

Source: Dun & Bradstreet. Data in this table are copyright (c) 1999 of Dun & Bradstreet. Reprinted by special arrangement with D&B. *Note:* UQ stands for "Upper Quartile" and represents the top 25 percent of sample; MED stands for "Median"; and LQ stands for "Lower Quartile" and represents the lowest 25 percent.

D&B INDUSTRY NORMS: SIC 3578 - CALCULATING AND ACCOUNTING EQUIPMENT

	1998 (26) Estab.		1997 (27) Estab.		1996 (20) Estab.	
	$	%	$	%	$	%
Cash	2,773,837	16.7	370,561	10.7	1,036,206	13.6
Accounts Receivable	4,634,134	27.9	1,142,853	33.0	1,904,791	25.0
Notes Receivable	-	-	20,779	.6	7,619	.1
Inventory	2,607,739	15.7	675,322	19.5	1,493,356	19.6
Other Current Assets	847,100	5.1	238,960	6.9	761,916	10.0
Total Current Assets	10,862,810	65.4	2,448,475	70.7	5,203,888	68.3
Fixed Assets	3,537,887	21.3	644,154	18.6	1,158,113	15.2
Other Non-current Assets	2,209,103	13.3	370,561	10.7	1,257,162	16.5
Total Assets	16,609,800	100.0	3,463,190	100.0	7,619,163	100.0
Accounts Payable	1,893,517	11.4	460,604	13.3	891,442	11.7
Bank Loans	83,049	.5	-	-	-	-
Notes Payable	448,465	2.7	117,748	3.4	175,241	2.3
Other Current Liabilities	3,255,521	19.6	574,890	16.6	1,158,113	15.2
Total Current Liabilities	5,680,552	34.2	1,153,242	33.3	2,224,796	29.2
Other Long Term	3,787,034	22.8	540,258	15.6	1,112,398	14.6
Deferred Credits	16,610	.1	6,926	.2	-	-
Net Worth	7,125,604	42.9	1,762,764	50.9	4,281,970	56.2
Total Liabilities & Net Worth	16,609,800	100.0	3,463,190	100.0	7,619,164	100.0
Net Sales	21,181,000	100.0	8,721,231	100.0	45,983,993	100.0
Gross Profits	7,836,970	37.0	3,104,758	35.6	16,508,253	35.9
Net Profit After Tax	381,258	1.8	558,159	6.4	1,747,392	3.8
Working Capital	5,182,257	-	1,295,233	-	2,979,092	-

Source: Dun & Bradstreet. Data in this table are copyright (c) 1999 of Dun & Bradstreet. Reprinted by special arrangement with D&B. *Notes:* Values in parentheses above columns indicate the number of establishments in the sample. Data shown are for all companies.

D&B KEY BUSINESS RATIOS: SIC 3578

	1998			1997			1996		
	UQ	MED	LQ	UQ	MED	LQ	UQ	MED	LQ
Solvency									
Quick ratio	1.9	1.3	.9	3.0	1.7	.8	2.8	1.7	.5
Current ratio	2.9	2.2	1.2	4.5	2.3	1.3	4.5	2.9	1.3
Current liabilities/Net worth (%)	36.9	58.1	91.9	19.1	48.4	108.8	13.5	32.3	107.0
Current liabilities/Inventory (%)	116.9	189.1	279.9	58.9	180.3	213.2	74.2	105.5	259.1
Total liabilities/Net worth (%)	48.2	64.9	130.4	31.6	72.6	128.0	15.0	32.8	137.3
Fixed assets/Net worth (%)	11.5	22.6	50.2	13.8	26.3	46.7	8.8	16.6	27.8
Efficiency									
Collection period (days)	35.4	62.8	114.1	40.4	54.6	93.8	33.9	59.4	87.0
Sales to Inventory	12.6	6.0	4.3	16.9	9.6	5.4	12.3	9.1	5.3
Assets/Sales (%)	39.4	75.3	118.5	31.4	62.2	85.6	58.3	72.1	85.2
Sales/Net Working Capital	9.7	3.7	1.9	9.1	5.2	3.1	6.6	4.2	2.6
Accounts payable/Sales (%)	5.0	8.2	10.9	4.7	6.6	8.4	4.6	7.7	9.5
Profitability									
Return - Sales (%)	9.8	2.5	-4.3	9.6	7.1	4.1	9.5	5.4	-2.4
Return - Assets (%)	11.8	4.9	-4.3	21.9	11.3	9.1	11.3	6.8	-2.9
Return - Net Worth (%)	32.4	11.8	-1.3	52.7	26.1	16.3	31.2	8.8	-7.0

Source: Dun & Bradstreet. Data in this table are copyright (c) 1999 of Dun & Bradstreet. Reprinted by special arrangement with D&B. *Note:* UQ stands for "Upper Quartile" and represents the top 25 percent of sample; MED stands for "Median"; and LQ stands for "Lower Quartile" and represents the lowest 25 percent.

D&B INDUSTRY NORMS: SIC 3672 - PRINTED CIRCUIT BOARDS

	1998 (258) Estab.		1997 (326) Estab.		1996 (282) Estab.	
	$	%	$	%	$	%
Cash	188,784	11.1	165,503	11.0	127,981	11.6
Accounts Receivable	513,629	30.2	473,941	31.5	348,637	31.6
Notes Receivable	5,102	.3	4,514	.3	4,413	.4
Inventory	311,239	18.3	245,246	16.3	178,732	16.2
Other Current Assets	74,833	4.4	67,706	4.5	52,958	4.8
Total Current Assets	1,093,587	64.3	956,910	63.6	712,721	64.6
Fixed Assets	513,629	30.2	481,464	32.0	339,811	30.8
Other Non-current Assets	93,542	5.5	66,201	4.4	50,751	4.6
Total Assets	1,700,758	100.0	1,504,575	100.0	1,103,283	100.0
Accounts Payable	280,625	16.5	237,723	15.8	178,732	16.2
Bank Loans	1,701	.1	1,505	.1	3,310	.3
Notes Payable	59,527	3.5	61,688	4.1	38,615	3.5
Other Current Liabilities	256,814	15.1	227,191	15.1	180,938	16.4
Total Current Liabilities	598,667	35.2	528,107	35.1	401,595	36.4
Other Long Term	290,830	17.1	276,842	18.4	188,661	17.1
Deferred Credits	3,402	.2	3,009	.2	2,207	.2
Net Worth	807,860	47.5	696,618	46.3	510,820	46.3
Total Liabilities & Net Worth	1,700,759	100.0	1,504,576	100.0	1,103,283	100.0
Net Sales	4,286,719	100.0	4,087,817	100.0	2,902,550	100.0
Gross Profits	1,247,435	29.1	1,340,804	32.8	911,401	31.4
Net Profit After Tax	184,329	4.3	188,040	4.6	162,543	5.6
Working Capital	494,920	-	428,804	-	311,126	-

Source: Dun & Bradstreet. Data in this table are copyright (c) 1999 of Dun & Bradstreet. Reprinted by special arrangement with D&B. *Notes:* Values in parentheses above columns indicate the number of establishments in the sample. Data shown are for all companies.

D&B KEY BUSINESS RATIOS: SIC 3672

	1998			1997			1996		
	UQ	MED	LQ	UQ	MED	LQ	UQ	MED	LQ
Solvency									
Quick ratio	2.2	1.1	.8	2.1	1.2	.8	2.2	1.2	.7
Current ratio	3.5	1.9	1.3	3.3	1.9	1.3	2.9	1.9	1.3
Current liabilities/Net worth (%)	27.2	73.4	151.6	27.8	65.0	142.1	29.9	67.4	166.0
Current liabilities/Inventory (%)	100.6	175.2	256.6	114.3	191.1	323.1	120.9	192.5	290.0
Total liabilities/Net worth (%)	44.9	110.2	218.1	52.0	107.6	228.6	51.0	113.9	224.5
Fixed assets/Net worth (%)	28.8	55.8	119.2	33.4	68.3	117.7	30.0	65.2	111.3
Efficiency									
Collection period (days)	36.4	45.7	57.3	36.5	47.3	58.8	38.0	47.3	57.7
Sales to Inventory	22.8	12.3	6.8	31.1	14.9	8.6	32.4	14.1	8.0
Assets/Sales (%)	32.2	45.4	62.6	30.1	41.5	58.7	30.3	42.2	55.5
Sales/Net Working Capital	13.5	7.6	4.3	14.8	7.6	4.7	14.6	7.5	5.3
Accounts payable/Sales (%)	3.7	6.7	10.5	3.5	6.4	9.1	4.1	6.4	9.7
Profitability									
Return - Sales (%)	8.3	3.6	.7	8.1	3.8	1.2	8.3	4.3	1.7
Return - Assets (%)	17.8	7.9	1.3	16.7	8.1	3.4	18.4	10.6	4.3
Return - Net Worth (%)	39.4	18.9	4.8	44.0	19.7	9.1	46.0	21.2	10.3

Source: Dun & Bradstreet. Data in this table are copyright (c) 1999 of Dun & Bradstreet. Reprinted by special arrangement with D&B. *Note:* UQ stands for "Upper Quartile" and represents the top 25 percent of sample; MED stands for "Median"; and LQ stands for "Lower Quartile" and represents the lowest 25 percent.

D&B INDUSTRY NORMS: SIC 3674 - SEMICONDUCTORS AND RELATED DEVICES

	1998 (272) Estab.		1997 (268) Estab.		1996 (237) Estab.	
	$	%	$	%	$	%
Cash	3,099,160	23.1	1,001,216	18.2	617,112	19.6
Accounts Receivable	2,777,170	20.7	1,171,752	21.3	755,647	24.0
Notes Receivable	-	-	5,501	.1	3,149	.1
Inventory	2,401,514	17.9	1,061,729	19.3	604,518	19.2
Other Current Assets	1,113,551	8.3	539,116	9.8	299,110	9.5
Total Current Assets	9,391,395	70.0	3,779,314	68.7	2,279,536	72.4
Fixed Assets	3,058,912	22.8	1,309,282	23.8	686,379	21.8
Other Non-current Assets	965,972	7.2	412,589	7.5	182,615	5.8
Total Assets	13,416,279	100.0	5,501,185	100.0	3,148,530	100.0
Accounts Payable	1,556,288	11.6	605,130	11.0	406,160	12.9
Bank Loans	13,416	.1	5,501	.1	-	-
Notes Payable	147,579	1.1	137,530	2.5	88,159	2.8
Other Current Liabilities	1,972,193	14.7	880,190	16.0	522,656	16.6
Total Current Liabilities	3,689,476	27.5	1,628,351	29.6	1,016,975	32.3
Other Long Term	1,462,374	10.9	638,137	11.6	321,150	10.2
Deferred Credits	26,833	.2	27,506	.5	3,149	.1
Net Worth	8,237,595	61.4	3,207,191	58.3	1,807,256	57.4
Total Liabilities & Net Worth	13,416,278	100.0	5,501,185	100.0	3,148,530	100.0
Net Sales	14,722,000	100.0	10,006,000	100.0	9,835,229	100.0
Gross Profits	5,299,920	36.0	3,882,328	38.8	3,924,256	39.9
Net Profit After Tax	426,938	2.9	410,246	4.1	816,324	8.3
Working Capital	5,701,918	-	2,150,963	-	1,262,560	-

Source: Dun & Bradstreet. Data in this table are copyright (c) 1999 of Dun & Bradstreet. Reprinted by special arrangement with D&B. *Notes:* Values in parentheses above columns indicate the number of establishments in the sample. Data shown are for all companies.

D&B KEY BUSINESS RATIOS: SIC 3674

	1998			1997			1996		
	UQ	MED	LQ	UQ	MED	LQ	UQ	MED	LQ
Solvency									
Quick ratio	3.0	1.6	.9	2.6	1.5	.8	2.3	1.3	.8
Current ratio	5.0	2.9	1.7	4.5	2.7	1.7	3.9	2.5	1.6
Current liabilities/Net worth (%)	18.9	33.1	66.3	19.7	36.5	86.0	23.9	39.0	96.5
Current liabilities/Inventory (%)	88.6	142.1	249.4	71.8	155.9	282.5	86.6	143.5	243.8
Total liabilities/Net worth (%)	23.2	48.7	100.7	25.7	55.7	114.9	28.3	57.4	116.8
Fixed assets/Net worth (%)	13.4	30.4	69.1	14.5	33.9	69.5	13.8	30.5	65.3
Efficiency									
Collection period (days)	43.6	55.1	73.2	36.5	48.4	63.3	40.4	53.7	69.1
Sales to Inventory	12.6	7.1	4.8	13.7	8.5	5.3	12.0	7.9	5.1
Assets/Sales (%)	53.9	94.4	147.2	48.1	72.7	113.9	44.7	70.0	106.1
Sales/Net Working Capital	4.6	2.6	1.6	6.1	3.8	2.2	5.6	3.6	2.0
Accounts payable/Sales (%)	4.4	7.9	14.4	3.8	6.9	9.9	3.9	8.0	11.9
Profitability									
Return - Sales (%)	11.5	4.2	-3.1	10.9	5.2	.4	13.8	7.2	2.2
Return - Assets (%)	14.3	6.4	-2.8	14.9	6.8	.1	19.8	10.6	3.4
Return - Net Worth (%)	23.0	13.0	-4.5	26.8	11.0	.2	28.6	16.8	6.0

Source: Dun & Bradstreet. Data in this table are copyright (c) 1999 of Dun & Bradstreet. Reprinted by special arrangement with D&B. *Note:* UQ stands for "Upper Quartile" and represents the top 25 percent of sample; MED stands for "Median"; and LQ stands for "Lower Quartile" and represents the lowest 25 percent.

D&B INDUSTRY NORMS: SIC 3675 - ELECTRONIC CAPACITORS

	1998 (14) Estab.		1997 (15) Estab.		1996 (16) Estab.	
	$	%	$	%	$	%
Cash	755,968	14.7	467,801	9.1	483,603	10.3
Accounts Receivable	1,244,519	24.2	1,244,041	24.2	1,093,977	23.3
Notes Receivable	15,428	.3	5,141	.1	28,171	.6
Inventory	1,198,235	23.3	1,351,995	26.3	1,380,383	29.4
Other Current Assets	149,137	2.9	195,345	3.8	122,075	2.6
Total Current Assets	3,363,287	65.4	3,264,323	63.5	3,108,209	66.2
Fixed Assets	1,491,365	29.0	1,408,542	27.4	1,155,014	24.6
Other Non-current Assets	287,988	5.6	467,801	9.1	431,956	9.2
Total Assets	5,142,640	100.0	5,140,666	100.0	4,695,179	100.0
Accounts Payable	766,253	14.9	411,253	8.0	511,775	10.9
Bank Loans	-	-	-	-	-	-
Notes Payable	35,998	.7	41,125	.8	18,781	.4
Other Current Liabilities	452,552	8.8	832,788	16.2	770,009	16.4
Total Current Liabilities	1,254,803	24.4	1,285,166	25.0	1,300,565	27.7
Other Long Term	1,126,238	21.9	771,100	15.0	713,667	15.2
Deferred Credits	10,285	.2	5,141	.1	-	-
Net Worth	2,751,312	53.5	3,079,259	59.9	2,680,947	57.1
Total Liabilities & Net Worth	5,142,638	100.0	5,140,666	100.0	4,695,179	100.0
Net Sales	11,497,579	100.0	12,723,484	100.0	8,001,214	100.0
Gross Profits	3,472,269	30.2	3,855,216	30.3	2,336,354	29.2
Net Profit After Tax	528,889	4.6	776,133	6.1	376,057	4.7
Working Capital	2,108,482	-	1,979,156	-	1,807,643	-

Source: Dun & Bradstreet. Data in this table are copyright (c) 1999 of Dun & Bradstreet. Reprinted by special arrangement with D&B. *Notes:* Values in parentheses above columns indicate the number of establishments in the sample. Data shown are for all companies.

D&B KEY BUSINESS RATIOS: SIC 3675

	1998			1997			1996		
	UQ	MED	LQ	UQ	MED	LQ	UQ	MED	LQ
Solvency									
Quick ratio	2.7	1.9	1.2	2.1	1.8	.7	2.3	1.3	.7
Current ratio	4.7	4.2	2.7	4.3	3.5	1.6	3.7	2.8	1.4
Current liabilities/Net worth (%)	19.9	24.3	56.1	20.4	28.1	54.7	25.9	57.7	75.8
Current liabilities/Inventory (%)	54.2	69.1	82.7	53.4	73.3	110.2	60.5	83.9	125.5
Total liabilities/Net worth (%)	31.4	36.2	96.4	38.9	46.7	82.3	41.1	76.7	121.2
Fixed assets/Net worth (%)	33.2	46.5	133.2	20.8	42.1	55.5	24.4	42.7	61.5
Efficiency									
Collection period (days)	40.2	46.7	51.1	40.0	47.8	50.3	43.4	52.0	55.8
Sales to Inventory	7.8	5.8	4.5	8.0	6.0	4.8	7.9	7.0	5.0
Assets/Sales (%)	47.6	53.7	74.2	55.1	69.5	94.4	40.2	65.9	80.3
Sales/Net Working Capital	5.8	4.7	3.1	6.7	5.8	3.7	9.1	5.5	4.0
Accounts payable/Sales (%)	2.8	4.9	7.0	2.4	4.1	7.3	3.5	5.5	8.8
Profitability									
Return - Sales (%)	8.0	4.0	1.1	8.7	5.5	4.2	6.7	5.2	1.7
Return - Assets (%)	12.1	7.5	1.8	9.4	8.5	7.0	11.5	7.6	3.6
Return - Net Worth (%)	15.5	9.8	2.4	15.6	14.0	12.5	19.3	12.1	6.5

Source: Dun & Bradstreet. Data in this table are copyright (c) 1999 of Dun & Bradstreet. Reprinted by special arrangement with D&B. *Note:* UQ stands for "Upper Quartile" and represents the top 25 percent of sample; MED stands for "Median"; and LQ stands for "Lower Quartile" and represents the lowest 25 percent.

D&B INDUSTRY NORMS: SIC 3677 - ELECTRONIC COILS AND TRANSFORMERS

	1998 (65) Estab.		1997 (79) Estab.		1996 (72) Estab.	
	$	%	$	%	$	%
Cash	217,019	15.9	167,075	14.5	164,153	14.0
Accounts Receivable	408,105	29.9	361,804	31.4	358,791	30.6
Notes Receivable	4,095	.3	5,761	.5	-	-
Inventory	298,913	21.9	276,538	24.0	303,682	25.9
Other Current Assets	80,529	5.9	59,917	5.2	38,693	3.3
Total Current Assets	1,008,661	73.9	871,095	75.6	865,319	73.8
Fixed Assets	281,169	20.6	200,490	17.4	216,916	18.5
Other Non-current Assets	75,070	5.5	80,657	7.0	90,284	7.7
Total Assets	1,364,900	100.0	1,152,242	100.0	1,172,519	100.0
Accounts Payable	133,760	9.8	149,792	13.0	146,565	12.5
Bank Loans	16,379	1.2	-	-	9,380	.8
Notes Payable	40,947	3.0	50,699	4.4	48,073	4.1
Other Current Liabilities	174,707	12.8	144,030	12.5	152,427	13.0
Total Current Liabilities	365,793	26.8	344,521	29.9	356,445	30.4
Other Long Term	174,707	12.8	188,968	16.4	131,322	11.2
Deferred Credits	-	-	1,152	.1	5,863	.5
Net Worth	824,400	60.4	617,602	53.6	678,888	57.9
Total Liabilities & Net Worth	1,364,900	100.0	1,152,243	100.0	1,172,518	100.0
Net Sales	3,056,060	100.0	4,189,223	100.0	3,689,982	100.0
Gross Profits	1,103,238	36.1	1,495,553	35.7	1,346,843	36.5
Net Profit After Tax	235,317	7.7	234,596	5.6	236,159	6.4
Working Capital	642,868	-	526,575	-	508,873	-

Source: Dun & Bradstreet. Data in this table are copyright (c) 1999 of Dun & Bradstreet. Reprinted by special arrangement with D&B. *Notes:* Values in parentheses above columns indicate the number of establishments in the sample. Data shown are for all companies.

D&B KEY BUSINESS RATIOS: SIC 3677

	1998			1997			1996		
	UQ	MED	LQ	UQ	MED	LQ	UQ	MED	LQ
Solvency									
Quick ratio	3.4	1.8	.9	3.4	1.6	.9	2.9	1.4	.8
Current ratio	5.0	3.4	1.8	5.9	2.6	1.8	5.2	2.8	1.6
Current liabilities/Net worth (%)	19.6	35.7	99.8	18.9	45.7	105.8	21.6	40.8	99.1
Current liabilities/Inventory (%)	52.7	91.0	168.9	59.5	96.3	172.7	59.9	104.1	161.2
Total liabilities/Net worth (%)	22.2	61.2	112.1	21.7	82.2	151.3	26.6	68.3	164.3
Fixed assets/Net worth (%)	12.8	28.4	54.7	8.8	25.5	53.4	8.8	25.6	51.1
Efficiency									
Collection period (days)	39.6	50.4	61.9	32.5	46.0	55.9	37.5	50.9	61.5
Sales to Inventory	15.4	7.8	5.3	20.2	8.4	5.2	11.5	7.6	4.9
Assets/Sales (%)	35.0	54.8	62.3	32.0	43.2	65.3	36.6	48.9	67.5
Sales/Net Working Capital	7.0	4.2	2.8	7.8	5.1	3.7	7.4	4.7	3.3
Accounts payable/Sales (%)	2.8	4.1	5.8	2.7	4.3	7.2	2.5	4.2	7.2
Profitability									
Return - Sales (%)	15.5	7.3	3.7	8.4	5.7	1.5	8.6	6.1	2.7
Return - Assets (%)	20.9	12.6	5.9	20.6	11.7	3.0	19.8	12.3	4.4
Return - Net Worth (%)	35.3	22.3	11.2	38.3	19.8	3.6	40.7	20.1	7.9

Source: Dun & Bradstreet. Data in this table are copyright (c) 1999 of Dun & Bradstreet. Reprinted by special arrangement with D&B. *Note:* UQ stands for "Upper Quartile" and represents the top 25 percent of sample; MED stands for "Median"; and LQ stands for "Lower Quartile" and represents the lowest 25 percent.

D&B INDUSTRY NORMS: SIC 3678 - ELECTRONIC CONNECTORS

	1998 (37) Estab.		1997 (52) Estab.		1996 (45) Estab.	
	$	%	$	%	$	%
Cash	738,775	13.5	421,885	12.3	375,303	12.8
Accounts Receivable	1,154,677	21.1	994,687	29.0	785,792	26.8
Notes Receivable	-	-	3,430	.1	11,728	.4
Inventory	1,450,187	26.5	843,769	24.6	733,015	25.0
Other Current Assets	355,706	6.5	198,937	5.8	143,671	4.9
Total Current Assets	3,699,345	67.6	2,462,708	71.8	2,049,509	69.9
Fixed Assets	1,417,353	25.9	758,020	22.1	750,607	25.6
Other Non-current Assets	355,706	6.5	209,227	6.1	131,943	4.5
Total Assets	5,472,404	100.0	3,429,955	100.0	2,932,059	100.0
Accounts Payable	558,185	10.2	500,774	14.6	489,654	16.7
Bank Loans	-	-	20,580	.6	8,796	.3
Notes Payable	82,086	1.5	58,309	1.7	126,078	4.3
Other Current Liabilities	749,719	13.7	504,204	14.7	469,129	16.0
Total Current Liabilities	1,389,990	25.4	1,083,867	31.6	1,093,657	37.3
Other Long Term	547,240	10.0	435,604	12.7	392,896	13.4
Deferred Credits	21,890	.4	6,860	.2	5,864	.2
Net Worth	3,513,283	64.2	1,903,626	55.5	1,439,640	49.1
Total Liabilities & Net Worth	5,472,403	100.0	3,429,957	100.0	2,932,057	100.0
Net Sales	6,006,566	100.0	20,112,832	100.0	6,558,645	100.0
Gross Profits	2,216,423	36.9	7,140,055	35.5	2,413,581	36.8
Net Profit After Tax	570,624	9.5	1,548,688	7.7	524,692	8.0
Working Capital	2,309,354	-	1,378,842	-	955,851	-

Source: Dun & Bradstreet. Data in this table are copyright (c) 1999 of Dun & Bradstreet. Reprinted by special arrangement with D&B. *Notes:* Values in parentheses above columns indicate the number of establishments in the sample. Data shown are for all companies.

D&B KEY BUSINESS RATIOS: SIC 3678

	1998			1997			1996		
	UQ	MED	LQ	UQ	MED	LQ	UQ	MED	LQ
Solvency									
Quick ratio	2.2	1.5	.7	2.2	1.2	.8	2.2	1.0	.7
Current ratio	4.9	2.8	1.9	4.1	2.4	1.5	3.4	2.1	1.2
Current liabilities/Net worth (%)	18.4	32.8	69.4	22.6	44.9	109.9	28.0	57.7	149.0
Current liabilities/Inventory (%)	47.6	84.8	162.8	66.6	121.4	187.0	89.4	136.6	205.8
Total liabilities/Net worth (%)	26.3	38.7	82.7	28.1	72.9	157.8	43.1	87.7	215.6
Fixed assets/Net worth (%)	20.8	38.6	65.1	23.8	44.1	66.5	34.5	54.1	79.5
Efficiency									
Collection period (days)	39.4	54.1	67.1	47.3	54.8	68.1	42.9	54.4	65.6
Sales to Inventory	7.9	6.0	3.6	9.1	7.0	4.5	9.9	7.3	5.4
Assets/Sales (%)	53.5	77.3	93.4	48.3	65.6	85.7	43.2	56.8	78.2
Sales/Net Working Capital	4.5	2.9	2.2	7.0	4.5	2.7	7.8	4.0	3.4
Accounts payable/Sales (%)	4.0	6.8	11.8	5.0	7.0	12.5	4.7	6.0	9.1
Profitability									
Return - Sales (%)	15.5	9.5	5.2	11.0	6.8	3.3	12.1	7.6	3.5
Return - Assets (%)	21.4	11.1	4.7	19.5	12.5	5.3	21.8	14.3	7.1
Return - Net Worth (%)	28.3	18.6	6.4	30.7	18.9	12.2	38.9	25.7	15.4

Source: Dun & Bradstreet. Data in this table are copyright (c) 1999 of Dun & Bradstreet. Reprinted by special arrangement with D&B. *Note:* UQ stands for "Upper Quartile" and represents the top 25 percent of sample; MED stands for "Median"; and LQ stands for "Lower Quartile" and represents the lowest 25 percent.

D&B INDUSTRY NORMS: SIC 3679 - ELECTRONIC COMPONENTS, NEC

	1998 (371) Estab.		1997 (427) Estab.		1996 (377) Estab.	
	$	%	$	%	$	%
Cash	227,792	14.2	196,487	15.4	168,622	15.9
Accounts Receivable	455,585	28.4	372,559	29.2	291,641	27.5
Notes Receivable	8,021	.5	6,379	.5	3,182	.3
Inventory	401,043	25.0	331,731	26.0	272,552	25.7
Other Current Assets	88,229	5.5	63,794	5.0	60,449	5.7
Total Current Assets	1,180,670	73.6	970,950	76.1	796,446	75.1
Fixed Assets	322,438	20.1	237,315	18.6	201,497	19.0
Other Non-current Assets	101,063	6.3	67,622	5.3	62,570	5.9
Total Assets	1,604,171	100.0	1,275,887	100.0	1,060,513	100.0
Accounts Payable	218,167	13.6	187,556	14.7	148,472	14.0
Bank Loans	1,604	.1	2,552	.2	-	-
Notes Payable	59,354	3.7	43,380	3.4	47,723	4.5
Other Current Liabilities	243,834	15.2	188,831	14.8	161,198	15.2
Total Current Liabilities	522,959	32.6	422,319	33.1	357,393	33.7
Other Long Term	205,334	12.8	167,141	13.1	133,625	12.6
Deferred Credits	3,208	.2	1,276	.1	2,121	.2
Net Worth	872,669	54.4	685,152	53.7	567,374	53.5
Total Liabilities & Net Worth	1,604,170	100.0	1,275,888	100.0	1,060,513	100.0
Net Sales	3,814,489	100.0	3,100,627	100.0	3,085,364	100.0
Gross Profits	1,323,628	34.7	1,072,817	34.6	1,113,816	36.1
Net Profit After Tax	217,426	5.7	145,729	4.7	169,695	5.5
Working Capital	657,710	-	548,632	-	439,052	-

Source: Dun & Bradstreet. Data in this table are copyright (c) 1999 of Dun & Bradstreet. Reprinted by special arrangement with D&B. *Notes:* Values in parentheses above columns indicate the number of establishments in the sample. Data shown are for all companies.

D&B KEY BUSINESS RATIOS: SIC 3679

	1998			1997			1996		
	UQ	MED	LQ	UQ	MED	LQ	UQ	MED	LQ
Solvency									
Quick ratio	2.4	1.4	.8	2.7	1.5	.9	2.4	1.4	.8
Current ratio	4.2	2.4	1.6	4.6	2.6	1.6	4.1	2.4	1.6
Current liabilities/Net worth (%)	21.8	49.9	106.9	21.6	48.2	121.9	23.0	54.4	129.6
Current liabilities/Inventory (%)	65.0	113.8	197.7	64.5	110.9	177.6	63.3	116.2	186.8
Total liabilities/Net worth (%)	30.9	77.3	159.6	31.1	75.6	166.8	28.1	84.3	177.6
Fixed assets/Net worth (%)	14.2	33.3	61.8	13.0	28.6	56.6	14.1	30.7	62.2
Efficiency									
Collection period (days)	35.4	47.5	62.3	33.6	46.0	60.6	30.3	45.3	58.4
Sales to Inventory	13.5	8.2	4.7	16.9	8.6	5.2	15.5	8.6	5.2
Assets/Sales (%)	33.1	47.7	70.4	33.0	44.1	64.6	32.1	43.2	62.8
Sales/Net Working Capital	8.6	4.9	2.7	9.0	5.4	3.1	9.7	5.4	3.3
Accounts payable/Sales (%)	3.2	5.4	9.0	2.9	5.3	8.5	3.2	4.9	8.4
Profitability									
Return - Sales (%)	10.7	5.0	1.9	9.1	4.5	1.2	8.7	4.8	1.9
Return - Assets (%)	20.2	9.2	2.7	18.8	7.9	2.6	19.6	11.1	4.0
Return - Net Worth (%)	39.5	18.5	6.2	34.1	17.7	6.3	46.2	22.1	8.8

Source: Dun & Bradstreet. Data in this table are copyright (c) 1999 of Dun & Bradstreet. Reprinted by special arrangement with D&B. *Note:* UQ stands for "Upper Quartile" and represents the top 25 percent of sample; MED stands for "Median"; and LQ stands for "Lower Quartile" and represents the lowest 25 percent.

D&B INDUSTRY NORMS: SIC 3694 - ENGINE ELECTRICAL EQUIPMENT

	1998 (39) Estab.		1997 (62) Estab.		1996 (55) Estab.	
	$	%	$	%	$	%
Cash	166,006	11.2	171,682	13.8	87,886	11.6
Accounts Receivable	346,835	23.4	273,695	22.0	198,501	26.2
Notes Receivable	11,858	.8	6,220	.5	15,153	2.0
Inventory	508,394	34.3	389,394	31.3	233,353	30.8
Other Current Assets	62,252	4.2	59,715	4.8	40,155	5.3
Total Current Assets	1,095,345	73.9	900,706	72.4	575,048	75.9
Fixed Assets	297,922	20.1	245,082	19.7	122,738	16.2
Other Non-current Assets	88,932	6.0	98,282	7.9	59,853	7.9
Total Assets	1,482,199	100.0	1,244,070	100.0	757,639	100.0
Accounts Payable	174,899	11.8	174,170	14.0	103,039	13.6
Bank Loans	-	-	1,244	.1	-	-
Notes Payable	32,608	2.2	43,542	3.5	40,913	5.4
Other Current Liabilities	219,365	14.8	197,807	15.9	103,039	13.6
Total Current Liabilities	426,872	28.8	416,763	33.5	246,991	32.6
Other Long Term	133,398	9.0	126,895	10.2	67,430	8.9
Deferred Credits	4,447	.3	2,488	.2	-	-
Net Worth	917,481	61.9	697,923	56.1	443,219	58.5
Total Liabilities & Net Worth	1,482,198	100.0	1,244,069	100.0	757,640	100.0
Net Sales	4,815,686	100.0	3,272,954	100.0	2,014,023	100.0
Gross Profits	1,348,392	28.0	873,879	26.7	704,908	35.0
Net Profit After Tax	226,337	4.7	94,916	2.9	142,996	7.1
Working Capital	668,472	-	483,944	-	328,058	-

Source: Dun & Bradstreet. Data in this table are copyright (c) 1999 of Dun & Bradstreet. Reprinted by special arrangement with D&B. *Notes:* Values in parentheses above columns indicate the number of establishments in the sample. Data shown are for all companies.

D&B KEY BUSINESS RATIOS: SIC 3694

	1998			1997			1996		
	UQ	MED	LQ	UQ	MED	LQ	UQ	MED	LQ
Solvency									
Quick ratio	2.7	1.6	.7	2.3	1.1	.7	1.7	1.1	.7
Current ratio	5.5	4.1	1.7	6.0	2.3	1.5	3.8	2.4	1.3
Current liabilities/Net worth (%)	13.8	29.3	70.7	15.0	55.6	145.2	16.0	40.3	71.4
Current liabilities/Inventory (%)	30.2	63.9	130.8	36.6	93.6	177.8	37.6	73.3	172.0
Total liabilities/Net worth (%)	15.7	54.9	125.2	17.9	81.8	192.7	16.6	44.2	97.7
Fixed assets/Net worth (%)	13.9	35.2	52.0	16.9	35.6	56.9	9.6	21.7	36.1
Efficiency									
Collection period (days)	28.4	35.6	47.7	21.2	29.9	46.2	31.0	38.0	52.6
Sales to Inventory	20.4	7.4	4.2	14.0	8.8	4.9	10.7	4.8	3.2
Assets/Sales (%)	26.5	44.1	60.6	30.2	41.1	60.3	30.7	41.8	56.2
Sales/Net Working Capital	6.6	4.2	3.0	14.4	6.0	4.2	6.4	4.7	3.0
Accounts payable/Sales (%)	2.5	3.9	5.7	2.6	7.3	10.6	3.5	4.8	6.6
Profitability									
Return - Sales (%)	8.5	6.0	2.1	8.0	3.1	.4	4.6	3.3	.9
Return - Assets (%)	21.2	12.5	4.0	14.1	7.4	1.2	9.7	6.3	.9
Return - Net Worth (%)	37.1	18.7	4.5	27.3	15.2	1.6	22.1	13.5	.8

Source: Dun & Bradstreet. Data in this table are copyright (c) 1999 of Dun & Bradstreet. Reprinted by special arrangement with D&B. *Note:* UQ stands for "Upper Quartile" and represents the top 25 percent of sample; MED stands for "Median"; and LQ stands for "Lower Quartile" and represents the lowest 25 percent.

D&B INDUSTRY NORMS: SIC 3695 - MAGNETIC AND OPTICAL RECORDING MEDIA

	1998 (22) Estab.		1997 (23) Estab.		1996 (19) Estab.	
	$	%	$	%	$	%
Cash	1,572,288	15.8	644,244	21.8	206,718	28.8
Accounts Receivable	2,179,311	21.9	768,364	26.0	175,136	24.4
Notes Receivable	9,951	.1	11,821	.4	718	.1
Inventory	1,243,899	12.5	449,198	15.2	67,470	9.4
Other Current Assets	398,048	4.0	227,554	7.7	58,139	8.1
Total Current Assets	5,403,497	54.3	2,101,181	71.1	508,181	70.8
Fixed Assets	3,562,527	35.8	594,005	20.1	160,063	22.3
Other Non-current Assets	985,168	9.9	260,062	8.8	49,526	6.9
Total Assets	9,951,192	100.0	2,955,248	100.0	717,770	100.0
Accounts Payable	815,998	8.2	434,421	14.7	116,997	16.3
Bank Loans	139,317	1.4	-	-	-	-
Notes Payable	49,756	.5	32,508	1.1	15,791	2.2
Other Current Liabilities	1,890,727	19.0	360,540	12.2	106,230	14.8
Total Current Liabilities	2,895,798	29.1	827,469	28.0	239,018	33.3
Other Long Term	1,532,484	15.4	431,466	14.6	51,679	7.2
Deferred Credits	-	-	14,776	.5	-	-
Net Worth	5,522,912	55.5	1,681,536	56.9	427,073	59.5
Total Liabilities & Net Worth	9,951,194	100.0	2,955,247	100.0	717,770	100.0
Net Sales	4,988,000	100.0	3,846,691	100.0	2,911,215	100.0
Gross Profits	1,561,244	31.3	1,615,610	42.0	1,278,023	43.9
Net Profit After Tax	64,844	1.3	276,962	7.2	-145,561	-
Working Capital	2,507,701	-	1,273,712	-	269,164	-

Source: Dun & Bradstreet. Data in this table are copyright (c) 1999 of Dun & Bradstreet. Reprinted by special arrangement with D&B. *Notes:* Values in parentheses above columns indicate the number of establishments in the sample. Data shown are for all companies.

D&B KEY BUSINESS RATIOS: SIC 3695

	1998			1997			1996		
	UQ	MED	LQ	UQ	MED	LQ	UQ	MED	LQ
Solvency									
Quick ratio	3.8	1.5	.7	5.6	1.7	1.2	3.3	1.6	1.1
Current ratio	5.2	2.4	1.0	7.5	2.8	1.7	4.5	2.5	1.4
Current liabilities/Net worth (%)	11.8	16.7	84.9	14.6	28.9	60.6	17.7	38.6	79.6
Current liabilities/Inventory (%)	99.9	127.3	273.9	72.2	175.8	356.1	155.9	266.3	334.5
Total liabilities/Net worth (%)	16.9	58.1	152.0	26.4	55.4	94.5	26.7	39.4	116.0
Fixed assets/Net worth (%)	16.7	94.1	135.9	11.6	29.3	56.2	16.7	24.0	50.2
Efficiency									
Collection period (days)	44.4	50.1	73.8	39.3	55.9	74.3	40.0	48.9	71.2
Sales to Inventory	15.3	9.0	4.3	13.2	7.6	4.9	17.9	14.8	9.0
Assets/Sales (%)	37.1	75.6	96.7	30.4	46.4	83.6	30.6	39.2	104.4
Sales/Net Working Capital	7.7	4.8	2.7	8.4	3.8	2.7	6.3	3.5	2.6
Accounts payable/Sales (%)	4.3	6.4	9.6	3.4	8.5	12.2	2.6	5.6	9.4
Profitability									
Return - Sales (%)	10.6	1.0	-16.5	13.0	6.0	2.1	13.5	4.2	-22.3
Return - Assets (%)	38.9	.8	-6.3	27.0	11.3	2.1	20.2	11.5	-22.2
Return - Net Worth (%)	138.9	11.0	-13.3	38.5	27.3	5.4	36.7	16.0	-29.8

Source: Dun & Bradstreet. Data in this table are copyright (c) 1999 of Dun & Bradstreet. Reprinted by special arrangement with D&B. *Note:* UQ stands for "Upper Quartile" and represents the top 25 percent of sample; MED stands for "Median"; and LQ stands for "Lower Quartile" and represents the lowest 25 percent.

D&B INDUSTRY NORMS: SIC 3699 - ELECTRICAL EQUIPMENT & SUPPLIES, NEC

	1998 (183) Estab.		1997 (208) Estab.		1996 (165) Estab.	
	$	%	$	%	$	%
Cash	306,613	15.3	167,073	13.8	174,486	15.2
Accounts Receivable	577,154	28.8	349,885	28.9	346,677	30.2
Notes Receivable	12,024	.6	10,896	.9	5,740	.5
Inventory	436,874	21.8	285,719	23.6	264,025	23.0
Other Current Assets	134,269	6.7	85,958	7.1	74,616	6.5
Total Current Assets	1,466,934	73.2	899,531	74.3	865,544	75.4
Fixed Assets	370,741	18.5	215,500	17.8	202,037	17.6
Other Non-current Assets	166,333	8.3	95,643	7.9	80,356	7.0
Total Assets	2,004,008	100.0	1,210,674	100.0	1,147,937	100.0
Accounts Payable	248,497	12.4	159,809	13.2	158,415	13.8
Bank Loans	8,016	.4	3,632	.3	-	-
Notes Payable	60,120	3.0	48,427	4.0	44,770	3.9
Other Current Liabilities	336,673	16.8	194,919	16.1	189,409	16.5
Total Current Liabilities	653,306	32.6	406,787	33.6	392,594	34.2
Other Long Term	248,497	12.4	141,649	11.7	135,456	11.8
Deferred Credits	2,004	.1	1,211	.1	1,148	.1
Net Worth	1,100,200	54.9	661,028	54.6	618,738	53.9
Total Liabilities & Net Worth	2,004,007	100.0	1,210,675	100.0	1,147,936	100.0
Net Sales	4,004,988	100.0	3,350,594	100.0	3,902,167	100.0
Gross Profits	1,533,910	38.3	1,266,525	37.8	1,541,356	39.5
Net Profit After Tax	208,259	5.2	174,231	5.2	277,054	7.1
Working Capital	813,627	-	492,745	-	472,950	-

Source: Dun & Bradstreet. Data in this table are copyright (c) 1999 of Dun & Bradstreet. Reprinted by special arrangement with D&B. *Notes:* Values in parentheses above columns indicate the number of establishments in the sample. Data shown are for all companies.

D&B KEY BUSINESS RATIOS: SIC 3699

	1998			1997			1996		
	UQ	MED	LQ	UQ	MED	LQ	UQ	MED	LQ
Solvency									
Quick ratio	2.7	1.4	.8	2.5	1.3	.8	2.8	1.3	.8
Current ratio	4.4	2.6	1.5	4.4	2.3	1.6	4.5	2.5	1.4
Current liabilities/Net worth (%)	21.1	47.0	100.6	17.4	50.9	103.7	21.5	48.6	111.2
Current liabilities/Inventory (%)	66.6	116.1	208.5	63.4	125.3	187.2	62.8	117.7	198.9
Total liabilities/Net worth (%)	33.5	66.2	129.2	28.1	69.1	134.6	26.1	72.6	156.0
Fixed assets/Net worth (%)	12.1	25.1	45.7	11.6	26.4	56.1	9.5	24.9	54.5
Efficiency									
Collection period (days)	36.3	52.4	78.5	29.1	49.1	66.1	34.9	52.6	73.0
Sales to Inventory	14.3	7.4	4.9	13.8	7.9	4.9	13.7	7.3	5.1
Assets/Sales (%)	34.3	49.8	83.9	30.2	44.4	73.0	35.2	50.1	77.5
Sales/Net Working Capital	8.7	5.0	2.8	10.5	5.4	3.1	9.1	5.2	2.8
Accounts payable/Sales (%)	3.1	5.3	8.8	3.3	4.7	9.3	3.0	5.4	8.5
Profitability									
Return - Sales (%)	10.8	5.6	1.4	8.9	3.7	1.8	13.4	4.7	1.4
Return - Assets (%)	22.0	8.1	1.0	16.3	8.6	3.4	28.4	8.6	1.8
Return - Net Worth (%)	33.0	14.0	2.7	32.2	15.7	6.6	55.3	16.8	3.8

Source: Dun & Bradstreet. Data in this table are copyright (c) 1999 of Dun & Bradstreet. Reprinted by special arrangement with D&B. *Note:* UQ stands for "Upper Quartile" and represents the top 25 percent of sample; MED stands for "Median"; and LQ stands for "Lower Quartile" and represents the lowest 25 percent.

D&B INDUSTRY NORMS: SIC 7371 - COMPUTER PROGRAMMING SERVICES

	1998 (1461) Estab.		1997 (1568) Estab.		1996 (1333) Estab.	
	$	%	$	%	$	%
Cash	148,340	26.6	133,747	25.7	92,959	25.2
Accounts Receivable	197,415	35.4	182,667	35.1	126,159	34.2
Notes Receivable	3,346	.6	3,643	.7	2,582	.7
Inventory	16,172	2.9	19,255	3.7	14,387	3.9
Other Current Assets	43,498	7.8	39,031	7.5	26,191	7.1
Total Current Assets	408,771	73.3	378,343	72.7	262,278	71.1
Fixed Assets	99,823	17.9	94,196	18.1	74,884	20.3
Other Non-current Assets	49,075	8.8	47,878	9.2	31,724	8.6
Total Assets	557,669	100.0	520,417	100.0	368,886	100.0
Accounts Payable	54,094	9.7	54,644	10.5	38,733	10.5
Bank Loans	1,115	.2	-	-	369	.1
Notes Payable	15,615	2.8	13,531	2.6	11,804	3.2
Other Current Liabilities	115,995	20.8	113,451	21.8	78,204	21.2
Total Current Liabilities	186,819	33.5	181,626	34.9	129,110	35.0
Other Long Term	46,844	8.4	47,878	9.2	35,782	9.7
Deferred Credits	3,346	.6	3,123	.6	2,951	.8
Net Worth	320,660	57.5	287,791	55.3	201,043	54.5
Total Liabilities & Net Worth	557,669	100.0	520,418	100.0	368,886	100.0
Net Sales	1,854,157	100.0	1,700,704	100.0	1,259,911	100.0
Gross Profits	1,079,119	58.2	983,007	57.8	734,528	58.3
Net Profit After Tax	98,270	5.3	105,444	6.2	86,934	6.9
Working Capital	221,953	-	196,718	-	133,168	-

Source: Dun & Bradstreet. Data in this table are copyright (c) 1999 of Dun & Bradstreet. Reprinted by special arrangement with D&B. *Notes:* Values in parentheses above columns indicate the number of establishments in the sample. Data shown are for all companies.

D&B KEY BUSINESS RATIOS: SIC 7371

	1998			1997			1996		
	UQ	MED	LQ	UQ	MED	LQ	UQ	MED	LQ
Solvency									
Quick ratio	4.4	1.9	1.1	4.4	1.8	1.0	4.2	1.8	1.0
Current ratio	5.3	2.4	1.4	5.3	2.2	1.3	5.2	2.3	1.3
Current liabilities/Net worth (%)	15.3	43.9	107.3	15.3	48.8	126.3	15.8	46.4	123.0
Current liabilities/Inventory (%)	112.6	245.8	571.8	95.3	254.9	533.0	88.3	217.9	473.7
Total liabilities/Net worth (%)	20.1	53.9	136.7	20.0	63.5	158.3	20.9	61.8	148.9
Fixed assets/Net worth (%)	10.2	22.7	50.3	12.0	26.4	60.9	11.5	28.5	62.8
Efficiency									
Collection period (days)	33.2	56.6	87.6	34.0	54.4	81.4	31.5	54.0	81.3
Sales to Inventory	129.7	50.5	15.8	124.8	49.4	20.8	99.4	37.8	17.8
Assets/Sales (%)	22.9	35.9	63.8	21.3	33.3	54.2	22.3	34.8	55.8
Sales/Net Working Capital	12.8	6.7	3.3	15.2	7.5	4.0	16.4	7.6	4.1
Accounts payable/Sales (%)	1.4	3.3	7.2	1.4	3.2	6.5	1.3	3.4	7.0
Profitability									
Return - Sales (%)	11.5	4.7	.9	13.0	4.9	.9	13.8	4.8	1.3
Return - Assets (%)	28.8	11.9	2.5	32.0	11.3	1.7	31.7	11.6	2.7
Return - Net Worth (%)	56.9	25.0	5.9	62.3	24.2	5.6	61.5	25.1	7.0

Source: Dun & Bradstreet. Data in this table are copyright (c) 1999 of Dun & Bradstreet. Reprinted by special arrangement with D&B. *Note:* UQ stands for "Upper Quartile" and represents the top 25 percent of sample; MED stands for "Median"; and LQ stands for "Lower Quartile" and represents the lowest 25 percent.

D&B INDUSTRY NORMS: SIC 7372 - PREPACKAGED SOFTWARE

	1998 (411) Estab.		1997 (387) Estab.		1996 (379) Estab.	
	$	%	$	%	$	%
Cash	867,714	27.6	290,330	23.9	226,881	26.3
Accounts Receivable	921,160	29.3	363,216	29.9	268,289	31.1
Notes Receivable	9,432	.3	8,503	.7	7,764	.9
Inventory	100,605	3.2	55,879	4.6	40,545	4.7
Other Current Assets	339,540	10.8	103,255	8.5	80,228	9.3
Total Current Assets	2,238,451	71.2	821,183	67.6	623,707	72.3
Fixed Assets	531,318	16.9	236,880	19.5	141,477	16.4
Other Non-current Assets	374,123	11.9	156,705	12.9	97,481	11.3
Total Assets	3,143,892	100.0	1,214,768	100.0	862,665	100.0
Accounts Payable	289,238	9.2	131,195	10.8	91,443	10.6
Bank Loans	-	-	2,430	.2	863	.1
Notes Payable	40,871	1.3	17,007	1.4	12,940	1.5
Other Current Liabilities	701,088	22.3	268,464	22.1	195,825	22.7
Total Current Liabilities	1,031,197	32.8	419,096	34.5	301,071	34.9
Other Long Term	286,094	9.1	119,047	9.8	74,189	8.6
Deferred Credits	18,863	.6	4,859	.4	2,588	.3
Net Worth	1,807,738	57.5	671,768	55.3	484,818	56.2
Total Liabilities & Net Worth	3,143,892	100.0	1,214,770	100.0	862,666	100.0
Net Sales	7,519,760	100.0	3,136,901	100.0	3,036,209	100.0
Gross Profits	4,587,054	61.0	2,038,986	65.0	1,888,522	62.2
Net Profit After Tax	353,429	4.7	128,613	4.1	157,883	5.2
Working Capital	1,207,254	-	402,089	-	322,638	-

Source: Dun & Bradstreet. Data in this table are copyright (c) 1999 of Dun & Bradstreet. Reprinted by special arrangement with D&B. *Notes:* Values in parentheses above columns indicate the number of establishments in the sample. Data shown are for all companies.

D&B KEY BUSINESS RATIOS: SIC 7372

	1998			1997			1996		
	UQ	MED	LQ	UQ	MED	LQ	UQ	MED	LQ
Solvency									
Quick ratio	3.6	1.8	1.0	3.7	1.5	.9	3.6	1.6	1.0
Current ratio	4.5	2.4	1.4	5.0	2.1	1.2	4.8	2.3	1.3
Current liabilities/Net worth (%)	19.8	41.5	94.8	17.5	42.1	109.0	20.4	44.4	121.4
Current liabilities/Inventory (%)	134.9	291.8	525.6	117.6	289.3	559.3	140.1	260.4	537.3
Total liabilities/Net worth (%)	25.0	51.5	126.0	20.2	60.3	139.3	22.4	54.1	135.8
Fixed assets/Net worth (%)	10.6	20.4	42.7	12.5	27.0	64.9	10.6	21.8	51.7
Efficiency									
Collection period (days)	39.3	72.3	103.3	37.4	61.2	87.7	46.3	68.5	93.3
Sales to Inventory	124.6	54.7	26.1	120.1	46.7	18.4	109.6	40.1	19.3
Assets/Sales (%)	34.7	66.0	108.9	29.4	48.1	83.5	33.8	54.6	84.2
Sales/Net Working Capital	10.4	4.0	2.1	12.5	5.8	2.9	11.4	5.3	2.6
Accounts payable/Sales (%)	2.3	4.6	8.2	2.3	4.6	7.9	2.3	4.4	7.0
Profitability									
Return - Sales (%)	12.6	6.1	.6	10.9	4.6	.4	12.3	4.9	.6
Return - Assets (%)	26.2	9.2	.7	20.6	7.9	.4	24.3	8.9	1.6
Return - Net Worth (%)	45.0	16.9	2.4	43.7	15.7	1.9	45.8	18.0	4.9

Source: Dun & Bradstreet. Data in this table are copyright (c) 1999 of Dun & Bradstreet. Reprinted by special arrangement with D&B. *Note:* UQ stands for "Upper Quartile" and represents the top 25 percent of sample; MED stands for "Median"; and LQ stands for "Lower Quartile" and represents the lowest 25 percent.

D&B INDUSTRY NORMS: SIC 7373 - COMPUTER INTEGRATED SYSTEMS DESIGN

	1998 (1380) Estab.		1997 (1547) Estab.		1996 (1231) Estab.	
	$	%	$	%	$	%
Cash	110,602	19.8	92,566	18.9	72,461	18.4
Accounts Receivable	237,961	42.6	214,028	43.7	166,187	42.2
Notes Receivable	2,234	.4	2,939	.6	2,757	.7
Inventory	45,805	8.2	44,569	9.1	41,350	10.5
Other Current Assets	36,309	6.5	28,406	5.8	24,416	6.2
Total Current Assets	432,911	77.5	382,508	78.1	307,171	78.0
Fixed Assets	87,141	15.6	77,383	15.8	62,615	15.9
Other Non-current Assets	38,543	6.9	29,876	6.1	24,022	6.1
Total Assets	558,595	100.0	489,767	100.0	393,808	100.0
Accounts Payable	100,547	18.0	96,974	19.8	75,217	19.1
Bank Loans	1,117	.2	490	.1	394	.1
Notes Payable	16,758	3.0	18,611	3.8	16,146	4.1
Other Current Liabilities	116,188	20.8	102,851	21.0	81,518	20.7
Total Current Liabilities	234,610	42.0	218,926	44.7	173,275	44.0
Other Long Term	51,949	9.3	45,059	9.2	37,412	9.5
Deferred Credits	1,117	.2	1,959	.4	1,181	.3
Net Worth	270,918	48.5	223,824	45.7	181,939	46.2
Total Liabilities & Net Worth	558,594	100.0	489,768	100.0	393,807	100.0
Net Sales	2,328,624	100.0	2,015,473	100.0	1,787,000	100.0
Gross Profits	884,877	38.0	769,911	38.2	714,800	40.0
Net Profit After Tax	93,145	4.0	84,650	4.2	87,563	4.9
Working Capital	198,301	-	163,582	-	133,894	-

Source: Dun & Bradstreet. Data in this table are copyright (c) 1999 of Dun & Bradstreet. Reprinted by special arrangement with D&B. *Notes:* Values in parentheses above columns indicate the number of establishments in the sample. Data shown are for all companies.

D&B KEY BUSINESS RATIOS: SIC 7373

	1998			1997			1996		
	UQ	MED	LQ	UQ	MED	LQ	UQ	MED	LQ
Solvency									
Quick ratio	2.7	1.5	1.0	2.5	1.4	.9	2.5	1.4	.9
Current ratio	3.5	1.9	1.3	3.2	1.7	1.2	3.2	1.8	1.2
Current liabilities/Net worth (%)	28.6	74.4	169.9	33.1	87.5	206.4	30.2	86.5	188.0
Current liabilities/Inventory (%)	129.1	282.6	514.5	134.6	271.9	501.4	131.1	238.8	428.9
Total liabilities/Net worth (%)	34.0	93.6	206.0	43.2	106.5	234.2	38.3	103.4	224.1
Fixed assets/Net worth (%)	11.4	25.5	54.5	11.6	26.7	62.1	11.8	26.5	58.4
Efficiency									
Collection period (days)	31.4	50.0	75.2	31.8	47.5	73.7	31.4	49.6	77.0
Sales to Inventory	80.0	33.1	15.7	87.1	33.1	14.2	62.3	25.9	14.3
Assets/Sales (%)	19.1	28.2	47.5	19.8	28.1	42.0	19.5	28.6	44.3
Sales/Net Working Capital	19.9	10.0	4.9	22.1	10.9	5.9	18.9	10.0	5.5
Accounts payable/Sales (%)	2.3	5.0	8.6	2.5	5.3	9.1	2.7	5.3	9.4
Profitability									
Return - Sales (%)	9.3	3.5	.9	8.5	3.4	.9	8.4	3.4	1.0
Return - Assets (%)	26.5	10.2	2.3	24.3	10.1	2.2	23.6	9.7	3.0
Return - Net Worth (%)	65.8	29.2	6.9	63.7	28.1	8.1	59.7	24.4	8.9

Source: Dun & Bradstreet. Data in this table are copyright (c) 1999 of Dun & Bradstreet. Reprinted by special arrangement with D&B. *Note:* UQ stands for "Upper Quartile" and represents the top 25 percent of sample; MED stands for "Median"; and LQ stands for "Lower Quartile" and represents the lowest 25 percent.

D&B INDUSTRY NORMS: SIC 7374 - DATA PROCESSING AND PREPARATION

	1998 (292) Estab.		1997 (315) Estab.		1996 (298) Estab.	
	$	%	$	%	$	%
Cash	267,226	18.9	205,312	21.4	125,870	19.1
Accounts Receivable	401,546	28.4	278,226	29.0	191,771	29.1
Notes Receivable	7,069	.5	9,594	1.0	7,908	1.2
Inventory	29,692	2.1	18,229	1.9	11,862	1.8
Other Current Assets	121,595	8.6	75,793	7.9	54,039	8.2
Total Current Assets	827,128	58.5	587,154	61.2	391,450	59.4
Fixed Assets	411,444	29.1	280,145	29.2	208,246	31.6
Other Non-current Assets	175,323	12.4	92,102	9.6	59,311	9.0
Total Assets	1,413,895	100.0	959,401	100.0	659,007	100.0
Accounts Payable	114,526	8.1	81,549	8.5	53,380	8.1
Bank Loans	7,069	.5	959	.1	-	-
Notes Payable	42,417	3.0	32,620	3.4	27,019	4.1
Other Current Liabilities	294,090	20.8	184,205	19.2	125,211	19.0
Total Current Liabilities	458,102	32.4	299,333	31.2	205,610	31.2
Other Long Term	188,048	13.3	115,128	12.0	84,353	12.8
Deferred Credits	11,311	.8	5,756	.6	3,954	.6
Net Worth	756,434	53.5	539,183	56.2	365,090	55.4
Total Liabilities & Net Worth	1,413,895	100.0	959,400	100.0	659,007	100.0
Net Sales	3,676,169	100.0	2,390,647	100.0	1,603,588	100.0
Gross Profits	1,764,561	48.0	1,224,011	51.2	832,262	51.9
Net Profit After Tax	209,542	5.7	131,486	5.5	96,215	6.0
Working Capital	369,027	-	287,820	-	185,840	-

Source: Dun & Bradstreet. Data in this table are copyright (c) 1999 of Dun & Bradstreet. Reprinted by special arrangement with D&B. *Notes:* Values in parentheses above columns indicate the number of establishments in the sample. Data shown are for all companies.

D&B KEY BUSINESS RATIOS: SIC 7374

	1998			1997			1996		
	UQ	MED	LQ	UQ	MED	LQ	UQ	MED	LQ
Solvency									
Quick ratio	2.9	1.5	1.0	3.4	1.7	.9	3.0	1.6	.9
Current ratio	3.7	1.9	1.2	4.3	2.1	1.2	3.9	2.0	1.2
Current liabilities/Net worth (%)	14.6	39.7	95.3	16.0	41.3	96.3	16.5	43.3	81.5
Current liabilities/Inventory (%)	168.3	276.0	525.0	146.3	248.3	561.2	157.5	335.6	629.2
Total liabilities/Net worth (%)	28.7	65.2	157.2	23.6	61.3	149.0	21.9	61.4	141.3
Fixed assets/Net worth (%)	17.5	40.5	89.8	16.0	46.1	92.5	20.2	55.1	99.3
Efficiency									
Collection period (days)	33.2	50.7	72.8	32.0	46.7	68.6	33.9	48.0	69.1
Sales to Inventory	123.9	61.8	30.5	151.5	83.3	40.7	132.8	50.9	31.7
Assets/Sales (%)	26.0	45.9	84.1	28.0	41.6	66.8	28.1	44.3	68.3
Sales/Net Working Capital	16.5	7.2	3.9	13.7	7.7	4.2	13.6	7.6	3.4
Accounts payable/Sales (%)	1.5	3.4	6.7	1.4	3.4	6.2	1.5	3.4	6.3
Profitability									
Return - Sales (%)	11.2	5.2	1.6	11.8	4.8	1.3	10.9	4.9	1.5
Return - Assets (%)	19.2	9.6	2.4	20.6	7.5	2.8	18.7	9.2	2.4
Return - Net Worth (%)	41.3	18.5	7.3	41.5	16.9	6.5	35.8	16.8	6.4

Source: Dun & Bradstreet. Data in this table are copyright (c) 1999 of Dun & Bradstreet. Reprinted by special arrangement with D&B. *Note:* UQ stands for "Upper Quartile" and represents the top 25 percent of sample; MED stands for "Median"; and LQ stands for "Lower Quartile" and represents the lowest 25 percent.

D&B INDUSTRY NORMS: SIC 7375 - INFORMATION RETRIEVAL SERVICES

	1998 (102) Estab.		1997 (116) Estab.		1996 (76) Estab.	
	$	%	$	%	$	%
Cash	244,524	21.9	99,166	20.8	136,613	16.8
Accounts Receivable	276,904	24.8	132,539	27.8	223,623	27.5
Notes Receivable	3,350	.3	1,907	.4	-	-
Inventory	25,681	2.3	8,105	1.7	17,890	2.2
Other Current Assets	99,373	8.9	29,082	6.1	86,196	10.6
Total Current Assets	649,832	58.2	270,799	56.8	464,322	57.1
Fixed Assets	362,878	32.5	156,853	32.9	248,018	30.5
Other Non-current Assets	103,839	9.3	49,106	10.3	100,834	12.4
Total Assets	1,116,549	100.0	476,758	100.0	813,174	100.0
Accounts Payable	108,305	9.7	69,130	14.5	91,889	11.3
Bank Loans	1,117	.1	-	-	813	.1
Notes Payable	21,214	1.9	12,396	2.6	21,143	2.6
Other Current Liabilities	232,242	20.8	82,002	17.2	143,932	17.7
Total Current Liabilities	362,878	32.5	163,528	34.3	257,777	31.7
Other Long Term	144,035	12.9	76,758	16.1	125,229	15.4
Deferred Credits	6,699	.6	954	.2	4,879	.6
Net Worth	602,936	54.0	235,518	49.4	425,290	52.3
Total Liabilities & Net Worth	1,116,548	100.0	476,758	100.0	813,175	100.0
Net Sales	2,205,956	100.0	1,156,853	100.0	3,297,478	100.0
Gross Profits	1,043,417	47.3	552,976	47.8	1,213,472	36.8
Net Profit After Tax	103,680	4.7	55,529	4.8	125,304	3.8
Working Capital	286,953	-	107,271	-	206,546	-

Source: Dun & Bradstreet. Data in this table are copyright (c) 1999 of Dun & Bradstreet. Reprinted by special arrangement with D&B. *Notes:* Values in parentheses above columns indicate the number of establishments in the sample. Data shown are for all companies.

D&B KEY BUSINESS RATIOS: SIC 7375

	1998			1997			1996		
	UQ	MED	LQ	UQ	MED	LQ	UQ	MED	LQ
Solvency									
Quick ratio	3.1	1.5	.8	3.3	1.2	.8	3.5	1.4	.9
Current ratio	3.9	1.9	1.2	3.8	1.7	1.0	4.2	1.7	1.1
Current liabilities/Net worth (%)	15.8	44.2	126.9	15.3	43.7	104.5	22.8	49.4	113.4
Current liabilities/Inventory (%)	131.2	249.9	466.7	167.9	438.6	540.3	64.8	222.9	510.2
Total liabilities/Net worth (%)	25.9	74.8	171.6	22.5	71.6	142.4	26.9	70.4	139.5
Fixed assets/Net worth (%)	24.7	60.1	98.1	24.0	58.1	95.5	24.8	55.8	96.7
Efficiency									
Collection period (days)	32.2	46.8	66.3	28.8	47.8	70.7	38.9	55.7	80.2
Sales to Inventory	171.4	32.2	16.2	194.9	50.2	26.4	276.2	99.7	60.7
Assets/Sales (%)	26.5	41.9	85.4	30.1	40.5	62.8	28.2	49.7	76.7
Sales/Net Working Capital	19.2	9.0	4.3	17.1	7.6	4.1	23.4	7.9	3.6
Accounts payable/Sales (%)	1.3	3.8	7.3	2.0	5.6	9.1	3.2	5.3	9.5
Profitability									
Return - Sales (%)	11.3	5.2	1.2	11.7	4.0	-1.0	8.4	3.4	.9
Return - Assets (%)	25.2	10.2	2.2	30.1	8.5	-.5	12.1	5.0	.7
Return - Net Worth (%)	55.8	20.3	3.9	50.4	19.9	-1.1	21.3	7.5	2.8

Source: Dun & Bradstreet. Data in this table are copyright (c) 1999 of Dun & Bradstreet. Reprinted by special arrangement with D&B. *Note:* UQ stands for "Upper Quartile" and represents the top 25 percent of sample; MED stands for "Median"; and LQ stands for "Lower Quartile" and represents the lowest 25 percent.

D&B INDUSTRY NORMS: SIC 7376 - COMPUTER FACILITIES MANAGEMENT

	1998 (21) Estab.		1997 (24) Estab.		1996 (27) Estab.	
	$	%	$	%	$	%
Cash	305,878	16.9	178,998	20.7	135,036	21.9
Accounts Receivable	678,723	37.5	356,266	41.2	237,391	38.5
Notes Receivable	-	-	-	-	617	.1
Inventory	47,058	2.6	21,618	2.5	14,182	2.3
Other Current Assets	320,357	17.7	74,366	8.6	39,462	6.4
Total Current Assets	1,352,016	74.7	631,248	73.0	426,688	69.2
Fixed Assets	211,762	11.7	172,945	20.0	128,870	20.9
Other Non-current Assets	246,150	13.6	60,531	7.0	61,043	9.9
Total Assets	1,809,928	100.0	864,724	100.0	616,601	100.0
Accounts Payable	329,407	18.2	103,767	12.0	62,893	10.2
Bank Loans	-	-	2,594	.3	1,850	.3
Notes Payable	45,248	2.5	44,101	5.1	16,032	2.6
Other Current Liabilities	287,779	15.9	198,022	22.9	159,700	25.9
Total Current Liabilities	662,434	36.6	348,484	40.3	240,475	39.0
Other Long Term	128,505	7.1	39,777	4.6	32,063	5.2
Deferred Credits	3,620	.2	6,053	.7	-	-
Net Worth	1,015,370	56.1	470,409	54.4	344,063	55.8
Total Liabilities & Net Worth	1,809,929	100.0	864,723	100.0	616,601	100.0
Net Sales	3,307,824	100.0	2,077,135	100.0	1,176,390	100.0
Gross Profits	1,250,357	37.8	847,471	40.8	556,432	47.3
Net Profit After Tax	92,619	2.8	29,080	1.4	44,703	3.8
Working Capital	689,583	-	282,765	-	186,214	-

Source: Dun & Bradstreet. Data in this table are copyright (c) 1999 of Dun & Bradstreet. Reprinted by special arrangement with D&B. *Notes:* Values in parentheses above columns indicate the number of establishments in the sample. Data shown are for all companies.

D&B KEY BUSINESS RATIOS: SIC 7376

	1998			1997			1996		
	UQ	MED	LQ	UQ	MED	LQ	UQ	MED	LQ
Solvency									
Quick ratio	2.9	1.6	1.1	3.4	2.0	1.1	2.7	1.8	.9
Current ratio	5.8	2.0	1.2	3.7	2.1	1.2	3.5	1.9	1.0
Current liabilities/Net worth (%)	15.6	70.5	114.1	14.6	45.1	249.6	18.9	75.9	110.5
Current liabilities/Inventory (%)	141.3	272.2	403.2	192.9	313.9	383.5	106.9	156.8	188.5
Total liabilities/Net worth (%)	18.2	87.4	137.1	14.6	64.2	280.6	32.3	76.2	172.1
Fixed assets/Net worth (%)	9.1	25.9	32.5	13.4	37.4	67.6	14.9	37.5	60.6
Efficiency									
Collection period (days)	18.1	49.7	85.9	48.9	66.8	84.3	46.8	50.9	60.5
Sales to Inventory	263.0	160.1	85.5	103.0	34.2	32.8	294.9	282.4	71.4
Assets/Sales (%)	20.0	25.6	51.2	24.1	30.2	39.7	21.7	28.6	36.3
Sales/Net Working Capital	19.4	9.7	7.7	26.7	14.4	7.1	15.3	9.2	6.4
Accounts payable/Sales (%)	1.8	3.4	9.2	1.9	3.0	9.5	.9	2.7	3.6
Profitability									
Return - Sales (%)	10.7	4.2	1.2	8.1	5.7	-.4	9.7	7.1	3.2
Return - Assets (%)	13.7	6.7	.1	21.9	10.8	2.2	28.4	9.3	4.9
Return - Net Worth (%)	34.0	19.2	3.0	38.2	25.6	3.6	48.7	24.4	7.8

Source: Dun & Bradstreet. Data in this table are copyright (c) 1999 of Dun & Bradstreet. Reprinted by special arrangement with D&B. *Note:* UQ stands for "Upper Quartile" and represents the top 25 percent of sample; MED stands for "Median"; and LQ stands for "Lower Quartile" and represents the lowest 25 percent.

D&B INDUSTRY NORMS: SIC 7377 - COMPUTER RENTAL & LEASING

	1998 (47) Estab.		1997 (63) Estab.		1996 (63) Estab.	
	$	%	$	%	$	%
Cash	177,275	8.3	210,320	11.6	134,788	12.4
Accounts Receivable	420,762	19.7	319,106	17.6	186,965	17.2
Notes Receivable	2,136	.1	7,252	.4	8,696	.8
Inventory	106,792	5.0	106,973	5.9	73,916	6.8
Other Current Assets	356,686	16.7	81,590	4.5	106,526	9.8
Total Current Assets	1,063,651	49.8	725,241	40.0	510,891	47.0
Fixed Assets	724,052	33.9	786,886	43.4	383,712	35.3
Other Non-current Assets	348,143	16.3	300,975	16.6	192,400	17.7
Total Assets	2,135,846	100.0	1,813,102	100.0	1,087,003	100.0
Accounts Payable	187,954	8.8	141,422	7.8	91,308	8.4
Bank Loans	-	-	-	-	-	-
Notes Payable	209,313	9.8	123,291	6.8	40,219	3.7
Other Current Liabilities	390,860	18.3	273,778	15.1	186,965	17.2
Total Current Liabilities	788,127	36.9	538,491	29.7	318,492	29.3
Other Long Term	397,267	18.6	424,266	23.4	218,488	20.1
Deferred Credits	2,136	.1	5,439	.3	1,087	.1
Net Worth	948,316	44.4	844,905	46.6	548,937	50.5
Total Liabilities & Net Worth	2,135,846	100.0	1,813,101	100.0	1,087,004	100.0
Net Sales	4,139,266	100.0	2,846,488	100.0	2,121,446	100.0
Gross Profits	1,966,151	47.5	1,400,472	49.2	1,101,030	51.9
Net Profit After Tax	318,723	7.7	298,881	10.5	267,302	12.6
Working Capital	275,524	-	186,749	-	192,399	-

Source: Dun & Bradstreet. Data in this table are copyright (c) 1999 of Dun & Bradstreet. Reprinted by special arrangement with D&B. *Notes:* Values in parentheses above columns indicate the number of establishments in the sample. Data shown are for all companies.

D&B KEY BUSINESS RATIOS: SIC 7377

	1998			1997			1996		
	UQ	MED	LQ	UQ	MED	LQ	UQ	MED	LQ
Solvency									
Quick ratio	1.2	.8	.5	2.2	.9	.3	2.2	.8	.4
Current ratio	1.9	1.3	.6	2.8	1.1	.5	4.4	1.6	.7
Current liabilities/Net worth (%)	21.2	93.1	207.8	17.5	47.9	94.1	14.1	46.1	102.5
Current liabilities/Inventory (%)	115.1	201.0	441.2	73.9	375.5	557.3	59.3	278.1	362.4
Total liabilities/Net worth (%)	30.2	145.1	287.6	41.8	95.7	250.8	31.1	73.7	218.2
Fixed assets/Net worth (%)	9.0	58.8	111.7	14.5	95.6	225.3	11.8	64.6	141.4
Efficiency									
Collection period (days)	30.7	40.5	54.2	21.0	29.4	52.0	20.5	32.3	55.7
Sales to Inventory	75.6	22.3	15.2	111.3	44.0	9.7	61.9	33.4	7.2
Assets/Sales (%)	44.5	75.5	128.5	48.3	54.7	108.2	44.6	83.1	165.4
Sales/Net Working Capital	23.9	11.7	2.7	14.3	8.1	4.3	8.5	4.0	1.3
Accounts payable/Sales (%)	1.8	4.8	8.7	1.4	4.1	8.5	1.8	4.1	8.6
Profitability									
Return - Sales (%)	13.9	5.3	1.1	20.7	6.3	2.3	24.3	13.7	4.7
Return - Assets (%)	15.1	5.6	1.1	24.0	10.5	3.1	33.2	12.6	3.6
Return - Net Worth (%)	44.0	23.8	3.4	49.9	24.5	8.8	67.1	37.7	15.2

Source: Dun & Bradstreet. Data in this table are copyright (c) 1999 of Dun & Bradstreet. Reprinted by special arrangement with D&B. *Note:* UQ stands for "Upper Quartile" and represents the top 25 percent of sample; MED stands for "Median"; and LQ stands for "Lower Quartile" and represents the lowest 25 percent.

D&B INDUSTRY NORMS: SIC 7378 - COMPUTER MAINTENANCE & REPAIR

	1998 (266) Estab.		1997 (342) Estab.		1996 (329) Estab.	
	$	%	$	%	$	%
Cash	47,058	17.9	48,962	19.1	35,927	14.4
Accounts Receivable	90,698	34.5	94,336	36.8	91,066	36.5
Notes Receivable	2,366	.9	1,794	.7	2,245	.9
Inventory	46,006	17.5	45,117	17.6	50,398	20.2
Other Current Assets	14,459	5.5	11,536	4.5	10,229	4.1
Total Current Assets	200,587	76.3	201,745	78.7	189,865	76.1
Fixed Assets	46,532	17.7	41,785	16.3	46,905	18.8
Other Non-current Assets	15,774	6.0	12,817	5.0	12,724	5.1
Total Assets	262,893	100.0	256,347	100.0	249,494	100.0
Accounts Payable	41,274	15.7	44,861	17.5	41,416	16.6
Bank Loans	526	.2	256	.1	-	-
Notes Payable	11,041	4.2	8,972	3.5	11,227	4.5
Other Current Liabilities	48,109	18.3	48,962	19.1	44,410	17.8
Total Current Liabilities	100,950	38.4	103,051	40.2	97,053	38.9
Other Long Term	24,449	9.3	26,660	10.4	31,935	12.8
Deferred Credits	1,314	.5	1,538	.6	998	.4
Net Worth	136,178	51.8	125,098	48.8	119,509	47.9
Total Liabilities & Net Worth	262,891	100.0	256,347	100.0	249,495	100.0
Net Sales	1,289,064	100.0	1,164,577	100.0	938,987	100.0
Gross Profits	558,165	43.3	493,781	42.4	399,069	42.5
Net Profit After Tax	59,297	4.6	65,216	5.6	40,376	4.3
Working Capital	99,636	-	98,694	-	92,812	-

Source: Dun & Bradstreet. Data in this table are copyright (c) 1999 of Dun & Bradstreet. Reprinted by special arrangement with D&B. *Notes:* Values in parentheses above columns indicate the number of establishments in the sample. Data shown are for all companies.

D&B KEY BUSINESS RATIOS: SIC 7378

	1998			1997			1996		
	UQ	MED	LQ	UQ	MED	LQ	UQ	MED	LQ
Solvency									
Quick ratio	2.8	1.4	.8	2.5	1.4	.9	2.5	1.3	.8
Current ratio	4.6	2.1	1.3	3.6	2.0	1.4	4.1	2.1	1.3
Current liabilities/Net worth (%)	22.7	61.2	157.5	29.8	69.8	152.6	23.8	63.8	143.8
Current liabilities/Inventory (%)	86.6	179.2	312.8	86.9	161.0	325.1	88.9	154.5	289.1
Total liabilities/Net worth (%)	25.2	79.0	194.4	41.1	89.6	190.8	34.1	89.9	191.5
Fixed assets/Net worth (%)	13.4	29.9	70.6	10.1	24.5	52.7	12.7	32.1	65.8
Efficiency									
Collection period (days)	22.1	35.0	51.8	20.9	36.1	50.4	24.1	34.0	51.3
Sales to Inventory	53.9	24.2	13.3	63.3	22.2	11.9	45.5	19.3	10.2
Assets/Sales (%)	16.4	23.0	38.3	17.0	23.9	35.9	17.7	25.4	36.2
Sales/Net Working Capital	22.6	11.2	6.2	18.4	10.1	6.5	18.3	10.3	6.4
Accounts payable/Sales (%)	2.3	3.8	7.5	2.3	4.0	6.2	1.9	4.4	7.4
Profitability									
Return - Sales (%)	8.8	4.0	1.0	7.2	3.5	1.0	8.3	2.6	.8
Return - Assets (%)	31.7	12.8	2.9	28.3	12.5	3.1	20.9	7.9	2.0
Return - Net Worth (%)	72.7	33.7	8.2	69.5	23.8	8.4	47.1	18.6	6.5

Source: Dun & Bradstreet. Data in this table are copyright (c) 1999 of Dun & Bradstreet. Reprinted by special arrangement with D&B. *Note:* UQ stands for "Upper Quartile" and represents the top 25 percent of sample; MED stands for "Median"; and LQ stands for "Lower Quartile" and represents the lowest 25 percent.

D&B INDUSTRY NORMS: SIC 7379 - COMPUTER RELATED SERVICES, NEC

	1998 (765) Estab.		1997 (800) Estab.		1996 (648) Estab.	
	$	%	$	%	$	%
Cash	70,556	24.7	66,270	24.7	50,216	24.0
Accounts Receivable	123,687	43.3	112,417	41.9	87,460	41.8
Notes Receivable	857	.3	1,073	.4	1,883	.9
Inventory	10,855	3.8	10,464	3.9	11,508	5.5
Other Current Assets	17,710	6.2	17,439	6.5	12,345	5.9
Total Current Assets	223,665	78.3	207,663	77.4	163,412	78.1
Fixed Assets	45,990	16.1	46,684	17.4	35,151	16.8
Other Non-current Assets	15,996	5.6	13,952	5.2	10,671	5.1
Total Assets	285,651	100.0	268,299	100.0	209,234	100.0
Accounts Payable	35,992	12.6	34,074	12.7	28,037	13.4
Bank Loans	571	.2	-	-	-	-
Notes Payable	8,284	2.9	9,659	3.6	8,788	4.2
Other Current Liabilities	59,130	20.7	61,440	22.9	47,287	22.6
Total Current Liabilities	103,977	36.4	105,173	39.2	84,112	40.2
Other Long Term	23,138	8.1	21,196	7.9	20,924	10.0
Deferred Credits	571	.2	805	.3	418	.2
Net Worth	157,965	55.3	141,125	52.6	103,781	49.6
Total Liabilities & Net Worth	285,651	100.0	268,299	100.0	209,235	100.0
Net Sales	1,545,704	100.0	1,494,128	100.0	1,151,146	100.0
Gross Profits	715,661	46.3	642,475	43.0	497,295	43.2
Net Profit After Tax	108,199	7.0	83,671	5.6	64,464	5.6
Working Capital	119,688	-	102,490	-	79,301	-

Source: Dun & Bradstreet. Data in this table are copyright (c) 1999 of Dun & Bradstreet. Reprinted by special arrangement with D&B. *Notes:* Values in parentheses above columns indicate the number of establishments in the sample. Data shown are for all companies.

D&B KEY BUSINESS RATIOS: SIC 7379

	1998			1997			1996		
	UQ	MED	LQ	UQ	MED	LQ	UQ	MED	LQ
Solvency									
Quick ratio	4.3	2.0	1.2	3.6	1.7	1.1	3.3	1.7	1.0
Current ratio	5.1	2.3	1.4	4.4	2.0	1.3	4.0	2.1	1.3
Current liabilities/Net worth (%)	16.7	50.2	136.8	21.6	62.4	159.2	25.7	70.2	160.8
Current liabilities/Inventory (%)	82.0	246.9	461.1	110.5	257.0	501.7	119.3	187.1	322.4
Total liabilities/Net worth (%)	20.4	59.8	172.1	24.9	73.4	186.1	33.0	80.5	194.8
Fixed assets/Net worth (%)	10.6	22.7	53.9	11.1	25.8	56.8	11.3	26.1	67.1
Efficiency									
Collection period (days)	31.8	50.8	71.7	32.8	50.6	77.0	32.1	49.6	74.1
Sales to Inventory	129.0	38.7	16.1	113.2	37.9	14.9	92.8	27.9	12.7
Assets/Sales (%)	17.0	25.5	36.6	17.8	25.3	36.4	17.4	25.1	36.0
Sales/Net Working Capital	20.1	10.2	5.8	19.5	10.1	5.6	17.6	9.5	5.5
Accounts payable/Sales (%)	1.4	3.3	6.4	1.3	3.8	6.9	1.6	3.5	7.1
Profitability									
Return - Sales (%)	12.0	5.2	1.8	9.6	3.9	1.1	10.6	4.1	1.3
Return - Assets (%)	43.5	16.1	6.3	34.6	13.4	3.6	35.2	14.0	4.2
Return - Net Worth (%)	80.8	37.5	13.7	71.3	31.3	8.0	67.5	33.9	10.5

Source: Dun & Bradstreet. Data in this table are copyright (c) 1999 of Dun & Bradstreet. Reprinted by special arrangement with D&B. *Note:* UQ stands for "Upper Quartile" and represents the top 25 percent of sample; MED stands for "Median"; and LQ stands for "Lower Quartile" and represents the lowest 25 percent.

CHAPTER 4 - PART I

COMPANY DIRECTORY

This chapter presents brief profiles of 1,000 companies in the Computers & Software sector. Companies are public, private, and elements of public companies ("public family members").

Each entry features the *D-U-N-S* access number for the company, the company name, its parent (if applicable), address, telephone, sales, employees, the company's primary SIC classification, a brief description of the company's business activity, and the name and title of its chairman, president, or other high-ranking officer. If the company is an exporter, importer, or both, the fact is indicated by the abbreviations EXP, IMP, and IMP EXP shown facing the *D-U-N-S* number.

Rankings of these companies are shown in Chapter 5. Additional financial data—on an aggregated, industry level—are shown in Chapter 3.

This product includes proprietary data of Dun & Bradstreet, Inc.

D-U-N-S 09-995-6906   EXP
3COM CORPORATION
5400 Bayfront Plz, Santa Clara, CA 95054
Phone: (408) 326-5000
Sales: $5,420,367,000   *Employees:* 12,920
Company Type: Public   *Employees here:* 285
SIC: 7373
   Computer networking systems
Eric A Benhamou, Chairman of the Board

D-U-N-S 17-357-4161   EXP
3D SYSTEMS INC.
   (Parent: 3D Systems (Canada) Inc)
26081 Avenue Hall, Santa Clarita, CA 91355
Phone: (661) 295-5600
Sales: $90,257,000   *Employees:* 400
Company Type: Public Family Member   *Employees here:* 200
SIC: 3571
   Mfg of solid imaging systems using stereolithography
     technology
Arthur B Sims, Chief Executive Officer

D-U-N-S 80-972-5336
4FRONT SOFTWARE INTERNATIONAL
5650 Greenwood Plaza Blvd, Englewood, CO 80111
Phone: (303) 721-7341
Sales: $84,145,000   *Employees:* 800
Company Type: Public   *Employees here:* 800
SIC: 7371
   Holding company
Anil Doshi, Chairman of the Board

D-U-N-S 02-018-8793
A C I WORLDWIDE INC.
   (Parent: Transaction Systems Architects)
330 S 108th Ave, Omaha, NE 68154
Phone: (402) 390-7600
Sales: $107,300,000   *Employees:* 1,055
Company Type: Public Family Member   *Employees here:* 760
SIC: 7372
   Computer programming systems design
William E Fisher, Chief Executive Officer

D-U-N-S 79-185-8012
A-PLUS MANUFACTURING CORP.
   (Parent: Harvard Custom Mfg Llc)
2381 Bering Dr, San Jose, CA 95131
Phone: (408) 435-7888
Sales: $60,000,000   *Employees:* 430
Company Type: Private   *Employees here:* 430
SIC: 3672
   Assembly of printed circuit boards
Steve Chen, President

D-U-N-S 00-309-0198   EXP
AAI CORPORATION
   (Parent: United Industrial Corporation)
York Rd & Industry Ln, Cockeysville, MD 21031
Phone: (410) 666-1400
Sales: $179,957,000   *Employees:* 1,500
Company Type: Public Family Member   *Employees here:* 1,200
SIC: 3699
   Mfg electronic equipment ammunition & ordnance
     equipment & handling equipment
Richard R Erkeneff, President

D-U-N-S 96-177-7455
AARDVARK, INC.
1408 Sandalwood Dr Apt K, Colorado Springs, CO 80916
Phone: (719) 574-9325

Sales: $143,600,000   *Employees:* 1,850
Company Type: Private   *Employees here:* 375
SIC: 7371
   Computer software development computer consulting &
     integration
Gary L Liggett, President

D-U-N-S 00-257-6817   EXP
AAVID THERMAL PRODUCTS, INC.
   (Parent: Aavid Thermal Technologies)
1 Kool Path Oshea Indust, Laconia, NH 03246
Phone: (603) 528-3400
Sales: $134,619,000   *Employees:* 1,088
Company Type: Public   *Employees here:* 1,088
SIC: 3679
   Mfg thermal electronic components
Ronald F Borelli, President

D-U-N-S 84-207-9949
AAVID THERMAL TECHNOLOGIES
1 Eagle Sq, Ste. 509, Concord, NH 03301
Phone: (603) 224-1117
Sales: $167,745,000   *Employees:* 1,797
Company Type: Private   *Employees here:* 27
SIC: 3699
   Thermal management for electronics
Ronald F Borelli, Chairman of the Board

D-U-N-S 06-748-2505
ABN AMRO SERVICES COMPANY INC.
   (Parent: La Salle National Corp Del)
5515 N East River Rd, Chicago, IL 60656
Phone: (773) 714-3000
Sales: $183,432,000   *Employees:* 2,300
Company Type: Private   *Employees here:* 1,600
SIC: 7374
   Data processing services
Harrison Tempest, Chairman of the Board

D-U-N-S 83-966-9652
ABR BENEFITS SERVICES, INC.
   (Parent: ABR Information Services Inc)
34125 Us Highway 19 N, Palm Harbor, FL 34684
Phone: (727) 785-2819
Sales: $77,700,000   *Employees:* 1,000
Company Type: Public Family Member   *Employees here:* 1,000
SIC: 7371
   Comprehensive benefits administration information and
     compliance services
James Macdougald, Chairman of the Board

D-U-N-S 17-726-0148   EXP
ACCLAIM ENTERTAINMENT
1 Acclaim Plz, Glen Cove, NY 11542
Phone: (516) 656-5000
Sales: $326,561,000   *Employees:* 660
Company Type: Public   *Employees here:* 200
SIC: 7372
   Devel mktg & dist of interactive entertainment pdts (video
     game computer software for home entertainment) &
     publishes comics
Gregory E Fischbach, Chairman of the Board

D-U-N-S 05-544-5860   EXP
ACE ELECTRIC, LLC
501 S East Ave, Columbus, KS 66725
Phone: (316) 429-1000
Sales: $60,000,000   *Employees:* 410
Company Type: Private   *Employees here:* 360
SIC: 3694
   Mfg & whol electrical auto equipment
Denis Desmond, President

D-U-N-S 11-329-1769   IMP EXP
ACER AMERICA CORPORATION
2641 Orchard Pkwy, San Jose, CA 95134
Phone: (408) 432-6200
Sales: $1,141,196,000   *Employees:* 1,348
Company Type: Private   *Employees here:* 686
SIC: 3571
    Mfg computers
Max Wu, President

D-U-N-S 80-837-9820   EXP
ACER LATIN AMERICA, INC.
1701 Nw 87th Ave, Miami, FL 33172
Phone: (305) 477-8119
Sales: $272,635,000   *Employees:* 100
Company Type: Private   *Employees here:* 100
SIC: 3571
    Mfg minicomputers & personal computers
Juan M Rojas, President

D-U-N-S 61-760-8476   EXP
ACS BUSINESS PROCESS SOLUTIONS
    (Parent: Affiliated Computer Services)
510 W Park Land Dr, Sandy, UT 84070
Phone: (801) 567-5000
Sales: $71,000,000   *Employees:* 4,000
Company Type: Public Family Member   *Employees here:* 1,000
SIC: 7374
    Data entry services
Lynn Blodgett, President

D-U-N-S 05-860-5858
ACS GOVERNMENT SOLUTIONS GROUP INC.
    (Parent: Affiliated Computer Services)
1 Curie Ct, Rockville, MD 20850
Phone: (301) 921-7000
Sales: $229,700,000   *Employees:* 3,900
Company Type: Public Family Member   *Employees here:* 550
SIC: 7379
    Computer consulting systems analysis and design data
      processing service and designs and markets business
      oriented software
Peter A Bracken, President

D-U-N-S 60-884-8982
ACS TECHNOLOGY SOLUTIONS, INC.
    (Parent: Affiliated Computer Services)
3030 LBJ Fwy, Ste. 910, Dallas, TX 75234
Phone: (972) 243-1020
Sales: $54,500,000   *Employees:* 450
Company Type: Public Family Member   *Employees here:* 230
SIC: 7371
    Computer programming services
Robert Brooks, Chairman of the Board

D-U-N-S 10-115-4839   EXP
ACT MANUFACTURING INC.
108 Forest Ave, Hudson, MA 01749
Phone: (978) 562-1200
Sales: $264,654,000   *Employees:* 985
Company Type: Public   *Employees here:* 300
SIC: 3672
    Mfg printed circuit board and electronic cable harness
      assemblies
John A Pino, Chairman of the Board

D-U-N-S 14-822-2045   EXP
ACTEL CORPORATION
955 E Arques Ave, Sunnyvale, CA 94086
Phone: (408) 739-1010

Sales: $155,858,000   *Employees:* 380
Company Type: Public   *Employees here:* 300
SIC: 3674
    Mfg integrated circuits & software development
John C East, President

D-U-N-S 05-196-4047
ACXIOM CORPORATION
301 Industrial Blvd, Conway, AR 72032
Phone: (501) 336-1000
Sales: $465,065,000   *Employees:* 3,600
Company Type: Public   *Employees here:* 1,500
SIC: 7375
    Computer based decision support information data
      processing and software development
Rodger S Kline, Chief Operating Officer

D-U-N-S 03-335-8581   IMP EXP
ADAPTEC INC.
691 S Milpitas Blvd, Milpitas, CA 95035
Phone: (408) 945-8600
Sales: $1,007,293,000   *Employees:* 3,276
Company Type: Public   *Employees here:* 1,100
SIC: 3577
    Mfg computer input/output components and custom
      integrated circuits
Robert N Graham, President

D-U-N-S 10-277-9337   EXP
ADEPT TECHNOLOGY INC.
150 Rose Orchard Way, San Jose, CA 95134
Phone: (408) 432-0888
Sales: $98,394,000   *Employees:* 394
Company Type: Public   *Employees here:* 259
SIC: 7373
    Mfg software & hardware for assembly material handling &
      packaging applications
Brian R Carlisle, Chairman of the Board

D-U-N-S 80-528-9451
ADFLEX SOLUTIONS, INC.
2001 W Chandler Blvd, Chandler, AZ 85224
Phone: (602) 963-4584
Sales: $213,878,000   *Employees:* 5,254
Company Type: Public   *Employees here:* 709
SIC: 3679
    Mfg electronic interconnection products
Rolando C Esteverena, Chairman of the Board

D-U-N-S 10-209-6559   EXP
ADOBE SYSTEMS INCORPORATED
345 Park Ave, San Jose, CA 95110
Phone: (408) 536-6000
Sales: $894,791,000   *Employees:* 2,680
Company Type: Public   *Employees here:* 700
SIC: 7372
    Software development
John E Warnock, Chairman of the Board

D-U-N-S 80-192-5199
ADP FINANCIAL INFORMATION SERVICES
    (Parent: Automatic Data Processing)
2 Journal Square Plz, Jersey City, NJ 07306
Phone: (201) 714-3000
Sales: $191,100,000   *Employees:* 3,000
Company Type: Public Family Member   *Employees here:* 700
SIC: 7374
    Electronic data processing for the brokerage industry
Richard J Daly, Co-President

D-U-N-S 10-350-7778   EXP
ADVANCED DIGITAL INFO CORP.
10201 Willows Rd NE, Redmond, WA 98052

Phone: (425) 881-8004
Sales: $114,557,000 *Employees:* 80
Company Type: Public *Employees here:* 60
SIC: 3577
   Mfg computer peripheral equipment
Charles Stonecipher, Chief Operating Officer

D-U-N-S 02-119-2422   EXP
ADVANCED ENERGY INDUSTRIES
1625 Sharp Point Dr, Fort Collins, CO 80525
Phone: (970) 407-4670
Sales: $141,923,000 *Employees:* 1,059
Company Type: Public *Employees here:* 900
SIC: 3679
   Mfg electronic power supplies & controls
Douglas A Schatz, Chairman of the Board

D-U-N-S 04-863-4059   EXP
ADVANCED MICRO DEVICES INC.
1 AMD Pl, Sunnyvale, CA 94086
Phone: (408) 732-2400
Sales: $2,542,141,000 *Employees:* 12,800
Company Type: Public *Employees here:* 3,100
SIC: 3674
   Mfg integrated circuits
Richard Previte, President

D-U-N-S 15-447-5537
ADVANCED QUICK CIRCUITS LP
200 East Dr, Melbourne, FL 32904
Phone: (407) 259-4700
Sales: $63,000,000 *Employees:* 585
Company Type: Private *Employees here:* 35
SIC: 3672
   Mfg printed electronic circuit boards
Bruce C Stevens, Managing Director

D-U-N-S 11-271-3128
ADVENT SOFTWARE INC.
301 Brannan St, Fl 6, San Francisco, CA 94107
Phone: (415) 543-7696
Sales: $70,998,000 *Employees:* 450
Company Type: Public *Employees here:* 285
SIC: 7372
   Develops investment software
Stephanie Dimarco, Chief Executive Officer

D-U-N-S 62-643-9228
AEG CAPITAL CORP
   (*Parent:* Daimler-Benz North Amer Corp)
375 Park Ave, Ste. 3001, New York, NY 10152
Phone: (212) 909-9700
Sales: $269,000,000 *Employees:* 1,800
Company Type: Private *Employees here:* 1
SIC: 3674
   Holding company through its subsidiary mfg semiconductor
      products
Hanspeter Eberhardt, Director

D-U-N-S 15-557-5095
AEROFLEX LABORATORIES INC.
   (*Parent:* Aeroflex Inc)
35 S Service Rd, Plainview, NY 11803
Phone: (516) 694-6700
Sales: $54,371,000 *Employees:* 425
Company Type: Public Family Member *Employees here:* 425
SIC: 3679
   Manufactures infrared scanning devices electric motors
      microcircuits synthesizers microprocessors & multichip
      modules
Leonard Borow, President

D-U-N-S 05-835-5629
AGENA CORPORATION
   (*Parent:* AMS Services Inc)
19015 N Creek Pkwy, Bothell, WA 98011
Phone: (425) 402-1005
Sales: $125,000,000 *Employees:* 1,100
Company Type: Public Family Member *Employees here:* 100
SIC: 7371
   Computer software development & whol computer hardware
Dick Eagle, Vice-President

D-U-N-S 93-841-1824
AII TECHNOLOGIES INC.
1414 Allen Bradley Dr, El Paso, TX 79936
Phone: (915) 626-2222
Sales: $361,775,000 *Employees:* 1,000
Company Type: Private *Employees here:* 950
SIC: 3571
   Assembles personal computers
Ken Su, President

D-U-N-S 02-146-0886
AJILON SERVICES INC.
   (*Parent:* Adecco Inc)
210 W Pennsylvania Ave, Baltimore, MD 21204
Phone: (410) 821-0435
Sales: $110,000,000 *Employees:* 2,600
Company Type: Private *Employees here:* 35
SIC: 7379
   Consulting for data processing & computers & general
      management consulting
Roy F Haggerty, President

D-U-N-S 13-943-7560   EXP
ALCOA FUJIKURA LTD.
   (*Parent:* Alcoa Inc)
105 Westpark Dr, Ste. 200, Brentwood, TN 37027
Phone: (615) 370-2100
Sales: $1,700,000,000 *Employees:* 35,000
Company Type: Public Family Member *Employees here:* 200
SIC: 3694
   Mfg wire harness sets & automotive electrical components &
      fiber optic cable
Robert S Hughes, President

D-U-N-S 62-142-0678   EXP
ALLEGRO MICROSYSTEMS INC.
115 Ne Cutoff, Worcester, MA 01606
Phone: (508) 853-5000
Sales: $210,000,000 *Employees:* 1,900
Company Type: Private *Employees here:* 980
SIC: 3674
   Mfg semiconductors
Allan Kimball, President

D-U-N-S 13-160-8663
ALLIANCE SEMICONDUCTOR CORP.
3099 N 1st St, San Jose, CA 95134
Phone: (408) 383-4900
Sales: $118,400,000 *Employees:* 129
Company Type: Public *Employees here:* 117
SIC: 3674
   Mfg solid-state memory chips
N D Reddy, Chairman of the Board

D-U-N-S 10-664-8652
ALLIED BUSINESS SYSTEMS INC.
   (*Parent:* Norwest Financial Inc)
139 Woodfield Dr, Macon, GA 31210
Phone: (912) 474-7601

Sales: $77,700,000   *Employees:* 1,000
Company Type: Public Family Member   *Employees here:* 36
SIC: 7371
   Ret computers and computer software & develops computer
      software programs
Royle R Duff, President

D-U-N-S 18-297-3172
ALLIED TELESYN INTERNATIONAL
950 Kifer Rd, Sunnyvale, CA 94086
Phone: (408) 730-0950
Sales: $163,039,000   *Employees:* 450
Company Type: Private   *Employees here:* 225
SIC: 3577
   Mfg local area network products
Takayoshi Oshima, Chairman of the Board

D-U-N-S 78-822-0119
ALLTEL FINANCIAL SERVICES INC.
   (Parent: Alltel Information Services)
4001 N Rodney Parham Rd, Little Rock, AR 72212
Phone: (501) 220-5100
Sales: $124,300,000   *Employees:* 1,600
Company Type: Public Family Member   *Employees here:* 1,600
SIC: 7371
   Data processing & financial management service
John E Steuri, Chairman of the Board

D-U-N-S 06-530-9544
ALLTEL INFORMATION SERVICES
   (Parent: Alltel Corporation)
4001 N Rodney Parham Rd, Little Rock, AR 72212
Phone: (501) 220-5100
Sales: $510,200,000   *Employees:* 8,000
Company Type: Public Family Member   *Employees here:* 4,000
SIC: 7374
   Data processing services application software and financial
      management services
William L Cravens, Chairman of the Board

D-U-N-S 00-103-0311
ALPHA INDUSTRIES INC.
20 Sylvan Rd, Woburn, MA 01801
Phone: (781) 935-5150
Sales: $116,881,000   *Employees:* 801
Company Type: Public   *Employees here:* 565
SIC: 3679
   Mfg microwave devices & components
George S Kariotis, Chairman of the Board

D-U-N-S 06-212-1363
ALPHA TECHNOLOGIES GROUP, INC.
1155 Dairy Ashford St, Houston, TX 77094
Phone: (281) 647-9941
Sales: $77,045,000   *Employees:* 987
Company Type: Public   *Employees here:* 10
SIC: 7373
   Designs manufactures and sells thermal management
      products and connectors
Marshall D Butler, Chairman of the Board

D-U-N-S 00-304-1597   EXP
ALTEC LANSING TECHNOLOGIES
Rr 6, Milford, PA 18337
Phone: (570) 296-6444
Sales: $53,900,000   *Employees:* 500
Company Type: Private   *Employees here:* 130
SIC: 3577
   Design mfg marketing & distribution of high end computer
      peripherals & audio products
Edward Anchel, Chairman of the Board

D-U-N-S 11-817-1834   EXP
ALTERA CORPORATION
101 Innovation Dr, San Jose, CA 95134
Phone: (408) 544-7000
Sales: $654,342,000   *Employees:* 915
Company Type: Public   *Employees here:* 750
SIC: 3674
   Mfg semiconductor chips & related development software &
      hardware
Rodney Smith, Chairman of the Board

D-U-N-S 05-178-2381   EXP
ALTRON INCORPORATED
   (Parent: Sanmina Corporation)
1 Jewel Dr, Wilmington, MA 01887
Phone: (978) 658-5800
Sales: $172,428,000   *Employees:* 1,210
Company Type: Public Family Member   *Employees here:* 864
SIC: 3672
   Mfg interconnect systems printed circuit backplanes
      multilayer printed circuit boards & complex surface mount
      assemblies
Jure Sola, Chairman of the Board

D-U-N-S 06-356-7820   EXP
AMDAHL CORPORATION
1250 E Arques Ave, Sunnyvale, CA 94086
Phone: (408) 746-6000
Sales: $948,800,000   *Employees:* 11,000
Company Type: Private   *Employees here:* 3,800
SIC: 7378
   Computer consulting & professional svcs systems maint &
      support software mfg mainframe & computer storage
      systems & servers
David B Wright, President

D-U-N-S 15-258-4223
AMDAHL FINANCE CORPORATION
   (Parent: Amdahl Corporation)
1250 E Arques Ave, Sunnyvale, CA 94086
Phone: (408) 746-6000
Sales: $294,400,000   *Employees:* 5,000
Company Type: Private   *Employees here:* 5,000
SIC: 7379
   Computer related services
David B Wright, President

D-U-N-S 15-258-4462
AMDAHL INTERNATIONAL CORP.
   (Parent: Amdahl Corporation)
1250 E Arques Ave, Sunnyvale, CA 94086
Phone: (408) 746-6000
Sales: $240,600,000   *Employees:* 2,000
Company Type: Private   *Employees here:* 3
SIC: 7379
   Computer related services
E J Zemke, President

D-U-N-S 04-675-0063
AMERICAN CENTURY SERVICES CORP.
   (Parent: American Century Companies)
4500 Main St, Ste. 1400, Kansas City, MO 64111
Phone: (816) 531-5575
Sales: $159,100,000   *Employees:* 2,500
Company Type: Private   *Employees here:* 1,952
SIC: 7374
   Data processing & related services
James E Stowers Jr, Chairman of the Board

D-U-N-S 00-727-0028
AMERICAN INTL GROUP DATA CTR
   (Parent: American International Group)
2 Peach Tree Hill Rd, Livingston, NJ 07039

Phone: (973) 533-3500
Sales: $115,000,000   *Employees:* 565
Company Type: Public Family Member   *Employees here:* 350
SIC: 7374
    Data processing service
Lawrence W English, President

D-U-N-S 06-927-8570   EXP
AMERICAN MGT SYSTEMS INC.
4050 Legato Rd, Ste. 1, Fairfax, VA 22033
Phone: (703) 267-8000
Sales: $872,300,000   *Employees:* 7,100
Company Type: Public   *Employees here:* 2,300
SIC: 7379
    Systems integration & consulting services software
Paul A Brands, Chairman of the Board

D-U-N-S 00-211-4643   EXP
AMERICAN PRECISION INDUSTRIES
2777 Walden Ave, Ste. 1, Buffalo, NY 14225
Phone: (716) 684-9700
Sales: $184,070,000   *Employees:* 2,043
Company Type: Public   *Employees here:* 244
SIC: 3677
    Mfr electronic coils inductors step motors industrl controls
      heat exchangers steam condensers & moisture separators
Kurt Wiedenhaupt, Chairman of the Board

D-U-N-S 03-005-4860
AMERICAN SOFTWARE, INC.
470 E Paces Ferry Rd NE, Atlanta, GA 30305
Phone: (404) 261-4381
Sales: $107,472,000   *Employees:* 701
Company Type: Public   *Employees here:* 440
SIC: 7372
    Develops and markets computer software
James C Edenfield, President

D-U-N-S 10-839-8462
AMERITECH LIBRARY SERVICES
    (Parent: Dynix Corporation)
400 Dynix Dr, Provo, UT 84604
Phone: (801) 223-5200
Sales: $88,000,000   *Employees:* 500
Company Type: Public Family Member   *Employees here:* 400
SIC: 7373
    Computer systems design whol computers/peripherals
Lana Porter, President

D-U-N-S 01-819-8205
AMKOR TECHNOLOGY, INC.
1345 Enterprise Dr, West Chester, PA 19380
Phone: (610) 431-9600
Sales: $1,455,761,000   *Employees:* 9,880
Company Type: Public   *Employees here:* 90
SIC: 3674
    Semiconductor packaging and test services
James J Kim, Chairman of the Board

D-U-N-S 00-301-2549   EXP
AMP INCORPORATED
470 Friendship Rd, Harrisburg, PA 17111
Phone: (717) 564-0100
Sales: $5,745,235,000   *Employees:* 46,526
Company Type: Public   *Employees here:* 177
SIC: 3678
    Mfg electronic & electrical connection devices & current
      carrying devices
James E Marley, Acting Head, Global Competencies

D-U-N-S 17-722-0647   EXP
AMPHENOL CORPORATION
    (Parent: KKR 1996 Fund LP)
358 Hall Ave, Wallingford, CT 06492

Phone: (203) 265-8900
Sales: $884,348,000   *Employees:* 6,900
Company Type: Public   *Employees here:* 47
SIC: 3678
    Mfg electronic and other connectors and cable assemblies
Martin H Loeffler, Chairman of the Board

D-U-N-S 08-609-7060
AMPLICON INC.
5 Hutton Centre Dr, Santa Ana, CA 92707
Phone: (714) 751-7551
Sales: $313,789,000   *Employees:* 236
Company Type: Private   *Employees here:* 196
SIC: 7377
    Leases & whol computer systems
Patrick E Paddon, Chairman of the Board

D-U-N-S 78-812-5870
AMS MANAGEMENT SYSTEMS GROUP INC.
    (Parent: AMS Services Inc)
3 Waterside Xing, Windsor, CT 06095
Phone: (860) 602-6000
Sales: $124,000,000   *Employees:* 1,187
Company Type: Public Family Member   *Employees here:* 437
SIC: 7371
    Software development
Christophe McGee, President

D-U-N-S 14-703-6602
AMS SERVICES INC.
    (Parent: Continental Casualty Company)
700 Longwater Dr, Ste. 1, Norwell, MA 02061
Phone: (781) 982-9400
Sales: $219,534,000   *Employees:* 1,600
Company Type: Public Family Member   *Employees here:* 85
SIC: 7372
    Develops business computer software & data processing
      service
David W Wroe, Chairman of the Board

D-U-N-S 13-967-8270   EXP
ANADIGICS INC.
35 Technology Dr, Warren, NJ 07059
Phone: (908) 668-5000
Sales: $102,536,000   *Employees:* 475
Company Type: Public   *Employees here:* 475
SIC: 3674
    Mfg semiconductors
Bami Bastani, President

D-U-N-S 00-141-8417   EXP
ANALOG DEVICES, INC.
1 Technology Way, Norwood, MA 02062
Phone: (781) 329-4700
Sales: $1,230,571,000   *Employees:* 7,200
Company Type: Public   *Employees here:* 1,000
SIC: 3674
    Mfg integrated circuits
Jerald G Fishman, President

D-U-N-S 06-478-0281
ANALYSTS INTERNATIONAL CORP.
7615 Metro Blvd, Minneapolis, MN 55439
Phone: (612) 835-5900
Sales: $587,411,000   *Employees:* 5,571
Company Type: Public   *Employees here:* 127
SIC: 7371
    Custom computer programming computer related services
      data processing school
Frederick W Lang, Chairman of the Board

D-U-N-S 10-792-8996
ANSTEC, INC.
1410 Spring Hill Rd, Mc Lean, VA 22102

Phone: (703) 848-7200
Sales: $52,306,000   *Employees:* 490
Company Type: Private   *Employees here:* 200
SIC: 7371
   Computer systems design & integration systems engineering
      computer facility management
Satyendra P Shrivastava, President

D-U-N-S 06-764-1597
ANTEON CORP.
   (Parent: Azimuth Technologies Inc)
3211 Jermantown Rd, Fairfax, VA 22030
Phone: (703) 246-0200
Sales: $176,292,000   *Employees:* 2,300
Company Type: Private   *Employees here:* 246
SIC: 7379
   Information technology services systems engineering
      computer network design & installation
Joseph M Kampf, President

D-U-N-S 19-558-3729
APEX DATA SERVICES INC.
198 Van Buren St, Herndon, VA 20170
Phone: (703) 709-3000
Sales: $76,200,000   *Employees:* 1,200
Company Type: Private   *Employees here:* 50
SIC: 7374
   Conversion indexing abstracting & transaction processing
Shashikant Gupta, President

D-U-N-S 06-070-4780   EXP
APPLE COMPUTER INC.
1 Infinite Loop, Cupertino, CA 95014
Phone: (408) 996-1010
Sales: $5,941,000,000   *Employees:* 6,658
Company Type: Public   *Employees here:* 2,000
SIC: 3571
   Mfg personal computers & peripheral products operating
      system & application computer software
Steven Jobs, Chief Executive Officer

D-U-N-S 06-163-3244   EXP
APPLIED AUTOMATION INC.
   (Parent: Bailey Elsag Inc)
Pawhuska Rd, Bartlesville, OK 74003
Phone: (918) 662-7000
Sales: $96,000,000   *Employees:* 398
Company Type: Private   *Employees here:* 290
SIC: 3577
   Mfg electronic hardware & develops computer software
Gary Waugh, President

D-U-N-S 18-984-1349
APPLIED CELLULAR TECHNOLOGY
400 Royal Palm Way, Palm Beach, FL 33480
Phone: (561) 366-4800
Sales: $103,159,000   *Employees:* 460
Company Type: Public   *Employees here:* 11
SIC: 7379
   Computer consulting & software development
Richard J Sullivan, Chairman of the Board

D-U-N-S 08-037-4150   EXP
APPLIED FILMS CORPORATION
9586 E I25 Frontage Rd, Longmont, CO 80504
Phone: (303) 774-3200
Sales: $53,041,000   *Employees:* 200
Company Type: Public   *Employees here:* 200
SIC: 3674
   Mfg thin film coatings
Cecil Van Alsburg, Chairman of the Board

D-U-N-S 00-834-2198   EXP
APPLIED MAGNETICS CORPORATION
75 Robin Hill Rd, Goleta, CA 93117
Phone: (805) 683-5353
Sales: $183,597,000   *Employees:* 4,700
Company Type: Public   *Employees here:* 1,000
SIC: 3679
   Mfg computer disk drive components
Craig Crisman, Chairman of the Board

D-U-N-S 09-853-8341
APPLIED MICRO CIRCUITS CORP.
6290 Sequence Dr, San Diego, CA 92121
Phone: (619) 450-9333
Sales: $76,618,000   *Employees:* 335
Company Type: Public   *Employees here:* 222
SIC: 3674
   Mfg integrated microcircuits
Roger A Smullen, Chairman of the Board

D-U-N-S 17-482-9663
APPLIED SCIENCE & TECHNOLOGY
35 Cabot Rd, Woburn, MA 01801
Phone: (781) 933-5560
Sales: $83,436,000   *Employees:* 355
Company Type: Public   *Employees here:* 105
SIC: 3679
   Mfg microwave components
Dr Richard S Post, President

D-U-N-S 10-318-7050   EXP
APPLIED SYSTEMS INC.
200 Applied Pkwy, University Park, IL 60466
Phone: (708) 534-5575
Sales: $76,068,000   *Employees:* 1,100
Company Type: Private   *Employees here:* 600
SIC: 7371
   Computer software design and service & whol computer
      hardware
Robert Eustace, Chairman of the Board

D-U-N-S 12-100-1887
ARDENT SOFTWARE INC.
50 Washington St, Westborough, MA 01581
Phone: (508) 366-3888
Sales: $119,260,000   *Employees:* 580
Company Type: Public   *Employees here:* 200
SIC: 7371
   Computer software development & prepackaged software
Peter Gyenes, Chairman of the Board

D-U-N-S 62-618-2463
ARIS CORPORATION
2229 112th Ave NE, Bellevue, WA 98004
Phone: (425) 372-2713
Sales: $62,550,000   *Employees:* 660
Company Type: Public   *Employees here:* 120
SIC: 7379
   Data base consulting & training software development
Paul Song, Chairman of the Board

D-U-N-S 60-659-6450   EXP
ARLON INC.
   (Parent: Bairnco Corporation)
2251 Lucien Way, Maitland, FL 32751
Phone: (407) 875-2222
Sales: $99,391,000   *Employees:* 505
Company Type: Public Family Member   *Employees here:* 4
SIC: 3674
   Mfg circuit board materials custom flexible laminates for the
      electrical industry & vinyl film
Luke Fichthorn III, Chairman of the Board

D-U-N-S 00-106-2942
ARROW AUTOMOTIVE INDUSTRIES
1 Arrow Dr, Morrilton, AR 72110
Phone: (501) 354-0111
Sales: $87,501,000   *Employees:* 300
Company Type: Private   *Employees here:* 300
SIC: 3694
   Remfg automotive electrical & mechanical components
W H Henderson, President

D-U-N-S 78-567-3716
ARSYS INNOTECH CORPORATION
45535 Northport Loop E, Fremont, CA 94538
Phone: (510) 661-2650
Sales: $95,171,000   *Employees:* 55
Company Type: Private   *Employees here:* 30
SIC: 3571
   Mfg personal computers and peripheral equipment
Chang-Lin Lin, President

D-U-N-S 13-161-4109   EXP
ARTECON, INC. ·
1656 McCarthy Blvd, Milpitas, CA 95035
Phone: (408) 954-0710
Sales: $66,340,000   *Employees:* 238
Company Type: Public   *Employees here:* 205
SIC: 3572
   Design & mfg disk & tape storage products
David Eeg, President

D-U-N-S 10-850-0810 .   EXP
ARTESYN NORTH AMERICA INC.
   (*Parent:* Artesyn Technologies Inc)
7575 Market Place Dr, Eden Prairie, MN 55344
Phone: (612) 941-1100
Sales: $228,168,000   *Employees:* 2,848
Company Type: Public Family Member   *Employees here:* 102
SIC: 3679
   Mfg electronic components electrical repair
Lou Debartelo, Chairman of the Board

D-U-N-S 04-493-0139   EXP
ARTESYN TECHNOLOGIES INC.
7900 Glades Rd, Ste. 500, Boca Raton, FL 33434
Phone: (561) 451-1000
Sales: $527,236,000   *Employees:* 6,900
Company Type: Public   *Employees here:* 16
SIC: 3679
   Mfg power conversion products
Joseph M O'Donnell, Chairman of the Board

D-U-N-S 60-345-8837   EXP
ASCEND COMMUNICATIONS INC.
1701 Harbor Bay Pkwy, Alameda, CA 94502
Phone: (510) 769-6001
Sales: $1,478,682,000   *Employees:* 1,644
Company Type: Public   *Employees here:* 140
SIC: 3577
   Mfg remote networking products
Mory Ejabat, President

D-U-N-S 15-344-5135   EXP
ASPECT TELECOMMUNICATIONS CORP.
1730 Fox Dr, San Jose, CA 95131
Phone: (408) 325-2200
Sales: $512,316,000   *Employees:* 1,600
Company Type: Public   *Employees here:* 670
SIC: 7372
   Mfg and support of telephone call distribution systems
James R Carreker, Chairman of the Board

D-U-N-S 04-430-6348
ASPEN SYSTEMS CORPORATION
2277 Research Blvd, Rockville, MD 20850
Phone: (301) 519-5000
Sales: $101,346,000   *Employees:* 1,501
Company Type: Private   *Employees here:* 1,200
SIC: 7374
   Data processing services
Albert Lampert, President

D-U-N-S 04-551-4031
ASPEN TECHNOLOGY INC.
10 Canal Park, Cambridge, MA 02141
Phone: (617) 577-0100
Sales: $252,555,000   *Employees:* 1,518
Company Type: Public   *Employees here:* 260
SIC: 7372
   Develops and markets application software
Lawrence B Evans, Chairman of the Board

D-U-N-S 01-876-8648
AST RESEARCH INC.
16215 Alton Pkwy, Irvine, CA 92618
Phone: (949) 727-4141
Sales: $2,103,643,000   *Employees:* 3,000
Company Type: Private   *Employees here:* 600
SIC: 3571
   Mfg personal computer systems
Soon-Taek Kim, President

D-U-N-S 07-358-0201   EXP
ASTEA INTERNATIONAL INC.
455 Business Center Dr, Horsham, PA 19044
Phone: (215) 682-2500
Sales: $60,934,000   *Employees:* 253
Company Type: Public   *Employees here:* 190
SIC: 7372
   Computer software development & computer consultants
Zack Bergreen, Chairman of the Board

D-U-N-S 60-543-8423
ASTEC AMERICA INC.
5810 Van Allen Way, Carlsbad, CA 92008
Phone: (760) 757-1880
Sales: $357,000,000   *Employees:* 2,000
Company Type: Private   *Employees here:* 110
SIC: 3679
   Mfg electronic equipment
Jay L Geldmacher, President

D-U-N-S 80-794-9532   EXP
ATL PRODUCTS, INC.
   (*Parent:* Quantum Corporation)
2801 Kelvin Ave, Irvine, CA 92614
Phone: (714) 774-6900
Sales: $97,627,000   *Employees:* 190
Company Type: Public Family Member   *Employees here:* 186
SIC: 3572
   Mfg digital data library storage products
Kevin C Daly, President

D-U-N-S 19-901-4358
ATLANTRON, INC.
Guanajibo Shopp Ctr, Mayaguez, PR 00680
Phone: (787) 834-1295
Sales: $94,234,000   *Employees:* 750
Company Type: Private   *Employees here:* 500
SIC: 3672
   Mfg printed circuit boards electromechanical and cable
     assembly
David Black, President

D-U-N-S 12-138-5264   EXP
ATMEL CORPORATION
2325 Orchard Pkwy, San Jose, CA 95131
Phone: (408) 441-0311
Sales: $958,282,000   *Employees:* 6,100
Company Type: Public   *Employees here:* 1,311
SIC: 3674
   Mfg integrated circuits
George Perlegos, Chairman of the Board

D-U-N-S 15-725-4749
ATMI, INC.
7 Commerce Dr, Danbury, CT 06810
Phone: (203) 794-1100
Sales: $101,877,000   *Employees:* 200
Company Type: Public   *Employees here:* 100
SIC: 3674
   Holding company
Eugene G Banucci, Chairman of the Board

D-U-N-S 10-337-7503   EXP
ATTACHMATE CORPORATION
3617 131st Ave SE, Bellevue, WA 98006
Phone: (425) 644-4010
Sales: $316,076,000   *Employees:* 1,600
Company Type: Private   *Employees here:* 700
SIC: 7373
   Computer integration systems design and development
Frank Pritt, Chairman of the Board

D-U-N-S 18-560-0632   EXP
AUSPEX SYSTEMS INC.
2300 Central Expy, Santa Clara, CA 95050
Phone: (408) 566-2000
Sales: $60,621,000   *Employees:* 612
Company Type: Public   *Employees here:* 400
SIC: 3577
   Mfg file/data servers
R M Case, Chief Financial Officer

D-U-N-S 02-810-8483
AUSTIN SAMSUNG SEMICDTR LLC
   (Parent: Samsung Semiconductor Inc)
12100 Samsung Blvd, Austin, TX 78754
Phone: (512) 672-1000
Sales: $73,100,000   *Employees:* 950
Company Type: Private   *Employees here:* 950
SIC: 3674
   Mfg semiconductors devices & microcomputer components
Sung W Lee, President

D-U-N-S 06-970-1282   EXP
AUTODESK INC.
111 Mcinnis Pkwy, San Rafael, CA 94903
Phone: (415) 507-5000
Sales: $617,126,000   *Employees:* 2,470
Company Type: Public   *Employees here:* 400
SIC: 7372
   Design and drafting software products
Carol A Bartz, Chairman of the Board

D-U-N-S 02-030-8367   EXP
AUTOMATA INTERNATIONAL INC.
   (Parent: Cornerstone Eqity Invstors Llc)
1200 Severn Way, Sterling, VA 20166
Phone: (703) 450-2600
Sales: $60,000,000   *Employees:* 480
Company Type: Private   *Employees here:* 462
SIC: 3672
   Mfg printed circuit boards
John W Milks, President

D-U-N-S 06-120-4988
AUTOMATED CONCEPTS INC.
1500 Broadway, New York, NY 10036
Phone: (212) 391-2100
Sales: $57,000,000   *Employees:* 540
Company Type: Private   *Employees here:* 94
SIC: 7379
   Computer consulting & training
Frederick B Harris, President

D-U-N-S 00-191-5172
AUTOMATIC DATA PROCESSING
1 Adp Blvd, Roseland, NJ 07068
Phone: (973) 994-5000
Sales: $4,798,061,000   *Employees:* 34,000
Company Type: Public   *Employees here:* 1,500
SIC: 7374
   Electronic data processing services
Arthur F Weinbach, Chairman of the Board

D-U-N-S 08-365-4616
AUTOMETRIC INC.
7700 Boston Blvd, Springfield, VA 22153
Phone: (703) 923-4000
Sales: $60,160,000   *Employees:* 481
Company Type: Private   *Employees here:* 272
SIC: 7373
   Computer software systems design & development
Christophe Haakon, Chief Executive Officer

D-U-N-S 00-145-5799   EXP
AUTOMOTIVE CONTROLS CORP.
   (Parent: Echlin Inc)
1 Echlin Rd, Branford, CT 06405
Phone: (203) 481-5771
Sales: $116,435,000   *Employees:* 1,100
Company Type: Public Family Member   *Employees here:* 800
SIC: 3694
   Mfg automotive parts
Robert W Daley, President

D-U-N-S 11-349-1252   EXP
AUTOTOTE CORPORATION
750 Lexington Ave, Fl 25, New York, NY 10022
Phone: (212) 754-2233
Sales: $159,313,000   *Employees:* 1,000
Company Type: Public   *Employees here:* 20
SIC: 3578
   Mfg pari-mutuel wagering systems lottery operation
A L Weil, Chairman of the Board

D-U-N-S 78-237-2858
AVANT CORPORATION
46871 Bayside Pkwy, Fremont, CA 94538
Phone: (510) 413-8000
Sales: $227,141,000   *Employees:* 800
Company Type: Public   *Employees here:* 550
SIC: 7371
   Icda software development
Gerald C Hsu, Chairman of the Board

D-U-N-S 01-390-0449
AVERSTAR INC.
23 4th Ave, Burlington, MA 01803
Phone: (781) 221-6990
Sales: $85,800,000   *Employees:* 1,000
Company Type: Private   *Employees here:* 120
SIC: 7373
   Computer software development & integration service
Michael B Alexander, Chairman of the Board

D-U-N-S 17-911-9268   EXP
AVEX ELECTRONICS INC.
(Parent: J M Huber Corporation)
4807 Bradford Dr NW, Huntsville, AL 35805
Phone: (256) 722-6000
Sales: $717,124,000   *Employees:* 3,600
Company Type: Private   *Employees here:* 1,100
SIC: 3699
    Contract mfg of electronic systems
Jeff Nesbitt, President

D-U-N-S 84-729-0418
AVG ADVANCED TECHNOLOGIES LP
343 Saint Paul Blvd, Carol Stream, IL 60188
Phone: (630) 668-3900
Sales: $78,100,000   *Employees:* 1,200
Company Type: Private   *Employees here:* 1
SIC: 3672
    Mfg printed circuit boards & electronics contract
      manufacturer
Shalabh Kumar, Chief Executive Officer

D-U-N-S 14-769-0283   EXP
AVX VANCOUVER CORPORATION
(Parent: AVX Corporation)
5701 E Fourth Plain Blvd, Vancouver, WA 98661
Phone: (360) 696-2840
Sales: $90,000,000   *Employees:* 720
Company Type: Public Family Member   *Employees here:* 720
SIC: 3675
    Mfg ceramic chip capacitors
Benedict P Rosen, President

D-U-N-S 87-978-0500
AXENT TECHNOLOGIES INC.
2400 Res Blvd, Ste. 200, Rockville, MD 20850
Phone: (301) 258-5043
Sales: $101,019,000   *Employees:* 185
Company Type: Public   *Employees here:* 160
SIC: 7371
    Computer security software
Richard A Lefebvre, Chairman of the Board

D-U-N-S 09-260-9023   EXP
AXIOHM TRANSACTION SOLUTIONS
16 Sentry Pkwy W, Ste. 450, Blue Bell, PA 19422
Phone: (215) 591-0940
Sales: $153,748,000   *Employees:* 1,513
Company Type: Public   *Employees here:* 50
SIC: 3577
    Mfg computer peripheral equipment
Nicolas Dourassoff, Chief Executive Officer

D-U-N-S 02-356-5471
AZTEC TECHNOLOGY PARTNERS
50 Braintree Hill Park, Braintree, MA 02184
Phone: (781) 849-1702
Sales: $256,000,000   *Employees:* 1,400
Company Type: Public   *Employees here:* 15
SIC: 7373
    Information technology
James Claypoole, Chairman of the Board

D-U-N-S 01-158-9751   EXP
B M C SOFTWARE INC.
2101 Citywest Blvd, Houston, TX 77042
Phone: (713) 918-8800
Sales: $730,634,000   *Employees:* 2,777
Company Type: Public   *Employees here:* 1,464
SIC: 7372
    Develops and markets utility software
Douglas J Erwin, Chief Operating Officer

D-U-N-S 02-999-1395
BA MERCHANT SERVICES, INC.
(Parent: Bank Of Amer Nat Tr Sav Assn)
1 S Van Ness Ave, Fl 5, San Francisco, CA 94103
Phone: (415) 241-3390
Sales: $160,975,000   *Employees:* 564
Company Type: Public   *Employees here:* 554
SIC: 7374
    Computer processing services
Sharif Bayyari, President

D-U-N-S 01-828-8621   EXP
BAIRNCO CORPORATION
2251 Lucien Way, Ste. 300, Maitland, FL 32751
Phone: (407) 875-2222
Sales: $158,708,000   *Employees:* 850
Company Type: Public   *Employees here:* 11
SIC: 3672
    Mfr engineered materials and components and band saw
      blades
Luke E Fichthorn III, Chairman of the Board

D-U-N-S 06-411-2683   EXP
BANCTEC, INC.
4851 LBJ Fwy, Fl 12, Dallas, TX 75244
Phone: (972) 341-4000
Sales: $603,534,000   *Employees:* 4,000
Company Type: Public   *Employees here:* 500
SIC: 7373
    Provides integrated processing systems and develops
      application software mfg processing equipment and offers
      support services
Grahame N Clark Jr, Chairman of the Board

D-U-N-S 60-900-7042
BANCTEC USA
(Parent: Banctec Inc)
4851 LBJ Fwy, Ste. 1100, Dallas, TX 75244
Phone: (972) 341-4000
Sales: $375,000,000   *Employees:* 3,000
Company Type: Public Family Member   *Employees here:* 60
SIC: 7373
    Systems integration/services also operates in network
      management & support services & mfg of document
      processing equipment
James E Uren, President

D-U-N-S 10-828-0991
BANYAN SYSTEMS INCORPORATED
120 Flanders Rd, Westborough, MA 01581
Phone: (508) 898-1000
Sales: $74,342,000   *Employees:* 386
Company Type: Public   *Employees here:* 215
SIC: 7373
    Computer systems integration
William P Ferry, Chairman of the Board

D-U-N-S 94-268-8797
BARDEN COMPANIES, INC.
400 Renaissance Ctr, Detroit, MI 48243
Phone: (313) 259-0050
Sales: $124,300,000   *Employees:* 1,600
Company Type: Private   *Employees here:* 5
SIC: 7371
    Through it's subsidiary develops prepackaged educational
      software
Don H Barden, Chairman of the Board

D-U-N-S 13-935-0813   EXP
BARRA, INC.
2100 Milvia St, Berkeley, CA 94704
Phone: (510) 548-5442

Sales: $137,377,000   *Employees:* 600
Company Type: Public   *Employees here:* 280
SIC: 7372
    Business oriented computer software development financial
      management for business investment consulting
Kamal Duggirala, President

D-U-N-S 00-400-6727
BAY DATA CONSULTANTS LLC
    (Parent: Bay Resources Inc)
1856 Corporate Dr, Ste. 170, Norcross, GA 30093
Phone: (770) 279-8188
Sales: $56,000,000   *Employees:* 127
Company Type: Private   *Employees here:* 127
SIC: 7373
    System integration
Steve Johnson, President

D-U-N-S 16-134-9923   EXP
BAY NETWORKS, INC.
    (Parent: Northern Telecom Limited)
4401 Great America Pkwy, Santa Clara, CA 95054
Phone: (408) 988-2400
Sales: $641,000,000   *Employees:* 5,960
Company Type: Private   *Employees here:* 2,200
SIC: 3577
    Mfg computer internetworking products
David L House, President

D-U-N-S 94-381-4541
BBN BARRNET INC.
    (Parent: GTE Internetworking Inc)
150 Cambridgepark Dr, Cambridge, MA 02140
Phone: (617) 873-2000
Sales: $91,500,000   *Employees:* 850
Company Type: Public Family Member   *Employees here:* 850
SIC: 3577
    Mfg computer peripheral equipment
Richard Edminstor, President

D-U-N-S 07-481-1357
BDM CORPORATION SAUDIA ARABIA
    (Parent: BDM International Inc)
1501 Bdm Way, Mc Lean, VA 22102
Phone: (703) 848-5000
Sales: $228,900,000   *Employees:* 2,671
Company Type: Public Family Member   *Employees here:* 2,671
SIC: 7373
    Systems design development & integration applied research
      diversified professional & technical services
William C Hoover, President

D-U-N-S 61-971-3282
BDM INTERNATIONAL INC.
    (Parent: TRW Inc)
1501 Bdm Way, Mc Lean, VA 22102
Phone: (703) 848-5000
Sales: $770,800,000   *Employees:* 9,000
Company Type: Public Family Member   *Employees here:* 830
SIC: 7373
    Information technology technical and other expert services
Philip A Odeen, President

D-U-N-S 83-755-6844
BEA SYSTEMS, INC.
2315 N 1st St, San Jose, CA 95131
Phone: (408) 570-8000
Sales: $157,189,000   *Employees:* 1,300
Company Type: Public   *Employees here:* 550
SIC: 7371
    Software development
William T Coleman III, Chairman of the Board

D-U-N-S 79-972-2327
BEI SENSORS & SYSTEMS COMPANY
    (Parent: BEI Technologies Inc)
13100 Telfair Ave, Sylmar, CA 91342
Phone: (818) 362-7151
Sales: $150,000,000   *Employees:* 977
Company Type: Public Family Member   *Employees here:* 150
SIC: 3679
    Mfg sensors other electronic components
Dr Asad Madni, President

D-U-N-S 17-759-9784   EXP
BEI TECHNOLOGIES INC.
1 Post St, Ste. 2500, San Francisco, CA 94104
Phone: (415) 956-4477
Sales: $101,539,000   *Employees:* 977
Company Type: Public   *Employees here:* 10
SIC: 3679
    Mfg advanced electronic products to control and drive the
      motion of machinery & equipment
Gary D Wrench, Chief Financial Officer

D-U-N-S 00-132-1389
BEL FUSE INC.
198 Van Vorst St 200, Jersey City, NJ 07302
Phone: (201) 432-0463
Sales: $73,531,000   *Employees:* 707
Company Type: Public   *Employees here:* 47
SIC: 3679
    Mfg electronic components electric fuses coils &
      transformers
Elliot Bernstein, Chairman of the Board

D-U-N-S 18-331-2321
BELL MICROPRODUCTS INC.
1941 Ringwood Ave, San Jose, CA 95131
Phone: (408) 451-9400
Sales: $533,736,000   *Employees:* 650
Company Type: Public   *Employees here:* 125
SIC: 3672
    Whol semiconductors computers & computer products &
      mfg printed circuit boards
W D Bell, Chairman of the Board

D-U-N-S 02-479-2194   EXP
BENCHMARK ELECTRONICS INC.
3000 Technology Dr, Angleton, TX 77515
Phone: (409) 849-6550
Sales: $325,229,000   *Employees:* 2,280
Company Type: Public   *Employees here:* 550
SIC: 3672
    Contract manufacturer of printed circuit boards
Donald E Nigbor, President

D-U-N-S 13-109-7651
BENTLEY SYSTEMS INCORPORATED
690 Pennsylvania Dr, Exton, PA 19341
Phone: (610) 458-5000
Sales: $154,888,000   *Employees:* 950
Company Type: Private   *Employees here:* 450
SIC: 7373
    Computer aided design software distribution maintenance &
      support
Keith Bentley, Chief Executive Officer

D-U-N-S 84-799-8572
BERG ELECTRONICS CORP.
    (Parent: Framatome Connectors Intl Inc)
101 S Hanley Rd, Ste. 700, Saint Louis, MO 63105
Phone: (314) 726-1323

Sales: $785,150,000
Company Type: Private
SIC: 3678
   Manufacturers electronic connectors
James N Mills, Chief Executive Officer

Employees: 7,000
Employees here: 25

D-U-N-S 05-806-6572   EXP
BERGER & CO.
   (*Parent:* Modis Professional Services)
1350 17th St, Ste. 300, Denver, CO 80202
Phone: (303) 571-4557
Sales: $54,192,000
Company Type: Public Family Member
SIC: 7379
   Data processing consultant
Wayne Berger, Chief Executive Officer

Employees: 440
Employees here: 170

D-U-N-S 07-541-2031
BESAM AUTOMATED ENTRANCE SYSTEMS
84 Twin Rivers Dr, Hightstown, NJ 08520
Phone: (609) 443-5800
Sales: $58,103,000
Company Type: Private
SIC: 3699
   Manufactures installs and services automatic doors
Joseph V Loria, President

Employees: 300
Employees here: 105

D-U-N-S 10-673-6614
BETAC INTERNATIONAL CORP.
   (*Parent:* Affiliated Computer Services)
2001 N Beauregard St, Alexandria, VA 22311
Phone: (703) 824-3100
Sales: $60,000,000
Company Type: Public Family Member
SIC: 7373
   Information engineering & design
Earl F Lockwood, Chairman of the Board

Employees: 430
Employees here: 430

D-U-N-S 78-328-4169   EXP
BINDCO CORPORATION
1089 Mills Way, Redwood City, CA 94063
Phone: (650) 363-2200
Sales: $63,804,000
Company Type: Private
SIC: 7379
   Software services
Keith Scott, Chief Executive Officer

Employees: 280
Employees here: 240

D-U-N-S 78-771-6331
BISYS GROUP INC.
150 Clove Rd, Ste. 7, Little Falls, NJ 07424
Phone: (973) 812-8600
Sales: $386,344,000
Company Type: Public
SIC: 7374
   Data processing services and financial fund administration
Dennis R Sheehan, Chief Financial Officer

Employees: 2,200
Employees here: 12

D-U-N-S 60-634-4489
BISYS, INC.
   (*Parent:* Bisys Group Inc)
11 E Greenway Plz, Houston, TX 77046
Phone: (713) 622-8911
Sales: $81,898,000
Company Type: Public Family Member
SIC: 7374
   Electronic data processing service
Paul Bourke, President

Employees: 450
Employees here: 280

D-U-N-S 17-779-4450
BOEING CORINTH COMPANY
   (*Parent:* The Boeing Company)
7801 S Stemmons Fwy, Lake Dallas, TX 75065

Phone: (940) 497-7600
Sales: $121,900,000
Company Type: Public Family Member
SIC: 3679
   Mfg electronic components
J B Self, General Manager

Employees: 2,100
Employees here: 2,100

D-U-N-S 80-745-3311
BOEING INFORMATION SVCS INC.
   (*Parent:* The Boeing Company)
7990 Boeing Ct, Vienna, VA 22182
Phone: (703) 847-1100
Sales: $78,100,000
Company Type: Public Family Member
SIC: 7374
   Computer support services & systems integration
William Delaney, President

Employees: 1,231
Employees here: 500

D-U-N-S 78-798-8641
BOLD DATA TECHNOLOGY INC.
48351 Fremont Blvd, Fremont, CA 94538
Phone: (510) 445-8800
Sales: $407,506,000
Company Type: Private
SIC: 3571
   Mfg computer systems
Eugene Kiang, President

Employees: 100
Employees here: 100

D-U-N-S 05-052-1574   EXP
BOOLE & BABBAGE INC.
3131 Zanker Rd, San Jose, CA 95134
Phone: (408) 526-3000
Sales: $218,236,000
Company Type: Public
SIC: 7372
   Computer software development & maintenance consulting
     and other computer services
Franklin P Johnson Jr, Chairman of the Board

Employees: 970
Employees here: 300

D-U-N-S 62-194-0311
BORN INFORMATION SERVICES
294 Grove Ln E, Ste. 100, Wayzata, MN 55391
Phone: (612) 404-4000
Sales: $54,358,000
Company Type: Private
SIC: 7371
   Custom computer programming services
Rick Born, Chief Executive Officer

Employees: 675
Employees here: 390

D-U-N-S 60-963-3300
BORTEC INCORPORATED
221 N Kansas St, Ste. 1205, El Paso, TX 79901
Phone: (915) 533-3153
Sales: $120,900,000
Company Type: Private
SIC: 3699
   Mfg electronic electro-mechanical and mechanical products
Anthony Azar, President

Employees: 1,500
Employees here: 1,500

D-U-N-S 04-920-5602
BOUNDLESS TECHNOLOGIES INC.
   (*Parent:* Boundless Corporation)
100 Marcus Blvd, Hauppauge, NY 11788
Phone: (516) 342-7400
Sales: $99,200,000
Company Type: Public Family Member
SIC: 3575
   Manufactures video display terminals & designs & markets
    windows based terminals
J G Combs, Chairman of the Board

Employees: 329
Employees here: 290

D-U-N-S 14-473-9059
BOWTHORPE INTERNATIONAL INC.
87 Modular Ave, Commack, NY 11725

Phone: (516) 864-3700
Sales: $120,900,000   *Employees:* 1,500
Company Type: Private   *Employees here:* 10
SIC: 3699
    Manufactures electrical binding & electronic components
C M Mc Carthy, President

D-U-N-S 19-616-9437   EXP
BOX HILL SYSTEMS CORP.
161 Avenue Of The America, New York, NY 10013
Phone: (212) 989-4455
Sales: $70,344,000   *Employees:* 160
Company Type: Public   *Employees here:* 150
SIC: 3572
    Designs manufactures markets and supports high
       performance data storage systems for the open systems
       computing environment
Philip Black, Chief Executive Officer

D-U-N-S 00-173-8699   EXP
BRANSON ULTRASONICS CORP.
    (Parent: Emerson Electric US Holdg Corp)
41 Eagle Rd, Danbury, CT 06810
Phone: (203) 796-0400
Sales: $129,000,000   *Employees:* 530
Company Type: Public Family Member   *Employees here:* 375
SIC: 3699
    Mfg electrical equipment/supplies
Anthony E Pajk, President

D-U-N-S 08-388-1672
BRC HOLDINGS, INC.
    (Parent: Affiliated Computer Services)
1111 W Mockingbird Ln, Dallas, TX 75247
Phone: (214) 905-2300
Sales: $107,487,000   *Employees:* 970
Company Type: Public Family Member   *Employees here:* 77
SIC: 7374
    Information technology services
Henry Braswell, President

D-U-N-S 02-421-2524
BROADWAY & SEYMOUR, INC.
128 S Tryon St, Ste. 1000, Charlotte, NC 28202
Phone: (704) 372-4281
Sales: $79,559,000   *Employees:* 475
Company Type: Public   *Employees here:* 200
SIC: 7373
    Computer integrated systems design and development
Alan C Stanford, Chairman of the Board

D-U-N-S 03-921-5454   EXP
BRODERBUND SOFTWARE INC.
    (Parent: Learning Company Inc)
500 Redwood Blvd, Novato, CA 94947
Phone: (415) 382-4400
Sales: $190,787,000   *Employees:* 1,129
Company Type: Public Family Member   *Employees here:* 351
SIC: 7372
    Personal computer software
Joseph P Durrett, Chief Executive Officer

D-U-N-S 13-085-5265   EXP
BROOKTROUT TECHNOLOGY INC.
410 1st Ave, Needham, MA 02494
Phone: (781) 449-4100
Sales: $72,192,000   *Employees:* 300
Company Type: Public   *Employees here:* 200
SIC: 7371
    Computer software development and mfg facsimile
       equipment
Eric R Giler, President

D-U-N-S 04-836-7528
BTG, INC.
3877 Fairfax Ridge Rd, Fairfax, VA 22030
Phone: (703) 383-8000
Sales: $588,909,000   *Employees:* 1,400
Company Type: Public   *Employees here:* 800
SIC: 7371
    Designs and develops software and applications and a value-
       added reseller
Dr Edward H Bersoff, Chairman of the Board

D-U-N-S 80-519-2614
B.T.N.Y. SERVICES, INC.
    (Parent: Bankers Trust Company)
130 Liberty St, New York, NY 10006
Phone: (212) 250-2500
Sales: $61,700,000   *Employees:* 973
Company Type: Public Family Member   *Employees here:* 973
SIC: 7374
    Data processing & office support
Gerard A Callaghan, Chief Executive Officer

D-U-N-S 78-246-7666
BULL DATA SYSTEMS INC.
3 Executive Park Dr, Fl 3, Bedford, NH 03110
Phone: (603) 641-9638
Sales: $314,961,000   *Employees:* 2,200
Company Type: Private   *Employees here:* 3
SIC: 3571
    Holding company which mfg & svcs computer hardware &
       components
Camille De Montalivet, President

D-U-N-S 00-647-7533   EXP
BUREAU ENGRAVING INCORPORATED
3400 Technology Dr, Minneapolis, MN 55418
Phone: (612) 788-1000
Sales: $107,000,000   *Employees:* 700
Company Type: Private   *Employees here:* 180
SIC: 3672
    Mfg printed circuit boards & lithographic printing
Tom Stuart, Chairman of the Board

D-U-N-S 00-839-4454   EXP
BURR-BROWN CORPORATION
6730 S Tucson Blvd, Tucson, AZ 85706
Phone: (520) 746-1111
Sales: $252,102,000   *Employees:* 1,300
Company Type: Public   *Employees here:* 1,068
SIC: 3674
    Mfg microelectronic components input/output products &
       terminals
Syrus P Madavi, President

D-U-N-S 05-740-3040
BUSINESS RECORDS CORPORATION
    (Parent: BRC Holdings Inc)
1111 W Mockingbird Ln, Dallas, TX 75247
Phone: (214) 688-1800
Sales: $90,000,000   *Employees:* 450
Company Type: Public Family Member   *Employees here:* 60
SIC: 7374
    Microfilm & recording of records also var of year 2000
       software & services
Jerrold Morrison, President

D-U-N-S 00-100-9901
C & K COMPONENTS INC.
57 Stanley Ave, Watertown, MA 02472
Phone: (617) 926-6400

Sales: $225,000,000
Company Type: Private
SIC: 3679
Employees: 1,000
Employees here: 400
  Mfg electronic switches
Charles A Coolidge Jr, Chairman of the Board

D-U-N-S 19-699-7332   EXP
C CUBE MICROSYSTEMS INC.
1778 McCarthy Blvd, Milpitas, CA 95035
Phone: (408) 944-6300
Sales: $337,012,000
Company Type: Public
SIC: 3674
Employees: 750
Employees here: 85
  Mfg digital compression and decompression integrated
    circuits & systems
Alexandre A Balkanski, President

D-U-N-S 14-425-9876   EXP
CABLETRON SYSTEMS INC.
35 Industrial Way, Rochester, NH 03867
Phone: (603) 332-9400
Sales: $1,377,330,000
Company Type: Public
SIC: 3577
Employees: 6,887
Employees here: 2,100
  Mfr local area network & wide area network connectivity
    hardware & software & other network pdts & network
    systems integration
Craig R Benson, President

D-U-N-S 04-553-4641
CACI INTERNATIONAL INC.
1100 N Glebe Rd, Ste. 200, Arlington, VA 22201
Phone: (703) 841-7800
Sales: $326,110,000
Company Type: Public
SIC: 7373
Employees: 4,600
Employees here: 4,600
  Professional & technical services
Gregory R Bradford, President

D-U-N-S 10-406-8093   EXP
CADENCE DESIGN SYSTEMS INC.
555 River Oaks Pkwy, San Jose, CA 95134
Phone: (408) 943-1234
Sales: $915,893,000
Company Type: Public
SIC: 7372
Employees: 5,102
Employees here: 1,102
  Development of computer-aided design software & related
    services
Jack R Harding, President

D-U-N-S 07-717-7368
CAERE CORPORATION
100 Cooper Ct, Los Gatos, CA 95032
Phone: (408) 395-7000
Sales: $55,018,000
Company Type: Public
SIC: 7372
Employees: 293
Employees here: 250
  Mfg information recognition software & systems products
Robert G Teresi, Chairman of the Board

D-U-N-S 06-135-9824   EXP
CALCOMP TECHNOLOGIES, INC.
  (Parent: Lockheed Martin Corporation)
2411 W La Palma Ave, Anaheim, CA 92801
Phone: (714) 821-2000
Sales: $200,158,000
Company Type: Public
SIC: 3577
Employees: 1,225
Employees here: 130
  Mfg digitizing tablets plotters & scanners
John C Batterton, President

D-U-N-S 78-220-3533
CAMBRIDGE TECHNOLOGY PARTNERS
304 Vassar St, Cambridge, MA 02139
Phone: (617) 374-9800
Sales: $406,672,000
Company Type: Public
SIC: 7371
Employees: 3,222
Employees here: 395
  Software development
James K Sims, President

D-U-N-S 07-037-9854
CAMELOT CORPORATION
2415 Midway Rd, Ste. 121, Carrollton, TX 75006
Phone: (972) 733-3005
Sales: $1,662,000,000
Company Type: Public
SIC: 7371
Employees: 95
Employees here: 39
  Software developers (publishers) ret & distribution of cd-
    rom software & internet access services
David D McCurley, Chief Financial Officer

D-U-N-S 08-718-3588   EXP
CANDLE CORPORATION
2425 Olympic Blvd 400, Santa Monica, CA 90404
Phone: (310) 829-5800
Sales: $300,000,000
Company Type: Private
SIC: 7372
Employees: 1,400
Employees here: 450
  Develops computer software
Aubrey G Chernick, Chairman of the Board

D-U-N-S 16-152-7502
CARIBBEAN DATA SERVICES, LTD.
  (Parent: AMR Services Corporation)
4255 Amon Carter Blvd, Fort Worth, TX 76155
Phone: (817) 963-3068
Sales: $101,700,000
Company Type: Public Family Member
SIC: 7374
Employees: 1,600
Employees here: 26
  Computer data entry
Tom Lofland, Vice-President

D-U-N-S 78-999-3474
CARLYLE PARTNERS LEVERAGED CAP
1001 Penn Ave Nw, Ste. 220, Washington, DC 20004
Phone: (202) 347-2626
Sales: $599,500,000
Company Type: Private
SIC: 7373
Employees: 7,000
Employees here: 4
  Capital investment company for a systems design integration
    & commercial research company
William E Conway Jr, Managing Director

D-U-N-S 95-811-3748
CASTLEWOOD SYSTEMS INC.
7133 Coll Cntr Pkwy 200, Pleasanton, CA 94566
Phone: (925) 461-5515
Sales: $300,000,000
Company Type: Private
SIC: 3572
Employees: 50
Employees here: 4
  Mfg & develops computer storage devices
Syed Iftikar, President

D-U-N-S 18-599-5750
CBOL CORP.
6200 Canoga Ave, Ste. 410, Woodland Hills, CA 91367
Phone: (818) 704-8200
Sales: $100,000,000
Company Type: Private
SIC: 3674
Employees: 35
Employees here: 35
  Mfg systems integrators for aerospace defense industries &
    high tech computer-defense mfg
S D Kim, President

D-U-N-S 79-057-1087
CCC INFORMATION SERICES GROUP
444 Merchandise Mart, Chicago, IL 60654
Phone: (312) 222-4636
Sales: $159,106,000　　　　　　　　　　　　*Employees:* 1,200
Company Type: Private　　　　　　　　　*Employees here:* 1,120
SIC: 7371
　　Computer software development
David M Phillips, Chairman of the Board

D-U-N-S 15-908-3948
CELESTICA COLORADO INC.
　　(Parent: Celestica North America Inc)
3450 E Harmony Rd Bldg 6, Fort Collins, CO 80528
Phone: (970) 207-5000
Sales: $350,000,000　　　　　　　　　　　　*Employees:* 600
Company Type: Private　　　　　　　　　*Employees here:* 600
SIC: 3674
　　Mfg circuit boards
Joe Mixsell, Vice-President

D-U-N-S 17-671-6025
CENDANT SOFTWARE
　　(Parent: Cendant Corporation)
19840 Pioneer Ave, Torrance, CA 90503
Phone: (310) 793-0600
Sales: $650,000,000　　　　　　　　　　　　*Employees:* 2,500
Company Type: Public Family Member　　*Employees here:* 1,806
SIC: 7372
　　Software development
Chris Mcleod, Chief Executive Officer

D-U-N-S 09-595-4814
CENTRON DPL COMPANY, INC.
　　(Parent: Gatx Capital Corporation)
6455 City West Pkwy, Eden Prairie, MN 55344
Phone: (612) 829-2800
Sales: $200,000,000　　　　　　　　　　　　*Employees:* 200
Company Type: Public Family Member　　*Employees here:* 135
SIC: 7373
　　Systems integration specialists for communication equipment
Richard N Soskin, President

D-U-N-S 12-162-3672
CENTURY ELECTRONICS MANUFACTURING
274 Cedar Hill St, Marlborough, MA 01752
Phone: (508) 485-0275
Sales: $143,000,000　　　　　　　　　　　　*Employees:* 220
Company Type: Private　　　　　　　　　*Employees here:* 220
SIC: 3672
　　Design assemble and test electronic printed circuit boards
　　and systems
Walter J Conroy, President

D-U-N-S 04-241-0688
CERNER CORPORATION
2800 Rock Creek Pkwy, Kansas City, MO 64117
Phone: (816) 221-1024
Sales: $245,057,000　　　　　　　　　　　　*Employees:* 1,400
Company Type: Public　　　　　　　　　*Employees here:* 800
SIC: 7372
　　Computer software design & development
Neal L Patterson, Chairman of the Board

D-U-N-S 61-503-1531　　　　　　　　　　　　EXP
CERPLEX, INC.
1382 Bell Ave, Tustin, CA 92780
Phone: (714) 258-5600
Sales: $141,408,000　　　　　　　　　　　　*Employees:* 1,350
Company Type: Public　　　　　　　　　*Employees here:* 200
SIC: 7378
　　Service maintenance repair & mfg of computer peripherals
Stephen J Hopkins, President

D-U-N-S 96-549-8454
CGG CANADA LTD.
16430 Park Ten Pl, Houston, TX 77084
Phone: (281) 646-2400
Sales: $52,657,000　　　　　　　　　　　　*Employees:* 135
Company Type: Private　　　　　　　　　*Employees here:* 35
SIC: 7374
　　Geophysical data processing & seismic surveying
Peer Norgard, President

D-U-N-S 00-528-4864
CHAMBERLAIN MANUFACTURING CORP.
　　(Parent: Duchossois Industries Inc)
845 N Larch Ave, Elmhurst, IL 60126
Phone: (630) 279-3600
Sales: $161,100,000　　　　　　　　　　　　*Employees:* 2,000
Company Type: Private　　　　　　　　　*Employees here:* 200
SIC: 3699
　　Mfg garage door devices ordnance small arms and operates
　　radio broadcasting station
Craig J Duchossois, Chairman of the Board

D-U-N-S 00-504-3443
CHAMPION SPARK PLUG COMPANY
　　(Parent: Federal-Mogul Corporation)
900 Upton Ave, Toledo, OH 43607
Phone: (419) 535-2567
Sales: $350,500,000　　　　　　　　　　　　*Employees:* 5,645
Company Type: Public Family Member　　*Employees here:* 440
SIC: 3694
　　Mfg spark plugs other ignition devices windshield wiper arms
　　blades & refills & oil fuel & air filters
Richard Snell, Chairman of the Board

D-U-N-S 80-980-1269
CHANNEL MASTER LLC
1315 Industrial Park Dr, Smithfield, NC 27577
Phone: (919) 934-9711
Sales: $166,000,000　　　　　　　　　　　　*Employees:* 850
Company Type: Private　　　　　　　　　*Employees here:* 850
SIC: 3679
　　Mfg receiving antennas
Harold E Mills, President

D-U-N-S 16-873-3814
CHATHAM TECHNOLOGIES INC.
12221 Merit Dr, Ste. 400, Dallas, TX 75251
Phone: (972) 991-5559
Sales: $300,000,000　　　　　　　　　　　　*Employees:* 2,400
Company Type: Private　　　　　　　　　*Employees here:* 25
SIC: 3699
　　Holding company through subsidiaries design manufacture &
　　integration of custom electronic enclosures & components
William Kidd, Chairman

D-U-N-S 04-033-7243
CHECKFREE HOLDINGS CORPORATION
4411 E Jones Bridge Rd, Norcross, GA 30092
Phone: (770) 441-3387
Sales: $233,864,000　　　　　　　　　　　　*Employees:* 1,700
Company Type: Private　　　　　　　　　*Employees here:* 145
SIC: 7374
　　Electronic data processing services
Peter J Kight, Chairman of the Board

D-U-N-S 06-184-4015　　　　　　　　　　　　EXP
CHECKPOINT SYSTEMS INC.
101 Wolf Dr, Thorofare, NJ 08086
Phone: (609) 848-1800

Sales: $335,964,000   *Employees:* 3,605
Company Type: Public   *Employees here:* 1,800
SIC: 3699
  Mfg electronic article merchandising systems
Kevin P Dowd, President

D-U-N-S 09-112-6037
CHECKPOINT SYSTEMS OF PR
  (Parent: Checkpoint Systems Inc)
Sabanetas Industrial Park, Ponce, PR 00731
Phone: (787) 844-7340
Sales: $78,572,000   *Employees:* 640
Company Type: Public Family Member   *Employees here:* 640
SIC: 3699
  Mfg security control equipment
Kevin Dowd, President

D-U-N-S 09-915-6259
CHEROKEE INTERNATIONAL LLC
2841 Dow Ave, Tustin, CA 92780
Phone: (714) 544-6665
Sales: $77,022,000 .   *Employees:* 868
Company Type: Private   *Employees here:* 389
SIC: 3679
  Mfg electronic power supplies & other electronic components
Ganpat Patel, President

D-U-N-S 05-805-8405   EXP
CHERRY SEMICONDUCTOR CORP.
  (Parent: Cherry Corporation)
2000 S County Trl, East Greenwich, RI 02818
Phone: (401) 885-3600
Sales: $113,035,000   *Employees:* 975
Company Type: Public Family Member   *Employees here:* 968
SIC: 3674
  Mfg semiconductor integrated microcircuits and circuit
  networks
Alfred Budnick, President

D-U-N-S 13-170-6137
CHEYENNE SOFTWARE INC.
  (Parent: Computer Associates Intl)
1 Computer Associates Plz, Hauppauge, NY 11788
Phone: (516) 342-5224
Sales: $60,500,000   *Employees:* 778
Company Type: Public Family Member   *Employees here:* 285
SIC: 7371
  Develops markets and supports software for lan and wan
  applications
Peter A Schwartz, President

D-U-N-S 17-862-2312
CHIPPAC, INC.
  (Parent: Hyundai Electronics America)
3151 Coronado Dr, Santa Clara, CA 95054
Phone: (408) 486-5900
Sales: $400,000,000   *Employees:* 4,000
Company Type: Private   *Employees here:* 3,983
SIC: 3674
  Mfg semiconductors/related devices
Dennis McKenna, President

D-U-N-S 07-278-1511
CIBER, INC.
5251 DTC Pkwy, Ste. 1400, Englewood, CO 80111
Phone: (303) 220-0100
Sales: $550,421,000   *Employees:* 5,700
Company Type: Public   *Employees here:* 100
SIC: 7379
  Computer consultants
Bobby G Stevenson, Chairman of the Board

D-U-N-S 10-355-6585
CINCINNATI BELL INFO SYSTEMS
  (Parent: Convergys Corporation)
600 Vine St, Ste. 700, Cincinnati, OH 45202
Phone: (513) 784-5900
Sales: $600,000,000   *Employees:* 2,500
Company Type: Public Family Member   *Employees here:* 1,200
SIC: 7373
  Computer integrated systems design & computer software
  development specializing in billing solutions
Robert Marino, President

D-U-N-S 05-648-7531   EXP
CINCOM SYSTEMS INC.
55 Merchant St, Cincinnati, OH 45246
Phone: (513) 612-2300
Sales: $161,589,000   *Employees:* 1,240
Company Type: Private   *Employees here:* 500
SIC: 7373
  Software development
Thomas M Nies, Chairman of the Board

D-U-N-S 04-657-6526   EXP
CIRCUIT SYSTEMS, INC.
2350 Lunt Ave, Elk Grove Village, IL 60007
Phone: (847) 439-1999
Sales: $74,973,000   *Employees:* 715
Company Type: Public   *Employees here:* 250
SIC: 3672
  Mfg printed circuit boards
D S Patel, Chairman of the Board

D-U-N-S 18-175-9077   EXP
CIRCUIT-WISE, INC.
400 Sackett Point Rd, North Haven, CT 06473
Phone: (203) 281-6511
Sales: $71,801,000   *Employees:* 591
Company Type: Private   *Employees here:* 485
SIC: 3672
  Manufactures print circuit boards
Rollin Mettler Jr, Chairman of the Board

D-U-N-S 95-899-4741
CIRENT SEMICONDUSTOR (JV)
9333 S John Young Pkwy, Orlando, FL 32819
Phone: (407) 371-6000
Sales: $123,200,000   *Employees:* 1,600
Company Type: Private   *Employees here:* 1,600
SIC: 3674
  Mfg micro computer chips
Peter Panousis, President

D-U-N-S 11-330-3614   EXP
CIRRUS LOGIC INC.
3100 W Warren Ave, Fremont, CA 94538
Phone: (510) 623-8300
Sales: $954,270,000   *Employees:* 2,135
Company Type: Public   *Employees here:* 550
SIC: 3674
  Mfg integrated circuits
David D French, President

D-U-N-S 15-380-4570
CISCO SYSTEMS INC.
170 W Tasman Dr, San Jose, CA 95134
Phone: (408) 526-4000
Sales: $8,458,777,000   *Employees:* 15,000
Company Type: Public   *Employees here:* 700
SIC: 3577
  Mfg internetworking systems
John T Chambers, President

D-U-N-S 05-734-8450   EXP
CITICORP DEVELOPMENT CENTER
(Parent: Citibank (New York State))
12731 W Jefferson Blvd, Los Angeles, CA 90066
Phone: (310) 302-4000
Sales: $51,600,000   *Employees:* 600
Company Type: Public Family Member   *Employees here:* 500
SIC: 7373
   Computer systems analysis and design
Thomas Gaspard, President

D-U-N-S 60-459-6346   EXP
CITRIX SYSTEMS INC.
6400 Nw 6th Way, Fort Lauderdale, FL 33309
Phone: (954) 267-3000
Sales: $123,933,000   *Employees:* 500
Company Type: Public   *Employees here:* 114
SIC: 7371
   Computer software development
Roger W Roberts, Chief Executive Officer

D-U-N-S 61-261-2168
CLAREMONT TECHNOLOGY GROUP
(Parent: Complete Business Solutions)
1600 Nw Compton Dr, Beaverton, OR 97006
Phone: (503) 748-8000
Sales: $83,600,000   *Employees:* 700
Company Type: Public Family Member   *Employees here:* 80
SIC: 7379
   Computer consulting services
Rajendra A Vattikuti, President

D-U-N-S 62-525-6763
CLARIFY INC.
2125 Onel Dr, San Jose, CA 95131
Phone: (408) 573-3000
Sales: $88,217,000   *Employees:* 488
Company Type: Public   *Employees here:* 400
SIC: 7372
   Computer software development
Anthony Zingale, President

D-U-N-S 00-655-4885   EXP
CLOVER TECHNOLOGIES INC.
(Parent: Ameritech Corporation)
1 Clover Ct, Wixom, MI 48393
Phone: (248) 449-4700
Sales: $79,000,000   *Employees:* 404
Company Type: Public Family Member   *Employees here:* 251
SIC: 7373
   Communications systems integrator
George F Riley, Chairman of the Board

D-U-N-S 61-336-2375
CMOS TECHNOLOGIES, INC.
3040 Coronado Dr, Santa Clara, CA 95054
Phone: (408) 982-0500
Sales: $96,103,000   *Employees:* 250
Company Type: Private   *Employees here:* 25
SIC: 3571
   Mfg personal computers & software development
Sushant Patnaik, President

D-U-N-S 07-361-2178
CODE-ALARM INC.
950 E Whitcomb Ave, Madison Heights, MI 48071
Phone: (248) 583-9620
Sales: $62,503,000   *Employees:* 457
Company Type: Public   *Employees here:* 160
SIC: 3699
   Mfg electronic vehicle security control systems
Rand W Mueller, Chairman of the Board

D-U-N-S 79-990-1301
COGNIZANT TECH SOLUTIONS CORP.
(Parent: IMS Health Incorporated)
500 Glenpointe Ctr W, Teaneck, NJ 07666
Phone: (201) 801-0233
Sales: $116,500,000   *Employees:* 1,500
Company Type: Public   *Employees here:* 1,500
SIC: 7371
   Software services
Kumar Mahadeva, Chief Executive Officer

D-U-N-S 61-344-1609
COLUMBIA/HCA INFORMATION SERVICES
(Parent: Columbia/HCA Healthcare Corp)
1 Park Plz, Nashville, TN 37203
Phone: (615) 344-9551
Sales: $63,400,000   *Employees:* 1,000
Company Type: Public Family Member   *Employees here:* 1,000
SIC: 7374
   Data information & systems support services
Noel Williams, President

D-U-N-S 05-066-7112
COMDATA NETWORK INC.
(Parent: Ceridian Corporation)
5301 Maryland Way, Brentwood, TN 37027
Phone: (615) 370-7000
Sales: $127,200,000   *Employees:* 2,000
Company Type: Public Family Member   *Employees here:* 1,000
SIC: 7374
   Operates nationwide money transfer service
Tony Holcome, President

D-U-N-S 05-431-8936
COMDISCO INC.
6111 N River Rd, Des Plaines, IL 60018
Phone: (847) 698-3000
Sales: $3,243,000,000   *Employees:* 2,800
Company Type: Public   *Employees here:* 900
SIC: 7377
   Lease whol & finance leasing new & used computer
    equipment & computer services
Nicholas K Pontikes, President

D-U-N-S 09-921-6798   EXP
COMMUNICATIONS INSTRUMENTS
(Parent: Code Hennessy & Simmons Lp)
1396 Charlotte Hwy, Fairview, NC 28730
Phone: (828) 628-1711
Sales: $89,436,000   *Employees:* 1,200
Company Type: Private   *Employees here:* 400
SIC: 3679
   Mfg electro-mechanical stepping switches and solenoids and
    electronic relays
Ramzi A Dabbagh, Chief Executive Officer

D-U-N-S 79-078-3310
COMP-SYS DESIGNS
11874 Iowa Ave, Los Angeles, CA 90025
Phone: (213) 700-6424
Sales: $125,400,000   *Employees:* NA
Company Type: Private   *Employees here:* 2,000
SIC: 7379
   Computer related consulting services & computer systems
    analysis & design
Sam Senev, Owner

D-U-N-S 00-389-7733   EXP
COMPAQ COMPUTER CORPORATION
20555 Sh 249, Houston, TX 77070
Phone: (281) 370-0670

Sales: $31,169,000,000   *Employees:* 80,000
Company Type: Public   *Employees here:* 7,800
SIC: 3571
   Mfg personal computers servers & related products
Benjamin M Rosen, Chairman of the Board

D-U-N-S 04-921-4112
COMPAQ FEDERAL LLC
   (Parent: Compaq Computer Corporation)
6406 Ivy Ln, Greenbelt, MD 20770
Phone: (301) 918-5800
Sales: $120,800,000   *Employees:* 1,000
Company Type: Public Family Member   *Employees here:* 1,000
SIC: 3571
   Electronic computers, nsk
Don Weatherson, President

D-U-N-S 55-739-3485
COMPAQ LATIN AMERICA CORP.
   (Parent: Compaq Computer Corporation)
20555 Sh 249, Houston, TX 77070
Phone: (281) 370-0670
Sales: $737,512,000   *Employees:* NA
Company Type: Public Family Member   *Employees here:* NA
SIC: 3571
   Mfg personal computers
Manuel J Parra, President

D-U-N-S 14-869-3484
COMPLETE BUSINESS SOLUTIONS
32605 W 12 Mile Rd, Farmington Hills, MI 48334
Phone: (248) 488-2088
Sales: $123,000,000   *Employees:* 1,600
Company Type: Public   *Employees here:* 250
SIC: 7371
   Contract computer programming services
Rajendra B Vattikuti, President

D-U-N-S 05-865-2231
COMPTEK RESEARCH, INC.
2732 Transit Rd, Buffalo, NY 14224
Phone: (716) 677-4070
Sales: $72,008,000   *Employees:* 620
Company Type: Public   *Employees here:* 75
SIC: 7373
   Computer systems analysis & design
John J Sciuto, Chairman of the Board

D-U-N-S 96-382-4859
COMPUSERVE CORPORATION
   (Parent: MCI Worldcom Inc)
5000 Arlington Centre Blv, Columbus, OH 43220
Phone: (614) 457-8600
Sales: $194,200,000   *Employees:* 3,050
Company Type: Public Family Member   *Employees here:* 500
SIC: 7374
   Data communications
Bernard J Reeves, President

D-U-N-S 07-372-7919
COMPUTER AID INC.
1390 Ridgeview Dr, Allentown, PA 18104
Phone: (610) 530-5000
Sales: $90,806,000   *Employees:* 1,525
Company Type: Private   *Employees here:* 300
SIC: 7371
   Computer programming consultant
Anthony J Salvaggio, President

D-U-N-S 08-039-9256   EXP
COMPUTER ASSOCIATES INTERNATIONAL
1 Computer Associates Plz, Hauppauge, NY 11788
Phone: (516) 342-5224

Sales: $4,719,000,000   *Employees:* 11,400
Company Type: Public   *Employees here:* 2,250
SIC: 7372
   Development of computer software products
Charles B Wang, Chairman of the Board

D-U-N-S 05-563-5791
COMPUTER CURRICULUM CORP.
   (Parent: Prentice-Hall Inc (de Corp))
1287 Lawrence Station Rd, Sunnyvale, CA 94089
Phone: (408) 745-6270
Sales: $150,000,000   *Employees:* 850
Company Type: Private   *Employees here:* 450
SIC: 7373
   Turnkey vendors of computer assisted educational systems
Ronald Fortune, President

D-U-N-S 13-134-4673
COMPUTER GENERATED SOLUTIONS
1675 Broadway, Fl 31, New York, NY 10019
Phone: (212) 408-3800
Sales: $100,000,000   *Employees:* 900
Company Type: Private   *Employees here:* 200
SIC: 7373
   Computer systems development programming consulting
   value added resellers help desk training services & y-2000
   remediation
Philip Friedman, President

D-U-N-S 05-355-4382
COMPUTER HORIZONS CORP.
49 Old Bloomfield Ave, Mountain Lakes, NJ 07046
Phone: (973) 402-7400
Sales: $334,729,000   *Employees:* 3,630
Company Type: Public   *Employees here:* 300
SIC: 7371
   Computer software systems development integration data
   processing and software training
John J Cassese, Chairman of the Board

D-U-N-S 13-195-6427
COMPUTER MANAGEMENT SCIENCES
8133 Baymeadows Way, Jacksonville, FL 32256
Phone: (904) 737-8955
Sales: $71,163,000   *Employees:* 760
Company Type: Public   *Employees here:* 195
SIC: 7379
   Computer consultants
R H Wise, President

D-U-N-S 04-635-3892
COMPUTER MERCHANT LTD.
80 Washington St, Ste. S, Norwell, MA 02061
Phone: (781) 878-1070
Sales: $70,655,000   *Employees:* 470
Company Type: Private   *Employees here:* 40
SIC: 7379
   Computer consultant & software engineering firm
John R Danieli, President

D-U-N-S 10-225-9322   EXP
COMPUTER NETWORK TECH CORP.
605 Highway 169 N, Ste. 800, Minneapolis, MN 55441
Phone: (612) 797-6000
Sales: $97,841,000   *Employees:* 626
Company Type: Public   *Employees here:* 150
SIC: 7373
   Develops and provides high performance extended channel
   computer networking systems
Thomas G Hudson, President

D-U-N-S 08-140-2224
COMPUTER SALES INTERNATIONAL
10845 Olive Blvd, Saint Louis, MO 63141
Phone: (314) 997-7010
Sales: $309,349,000
Company Type: Private
SIC: 7377
   Leasing of computers
Kenneth B Steinback, Chairman of the Board

       Employees: 160
       Employees here: 100

D-U-N-S 00-958-1091   EXP
COMPUTER SCIENCES CORPORATION
2100 E Grand Ave, El Segundo, CA 90245
Phone: (310) 615-0311
Sales: $6,600,838,000
Company Type: Public
SIC: 7379
   Computer related consulting facilities management claims
     processing & credit investigation services systems
     integration
Michael Beebe, President

       Employees: 45,000
       Employees here: 250

D-U-N-S 06-364-0072   EXP
COMPUTER TASK GROUP INC.
800 Delaware Ave, Buffalo, NY 14209
Phone: (716) 882-8000
Sales: $407,588,000
Company Type: Public
SIC: 7371
   Software services computer related consulting services
Gale S Fitzgerald, Chairman of the Board

       Employees: 6,000
       Employees here: 113

D-U-N-S 07-773-4499
COMPUTRON SOFTWARE INC.
301 Route 17, Rutherford, NJ 07070
Phone: (201) 935-3400
Sales: $67,591,000
Company Type: Public
SIC: 7372
   Designs develops markets and supports business oriented
     software
John A Rade, President

       Employees: 454
       Employees here: 220

D-U-N-S 07-277-3849
COMPUWARE CORPORATION
31440 Northwestern Hwy, Farmington Hills, MI 48334
Phone: (248) 737-7300
Sales: $1,139,318,000
Company Type: Public
SIC: 7371
   Computer software development
Peter Karmanos Jr, Chairman of the Board

       Employees: 8,663
       Employees here: 1,805

D-U-N-S 04-243-6121
COMSHARE INCORPORATED
555 Briarwood Cir, Ste. 200, Ann Arbor, MI 48108
Phone: (734) 994-4800
Sales: $89,753,000
Company Type: Public
SIC: 7372
   Develops & markets business oriented computer software
Dennis G Ganster, President

       Employees: 405
       Employees here: 170

D-U-N-S 04-008-8999   EXP
COMTEC INFORMATION SYSTEMS
30 Plan Way, Warwick, RI 02886
Phone: (401) 739-5800
Sales: $60,000,000
Company Type: Private
SIC: 3577
   Mfr electronic id systems
Alfred Petteruti, Chairman of the Board

       Employees: 200
       Employees here: 200

D-U-N-S 13-020-5297   EXP
COMVERSE TECHNOLOGY INC.
170 Crossways Park Dr, Woodbury, NY 11797
Phone: (516) 677-7200
Sales: $488,940,000
Company Type: Public
SIC: 3571
   Designs manufactures & markets computer &
     telecommunications systems and software
Kobi Alexander, Chairman of the Board

       Employees: 2,823
       Employees here: 75

D-U-N-S 06-351-0622   EXP
CONCURRENT COMPUTER CORP.
2101 W Cypress Creek Rd, Fort Lauderdale, FL 33309
Phone: (954) 974-1700
Sales: $82,215,000
Company Type: Public
SIC: 3571
   Mfg & svcs real time computer systems
E C Siegel, Chairman of the Board

       Employees: 530
       Employees here: 250

D-U-N-S 00-388-8562
CONDOR TECHNOLOGY SOLUTIONS
170 Jennifer Rd, Ste. 325, Annapolis, MD 21401
Phone: (410) 266-8700
Sales: $92,100,000
Company Type: Public
SIC: 7373
   Systems software development systems integration ret and
     maint of computers and peripheral equip
Kennard F Hill, Chairman of the Board

       Employees: 1,073
       Employees here: 15

D-U-N-S 07-140-9460   EXP
CONFEDERATED SLISH KTNAI TRIBES
Hwy 93, Pablo, MT 59855
Phone: (406) 675-2700
Sales: $61,975,000
Company Type: Private
SIC: 3679
   Tribal management mfg electronic circuits & harness
     assemblies & information technical services & document
     scanning
Vern Clairmont, Executive

       Employees: 800
       Employees here: 550

D-U-N-S 78-706-9772
CONSIST INTERNATIONAL, INC.
10 E 53rd St, Fl 27, New York, NY 10022
Phone: (212) 759-2100
Sales: $100,000,000
Company Type: Private
SIC: 7371
   Develops & markets integrated financial software & imaging
     applications
Natalio S Fridman, President

       Employees: 900
       Employees here: 8

D-U-N-S 07-347-1476
CONSULTEC INC.
   (*Parent:* General American Life Insur Co)
9040 Roswell Rd, Ste. 700, Atlanta, GA 30350
Phone: (770) 594-7799
Sales: $74,000,000
Company Type: Private
SIC: 7373
   Computer facility management & computer integrated
     systems design
Gray J Arnold, President

       Employees: 800
       Employees here: 500

D-U-N-S 79-131-3109   EXP
CONTROL DATA SYSTEMS, INC.
   (*Parent:* CDSI Holding Coporation)
4201 Lexington Ave N, Saint Paul, MN 55126
Phone: (651) 415-2999

Sales: $200,000,000   *Employees:* 1,750
Company Type: Private   *Employees here:* 750
SIC: 7373
   Messaging and web services
James E Ousley, President

D-U-N-S 08-959-1317   EXP
COOPERATIVE COMPUTING INC.
   (Parent: Cooperative Computing Holdg Co)
6207 Bee Caves Rd, Austin, TX 78746
Phone: (512) 328-2300
Sales: $220,000,000   *Employees:* 1,800
Company Type: Private   *Employees here:* 650
SIC: 7371
   Provides computer software services & installs & operates
     computer systems
Glenn E Staats, President

D-U-N-S 00-214-8989
CORNELL-DUBILIER ELECTRONICS
1700 Route 23, Wayne, NJ 07470
Phone: (973) 694-8600
Sales: $52,000,000   *Employees:* 850
Company Type: Private   *Employees here:* 13
SIC: 3675
   Manufactures electronic capacitors and electrical mechanical
     devices
James R Kaplan, Chairman of the Board

D-U-N-S 00-324-9542
CORPORATE SOFTWARE & TECH
   (Parent: R R Donnelley & Sons Company)
2 Edgewater Dr, Norwood, MA 02062
Phone: (781) 440-1000
Sales: $85,800,000   *Employees:* 1,000
Company Type: Public Family Member   *Employees here:* 1,000
SIC: 7373
   Software development & consulting
Howard S Diamond, Chief Executive Officer

D-U-N-S 92-982-8176
COTELLIGENT, INC.
101 California St, San Francisco, CA 94111
Phone: (415) 439-6400
Sales: $244,683,000   *Employees:* 2,900
Company Type: Public   *Employees here:* 15
SIC: 7371
   Computer consulting & contract programming services
James R Lavelle, Chairman of the Board

D-U-N-S 02-719-7586
COVENANT COMPUTER LABORATORY
3263 Kifer Rd, Santa Clara, CA 95051
Phone: (408) 774-3581
Sales: $100,000,000   *Employees:* 25
Company Type: Private   *Employees here:* 25
SIC: 7371
   Computer networking server and desktop oem provider
James Lin, President

D-U-N-S 02-013-2973
CRA INC.
   (Parent: Newcourt Financial USA Inc)
11011 N 23rd Ave, Phoenix, AZ 85029
Phone: (602) 944-1548
Sales: $68,286,000   *Employees:* 38
Company Type: Private   *Employees here:* 34
SIC: 7377
   Computer equipment leasing wholesale & refurbishing
Rob Mac Farlane, Executive Vice-President

D-U-N-S 05-903-5543
CRAY RESEARCH, INC.
   (Parent: Silicon Graphics Inc)
655a Lone Oak Dr, Saint Paul, MN 55121
Phone: (612) 452-6650
Sales: $372,300,000   *Employees:* 3,100
Company Type: Public Family Member   *Employees here:* 800
SIC: 3571
   Mfg supercomputers & magnetic storage devices produces
     software products
Robert H Ewald, President

D-U-N-S 06-242-7778
CRYSTAL SEMICONDUCTOR CORP.
   (Parent: Cirrus Logic Inc)
4210 S Industrial Dr, Austin, TX 78744
Phone: (512) 445-7222
Sales: $65,400,000   *Employees:* 850
Company Type: Public Family Member   *Employees here:* 800
SIC: 3674
   Mfg integrated circuits
James H Clardy, Vice-President

D-U-N-S 87-825-0059
CSG SYSTEMS INCORPORATED
   (Parent: CSG Systems International)
2525 N 117th Ave, Omaha, NE 68164
Phone: (402) 431-7000
Sales: $156,048,000   *Employees:* 1,119
Company Type: Public Family Member   *Employees here:* 837
SIC: 7374
   Data processing
Neal Hansen, Chairman of the Board

D-U-N-S 87-811-5161
CSG SYSTEMS INTERNATIONAL
7887 E Belleview Ave, Englewood, CO 80111
Phone: (303) 796-2850
Sales: $171,801,000   *Employees:* 1,179
Company Type: Public   *Employees here:* 5
SIC: 7374
   Data processing
Neal Hansen, Chairman of the Board

D-U-N-S 04-589-7659   EXP
CSP INC.
40 Linnell Cir, Billerica, MA 01821
Phone: (978) 663-7598
Sales: $63,468,000   *Employees:* 247
Company Type: Public   *Employees here:* 62
SIC: 3577
   Mfg computer processors software & hardware packages
Alexander R Lupinetti, Chairman of the Board

D-U-N-S 18-763-2385
CSX TECHNOLOGY INC.
   (Parent: CSX Corporation)
500 Water St, Fl 15, Jacksonville, FL 32202
Phone: (904) 359-3100
Sales: $228,726,000   *Employees:* 780
Company Type: Public Family Member   *Employees here:* 215
SIC: 7371
   Holding company developing computer software & providing
     data processing services
John Andrews, President

D-U-N-S 09-991-0788
CTA INCORPORATED
6903 Rockledge Dr, Ste. 800, Bethesda, MD 20817
Phone: (301) 581-3200

Sales: $92,239,000
Employees: 1,250
Company Type: Private
Employees here: 125
SIC: 7373

Aerospace computer systems analysis design flight simulator mfg & training & consulting state org on year 2000 conversion

C E Velez, Chairman of the Board

D-U-N-S 86-862-4214
CUBIC APPLICATIONS INC.
(Parent: Cubic Corporation)
4550 3rd Ave SE, Lacey, WA 98503
Phone: (360) 493-6275
Sales: $63,000,000
Employees: 810
Company Type: Public Family Member
Employees here: 45
SIC: 7373

Military systems design and battlefield readiness training

Jack Walker, President

D-U-N-S 00-838-2293
EXP
CUBIC CORPORATION
9333 Balboa Ave, San Diego, CA 92123
Phone: (619) 277-6780
Sales: $414,136,000
Employees: 3,700
Company Type: Public
Employees here: 1,243
SIC: 3699

Mfg electronic training devices radio communications equip object detection equip & automatic revenue collection equip

William W Boyle, Chief Financial Officer

D-U-N-S 18-606-4960
EXP
CUBIC DEFENSE SYSTEMS INC.
(Parent: Cubic Corporation)
9333 Balboa Ave, San Diego, CA 92123
Phone: (619) 277-6780
Sales: $108,751,000
Employees: 768
Company Type: Public Family Member
Employees here: 753
SIC: 3699

Mfg electronic training devices communication & surveillance systems avionics systems and rf/digital products

Bruce D Roberts, President

D-U-N-S 11-414-8190
CURRENT ELECTRONICS INC.
(Parent: EFTC Corporation)
125 Elliott Rd, Newberg, OR 97132
Phone: (503) 538-0626
Sales: $55,000,000
Employees: 390
Company Type: Public Family Member
Employees here: 370
SIC: 3679

Mfg electronic circuitry

Greg Hewitson, President

D-U-N-S 09-077-3847
CVSI INC.
4g Crosby Dr, Bedford, MA 01730
Phone: (781) 275-2600
Sales: $135,000,000
Employees: 500
Company Type: Private
Employees here: 80
SIC: 7371

Computer services

James Regan, President

D-U-N-S 87-433-1564
CYBERMAX INC.
133 N 5th St, Allentown, PA 18102
Phone: (610) 770-1808
Sales: $96,800,000
Employees: NA
Company Type: Private
Employees here: NA
SIC: 3571

Manufactures & wholesales personal computers

Tom Watkins, Office Manager

D-U-N-S 06-690-5928
CYBERNETICS & SYSTEMS INC.
(Parent: CSX Technology Inc)
550 Water St, Fl 12, Jacksonville, FL 32202
Phone: (904) 359-7460
Sales: $91,904,000
Employees: 490
Company Type: Public Family Member
Employees here: 490
SIC: 7371

Custom computer programming service

Charles Wodehouse, President

D-U-N-S 07-440-7800
EXP
CYBORG SYSTEMS INC.
2 N Riverside Plz, Fl 12th, Chicago, IL 60606
Phone: (312) 454-1865
Sales: $59,030,000
Employees: 575
Company Type: Private
Employees here: 250
SIC: 7372

Computer software programs

Michael D Blair, Chairman of the Board

D-U-N-S 17-714-0688
CYMER INC.
16750 Via Del Campo Ct, San Diego, CA 92127
Phone: (619) 451-7300
Sales: $57,500,000
Employees: 712
Company Type: Public
Employees here: 555
SIC: 3699

Mfg laser systems & equipment

Robert P Akins, President

D-U-N-S 10-210-8446
EXP
CYPRESS SEMICONDUCTOR CORP.
3901 N 1st St, San Jose, CA 95134
Phone: (408) 943-2600
Sales: $544,356,000
Employees: 2,770
Company Type: Public
Employees here: 930
SIC: 3674

Mfr integrated circuits

T J Rodgers, President

D-U-N-S 11-331-2730
EXP
DALLAS SEMICONDUCTOR CORP.
4401 S Beltwood Pkwy, Dallas, TX 75244
Phone: (972) 371-4000
Sales: $342,608,000
Employees: 1,530
Company Type: Public
Employees here: 700
SIC: 3674

Mfg integrated circuits

C V Prothro, Chairman of the Board

D-U-N-S 04-590-3218
EXP
DATA GENERAL CORPORATION
4400 Computer Dr, Westborough, MA 01580
Phone: (508) 898-5000
Sales: $1,462,100,000
Employees: 4,700
Company Type: Public
Employees here: 1,200
SIC: 3571

Mfg minicomputers microcomputers & peripheral equipment

Ronald L Skates, President

D-U-N-S 16-102-9939
DATA PROCESSING RESOURCES CORP.
4400 Macarthur Blvd, Newport Beach, CA 92660
Phone: (949) 553-1102
Sales: $210,568,000
Employees: 2,010
Company Type: Public
Employees here: 124
SIC: 7373

Data system design system engineering data processing & online services consulting

Mary E Weaver, Chairman of the Board

D-U-N-S 14-423-6676
DATA SYSTEMS NETWORK CORP.
34705 W 12 Mile Rd, Farmington Hills, MI 48331
Phone: (248) 489-7117
Sales: $88,010,000   *Employees:* 285
Company Type: Public   *Employees here:* 70
SIC: 7373
  Computer network integration and fulfillment
Diane L Grieves, Executive Vice-President

D-U-N-S 12-202-3757
DATA TRANSMISSION NETWORK CORP.
9110 W Dodge Rd, Ste. 200, Omaha, NE 68114
Phone: (402) 390-2328
Sales: $126,374,000   *Employees:* 1,000
Company Type: Public   *Employees here:* 600
SIC: 7375
  Satellite delivery of electronic information and
    communication services
Roger R Brodersen, Chairman of the Board

D-U-N-S 02-112-0191
DATAMAX INTERNATIONAL CORP.
  (Parent: Liberty Partners Lp)
4501 Parkway Commerce Blv, Orlando, FL 32808
Phone: (407) 578-8007
Sales: $98,229,000   *Employees:* 500
Company Type: Private   *Employees here:* 370
SIC: 3577
  Designer of thermal barcode printers & labels
Marvin Davis, Chief Executive Officer

D-U-N-S 04-701-3966
DATAPOINT CORPORATION
8410 Datapoint Dr, San Antonio, TX 78229
Phone: (210) 593-7000
Sales: $151,445,000   *Employees:* 652
Company Type: Public   *Employees here:* 100
SIC: 7373
  Systems integration mfg computing equipment & software
    technology licensing
Asher B Edelman, Chairman of the Board

D-U-N-S 00-839-1047
DATAPRODUCTS CORPORATION
1757 Tapo Canyon Rd, Simi Valley, CA 93063
Phone: (805) 578-4000
Sales: $107,600,000   *Employees:* 1,000
Company Type: Private   *Employees here:* 400
SIC: 3577
  Mfg computer printers
Richard L Roll, President

D-U-N-S 04-225-5927   EXP
DATARAM CORPORATION
Princeton Rd Rr 571, Princeton, NJ 08543
Phone: (609) 799-0071
Sales: $77,286,000   *Employees:* 138
Company Type: Public   *Employees here:* 88
SIC: 3572
  Mfg computer memory products
Robert V Tarantino, Chairman of the Board

D-U-N-S 15-187-8097
DATASTREAM SYSTEMS INC.
50 Datastream Plz, Greenville, SC 29605
Phone: (864) 422-5001
Sales: $69,768,000   *Employees:* 600
Company Type: Public   *Employees here:* 450
SIC: 7372
  Computer software
Larry G Blackwell, Chairman of the Board

D-U-N-S 11-818-8119
DATATEC SYSTEMS, INC.
20c Commerce Way, Totowa, NJ 07512
Phone: (973) 890-4800
Sales: $76,804,000   *Employees:* 585
Company Type: Public   *Employees here:* 80
SIC: 7373
  Integration configuration and implementation of enterprise
    wide information communication networks
Isaac Gaon, Chief Executive Officer

D-U-N-S 08-092-0929
DATAWORKS CORPORATION
5910 Pcf Ctr Blvd, Ste. 300, San Diego, CA 92121
Phone: (619) 546-9600
Sales: $146,963,000   *Employees:* 300
Company Type: Public   *Employees here:* 120
SIC: 7373
  Designs and develops computer integrated systems
Stuart Clifton, President

D-U-N-S 06-514-2986
DAVIDSON & ASSOCIATES INC.
  (Parent: Cendant Corporation)
19840 Pioneer Ave, Torrance, CA 90503
Phone: (310) 793-0600
Sales: $68,900,000   *Employees:* 679
Company Type: Public Family Member   *Employees here:* 300
SIC: 7372
  Develops educational and entertainment software
Christophe McLeod, Chief Executive Officer

D-U-N-S 05-780-2209
DAVOX CORPORATION
6 Technology Park Dr, Westford, MA 01886
Phone: (978) 952-0200
Sales: $88,948,000   *Employees:* 398
Company Type: Public   *Employees here:* 115
SIC: 7373
  Systems integrator
Alphonse M Lucchese, Chairman of the Board

D-U-N-S 60-523-4442   EXP
DAW TECHNOLOGIES INC.
2700 S 900 W, Salt Lake City, UT 84119
Phone: (801) 977-3100
Sales: $52,541,000   *Employees:* 200
Company Type: Public   *Employees here:* 150
SIC: 3674
  Mfg clean room systems
Ronald W Daw, Chairman of the Board

D-U-N-S 79-066-9998
DBC HOLDING CORP.
  (Parent: Geac Computers Inc)
66 Perimeter Ctr E, Atlanta, GA 30346
Phone: (404) 239-2000
Sales: $101,000,000   *Employees:* 1,300
Company Type: Private   *Employees here:* 1,300
SIC: 7371
  Provides business applications software
Stephen Sadler, President

D-U-N-S 15-052-0344   EXP
DE LA RUE SYSTEMS AMRICAS CORP.
  (Parent: De La Rue Inc)
2441 Warrenville Rd, Lisle, IL 60532
Phone: (630) 245-0100
Sales: $140,900,000   *Employees:* 1,700
Company Type: Private   *Employees here:* 250
SIC: 3578
  Mfg bank equipment
Joseph Patten, President

D-U-N-S 04-683-5062
DECISION CONSULTANTS INC.
28411 Northwestern Hwy, Southfield, MI 48034
Phone: (248) 352-8650
Sales: $200,000,000   *Employees:* 1,900
Company Type: Private   *Employees here:* 400
SIC: 7371
   Information technology consulting service
Alphonse S Lucarelli, President

D-U-N-S 19-500-7570
DECISIONONE CORPORATION
   (Parent: Decisionone Holdings Corp)
50 Swedesford Rd, Malvern, PA 19355
Phone: (610) 296-6000
Sales: $805,717,000   *Employees:* 6,500
Company Type: Public Family Member   *Employees here:* 500
SIC: 7378
   Computer services including hardware support repair &
      refurbishing & network support
Karl Wyss, Chief Executive Officer

D-U-N-S 00-121-0186   EXP
DEL GLOBAL TECHNOLOGIES CORP.
1 Commerce Park, Valhalla, NY 10595
Phone: (914) 686-3600
Sales: $62,305,000   *Employees:* 466
Company Type: Public   *Employees here:* 68
SIC: 3679
   Mfg power supplies electronic filters power transformers
      capacitors & radiographic & mammography equipment
Leonard A Trugman, Chairman of the Board

D-U-N-S 11-431-5195   EXP
DELL COMPUTER CORPORATION
1 Dell Way, Round Rock, TX 78682
Phone: (512) 338-4400
Sales: $12,327,000,000   *Employees:* 13,500
Company Type: Public   *Employees here:* 5,500
SIC: 3571
   Manufactures & markets computer systems systems
      integration
Michael S Dell, Chairman of the Board

D-U-N-S 80-008-5763
DELL PRODUCTS LP
1 Dell Way, Round Rock, TX 78682
Phone: (512) 338-4400
Sales: $1,198,800,000   *Employees:* 10,000
Company Type: Private   *Employees here:* 10,000
SIC: 3571
   Mfg computers
Michael S Dell, Chairman of the Board

D-U-N-S 11-885-3779
DELPHAX SYSTEMS
   (Parent: Xerox Corporation)
5 Campanelli Cir, Canton, MA 02021
Phone: (781) 828-9917
Sales: $60,000,000   *Employees:* 400
Company Type: Public Family Member   *Employees here:* 75
SIC: 3577
   Mfg computer printers
Rogers Parson, President

D-U-N-S 18-504-6869   EXP
DELTA PRODUCTS CORPORATION
   (Parent: Delta America Ltd)
1650 W Calle Plata, Nogales, AZ 85621
Phone: (520) 294-8400

Sales: $52,200,000   *Employees:* 900
Company Type: Private   *Employees here:* 9
SIC: 3679
   Mfg electronic parts and peripherals
Bruce C Cheng, President

D-U-N-S 94-901-6539
DELTA TECHNOLOGIES INC.
   (Parent: Delta Air Lines Inc)
1001 International Blvd, Atlanta, GA 30354
Phone: (404) 714-1500
Sales: $171,500,000   *Employees:* 2,000
Company Type: Public Family Member   *Employees here:* 2,000
SIC: 7373
   Technology services
Leo Mullin, President

D-U-N-S 15-367-3595
DELTEC ELECTRONICS CORPORATION
   (Parent: Exide Electronics Group Inc)
2727 Kurtz St, San Diego, CA 92110
Phone: (619) 291-4211
Sales: $145,000,000   *Employees:* 1,300
Company Type: Private   *Employees here:* 250
SIC: 3679
   Mfg electronic circuits and power supplies
Raymond E Meyer, President

D-U-N-S 16-102-0151   EXP
DELUXE ELECTRONIC PAYMENT SYSTEMS
   (Parent: Deluxe Corporation)
400 W Deluxe Pkwy, Milwaukee, WI 53212
Phone: (414) 963-5000
Sales: $140,000,000   *Employees:* 1,200
Company Type: Public Family Member   *Employees here:* 650
SIC: 7374
   Data process & computer software services
Debra A Janssen, President

D-U-N-S 87-978-3900
DENDRITE INTERNATIONAL INC.
1200 Mount Kemble Ave, Morristown, NJ 07960
Phone: (973) 425-1200
Sales: $78,446,000   *Employees:* 725
Company Type: Public   *Employees here:* 725
SIC: 7371
   Computer software development & support services
John E Bailye, Chairman of the Board

D-U-N-S 04-561-0110
DETECTION SYSTEMS INC.
130 Perinton Pkwy, Fairport, NY 14450
Phone: (716) 223-4060
Sales: $126,343,000   *Employees:* 395
Company Type: Public   *Employees here:* 288
SIC: 3699
   Mfg security control & fire protection systems and
      equipment
Lawrence Tracey, President

D-U-N-S 10-653-9174
DIALIGHT CORP.
   (Parent: Roxboro Holdings Inc)
1913 Atlantic Ave, Manasquan, NJ 08736
Phone: (732) 223-9400
Sales: $70,000,000   *Employees:* 430
Company Type: Private   *Employees here:* 80
SIC: 3679
   Mfg electronic components and optoelectronics
Michael J Kirchoff, Chief Executive Officer

D-U-N-S 01-292-4460
DIALOG CORPORATION
2440 W El Camino Real, Mountain View, CA 94040
Phone: (650) 254-7000
Sales: $71,000,000   *Employees:* 1,000
Company Type: Private   *Employees here:* 500
SIC: 7375
  Information retrieval services
Jason Molle, President

D-U-N-S 10-210-1888   EXP
DIAMOND MULTIMEDIA SYSTEMS
2880 Junction Ave, San Jose, CA 95134
Phone: (408) 325-7000
Sales: $608,581,000   *Employees:* 841
Company Type: Public   *Employees here:* 290
SIC: 3672
  Mfg multimedia add-in computer subsystems and modems
William J Schroeder, Chairman of the Board

D-U-N-S 00-446-9300   EXP
DIEBOLD INCORPORATED
5995 Mayfair Rd, Canton, OH 44720
Phone: (330) 489-4000
Sales: $1,185,707,000   *Employees:* 6,489
Company Type: Public   *Employees here:* 900
SIC: 3578
  Mfg bank teller machines terminals elec detection apparatus
    safes vaults
Robert W Mahoney, Chairman of the Board

D-U-N-S 14-465-5669   EXP
DIGI INTERNATIONAL INC.
11001 Bren Rd E, Hopkins, MN 55343
Phone: (612) 912-3444
Sales: $182,932,000   *Employees:* 703
Company Type: Public   *Employees here:* 125
SIC: 3577
  Mfg computer input-output equipment software
John P Schinas, Chairman of the Board

D-U-N-S 17-424-3907
DIGICON CORPORATION
6903 Rockledge Dr, Ste. 600, Bethesda, MD 20817
Phone: (301) 564-6400
Sales: $62,885,000   *Employees:* 300
Company Type: Private   *Employees here:* 70
SIC: 7371
  Software design & development telecomm systems
    integration info engineering management services &
    network engineering
John J Wu, President

D-U-N-S 10-363-1131   EXP
DIGITAL AUDIO DISC CORPORATION
  (Parent: Sony Corporation Of America)
1800 N Fruitridge Ave, Terre Haute, IN 47804
Phone: (812) 462-8100
Sales: $115,200,000   *Employees:* 1,200
Company Type: Private   *Employees here:* 1,200
SIC: 3695
  Mfg optical and compact discs
James M Frische, Chairman of the Board

D-U-N-S 06-514-6854   EXP
DIGITAL EQUIPMENT CORP INTERNATIONAL
  (Parent: Digital Equipment Corporation)
100 Nagog Park, Acton, MA 01720
Phone: (978) 264-5993

Sales: $1,198,800,000   *Employees:* 10,000
Company Type: Public Family Member   *Employees here:* 6
SIC: 3571
  Mfg repairs & services computers
Abdul F Choonvala, President

D-U-N-S 00-103-8066   EXP
DIGITAL EQUIPMENT CORPORATION
  (Parent: Compaq Computer Corporation)
111 Powder Mill Rd, Maynard, MA 01754
Phone: (978) 493-5111
Sales: $5,989,900,000   *Employees:* 50,000
Company Type: Public Family Member   *Employees here:* 2,500
SIC: 3571
  Mfg computers & storage devices microprocessors peripheral
    equip maintenance & other services
Robert B Palmer, Chairman of the Board

D-U-N-S 80-480-0266   EXP
DII GROUP, INC.
6273 Monarch Park Pl, Longmont, CO 80503
Phone: (303) 652-2221
Sales: $779,603,000   *Employees:* 6,350
Company Type: Public   *Employees here:* 8
SIC: 3679
  Contract electronics manufacturer mfr printed circuit boards
    software development mfr electronic test equip
Ronald R Budacz, Chairman of the Board

D-U-N-S 05-978-2060
DIRECT MARKETING TECH INC.
  (Parent: Experian Corporation)
955 American Ln, Schaumburg, IL 60173
Phone: (847) 517-5600
Sales: $80,000,000   *Employees:* 640
Company Type: Private   *Employees here:* 620
SIC: 7374
  Data processing services
R S Thomas, President

D-U-N-S 18-634-8926
DISCLOSURE INCORPORATED
  (Parent: Primark Holding Corporation)
5161 River Rd, Ste. 1, Bethesda, MD 20816
Phone: (301) 951-1300
Sales: $67,500,000   *Employees:* 950
Company Type: Public Family Member   *Employees here:* 600
SIC: 7375
  Business information service
Steve Schneider, Chief Executive Officer

D-U-N-S 62-093-2178
DIVERSIFIED PHRM SERVICES
  (Parent: Smithkline Beecham Corporation)
7760 France Ave S, Ste. 500, Minneapolis, MN 55435
Phone: (612) 820-7000
Sales: $500,000,000   *Employees:* 1,000
Company Type: Private   *Employees here:* 400
SIC: 7375
  Prescription drug & claims management services
Mark O Johnson, President

D-U-N-S 13-049-3794
DMR CONSULTING GROUP INC.
  (Parent: Amdahl Corporation)
333 Thornall St, Edison, NJ 08837
Phone: (732) 549-4100
Sales: $400,000,000   *Employees:* 3,633
Company Type: Private   *Employees here:* 700
SIC: 7371
  Computer software services systems integration and
    management consulting services
Michael J Poehner, Chief Executive Officer

D-U-N-S 78-933-5809   EXP
DOCUMENTUM, INC.
5671 Gibraltar Dr, Pleasanton, CA 94588
Phone: (925) 463-6800
Sales: $75,635,000   *Employees:* 600
Company Type: Public   *Employees here:* 160
SIC: 7372
    Computer software development
Jeffrey A Miller, President

D-U-N-S 93-894-7546   EXP
DOMINION SEMICONDUCTORS L.L.C.
9600 Godwin Dr, Manassas, VA 20110
Phone: (703) 396-1000
Sales: $64,600,000   *Employees:* 600
Company Type: Private   *Employees here:* 600
SIC: 3577
    Mfgs 64-megabit memory chips
M A Graham, President

D-U-N-S 62-706-6269
DOVATRON INTERNATIONAL, INC.
    (Parent: DII Group Inc)
5405 Spine Rd, Boulder, CO 80301
Phone: (303) 581-1400
Sales: $274,651,000   *Employees:* 900
Company Type: Public Family Member   *Employees here:* 10
SIC: 3679
    Contract electronics manufacturer
Ronald R Budacz, Chairman of the Board

D-U-N-S 14-860-6767   EXP
DOVER TECHNOLOGIES INTERNATIONAL
    (Parent: Delaware Capital Holdings Inc)
1 Marine Midland Plz, Binghamton, NY 13901
Phone: (607) 773-2290
Sales: $435,400,000   *Employees:* 7,500
Company Type: Public Family Member   *Employees here:* 6
SIC: 3679
    Holding company (see operations)
John Pomeroy, President

D-U-N-S 04-914-9834
DOW JONES TELERATE, INC.
    (Parent: Telerate Holdings Inc)
200 Liberty St, New York, NY 10281
Phone: (212) 416-2000
Sales: $85,300,000   *Employees:* 1,200
Company Type: Private   *Employees here:* 7
SIC: 7375
    Computerized financial information service
Kenneth L Burenga, President

D-U-N-S 80-971-7481
DSP COMMUNICATIONS, INC.
20300 Stevens Creek Blvd, Cupertino, CA 95014
Phone: (408) 777-2700
Sales: $131,097,000   *Employees:* 35
Company Type: Public   *Employees here:* 30
SIC: 3674
    Mfg baseband chip sets
Nathan Hod, Chief Executive Officer

D-U-N-S 07-303-1197   EXP
DST SYSTEMS, INC.
333 W 11th St, Kansas City, MO 64105
Phone: (816) 435-1000
Sales: $650,678,000   *Employees:* 6,000
Company Type: Public   *Employees here:* 2,200
SIC: 7374
    Data processing service computer software applications
      printing and mailing service
Thomas A Mc Donnell, President

D-U-N-S 10-179-8296
DU PONT ELECTRONIC MATERIALS
    (Parent: Du Pont E I De Nemours And Co)
Km 2 Hm 3 Rr 686, Manati, PR 00674
Phone: (787) 854-1105
Sales: $135,286,000   *Employees:* 100
Company Type: Public Family Member   *Employees here:* 100
SIC: 3677
    Mfg electronic filtration devices
Thomas P McCarthy, President

D-U-N-S 10-693-7436
DUCHOSSOIS INDUSTRIES INC.
845 N Larch Ave, Elmhurst, IL 60126
Phone: (630) 279-3600
Sales: $241,500,000   *Employees:* 7,500
Company Type: Private   *Employees here:* 300
SIC: 3699
    Mfg garage door devices ordnance & small arms contract r &
      d & operates race track
Richard L Duchossois, Chairman of the Board

D-U-N-S 84-764-3319
DURANT ELECTRIC COMPANY
703 Highway 80 W, Clinton, MS 39056
Phone: (601) 924-3600
Sales: $65,496,000   *Employees:* 725
Company Type: Private   *Employees here:* 15
SIC: 3694
    Mfg auto parts
Frank X Lauritzen, Chairman of the Board

D-U-N-S 09-915-6523
DYNAMIC DETAILS, INC.
1220 N Simon Cir, Anaheim, CA 92806
Phone: (714) 688-7200
Sales: $68,000,000   *Employees:* 2,000
Company Type: Private   *Employees here:* 183
SIC: 3672
    Mfg printed circuit boards
Bruce McMaster, Chief Executive Officer

D-U-N-S 00-101-4182
DYNAMICS RESEARCH CORPORATION
60 Frontage Rd, Andover, MA 01810
Phone: (978) 475-9090
Sales: $159,377,000   *Employees:* 1,455
Company Type: Public   *Employees here:* 400
SIC: 7373
    Computer integrated systems design services mfg digital
      encoders & high precision components
Albert Rand, President

D-U-N-S 00-324-2013
DYNCORP
2000 Edmund Halley Dr, Reston, VA 20191
Phone: (703) 264-0330
Sales: $1,145,937,000   *Employees:* 16,100
Company Type: Private   *Employees here:* 135
SIC: 7373
    Management technical & professional services
Dan R Bannister, Chairman of the Board

D-U-N-S 10-648-7762
E-TEK DYNAMICS INC.
1865 Lundy Ave, San Jose, CA 95131
Phone: (408) 546-5000
Sales: $106,924,000   *Employees:* 787
Company Type: Public   *Employees here:* 787
SIC: 3674
    Mfg passive components & modules for fiber optic networks
Michael J Fitzpatrick, President

D-U-N-S 00-246-1838   EXP
EA INDUSTRIES
185 Monmouth Rd, West Long Branch, NJ 07764
Phone: (732) 229-1100
Sales: $76,511,000   *Employees:* 430
Company Type: Public   *Employees here:* 1
SIC: 3571
    Contract mfg services
Frank Brandenberg, President

D-U-N-S 87-907-4276
EARTHLINK NETWORK, INC.
3100 New York Dr, Pasadena, CA 91107
Phone: (626) 296-2400
Sales: $79,174,000   *Employees:* 1,329
Company Type: Public   *Employees here:* 1,329
SIC: 7375
    Internet access provider
Charles G Betty, President

D-U-N-S 96-889-7405
EASTMAN SOFTWARE, INC.
    (Parent: Eastman Kodak Company)
296 Concord Rd, Billerica, MA 01821
Phone: (978) 967-8000
Sales: $71,000,000   *Employees:* 700
Company Type: Public Family Member   *Employees here:* 700
SIC: 7372
    Develops software programs
Gerry Sutton, President

D-U-N-S 04-859-1648   EXP
ECC INTERNATIONAL CORP.
2001 W Oak Ridge Rd, Orlando, FL 32809
Phone: (407) 859-7410
Sales: $52,618,000   *Employees:* 538
Company Type: Public   *Employees here:* 538
SIC: 3699
    Mfg electronic simulators
Jerome Pogorzelski, Vice-President

D-U-N-S 03-696-8709
ECLIPSYS CORPORATION
777 E Atlantic Ave, Delray Beach, FL 33483
Phone: (561) 243-1440
Sales: $94,077,000   *Employees:* 997
Company Type: Public   *Employees here:* 471
SIC: 7371
    Computer software development
Harvey J Wilson, President

D-U-N-S 79-803-3627
EDGEMARK SYSTEMS INC.
11921 Bournefield Way, Silver Spring, MD 20904
Phone: (301) 625-1000
Sales: $104,604,000   *Employees:* 120
Company Type: Private   *Employees here:* 89
SIC: 7373
    Computer system selling service
Raymond Tuchman, Chairman of the Board

D-U-N-S 61-839-2682
EDIFY CORPORATION
2840 San Tomas Expy, Santa Clara, CA 95051
Phone: (408) 982-2000
Sales: $57,052,000   *Employees:* 425
Company Type: Public   *Employees here:* 260
SIC: 7372
    Business software development
Jeffrey M Crowe, President

D-U-N-S 17-715-3319
EER SYSTEMS, INC.
10289 Aerospace Rd, Lanham, MD 20706
Phone: (301) 577-8900
Sales: $75,000,000   *Employees:* 657
Company Type: Private   *Employees here:* 110
SIC: 7373
    Systems engineering design and integration provides space
    launch vehicles
Jai N Gupta, President

D-U-N-S 05-982-9226
EFTC CORPORATION
9351 Grant St, Fl 6, Denver, CO 80229
Phone: (303) 451-8200
Sales: $113,244,000   *Employees:* 1,120
Company Type: Public   *Employees here:* 575
SIC: 3672
    Mfg circuit board assemblies computer cables & subsystems
Jack Calderon, Chairman of the Board

D-U-N-S 19-371-5463   EXP
EL CAMINO RESOURCES INTERNATIONAL
21051 Warner Center Ln, Woodland Hills, CA 91367
Phone: (818) 226-6600
Sales: $678,186,000   *Employees:* 548
Company Type: Private   *Employees here:* 400
SIC: 7377
    Finance and operating leasing whol and ret computers &
    peripherals
David E Harmon, Chairman of the Board

D-U-N-S 03-766-1667   EXP
ELECTION SYSTEMS & SOFTWARE
11208 John Galt Blvd, Omaha, NE 68137
Phone: (402) 593-0101
Sales: $63,000,000   *Employees:* 310
Company Type: Private   *Employees here:* 70
SIC: 3577
    Computer peripheral equipment, nec
Bill Welsh, President

D-U-N-S 00-903-1485   EXP
ELECTRO SCIENTIFIC INDUSTRIES
13900 Nw Science Park Dr, Portland, OR 97229
Phone: (503) 641-4141
Sales: $229,619,000   *Employees:* 900
Company Type: Public   *Employees here:* 355
SIC: 3699
    Mfg electronics manufacturing machinery equipment
Donald R Vanluvanee, President

D-U-N-S 07-319-9531
ELECTRONIC ARTS
209 Redwood Shores Pkwy, Redwood City, CA 94065
Phone: (650) 571-7171
Sales: $908,852,000   *Employees:* 2,100
Company Type: Public   *Employees here:* 475
SIC: 7372
    Develops and markets computer video game software
John S Riccitiello, President

D-U-N-S 09-436-5772   EXP
ELECTRONIC ASSEMBLY CORP.
    (Parent: Plexus Corp)
2121 Harrison St, Neenah, WI 54956
Phone: (920) 722-2826
Sales: $437,000,000   *Employees:* 2,140
Company Type: Public Family Member   *Employees here:* 400
SIC: 3672
    Mfg electronic products
Peter Strandwitz, President

D-U-N-S 79-586-3646
ELECTRONIC DATA MANAGEMENT
1831 E Mills Ave 2500, El Paso, TX 79901
Phone: (915) 532-0097
Sales: $101,400,000   *Employees:* NA
Company Type: Private   *Employees here:* 1,800
SIC: 7374
   Data processing
Danny Vickers, President

D-U-N-S 04-666-7523
ELECTRONIC DATA SYSTEMS CORP.
5400 Legacy Dr, Plano, TX 75024
Phone: (972) 604-6000
Sales: $15,235,600,000   *Employees:* 110,000
Company Type: Public   *Employees here:* 11,118
SIC: 7374
   Data processing telecommunications & computer
      programming services
Richard Brown, Chairman of the Board

D-U-N-S 03-631-7738
ELECTRONIC MANUFACTURING SYSTEMS
120 9th Ave, Longmont, CO 80501
Phone: (303) 772-9081
Sales: $157,376,000   *Employees:* 1,600
Company Type: Private   *Employees here:* 2
SIC: 3571
   Contract manufacturing & systems integration
Mark J Stevenson, Chairman of the Board

D-U-N-S 60-232-5755   EXP
ELECTRONICS FOR IMAGING INC.
2855 Campus Dr, San Mateo, CA 94403
Phone: (650) 286-8600
Sales: $430,723,000   *Employees:* 556
Company Type: Public   *Employees here:* 409
SIC: 3577
   Mfg computer peripheral products & software
Dan Avida, President

D-U-N-S 00-834-4285   EXP
ELEXSYS INTERNATIONAL, INC.
   (Parent: Sanmina Corporation)
4405 Fortran Ct, San Jose, CA 95134
Phone: (408) 743-5400
Sales: $84,700,000   *Employees:* 1,300
Company Type: Public Family Member   *Employees here:* 300
SIC: 3672
   Mfg printed circuit boards
Jure Sola, Chairman of the Board

D-U-N-S 00-969-2351
ELGAR ELECTRONICS CORPORATION
   (Parent: Elgar Holdings Inc)
9250 Brown Deer Rd, San Diego, CA 92121
Phone: (619) 450-0085
Sales: $62,500,000   *Employees:* 433
Company Type: Private   *Employees here:* 290
SIC: 3679
   Mfg precision power supplies
Kenneth Kilpatrick, President

D-U-N-S 60-645-1565   EXP
ELTRON INTERNATIONAL INC.
41 Moreland Rd, Simi Valley, CA 93065
Phone: (805) 579-1800
Sales: $105,029,000   *Employees:* 409
Company Type: Private   *Employees here:* 104
SIC: 3577
   Mfg bar code label printers
Donald K Skinner, Chairman of the Board

D-U-N-S 09-744-7148   IMP EXP
EMC CORPORATION
171 South St, Hopkinton, MA 01748
Phone: (508) 435-1000
Sales: $2,937,860,000   *Employees:* 6,400
Company Type: Private   *Employees here:* 500
SIC: 3572
   Mfg computer storage products software
Michael C Ruettgers, President

D-U-N-S 10-168-0544
EMTEC INC.
817 E Gate Dr, Mount Laurel, NJ 08054
Phone: (609) 235-2121
Sales: $85,539,000   *Employees:* 250
Company Type: Private   *Employees here:* 100
SIC: 7373
   Full systems integrator
Thomas Dresser, Chairman

D-U-N-S 06-908-5777   EXP
ENCAD INC.
6059 Cornerstone Ct W, San Diego, CA 92121
Phone: (619) 452-0882
Sales: $110,055,000   *Employees:* 420
Company Type: Public   *Employees here:* 415
SIC: 3577
   Mfg computer printers
David A Purcell, Chairman of the Board

D-U-N-S 10-118-8514
ENTEX INFORMATION SERVICES
6 International Dr, Port Chester, NY 10573
Phone: (914) 935-3600
Sales: $2,456,632,000   *Employees:* 8,000
Company Type: Private   *Employees here:* 250
SIC: 7373
   PC systems integrator
John A McKenna Jr, President

D-U-N-S 04-742-1003
ENVOY CORPORATION
2 Lakeview Pl, Nashville, TN 37214
Phone: (615) 885-3700
Sales: $137,605,000   *Employees:* 583
Company Type: Public   *Employees here:* 205
SIC: 7374
   Data processing/preparation
Fred C Goad, Chairman of the Board

D-U-N-S 06-215-8480
EPSILON DATA MANAGEMENT INC.
   (Parent: DMDA Inc)
50 Cambridge St, Burlington, MA 01803
Phone: (781) 273-0250
Sales: $68,700,000   *Employees:* 800
Company Type: Private   *Employees here:* 600
SIC: 7373
   Marketing service develops software turnkey mini computer
      systems
Michael Iaccarino, Chief Executive Officer

D-U-N-S 15-116-0934
EPSON PORTLAND INC.
   (Parent: U S Epson Inc)
3950 Nw Aloclek Pl, Hillsboro, OR 97124
Phone: (503) 645-1118
Sales: $250,000,000   *Employees:* 1,500
Company Type: Private   *Employees here:* 1,450
SIC: 3577
   Mfg computer printers
Akio Mitsuishi, President

D-U-N-S 02-898-5245
ERICSSON HEWLETT-PACKARD
10440 N Central Expy, Dallas, TX 75231
Phone: (972) 583-0207
Sales: $81,200,000
Company Type: Private
SIC: 7372
 Prepackaged software services
Denise Harvey, Branch Manager
          Employees: NA
         Employees here: 900

D-U-N-S 78-956-7815
ESG CONSULTING INC.
3333 Bowers Ave, Ste. 200, Santa Clara, CA 95054
Phone: (408) 970-8595
Sales: $100,000,000
Company Type: Private
SIC: 7379
 High tech resources & consulting
Sal Shafi, President
          Employees: 90
         Employees here: 20

D-U-N-S 03-885-4584   EXP
ESS TECHNOLOGY INC.
48401 Fremont Blvd, Fremont, CA 94538
Phone: (510) 226-1088
Sales: $249,517,000
Company Type: Public
SIC: 3674
 Mfg semiconductors
Fred S Chan, Chairman of the Board
          Employees: 447
         Employees here: 341

D-U-N-S 61-158-0002   EXP
ETEC SYSTEMS INC.
26460 Corporate Ave, Hayward, CA 94545
Phone: (510) 783-9210
Sales: $288,327,000
Company Type: Public
SIC: 3699
 Mfg equip for the semiconductor industry
Stephen E Cooper, Chairman of the Board
          Employees: 1,119
         Employees here: 200

D-U-N-S 04-526-3035   EXP
EVANS & SUTHERLAND CMPT CORP.
600 Komas Dr, Salt Lake City, UT 84108
Phone: (801) 588-1000
Sales: $159,353,000
Company Type: Public
SIC: 3571
 Mfg interactive computing systems & application software
James R Oyler, President
          Employees: 831
         Employees here: 781

D-U-N-S 80-939-0834   EXP
EVEREX SYSTEMS, INC.
5020 Brandin Ct, Fremont, CA 94538
Phone: (510) 498-1111
Sales: $160,000,000
Company Type: Private
SIC: 3571
 Mfg personal computer peripherals
Cher Wang, Chairman of the Board
          Employees: 190
         Employees here: 180

D-U-N-S 14-428-9006   EXP
EXABYTE CORPORATION
1685 38th St, Boulder, CO 80301
Phone: (303) 442-4333
Sales: $286,505,000
Company Type: Public
SIC: 3572
 Mfg computer tape storage units
William Marriner, President
          Employees: 1,323
         Employees here: 850

D-U-N-S 05-949-5325   EXP
EXAR CORPORATION
48720 Kato Rd, Fremont, CA 94538

Phone: (510) 668-7000
Sales: $102,015,000
Company Type: Public
SIC: 3674
 Designs develops and markets analog and mixed-signal
  integrated circuits
Raimon L Conlisk, Chairman of the Board
          Employees: 347
         Employees here: 200

D-U-N-S 18-974-0558
FACTSET RESEARCH SYSTEMS, INC.
1 Greenwich Plz, Greenwich, CT 06830
Phone: (203) 863-1500
Sales: $78,911,000
Company Type: Public
SIC: 7374
 Online database services
Howard E Wille, Chairman of the Board
          Employees: 265
         Employees here: 175

D-U-N-S 00-489-5751
FAIRCHILD SEMICONDUCTOR CORP.
 (*Parent:* Fsc Semiconductor Corporation)
333 Western Ave, South Portland, ME 04106
Phone: (207) 775-8100
Sales: $789,200,000
Company Type: Private
SIC: 3674
 Mfg semiconductors & related devices
Kirk P Pond, Chairman of the Board
          Employees: 6,927
         Employees here: 1,800

D-U-N-S 08-908-2408
FANUC AMERICA CORPORATION
1800 Lakewood Blvd, Hoffman Estates, IL 60195
Phone: (847) 898-5000
Sales: $60,000,000
Company Type: Private
SIC: 7378
 Services cnc controls
Shigeaki Koyama, Chairman of the Board
          Employees: 210
         Employees here: 135

D-U-N-S 05-859-5174   EXP
FEDERAL DATA CORPORATION
 (*Parent:* Carlyle Group)
4800 Hampden Ln, Ste. 1100, Bethesda, MD 20814
Phone: (301) 986-0800
Sales: $336,306,000
Company Type: Private
SIC: 7373
 Computer integrated systems design & computer leasing
C R Hanley, Chairman of the Board
          Employees: 1,036
         Employees here: 230

D-U-N-S 61-496-9707
FICO AMERICA INC.
7755 S Research Dr, Tempe, AZ 85284
Phone: (602) 831-6600
Sales: $416,972,000
Company Type: Private
SIC: 7373
 Systems integrator & semiconductor manufacturing
  machinery service company
Gjalt Smit, President
          Employees: 30
         Employees here: 30

D-U-N-S 18-056-3058
FILEMAKER, INC.
 (*Parent:* Apple Computer Inc)
5201 Patrick Henry Dr, Santa Clara, CA 95054
Phone: (408) 987-7000
Sales: $281,703,000
Company Type: Public Family Member
SIC: 7372
 Mfg prepackaged software
Dominique P Goupil, President
          Employees: 800
         Employees here: 400

D-U-N-S 07-495-8679
FILENET CORPORATION
3565 Harbor Blvd, Costa Mesa, CA 92626
Phone: (714) 966-3400
Sales: $251,425,000   *Employees:* 1,675
Company Type: Public   *Employees here:* 650
SIC: 7372
    Computer software mfg computer automated document
        storage & retrieval systems
Lee D Roberts, President

D-U-N-S 80-014-3497   EXP
FILTRONIC COMTEK INC.
31901 Comteck Ln, Salisbury, MD 21804
Phone: (410) 546-7700
Sales: $73,159,000   *Employees:* 509
Company Type: Private   *Employees here:* 307
SIC: 3679
    Manufactures commercial uhf vhf & microwave components
        & sub systems
Thomas A Lambalot, President

D-U-N-S 08-033-8262
FINANCIAL INSTITUTIONS INC.
220 Liberty St, Warsaw, NY 14569
Phone: (716) 786-1100
Sales: $67,168,000   *Employees:* 419
Company Type: Private   *Employees here:* 48
SIC: 7374
    Data processing & state bank
Peter G Humphrey, President

D-U-N-S 12-094-4665   EXP
FIREARMS TRAINING SYSTEMS INC.
7340 Mcginnis Ferry Rd, Suwanee, GA 30024
Phone: (770) 813-0180
Sales: $73,547,000   *Employees:* 362
Company Type: Public   *Employees here:* 3
SIC: 3699
    Mfg computerized training and simulator systems
Emory O Berry, Chief Financial Officer

D-U-N-S 60-436-0081
FIRST DATA CORPORATION
401 Hackensack Ave, Hackensack, NJ 07601
Phone: (201) 525-4700
Sales: $5,234,500,000   *Employees:* 36,000
Company Type: Public   *Employees here:* 15
SIC: 7374
    Info processing services and communication services
James R Gudmens, President

D-U-N-S 05-897-0807
FIRST DATA RESOURCES INC.
    (*Parent:* First Data Corporation)
10825 Farnam Dr, Omaha, NE 68154
Phone: (402) 222-2000
Sales: $1,013,243,000   *Employees:* 6,000
Company Type: Public Family Member   *Employees here:* 4,000
SIC: 7374
    Data processing services credit and debit card transaction
        processing
Rich A Zehnacker, President

D-U-N-S 55-651-7258
FIRST DATA TECHNOLOGIES, INC.
    (*Parent:* First Data Corporation)
6200 S Quebec St, Ste. 170, Englewood, CO 80111
Phone: (303) 488-8000

Sales: $191,100,000   *Employees:* 3,000
Company Type: Public Family Member   *Employees here:* 3,000
SIC: 7374
    Data processing servicing agent
Charles T Fote, President

D-U-N-S 12-159-4832
FISERV INC.
255 Fiserv Dr, Brookfield, WI 53045
Phone: (414) 879-5000
Sales: $1,233,670,000   *Employees:* 12,500
Company Type: Public   *Employees here:* 65
SIC: 7374
    Data processing services & trust administration management
        services
Leslie M Muma, President

D-U-N-S 15-731-7009
FLEET SERVICES CORPORATION
    (*Parent:* Fleet Financial Group Inc)
111 Westminster St, Providence, RI 02903
Phone: (401) 278-6000
Sales: $382,600,000   *Employees:* 6,000
Company Type: Public Family Member   *Employees here:* 1
SIC: 7374
    Data processing service
Robert Drum, President

D-U-N-S 01-460-7886
FLEXTRONICS INTERNATIONAL LTD.
2090 Fortune Dr, San Jose, CA 95131
Phone: (408) 576-7000
Sales: $1,113,071,000   *Employees:* 11,300
Company Type: Private   *Employees here:* 1,000
SIC: 3672
    Contract manufacturer
Michael E Marks, Chairman of the Board

D-U-N-S 94-171-4834
FLEXTRONICS INTERNATIONAL USA
    (*Parent:* Flextronics International Ltd)
2090 Fortune Dr, San Jose, CA 95131
Phone: (408) 428-1300
Sales: $195,700,000   *Employees:* 3,000
Company Type: Private   *Employees here:* 2,500
SIC: 3672
    Advanced electronics manufacturing services
Michael Marks, Chairman of the Board

D-U-N-S 55-605-4591
FORCE 3 INC.
2147 Priest Bridge Dr, Crofton, MD 21114
Phone: (301) 261-0204
Sales: $76,198,000   *Employees:* 119
Company Type: Private   *Employees here:* 104
SIC: 3571
    Distributes computers & computer peripheral equipment
Rocky D Cintron, President

D-U-N-S 10-211-1804   EXP
FORCE COMPUTERS INC.
    (*Parent:* Solectron Corporation)
2001 Logic Dr, San Jose, CA 95124
Phone: (408) 371-5900
Sales: $60,900,000   *Employees:* 500
Company Type: Public Family Member   *Employees here:* 170
SIC: 3571
    Develops & mfg computer board computers & systems
Erika Williams, President

D-U-N-S 61-474-0785
FORE SYSTEMS, INC.
1000 Fore Dr, Warrendale, PA 15086

Phone: (724) 742-7618
Sales: $458,369,000   *Employees:* 1,592
Company Type: Public   *Employees here:* 300
SIC: 3577
   Mfg asynchronous transfer mode products
Thomas J Gill, President

D-U-N-S 00-771-0825   EXP
FORSYTHE TECHNOLOGY, INC.
7500 Frontage Rd, Skokie, IL 60077
Phone: (847) 675-8000
Sales: $280,500,000   *Employees:* 324
Company Type: Private   *Employees here:* 256
SIC: 7377
   Product distribution consulting services & technology leasing
Richard A Forsythe, President

D-U-N-S 95-672-4389
FORT LAUDERDALE NETWORK CORP.
1299 E Commercial Blvd, Fort Lauderdale, FL 33334
Phone: (954) 489-3981
Sales: $140,000,000   *Employees:* 30
Company Type: Private   *Employees here:* 30
SIC: 7375
   Internet provider
Paula Gambrill, President

D-U-N-S 62-309-4232
FORTE SOFTWARE, INC.
1800 Harrison St, Fl 15, Oakland, CA 94612
Phone: (510) 834-1501
Sales: $71,328,000   *Employees:* 431
Company Type: Public   *Employees here:* 250
SIC: 7372
   Software development
Martin Sprinzen, President

D-U-N-S 11-621-6821   EXP
FOURTH SHIFT CORPORATION
2 Meridian Crossings, Minneapolis, MN 55423
Phone: (612) 851-1500
Sales: $68,204,000   *Employees:* 450
Company Type: Public   *Employees here:* 200
SIC: 7372
   Prepackaged application software
Marion M Stuckey, Chairman of the Board

D-U-N-S 02-441-4026
FOXCONN CORPORATION
6455 Clara Rd, Ste. 300, Houston, TX 77041
Phone: (713) 937-8933
Sales: $52,192,000   *Employees:* 550
Company Type: Private   *Employees here:* 250
SIC: 7371
   Computer server integration
Jim Chang, President

D-U-N-S 08-292-1644   IMP
FUJITSU AMERICA INC.
3055 Orchard Dr, San Jose, CA 95134
Phone: (408) 432-1300
Sales: $2,000,000,000   *Employees:* 4,047
Company Type: Private   *Employees here:* 105
SIC: 3577
   Mfg computer peripherals fiber optic communication
     equipment radio transmission equipment & cellular phones
     & accessories
Motoyasu Matsuzaki, Chief Administrator

D-U-N-S 79-178-0133
FUJITSU-ICL SYSTEMS INC.
   (Parent: I C L Inc)
5429 LBJ Fwy, Dallas, TX 75240
Phone: (972) 716-8300

Sales: $308,225,000   *Employees:* 1,400
Company Type: Private   *Employees here:* 300
SIC: 7373
   Sells integrates supports information technology systems
Rod Powell, President

D-U-N-S 06-473-5566   EXP
FUJITSU MICROELECTRONICS INC.
3545 N 1st St, San Jose, CA 95134
Phone: (408) 922-9000
Sales: $500,000,000   *Employees:* 1,200
Company Type: Private   *Employees here:* 500
SIC: 3674
   Mfg semiconductors
Yuji Ezura, President

D-U-N-S 93-973-9041
FUJITSU PC CORPORATION
598 Gibraltar Dr, Milpitas, CA 95035
Phone: (408) 935-8800
Sales: $500,000,000   *Employees:* 200
Company Type: Private   *Employees here:* 175
SIC: 3571
   Mfg laptop computers
George Everhart, Chief Executive Officer

D-U-N-S 01-028-4797
G-TECH USA, INC.
6262a Katella Ave, Cypress, CA 90630
Phone: (714) 899-5688
Sales: $120,000,000   *Employees:* 100
Company Type: Private   *Employees here:* 100
SIC: 3577
   Mfg computer peripheral equipment
Ray Wang, President

D-U-N-S 87-924-8201
GALE GROUP
   (Parent: THI Holdings Corp)
27500 Drake Rd, Farmington Hills, MI 48331
Phone: (248) 669-4253
Sales: $63,900,000   *Employees:* 1,200
Company Type: Private
SIC: 7375
   Database information providers
Allen Paschal, President

D-U-N-S 15-984-7458
GALILEO INTERNATIONAL INC.
9700 W Higgins Rd, Ste. 400, Des Plaines, IL 60018
Phone: (847) 518-4000
Sales: $1,070,000,000   *Employees:* 1,909
Company Type: Public   *Employees here:* 400
SIC: 7375
   Travel reservation retrieval system
James E Barlett, Chairman of the Board

D-U-N-S 15-207-2849   EXP
GATEWAY, INC.
610 Gateway Dr, North Sioux City, SD 57049
Phone: (605) 232-2000
Sales: $6,293,680,000   *Employees:* 13,300
Company Type: Public   *Employees here:* 4,500
SIC: 3571
   Mfr and directly markets personal computers
Theodore W Waitt, Chairman of the Board

D-U-N-S 92-716-6082
GE INFORMATION SERVICES, INC.
   (Parent: General Electric Company)
401 N Washington St, Rockville, MD 20850
Phone: (301) 340-4000

Sales: $700,000,000
Company Type: Public Family Member　　　*Employees:* 2,400
SIC: 7374　　　　　　　　　　　　　　　　　*Employees here:* 2,360
　　　Network teleprocessing
Harvey Seegers, President

D-U-N-S 60-951-0490
GEAC COMPUTER SYSTEMS, INC.
　　　(Parent: DBC Holding Corp)
66 Perimeter Ctr E, Atlanta, GA 30346
Phone: (404) 239-2000
Sales: $101,000,000　　　　　　　　　　　*Employees:* 1,300
Company Type: Private　　　　　　　　　*Employees here:* 1,300
SIC: 7371
　　　Provides business applications software
Stephen Sadler, President

D-U-N-S 03-698-2734
GENAMERICA CORPORATION
　　　(Parent: General American Mutl Holdg Co)
700 Market St, Saint Louis, MO 63101
Phone: (314) 231-1700
Sales: $178,900,000　　　　　　　　　　　*Employees:* 4,250
Company Type: Private　　　　　　　　　*Employees here:* NA
SIC: 7376
　　　Computer facilities management
Richard A Liddy, Chairman of the Board

D-U-N-S 05-459-7455
GENERAL ELECTRIC CAPITAL
　　　(Parent: General Electric Capital Corp)
2000 Powell St, Ste. 200, Emeryville, CA 94608
Phone: (510) 450-4900
Sales: $300,000,000　　　　　　　　　　　*Employees:* 60
Company Type: Public Family Member　　*Employees here:* 57
SIC: 7377
　　　Computer equipment leasing
Kenneth Preble, Executive Vice-President

D-U-N-S 04-591-4165　　　　　　　　　　　　　　　EXP
GENERAL SCANNING INC.
500 Arsenal St, Watertown, MA 02472
Phone: (617) 924-1010
Sales: $181,530,000　　　　　　　　　　　*Employees:* 915
Company Type: Public　　　　　　　　　*Employees here:* 275
SIC: 3699
　　　Mfg laser system & components & thermal printers
Charles D Winston, President

D-U-N-S 11-995-8049
GENERAL SEMICONDUCTOR INC.
10 Melville Park Rd, Melville, NY 11747
Phone: (516) 847-3000
Sales: $361,891,000　　　　　　　　　　　*Employees:* 3,000
Company Type: Public　　　　　　　　　*Employees here:* 123
SIC: 3679
　　　Mfg rectifiers & transient voltage suppression components
Ronald A Ostertag, Chairman of the Board

D-U-N-S 62-228-6318　　　　　　　　　　　　　　　EXP
GENESYS TELECOM LABS
1155 Market St, Fl 11, San Francisco, CA 94103
Phone: (415) 437-1100
Sales: $84,668,000　　　　　　　　　　　*Employees:* 550
Company Type: Public　　　　　　　　　*Employees here:* 322
SIC: 7371
　　　Software development
Ori Sasson, Chief Executive Officer

D-U-N-S 10-629-0422　　　　　　　　　　　　　　　EXP
GENICOM CORPORATION
14800 Conference Center D, Chantilly, VA 20151
Phone: (703) 802-9200

Sales: $421,128,000　　　　　　　　　　　*Employees:* 1,700
Company Type: Public　　　　　　　　　*Employees here:* 97
SIC: 3577
　　　Mfg & services computer printers systems integration
Paul T Winn, President

D-U-N-S 01-726-9742
GEORGIA SOLECTRON CORPORATION
　　　(Parent: Solectron Corporation)
2651 Satellite Blvd, Duluth, GA 30096
Phone: (770) 623-7000
Sales: $108,500,000　　　　　　　　　　　*Employees:* 1,309
Company Type: Public Family Member　　*Employees here:* 800
SIC: 3578
　　　Mfg retail point-of-sale terminals & scanners
Koichi Nishimura, Chairman of the Board

D-U-N-S 94-725-2193
GEOSCIENCE CORP.
　　　(Parent: Tech-Sym Corporation)
10500 Wstffice Dr, Ste. 200, Houston, TX 77042
Phone: (713) 785-7790
Sales: $94,451,000　　　　　　　　　　　*Employees:* 589
Company Type: Public　　　　　　　　　*Employees here:* 1
SIC: 7371
　　　Develops seismic processing systems software & mfg
　　　　electronic geophysical instrumentation
Richard F Miles, President

D-U-N-S 04-771-3581
GERBER GARMENT TECHNOLOGY
　　　(Parent: Gerber Scientific Inc)
24 Industrial Park Rd W, Tolland, CT 06084
Phone: (860) 871-8082
Sales: $83,900,000　　　　　　　　　　　*Employees:* 850
Company Type: Public Family Member　　*Employees here:* 500
SIC: 7371
　　　Develops mfg computer aided design equipment computer
　　　　driven cutting machinery & robotic conveyor systems
Fredric K Rosen, President

D-U-N-S 00-115-8195　　　　　　　　　　　　　　　EXP
GERBER SCIENTIFIC INC.
83 Gerber Rd W, South Windsor, CT 06074
Phone: (860) 644-1551
Sales: $430,480,000　　　　　　　　　　　*Employees:* 2,200
Company Type: Public　　　　　　　　　*Employees here:* 200
SIC: 7373
　　　Mfg computer-aided & controlled manufacturing and
　　　　production systems
Gary K Bennett, Chief Financial Officer

D-U-N-S 02-846-4894
GETTY IMAGES INC.
2101 4th Ave, Fl 5, Seattle, WA 98121
Phone: (206) 695-3400
Sales: $76,100,000　　　　　　　　　　　*Employees:* 750
Company Type: Private　　　　　　　　　*Employees here:* 150
SIC: 7372
　　　Investment holding company
John Klein, President

D-U-N-S 94-625-7789　　　　　　　　　　　　　　　EXP
GLOBAL INTELLICOM, INC.
747 3rd Ave, Fl 17, New York, NY 10017
Phone: (212) 750-3772
Sales: $51,235,000　　　　　　　　　　　*Employees:* 204
Company Type: Public　　　　　　　　　*Employees here:* 36
SIC: 7373
　　　Develops computer information systems/hardware &
　　　　software
N N Muller, Chairman of the Board

D-U-N-S 79-832-3796
GOLDLEAF TECHNOLOGIES, INC.
   (*Parent:* Equifax Payment Services Inc)
100 W Main St, Hahira, GA 31632
Phone: (912) 794-2160
Sales: $1,366,087,000   *Employees:* 70
Company Type: Public Family Member   *Employees here:* 60
SIC: 7371
   Develops financial software
David L Peterson, President

D-U-N-S 13-019-9433
GOODTIMES HOME VIDEO CORP.
16 E 40th St, New York, NY 10016
Phone: (212) 951-3000
Sales: $62,400,000   *Employees:* 650
Company Type: Private   *Employees here:* 180
SIC: 3695
   Mfg whol & distributes video tapes
Joseph Cayre, President

D-U-N-S 95-999-1290   EXP
GORES TECHNOLOGY GROUP
10877 W Blvd 1805, Los Angeles, CA 90024
Phone: (310) 209-3010
Sales: $125,000,000   *Employees:* 30
Company Type: Private   *Employees here:* 8
SIC: 7372
   Computer software application
Alec Gores, Chairman of the Board

D-U-N-S 18-664-5461
GOVERNMENT COMPUTER SALES INC.
710 Nw Juniper St, Ste. 100, Issaquah, WA 98027
Phone: (425) 313-5000
Sales: $91,932,000   *Employees:* 100
Company Type: Private   *Employees here:* 55
SIC: 7373
   Computer value added reseller
Robert Fowler, President

D-U-N-S 04-838-2386
GOVERNMENT MICRO RESOURCES
7203 Gateway Ct, Manassas, VA 20109
Phone: (703) 330-1199
Sales: $115,085,000   *Employees:* 196
Company Type: Private   *Employees here:* 150
SIC: 3571
   Mfg computers software & peripheral equipment
Humberto A Pujals, Chief Executive Officer

D-U-N-S 03-624-4911
GREAT PLAINS SOFTWARE INC.
1701 38th St Sw, Ste. 1, Fargo, ND 58103
Phone: (701) 281-0550
Sales: $85,659,000   *Employees:* 755
Company Type: Public   *Employees here:* 260
SIC: 7372
   Whol and develop accounting software
Douglas J Burgum, Chairman of the Board

D-U-N-S 60-181-4502   EXP
GREENLEAF DISTRIBUTION INC.
4900 Patrick Henry Dr, Santa Clara, CA 95054
Phone: (408) 327-0388
Sales: $340,000,000   *Employees:* 150
Company Type: Private   *Employees here:* 120
SIC: 3571
   Mfg & distributor of personal computer hardware
James Lee, President

D-U-N-S 55-549-1489
GROUP TECHNOLOGIES CORPORATION
   (*Parent:* Sypris Solutions Inc)
10901 Malcolm Mckinley Dr, Tampa, FL 33612
Phone: (813) 972-6000
Sales: $113,356,000   *Employees:* 700
Company Type: Public   *Employees here:* 700
SIC: 3672
   Contract mfg of electronic products
Thomas Lovelock, President

D-U-N-S 07-779-8122
GRUMMAN SYSTEMS SUPPORT CORP.
   (*Parent:* Northrop Grumman Corporation)
10 Orville Dr, Bohemia, NY 11716
Phone: (516) 563-6800
Sales: $51,600,000   *Employees:* 600
Company Type: Public Family Member   *Employees here:* 100
SIC: 7373
   Computer systems integration services engineering and
      maintenance
Joseph Mulderig, President

D-U-N-S 06-470-3994
GSS ARRAY TECHNOLOGY, INC.
6835 Via Del Oro, San Jose, CA 95119
Phone: (408) 229-6100
Sales: $94,793,000   *Employees:* 500
Company Type: Private   *Employees here:* 400
SIC: 3672
   Provides electronic mfg services including printed circuit
      board assembly & chip-on-board assembly
Robert Zinn, President

D-U-N-S 80-918-5903   EXP
GT INTERACTIVE SOFTWARE CORP.
417 5th Ave, New York, NY 10016
Phone: (212) 726-6500
Sales: $530,677,000   *Employees:* 1,337
Company Type: Public   *Employees here:* 200
SIC: 7372
   Publisher & distributor of entertainment computer software
Thomas Heymann, Chairman of the Board

D-U-N-S 05-350-3983
GTE DATA SERVICES INC.
   (*Parent:* GTE Corporation)
1 E Telecom Pkwy, Tampa, FL 33637
Phone: (813) 978-4000
Sales: $753,489,000   *Employees:* 3,800
Company Type: Public Family Member *Employees here:* 2,500
SIC: 7374
   Data processing & software development
Michael Crawford, President

D-U-N-S 19-557-4835
GTE INFORMATION SERVICES INC.
   (*Parent:* GTE Corporation)
201 N Franklin St, Ste. 800, Tampa, FL 33602
Phone: (813) 273-4700
Sales: $426,300,000   *Employees:* 6,000
Company Type: Public Family Member   *Employees here:* 48
SIC: 7375
   Information retrieval & billing services
Thomas F Lysaught, President

D-U-N-S 00-176-3499
GTE INTERNETWORKING INC.
   (*Parent:* GTE Corporation)
150 Cambridgepark Dr, Cambridge, MA 02140
Phone: (617) 873-2000

Sales: $234,339,000   *Employees:* 2,000
Company Type: Public Family Member   *Employees here:* 1,100
SIC: 7373
   Systems integration services research development &
     consulting svcs applic software mfg sonar systems
Paul R Gudonis, President

D-U-N-S 05-180-2627   EXP
H N BULL INFORMATION SYSTEMS
   (Parent: Bull Data Systems Inc)
300 Concord Rd, Billerica, MA 01821
Phone: (978) 294-6000
Sales: $372,520,000   *Employees:* 1,350
Company Type: Private   *Employees here:* 350
SIC: 3571
   Mfg sales & maintenance of computers & related equipment
     systems integration/software services
Donald Zereski, President

D-U-N-S 17-591-5925
H T E INC.
1000 Business Center Dr, Lake Mary, FL 32746
Phone: (407) 904-3235
Sales: $54,500,000   *Employees:* 700
Company Type: Private   *Employees here:* 700
SIC: 7371
   Computer software development
Dennis J Howard, President

D-U-N-S 04-631-2559
HADCO CORPORATION
12a Manor Pkwy, Salem, NH 03079
Phone: (603) 898-8000
Sales: $826,359,000   *Employees:* 7,673
Company Type: Public   *Employees here:* 282
SIC: 3672
   Mfg printed circuits
Andrew E Lietz, President

D-U-N-S 06-327-4609
HADCO PHOENIX, INC.
   (Parent: Hadco Corporation)
5020 S 36th St, Phoenix, AZ 85040
Phone: (602) 268-3461
Sales: $78,100,000   *Employees:* 1,200
Company Type: Public Family Member   *Employees here:* 1,200
SIC: 3672
   Mfg surface mount multilayer circuit boards
Frederick G McNamee III, Chairman of the Board

D-U-N-S 07-047-1875   EXP
HADCO SANTA CLARA INC.
   (Parent: Hadco Corporation)
425 El Camino Real, Santa Clara, CA 95050
Phone: (408) 241-9900
Sales: $110,800,000   *Employees:* 1,700
Company Type: Public Family Member   *Employees here:* 1,600
SIC: 3672
   Mfg printed circuit boards
Chris Mastrogiacomo, Senior Vice-President

D-U-N-S 60-898-1833
HARBINGER CORPORATION
1277 Lenox Park Blvd NE, Atlanta, GA 30319
Phone: (404) 467-3000
Sales: $120,675,000   *Employees:* 1,044
Company Type: Public   *Employees here:* 190
SIC: 7372
   Application computer software development
C T Howle, Chairman of the Board

D-U-N-S 08-267-2197
HARBOR ELECTRONICS INC.
   (Parent: Berg Electronics Group Inc)
825 Old Trail Rd, Etters, PA 17319
Phone: (717) 938-7200
Sales: $57,000,000   *Employees:* 720
Company Type: Private   *Employees here:* 20
SIC: 3679
   Mfg electronic cable harness assemblies
Timothy Conlon, President

D-U-N-S 55-608-4655
HARRIS DATA SERVICES CORP.
   (Parent: Harris Corporation)
1201 E Abingdon Dr, Alexandria, VA 22314
Phone: (703) 548-9200
Sales: $51,600,000   *Employees:* 600
Company Type: Public Family Member   *Employees here:* 600
SIC: 7373
   Computer systems design
John T Hartley, President

D-U-N-S 06-513-5295   EXP
HARTE-HANKS DATA TECHNOLOGIES
   (Parent: Harte-Hanks Inc)
25 Linnell Cir, Billerica, MA 01821
Phone: (978) 663-9955
Sales: $76,954,000   *Employees:* 350
Company Type: Public Family Member   *Employees here:* 325
SIC: 7374
   Data processing service
Randall L Bean, Sr VP, Business Development

D-U-N-S 08-860-8807   EXP
HAYES MICROCOMPUTER PRODUCTS
   (Parent: Hayes Corporation)
5835 Peachtree Cors E, Norcross, GA 30092
Phone: (770) 840-9200
Sales: $75,400,000   *Employees:* 700
Company Type: Public Family Member   *Employees here:* 600
SIC: 3577
   Mfg communications peripherals
Dennis C Hayes, Chairman

D-U-N-S 07-915-8325
HBO & COMPANY
301 Perimeter Ctr N, Atlanta, GA 30346
Phone: (770) 393-6000
Sales: $1,203,204,000   *Employees:* 6,286
Company Type: Public   *Employees here:* 900
SIC: 7372
   Design and install application software for the medical
     industry and provide data processing services
Charles W Mccall, Chairman of the Board

D-U-N-S 87-300-9211   EXP
HEADWAY TECHNOLOGIES INC.
678 S Hillview Dr, Milpitas, CA 95035
Phone: (408) 934-5300
Sales: $175,000,000   *Employees:* 600
Company Type: Private   *Employees here:* 100
SIC: 3572
   Mfg magnetic recording heads
Michael Chang, President

D-U-N-S 07-526-6346
HEALTH MANAGEMENT SYSTEMS INC.
401 Park Ave S, Fl 4, New York, NY 10016
Phone: (212) 685-4545

Sales: $105,252,000   *Employees:* 837
Company Type: Public   *Employees here:* 375
SIC: 7374
    Specialized data processing & computer software developer
Paul J Kerz, Chairman of the Board

D-U-N-S 00-912-2532   EXP
HEWLETT-PACKARD COMPANY
3000 Hanover St, Palo Alto, CA 94304
Phone: (650) 857-1501
Sales: $47,061,000,000   *Employees:* 124,600
Company Type: Public   *Employees here:* 2,500
SIC: 3571
    Mfg computer equipment & systems software digital
    photography pdts computer peripheral pdts & other
    computer services
Lewis E Platt, Chairman of the Board

D-U-N-S 61-060-6832   EXP
HI-TECH MANUFACTURING, INC.
12520 Grant Dr, Thornton, CO 80241
Phone: (303) 280-9001
Sales: $59,031,000 ·   *Employees:* 500
Company Type: Private   *Employees here:* 500
SIC: 3672
    Assembles circuit boards
Edward Johnson, President

D-U-N-S 13-035-8682   EXP
HITACHI AUTOMOTIVE PRODUCTS USA
    (Parent: Hitachi America Ltd)
955 Warwick Rd, Harrodsburg, KY 40330
Phone: (606) 734-9451
Sales: $70,700,000   *Employees:* 1,140
Company Type: Private   *Employees here:* 940
SIC: 3694
    Mfg engine electrical equipment
T Hasagawa, President

D-U-N-S 11-331-4264
HITACHI SEMICONDUCTOR AMERICA
    (Parent: Hitachi America Ltd)
2000 Sierra Point Pkwy, Brisbane, CA 94005
Phone: (650) 589-8300
Sales: $205,024,000   *Employees:* 1,448
Company Type: Private   *Employees here:* 609
SIC: 3674
    Mfg semiconductors
Kosei Namiya, President

D-U-N-S 61-466-6592   EXP
HMT TECHNOLOGY CORPORATION
1055 Page Ave, Fremont, CA 94538
Phone: (510) 490-3100
Sales: $356,194,000   *Employees:* 2,248
Company Type: Public   *Employees here:* 1,348
SIC: 3572
    Mfg computer storage devices
Peter S Norris, Chief Financial Officer

D-U-N-S 17-323-4758
HNC SOFTWARE INC.
5930 Cornerstone Ct W, San Diego, CA 92121
Phone: (619) 546-8877
Sales: $113,735,000   *Employees:* 750
Company Type: Public   *Employees here:* 250
SIC: 7371
    Computer neural-network software development company
Robert L North, President

D-U-N-S 80-010-5793   EXP
HOLLAND AMERICA INV CORP.
565 5th Ave, Fl 17, New York, NY 10017

Phone: (212) 850-8500
Sales: $510,500,000   *Employees:* 5,000
Company Type: Private   *Employees here:* 25
SIC: 7372
    Provides computerized innformation mfg extruded brass &
    rolled form metal products & provides management
    services
John E Haegele, President

D-U-N-S 09-491-3647
HOOD CABLE COMPANY
6633 U S Highway 49, Hattiesburg, MS 39401
Phone: (601) 268-7202
Sales: $70,000,000   *Employees:* 1,000
Company Type: Private   *Employees here:* 160
SIC: 3694
    Mfg automotive wiring harnesses
James Hood, Chairman of the Board

D-U-N-S 08-042-0862
HOWARD SYSTEMS INTL INC.
695 Main St, Stamford, CT 06901
Phone: (203) 324-4600
Sales: $65,000,000   *Employees:* 436
Company Type: Private   *Employees here:* 30
SIC: 7371
    Computer applications programming database design systems
    design networking project management & client-server
    consultants
Howard Persky, President

D-U-N-S 15-531-7522   EXP
HUBER & SUHNER INC.
    (Parent: Huber & Suhner North Amer Corp)
19 Thompson Dr, Essex Junction, VT 05452
Phone: (802) 878-0555
Sales: $60,000,000   *Employees:* 160
Company Type: Private   *Employees here:* 140
SIC: 3679
    Mfg & whol r f and microwave components as well as sub
    systems
George Powch, President

D-U-N-S 55-622-0853
HUGHES AIRCRAFT MISSISSIPPI
    (Parent: Raytheon Company)
19859 Highway 80, Forest, MS 39074
Phone: (601) 469-3730
Sales: $65,000,000   *Employees:* 280
Company Type: Public Family Member   *Employees here:* 280
SIC: 3699
    Assembly & testing of electronic equipment & sheet metal
    processing & assembly
William Meyer, President

D-U-N-S 78-808-3368
HUNTINGTON SERVICE COMPANY
    (Parent: Huntington Bancshares Inc)
2361 Morse Rd, Columbus, OH 43229
Phone: (614) 480-8300
Sales: $143,200,000   *Employees:* 2,250
Company Type: Public Family Member   *Employees here:* 2,000
SIC: 7374
    Computer processing and data preparation and processing
    services
Douglas J Spence, President

D-U-N-S 95-912-0924
HUSKO INC.
100 S Milpitas Blvd, Milpitas, CA 95035
Phone: (408) 956-7100

Sales: $219,177,000   *Employees:* 49
Company Type: Private   *Employees here:* 19
SIC: 3679
  Mfg magnetic recording heads
Wai H Ng, President

D-U-N-S 00-645-6768   EXP
HUTCHINSON TECHNOLOGY INC.
40 W Highland Park Dr NE, Hutchinson, MN 55350
Phone: (320) 587-3797
Sales: $407,616,000   *Employees:* 8,293
Company Type: Public   *Employees here:* 3,891
SIC: 3679
  Mfg disk drive electronic components
Wayne M Fortun, President

D-U-N-S 18-179-2714   EXP
HYPERCOM CORPORATION
2851 W Kathleen Rd, Phoenix, AZ 85053
Phone: (602) 504-5000
Sales: $257,227,000   *Employees:* 893
Company Type: Public   *Employees here:* 400
SIC: 3577
  Mfg data communication networking equipment
Al Irato, President

D-U-N-S 07-789-3915
HYPERION SOFTWARE CORPORATION
  (*Parent:* Hyperion Solutions Corp)
1344 Crossman Ave, Sunnyvale, CA 94089
Phone: (408) 744-9500
Sales: $193,600,000   *Employees:* 1,900
Company Type: Public Family Member   *Employees here:* 1,000
SIC: 7372
  Develops and markets business oriented computer software
John Dillon, President

D-U-N-S 78-313-6906
HYPERION SOLUTIONS CORP.
1344 Crossman Ave, Sunnyvale, CA 94089
Phone: (408) 744-9500
Sales: $353,382,000   *Employees:* 1,800
Company Type: Public   *Employees here:* 300
SIC: 7371
  Computer software development
John Dillon, President

D-U-N-S 62-232-6684
I2 TECHNOLOGIES INC.
909 Las Colinas Blvd E, Irving, TX 75039
Phone: (214) 860-6000
Sales: $361,916,000   *Employees:* 2,244
Company Type: Public   *Employees here:* 550
SIC: 7372
  Develops & markets supply chain management software
Sanjiv S Sidhu, Chairman of the Board

D-U-N-S 78-727-3457
IBM WORLD TRADE EUROPE
  (*Parent:* IBM World Trade Corporation)
New Orchard Rd, Armonk, NY 10504
Phone: (914) 499-1900
Sales: $10,742,900,000   *Employees:* 99,900
Company Type: Public Family Member   *Employees here:* 400
SIC: 3577
  Mfr info handling systems equip includ data proc equip
    rentals svcs office products and related services
    telecommunications
Lucio Stanca, President

D-U-N-S 78-485-2147
IBS CONVERSIONS INC.
  (*Parent:* Interactive Business Systems)
2625 Butterfield Rd, Ste. 114W, Oak Brook, IL 60523
Phone: (630) 571-9100
Sales: $100,000,000   *Employees:* 150
Company Type: Private   *Employees here:* 75
SIC: 3577
  Mfg & service computer conversions
Daniel T Williams, President

D-U-N-S 02-066-6681
IDX SYSTEMS CORPORATION
1400 Shelburne Rd, South Burlington, VT 05403
Phone: (802) 862-1022
Sales: $251,417,000   *Employees:* 1,833
Company Type: Public   *Employees here:* 440
SIC: 7371
  Healthcare related custom computer programming
Richard E Tarrant, President

D-U-N-S 00-246-3305   EXP
IEC ELECTRONICS CORP.
105 Norton St, Newark, NY 14513
Phone: (315) 331-7742
Sales: $248,159,000   *Employees:* 1,536
Company Type: Public   *Employees here:* 1,000
SIC: 3672
  Mfg printed circuit board assemblies & electronic products &
    systems
Russell E Stingel, Chairman of the Board

D-U-N-S 93-358-8691
IMATION CORP.
1 Imation Pl, Saint Paul, MN 55128
Phone: (651) 704-4000
Sales: $2,046,500,000   *Employees:* 9,800
Company Type: Public   *Employees here:* 100
SIC: 3695
  Mfg data storage discs & cassettes & photo imaging systems
Barbara M Cederberg, President

D-U-N-S 78-373-2159
IMPACT INNOVATIONS HOLDINGS
  (*Parent:* Medaphis Corporation)
11 E Greenway Plz, Ste. 900, Houston, TX 77046
Phone: (713) 965-9000
Sales: $74,800,000   *Employees:* 1,265
Company Type: Public Family Member   *Employees here:* 300
SIC: 7379
  Computer consultants computer network educational service
    & magazine publisher
David McDowell, Chairman of the Board

D-U-N-S 55-696-7347
INCYTE PHARMACEUTICALS, INC.
3174 Porter Dr, Palo Alto, CA 94304
Phone: (650) 855-0555
Sales: $88,351,000   *Employees:* 676
Company Type: Public   *Employees here:* 550
SIC: 7375
  Genomic database products & services
Roy A Whitfield, Chief Executive Officer

D-U-N-S 00-833-4117
INDUS INTERNATIONAL INC.
60 Spear St, San Francisco, CA 94105
Phone: (415) 904-5000
Sales: $177,034,000   *Employees:* 650
Company Type: Public   *Employees here:* 300
SIC: 7372
  Software development and computer services
William Grabske, President

D-U-N-S 83-540-9921
INDUSTRI-MATEMATIK INTERNATIONAL
560 White Plains Rd, Tarrytown, NY 10591
Phone: (914) 631-2700
Sales: $59,612,000   *Employees:* 317
Company Type: Private   *Employees here:* 314
SIC: 7371
   Computer software development
Martin Leimdorfer, Chairman of the Board

D-U-N-S 14-739-0793
INDUSTRIAL COMPUTER SOURCE
   (Parent: Dynatech Corporation)
6260 Sequence Dr, San Diego, CA 92121
Phone: (619) 677-0877
Sales: $100,000,000   *Employees:* 323
Company Type: Public Family Member   *Employees here:* 309
SIC: 3571
   Mfg and wholesales computers and computer peripheral
     equipment
Steven Peltier, President

D-U-N-S 05-540-2754
INFINIUM SOFTWARE INC.
25 Communication Way, Hyannis, MA 02601
Phone: (508) 778-2000
Sales: $114,380,000   *Employees:* 658
Company Type: Public   *Employees here:* 350
SIC: 7372
   Computer software development
Robert A Pemberton, Chairman of the Board

D-U-N-S 19-342-5923   EXP
INFONET SERVICES CORPORATION
2100 E Grand Ave, El Segundo, CA 90245
Phone: (310) 335-2600
Sales: $76,200,000   *Employees:* 1,200
Company Type: Private   *Employees here:* 600
SIC: 7374
   Computer & communication services
Jose A Collazo, Chairman of the Board

D-U-N-S 07-885-1615
INFORMATION BUILDERS INC.
1250 Broadway, New York, NY 10001
Phone: (212) 736-4433
Sales: $290,000,000   *Employees:* 1,800
Company Type: Private   *Employees here:* 900
SIC: 7373
   Computer software services & licenses computer software
Gerald D Cohen, President

D-U-N-S 60-563-2298   EXP
INFORMATION MGT RESOURCES
26750 Us Highway 19 N, Clearwater, FL 33761
Phone: (727) 797-7080
Sales: $83,550,000   *Employees:* 955
Company Type: Public   *Employees here:* 45
SIC: 7379
   Computer related consulting services
Satish K Sanan, President

D-U-N-S 17-812-1273
INFORMATION TECH SOLUTIONS
   (Parent: Computer Sciences Corporation)
2 Eaton St, Ste. 908, Hampton, VA 23669
Phone: (757) 723-3544
Sales: $88,000,000   *Employees:* 1,100
Company Type: Public Family Member   *Employees here:* 500
SIC: 7373
   Systems analysis design engineering including logistics and
     engineers support services
Henry L Ellison, President

D-U-N-S 16-087-0648
INFORMIX CORPORATION
4100 Bohannon Dr, Menlo Park, CA 94025
Phone: (650) 926-6300
Sales: $662,298,000   *Employees:* 3,800
Company Type: Public   *Employees here:* 5
SIC: 7371
   Develops computer software
Robert J Finocchio Jr, Chairman of the Board

D-U-N-S 05-709-3734
INNOVEX PRECISION COMPONENTS
   (Parent: Innovex Inc)
530 11th Ave S, Hopkins, MN 55343
Phone: (612) 938-4155
Sales: $133,436,000   *Employees:* 600
Company Type: Public Family Member   *Employees here:* 2
SIC: 3679
   Mfg electronic components
Thomas W Haley, Chief Executive Officer

D-U-N-S 10-276-0501   EXP
INPRISE CORPORATION
100 Enterprise Way, Scotts Valley, CA 95066
Phone: (831) 431-1000
Sales: $174,000,000   *Employees:* 821
Company Type: Public   *Employees here:* 400
SIC: 7372
   Develops & markets business oriented computer software
Delbert W Yocam, Chairman of the Board

D-U-N-S 83-810-9213
INSPIRE INSURANCE SOLUTIONS
300 Burnett St, Fort Worth, TX 76102
Phone: (817) 332-7761
Sales: $56,569,000   *Employees:* 550
Company Type: Public   *Employees here:* 196
SIC: 7371
   Software developer & outsourcer
F G Dunham III, Chief Executive Officer

D-U-N-S 14-485-1409   EXP
INSTINET CORPORATION
   (Parent: Reuters America Holdings Inc)
875 3rd Ave, Fl 28, New York, NY 10022
Phone: (212) 310-9500
Sales: $600,000,000   *Employees:* 700
Company Type: Private   *Employees here:* 600
SIC: 7379
   Computerized securities brokerage services
Michael O Sanderson, President

D-U-N-S 60-796-0507   EXP
INSYNC SYSTEMS, INC.
1463 Centre Pointe Dr, Milpitas, CA 95035
Phone: (408) 946-3100
Sales: $86,099,000   *Employees:* 300
Company Type: Private   *Employees here:* 200
SIC: 3674
   Mfg stainless steel components & systems for gas control
     systems
Stan Leopard, Chairman of the Board

D-U-N-S 13-754-1504
INTEC SYSTEMS INC.
1140 Cypress Station Dr, Houston, TX 77090
Phone: (281) 444-5566
Sales: $116,000,000   *Employees:* 175
Company Type: Private   *Employees here:* 75
SIC: 7373
   Computer system selling services services computers
     consulting training & offers computer classes
Shirley Ding, President

D-U-N-S 08-325-1876   EXP
INTEGRATED CIRCUIT SYSTEMS
2435 Blvd Of The Generals, Norristown, PA 19403
Phone: (610) 630-5300
Sales: $160,634,000   *Employees:* 200
Company Type: Public   *Employees here:* 90
SIC: 3674
    Mfg integrated circuits
Boreen Henry I, Chairman of the Board

D-U-N-S 03-814-2600   EXP
INTEGRATED DEVICE TECHNOLOGY
2975 Stender Way, Santa Clara, CA 95054
Phone: (408) 727-6116
Sales: $587,136,000   *Employees:* 5,000
Company Type: Public   *Employees here:* 450
SIC: 3674
    Mfg integrated circuits
Leonard C Perham, President

D-U-N-S 60-820-8245   EXP
INTEGRATED SILICON SOLUTION
2231 Lawson Ln, Santa Clara, CA 95054
Phone: (408) 588-0800
Sales: $131,132,000   *Employees:* 175
Company Type: Public   *Employees here:* 150
SIC: 3674
    Mfg memory devices
Jimmy Lee, President

D-U-N-S 03-813-8392
INTEGRATED SYSTEMS INC.
201 Moffett Park Dr, Sunnyvale, CA 94089
Phone: (408) 542-1500
Sales: $120,469,000   *Employees:* 584
Company Type: Public   *Employees here:* 420
SIC: 7373
    Software services
Charles M Boesenberg, President

D-U-N-S 04-789-7855   EXP
INTEL CORPORATION
2200 Mission College Blvd, Santa Clara, CA 95054
Phone: (408) 765-8080
Sales: $26,273,000,000   *Employees:* 63,700
Company Type: Public   *Employees here:* 5,700
SIC: 3674
    Mfg semiconductor devices and microcomputer components
Craig R Barrett, President

D-U-N-S 17-309-4004   EXP
INTEL NETWORKS INCORPORATED
28 Crosby Dr, Bedford, MA 01730
Phone: (781) 270-8300
Sales: $139,576,000   *Employees:* 610
Company Type: Public   *Employees here:* 160
SIC: 3577
    Mfg computer networking products
Cary I Klafter, President

D-U-N-S 09-116-4442
INTEL PUERTO RICO INC.
    (Parent: Intel Corporation)
S Indus Park Rr 183, Las Piedras, PR 00771
Phone: (787) 733-8080
Sales: $1,500,000,000   *Employees:* 2,600
Company Type: Public Family Member   *Employees here:* 2,600
SIC: 3674
    Mfg of board products/related devices
Robert Perlman, Vice-President

D-U-N-S 04-527-8264
INTELIANT CORPORATION
    (Parent: SOS Staffing Services Inc)
5325 Wyoming Blvd NE, Albuquerque, NM 87109
Phone: (505) 821-9336
Sales: $75,000,000   *Employees:* 100
Company Type: Public Family Member   *Employees here:* 40
SIC: 7379
    Data systems consultants designers and information
       technology staffing
Curtis L Wolfe, President

D-U-N-S 80-226-5629
INTELLIGROUP INC.
499 Thornall St, Edison, NJ 08837
Phone: (732) 590-1600
Sales: $80,189,000   *Employees:* 425
Company Type: Public   *Employees here:* 40
SIC: 7371
    Computer software development & computer consulting
       service
Stephen A Carns, President

D-U-N-S 02-740-0899
INTELLISOURCE HOLDINGS INC.
1595 Spring Hill Rd, Vienna, VA 22182
Phone: (703) 873-1740
Sales: $100,000,000   *Employees:* 1,000
Company Type: Private   *Employees here:* 5
SIC: 7374
    Computer facilities network management & desktop
       outsourcing service
Michael Berta, President

D-U-N-S 96-541-7512
INTELLISOURCE INFO SYSTEMS
    (Parent: Intellisource Holdings Inc)
1595 Spring Hill Rd, Vienna, VA 22182
Phone: (703) 873-1740
Sales: $89,000,000   *Employees:* 1,000
Company Type: Private   *Employees here:* 60
SIC: 7374
    Computer facilities network management & desktop
       outsourcing services
Michael Berta, President

D-U-N-S 02-029-8246
INTER-NATIONAL RESEARCH INST
12200 Sunrise Valley Dr, Reston, VA 20191
Phone: (703) 715-9605
Sales: $53,402,000   *Employees:* 420
Company Type: Private   *Employees here:* 110
SIC: 7371
    Computer software engineering & development
Frank Engel, President

D-U-N-S 11-365-5468
INTERACTIVE BUSINESS SYSTEMS
2625 Bttrfeld Rd, Ste. 114w, Oak Brook, IL 60523
Phone: (630) 571-9100
Sales: $100,000,000   *Employees:* 1,200
Company Type: Private   *Employees here:* 350
SIC: 7379
    Data processing consulting
Daniel Williams, President

D-U-N-S 04-926-2835   EXP
INTERFACE SYSTEMS INC.
5855 Interface Dr, Ann Arbor, MI 48103
Phone: (734) 769-5900

Sales: $81,845,000   *Employees:* 170
Company Type: Public   *Employees here:* 125
SIC: 7373
  Mfg computer equipment
Robert A Nero, President

D-U-N-S 05-515-7903   EXP
INTERGRAPH CORPORATION
1 Madison Industrial Park, Huntsville, AL 35894
Phone: (256) 730-2000
Sales: $1,124,305,000   *Employees:* 7,700
Company Type: Public   *Employees here:* 4,000
SIC: 7373
  Interactive computer graphics systems software
James W Meadlock, Chairman of the Board

D-U-N-S 94-140-0228
INTERIM TECHNOLOGY INC.
  (*Parent:* Interim Services Inc)
823 Commerce Dr, Oak Brook, IL 60523
Phone: (630) 574-3030
Sales: $133,600,000   *Employees:* 1,720
Company Type: Public Family Member   *Employees here:* 80
SIC: 7371
  Computer software design implementation and development
Stuart Emanuel, President

D-U-N-S 06-125-3076   EXP
INTERLEAF INC.
62 4th Ave, Waltham, MA 02451
Phone: (781) 290-0710
Sales: $52,577,000   *Employees:* 350
Company Type: Public   *Employees here:* 100
SIC: 7372
  Document management software
Peter J Rice, Treasurer

D-U-N-S 80-186-6716   EXP
INTERMAG, INC.
4910 Raley Blvd, Sacramento, CA 95838
Phone: (916) 568-6744
Sales: $52,503,000   *Employees:* 222
Company Type: Private   *Employees here:* 222
SIC: 3695
  Mfg magnetic/optical recording media
T C Lin, President

D-U-N-S 00-490-8729   EXP
INTERMEC TECHNOLOGIES CORP.
  (*Parent:* Unova Inc)
6001 36th Ave W, Everett, WA 98203
Phone: (425) 348-2600
Sales: $387,200,000   *Employees:* 3,600
Company Type: Public Family Member   *Employees here:* 950
SIC: 3577
  Mfg computer bar code data collection products labels
    application software
Michael Ohanian, President

D-U-N-S 00-136-8083   EXP
INTERNATIONAL BUSINESS MACHINES CORP.
New Orchard Rd, Armonk, NY 10504
Phone: (914) 765-1900
Sales: $78,508,000,000   *Employees:* 269,465
Company Type: Public   *Employees here:* 850
SIC: 3571
  Mfg info processing systems software maintenance svcs mfg
    peripherals other related pdts & svcs
Louis V Gerstner Jr, Chairman of the Board

D-U-N-S 13-174-0839   EXP
INTERNATIONAL FUEL CELLS, LLC
  (*Parent:* United Technologies Corp)
195 Governors Hwy, South Windsor, CT 06074
Phone: (860) 727-2200
Sales: $60,000,000   *Employees:* 450
Company Type: Public Family Member   *Employees here:* 430
SIC: 3674
  Mfg semiconductors/related devices
R Suttmiller, President

D-U-N-S 87-806-1621
INTERNATIONAL MANUFACTURING SERVICES
2222 Qume Dr, San Jose, CA 95131
Phone: (408) 953-1000
Sales: $312,511,000   *Employees:* 3,600
Company Type: Public   *Employees here:* 150
SIC: 3674
  Mfg surface mount products & provides in-circuit and
    functional testing services
Robert G Behlman, Chairman of the Board

D-U-N-S 79-311-1006
INTERNATIONAL NETWORK SVCS
1213 Innsbruck Dr, Sunnyvale, CA 94089
Phone: (408) 542-0100
Sales: $169,678,000   *Employees:* 1,353
Company Type: Public   *Employees here:* 300
SIC: 7379
  Network services
Donald K McKinney, Chairman of the Board

D-U-N-S 04-167-4912   EXP
INTERNATIONAL RECTIFIER CORP.
233 Kansas St, El Segundo, CA 90245
Phone: (310) 322-3331
Sales: $551,891,000   *Employees:* 4,395
Company Type: Public   *Employees here:* 900
SIC: 3674
  Mfg semiconductors & related devices
Eric Lidow, Chairman of the Board

D-U-N-S 12-594-8000   EXP
INTERNATIONAL RESISTIVE CO.
736 Greenway Rd, Boone, NC 28607
Phone: (828) 264-8861
Sales: $80,000,000   *Employees:* 600
Company Type: Private   *Employees here:* 250
SIC: 3676
  Mfg electronic resistive products
Jerry August, President

D-U-N-S 07-933-8869   EXP
INTERPHASE CORPORATION
13800 Senlac Dr, Dallas, TX 75234
Phone: (214) 654-5000
Sales: $66,004,000   *Employees:* 222
Company Type: Public   *Employees here:* 135
SIC: 3577
  Mfg & design high performance networking & mass storage
    controller & stand-alone networking products for high-end
    microcomputers
Gregory B Kalush, Chief Financial Officer

D-U-N-S 02-030-6338
INTERSOLV, INC.
9420 Key West Ave, Ste. 100, Rockville, MD 20850
Phone: (301) 838-5000
Sales: $109,100,000   *Employees:* 1,073
Company Type: Public   *Employees here:* 300
SIC: 7372
  Computer software
Gary G Greenfield, President

D-U-N-S 11-329-0969
INTUIT INC.
2535 Garcia Ave, Mountain View, CA 94043
Phone: (650) 944-6000
Sales: $592,736,000   *Employees:* 2,860
Company Type: Public   *Employees here:* 70
SIC: 7372
   Develops small business and consumer software
William H Harris Jr, President

D-U-N-S 02-153-7865   EXP
IOMEGA CORPORATION
1821 Iomega Way, Roy, UT 84067
Phone: (801) 778-1000
Sales: $1,739,972,000   *Employees:* 4,816
Company Type: Public   *Employees here:* 800
SIC: 3572
   Mfg computer storage devices
Jodie Glore, President

D-U-N-S 07-898-8110   EXP
IPEC-PLANAR, INC.
   (Parent: Integrated Process Eqp Corp)
4717 E Hilton Ave, Phoenix, AZ 85034
Phone: (602) 517-7200
Sales: $125,000,000   *Employees:* 800
Company Type: Public Family Member   *Employees here:* 600
SIC: 3695
   Mfg semiconductor production control equipment
Sanjeev Chitre, Chairman of the Board

D-U-N-S 62-315-9316
IPM SERVICE CORPORATION
   (Parent: PPM America Inc)
2700 Lone Star Dr, Dallas, TX 75212
Phone: (214) 951-0010
Sales: $91,000,000   *Employees:* 1,467
Company Type: Private   *Employees here:* 92
SIC: 3694
   Manufactures & distributes automotive electrical equipment
      & parts
John Horton, Chief Executive Officer

D-U-N-S 11-524-6688   EXP
IRIS GRAPHICS INC.
   (Parent: Scitex Development Corp)
6 Crosby Dr, Bedford, MA 01730
Phone: (781) 275-8777
Sales: $75,000,000   *Employees:* 277
Company Type: Private   *Employees here:* 277
SIC: 3577
   Mfg high resolution color computer printers
Bruce Harrison, President

D-U-N-S 07-466-4715
ISAAC FAIR AND COMPANY INC.
120 N Redwood Dr, San Rafael, CA 94903
Phone: (415) 472-2211
Sales: $245,545,000   *Employees:* 1,487
Company Type: Public   *Employees here:* 355
SIC: 7372
   Decision-making computer software
Kenneth M Rapp, President

D-U-N-S 79-342-4367   EXP
ITI TECHNOLOGIES, INC.
2266 2nd St N, Saint Paul, MN 55109
Phone: (651) 777-2690

Sales: $100,999,000   *Employees:* 1,124
Company Type: Public   *Employees here:* 459
SIC: 3699
   Through subsidiary mfg wireless security systems &
      monitoring equipment
Thomas L Auth, President

D-U-N-S 80-103-9371
ITT DEFENSE & ELECTRONICS
   (Parent: ITT Industries Inc)
1650 Tysons Blvd, Mc Lean, VA 22102
Phone: (703) 790-6300
Sales: $812,900,000   *Employees:* 14,000
Company Type: Public Family Member   *Employees here:* 50
SIC: 3679
   Mfg electronic components
Louis J Giuliano, President

D-U-N-S 96-847-5962
IXL ENTERPRISES INC.
1888 Emery St Nw, Ste. 400, Atlanta, GA 30318
Phone: (404) 267-3800
Sales: $64,767,000   *Employees:* 1,300
Company Type: Private   *Employees here:* 4
SIC: 7374
   Web page design services
William C Nussey, President

D-U-N-S 00-255-4459   EXP
J M HUBER CORPORATION
333 Thornall St, Edison, NJ 08837
Phone: (732) 549-8600
Sales: $1,298,550,000   *Employees:* 5,153
Company Type: Private   *Employees here:* 140
SIC: 3699
   Electronic mfg services mines kaolin mfg inorganic chemicals
      & oriented strand board oil & gas expl & prod
Peter T Francis, Chairman of the Board

D-U-N-S 03-847-4342
J P MORGAN SERVICES INC.
   (Parent: J P Morgan & Company Inc)
500 Stanton Christiana Rd, Newark, DE 19713
Phone: (302) 634-1000
Sales: $63,400,000   *Employees:* 1,000
Company Type: Public Family Member   *Employees here:* 1,000
SIC: 7374
   Data processing services
Rich J Jhonson, President

D-U-N-S 04-181-0979   EXP
JABIL CIRCUIT INC.
10800 Roosevelt Blvd N, Saint Petersburg, FL 33716
Phone: (727) 577-9749
Sales: $1,277,374,000   *Employees:* 3,661
Company Type: Public   *Employees here:* 1,344
SIC: 3672
   Mfr circuit board assemblies and systems
William D Morean, Chairman of the Board

D-U-N-S 07-668-6112
JACOM COMPUTER SERVICES, INC.
   (Parent: Unicapital Corporation)
207 Washington St, Northvale, NJ 07647
Phone: (201) 767-4040
Sales: $90,071,000   *Employees:* 25
Company Type: Public Family Member   *Employees here:* 25
SIC: 7377
   Leases & whol computers peripheral equipment software &
      telecommunication equipment
John Alfano, President

D-U-N-S 83-469-2162
JANIS GROUP INC.
201 W Passaic St, Ste. 403, Rochelle Park, NJ 07662
Phone: (201) 712-0505
Sales: $62,000,000   *Employees:* 262
Company Type: Private   *Employees here:* 155
SIC: 7373
    Systems integration services & computer consulting service
Michael G Janis, President

D-U-N-S 60-304-9685   EXP
JATON CORP.
556 S Milpitas Blvd, Milpitas, CA 95035
Phone: (408) 942-9888
Sales: $116,000,000   *Employees:* 255
Company Type: Private   *Employees here:* 250
SIC: 3672
    Mfg vga cards memory modules mother boards modems &
     multimedia products
Vicky Hong, President

D-U-N-S 08-634-9982
J.D. EDWARDS & COMPANY
1 Technology Way, Denver, CO 80237
Phone: (303) 334-4000
Sales: $933,982,000   *Employees:* 4,950
Company Type: Public   *Employees here:* 2,400
SIC: 7372
    Financial and business application computer software
Douglas S Massingill, President

D-U-N-S 95-883-6777   EXP
J.D. EDWARDS WORLD SOLUTIONS CO.
    (Parent: JD Edwards & Company)
8055 E Tufts Ave, Ste. 1331, Denver, CO 80237
Phone: (303) 488-4000
Sales: $275,400,000   *Employees:* 2,700
Company Type: Public Family Member   *Employees here:* 2,700
SIC: 7372
    Conduct sales service & contracts for parent company
C E Mc Vaney, Chairman of the Board

D-U-N-S 94-260-3325
JDA SOFTWARE GROUP, INC.
11811 N Tatum Blvd, Phoenix, AZ 85028
Phone: (602) 404-5500
Sales: $138,463,000   *Employees:* 1,100
Company Type: Public   *Employees here:* 270
SIC: 7373
    Computer software & services
James D Armstrong, Chairman of the Board

D-U-N-S 95-739-2467
JLC HOLDING INC.
9920 Pcf Hts Blvd   500, San Diego, CA 92121
Phone: (619) 587-0087
Sales: $131,500,000   *Employees:* 1,000
Company Type: Private   *Employees here:* 7
SIC: 7377
    Prepackaged educational software/educational consulting
     services/computer hardware leasing
Stan Sanderson, President

D-U-N-S 04-265-1687   EXP
JOHNSON MATTHEY ADVANCED CIRCUITS
    (Parent: Matthey Johnson Investments)
6442 City West Pkwy, Eden Prairie, MN 55344
Phone: (612) 988-8700
Sales: $210,000,000   *Employees:* 1,710
Company Type: Private   *Employees here:* 30
SIC: 3672
    Mfg printed circuits
Malcolm Baxter, President

D-U-N-S 06-742-0703
JOSTENS LEARNING CORPORATION
    (Parent: Jlc Holding Inc)
9920 Pcf Hts Blvd 500, San Diego, CA 92121
Phone: (619) 587-0087
Sales: $100,000,000   *Employees:* 750
Company Type: Private   *Employees here:* 250
SIC: 7377
    Prepackaged educational software and computer hardware
     leasing
Terry Crane, President

D-U-N-S 14-463-4367   EXP
JOURNAL OF COMMERCE INC.
2 World Trade Ctr, New York, NY 10048
Phone: (212) 837-7000
Sales: $52,000,000   *Employees:* 450
Company Type: Private   *Employees here:* 200
SIC: 7375
    Data base information services & newspaper & magazine
     publishers
Willy Morgan, Publisher

D-U-N-S 00-301-6342   EXP
JPM COMPANY
155 N 15th St, Lewisburg, PA 17837
Phone: (570) 524-8225
Sales: $128,351,000   *Employees:* 2,800
Company Type: Public   *Employees here:* 15
SIC: 3679
    Mfg wire & cable harness assemblies
John H Mathias, Chairman of the Board

D-U-N-S 82-617-9970
JTS CORPORATION
166 Baypointe Pkwy, San Jose, CA 95134
Phone: (408) 468-1800
Sales: $145,919,000   *Employees:* 6,000
Company Type: Private   *Employees here:* 175
SIC: 3572
    Mfg disk drives
David T Mitchell, President

D-U-N-S 15-530-0924   EXP
JVC AMERICA INC.
1 JVC Rd, Tuscaloosa, AL 35405
Phone: (205) 556-7111
Sales: $175,000,000   *Employees:* 700
Company Type: Private   *Employees here:* 600
SIC: 3695
    Mfg magnetic tapes and compact disks
M Ichawaka, President

D-U-N-S 10-113-4864
K-N HOLDINGS INC.
    (Parent: Kearney-National Inc)
108 Corporate Park Dr, White Plains, NY 10604
Phone: (914) 694-6700
Sales: $58,900,000   *Employees:* 950
Company Type: Private   *Employees here:* 8
SIC: 3694
    Manufactures automotive electrical equipment & electrical
     switches
Joseph L Aurechio, President

D-U-N-S 08-013-9223   EXP
K SYSTEMS INC.
950 Tower Ln, Ste. 800, Foster City, CA 94404
Phone: (650) 349-7400

Sales: $259,191,000 Employees: 1,600
Company Type: Private Employees here: 5
SIC: 3679
  Mfg electronic components nose cones & guided missile
    engine parts
Dr Harold J Smead, Chairman of the Board

D-U-N-S 00-513-7810
KANBAY LLC
6400 Schafer Ct, Ste. 100, Des Plaines, IL 60018
Phone: (847) 384-6100
Sales: $426,600,000 Employees: 550
Company Type: Private Employees here: 35
SIC: 7371
  Consultants
Raymond Spencer, Chairman of the Board

D-U-N-S 19-143-6245 EXP
KAO INFO SYSTEMS COMPANY
  (*Parent:* Kao Corp Of America)
40 Grissom Rd, Plymouth, MA 02360
Phone: (508) 747-5520
Sales: $400,000,000 Employees: 1,400
Company Type: Private Employees here: 420
SIC: 3695
  Mfg floppy disks computer software duplication services &
    mfg compact discs
Peter Mc Guirk, President

D-U-N-S 00-826-7262 EXP
KAVLICO CORPORATION
14501 E Los Angeles Ave, Moorpark, CA 93021
Phone: (805) 523-2000
Sales: $75,400,000 Employees: 1,300
Company Type: Private Employees here: 1,293
SIC: 3679
  Mfg electronic components
Fred Kavli, Chairman of the Board

D-U-N-S 61-528-4569
KAWASAKI STEEL HOLDINGS (USA)
55 E 52nd St, Fl 31, New York, NY 10022
Phone: (212) 935-8710
Sales: $51,400,000 Employees: 668
Company Type: Private Employees here: 1
SIC: 3674
  Mfg semi-conductors
Akio Shimizu, President

D-U-N-S 07-170-7764
KEANE INC.
10 City Sq, Boston, MA 02129
Phone: (617) 241-9200
Sales: $654,395,000 Employees: 8,008
Company Type: Public Employees here: 200
SIC: 7373
  Computer integrated systems design
John F Keane, President

D-U-N-S 04-319-0198 IMP EXP
KEARNEY-NATIONAL INC.
  (*Parent:* The Dyson-Kissner-Moran)
108 Corporate Park Dr, White Plains, NY 10604
Phone: (914) 694-6700
Sales: $200,000,000 Employees: 1,780
Company Type: Private Employees here: 10
SIC: 3679
  Mfg sensors electronic & electrical systems
Robert R Dyson, Chairman

D-U-N-S 78-842-1808 EXP
KEMET CORPORATION
2835 Kemet Way, Simpsonville, SC 29681

Phone: (864) 963-6300
Sales: $667,721,000 Employees: 10,300
Company Type: Public Employees here: 1,529
SIC: 3675
  Mfg capacitors
D R Cash, Treasurer

D-U-N-S 15-750-2634 EXP
KEMET ELECTRONICS CORPORATION
  (*Parent:* Kemet Corporation)
2835 Kemet Way, Simpsonville, SC 29681
Phone: (864) 963-6300
Sales: $667,721,000 Employees: 11,000
Company Type: Public Family Member Employees here: 1,400
SIC: 3675
  Mfg capacitors
David E Maguire, Chairman of the Board

D-U-N-S 11-294-0978
KENAN SYSTEMS CORPORATION
1 Main St, Cambridge, MA 02142
Phone: (617) 225-2200
Sales: $83,845,000 Employees: 750
Company Type: Private Employees here: 250
SIC: 7371
  Provider of software products and services including mobile
    and wireline voice and data services broadband and internet
Dr Kenan E Sahin, President

D-U-N-S 14-425-9819
KENDA SYSTEMS INC.
1 Stiles Rd, Ste. 106, Salem, NH 03079
Phone: (603) 898-7884
Sales: $58,365,000 Employees: 96
Company Type: Private Employees here: 11
SIC: 7371
  Computer programming services
Stephen K Kenda, President

D-U-N-S 06-680-0475
KEY SERVICES CORPORATION
  (*Parent:* Keycorp)
127 Public Sq, Cleveland, OH 44114
Phone: (216) 689-3802
Sales: $269,600,000 Employees: 4,230
Company Type: Public Family Member Employees here: 1,300
SIC: 7374
  Computer and data processing services
Allen J Gula Jr, Chairman of the Board

D-U-N-S 04-844-0424 EXP
KEY TRONIC CORPORATION
4424 N Sullivan Rd, Spokane, WA 99216
Phone: (509) 928-8000
Sales: $170,050,000 Employees: 2,685
Company Type: Public Employees here: 280
SIC: 3575
  Mfg computer keyboards
Jack W Oehlke, President

D-U-N-S 13-152-2401 EXP
KIMBALL ELECTRONICS INC.
  (*Parent:* Kimball International Inc)
1038 E 15th St, Jasper, IN 47546
Phone: (812) 634-4200
Sales: $300,000,000 Employees: 2,390
Company Type: Public Family Member Employees here: 750
SIC: 3672
  Mfg printed circuit boards & electronic assemblies
Douglas A Habig, Chairman of the Board

D-U-N-S 19-781-9683 EXP
KINGSTON TECHNOLOGY COMPANY
17600 Newhope St, Fountain Valley, CA 92708

Phone: (714) 435-2600
Sales: $365,686,000   *Employees:* 734
Company Type: Private   *Employees here:* 634
SIC: 3577
    Mfg computer peripheral equipment
John Tu, President

D-U-N-S 10-694-6676
KIRCHMAN CORPORATION
711 E Altamonte Dr, Altamonte Springs, FL 32701
Phone: (407) 831-3001
Sales: $60,000,000   *Employees:* 470
Company Type: Private   *Employees here:* 200
SIC: 7371
    Computer software development & applications
Kenneth P Kirchman, Chairman of the Board

D-U-N-S 00-511-5902   EXP
KNOWLES ELECTRONICS
1151 Maplewood Dr, Itasca, IL 60143
Phone: (630) 250-5100
Sales: $100,000,000   *Employees:* 641
Company Type: Private   *Employees here:* 204
SIC: 3679
    Mfg acoustic transducers and solenoid switches
Reginald G Garratt, Chairman of the Board

D-U-N-S 18-341-1651
KOBE PRECISION INC.
    (Parent: Kobe Stl USA Holdings De Corp)
31031 Huntwood Ave, Hayward, CA 94544
Phone: (510) 487-3200
Sales: $125,000,000   *Employees:* 450
Company Type: Private   *Employees here:* 450
SIC: 3674
    Mfg aluminum substrate for computer disks
Masayoshi Takebayashi, President

D-U-N-S 10-277-8750   EXP
KOMAG INCORPORATED
1704 Automation Pkwy, San Jose, CA 95131
Phone: (408) 576-2000
Sales: $631,082,000   *Employees:* 4,738
Company Type: Public   *Employees here:* 240
SIC: 3695
    Mfg thin-film media for use in hard disk drives
Stephen C Johnson, President

D-U-N-S 80-991-9996
KOREA DATA SYSTEMS (USA) INC.
12300 Edison Way, Garden Grove, CA 92841
Phone: (714) 379-5599
Sales: $250,000,000   *Employees:* 45
Company Type: Private   *Employees here:* 45
SIC: 3577
    Whol computers computer peripherals and software
John Hui, President

D-U-N-S 09-427-3653   EXP
KRONOS INCORPORATED
400 5th Ave, Ste. 3, Waltham, MA 02451
Phone: (781) 890-3232
Sales: $202,469,000   *Employees:* 1,538
Company Type: Public   *Employees here:* 300
SIC: 7372
    Mfg time attendance & data collection software and systems
W P Decker, President

D-U-N-S 17-451-9678
KYOCERA AMERICA INC.
    (Parent: Kyocera International Inc)
8611 Balboa Ave, San Diego, CA 92123
Phone: (619) 576-2600

Sales: $65,400,000   *Employees:* 850
Company Type: Private   *Employees here:* 775
SIC: 3674
    Mfg integrated circuits
David Grooms, President

D-U-N-S 04-789-6097
KYOCERA INTERNATIONAL INC.
8611 Balboa Ave, San Diego, CA 92123
Phone: (619) 576-2600
Sales: $142,500,000   *Employees:* 1,850
Company Type: Private   *Employees here:* 50
SIC: 3674
    Mfg semiconductor components whol photographic equip
      mfg telecommunication equip and laser printers
Rodney Lanthorne, President

D-U-N-S 93-830-6578
L H S GROUP INC.
6 Concourse Pkwy NE, Atlanta, GA 30328
Phone: (770) 280-3100
Sales: $105,411,000   *Employees:* 900
Company Type: Public   *Employees here:* 10
SIC: 7371
    Holding company
Hartmut Lademacher, Chairman of the Board

D-U-N-S 17-772-7617
LA CIE LTD.
22985 Nw Evergreen Pkwy, Hillsboro, OR 97124
Phone: (503) 844-4500
Sales: $62,000,000   *Employees:* 120
Company Type: Private   *Employees here:* 114
SIC: 3572
    Mfg computer disk drives & computer software development
Lyman Potts, President

D-U-N-S 09-602-1027
LACERTE SOFTWARE CORPORATION
    (Parent: Intuit Inc)
13155 Noel Rd, Fl 22, Dallas, TX 75240
Phone: (972) 490-8500
Sales: $65,000,000   *Employees:* 300
Company Type: Public Family Member   *Employees here:* 300
SIC: 7371
    Computer software development
Randall C Zeller, President

D-U-N-S 80-598-1073
LAMBDA HOLDINGS INC.
515 Broadhollow Rd, Melville, NY 11747
Phone: (516) 694-4200
Sales: $87,100,000   *Employees:* 1,500
Company Type: Private   *Employees here:* 200
SIC: 3679
    Manufactures electronic power supplies
Joshua A Hauser, President

D-U-N-S 06-722-1796
LANDMARK GRAPHICS CORPORATION
    (Parent: Halliburton Delaware Inc)
15150 Memorial Dr, Houston, TX 77079
Phone: (281) 560-1000
Sales: $70,800,000   *Employees:* 910
Company Type: Public Family Member   *Employees here:* 300
SIC: 7371
    Design application computer software and integrated system
      design
Robert P Peebler, President

D-U-N-S 14-433-4745
LASON, INC.
1305 Stephenson Hwy, Troy, MI 48083

Phone: (248) 597-5800
Sales: $120,337,000   *Employees:* 1,250
Company Type: Public   *Employees here:* 300
SIC: 7374
   Computer printing and photocopying
Gary Monroe, Chairman of the Board

   D-U-N-S 10-301-7299   EXP
LATTICE SEMICONDUCTOR CORP.
5555 Ne Moore Ct, Hillsboro, OR 97124
Phone: (503) 681-0118
Sales: $245,894,000   *Employees:* 569
Company Type: Public   *Employees here:* 237
SIC: 3674
   Mfg integrated circuits & related development system
      software
Steven A Laub, Chief Operating Officer

   D-U-N-S 09-528-6985
LAWSON ASSOCIATES, INC.
1300 Godward St NE, Minneapolis, MN 55413
Phone: (612) 379-2633
Sales: $199,000,000   *Employees:* 1,400
Company Type: Private   *Employees here:* 800
SIC: 7372
   Application computer software development services
Richard Lawson, Chairman of the Board

   D-U-N-S 09-309-5867
LEARNING COMPANY INC.
1 Athenaeum St, Cambridge, MA 02142
Phone: (617) 494-1200
Sales: $392,438;000   *Employees:* 1,525
Company Type: Public   *Employees here:* 250
SIC: 7372
   Develops consumer software
Michael J Perik, Chairman of the Board

   D-U-N-S 60-206-8561
LEGATO SYSTEMS, INC.
3210 Porter Dr, Palo Alto, CA 94304
Phone: (650) 812-6000
Sales: $143,178,000   *Employees:* 457
Company Type: Public   *Employees here:* 300
SIC: 7372
   Computer software development
Louis C Cole, Chairman of the Board

   D-U-N-S 15-207-3383   EXP
LEVEL ONE COMMUNICATIONS INC.
9750 Goethe Rd, Sacramento, CA 95827
Phone: (916) 855-5000
Sales: $262,988,000   *Employees:* 410
Company Type: Public   *Employees here:* 216
SIC: 3674
   Mfg integrated circuits
Robert S Pepper, Chairman of the Board

   D-U-N-S 03-840-9868   EXP
LEVI RAY & SHOUP INC.
2401 W Monroe St, Springfield, IL 62704
Phone: (217) 793-3800
Sales: $79,212,000   *Employees:* 405
Company Type: Private   *Employees here:* 288
SIC: 7373
   Designer of computer utility software computer consulting
      develops & markets application software programs
David R Blair, Sr Consultant

   D-U-N-S 55-606-9730   EXP
LEXMARK INTERNATIONAL GROUP
740 W New Circle Rd, Lexington, KY 40511
Phone: (606) 232-2000

Sales: $3,020,600,000   *Employees:* 8,000
Company Type: Public   *Employees here:* 5,000
SIC: 3577
   Mfg computer printers typewriters & supplies
Paul J Curlander, President

   D-U-N-S 03-253-3788   EXP
LINEAR TECHNOLOGY CORPORATION
1630 McCarthy Blvd, Milpitas, CA 95035
Phone: (408) 432-1900
Sales: $484,799,000   *Employees:* 2,155
Company Type: Public   *Employees here:* 900
SIC: 3674
   Mfg linear integrated circuits
Clive B Davies, Chief Operating Officer

   D-U-N-S 04-153-0627
LOCKHEED MARTIN IMS CORP.
   (Parent: Lockheed Martin Corporation)
300 Frank W Burr Blvd, Teaneck, NJ 07666
Phone: (201) 692-2900
Sales: $204,000,000   *Employees:* 3,203
Company Type: Public Family Member   *Employees here:* 113
SIC: 7374
   Data processing & other services
John M Brophy, President

   D-U-N-S 79-967-3389
LOGICARE INC.
85a Marcus Dr, Melville, NY 11747
Phone: (516) 420-0700
Sales: $181,340,000   *Employees:* 35
Company Type: Private   *Employees here:* 35
SIC: 7373
   Systems integration wholesales computer parts hardware and
      software
Kishor Chinchwadkar, President

   D-U-N-S 09-410-8503
LOGICON EAGLE TECHNOLOGY, INC.
   (Parent: Logicon Inc)
2100 Washington Blvd, Arlington, VA 22204
Phone: (703) 486-3500
Sales: $53,700,000   *Employees:* 625
Company Type: Public Family Member   *Employees here:* 55
SIC: 7373
   Computer systems design engineering & analysis
James F Harvey, President

   D-U-N-S 05-227-2044   EXP
LOGICON INC.
   (Parent: Northrop Grumman Corporation)
2411 Dallas Cornr Park, Herndon, VA 20171
Phone: (703) 713-4000
Sales: $650,000,000   *Employees:* 5,000
Company Type: Public Family Member   *Employees here:* 55
SIC: 7373
   Information technology services
Herbert W Anderson, President

   D-U-N-S 10-922-0202
LOGICON SPACE & INFORMATION
   (Parent: Logicon Inc)
12015 Lee Jackson Memoria, Fairfax, VA 22033
Phone: (703) 691-3600
Sales: $54,500,000   *Employees:* 700
Company Type: Public Family Member   *Employees here:* 250
SIC: 7371
   Software development & systems development & integration
Donald G Hard, Vice-President

D-U-N-S 05-518-2869
LOGICON SYSCON INC.
    (Parent: Logicon Inc)
8110 Gatehouse Rd, Falls Church, VA 22042
Phone: (703) 205-3100
Sales: $124,300,000   *Employees:* 1,600
Company Type: Public Family Member   *Employees here:* 100
SIC: 7371
    Computer system development and engineering
John R, President/CEO

D-U-N-S 02-423-7877   EXP
LOGITECH INC.
6505 Kaiser Dr, Fremont, CA 94555
Phone: (510) 795-8500
Sales: $413,000,000   *Employees:* NA
Company Type: Private   *Employees here:* NA
SIC: 3577
    Mfg computer interface devices
Guerrino De Luca, President

D-U-N-S 01-185-0484
LOTUS DEVELOPMENT CORPORATION
    (Parent: International Bus Mchs Corp)
55 Cambridge Pkwy, Ste. 5, Cambridge, MA 02142
Phone: (617) 577-8500
Sales: $807,800,000   *Employees:* 7,909
Company Type: Public Family Member   *Employees here:* 875
SIC: 7372
    Design & production of application software computer
      related consulting services
Jeff Papows, President

D-U-N-S 01-244-4253   EXP
LSI LOGIC CORPORATION
1551 McCarthy Blvd, Milpitas, CA 95035
Phone: (408) 433-8000
Sales: $1,490,701,000   *Employees:* 4,443
Company Type: Public   *Employees here:* 2,400
SIC: 3674
    Mfg application-specific integrated circuits
Wilfred J Corrigan, Chairman of the Board

D-U-N-S 79-405-6713
LUCAS AUTOMATION & CTRL ENGRG
    (Parent: Kelsey-Hayes Company)
1000 Lucas Way, Hampton, VA 23666
Phone: (757) 766-1500
Sales: $119,000,000   *Employees:* 2,955
Company Type: Private   *Employees here:* 265
SIC: 3571
    Mfrs & sells microcomputer development systems graphic
      control boards display panels infrared touch screens
Robert J Davies, President

D-U-N-S 92-781-7601
LYCOS INC.
    (Parent: CMGI Inc)
400-2 Totten Pond Rd, Waltham, MA 02451
Phone: (781) 370-2700
Sales: $56,060,000   *Employees:* 600
Company Type: Public   *Employees here:* 200
SIC: 7375
    Internet site
Robert Davis, President

D-U-N-S 78-027-4155
LYNK SYSTEMS INC.
600 Morgan Falls Rd, Atlanta, GA 30350
Phone: (770) 396-1616

Sales: $87,000,000   *Employees:* 290
Company Type: Private   *Employees here:* 250
SIC: 7374
    Computer processing & data preparation & processing
      services
Edward R Uzialko, President

D-U-N-S 78-834-0743
M C M S, INC.
    (Parent: Cornerstone Eqity Invstors Llc)
16399 Franklin Rd, Nampa, ID 83687
Phone: (208) 893-3434
Sales: $333,920,000   *Employees:* 1,800
Company Type: Private   *Employees here:* 1,100
SIC: 3672
    Mfg printed circuit boards
Robert F Subia, Chairman of the Board

D-U-N-S 62-153-2936
M R J GROUP, INC.
10560 Arrowhead Dr, Fairfax, VA 22030
Phone: (703) 385-0700
Sales: $127,000,000   *Employees:* 850
Company Type: Private   *Employees here:* 1
SIC: 7373
    Holding company
J K Driessen, President

D-U-N-S 00-508-6376   EXP
MAC LEAN-FOGG COMPANY
1026 Allanson Rd, Mundelein, IL 60060
Phone: (847) 566-0010
Sales: $230,000,000   *Employees:* 1,520
Company Type: Private   *Employees here:* 30
SIC: 3678
    Mfg & distributes connectors for wire & cable industrial
      fasteners industrial plastic and thermo plastic products
Barry L Mac Lean, President

D-U-N-S 93-203-8961
MACDERMID INC.
    (Parent: MacDermid Incorporated)
1 Norman Dr, Wilmington, DE 19808
Phone: (302) 995-3563
Sales: $80,500,000   *Employees:* 152
Company Type: Public Family Member   *Employees here:* 67
SIC: 3679
    Design
Patricia Janssen, President

D-U-N-S 80-789-5362
MACK TECHNOLOGIES, INC.
    (Parent: Mack Molding Company Inc)
27 Carlisle Rd, Westford, MA 01886
Phone: (978) 392-5500
Sales: $255,727,000   *Employees:* 180
Company Type: Private   *Employees here:* 140
SIC: 3577
    Turnkey manufacturing
Ronald A Jellison, President

D-U-N-S 00-965-3148
MACNEAL-SCHWENDLER CORPORATION
815 Colorado Blvd, Ste. 601, Los Angeles, CA 90041
Phone: (323) 258-9111
Sales: $134,850,000   *Employees:* 700
Company Type: Public   *Employees here:* 186
SIC: 7373
    Computer-aided engineering (cae) systems service
Frank Perna Jr, Chairman of the Board

D-U-N-S 17-481-3634
MACROMEDIA INC.
600 Townsend St, Ste. 310w, San Francisco, CA 94103
Phone: (415) 252-2000
Sales: $113,086,000   *Employees:* 300
Company Type: Public   *Employees here:* 175
SIC: 7372
    Computer software development
Robert K Burgess, President

D-U-N-S 05-171-1901   EXP
MAGNETIC DATA, INC.
    (Parent: Magnetic Data Technologies Llc)
6754 Shady Oak Rd, Eden Prairie, MN 55344
Phone: (612) 942-4300
Sales: $57,000,000   *Employees:* 530
Company Type: Public Family Member   *Employees here:* 300
SIC: 3572
    Remanufacturers & repairs computer storage devices
Brian Stone, President

D-U-N-S 12-084-8312   EXP
MAI SYSTEMS CORPORATION
9601 Jeronimo Rd, Irvine, CA 92618
Phone: (949) 598-6000
Sales: $70,978,000   *Employees:* 467
Company Type: Public   *Employees here:* 200
SIC: 7373
    Computer systems integration services
George G Bayz, President

D-U-N-S 05-351-8312
MANTECH INTERNATIONAL CORP.
12015 Lee Jackson Hwy, Fairfax, VA 22033
Phone: (703) 218-6000
Sales: $337,169,000   *Employees:* 4,194
Company Type: Private   *Employees here:* 121
SIC: 7373
    System engineering and other engineering services
George J Pedersen, Chairman of the Board

D-U-N-S 04-901-9052
MANU-TRONICS INC.
8701 100th St, Pleasant Prairie, WI 53158
Phone: (414) 947-7700
Sales: $70,000,000   *Employees:* 450
Company Type: Private   *Employees here:* 450
SIC: 3672
    Mfg circuit board assemblies & electronic products
Roger R Mayer, President

D-U-N-S 86-938-0840   EXP
MANUFACTURERS SERVICES LTD.
200 Baker Ave, Concord, MA 01742
Phone: (978) 287-5630
Sales: $800,000,000   *Employees:* 2,800
Company Type: Private   *Employees here:* 50
SIC: 3577
    Custom computer manufacturer
Kevin C Melia, Chief Executive Officer

D-U-N-S 60-245-6402   EXP
MANUGISTICS GROUP INC.
2115 E Jefferson St, Rockville, MD 20852
Phone: (301) 984-5000
Sales: $175,666,000   *Employees:* 1,300
Company Type: Public   *Employees here:* 500
SIC: 7371
    Develops & dist computer software pdts & programming
        services computer consulting & computer facilities
        management
William M Gibson, Chairman of the Board

D-U-N-S 06-927-8166   EXP
MANUGISTICS, INC.
    (Parent: Manugistics Group Inc)
2115 E Jefferson St, Rockville, MD 20852
Phone: (301) 984-5000
Sales: $200,000,000   *Employees:* 1,400
Company Type: Public Family Member   *Employees here:* 800
SIC: 7371
    Dev whol mainframe mini micro computer software
        computer consulting computer facilities management &
        prepackages software
William M Gibson, President

D-U-N-S 05-409-2119
MAPICS, INC.
5775-D Glenbridge Dr, Atlanta, GA 30328
Phone: (404) 705-3000
Sales: $129,741,000   *Employees:* 400
Company Type: Public   *Employees here:* 259
SIC: 7372
    Develops applications software
William J Gilmour, Chief Financial Officer

D-U-N-S 15-144-4767
MAPINFO CORPORATION
1 Global Vw, Troy, NY 12180
Phone: (518) 285-6000
Sales: $60,603,000   *Employees:* 400
Company Type: Public   *Employees here:* 300
SIC: 7372
    Develops markets licenses and supports mapping software
        products application development tools and data products
John C Cavalier, President

D-U-N-S 17-614-9334
MARCAM SOLUTIONS INC.
95 Wells Ave, Newton, MA 02459
Phone: (617) 965-0220
Sales: $124,520,000   *Employees:* 805
Company Type: Public   *Employees here:* 400
SIC: 7372
    Software development and applications
Jonathan C Crane, President

D-U-N-S 96-967-3995
MARTIN COLLIER
6711 Rolling Vista Dr, Dallas, TX 75248
Phone: (214) 987-3952
Sales: $220,000,000   *Employees:* 13
Company Type: Private   *Employees here:* 3
SIC: 7371
    Software development/whol advertising specialties
Martin Collier, Owner

D-U-N-S 11-263-0504
MARTIN JAMES & CO INC.
3050 Chain Bridge Rd, Fairfax, VA 22030
Phone: (703) 352-0900
Sales: $55,000,000   *Employees:* 300
Company Type: Private   *Employees here:* 150
SIC: 7373
    Computer systems engineers
Ben Levitan, President

D-U-N-S 18-175-9119   EXP
MASTECH CORPORATION
1004 Mckee Rd, Oakdale, PA 15071
Phone: (412) 787-2100

Sales: $195,967,000 *Employees:* 1,800
Company Type: Public *Employees here:* 500
SIC: 7371
  Custom computer programing engineering services data
    processing/preparation information retrieval services
Sunil Wadhwani, Chairman of the Board

D-U-N-S 00-277-4532
MATCO ELECTRONICS GROUP INC.
320 N Jensen Rd, Ste. 3, Vestal, NY 13850
Phone: (607) 729-8973
Sales: $400,000,000 *Employees:* 2,400
Company Type: Private *Employees here:* 25
SIC: 3672
  Umbrella corporation for subsidiaries
James F Matthews, President

D-U-N-S 60-701-7449 EXP
MATTHEY JOHNSON ELECTRONICS
  (Parent: Matthey Johnson Investments)
15128 E Euclid Ave, Spokane, WA 99216
Phone: (509) 924-2200
Sales: $130,000,000 *Employees:* 1,100
Company Type: Private *Employees here:* 1,000
SIC: 3679
  Mfg electronic components
Dr Michael Cleare, President

D-U-N-S 62-063-8312
MAXI SWITCH, INC.
2901 E Elvira Rd, Tucson, AZ 85706
Phone: (520) 294-5450
Sales: $77,691,000 *Employees:* 140
Company Type: Private *Employees here:* 140
SIC: 3575
  Mfg computer input devices
Syed Hasan, President

D-U-N-S 10-211-2489 EXP
MAXIM INTEGRATED PRODUCTS
120 San Gabriel Dr, Sunnyvale, CA 94086
Phone: (408) 737-7600
Sales: $560,220,000 *Employees:* 3,066
Company Type: Public *Employees here:* 956
SIC: 3674
  Mfg integrated circuits
John F Gifford, Chairman of the Board

D-U-N-S 17-766-7219 EXP
MAXTOR CORPORATION
510 Cottonwood Dr, Milpitas, CA 95035
Phone: (408) 432-1700
Sales: $1,424,320,000 *Employees:* 5,700
Company Type: Public *Employees here:* 800
SIC: 3572
  Mfg computer mass-storage products
Michael R Cannon, President

D-U-N-S 00-956-7942 EXP
MAXWELL TECHNOLOGIES, INC.
9275 Sky Park Ct, San Diego, CA 92123
Phone: (619) 279-5100
Sales: $125,308,000 *Employees:* 600
Company Type: Public *Employees here:* 30
SIC: 3571
  Mfg computer systems research pulsed power systems design
    power conversion equipment application software
Kenneth F Potashner, Chairman of the Board

D-U-N-S 07-313-4553
MBNA HALLMARK INFORMATION SERVICES
  (Parent: Mbna America Bank Na)
16001 Dallas Pkwy, Dallas, TX 75248

Phone: (972) 233-7101
Sales: $300,000,000 *Employees:* 2,200
Company Type: Public Family Member *Employees here:* 1,400
SIC: 7374
  Data processing services
Ronald W Davies, Chairman of the Board

D-U-N-S 93-364-4510
MCE COMPANIES, INC.
310 Depot St, Ann Arbor, MI 48104
Phone: (734) 761-8191
Sales: $81,000,000 *Employees:* 660
Company Type: Private *Employees here:* 5
SIC: 3679
  Holding company
John L Smucker, President

D-U-N-S 09-733-6259
MCHUGH SOFTWARE INTERNATIONAL
  (Parent: Alvey Systems Inc)
20700 Swenson Dr, Ste. 400, Waukesha, WI 53186
Phone: (414) 317-2000
Sales: $69,442,000 *Employees:* 418
Company Type: Private *Employees here:* 305
SIC: 7373
  Warehouse mgt systems software & related hardware
Ritch Durheim, President

D-U-N-S 05-417-4008
MCI SYSTEMHOUSE CORP.
  (Parent: MCI Communications Corporation)
1768 Bus Ctr Dr, Ste. 200, Reston, VA 20191
Phone: (703) 438-7300
Sales: $145,800,000 *Employees:* 1,700
Company Type: Public Family Member *Employees here:* 200
SIC: 7373
  Computer systems design engineering and software
    development and design total systems integrator
Scott B Ross, President

D-U-N-S 80-990-7009 EXP
MDL INFORMATION SYSTEMS, INC.
14600 Catalina St, San Leandro, CA 94577
Phone: (510) 895-1313
Sales: $61,506,000 *Employees:* 390
Company Type: Private *Employees here:* 275
SIC: 7372
  Software development
Steven D Goldby, Chairman of the Board

D-U-N-S 07-875-3092
MEDIC COMPUTER SYSTEMS INC.
8601 Six Forks Rd, Ste. 300, Raleigh, NC 27615
Phone: (919) 847-8102
Sales: $71,300,000 *Employees:* 830
Company Type: Private *Employees here:* 350
SIC: 7373
  Systems integration services
John P Mc Connell, President

D-U-N-S 06-515-2530
MEDICAL INFORMATION TECHNOLOGY
Meditech Cir, Westwood, MA 02090
Phone: (781) 821-3000
Sales: $193,805,000 *Employees:* 1,500
Company Type: Private *Employees here:* 250
SIC: 7371
  Computer software development & services
A N Pappalardo, Chairman of the Board

D-U-N-S 96-646-2111
MEDICAL MANAGER CORPORATION
3001 N Rocky Point Dr E, Tampa, FL 33607
Phone: (813) 287-2990

Sales: $78,127,000
Company Type: Public
SIC: 7372

Employees: 1,085
Employees here: 37

    Medical management software
Michael A Singer, Chairman of the Board

D-U-N-S 04-716-7556
MEDQUIST INC.
5 Greentree Ctr, Ste. 311, Marlton, NJ 08053
Phone: (609) 596-8877
Sales: $84,590,000
Company Type: Public
SIC: 7374

Employees: 857
Employees here: 42

    Electronic transcription & document management services
David A Cohen, Chairman of the Board

D-U-N-S 02-922-1710
MEDSTAT HOLDINGS INC.
    (Parent: The Thomson Corporation)
777 E Eisenhower Pkwy, Ann Arbor, MI 48108
Phone: (734) 996-1180
Sales: $81,200,000
Company Type: Private
SIC: 7372

Employees: 800
Employees here: 400

    Computer software & market research and information
      systems
Laurence J Hagerty, President

D-U-N-S 19-372-3756
MEKTEC CORP.
4211 Starboard Dr, Fremont, CA 94538
Phone: (510) 413-2400
Sales: $55,000,000
Company Type: Private
SIC: 3672

Employees: 560
Employees here: 530

    Mfg flexible printed circuits
Tsutomu Takeda, President

D-U-N-S 09-779-4390
MELITA INTERNATIONAL CORP.
5051 Peachtree Corners Ci, Norcross, GA 30092
Phone: (770) 446-7800
Sales: $65,790,000
Company Type: Public
SIC: 7371

Employees: 325
Employees here: 200

    Software development specializing in customer contact and
      call management systems
Aleksander Szlam, Chairman of the Board

D-U-N-S 36-183-4617   EXP
MEMC ELECTRONIC MATERIALS
    (Parent: Huls Corporation)
501 Pearl Dr, O'Fallon, MO 63366
Phone: (314) 279-5500
Sales: $758,916,000
Company Type: Public
SIC: 3674

Employees: 6,100
Employees here: 1,770

    Mfg silicon wafers
Klaus R Von Horde, President

D-U-N-S 92-677-5180   EXP
MEMC SOUTHWEST INC.
    (Parent: MEMC Electronic Materials)
6416 S Highway 75, Sherman, TX 75090
Phone: (903) 891-5000
Sales: $172,036,000
Company Type: Public Family Member
SIC: 3674

Employees: 1,400
Employees here: 1,400

    Manufactures chemically doped silicon wafers
Dr John Robinson, President

D-U-N-S 03-137-4879
MENTOR GRAPHICS CORPORATION
8005 Sw Boeckman Rd, Wilsonville, OR 97070
Phone: (503) 685-7000
Sales: $454,727,000
Company Type: Public
SIC: 7373

Employees: 2,570
Employees here: 1,000

    Electronic design automation (EDA) software and systems
Walden C Rhines, President

D-U-N-S 10-676-0549   EXP
MERCURY COMPUTER SYSTEMS INC.
199 Riverneck Rd, Chelmsford, MA 01824
Phone: (978) 256-1300
Sales: $85,544,000
Company Type: Public
SIC: 3571

Employees: 378
Employees here: 211

    Mfg multi-computer digital signal processing computer
      systems
James Bertelli, President

D-U-N-S 82-619-6388
MERIX CORPORATION
1521 Poplar Ln, Forest Grove, OR 97116
Phone: (503) 359-9300
Sales: $178,620,000
Company Type: Public
SIC: 3672

Employees: 1,454
Employees here: 801

    Mfg printed circuit boards
Deborah A Coleman, Chairman of the Board

D-U-N-S 01-641-0789
METAMOR INFORMATION TECH SERVICES
    (Parent: Metamor Worldwide Inc)
4400 Post Oak Pkwy, Fl 23, Houston, TX 77027
Phone: (713) 961-0888
Sales: $310,300,000
Company Type: Public Family Member
SIC: 7371

Employees: 4,000
Employees here: 500

    Computer software services & data processing services
George Fink, President

D-U-N-S 82-466-1086
METAMOR WORLDWIDE INC.
4400 Post Oak Pkwy, Houston, TX 77027
Phone: (713) 961-3633
Sales: $1,008,059,000
Company Type: Public
SIC: 7371

Employees: 33,650
Employees here: 25

    Computer programming services
Michael T Willis, Chairman of the Board

D-U-N-S 00-509-2135   EXP
METHODE ELECTRONICS INC.
7444 W Wilson Ave, Chicago, IL 60656
Phone: (708) 867-9600
Sales: $385,106,000
Company Type: Public
SIC: 3678

Employees: 3,800
Employees here: 300

    Mfg electronic components connectors & controls circuit
      boards distribution systems & test equipment
William J Mcginley, Chairman of the Board

D-U-N-S 09-741-6796
METRO INFORMATION SERVICES
200 Golden Oak Ct, Virginia Beach, VA 23452
Phone: (757) 486-1900
Sales: $165,400,000
Company Type: Public
SIC: 7371

Employees: 2,131
Employees here: 104

    Consulting software contract services
John H Fain, President

D-U-N-S 04-862-0462 EXP
METROLOGIC INSTRUMENTS INC.
Coles Road At Rt 42, Blackwood, NJ 08012
Phone: (609) 228-8100
Sales: $53,495,000 *Employees:* 465
Company Type: Public *Employees here:* 420
SIC: 3699
 Mfg bar code scanning devices
C H Knowles, Chairman of the Board

D-U-N-S 00-959-4495
METRUM-DATATAPE INC.
 (Parent: Sypris Solutions Inc)
4800 E Dry Creek Rd, Littleton, CO 80122
Phone: (303) 773-4700
Sales: $52,000,000 *Employees:* 300
Company Type: Private *Employees here:* 140
SIC: 3572
 Mfg electronic storage devices
John B Krauss, President

D-U-N-S 60-623-9481
MFP TECHNOLOGY SERVICES INC.
 (Parent: MFP Technology Services Ltd)
35 Technology Pkwy S, Norcross, GA 30092
Phone: (770) 613-5357
Sales: $200,000,000 *Employees:* 90
Company Type: Private *Employees here:* 3
SIC: 7377
 Computer rental/leasing whol computers/peripherals
  computer systems design
Peter Wolfraim, President

D-U-N-S 60-890-5451
MGV INTERNATIONAL INC.
29b Technology Dr, Ste. 100, Irvine, CA 92618
Phone: (949) 453-1965
Sales: $160,000,000 *Employees:* 35
Company Type: Private *Employees here:* 35
SIC: 3577
 Mfg computer peripherals & whol electronic computer
  peripherals
Marc V Ganouna, President

D-U-N-S 09-260-9585
MICREL, INCORPORATED
1849 Fortune Dr, San Jose, CA 95131
Phone: (408) 944-0800
Sales: $104,158,000 *Employees:* 546
Company Type: Public *Employees here:* 350
SIC: 3674
 Mfg analog integrated circuits
Raymond D Zinn, President

D-U-N-S 10-276-4784
MICRO LINEAR CORPORATION
2092 Concourse Dr, San Jose, CA 95131
Phone: (408) 433-5200
Sales: $65,759,000 *Employees:* 252
Company Type: Public *Employees here:* 235
SIC: 3674
 Mfg integrated circuits
David L Gellatly, President

D-U-N-S 60-700-0288
MICRO MODELING ASSOCIATES INC.
115 Broadway, Fl 14, New York, NY 10006
Phone: (212) 233-9890
Sales: $51,000,000 *Employees:* 280
Company Type: Private *Employees here:* 150
SIC: 7379
 Computer software consultants
Roy Wetterstrom, President

D-U-N-S 61-105-8140 EXP
MICRO VOICE APPLICATIONS INC.
5100 Gamble Dr, Ste. 400, Minneapolis, MN 55416
Phone: (612) 373-9300
Sales: $63,950,000 *Employees:* 220
Company Type: Private *Employees here:* 210
SIC: 7371
 Custom voice mail software
Wayne Miller, President

D-U-N-S 18-691-7969 EXP
MICROCHIP TECHNOLOGY INC.
2355 W Chandler Blvd, Chandler, AZ 85224
Phone: (602) 786-7200
Sales: $396,894,000 *Employees:* 2,153
Company Type: Public *Employees here:* 1,250
SIC: 3674
 Mfg semiconductors
Steve Sanghi, Chairman of the Board

D-U-N-S 10-262-6405
MICROGRAFX, INC.
1303 E Arapaho Rd, Richardson, TX 75081
Phone: (972) 234-1769
Sales: $71,792,000 *Employees:* 302
Company Type: Public *Employees here:* 180
SIC: 7372
 Develops computer graphics software
Douglas Richard, President

D-U-N-S 06-265-1997
MICRON ELECTRONICS, INC.
 (Parent: Micron Technology Inc)
900 E Karcher Rd, Nampa, ID 83687
Phone: (208) 893-3434
Sales: $1,733,432,000 *Employees:* 2,750
Company Type: Public *Employees here:* 600
SIC: 3571
 Mfg personal computer systems memory products & modules
Joel Kocher, Chairman of the Board

D-U-N-S 09-312-0871 EXP
MICRON TECHNOLOGY INC.
8000 Federal Way, Boise, ID 83716
Phone: (208) 368-4000
Sales: $3,011,900,000 *Employees:* 15,300
Company Type: Public *Employees here:* 7,000
SIC: 3571
 Mfg personal computers semiconductor random access
  memory components
Steven R Appleton, Chairman of the Board

D-U-N-S 15-082-2823 EXP
MICRONICS COMPUTERS INC.
 (Parent: Diamond Multimedia Systems)
45365 Northport Loop W, Fremont, CA 94538
Phone: (510) 651-2300
Sales: $99,276,000 *Employees:* 122
Company Type: Public Family Member *Employees here:* 100
SIC: 3672
 Mfg system boards & computer peripherals
Charles J Hart, President

D-U-N-S 09-240-2726 EXP
MICROS SYSTEMS INC.
12000 Baltimore Ave, Beltsville, MD 20705
Phone: (301) 210-6000
Sales: $280,245,000 *Employees:* 1,754
Company Type: Public *Employees here:* 600
SIC: 3578
 Mfr point-of-sale electronic information systems & software
  products
Louis M Brown Jr, Chairman of the Board

D-U-N-S 15-772-7991
MICROS-TO-MAINFRAMES, INC.
614 Corporate Way, Valley Cottage, NY 10989
Phone: (914) 268-5000
Sales: $69,601,000   *Employees:* 160
Company Type: Public   *Employees here:* 55
SIC: 7379
    Computer consultants & whol microcomputers peripheral
        equipment accessories & software
Steven H Rothman, President

D-U-N-S 05-155-0838   EXP
MICROSEMI CORPORATION
2830 S Fairview St, Santa Ana, CA 92704
Phone: (714) 979-8220
Sales: $164,710,000   *Employees:* 1,750
Company Type: Public   *Employees here:* 400
SIC: 3674
    Mfg semiconductors
Philip Frey Jr, Chairman of the Board

D-U-N-S 08-146-6849   EXP
MICROSOFT CORPORATION
1 Microsoft Way, Redmond, WA 98052
Phone: (425) 882-8080
Sales: $14,484,000,000   *Employees:* 27,320
Company Type: Public   *Employees here:* 3,800
SIC: 7372
    Mfg microcomputer software computer peripheral devices
        publishes books
William H Gates III, Chairman of the Board

D-U-N-S 60-896-3906
MICROSOFT PUERTO RICO INC.
    (Parent: Microsoft Corporation)
Km 77 Hm 8 Rr 3, Humacao, PR 00791
Phone: (787) 850-1600
Sales: $201,090,000   *Employees:* 250
Company Type: Public Family Member   *Employees here:* 250
SIC: 7372
    Prepackaged software services
Rodolfo Acevedo, General Manager

D-U-N-S 62-289-5613
MICROSTRATEGY INCORPORATED
8000 Towers Crescent Dr, Vienna, VA 22182
Phone: (703) 848-8600
Sales: $70,699,000   *Employees:* 907
Company Type: Public   *Employees here:* 450
SIC: 7372
    Prepackaged software & computer software systems analysis
        design development
Michael J Saylor, President

D-U-N-S 06-773-8997   EXP
MICROTOUCH SYSTEMS INC.
300 Griffin Park, Methuen, MA 01844
Phone: (978) 659-9000
Sales: $144,370,000   *Employees:* 682
Company Type: Public   *Employees here:* 325
SIC: 3577
    Mfg computer peripheral equipment
Geoffrey P Clear, Chief Financial Officer

D-U-N-S 88-447-5807
MICRUS
1580 Route 52, Hopewell Junction, NY 12533
Phone: (914) 894-6001
Sales: $390,000,000   *Employees:* 1,100
Company Type: Private   *Employees here:* 1,100
SIC: 3674
    Semiconductor manufacturing
Gary R Ricks, Treasurer

D-U-N-S 09-077-9422   EXP
MID-SOUTH ELECTRICS INC.
    (Parent: Mid-South Industries Inc)
Hwy 30, Annville, KY 40402
Phone: (606) 364-5142
Sales: $123,799,000   *Employees:* 800
Company Type: Private   *Employees here:* 750
SIC: 3672
    Circuit board assembly injection molding and
        electromechanical assembly
Jerry Weaver, Chairman of the Board

D-U-N-S 00-440-2301   EXP
MID-SOUTH INDUSTRIES INC.
2600 E Meighan Blvd, Gadsden, AL 35903
Phone: (256) 442-3287
Sales: $178,145,000   *Employees:* 1,400
Company Type: Private   *Employees here:* 12
SIC: 3672
    Holding company for its subsidiaries
Jerry Weaver, Chairman of the Board

D-U-N-S 17-469-1527
MIDWEST PAYMENT SYSTEMS, INC.
    (Parent: The Fifth Third Bank)
38 Fountain Square Plz, Cincinnati, OH 45202
Phone: (513) 579-5447
Sales: $167,000,000   *Employees:* 258
Company Type: Public Family Member   *Employees here:* 256
SIC: 7374
    Data processing service
George A Schafer Jr, President

D-U-N-S 36-160-1289
MILESTONE TECHNOLOGIES INC.
    (Parent: Ablest Service Corp)
1600 W Broadway Rd, Tempe, AZ 85282
Phone: (602) 894-5110
Sales: $119,516,000   *Employees:* 90
Company Type: Public Family Member   *Employees here:* 90
SIC: 7374
    Data processing consultants
Charles Heist, Chairman of the Board

D-U-N-S 03-966-4859   EXP
MINDSCAPE, INC.
    (Parent: Learning Company Inc)
88 Rowland Way, Novato, CA 94945
Phone: (415) 897-9900
Sales: $140,000,000   *Employees:* 500
Company Type: Public Family Member   *Employees here:* 250
SIC: 7372
    Develops packaged computer software
John Moore, Chief Executive Officer

D-U-N-S 84-741-2368
MINDSPRING ENTERPRISES, INC.
1430 W Peachtree St NW, Atlanta, GA 30309
Phone: (404) 815-0770
Sales: $52,557,000   *Employees:* 502
Company Type: Public   *Employees here:* 400
SIC: 7374
    Internet service provider
Charles M Brewer, Chief Executive Officer

D-U-N-S 07-764-6446
MISSISSPPI BAND CHOCTAW INDIANS
Hwy 16 W, Philadelphia, MS 39350
Phone: (601) 656-5251

Sales: $261,300,000
Employees: 4,500
Company Type: Private
Employees here: 2,000
SIC: 3679

Mfg wiring harnesses car speakers and computer component boards and leases commercial real estate

Phillip Martin, Chief

D-U-N-S 18-311-7860
MITSUBISHI ELECTRIC AUTO AMER
(Parent: Mitsubishi Electric America)
4773 Bethany Rd, Mason, OH 45040
Phone: (513) 398-2220
Sales: $430,000,000
Employees: 600
Company Type: Private
Employees here: 300
SIC: 3694

Mfg electrical automotive parts & car radios

Yasuo Iwamoto, President

D-U-N-S 04-738-8236 EXP
MITSUBISHI SILICON AMERICA
1351 Tandem Ave NE, Salem, OR 97303
Phone: (503) 371-0041
Sales: $170,000,000
Employees: 1,290
Company Type: Private
Employees here: 1,260
SIC: 3674

Mfg silicon wafers

Jim Ellick, President

D-U-N-S 79-362-0428
MKE-QUANTUM COMPONENTS, LLC
(Parent: Quantum Corporation)
1450 Infinite Dr, Louisville, CO 80027
Phone: (303) 604-4000
Sales: $64,600,000
Employees: 600
Company Type: Public Family Member
Employees here: 600
SIC: 3577

Mfg thin-film heads

Mark Jackson, President

D-U-N-S 96-152-3214
MLC HOLDINGS INC.
11150 Sunset Hills Rd, Reston, VA 20190
Phone: (703) 834-5710
Sales: $118,442,000
Employees: 186
Company Type: Public
Employees here: 44
SIC: 7377

Holding company

Phillip G Norton, Chairman of the Board

D-U-N-S 00-980-6857
MMC TECHNOLOGY
(Parent: Hyundai Electronics America)
2001 Fortune Dr, San Jose, CA 95131
Phone: (408) 232-8600
Sales: $70,500,000
Employees: 655
Company Type: Private
Employees here: 655
SIC: 3577

Mfg & whol computer equipment

Nic Pignati, President

D-U-N-S 02-468-3880 EXP
MOBIUS MANAGEMENT SYSTEMS INC.
120 Old Post Rd, Rye, NY 10580
Phone: (914) 921-7200
Sales: $56,527,000
Employees: 360
Company Type: Public
Employees here: 175
SIC: 7371

Computer software development licensing & maintenance

Mitchell Gross, President

D-U-N-S 17-852-5879
MODUS MEDIA INTERNATIONAL INC.
690 Canton St, Westwood, MA 02090

Phone: (781) 407-2000
Sales: $212,000,000
Employees: 3,600
Company Type: Private
Employees here: 40
SIC: 7379

Systems software development services

Terence M Leahy, Chairman of the Board

D-U-N-S 00-524-6673 EXP
MOLEX INCORPORATED
2222 Wellington Ct, Lisle, IL 60532
Phone: (630) 969-4550
Sales: $1,622,975,000
Employees: 13,000
Company Type: Public
Employees here: 800
SIC: 3678

Mfg electronic connectors terminals & switches cable & other

John H Krehbiel Jr, President

D-U-N-S 55-709-3556
MOLEX INTERNATIONAL INC.
(Parent: Molex Incorporated)
2222 Wellington Ct, Lisle, IL 60532
Phone: (630) 969-4550
Sales: $540,500,000
Employees: 7,671
Company Type: Public Family Member
Employees here: 98
SIC: 3678

Holding company

F A Krehbiel Sr, President

D-U-N-S 12-254-8027
MOSLER INC.
(Parent: Kelso Investment Assoc Iv Lp)
8509 Berk Blvd, Hamilton, OH 45015
Phone: (513) 870-1900
Sales: $226,800,000
Employees: 1,688
Company Type: Private
Employees here: 300
SIC: 3699

Mfr electronic security systems & apparatus & physical security products

Michel Rapoport, President

D-U-N-S 04-447-7123 EXP
MOTORCAR PARTS & ACCESSORIES
2727 Maricopa St, Torrance, CA 90503
Phone: (310) 212-7910
Sales: $112,952,000
Employees: 690
Company Type: Public
Employees here: 640
SIC: 3694

Remanufacturer & distributor replacement alternators & starters

Richard Marks, President

D-U-N-S 19-587-0118
MOTOROLA AUTOMOTIVE PRODUCTS
(Parent: Motorola Inc)
4000 Commercial Ave, Northbrook, IL 60062
Phone: (847) 480-8000
Sales: $100,000,000
Employees: 800
Company Type: Public Family Member
Employees here: 800
SIC: 3694

Mfg automotive electronics

Frederick T Tucker, Co-President

D-U-N-S 19-202-1608 EXP
MRV COMMUNICATIONS, INC.
20415 Nordhoff St, Chatsworth, CA 91311
Phone: (818) 773-9044
Sales: $165,471,000
Employees: 438
Company Type: Public
Employees here: 150
SIC: 3674

Mfr semiconductor devices

Noam Lotan, President

D-U-N-S 03-485-1535   EXP
MTI TECHNOLOGY CORPORATION
4905 E La Palma Ave, Anaheim, CA 92807
Phone: (714) 970-0300
Sales: $200,011,000
Company Type: Public   *Employees:* 562
SIC: 3572   *Employees here:* 200
  Mfg computer storage systems related products & software
Earl Pearlman, President

D-U-N-S 09-269-0833   EXP
MULTICRAFT INTERNATIONAL LTD
148 Michel Dr, Brandon, MS 39042
Phone: (601) 825-3054
Sales: $100,000,000
Company Type: Private   *Employees:* 1,742
SIC: 3694   *Employees here:* 32
  Mfg automotive electrical equipment & automotive
  stampings
Hans Post, Chief Executive Officer

D-U-N-S 09-225-9563
MULTILAYER TECHNOLOGY INC.
  (*Parent:* DII Group Inc)
16 Hammond, Irvine, CA 92618
Phone: (949) 951-3388
Sales: $94,600,000
Company Type: Public Family Member   *Employees:* 1,452
SIC: 3672   *Employees here:* 450
  Mfg multilayer printed circuit boards
Steve Schlepp, President

D-U-N-S 10-668-8070   EXP
MYLEX CORPORATION
34551 Ardenwood Blvd, Fremont, CA 94555
Phone: (510) 796-6100
Sales: $135,726,000
Company Type: Public   *Employees:* 373
SIC: 3577   *Employees here:* 155
  Mfg computer peripheral equipment
Ismael Dudhia, Chairman of the Board

D-U-N-S 00-204-3958   EXP
N A I TECHNOLOGIES, INC.
282 New York Ave, Huntington, NY 11743
Phone: (516) 271-5675
Sales: $51,864,000
Company Type: Public   *Employees:* 194
SIC: 7373   *Employees here:* 7
  Mfg rugged computer terminals & computer peripheral equip
  systems integration mfg telecommunications equip
Robert A Carlson, Chairman of the Board

D-U-N-S 05-459-1813
N B S G III
27 Maiden Ln, Ste. 300, San Francisco, CA 94108
Phone: (415) 788-8488
Sales: $100,000,000
Company Type: Private   *Employees:* 400
SIC: 7379   *Employees here:* 30
  Computer consultants
Joesph Strong, President

D-U-N-S 84-937-8039   EXP
NACOM CORPORATION
  (*Parent:* Yazaki International Corp)
375 Airport Rd, Griffin, GA 30224
Phone: (770) 467-9545
Sales: $145,466,000
Company Type: Private   *Employees:* 1,000
SIC: 3672   *Employees here:* 1,000
  Mfg electrical modules and junction boxes
Thomas Parker, President

D-U-N-S 04-385-6723
NATIONAL COMPUTER SYSTEMS
11000 Prairie Lakes Dr, Eden Prairie, MN 55344
Phone: (612) 829-3000
Sales: $406,015,000
Company Type: Public   *Employees:* 3,500
SIC: 3577   *Employees here:* 60
  Mfg optical scanning equipment computer forms application
  software optical scanning testing and systems integration
  services
Russell A Gullotti, Chairman of the Board

D-U-N-S 04-297-8528
NATIONAL DATA CORPORATION
National Data Plz, Atlanta, GA 30329
Phone: (404) 728-2000
Sales: $649,044,000
Company Type: Public   *Employees:* 6,100
SIC: 7374   *Employees here:* 500
  Data processing services
Robert A Yellowlees, Chairman of the Board

D-U-N-S 07-048-7657   EXP
NATIONAL INSTRUMENTS CORP.
6504 Bridge Point Pkwy, Austin, TX 78730
Phone: (512) 338-9119
Sales: $240,879,000
Company Type: Public   *Employees:* 1,465
SIC: 3577   *Employees here:* 762
  Mfg computer equip consisting of computer & measuring
  equip interface boards & computer-based instrumentation
  software
James J Truchard PhD, Chairman of the Board

D-U-N-S 11-595-9744
NATIONAL PROCESSING, INC.
  (*Parent:* National City Corporation)
1 Oxmore Pl, Louisville, KY 40222
Phone: (502) 326-7000
Sales: $405,661,000
Company Type: Public   *Employees:* 10,640
SIC: 7374   *Employees here:* 50
  Data processing
Jim W Cate, Chief Financial Officer

D-U-N-S 04-147-2986   EXP
NATIONAL SEMICONDUCTOR CORP.
2900 Semiconductor Dr, Santa Clara, CA 95051
Phone: (408) 721-5000
Sales: $2,536,700,000
Company Type: Public   *Employees:* 13,000
SIC: 3674   *Employees here:* 5,100
  Mfg integrated circuits
Brian Halla, Chairman of the Board

D-U-N-S 10-116-4879   EXP
NATURAL MICROSYSTEMS CORP.
100 Crossing Blvd, Framingham, MA 01702
Phone: (508) 271-1000
Sales: $75,363,000
Company Type: Public   *Employees:* 260
SIC: 3577   *Employees here:* 170
  Mfg hardware & software packages for micro computers
Robert Schechter, Chairman of the Board

D-U-N-S 62-086-4504
NCI INFORMATION SYSTEMS INC.
8260 Greensboro Dr, Mc Lean, VA 22102
Phone: (703) 903-0325

Sales: $92,500,000　　　　　　　*Employees:* 1,000
Company Type: Private　　　　*Employees here:* 150
SIC: 7371
　　Information & telecommunication systems design
　　　development integration & technical support
Charles K Narang, President

D-U-N-S 00-131-6090　　　　　　　　　　　EXP
NCR CORPORATION
1700 S Patterson Blvd, Dayton, OH 45479
Phone: (937) 445-5000
Sales: $6,505,000,000　　　　　*Employees:* 38,300
Company Type: Public　　　　*Employees here:* 3,500
SIC: 3571
　　Mfg & service information processing systems
Lars Nyberg, Chairman of the Board

D-U-N-S 09-853-0603　　　　　　　　　　　EXP
NEC ELECTRONICS INC.
　　(Parent: NEC USA Inc)
2880 Scott Blvd, Santa Clara, CA 95050
Phone: (408) 588-6000
Sales: $1,738,000,000　　　　　*Employees:* 2,800
Company Type: Private　　　　*Employees here:* 450
SIC: 3674
　　Designs mfg & distributes semiconductor components
Hirokazu Hashimoto, President

D-U-N-S 80-895-9027　　　　　　　　　　　EXP
NEOMAGIC CORPORATION
3260 Jay St, Santa Clara, CA 95054
Phone: (408) 988-7020
Sales: $124,654,000　　　　　*Employees:* 162
Company Type: Public　　　　*Employees here:* 125
SIC: 3674
　　Mfg multimedia accelerators
Prakash Agarwal, President

D-U-N-S 05-326-9049　　　　　　　　　　　EXP
NER DATA PRODUCTS INC.
　　(Parent: NER Holdings Inc)
307 Delsea Dr S, Glassboro, NJ 08028
Phone: (609) 881-5524
Sales: $65,000,000　　　　　*Employees:* 550
Company Type: Private　　　　*Employees here:* 40
SIC: 3577
　　Mfg computer printer & ink jet supplies ribbons & toners
　　　data storage systems & network furniture
Francis C Oatway, Chairman of the Board

D-U-N-S 62-339-7494
NETMANAGE, INC.
10725 N Deanza Blvd, Cupertino, CA 95014
Phone: (408) 973-7171
Sales: $61,524,000　　　　　*Employees:* 440
Company Type: Public　　　　*Employees here:* 200
SIC: 7371
　　Develops inter-networking applications & software
Zvi Alon, Chairman of the Board

D-U-N-S 84-850-0666
NETSCAPE COMMUNICATIONS CORP.
501 E Middlefield Rd, Mountain View, CA 94043
Phone: (650) 254-1900
Sales: $533,851,000　　　　　*Employees:* 2,936
Company Type: Public　　　　*Employees here:* 500
SIC: 7372
　　Develops application software for the internet
James L Barksdale, President

D-U-N-S 14-795-1230
NETSCOUT SYSTEMS INC.
4 Technology Park Dr, Westford, MA 01886

Phone: (978) 614-4000
Sales: $70,000,000　　　　　*Employees:* 200
Company Type: Private　　　　*Employees here:* 150
SIC: 7371
　　Software development and sales
Narendra Popat, President

D-U-N-S 80-205-4742　　　　　　　　　　　EXP
NETWORK APPLIANCE, INC.
2770 San Tomas Expy, Santa Clara, CA 95051
Phone: (408) 367-3000
Sales: $166,163,000　　　　　*Employees:* 450
Company Type: Public　　　　*Employees here:* 300
SIC: 7373
　　Computer integrated systems design
Daniel J Warmenhoven, President

D-U-N-S 60-620-5433
NETWORK ASSOCIATES INC.
3965 Freedom Cir, Santa Clara, CA 95054
Phone: (408) 988-3832
Sales: $612,193,000　　　　　*Employees:* 1,600
Company Type: Public　　　　*Employees here:* 600
SIC: 7371
　　Computer software development
William L Larson, Chairman of the Board

D-U-N-S 18-696-7097　　　　　　　　　　　EXP
NETWORK COMPUTING DEVICES
350 Bernardo Ave, Mountain View, CA 94043
Phone: (650) 694-0650
Sales: $133,400,000　　　　　*Employees:* 352
Company Type: Public　　　　*Employees here:* 200
SIC: 3575
　　Mfg computer terminals produce application software
Robert G Gilbertson, President

D-U-N-S 17-543-0818
NETWORK GENERAL CORPORATION
　　(Parent: Network Associates Inc)
2805 Bowers Ave, Santa Clara, CA 95051
Phone: (408) 988-3832
Sales: $240,668,000　　　　　*Employees:* 818
Company Type: Public Family Member　　*Employees here:* 375
SIC: 7373
　　Design develop and market software based analysis &
　　　monitoring tools
William L Larson, Chairman of the Board

D-U-N-S 60-251-2642
NEW RESOURCES CORPORATION
3315 Algonquin Rd, Ste. 500, Rolling Meadows, IL 60008
Phone: (847) 797-5800
Sales: $60,987,000　　　　　*Employees:* 700
Company Type: Private　　　　*Employees here:* 250
SIC: 7376
　　Management consulting
Gregg Novosad, Chief Executive Officer

D-U-N-S 78-723-5894　　　　　　　　　　　IMP
NEXTREND TECHNOLOGY, INC.
47560 Seabridge Dr, Fremont, CA 94538
Phone: (510) 659-8500
Sales: $114,994,000　　　　　*Employees:* 70
Company Type: Private　　　　*Employees here:* 70
SIC: 7373
　　Computer integrated systems design and whol computer
　　　components & peripherals
Donald Y Chang, Chairman of the Board

D-U-N-S 87-851-6160
NGK SPARK PLUG MANUFACTURING (U.S.A.)
1 Ngk Dr, Sissonville, WV 25320
Phone: (304) 988-0060

Sales: $200,000,000 *Employees:* 225
Company Type: Private *Employees here:* 200
SIC: 3694
  Mfg & whol oxygen sensors for the automotive industry
Toshio Hattori, President

D-U-N-S 14-494-3271
NOMA APPLIANCE & ELECTRONICS
11130 Rojas Dr, Ste. A, El Paso, TX 79935
Phone: (915) 591-6631
Sales: $99,300,000 *Employees:* 1,600
Company Type: Private *Employees here:* 10
SIC: 3694
  Mfg wiring harness sets
Steve Ferguson, Chairman of the Board

D-U-N-S 08-190-0615 EXP
NORTHERN COMPUTERS INC.
  (Parent: American Trading And Prod Corp)
5007 S Howell Ave, Milwaukee, WI 53207
Phone: (414) 769-5980
Sales: $65,000,000 *Employees:* 250
Company Type: Private *Employees here:* 131
SIC: 3699
  Mfg security access control equipment
Joel Konicek, President

D-U-N-S 07-177-7841
NORWEST SERVICES, INC.
  (Parent: Wells Fargo & Company)
255 2nd Ave S, Minneapolis, MN 55401
Phone: (612) 667-1234
Sales: $73,700,000 *Employees:* 1,161
Company Type: Public Family Member *Employees here:* 760
SIC: 7374
  Data processing services
C W Edwards, President

D-U-N-S 62-489-7013
NOVA INFORMATION SYSTEMS INC.
  (Parent: Nova Corporation)
1 Concourse Pkwy, Ste. 300, Atlanta, GA 30328
Phone: (770) 396-1456
Sales: $335,625,000 *Employees:* 480
Company Type: Public Family Member *Employees here:* 120
SIC: 7375
  Electronic information processing
Edward Grzedzinski, Chairman of the Board

D-U-N-S 03-778-7298
NOVELL, INC.
122 E 1700 S, Provo, UT 84606
Phone: (801) 861-7000
Sales: $1,083,887,000 *Employees:* 4,510
Company Type: Public *Employees here:* 1,108
SIC: 7373
  Designs markets and services local area network (LAN)
    software systems & other related connectivity products
Eric E Schmidt, Chairman of the Board

D-U-N-S 00-637-3377 EXP
NUGENT ROBINSON INC.
800 E 8th St, New Albany, IN 47150
Phone: (812) 945-0211
Sales: $74,146,000 *Employees:* 674
Company Type: Public *Employees here:* 90
SIC: 3678
  Mfr electronic connectors
Robert L Knabel, Chief Financial Officer

D-U-N-S 18-150-4507 EXP
OAK TECHNOLOGY INC.
139 Kifer Ct, Sunnyvale, CA 94086

Phone: (408) 737-0888
Sales: $157,106,000 *Employees:* 511
Company Type: Public *Employees here:* 300
SIC: 3674
  Mfg multimedia semiconductors & related software
Young K Sohn, President

D-U-N-S 07-483-0209
OAO CORPORATION
7500 Greenway Center Dr, Greenbelt, MD 20770
Phone: (301) 345-0750
Sales: $196,435,000 *Employees:* 1,457
Company Type: Private *Employees here:* 330
SIC: 7371
  Computer software development aerospace engineering
    services thermal systems suppliers & robotics
Cecile D Barker, Chairman of the Board

D-U-N-S 60-667-2962 EXP
OBJECTIVE SYSTEMS INTEGRATORS
100 Blue Ravine Rd, Folsom, CA 95630
Phone: (916) 353-2400
Sales: $60,575,000 *Employees:* 425
Company Type: Public *Employees here:* 220
SIC: 7371
  Software development for computer network management
    systems
Tom Johnson, Co-Chief Executive Officer

D-U-N-S 06-358-7745 EXP
OCLC ONLINE CMPT LIB CTR INC.
6565 Frantz Rd, Dublin, OH 43017
Phone: (614) 764-6000
Sales: $130,939,000 *Employees:* 950
Company Type: Private *Employees here:* 825
SIC: 7375
  Computerized library services
Robert L Jordan, President

D-U-N-S 10-399-1584 EXP
ODS NETWORKS, INC.
1101 E Arapaho Rd, Richardson, TX 75081
Phone: (972) 234-6400
Sales: $92,327,000 *Employees:* 389
Company Type: Public *Employees here:* 300
SIC: 3577
  Mfg computer networking & internetworking products &
    systems integration services
G W Paxton Jr, Chairman of the Board

D-U-N-S 00-902-4233
OECO CORPORATION
4607 Se International Way, Milwaukie, OR 97222
Phone: (503) 659-5999
Sales: $83,356,000 *Employees:* 865
Company Type: Private *Employees here:* 865
SIC: 3679
  Mfg electronic components
John F Lillicrop, President

D-U-N-S 18-176-4192
OLIN-ASAHI INTERCONNECT TECH
  (Parent: Olin Corporation)
501 Merritt 7, Norwalk, CT 06851
Phone: (203) 750-3000
Sales: $2,638,000,000 *Employees:* 220
Company Type: Public Family Member *Employees here:* 1
SIC: 3674
  Mfg microcircuits
Olin Corporation, Principal

D-U-N-S 03-067-8494
OMNI TECH CORPORATION
N27w23676 Paul Rd, Pewaukee, WI 53072

Phone: (414) 523-3300
Sales: $73,543,000 *Employees:* 200
Company Type: Private *Employees here:* 180
SIC: 3571
  Mfg electronic computers reseller of computer peripheral
    equipment & provider of technology services
Terry Anderson, President

D-U-N-S 84-865-4943
ONIX SYSTEMS INC.
  (Parent: Thermo Instrument Systems Inc)
22001 Northpark Dr, Kingwood, TX 77339
Phone: (281) 348-1112
Sales: $121,525,000 *Employees:* 845
Company Type: Public *Employees here:* 661
SIC: 7371
  Custom computer programming
William J Zolner, President

D-U-N-S 86-859-7212
OPEN MARKET INC.
1 Wayside Rd, Burlington, MA 01803
Phone: (781) 359-7572
Sales: $61,260,000 *Employees:* 347
Company Type: Public *Employees here:* 281
SIC: 7373
  Computer software products
Gary B Eichhorn, President

D-U-N-S 09-971-0451   IMP EXP
OPTEK TECHNOLOGY, INC.
1215 W Crosby Rd, Carrollton, TX 75006
Phone: (972) 323-2200
Sales: $87,229,000 *Employees:* 2,145
Company Type: Public *Employees here:* 350
SIC: 3674
  Mfg semiconductors & related devices
Thomas R Filesi, Chairman of the Board

D-U-N-S 14-470-9193   EXP
ORACLE CORPORATION
500 Oracle Pkwy, Redwood City, CA 94065
Phone: (650) 506-7000
Sales: $7,143,866,000 *Employees:* 36,802
Company Type: Public *Employees here:* 2,300
SIC: 7372
  Software systems consulting & education services
Lawrence J Ellison, Chairman of the Board

D-U-N-S 62-141-1289
ORIGIN TECHNOLOGY IN BUSINESS
1764 A Durham Rd, South Plainfield, NJ 07080
Phone: (732) 572-4900
Sales: $290,000,000 *Employees:* 1,500
Company Type: Private *Employees here:* 40
SIC: 7373
  Computer integrated system design computer processing
    computer facility management services and computer
    consulting
Jim Curham, Chief Financial Officer

D-U-N-S 17-829-5812
OSI SYSTEMS INC.
12525 Chadron Ave, Hawthorne, CA 90250
Phone: (310) 978-0516
Sales: $77,628,000 *Employees:* 725
Company Type: Public *Employees here:* 325
SIC: 3674
  Mfg photo electric cells & x-ray baggage scanners
Deepak Chopra, President

D-U-N-S 03-221-0858
OVERLAND DATA INC.
8975 Balboa Ave, San Diego, CA 92123

Phone: (619) 571-5555
Sales: $75,164,000 *Employees:* 233
Company Type: Public *Employees here:* 210
SIC: 3577
  Designs storage systems
Vernon A Loforti, Chief Financial Officer

D-U-N-S 94-858-1855
OYO CORPORATION USA
9777 W Gulf Bank Rd, Houston, TX 77040
Phone: (713) 849-0804
Sales: $113,088,000 *Employees:* 712
Company Type: Private *Employees here:* 331
SIC: 3678
  Mfg geophysical electronic equipment
Chris Nishawaki, Treasurer

D-U-N-S 09-426-7416
P S I HOLDING GROUP INC.
257 Cedar Hill St, Marlborough, MA 01752
Phone: (508) 485-2636
Sales: $57,500,000 *Employees:* 175
Company Type: Private *Employees here:* 2
SIC: 7371
  Computer maintenance & repair software training & support
Thomas D Willson, President

D-U-N-S 09-228-0015
PACIFIC CIRCUITS INC.
17550 Ne 67th Ct, Redmond, WA 98052
Phone: (425) 883-7575
Sales: $80,000,000 *Employees:* 650
Company Type: Private *Employees here:* 350
SIC: 3672
  Mfg printed circuit boards
Lewis Coley III, President

D-U-N-S 00-839-2391
PACIFIC ELECTRICORD COMPANY
  (Parent: Leviton Manufacturing Co Inc)
747 W Redondo Beach Blvd, Gardena, CA 90247
Phone: (310) 532-6600
Sales: $92,800,000 *Employees:* 1,150
Company Type: Private *Employees here:* 600
SIC: 3699
  Mfg electric cords
Edwin B Kanner, President

D-U-N-S 15-539-1121
PACKARD BELL NEC
1 Packard Bell Way, Sacramento, CA 95828
Phone: (916) 388-0101
Sales: $959,200,000 *Employees:* 8,000
Company Type: Private *Employees here:* 5,000
SIC: 3571
  Mfg personal computers and computer peripheral equipment
Alain Couder, President

D-U-N-S 80-534-5337
PACKARD-HUGHES INTERCONNECT CO
  (Parent: General Motors Corporation)
17150 Von Karman Ave, Irvine, CA 92614
Phone: (949) 660-5701
Sales: $98,700,000 *Employees:* 1,700
Company Type: Public Family Member *Employees here:* 400
SIC: 3679
  Mfg & assembles electronic components & provides
    engineering services
David Schramm, President

D-U-N-S 12-873-7350
PACKARD-HUGHES INTRCNCT WR SYS
  (Parent: Packard-Hghes Interconnect Co)
17195 Us Highway 98, Foley, AL 36535

Phone: (334) 943-1623
Sales: $75,000,000   *Employees:* 600
Company Type: Public Family Member   *Employees here:* 400
SIC: 3679
    Mfg electronic components
David J Schramm, President

D-U-N-S 96-157-1676
PANURGY CORPORATION
9881 Broken Land Pkwy, Columbia, MD 21046
Phone: (410) 309-9800
Sales: $124,500,000   *Employees:* 1,451
Company Type: Private   *Employees here:* 735
SIC: 7373
    Computer systems design
Daniel J Klein, Chairman of the Board

D-U-N-S 15-193-1508
PAR COMPUTER-LEASING
2905 Wilson Ave SW, Grandville, MI 49418
Phone: (616) 532-5555
Sales: $262,900,000   *Employees:* 2,000
Company Type: Private   *Employees here:* 2,000
SIC: 7377
    Computer leasing
Phillip Bennett, Partner

D-U-N-S 05-527-1183   EXP
PAR TECHNOLOGY CORPORATION
8383 Seneca Tpke, Ste. 2, New Hartford, NY 13413
Phone: (315) 738-0600
Sales: $100,020,000   *Employees:* 894
Company Type: Public   *Employees here:* 59
SIC: 7373
    Computer integrated systems design
Dr John W Sammon Jr, Chairman of the Board

D-U-N-S 11-279-3336
PARAGON COMPUTER PROFESSIONALS
20 Commerce Dr, Ste. 226, Cranford, NJ 07016
Phone: (908) 709-6767
Sales: $71,000,000   *Employees:* 1,000
Company Type: Private   *Employees here:* 100
SIC: 7379
    Computer consultants
Daniel O Connor, President

D-U-N-S 17-574-9431
PARAMETRIC TECHNOLOGY CORP.
128 Technology Dr, Waltham, MA 02453
Phone: (781) 398-5000
Sales: $1,017,970,000   *Employees:* 4,911
Company Type: Public   *Employees here:* 1,300
SIC: 7372
    Prepackaged software services custom software programming
Steven C Walske, Chairman of the Board

D-U-N-S 04-447-6224   EXP
PARK ELECTROCHEMICAL CORP.
5 Dakota Dr, New Hyde Park, NY 11042
Phone: (516) 354-4100
Sales: $376,158,000   *Employees:* 2,500
Company Type: Public   *Employees here:* 15
SIC: 3672
    Mfg printed circuitry materials printed circuits adhesive tape
      bonding films plastic resin coated fabrics plumbing fixtures
Brian E Shore, President

D-U-N-S 05-177-8934   EXP
PARLEX CORPORATION
145 Milk St, Methuen, MA 01844
Phone: (978) 685-4341

Sales: $60,275,000   *Employees:* 558
Company Type: Public   *Employees here:* 275
SIC: 3672
    Mfr printed circuits & related laminated cables
Herbert W Pollack, Chairman of the Board

D-U-N-S 09-557-6989   EXP
PARTECH, INC.
    (Parent: Par Technology Corporation)
8383 Seneca Tpke, Ste. 2, New Hartford, NY 13413
Phone: (315) 738-0600
Sales: $73,817,000   *Employees:* 539
Company Type: Public Family Member   *Employees here:* 305
SIC: 7373
    Mfg point-of-sale devices
Dr John W Sammon Jr, N/A

D-U-N-S 09-439-9359
PAYCHEX, INC.
911 Panorama Trl S, Rochester, NY 14625
Phone: (716) 385-6666
Sales: $993,445,000   *Employees:* 4,440
Company Type: Public   *Employees here:* 900
SIC: 7374
    Computerized payroll accounting and employee leasing
      service
B T Golisano, Chairman of the Board

D-U-N-S 07-245-8813
PCS HEALTH SYSTEMS, INC.
    (Parent: Rite Aid Corporation)
9501 E Shea Blvd, Scottsdale, AZ 85260
Phone: (602) 391-4600
Sales: $152,800,000   *Employees:* 2,400
Company Type: Public Family Member   *Employees here:* 1,800
SIC: 7374
    Data processing services
Jean-Pierr Millon, President

D-U-N-S 09-264-7197
PEACHTREE SOFTWARE INC.
    (Parent: ADP Atlantic Inc)
1505 Pavilion Pl, Ste. C, Norcross, GA 30093
Phone: (770) 724-4000
Sales: $55,000,000   *Employees:* 300
Company Type: Public Family Member   *Employees here:* 285
SIC: 7372
    Develops & markets business oriented software packages for
      microcomputers
Ron Berni, President

D-U-N-S 94-330-1507
PEGASUS CONSULTING GROUP INC.
90 Woodbridge Ctr Dr, Woodbridge, NJ 07095
Phone: (732) 726-0800
Sales: $84,687,000   *Employees:* 340
Company Type: Private   *Employees here:* 230
SIC: 7371
    Software development & consulting
Paul Parmer, President

D-U-N-S 82-637-4092
PEMSTAR INC.
3535 Technology Dr NW, Rochester, MN 55901
Phone: (507) 288-6720
Sales: $165,049,000   *Employees:* 580
Company Type: Private   *Employees here:* 300
SIC: 3571
    Precision electromechanical manufacturing
Allen Berning, Chief Executive Officer

D-U-N-S 19-467-8116
PEOPLESOFT, INC.
4460 Hacienda Dr, Pleasanton, CA 94588
Phone: (925) 225-3000
Sales: $815,651,000   *Employees:* 4,452
Company Type: Public   *Employees here:* 800
SIC: 7372
  Computer software development
David A Duffield, Chairman of the Board

D-U-N-S 09-946-0552
PEREGRINE SYSTEMS INC.
12670 High Bluff Dr, San Diego, CA 92130
Phone: (619) 481-5000
Sales: $61,877,000   *Employees:* 350
Company Type: Public   *Employees here:* 200
SIC: 7371
  Development of computer software and systems
Stephen P Gardner, Chief Executive Officer

D-U-N-S 19-169-2813
PEROT SYSTEMS CORPORATION
12377 Merit Dr, Ste: 1100, Dallas, TX 75251
Phone: (972) 383-5600
Sales: $599,438,000   *Employees:* 5,600
Company Type: Public   *Employees here:* 2,811
SIC: 7376
  Computer facilities management & computer consulting
Ross Perot, Chairman of the Board

D-U-N-S 96-777-5453   EXP
PETROLEUM INFRMTON/DWIGHTS LLC
  (Parent: Information Handling Services)
5333 Westheimer Rd, Houston, TX 77056
Phone: (713) 840-8282
Sales: $72,000,000   *Employees:* 565
Company Type: Private   *Employees here:* 180
SIC: 7375
  Provider of well production & seismic data data management
   solutions & software
R C Ivey, President

D-U-N-S 60-278-0637
PHASE METRICS, INC.
10260 Sorrento Valley Rd, San Diego, CA 92121
Phone: (619) 646-4800
Sales: $71,400,000   *Employees:* 668
Company Type: Private   *Employees here:* 204
SIC: 3572
  Mfg computer storage devices
John Schaefer, Chairman of the Board

D-U-N-S 88-340-5920
PHILIPS COMM & SEC SYSTEMS
  (Parent: Philips Electronics North Amer)
1004 New Holland Ave, Lancaster, PA 17601
Phone: (717) 295-2900
Sales: $125,000,000   *Employees:* 475
Company Type: Private   *Employees here:* 400
SIC: 3699
  Mfg electrical equipment & supplies
Jerry Gabbard, President

D-U-N-S 80-000-8286   EXP
PHILIPS SEMICONDUCTORS, INC.
  (Parent: Philips Electronics North Amer)
811 E Arques Ave, Sunnyvale, CA 94086
Phone: (408) 991-2000
Sales: $215,600,000   *Employees:* 2,800
Company Type: Private   *Employees here:* 1,500
SIC: 3674
  Designs integrated circuits
Ross Anderson, Management

D-U-N-S 10-885-8044
PHOENIX TECHNOLOGIES LTD.
411 E Plumeria Dr, San Jose, CA 95134
Phone: (408) 570-1000
Sales: $73,655,000   *Employees:* 572
Company Type: Public   *Employees here:* 300
SIC: 7371
  Software development
Jack Kay, President

D-U-N-S 15-208-7847
PHOTOCIRCUITS CORPORATION
31 Sea Cliff Ave, Glen Cove, NY 11542
Phone: (516) 674-1000
Sales: $320,665,000   *Employees:* 3,364
Company Type: Private   *Employees here:* 2,179
SIC: 3672
  Manufactures printed circuit boards
John Endee, President

D-U-N-S 18-165-2678
PHYSICIAN COMPUTER NETWORK
1200 The American Rd, Morris Plains, NJ 07950
Phone: (973) 490-3100
Sales: $95,797,000   *Employees:* 530
Company Type: Private   *Employees here:* 80
SIC: 7373
  Develops & markets practice management & clinical
   information software products
Carter Evans, President

D-U-N-S 06-570-3209
PINKERTON COMPUTER CONSULTANTS
4 Neshaminy Interplex, Langhorne, PA 19053
Phone: (215) 639-8853
Sales: $91,926,000   *Employees:* 572
Company Type: Private   *Employees here:* 8
SIC: 7379
  Computer consultants
William D Pinkerton, President

D-U-N-S 61-866-3850
PKS INFORMATION SERVICES LLC
  (Parent: Level 3 Communications Inc)
13710 Fnb Pkwy, Omaha, NE 68154
Phone: (402) 498-8250
Sales: $182,700,000   *Employees:* 3,100
Company Type: Private   *Employees here:* 550
SIC: 7379
  Computer processing services
Jimmy D Byrd, Chief Executive Officer

D-U-N-S 10-301-7166   EXP
PLANAR SYSTEMS INC.
1400 Nw Compton Dr, Beaverton, OR 97006
Phone: (503) 690-1100
Sales: $129,015,000   *Employees:* 900
Company Type: Public   *Employees here:* 250
SIC: 3575
  Mfg high performance information displays
James M Hurd, President

D-U-N-S 61-982-6159   EXP
PLATINUM SOFTWARE CORPORATION
195 Technology Dr, Irvine, CA 92618
Phone: (949) 453-4000
Sales: $98,488,000   *Employees:* 650
Company Type: Public   *Employees here:* 200
SIC: 7372
  Business oriented computer software
L G Klaus, Chairman of the Board

D-U-N-S 16-197-5909
PLATINUM TECHNOLOGY INTERNATIONAL
1815 S Meyers Rd, Ste. 1000, Villa Park, IL 60181
Phone: (630) 620-5000
Sales: $738,880,000   *Employees:* 5,000
Company Type: Public   *Employees here:* 2,000
SIC: 7372
    Develops markets and supports system software products
Andrew J Filipowski, Chairman of the Board

D-U-N-S 05-101-1443
PLATINUM TECHNOLOGY SOLUTIONS
    (Parent: Platinum Technology Intl)
9800 S La Cienega Blvd, Inglewood, CA 90301
Phone: (310) 670-6500
Sales: $93,300,000   *Employees:* 1,200
Company Type: Public Family Member   *Employees here:* 150
SIC: 7371
    Computer software development & prepackaged software
Andrew J Filipowski, Chairman of the Board

D-U-N-S 09-854-4398
PLEXUS CORP.
55 Jewelers Park Dr, Neenah, WI 54956
Phone: (920) 722-3451
Sales: $396,815,000   *Employees:* 2,345
Company Type: Public   *Employees here:* 100
SIC: 3672
    Mfg electronic products
John L Nussbaum, President

D-U-N-S 06-253-0894
POLICY MANAGEMENT SYSTEMS CORP.
1 Pmsc Ctr, Blythewood, SC 29016
Phone: (803) 735-4000
Sales: $582,782,000   *Employees:* 6,017
Company Type: Public   *Employees here:* 2,300
SIC: 7372
    Software computer systems & other
G L Wilson, Chairman of the Board

D-U-N-S 17-424-2511
POLYGRAM MANUFACTURING & DIST CENTERS
    (Parent: Polygram Holding Inc)
700 S Battleground Ave, Grover, NC 28073
Phone: (704) 734-4100
Sales: $115,000,000   *Employees:* 700
Company Type: Private   *Employees here:* 700
SIC: 3695
    Mfg optical discs
Henny Jorgensen, President

D-U-N-S 06-458-5565   EXP
POWER-ONE INC.
740 Calle Plano, Camarillo, CA 93012
Phone: (805) 987-8741
Sales: $91,583,000   *Employees:* 1,704
Company Type: Public   *Employees here:* 194
SIC: 3679
    Mfg direct current power supplies
Steven J Goldman, Chairman of the Board

D-U-N-S 14-817-9625   EXP
POWEREX INC.
200 E Hillis St, Youngwood, PA 15697
Phone: (724) 925-7272
Sales: $96,582,000   *Employees:* 330
Company Type: Private   *Employees here:* 326
SIC: 3674
    Mfg high power semi-conductors
Stanley R Hunt, President

D-U-N-S 78-110-5069
POWERHOUSE TECHNOLOGIES INC.
2311 S 7th Ave, Bozeman, MT 59715
Phone: (406) 585-6600
Sales: $196,935,000   *Employees:* 1,380
Company Type: Public   *Employees here:* 200
SIC: 3575
    Mfg lottery systems oper on-line lotteries mfg wagering
        systems & oper coin-operated mach routes
Richard M Haddrill, President

D-U-N-S 04-937-6189   EXP
PRAEGITZER INDUSTRIES INC.
1270 Se Mnmuth Cutoff Rd, Dallas, OR 97338
Phone: (503) 623-9273
Sales: $182,773,000   *Employees:* 2,000
Company Type: Public   *Employees here:* 700
SIC: 3672
    Mfg & design printed circuit boards
Robert L Praegitzer, Chairman of the Board

D-U-N-S 00-959-2056
PRC INC.
    (Parent: Litton Industries Inc)
1500 Prc Dr, Mc Lean, VA 22102
Phone: (703) 556-1111
Sales: $426,600,000   *Employees:* 5,500
Company Type: Public Family Member   *Employees here:* 1,300
SIC: 7371
    Information technology based systems
Leonard Pomata, President

D-U-N-S 60-643-9628   EXP
PRECISMETALS INC.
    (Parent: Electronic Mfg Systems)
120 9th Ave, Longmont, CO 80501
Phone: (303) 772-9081
Sales: $192,700,000   *Employees:* 1,600
Company Type: Private   *Employees here:* 2
SIC: 3571
    Contract manufacturing & systems integration
Mark J Stevenson, Chairman of the Board

D-U-N-S 15-136-2019   EXP
PRESTOLITE WIRE CORPORATION
200 Galleria, Ste. 200, Southfield, MI 48034
Phone: (248) 355-4422
Sales: $228,000,000   *Employees:* 1,255
Company Type: Private   *Employees here:* 60
SIC: 3694
    Mfg automotive engine electrical wiring products &
        nonferrous insulated wire cable & telecommunication
        products
Gasper Buffa, President

D-U-N-S 13-137-5685
PRINCETON INFORMATION LTD.
2 Penn Plz, Fl 24, New York, NY 10121
Phone: (212) 563-5030
Sales: $60,358,000   *Employees:* 800
Company Type: Private   *Employees here:* 175
SIC: 7379
    Computer consultants
Noel Marcus, President

D-U-N-S 00-925-4095   EXP
PRINT NORTHWEST CO LP
4918 20th St E, Tacoma, WA 98424
Phone: (253) 922-9393

Sales: $89,000,000   *Employees:* 685
Company Type: Private   *Employees here:* 500
SIC: 7372
    Computer software fulfillment services & lithographic
      printing
Kurt B Dammeier, President

D-U-N-S 04-607-9802
PRINTRAK INTERNATIONAL INC.
1250 N Tustin Ave, Anaheim, CA 92807
Phone: (714) 666-2700
Sales: $71,876,000   *Employees:* 430
Company Type: Public   *Employees here:* 270
SIC: 7371
    Designs assemblies installs and maintains computerized
      fingerprint and photograph identification systems
Richard D Giles, President

D-U-N-S 06-617-7007   EXP
PRINTRONIX INC.
17500 Cartwright Rd, Irvine, CA 92614
Phone: (949) 863-1900
Sales: $170,391,000   *Employees:* 992
Company Type: Public   *Employees here:* 247
SIC: 3577
    Mfg computer printers
Robert A Kleist, President

D-U-N-S 05-886-6203   EXP
PROCESSORS UNLIMITED COMPANY
5339 Alpha Rd, Ste. 200, Dallas, TX 75240
Phone: (972) 980-7825
Sales: $101,700,000   *Employees:* 1,000
Company Type: Private   *Employees here:* 70
SIC: 7372
    Computer software services & inventory computing services
Steve Svanda, General Partner

D-U-N-S 17-437-9875   EXP
PROCOM TECHNOLOGY INC.
1821 E Dyer Rd, Santa Ana, CA 92705
Phone: (949) 852-1000
Sales: $111,886,000   *Employees:* 308
Company Type: Public   *Employees here:* 200
SIC: 3577
    Mfg computer peripheral equipment and storage devices
Alex Razmjoo, Chairman of the Board

D-U-N-S 10-885-4894
PROGRESS SOFTWARE CORPORATION
14 Oak Park Dr, Bedford, MA 01730
Phone: (781) 280-4000
Sales: $239,890,000   *Employees:* 1,201
Company Type: Public   *Employees here:* 600
SIC: 7371
    Computer software development
Joseph W Alsop, President

D-U-N-S 80-441-2914
PROHEALTH CARE INC.
725 American Ave, Waukesha, WI 53188
Phone: (414) 544-2011
Sales: $175,450,000   *Employees:* 2,840
Company Type: Private   *Employees here:* 6
SIC: 7374
    Business services for the health care industry
Donald W Fundingsland, President

D-U-N-S 06-514-1517
PROJECT SOFTWARE & DEVELOPMENT
100 Crosby Dr, Bedford, MA 01730
Phone: (781) 280-2000

Sales: $73,329,000   *Employees:* 619
Company Type: Public   *Employees here:* 231
SIC: 7372
    Develops application computer software
Norman E Drapeau Jr, President

D-U-N-S 00-844-1347
PROQUIRE LLC
100 S Wacker Dr, Chicago, IL 60606
Phone: (312) 693-7052
Sales: $200,000,000   *Employees:* 150
Company Type: Private   *Employees here:* 150
SIC: 7373
    Computer reseller
Pat Cain, Sales & Marketing

D-U-N-S 06-410-0076
PROXIMA CORPORATION
9440 Carroll Park Dr, San Diego, CA 92121
Phone: (619) 457-5500
Sales: $154,665,000   *Employees:* 444
Company Type: Private   *Employees here:* 246
SIC: 3679
    Mfg liquid crystal display products
Kenneth E Olsen, Chairman of the Board

D-U-N-S 19-240-3269   EXP
PSC AUTOMATION, INC.
    (Parent: PSC Inc)
675 Basket Rd, Webster, NY 14580
Phone: (716) 265-1600
Sales: $230,000,000   *Employees:* 65
Company Type: Public Family Member   *Employees here:* 56
SIC: 3699
    Mfg laser scanners
William J Woodward, Treasurer

D-U-N-S 04-922-3357   EXP
PSC INC.
675 Basket Rd, Webster, NY 14580
Phone: (716) 265-1600
Sales: $207,840,000   *Employees:* 1,150
Company Type: Public   *Employees here:* 500
SIC: 3577
    Mfg bar code readers verifiers integrated sortation scanning
      systems
Robert C Strandberg, President

D-U-N-S 60-726-1369
PSINET INC.
510 Huntmar Park Dr, Herndon, VA 20170
Phone: (703) 904-4100
Sales: $121,900,000   *Employees:* 1,000
Company Type: Public   *Employees here:* 300
SIC: 7373
    Internet services provider
William L Schrader, Chairman of the Board

D-U-N-S 19-781-7497   EXP
PYXIS CORPORATION
    (Parent: Cardinal Health Inc)
3750 Torrey View Ct, San Diego, CA 92130
Phone: (619) 480-6000
Sales: $82,000,000   *Employees:* 1,300
Company Type: Public Family Member   *Employees here:* 600
SIC: 7373
    Computer integrated systems
Robert D Walter, Chairman of the Board

D-U-N-S 03-956-1725
QAD INC.
6450 Via Real, Carpinteria, CA 93013
Phone: (805) 566-4997

Sales: $91,549,000
Company Type: Public
SIC: 7371
   Computer software development and programming
     applications
Pamela M Lopker, Chairman of the Board
Employees: 1,156
Employees here: 500

D-U-N-S 08-654-7338
QMS INC.
1 Magnum Pass, Mobile, AL 36618
Phone: (334) 633-4300
Sales: $133,491,000
Company Type: Public
SIC: 3577
   Mfg nonimpact print systems interfaces & other components
     application software
James A Wallace, Chief Financial Officer
Employees: 674
Employees here: 428

D-U-N-S 12-081-2854 EXP
QRS CORPORATION
1400 Marina Way S, Richmond, CA 94804
Phone: (510) 215-5000
Sales: $71,632,000
Company Type: Public
SIC: 7375
   Information database & electronic data interchange services
John S Simon, Chief Executive Officer
Employees: 270
Employees here: 220

D-U-N-S 61-163-1912
QUAD SYSTEMS TECHNOLOGIES INC.
7200 N Serenoa Dr, Sarasota, FL 34241
Phone: (941) 921-1363
Sales: $500,000;000
Company Type: Private
SIC: 7373
   Computer systems integration
Glenn R Mc Caughey, President
Employees: 2
Employees here: 2

D-U-N-S 36-440-6074
QUANTEGY INC.
   (Parent: Equitable Life Assur Soc Of US)
800 Commerce Dr, Peachtree City, GA 30269
Phone: (770) 486-2800
Sales: $105,600,000
Company Type: Public Family Member
SIC: 3695
   Mfg magnetic tapes
Alex Sorokin, President
Employees: 1,100
Employees here: 45

D-U-N-S 02-119-5540 EXP
QUANTUM CORPORATION
500 McCarthy Blvd, Milpitas, CA 95035
Phone: (408) 894-4000
Sales: $5,803,235,000
Company Type: Public
SIC: 3572
   Mfg computer storage products
Michael A Brown, Chairman of the Board
Employees: 6,219
Employees here: 2,295

D-U-N-S 05-736-4507
QUESTECH, INC.
7600w Leesburg Pike, Falls Church, VA 22043
Phone: (703) 760-1000
Sales: $78,476,000
Company Type: Private
SIC: 7373
   System engineering analysis & design technical field
     engineering
Vincent L Salvatori, Chairman of the Board
Employees: 800
Employees here: 71

D-U-N-S 96-202-1531
QUESTPOINT
401 Market St, Philadelphia, PA 19106

Phone: (215) 973-1294
Sales: $286,800,000
Company Type: Private
SIC: 7374
   Check processing & remittance services
Joseph Loughry III, President
Employees: 4,500
Employees here: 4,000

D-U-N-S 17-841-7929
QUICKTURN DESIGN SYSTEMS INC.
55 W Trimble Rd, San Jose, CA 95131
Phone: (408) 914-6000
Sales: $104,109,000
Company Type: Public
SIC: 7373
   Mfg electronic design verification systems
Keith R Lobo, President
Employees: 388
Employees here: 300

D-U-N-S 03-940-0106
R C G INFORMATION TECHNOLOGY
   (Parent: R C G International Inc)
379 Thornall St, Ste. 60, Edison, NJ 08837
Phone: (732) 744-3500
Sales: $191,886,000
Company Type: Public Family Member
SIC: 7379
   Data processing solution and data processing supplemental
     staffing services
Robert P Buttacavoli, President
Employees: 1,600
Employees here: 75

D-U-N-S 00-111-4867
R E PHELON COMPANY INC.
895 University Pkwy, Aiken, SC 29801
Phone: (803) 649-1381
Sales: $65,000,000
Company Type: Private
SIC: 3694
   Mfg electrical magnetos & parts electronic testing equipment
Russell D Phelon, President
Employees: 565
Employees here: 405

D-U-N-S 86-894-6922
R EMASS INC.
   (Parent: Raytheon E-Systems Inc)
10949 E Peakview Ave, Englewood, CO 80111
Phone: (303) 792-9700
Sales: $81,000,000
Company Type: Public Family Member
SIC: 3572
   Mfg computer storage unit devices & radio & TV
     communication equipment
Mitchell D Bohn, President
Employees: 300
Employees here: 156

D-U-N-S 09-681-7002 EXP
R F MONOLITHICS INC.
4347 Sigma Rd, Dallas, TX 75244
Phone: (972) 448-3700
Sales: $55,172,000
Company Type: Public
SIC: 3679
   Mfg radio frequency transmitting components
Sam L Densmore, President
Employees: 600
Employees here: 524

D-U-N-S 17-724-2435
RADIANT SYSTEMS INC.
1000 Alderman Dr, Ste. A, Alpharetta, GA 30005
Phone: (770) 772-3000
Sales: $78,003,000
Company Type: Public
SIC: 7373
   Computer integrated systems design
Erez Goren, Chairman of the Board
Employees: 581
Employees here: 297

D-U-N-S 18-107-4055 EXP
RADISYS CORPORATION
5445 Ne Dawson Creek Dr, Hillsboro, OR 97124

Phone: (503) 615-1100
Sales: $125,442,000
Company Type: Public
SIC: 3577
   Mfg computer systems
Dr Glen Myers, Chairman of the Board

Employees: 458
Employees here: 400

D-U-N-S 10-872-7819
RAINBOW TECHNOLOGIES INC.
50 Technology Dr, Irvine, CA 92618
Phone: (949) 450-7300
Sales: $94,724,000
Company Type: Public
SIC: 3577
   Mfg computer software protection products
Walter W Straub, Chairman of the Board

Employees: 300
Employees here: 150

D-U-N-S 11-812-7729   EXP
RALTRON ELECTRONICS CORP.
10651 Nw 19th St, Miami, FL 33172
Phone: (305) 593-6033
Sales: $75,000,000
Company Type: Private
SIC: 3679
   Manufacturer and supplier of passive electronic components
Alexander Wolloch, President

Employees: 275
Employees here: 210

D-U-N-S 60-666-2757
RAND MCNALLY MEDIA SVCS INC.
   (Parent: Rand McNally Holdings II Inc)
8255 Central Park Ave, Skokie, IL 60076
Phone: (847) 673-9100
Sales: $68,800,000
Company Type: Private
SIC: 7373
   Computer disk duplication
Jim Thaden, President

Employees: 801
Employees here: NA

D-U-N-S 07-497-8693
RAPIDIGM INC.
4400 Campbells Run Rd, Pittsburgh, PA 15205
Phone: (412) 494-9800
Sales: $196,000,000
Company Type: Private
SIC: 7373
   Computer system design & programming service
Lewis P Wheeler, Chairman of the Board

Employees: 1,800
Employees here: 35

D-U-N-S 08-124-4378
RATIONAL SOFTWARE CORPORATION
18880 Homestead Rd, Cupertino, CA 95014
Phone: (408) 863-9900
Sales: $310,670,000
Company Type: Public
SIC: 7372
   Computer systems software development
Paul D Levy, Chairman of the Board

Employees: 1,743
Employees here: 200

D-U-N-S 00-912-5527   EXP
RAYCHEM CORPORATION
300 Constitution Dr, Menlo Park, CA 94025
Phone: (650) 361-3333
Sales: $1,798,456,000
Company Type: Public
SIC: 3678
   Mfg electronic connectors insulation material (plastic)
   electric heating equip electronic resistors & power
   connectors
Raymond J Sims, Chief Financial Officer

Employees: 9,036
Employees here: 3,000

D-U-N-S 04-341-2618
RAYTHEON SERVICE COMPANY
   (Parent: Raytheon Engneers Constrs Intl)
2 Wayside Rd, Burlington, MA 01803

Phone: (781) 238-3000
Sales: $817,000,000
Company Type: Public Family Member
SIC: 7376
   Provides management support repair & engineering services
   for electronic computer equipment & runs government
   facilities
Herbert Deitcher, Treasurer

Employees: 6,200
Employees here: 700

D-U-N-S 14-722-9132
RAYTHEON STX CORPORATION
   (Parent: Raytheon Technical Svcs Co)
4400 Forbes Blvd, Lanham, MD 20706
Phone: (301) 794-5000
Sales: $120,000,000
Company Type: Public Family Member
SIC: 7373
   Information technology science engineering/computer
   systems design development & integration software
   development
Ashok Kaveeshwar, President

Employees: 1,700
Employees here: 200

D-U-N-S 05-654-6583
RAYTHEON TRAINING INC.
   (Parent: Raytheon Company)
621 Six Flags Dr, Arlington, TX 76011
Phone: (817) 619-2000
Sales: $330,000,000
Company Type: Public Family Member
SIC: 3699
   Mfg flight simulators & flight training devices
Philip T Le Pore, President

Employees: 4,100
Employees here: 900

D-U-N-S 10-276-2192   EXP
READ-RITE CORPORATION
345 Los Coches St, Milpitas, CA 95035
Phone: (408) 262-6700
Sales: $808,622,000
Company Type: Public
SIC: 3679
   Mfg thin film magnetic recording heads
Cyril J Yansouni, Chairman of the Board

Employees: 18,000
Employees here: 1,500

D-U-N-S 08-002-2015
REFLECTONE INC.
   (Parent: British Aerospace N Amer Inc)
4908 Tampa West Blvd, Tampa, FL 33634
Phone: (813) 885-7481
Sales: $64,600,000
Company Type: Private
SIC: 3699
   Mfg aircraft training devices & provides flight training
   services
John Pitts, President

Employees: 800
Employees here: 345

D-U-N-S 78-292-2561
REMEDY CORPORATION
1505 Salado Dr, Mountain View, CA 94043
Phone: (650) 903-5200
Sales: $129,184,000
Company Type: Public
SIC: 7371
   Computer software development
Lawrence L Garlick, Chairman of the Board

Employees: 450
Employees here: 250

D-U-N-S 09-077-5891
RMS HOLDINGS, INCORPORATED
4221 Forbes Blvd, Fl 1, Lanham, MD 20706
Phone: (301) 306-4460
Sales: $90,946,000
Company Type: Private
SIC: 7374
   Computer facilities and network management
Michael A D, President

Employees: 1,000
Employees here: 60

D-U-N-S 00-431-8994   EXP
ROBROY INDUSTRIES INC.
River Rd, Verona, PA 15147
Phone: (412) 828-2100
Sales: $126,112,000   *Employees:* 755
Company Type: Private   *Employees here:* 25
SIC: 3572
   Mfg computer packaging conduit enclosure and oil field
    products
Peter McIlroy II, Chairman of the Board

D-U-N-S 96-066-1775
ROFIN-SINAR TECHNOLOGIES INC.
45701 Mast St, Plymouth, MI 48170
Phone: (734) 455-5400
Sales: $117,583,000   *Employees:* 500
Company Type: Public   *Employees here:* 105
SIC: 3699
   Manufactures laser products
Dr Peter Wirth, President

D-U-N-S 07-187-1586   IMP EXP
ROSS SYSTEMS, INC.
2 Cncourse Pkwy, Ste. 800, Atlanta, GA 30328
Phone: (770) 351-9600
Sales: $91,684,000   *Employees:* 582
Company Type: Public   *Employees here:* 170
SIC: 7372
   Business oriented software computer related consulting
    education & maintenance services
Dennis V Vohs, Chief Executive Officer

D-U-N-S 62-268-0130   EXP
ROXBORO HOLDINGS INC.
1913 Atlantic Ave, Manasquan, NJ 08736
Phone: (732) 223-9400
Sales: $100,000,000   *Employees:* 600
Company Type: Private   *Employees here:* 3
SIC: 3679
   Holding company
Peter Timms, President

D-U-N-S 07-616-2676
S C DATA CENTER INC.
1112 7th Ave, Monroe, WI 53566
Phone: (608) 328-8600
Sales: $250,000,000   *Employees:* 1,200
Company Type: Private   *Employees here:* 1,200
SIC: 7374
   Data processing service
John Baumann, President

D-U-N-S 19-855-7092   EXP
S3 INCORPORATED
2801 Mission College Blvd, Santa Clara, CA 95054
Phone: (408) 588-8000
Sales: $436,359,000   *Employees:* 450
Company Type: Public   *Employees here:* 450
SIC: 3577
   Mfg high performance multimedia acceleration products
Kenneth F Potashner, Chairman of the Board

D-U-N-S 16-144-4740
SABRE GROUP, INC.
   (Parent: Sabre Group Holdings Inc)
4255 Amon Carter Blvd, Fort Worth, TX 76155
Phone: (817) 963-1234
Sales: $1,783,547,000   *Employees:* 10,300
Company Type: Public Family Member   *Employees here:* 5,800
SIC: 7371
   Custom computer programming data processing/preparation
    business services business consulting services
Donald J Carty, Chairman of the Board

D-U-N-S 79-338-5535
SAEHAN MEDIA AMERICA INC.
1989 Palomar Oaks Way, Carlsbad, CA 92009
Phone: (760) 929-7770
Sales: $139,819,000   *Employees:* 40
Company Type: Private   *Employees here:* 24
SIC: 3695
   Mfg blank video and audio tapes
Myung S Hong, President

D-U-N-S 17-388-5450
SAGA SOFTWARE, INC.
   (Parent: Thayer Capital Partners)
11190 Sunrise Valley Dr, Reston, VA 20191
Phone: (703) 860-5050
Sales: $81,200,000   *Employees:* 800
Company Type: Private   *Employees here:* 300
SIC: 7372
   Computer software developer
Daniel F Gillis, President

D-U-N-S 36-240-7041   EXP
SANDISK CORPORATION
140 Caspian Ct, Sunnyvale, CA 94089
Phone: (408) 542-0500
Sales: $125,253,000   *Employees:* 445
Company Type: Public   *Employees here:* 400
SIC: 3572
   Mfg computer storage devices
Dr Eli Harari, President

D-U-N-S 79-877-8395   EXP
SANMINA CORPORATION
355 Trimble Rd, San Jose, CA 95131
Phone: (408) 954-5500
Sales: $923,788,000   *Employees:* 5,477
Company Type: Public   *Employees here:* 318
SIC: 3672
   Mfg printed circuit boards backplane assemblies & cable &
    wire harness assemblies
Jure Sola, Chairman of the Board

D-U-N-S 00-261-7819
SANTA CRUZ OPERATION INC.
425 Encinal St, Santa Cruz, CA 95060
Phone: (831) 425-7222
Sales: $171,900,000   *Employees:* 1,136
Company Type: Public   *Employees here:* 149
SIC: 7371
   Design and develop computer software
Doug Michels, President

D-U-N-S 18-361-6317
SAP AMERICA INC.
3999 W Chester Pike, Newtown Square, PA 19073
Phone: (610) 355-2500
Sales: $317,300,000   *Employees:* 4,090
Company Type: Private   *Employees here:* 396
SIC: 7371
   Provides software sales training & consulting services
Kevin McKay, Chief Executive Officer

D-U-N-S 02-683-5731
SAP AMERICA PUBIC SECTOR, INC.
   (Parent: SAP America Inc)
300 Stevens Dr, Philadelphia, PA 19113
Phone: (610) 595-4900
Sales: $65,000,000   *Employees:* 150
Company Type: Private   *Employees here:* 150
SIC: 7371
   Software sales training & consulting
Robert M Salvucci, President

D-U-N-S 79-016-6219
SAPIENT CORPORATION
1 Memorial Dr, Cambridge, MA 02142
Phone: (617) 621-0200
Sales: $90,360,000   *Employees:* 924
Company Type: Public   *Employees here:* 350
SIC: 7371
    Computer software applications
Jerry A Greenberg, Co-Chairman of the Board

D-U-N-S 04-004-6724   EXP
SAS INSTITUTE INC.
S A S Campus Dr, Cary, NC 27513
Phone: (919) 677-8000
Sales: $747,741,000   *Employees:* 5,285
Company Type: Private   *Employees here:* 2,585
SIC: 7372
    Prepackaged software
James H Goodnight, President

D-U-N-S 14-424-0850   EXP
SATURN ELECTRONICS & ENGRG
255 Rex Blvd, Auburn Hills, MI 48326
Phone: (248) 853-5724
Sales: $161,048,000   *Employees:* 1,538
Company Type: Private   *Employees here:* 82
SIC: 3672
    Mfg electronic printed circuit boards and motor vehicle parts
Wallace K Tsuha Jr, Chairman of the Board

D-U-N-S 07-659-2641 .
SAVINGS BNK LF INSUR OF MASS
1 Linscott Rd, Woburn, MA 01801
Phone: (781) 938-3500
Sales: $198,331,000   *Employees:* 150
Company Type: Private   *Employees here:* 125
SIC: 7374
    Life insurance products
Robert K Sheridan, President

D-U-N-S 09-360-6747   EXP
SAWTEK INC.
1818 S Hwy 441, Apopka, FL 32703
Phone: (407) 886-8860
Sales: $97,700,000   *Employees:* 549
Company Type: Public   *Employees here:* 388
SIC: 3677
    Mfg electronic signal processing components
Steven P Miller, Chairman of the Board

D-U-N-S 18-061-0958   EXP
SBS TECHNOLOGIES INC.
2400 La Ne, Ste. 600, Albuquerque, NM 87110
Phone: (505) 875-0600
Sales: $74,214,000   *Employees:* 300
Company Type: Public   *Employees here:* 75
SIC: 7373
    Develops computer interface equipment mfg telemetry
        equipment mfg input/output computer equipment
Christophe Amenson, Chief Executive Officer

D-U-N-S 04-623-3862   EXP
SCAN-OPTICS, INC.
169 Progress Dr, Manchester, CT 06040
Phone: (860) 645-7878
Sales: $56,608,000   *Employees:* 324
Company Type: Public   *Employees here:* 250
SIC: 3577
    Mfr & service information processing systems
James C Mavel, Chairman of the Board

D-U-N-S 03-041-8610
SCB COMPUTER TECHNOLOGY INC.
1365 W Brierbrook Rd, Memphis, TN 38138
Phone: (901) 754-6577
Sales: $109,472,000   *Employees:* 1,100
Company Type: Public   *Employees here:* 150
SIC: 7371
    Information technology consulting service outsourcing and
        professional staffing
Ben C Bryant Jr, President

D-U-N-S 09-498-3046
SCHLUMBERGER TECHNOLOGIES INC.
    (Parent: Schlumberger Technology Corp)
277 Park Ave, Fl 41, New York, NY 10172
Phone: (212) 350-9400
Sales: $171,500,000   *Employees:* 2,000
Company Type: Public Family Member   *Employees here:* 300
SIC: 7373
    Computer integrated systems design & testing
Clermont Matton, President

D-U-N-S 00-401-6960   EXP
SCI SYSTEMS INC.
2101 Clinton Ave W, Huntsville, AL 35805
Phone: (256) 882-4800
Sales: $6,805,893,000   *Employees:* 22,324
Company Type: Public   *Employees here:* 400
SIC: 3571
    Mfg computers printed circuit boards telecommunications
        equip computer peripheral equip & patient monitoring
        equip
Olin B King, Chairman of the Board

D-U-N-S 87-949-2916
SCT SOFTWARE & RESOURCES MGT
    (Parent: Systems & Computer Tech Corp)
4 Country View Rd, Malvern, PA 19355
Phone: (610) 647-5930
Sales: $73,600,000   *Employees:* 946
Company Type: Public Family Member   *Employees here:* 750
SIC: 7371
    Software resource management & onsite facility management
Michael J Emmi, Chairman of the Board

D-U-N-S 10-277-0260   EXP
SDL, INC.
80 Rose Orchard Way, San Jose, CA 95134
Phone: (408) 943-9411
Sales: $91,364,000   *Employees:* 650
Company Type: Public   *Employees here:* 235
SIC: 3674
    Mfg semiconductors & related devices
Donald R Scifres, Chairman of the Board

D-U-N-S 60-547-2570
SEAGATE SFTWR STOR MGT GROUP
    (Parent: Seagate Technology Inc)
708 Fiero Ln, Ste. 5, San Luis Obispo, CA 93401
Phone: (805) 544-1496
Sales: $293,226,000   *Employees:* 325
Company Type: Public Family Member   *Employees here:* 150
SIC: 7371
    Computer software development
Terry Cunningham, President

D-U-N-S 84-909-8637
SEAGATE SOFTWARE, INC.
    (Parent: Seagate Technology Inc)
3061 Zanker Rd, San Jose, CA 95134
Phone: (408) 456-4500

Sales: $293,000,000   *Employees:* 1,700
Company Type: Public Family Member   *Employees here:* 4
SIC: 7372
   Prepackaged software
Terry Cunningham, President

D-U-N-S 09-853-3326   EXP
SEAGATE TECHNOLOGY INC.
920 Disc Dr Bldg 1, Scotts Valley, CA 95066
Phone: (831) 438-6550
Sales: $6,819,000,000   *Employees:* 87,000
Company Type: Public   *Employees here:* 1,400
SIC: 3572
   Mfg magnetic disk drives
William D Watkins, Chief Operating Officer

D-U-N-S 05-628-0555
SEARS HOME SERVICES GROUP
   (Parent: Sears Roebuck And Co)
1300 Louis Henna Blvd, Round Rock, TX 78664
Phone: (512) 834-8341
Sales: $147,400,000   *Employees:* 2,500
Company Type: Public Family Member   *Employees here:* 900
SIC: 7379
   Computer technical service
Arthur C Martinez, Chairman of the Board

D-U-N-S 12-161-5538
SECURITY DYNAMICS TECH INC.
20 Crosby Dr, Bedford, MA 01730
Phone: (781) 687-7000
Sales: $135,930,000   *Employees:* 360
Company Type: Public   *Employees here:* 220
SIC: 3577
   Designs develops and markets computer security access
      hardware and software
Charles R Stuckey, Chairman of the Board

D-U-N-S 61-033-1217
SEER TECHNOLOGIES INC.
   (Parent: Level 8 Systems Inc)
8000 Regency Pkwy, Cary, NC 27511
Phone: (919) 380-5000
Sales: $63,964,000   *Employees:* 411
Company Type: Public   *Employees here:* 125
SIC: 7371
   Computer software development
Michael A Reiff, Senior Vice-President

D-U-N-S 06-437-8086
SEI INVESTMENT COMPANY
1 Freedom Valley Dr, Oaks, PA 19456
Phone: (610) 676-1000
Sales: $292,749,000   *Employees:* 1,133
Company Type: Public   *Employees here:* 80
SIC: 7372
   Provides information processing software service computer
      facilities management operates open-end funds
      management consulting
Alfred P West Jr, Chairman of the Board

D-U-N-S 00-847-9941   EXP
SEMTECH CORPORATION
652 Mitchell Rd, Newbury Park, CA 91320
Phone: (805) 498-2111
Sales: $102,808,000   *Employees:* 503
Company Type: Public   *Employees here:* 180
SIC: 3674
   Mfg semiconductors/related devices
John D Poe, President

D-U-N-S 60-663-0754   EXP
SEQUEL INC.
6341 San Ignacio Ave, San Jose, CA 95119
Phone: (408) 361-4600
Sales: $85,846,000   *Employees:* 700
Company Type: Private   *Employees here:* 300
SIC: 7378
   Provider of integrated support services
William Mitchell, President

D-U-N-S 10-301-0260
SEQUENT COMPUTER SYSTEMS INC.
15450 Sw Koll Pkwy, Beaverton, OR 97006
Phone: (503) 626-5700
Sales: $833,886,000   *Employees:* 2,818
Company Type: Public   *Employees here:* 1,200
SIC: 3571
   Mfg computer systems
Karl C Powell Jr, Chairman of the Board

D-U-N-S 17-532-0761
SETA CORP.
6862 Elm St, Ste. 600, Mc Lean, VA 22101
Phone: (703) 821-8178
Sales: $60,000,000   *Employees:* 480
Company Type: Private   *Employees here:* 430
SIC: 7373
   Computer systems engineers & integration services
Ranvir Trehan, President

D-U-N-S 87-840-4219
SHAPE GLOBAL TECHNOLOGY INC.
7 Shape Dr, Kennebunk, ME 04043
Phone: (207) 985-4972
Sales: $90,000,000   *Employees:* 600
Company Type: Private   *Employees here:* 2
SIC: 3695
   Through subsidiary mfg audio and video cassettes micro disc
      catridges and blank magnetic tapes
Peter Ciriello, Chief Executive Officer

D-U-N-S 80-905-0230   EXP
SHAPE INC.
   (Parent: Shape Global Technology Inc)
7 Shape Dr, Kennebunk, ME 04043
Phone: (207) 985-4972
Sales: $90,000,000   *Employees:* 600
Company Type: Private   *Employees here:* 250
SIC: 3695
   Mfg audio and video cassettes micro disc cartridges and
      blank magnetic tapes
Peter Ciriello, President

D-U-N-S 18-839-7921   EXP
SHARP MICROELECTRONICS TECH
5700 Nw Pacific Rim Blvd, Camas, WA 98607
Phone: (360) 834-8700
Sales: $67,276,000   *Employees:* 340
Company Type: Private   *Employees here:* 300
SIC: 3674
   Microchip development mfg & service liquid crystal displays
      imaging & data communication products
Dr John Manning, President

D-U-N-S 00-614-7268   EXP
SHELDAHL, INC.
1150 Sheldahl Rd, Northfield, MN 55057
Phone: (507) 663-8000
Sales: $117,045,000   *Employees:* 922
Company Type: Public   *Employees here:* 701
SIC: 3672
   Mfg circuitry & flexible laminates
Edward L Lundstrom, President

D-U-N-S 09-598-3334   EXP
SHIN-ETSU HANDOTAI AMERICA
4111 Ne 112th Ave, Vancouver, WA 98682
Phone: (360) 883-7000
Sales: $400,000,000   *Employees:* 1,700
Company Type: Private   *Employees here:* 1,690
SIC: 3674
   Mfg electronic grade silicon
Isao Iwashita, President

D-U-N-S 80-885-6512
SIEBEL SYSTEMS, INC.
1855 S Grant St, San Mateo, CA 94402
Phone: (650) 295-5000
Sales: $118,775,000   *Employees:* 473
Company Type: Public   *Employees here:* 160
SIC: 7372
   Application computer software
Thomas M Siebel, Chairman of the Board

D-U-N-S 10-323-1692   EXP
SIEMENS MICROELECTRONICS, INC.
   (*Parent:* Siemens Corporation)
10950 N Tantau Ave, Cupertino, CA 95014
Phone: (408) 777-4500
Sales: $738,000,000   *Employees:* 2,750
Company Type: Private   *Employees here:* 350
SIC: 3674
   Mfg semiconductors & other electronic components
Peter Bauer, President

D-U-N-S 02-961-6877
SIEMENS PYRAMID INFO SYSTEMS
   (*Parent:* Siemens Nixdorf Info Systems)
3860 N 1st St, San Jose, CA 95134
Phone: (408) 428-9000
Sales: $108,800,000   *Employees:* 900
Company Type: Private   *Employees here:* 600
SIC: 3571
   Mfg super mini & mini mainframe computer systems &
      related software
Dr Raj Nathan, President

D-U-N-S 03-786-2398
SIERRA ON-LINE INC.
   (*Parent:* Cendant Corporation)
3380 146th Pl Se, Ste. 300, Bellevue, WA 98007
Phone: (425) 649-9800
Sales: $111,900,000   *Employees:* 1,100
Company Type: Public Family Member   *Employees here:* 200
SIC: 7372
   Computer software development & publishing
Kenneth A Williams, Chief Executive Officer

D-U-N-S 06-913-5846
SIGMA CIRCUITS INC.
   (*Parent:* Tyco Printed Circuit Group)
400 Mathew St, Santa Clara, CA 95050
Phone: (408) 727-9169
Sales: $79,980,000   *Employees:* 785
Company Type: Private   *Employees here:* 400
SIC: 3672
   Mfg electronic interconnects
Steve Gardner, President

D-U-N-S 82-562-2327   EXP
SIGMATRON INTERNATIONAL
2201 Landmeier Rd, Elk Grove Village, IL 60007
Phone: (847) 956-8000

Sales: $85,651,000   *Employees:* 1,700
Company Type: Public   *Employees here:* 275
SIC: 3672
   Mfg printed circuit boards and electronic components
Gary R Fairhead, President

D-U-N-S 18-198-6670
SIGNAL CORPORATION
3040 Williams Dr, Ste. 200, Fairfax, VA 22031
Phone: (703) 205-0500
Sales: $91,535,000   *Employees:* 1,250
Company Type: Private   *Employees here:* 1,000
SIC: 7379
   High technology services
Roger Mody, Chairman of the Board

D-U-N-S 07-838-8451
SIGNAL TECHNOLOGY CORPORATION
222 Rosewood Dr, Danvers, MA 01923
Phone: (978) 774-2281
Sales: $102,279,000   *Employees:* 820
Company Type: Public   *Employees here:* 175
SIC: 3679
   Mfg electronic components & subsystems
George Lombard, President

D-U-N-S 02-403-9778   EXP
SILICON GRAPHICS INC.
2011 N Shoreline Blvd, Mountain View, CA 94043
Phone: (650) 960-1980
Sales: $3,100,610,000   *Employees:* 10,286
Company Type: Public   *Employees here:* 1,600
SIC: 3571
   Mfg computer systems processors & microprocessors
      application software
Richard Belluzzo, Chairman of the Board

D-U-N-S 06-446-9679   EXP
SILICON SYSTEMS INC.
   (*Parent:* Texas Instruments Incorporated)
14351 Myford Rd, Tustin, CA 92780
Phone: (714) 731-7110
Sales: $500,000,000   *Employees:* 2,039
Company Type: Public Family Member   *Employees here:* 650
SIC: 3674
   Mfg integrated circuits
Fredrick Goerner, President

D-U-N-S 00-913-1392   EXP
SILICONIX INCORPORATED
   (*Parent:* Vishay Temic Semicon Acq Holdi)
2201 Laurelwood Rd, Santa Clara, CA 95054
Phone: (408) 988-8000
Sales: $321,551,000   *Employees:* 1,226
Company Type: Public   *Employees here:* 860
SIC: 3674
   Mfg semiconductor products
King Owyang, President

D-U-N-S 04-589-7097
SIPEX CORPORATION
22 Linnell Cir, Billerica, MA 01821
Phone: (978) 667-8700
Sales: $51,210,000   *Employees:* 435
Company Type: Public   *Employees here:* 156
SIC: 3674
   Mfg electronic data acquisition components
James E Donegan, Chairman of the Board

D-U-N-S 19-596-2543   EXP
SMART MODULAR TECHNOLOGIES
4305 Cushing Pkwy, Fremont, CA 94538
Phone: (510) 623-1231

Sales: $714,651,000   *Employees:* 831
Company Type: Public   *Employees here:* 300
SIC: 3674
   Mfg memory modules & pc card products
Ajay B Shah, Chairman of the Board

D-U-N-S 18-108-2686   EXP
SMARTFLEX SYSTEMS INC.
14312 Franklin Ave, Tustin, CA 92780
Phone: (714) 838-8737
Sales: $133,347,000   *Employees:* 1,169
Company Type: Public   *Employees here:* 137
SIC: 3678
   Mfg flexible interconnect assemblies
William L Healey, Chairman of the Board

D-U-N-S 96-835-4936
SMITH WALL ASSOCIATES LLC
100 Wood Ave S, Ste. 400, Iselin, NJ 08830
Phone: (732) 906-1800
Sales: $100,000,000   *Employees:* 25
Company Type: Private   *Employees here:* 25
SIC: 7371
   Software dev
Jeffrey Citron, President

D-U-N-S 94-340-6488
SMT CENTRE OF TEXAS, INC.
15508 Bratton Ln, Austin, TX 78728
Phone: (512) 310-4300
Sales: $60,000,000   *Employees:* 350
Company Type: Private   *Employees here:* 350
SIC: 3672
   Electronic assembly
Paul Walker, President

D-U-N-S 02-404-4468
SOFTCHOICE CORPORATION
3 Quincy St, Norwalk, CT 06850
Phone: (203) 797-9000
Sales: $120,000,000   *Employees:* 220
Company Type: Private   *Employees here:* 25
SIC: 7372

Chandran Rajaratnam, President

D-U-N-S 06-677-4357
SOFTWARE AG SYSTEMS, INC.
11190 Sunrise Valley Dr, Reston, VA 20191
Phone: (703) 860-5050
Sales: $181,224,000   *Employees:* 950
Company Type: Public   *Employees here:* 330
SIC: 7372
   Computer systems software development & packaging
Daniel Gillis, President

D-U-N-S 08-701-1003   EXP
SOLECTRON CORPORATION
847 Gibraltar Dr, Milpitas, CA 95035
Phone: (408) 957-8500
Sales: $5,288,294,000   *Employees:* 24,857
Company Type: Public   *Employees here:* 5,700
SIC: 3672
   Printed circuit board assembly electrical engineering services
      computer equip maintenance packaging & labeling services
Dr Koichi Nishimura, Chairman of the Board

D-U-N-S 96-589-7994
SOLECTRON MASSACHUSSETS CORP.
   (Parent: Solectron Corporation)
1 Solectron Dr, Westborough, MA 01581
Phone: (508) 616-6000

Sales: $75,000,000   *Employees:* 300
Company Type: Public Family Member   *Employees here:* 300
SIC: 3679
   Printed circuit board assembly electrical engineering services
      computer equip maintenance packaging & labeling services
Walter Wilson, President

D-U-N-S 79-300-4920
SOLECTRON TECHNOLOGY, INC.
   (Parent: Solectron Corporation)
6800 Solectron Dr, Charlotte, NC 28262
Phone: (704) 598-3300
Sales: $163,100,000   *Employees:* 2,500
Company Type: Public Family Member   *Employees here:* 1,200
SIC: 3672
   Mfg printed circuit boards
Robert Bradshaw, President

D-U-N-S 93-771-5779
SOLECTRON TEXAS LP
12455 Research Blvd, Austin, TX 78759
Phone: (512) 425-4100
Sales: $600,000,000   *Employees:* 3,600
Company Type: Private   *Employees here:* 2,300
SIC: 3571
   Mfg electronic computers
Ron Shelly, President

D-U-N-S 04-065-3636   EXP
SONY MAGNETIC PRODUCTS INC.
   (Parent: Sony Electronics Inc)
36305 W Main St, Dothan, AL 36305
Phone: (334) 793-7655
Sales: $118,100,000   *Employees:* 1,230
Company Type: Private   *Employees here:* 1,200
SIC: 3695
   Mfg audio and video recording tapes and floppy diskettes
William B Singletary, President

D-U-N-S 18-351-6160
SOUTHLAND MICRO SYSTEMS INC.
7 Morgan, Irvine, CA 92618
Phone: (949) 380-1958
Sales: $170,000,000   *Employees:* 210
Company Type: Private   *Employees here:* 210
SIC: 3577
   Manufactures computer memory upgrades
John Meehan, President

D-U-N-S 00-433-4694
SPANG & COMPANY
Brugh Ave, Butler, PA 16001
Phone: (724) 287-8781
Sales: $100,000,000   *Employees:* 1,200
Company Type: Private   *Employees here:* 200
SIC: 3672
   Mfg electronic components toys power transformers
      panelboards
Frank E Rath Jr, Chairman of the Board

D-U-N-S 78-661-2481
SPECTRA-PHYSICS LASERS, INC.
   (Parent: Spectr-Physics Hldings USA Inc)
1335 Terra Bella Ave, Mountain View, CA 94043
Phone: (650) 961-2550
Sales: $159,174,000   *Employees:* 895
Company Type: Public   *Employees here:* 400
SIC: 3699
   Mfg lasers & laser systems
Patrick Edsell, Chairman of the Board

D-U-N-S 62-319-3323
SPECTRA PRECISION INC.
  (*Parent:* Spectra-Physics Inc)
5475 Kellenburger Rd, Dayton, OH 45424
Phone: (937) 233-8921
Sales: $130,000,000
Company Type: Private
Employees: 800
Employees here: 600
SIC: 3699
  Mfg lasers & machine control devices
Steve Berglund, President

D-U-N-S 00-826-2602   EXP
SPECTROLAB INC.
  (*Parent:* Hughes Electronics Corporation)
12500 Gladstone Ave, Sylmar, CA 91342
Phone: (818) 365-4611
Sales: $60,000,000
Company Type: Public Family Member
Employees: 780
Employees here: 780
SIC: 3674
  Mfg solar cells & other power supplies
Dieter Zemmrich, President

D-U-N-S 04-576-4453   EXP
SPECTRUM CONTROL INC.
6000 W Ridge Rd, Erie, PA 16506
Phone: (814) 835-4000
Sales: $59,868,000
Company Type: Public
Employees: 763
Employees here: 56
SIC: 3677
  Manufactures electronic filtration devices and electronic
    capacitors
Richard A Southworth, President

D-U-N-S 03-859-0899
SPECTRUM TECHNOLOGY GROUP INC.
  (*Parent:* Ciber Inc)
3421 Us Highway 22, Ste. 1, Somerville, NJ 08876
Phone: (908) 725-4000
Sales: $70,000,000
Company Type: Public Family Member
Employees: 450
Employees here: 150
SIC: 7379
  Computer consultants
Robert Nonni, President

D-U-N-S 00-863-0097
SPLASH TECHNOLOGY, INC.
  (*Parent:* Splash Technology Holdings)
555 Del Rey Ave, Sunnyvale, CA 94086
Phone: (408) 328-6300
Sales: $76,000,000
Company Type: Public Family Member
Employees: 163
Employees here: 163
SIC: 3577
  Mfg printer server equipment
Kevin K MacGillivray, President

D-U-N-S 15-179-2389
SPS PAYMENT SYSTEMS, INC.
  (*Parent:* Associates First Capital Corp)
2500 Lake Cook Rd, Riverwoods, IL 60015
Phone: (847) 405-3400
Sales: $223,000,000
Company Type: Public Family Member
Employees: 3,500
Employees here: 290
SIC: 7374
  Electronic processing of credit card transactions admin of
    private label credit card programs and operational out-
    sourcing
Robert L Wieseneck, President

D-U-N-S 03-088-0488   EXP
SPSS INC.
233 S Wacker Dr, Chicago, IL 60606
Phone: (312) 651-3000
Sales: $110,644,000
Company Type: Public
Employees: 800
Employees here: 400
SIC: 7372
  Statistical computing software programs
Jack Noonan, President

D-U-N-S 05-498-8506   EXP
STANDARD MICROSYSTEMS CORP.
80 Arkay Dr, Hauppauge, NY 11788
Phone: (516) 434-4600
Sales: $155,747,000
Company Type: Public
Employees: 500
Employees here: 402
SIC: 3674
  Mfg integrated circuits
Paul Richman, Chairman of the Board

D-U-N-S 80-909-6902
STARGATE SYSTEMS, INC.
1810 W Touhy Ave, Chicago, IL 60626
Phone: (773) 274-6080
Sales: $775,400,000
Company Type: Private
Employees: 10,000
Employees here: 10,000
SIC: 7371
  Computer programming and consulting
Kurt Fujio, President

D-U-N-S 15-466-7125   EXP
STARTEK USA INC.
  (*Parent:* Startek Inc)
111 Havana St, Aurora, CO 80010
Phone: (303) 361-6000
Sales: $79,011,000
Company Type: Public Family Member
Employees: 1,000
Employees here: 550
SIC: 7372
  Prepackaged software & fulfillment service & computer
    support
A E Stephenson Jr, Chairman of the Board

D-U-N-S 03-049-0445
STAVELEY INC.
  (*Parent:* Staveley Investments Inc)
50 Main St, White Plains, NY 10606
Phone: (914) 682-6830
Sales: $91,000,000
Company Type: Private
Employees: 1,568
Employees here: 15
SIC: 3679
  Mfg ultrasonic transducers & test equip industrial weighing
    machines & sales distributor of parts for coal crushing
    machines
Sal Busciolano, Principal

D-U-N-S 05-108-8987   EXP
STB SYSTEMS INC.
3400 Waterview Pkwy, Richardson, TX 75080
Phone: (972) 234-8750
Sales: $266,270,000
Company Type: Public
Employees: 2,156
Employees here: 240
SIC: 3672
  Mfg multimedia and specialized technology products
William E Ogel, Chairman of the Board

D-U-N-S 01-585-5612
STEALTHSOFT CORPORATION
14725 Alton Pkwy, Irvine, CA 92618
Phone: (949) 855-0234
Sales: $200,000,000
Company Type: Private
Employees: 150
Employees here: 12
SIC: 7371
  Software sales installation & maintenance
Robert F Conley, President

D-U-N-S 79-945-0473
STELLEX MICROWAVE SYSTEMS
(Parent: Stellex Industries Inc)
3333 Hillview Ave, Palo Alto, CA 94304
Phone: (650) 813-2000
Sales: $89,000,000   *Employees:* 504
Company Type: Private   *Employees here:* 504
SIC: 3679
   Mfg electronic components
Keith Gilbert, President

D-U-N-S 93-770-4302   EXP
STERLING COMMERCE INC.
300 Crescent Ct, Ste. 1200, Dallas, TX 75201
Phone: (214) 981-1000
Sales: $490,302,000   *Employees:* 600
Company Type: Public   *Employees here:* 10
SIC: 7372
   Computer software & systems
Warner C Blow, President

D-U-N-S 01-317-5161   EXP
STERLING SOFTWARE INC.
300 Crescent Ct, Ste. 1200, Dallas, TX 75201
Phone: (214) 981-1000
Sales: $719,943,000   *Employees:* 3,600
Company Type: Public   *Employees here:* 50
SIC: 7372
   Develops computer software provides information
      technology services to the federal government
Sam Wyly, Chairman of the Board

D-U-N-S 04-803-0902
STERLING SOFTWARE U S AMER INC.
(Parent: Sterling Software Inc)
1800 Alexander Bell Dr, Reston, VA 20191
Phone: (703) 264-8000
Sales: $88,800,000   *Employees:* 874
Company Type: Public Family Member   *Employees here:* 360
SIC: 7372
   Systems software products
Maria Smith, President

D-U-N-S 18-121-1046   EXP
STEWART CONNECTOR SYSTEMS INC.
(Parent: Insilco Corporation)
1118 Susquehanna Trl, Glen Rock, PA 17327
Phone: (717) 235-7512
Sales: $56,276,000   *Employees:* 650
Company Type: Private   *Employees here:* 300
SIC: 3678
   Mfg electronic connectors
George Jadosh, Executive Vice-President

D-U-N-S 06-496-4836
STONEBRIDGE TECHNOLOGIES, INC.
14800 Landmark Blvd, Dallas, TX 75240
Phone: (972) 404-9755
Sales: $106,145,000   *Employees:* 175
Company Type: Private   *Employees here:* 90
SIC: 7373
   Computer integrated systems design
James W Sherriff, Chief Executive Officer

D-U-N-S 60-628-0873   EXP
STONERIDGE, INC.
9400 E Market St, Warren, OH 44484
Phone: (330) 856-2443

Sales: $449,506,000   *Employees:* 4,400
Company Type: Public   *Employees here:* 7
SIC: 3679
   Mfr vehicle elec power & distribution systems electron & elec
      switch pdts elec instrumentation & info display pdts
David M Draime, Chairman

D-U-N-S 05-122-2065
STORAGE TECHNOLOGY CORPORATION
2270 S 88th St, Louisville, CO 80028
Phone: (303) 673-5151
Sales: $2,258,222,000   *Employees:* 8,300
Company Type: Public   *Employees here:* 3,400
SIC: 3572
   Mfg computer storage devices & other computer-related
      products consulting & other services
David E Weiss, Chairman of the Board

D-U-N-S 84-741-5486   IMP
STORMEDIA INCORPORATED
385 Reed St, Santa Clara, CA 95050
Phone: (408) 327-8400
Sales: $230,400,000   *Employees:* 2,400
Company Type: Public   *Employees here:* 2,400
SIC: 3695
   Mfg thin film magnetic media
William J Almon, Chairman of the Board

D-U-N-S 02-171-8481   EXP
STRATUS COMPUTER, INC.
(Parent: Ascend Communications Inc)
55 Fairbanks Blvd, Marlborough, MA 01752
Phone: (508) 460-2000
Sales: $688,275,000   *Employees:* 2,487
Company Type: Public Family Member   *Employees here:* 1,052
SIC: 3571
   Mfg & service online transaction processing computer
      systems & related software and services
Bruce L Sachs, President

D-U-N-S 88-321-9149
STREAM INTERNATIONAL INC.
(Parent: R R Donnelley & Sons Company)
275 Dan Rd, Canton, MA 02021
Phone: (781) 575-6800
Sales: $186,846,000   *Employees:* 5,000
Company Type: Public Family Member   *Employees here:* 800
SIC: 7373
   Technical support services
Stephen D Moore, Chairman of the Board

D-U-N-S 05-839-5070   EXP
STRUCTURAL DYNAMICS RES CORP.
2000 Eastman Dr, Milford, OH 45150
Phone: (513) 576-2400
Sales: $403,025,000   *Employees:* 2,200
Company Type: Public   *Employees here:* 838
SIC: 7372
   Mechanical design automation business oriented engineering
      software & engineering consulting services
William J Weyand, Chairman of the Board

D-U-N-S 03-724-8267   EXP
SULCUS HOSPITALITY TECH
41 N Main Stor, Greensburg, PA 15601
Phone: (724) 836-2000
Sales: $52,145,000   *Employees:* 430
Company Type: Public   *Employees here:* 72
SIC: 3578
   Prepackaged software services
Leon Harris, Chairman of the Board

D-U-N-S 61-496-2298   EXP
SUMITOMO SITIX SILICON INC.
49090 Milmont Dr, Fremont, CA 94538
Phone: (510) 651-3778
Sales: $510,000,000   *Employees:* 1,500
Company Type: Private   *Employees here:* 50
SIC: 3674
  Mfg silicon wafer material
Junichi Ishida, Chairman of the Board

D-U-N-S 60-142-5960
SUMMIT GROUP INC.
  (*Parent:* Ciber Inc)
4215 Edison Lakes Pkwy, Mishawaka, IN 46545
Phone: (219) 272-8500
Sales: $75,000,000   *Employees:* 425
Company Type: Public Family Member   *Employees here:* 130
SIC: 7379
  Computer consulting service
David Jones, Chief Executive Officer

D-U-N-S 78-765-9432
SUMMIT SERVICE CORPORATION
  (*Parent:* Summit Bancorp)
55 Challenger Rd, Ridgefield Park, NJ 07660
Phone: (201) 296-3000
Sales: $82,500,000   *Employees:* 1,300
Company Type: Public Family Member   *Employees here:* 1,000
SIC: 7374
  Provides data and item processing services and other
    administrative services
Alan N Posencheg, President

D-U-N-S 01-304-4532   EXP
SUN MICROSYSTEMS INC.
901 San Antonio Rd, Palo Alto, CA 94303
Phone: (650) 960-1300
Sales: $9,790,840,000   *Employees:* 26,300
Company Type: Public   *Employees here:* 3,500
SIC: 3571
  Mfg computing systems computer related services operating
    system software mfg microprocessors
Scott Mc Nealy, Chairman of the Board

D-U-N-S 10-142-2731
SUNGARD DATA SYSTEMS INC.
1285 Drummers Ln, Wayne, PA 19087
Phone: (610) 341-8700
Sales: $862,151,000   *Employees:* 4,500
Company Type: Public   *Employees here:* 37
SIC: 7374
  Data processing services disaster recovery services and
    computer software development
James L Mann, Chairman of the Board

D-U-N-S 15-729-3853
SUNGARD INVESTMENT VENTURES
  (*Parent:* Sungard Data Systems Inc)
103 Springer Building, Wilmington, DE 19810
Phone: (302) 478-6160
Sales: $101,700,000   *Employees:* 1,600
Company Type: Public Family Member   *Employees here:* 3
SIC: 7374
  Holding company which through subsidiaries active in data
    processing services on remote
Michael J Ruane, President

D-U-N-S 08-476-4836   EXP
SUNGARD RECOVERY SERVICES INC.
  (*Parent:* Sungard Investment Ventures)
1285 Drummers Ln, Wayne, PA 19087
Phone: (610) 341-8700

Sales: $150,000,000   *Employees:* 500
Company Type: Public Family Member   *Employees here:* 125
SIC: 7374
  Comprehensive business recovery services
Michael F Mulholland, Chairman of the Board

D-U-N-S 05-293-4841
SUNQUEST INFO SYSTEMS INC.
4801 E Broadway Blvd, Tucson, AZ 85711
Phone: (520) 570-2000
Sales: $102,337,000   *Employees:* 828
Company Type: Public   *Employees here:* 630
SIC: 7373
  Health care computer systems
Sidney A Goldblatt, President

D-U-N-S 62-212-6118
SUNSOFT, INC.
  (*Parent:* Sun Microsystems Inc)
2550 Garcia Ave, Mountain View, CA 94043
Phone: (650) 960-1300
Sales: $217,300,000   *Employees:* 2,800
Company Type: Public Family Member   *Employees here:* 2,000
SIC: 7371
  Computer software development
Janpieter Scheerder, President

D-U-N-S 96-008-0216
SUPERIOR CONSLT HOLDINGS CORP.
4000 Town Ctr, Ste. 1100, Southfield, MI 48075
Phone: (248) 386-8300
Sales: $76,895,000   *Employees:* 300
Company Type: Public   *Employees here:* 100
SIC: 7379
  Healthcare information technology consulting services
Richard Helppie, Chairman of the Board

D-U-N-S 01-093-8538   EXP
SUPERTEX INC.
1235 Bordeaux Dr, Sunnyvale, CA 94089
Phone: (408) 744-0100
Sales: $52,706,000   *Employees:* 450
Company Type: Public   *Employees here:* 350
SIC: 3674
  Mfg semiconductor components
Richard E Siegel, Executive Vice-President

D-U-N-S 17-329-3085
SUTHERLAND GROUP LTD INC.
1160 Pittsford Victor Rd, Pittsford, NY 14534
Phone: (716) 586-5757
Sales: $99,500,000   *Employees:* 1,400
Company Type: Private   *Employees here:* 1,330
SIC: 7375
  Information retrieval services commercial nonphysical
    research management consulting services
Dilip Vellodi, Chief Executive Officer

D-U-N-S 13-156-3215   EXP
SYBASE, INC.
6475 Christie Ave, Emeryville, CA 94608
Phone: (510) 596-3500
Sales: $903,937,000   *Employees:* 5,484
Company Type: Public   *Employees here:* 600
SIC: 7372
  Computer software development computer related services
John Chen, Chairman of the Board

D-U-N-S 04-175-9564
SYKES ENTERPRISES INCORPORATED
100 N Tampa St, Ste. 3900, Tampa, FL 33602
Phone: (813) 274-1000

Sales: $469,462,000   *Employees:* 8,700
Company Type: Public   *Employees here:* 200
SIC: 7371
   Computer hardware and software and integration services
John H Sykes, Chairman of the Board

D-U-N-S 17-715-5645
SYLVEST MANAGEMENT SYSTEM
   (Parent: Federal Data Corporation)
7501 Greenway Center Dr, Greenbelt, MD 20770
Phone: (301) 986-0800
Sales: $305,000,000   *Employees:* 155
Company Type: Private   *Employees here:* 120
SIC: 3571
   Computer system integration
Charles Mathews, Vice-President

D-U-N-S 06-469-6941
SYMANTEC CORPORATION
10201 Torre Ave, Cupertino, CA 95014
Phone: (408) 253-9600
Sales: $578,361,000   *Employees:* 2,300
Company Type: Public   *Employees here:* 400
SIC: 7372
   Develops markets and supports a diversified line of
     application and system software products
Gordon E Eubanks Jr, President

D-U-N-S 06-597-3067   EXP
SYMBOL TECHNOLOGIES INC.
1 Symbol Plz, Holtsville, NY 11742
Phone: (516) 738-2400
Sales: $774,345,000   *Employees:* 3,200
Company Type: Public   *Employees here:* 1,800
SIC: 3577
   Manufactures bar code optical scanning devices and other
Jerome Swartz, Chairman of the Board

D-U-N-S 16-149-9579
SYNOPSYS, INC.
700 E Middlefield Rd, Mountain View, CA 94043
Phone: (650) 962-5000
Sales: $717,940,000   *Employees:* 2,592
Company Type: Public   *Employees here:* 500
SIC: 7371
   Custom computer programming
Aart J De Geus, Chairman of the Board

D-U-N-S 10-844-4944   EXP
SYNTEL, INC.
2800 Livernois Rd, Ste. 400, Troy, MI 48083
Phone: (248) 619-2800
Sales: $124,338,000   *Employees:* 2,000
Company Type: Public   *Employees here:* 120
SIC: 7371
   Computer software systems programming services
Bharat Desai, President

D-U-N-S 14-847-9967
SYPRIS SOLUTIONS INC.
350 Starks Building, Louisville, KY 40202
Phone: (502) 585-5544
Sales: $217,355,000   *Employees:* 1,600
Company Type: Private   *Employees here:* 12
SIC: 3672
   Diversified industrial manufacturer and service company
Jeffrey T Gill, President

D-U-N-S 15-216-9884
SYSTEM RESOURCES CORPORATION
128 Wheeler Rd, Burlington, MA 01803
Phone: (781) 270-9228

Sales: $58,053,000   *Employees:* 500
Company Type: Private   *Employees here:* 100
SIC: 7373
   Engineering systems software development
Samir A Desai, President

D-U-N-S 07-339-8414
SYSTEM SOFTWARE ASSOCIATES
500 W Madison St, Chicago, IL 60661
Phone: (312) 258-6000
Sales: $420,800,000   *Employees:* 2,200
Company Type: Public   *Employees here:* 850
SIC: 7372
   Develops computer software
William M Stuek, Chairman of the Board

D-U-N-S 07-554-3579
SYSTEMS & COMPUTER TECH CORP.
4 Country View Rd, Malvern, PA 19355
Phone: (610) 647-5930
Sales: $403,668,000   *Employees:* 3,400
Company Type: Public   *Employees here:* 845
SIC: 7373
   Develops and packages software applications and onsite
     computer facilities management
Michael D Chamberlain, President

D-U-N-S 16-151-1795   EXP
SYSTEMS IN FOCUS INC.
27700b Sw Parkway Ave, Wilsonville, OR 97070
Phone: (503) 685-8888
Sales: $306,663,000   *Employees:* 525
Company Type: Public   *Employees here:* 475
SIC: 3577
   Mfg multimedia projection products
John V Harker, Chairman of the Board

D-U-N-S 78-041-7580
T D K COMPONENTS USA
   (Parent: T D K USA Corporation)
1 T D K Blvd, Peachtree City, GA 30269
Phone: (770) 631-0410
Sales: $70,000,000   *Employees:* 220
Company Type: Private   *Employees here:* 220
SIC: 3675
   Mfg capacitors
Noburo Nakamura, President

D-U-N-S 00-926-0894   EXP
TALLY PRINTER CORPORATION
8301 S 180th St, Kent, WA 98032
Phone: (425) 251-5500
Sales: $75,000,000   *Employees:* 350
Company Type: Private   *Employees here:* 300
SIC: 3577
   Mfg computer printers
William Munro, President

D-U-N-S 19-967-1074   EXP
TANGENT COMPUTER INC.
197 Airport Blvd, Burlingame, CA 94010
Phone: (650) 342-9388
Sales: $108,023,000   *Employees:* 187
Company Type: Private   *Employees here:* 107
SIC: 3571
   Mfg computers
Doug Monsour, President

D-U-N-S 06-934-1972
TASC, INC.
   (Parent: Litton Industries Inc)
55 Walkers Brook Dr, Reading, MA 01867
Phone: (781) 942-2000

       D&B/Gale Industry Handbook

Sales: $240,000,000   *Employees:* 2,800
Company Type: Public Family Member   *Employees here:* 500
SIC: 7373
    Applied information technology services
R E Hineman, President

D-U-N-S 06-459-8188   EXP
TATUNG COMPANY OF AMERICA INC.
2850 E El Presidio St, Long Beach, CA 90810
Phone: (310) 637-2105
Sales: $141,996,000   *Employees:* 360
Company Type: Private   *Employees here:* 270
SIC: 3571
    Mfg computers monitors televisions vcr's refrigerators &
      microwave ovens
Hsin-Chu Liu, President

D-U-N-S 00-735-9524   EXP
TECCOR ELECTRONICS INC.
    (Parent: Ranco Incorporated Delaware)
1800 Hurd Dr, Irving, TX 75038
Phone: (972) 580-1515
Sales: $105,000,000   *Employees:* 1,300
Company Type: Private   *Employees here:* 1,129
SIC: 3674
    Mfg semiconductors
Alfred G Lapierre, President

D-U-N-S 00-230-0556   EXP
TECHNITROL INC.
1210 Northbrook Dr, Langhorne, PA 19053
Phone: (215) 355-2900
Sales: $397,067,000   *Employees:* 14,400
Company Type: Public   *Employees here:* 10
SIC: 3679
    Mfg electronic components & modules electrical contacts
      laminating metal pdts
James M Papada III, Chief Executive Officer

D-U-N-S 80-945-9969
TECHNOLOGY SERVICE SOLUTIONS
1585 Paoli Pike, West Chester, PA 19380
Phone: (610) 344-3650
Sales: $534,700,000   *Employees:* 6,200
Company Type: Private   *Employees here:* 150
SIC: 7378
    Multivendor desktop service provider including maintenance
      software & network support
Marianne W Crew, Chief Executive Officer

D-U-N-S 18-776-9278
TECHNOLOGY SOLUTIONS COMPANY
205 N Michigan Ave, Chicago, IL 60601
Phone: (312) 228-4500
Sales: $271,875,000   *Employees:* 1,572
Company Type: Public   *Employees here:* 100
SIC: 7373
    System software development services & consulting
John T Kohler, President

D-U-N-S 05-590-6002   EXP
TECHSONIC INDUSTRIES INC.
    (Parent: Teleflex Incorporated)
5 Humminbird Ln, Eufaula, AL 36027
Phone: (334) 687-6613
Sales: $52,000,000   *Employees:* 285
Company Type: Public Family Member   *Employees here:* 255
SIC: 3679
    Mfg marine information systems
Steven Duvall, N/A

D-U-N-S 17-758-3390   EXP
TECHWORKS INC.
4030 W Braker Ln, Ste. 500, Austin, TX 78759
Phone: (512) 794-8533
Sales: $100,000,000   *Employees:* 75
Company Type: Private   *Employees here:* 60
SIC: 3674
    Mfg memory boards specifically d-ram
Yoshio Takahara, President

D-U-N-S 09-745-6099
TECSTAR, INC.
15251 Don Julian Rd, City Of Industry, CA 91745
Phone: (626) 968-3000
Sales: $140,000,000   *Employees:* 980
Company Type: Private   *Employees here:* 550
SIC: 3674
    Manufactures solar panel arrays and electromechanical
      components for aircraft
David M Van Buren, President

D-U-N-S 09-949-1235
TEKMARK GLOBAL SOLUTIONS LLC
100 Metroplex Dr, Ste. 102, Edison, NJ 08817
Phone: (732) 572-5400
Sales: $98,326,000   *Employees:* 900
Company Type: Private   *Employees here:* 650
SIC: 7379
    Supplemental staffing services
Guy Delgrande, President

D-U-N-S 80-996-6146   EXP
TELCOM SEMICONDUCTOR, INC.
1300 Terra Bella Ave, Mountain View, CA 94043
Phone: (650) 968-9252
Sales: $55,435,000   *Employees:* 321
Company Type: Public   *Employees here:* 175
SIC: 3674
    Mfg integrated circuits
Phillip M Drayer, President

D-U-N-S 10-864-9864   EXP
TELCORDIA TECHNOLOGIES INC.
    (Parent: Science Applications Intl Corp)
445 S St Morris Corp, Morristown, NJ 07960
Phone: (973) 740-3000
Sales: $477,200,000   *Employees:* 6,154
Company Type: Private   *Employees here:* 610
SIC: 7371
    Computer software development computer-related systems
      engineering applied & marketing research & training/
      consulting
Richard C Smith, Chief Executive Officer

D-U-N-S 08-237-2996
TELOS FIELD ENGINEERING INC.
    (Parent: Telos Corporation (california))
530 W 1500 S, Woods Cross, UT 84087
Phone: (801) 298-8000
Sales: $94,600,000   *Employees:* 1,100
Company Type: Public Family Member   *Employees here:* 25
SIC: 7378
    Repair services for computer sub-assemblies manufactures
      replacement memory systems & test equipment &
      equipment broker
Mark Hester, President

D-U-N-S 04-112-7879   EXP
TELXON CORPORATION
3330 W Market St, Akron, OH 44333
Phone: (330) 867-3700

Sales: $465,870,000   *Employees:* 1,550
Company Type: Public   *Employees here:* 255
SIC: 3571
    Mfg portable microcomputer systems systems integration
      services
Frank E Brick, President

D-U-N-S 60-226-2990   EXP
TENNESSEE DENSO MANUFACTURING
    (Parent: Denso International America)
1720 Robert C Jackson Dr, Maryville, TN 37801
Phone: (423) 982-7000
Sales: $800,000,000   *Employees:* 2,552
Company Type: Private   *Employees here:* 1,600
SIC: 3694
    Mfg automotive parts & accessories
Kiyohiro Shimotsu, President

D-U-N-S 00-732-1904   EXP
TEXAS INSTRUMENTS INCORPORATED
8505 Forest Ln, Dallas, TX 75243
Phone: (972) 995-2011
Sales: $8,460,000,000   *Employees:* 36,400
Company Type: Public   *Employees here:* 9,900
SIC: 3674
    Mfg semiconductors & related devices electronic circuits &
      connectors clad metals calculators
Thomas J Engibous, Chairman of the Board

D-U-N-S 07-389-6714
TEXAS MICROSYSTEMS INC.
    (Parent: Texas Micro Inc)
5959 Corporate Dr, Houston, TX 77036
Phone: (713) 541-8200
Sales: $70,940,000   *Employees:* 350
Company Type: Public Family Member   *Employees here:* 300
SIC: 3577
    Mfg computer peripheral equipment
John C Leonardo Jr, Chief Operating Officer

D-U-N-S 14-836-6677   EXP
THREE-FIVE SYSTEMS, INC.
1600 N Desert Dr, Tempe, AZ 85281
Phone: (602) 389-8600
Sales: $84,642,000   *Employees:* 459
Company Type: Public   *Employees here:* 174
SIC: 3577
    Mfg integrated graphic display systems light emitting diodes
      & liquid crystal displays
David R Buchanan, Chairman of the Board

D-U-N-S 18-665-4752
TIBCO FINANCE TECHNOLOGY INC.
3165 Porter Dr, Palo Alto, CA 94304
Phone: (650) 846-5000
Sales: $100,000,000   *Employees:* 500
Company Type: Private   *Employees here:* 200
SIC: 7373
    Systems integration
Vivek Y Ranadive, Chairman of the Board

D-U-N-S 82-511-2915   EXP
TIER TECHNOLOGIES, INC.
1350 Treat Blvd, Ste. 250, Walnut Creek, CA 94596
Phone: (925) 937-3950
Sales: $57,725,000   *Employees:* 308
Company Type: Public   *Employees here:* 200
SIC: 7373
    Professional information technology (it) consulting
      application development & software engineering services
James L Bildner, Chairman of the Board

D-U-N-S 62-165-3245   EXP
TIVOLI SYSTEMS INC.
    (Parent: International Bus Mchs Corp)
9442 N Capital Of Texas H, Austin, TX 78759
Phone: (512) 436-8000
Sales: $1,400,000,000   *Employees:* 3,600
Company Type: Public Family Member   *Employees here:* 1,800
SIC: 7371
    Computer software development
Jan Lindelow, Chairman of the Board

D-U-N-S 79-617-2583
TOPPAN ELECTRONICS INC.
7770 Miramar Rd, San Diego, CA 92126
Phone: (619) 695-2222
Sales: $135,000,000   *Employees:* 500
Company Type: Private   *Employees here:* 500
SIC: 3672
    Mfg printed circuit boards
Noaki Iwata, President

D-U-N-S 60-645-6119
TOSHIBA AMER ELCTRNIC CMPNENTS
    (Parent: Toshiba America Inc)
9775 Toledo Way, Irvine, CA 92618
Phone: (949) 455-2000
Sales: $116,100,000   *Employees:* 2,000
Company Type: Private   *Employees here:* 300
SIC: 3679
    Mfg and whol electronic components
Hideo Ito, Chairman of the Board

D-U-N-S 19-409-6525
TOSHIBA AMER INFO SYSTEMS INC.
    (Parent: Toshiba America Inc)
9740 Irvine Blvd, Irvine, CA 92618
Phone: (949) 583-3000
Sales: $4,104,584,000   *Employees:* 3,600
Company Type: Private   *Employees here:* 2,500
SIC: 3571
    Mfg electronic computers computer peripheral equipment
      photocopy machines computer disk drives telephone
      systems & facsimile
Atsutoshi Nishida, President

D-U-N-S 60-408-5944
TOTAL PERIPHERALS, INC.
102 Otis St, Northborough, MA 01532
Phone: (508) 393-1777
Sales: $90,502,000   *Employees:* 130
Company Type: Private   *Employees here:* 80
SIC: 3571
    Mfg & whol computers & peripheral equipment
Rex Chen, President

D-U-N-S 10-199-1222
TOTAL SYSTEM SERVICES INC.
    (Parent: Columbus Bank & Trust Company)
1200 6th Ave, Columbus, GA 31901
Phone: (706) 649-2310
Sales: $187,787,000   *Employees:* 2,500
Company Type: Public   *Employees here:* 27
SIC: 7374
    Data processing services
Richard W Ussery, Chairman of the Board

D-U-N-S 10-393-3453
TRACOR SYSTEM TECHNOLOGIES
    (Parent: Tracor Inc)
1601 Research Blvd, Rockville, MD 20850
Phone: (301) 738-4000

Sales: $400,000,000   *Employees:* 4,500
Company Type: Private   *Employees here:* 1,700
SIC: 7373
   Systems design systems engineering & systems integration
Barry G Campbell, Chief Executive Officer

D-U-N-S 95-839-2557
TRANSACT TECHNOLOGIES INC.
7 Laser Ln, Wallingford, CT 06492
Phone: (203) 269-1198
Sales: $58,400,000   *Employees:* 240
Company Type: Public   *Employees here:* 4
SIC: 3577
   Mfg transaction based printers and printer peripherals
Bart C Shuldman, President

D-U-N-S 84-748-6990
TRANSACTION SYSTEMS ARCHITECTS
224 S 108th Ave, Ste. 7, Omaha, NE 68154
Phone: (402) 334-5101
Sales: $289,761,000   *Employees:* 2,054
Company Type: Public   *Employees here:* 15
SIC: 7372   ·
   Software development
David C Russell, Chief Operating Officer

D-U-N-S 15-074-2583
TRANSCORE
   (Parent: Science Applications Intl Corp)
7611 Derry St, Harrisburg, PA 17111
Phone: (717) 561-2400
Sales: $75,000,000   *Employees:* 365
Company Type: Private   *Employees here:* 70
SIC: 7373
   Systerm intergration of telecommunication equipment
Russell S Lewis, Chief Executive Officer

D-U-N-S 09-271-3148   EXP
TRANSPO ELECTRONICS INC.
2150 Brengle Ave, Orlando, FL 32808
Phone: (407) 298-4563
Sales: $72,015,000   *Employees:* 750
Company Type: Private   *Employees here:* 720
SIC: 3694
   Mfg voltage regulators & whol automotive parts
Frank C Oropeza, President

D-U-N-S 87-890-3145
TRANSQUEST HOLDINGS INC.
   (Parent: Delta Air Lines Inc)
1001 International Blvd, Atlanta, GA 30354
Phone: (404) 714-1500
Sales: $124,300,000   *Employees:* 1,600
Company Type: Public Family Member   *Employees here:* 1,568
SIC: 7371
   Technology services
Bill Belew, President

D-U-N-S 14-688-1875
TRI-COR INDUSTRIES INC.
2900 Eisenhower Ave, Alexandria, VA 22314
Phone: (703) 682-2000
Sales: $53,179,000   *Employees:* 576
Company Type: Private   *Employees here:* 30
SIC: 7373
   Data processing support systems integrators
Louis Gonzalez, President

D-U-N-S 17-431-0763   EXP
TRIAD DATA INC.
   (Parent: Renaissance Worldwide Inc)
515 Madison Ave, Fl 1810, New York, NY 10022
Phone: (212) 758-1010

Sales: $77,000,000   *Employees:* 500
Company Type: Public Family Member   *Employees here:* 175
SIC: 7379
   Computer consultants
Harley Lippman, President

D-U-N-S 09-401-2242
TRIDENT DATA SYSTEMS INC.
5933 W Century Blvd, Ste. 7, Los Angeles, CA 90045
Phone: (310) 645-6483
Sales: $94,000,000   *Employees:* 936
Company Type: Private   *Employees here:* 80
SIC: 7379
   Computer system consultant provider of systems integration
     services and application development
Joe Parks Jr, Chief Executive Officer

D-U-N-S 18-105-9304
TRIDENT MICROSYSTEMS INC.
189 Bernardo Ave, Mountain View, CA 94043
Phone: (650) 691-9211
Sales: $113,002,000   *Employees:* 439
Company Type: Public   *Employees here:* 210
SIC: 3674
   Mfg very large scale integrated circuit graphics & multimedia
     products
Jung-Herng Chang, Senior Vice-President

D-U-N-S 79-110-1728   EXP
TRIGEM AMERICA CORPORATION
14350 Myford Rd, Irvine, CA 92606
Phone: (714) 481-3636
Sales: $126,193,000   *Employees:* 50
Company Type: Private   *Employees here:* 50
SIC: 3571
   Mfg personal computers
Chung Chul, Chief Executive Officer

D-U-N-S 00-509-4099   EXP
TRIPPE MANUFACTURING COMPANY
1111 W 35th St, Chicago, IL 60609
Phone: (312) 755-5400
Sales: $125,000,000   *Employees:* 400
Company Type: Private   *Employees here:* 398
SIC: 3679
   Mfg electronic power supplies
Elbert Howell, Chief Executive Officer

D-U-N-S 04-544-4635
TRIQUINT SEMICONDUCTOR, INC.
2300 Ne Brookwood Pkwy, Hillsboro, OR 97124
Phone: (503) 615-9000
Sales: $71,367,000   *Employees:* 361
Company Type: Public   *Employees here:* 356
SIC: 3674
   Mfg semiconductors
Steve Sharp, President

D-U-N-S 12-420-5352
TSR CONSULTING SERVICES INC.
   (Parent: TSR Inc)
400 Oser Ave, Ste. 400, Hauppauge, NY 11788
Phone: (516) 231-0333
Sales: $60,000,000   *Employees:* 200
Company Type: Public Family Member   *Employees here:* 20
SIC: 7379
   Computer consultants
Ernie Bago, President

D-U-N-S 04-308-1405
TSR, INC.
400 Oser Ave, Ste. 400, Hauppauge, NY 11788
Phone: (516) 231-0333

Sales: $70,435,000
Company Type: Public
SIC: 7371
   Computer programming
Joseph F Hughes, Chairman of the Board

Employees: 350
Employees here: 55

D-U-N-S 07-326-8039
TULLETT & TOKYO FOREX INC.
80 Pine St, New York, NY 10005
Phone: (212) 208-2000
Sales: $232,800,000
Company Type: Private
SIC: 7371
   Computer programming services & depository banking
    services commodity contract broker
Timothy Boyle, President

Employees: 3,000
Employees here: 500

D-U-N-S 88-402-5834
TYCO PRINTED CIRCUIT GROUP
   (Parent: Tyco International (US) Inc)
4 Old Monson Rd, Stafford Springs, CT 06076
Phone: (860) 684-5881
Sales: $78,100,000
Company Type: Private
SIC: 3672
   Mfg printed circuit boards & assembles backplanes
L D Kozlowski, President

Employees: 1,200
Employees here: 300

D-U-N-S 11-871-7529
U M I & COMPANY
   (Parent: Bell & Howell Company)
300 N Zeeb Rd, Ann Arbor, MI 48103
Phone: (734) 761-4700
Sales: $94,800,000
Company Type: Public Family Member
SIC: 7375
   Information retrieval services
Joseph P Reynolds, President

Employees: 1,335
Employees here: 800

D-U-N-S 83-750-1725
U S CAPITAL EQUIPMENT LESSORS
4010 Barranca Pkwy, Irvine, CA 92604
Phone: (949) 451-1600
Sales: $150,000,000
Company Type: Private
SIC: 7377
   Capital equipment & computer equipment leasing
Monty Ruff, President

Employees: 25
Employees here: 20

D-U-N-S 87-842-3110
U S EPSON INC.
20770 Madrona Ave, Torrance, CA 90503
Phone: (310) 782-0770
Sales: $175,400,000
Company Type: Private
SIC: 3577
   Holding company
Akihiko Sakai, President

Employees: 1,630
Employees here: 1

D-U-N-S 78-894-1474
UNICOMP INC.
1850 Parkway Pl SE, Marietta, GA 30067
Phone: (770) 424-3684
Sales: $52,106,000
Company Type: Public
SIC: 7372
   Computer hardware & software design
Stephen A Hafer, President

Employees: 360
Employees here: 313

D-U-N-S 01-071-2847
UNIGRAPHICS SOLUTIONS INC.
   (Parent: Electronic Data Systems Corp)
13736 Riverport Dr, Maryland Heights, MO 63043

Phone: (314) 344-5900
Sales: $400,000,000
Company Type: Public
SIC: 3695
   Manufacture computer software
John Mazzola, President

Employees: 2,000
Employees here: 400

D-U-N-S 02-281-0311
UNIPHASE CORPORATION
163 Baypointe Pkwy, San Jose, CA 95134
Phone: (408) 434-1800
Sales: $175,801,000
Company Type: Public
SIC: 3674
   Mfg semiconductors & related devices
Kevin N Kalkhoven, Chairman of the Board

Employees: 976
Employees here: 350

D-U-N-S 36-402-4828
UNISON INDUSTRIES LTD PARTNR
7575 Baymeadows Way, Jacksonville, FL 32256
Phone: (904) 739-4000
Sales: $150,000,000
Company Type: Private
SIC: 3694
   Mfg ignition & other electrical components
Frederick B Sontag, President

Employees: 1,150
Employees here: 450

D-U-N-S 00-535-8932   EXP
UNISYS CORPORATION
Township Ln Nion Mtg Rads, Blue Bell, PA 19422
Phone: (215) 986-4011
Sales: $7,208,400,000
Company Type: Public
SIC: 7373
   Mfg computers systems servers & software peripherals
    systems integration & outsourcing svcs computer equip
    maintenance
Lawrence A Weinbach, Chairman of the Board

Employees: 33,200
Employees here: 3,400

D-U-N-S 08-139-8612   EXP
UNIT PARTS COMPANY
4600 Se 59th St, Oklahoma City, OK 73135
Phone: (405) 677-3361
Sales: $93,100,000
Company Type: Private
SIC: 3694
   Remanufactures automotive alternators & starters
Jack D Vollbrecht Jr, President

Employees: 1,500
Employees here: 1,480

D-U-N-S 00-152-7852   EXP
UNITED INDUSTRIAL CORPORATION
570 Lexington Ave, New York, NY 10022
Phone: (212) 752-8787
Sales: $235,183,000
Company Type: Public
SIC: 3699
   Mfr electronic training devices & detection equip
    ammunition industrial stokers
Richard R Erkeneff, President

Employees: 1,800
Employees here: 9

D-U-N-S 00-613-2828
UNITED OPTICAL TECH CORP.
1555 Williams Dr, Ste. 102, Marietta, GA 30066
Phone: (770) 426-4700
Sales: $100,000,000
Company Type: Private
SIC: 3699
   Design develop mfg electro optical long range surveillance
    systems
Alan E Rand, President

Employees: 5
Employees here: 5

D-U-N-S 00-141-4879   EXP
UNITRODE CORPORATION
7 Continental Blvd, Merrimack, NH 03054

Phone: (603) 424-2410
Sales: $177,603,000   *Employees:* 668
Company Type: Public   *Employees here:* 500
SIC: 3674
  Mfg integrated circuits
Robert J Richardson, Chairman of the Board

D-U-N-S 13-755-7450
UNIVERSAL COMPUTER NETWORK
6700 Hollister St, Houston, TX 77040
Phone: (713) 718-1800
Sales: $78,900,000   *Employees:* 600
Company Type: Private   *Employees here:* 600
SIC: 7377
  Leases computer data circuit lines and telephone lines
Robert Brockman, President

D-U-N-S 60-324-6695
UNIVERSAL SYSTEMS INC.
14585 Avion Pkwy, Chantilly, VA 20151
Phone: (703) 222-2840
Sales: $78,123,000   *Employees:* 340
Company Type: Private   *Employees here:* 225
SIC: 7373
  Computer systems integration
Robert E La Rose, President

D-U-N-S 06-653-7309
US BANCORP INFO SVCS CORP.
  (*Parent:* U S Bancorp)
332 Minnesota St, Saint Paul, MN 55101
Phone: (612) 973-1111
Sales: $143,000,000   *Employees:* 2,247
Company Type: Public Family Member   *Employees here:* 848
SIC: 7374
  Data processing services
Phil Heasley, Chairman of the Board

D-U-N-S 07-155-5254   EXP
USCS INTERNATIONAL, INC.
2969 Prospect Park Dr, Rancho Cordova, CA 95670
Phone: (916) 636-4500
Sales: $299,346,000   *Employees:* 2,038
Company Type: Public   *Employees here:* 146
SIC: 7371
  Computer programming services/fulfillment services
James C Castle, Chairman of the Board

D-U-N-S 17-517-3293
USER TECHNOLOGY ASSOCIATES
950 N Glebe Rd, Arlington, VA 22203
Phone: (703) 522-5132
Sales: $57,437,000   *Employees:* 760
Company Type: Private   *Employees here:* 100
SIC: 7373
  Computer systems engineering
Yong K Kim, President

D-U-N-S 36-163-2342
USG INTERIORS INTERNATIONAL
  (*Parent:* Usg Interiors Inc (del))
125 S Franklin St, Chicago, IL 60606
Phone: (312) 606-4000
Sales: $109,800,000   *Employees:* NA
Company Type: Public Family Member   *Employees here:* NA
SIC: 3699
  Mfg grids
J B James, President

D-U-N-S 79-548-0698
UTMC MICROELECTRONIC SYSTEMS
  (*Parent:* United Technologies Corp)
4350 Centennial Blvd, Colorado Springs, CO 80907
Phone: (719) 594-8000

Sales: $74,800,000   *Employees:* 340
Company Type: Public Family Member   *Employees here:* 330
SIC: 3674
  Mfg semiconductors
Charles H Ide, Chief Executive Officer

D-U-N-S 02-118-8396   EXP
V L S I TECHNOLOGY INC.
1240 Mc Kay Dr, San Jose, CA 95131
Phone: (408) 434-3000
Sales: $712,653,000   *Employees:* 2,500
Company Type: Public   *Employees here:* 1,250
SIC: 3674
  Mfg integrated circuits
Alfred J Stein, Chairman of the Board

D-U-N-S 78-694-0056   EXP
VANTIVE CORPORATION
2455 Augustine Dr, Santa Clara, CA 95054
Phone: (408) 982-5700
Sales: $117,346,000   *Employees:* 451
Company Type: Public   *Employees here:* 250
SIC: 7372
  Business oriented computer software
John R Luongo, Chairman of the Board

D-U-N-S 06-334-4022
VEBA CORPORATION
605 3rd Ave, Fl 44, New York, NY 10158
Phone: (212) 922-2700
Sales: $4,000,000,000   *Employees:* 9,100
Company Type: Private   *Employees here:* 12
SIC: 3674
  Mfg silicon wafers & chemical products & whol industrial
    chemicals petroleum products industrial supplies ferroalloys
    & coal
H H Putthoff, President

D-U-N-S 01-562-5890   EXP
VECTRON TECHNOLOGIES INC.
  (*Parent:* Dover Technologies Intl)
267 Lowell Rd, Hudson, NH 03051
Phone: (603) 598-0070
Sales: $60,000,000   *Employees:* 225
Company Type: Public Family Member   *Employees here:* 225
SIC: 3679
  Mfg electronic components
Terence Ede, President

D-U-N-S 05-051-5022   EXP
VERBATIM CORPORATION
  (*Parent:* Mitsubishi Chemical Amer Inc)
1200 W Wt Harris Blvd, Charlotte, NC 28262
Phone: (704) 547-6500
Sales: $400,000,000   *Employees:* 1,100
Company Type: Private   *Employees here:* 120
SIC: 3695
  Mfg magnetic storage disks tape digital data cassettes &
    cartridges optical disks imaging products cd-rom &
    transparencies
Naoto Wada, President

D-U-N-S 01-446-6825   EXP
VERIFONE INC.
  (*Parent:* Hewlett-Packard Company)
4988 Gr America Pkwy, Santa Clara, CA 95054
Phone: (408) 496-0444
Sales: $273,400,000   *Employees:* 3,300
Company Type: Public Family Member   *Employees here:* 190
SIC: 3578
  Mfg transaction automation systems produce software mfg
    computer peripherals
Robin Abrams, President

D-U-N-S 06-475-9079
VERITAS SOFTWARE CORPORATION
1600 Plymouth St, Mountain View, CA 94043
Phone: (650) 335-8000
Sales: $121,125,000   *Employees:* 579
Company Type: Public   *Employees here:* 350
SIC: 7372
    Business oriented computer software
Mark Leslie, Chairman of the Board

D-U-N-S 19-744-1496
VERSYSS INCORPORATED
    (Parent: Physician Computer Network)
1200 The American Rd, Morris Plains, NJ 07950
Phone: (973) 490-3200
Sales: $60,000,000   *Employees:* 145
Company Type: Private   *Employees here:* 80
SIC: 7371
    Computer software and hardware development & turnkey
    business solutions
Henry Green, President

D-U-N-S 10-276-8504   EXP
VIASOFT, INC.
3033 N 44th St, Ste. 101, Phoenix, AZ 85018
Phone: (602) 952-0050
Sales: $113,687,000   *Employees:* 450
Company Type: Public   *Employees here:* 200
SIC: 7371
    Application computer software
Steven D Whiteman, President

D-U-N-S 00-664-4199
VIASYSTEMS GROUP INC.
101 S Hanley Rd, Saint Louis, MO 63105
Phone: (314) 727-2087
Sales: $600,000,000   *Employees:* 2,100
Company Type: Private   *Employees here:* 5
SIC: 3672
    Mfg printed circuit boards
James N Mills, Chairman of the Board

D-U-N-S 12-977-4279
VIASYSTEMS INC.
    (Parent: Viasystems Group Inc)
101 S Hanley Rd, Saint Louis, MO 63105
Phone: (314) 727-2087
Sales: $136,900,000   *Employees:* 2,100
Company Type: Private   *Employees here:* 5
SIC: 3672
    Mfgs circuit boards and backpanels
James N Mills, Chairman of the Board

D-U-N-S 04-852-4081   EXP
VIASYSTEMS TECHNOLOGIES LLC
4500 S Laburnum Ave, Richmond, VA 23231
Phone: (804) 226-5000
Sales: $390,000,000   *Employees:* 2,468
Company Type: Private   *Employees here:* 2,060
SIC: 3672
    Mfgs printed circuit boards and backpanels
James N Mills, Chief Executive Officer

D-U-N-S 11-329-6784
VICTRON INC.
6600 Stevenson Blvd, Fremont, CA 94538
Phone: (510) 360-2222
Sales: $109,461,000   *Employees:* 450
Company Type: Private   *Employees here:* 450
SIC: 3672
    Printed circuit board assembly
Doo S Yun, President

D-U-N-S 96-660-2682   EXP
VIDEO MONITORING SVCS AMER LP
330 W 42nd St, Fl 28, New York, NY 10036
Phone: (212) 736-2010
Sales: $56,800,000   *Employees:* 800
Company Type: Private   *Employees here:* 300
SIC: 7375
    Broadcast information retrieval service
Robert Cohen, President

D-U-N-S 78-040-4067
VIDEOSERVER INC.
63 3rd Ave, Burlington, MA 01803
Phone: (781) 229-2000
Sales: $53,495,000   *Employees:* 98
Company Type: Public   *Employees here:* 98
SIC: 3571
    Mfg networking equipment
Khoa Nguyen, President

D-U-N-S 12-161-8110
VIEWLOGIC SYSTEMS INC.
293 Boston Post Rd W, Marlborough, MA 01752
Phone: (508) 480-0881
Sales: $62,000,000   *Employees:* 240
Company Type: Public   *Employees here:* 125
SIC: 7373
    Designs develops & markets software for computer aided
    engineering (cae)
William J Herman, President

D-U-N-S 60-304-6483
VIKING COMPONENTS INC.
30200 Avenida De Las, Rancho Santa Margari, CA 92688
Phone: (949) 643-7255
Sales: $260,652,000   *Employees:* 500
Company Type: Private   *Employees here:* 417
SIC: 3577
    Mfg computer peripheral equipment
Glenn Mc Cusker, President

D-U-N-S 60-251-5140   EXP
VIRTUALFUND.COM, INC.
7156 Shady Oak Rd, Eden Prairie, MN 55344
Phone: (612) 941-8687
Sales: $80,732,000   *Employees:* 404
Company Type: Public   *Employees here:* 10
SIC: 3577
    Mfg color printers typesetters filmsetters and related supplies
Robert J Wenzel, President

D-U-N-S 00-726-5382   EXP
VISHAY-DALE ELECTRONICS, INC.
    (Parent: Vishay-Dale Holdings Inc)
1122 23rd St, Columbus, NE 68601
Phone: (402) 564-3131
Sales: $230,751,000   *Employees:* 4,000
Company Type: Public Family Member   *Employees here:* 800
SIC: 3676
    Mfg resistors
Roland Reuschoff, Vice-President

D-U-N-S 14-758-0914   EXP
VISHAY-DALE HOLDINGS INC.
    (Parent: Vishay Intertechnology Inc)
1122 23rd St, Columbus, NE 68601
Phone: (402) 564-3131
Sales: $244,735,000   *Employees:* 4,129
Company Type: Public Family Member   *Employees here:* 7
SIC: 3676
    Mfg resistors
Dr Felix Zandman, Chairman of the Board

D-U-N-S 00-232-7484   EXP
VISHAY INTERTECHNOLOGY INC.
63 Lincoln Hwy, Malvern, PA 19355
Phone: (610) 644-1300
Sales: $1,125,219,000   *Employees:* 17,400
Company Type: Public   *Employees here:* 250
SIC: 3676
   Mfg electronic resistors
Felix Zandman, Chairman of the Board

D-U-N-S 00-118-6212   EXP
VISHAY VITRAMON INCORPORATED
   (*Parent:* Vishay Intertechnology Inc)
10 Main St, Monroe, CT 06468
Phone: (203) 268-6261
Sales: $66,000,000   *Employees:* 1,368
Company Type: Public Family Member   *Employees here:* 400
SIC: 3675
   Mfg & dist electronic capacitors
Michael J Smith, Vice-President

D-U-N-S 61-985-7147
VISIO CORP.
520 Pike St, Ste. 1800, Seattle, WA 98101
Phone: (206) 521-4500
Sales: $165,995,000   *Employees:* 555
Company Type: Public   *Employees here:* 300
SIC: 7372
   Business oriented computer software
Steve Gordon, Chief Financial Officer

D-U-N-S 18-815-7127   EXP
VISIONTEK, INC.
1175 Lakeside Dr, Gurnee, IL 60031
Phone: (847) 360-7500
Sales: $121,530,000   *Employees:* 200
Company Type: Private   *Employees here:* 175
SIC: 3577
   Mfg computer memory & related products
Allen Sutker, President

D-U-N-S 80-918-6331   EXP
VITECH AMERICA, INC.
8807 Nw 23rd St, Miami, FL 33172
Phone: (305) 477-1161
Sales: $117,537,000   *Employees:* 650
Company Type: Public   *Employees here:* 30
SIC: 3571
   Manufactures personal computers and consumer electronics
Georges C St Laurent III, Chairman of the Board

D-U-N-S 17-356-6738   EXP
VITESSE SEMICONDUCTOR CORP.
741 Calle Plano, Camarillo, CA 93012
Phone: (805) 388-3700
Sales: $175,082,000   *Employees:* 590
Company Type: Public   *Employees here:* 375
SIC: 3674
   Mfg gallium arsenide integrated microcircuits
Eugene F Hovanec, Chief Financial Officer

D-U-N-S 03-936-9749
VOLT DELTA RESOURCES, INC.
   (*Parent:* Volt Information Sciences Inc)
1221 Avenue Of The Americ, New York, NY 10020
Phone: (212) 827-2600
Sales: $60,500,000   *Employees:* 481
Company Type: Public Family Member   *Employees here:* 70
SIC: 7373
   Design installation & maintenance of computer systems
William Shaw, Chairman of the Board

D-U-N-S 62-194-8884   EXP
VTC INC.
2800 E Old Shakopee Rd, Minneapolis, MN 55425
Phone: (612) 853-5100
Sales: $174,000,000   *Employees:* 600
Company Type: Private   *Employees here:* 599
SIC: 3674
   Mfg integrated circuits
Larry Jodsaas, President

D-U-N-S 06-767-1362   EXP
W R Q INC.
1500 Dexter Ave N, Seattle, WA 98109
Phone: (206) 217-7500
Sales: $138,534,000   *Employees:* 710
Company Type: Private   *Employees here:* 650
SIC: 7372
   Computer software/host access software/unix/nt integration
     software & software management
Douglas Walker, President

D-U-N-S 13-266-9656   EXP
WABASH TECHNOLOGIES
   (*Parent:* Kearney-National Inc)
1375 Swan St, Huntington, IN 46750
Phone: (219) 356-8300
Sales: $140,000,000   *Employees:* 1,338
Company Type: Private   *Employees here:* 520
SIC: 3677
   Mfg electronic coils and industrial controls
Jerry Gallagher, Chief Executive Officer

D-U-N-S 16-176-1184   EXP
WACKER SEMICONDUCTOR HOLDING CORP.
7200 Nw Front Ave, Portland, OR 97210
Phone: (503) 243-2020
Sales: $123,200,000   *Employees:* 1,600
Company Type: Private   *Employees here:* 2
SIC: 3674
   Holding company
James Ellis, President

D-U-N-S 09-625-3737   EXP
WACKER SILTRONIC CORPORATION
   (*Parent:* Wacker Semicdtr Holdg Corp)
7200 Nw Front Ave, Portland, OR 97210
Phone: (503) 243-2020
Sales: $107,800,000   *Employees:* 1,400
Company Type: Private   *Employees here:* 1,385
SIC: 3674
   Mfg silicon wafers
James Ellis, President

D-U-N-S 07-295-1569
WALKER INTERACTIVE SYSTEMS
303 2nd St, San Francisco, CA 94107
Phone: (415) 495-8811
Sales: $71,409,000   *Employees:* 520
Company Type: Public   *Employees here:* 250
SIC: 7371
   Computer software development
Leonard Y Liu, Chairman of the Board

D-U-N-S 06-737-1542
WALL DATA INCORPORATED
11332 Ne 122nd Way, Kirkland, WA 98034
Phone: (425) 814-9255
Sales: $140,851,000   *Employees:* 793
Company Type: Public   *Employees here:* 250
SIC: 7372
   Business application software
John Wall, President

D-U-N-S 17-530-1720
WANG GOVERNMENT SERVICES INC.
  (Parent: Wang Laboratories Inc)
7900 Westpark Dr, Mc Lean, VA 22102
Phone: (703) 827-3000
Sales: $300,000,000   *Employees:* 1,000
Company Type: Public Family Member   *Employees here:* 700
SIC: 7373
    Computer systems integration systems design & engineering
    & whol computer hardware & software computer
    maintenance
James Hogan, President

D-U-N-S 00-101-8167   EXP
WANG LABORATORIES, INC.
290 Concord Rd, Billerica, MA 01821
Phone: (978) 967-5000
Sales: $1,887,000,000   *Employees:* 20,000
Company Type: Public   *Employees here:* 950
SIC: 7378
    Hardware maintenance network integration & support
    services
Joseph M Tucci, Chairman of the Board

D-U-N-S 00-912-1534   EXP
WATKINS-JOHNSON COMPANY
3333 Hillview Ave, Palo Alto, CA 94304
Phone: (650) 493-4141
Sales: $291,271,000   *Employees:* 2,400
Company Type: Public   *Employees here:* 900
SIC: 3674   .
    Mfg electronic systems semiconductor equipment
Dr W K Kennedy Jr, President

D-U-N-S 96-423-9990
WELLCOR AMERICA INC.
3030 Nw Expwy, Ste. 1500, Oklahoma City, OK 73112
Phone: (405) 951-4700
Sales: $75,000,000   *Employees:* 168
Company Type: Private   *Employees here:* 160
SIC: 7373
    Investment holding company
Jon Frieson, President

D-U-N-S 05-198-3567   EXP
WESTERN DIGITAL CORPORATION
8105 Irvine Center Dr, Irvine, CA 92618
Phone: (949) 932-5000
Sales: $3,541,225,000   *Employees:* 13,045
Company Type: Public   *Employees here:* 900
SIC: 3572
    Mfg computer disk drives
Charles A Haggerty, Chairman of the Board

D-U-N-S 13-187-4224
WHITTMAN-HART INC.
311 S Wacker Dr, Chicago, IL 60606
Phone: (312) 922-9200
Sales: $307,613,000   *Employees:* 1,674
Company Type: Public   *Employees here:* 700
SIC: 7371
    Information technology services
Robert F Bernard, Chairman of the Board

D-U-N-S 19-846-0511   EXP
WILLIAMS CONTROLS INC.
14100 Sw 72nd Ave, Portland, OR 97224
Phone: (503) 684-8600

Sales: $57,646,000   *Employees:* 511
Company Type: Public   *Employees here:* 175
SIC: 3679
    Mfg heavy vehicle agricultural equipment and electrical
    products
Gerard A Herlihy, Chief Financial Officer

D-U-N-S 15-170-8575   EXP
WIN LABORATORIES, LTD.
11090 Industrial Rd, Manassas, VA 20109
Phone: (703) 330-1426
Sales: $63,903,000   *Employees:* 180
Company Type: Private   *Employees here:* 120
SIC: 3571
    Mfg personal computers
Winfred V Wu, President

D-U-N-S 10-297-5448   EXP
WIND RIVER SYSTEMS INC.
500 Wind River Way, Alameda, CA 94501
Phone: (510) 748-4100
Sales: $92,400,000   *Employees:* 563
Company Type: Public   *Employees here:* 250
SIC: 7372
    Computer software development
Ronald A Abelmann, President

D-U-N-S 18-682-4231   EXP
WINTEC INDUSTRIES INC.
4280 Technology Dr, Fremont, CA 94538
Phone: (510) 770-9239
Sales: $700,000,000   *Employees:* 160
Company Type: Private   *Employees here:* 160
SIC: 3577
    Mfg computer peripheral equip & whol electronic parts &
    equip
William Jeng, President

D-U-N-S 62-536-4443   EXP
WIREKRAFT INDUSTRIES, INC.
  (Parent: International Wire Group Inc)
101 S Hanley Rd, Ste. 1075, Saint Louis, MO 63105
Phone: (314) 719-1000
Sales: $310,400,000   *Employees:* 5,000
Company Type: Private   *Employees here:* 22
SIC: 3694
    Mfg copper wire and cable and electric harness assemblies
James N Mills, Chairman of the Board

D-U-N-S 00-642-1051
WOODS INDUSTRIES INC.
  (Parent: Katy Industries Inc)
510 3rd Ave SW, Carmel, IN 46032
Phone: (317) 844-7261
Sales: $180,000,000   *Employees:* 900
Company Type: Public Family Member   *Employees here:* 250
SIC: 3699
    Mfg electrical equipment
Daniel Esposito, President

D-U-N-S 07-091-2811   EXP
WORLD WIDE AUTOMOTIVE INC.
  (Parent: Delco Remy International Inc)
130 W Brooke Rd, Winchester, VA 22603
Phone: (540) 667-9100
Sales: $102,000,000   *Employees:* 375
Company Type: Public Family Member   *Employees here:* 150
SIC: 3694
    Mfg rebuilt electrical auto equipment
Richard Keister, President

D-U-N-S 03-126-4307
WORLDCOM ADVANCED NETWORKS INC.
(*Parent:* MCI Worldcom Inc)
5000 Britton Rd, Hilliard, OH 43026
Phone: (614) 723-1741
Sales: $128,700,000   *Employees:* 1,500
Company Type: Public Family Member   *Employees here:* 1,500
SIC: 7373
    Computer systems design
Peter Van Camp, President

D-U-N-S 04-863-4331   EXP
XEROX COLORGRAFX SYSTEMS INC.
(*Parent:* Xerox Corporation)
5853 Rue Ferrari, San Jose, CA 95138
Phone: (408) 225-2800
Sales: $156,199,000   *Employees:* 310
Company Type: Public Family Member   *Employees here:* 280
SIC: 3577
    Designs & mfg plotters & printers
Barry R Lathan, President

D-U-N-S 11-431-9213
XETEL CORPORATION
2105 Gracy Farms Ln, Austin, TX 78758
Phone: (512) 435-1000
Sales: $112,685,000   *Employees:* 650
Company Type: Public   *Employees here:* 515
SIC: 3672
    Mfg custom design surface mount assemblies & engineering
      services
Angelo A Decaro Jr, President

D-U-N-S 09-701-6364   EXP
XICOR INC.
1511 Buckeye Dr, Milpitas, CA 95035
Phone: (408) 432-8888
Sales: $122,453,000   *Employees:* 738
Company Type: Public   *Employees here:* 700
SIC: 3674
    Mfg semiconductors
Raphael Klein, Chairman of the Board

D-U-N-S 11-816-8293   EXP
XILINX, INC.
2100 Logic Dr, San Jose, CA 95124
Phone: (408) 559-7778
Sales: $613,593,000   *Employees:* 1,391
Company Type: Public   *Employees here:* 988
SIC: 3674
    Mfg programmable logic devices & related development
      software
Willem Roelandts, President

D-U-N-S 19-935-7773   EXP
XIRCOM INC.
2300 Corporate Center Dr, Thousand Oaks, CA 91320
Phone: (805) 376-9300
Sales: $276,056,000   *Employees:* 1,000
Company Type: Public   *Employees here:* 163
SIC: 3577
    Designs develops and mfg computer network and
      connectivity products
Gates Dirk I, Chairman of the Board

D-U-N-S 94-598-1819
XLCONNECT SYSTEMS, INC.
(*Parent:* Xlconnect Solutions Inc)
411 Eagleview Blvd, Exton, PA 19341
Phone: (610) 458-5500

Sales: $170,000,000   *Employees:* 1,400
Company Type: Public Family Member   *Employees here:* 1,400
SIC: 7379
    Systems aggregator & value added consulting
Robert J Couture, Chairman of the Board

D-U-N-S 80-878-6461   EXP
XYLAN CORPORATION
26707 Agoura Rd, Calabasas, CA 91302
Phone: (818) 880-3500
Sales: $210,849,000   *Employees:* 721
Company Type: Public   *Employees here:* 239
SIC: 3577
    Mfg computer networking switching systems
Steve Y Kim, Chairman of the Board

D-U-N-S 04-901-5696   EXP
ZEBRA TECHNOLOGIES CORP.
333 Corporate Woods Pkwy, Vernon Hills, IL 60061
Phone: (847) 634-6700
Sales: $192,071,000   *Employees:* 745
Company Type: Public   *Employees here:* 600
SIC: 3577
    Mfg bar code printers supplies and software
Edward L Kaplan, Chairman of the Board

D-U-N-S 02-163-7293
ZENITH DATA SYSTEMS CORP.
(*Parent:* Packard Bell Nec)
2150 E Lake Cook Rd, Buffalo Grove, IL 60089
Phone: (000) 000-0000
Sales: $156,700,000   *Employees:* 1,300
Company Type: Private   *Employees here:* 1,300
SIC: 3571
    Mfg computers
Clifford Jenks, Chief Operating Officer

D-U-N-S 07-631-4459   EXP
ZILOG INC.
(*Parent:* Tpg Partners II Lp)
910 E Hamilton Ave, Campbell, CA 95008
Phone: (408) 558-8500
Sales: $204,738,000   *Employees:* 1,270
Company Type: Public   *Employees here:* 250
SIC: 3674
    Mfg integrated circuit products
Curtis J Crawford, President

RANKINGS AND COMPANIES

The companies presented in Chapter 4 - Company Directory are arranged in this chapter in rank order: by sales and by number of employees. Each company's name, rank, location, type, sales, employment figure, and primary SIC are shown. Only companies with reported sales data are included in the "rankings by sales" table; similarly, only companies that report employment data are ranked in the "rankings by employment" table.

Company type is either Public, Private, or Public Family Member. The last category is used to label corporate entities that belong to a group of companies, the relationship being that of a subsidiary or element of a parent. The parents of Public Family Member companies can be found in the company's directory entry presented in Chapter 4.

This product includes proprietary data of Dun & Bradstreet, Inc.

D&B COMPANY RANKINGS BY SALES

Company	Rank	Location	Type	Sales ($ mil.)	Employ- ment	Primary SIC
International Business Machines Corp.	1	Armonk, NY	Public	78,508.0	269,465	3571
Hewlett-Packard Company	2	Palo Alto, CA	Public	47,061.0	124,600	3571
Compaq Computer Corporation	3	Houston, TX	Public	31,169.0	80,000	3571
Intel Corporation	4	Santa Clara, CA	Public	26,273.0	63,700	3674
Electronic Data Systems Corp.	5	Plano, TX	Public	15,235.6	110,000	7374
Microsoft Corporation	6	Redmond, WA	Public	14,484.0	27,320	7372
Dell Computer Corporation	7	Round Rock, TX	Public	12,327.0	13,500	3571
IBM World Trade Europe	8	Armonk, NY	Public Family Member	10,742.9	99,900	3577
Sun Microsystems Inc.	9	Palo Alto, CA	Public	9,790.8	26,300	3571
Texas Instruments Incorporated	10	Dallas, TX	Public	8,460.0	36,400	3674
Cisco Systems Inc.	11	San Jose, CA	Public	8,458.8	15,000	3577
Unisys Corporation	12	Blue Bell, PA	Public	7,208.4	33,200	7373
Oracle Corporation	13	Redwood City, CA	Public	7,143.9	36,802	7372
Seagate Technology Inc.	14	Scotts Valley, CA	Public	6,819.0	87,000	3572
SCI Systems Inc.	15	Huntsville, AL	Public	6,805.9	22,324	3571
Computer Sciences Corporation	16	El Segundo, CA	Public	6,600.8	45,000	7379
NCR Corporation	17	Dayton, OH	Public	6,505.0	38,300	3571
Gateway, Inc.	18	North Sioux City, SD	Public	6,293.7	13,300	3571
Digital Equipment Corporation	19	Maynard, MA	Public Family Member	5,989.9	50,000	3571
Apple Computer Inc.	20	Cupertino, CA	Public	5,941.0	6,658	3571
Quantum Corporation	21	Milpitas, CA	Public	5,803.2	6,219	3572
AMP Incorporated	22	Harrisburg, PA	Public	5,745.2	46,526	3678
3Com Corporation	23	Santa Clara, CA	Public	5,420.4	12,920	7373
Solectron Corporation	24	Milpitas, CA	Public	5,288.3	24,857	3672
First Data Corporation	25	Hackensack, NJ	Public	5,234.5	36,000	7374
Automatic Data Processing	26	Roseland, NJ	Public	4,798.1	34,000	7374
Computer Associates International	27	Hauppauge, NY	Public	4,719.0	11,400	7372
Toshiba Amer Info Systems Inc.	28	Irvine, CA	Private	4,104.6	3,600	3571
Veba Corporation	29	New York, NY	Private	4,000.0	9,100	3674
Western Digital Corporation	30	Irvine, CA	Public	3,541.2	13,045	3572
Comdisco Inc.	31	Des Plaines, IL	Public	3,243.0	2,800	7377
Silicon Graphics Inc.	32	Mountain View, CA	Public	3,100.6	10,286	3571
Lexmark International Group	33	Lexington, KY	Public	3,020.6	8,000	3577
Micron Technology Inc.	34	Boise, ID	Public	3,011.9	15,300	3571
Emc Corporation	35	Hopkinton, MA	Private	2,937.9	6,400	3572
Olin-Asahi Interconnect Tech	36	Norwalk, CT	Public Family Member	2,638.0	220	3674
Advanced Micro Devices Inc.	37	Sunnyvale, CA	Public	2,542.1	12,800	3674
National Semiconductor Corp.	38	Santa Clara, CA	Public	2,536.7	13,000	3674
Entex Information Services	39	Port Chester, NY	Private	2,456.6	8,000	7373
Storage Technology Corporation	40	Louisville, CO	Public	2,258.2	8,300	3572
AST Research, Inc.	41	Irvine, CA	Private	2,103.6	3,000	3571
Imation Corp.	42	Saint Paul, MN	Public	2,046.5	9,800	3695
Fujitsu America Inc.	43	San Jose, CA	Private	2,000.0	4,047	3577
Wang Laboratories, Inc.	44	Billerica, MA	Public	1,887.0	20,000	7378
Raychem Corporation	45	Menlo Park, CA	Public	1,798.5	9,036	3678
Sabre Group, Inc.	46	Fort Worth, TX	Public Family Member	1,783.5	10,300	7371
Iomega Corporation	47	Roy, UT	Public	1,740.0	4,816	3572
NEC Electronics Inc.	48	Santa Clara, CA	Private	1,738.0	2,800	3674
Micron Electronics, Inc.	49	Nampa, ID	Public	1,733.4	2,750	3571
Alcoa Fujikura Ltd.	50	Brentwood, TN	Public Family Member	1,700.0	35,000	3694
Camelot Corporation	51	Carrollton, TX	Public	1,662.0	95	7371
Molex Incorporated	52	Lisle, IL	Public	1,623.0	13,000	3678
Intel Puerto Rico Inc.	53	Las Piedras, PR	Public Family Member	1,500.0	2,600	3674
LSI Logic Corporation	54	Milpitas, CA	Public	1,490.7	4,443	3674
Ascend Communications Inc.	55	Alameda, CA	Public	1,478.7	1,644	3577
Data General Corporation	56	Westborough, MA	Public	1,462.1	4,700	3571
Amkor Technology, Inc.	57	West Chester, PA	Public	1,455.8	9,880	3674
Maxtor Corporation	58	Milpitas, CA	Public	1,424.3	5,700	3572
Tivoli Systems Inc.	59	Austin, TX	Public Family Member	1,400.0	3,600	7371
Cabletron Systems Inc.	60	Rochester, NH	Public	1,377.3	6,887	3577
Goldleaf Technologies, Inc.	61	Hahira, GA	Public Family Member	1,366.1	70	7371
J M Huber Corporation	62	Edison, NJ	Private	1,298.6	5,153	3699
Jabil Circuit Inc.	63	Saint Petersburg, FL	Public	1,277.4	3,661	3672
Fiserv Inc.	64	Brookfield, WI	Public	1,233.7	12,500	7374
Analog Devices, Inc.	65	Norwood, MA	Public	1,230.6	7,200	3674
HBO & Company	66	Atlanta, GA	Public	1,203.2	6,286	7372
Digital Equipment Corp International	67	Acton, MA	Public Family Member	1,198.8	10,000	3571
Dell Products LP	68	Round Rock, TX	Private	1,198.8	10,000	3571
Diebold Incorporated	69	Canton, OH	Public	1,185.7	6,489	3578
Dyncorp	70	Reston, VA	Private	1,145.9	16,100	7373

D&B COMPANY RANKINGS BY SALES

Company	Rank	Location	Type	Sales ($ mil.)	Employ- ment	Primary SIC
Acer America Corporation	71	San Jose, CA	Private	1,141.2	1,348	3571
Compuware Corporation	72	Farmington Hills, MI	Public	1,139.3	8,663	7371
Vishay Intertechnology Inc.	73	Malvern, PA	Public	1,125.2	17,400	3676
Intergraph Corporation	74	Huntsville, AL	Public	1,124.3	7,700	7373
Flextronics International Ltd.	75	San Jose, CA	Private	1,113.1	11,300	3672
Novell, Inc.	76	Provo, UT	Public	1,083.9	4,510	7373
Galileo International Inc.	77	Des Plaines, IL	Public	1,070.0	1,909	7375
Parametric Technology Corp.	78	Waltham, MA	Public	1,018.0	4,911	7372
First Data Resources Inc.	79	Omaha, NE	Public Family Member	1,013.2	6,000	7374
Metamor Worldwide Inc.	80	Houston, TX	Public	1,008.1	33,650	7371
Adaptec Inc.	81	Milpitas, CA	Public	1,007.3	3,276	3577
Paychex, Inc.	82	Rochester, NY	Public	993.4	4,440	7374
Packard Bell Nec	83	Sacramento, CA	Private	959.2	8,000	3571
Atmel Corporation	84	San Jose, CA	Public	958.3	6,100	3674
Cirrus Logic Inc.	85	Fremont, CA	Public	954.3	2,135	3674
Amdahl Corporation	86	Sunnyvale, CA	Private	948.8	11,000	7378
J.D. Edwards & Company	87	Denver, CO	Public	934.0	4,950	7372
Sanmina Corporation	88	San Jose, CA	Public	923.8	5,477	3672
Cadence Design Systems Inc.	89	San Jose, CA	Public	915.9	5,102	7372
Electronic Arts	90	Redwood City, CA	Public	908.9	2,100	7372
Sybase, Inc.	91	Emeryville, CA	Public	903.9	5,484	7372
Adobe Systems Incorporated	92	San Jose, CA	Public	894.8	2,680	7372
Amphenol Corporation	93	Wallingford, CT	Public	884.3	6,900	3678
American Mgt Systems Inc.	94	Fairfax, VA	Public	872.3	7,100	7379
Sungard Data Systems Inc.	95	Wayne, PA	Public	862.2	4,500	7374
Sequent Computer Systems Inc.	96	Beaverton, OR	Public	833.9	2,818	3571
Hadco Corporation	97	Salem, NH	Public	826.4	7,673	3672
Raytheon Service Company	98	Burlington, MA	Public Family Member	817.0	6,200	7376
Peoplesoft, Inc.	99	Pleasanton, CA	Public	815.7	4,452	7372
ITT Defense & Electronics	100	Mc Lean, VA	Public Family Member	812.9	14,000	3679
Read-Rite Corporation	101	Milpitas, CA	Public	808.6	18,000	3679
Lotus Development Corporation	102	Cambridge, MA	Public Family Member	807.8	7,909	7372
DecisionOne Corporation	103	Malvern, PA	Public Family Member	805.7	6,500	7378
Tennessee Denso Manufacturing	104	Maryville, TN	Private	800.0	2,552	3694
Manufacturers Services Ltd.	105	Concord, MA	Private	800.0	2,800	3577
Fairchild Semiconductor Corp.	106	South Portland, ME	Private	789.2	6,927	3674
Berg Electronics Corp.	107	Saint Louis, MO	Private	785.2	7,000	3678
DII Group, Inc.	108	Longmont, CO	Public	779.6	6,350	3679
Stargate Systems, Inc.	109	Chicago, IL	Private	775.4	10,000	7371
Symbol Technologies Inc.	110	Holtsville, NY	Public	774.3	3,200	3577
BDM International Inc.	111	Mc Lean, VA	Public Family Member	770.8	9,000	7373
MEMC Electronic Materials	112	O'Fallon, MO	Public	758.9	6,100	3674
GTE Data Services Inc.	113	Tampa, FL	Public Family Member	753.5	3,800	7374
SAS Institute Inc.	114	Cary, NC	Private	747.7	5,285	7372
Platinum Technology International	115	Villa Park, IL	Public	738.9	5,000	7372
Siemens Microelectronics, Inc.	116	Cupertino, CA	Private	738.0	2,750	3674
Compaq Latin America Corp.	117	Houston, TX	Public Family Member	737.5	NA	3571
B M C Software Inc.	118	Houston, TX	Public	730.6	2,777	7372
Sterling Software Inc.	119	Dallas, TX	Public	719.9	3,600	7372
Synopsys, Inc.	120	Mountain View, CA	Public	717.9	2,592	7371
Avex Electronics Inc.	121	Huntsville, AL	Private	717.1	3,600	3699
Smart Modular Technologies	122	Fremont, CA	Public	714.7	831	3674
V L S I Technology Inc.	123	San Jose, CA	Public	712.7	2,500	3674
Wintec Industries Inc.	124	Fremont, CA	Private	700.0	160	3577
GE Information Services, Inc.	125	Rockville, MD	Public Family Member	700.0	2,400	7374
Stratus Computer, Inc.	126	Marlborough, MA	Public Family Member	688.3	2,487	3571
El Camino Resources International	127	Woodland Hills, CA	Private	678.2	548	7377
Kemet Electronics Corporation	128	Simpsonville, SC	Public Family Member	667.7	11,000	3675
Kemet Corporation	129	Simpsonville, SC	Public	667.7	10,300	3675
Informix Corporation	130	Menlo Park, CA	Public	662.3	3,800	7371
Keane Inc.	131	Boston, MA	Public	654.4	8,008	7373
Altera Corporation	132	San Jose, CA	Public	654.3	915	3674
DST Systems, Inc.	133	Kansas City, MO	Public	650.7	6,000	7374
Logicon Inc.	134	Herndon, VA	Public Family Member	650.0	5,000	7373
Cendant Software	135	Torrance, CA	Public Family Member	650.0	2,500	7372
National Data Corporation	136	Atlanta, GA	Public	649.0	6,100	7374
Bay Networks, Inc.	137	Santa Clara, CA	Private	641.0	5,960	3577
Komag Incorporated	138	San Jose, CA	Public	631.1	4,738	3695
Autodesk Inc.	139	San Rafael, CA	Public	617.1	2,470	7372
Xilinx, Inc.	140	San Jose, CA	Public	613.6	1,391	3674

D&B COMPANY RANKINGS BY SALES

Company	Rank	Location	Type	Sales ($ mil.)	Employ-ment	Primary SIC
Network Associates Inc.	141	Santa Clara, CA	Public	612.2	1,600	7371
Diamond Multimedia Systems	142	San Jose, CA	Public	608.6	841	3672
Banctec, Inc.	143	Dallas, TX	Public	603.5	4,000	7373
Viasystems Group Inc.	144	Saint Louis, MO	Private	600.0	2,100	3672
Solectron Texas LP	145	Austin, TX	Private	600.0	3,600	3571
Instinet Corporation	146	New York, NY	Private	600.0	700	7379
Cincinnati Bell Info Systems	147	Cincinnati, OH	Public Family Member	600.0	2,500	7373
Carlyle Partners Leveraged Cap	148	Washington, DC	Private	599.5	7,000	7373
Perot Systems Corporation	149	Dallas, TX	Public	599.4	5,600	7376
Intuit Inc.	150	Mountain View, CA	Public	592.7	2,860	7372
BTG, Inc.	151	Fairfax, VA	Public	588.9	1,400	7371
Analysts International Corp.	152	Minneapolis, MN	Public	587.4	5,571	7371
Integrated Device Technology	153	Santa Clara, CA	Public	587.1	5,000	3674
Policy Management Systems Corp.	154	Blythewood, SC	Public	582.8	6,017	7372
Symantec Corporation	155	Cupertino, CA	Public	578.4	2,300	7372
Maxim Integrated Products	156	Sunnyvale, CA	Public	560.2	3,066	3674
International Rectifier Corp.	157	El Segundo, CA	Public	551.9	4,395	3674
Ciber, Inc.	158	Englewood, CO	Public	550.4	5,700	7379
Cypress Semiconductor Corp.	159	San Jose, CA	Public	544.4	2,770	3674
Molex International Inc.	160	Lisle, IL	Public Family Member	540.5	7,671	3678
Technology Service Solutions	161	West Chester, PA	Private	534.7	6,200	7378
Netscape Communications Corp.	162	Mountain View, CA	Public	533.9	2,936	7372
Bell Microproducts Inc.	163	San Jose, CA	Public	533.7	650	3672
GT Interactive Software Corp.	164	New York, NY	Public	530.7	1,337	7372
Artesyn Technologies Inc.	165	Boca Raton, FL	Public	527.2	6,900	3679
Aspect Telecommunications Corp.	166	San Jose, CA	Public	512.3	1,600	7372
Holland America Inv Corp.	167	New York, NY	Private	510.5	5,000	7372
Alltel Information Services	168	Little Rock, AR	Public Family Member	510.2	8,000	7374
Sumitomo Sitix Silicon Inc.	169	Fremont, CA	Private	510.0	1,500	3674
Silicon Systems Inc.	170	Tustin, CA	Public Family Member	500.0	2,039	3674
Quad Systems Technologies Inc.	171	Sarasota, FL	Private	500.0	2	7373
Fujitsu PC Corporation	172	Milpitas, CA	Private	500.0	200	3571
Fujitsu Microelectronics Inc.	173	San Jose, CA	Private	500.0	1,200	3674
Diversified Phrm Services	174	Minneapolis, MN	Private	500.0	1,000	7375
Sterling Commerce Inc.	175	Dallas, TX	Public	490.3	600	7372
Comverse Technology Inc.	176	Woodbury, NY	Public	488.9	2,823	3571
Linear Technology Corporation	177	Milpitas, CA	Public	484.8	2,155	3674
Telcordia Technologies Inc.	178	Morristown, NJ	Private	477.2	6,154	7371
Sykes Enterprises Incorporated	179	Tampa, FL	Public	469.5	8,700	7371
Telxon Corporation	180	Akron, OH	Public	465.9	1,550	3571
Acxiom Corporation	181	Conway, AR	Public	465.1	3,600	7375
Fore Systems, Inc.	182	Warrendale, PA	Public	458.4	1,592	3577
Mentor Graphics Corporation	183	Wilsonville, OR	Public	454.7	2,570	7373
Stoneridge, Inc.	184	Warren, OH	Public	449.5	4,400	3679
Electronic Assembly Corp.	185	Neenah, WI	Public Family Member	437.0	2,140	3672
S3 Incorporated	186	Santa Clara, CA	Public	436.4	450	3577
Dover Technologies International	187	Binghamton, NY	Public Family Member	435.4	7,500	3679
Electronics For Imaging Inc.	188	San Mateo, CA	Public	430.7	556	3577
Gerber Scientific Inc.	189	South Windsor, CT	Public	430.5	2,200	7373
Mitsubishi Electric Auto Amer	190	Mason, OH	Private	430.0	600	3694
PRC Inc.	191	Mc Lean, VA	Public Family Member	426.6	5,500	7371
Kanbay LLC	192	Des Plaines, IL	Private	426.6	550	7371
GTE Information Services Inc.	193	Tampa, FL	Public Family Member	426.3	6,000	7375
Genicom Corporation	194	Chantilly, VA	Public	421.1	1,700	3577
System Software Associates	195	Chicago, IL	Public	420.8	2,200	7372
FICO America Inc.	196	Tempe, AZ	Private	417.0	30	7373
Cubic Corporation	197	San Diego, CA	Public	414.1	3,700	3699
Logitech Inc.	198	Fremont, CA	Private	413.0	NA	3577
Hutchinson Technology Inc.	199	Hutchinson, MN	Public	407.6	8,293	3679
Computer Task Group Inc.	200	Buffalo, NY	Public	407.6	6,000	7371
Bold Data Technology Inc.	201	Fremont, CA	Private	407.5	100	3571
Cambridge Technology Partners	202	Cambridge, MA	Public	406.7	3,222	7371
National Computer Systems	203	Eden Prairie, MN	Public	406.0	3,500	3577
National Processing, Inc.	204	Louisville, KY	Public	405.7	10,640	7374
Systems & Computer Tech Corp.	205	Malvern, PA	Public	403.7	3,400	7373
Structural Dynamics Res Corp.	206	Milford, OH	Public	403.0	2,200	7372
Verbatim Corporation	207	Charlotte, NC	Public	400.0	1,100	3695
Unigraphics Solutions Inc.	208	Maryland Heights, MO	Public	400.0	2,000	3695
Tracor System Technologies	209	Rockville, MD	Private	400.0	4,500	7373
Shin-Etsu Handotai America	210	Vancouver, WA	Private	400.0	1,700	3674

D&B COMPANY RANKINGS BY SALES

Company	Rank	Location	Type	Sales ($ mil.)	Employ- ment	Primary SIC
Matco Electronics Group Inc.	211	Vestal, NY	Private	400.0	2,400	3672
KAO Info Systems Company	212	Plymouth, MA	Private	400.0	1,400	3695
DMR Consulting Group Inc.	213	Edison, NJ	Private	400.0	3,633	7371
Chippac, Inc.	214	Santa Clara, CA	Private	400.0	4,000	3674
Technitrol Inc.	215	Langhorne, PA	Public	397.1	14,400	3679
Microchip Technology Inc.	216	Chandler, AZ	Public	396.9	2,153	3674
Plexus Corp.	217	Neenah, WI	Public	396.8	2,345	3672
Learning Company Inc.	218	Cambridge, MA	Public	392.4	1,525	7372
Viasystems Technologies LLC	219	Richmond, VA	Private	390.0	2,468	3672
Micrus	220	Hopewell Junction, NY	Private	390.0	1,100	3674
Intermec Technologies Corp.	221	Everett, WA	Public Family Member	387.2	3,600	3577
Bisys Group Inc.	222	Little Falls, NJ	Public	386.3	2,200	7374
Methode Electronics Inc.	223	Chicago, IL	Public	385.1	3,800	3678
Fleet Services Corporation	224	Providence, RI	Public Family Member	382.6	6,000	7374
Park Electrochemical Corp.	225	New Hyde Park, NY	Public	376.2	2,500	3672
Banctec USA	226	Dallas, TX	Public Family Member	375.0	3,000	7373
H N Bull Information Systems	227	Billerica, MA	Private	372.5	1,350	3571
Cray Research, Inc.	228	Saint Paul, MN	Public Family Member	372.3	3,100	3571
Kingston Technology Company	229	Fountain Valley, CA	Private	365.7	734	3577
I2 Technologies Inc.	230	Irving, TX	Public	361.9	2,244	7372
General Semiconductor Inc.	231	Melville, NY	Public	361.9	3,000	3679
AII Technologies Inc.	232	El Paso, TX	Private	361.8	1,000	3571
Astec America Inc.	233	Carlsbad, CA	Private	357.0	2,000	3679
HMT Technology Corporation	234	Fremont, CA	Public	356.2	2,248	3572
Hyperion Solutions Corp.	235	Sunnyvale, CA	Public	353.4	1,800	7371
Champion Spark Plug Company	236	Toledo, OH	Public Family Member	350.5	5,645	3694
Celestica Colorado Inc.	237	Fort Collins, CO	Private	350.0	600	3674
Dallas Semiconductor Corp.	238	Dallas, TX	Public	342.6	1,530	3674
Greenleaf Distribution Inc.	239	Santa Clara, CA	Private	340.0	150	3571
Mantech International Corp.	240	Fairfax, VA	Private	337.2	4,194	7373
C Cube Microsystems Inc.	241	Milpitas, CA	Public	337.0	750	3674
Federal Data Corporation	242	Bethesda, MD	Private	336.3	1,036	7373
Checkpoint Systems Inc.	243	Thorofare, NJ	Public	336.0	3,605	3699
Nova Information Systems Inc.	244	Atlanta, GA	Public Family Member	335.6	480	7375
Computer Horizons Corp.	245	Mountain Lakes, NJ	Public	334.7	3,630	7371
M C M S, Inc.	246	Nampa, ID	Private	333.9	1,800	3672
Raytheon Training Inc.	247	Arlington, TX	Public Family Member	330.0	4,100	3699
Acclaim Entertainment	248	Glen Cove, NY	Public	326.6	660	7372
CACI International Inc.	249	Arlington, VA	Public	326.1	4,600	7373
Benchmark Electronics Inc.	250	Angleton, TX	Public	325.2	2,280	3672
Siliconix Incorporated	251	Santa Clara, CA	Public	321.6	1,226	3674
Photocircuits Corporation	252	Glen Cove, NY	Private	320.7	3,364	3672
SAP America Inc.	253	Newtown Square, PA	Private	317.3	4,090	7371
Attachmate Corporation	254	Bellevue, WA	Private	316.1	1,600	7373
Bull Data Systems Inc.	255	Bedford, NH	Private	315.0	2,200	3571
Amplicon Inc.	256	Santa Ana, CA	Private	313.8	236	7377
International Manufacturing Services	257	San Jose, CA	Public	312.5	3,600	3674
Rational Software Corporation	258	Cupertino, CA	Public	310.7	1,743	7372
Wirekraft Industries, Inc.	259	Saint Louis, MO	Private	310.4	5,000	3694
Metamor Information Tech Services	260	Houston, TX	Public Family Member	310.3	4,000	7371
Computer Sales International	261	Saint Louis, MO	Private	309.3	160	7377
Fujitsu-ICL Systems Inc.	262	Dallas, TX	Private	308.2	1,400	7373
Whittman-Hart Inc.	263	Chicago, IL	Public	307.6	1,674	7371
Systems In Focus Inc.	264	Wilsonville, OR	Public	306.7	525	3577
Sylvest Management System	265	Greenbelt, MD	Private	305.0	155	3571
Wang Government Services Inc.	266	Mc Lean, VA	Public Family Member	300.0	1,000	7373
MBNA Hallmark Information Services	267	Dallas, TX	Public Family Member	300.0	2,200	7374
Kimball Electronics Inc.	268	Jasper, IN	Public Family Member	300.0	2,390	3672
General Electric Capital	269	Emeryville, CA	Public Family Member	300.0	60	7377
Chatham Technologies Inc.	270	Dallas, TX	Private	300.0	2,400	3699
Castlewood Systems Inc.	271	Pleasanton, CA	Private	300.0	50	3572
Candle Corporation	272	Santa Monica, CA	Private	300.0	1,400	7372
USCS International, Inc.	273	Rancho Cordova, CA	Public	299.3	2,038	7371
Amdahl Finance Corporation	274	Sunnyvale, CA	Private	294.4	5,000	7379
Seagate Sftwr Stor Mgt Group	275	San Luis Obispo, CA	Public Family Member	293.2	325	7371
Seagate Software, Inc.	276	San Jose, CA	Public Family Member	293.0	1,700	7372
SEI Investment Company	277	Oaks, PA	Public	292.7	1,133	7372
Watkins-Johnson Company	278	Palo Alto, CA	Public	291.3	2,400	3674
Origin Technology In Business	279	South Plainfield, NJ	Private	290.0	1,500	7373
Information Builders Inc.	280	New York, NY	Private	290.0	1,800	7373

D&B COMPANY RANKINGS BY SALES

Company	Rank	Location	Type	Sales ($ mil.)	Employ-ment	Primary SIC
Transaction Systems Architects	281	Omaha, NE	Public	289.8	2,054	7372
Etec Systems Inc.	282	Hayward, CA	Public	288.3	1,119	3699
Questpoint	283	Philadelphia, PA	Private	286.8	4,500	7374
Exabyte Corporation	284	Boulder, CO	Public	286.5	1,323	3572
Filemaker, Inc.	285	Santa Clara, CA	Public Family Member	281.7	800	7372
Forsythe Technology, Inc.	286	Skokie, IL	Private	280.5	324	7377
Micros Systems Inc.	287	Beltsville, MD	Public	280.2	1,754	3578
Xircom Inc.	288	Thousand Oaks, CA	Public	276.1	1,000	3577
J.D. Edwards World Solutions Co.	289	Denver, CO	Public Family Member	275.4	2,700	7372
Dovatron International, Inc.	290	Boulder, CO	Public Family Member	274.7	900	3679
Verifone Inc.	291	Santa Clara, CA	Public Family Member	273.4	3,300	3578
Acer Latin America, Inc.	292	Miami, FL	Private	272.6	100	3571
Technology Solutions Company	293	Chicago, IL	Public	271.9	1,572	7373
Key Services Corporation	294	Cleveland, OH	Public Family Member	269.6	4,230	7374
AEG Capital Corp	295	New York, NY	Private	269.0	1,800	3674
STB Systems Inc.	296	Richardson, TX	Public	266.3	2,156	3672
Act Manufacturing Inc.	297	Hudson, MA	Public	264.7	985	3672
Level One Communications Inc.	298	Sacramento, CA	Public	263.0	410	3674
Par Computer-Leasing	299	Grandville, MI	Private	262.9	2,000	7377
Mississppi Band Choctaw Indians	300	Philadelphia, MS	Private	261.3	4,500	3679
Viking Components Inc.	301	Rancho S Margari,, CA	Private	260.7	500	3577
K Systems Inc.	302	Foster City, CA	Private	259.2	1,600	3679
Hypercom Corporation	303	Phoenix, AZ	Public	257.2	893	3577
Aztec Technology Partners	304	Braintree, MA	Public	256.0	1,400	7373
Mack Technologies, Inc.	305	Westford, MA	Private	255.7	180	3577
Aspen Technology Inc.	306	Cambridge, MA	Public	252.6	1,518	7372
Burr-Brown Corporation	307	Tucson, AZ	Public	252.1	1,300	3674
Filenet Corporation	308	Costa Mesa, CA	Public	251.4	1,675	7372
IDX Systems Corporation	309	South Burlington, VT	Public	251.4	1,833	7371
S C Data Center Inc.	310	Monroe, WI	Private	250.0	1,200	7374
Korea Data Systems (USA) Inc.	311	Garden Grove, CA	Private	250.0	45	3577
Epson Portland Inc.	312	Hillsboro, OR	Private	250.0	1,500	3577
ESS Technology Inc.	313	Fremont, CA	Public	249.5	447	3674
IEC Electronics Corp.	314	Newark, NY	Public	248.2	1,536	3672
Lattice Semiconductor Corp.	315	Hillsboro, OR	Public	245.9	569	3674
Isaac Fair And Company Inc.	316	San Rafael, CA	Public	245.5	1,487	7372
Cerner Corporation	317	Kansas City, MO	Public	245.1	1,400	7372
Vishay-Dale Holdings Inc.	318	Columbus, NE	Public Family Member	244.7	4,129	3676
Cotelligent, Inc.	319	San Francisco, CA	Public	244.7	2,900	7371
Duchossois Industries Inc.	320	Elmhurst, IL	Private	241.5	7,500	3699
National Instruments Corp.	321	Austin, TX	Public	240.9	1,465	3577
Network General Corporation	322	Santa Clara, CA	Public Family Member	240.7	818	7373
Amdahl International Corp.	323	Sunnyvale, CA	Private	240.6	2,000	7379
Tasc, Inc.	324	Reading, MA	Public Family Member	240.0	2,800	7373
Progress Software Corporation	325	Bedford, MA	Public	239.9	1,201	7371
United Industrial Corporation	326	New York, NY	Public	235.2	1,800	3699
GTE Internetworking Inc.	327	Cambridge, MA	Public Family Member	234.3	2,000	7373
Checkfree Holdings Corporation	328	Norcross, GA	Private	233.9	1,700	7374
Tullett & Tokyo Forex Inc.	329	New York, NY	Private	232.8	3,000	7371
Vishay-Dale Electronics, Inc.	330	Columbus, NE	Public Family Member	230.8	4,000	3676
Stormedia Incorporated	331	Santa Clara, CA	Public	230.4	2,400	3695
PSC Automation, Inc.	332	Webster, NY	Public Family Member	230.0	65	3699
Mac Lean-Fogg Company	333	Mundelein, IL	Private	230.0	1,520	3678
ACS Government Solutions Group Inc.	334	Rockville, MD	Public Family Member	229.7	3,900	7379
Electro Scientific Industries	335	Portland, OR	Public	229.6	900	3699
BDM Corporation Saudia Arabia	336	Mc Lean, VA	Public Family Member	228.9	2,671	7373
CSX Technology Inc.	337	Jacksonville, FL	Public Family Member	228.7	780	7371
Artesyn North America Inc.	338	Eden Prairie, MN	Public Family Member	228.2	2,848	3679
Prestolite Wire Corporation	339	Southfield, MI	Private	228.0	1,255	3694
Avant Corporation	340	Fremont, CA	Public	227.1	800	7371
Mosler Inc.	341	Hamilton, OH	Private	226.8	1,688	3699
C & K Components Inc.	342	Watertown, MA	Private	225.0	1,000	3679
SPS Payment Systems, Inc.	343	Riverwoods, IL	Public Family Member	223.0	3,500	7374
Martin Collier	344	Dallas, TX	Private	220.0	13	7371
Cooperative Computing Inc.	345	Austin, TX	Private	220.0	1,800	7371
AMS Services Inc.	346	Norwell, MA	Public Family Member	219.5	1,600	7372
Husko Inc.	347	Milpitas, CA	Private	219.2	49	3679
Boole & Babbage Inc.	348	San Jose, CA	Public	218.2	970	7372
Sypris Solutions Inc.	349	Louisville, KY	Private	217.4	1,600	3672
Sunsoft, Inc.	350	Mountain View, CA	Public Family Member	217.3	2,800	7371

D&B COMPANY RANKINGS BY SALES

Company	Rank	Location	Type	Sales ($ mil.)	Employ-ment	Primary SIC
Philips Semiconductors, Inc.	351	Sunnyvale, CA	Private	215.6	2,800	3674
Adflex Solutions, Inc.	352	Chandler, AZ	Public	213.9	5,254	3679
Modus Media International Inc.	353	Westwood, MA	Private	212.0	3,600	7379
Xylan Corporation	354	Calabasas, CA	Public	210.8	721	3577
Data Processing Resources Corp.	355	Newport Beach, CA	Public	210.6	2,010	7373
Johnson Matthey Advanced Circuits	356	Eden Prairie, MN	Private	210.0	1,710	3672
Allegro Microsystems Inc.	357	Worcester, MA	Private	210.0	1,900	3674
PSC Inc.	358	Webster, NY	Public	207.8	1,150	3577
Hitachi Semiconductor America	359	Brisbane, CA	Private	205.0	1,448	3674
Zilog Inc.	360	Campbell, CA	Public	204.7	1,270	3674
Lockheed Martin IMS Corp.	361	Teaneck, NJ	Public Family Member	204.0	3,203	7374
Kronos Incorporated	362	Waltham, MA	Public	202.5	1,538	7372
Microsoft Puerto Rico Inc.	363	Humacao, PR	Public Family Member	201.1	250	7372
Calcomp Technologies, Inc.	364	Anaheim, CA	Public	200.2	1,225	3577
MTI Technology Corporation	365	Anaheim, CA	Public	200.0	562	3572
Stealthsoft Corporation	366	Irvine, CA	Private	200.0	150	7371
Proquire LLC	367	Chicago, IL	Private	200.0	150	7373
NGK Spark Plug Manufacturing	368	Sissonville, WV	Private	200.0	225	3694
MFP Technology Services Inc.	369	Norcross, GA	Private	200.0	90	7377
Manugistics, Inc.	370	Rockville, MD	Public Family Member	200.0	1,400	7371
Kearney-National Inc.	371	White Plains, NY	Private	200.0	1,780	3679
Decision Consultants Inc.	372	Southfield, MI	Private	200.0	1,900	7371
Control Data Systems, Inc.	373	Saint Paul, MN	Private	200.0	1,750	7373
Centron Dpl Company, Inc.	374	Eden Prairie, MN	Public Family Member	200.0	200	7373
Lawson Associates, Inc.	375	Minneapolis, MN	Private	199.0	1,400	7372
Savings Bnk Lf Insur Of Mass	376	Woburn, MA	Private	198.3	150	7374
Powerhouse Technologies Inc.	377	Bozeman, MT	Public	196.9	1,380	3575
OAO Corporation	378	Greenbelt, MD	Private	196.4	1,457	7371
Rapidigm Inc.	379	Pittsburgh, PA	Private	196.0	1,800	7373
Mastech Corporation	380	Oakdale, PA	Public	196.0	1,800	7371
Flextronics International USA	381	San Jose, CA	Private	195.7	3,000	3672
Compuserve Corporation	382	Columbus, OH	Public Family Member	194.2	3,050	7374
Medical Information Technology	383	Westwood, MA	Private	193.8	1,500	7371
Hyperion Software Corporation	384	Sunnyvale, CA	Public Family Member	193.6	1,900	7372
Precismetals Inc.	385	Longmont, CO	Private	192.7	1,600	3571
Zebra Technologies Corp.	386	Vernon Hills, IL	Public	192.1	745	3577
R C G Information Technology	387	Edison, NJ	Public Family Member	191.9	1,600	7379
First Data Technologies, Inc.	388	Englewood, CO	Public Family Member	191.1	3,000	7374
ADP Financial Information Services	389	Jersey City, NJ	Public Family Member	191.1	3,000	7374
Broderbund Software Inc.	390	Novato, CA	Public Family Member	190.8	1,129	7372
Total System Services Inc.	391	Columbus, GA	Public	187.8	2,500	7374
Stream International Inc.	392	Canton, MA	Public Family Member	186.8	5,000	7373
American Precision Industries	393	Buffalo, NY	Public	184.1	2,043	3677
Applied Magnetics Corporation	394	Goleta, CA	Public	183.6	4,700	3679
ABN Amro Services Company Inc.	395	Chicago, IL	Private	183.4	2,300	7374
Digi International Inc.	396	Hopkins, MN	Public	182.9	703	3577
Praegitzer Industries Inc.	397	Dallas, OR	Public	182.8	2,000	3672
PKS Information Services LLC	398	Omaha, NE	Private	182.7	3,100	7379
General Scanning Inc.	399	Watertown, MA	Public	181.5	915	3699
Logicare Inc.	400	Melville, NY	Private	181.3	35	7373
Software Ag Systems, Inc.	401	Reston, VA	Public	181.2	950	7372
Woods Industries Inc.	402	Carmel, IN	Public Family Member	180.0	900	3699
AAI Corporation	403	Cockeysville, MD	Public Family Member	180.0	1,500	3699
GenAmerica Corporation	404	Saint Louis, MO	Private	178.9	4,250	7376
Merix Corporation	405	Forest Grove, OR	Public	178.6	1,454	3672
Mid-South Industries Inc.	406	Gadsden, AL	Private	178.1	1,400	3672
Unitrode Corporation	407	Merrimack, NH	Public	177.6	668	3674
Indus International Inc.	408	San Francisco, CA	Public	177.0	650	7372
Anteon Corp.	409	Fairfax, VA	Private	176.3	2,300	7379
Uniphase Corporation	410	San Jose, CA	Public	175.8	976	3674
Manugistics Group Inc.	411	Rockville, MD	Public	175.7	1,300	7371
Prohealth Care Inc.	412	Waukesha, WI	Private	175.4	2,840	7374
U S Epson Inc.	413	Torrance, CA	Private	175.4	1,630	3577
Vitesse Semiconductor Corp.	414	Camarillo, CA	Public	175.1	590	3674
JVC America Inc.	415	Tuscaloosa, AL	Private	175.0	700	3695
Headway Technologies Inc.	416	Milpitas, CA	Private	175.0	600	3572
VTC Inc.	417	Minneapolis, MN	Private	174.0	600	3674
Inprise Corporation	418	Scotts Valley, CA	Public	174.0	821	7372
Altron Incorporated	419	Wilmington, MA	Public Family Member	172.4	1,210	3672
MEMC Southwest Inc.	420	Sherman, TX	Public Family Member	172.0	1,400	3674

D&B COMPANY RANKINGS BY SALES

Company	Rank	Location	Type	Sales ($ mil.)	Employ- ment	Primary SIC
Santa Cruz Operation Inc.	421	Santa Cruz, CA	Public	171.9	1,136	7371
CSG Systems International	422	Englewood, CO	Public	171.8	1,179	7374
Schlumberger Technologies Inc.	423	New York, NY	Public Family Member	171.5	2,000	7373
Delta Technologies Inc.	424	Atlanta, GA	Public Family Member	171.5	2,000	7373
Printronix Inc.	425	Irvine, CA	Public	170.4	992	3577
Key Tronic Corporation	426	Spokane, WA	Public	170.1	2,685	3575
Xlconnect Systems, Inc.	427	Exton, PA	Public Family Member	170.0	1,400	7379
Southland Micro Systems Inc.	428	Irvine, CA	Private	170.0	210	3577
Mitsubishi Silicon America	429	Salem, OR	Private	170.0	1,290	3674
International Network Svcs	430	Sunnyvale, CA	Public	169.7	1,353	7379
Aavid Thermal Technologies	431	Concord, NH	Private	167.7	1,797	3699
Midwest Payment Systems, Inc.	432	Cincinnati, OH	Public Family Member	167.0	258	7374
Network Appliance, Inc.	433	Santa Clara, CA	Public	166.2	450	7373
Channel Master LLC	434	Smithfield, NC	Private	166.0	850	3679
Visio Corp.	435	Seattle, WA	Public	166.0	555	7372
MRV Communications, Inc.	436	Chatsworth, CA	Public	165.5	438	3674
Metro Information Services	437	Virginia Beach, VA	Public	165.4	2,131	7371
Pemstar Inc.	438	Rochester, MN	Private	165.0	580	3571
Microsemi Corporation	439	Santa Ana, CA	Public	164.7	1,750	3674
Solectron Technology, Inc.	440	Charlotte, NC	Public Family Member	163.1	2,500	3672
Allied Telesyn International	441	Sunnyvale, CA	Private	163.0	450	3577
Cincom Systems Inc.	442	Cincinnati, OH	Private	161.6	1,240	7373
Chamberlain Manufacturing Corp.	443	Elmhurst, IL	Private	161.1	2,000	3699
Saturn Electronics & Engrg	444	Auburn Hills, MI	Private	161.0	1,538	3672
BA Merchant Services, Inc.	445	San Francisco, CA	Public	161.0	564	7374
Integrated Circuit Systems	446	Norristown, PA	Public	160.6	200	3674
MGV International Inc.	447	Irvine, CA	Private	160.0	35	3577
Everex Systems, Inc.	448	Fremont, CA	Private	160.0	190	3571
Dynamics Research Corporation	449	Andover, MA	Public	159.4	1,455	7373
Evans & Sutherland Cmpt Corp.	450	Salt Lake City, UT	Public	159.4	831	3571
Autotote Corporation	451	New York, NY	Public	159.3	1,000	3578
Spectra-Physics Lasers, Inc.	452	Mountain View, CA	Public	159.2	895	3699
CCC Information Serices Group	453	Chicago, IL	Private	159.1	1,200	7371
American Century Services Corp.	454	Kansas City, MO	Private	159.1	2,500	7374
Bairnco Corporation	455	Maitland, FL	Public	158.7	850	3672
Electronic Manufacturing Systems	456	Longmont, CO	Private	157.4	1,600	3571
Bea Systems, Inc.	457	San Jose, CA	Public	157.2	1,300	7371
Oak Technology Inc.	458	Sunnyvale, CA	Public	157.1	511	3674
Zenith Data Systems Corp.	459	Buffalo Grove, IL	Private	156.7	1,300	3571
Xerox Colorgrafx Systems Inc.	460	San Jose, CA	Public Family Member	156.2	310	3577
CSG Systems Incorporated	461	Omaha, NE	Public Family Member	156.0	1,119	7374
Actel Corporation	462	Sunnyvale, CA	Public	155.9	380	3674
Standard Microsystems Corp.	463	Hauppauge, NY	Public	155.7	500	3674
Bentley Systems Incorporated	464	Exton, PA	Private	154.9	950	7373
Proxima Corporation	465	San Diego, CA	Private	154.7	444	3679
Axiohm Transaction Solutions	466	Blue Bell, PA	Public	153.7	1,513	3577
Pcs Health Systems, Inc.	467	Scottsdale, AZ	Public Family Member	152.8	2,400	7374
Datapoint Corporation	468	San Antonio, TX	Public	151.4	652	7373
Unison Industries Ltd Partnr	469	Jacksonville, FL	Private	150.0	1,150	3694
U S Capital Equipment Lessors	470	Irvine, CA	Private	150.0	25	7377
Sungard Recovery Services Inc.	471	Wayne, PA	Public Family Member	150.0	500	7374
Computer Curriculum Corp.	472	Sunnyvale, CA	Private	150.0	850	7373
BEI Sensors & Systems Company	473	Sylmar, CA	Public Family Member	150.0	977	3679
Sears Home Services Group	474	Round Rock, TX	Public Family Member	147.4	2,500	7379
Dataworks Corporation	475	San Diego, CA	Public	147.0	300	7373
JTS Corporation	476	San Jose, CA	Private	145.9	6,000	3572
MCI Systemhouse Corp.	477	Reston, VA	Public Family Member	145.8	1,700	7373
Nacom Corporation	478	Griffin, GA	Private	145.5	1,000	3672
Deltec Electronics Corporation	479	San Diego, CA	Private	145.0	1,300	3679
Microtouch Systems Inc.	480	Methuen, MA	Public	144.4	682	3577
Aardvark, Inc.	481	Colorado Springs, CO	Private	143.6	1,850	7371
Huntington Service Company	482	Columbus, OH	Public Family Member	143.2	2,250	7374
Legato Systems, Inc.	483	Palo Alto, CA	Public	143.2	457	7372
US Bancorp Info Svcs Corp.	484	Saint Paul, MN	Public Family Member	143.0	2,247	7374
Century Electronics Manufacturing	485	Marlborough, MA	Private	143.0	220	3672
Kyocera International Inc.	486	San Diego, CA	Private	142.5	1,850	3674
Tatung Company Of America Inc.	487	Long Beach, CA	Private	142.0	360	3571
Advanced Energy Industries	488	Fort Collins, CO	Public	141.9	1,059	3679
Cerplex, Inc.	489	Tustin, CA	Public	141.4	1,350	7378
De La Rue Systems Amricas Corp.	490	Lisle, IL	Private	140.9	1,700	3578

D&B COMPANY RANKINGS BY SALES

Company	Rank	Location	Type	Sales ($ mil.)	Employ-ment	Primary SIC
Wall Data Incorporated	491	Kirkland, WA	Public	140.9	793	7372
Wabash Technologies	492	Huntington, IN	Private	140.0	1,338	3677
Tecstar, Inc.	493	City Of Industry, CA	Private	140.0	980	3674
Mindscape, Inc.	494	Novato, CA	Public Family Member	140.0	500	7372
Fort Lauderdale Network Corp.	495	Fort Lauderdale, FL	Private	140.0	30	7375
Deluxe Electronic Payment Systems	496	Milwaukee, WI	Public Family Member	140.0	1,200	7374
Saehan Media America Inc.	497	Carlsbad, CA	Private	139.8	40	3695
Intel Networks Incorporated	498	Bedford, MA	Public	139.6	610	3577
W R Q Inc.	499	Seattle, WA	Private	138.5	710	7372
JDA Software Group, Inc.	500	Phoenix, AZ	Public	138.5	1,100	7373
Envoy Corporation	501	Nashville, TN	Public	137.6	583	7374
Barra, Inc.	502	Berkeley, CA	Public	137.4	600	7372
Viasystems Inc.	503	Saint Louis, MO	Private	136.9	2,100	3672
Security Dynamics Tech Inc.	504	Bedford, MA	Public	135.9	360	3577
Mylex Corporation	505	Fremont, CA	Public	135.7	373	3577
Du Pont Electronic Materials	506	Manati, PR	Public Family Member	135.3	100	3677
Toppan Electronics Inc.	507	San Diego, CA	Private	135.0	500	3672
CVSI Inc.	508	Bedford, MA	Private	135.0	500	7371
MacNeal-Schwendler Corporation	509	Los Angeles, CA	Public	134.9	700	7373
Aavid Thermal Products, Inc.	510	Laconia, NH	Public	134.6	1,088	3679
Interim Technology Inc.	511	Oak Brook, IL	Public Family Member	133.6	1,720	7371
QMS Inc.	512	Mobile, AL	Public	133.5	674	3577
Innovex Precision Components	513	Hopkins, MN	Public Family Member	133.4	600	3679
Network Computing Devices	514	Mountain View, CA	Public	133.4	352	3575
Smartflex Systems Inc.	515	Tustin, CA	Public	133.3	1,169	3678
JLC Holding Inc.	516	San Diego, CA	Private	131.5	1,000	7377
Integrated Silicon Solution	517	Santa Clara, CA	Public	131.1	175	3674
DSP Communications, Inc.	518	Cupertino, CA	Public	131.1	35	3674
OCLC Online Cmpt Lib Ctr Inc.	519	Dublin, OH	Private	130.9	950	7375
Spectra Precision Inc.	520	Dayton, OH	Private	130.0	800	3699
Matthey Johnson Electronics	521	Spokane, WA	Private	130.0	1,100	3679
Mapics, Inc.	522	Atlanta, GA	Public	129.7	400	7372
Remedy Corporation	523	Mountain View, CA	Public	129.2	450	7371
Planar Systems Inc.	524	Beaverton, OR	Public	129.0	900	3575
Branson Ultrasonics Corp.	525	Danbury, CT	Public Family Member	129.0	530	3699
Worldcom Advanced Networks Inc.	526	Hilliard, OH	Public Family Member	128.7	1,500	7373
JPM Company	527	Lewisburg, PA	Public	128.4	2,800	3679
Comdata Network Inc.	528	Brentwood, TN	Public Family Member	127.2	2,000	7374
M R J Group, Inc.	529	Fairfax, VA	Private	127.0	850	7373
Data Transmission Network Corp.	530	Omaha, NE	Public	126.4	1,000	7375
Detection Systems Inc.	531	Fairport, NY	Public	126.3	395	3699
Trigem America Corporation	532	Irvine, CA	Private	126.2	50	3571
Robroy Industries Inc.	533	Verona, PA	Private	126.1	755	3572
Radisys Corporation	534	Hillsboro, OR	Public	125.4	458	3577
Comp-Sys Designs	535	Los Angeles, CA	Private	125.4	NA	7379
Maxwell Technologies, Inc.	536	San Diego, CA	Public	125.3	600	3571
Sandisk Corporation	537	Sunnyvale, CA	Public	125.3	445	3572
Trippe Manufacturing Company	538	Chicago, IL	Private	125.0	400	3679
Philips Comm & Sec Systems	539	Lancaster, PA	Private	125.0	475	3699
Kobe Precision Inc.	540	Hayward, CA	Private	125.0	450	3674
Ipec-Planar, Inc.	541	Phoenix, AZ	Public Family Member	125.0	800	3695
Gores Technology Group	542	Los Angeles, CA	Private	125.0	30	7372
Agena Corporation	543	Bothell, WA	Public Family Member	125.0	1,100	7371
Neomagic Corporation	544	Santa Clara, CA	Public	124.7	162	3674
Marcam Solutions Inc.	545	Newton, MA	Public	124.5	805	7372
Panurgy Corporation	546	Columbia, MD	Private	124.5	1,451	7373
Syntel, Inc.	547	Troy, MI	Public	124.3	2,000	7371
Transquest Holdings Inc.	548	Atlanta, GA	Public Family Member	124.3	1,600	7371
Logicon Syscon Inc.	549	Falls Church, VA	Public Family Member	124.3	1,600	7371
Barden Companies, Inc.	550	Detroit, MI	Private	124.3	1,600	7371
Alltel Financial Services Inc.	551	Little Rock, AR	Public Family Member	124.3	1,600	7371
AMS Management Systems Group Inc.	552	Windsor, CT	Public Family Member	124.0	1,187	7371
Citrix Systems Inc.	553	Fort Lauderdale, FL	Public	123.9	500	7371
Mid-South Electrics Inc.	554	Annville, KY	Private	123.8	800	3672
Wacker Semiconductor Holding Corp.	555	Portland, OR	Private	123.2	1,600	3674
Cirent Semicondustor (JV)	556	Orlando, FL	Private	123.2	1,600	3674
Complete Business Solutions	557	Farmington Hills, MI	Public	123.0	1,600	7371
Xicor Inc.	558	Milpitas, CA	Public	122.5	738	3674
PSInet Inc.	559	Herndon, VA	Public	121.9	1,000	7373
Boeing Corinth Company	560	Lake Dallas, TX	Public Family Member	121.9	2,100	3679

D&B COMPANY RANKINGS BY SALES

Company	Rank	Location	Type	Sales ($ mil.)	Employ-ment	Primary SIC
Visiontek, Inc.	561	Gurnee, IL	Private	121.5	200	3577
Onix Systems Inc.	562	Kingwood, TX	Public	121.5	845	7371
Veritas Software Corporation	563	Mountain View, CA	Public	121.1	579	7372
Bowthorpe International Inc.	564	Commack, NY	Private	120.9	1,500	3699
Bortec Incorporated	565	El Paso, TX	Private	120.9	1,500	3699
Compaq Federal LLC	566	Greenbelt, MD	Public Family Member	120.8	1,000	3571
Harbinger Corporation	567	Atlanta, GA	Public	120.7	1,044	7372
Integrated Systems Inc.	568	Sunnyvale, CA	Public	120.5	584	7373
Lason, Inc.	569	Troy, MI	Public	120.3	1,250	7374
Softchoice Corporation	570	Norwalk, CT	Private	120.0	220	7372
Raytheon STX Corporation	571	Lanham, MD	Public Family Member	120.0	1,700	7373
G-Tech USA, Inc.	572	Cypress, CA	Private	120.0	100	3577
Milestone Technologies Inc.	573	Tempe, AZ	Public Family Member	119.5	90	7374
Ardent Software Inc.	574	Westborough, MA	Public	119.3	580	7371
Lucas Automation & Ctrl Engrg	575	Hampton, VA	Private	119.0	2,955	3571
Siebel Systems, Inc.	576	San Mateo, CA	Public	118.8	473	7372
MLC Holdings Inc.	577	Reston, VA	Public	118.4	186	7377
Alliance Semiconductor Corp.	578	San Jose, CA	Public	118.4	129	3674
Sony Magnetic Products Inc.	579	Dothan, AL	Private	118.1	1,230	3695
Rofin-Sinar Technologies Inc.	580	Plymouth, MI	Public	117.6	500	3699
Vitech America, Inc.	581	Miami, FL	Public	117.5	650	3571
Vantive Corporation	582	Santa Clara, CA	Public	117.3	451	7372
Sheldahl, Inc.	583	Northfield, MN	Public	117.0	922	3672
Alpha Industries Inc.	584	Woburn, MA	Public	116.9	801	3679
Cognizant Tech Solutions Corp.	585	Teaneck, NJ	Public	116.5	1,500	7371
Automotive Controls Corp.	586	Branford, CT	Public Family Member	116.4	1,100	3694
Toshiba Amer Elctrnic Cmpnents	587	Irvine, CA	Private	116.1	2,000	3679
Jaton Corp.	588	Milpitas, CA	Private	116.0	255	3672
Intec Systems Inc.	589	Houston, TX	Private	116.0	175	7373
Digital Audio Disc Corporation	590	Terre Haute, IN	Private	115.2	1,200	3695
Government Micro Resources	591	Manassas, VA	Private	115.1	196	3571
Polygram Manufacturing & Dist	592	Grover, NC	Private	115.0	700	3695
American Intl Group Data Ctr	593	Livingston, NJ	Public Family Member	115.0	565	7374
Nextrend Technology, Inc.	594	Fremont, CA	Private	115.0	70	7373
Advanced Digital Info Corp.	595	Redmond, WA	Public	114.6	80	3577
Infinium Software Inc.	596	Hyannis, MA	Public	114.4	658	7372
HNC Software Inc.	597	San Diego, CA	Public	113.7	750	7371
Viasoft, Inc.	598	Phoenix, AZ	Public	113.7	450	7371
Group Technologies Corporation	599	Tampa, FL	Public	113.4	700	3672
EFTC Corporation	600	Denver, CO	Public	113.2	1,120	3672
Oyo Corporation USA	601	Houston, TX	Private	113.1	712	3678
Macromedia Inc.	602	San Francisco, CA	Public	113.1	300	7372
Cherry Semiconductor Corp.	603	East Greenwich, RI	Public Family Member	113.0	975	3674
Trident Microsystems Inc.	604	Mountain View, CA	Public	113.0	439	3674
Motorcar Parts & Accessories	605	Torrance, CA	Public	113.0	690	3694
Xetel Corporation	606	Austin, TX	Public	112.7	650	3672
Sierra On-Line Inc.	607	Bellevue, WA	Public Family Member	111.9	1,100	7372
Procom Technology Inc.	608	Santa Ana, CA	Public	111.9	308	3577
Hadco Santa Clara Inc.	609	Santa Clara, CA	Public Family Member	110.8	1,700	3672
SPSS Inc.	610	Chicago, IL	Public	110.6	800	7372
Encad Inc.	611	San Diego, CA	Public	110.1	420	3577
Ajilon Services Inc.	612	Baltimore, MD	Private	110.0	2,600	7379
USG Interiors International	613	Chicago, IL	Public Family Member	109.8	NA	3699
SCB Computer Technology Inc.	614	Memphis, TN	Public	109.5	1,100	7371
Victron Inc.	615	Fremont, CA	Private	109.5	450	3672
Intersolv, Inc.	616	Rockville, MD	Public	109.1	1,073	7372
Siemens Pyramid Info Systems	617	San Jose, CA	Private	108.8	900	3571
Cubic Defense Systems Inc.	618	San Diego, CA	Public Family Member	108.8	768	3699
Georgia Solectron Corporation	619	Duluth, GA	Public Family Member	108.5	1,309	3578
Tangent Computer Inc.	620	Burlingame, CA	Private	108.0	187	3571
Wacker Siltronic Corporation	621	Portland, OR	Private	107.8	1,400	3674
Dataproducts Corporation	622	Simi Valley, CA	Private	107.6	1,000	3577
BRC Holdings, Inc.	623	Dallas, TX	Public Family Member	107.5	970	7374
American Software, Inc.	624	Atlanta, GA	Public	107.5	701	7372
A C I Worldwide Inc.	625	Omaha, NE	Public Family Member	107.3	1,055	7372
Bureau Engraving Incorporated	626	Minneapolis, MN	Private	107.0	700	3672
E-Tek Dynamics Inc.	627	San Jose, CA	Public	106.9	787	3674
Stonebridge Technologies, Inc.	628	Dallas, TX	Private	106.1	175	7373
Quantegy Inc.	629	Peachtree City, GA	Public Family Member	105.6	1,100	3695
L H S Group Inc.	630	Atlanta, GA	Public	105.4	900	7371

D&B COMPANY RANKINGS BY SALES

Company	Rank	Location	Type	Sales ($ mil.)	Employ- ment	Primary SIC
Health Management Systems Inc.	631	New York, NY	Public	105.3	837	7374
Eltron International Inc.	632	Simi Valley, CA	Private	105.0	409	3577
Teccor Electronics Inc.	633	Irving, TX	Private	105.0	1,300	3674
Edgemark Systems Inc.	634	Silver Spring, MD	Private	104.6	120	7373
Micrel, Incorporated	635	San Jose, CA	Public	104.2	546	3674
Quickturn Design Systems Inc.	636	San Jose, CA	Public	104.1	388	7373
Applied Cellular Technology	637	Palm Beach, FL	Public	103.2	460	7379
Semtech Corporation	638	Newbury Park, CA	Public	102.8	503	3674
Anadigics Inc.	639	Warren, NJ	Public	102.5	475	3674
Sunquest Info Systems Inc.	640	Tucson, AZ	Public	102.3	828	7373
Signal Technology Corporation	641	Danvers, MA	Public	102.3	820	3679
Exar Corporation	642	Fremont, CA	Public	102.0	347	3674
World Wide Automotive Inc.	643	Winchester, VA	Public Family Member	102.0	375	3694
ATMI, Inc.	644	Danbury, CT	Public	101.9	200	3674
Sungard Investment Ventures	645	Wilmington, DE	Public Family Member	101.7	1,600	7374
Processors Unlimited Company	646	Dallas, TX	Private	101.7	1,000	7372
Caribbean Data Services, Ltd.	647	Fort Worth, TX	Public Family Member	101.7	1,600	7374
BEI Technologies Inc.	648	San Francisco, CA	Public	101.5	977	3679
Electronic Data Management	649	El Paso, TX	Private	101.4	NA	7374
Aspen Systems Corporation	650	Rockville, MD	Private	101.3	1,501	7374
Axent Technologies Inc.	651	Rockville, MD	Public	101.0	185	7371
GEAC Computer Systems, Inc.	652	Atlanta, GA	Private	101.0	1,300	7371
DBC Holding Corp.	653	Atlanta, GA	Private	101.0	1,300	7371
ITI Technologies, Inc.	654	Saint Paul, MN	Public	101.0	1,124	3699
Par Technology Corporation	655	New Hartford, NY	Public	100.0	894	7373
United Optical Tech Corp.	656	Marietta, GA	Private	100.0	5	3699
Tibco Finance Technology Inc.	657	Palo Alto, CA	Private	100.0	500	7373
Techworks Inc.	658	Austin, TX	Private	100.0	75	3674
Spang & Company	659	Butler, PA	Private	100.0	1,200	3672
Smith Wall Associates LLC	660	Iselin, NJ	Private	100.0	25	7371
Roxboro Holdings Inc.	661	Manasquan, NJ	Private	100.0	600	3679
N B S G III	662	San Francisco, CA	Private	100.0	400	7379
Multicraft International Ltd	663	Brandon, MS	Private	100.0	1,742	3694
Motorola Automotive Products	664	Northbrook, IL	Public Family Member	100.0	800	3694
Knowles Electronics	665	Itasca, IL	Private	100.0	641	3679
Jostens Learning Corporation	666	San Diego, CA	Private	100.0	750	7377
Interactive Business Systems	667	Oak Brook, IL	Private	100.0	1,200	7379
Intellisource Holdings Inc.	668	Vienna, VA	Private	100.0	1,000	7374
Industrial Computer Source	669	San Diego, CA	Public Family Member	100.0	323	3571
IBS Conversions Inc.	670	Oak Brook, IL	Private	100.0	150	3577
ESG Consulting Inc.	671	Santa Clara, CA	Private	100.0	90	7379
Covenant Computer Laboratory	672	Santa Clara, CA	Private	100.0	25	7371
Consist International, Inc.	673	New York, NY	Private	100.0	900	7371
Computer Generated Solutions	674	New York, NY	Private	100.0	900	7373
CBOL Corp.	675	Woodland Hills, CA	Private	100.0	35	3674
Sutherland Group Ltd Inc.	676	Pittsford, NY	Private	99.5	1,400	7375
Arlon Inc.	677	Maitland, FL	Public Family Member	99.4	505	3674
Noma Appliance & Electronics	678	El Paso, TX	Private	99.3	1,600	3694
Micronics Computers Inc.	679	Fremont, CA	Public Family Member	99.3	122	3672
Boundless Technologies Inc.	680	Hauppauge, NY	Public Family Member	99.2	329	3575
Packard-Hughes Interconnect Co	681	Irvine, CA	Public Family Member	98.7	1,700	3679
Platinum Software Corporation	682	Irvine, CA	Public	98.5	650	7372
Adept Technology Inc.	683	San Jose, CA	Public	98.4	394	7373
Tekmark Global Solutions LLC	684	Edison, NJ	Private	98.3	900	7379
Datamax International Corp.	685	Orlando, FL	Private	98.2	500	3577
Computer Network Tech Corp.	686	Minneapolis, MN	Public	97.8	626	7373
Sawtek Inc.	687	Apopka, FL	Public	97.7	549	3677
ATL Products, Inc.	688	Irvine, CA	Public Family Member	97.6	190	3572
Cybermax Inc.	689	Allentown, PA	Private	96.8	NA	3571
Powerex Inc.	690	Youngwood, PA	Private	96.6	330	3674
CMOS Technologies, Inc.	691	Santa Clara, CA	Private	96.1	250	3571
Applied Automation Inc.	692	Bartlesville, OK	Private	96.0	398	3577
Physician Computer Network	693	Morris Plains, NJ	Private	95.8	530	7373
Arsys Innotech Corporation	694	Fremont, CA	Private	95.2	55	3571
U M I & Company	695	Ann Arbor, MI	Public Family Member	94.8	1,335	7375
GSS Array Technology, Inc.	696	San Jose, CA	Private	94.8	500	3672
Rainbow Technologies Inc.	697	Irvine, CA	Public	94.7	300	3577
Telos Field Engineering Inc.	698	Woods Cross, UT	Public Family Member	94.6	1,100	7378
Multilayer Technology Inc.	699	Irvine, CA	Public Family Member	94.6	1,452	3672
Geoscience Corp.	700	Houston, TX	Public	94.5	589	7371

D&B COMPANY RANKINGS BY SALES

Company	Rank	Location	Type	Sales ($ mil.)	Employ-ment	Primary SIC
Atlantron, Inc.	701	Mayaguez, PR	Private	94.2	750	3672
Eclipsys Corporation	702	Delray Beach, FL	Public	94.1	997	7371
Trident Data Systems Inc.	703	Los Angeles, CA	Private	94.0	936	7379
Platinum Technology Solutions	704	Inglewood, CA	Public Family Member	93.3	1,200	7371
Unit Parts Company	705	Oklahoma City, OK	Private	93.1	1,500	3694
Pacific Electricord Company	706	Gardena, CA	Private	92.8	1,150	3699
NCI Information Systems Inc.	707	Mc Lean, VA	Private	92.5	1,000	7371
Wind River Systems Inc.	708	Alameda, CA	Public	92.4	563	7372
ODS Networks, Inc.	709	Richardson, TX	Public	92.3	389	3577
CTA Incorporated	710	Bethesda, MD	Private	92.2	1,250	7373
Condor Technology Solutions	711	Annapolis, MD	Public	92.1	1,073	7373
Government Computer Sales Inc.	712	Issaquah, WA	Private	91.9	100	7373
Pinkerton Computer Consultants	713	Langhorne, PA	Private	91.9	572	7379
Cybernetics & Systems Inc.	714	Jacksonville, FL	Public Family Member	91.9	490	7371
Ross Systems, Inc.	715	Atlanta, GA	Public	91.7	582	7372
Power-One Inc.	716	Camarillo, CA	Public	91.6	1,704	3679
Qad Inc.	717	Carpinteria, CA	Public	91.5	1,156	7371
Signal Corporation	718	Fairfax, VA	Private	91.5	1,250	7379
BBN Barrnet Inc.	719	Cambridge, MA	Public Family Member	91.5	850	3577
SDL, Inc.	720	San Jose, CA	Public	91.4	650	3674
Staveley Inc.	721	White Plains, NY	Private	91.0	1,568	3679
IPM Service Corporation	722	Dallas, TX	Private	91.0	1,467	3694
RMS Holdings, Incorporated	723	Lanham, MD	Private	90.9	1,000	7374
Computer Aid Inc.	724	Allentown, PA	Private	90.8	1,525	7371
Total Peripherals, Inc.	725	Northborough, MA	Private	90.5	130	3571
Sapient Corporation	726	Cambridge, MA	Public	90.4	924	7371
3D Systems Inc.	727	Santa Clarita, CA	Public Family Member	90.3	400	3571
Jacom Computer Services, Inc.	728	Northvale, NJ	Public Family Member	90.1	25	7377
Shape Inc.	729	Kennebunk, ME	Private	90.0	600	3695
Shape Global Technology Inc.	730	Kennebunk, ME	Private	90.0	600	3695
Business Records Corporation	731	Dallas, TX	Public Family Member	90.0	450	7374
AVX Vancouver Corporation	732	Vancouver, WA	Public Family Member	90.0	720	3675
Comshare Incorporated	733	Ann Arbor, MI	Public	89.8	405	7372
Communications Instruments	734	Fairview, NC	Private	89.4	1,200	3679
Stellex Microwave Systems	735	Palo Alto, CA	Private	89.0	504	3679
Print Northwest Co LP	736	Tacoma, WA	Private	89.0	685	7372
Intellisource Info Systems	737	Vienna, VA	Private	89.0	1,000	7374
Davox Corporation	738	Westford, MA	Public	88.9	398	7373
Sterling Software U S Amer Inc.	739	Reston, VA	Public Family Member	88.8	874	7372
Incyte Pharmaceuticals, Inc.	740	Palo Alto, CA	Public	88.4	676	7375
Clarify Inc.	741	San Jose, CA	Public	88.2	488	7372
Data Systems Network Corp.	742	Farmington Hills, MI	Public	88.0	285	7373
Information Tech Solutions	743	Hampton, VA	Public Family Member	88.0	1,100	7373
Ameritech Library Services	744	Provo, UT	Public Family Member	88.0	500	7373
Arrow Automotive Industries	745	Morrilton, AR	Private	87.5	300	3694
Optek Technology, Inc.	746	Carrollton, TX	Public	87.2	2,145	3674
Lambda Holdings Inc.	747	Melville, NY	Private	87.1	1,500	3679
Lynk Systems Inc.	748	Atlanta, GA	Private	87.0	290	7374
Insync Systems, Inc.	749	Milpitas, CA	Private	86.1	300	3674
Sequel Inc.	750	San Jose, CA	Private	85.8	700	7378
Corporate Software & Tech	751	Norwood, MA	Public Family Member	85.8	1,000	7373
Averstar Inc.	752	Burlington, MA	Private	85.8	1,000	7373
Great Plains Software Inc.	753	Fargo, ND	Public	85.7	755	7372
Sigmatron International	754	Elk Grove Village, IL	Public	85.7	1,700	3672
Mercury Computer Systems Inc.	755	Chelmsford, MA	Public	85.5	378	3571
Emtec Inc.	756	Mount Laurel, NJ	Private	85.5	250	7373
Dow Jones Telerate, Inc.	757	New York, NY	Private	85.3	1,200	7375
Elexsys International, Inc.	758	San Jose, CA	Public Family Member	84.7	1,300	3672
Pegasus Consulting Group Inc.	759	Woodbridge, NJ	Private	84.7	340	7371
Genesys Telecom Labs	760	San Francisco, CA	Public	84.7	550	7371
Three-Five Systems, Inc.	761	Tempe, AZ	Public	84.6	459	3577
Medquist Inc.	762	Marlton, NJ	Public	84.6	857	7374
4Front Software International	763	Englewood, CO	Public	84.1	800	7371
Gerber Garment Technology	764	Tolland, CT	Public Family Member	83.9	850	7371
Kenan Systems Corporation	765	Cambridge, MA	Private	83.8	750	7371
Claremont Technology Group	766	Beaverton, OR	Public Family Member	83.6	700	7379
Information Mgt Resources	767	Clearwater, FL	Public	83.5	955	7379
Applied Science & Technology	768	Woburn, MA	Public	83.4	355	3679
OECO Corporation	769	Milwaukie, OR	Private	83.4	865	3679
Summit Service Corporation	770	Ridgefield Park, NJ	Public Family Member	82.5	1,300	7374

D&B COMPANY RANKINGS BY SALES

Company	Rank	Location	Type	Sales ($ mil.)	Employ- ment	Primary SIC
Concurrent Computer Corp.	771	Fort Lauderdale, FL	Public	82.2	530	3571
Pyxis Corporation	772	San Diego, CA	Public Family Member	82.0	1,300	7373
Bisys, Inc.	773	Houston, TX	Public Family Member	81.9	450	7374
Interface Systems Inc.	774	Ann Arbor, MI	Public	81.8	170	7373
Saga Software, Inc.	775	Reston, VA	Private	81.2	800	7372
Medstat Holdings Inc.	776	Ann Arbor, MI	Private	81.2	800	7372
Ericsson Hewlett-Packard	777	Dallas, TX	Private	81.2	NA	7372
R Emass Inc.	778	Englewood, CO	Public Family Member	81.0	300	3572
MCE Companies, Inc.	779	Ann Arbor, MI	Private	81.0	660	3679
Virtualfund.Com, Inc.	780	Eden Prairie, MN	Public	80.7	404	3577
MacDermid Inc.	781	Wilmington, DE	Public Family Member	80.5	152	3679
Intelligroup Inc.	782	Edison, NJ	Public	80.2	425	7371
Pacific Circuits Inc.	783	Redmond, WA	Private	80.0	650	3672
International Resistive Co.	784	Boone, NC	Private	80.0	600	3676
Direct Marketing Tech Inc.	785	Schaumburg, IL	Private	80.0	640	7374
Sigma Circuits Inc.	786	Santa Clara, CA	Private	80.0	785	3672
Broadway & Seymour, Inc.	787	Charlotte, NC	Public	79.6	475	7373
Levi Ray & Shoup Inc.	788	Springfield, IL	Private	79.2	405	7373
Earthlink Network, Inc.	789	Pasadena, CA	Public	79.2	1,329	7375
Startek USA Inc.	790	Aurora, CO	Public Family Member	79.0	1,000	7372
Clover Technologies Inc.	791	Wixom, MI	Public Family Member	79.0	404	7373
Factset Research Systems, Inc.	792	Greenwich, CT	Public	78.9	265	7374
Universal Computer Network	793	Houston, TX	Private	78.9	600	7377
Checkpoint Systems Of PR	794	Ponce, PR	Public Family Member	78.6	640	3699
Questech, Inc.	795	Falls Church, VA	Private	78.5	800	7373
Dendrite International Inc.	796	Morristown, NJ	Public	78.4	725	7371
Medical Manager Corporation	797	Tampa, FL	Public	78.1	1,085	7372
Universal Systems Inc.	798	Chantilly, VA	Private	78.1	340	7373
Tyco Printed Circuit Group	799	Stafford Springs, CT	Private	78.1	1,200	3672
Hadco Phoenix, Inc.	800	Phoenix, AZ	Public Family Member	78.1	1,200	3672
Boeing Information Svcs Inc.	801	Vienna, VA	Public Family Member	78.1	1,231	7374
AVG Advanced Technologies LP	802	Carol Stream, IL	Private	78.1	1,200	3672
Radiant Systems Inc.	803	Alpharetta, GA	Public	78.0	581	7373
Allied Business Systems Inc.	804	Macon, GA	Public Family Member	77.7	1,000	7371
ABR Benefits Services, Inc.	805	Palm Harbor, FL	Public Family Member	77.7	1,000	7371
Maxi Switch, Inc.	806	Tucson, AZ	Private	77.7	140	3575
OSI Systems Inc.	807	Hawthorne, CA	Public	77.6	725	3674
Dataram Corporation	808	Princeton, NJ	Public	77.3	138	3572
Alpha Technologies Group, Inc.	809	Houston, TX	Public	77.0	987	7373
Cherokee International LLC	810	Tustin, CA	Private	77.0	868	3679
Triad Data Inc.	811	New York, NY	Public Family Member	77.0	500	7379
Harte-Hanks Data Technologies	812	Billerica, MA	Public Family Member	77.0	350	7374
Superior Conslt Holdings Corp.	813	Southfield, MI	Public	76.9	300	7379
Datatec Systems, Inc.	814	Totowa, NJ	Public	76.8	585	7373
Applied Micro Circuits Corp.	815	San Diego, CA	Public	76.6	335	3674
EA Industries	816	West Long Branch, NJ	Public	76.5	430	3571
Infonet Services Corporation	817	El Segundo, CA	Private	76.2	1,200	7374
Apex Data Services Inc.	818	Herndon, VA	Private	76.2	1,200	7374
Force 3 Inc.	819	Crofton, MD	Private	76.2	119	3571
Getty Images Inc.	820	Seattle, WA	Private	76.1	750	7372
Applied Systems Inc.	821	University Park, IL	Private	76.1	1,100	7371
Splash Technology, Inc.	822	Sunnyvale, CA	Public Family Member	76.0	163	3577
Documentum, Inc.	823	Pleasanton, CA	Public	75.6	600	7372
Kavlico Corporation	824	Moorpark, CA	Private	75.4	1,300	3679
Hayes Microcomputer Products	825	Norcross, GA	Public Family Member	75.4	700	3577
Natural Microsystems Corp.	826	Framingham, MA	Public	75.4	260	3577
Overland Data Inc.	827	San Diego, CA	Public	75.2	233	3577
Wellcor America Inc.	828	Oklahoma City, OK	Private	75.0	168	7373
Transcore	829	Harrisburg, PA	Private	75.0	365	7373
Tally Printer Corporation	830	Kent, WA	Private	75.0	350	3577
Summit Group Inc.	831	Mishawaka, IN	Public Family Member	75.0	425	7379
Solectron Massachussets Corp.	832	Westborough, MA	Public Family Member	75.0	300	3679
Raltron Electronics Corp.	833	Miami, FL	Private	75.0	275	3679
Packard-Hughes Intrcnct Wr Sys	834	Foley, AL	Public Family Member	75.0	600	3679
Iris Graphics Inc.	835	Bedford, MA	Private	75.0	277	3577
Inteliant Corporation	836	Albuquerque, NM	Public Family Member	75.0	100	7379
EER Systems, Inc.	837	Lanham, MD	Private	75.0	657	7373
Circuit Systems, Inc.	838	Elk Grove Village, IL	Public	75.0	715	3672
UTMC Microelectronic Systems	839	Colorado Springs, CO	Public Family Member	74.8	340	3674
Impact Innovations Holdings	840	Houston, TX	Public Family Member	74.8	1,265	7379

D&B COMPANY RANKINGS BY SALES

Company	Rank	Location	Type	Sales ($ mil.)	Employ-ment	Primary SIC
Banyan Systems Incorporated	841	Westborough, MA	Public	74.3	386	7373
SBS Technologies Inc.	842	Albuquerque, NM	Public	74.2	300	7373
Nugent Robinson Inc.	843	New Albany, IN	Public	74.1	674	3678
Consultec Inc.	844	Atlanta, GA	Private	74.0	800	7373
Partech, Inc.	845	New Hartford, NY	Public Family Member	73.8	539	7373
Norwest Services, Inc.	846	Minneapolis, MN	Public Family Member	73.7	1,161	7374
Phoenix Technologies Ltd.	847	San Jose, CA	Public	73.7	572	7371
SCT Software & Resources Mgt	848	Malvern, PA	Public Family Member	73.6	946	7371
Firearms Training Systems Inc.	849	Suwanee, GA	Public	73.5	362	3699
Omni Tech Corporation	850	Pewaukee, WI	Private	73.5	200	3571
Bel Fuse Inc.	851	Jersey City, NJ	Public	73.5	707	3679
Project Software & Development	852	Bedford, MA	Public	73.3	619	7372
Filtronic Comtek Inc.	853	Salisbury, MD	Private	73.2	509	3679
Austin Samsung Semicdtr LLC	854	Austin, TX	Private	73.1	950	3674
Brooktrout Technology Inc.	855	Needham, MA	Public	72.2	300	7371
Transpo Electronics Inc.	856	Orlando, FL	Private	72.0	750	3694
Comptek Research, Inc.	857	Buffalo, NY	Public	72.0	620	7373
Petroleum Infrmton/Dwights LLC	858	Houston, TX	Private	72.0	565	7375
Printrak International Inc.	859	Anaheim, CA	Public	71.9	430	7371
Circuit-Wise, Inc.	860	North Haven, CT	Private	71.8	591	3672
Micrografx, Inc.	861	Richardson, TX	Public	71.8	302	7372
QRS Corporation	862	Richmond, CA	Public	71.6	270	7375
Walker Interactive Systems	863	San Francisco, CA	Public	71.4	520	7371
Phase Metrics, Inc.	864	San Diego, CA	Private	71.4	668	3572
Triquint Semiconductor, Inc.	865	Hillsboro, OR	Public	71.4	361	3674
Forte Software, Inc.	866	Oakland, CA	Public	71.3	431	7372
Medic Computer Systems Inc.	867	Raleigh, NC	Private	71.3	830	7373
Computer Management Sciences	868	Jacksonville, FL	Public	71.2	760	7379
Paragon Computer Professionals	869	Cranford, NJ	Private	71.0	1,000	7379
Eastman Software, Inc.	870	Billerica, MA	Public Family Member	71.0	700	7372
Dialog Corporation	871	Mountain View, CA	Private	71.0	1,000	7375
ACS Business Process Solutions	872	Sandy, UT	Public Family Member	71.0	4,000	7374
Advent Software Inc.	873	San Francisco, CA	Public	71.0	450	7372
MAI Systems Corporation	874	Irvine, CA	Public	71.0	467	7373
Texas Microsystems Inc.	875	Houston, TX	Public Family Member	70.9	350	3577
Landmark Graphics Corporation	876	Houston, TX	Public Family Member	70.8	910	7371
Hitachi Automotive Products USA	877	Harrodsburg, KY	Private	70.7	1,140	3694
Microstrategy Incorporated	878	Vienna, VA	Public	70.7	907	7372
Computer Merchant Ltd.	879	Norwell, MA	Private	70.7	470	7379
MMC Technology	880	San Jose, CA	Private	70.5	655	3577
TSR, Inc.	881	Hauppauge, NY	Public	70.4	350	7371
Box Hill Systems Corp.	882	New York, NY	Public	70.3	160	3572
T D K Components USA	883	Peachtree City, GA	Private	70.0	220	3675
Spectrum Technology Group Inc.	884	Somerville, NJ	Public Family Member	70.0	450	7379
Netscout Systems Inc.	885	Westford, MA	Private	70.0	200	7371
Manu-Tronics Inc.	886	Pleasant Prairie, WI	Private	70.0	450	3672
Hood Cable Company	887	Hattiesburg, MS	Private	70.0	1,000	3694
Dialight Corp.	888	Manasquan, NJ	Private	70.0	430	3679
Datastream Systems Inc.	889	Greenville, SC	Public	69.8	600	7372
Micros-To-Mainframes, Inc.	890	Valley Cottage, NY	Public	69.6	160	7379
McHugh Software International	891	Waukesha, WI	Private	69.4	418	7373
Davidson & Associates Inc.	892	Torrance, CA	Public Family Member	68.9	679	7372
Rand McNally Media Svcs Inc.	893	Skokie, IL	Private	68.8	801	7373
Epsilon Data Management Inc.	894	Burlington, MA	Private	68.7	800	7373
CRA Inc.	895	Phoenix, AZ	Private	68.3	38	7377
Fourth Shift Corporation	896	Minneapolis, MN	Public	68.2	450	7372
Dynamic Details, Inc.	897	Anaheim, CA	Private	68.0	2,000	3672
Computron Software Inc.	898	Rutherford, NJ	Public	67.6	454	7372
Disclosure Incorporated	899	Bethesda, MD	Public Family Member	67.5	950	7375
Sharp Microelectronics Tech	900	Camas, WA	Private	67.3	340	3674
Financial Institutions Inc.	901	Warsaw, NY	Private	67.2	419	7374
Artecon, Inc.	902	Milpitas, CA	Public	66.3	238	3572
Interphase Corporation	903	Dallas, TX	Public	66.0	222	3577
Vishay Vitramon Incorporated	904	Monroe, CT	Public Family Member	66.0	1,368	3675
Melita International Corp.	905	Norcross, GA	Public	65.8	325	7371
Micro Linear Corporation	906	San Jose, CA	Public	65.8	252	3674
Durant Electric Company	907	Clinton, MS	Private	65.5	725	3694
Kyocera America Inc.	908	San Diego, CA	Private	65.4	850	3674
Crystal Semiconductor Corp.	909	Austin, TX	Public Family Member	65.4	850	3674
SAP America Pubic Sector, Inc.	910	Philadelphia, PA	Private	65.0	150	7371

D&B COMPANY RANKINGS BY SALES

Company	Rank	Location	Type	Sales ($ mil.)	Employ-ment	Primary SIC
R E Phelon Company Inc.	911	Aiken, SC	Private	65.0	565	3694
Northern Computers Inc.	912	Milwaukee, WI	Private	65.0	250	3699
NER Data Products Inc.	913	Glassboro, NJ	Private	65.0	550	3577
Lacerte Software Corporation	914	Dallas, TX	Public Family Member	65.0	300	7371
Hughes Aircraft Mississippi	915	Forest, MS	Public Family Member	65.0	280	3699
Howard Systems Intl Inc.	916	Stamford, CT	Private	65.0	436	7371
IXL Enterprises Inc.	917	Atlanta, GA	Private	64.8	1,300	7374
Reflectone Inc.	918	Tampa, FL	Private	64.6	800	3699
MKE-Quantum Components, LLC	919	Louisville, CO	Public Family Member	64.6	600	3577
Dominion Semiconductors L.L.C.	920	Manassas, VA	Private	64.6	600	3577
Seer Technologies Inc.	921	Cary, NC	Public	64.0	411	7371
Micro Voice Applications Inc.	922	Minneapolis, MN	Private	64.0	220	7371
Win Laboratories, Ltd.	923	Manassas, VA	Private	63.9	180	3571
Gale Group	924	Farmington Hills, MI	Private	63.9	1,200	7375
Bindco Corporation	925	Redwood City, CA	Private	63.8	280	7379
CSP Inc.	926	Billerica, MA	Public	63.5	247	3577
J P Morgan Services Inc.	927	Newark, DE	Public Family Member	63.4	1,000	7374
Columbia/HCA Information Services	928	Nashville, TN	Public Family Member	63.4	1,000	7374
Election Systems & Software	929	Omaha, NE	Private	63.0	310	3577
Cubic Applications Inc.	930	Lacey, WA	Public Family Member	63.0	810	7373
Advanced Quick Circuits LP	931	Melbourne, FL	Private	63.0	585	3672
Digicon Corporation	932	Bethesda, MD	Private	62.9	300	7371
Aris Corporation	933	Bellevue, WA	Public	62.5	660	7379
Code-Alarm Inc.	934	Madison Heights, MI	Public	62.5	457	3699
Elgar Electronics Corporation	935	San Diego, CA	Private	62.5	433	3679
Goodtimes Home Video Corp.	936	New York, NY	Private	62.4	650	3695
Del Global Technologies Corp.	937	Valhalla, NY	Public	62.3	466	3679
Viewlogic Systems Inc.	938	Marlborough, MA	Public	62.0	240	7373
La Cie Ltd.	939	Hillsboro, OR	Private	62.0	120	3572
Janis Group Inc.	940	Rochelle Park, NJ	Private	62.0	262	7373
Confederated Slish Ktnai Tribes	941	Pablo, MT	Private	62.0	800	3679
Peregrine Systems Inc.	942	San Diego, CA	Public	61.9	350	7371
B.T.N.Y. Services, Inc.	943	New York, NY	Public Family Member	61.7	973	7374
Netmanage, Inc.	944	Cupertino, CA	Public	61.5	440	7371
MDL Information Systems, Inc.	945	San Leandro, CA	Private	61.5	390	7372
Open Market Inc.	946	Burlington, MA	Public	61.3	347	7373
New Resources Corporation	947	Rolling Meadows, IL	Private	61.0	700	7376
Astea International Inc.	948	Horsham, PA	Public	60.9	253	7372
Force Computers Inc.	949	San Jose, CA	Public Family Member	60.9	500	3571
Auspex Systems Inc.	950	Santa Clara, CA	Public	60.6	612	3577
Mapinfo Corporation	951	Troy, NY	Public	60.6	400	7372
Objective Systems Integrators	952	Folsom, CA	Public	60.6	425	7371
Volt Delta Resources, Inc.	953	New York, NY	Public Family Member	60.5	481	7373
Cheyenne Software Inc.	954	Hauppauge, NY	Public Family Member	60.5	778	7371
Princeton Information Ltd.	955	New York, NY	Private	60.4	800	7379
Parlex Corporation	956	Methuen, MA	Public	60.3	558	3672
Autometric Inc.	957	Springfield, VA	Private	60.2	481	7373
Versyss Incorporated	958	Morris Plains, NJ	Private	60.0	145	7371
Vectron Technologies Inc.	959	Hudson, NH	Public Family Member	60.0	225	3679
TSR Consulting Services Inc.	960	Hauppauge, NY	Public Family Member	60.0	200	7379
Spectrolab Inc.	961	Sylmar, CA	Public Family Member	60.0	780	3674
SMT Centre Of Texas, Inc.	962	Austin, TX	Private	60.0	350	3672
Seta Corp.	963	Mc Lean, VA	Private	60.0	480	7373
Kirchman Corporation	964	Altamonte Springs, FL	Private	60.0	470	7371
International Fuel Cells, LLC	965	South Windsor, CT	Public Family Member	60.0	450	3674
Huber & Suhner Inc.	966	Essex Junction, VT	Private	60.0	160	3679
Fanuc America Corporation	967	Hoffman Estates, IL	Private	60.0	210	7378
Delphax Systems	968	Canton, MA	Public Family Member	60.0	400	3577
Comtec Information Systems	969	Warwick, RI	Private	60.0	200	3577
Betac International Corp.	970	Alexandria, VA	Public Family Member	60.0	430	7373
Automata International Inc.	971	Sterling, VA	Private	60.0	480	3672
Ace Electric, LLC	972	Columbus, KS	Private	60.0	410	3694
A-Plus Manufacturing Corp.	973	San Jose, CA	Private	60.0	430	3672
Spectrum Control Inc.	974	Erie, PA	Public	59.9	763	3677
Industri-Matematik International	975	Tarrytown, NY	Private	59.6	317	7371
Hi-Tech Manufacturing, Inc.	976	Thornton, CO	Private	59.0	500	3672
Cyborg Systems Inc.	977	Chicago, IL	Private	59.0	575	7372
K-N Holdings Inc.	978	White Plains, NY	Private	58.9	950	3694
Transact Technologies Inc.	979	Wallingford, CT	Public	58.4	240	3577
Kenda Systems Inc.	980	Salem, NH	Private	58.4	96	7371

D&B COMPANY RANKINGS BY SALES

Company	Rank	Location	Type	Sales ($ mil.)	Employ-ment	Primary SIC
Besam Automated Entrance Systems	981	Hightstown, NJ	Private	58.1	300	3699
System Resources Corporation	982	Burlington, MA	Private	58.1	500	7373
Tier Technologies, Inc.	983	Walnut Creek, CA	Public	57.7	308	7373
Williams Controls Inc.	984	Portland, OR	Public	57.6	511	3679
P S I Holding Group Inc.	985	Marlborough, MA	Private	57.5	175	7371
Cymer Inc.	986	San Diego, CA	Public	57.5	712	3699
User Technology Associates	987	Arlington, VA	Private	57.4	760	7373
Edify Corporation	988	Santa Clara, CA	Public	57.1	425	7372
Magnetic Data, Inc.	989	Eden Prairie, MN	Public Family Member	57.0	530	3572
Harbor Electronics Inc.	990	Etters, PA	Private	57.0	720	3679
Automated Concepts Inc.	991	New York, NY	Private	57.0	540	7379
Video Monitoring Svcs Amer LP	992	New York, NY	Private	56.8	800	7375
Scan-Optics, Inc.	993	Manchester, CT	Public	56.6	324	3577
Inspire Insurance Solutions	994	Fort Worth, TX	Public	56.6	550	7371
Mobius Management Systems Inc.	995	Rye, NY	Public	56.5	360	7371
Stewart Connector Systems Inc.	996	Glen Rock, PA	Private	56.3	650	3678
Lycos Inc.	997	Waltham, MA	Public	56.1	600	7375
Bay Data Consultants LLC	998	Norcross, GA	Private	56.0	127	7373
Telcom Semiconductor, Inc.	999	Mountain View, CA	Public	55.4	321	3674
R F Monolithics Inc.	1000	Dallas, TX	Public	55.2	600	3679
Caere Corporation	1001	Los Gatos, CA	Public	55.0	293	7372
Peachtree Software Inc.	1002	Norcross, GA	Public Family Member	55.0	300	7372
Mektec Corp.	1003	Fremont, CA	Private	55.0	560	3672
Martin James & Co Inc.	1004	Fairfax, VA	Private	55.0	300	7373
Current Electronics Inc.	1005	Newberg, OR	Public Family Member	55.0	390	3679
Logicon Space & Information	1006	Fairfax, VA	Public Family Member	54.5	700	7371
H T E Inc.	1007	Lake Mary, FL	Private	54.5	700	7371
ACS Technology Solutions, Inc.	1008	Dallas, TX	Public Family Member	54.5	450	7371
Aeroflex Laboratories Inc.	1009	Plainview, NY	Public Family Member	54.4	425	3679
Born Information Services	1010	Wayzata, MN	Private	54.4	675	7371
Berger & Co.	1011	Denver, CO	Public Family Member	54.2	440	7379
Altec Lansing Technologies	1012	Milford, PA	Private	53.9	500	3577
Logicon Eagle Technology, Inc.	1013	Arlington, VA	Public Family Member	53.7	625	7373
Videoserver Inc.	1014	Burlington, MA	Public	53.5	98	3571
Metrologic Instruments Inc.	1015	Blackwood, NJ	Public	53.5	465	3699
Inter-National Research Inst	1016	Reston, VA	Private	53.4	420	7371
Tri-Cor Industries Inc.	1017	Alexandria, VA	Private	53.2	576	7373
Applied Films Corporation	1018	Longmont, CO	Public	53.0	200	3674
Supertex Inc.	1019	Sunnyvale, CA	Public	52.7	450	3674
CGG Canada Ltd.	1020	Houston, TX	Private	52.7	135	7374
ECC International Corp.	1021	Orlando, FL	Public	52.6	538	3699
Interleaf Inc.	1022	Waltham, MA	Public	52.6	350	7372
Mindspring Enterprises, Inc.	1023	Atlanta, GA	Public	52.6	502	7374
Daw Technologies Inc.	1024	Salt Lake City, UT	Public	52.5	200	3674
Intermag, Inc.	1025	Sacramento, CA	Private	52.5	222	3695
Anstec, Inc.	1026	Mc Lean, VA	Private	52.3	490	7371
Delta Products Corporation	1027	Nogales, AZ	Private	52.2	900	3679
Foxconn Corporation	1028	Houston, TX	Private	52.2	550	7371
Sulcus Hospitality Tech	1029	Greensburg, PA	Public	52.1	430	3578
Unicomp Inc.	1030	Marietta, GA	Public	52.1	360	7372
Techsonic Industries Inc.	1031	Eufaula, AL	Public Family Member	52.0	285	3679
Metrum-Datatape Inc.	1032	Littleton, CO	Private	52.0	300	3572
Journal Of Commerce Inc.	1033	New York, NY	Private	52.0	450	7375
Cornell-Dubilier Electronics	1034	Wayne, NJ	Private	52.0	850	3675
N A I Technologies, Inc.	1035	Huntington, NY	Public	51.9	194	7373
Harris Data Services Corp.	1036	Alexandria, VA	Public Family Member	51.6	600	7373
Grumman Systems Support Corp.	1037	Bohemia, NY	Public Family Member	51.6	600	7373
Citicorp Development Center	1038	Los Angeles, CA	Public Family Member	51.6	600	7373
Kawasaki Steel Holdings (USA)	1039	New York, NY	Private	51.4	668	3674
Global Intellicom, Inc.	1040	New York, NY	Public	51.2	204	7373
Sipex Corporation	1041	Billerica, MA	Public	51.2	435	3674
Micro Modeling Associates Inc.	1042	New York, NY	Private	51.0	280	7379

D&B COMPANY RANKINGS BY EMPLOYMENT

Company	Rank	Location	Type	Sales ($ mil.)	Employ-ment	Primary SIC
International Business Machines Corp.	1	Armonk, NY	Public	78,508.0	269,465	3571
Hewlett-Packard Company	2	Palo Alto, CA	Public	47,061.0	124,600	3571
Electronic Data Systems Corp.	3	Plano, TX	Public	15,235.6	110,000	7374
IBM World Trade Europe	4	Armonk, NY	Public Family Member	10,742.9	99,900	3577
Seagate Technology Inc.	5	Scotts Valley, CA	Public	6,819.0	87,000	3572
Compaq Computer Corporation	6	Houston, TX	Public	31,169.0	80,000	3571
Intel Corporation	7	Santa Clara, CA	Public	26,273.0	63,700	3674
Digital Equipment Corporation	8	Maynard, MA	Public Family Member	5,989.9	50.000	3571
AMP Incorporated	9	Harrisburg, PA	Public	5,745.2	46,526	3678
Computer Sciences Corporation	10	El Segundo, CA	Public	6,600.8	45,000	7379
NCR Corporation	11	Dayton, OH	Public	6,505.0	38,300	3571
Oracle Corporation	12	Redwood City, CA	Public	7,143.9	36,802	7372
Texas Instruments Incorporated	13	Dallas, TX	Public	8,460.0	36,400	3674
First Data Corporation	14	Hackensack, NJ	Public	5,234.5	36,000	7374
Alcoa Fujikura Ltd.	15	Brentwood, TN	Public Family Member	1,700.0	35,000	3694
Automatic Data Processing	16	Roseland, NJ	Public	4,798.1	34,000	7374
Metamor Worldwide Inc.	17	Houston, TX	Public	1,008.1	33,650	7371
Unisys Corporation	18	Blue Bell, PA	Public	7,208.4	33,200	7373
Microsoft Corporation	19	Redmond, WA	Public	14,484.0	27,320	7372
Sun Microsystems Inc.	20	Palo Alto, CA	Public	9,790.8	26,300	3571
Solectron Corporation	21	Milpitas, CA	Public	5,288.3	24,857	3672
SCI Systems Inc.	22	Huntsville, AL	Public	6,805.9	22,324	3571
Wang Laboratories, Inc.	23	Billerica, MA	Public	1,887.0	20,000	7378
Read-Rite Corporation	24	Milpitas, CA	Public	808.6	18,000	3679
Vishay Intertechnology Inc.	25	Malvern, PA	Public	1,125.2	17,400	3676
Dyncorp	26	Reston, VA	Private	1,145.9	16,100	7373
Micron Technology Inc.	27	Boise, ID	Public	3,011.9	15,300	3571
Cisco Systems Inc.	28	San Jose, CA	Public	8,458.8	15,000	3577
Technitrol Inc.	29	Langhorne, PA	Public	397.1	14,400	3679
ITT Defense & Electronics	30	Mc Lean, VA	Public Family Member	812.9	14,000	3679
Dell Computer Corporation	31	Round Rock, TX	Public	12,327.0	13,500	3571
Gateway, Inc.	32	North Sioux City, SD	Public	6,293.7	13,300	3571
Western Digital Corporation	33	Irvine, CA	Public	3,541.2	13,045	3572
National Semiconductor Corp.	34	Santa Clara, CA	Public	2,536.7	13,000	3674
Molex Incorporated	35	Lisle, IL	Public	1,623.0	13,000	3678
3Com Corporation	36	Santa Clara, CA	Public	5,420.4	12,920	7373
Advanced Micro Devices Inc.	37	Sunnyvale, CA	Public	2,542.1	12,800	3674
Fiserv Inc.	38	Brookfield, WI	Public	1,233.7	12,500	7374
Computer Associates International	39	Hauppauge, NY	Public	4,719.0	11,400	7372
Flextronics International Ltd.	40	San Jose, CA	Private	1,113.1	11,300	3672
Kemet Electronics Corporation	41	Simpsonville, SC	Public Family Member	667.7	11,000	3675
Amdahl Corporation	42	Sunnyvale, CA	Private	948.8	11,000	7378
National Processing, Inc.	43	Louisville, KY	Public	405.7	10,640	7374
Sabre Group, Inc.	44	Fort Worth, TX	Public Family Member	1,783.5	10,300	7371
Kemet Corporation	45	Simpsonville, SC	Public	667.7	10,300	3675
Silicon Graphics Inc.	46	Mountain View, CA	Public	3,100.6	10,286	3571
Stargate Systems, Inc.	47	Chicago, IL	Private	775.4	10,000	7371
Digital Equipment Corp International	48	Acton, MA	Public Family Member	1,198.8	10,000	3571
Dell Products LP	49	Round Rock, TX	Private	1,198.8	10,000	3571
Amkor Technology, Inc.	50	West Chester, PA	Public	1,455.8	9,880	3674
Imation Corp.	51	Saint Paul, MN	Public	2,046.5	9,800	3695
Veba Corporation	52	New York, NY	Private	4,000.0	9,100	3674
Raychem Corporation	53	Menlo Park, CA	Public	1,798.5	9,036	3678
BDM International Inc.	54	Mc Lean, VA	Public Family Member	770.8	9,000	7373
Sykes Enterprises Incorporated	55	Tampa, FL	Public	469.5	8,700	7371
Compuware Corporation	56	Farmington Hills, MI	Public	1,139.3	8,663	7371
Storage Technology Corporation	57	Louisville, CO	Public	2,258.2	8,300	3572
Hutchinson Technology Inc.	58	Hutchinson, MN	Public	407.6	8,293	3679
Keane Inc.	59	Boston, MA	Public	654.4	8,008	7373
Packard Bell Nec	60	Sacramento, CA	Private	959.2	8,000	3571
Lexmark International Group	61	Lexington, KY	Public	3,020.6	8,000	3577
Entex Information Services	62	Port Chester, NY	Private	2,456.6	8,000	7373
Alltel Information Services	63	Little Rock, AR	Public Family Member	510.2	8,000	7374
Lotus Development Corporation	64	Cambridge, MA	Public Family Member	807.8	7,909	7372
Intergraph Corporation	65	Huntsville, AL	Public	1,124.3	7,700	7373
Hadco Corporation	66	Salem, NH	Public	826.4	7,673	3672
Molex International Inc.	67	Lisle, IL	Public Family Member	540.5	7,671	3678
Duchossois Industries Inc.	68	Elmhurst, IL	Private	241.5	7,500	3699
Dover Technologies International	69	Binghamton, NY	Public Family Member	435.4	7,500	3679
Analog Devices, Inc.	70	Norwood, MA	Public	1,230.6	7,200	3674

D&B COMPANY RANKINGS BY EMPLOYMENT

Company	Rank	Location	Type	Sales ($ mil.)	Employ- ment	Primary SIC
American Mgt Systems Inc.	71	Fairfax, VA	Public	872.3	7,100	7379
Carlyle Partners Leveraged Cap	72	Washington, DC	Private	599.5	7,000	7373
Berg Electronics Corp.	73	Saint Louis, MO	Private	785.2	7,000	3678
Fairchild Semiconductor Corp.	74	South Portland, ME	Private	789.2	6,927	3674
Artesyn Technologies Inc.	75	Boca Raton, FL	Public	527.2	6,900	3679
Amphenol Corporation	76	Wallingford, CT	Public	884.3	6,900	3678
Cabletron Systems Inc.	77	Rochester, NH	Public	1,377.3	6,887	3577
Apple Computer Inc.	78	Cupertino, CA	Public	5,941.0	6,658	3571
DecisionOne Corporation	79	Malvern, PA	Public Family Member	805.7	6,500	7378
Diebold Incorporated	80	Canton, OH	Public	1,185.7	6,489	3578
Emc Corporation	81	Hopkinton, MA	Private	2,937.9	6,400	3572
DII Group, Inc.	82	Longmont, CO	Public	779.6	6,350	3679
HBO & Company	83	Atlanta, GA	Public	1,203.2	6,286	7372
Quantum Corporation	84	Milpitas, CA	Public	5,803.2	6,219	3572
Technology Service Solutions	85	West Chester, PA	Private	534.7	6,200	7378
Raytheon Service Company	86	Burlington, MA	Public Family Member	817.0	6,200	7376
Telcordia Technologies Inc.	87	Morristown, NJ	Private	477.2	6,154	7371
National Data Corporation	88	Atlanta, GA	Public	649.0	6,100	7374
MEMC Electronic Materials	89	O'Fallon, MO	Public	758.9	6,100	3674
Atmel Corporation	90	San Jose, CA	Public	958.3	6,100	3674
Policy Management Systems Corp.	91	Blythewood, SC	Public	582.8	6,017	7372
JTS Corporation	92	San Jose, CA	Private	145.9	6,000	3572
GTE Information Services Inc.	93	Tampa, FL	Public Family Member	426.3	6,000	7375
Fleet Services Corporation	94	Providence, RI	Public Family Member	382.6	6,000	7374
First Data Resources Inc.	95	Omaha, NE	Public Family Member	1,013.2	6,000	7374
DST Systems, Inc.	96	Kansas City, MO	Public	650.7	6,000	7374
Computer Task Group Inc.	97	Buffalo, NY	Public	407.6	6,000	7371
Bay Networks, Inc.	98	Santa Clara, CA	Private	641.0	5,960	3577
Maxtor Corporation	99	Milpitas, CA	Public	1,424.3	5,700	3572
Ciber, Inc.	100	Englewood, CO	Public	550.4	5,700	7379
Champion Spark Plug Company	101	Toledo, OH	Public Family Member	350.5	5,645	3694
Perot Systems Corporation	102	Dallas, TX	Public	599.4	5,600	7376
Analysts International Corp.	103	Minneapolis, MN	Public	587.4	5,571	7371
PRC Inc.	104	Mc Lean, VA	Public Family Member	426.6	5,500	7371
Sybase, Inc.	105	Emeryville, CA	Public	903.9	5,484	7372
Sanmina Corporation	106	San Jose, CA	Public	923.8	5,477	3672
SAS Institute Inc.	107	Cary, NC	Private	747.7	5,285	7372
Adflex Solutions, Inc.	108	Chandler, AZ	Public	213.9	5,254	3679
J M Huber Corporation	109	Edison, NJ	Private	1,298.6	5,153	3699
Cadence Design Systems Inc.	110	San Jose, CA	Public	915.9	5,102	7372
Wirekraft Industries, Inc.	111	Saint Louis, MO	Private	310.4	5,000	3694
Stream International Inc.	112	Canton, MA	Public Family Member	186.8	5,000	7373
Platinum Technology International	113	Villa Park, IL	Public	738.9	5,000	7372
Logicon Inc.	114	Herndon, VA	Public Family Member	650.0	5,000	7373
Integrated Device Technology	115	Santa Clara, CA	Public	587.1	5,000	3674
Holland America Inv Corp.	116	New York, NY	Private	510.5	5,000	7372
Amdahl Finance Corporation	117	Sunnyvale, CA	Private	294.4	5,000	7379
J.D. Edwards & Company	118	Denver, CO	Public	934.0	4,950	7372
Parametric Technology Corp.	119	Waltham, MA	Public	1,018.0	4,911	7372
Iomega Corporation	120	Roy, UT	Public	1,740.0	4,816	3572
Komag Incorporated	121	San Jose, CA	Public	631.1	4,738	3695
Data General Corporation	122	Westborough, MA	Public	1,462.1	4,700	3571
Applied Magnetics Corporation	123	Goleta, CA	Public	183.6	4,700	3679
CACI International Inc.	124	Arlington, VA	Public	326.1	4,600	7373
Novell, Inc.	125	Provo, UT	Public	1,083.9	4,510	7373
Tracor System Technologies	126	Rockville, MD	Private	400.0	4,500	7373
Sungard Data Systems Inc.	127	Wayne, PA	Public	862.2	4,500	7374
Questpoint	128	Philadelphia, PA	Private	286.8	4,500	7374
Mississppi Band Choctaw Indians	129	Philadelphia, MS	Private	261.3	4,500	3679
Peoplesoft, Inc.	130	Pleasanton, CA	Public	815.7	4,452	7372
LSI Logic Corporation	131	Milpitas, CA	Public	1,490.7	4,443	3674
Paychex, Inc.	132	Rochester, NY	Public	993.4	4,440	7374
Stoneridge, Inc.	133	Warren, OH	Public	449.5	4,400	3679
International Rectifier Corp.	134	El Segundo, CA	Public	551.9	4,395	3674
GenAmerica Corporation	135	Saint Louis, MO	Private	178.9	4,250	7376
Key Services Corporation	136	Cleveland, OH	Public Family Member	269.6	4,230	7374
Mantech International Corp.	137	Fairfax, VA	Private	337.2	4,194	7373
Vishay-Dale Holdings Inc.	138	Columbus, NE	Public Family Member	244.7	4,129	3676
Raytheon Training Inc.	139	Arlington, TX	Public Family Member	330.0	4,100	3699
SAP America Inc.	140	Newtown Square, PA	Private	317.3	4,090	7371

D&B COMPANY RANKINGS BY EMPLOYMENT

Company	Rank	Location	Type	Sales ($ mil.)	Employ- ment	Primary SIC
Fujitsu America Inc.	141	San Jose, CA	Private	2,000.0	4,047	3577
Vishay-Dale Electronics, Inc.	142	Columbus, NE	Public Family Member	230.8	4,000	3676
Metamor Information Tech Services	143	Houston, TX	Public Family Member	310.3	4,000	7371
Chippac, Inc.	144	Santa Clara, CA	Private	400.0	4,000	3674
Banctec, Inc.	145	Dallas, TX	Public	603.5	4,000	7373
ACS Business Process Solutions	146	Sandy, UT	Public Family Member	71.0	4,000	7374
ACS Government Solutions Group Inc.	147	Rockville, MD	Public Family Member	229.7	3,900	7379
Methode Electronics Inc.	148	Chicago, IL	Public	385.1	3,800	3678
Informix Corporation	149	Menlo Park, CA	Public	662.3	3,800	7371
GTE Data Services Inc.	150	Tampa, FL	Public Family Member	753.5	3,800	7374
Cubic Corporation	151	San Diego, CA	Public	414.1	3,700	3699
Jabil Circuit Inc.	152	Saint Petersburg, FL	Public	1,277.4	3,661	3672
DMR Consulting Group Inc.	153	Edison, NJ	Private	400.0	3,633	7371
Computer Horizons Corp.	154	Mountain Lakes, NJ	Public	334.7	3,630	7371
Checkpoint Systems Inc.	155	Thorofare, NJ	Public	336.0	3,605	3699
Toshiba Amer Info Systems Inc.	156	Irvine, CA	Private	4,104.6	3,600	3571
Tivoli Systems Inc.	157	Austin, TX	Public Family Member	1,400.0	3,600	7371
Sterling Software Inc.	158	Dallas, TX	Public	719.9	3,600	7372
Solectron Texas LP	159	Austin, TX	Private	600.0	3,600	3571
Modus Media International Inc.	160	Westwood, MA	Private	212.0	3,600	7379
International Manufacturing Services	161	San Jose, CA	Public	312.5	3,600	3674
Intermec Technologies Corp.	162	Everett, WA	Public Family Member	387.2	3,600	3577
Avex Electronics Inc.	163	Huntsville, AL	Private	717.1	3,600	3699
Acxiom Corporation	164	Conway, AR	Public	465.1	3,600	7375
SPS Payment Systems, Inc.	165	Riverwoods, IL	Public Family Member	223.0	3,500	7374
National Computer Systems	166	Eden Prairie, MN	Public	406.0	3,500	3577
Systems & Computer Tech Corp.	167	Malvern, PA	Public	403.7	3,400	7373
Photocircuits Corporation	168	Glen Cove, NY	Private	320.7	3,364	3672
Verifone Inc.	169	Santa Clara, CA	Public Family Member	273.4	3,300	3578
Adaptec Inc.	170	Milpitas, CA	Public	1,007.3	3,276	3577
Cambridge Technology Partners	171	Cambridge, MA	Public	406.7	3,222	7371
Lockheed Martin IMS Corp.	172	Teaneck, NJ	Public Family Member	204.0	3,203	7374
Symbol Technologies Inc.	173	Holtsville, NY	Public	774.3	3,200	3577
PKS Information Services LLC	174	Omaha, NE	Private	182.7	3,100	7379
Cray Research, Inc.	175	Saint Paul, MN	Public Family Member	372.3	3,100	3571
Maxim Integrated Products	176	Sunnyvale, CA	Public	560.2	3,066	3674
Compuserve Corporation	177	Columbus, OH	Public Family Member	194.2	3,050	7374
Tullett & Tokyo Forex Inc.	178	New York, NY	Private	232.8	3,000	7371
General Semiconductor Inc.	179	Melville, NY	Public	361.9	3,000	3679
Flextronics International USA	180	San Jose, CA	Private	195.7	3,000	3672
First Data Technologies, Inc.	181	Englewood, CO	Public Family Member	191.1	3,000	7374
Banctec USA	182	Dallas, TX	Public Family Member	375.0	3,000	7373
AST Research, Inc.	183	Irvine, CA	Private	2,103.6	3,000	3571
ADP Financial Information Services	184	Jersey City, NJ	Public Family Member	191.1	3,000	7374
Lucas Automation & Ctrl Engrg	185	Hampton, VA	Private	119.0	2,955	3571
Netscape Communications Corp.	186	Mountain View, CA	Public	533.9	2,936	7372
Cotelligent, Inc.	187	San Francisco, CA	Public	244.7	2,900	7371
Intuit Inc.	188	Mountain View, CA	Public	592.7	2,860	7372
Artesyn North America Inc.	189	Eden Prairie, MN	Public Family Member	228.2	2,848	3679
Prohealth Care Inc.	190	Waukesha, WI	Private	175.4	2,840	7374
Comverse Technology Inc.	191	Woodbury, NY	Public	488.9	2,823	3571
Sequent Computer Systems Inc.	192	Beaverton, OR	Public	833.9	2,818	3571
Tasc, Inc.	193	Reading, MA	Public Family Member	240.0	2,800	7373
Sunsoft, Inc.	194	Mountain View, CA	Public Family Member	217.3	2,800	7371
Philips Semiconductors, Inc.	195	Sunnyvale, CA	Private	215.6	2,800	3674
NEC Electronics Inc.	196	Santa Clara, CA	Private	1,738.0	2,800	3674
Manufacturers Services Ltd.	197	Concord, MA	Private	800.0	2,800	3577
JPM Company	198	Lewisburg, PA	Public	128.4	2,800	3679
Comdisco Inc.	199	Des Plaines, IL	Public	3,243.0	2,800	7377
B M C Software Inc.	200	Houston, TX	Public	730.6	2,777	7372
Cypress Semiconductor Corp.	201	San Jose, CA	Public	544.4	2,770	3674
Siemens Microelectronics, Inc.	202	Cupertino, CA	Private	738.0	2,750	3674
Micron Electronics, Inc.	203	Nampa, ID	Public	1,733.4	2,750	3571
J.D. Edwards World Solutions Co.	204	Denver, CO	Public Family Member	275.4	2,700	7372
Key Tronic Corporation	205	Spokane, WA	Public	170.1	2,685	3575
Adobe Systems Incorporated	206	San Jose, CA	Public	894.8	2,680	7372
BDM Corporation Saudia Arabia	207	Mc Lean, VA	Public Family Member	228.9	2,671	7373
Intel Puerto Rico Inc.	208	Las Piedras, PR	Public Family Member	1,500.0	2,600	3674
Ajilon Services Inc.	209	Baltimore, MD	Private	110.0	2,600	7379
Synopsys, Inc.	210	Mountain View, CA	Public	717.9	2,592	7371

D&B COMPANY RANKINGS BY EMPLOYMENT

Company	Rank	Location	Type	Sales ($ mil.)	Employ-ment	Primary SIC
Mentor Graphics Corporation	211	Wilsonville, OR	Public	454.7	2,570	7373
Tennessee Denso Manufacturing	212	Maryville, TN	Private	800.0	2,552	3694
V L S I Technology Inc.	213	San Jose, CA	Public	712.7	2,500	3674
Total System Services Inc.	214	Columbus, GA	Public	187.8	2,500	7374
Solectron Technology, Inc.	215	Charlotte, NC	Public Family Member	163.1	2,500	3672
Sears Home Services Group	216	Round Rock, TX	Public Family Member	147.4	2,500	7379
Park Electrochemical Corp.	217	New Hyde Park, NY	Public	376.2	2,500	3672
Cincinnati Bell Info Systems	218	Cincinnati, OH	Public Family Member	600.0	2,500	7373
Cendant Software	219	Torrance, CA	Public Family Member	650.0	2,500	7372
American Century Services Corp.	220	Kansas City, MO	Private	159.1	2,500	7374
Stratus Computer, Inc.	221	Marlborough, MA	Public Family Member	688.3	2,487	3571
Autodesk Inc.	222	San Rafael, CA	Public	617.1	2,470	7372
Viasystems Technologies LLC	223	Richmond, VA	Private	390.0	2,468	3672
Watkins-Johnson Company	224	Palo Alto, CA	Public	291.3	2,400	3674
Stormedia Incorporated	225	Santa Clara, CA	Public	230.4	2,400	3695
Pcs Health Systems, Inc.	226	Scottsdale, AZ	Public Family Member	152.8	2,400	7374
Matco Electronics Group Inc.	227	Vestal, NY	Private	400.0	2,400	3672
GE Information Services, Inc.	228	Rockville, MD	Public Family Member	700.0	2,400	7374
Chatham Technologies Inc.	229	Dallas, TX	Private	300.0	2,400	3699
Kimball Electronics Inc.	230	Jasper, IN	Public Family Member	300.0	2,390	3672
Plexus Corp.	231	Neenah, WI	Public	396.8	2,345	3672
Symantec Corporation	232	Cupertino, CA	Public	578.4	2,300	7372
Anteon Corp.	233	Fairfax, VA	Private	176.3	2,300	7379
ABN Amro Services Company Inc.	234	Chicago, IL	Private	183.4	2,300	7374
Benchmark Electronics Inc.	235	Angleton, TX	Public	325.2	2,280	3672
Huntington Service Company	236	Columbus, OH	Public Family Member	143.2	2,250	7374
HMT Technology Corporation	237	Fremont, CA	Public	356.2	2,248	3572
US Bancorp Info Svcs Corp.	238	Saint Paul, MN	Public Family Member	143.0	2,247	7374
I2 Technologies Inc.	239	Irving, TX	Public	361.9	2,244	7372
System Software Associates	240	Chicago, IL	Public	420.8	2,200	7372
Structural Dynamics Res Corp.	241	Milford, OH	Public	403.0	2,200	7372
MBNA Hallmark Information Services	242	Dallas, TX	Public Family Member	300.0	2,200	7374
Gerber Scientific Inc.	243	South Windsor, CT	Public	430.5	2,200	7373
Bull Data Systems Inc.	244	Bedford, NH	Private	315.0	2,200	3571
Bisys Group Inc.	245	Little Falls, NJ	Public	386.3	2,200	7374
STB Systems Inc.	246	Richardson, TX	Public	266.3	2,156	3672
Linear Technology Corporation	247	Milpitas, CA	Public	484.8	2,155	3674
Microchip Technology Inc.	248	Chandler, AZ	Public	396.9	2,153	3674
Optek Technology, Inc.	249	Carrollton, TX	Public	87.2	2,145	3674
Electronic Assembly Corp.	250	Neenah, WI	Public Family Member	437.0	2,140	3672
Cirrus Logic Inc.	251	Fremont, CA	Public	954.3	2,135	3674
Metro Information Services	252	Virginia Beach, VA	Public	165.4	2,131	7371
Viasystems Inc.	253	Saint Louis, MO	Private	136.9	2,100	3672
Viasystems Group Inc.	254	Saint Louis, MO	Private	600.0	2,100	3672
Electronic Arts	255	Redwood City, CA	Public	908.9	2,100	7372
Boeing Corinth Company	256	Lake Dallas, TX	Public Family Member	121.9	2,100	3679
Transaction Systems Architects	257	Omaha, NE	Public	289.8	2,054	7372
American Precision Industries	258	Buffalo, NY	Public	184.1	2,043	3677
Silicon Systems Inc.	259	Tustin, CA	Public Family Member	500.0	2,039	3674
USCS International, Inc.	260	Rancho Cordova, CA	Public	299.3	2,038	7371
Data Processing Resources Corp.	261	Newport Beach, CA	Public	210.6	2,010	7373
Unigraphics Solutions Inc.	262	Maryland Heights, MO	Public	400.0	2,000	3695
Toshiba Amer Elctrnic Cmpnents	263	Irvine, CA	Private	116.1	2,000	3679
Syntel, Inc.	264	Troy, MI	Public	124.3	2,000	7371
Schlumberger Technologies Inc.	265	New York, NY	Public Family Member	171.5	2,000	7373
Praegitzer Industries Inc.	266	Dallas, OR	Public	182.8	2,000	3672
Par Computer-Leasing	267	Grandville, MI	Private	262.9	2,000	7377
GTE Internetworking Inc.	268	Cambridge, MA	Public Family Member	234.3	2,000	7373
Dynamic Details, Inc.	269	Anaheim, CA	Private	68.0	2,000	3672
Delta Technologies Inc.	270	Atlanta, GA	Public Family Member	171.5	2,000	7373
Comdata Network Inc.	271	Brentwood, TN	Public Family Member	127.2	2,000	7374
Chamberlain Manufacturing Corp.	272	Elmhurst, IL	Private	161.1	2,000	3699
Astec America Inc.	273	Carlsbad, CA	Private	357.0	2,000	3679
Amdahl International Corp.	274	Sunnyvale, CA	Private	240.6	2,000	7379
Galileo International Inc.	275	Des Plaines, IL	Public	1,070.0	1,909	7375
Hyperion Software Corporation	276	Sunnyvale, CA	Public Family Member	193.6	1,900	7372
Decision Consultants Inc.	277	Southfield, MI	Private	200.0	1,900	7371
Allegro Microsystems Inc.	278	Worcester, MA	Private	210.0	1,900	3674
Kyocera International Inc.	279	San Diego, CA	Private	142.5	1,850	3674
Aardvark, Inc.	280	Colorado Springs, CO	Private	143.6	1,850	7371

D&B COMPANY RANKINGS BY EMPLOYMENT

Company	Rank	Location	Type	Sales ($ mil.)	Employ-ment	Primary SIC
IDX Systems Corporation	281	South Burlington, VT	Public	251.4	1,833	7371
United Industrial Corporation	282	New York, NY	Public	235.2	1,800	3699
Rapidigm Inc.	283	Pittsburgh, PA	Private	196.0	1,800	7373
Mastech Corporation	284	Oakdale, PA	Public	196.0	1,800	7371
M C M S, Inc.	285	Nampa, ID	Private	333.9	1,800	3672
Information Builders Inc.	286	New York, NY	Private	290.0	1,800	7373
Hyperion Solutions Corp.	287	Sunnyvale, CA	Public	353.4	1,800	7371
Cooperative Computing Inc.	288	Austin, TX	Private	220.0	1,800	7371
AEG Capital Corp	289	New York, NY	Private	269.0	1,800	3674
Aavid Thermal Technologies	290	Concord, NH	Private	167.7	1,797	3699
Kearney-National Inc.	291	White Plains, NY	Private	200.0	1,780	3679
Micros Systems Inc.	292	Beltsville, MD	Public	280.2	1,754	3578
Microsemi Corporation	293	Santa Ana, CA	Public	164.7	1,750	3674
Control Data Systems, Inc.	294	Saint Paul, MN	Private	200.0	1,750	7373
Rational Software Corporation	295	Cupertino, CA	Public	310.7	1,743	7372
Multicraft International Ltd	296	Brandon, MS	Private	100.0	1,742	3694
Interim Technology Inc.	297	Oak Brook, IL	Public Family Member	133.6	1,720	7371
Johnson Matthey Advanced Circuits	298	Eden Prairie, MN	Private	210.0	1,710	3672
Power-One Inc.	299	Camarillo, CA	Public	91.6	1,704	3679
Sigmatron International	300	Elk Grove Village, IL	Public	85.7	1,700	3672
Shin-Etsu Handotai America	301	Vancouver, WA	Private	400.0	1,700	3674
Seagate Software, Inc.	302	San Jose, CA	Public Family Member	293.0	1,700	7372
Raytheon STX Corporation	303	Lanham, MD	Public Family Member	120.0	1,700	7373
Packard-Hughes Interconnect Co	304	Irvine, CA	Public Family Member	98.7	1,700	3679
MCI Systemhouse Corp.	305	Reston, VA	Public Family Member	145.8	1,700	7373
Hadco Santa Clara Inc.	306	Santa Clara, CA	Public Family Member	110.8	1,700	3672
Genicom Corporation	307	Chantilly, VA	Public	421.1	1,700	3577
De La Rue Systems Amricas Corp.	308	Lisle, IL	Private	140.9	1,700	3578
Checkfree Holdings Corporation	309	Norcross, GA	Private	233.9	1,700	7374
Mosler Inc.	310	Hamilton, OH	Private	226.8	1,688	3699
Filenet Corporation	311	Costa Mesa, CA	Public	251.4	1,675	7372
Whittman-Hart Inc.	312	Chicago, IL	Public	307.6	1,674	7371
Ascend Communications Inc.	313	Alameda, CA	Public	1,478.7	1,644	3577
U S Epson Inc.	314	Torrance, CA	Private	175.4	1,630	3577
Wacker Semiconductor Holding Corp.	315	Portland, OR	Private	123.2	1,600	3674
Transquest Holdings Inc.	316	Atlanta, GA	Public Family Member	124.3	1,600	7371
Sypris Solutions Inc.	317	Louisville, KY	Private	217.4	1,600	3672
Sungard Investment Ventures	318	Wilmington, DE	Public Family Member	101.7	1,600	7374
R C G Information Technology	319	Edison, NJ	Public Family Member	191.9	1,600	7379
Precismetals Inc.	320	Longmont, CO	Private	192.7	1,600	3571
Noma Appliance & Electronics	321	El Paso, TX	Private	99.3	1,600	3694
Network Associates Inc.	322	Santa Clara, CA	Public	612.2	1,600	7371
Logicon Syscon Inc.	323	Falls Church, VA	Public Family Member	124.3	1,600	7371
K Systems Inc.	324	Foster City, CA	Private	259.2	1,600	3679
Electronic Manufacturing Systems	325	Longmont, CO	Private	157.4	1,600	3571
Complete Business Solutions	326	Farmington Hills, MI	Public	123.0	1,600	7371
Cirent Semicondustor (JV)	327	Orlando, FL	Private	123.2	1,600	3674
Caribbean Data Services, Ltd.	328	Fort Worth, TX	Public Family Member	101.7	1,600	7374
Barden Companies, Inc.	329	Detroit, MI	Private	124.3	1,600	7371
Attachmate Corporation	330	Bellevue, WA	Private	316.1	1,600	7373
Aspect Telecommunications Corp.	331	San Jose, CA	Public	512.3	1,600	7372
AMS Services Inc.	332	Norwell, MA	Public Family Member	219.5	1,600	7372
Alltel Financial Services Inc.	333	Little Rock, AR	Public Family Member	124.3	1,600	7371
Fore Systems, Inc.	334	Warrendale, PA	Public	458.4	1,592	3577
Technology Solutions Company	335	Chicago, IL	Public	271.9	1,572	7373
Staveley Inc.	336	White Plains, NY	Private	91.0	1,568	3679
Telxon Corporation	337	Akron, OH	Public	465.9	1,550	3571
Saturn Electronics & Engrg	338	Auburn Hills, MI	Private	161.0	1,538	3672
Kronos Incorporated	339	Waltham, MA	Public	202.5	1,538	7372
IEC Electronics Corp.	340	Newark, NY	Public	248.2	1,536	3672
Dallas Semiconductor Corp.	341	Dallas, TX	Public	342.6	1,530	3674
Learning Company Inc.	342	Cambridge, MA	Public	392.4	1,525	7372
Computer Aid Inc.	343	Allentown, PA	Private	90.8	1,525	7371
Mac Lean-Fogg Company	344	Mundelein, IL	Private	230.0	1,520	3678
Aspen Technology Inc.	345	Cambridge, MA	Public	252.6	1,518	7372
Axiohm Transaction Solutions	346	Blue Bell, PA	Public	153.7	1,513	3577
Aspen Systems Corporation	347	Rockville, MD	Private	101.3	1,501	7374
Worldcom Advanced Networks Inc.	348	Hilliard, OH	Public Family Member	128.7	1,500	7373
Unit Parts Company	349	Oklahoma City, OK	Private	93.1	1,500	3694
Sumitomo Sitix Silicon Inc.	350	Fremont, CA	Private	510.0	1,500	3674

D&B COMPANY RANKINGS BY EMPLOYMENT

Company	Rank	Location	Type	Sales ($ mil.)	Employ- ment	Primary SIC
Origin Technology In Business	351	South Plainfield, NJ	Private	290.0	1,500	7373
Medical Information Technology	352	Westwood, MA	Private	193.8	1,500	7371
Lambda Holdings Inc.	353	Melville, NY	Private	87.1	1,500	3679
Epson Portland Inc.	354	Hillsboro, OR	Private	250.0	1,500	3577
Cognizant Tech Solutions Corp.	355	Teaneck, NJ	Public	116.5	1,500	7371
Bowthorpe International Inc.	356	Commack, NY	Private	120.9	1,500	3699
Bortec Incorporated	357	El Paso, TX	Private	120.9	1,500	3699
AAI Corporation	358	Cockeysville, MD	Public Family Member	180.0	1,500	3699
Isaac Fair And Company Inc.	359	San Rafael, CA	Public	245.5	1,487	7372
IPM Service Corporation	360	Dallas, TX	Private	91.0	1,467	3694
National Instruments Corp.	361	Austin, TX	Public	240.9	1,465	3577
OAO Corporation	362	Greenbelt, MD	Private	196.4	1,457	7371
Dynamics Research Corporation	363	Andover, MA	Public	159.4	1,455	7373
Merix Corporation	364	Forest Grove, OR	Public	178.6	1,454	3672
Multilayer Technology Inc.	365	Irvine, CA	Public Family Member	94.6	1,452	3672
Panurgy Corporation	366	Columbia, MD	Private	124.5	1,451	7373
Hitachi Semiconductor America	367	Brisbane, CA	Private	205.0	1,448	3674
Xlconnect Systems, Inc.	368	Exton, PA	Public Family Member	170.0	1,400	7379
Wacker Siltronic Corporation	369	Portland, OR	Private	107.8	1,400	3674
Sutherland Group Ltd Inc.	370	Pittsford, NY	Private	99.5	1,400	7375
Mid-South Industries Inc.	371	Gadsden, AL	Private	178.1	1,400	3672
MEMC Southwest Inc.	372	Sherman, TX	Public Family Member	172.0	1,400	3674
Manugistics, Inc.	373	Rockville, MD	Public Family Member	200.0	1,400	7371
Lawson Associates, Inc.	374	Minneapolis, MN	Private	199.0	1,400	7372
KAO Info Systems Company	375	Plymouth, MA	Private	400.0	1,400	3695
Fujitsu-ICL Systems Inc.	376	Dallas, TX	Private	308.2	1,400	7373
Cerner Corporation	377	Kansas City, MO	Public	245.1	1,400	7372
Candle Corporation	378	Santa Monica, CA	Private	300.0	1,400	7372
BTG, Inc.	379	Fairfax, VA	Public	588.9	1,400	7371
Aztec Technology Partners	380	Braintree, MA	Public	256.0	1,400	7373
Xilinx, Inc.	381	San Jose, CA	Public	613.6	1,391	3674
Powerhouse Technologies Inc.	382	Bozeman, MT	Public	196.9	1,380	3575
Vishay Vitramon Incorporated	383	Monroe, CT	Public Family Member	66.0	1,368	3675
International Network Svcs	384	Sunnyvale, CA	Public	169.7	1,353	7379
H N Bull Information Systems	385	Billerica, MA	Private	372.5	1,350	3571
Cerplex, Inc.	386	Tustin, CA	Public	141.4	1,350	7378
Acer America Corporation	387	San Jose, CA	Private	1,141.2	1,348	3571
Wabash Technologies	388	Huntington, IN	Private	140.0	1,338	3677
GT Interactive Software Corp.	389	New York, NY	Public	530.7	1,337	7372
U M I & Company	390	Ann Arbor, MI	Public Family Member	94.8	1,335	7375
Earthlink Network, Inc.	391	Pasadena, CA	Public	79.2	1,329	7375
Exabyte Corporation	392	Boulder, CO	Public	286.5	1,323	3572
Georgia Solectron Corporation	393	Duluth, GA	Public Family Member	108.5	1,309	3578
Zenith Data Systems Corp.	394	Buffalo Grove, IL	Private	156.7	1,300	3571
Teccor Electronics Inc.	395	Irving, TX	Private	105.0	1,300	3674
Summit Service Corporation	396	Ridgefield Park, NJ	Public Family Member	82.5	1,300	7374
Pyxis Corporation	397	San Diego, CA	Public Family Member	82.0	1,300	7373
Manugistics Group Inc.	398	Rockville, MD	Public	175.7	1,300	7371
Kavlico Corporation	399	Moorpark, CA	Private	75.4	1,300	3679
IXL Enterprises Inc.	400	Atlanta, GA	Private	64.8	1,300	7374
GEAC Computer Systems, Inc.	401	Atlanta, GA	Private	101.0	1,300	7371
Elexsys International, Inc.	402	San Jose, CA	Public Family Member	84.7	1,300	3672
Deltec Electronics Corporation	403	San Diego, CA	Private	145.0	1,300	3679
DBC Holding Corp.	404	Atlanta, GA	Private	101.0	1,300	7371
Burr-Brown Corporation	405	Tucson, AZ	Public	252.1	1,300	3674
Bea Systems, Inc.	406	San Jose, CA	Public	157.2	1,300	7371
Mitsubishi Silicon America	407	Salem, OR	Private	170.0	1,290	3674
Zilog Inc.	408	Campbell, CA	Public	204.7	1,270	3674
Impact Innovations Holdings	409	Houston, TX	Public Family Member	74.8	1,265	7379
Prestolite Wire Corporation	410	Southfield, MI	Private	228.0	1,255	3694
Signal Corporation	411	Fairfax, VA	Private	91.5	1,250	7379
Lason, Inc.	412	Troy, MI	Public	120.3	1,250	7374
CTA Incorporated	413	Bethesda, MD	Private	92.2	1,250	7373
Cincom Systems Inc.	414	Cincinnati, OH	Private	161.6	1,240	7373
Boeing Information Svcs Inc.	415	Vienna, VA	Public Family Member	78.1	1,231	7374
Sony Magnetic Products Inc.	416	Dothan, AL	Private	118.1	1,230	3695
Siliconix Incorporated	417	Santa Clara, CA	Public	321.6	1,226	3674
Calcomp Technologies, Inc.	418	Anaheim, CA	Public	200.2	1,225	3577
Altron Incorporated	419	Wilmington, MA	Public Family Member	172.4	1,210	3672
Progress Software Corporation	420	Bedford, MA	Public	239.9	1,201	7371

D&B COMPANY RANKINGS BY EMPLOYMENT

Company	Rank	Location	Type	Sales ($ mil.)	Employ-ment	Primary SIC
Tyco Printed Circuit Group	421	Stafford Springs, CT	Private	78.1	1,200	3672
Spang & Company	422	Butler, PA	Private	100.0	1,200	3672
S C Data Center Inc.	423	Monroe, WI	Private	250.0	1,200	7374
Platinum Technology Solutions	424	Inglewood, CA	Public Family Member	93.3	1,200	7371
Interactive Business Systems	425	Oak Brook, IL	Private	100.0	1,200	7379
Infonet Services Corporation	426	El Segundo, CA	Private	76.2	1,200	7374
Hadco Phoenix, Inc.	427	Phoenix, AZ	Public Family Member	78.1	1,200	3672
Gale Group	428	Farmington Hills, MI	Private	63.9	1,200	7375
Fujitsu Microelectronics Inc.	429	San Jose, CA	Private	500.0	1,200	3674
Dow Jones Telerate, Inc.	430	New York, NY	Private	85.3	1,200	7375
Digital Audio Disc Corporation	431	Terre Haute, IN	Private	115.2	1,200	3695
Deluxe Electronic Payment Systems	432	Milwaukee, WI	Public Family Member	140.0	1,200	7374
Communications Instruments	433	Fairview, NC	Private	89.4	1,200	3679
CCC Information Serices Group	434	Chicago, IL	Private	159.1	1,200	7371
AVG Advanced Technologies LP	435	Carol Stream, IL	Private	78.1	1,200	3672
Apex Data Services Inc.	436	Herndon, VA	Private	76.2	1,200	7374
AMS Management Systems Group Inc.	437	Windsor, CT	Public Family Member	124.0	1,187	7371
CSG Systems International	438	Englewood, CO	Public	171.8	1,179	7374
Smartflex Systems Inc.	439	Tustin, CA	Public	133.3	1,169	3678
Norwest Services, Inc.	440	Minneapolis, MN	Public Family Member	73.7	1,161	7374
Qad Inc.	441	Carpinteria, CA	Public	91.5	1,156	7371
Unison Industries Ltd Partnr	442	Jacksonville, FL	Private	150.0	1,150	3694
PSC Inc.	443	Webster, NY	Public	207.8	1,150	3577
Pacific Electricord Company	444	Gardena, CA	Private	92.8	1,150	3699
Hitachi Automotive Products USA	445	Harrodsburg, KY	Private	70.7	1,140	3694
Santa Cruz Operation Inc.	446	Santa Cruz, CA	Public	171.9	1,136	7371
SEI Investment Company	447	Oaks, PA	Public	292.7	1,133	7372
Broderbund Software Inc.	448	Novato, CA	Public Family Member	190.8	1,129	7372
ITI Technologies, Inc.	449	Saint Paul, MN	Public	101.0	1,124	3699
EFTC Corporation	450	Denver, CO	Public	113.2	1,120	3672
Etec Systems Inc.	451	Hayward, CA	Public	288.3	1,119	3699
CSG Systems Incorporated	452	Omaha, NE	Public Family Member	156.0	1,119	7374
Verbatim Corporation	453	Charlotte, NC	Private	400.0	1,100	3695
Telos Field Engineering Inc.	454	Woods Cross, UT	Public Family Member	94.6	1,100	7378
Sierra On-Line Inc.	455	Bellevue, WA	Public Family Member	111.9	1,100	7372
SCB Computer Technology Inc.	456	Memphis, TN	Public	109.5	1,100	7371
Quantegy Inc.	457	Peachtree City, GA	Public Family Member	105.6	1,100	3695
Micrus	458	Hopewell Junction, NY	Private	390.0	1,100	3674
Matthey Johnson Electronics	459	Spokane, WA	Private	130.0	1,100	3679
JDA Software Group, Inc.	460	Phoenix, AZ	Public	138.5	1,100	7373
Information Tech Solutions	461	Hampton, VA	Public Family Member	88.0	1,100	7373
Automotive Controls Corp.	462	Branford, CT	Public Family Member	116.4	1,100	3694
Applied Systems Inc.	463	University Park, IL	Private	76.1	1,100	7371
Agena Corporation	464	Bothell, WA	Public Family Member	125.0	1,100	7371
Aavid Thermal Products, Inc.	465	Laconia, NH	Public	134.6	1,088	3679
Medical Manager Corporation	466	Tampa, FL	Public	78.1	1,085	7372
Intersolv, Inc.	467	Rockville, MD	Public	109.1	1,073	7372
Condor Technology Solutions	468	Annapolis, MD	Public	92.1	1,073	7373
Advanced Energy Industries	469	Fort Collins, CO	Public	141.9	1,059	3679
A C I Worldwide Inc.	470	Omaha, NE	Public Family Member	107.3	1,055	7372
Harbinger Corporation	471	Atlanta, GA	Public	120.7	1,044	7372
Federal Data Corporation	472	Bethesda, MD	Private	336.3	1,036	7373
Xircom Inc.	473	Thousand Oaks, CA	Public	276.1	1,000	3577
Wang Government Services Inc.	474	Mc Lean, VA	Public Family Member	300.0	1,000	7373
Startek USA Inc.	475	Aurora, CO	Public Family Member	79.0	1,000	7372
RMS Holdings, Incorporated	476	Lanham, MD	Private	90.9	1,000	7374
PSInet Inc.	477	Herndon, VA	Public	121.9	1,000	7373
Processors Unlimited Company	478	Dallas, TX	Private	101.7	1,000	7372
Paragon Computer Professionals	479	Cranford, NJ	Private	71.0	1,000	7379
NCI Information Systems Inc.	480	Mc Lean, VA	Private	92.5	1,000	7371
Nacom Corporation	481	Griffin, GA	Private	145.5	1,000	3672
JLC Holding Inc.	482	San Diego, CA	Private	131.5	1,000	7377
J P Morgan Services Inc.	483	Newark, DE	Public Family Member	63.4	1,000	7374
Intellisource Info Systems	484	Vienna, VA	Private	89.0	1,000	7374
Intellisource Holdings Inc.	485	Vienna, VA	Private	100.0	1,000	7374
Hood Cable Company	486	Hattiesburg, MS	Private	70.0	1,000	3694
Diversified Phrm Services	487	Minneapolis, MN	Private	500.0	1,000	7375
Dialog Corporation	488	Mountain View, CA	Private	71.0	1,000	7375
Dataproducts Corporation	489	Simi Valley, CA	Private	107.6	1,000	3577
Data Transmission Network Corp.	490	Omaha, NE	Public	126.4	1,000	7375

D&B COMPANY RANKINGS BY EMPLOYMENT

Company	Rank	Location	Type	Sales ($ mil.)	Employ-ment	Primary SIC
Corporate Software & Tech	491	Norwood, MA	Public Family Member	85.8	1,000	7373
Compaq Federal LLC	492	Greenbelt, MD	Public Family Member	120.8	1,000	3571
Columbia/HCA Information Services	493	Nashville, TN	Public Family Member	63.4	1,000	7374
C & K Components Inc.	494	Watertown, MA	Private	225.0	1,000	3679
Averstar Inc.	495	Burlington, MA	Private	85.8	1,000	7373
Autotote Corporation	496	New York, NY	Public	159.3	1,000	3578
Allied Business Systems Inc.	497	Macon, GA	Public Family Member	77.7	1,000	7371
AII Technologies Inc.	498	El Paso, TX	Private	361.8	1,000	3571
ABR Benefits Services, Inc.	499	Palm Harbor, FL	Public Family Member	77.7	1,000	7371
Eclipsys Corporation	500	Delray Beach, FL	Public	94.1	997	7371
Printronix Inc.	501	Irvine, CA	Public	170.4	992	3577
Alpha Technologies Group, Inc.	502	Houston, TX	Public	77.0	987	7373
Act Manufacturing Inc.	503	Hudson, MA	Public	264.7	985	3672
Tecstar, Inc.	504	City Of Industry, CA	Private	140.0	980	3674
BEI Technologies Inc.	505	San Francisco, CA	Public	101.5	977	3679
BEI Sensors & Systems Company	506	Sylmar, CA	Public Family Member	150.0	977	3679
Uniphase Corporation	507	San Jose, CA	Public	175.8	976	3674
Cherry Semiconductor Corp.	508	East Greenwich, RI	Public Family Member	113.0	975	3674
B.T.N.Y. Services, Inc.	509	New York, NY	Public Family Member	61.7	973	7374
BRC Holdings, Inc.	510	Dallas, TX	Public Family Member	107.5	970	7374
Boole & Babbage Inc.	511	San Jose, CA	Public	218.2	970	7372
Information Mgt Resources	512	Clearwater, FL	Public	83.5	955	7379
Software Ag Systems, Inc.	513	Reston, VA	Public	181.2	950	7372
OCLC Online Cmpt Lib Ctr Inc.	514	Dublin, OH	Private	130.9	950	7375
K-N Holdings Inc.	515	White Plains, NY	Private	58.9	950	3694
Disclosure Incorporated	516	Bethesda, MD	Public Family Member	67.5	950	7375
Bentley Systems Incorporated	517	Exton, PA	Private	154.9	950	7373
Austin Samsung Semicdtr LLC	518	Austin, TX	Private	73.1	950	3674
SCT Software & Resources Mgt	519	Malvern, PA	Public Family Member	73.6	946	7371
Trident Data Systems Inc.	520	Los Angeles, CA	Private	94.0	936	7379
Sapient Corporation	521	Cambridge, MA	Public	90.4	924	7371
Sheldahl, Inc.	522	Northfield, MN	Public	117.0	922	3672
General Scanning Inc.	523	Watertown, MA	Public	181.5	915	3699
Altera Corporation	524	San Jose, CA	Public	654.3	915	3674
Landmark Graphics Corporation	525	Houston, TX	Public Family Member	70.8	910	7371
Microstrategy Incorporated	526	Vienna, VA	Public	70.7	907	7372
Woods Industries Inc.	527	Carmel, IN	Public Family Member	180.0	900	3699
Tekmark Global Solutions LLC	528	Edison, NJ	Private	98.3	900	7379
Siemens Pyramid Info Systems	529	San Jose, CA	Private	108.8	900	3571
Planar Systems Inc.	530	Beaverton, OR	Public	129.0	900	3575
L H S Group Inc.	531	Atlanta, GA	Public	105.4	900	7371
Electro Scientific Industries	532	Portland, OR	Public	229.6	900	3699
Dovatron International, Inc.	533	Boulder, CO	Public Family Member	274.7	900	3679
Delta Products Corporation	534	Nogales, AZ	Private	52.2	900	3679
Consist International, Inc.	535	New York, NY	Private	100.0	900	7371
Computer Generated Solutions	536	New York, NY	Private	100.0	900	7373
Spectra-Physics Lasers, Inc.	537	Mountain View, CA	Public	159.2	895	3699
Par Technology Corporation	538	New Hartford, NY	Public	100.0	894	7373
Hypercom Corporation	539	Phoenix, AZ	Public	257.2	893	3577
Sterling Software U S Amer Inc.	540	Reston, VA	Public Family Member	88.8	874	7372
Cherokee International LLC	541	Tustin, CA	Private	77.0	868	3679
OECO Corporation	542	Milwaukie, OR	Private	83.4	865	3679
Medquist Inc.	543	Marlton, NJ	Public	84.6	857	7374
M R J Group, Inc.	544	Fairfax, VA	Private	127.0	850	7373
Kyocera America Inc.	545	San Diego, CA	Private	65.4	850	3674
Gerber Garment Technology	546	Tolland, CT	Public Family Member	83.9	850	7371
Crystal Semiconductor Corp.	547	Austin, TX	Public Family Member	65.4	850	3674
Cornell-Dubilier Electronics	548	Wayne, NJ	Private	52.0	850	3675
Computer Curriculum Corp.	549	Sunnyvale, CA	Private	150.0	850	7373
Channel Master LLC	550	Smithfield, NC	Private	166.0	850	3679
BBN Barrnet Inc.	551	Cambridge, MA	Public Family Member	91.5	850	3577
Bairnco Corporation	552	Maitland, FL	Public	158.7	850	3672
Onix Systems Inc.	553	Kingwood, TX	Public	121.5	845	7371
Diamond Multimedia Systems	554	San Jose, CA	Public	608.6	841	3672
Health Management Systems Inc.	555	New York, NY	Public	105.3	837	7374
Smart Modular Technologies	556	Fremont, CA	Public	714.7	831	3674
Evans & Sutherland Cmpt Corp.	557	Salt Lake City, UT	Public	159.4	831	3571
Medic Computer Systems Inc.	558	Raleigh, NC	Private	71.3	830	7373
Sunquest Info Systems Inc.	559	Tucson, AZ	Public	102.3	828	7373
Inprise Corporation	560	Scotts Valley, CA	Public	174.0	821	7372

D&B COMPANY RANKINGS BY EMPLOYMENT

Company	Rank	Location	Type	Sales ($ mil.)	Employ-ment	Primary SIC
Signal Technology Corporation	561	Danvers, MA	Public	102.3	820	3679
Network General Corporation	562	Santa Clara, CA	Public Family Member	240.7	818	7373
Cubic Applications Inc.	563	Lacey, WA	Public Family Member	63.0	810	7373
Marcam Solutions Inc.	564	Newton, MA	Public	124.5	805	7372
Rand McNally Media Svcs Inc.	565	Skokie, IL	Private	68.8	801	7373
Alpha Industries Inc.	566	Woburn, MA	Public	116.9	801	3679
Video Monitoring Svcs Amer LP	567	New York, NY	Private	56.8	800	7375
SPSS Inc.	568	Chicago, IL	Public	110.6	800	7372
Spectra Precision Inc.	569	Dayton, OH	Private	130.0	800	3699
Saga Software, Inc.	570	Reston, VA	Private	81.2	800	7372
Reflectone Inc.	571	Tampa, FL	Private	64.6	800	3699
Questech, Inc.	572	Falls Church, VA	Private	78.5	800	7373
Princeton Information Ltd.	573	New York, NY	Private	60.4	800	7379
Motorola Automotive Products	574	Northbrook, IL	Public Family Member	100.0	800	3694
Mid-South Electrics Inc.	575	Annville, KY	Private	123.8	800	3672
Medstat Holdings Inc.	576	Ann Arbor, MI	Private	81.2	800	7372
Ipec-Planar, Inc.	577	Phoenix, AZ	Public Family Member	125.0	800	3695
Filemaker, Inc.	578	Santa Clara, CA	Public Family Member	281.7	800	7372
Epsilon Data Management Inc.	579	Burlington, MA	Private	68.7	800	7373
Consultec Inc.	580	Atlanta, GA	Private	74.0	800	7373
Confederated Slish Ktnai Tribes	581	Pablo, MT	Private	62.0	800	3679
Avant Corporation	582	Fremont, CA	Public	227.1	800	7371
4Front Software International	583	Englewood, CO	Public	84.1	800	7371
Wall Data Incorporated	584	Kirkland, WA	Public	140.9	793	7372
E-Tek Dynamics Inc.	585	San Jose, CA	Public	106.9	787	3674
Sigma Circuits Inc.	586	Santa Clara, CA	Private	80.0	785	3672
Spectrolab Inc.	587	Sylmar, CA	Public Family Member	60.0	780	3674
CSX Technology Inc.	588	Jacksonville, FL	Public Family Member	228.7	780	7371
Cheyenne Software Inc.	589	Hauppauge, NY	Public Family Member	60.5	778	7371
Cubic Defense Systems Inc.	590	San Diego, CA	Public Family Member	108.8	768	3699
Spectrum Control Inc.	591	Erie, PA	Public	59.9	763	3677
User Technology Associates	592	Arlington, VA	Private	57.4	760	7373
Computer Management Sciences	593	Jacksonville, FL	Public	71.2	760	7379
Robroy Industries Inc.	594	Verona, PA	Private	126.1	755	3572
Great Plains Software Inc.	595	Fargo, ND	Public	85.7	755	7372
Transpo Electronics Inc.	596	Orlando, FL	Private	72.0	750	3694
Kenan Systems Corporation	597	Cambridge, MA	Private	83.8	750	7371
Jostens Learning Corporation	598	San Diego, CA	Private	100.0	750	7377
HNC Software Inc.	599	San Diego, CA	Public	113.7	750	7371
Getty Images Inc.	600	Seattle, WA	Private	76.1	750	7372
C Cube Microsystems Inc.	601	Milpitas, CA	Public	337.0	750	3674
Atlantron, Inc.	602	Mayaguez, PR	Private	94.2	750	3672
Zebra Technologies Corp.	603	Vernon Hills, IL	Public	192.1	745	3577
Xicor Inc.	604	Milpitas, CA	Public	122.5	738	3674
Kingston Technology Company	605	Fountain Valley, CA	Private	365.7	734	3577
OSI Systems Inc.	606	Hawthorne, CA	Public	77.6	725	3674
Durant Electric Company	607	Clinton, MS	Private	65.5	725	3694
Dendrite International Inc.	608	Morristown, NJ	Public	78.4	725	7371
Xylan Corporation	609	Calabasas, CA	Public	210.8	721	3577
Harbor Electronics Inc.	610	Etters, PA	Private	57.0	720	3679
AVX Vancouver Corporation	611	Vancouver, WA	Public Family Member	90.0	720	3675
Circuit Systems, Inc.	612	Elk Grove Village, IL	Public	75.0	715	3672
Oyo Corporation USA	613	Houston, TX	Private	113.1	712	3678
Cymer Inc.	614	San Diego, CA	Public	57.5	712	3699
W R Q Inc.	615	Seattle, WA	Private	138.5	710	7372
Bel Fuse Inc.	616	Jersey City, NJ	Public	73.5	707	3679
Digi International Inc.	617	Hopkins, MN	Public	182.9	703	3577
American Software, Inc.	618	Atlanta, GA	Public	107.5	701	7372
Sequel Inc.	619	San Jose, CA	Private	85.8	700	7378
Polygram Manufacturing & Dist	620	Grover, NC	Private	115.0	700	3695
New Resources Corporation	621	Rolling Meadows, IL	Private	61.0	700	7376
MacNeal-Schwendler Corporation	622	Los Angeles, CA	Public	134.9	700	7373
Logicon Space & Information	623	Fairfax, VA	Public Family Member	54.5	700	7371
JVC America Inc.	624	Tuscaloosa, AL	Private	175.0	700	3695
Instinet Corporation	625	New York, NY	Private	600.0	700	7379
Hayes Microcomputer Products	626	Norcross, GA	Public Family Member	75.4	700	3577
H T E Inc.	627	Lake Mary, FL	Private	54.5	700	7371
Group Technologies Corporation	628	Tampa, FL	Public	113.4	700	3672
Eastman Software, Inc.	629	Billerica, MA	Public Family Member	71.0	700	7372
Claremont Technology Group	630	Beaverton, OR	Public Family Member	83.6	700	7379

D&B COMPANY RANKINGS BY EMPLOYMENT

Company	Rank	Location	Type	Sales ($ mil.)	Employ- ment	Primary SIC
Bureau Engraving Incorporated	631	Minneapolis, MN	Private	107.0	700	3672
Motorcar Parts & Accessories	632	Torrance, CA	Public	113.0	690	3694
Print Northwest Co LP	633	Tacoma, WA	Private	89.0	685	7372
Microtouch Systems Inc.	634	Methuen, MA	Public	144.4	682	3577
Davidson & Associates Inc.	635	Torrance, CA	Public Family Member	68.9	679	7372
Incyte Pharmaceuticals, Inc.	636	Palo Alto, CA	Public	88.4	676	7375
Born Information Services	637	Wayzata, MN	Private	54.4	675	7371
QMS Inc.	638	Mobile, AL	Public	133.5	674	3577
Nugent Robinson Inc.	639	New Albany, IN	Public	74.1	674	3678
Unitrode Corporation	640	Merrimack, NH	Public	177.6	668	3674
Phase Metrics, Inc.	641	San Diego, CA	Private	71.4	668	3572
Kawasaki Steel Holdings (USA)	642	New York, NY	Private	51.4	668	3674
MCE Companies, Inc.	643	Ann Arbor, MI	Private	81.0	660	3679
Aris Corporation	644	Bellevue, WA	Public	62.5	660	7379
Acclaim Entertainment	645	Glen Cove, NY	Public	326.6	660	7372
Infinium Software Inc.	646	Hyannis, MA	Public	114.4	658	7372
EER Systems, Inc.	647	Lanham, MD	Private	75.0	657	7373
MMC Technology	648	San Jose, CA	Private	70.5	655	3577
Datapoint Corporation	649	San Antonio, TX	Public	151.4	652	7373
Xetel Corporation	650	Austin, TX	Public	112.7	650	3672
Vitech America, Inc.	651	Miami, FL	Public	117.5	650	3571
Stewart Connector Systems Inc.	652	Glen Rock, PA	Private	56.3	650	3678
SDL, Inc.	653	San Jose, CA	Public	91.4	650	3674
Platinum Software Corporation	654	Irvine, CA	Public	98.5	650	7372
Pacific Circuits Inc.	655	Redmond, WA	Private	80.0	650	3672
Indus International Inc.	656	San Francisco, CA	Public	177.0	650	7372
Goodtimes Home Video Corp.	657	New York, NY	Private	62.4	650	3695
Bell Microproducts Inc.	658	San Jose, CA	Public	533.7	650	3672
Knowles Electronics	659	Itasca, IL	Private	100.0	641	3679
Direct Marketing Tech Inc.	660	Schaumburg, IL	Private	80.0	640	7374
Checkpoint Systems Of PR	661	Ponce, PR	Public Family Member	78.6	640	3699
Computer Network Tech Corp.	662	Minneapolis, MN	Public	97.8	626	7373
Logicon Eagle Technology, Inc.	663	Arlington, VA	Public Family Member	53.7	625	7373
Comptek Research, Inc.	664	Buffalo, NY	Public	72.0	620	7373
Project Software & Development	665	Bedford, MA	Public	73.3	619	7372
Auspex Systems Inc.	666	Santa Clara, CA	Public	60.6	612	3577
Intel Networks Incorporated	667	Bedford, MA	Public	139.6	610	3577
VTC Inc.	668	Minneapolis, MN	Private	174.0	600	3674
Universal Computer Network	669	Houston, TX	Private	78.9	600	7377
Sterling Commerce Inc.	670	Dallas, TX	Public	490.3	600	7372
Shape Inc.	671	Kennebunk, ME	Private	90.0	600	3695
Shape Global Technology Inc.	672	Kennebunk, ME	Private	90.0	600	3695
Roxboro Holdings Inc.	673	Manasquan, NJ	Private	100.0	600	3679
R F Monolithics Inc.	674	Dallas, TX	Public	55.2	600	3679
Packard-Hughes Intrcnct Wr Sys	675	Foley, AL	Public Family Member	75.0	600	3679
MKE-Quantum Components, LLC	676	Louisville, CO	Public Family Member	64.6	600	3577
Mitsubishi Electric Auto Amer	677	Mason, OH	Private	430.0	600	3694
Maxwell Technologies, Inc.	678	San Diego, CA	Public	125.3	600	3571
Lycos Inc.	679	Waltham, MA	Public	56.1	600	7375
International Resistive Co.	680	Boone, NC	Private	80.0	600	3676
Innovex Precision Components	681	Hopkins, MN	Public Family Member	133.4	600	3679
Headway Technologies Inc.	682	Milpitas, CA	Private	175.0	600	3572
Harris Data Services Corp.	683	Alexandria, VA	Public Family Member	51.6	600	7373
Grumman Systems Support Corp.	684	Bohemia, NY	Public Family Member	51.6	600	7373
Dominion Semiconductors L.L.C.	685	Manassas, VA	Private	64.6	600	3577
Documentum, Inc.	686	Pleasanton, CA	Public	75.6	600	7372
Datastream Systems Inc.	687	Greenville, SC	Public	69.8	600	7372
Citicorp Development Center	688	Los Angeles, CA	Public Family Member	51.6	600	7373
Celestica Colorado Inc.	689	Fort Collins, CO	Private	350.0	600	3674
Barra, Inc.	690	Berkeley, CA	Public	137.4	600	7372
Circuit-Wise, Inc.	691	North Haven, CT	Private	71.8	591	3672
Vitesse Semiconductor Corp.	692	Camarillo, CA	Public	175.1	590	3674
Geoscience Corp.	693	Houston, TX	Public	94.5	589	7371
Datatec Systems, Inc.	694	Totowa, NJ	Public	76.8	585	7373
Advanced Quick Circuits LP	695	Melbourne, FL	Private	63.0	585	3672
Integrated Systems Inc.	696	Sunnyvale, CA	Public	120.5	584	7373
Envoy Corporation	697	Nashville, TN	Public	137.6	583	7374
Ross Systems, Inc.	698	Atlanta, GA	Public	91.7	582	7372
Radiant Systems Inc.	699	Alpharetta, GA	Public	78.0	581	7373
Pemstar Inc.	700	Rochester, MN	Private	165.0	580	3571

D&B COMPANY RANKINGS BY EMPLOYMENT

Company	Rank	Location	Type	Sales ($ mil.)	Employ- ment	Primary SIC
Ardent Software Inc.	701	Westborough, MA	Public	119.3	580	7371
Veritas Software Corporation	702	Mountain View, CA	Public	121.1	579	7372
Tri-Cor Industries Inc.	703	Alexandria, VA	Private	53.2	576	7373
Cyborg Systems Inc.	704	Chicago, IL	Private	59.0	575	7372
Pinkerton Computer Consultants	705	Langhorne, PA	Private	91.9	572	7379
Phoenix Technologies Ltd.	706	San Jose, CA	Public	73.7	572	7371
Lattice Semiconductor Corp.	707	Hillsboro, OR	Public	245.9	569	3674
R E Phelon Company Inc.	708	Aiken, SC	Private	65.0	565	3694
Petroleum Infrmton/Dwights LLC	709	Houston, TX	Private	72.0	565	7375
American Intl Group Data Ctr	710	Livingston, NJ	Public Family Member	115.0	565	7374
BA Merchant Services, Inc.	711	San Francisco, CA	Public	161.0	564	7374
Wind River Systems Inc.	712	Alameda, CA	Public	92.4	563	7372
MTI Technology Corporation	713	Anaheim, CA	Public	200.0	562	3572
Mektec Corp.	714	Fremont, CA	Private	55.0	560	3672
Parlex Corporation	715	Methuen, MA	Public	60.3	558	3672
Electronics For Imaging Inc.	716	San Mateo, CA	Public	430.7	556	3577
Visio Corp.	717	Seattle, WA	Public	166.0	555	7372
NER Data Products Inc.	718	Glassboro, NJ	Private	65.0	550	3577
Kanbay LLC	719	Des Plaines, IL	Private	426.6	550	7371
Inspire Insurance Solutions	720	Fort Worth, TX	Public	56.6	550	7371
Genesys Telecom Labs	721	San Francisco, CA	Public	84.7	550	7371
Foxconn Corporation	722	Houston, TX	Private	52.2	550	7371
Sawtek Inc.	723	Apopka, FL	Public	97.7	549	3677
El Camino Resources International	724	Woodland Hills, CA	Private	678.2	548	7377
Micrel, Incorporated	725	San Jose, CA	Public	104.2	546	3674
Automated Concepts Inc.	726	New York, NY	Private	57.0	540	7379
Partech, Inc.	727	New Hartford, NY	Public Family Member	73.8	539	7373
ECC International Corp.	728	Orlando, FL	Public	52.6	538	3699
Physician Computer Network	729	Morris Plains, NJ	Private	95.8	530	7373
Magnetic Data, Inc.	730	Eden Prairie, MN	Public Family Member	57.0	530	3572
Concurrent Computer Corp.	731	Fort Lauderdale, FL	Public	82.2	530	3571
Branson Ultrasonics Corp.	732	Danbury, CT	Public Family Member	129.0	530	3699
Systems In Focus Inc.	733	Wilsonville, OR	Public	306.7	525	3577
Walker Interactive Systems	734	San Francisco, CA	Public	71.4	520	7371
Williams Controls Inc.	735	Portland, OR	Public	57.6	511	3679
Oak Technology Inc.	736	Sunnyvale, CA	Public	157.1	511	3674
Filtronic Comtek Inc.	737	Salisbury, MD	Private	73.2	509	3679
Arlon Inc.	738	Maitland, FL	Public Family Member	99.4	505	3674
Stellex Microwave Systems	739	Palo Alto, CA	Private	89.0	504	3679
Semtech Corporation	740	Newbury Park, CA	Public	102.8	503	3674
Mindspring Enterprises, Inc.	741	Atlanta, GA	Public	52.6	502	7374
Viking Components Inc.	742	Rancho S Margari, CA	Private	260.7	500	3577
Triad Data Inc.	743	New York, NY	Public Family Member	77.0	500	7379
Toppan Electronics Inc.	744	San Diego, CA	Private	135.0	500	3672
Tibco Finance Technology Inc.	745	Palo Alto, CA	Private	100.0	500	7373
System Resources Corporation	746	Burlington, MA	Private	58.1	500	7373
Sungard Recovery Services Inc.	747	Wayne, PA	Public Family Member	150.0	500	7374
Standard Microsystems Corp.	748	Hauppauge, NY	Public	155.7	500	3674
Rofin-Sinar Technologies Inc.	749	Plymouth, MI	Public	117.6	500	3699
Mindscape, Inc.	750	Novato, CA	Public Family Member	140.0	500	7372
Hi-Tech Manufacturing, Inc.	751	Thornton, CO	Private	59.0	500	3672
GSS Array Technology, Inc.	752	San Jose, CA	Private	94.8	500	3672
Force Computers Inc.	753	San Jose, CA	Public Family Member	60.9	500	3571
Datamax International Corp.	754	Orlando, FL	Private	98.2	500	3577
CVSI Inc.	755	Bedford, MA	Private	135.0	500	7371
Citrix Systems Inc.	756	Fort Lauderdale, FL	Public	123.9	500	7371
Ameritech Library Services	757	Provo, UT	Public Family Member	88.0	500	7373
Altec Lansing Technologies	758	Milford, PA	Private	53.9	500	3577
Cybernetics & Systems Inc.	759	Jacksonville, FL	Public Family Member	91.9	490	7371
Anstec, Inc.	760	Mc Lean, VA	Private	52.3	490	7371
Clarify Inc.	761	San Jose, CA	Public	88.2	488	7372
Volt Delta Resources, Inc.	762	New York, NY	Public Family Member	60.5	481	7373
Autometric Inc.	763	Springfield, VA	Private	60.2	481	7373
Seta Corp.	764	Mc Lean, VA	Private	60.0	480	7373
Nova Information Systems Inc.	765	Atlanta, GA	Public Family Member	335.6	480	7375
Automata International Inc.	766	Sterling, VA	Private	60.0	480	3672
Philips Comm & Sec Systems	767	Lancaster, PA	Private	125.0	475	3699
Broadway & Seymour, Inc.	768	Charlotte, NC	Public	79.6	475	7373
Anadigics Inc.	769	Warren, NJ	Public	102.5	475	3674
Siebel Systems, Inc.	770	San Mateo, CA	Public	118.8	473	7372

D&B COMPANY RANKINGS BY EMPLOYMENT

Company	Rank	Location	Type	Sales ($ mil.)	Employ-ment	Primary SIC
Kirchman Corporation	771	Altamonte Springs, FL	Private	60.0	470	7371
Computer Merchant Ltd.	772	Norwell, MA	Private	70.7	470	7379
MAI Systems Corporation	773	Irvine, CA	Public	71.0	467	7373
Del Global Technologies Corp.	774	Valhalla, NY	Public	62.3	466	3679
Metrologic Instruments Inc.	775	Blackwood, NJ	Public	53.5	465	3699
Applied Cellular Technology	776	Palm Beach, FL	Public	103.2	460	7379
Three-Five Systems, Inc.	777	Tempe, AZ	Public	84.6	459	3577
Radisys Corporation	778	Hillsboro, OR	Public	125.4	458	3577
Legato Systems, Inc.	779	Palo Alto, CA	Public	143.2	457	7372
Code-Alarm Inc.	780	Madison Heights, MI	Public	62.5	457	3699
Computron Software Inc.	781	Rutherford, NJ	Public	67.6	454	7372
Vantive Corporation	782	Santa Clara, CA	Public	117.3	451	7372
Victron Inc.	783	Fremont, CA	Private	109.5	450	3672
Viasoft, Inc.	784	Phoenix, AZ	Public	113.7	450	7371
Supertex Inc.	785	Sunnyvale, CA	Public	52.7	450	3674
Spectrum Technology Group Inc.	786	Somerville, NJ	Public Family Member	70.0	450	7379
S3 Incorporated	787	Santa Clara, CA	Public	436.4	450	3577
Remedy Corporation	788	Mountain View, CA	Public	129.2	450	7371
Network Appliance; Inc.	789	Santa Clara, CA	Public	166.2	450	7373
Manu-Tronics Inc.	790	Pleasant Prairie, WI	Private	70.0	450	3672
Kobe Precision Inc.	791	Hayward, CA	Private	125.0	450	3674
Journal Of Commerce Inc.	792	New York, NY	Private	52.0	450	7375
International Fuel Cells, LLC	793	South Windsor, CT	Public Family Member	60.0	450	3674
Fourth Shift Corporation	794	Minneapolis, MN	Public	68.2	450	7372
Business Records Corporation	795	Dallas, TX	Public Family Member	90.0	450	7374
Bisys, Inc.	796	Houston, TX	Public Family Member	81.9	450	7374
Allied Telesyn International	797	Sunnyvale, CA	Private	163.0	450	3577
Advent Software Inc.	798	San Francisco, CA	Public	71.0	450	7372
ACS Technology Solutions, Inc.	799	Dallas, TX	Public Family Member	54.5	450	7371
ESS Technology Inc.	800	Fremont, CA	Public	249.5	447	3674
Sandisk Corporation	801	Sunnyvale, CA	Public	125.3	445	3572
Proxima Corporation	802	San Diego, CA	Private	154.7	444	3679
Netmanage, Inc.	803	Cupertino, CA	Public	61.5	440	7371
Berger & Co.	804	Denver, CO	Public Family Member	54.2	440	7379
Trident Microsystems Inc.	805	Mountain View, CA	Public	113.0	439	3674
MRV Communications, Inc.	806	Chatsworth, CA	Public	165.5	438	3674
Howard Systems Intl Inc.	807	Stamford, CT	Private	65.0	436	7371
Sipex Corporation	808	Billerica, MA	Public	51.2	435	3674
Elgar Electronics Corporation	809	San Diego, CA	Private	62.5	433	3679
Forte Software, Inc.	810	Oakland, CA	Public	71.3	431	7372
Sulcus Hospitality Tech	811	Greensburg, PA	Public	52.1	430	3578
Printrak International Inc.	812	Anaheim, CA	Public	71.9	430	7371
EA Industries	813	West Long Branch, NJ	Public	76.5	430	3571
Dialight Corp.	814	Manasquan, NJ	Private	70.0	430	3679
Betac International Corp.	815	Alexandria, VA	Public Family Member	60.0	430	7373
A-Plus Manufacturing Corp.	816	San Jose, CA	Private	60.0	430	3672
Summit Group Inc.	817	Mishawaka, IN	Public Family Member	75.0	425	7379
Objective Systems Integrators	818	Folsom, CA	Public	60.6	425	7371
Intelligroup Inc.	819	Edison, NJ	Public	80.2	425	7371
Edify Corporation	820	Santa Clara, CA	Public	57.1	425	7372
Aeroflex Laboratories Inc.	821	Plainview, NY	Public Family Member	54.4	425	3679
Inter-National Research Inst	822	Reston, VA	Private	53.4	420	7371
Encad Inc.	823	San Diego, CA	Public	110.1	420	3577
Financial Institutions Inc.	824	Warsaw, NY	Private	67.2	419	7374
McHugh Software International	825	Waukesha, WI	Private	69.4	418	7373
Seer Technologies Inc.	826	Cary, NC	Public	64.0	411	7371
Level One Communications Inc.	827	Sacramento, CA	Public	263.0	410	3674
Ace Electric, LLC	828	Columbus, KS	Private	60.0	410	3694
Eltron International Inc.	829	Simi Valley, CA	Private	105.0	409	3577
Levi Ray & Shoup Inc.	830	Springfield, IL	Private	79.2	405	7373
Comshare Incorporated	831	Ann Arbor, MI	Public	89.8	405	7372
Virtualfund.Com, Inc.	832	Eden Prairie, MN	Public	80.7	404	3577
Clover Technologies Inc.	833	Wixom, MI	Public Family Member	79.0	404	7373
Trippe Manufacturing Company	834	Chicago, IL	Private	125.0	400	3679
N B S G III	835	San Francisco, CA	Private	100.0	400	7379
Mapinfo Corporation	836	Troy, NY	Public	60.6	400	7372
Mapics, Inc.	837	Atlanta, GA	Public	129.7	400	7372
Delphax Systems	838	Canton, MA	Public Family Member	60.0	400	3577
3D Systems Inc.	839	Santa Clarita, CA	Public Family Member	90.3	400	3571
Davox Corporation	840	Westford, MA	Public	88.9	398	7373

D&B COMPANY RANKINGS BY EMPLOYMENT

Company	Rank	Location	Type	Sales ($ mil.)	Employ-ment	Primary SIC
Applied Automation Inc.	841	Bartlesville, OK	Private	96.0	398	3577
Detection Systems Inc.	842	Fairport, NY	Public	126.3	395	3699
Adept Technology Inc.	843	San Jose, CA	Public	98.4	394	7373
MDL Information Systems, Inc.	844	San Leandro, CA	Private	61.5	390	7372
Current Electronics Inc.	845	Newberg, OR	Public Family Member	55.0	390	3679
ODS Networks, Inc.	846	Richardson, TX	Public	92.3	389	3577
Quickturn Design Systems Inc.	847	San Jose, CA	Public	104.1	388	7373
Banyan Systems Incorporated	848	Westborough, MA	Public	74.3	386	7373
Actel Corporation	849	Sunnyvale, CA	Public	155.9	380	3674
Mercury Computer Systems Inc.	850	Chelmsford, MA	Public	85.5	378	3571
World Wide Automotive Inc.	851	Winchester, VA	Public Family Member	102.0	375	3694
Mylex Corporation	852	Fremont, CA	Public	135.7	373	3577
Transcore	853	Harrisburg, PA	Private	75.0	365	7373
Firearms Training Systems Inc.	854	Suwanee, GA	Public	73.5	362	3699
Triquint Semiconductor, Inc.	855	Hillsboro, OR	Public	71.4	361	3674
Unicomp Inc.	856	Marietta, GA	Public	52.1	360	7372
Tatung Company Of America Inc.	857	Long Beach, CA	Private	142.0	360	3571
Security Dynamics Tech Inc.	858	Bedford, MA	Public	135.9	360	3577
Mobius Management Systems Inc.	859	Rye, NY	Public	56.5	360	7371
Applied Science & Technology	860	Woburn, MA	Public	83.4	355	3679
Network Computing Devices	861	Mountain View, CA	Public	133.4	352	3575
TSR, Inc.	862	Hauppauge, NY	Public	70.4	350	7371
Texas Microsystems Inc.	863	Houston, TX	Public Family Member	70.9	350	3577
Tally Printer Corporation	864	Kent, WA	Private	75.0	350	3577
SMT Centre Of Texas, Inc.	865	Austin, TX	Private	60.0	350	3672
Peregrine Systems Inc.	866	San Diego, CA	Public	61.9	350	7371
Interleaf Inc.	867	Waltham, MA	Public	52.6	350	7372
Harte-Hanks Data Technologies	868	Billerica, MA	Public Family Member	77.0	350	7374
Open Market Inc.	869	Burlington, MA	Public	61.3	347	7373
Exar Corporation	870	Fremont, CA	Public	102.0	347	3674
UTMC Microelectronic Systems	871	Colorado Springs, CO	Public Family Member	74.8	340	3674
Universal Systems Inc.	872	Chantilly, VA	Private	78.1	340	7373
Sharp Microelectronics Tech	873	Camas, WA	Private	67.3	340	3674
Pegasus Consulting Group Inc.	874	Woodbridge, NJ	Private	84.7	340	7371
Applied Micro Circuits Corp.	875	San Diego, CA	Public	76.6	335	3674
Powerex Inc.	876	Youngwood, PA	Private	96.6	330	3674
Boundless Technologies Inc.	877	Hauppauge, NY	Public Family Member	99.2	329	3575
Seagate Sftwr Stor Mgt Group	878	San Luis Obispo, CA	Public Family Member	293.2	325	7371
Melita International Corp.	879	Norcross, GA	Public	65.8	325	7371
Scan-Optics, Inc.	880	Manchester, CT	Public	56.6	324	3577
Forsythe Technology, Inc.	881	Skokie, IL	Private	280.5	324	7377
Industrial Computer Source	882	San Diego, CA	Public Family Member	100.0	323	3571
Telcom Semiconductor, Inc.	883	Mountain View, CA	Public	55.4	321	3674
Industri-Matematik International	884	Tarrytown, NY	Private	59.6	317	7371
Xerox Colorgrafx Systems Inc.	885	San Diego, CA	Public Family Member	156.2	310	3577
Election Systems & Software	886	Omaha, NE	Private	63.0	310	3577
Tier Technologies, Inc.	887	Walnut Creek, CA	Public	57.7	308	7373
Procom Technology Inc.	888	Santa Ana, CA	Public	111.9	308	3577
Micrografx, Inc.	889	Richardson, TX	Public	71.8	302	7372
Superior Conslt Holdings Corp.	890	Southfield, MI	Public	76.9	300	7379
Solectron Massachussets Corp.	891	Westborough, MA	Public Family Member	75.0	300	3679
SBS Technologies Inc.	892	Albuquerque, NM	Public	74.2	300	7373
Rainbow Technologies Inc.	893	Irvine, CA	Public	94.7	300	3577
R Emass Inc.	894	Englewood, CO	Public Family Member	81.0	300	3572
Peachtree Software Inc.	895	Norcross, GA	Public Family Member	55.0	300	7372
Metrum-Datatape Inc.	896	Littleton, CO	Private	52.0	300	3572
Martin James & Co Inc.	897	Fairfax, VA	Private	55.0	300	7373
Macromedia Inc.	898	San Francisco, CA	Public	113.1	300	7372
Lacerte Software Corporation	899	Dallas, TX	Public Family Member	65.0	300	7371
Insync Systems, Inc.	900	Milpitas, CA	Private	86.1	300	3674
Digicon Corporation	901	Bethesda, MD	Private	62.9	300	7371
Dataworks Corporation	902	San Diego, CA	Public	147.0	300	7373
Brooktrout Technology Inc.	903	Needham, MA	Public	72.2	300	7371
Besam Automated Entrance Systems	904	Hightstown, NJ	Private	58.1	300	3699
Arrow Automotive Industries	905	Morrilton, AR	Private	87.5	300	3694
Caere Corporation	906	Los Gatos, CA	Public	55.0	293	7372
Lynk Systems Inc.	907	Atlanta, GA	Private	87.0	290	7374
Techsonic Industries Inc.	908	Eufaula, AL	Public Family Member	52.0	285	3679
Data Systems Network Corp.	909	Farmington Hills, MI	Public	88.0	285	7373
Micro Modeling Associates Inc.	910	New York, NY	Private	51.0	280	7379

D&B COMPANY RANKINGS BY EMPLOYMENT

Company	Rank	Location	Type	Sales ($ mil.)	Employment	Primary SIC
Hughes Aircraft Mississippi	911	Forest, MS	Public Family Member	65.0	280	3699
Bindco Corporation	912	Redwood City, CA	Private	63.8	280	7379
Iris Graphics Inc.	913	Bedford, MA	Private	75.0	277	3577
Raltron Electronics Corp.	914	Miami, FL	Private	75.0	275	3679
QRS Corporation	915	Richmond, CA	Public	71.6	270	7375
Factset Research Systems, Inc.	916	Greenwich, CT	Public	78.9	265	7374
Janis Group Inc.	917	Rochelle Park, NJ	Private	62.0	262	7373
Natural Microsystems Corp.	918	Framingham, MA	Public	75.4	260	3577
Midwest Payment Systems, Inc.	919	Cincinnati, OH	Public Family Member	167.0	258	7374
Jaton Corp.	920	Milpitas, CA	Private	116.0	255	3672
Astea International Inc.	921	Horsham, PA	Public	60.9	253	7372
Micro Linear Corporation	922	San Jose, CA	Public	65.8	252	3674
Northern Computers Inc.	923	Milwaukee, WI	Private	65.0	250	3699
Microsoft Puerto Rico Inc.	924	Humacao, PR	Public Family Member	201.1	250	7372
Emtec Inc.	925	Mount Laurel, NJ	Private	85.5	250	7373
CMOS Technologies, Inc.	926	Santa Clara, CA	Private	96.1	250	3571
CSP Inc.	927	Billerica, MA	Public	63.5	247	3577
Viewlogic Systems Inc.	928	Marlborough, MA	Public	62.0	240	7373
Transact Technologies Inc.	929	Wallingford, CT	Public	58.4	240	3577
Artecon, Inc.	930	Milpitas, CA	Public	66.3	238	3572
Amplicon Inc.	931	Santa Ana, CA	Private	313.8	236	7377
Overland Data Inc.	932	San Diego, CA	Public	75.2	233	3577
Vectron Technologies Inc.	933	Hudson, NH	Public Family Member	60.0	225	3679
NGK Spark Plug Manufacturing	934	Sissonville, WV	Private	200.0	225	3694
Interphase Corporation	935	Dallas, TX	Public	66.0	222	3577
Intermag, Inc.	936	Sacramento, CA	Private	52.5	222	3695
T D K Components USA	937	Peachtree City, GA	Private	70.0	220	3675
Softchoice Corporation	938	Norwalk, CT	Private	120.0	220	7372
Olin-Asahi Interconnect Tech	939	Norwalk, CT	Public Family Member	2,638.0	220	3674
Micro Voice Applications Inc.	940	Minneapolis, MN	Private	64.0	220	7371
Century Electronics Manufacturing	941	Marlborough, MA	Private	143.0	220	3672
Southland Micro Systems Inc.	942	Irvine, CA	Private	170.0	210	3577
Fanuc America Corporation	943	Hoffman Estates, IL	Private	60.0	210	7378
Global Intellicom, Inc.	944	New York, NY	Public	51.2	204	7373
Visiontek, Inc.	945	Gurnee, IL	Private	121.5	200	3577
TSR Consulting Services Inc.	946	Hauppauge, NY	Public Family Member	60.0	200	7379
Omni Tech Corporation	947	Pewaukee, WI	Private	73.5	200	3571
Netscout Systems Inc.	948	Westford, MA	Private	70.0	200	7371
Integrated Circuit Systems	949	Norristown, PA	Public	160.6	200	3674
Fujitsu PC Corporation	950	Milpitas, CA	Private	500.0	200	3571
Daw Technologies Inc.	951	Salt Lake City, UT	Public	52.5	200	3674
Comtec Information Systems	952	Warwick, RI	Private	60.0	200	3577
Centron Dpl Company, Inc.	953	Eden Prairie, MN	Public Family Member	200.0	200	7373
ATMI, Inc.	954	Danbury, CT	Public	101.9	200	3674
Applied Films Corporation	955	Longmont, CO	Public	53.0	200	3674
Government Micro Resources	956	Manassas, VA	Private	115.1	196	3571
N A I Technologies, Inc.	957	Huntington, NY	Public	51.9	194	7373
Everex Systems, Inc.	958	Fremont, CA	Private	160.0	190	3571
ATL Products, Inc.	959	Irvine, CA	Public Family Member	97.6	190	3572
Tangent Computer Inc.	960	Burlingame, CA	Private	108.0	187	3571
MLC Holdings Inc.	961	Reston, VA	Public	118.4	186	7377
Axent Technologies Inc.	962	Rockville, MD	Public	101.0	185	7371
Win Laboratories, Ltd.	963	Manassas, VA	Private	63.9	180	3571
Mack Technologies, Inc.	964	Westford, MA	Private	255.7	180	3577
Stonebridge Technologies, Inc.	965	Dallas, TX	Private	106.1	175	7373
P S I Holding Group Inc.	966	Marlborough, MA	Private	57.5	175	7371
Integrated Silicon Solution	967	Santa Clara, CA	Public	131.1	175	3674
Intec Systems Inc.	968	Houston, TX	Private	116.0	175	7373
Interface Systems Inc.	969	Ann Arbor, MI	Public	81.8	170	7373
Wellcor America Inc.	970	Oklahoma City, OK	Private	75.0	168	7373
Splash Technology, Inc.	971	Sunnyvale, CA	Public Family Member	76.0	163	3577
Neomagic Corporation	972	Santa Clara, CA	Public	124.7	162	3674
Wintec Industries Inc.	973	Fremont, CA	Private	700.0	160	3577
Micros-To-Mainframes, Inc.	974	Valley Cottage, NY	Public	69.6	160	7379
Huber & Suhner Inc.	975	Essex Junction, VT	Private	60.0	160	3679
Computer Sales International	976	Saint Louis, MO	Private	309.3	160	7377
Box Hill Systems Corp.	977	New York, NY	Public	70.3	160	3572
Sylvest Management System	978	Greenbelt, MD	Private	305.0	155	3571
MacDermid Inc.	979	Wilmington, DE	Public Family Member	80.5	152	3679
Stealthsoft Corporation	980	Irvine, CA	Private	200.0	150	7371

D&B COMPANY RANKINGS BY EMPLOYMENT

Company	Rank	Location	Type	Sales ($ mil.)	Employ- ment	Primary SIC
Savings Bnk Lf Insur Of Mass	981	Woburn, MA	Private	198.3	150	7374
SAP America Pubic Sector, Inc.	982	Philadelphia, PA	Private	65.0	150	7371
Proquire LLC	983	Chicago, IL	Private	200.0	150	7373
IBS Conversions Inc.	984	Oak Brook, IL	Private	100.0	150	3577
Greenleaf Distribution Inc.	985	Santa Clara, CA	Private	340.0	150	3571
Versyss Incorporated	986	Morris Plains, NJ	Private	60.0	145	7371
Maxi Switch, Inc.	987	Tucson, AZ	Private	77.7	140	3575
Dataram Corporation	988	Princeton, NJ	Public	77.3	138	3572
CGG Canada Ltd.	989	Houston, TX	Private	52.7	135	7374
Total Peripherals, Inc.	990	Northborough, MA	Private	90.5	130	3571
Alliance Semiconductor Corp.	991	San Jose, CA	Public	118.4	129	3674
Bay Data Consultants LLC	992	Norcross, GA	Private	56.0	127	7373
Micronics Computers Inc.	993	Fremont, CA	Public Family Member	99.3	122	3672
La Cie Ltd.	994	Hillsboro, OR	Private	62.0	120	3572
Edgemark Systems Inc.	995	Silver Spring, MD	Private	104.6	120	7373
Force 3 Inc.	996	Crofton, MD	Private	76.2	119	3571
Inteliant Corporation	997	Albuquerque, NM	Public Family Member	75.0	100	7379
Government Computer Sales Inc.	998	Issaquah, WA	Private	91.9	100	7373
G-Tech USA, Inc.	999	Cypress, CA	Private	120.0	100	3577
Du Pont Electronic Materials	1000	Manati, PR	Public Family Member	135.3	100	3677
Bold Data Technology Inc.	1001	Fremont, CA	Private	407.5	100	3571
Acer Latin America, Inc.	1002	Miami, FL	Private	272.6	100	3571
Videoserver Inc.	1003	Burlington, MA	Public	53.5	98	3571
Kenda Systems Inc.	1004	Salem, NH	Private	58.4	96	7371
Camelot Corporation	1005	Carrollton, TX	Public	1,662.0	95	7371
Milestone Technologies Inc.	1006	Tempe, AZ	Public Family Member	119.5	90	7374
MFP Technology Services Inc.	1007	Norcross, GA	Private	200.0	90	7377
ESG Consulting Inc.	1008	Santa Clara, CA	Private	100.0	90	7379
Advanced Digital Info Corp.	1009	Redmond, WA	Public	114.6	80	3577
Techworks Inc.	1010	Austin, TX	Private	100.0	75	3674
Nextrend Technology, Inc.	1011	Fremont, CA	Private	115.0	70	7373
Goldleaf Technologies, Inc.	1012	Hahira, GA	Public Family Member	1,366.1	70	7371
PSC Automation, Inc.	1013	Webster, NY	Public Family Member	230.0	65	3699
General Electric Capital	1014	Emeryville, CA	Public Family Member	300.0	60	7377
Arsys Innotech Corporation	1015	Fremont, CA	Private	95.2	55	3571
Trigem America Corporation	1016	Irvine, CA	Private	126.2	50	3571
Castlewood Systems Inc.	1017	Pleasanton, CA	Private	300.0	50	3572
Husko Inc.	1018	Milpitas, CA	Private	219.2	49	3679
Korea Data Systems (USA) Inc.	1019	Garden Grove, CA	Private	250.0	45	3577
Saehan Media America Inc.	1020	Carlsbad, CA	Private	139.8	40	3695
CRA Inc.	1021	Phoenix, AZ	Private	68.3	38	7377
MGV International Inc.	1022	Irvine, CA	Private	160.0	35	3577
Logicare Inc.	1023	Melville, NY	Private	181.3	35	7373
DSP Communications, Inc.	1024	Cupertino, CA	Public	131.1	35	3674
CBOL Corp.	1025	Woodland Hills, CA	Private	100.0	35	3674
Gores Technology Group	1026	Los Angeles, CA	Private	125.0	30	7372
Fort Lauderdale Network Corp.	1027	Fort Lauderdale, FL	Private	140.0	30	7375
FICO America Inc.	1028	Tempe, AZ	Private	417.0	30	7373
U S Capital Equipment Lessors	1029	Irvine, CA	Private	150.0	25	7377
Smith Wall Associates LLC	1030	Iselin, NJ	Private	100.0	25	7371
Jacom Computer Services, Inc.	1031	Northvale, NJ	Public Family Member	90.1	25	7377
Covenant Computer Laboratory	1032	Santa Clara, CA	Private	100.0	25	7371
Martin Collier	1033	Dallas, TX	Private	220.0	13	7371
United Optical Tech Corp.	1034	Marietta, GA	Private	100.0	5	3699
Quad Systems Technologies Inc.	1035	Sarasota, FL	Private	500.0	2	7373

CHAPTER 6 - PART I

MERGERS & ACQUISITIONS

The following essay presents a look at merger and acquisition activity in the Computers & Software sector. A general overview of M&A activity is followed by a listing of actual merger and acquisition events. Purchasing companies are listed in alphabetical order, with a paragraph set aside for each acquisition.

This essay discusses recent merger and acquisition activity in the industry and its effect on the industry. The essay is followed by a list of significant acquisitions and mergers.

The late 1990s saw merger and acquisition fever among computer hardware and software companies. High-profile companies, such as Microsoft Corp, IBM, Cisco Systems, Compaq Computer Corp., and American Online Inc. made strategic purchases throughout 1998 and 1999 to diversify their product lines. In many cases, consolidation provides a way for company to offer compatible end-to-end services and products to their customers. But life after a merger for a high-tech firm isn't always easy, according to the consulting firm Hay Group Inc. As reported in February of 1999, the Hay Group surveyed 60 senior executives from leading high-tech firms, who revealed that following a merger there were often problems delivering new products or an exodus of top- performing personnel. To avert these types of problems, some companies, such as Cisco, which has acquired over 30 businesses since 1993, have begun taking minority stakes in a business so that they can learn about the business and its technology before making an acquisition.

The reason for the intense merger and acquisition activity in the software industry is simple: it is cheaper and more efficient for many established firms to buy small businesses with cutting edge technology than to plan, design, and test new software on their own. A firm planning to enter a niche market can usually purchase a small company already developing software for that market for less money and in less time than it would cost to develop a new product. Analysts also point to the fact that the industry is overcrowded and that too many companies are vying for the same customers. This creates a willingness on the part of small software businesses to be acquired in hopes that they can capitalize on the marketing and distribution dollars of larger businesses.

The network security and antivirus market has been an active segment in the software arena. In December of 1997, McAfee Associates Inc. and Network General Corp. joined forces to form Network Associates Inc., which immediately acquired Pretty Good Privacy Inc. and a few months later bought Secure Networks Inc. In an effort to compete in this tightening arena, Symantec Corp., maker of the Norton antivirus software, agreed to purchase and license the antivirus software manufactured by IBM Corp. in May of 1998.

Analytical applications software is another burgeoning niche market in the software industry; analysts predict that it will grow from a $1 billion market in 1997 into a $2.65 billion market by 2001. Recent merger and acquisition activity in the market offers a prime example of how penetration by a major player forces smaller firms to buy or be bought simply to remain competitive. The 1998 announcement by Microsoft Corp. that it intends to enter the market spurred plans for a major merger between two leading business analysis software vendors; Arbor Software Corp. and Hyperion Software Corp. announced plans to merge in June of 1998, hoping to capture additional market share before Microsoft releases its online analytical processing server software. The new company, which will be called Hyperion Solutions, will boast a market capitalization of $1.3 billion.

Following a failed $9.8 billion takeover bid for Computer Sciences Corp. in 1998, Computer Associates International Inc. (CAI) successfully bought Platinum Technology International for $3.5 billion in 1999. The acquisition helped bolster CAI's service business. CAI, which is the fourth-largest software maker, had been looking to merge with a product manufacturing and selling operations as a means of competing with IBM Corp., which had already penetrated the services marketplace. It had originally wanted to buy Computer Sciences because it is a leading computer-services company. Computer Sciences narrowly avoided the hostile threat, but the attempted merger reflects the growing trend among product vendors to seek out alliances with services firms in an effort to broaden customer bases and offer clients more a more comprehensive line of technology wares that includes services.

Merger and acquisition activity has also heated up in other computer industry segments. In fact, the networking sector saw its two largest acquisitions in history take place in 1997 with the $6.6 billion merger of 3COM Corp. and U.S. Robotics Corp., which joined the LAN and WAN vendors, allowing for end-to-end networking capabilities, and the $3.7 billion merger of Ascend Communications Inc. and Cascade Communications Inc., which combined a WAN access provider with a WAN core switching technology provider. The reason for such consolidation is market driven: network equipment providers continue to scramble to offer Internet Service Providers (ISPs) comprehensive and integrated technologies, allowing the ISPs to distinguish their services from the growing numbers of start-ups. Looking to expand its data-networking operations, Lucent Technologies Inc. bought Ascend for $24 billion in 1999.

Like many firms in the software and computer services markets, many networking technology companies are also finding it less expensive and less time consuming to acquire existing businesses than to develop their own new technology. Aggressive acquisition campaigns over the five years have established Cisco Systems Inc., which agreed to a partnerships in 1997 with Alcatel and GTE as a means of gaining access to the emerging voice technology market, and 3COM Corp. as clear market leaders, with revenues more than double those of their two largest competitors: Cabletron Systems and Bay Networks.

In the Internet Service Provider market itself, growth has been phenomenal. The ability of small ISPs to effectively and cheaply serve local markets has fueled the consolidation that has taken place in the national ISP market over the past year. America Online Inc. (AOL) led the charge with the purchase of the consumer online service of CompuServe Corp. from WorldCom Inc. in September of 1997. Hoping to gain a stronger Internet presence, AOL bought Netscape Communications, the developer of the leading Internet browser. For much of the mid- to late 1990s, Microsoft Corp. and Netscape Communications Corp. have vied to have the dominant browser portal. In 1997, Netscape spent hundreds of millions of dollars to purchase KIVA Software Corp., producers of a high-end World Wide Web server; Actra, an Internet commerce solutions provider; Digital Style Corp., a World Wide Web graphics tools provider; and Portola Communications, Inc., a messaging-server technology provider.

In the late 1990s, Microsoft showed its intentions to expand beyond computer software. Investments in 1999 included a wireless communications firm and a fiber-optic network company. In 1997 Microsoft Corp. bought Hotmail, the award-winning World Wide Web-based free email service; Vxtreme Inc., a video streaming technology maker; WebTV Networks Inc., a set-top box maker that will allow Microsoft to produce a box version for Windows CE; Dimension X Inc., a

Java-based multimedia tools manufacturer; and Interse Corp., a manufacturer of Internet usage monitoring software. The industry behemoth also invested $1 billion in Comcast Cable Communications, Inc. to bolster the market for its WebTV venture.

Comparable to the consolidation trends in the networking, ISP, and other Internet-related industries has been the activity in the telecommunications industry as the giants grow even larger in their quest to offer a full range of telecommunications services to clients, including Internet access and related online services. In 1997, SBC Communications Inc. joined forces with Pacific Telesis Group in a $16.5 billion deal, and Bell Atlantic Corp. and Nynex Corp. merged for $25.6 billion. In July 1998, WorldCom Inc. and MCI Communications Corp. came together for an unprecedented $37 billion.

During 1997 and 1998 WorldCom Inc. made several major purchases aimed at growing its Internet-related holdings, including H&R Block's CompuServe and America Online's network subsidiary, ANS Communications Inc. These purchases, coupled with the MCI Communications merger, leave MCI-WorldCom in control of more than one-half of worldwide Internet traffic and a leader in the continual push towards globalization in the telecommunications market.

Second only to WorldCom in news making deals over the past two years has been Compaq Computer Corp., which completed many major acquisitions in the in the late 1990s. In 1999, Compaq looked outside the computer hardware market to purchase Shopping.com, an Internet shopping site, and Zip2, a provider of Internet platform solutions. Its $3 billion purchase of Tandem Computers Inc. was the largest transaction in the computer hardware industry in 1997. The acquisition doubled Compaq's sales force and secured Windows NT server technology, which allowed the company to begin offering clients more fully integrated products. Little more than a year later, in June of 1998, Compaq paid $9 billion for Digital Equipment Corp., in the largest acquisition ever completed in the computer hardware industry, to become the worldwide leader in multi-user storage systems. Both deals reflect the growing trends in the marketplace for consolidation and diversification, which are the result of growing demand for fully integrated products and the increasing tendency, particularly on the part of business clients, to seek dealers who can services all of their computing needs.

Other major players in the computer hardware industry have been seeking growth via acquisition over the past two years, including Gateway 2000 Inc., which diversified into server technology in 1997 with the acquisition of Advanced Logic Research Inc. and Intel Corp., which moved into the notebook graphics chips market with its $420 million purchase of Chips and Technologies Inc. in early 1998 and branched into the microprocessor server technology arena by buying Corollary, Inc. in late 1997.

Some industry analysts believe that the acquisitions and mega-mergers taking place bode well for those involved, while skeptics point out that, historically, anticipated synergies are quite often overblown. While these analysts may disagree on the outcome all this activity will produce for the businesses at hand, as well as the customer they serve, they seem to be in agreement that the merger and acquisition flurries that have taken place in all segments of the computer industry will at least continue, if not escalate to new record breaking levels.

Mergers and Acquisitions

3COM Corp. bought **U.S. Robotics Corp.,** a remote access vendor, in the largest merger in the networking industry to date, for $8.5 billion on June 12, 1998. [*PC Week,* 6/23/97, p.129.]

Activision, Inc. bought **Centre Soft Limited,** an interactive entertainment software distributor located in the United Kingdom, for 2.8 million shares on December 1, 1997. [*Next Wave Stocks: Mergers & Acquisitions,* 12/97.]

—bought **NBG Distribution,** an entertainment software distributor located in Germany, for 281,000 shares on December 1, 1997. [*Next Wave Stocks: Mergers & Acquisitions,* 12/97.]

ADE Corp. bought **Phase Shift Technology, Inc.,** a maker of metrology products for the semiconductor and computer hard disk industries, for two million shares on June 15, 1998. [*Next Wave Stocks: Mergers & Acquisitions,* 6/98.]

America Online, Inc. bought **Netscape Communications,** which developed the leading Internet browser, in a $4.2 billion stock swap in November of 1998. [*Computerworld,* 11/30/98, p.1.]

—bought **Mirabilis Ltd.,** an Internet service provider based in Tel Aviv, Israel, for $287 million in cash on June 5, 1998. [*Edge: Work-Group Computing Report,* 6/15/98, p. 9.]

—bought **Personal Library Software Inc.,** a privately held developer of searching and information indexing technologies located in Rockville, Maryland, on January 21, 1998. [*Information Today,* 3/98, p. 7.]

—bought the consumer online service of **CompuServe** from **WorldCom** on September 9, 1997. In exchange for the CompuServe service and $175 million in cash, AOL transferred **ANS Communications Inc.,** its network subsidiary, to WorldCom. [*Online,* 3/98, p. 77.]

Andrea Electronics Corporation bought **Lamar Signal Processing, Ltd.,** a digital signal processing noise cancellation technology developer located in Israel, for $3 million in cash and 1.8 million common shares on April 7, 1998. [*Next Wave Stocks: Mergers & Acquisitions,* 4/98.]

Apertus Technologies Inc. bought **Carleton Corp.,** a privately owned data warehousing operation, for $5 million in stock and $2 million in cash on November 4, 1997. [*Computergram International,* 11/4/97.]

Ardent Software Inc. bought **Dovetail Software Inc.,** a data translation software maker located in Burlington, Massachusetts, on June 5, 1998. [*PC Week,* 6/22/98, p. 61.]

Ascend Communications Inc. bought **Cascade Communications Corp.,** a manufacturer of WAN switches, in the second largest merger to date in the networking industry, for $3.6 billion on June 30, 1997. [*InfoWorld,* 12/22/97, p.181.]

Aspect Telecommunications bought **Voicetek Corporation,** a software platforms and applications solutions provider located in Chelmsford, Massachusetts, for $71 million in cash in April of 1998. [*Next Wave Stocks: Mergers & Acquisitions,* 4/98.]

Aspen Technology, Inc. bought **Treiber Controls, Inc.**, a provider of process control technologies and services based in Toronto, Ontario, Canada, on June 3, 1998. [*Business Wire, 6/3/98.*]

—bought **Zyquad Limited,** an engineering workflow management software developer located in Nottingham, England, for 218,000 shares on April 23, 1998. [*Next Wave Stocks: Mergers & Acquisitions, 4/98.*]

Avid Technology bought **Softimage Inc.**, an animation and video production application manufacturer located in Montreal, Quebec, Canada, for $285 million on June 15, 1998. [*MacWEEK, 6/29/98, p. 3.*]

Axiom Inc. bought **Innovative Data Technology,** a billing mediation systems supplier located in San Diego, California, for $8 million in cash and stock, on May 18, 1998. [*Next Wave Stocks: Mergers & Acquisitions, 5/98.*]

Barringer Technologies Inc. bought **DigiVision Inc.**, a real time video enhancement technology developer located in San Diego, California, for $750,000 in cash on May 4, 1998. [*Next Wave Stocks: Mergers & Acquisitions, 5/98.*]

Bay Networks bought **Rapid City Communications,** a Gigabit Ethernet start-up firm, in June of 1997. [*Next Wave Stocks: Mergers & Acquisitions, 6/97.*]

Bell Atlantic Corp. and **Nynex Corp.** merged into the largest regional Bell company and the second largest telecommunications company in the U.S., with estimated annual operating revenues of $29.2 billion, in a deal valued at $25.6 billion in August of 1997. The company retained the Bell Atlantic name. [*InternetWeek, 9/1/97, p. S7.*]

Borland International Inc. bought **Visigenic Software Inc.**, a distributed object technology provider, for $111 million in March of 1998. [*Computer Dealer News, 3/16/98, p. 6.*]

Bowne & Company Inc. bought **Open Sesame,** an Internet service provider based in Cambridge, Massachusetts, in June of 1998. *Computerworld, 6/22/98, p. 41.*]

—bought **Mountain Lake Software Corp.**, a computer software manufacturer located in Toronto, Ontario, Canada, in June of 1998. [*Computerworld, 6/22/98, p. 41.*]

Cable and Wireless bought all of the Internet assets of **MCI Communications Corp.**, the world's second largest long distance telephone company, for $1.6 billion, in July of 1998. [*The Wall Street Journal, 7/15/98, p. B6.*]

Cabletron Systems Inc. bought **OASys Group Inc.**, a telecommunications software developer located Los Gatos, California, for 240,000 shares on February 7, 1997. [*Business Wire, 2/7/97.*]

CACI International, Inc. bought **AnaData Limited,** a database marketing software products firm located in the United Kingdom, for $2 million on December 3, 1997. [*Next Wave Stocks: Mergers & Acquisitions, 12/97.*]

Celerity Solutions, Inc. bought **Somerset Automation, Inc.**, a privately owned warehouse management software developer located in Irvine, California, for $2.845 million in cash and notes and 1.95 million shares on December 10, 1997. [*Next Wave Stocks: Mergers & Acquisitions, 12/97.*]

Checkmate Electronics, Inc. bought **Total Retail Solutions, Inc.**, a software development and consulting business located in Brandon, Florida, on December 9, 1997. [*Next Wave Stocks: Mergers & Acquisitions, 12/97.*]

Cisco Systems, Inc. bought **GeoTel Communications Corp**, a Lowell, Massachusetts-based company that produces voice call-center software, for $2 billion in stock in June of 1999. [*Business Wire, 6/24/99.*]

—bought **Sentient Networks, Inc.,** a privately held company located in Milpitas, California, that produces high-density ATM circuit technology, in June of 1999. [*Business Wire, 6/24/99.*]

—bought Petulman, California-based **Fibex Systems** and Glen Allen, Virginia-based **Amteva Technology,** two companies that produce voice-service products and devices, in June of 1999. [*Business Wire, 6/18/99.*]

—bought **NetSpeed Inc.,** a Digital Subscriber Line technology manufacturer located in Austin, Texas, for roughly $236 million in stock in March of 1998. [*EDGE, on & about AT&T,* 3/16/98, p. 7.]

—bought **LightSpeed Software,** a voice signaling translation technology manufacturer located in Sterling, Virginia, for roughly $160 million in stock in January of 1998. [*PC Week,* 1/5/98, p. 95.]

—bought **Ardent Communications Corp.,** a compressed voice, LAN, and data and video traffic transmission technology provider located in San Jose, California, for $156 million in stock in July of 1997. [*EDGE, on & about AT&T,* 6/30/97, p. 6.]

—bought **Global Internet Software Group,** based in Palo Alto, California, for $40.25 million in cash in July of 1997. [*EDGE: Work-Group Computing Report,* 6/30/97, p. 10.]

—bought **Skystone Systems Corp.,** a privately owned Synchronous Optical Networking/Synchronous Digital Hierarchy technology provider based in Ottawa, Ontario, Canada, for $22.6 million in cash and one million shares in July of 1997. [*EDGE, on & about AT&T,* 6/16/97, p. 24.]

—bought **Stratacom Inc.,** a WAN switching technology provider, for $4 billion in July of 1996. The purchase was Cisco's largest ever, and it established the company as the network equipment industry's pacesetter. [*Electronic News,* 4/7/97, p. 1.]

CNET, Inc. bought **U.Vision, Inc.,** an Internet pricing and availability technology developer, for 545,000 shares on May 12, 1998. [*Next Wave Stocks: Mergers & Acquisitions,* 5/98.]

COGNICASE Inc. bought **Informatique B.F.G. Ltd.,** a computer systems management outsourcing firm, for $2.8 million in cash and 46,377 shares on April 9, 1998. [*Next Wave Stocks: Mergers & Acquisitions,* 4/98.]

Compaq Computer Corp. bought 9,935,449 share or 95.91 percent of the outstanding shares of common stock of **Shopping.com,** an Internet shopping site, for $18.25 per share in cash on February 16, 1999.

[Compaq press release. Available from http://www1.compaq.com.]

—bought **Zip2 Corp.,** a leading provider of Internet platform solutions, on February 16, 1999. [Compaq press release. Available from http://www1.compaq.com.]

—bought **Digital Equipment Corp.,** for $9 billion on June 15, 1998. It was the largest acquisition ever completed in the information technology industry. [*Business Week,* 6/22/98, p. 44.]

—bought **Tandem Computers Inc.,** a manufacturer of computer systems used in stock exchanges and phone companies, for $3 billion in stock in June of 1997. The acquisition was the largest in the PC industry in 1997. [*The Wall Street Journal,* 6/24/97, p. A3.]

Compressent Corp. bought **Softlink, Inc.** a privately owned e-mail upgrading products developer based in California, for 450,000 shares on December 22, 1997. [*Next Wave Stocks: Mergers & Acquisitions,* 12/97.]

CompuCom Systems, Inc. bought **Dataflex Corp.,** based in Clearwater, Florida, for $24 million in stock and cash in May of 1998. [*Computer Reseller News,* 6/1/98, p. 59.]

—bought **Computer Integration Corp.,** based in Charlotte, North Carolina, for $17 million in cash on May 13, 1998. [*Business Wire,* 5/13/98.]

Computer Associates International Inc. bought **Platinum Technology International Inc.,** which makes software and information systems based in Oakbrook Terrace, Illinois, for $3.5 billion in March of 1999. [*New York Times on the Web,* 3/30/99.]

Computer Sciences Corp. bought **KOBRA Beheer BV,** a BAAN enterprise software consultant located in Rotterdam, The Netherlands, in November of 1997. [*Software Industry Report,* 11/3/97, p. 3.]

—bought **Pinnacle Group Inc.,** a systems integrator located in Athens, Georgia, in January of 1997. [*Business Wire,* 1/21/97.]

Compuware Corp. bought **NuMega Technologies, Inc.,** a developer of error detection and debugging software, on December 15, 1997. [*Next Wave Stocks: Mergers & Acquisitions,* 12/97.]

Concentric Network Corp. bought **Delta Internet Services Inc.,**, a dial-up, dedicated access, and World Wide Web hosting services provider based in California, on June 5, 1998. [*Next Wave Stocks: Mergers & Acquisitions,* 6/98.]

Creative Technology Ltd. bought **Silicon Engineering, Inc.,** a Scotts Valley, California-based developer of integrated circuits for multimedia, storage and communications industries, for 921,271 shares on May 26, 1998. [*Next Wave Stocks: Mergers & Acquisitions,* 5/98.] .

—bought **Ensoniq,** an audio technology hardware and software developer based in Malvern, Pennsylvania, for $77 million on December 10, 1997. [*Next Wave Stocks: Mergers & Acquisitions,* 12/97.]

Cybex Computer Products Corp. bought **Elsner Computertechnic GmbH** and **PolyCon Data Systems GmbH**, both privately owned firms based in Steinhagen, Germany, for $8 million on December 30, 1997. [*Next Wave Stocks: Mergers & Acquisitions,* 12/97.]

DAOU Systems Inc. bought **Technology Management Inc.,** an information technology consulting company located in Indianapolis, Indiana, for $22.5 million on June 17, 1998. [*Business Wire,* 6/17/98.]

Dell Computer Corporation bought **ConvergeNet Technologies,** a network storage company, for $340 million in stock in September of 1999. [*Wired News,* 9/9/99.]

DocuCorp International bought **EZ Power Systems Inc.,** a document management software system developer located in Philadelphia, Pennsylvania, on April 30, 1998. [*Next Wave Stocks: Mergers & Acquisitions,* 4/98.]

DynamicWeb Enterprises Inc. bought **Design Crafting Inc.,** an information technology services firm located in Millburn, New Jersey, for 100,000 shares on May 7, 1998. [*Next Wave Stocks: Mergers & Acquisitions,* 5/98.]

Electronic Arts bought **Tiberon Entertainment, Inc.,** an entertainment software developer located in Maitland, Florida, on April 2, 1998. [*Next Wave Stocks: Mergers & Acquisitions,* 4/98.]

EMC bought **Data General,** a dot-com business storage provider, for $1 billion in August of 1999. [*Redherring.com,* 8/10/99.]

Engineering Animation, Inc. bought **Sense8 Corp.,** a privately owned simulation and 3D products developer located in Mill Valley, California, on June 17, 1998. [*Next Wave Stocks: Mergers & Acquisitions,* 6/98.]

Entrust Technologies Inc. bought **R3 Security Engineering AG,** a security technology research, consulting, and engineering company located in Switzerland on June 22, 1998. [*Information Week,* 6/22/98, p. 32.]

Evans & Sutherland Computer Corp. bought **AccelGraphics, Inc.,** a 2D and 3D graphics technology supplier, for $52 million in cash and stock on June 29, 1998. [*Next Wave Stocks: Mergers & Acquisitions,* 6/98.]

—bought **Silicon Reality Inc.,** a 3D graphics hardware and software products designer and manufacturer located in Federal Way, Washington, on July 6, 1998. [*Business Wire,* 7/6/98.]

Gateway 2000 Inc. bought **Advanced Logic Research Inc.,** a multiprocessing system technology supplier located in Irvine, Texas, for $15.50 per share, or $194 million, on June 23, 1997. [*Computergram International,* 6/23/97.]

Getronics bought **Wang Global,** a leading international network technology services and solutions company, in a stock transaction on June 8, 1999. [Getronics press release. Available from http://www.getronics.com.]

Gibson Musical Instruments Corp. bought **Opcode Systems Inc.,** a music software and MIDI hardware developer located in Palo Alto, California, in May of 1998. [*MacWEEK,* 6/15/98, p. 13.]

GTE Corp. bought **BBN Corp.,** an Internet service provider, in May of 1997. GTE Corp. changed the name of BBN Corp. to GTE Internetworking. [*Next Wave Stocks: Mergers & Acquisitions,* 5/97.]

Hewlett-Packard Co. bought **Qosnetics,** a Portsmouth, New Hampshire-based company that develops IP-based conformance verification and performance stressing tools for Internet networks, on September 20, 1999. [HP press release. Available from http://www.hp.com.]

—bought **Security Force Software, Inc.,** a startup company based in Research Triangle Park, North Carolina that develops risk-assessment technology for enterprise networks, on August 2, 1999. [HP press release. Available from http://www.hp.com.]

—bought **Dazel Corp.,** an Austin, Texas-based privately held company that develops electronic information delivery software, on May 5, 1999. [HP press release. Available from http://www.hp.com.]

—bought **PROLIN,** a service management software provider located in Amsterdam, The Netherlands, on June 6, 1997. [*Business Wire,* 6/6/97.]

—bought **VeriFone, Inc.,** one of the world's largest electronic commerce companies, in a stock transaction worth $1.29 billion on June 25, 1997. [*Business Wire,* 6/25/97.]

—bought **Vital Technology Pte. Ltd.,** a printed circuit board assembly and IC packaging machine vision inspection systems developer based in Singapore, in late 1997. [*Electronic News,* 10/13/97, p. 40.]

—bought **Optimization Systems Associates Inc.,** a privately owned computer-aided engineering software developer based in Ontario, Canada, on November 25, 1997. [*Business Wire,* 11/25/97.]

HNC Software Inc. bought **Financial Technology Inc.,** a Chicago, Illinois-based developer and marketer of information systems for financial institutions, for $1.5 million in cash and 397,000 shares on April 8, 1998. [*Next Wave Stocks: Mergers & Acquisitions,* 4/98.]

—bought **CompReview Inc.,** an insurance information technology services provider located in Costa Me-

sa, California, on December 1, 1997. [*Next Wave Stocks: Mergers & Acquisitions,* 12/97.]

IBM bought **DASCOM, Inc.,** a developer of Web-based and enterprise security technology, on September 22, 1999. [IBM press release. Available from http://www.ibm.com.]

—bought **Mylex Corp.,** a developer of technology for moving, storing, protecting, and managing data in desktop and networked environments, for $240 million on July 27, 1999. [IBM press release. Available from http://www.ibm.com.]

—and **Sequent Computer Systems,** a Beaverton, Oregon-based company that specializes in data-center solutions, agreed to merge in a transaction valued at $810 million on July 12, 1999. [IBM press release. Available from http://www.ibm.com.]

—bought **Whistle Communications, Inc.,** a developer of e-business products for small businesses based in Foster City, California, on June 9, 1999. [IBM press release. Available from http://www.ibm.com.]

ICC Technologies, Inc. bought **Rare Medium, Inc.,** an Internet services firm located in Manhattan, New York, for $45 million on April 15, 1998. [*Next Wave Stocks: Mergers & Acquisitions,* 4/98.]

ICG Communications Inc. bought **Netcom Online Communications Service Inc.,** the fifth largest Internet service provider in the U.S., in October of 1997. [*Next Wave Stocks: Mergers & Acquisitions,* 10/97.]

Infinium Software, Inc. bought **Cort Directions, Inc.,** a payroll software developer, on June 12, 1998. [*Business Wire,* 6/12/98.]

Intel Corp. bought **Chips and Technologies Inc.,** a PC notebook graphics controller and accelerator manufacturer, for $420 million in January of 1998. [*PC Week,* 2/2/98, p. 47.]

—bought **Corollary, Inc.,** a privately owned microprocessor server technology developer based in Irvine, California, in October of 1997. [*Computerworld,* 10/6/97, p. 72.]

Integrated Silicon Solution, Inc. bought **Nexcom Technology Inc.,** a privately owned Flash memory cell and design technology developer located in Sunnyvale, California, for $500,000 and 772,693 shares of common stock on December 9, 1997. [*Next Wave Stocks: Mergers & Acquisitions,* 12/97.]

Intermedia Communications bought Monroe, Louisiana-based **LDS Communications Group,** a provider of long distance voice and data telecommunications services, including Internet and World Wide Web access, for $151 million in stock and cash on December 17, 1997. [*Next Wave Stocks: Mergers & Acquisitions,* 12/97.]

Keane, Inc. bought **GSE Erudite Software, Inc.,** an information technology consultant located in Salt Lake City, Utah, on May 4, 1998. [*Next Wave Stocks: Mergers & Acquisitions,* 5/98.]

Larscom Inc. bought Research Triangle Park, North Carolina-based **NetEdge Systems, Inc.,** a privately owned ATM access equipment maker, for $26 million in cash and $9 million in debt assumption on December 31, 1997. [*Next Wave Stocks: Mergers & Acquisitions,* 12/97.]

LHS Group bought **InfoCellular, Inc.,** a provider of point-of-sale software and services located in Marlborough, Massachusetts, for $8.4 million in common stock on June 15, 1998. [*Communications Daily,* 6/15/98, p. 1.]

Lucent Technologies Inc. bought **Internal Network Services Inc.,** a network designer located in Sunnyvale, California, for $3.7 billion in stock in August of 1999. [*CFO Magazine,* 9/99.]

—bought **Ascend Communications,** a data-networking equipment supplier located in Alameda, California, for $24 billion in June of 1999. [*CFO Magazine,* 9/99.]

—bought **Livingston Enterprises Inc.,** a remote access data-networking software and services provider located in Pleasanton, California, for $650 million on December 17, 1997. [*Communications Daily,* 12/17/97, p. 6.]

—bought **Octel Communications Corp.,** a messaging technology provider based in Milpitas, California, for

$1.8 billion on September 30, 1997. [*Communications Daily,* 9/30/97, p. 7.]

Mastech Corp. bought **MC Computer Services Pty. Ltd.,** a privately owned information technology services provider located in Canberra, Australia, on June 30, 1998. [*Next Wave Stocks: Mergers & Acquisitions,* 6/98.]

Mattel bought **The Learning Company,** a consumer software company that has developed software titles such as Carmen Sandiego and Riven, for $3.8 billion in December of 1998. [The New York Times on the Web, *12/14/98.*]

McAfee Associates Inc., located in Santa Clara, California, and **Network General Corp.,** located in Menlo Park, California, merged to form **Network Associates Inc.,** a network security and management software developer, on December 1, 1997. [*MacWeek,* 12/8/97, p. 8.]

MEMCO Software, Ltd. bought **AbirNet Ltd.,** a network protection and intrusion detection software developer based in Israel, and **Network Information Technology, Inc.,** a server security software provider based in Saratoga, California, for a total of $43.7 million in stock and $11.3 million in cash in June of 1998. [*Business Wire,* 6/10/98.]

Micro-Integration Corp. bought **SuiteOne Computer Services, Inc.,** a UNIX services provider located in Pittsburgh, Pennsylvania, on December 15, 1997. [*Next Wave Stocks: Mergers & Acquisitions,* 12/97.]

Micron Electronics Inc. bought **Netframe Systems Inc.** on July 15, 1997. [*Computergram International,* 9/25/97.]

Microsoft Corp. bought 4 percent of **Nextel Communications Inc.,** a national provider of wireless communications, for $600 million in May of 1999. [*The New York Times on the Web,* 5/11/99.]

—bought a 1.3 percent stake in **Qwest Communications,** a fiber-optic network company, for $200 million in December of 1998. [*Red Herring,* 12/14/98.]

—bought **Firefly Network Inc.,** a privately owned Internet commerce technology developer located in

Cambridge, Massachusetts, in April of 1998. [*Next Wave Stocks: Mergers & Acquisitions, 4/98.*]

—bought **Hotmail,** an award-winning Web-based free email service, on December 31, 1997. [*PR Newswire,* 12/31/97.]

—bought **VXtreme Inc.,** an Internet streaming company located in Sunnyvale, California, for $75 million on August 6, 1997. [*Computergram International,* 8/6/97.]

—bought **WebTV Networks Inc.,** a Palo Alto, California-based provider of systems which allow Internet access via television, for $425 million on August 1, 1997. [*Communications Daily,* 8/4/97, p. 7.]

—bought **Dimension X Inc.,** a Java-based multimedia tools manufacturer located in San Francisco, California, in May of 1997. [*MacWEEK,* 5/12/97, p.3.]

—bought **Interse Corp.,** a manufacturer of Internet usage monitoring software, in March of 1997. [*InfoWorld,* 3/10/97.]

National Semiconductor Corp. bought **Cyrix Corp.,** a microprocessor manufacturer located in Dallas, Texas, in a stock transaction on November 17, 1997. [*Business Wire,* 11/17/97.]

NetManage, Inc. bought **Relay Technology, Inc.,** a network connectivity, file transfer, and terminal emulation services provider located in Vienna, Virginia, on December 8, 1997. [*Next Wave Stocks: Mergers & Acquisitions,* 12/97.]

Netscape Communications Corp. bought **KIVA Software Corp.,** an application server software maker located in Mountain View, California, for $180 million in stock in November of 1997. [*Computerworld,* 12/1/97, p. 16.]

—bought **Actra,** an Internet commerce software maker, for $56.1 million in stock in late 1997. [*Computerworld,* 11/10/97, p. 8.]

—bought **DigitalStyle Corp.,** a World Wide Web graphics tools provider, on June 17, 1997. [*PR Newswire,* 6/17/97.]

—bought **Portola Communications, Inc.,** a messaging systems manufacturer, for $56 million on June 17, 1997. [*PR Newswire,* 6/17/97.]

Network Associates Inc. bought **Secure Networks Inc.** for $25 million in May of 1998. [*InternetWeek,* 5/18/98, p. 16.]

—bought **Pretty Good Privacy Inc.,** an encryption tools developer located in San Mateo, California, for $36 million on December 1, 1997. [*MacWeek,* 12/8/97, p. 8.]

OAO Technology Solutions, Inc. bought **DHR Technologies, Inc.,** a software and information technology services developer located in Columbia, Maryland, on April 2, 1998. [*Next Wave Stocks: Mergers & Acquisitions,* 4/98.]

Open Text Corp. bought **Information Dimensions, Inc.,** an enterprise document management firm based in Dublin, Ohio, on June 3, 1998. [*Next Wave Stocks: Mergers & Acquisitions,* 6/98.]

Parametric Technology Corp. bought **ICEM Technologies,** a surfacing and reverse engineering software tools developer based in Frankfurt, Germany, on June 10, 1998. [*Business Wire,* 6/10/98.]

Peritus Software Inc. bought **Millennium Dynamics, Inc.,** based in Cincinnati, Ohio, for $30 million and 2.175 million shares on December 3, 1997. [*Next Wave Stocks: Mergers & Acquisitions,* 12/97.]

Planning & Logic, Inc. and **Forum Systems, Inc.** merged to form **PowerPlan Corporation** on May 19, 1998. [*PR Newswire,* 5/19/98.]

Preview Software Inc., of Cupertino, California, and **Portland Software Inc.,** of Portland, Oregon, merged to form **Preview Systems,** a provider of ESD transactions technology, in June of 1998. [*Computer Reseller News,* 6/15/98, p. 334.]

Prism Solutions, Inc. bought **Systems Techniques, Inc.,** an Atlanta, Georgia-based data warehousing firm serving the healthcare industry, on May 14, 1998. [*Next Wave Stocks: Mergers & Acquisitions,* 5/98.]

Qwest bought **EUnet International,** a European Internet services provider based in Amsterdam, The Netherlands, for $4.5 million in cash, $135.5 million in shares, and an additional $14.4 million in cash or shares, to be determined by Quest, on April 15, 1998. [*Next Wave Stocks: Mergers & Acquisitions, 4/98.*]

SBC Communications Inc. bought **Pacific Telesis Group** for $16.5 billion on April 2, 1997. The acquisition made SBC Communications the second largest telecommunications company in the U. S. *Communications Daily, 4/2/97, p.1.*]

Scan-Optics, Inc. bought **Southern Computer Systems,** a data entry and document automation software firm located in Birmingham, Alabama, for $7 million in cash on June 16, 1998. [*PR Newswire, 6/18/98.*]

SCM Microsystems, Inc. bought **Intellicard Systems Pte. Ltd.,** based in Singapore, for $7 million in cash and stock on June 8, 1998. [*PR Newswire, 6/8/98.*]

—bought **Intermart Systems K.K.,** a Japanese manufacturer of PC-based access devices, for $8 million in cash and stock on May 21, 1998. [*Next Wave Stocks: Mergers & Acquisitions, 5/98.*]

Silicon Valley Research, Inc. bought **Quality I.C. Corporation,** an integrated circuit design consultant based in Austin, Texas, for $200,000 in cash and 3.15 million shares on April 1, 1998. [*Next Wave Stocks: Mergers & Acquisitions, 4/98.*]

Sun Microsystems, Inc. bought **Forte Software, Inc.** a developer of enterprise-class distributed applications, for $540 million in August of 1999. [*PR Newswire, 8/23/99.*]

—bought **MAXSTRAT Corp.,** a supplier of high-performance computing storage systems, in January of 1999. [*PR Newswire, 1/25/99.*]

—bought **Beduin Communications,** a privately held Canadian company specializing in Java application products, in October of 1998. [*PR Newswire, 10/20/98.*]

—bought **i-Planet,** a privately held developer of secure-access software, in October of 1998. [*PR Newswire, 10/5/98.*]

—bought **Dakota Scientific Software Inc.,** a developer of scientific and engineering software components, on June 24, 1998. [*Business Wire, 6/24/98.*]

—bought **Chorus Systems SA,** a telecommunications equipment operating systems manufacturer based in France, in September of 1997. [*Computing Canada, 9/29/97, p. 6.*]

—bought **Diba, Inc.,** a supplier of technology to the information appliance industry, on August 25, 1997. [*Business Wire, 8/25/97.*]

—bought **LongView Technologies LLC,** a Palo Alto, California-based software company specializing in dynamic-language research, on February 18, 1997. [*EDGE: Work-Group Computing Report, 2/24/97, p. 18.*]

Take-Two Interactive Software, Inc. bought **DirectSoft Australia Pty. Ltd.,** a PC and video game software manufacturer and distributor based in Sydney, Australia, on June 11, 1998. [*Business Wire, 6/11/98.*]

TechWave Inc. bought **CyberTrust Inc.,** an online transaction processor, in June of 1998. [*Computer Reseller News, 6/15/98, p. 334.*]

—bought **eWarehouse Inc.,** an online reseller based in Montreal, Quebec, Canada, in June of 1998. [*Computer Reseller News, 6/15/98, p. 334.*]

Tekgraf, Inc. bought **Computer Graphics Technology,** a graphics equipment and software distributor located in Greenville, South Carolina, on April 1, 1998. [*Next Wave Stocks: Mergers & Acquisitions, 4/98.*]

Teleport Communications Group, Inc. bought **Kansas City Fiber Network, LP,** a local exchange carrier, on December 2, 1997. The acquisition makes Teleport Communications Group the first and largest U.S.-based local telecommunications services provider to use both fiber optic and broadband wireless technology. [*Next Wave Stocks: Mergers & Acquisitions, 12/97.*]

Template Software Inc. bought **Milestone Austria,** a software developer, on April 1, 1998. [*Next Wave Stocks: Mergers & Acquisitions,* 4/98.]

THQ, Inc. bought **GameFX Inc.,** an Arlington, Massachusetts-based applied technology developer serving the interactive entertainment software industry, on May 4, 1998. [*Next Wave Stocks: Mergers & Acquisitions,* 5/98.]

Transaction Systems Architects, Inc. bought **Edgeware, Inc.,** a privately owned retail software business located in Clearwater, Florida, for 143,436 shares on May 6, 1998. [*Next Wave Stocks: Mergers & Acquisitions,* 5/98.]

Tridex Corporation bought **Progressive Software, Inc.,** a privately owned software and systems services provider based in Charlotte, North Carolina, for $33.9 million in cash, $5 million in stock, and $9.6 million in debt assumption on April 20, 1998. [*Next Wave Stocks: Mergers & Acquisitions,* 4/98.]

Vignette Corp. bought **RandomNoise Inc.,** a Java authoring tools developer, in May of 1998. [*MacWEEK,* 5/18/98, p. 19.]

Voice Control Systems, Inc. bought **PureSpeech,** a privately owned speech recognition technology provider based in Cambridge, Massachusetts, on May 12, 1998. [*Next Wave Stocks: Mergers & Acquisitions,* 5/98.]

WorldCom Inc. and **MCI Communications Corp.,** the second largest long distance phone company in the world, merged to form **MCI WorldCom,** a telecommunications giant with more $30 billion in sales, in July of 1998. The transaction, valued at roughly $37 billion, was the largest to date in the telecommunications and computer industries. [*Computer Reseller News,* 7/20/98, p. 192.]

—bought **Brooks Fiber,** a nationwide Internet service provider, for $2.9 billion in January of 1998. [*Online,* 3/98, p. 77.]

—bought **CompuServe,** an online service provider, in a $1.2 billion stock swap on September 9, 1997. WorldCom then transferred the CompuServe consumer online service to **America Online, Inc.** in exchange for AOL's network subsidiary, **ANS Communications Inc.,** and $175 million in cash. [*Online,* 3/98, p. 77.]

Yahoo! Inc. bought **Viaweb Inc.,** an Internet commerce software distributor, for $49 million in stock in June of 1998. The acquisition was the largest in Yahoo's history. [*InformationWeek,* 6/15/98, p. 196.]

Yurie Systems bought **Data Labs, Inc.,** an ATM access equipment manufacturer based in Gaithersburg, Maryland, for 358,412 shares on December 2, 1997. [*Next Wave Stocks: Mergers & Acquisitions,* 12/97.]

Bibliography

Barker, Robert. "How to Be in the Right Spot to Catch a Merger Wave." *Business Week,* 6/15/98, p. 88.

Champy, Jim. "Why the CA/CSC Merger Was Doomed From the Start." *Computerworld,* 3/23/98, p. 76.

Cohen, Sarah. "Ascend, Cascade to Merge." *Electronic News,* 4/7/97, p. 1.

Collett, Stacy. "Study: High-Tech Megers Often Lead to Paralysis." *Computerworld,* 2/8/99, p.33.

Donnelly, George. "Acquiring Minds." *CFO Magazine,* 9/99.

Gant, Joanna. "Power Surge Promotes M&A Hot Spot." *Acquisitions Monthly,* 6/98, p. 18.

Gillooly, Brian. "Be Ready for the Merger Monster." *InformationWeek,* 6/1/98, p.147.

Hausman, Eric. "Mergers and Acquisitions." *Computer Reseller News,* 4/20/98, p.132.

Krill, Paul. "LAP Market Heats Up With Arbor-Hyperion Merge." *InfoWorld,* 6/1/98, p. 11.

Olsen, Florence. "Major Mergers Shrink Size of Server Industry." *Government Computer News,* 7/14/97, p. 56.

Pender, Lee. "Antivirus Merger Contagious." *Computer Reseller News,* 6/22/98, p.105.

Pender, Lee. "Techwave Buy Signals Change in ESD Market." *Computer Reseller News,* 6/15/98, p. 334.

Schwartz, Ephriam. "To Merge or Be Bought?" *InfoWorld,* 12/22/97, p. 18.

Wilson, Tim. "Merger Mania." *InternetWeek,* 5/18/98, p. 16.

—AnnaMarie L. Sheldon, updated by Katherine Wagner.

ASSOCIATIONS

This chapter presents a selection of business and professional associations active in the Computer & Software sector. The information shown is adapted from Gale's *Encyclopedia of Associations* series and provides detailed and comprehensive information on nonprofit membership organizations.

Entries are arranged in alphabetical order. Categories included are name, address, contact person, telephone, toll-free number, fax number, E-mail address and web site URL (when provided). A text block shows founding date, staff, number of members, budget, and a general description of activities.

AMERICAN COMPUTER SCIENCE LEAGUE
PO Box 40118
Providence, RI 02940
Founded: 1978. Secondary schools. Seeks to develop computer science education at the secondary school level. Works to provide educational opportunities for computer enthusiasts and motivate students to pursue classroom computer topics in-depth as well as to study computer subjects not covered in school curricula. Administers the annual Invitational Team All-Star Contest for junior and senior high school students; including computers, trophies, and computer-related materials.

AMERICAN COMPUTER SCIENTISTS ASSOCIATION
11 Commerce Dr., 3rd Fl.
Cranford, NJ 07016-3531
Daniel Louis Grossman, Esq.
PH: (908)272-0016
FX: (908)272-6297
URL: www.acsa2000.net/1996b2.html
Founded: 1993. **Members:** 59,800. Works for computer scientists.

AMERICAN VOICE INPUT/OUTPUT SOCIETY
PO Box 20817
San Jose, CA 95160
Peggie Johnson, Contact
PH: (408)323-1783
FX: (408)323-1782
Founded: 1982. **Members:** 470. Academics, researchers, management personnel, vendors, and engineers (450); corporations (20). Seeks to: facilitate communication among potential users of voice technology and the developers and suppliers of this technology; offer information to researchers, technologists, and users on current and future voice input/output technology and its applications. (Voice input/output technology is concerned with the applications of voice recognition and synthesis with and through computers.) Provides information to current and potential users through demonstrations of practical applications of voice systems; offers users opportunities to meet with voice technology researchers, technologists, and service and product providers.

ASSOCIATION FOR AUTOMATED REASONING
c/o Lawrence Wos
9700 S. Cass Ave.
Math and Computer Science Division
Argonne National Lab
Argonne, IL 60439
Lawrence Wos, Pres.
PH: (630)252-7224
FX: (630)252-5986
Founded: 1984. **Members:** 400. Scientists united to promote research in the field of automated reasoning programs for computer systems.

ASSOCIATION FOR COMPUTER-AIDED DESIGN ON ARCHITECTURE
PO Box 210016
Cincinnati, OH 45221-0016
PH: (513)556-0487
E-mail: anton.harfmann@uc.edu
URL: www.acadia.org
Founded: 1980. **Staff:** 20. **Members:** 300. Educators, students, and professionals. Provides quality education in the area of computer-aided design.

ASSOCIATION FOR INFORMATION SYSTEMS
PO Box 2712
Atlanta, GA 30301-2712
Ephraim R. McLean, Exec.Dir.
PH: (404)651-0258
FX: (404)651-4938
E-mail: ais@gsu.edu
URL: www.aisnet.org
Founded: 1995. **Staff:** 3. **Members:** 1,700. Academics engaged in the study of information systems and related fields. Represents and promotes members' interests; encourages research and study in information systems and management. Conducts continuing education programs for members; establishes and maintains standards for research and practice in information systems.

ASSOCIATION FOR THE ADVANCEMENT OF CAT TECHNOLOGY
PO Box 813
Mechanicsburg, PA 17055
TF: (800)254-5481
FX: (877)795-0004
Founded: 1995. **Staff:** 3. **Members:** 600. **Budget:** 100,000. Individuals who use software for court and deposition reporting. Provides enhancement suggestions to software vendors. Conducts educational and research programs.

ASSOCIATION OF INFORMATION TECHNOLOGY PROFESSIONALS
315 South Northwest Highway, Ste. 200
Park Ridge, IL 60068-4278
Jay Fitzgerald, Dir. of Finance
PH: (847)825-8124
TF: (800)224-9371
FX: (847)825-1693
E-mail: 70430.35@compuserve.com
URL: www.aitp.org
Founded: 1951. **Staff:** 7. **Members:** 9,000. **Budget:** 800,000. Managerial personnel, staff, educators, and individuals interested in the management of information resources. Founder of the Certificate in Data Processing examination program, now administered by an intersociety organization. Maintains Legislative Communications Network. Professional education programs include EDP-oriented business and management principles, self-study courses and a series of videotaped management development seminars. Sponsors student organizations around the country interested in data processing and encourages members to serve as counselors for the Scout computer merit badge. Conducts research projects, including a business information systems curriculum for two- and four-year colleges.

ASSOCIATION OF ONLINE PROFESSIONALS
6096 Franconia Rd., Ste. D
Alexandria, VA 22310
Dave McClure, Exec.Dir.
PH: (703)924-5800
FX: (703)924-5801
E-mail: info@aop.org
URL: www.aop.org
Founded: 1994. **Staff:** 2. **Members:** 1,000. **Budget:** 300,000. Works to foster and promote the growth of online communication and electronic commerce worldwide through legislative advocacy and professional services. Works with individuals and companies involved in the creation, management and growth of computer-based, remote-access communication systems, including Internet and online services.

ASSOCIATION OF SERVICE AND COMPUTER DEALERS INTERNATIONAL
1045 E. Atlantic Ave.
Delray Beach, FL 33483
Joseph Marion, Pres.
PH: (561)266-9016
FX: (561)266-9017
URL: www.ascdi.com
Founded: 1981. **Staff:** 3. **Members:** 160. Dealers, brokers, and lessors of computer hardware, who emphasize mid-range systems such as the IBM AS/400, S/38, and S/36. Enforces the code of ethics established by the Computer Dealers and Lessors Association.

ASSOCIATION OF SHAREWARE PROFESSIONALS
157-F Love Ave.
Greenwood, IN 46142
Richard Holler, Exec.Dir.

PH: (317)888-2194
FX: (317)888-2195
E-mail: execdir@asp-shareware.org
URL: www.asp-shareware.org
A trade association for computer software developers and distributors, providing resources, aid, and assistance in improving their products and their business operations.

CDLA, THE COMPUTER LEASING AND REMARKETING ASSOCIATION
11921 Freedom Dr., Ste. 550
Reston, VA 20190-5608
David E. Poisson, Exec.VP
PH: (703)904-4337
FX: (703)904-4339
E-mail: info@itra.net
URL: www.itra.net
Founded: 1967. **Staff:** 2. **Members:** 120. **Budget:** 250,000. Companies that buy, sell, and lease new and used computer equipment, including central processing units and peripheral devices; associate members are companies that are actively engaged in business related to the computer industry. Promotes enhanced status of computer lessors and dealers; assures ethical business dealings for the benefit of members and their customers.

CENTER FOR OFFICE TECHNOLOGY
301 N. Fairfax St., Ste. 102
Alexandria, VA 22314
PJ Edington, Exec.Dir.
PH: (703)684-7760
FX: (703)684-4554
URL: www.cot.org
Founded: 1985. **Staff:** 23. **Members:** 20. **Budget:** 400,000. Employers, manufacturers, and organizations interested in comfort, health, and safety concerns associated with the occupational use of office equipment. Seeks to address public policy and workplace issues arising from the use of information processing equipment, especially those involving video display terminals (VDTs). Functions as a clearinghouse of scientific information for policy makers and the media; conducts educational programs for employees and employers.

COMMERCIAL INTERNET EXCHANGE ASSOCIATION
1041 Sterling Rd., Ste. 104A
Herndon, VA 20170
Barbro Dooley, Ph.D., Exec.Dir.
PH: (703)709-8200
FX: (703)709-5249
E-mail: washburn@cix.org
URL: www.cix.org
Founded: 1991. **Members:** 40. Public Data Internetwork service providers united to promote and encourage development of the public data communications internetworking services industry. Provides a neutral forum for the exchange of ideas and information. Serves as a clearinghouse of resources. Develops positions on legislative and policy issues of interest to members. Assists member networks in the establishment of, and adherence to, operational, technical, and administrative policies and standards necessary to ensure fair, open, and competitive operations and communication. **Publications:** none.

COMPUTER AND AUTOMATED SYSTEMS ASSOCIATION OF SOCIETY OF MANUFACTURING ENGINEERS
One SME Dr.
PO Box 930
Dearborn, MI 48121-0930
Sandra B. Marshall, Manager
PH: (313)271-1500
FX: (313)271-2861
URL: www.sme.org/casa
Founded: 1975. **Staff:** 2. **Members:** 7,000. Sponsored by Society of Manufacturing Engineers. Automation implementation professionals, manufacturers, consultants, vendors, academics, and students in 35 countries. Promotes computer automation and enterprise integration for the advancement of research, design, installation, operation, maintenance, and communication in manufacturing. Acts as liaison between industry, government, and academia to identify areas that need further technological development; encourages companies to develop completely integrated manufacturing facilities. Conducts seminars and workshops on automated manufacturing.

COMPUTER GAME DEVELOPERS ASSOCIATION
1421 El Miradero Ave.
Glendale, CA 91201
Annie Van Bebber, Bd.Chm.
PH: (818)548-5047
FX: (818)548-5162
E-mail: info@cgda.org
URL: www.cgda.org/
Staff: 1. **Members:** 1,200. Individuals with a professional interest in the interactive entertainment, educational software, and multimedia industries. Promotes development of new entertainment programs and media. Facilitates exchange of information among members; conducts promotional activities.

COMPUTER MEASUREMENT GROUP
151 Fries Mill Rd., Ste. 104
Turnersville, NJ 08012-2016
Judith Keel, Exec.Dir.
Founded: 1969. **Staff:** 7. **Members:** 3,000. **Budget:** 2,000,000. Computer professionals. Acts as an information clearinghouse and provides educational programs for those involved in evaluating computer performance.

COMPUTING RESEARCH ASSOCIATION
1100 Seventeenth St. NW, Ste. 507
Washington, DC 20036
PH: (202)234-2111
FX: (202)667-1066
E-mail: info@cra.org
URL: www.cra.org/
Founded: 1972. **Members:** 185. Computer science and computer engineering academic departments, industrial laboratories. Seeks to strengthen research and education in the computing fields, expand opportunites for women and minorities and educate the public and policy makers on the importance of computing research. Represents the computing research community; advocates on behalf of the community in science and technology policy-making; conducts employment studies and educational programs.

COMPUTING TECHNOLOGY INDUSTRY ASSOCIATION
450 E. 22nd St., Ste. 230
Lombard, IL 60148-6158
John Venator, CEO & Exec.VP
PH: (630)268-1818
FX: (630)268-1384
E-mail: info@comptia.org
URL: www.comptia.org
Founded: 1982. **Staff:** 50. **Members:** 7,500. Computer equipment resellers, manufacturers, distributors, software publishers, and other companies doing business with the computer industry. Increases professional and ethical standards in the industry; protect consumers from inept or nonservicing dealers; help the consumer to easily identify better dealers and obtain an appropriate system for their needs; provide for the exchange of ideas for improvement within the reseller channel; promote a consistent level of service and ethical standards. Members are required to provide fully staffed service departments and offer customers maintenance contracts guaranteeing prompt response time. Conducts technical professional development and training programs in areas such as management, sales, and channel development. Serves as information clearinghouse and for resource the industry; sponsors educational programs; and bestows Golden Screen Award and Awards of Excellence.

CREATIVE MUSICIANS COALITION
1024 W. Willcox Ave.
Peoria, IL 61604
Ronald A. Wallace, Pres.

PH: (309)685-4843
TF: (800)882-4262
FX: (309)685-4878
E-mail: aimcmc@pan.com
URL: www.aimcmc.com
Founded: 1984. **Members:** 500. Members come from all walks of life, but have the same desire to experience, appreciate, and participate in the advancement of independent music composition, production, arrangement, performance, promotion, and distribution. Dedicated to the advancement of independent music and the success of independent musicians. Promotes and distributes independent music to the general public.

DDA, ASSOCIATION OF THE DEC MARKETPLACE

107 S. Main St.
Chelsea, MI 48118
Greg Casto, Pres.
PH: (734)475-8333
TF: (800)332-1130
FX: (734)475-4671
E-mail: admin@dda.org
Founded: 1982. **Staff:** 3. **Members:** 80. **Budget:** 200,000. Dealers engaged in sale of 'Digital Equipment Corporation and compatible products. Goal is to promote a structured market for DEC products. Establishes and enforces high ethical and professional standards for members. Works to ensure uniformity of policy and procedure regarding the sale and service of DEC products. Educates end-users and other dealers on the benefits of associations.

FORTH INTEREST GROUP

100 Dolores St., No. 183
Carmel, CA 93923-8665 .
John D. Hall, President
Founded: 1978. **Staff:** 2. **Members:** 1,200. Individuals interested in learning and/or programming in the computer language FORTH. (FORTH is a threaded interpretative computer language that allows the operator programming flexibility.) Promotes the utilization and modification of FORTH. Conducts specialized education programs.

FREE SOFTWARE FOUNDATION

59 Temple Pl., Ste. 330
Boston, MA 02111-1307
Richard M. Stallman, Pres.
PH: (617)542-5942
FX: (617)542-2652
URL: www.gnu.org
Founded: 1985. **Staff:** 10. Works to eliminate restrictions on people's abilities and rights to copy, redistribute, understand, and modify computer programs. Promotes the development and use of free software in all areas of computer use (free refers to freedom of use, not necessarily price). Concentrates efforts on the development of new software, specifically a system called GNU, which would eliminate the necessity of purchasing a proprietary system. FSF uses its General Public License to copyright its software in a way that allows interested users to access, copy, or alter the software without limiting its access to others.

GEOSPATIAL INFORMATION AND TECHNOLOGY ASSOCIATION

14456 E. Evans Ave.
Aurora, CO 80014
Robert M. Samborski, Exec.Dir.
PH: (303)337-0513
FX: (303)337-1001
E-mail: staff@gita.org
URL: www.gita.org
Founded: 1982. **Staff:** 14. **Members:** 2,200. **Budget:** 2,000,000. Representatives from utilities, municipalities, and the telecommunications industry; vendors, service companies, and consultants. Focuses on "excellence in geospatial information techniques". Promotes education and the exchange of information in the AM/FM/GIS industry. Maintains speakers' bureau.

IEEE COMPUTER SOCIETY

1730 Massachusetts Ave. NW
Washington, DC 20036
T. Michael Elliott, Exec.Dir.
PH: (202)371-0101
FX: (202)728-9614
E-mail: csinfo@computer.org
URL: www.computer.org
Founded: 1946. **Staff:** 109. **Members:** 98,000. **Budget:** 26,000,000. Computer professionals. Promotes the development of computer and information sciences and fosters communication within the information processing community. Sponsors conferences, symposia, workshops, tutorials, technical meetings, and seminars. Operates Computer Society Press. Presents scholarships; bestows technical achievement and service awards and certificates.

IEEE SYSTEMS, MAN, AND CYBERNETICS SOCIETY

3 Park Ave., 17th Fl.
New York, NY 10016-5997
Dr. Richard Saeks, Pres.
PH: (212)419-7900
URL: www.ieee.org
Members: 4,269. A society of the Institute of Electrical and Electronics Engineers. Serves as a forum on the theoretical and practical considerations of systems engineering, human machine systems, and cybernetics—with a particular focus on synthetic and natural systems involving humans and machines.

IMAGE SOCIETY

PO Box 6221
Chandler, AZ 85246-6221
Eric G. Monroe, Pres. & Bd.Chm.
PH: (602)839-8709
E-mail: image@asu.edu
URL: www.public.asu.edu/~image
Founded: 1987. **Members:** 600. Individuals and organizations interested in the technological advancement and application of real-time visual simulation (medical, virtual reality, telepresence, aeronautical, and automotive) and other related virtual reality technologies.

INDEPENDENT CASH REGISTER DEALERS ASSOCIATION

1900 Crossbeam Dr.
Charlotte, NC 28217
Bill Bussard, Mgt.Exec.
PH: (704)357-3124
FX: (704)357-3127
E-mail: info@icrda.org
URL: www.icrda.org
Founded: 1945. **Members:** 450. Independent dealers who sell and service cash registers and computerized point-of-sale systems. Seeks to have manufacturers distribute their products through dealer organizations, rather than through individually established sales organizations. Furnishes sales and service aids to members; conducts management, sales, and service seminars; maintains speakers' bureau. Operates Parts Center, which offers cash register equipment and parts to members and non-members.

INDEPENDENT COMPUTER CONSULTANTS ASSOCIATION

11131 S. Towne Sq., Ste. F
St. Louis, MO 63123
Joyce Burkard, Exec. Dir.
PH: (314)892-1675
TF: (800)774-4222
FX: (314)487-1345
URL: www.icca.org
Founded: 1976. **Staff:** 3. **Members:** 1,500. Since 1976, the ICCA has provided a national network of independent computer consultants. ICCA's mission is to support the success of independent computer consultants in providing professional services to their clients. Members objectively support the best computer or software solutions in all areas of the computer industry, from hardware design to

systems integration to employee training. Membership is open to individuals, partnerships, and corporations providing consulting assistance in computer related areas.

INFORMATION TECHNOLOGY ASSOCIATION OF AMERICA
c/o ITAA
1616 N. Fort Meyer Dr., Ste. 1300
Arlington, VA 22209-9998
Harris Miller, President
PH: (703)522-5055
FX: (703)525-2279
Founded: 1982. **Staff:** 30. **Members:** 306. **Budget:** 4,500,000. A division of the Information Technology Association of America. Software companies involved in the development or marketing of software for personal, midrange, and mainframe computers. Promotes the software industry and addresses specific problems of the industry. Represents the industry before various governmental units; provides educational programs to members; conducts research and makes available legal services. Is currently developing standards.

INFORMATION TECHNOLOGY INDUSTRY COUNCIL
1250 Eye St. NW, Ste. 200
Washington, DC 20005
Rhett B. Dawson, Pres.
PH: (202)737-8888
FX: (202)638-4922
E-mail: webmaster@itic.org
URL: www.itic.org
Founded: 1916. **Staff:** 30. **Members:** 28. **Budget:** 3,000,000. Represents manufacturers of information technology products. Serves as secretariat and technology for ANSI-accredited standards committee x3 information technology group. Conducts public policy programs; compiles industry statistics.

INSTITUTE FOR CERTIFICATION OF COMPUTING PROFESSIONALS
2200 E. Devon Ave., Ste. 247
Des Plaines, IL 60018
Cynthia A. Blaese, Contact
PH: (847)299-4227
TF: (800)843-8227
FX: (847)299-4280
E-mail: 74040.3722@compuserve.com
URL: www.iccp.org
Founded: 1973. **Staff:** 5. **Members:** 50,000. **Budget:** 1,000,000. Professional societies united to promote the development of computer examinations which are of high quality, directed toward information technology professionals, and designed to encourage competence and professionalism. Individuals passing the exams automatically become members of the Institute for Certification of Computing Professionals. Individuals passing exams become certified as CCP or ACP. Has developed code of ethics and good practice to which those taking the exams promise to adhere. Maintains speakers' bureau; compiles statistics.

INTERACTIVE DIGITAL SOFTWARE ASSOCIATION
1400 Providence Hwy.
Norwood, MA 02062
Douglas Lowenstein, Pres.
E-mail: info@idsa.com
URL: www.e3expo.com
Founded: 1994. **Members:** 46. Represents the interactive entertainment software publishing industry. Established an autonomous rating board to rate interactive entertainment software. Established a program to combat piracy in the United States and around the world. Represents members on industry issues at the federal and state level. Provides market research and information. **Publications:** none.

INTERNATIONAL ASSOCIATION FOR COMPUTER INFORMATION SYSTEMS
Oklahoma State University
College of Business Administration
Stillwater, OK 74078
Dr. G. Daryl Nord, Mng.Dir.
PH: (405)744-8632
FX: (405)744-5180
E-mail: dnord@okway.okstate.edu
URL: www.iacis.org
Founded: 1960. **Members:** 700. Educators and computer professionals. Seeks to promote the knowledge, use, and teaching of computers, and technology. Dedicated to the improvement of information systems and computer professionals.

INTERNATIONAL ASSOCIATION FOR COMPUTER SYSTEMS SECURITY
6 Swathmore Ln.
Dix Hills, NY 11746
Robert J. Wilk, Founder & Pres.
PH: (516)499-1616
FX: (516)462-9178
Founded: 1981. **Staff:** 14. **Members:** 800. **Budget:** 400,000. Organizations and individuals in 32 countries interested in the security of their computerized information systems. Offers a testing program to certify individuals as Computer Systems Security Professionals; upholds a code of professional ethics. Supports continuing education through workshops; furthers awareness of security issues both within the industry and the government. Conducts in-house management security awareness programs and monthly seminars and workshops; distributes information on state-of-the-art methods of protecting computer and communication resources. Maintains speakers' bureau, sponsors lectures, and compiles statistics. Presents Distinguished Service Award.

INTERNATIONAL COUNCIL FOR COMPUTER COMMUNICATION
PO Box 9745
Washington, DC 20016-9745
Pramode K. Verma, President
PH: (703)836-7787
FX: (703)836-7787
E-mail: iccc@icccgovernors.org
URL: www.icccgovernors.org
Founded: 1972. **Staff:** 1. **Members:** 125. **Budget:** 60,000. Distinguished computer communication scientists (membership by invitation only). Promotes scientific research, development, and application of computer communication. Fosters progress in evaluation of applications of computer communication. Encourages the study of potential social and economic impacts on the field and of policies influencing those impacts. Seeks to improve public understanding of computer communication.

INTERNATIONAL DATA WAREHOUSING ASSOCIATION
PO Box 2001
Andover, MA 01810
Sid Adelman, Contact
PH: (978)470-3380
FX: (978)470-0526
E-mail: association@idwa.org
URL: www.idwa.org
Founded: 1996. **Staff:** 2. **Members:** 2,610. **Budget:** 150,000. Seeks to advance the knowledge, theory and advancement of data warehousing. Conducts educational programs.

INTERNATIONAL DISK DRIVE EQUIPMENT AND MATERIALS ASSOCIATION
3255 Scott Blvd., Ste. 2-102
Santa Clara, CA 95054-3013
Debbie Lee, Program Mgr.
PH: (408)330-8100
FX: (408)492-1425
E-mail: idema@idema.org
URL: www.idema.org

Founded: 1986. **Staff:** 10. **Members:** 832. **Budget:** 4,000,000. Corporations (720), individuals (100), and universities (12) with an interest in data storage technologies. Promotes the technological, manufacturing, marketing, and business progress of the data storage industry.

INTERNATIONAL SOCIETY FOR TECHNOLOGY IN EDUCATION
1787 Agate St.
Eugene, OR 97403-1923
Maia S. Howes, Exec.Sec.
PH: (541)346-4414
TF: (800)336-5191
FX: (541)346-5890
E-mail: iste@oregon.uoregon.edu
URL: www.iste.org
Founded: 1979. **Staff:** 32. **Members:** 10,000. Teachers, administrators, computer and curriculum coordinators, and others interested in improving the quality of education through the innovative use of technology. Facilitates exchange of information and resources between international policy makers and professional organizations; encourages research and evaluation relating to the use of technology in education. Maintains the Private Sector Council to promote cooperation among private sector organizations to identify needs and establish standards for hardware, software, and other technology-based educational systems, products, and services.

INTERNATIONAL SOCIETY OF PARAMETRIC ANALYSTS
PO Box 6402
Town & Country Branch
Chesterfield, MO 63006-6402
Jack Grueza, Chm.
PH: (314)527-2955
FX: (314)256-8358
E-mail: clydeperry@aol.com
Founded: 1979. **Members:** 400. Engineers, designers, statisticians, estimators, and managers in industry, the military, and government who develop and use computerized, parametric cost-estimating models. Conducts educational activities aimed at promoting usage of parametric modeling techniques for purposes of cost estimating, risk analysis, and technology forecasting. Sponsors placement service.

INTERNET SOCIETY
12020 Sunrise Valley Dr., Ste. 210
Reston, VA 20191-3429
Donald M. Heath, Pres.
PH: (703)648-9888
FX: (703)648-9887
E-mail: membership@isoc.org
URL: www.isoc.org
Founded: 1992. **Staff:** 10. **Members:** 6,500. **Budget:** 5,000,000. Technologists, developers, educators, researchers, government representatives, and business people. Seeks to ensure global cooperation and coordination for the Internet and related internetworking technologies and applications. Supports the development and dissemination of standards for the Internet. Promotes the growth of Internet architecture and Internet-related education and research. Encourages assistance to technologically developing countries in implementing local Internet infrastructures.

M TECHNOLOGY ASSOCIATION
1738 Elton Rd., No. 205
Silver Spring, MD 20903-1725
Maureen Lilly, Exec. Officer
PH: (301)431-4070
FX: (301)431-0017
E-mail: mta@mtechnology.org
URL: www.mtechnology.org
Founded: 1971. **Staff:** 5. **Members:** 1,300. Professionals and organizations from the academic, business, medical, and scientific communities; others interested in Standard M (also known as MUMPS). (The M programming language was originally developed for medical applications, but is now also used for business applica-tions.) Provides a forum for dissemination of information, discussion of common problems, and introduction of technical and managerial innovations in the use and application of Standard M. Operates placement service. Sponsors competitions; conducts educational programs.

NATIONAL COMPUTER SECURITY ASSOCIATION
1200 Walnut Bottom Rd.
Carlisle, PA 17013
Peter Tippett, Pres.
PH: (717)258-1816
TF: (800)488-4595
FX: (717)243-8642
E-mail: office@ncsa.com
URL: www.icsa.net
Founded: 1989. **Staff:** 100. **Members:** 3,500. Works to improve security and confidence in global computing through awareness and the continuous education of products, systems, and people. Services include security-related research, conferences, publications, professional membership, and vendor and user based consortia and certification.

NATIONAL STORAGE INDUSTRY CONSORTIUM
9888 Carroll Center Rd., Ste. 115
San Diego, CA 92126-4580
Barry Schechtman, Exec.Dir.
PH: (619)621-2550
FX: (619)621-2551
E-mail: nsic@nsic.org
URL: www.nsic.org
Founded: 1991. **Staff:** 7. Companies and universities involved in computer data storage research united to accomplish mutual goals. Creates and manages joint precompetitive research programs among its members. Performs studies to develop long term roadmaps for various data storage technologies.

NATIONAL TRAINING SYSTEMS ASSOCIATION
2111 Wilson Blvd., Ste. 400
Arlington, VA 22201-3001
Fred Lewis, Exec.Dir.
PH: (703)247-2569
TF: (800)677-6897
FX: (703)243-1659
URL: www.trainingsystems.org
Founded: 1988. **Staff:** 3. **Members:** 300. **Budget:** 750,000. Represents the business interests of manufacturers of simulation systems, computer-based training systems, and training support systems; providers of contract training and other related training support services. Promotes the growth, development, and application of military training systems, products, and services. Seeks to: contribute to the operational readiness and combat effectiveness of the armed forces of the U.S. and its allies; assist in fulfilling the training requirements of related federal agencies; enhance public education and training; increase understanding and appreciation of training systems technologies and services. Fosters communication between government and industry regarding requirements and procurement issues and policies; promotes responsibility and integrity among members. Compiles statistics; conducts research and educational programs.

NETWORK PROFESSIONAL ASSOCIATION
710 Ogden Ave., Ste. 600
Naperville, IL 60563
Randy Jackson, MCNE, Chrmn.
PH: (630)579-3282
E-mail: npa@npa.org
URL: www.npa.org
Founded: 1990. **Staff:** 14. **Members:** 7,000. **Budget:** 1,000,000. Computing professionals. Advances the network computing profession. Unites the members in a worldwide association. Offers programs and services.

**NORTH AMERICAN COMPUTER SERVICE
  ASSOCIATION**
1 S Orange Ave., Ste. 500
Orlando, FL 32801-2627
David G. Glascock, Dir.
PH: (407)206-1111
TF: (888)666-1160
FX: (407)206-1114
Founded: 1982. **Staff:** 10. **Members:** 1,000. **Budget:** 250,000.
Computer service and repair companies; suppliers to the industry;
computer repair schools; professional consultants. Promotes orderly
growth for the computer service industry and assists members with
tasks such as contract negotiation, training, legislative liaison, and
parts and supplies purchasing. Maintains placement service mem-
bers and acquisition.

**NORTH AMERICAN FUZZY INFORMATION
  PROCESSING SOCIETY**
1000 Chastain Rd.
Kennesaw, GA 30144-5591
Prof. Nancy Green-Hall, Sec.-Treas.
PH: (770)423-6042
FX: (770)423-6539
E-mail: nachll@y.sunmail.kennesau.edu
Founded: 1981. **Members:** 150. Civil and electrical engineers, sys-
tems scientists, mathematicians, operations researchers, computer
scientists, knowledge engineers, and logicians. Promotes scientific
study and dissemination of applications and theories of fuzzy sets,
logic, and measures.

OBJECT MANAGEMENT GROUP
492 Old Connecticut Path
Framingham, MA 01701
PH: (508)820-4300
FX: (508)820-4303
Founded: 1989. **Members:** 250. Information systems vendors, software developers, and computer users. Promotes the theory and practice of object management technology in software development.
Works for the development of standards within the industry for the
purpose of forming a heterogeneous applications environment across
all major hardware and operating systems. (Object management is
defined by OMG as a type of software development environment
that models the real world through the representation of software
"objects" or capsules of code with distinct functions.)

**PERSONAL COMPUTER MANAGEMENT
  ASSOCIATION**
31832 Poole Ct.
Temecula, CA 92591
Ronald Henderson, President
PH: (909)694-1936
Founded: 1982. **Staff:** 5. Provides training packages, self-study
books, and cassettes. Presently inactive.

**PERSONAL COMPUTER MEMORY CARD
  INTERNATIONAL ASSOCIATION**
2635 N. First St., Ste. 209
San Jose, CA 95134-2044
Patrick Maher, Exec. Officer
PH: (408)433-2273
FX: (408)433-9558
E-mail: office@pcmcia.org
URL: www.pc-card.com
Founded: 1989. **Staff:** 5. **Members:** 300. Computer industry pro-
fessionals. Promotes technological development of PC Cards (credit
card sized peripheral devices that add capabilities such as memory,
mass storage, and I/O to computers). Sets standards and defines
technical specifications. Sponsors educational events, research pro-
grams, and speakers' bureau.

**PORTABLE COMPUTER AND COMMUNICATIONS
  ASSOCIATION**
PO Box 2460
Boulder Creek, CA 95006
Robert Venter, Exec.Dir.
PH: (831)338-0924
FX: (831)338-7806
E-mail: pcca@pcca.org
URL: www.pcca.org
Founded: 1993. Messaging, paging, and wireless networks; soft-
ware developers and vendors. Promotes development of software
and hardware standards for interoperable mobile computing and
communications. Represents members' interests. Conducts research
and educational programs.

SALUTATION CONSORTIUM
4321 Granby Way
Marietta, GA 30062
Robert F. Pecora, Mng.Dir.
PH: (770)642-8565
FX: (770)642-7875
E-mail: director@salutation.org
URL: www.salutation.org
Founded: 1995. **Members:** 24. Manufacturers of computers, net-
work services information management solutions, and office equip-
ment. Develops interoperability specifications that will link office
equipment to computers over a network.

**SERIAL STORAGE ARCHITECTURE INDUSTRY
  ASSOCIATION**
5600 Cottle Rd.
San Jose, CA 95193-0001
Lee Steckmest, Sec.
FX: (408)256-0595
Founded: 1995. **Members:** 40. **Budget:** 250,000. Companies with-
in the computer industry who promote Serial Storage Architecture
(SSA). Goals are to promote the technical and economic benefits of
SSA; to accelerate the adoption and proliferation of SSA products
and services; to develop an infrastructure that enables the technical
excellence of SSA; to foster the continuing evolution of the SSA
standards; and to encourage cooperation between members of the
computer and storage industry.

**SOCIETY FOR COMPUTER SIMULATION
  INTERNATIONAL**
PO Box 17900
San Diego, CA 92177-7900
William Gallagher, Exec.Dir.
PH: (619)277-3888
FX: (619)277-3930
E-mail: info@scs.org
URL: www.scs.org
Founded: 1952. **Staff:** 9. **Members:** 2,000. **Budget:** 1,000,000.
Persons professionally engaged in simulation, particularly through
the use of computers and similar devices that employ mathematical
or physical analogies. Maintains speakers' bureau.

SOCIETY FOR COMPUTERS IN PSYCHOLOGY
Cal State University
PO Box 6846
Fullerton, CA 92834-6846
Sarah Ransdell, Ph.D., Contact
URL: www.lafayette.edu/allanr/scip.hmtl
Founded: 1971. Researchers and students interested in the applica-
tion of computers to psychology. Works to "increase and diffuse
knowledge of the use of computers in psychological research." As-
sists psychologists in using microcomputers in teaching and re-
search.

SOCIETY FOR INFORMATION DISPLAY
31 E Julian St.
San Jose, CA 95112-4006
Dee Dumont, Exec.Dir.

PH: (408)977-1013
FX: (408)977-1531
E-mail: office@sid.org
URL: www.sid.org
Founded: 1962. Staff: 2. Members: 4,000. Budget: 1,500,000. Scientists, engineers, students, others, and business firms dealing with information display problems. Encourages scientific, literary, and educational advancement of information display and its allied arts and sciences, including the disciplines of display theory, display device and systems development, and the psychological and physiological effects of display systems on the human senses. Plans to establish central repository for information and to develop definitions and standards in the field. Maintains speakers' bureau.

SOCIETY FOR SOFTWARE QUALITY

PO Box 86958
San Diego, CA 92138-6958
Wililam Swain, Sec CFO
PH: (619)571-3112
E-mail: ssq@ssq.org
URL: www.ssq.org/
Founded: 1984. Members: 250. Budget: 87,700. Software professionals. Seeks to advance the art, science, and technology of software quality assurance. Promotes professional development of members and encourages high standards in the field. Fosters communication between the public and the industry. Assists colleges and universities in developing and implementing curricula in quality evaluation and methodologies. Operates speakers' bureau.

SOFTWARE TESTING INSTITUTE

PO Box 831056
Richardson, TX 75080-3124
Susan Archer, Dir.
PH: (972)680-8507
FX: (972)680-8905
URL: www.ondaweb.com/sti/
Founded: 1995. Members: 50. Software development and testing professionals. Works to provide members with expertise to work more productively and efficiently. Provides access to industry publications and research; offers online services; conducts educational programs; compiles statistics.

SPECIAL INTEREST GROUP FOR ARCHITECTURE OF COMPUTER SYSTEMS

1515 Broadway, 17th Fl.
New York, NY 10036
Jean-Loup Baer, Chm.
PH: (212)869-7440
FX: (212)302-5826
E-mail: sigs@acm.org
URL: www.acm.org/sigarch/
Members: 5,000. A special interest group of the Association for Computing Machinery. Computer professionals interested in the architecture of computers. (Computer architecture is the study of the arrangement of physical resources of computer systems, their partitioning, and the organization of a processor.) Disseminates technical information on the architecture of computer systems. Sponsors educational and research programs.

SPECIAL INTEREST GROUP FOR COMPUTER PERSONNEL RESEARCH

University of Dayton
College of Business
Department of MIS Decision Sciences
Dayton, OH 45469-2130
Thomas W. Ferratt, Sig. Chairman
PH: (937)229-2728
FX: (937)229-4000
Founded: 1962. Members: 200. A special interest group of the Association for Computing. Computer managers, MIS academicians, and human resource specialists. Conducts research into selection, training, evaluation, and management of computer personnel; identifies specific research problems; promotes and coordinates investigations pertaining to the nature of computer personnel and their jobs.

SPECIAL INTEREST GROUP FOR COMPUTER SCIENCE EDUCATION

Grand Valley State University
One Campus Dr.
Allendale, MI 49401
Bruce Klein, Chm.
PH: (616)895-6611
FX: (616)895-2106
Founded: 1970. Members: 2,000. A special interest group of the Association for Computing Machinery. Seeks to provide a forum for the solution of problems common to professionals in developing, implementing, and evaluating computer science programs, courses, and materials; to encourage and assist in the development of effective academic programs and courses in computer science; and to promote research in computer science education. Collects and disseminates information concerning courses and programs offered in secondary, associate, undergraduate, and graduate degree programs. Organizes and presents sessions at national meetings and disseminates information to computer science professionals.

SPECIAL INTEREST GROUP FOR COMPUTERS AND SOCIETY

1515 Broadway, 17th Fl.
New York, NY 10036
Heather Levell, Program Dir.
PH: (212)626-0613
FX: (302)302-5826
Staff: 1. Members: 1,289. Budget: 60,000. A special interest group of the Association for Computing Machinery. Computer and physical scientists, professionals, and other individuals interested in issues and applications of computers in society. Informs the public of issues concerning computers and society. Conducts computer literacy symposia.

SPECIAL INTEREST GROUP FOR DESIGN AUTOMATION

University of Virginia
Thorton Hall
Department of Computer Science
Charlottesville, VA 22903
Dr. James Cohoon, Chm.
PH: (804)982-2210
FX: (804)982-2214
Founded: 1965. Members: 1,200. A special interest group of the Association for Computing Machinery. Professionals interested in the application of computers to engineering design function, especially in the electronic engineering field. Areas of concern include: theoretic, analytic, and heuristic methods for performing and assisting in design tasks; use of computer techniques, algorithms, and programs to provide design documentation, control manufacturing processes, evaluate design through simulation, and facilitate communication between designers and design tasks. Holds panel and technical meetings.

SPECIAL INTEREST GROUP ON ADA

c/o Benjamin Brosgol
200 Wheeler Rd.
Aonix
Burlington, MA 01803-5500
Benjamin Brosgol, Chm.
PH: (781)270-0030
FX: (781)270-6882
Founded: 1981. Members: 3,707. Special interest group of the Association for Computing Machinery made up of computer professionals. Disseminates information about Ada (a programming language) including its usage, environment, standardization, and implementation.

SPECIAL INTEREST GROUP ON ALGORITHMS COMPUTABILITY THEORY
c/o Association for Computing Machinery
1515 Broadway
New York, NY 10036
Jeff Vitter, Chm.
PH: (212)869-7440
FX: (212)302-5826
URL: sigact.acm.org/sigact
Founded: 1969. **Members:** 2,242. **Budget:** 96,000. Individuals interested in theories of computer sciences and analysis of algorithms (step-by-step procedures for solving mathematical problems). Is concerned with automata and formal languages and their applications, formal semantics of programming languages, theories of computing and computational models, computational complexity, and theoretical principles of programming language design and implementation. Bestows awards.

SPECIAL INTEREST GROUP ON COMPUTER GRAPHICS AND INTERACTIVE TECHNIQUES
Association for Computing Machinery
1515 Broadway, 17th Fl.
New York, NY 10036
Patrick McCarren, Assoc.Dir.
PH: (212)869-7440
FX: (212)302-5826
E-mail: acmhelp@acm.org
URL: www.siggraph.org
Founded: 1968. **Members:** 8,000. Special interest group of the Association of Computing Machinery. Computer graphics professionals and students. Disseminates technical information on computer graphics and interactive techniques such as man-machine communication, image processing, and manipulation.

SPECIAL INTEREST GROUP ON MEASUREMENT AND EVALUATION
University of Washington
Box 352350
Department of Computer Science
Seattle, WA 98195-2350
Edward D. Lazowska, Chm.
PH: (206)543-1695
FX: (206)543-2969
E-mail: lazowska@cs.washington.edu
URL: www.cs.washington.edu
Members: 1,886. A special interest group of the Association for Computing Machinery. Individuals interested in the problems related to measuring and evaluating computer system performance, including applying and adapting existing methods and developing new ones. Provides a forum for discussion of the role of simulation, design, and interpretation of benchmarks (standards by which systems are measured); analysis of hardware and software monitor output; development of suitable analytical models.

SPECIAL INTEREST GROUP ON MICROPROGRAMMING AND MICROARCHITECTURE
MICROSOFT
1 Microsoft Way
Redmond, WA 98052-6399
James O. Bondi, Chm.
PH: (425)882-8080
FX: (425)936-7329
Founded: 1968. **Members:** 650. A special interest group of the Association for Computing Machinery. Individuals involved in the development of microprogrammed computers; educators teaching microprogramming and development of firmware (programming codes that are physically burned into the hardware). Promotes the exchange of information on microprogramming. Conducts tutorials.

SPECIAL INTEREST GROUP ON OPERATING SYSTEMS
c/o Henry M. Levy
FR-35
Department of Computer Science
University of Washington
Seattle, WA 98195
Henry M. Levy, Chm.
PH: (919)660-6523
Members: 8,058. A special interest group of the Association for Computing Machinery. Individuals interested in computer operating systems. Areas of interest include architecture for multiprogramming, multiprocessing, time-sharing, and distributed systems; resource management, evaluation, and simulation; reliability, integrity, and security of data; communications among computing processes.

SPECIAL INTEREST GROUP ON PROGRAMMING LANGUAGES
Association for Computing Machinery
1515 Broadway
New York, NY 10036
Mary Lou Soffa, Chm.
PH: (212)869-7440
FX: (212)302-5826
URL: www.acm.org/sigplan/
Founded: 1966. **Staff:** 1. **Members:** 6,500. A special interest group of the Association for Computing Machinery. Computer professionals. Promotes the advancement of the state of the art in computer programming languages. Areas of interest include: programming methodology; programming language definition; principles and techniques of compiler implementation; general purpose and application oriented languages; programming language design; teaching of programming languages; standards.

SPECIAL INTEREST GROUP ON SECURITY, AUDIT AND CONTROL
Association for Computing Machinery
1515 Broadway
New York, NY 10036
Ravi Sandhu, SIG Chair
PH: (212)869-7440
FX: (212)302-5826
Founded: 1980. **Members:** 1,120. A special interest group of the Association for Computing Machinery. Information processing security personnel; auditors; accountants; computer technicians. Purpose is to maintain high levels of skill and awareness regarding technology and practice in the fields of computer security, audit, and control. Examines issues including control of access to resources, identity verification, risk analysis, logging of transactions, data reduction, analysis and certification of programs, and architectural foundations for security systems.

SPECIAL INTEREST GROUP ON SOFTWARE ENGINEERING
1515 Broadway
New York, NY 10036
Dick Taylor, Chm.
PH: (212)869-7440
FX: (212)302-5826
Founded: 1976. **Members:** 10,424. A special interest group of the Association for Computing Machinery. Computer professionals interested in the technology of software creation and evolution. Promotes exchange of ideas and information.

SPECIAL INTEREST GROUPWARE AND GROUPWORK
749 SLIS
University of Pittsburgh
Pittsburgh, PA 15260
E-mail: mahling@sis.pitt.edu
Founded: 1981. **Members:** 1,700. **Budget:** 110,000. A special interest group of the Association for Computing Machinery (see separate entry). Individuals involved in industry, academia, and government interested in office information systems. (Office information systems use computer and communications technologies to make offices more efficient.) Seeks to foster and conduct research on offi-

ce information systems and groupware and encourage companies manufacturing information systems components to make use of the findings. Maintains speakers' bureau.

SYSTEM INDEPENDENT DATA FORMAT ASSOCIATION
3335 N. Arlington Heights Rd., Ste. E
Arlington Heights, VA 60004
C. Andrew Larsen, Exec.Dir.
PH: (847)577-7200
FX: (847)577-7276
E-mail: sidf@sidf.org
URL: www.sidf.org
Founded: 1993. **Staff:** 3. **Members:** 20. **Budget:** 75,000. Back-up tape hardware and software companies. Promotes "a universally accpeted standard for back-up tape drives to allow cross-platform migration".

TRANSACTION PROCESSING PERFORMANCE COUNCIL
777 N. 1st St., Ste. 600
San Jose, CA 95112
Mr. Kim Shanley, Admin.
PH: (408)295-8894
FX: (408)295-9768
Founded: 1988. **Members:** 46. Computer hardware and software companies, computer users and vendors, and industry organizations. Defines transaction processing benchmarks for measuring database performance; disseminates performance data.

UPSILON PI EPSILON ASSOCIATION
California State University, Chico
Department of Computer Science
Chico, CA 95929-0410
Orlando S. Madrigal, Ph.D., Sec.
PH: (530)898-6442
FX: (530)898-5995
E-mail: osm@csuchico.edu
URL: www.acm.org/upe/
Founded: 1967. **Members:** 1,800. **Budget:** 48,000. Honor society - computing sciences. Students and faculty involved in computing science programs worldwide. Recognizes academic excellence in computing science at both the undergraduate and graduate levels; provides speakers. Cosponsors National Scholastic Programming Contest, the International Science and Engineering Fair, and other student activities in conjunction with other computer-related organizations. Bestows UPE Chapter Advisor of the Year Award; offers scholarships.

VMEBUS INTERNATIONAL TRADE ASSOCIATION
7825 E. Gelding St., No. 104
Scottsdale, AZ 85260-3415
Ray Alderman, Exec.Dir.
PH: (602)951-8866
FX: (602)951-0720
E-mail: info@vita.com
URL: www.vita.com
Founded: 1984. **Staff:** 6. **Members:** 140. **Budget:** 1,000,000. Manufacturers, users, consultants, integrators, and distributors interested in VMEbus microprocessor boards, subsystems, and systems. Promotes the technical and commercial success of the VMEbus Conducts technical seminars. ANSI-accredited standards development organization.

WORLD COMPUTER GRAPHICS ASSOCIATION
6121 Lincolnia Rd., Ste. 302
Alexandria, VA 22312
Caby Smith, Pres.
PH: (703)642-3050
FX: (703)642-1663
Founded: 1981. Goals are to: promote the growth and serve the needs of the global computer graphics community; improve international productivity and technological advancement through the use of computer graphics; assist computer graphics development activities.

CONSULTANTS

Consultants and consulting organizations active in the Computer & Software sector are featured in this chapter. Entries are adapted from Gale's *Consultants and Consulting Organizations Directory* (*CCOD*). Each entry represents an expertise which may be of interest to business organizations, government agencies, nonprofit institutions, and individuals requiring technical and other support. The listees shown are located in the United States and Canada.

In Canada, the use of the term "consultant" is restricted. The use of the word, in this chapter, does not necessarily imply that the firm has been granted the "consultant" designation in Canada.

Entries are arranged in alphabetical order. Categories include contact information (address, phone, fax, web site, E-mail); names and titles of executive officers; and a descriptive block that begins with founding year and staff.

4-SERV INC.
4700 Rochester Rd.
Troy, MI 48098
PH: (248)680-9400
FX: (248)680-9403
URL: www.4-serv.com
Founded: 1985. **Staff:** 50. Activities: Specialists in client/server systems integration. Also offers counsel in business analysis, design, and development; implementation of client/server applications; and GUI systems.

A & T SYSTEMS, INC.
12520 Prosperity Dr., Ste. 300
Silver Spring, MD 20904
Ashok K. Thareja, CEO & President
PH: (301)384-1425
TF: (800)933-1425
FX: (301)384-1405
E-mail: hareja@.com
URL: www.ats.com
Founded: 1984. **Staff:** 40. Activities: Data processing consultants providing services in research and development support, internet & internet software &' services. Internet security, education and training; RFP or proposal writing; and design analysis and evaluation in the areas of: performance analysis and modeling, computer systems procurement and planning, information technology consulting, systems integration, software design and development, and UNIX systems. Industries served: computer manufacturers, federal government, and computer consulting companies.

AAONTON GROUP
1322 Rivercrest Blvd., Ste. 412
Allen, TX 75002-2921
Jack D. Harper, BBA
PH: (214)390-2444
TF: (888)390-2444
FX: (214)390-7317
E-mail: jharper@flash.net
Founded: 1981. **Staff:** 18. Activities: Specialists in marketing services and products. Industries served: financial, trading, real estate, oil and gas, manufacturing, healthcare products and services, and international trade.

A.B. DATA, LTD.
8050 N. Port Washington Rd.
Milwaukee, WI 53217
Bruce Arbit, Co-Managing Director
PH: (414)352-4404
TF: (800)558-6908
FX: (414)352-3994
E-mail: barbit@abdata.com
Founded: 1977. **Staff:** 90. Activities: Provides information management and direct marketing services to nonprofit organizations, political campaigns, direct mail marketers and publishers. Emphasis is on data base management and custom data processing services for marketing purposes.

ABACUS TECHNOLOGY CORP.
5454 Wisconsin Ave., Ste. 1100
Chevy Chase, MD 20815-6901
Dennis J. Yee, President
PH: (301)907-8500
FX: (301)907-8508
URL: www.abacustech.com
Founded: 1983. **Staff:** 241. Activities: Information management and technology consultants.

ACAP INC.
9717 E. 42nd St., Ste. 125
Tulsa, OK 74146-3655
Larry Rayner, President
PH: (918)663-2828
FX: (918)663-0556
E-mail: acap@acap.com
URL: www.acap.com
Founded: 1983. **Staff:** 23. Activities: Firm offers expertise in computer technology and programming.

ACC DOT COM
10078 Tyler Ct., Ste. D
Ijamsville, MD 21754
Roland F. Bryan, CEO & President
PH: (301)831-8288
TF: (800)242-0739
FX: (301)831-8289
E-mail: info@accsystems.com
URL: www.acc.systems.com
Founded: 1975. **Staff:** 100. Activities: Engineering consulting firm specializing in system integrators for networks, telecommunications, and networking.

ACCESS INNOVATIONS, INC.
PO Box 8640
Albuquerque, NM 87198-8640
Jay Ven Eman, Ph.D., CEO
PH: (505)265-3591
FX: (505)256-1080
E-mail: marketing@accessinn.com
URL: www.accessinn.com
Founded: 1978. **Staff:** 48. Activities: An information management firm providing consulting, support, and project management services in the expert areas of: (1) database design and construction; (2) editorial abstracting and indexing, specializing in sci-tech information; (3) development of customized machine-aided indexing software; (4) data capture via keying, scanning, and/or OCR (domestic or offshore services); (5) CD-ROM data preparation; (6) CD-ROM database production; (7) Internet and intranet production; (8) Web site design; (9) SGML and HTML tagging; (10) conversion of magnetic media from one system or application format to another, and (11) workflow and production methodology assessment. Serves the private and public sectors.

ADAPTIVE RESEARCH, A DIV. OF PACIFIC-SIERRA RESEARCH CORP.
4960 Corporate Dr. NW
Huntsville, AL 35805-6229
Dr. Ed Field
PH: (205)830-2620
FX: (205)830-2628
URL: www.adaptive-research.com
Founded: 1971. **Staff:** 305. Activities: Computer consulting firm specializes in research and development of computational fluid dynamics software.

ADAQ SYSTEMS CORP.
1333 Bordeaux Dr.
Sunnyvale, CA 94089
Matt Lezin
PH: (408)541-8520
FX: (408)541-0114
E-mail: info@adaq.com
Founded: 1987. **Staff:** 22. Activities: Consulting firm specializes in software for the air freight, modal independent, and courier industries.

ADSYSTECH INC.
8401 Colesville Rd., Ste. 450
Silver Spring, MD 20910
Arnold Avant, President
PH: (301)589-3434
FX: (301)589-9254
URL: www.adsystec.com
Founded: 1986. **Staff:** 99. Activities: Offers systems engineering and integration, software and information engineering, BPR, and communications.

ADVANCE TECHNOLOGY CONSULTANTS
5 Concourse Pky., NE, Ste. 2800
Atlanta, GA 30328
Cyrus W. Smith, C.E.O.
PH: (770)512-4080
FX: (770)512-4096
URL: www.atc-usa.com
Founded: 1988. **Staff:** 22. Activities: Firm offers expertise in the field of computer technology.

ADVANCED BUSINESS CONSULTANTS INC.
5960 Dearborn St., Ste. 200
Shawnee Mission, KS 66202-3316
Douglas Haynes, President
PH: (913)831-2121
FX: (913)831-0149
E-mail: abc-adm@swv.com.net
URL: www.abc-inc.com
Founded: 1986. **Staff:** 175. Activities: Firm offers services in the areas of computer technology and information systems.

ADVANCED COMPUTER TECHNOLOGIES INC.
108 Main St.
Norwalk, CT 06851-4640
James Dunleavey, President/Treasurer
PH: (203)847-9433
FX: (203)847-2475
Founded: 1982. **Staff:** 31. Activities: Computer technology firm emphasizes telecommunications services.

ADVANCED ENGINEERING SERVICES
1675 Walsh Ave., Bldg. SE
Santa Clara, CA 95051-2626
Solomon Shatz, President
PH: (408)988-3840
FX: (408)988-3938
Founded: 1976. **Staff:** 104. Activities: Offers consulting to management. Provides complete reliability improvement engineering services for computers, computer peripherals (disc drives, printers, displays, tape drives, etc.), telecommunications equipment, electronic and electro-mechanical components including connectors and subsystems. Additional services include evaluation and testing services for products, 5000 square foot evaluation and testing laboratory, failure analysis, surface analysis, and material evaluation. Provides technical expertise in electronic and microelectronic packaging and assembly engineering, equipment evaluation and selection, and expert witness services. Industries served: computer, electronic systems, aerospace, and aviation.

ADVANCED INFO SOLUTIONS
5000 SW Meadows Rd., Ste. 131
Lake Oswego, OR 97035-3230
David A. Bates, Vice President
PH: (503)684-9779
FX: (503)635-8236
URL: www.A-I-S.com
Founded: 1978. **Staff:** 55. Activities: Computer consultants for commercial accounts in Oregon and Washington.

ADVANCED NETWORK CONSULTING
475 Park Ave. S., 9th Fl.
New York, NY 10016
PH: (212)378-4109
FX: (212)376-6782
E-mail: sales@a-n-c.com
URL: www.a-n-c.com
Founded: 1990. **Staff:** 20. Activities: A provider of LAN consulting as well as hardware and software services. Server-based solutions include backup, antivirus LAN/WAN design, implementation and support, system administration and hardware warrantee contracts, and office automation for small businesses.

ADVANCED SYSTEMS DEVELOPMENT, INC.
2800 Shirlington Rd., Ste. 800
Arlington, VA 22206
Richard L. Bennett, President
PH: (703)998-3900
FX: (703)824-5699
Founded: 1979. **Staff:** 80. Activities: Provides management and technical support to private industry and government in the development and implementation of user-oriented computer systems. Expert LAN operation, administration, and user support. Specialists in optical disk technology, including CD-ROM and other image-based optical information systems.

AERIAL IMAGE TECHNOLOGY
5515 SE Milwaukee Ave.
Portland, OR 97202
Brian Huberty, President
PH: (503)239-0757
TF: (800)547-6730
FX: (503)239-0432
Founded: 1992. **Staff:** 12. Activities: Provides state-of-the-art technology and consulting for computer-based map or "spatial information" systems required by businesses and governments worldwide. City managers, foresters, farmers, wildlife managers, land managers need to know the "who, what, where, when, why and how much" of the resources they administer. AIT provides the expertise to design, develop, acquire, manage, and maintain spatial information systems for land and resource mapping. Products and services include: aerial photo reconnaissance and mapping services; aerial video reconnaissance and mapping services; image processing and analysis hardware and software; geographic information systems (GIS) hardware and software; global positioning systems (GPS) hardware and software; aerial photography and satellite imagery historical searches; digital mapping; as well as GIS and GPS training and consulting. Industries served: private groups; county, city, state, and federal government agencies; and international organizations.

**AEROSPACE INTERNATIONAL MANAGEMENT
  SYSTEMS INC.**
911 St. Andrews Dr.
Upland, CA 91784-9143
Raoul Castro, President
PH: (909)985-9316
FX: (909)988-0271
E-mail: aims-inc@worldnet.att.net
Founded: 1978. **Staff:** 12. Activities: Consultants to practically all phases of the aviation industry (corporate aircraft operations and commuter airlines). Recent experience in computerized aviation management programs, and preparation of computerized aviation manuals (operations, training, maintenance). Book "Corporate Aviation Management" Southern Illinois University.

AGENCY.COM
665 Broadway
New York, NY 10012
PH: (212)358-8220
FX: (212)358-8255
E-mail: info@agency.com
URL: www.agency.com
Founded: 1995. **Staff:** 650. Activities: Develops solutions and applications for every interactive platform including the Internet, proprietary intranets and extranets, CD-ROMs and Web-ROMs, kiosks and iTV.

AGPRO, INC.
Rte. 7, Box 100
Paris, TX 75462
D. Joe Gribble, President
PH: (903)785-5531
TF: (800)527-1030
FX: (903)784-7895
E-mail: agpro@neto.com
URL: www.agprousa.com
Founded: 1962. **Staff:** 14. Activities: Offers agricultural engineer-

ing design consultation for animal raising facilities including dairies, beef feedlots, swine operations, and embryo transplant facilities. Services include land utilization, plot plans, building design, equipment selection, integration with other farm and commercial activities, pollution control systems, genetic engineering systems, and computer applications. Also offers computer control and automation consultation, as well as consultation for waste management and control for food processing plants.

AGRA MONENCO INC.
2010 Winston Park Dr., Ste. 100
Oakville, Canada L6H 6A3
Bob Van Adel, President
PH: (905)829-5400
FX: (905)829-5625
URL: www.agra.com
Founded: 1907. **Staff:** 1320. Activities: International corporation specialized in engineering, construction, project development and management, information systems and the environment for power, process and infrastructure industries. Services include: economic, financial and technical feasibility studies; exploration and site selection; project planning and financing; conceptual and detailed design; process design; estimating; project management; procurement and logistics support; specifications and equipment selection; construction management; commissioning and operations assistance; maintenance and rehabilitation; management consulting; resource planning and development; socioeconomic impact assessments; system planning, development and implementation; computer software development and hardware selection; training and transfer of technology; and research. Industries served: utilities, private power, financing institutions, governments, and private companies.

AJILON
210 W. Pennsylvania Ave., Ste. 650
Towson, MD 21204-5348
Roy Haggerty, President
PH: (410)821-0435
TF: (800)626-8082
FX: (410)828-0106
Founded: 1978. **Staff:** 1200. Activities: Offers a full range of data processing professional services including application support, technical support, operations support, management/MIS consulting, productivity services and education/training. Specific consulting services cover business planning assistance, data processing organizational analysis, data processing operational analysis, data processing project and program management, and data communications planning. Clients primarily utilize large scale mainframes, integrated micro computers and networked micros in a variety of industries including banking, insurance, manufacturing, healthcare, government and services.

ALFORD & PARTNERS INC.
146-23 61 Rd.
Flushing, NY 11367-1203
Ron Alford, President
PH: (718)939-5800
TF: (800)843-7526
FX: (718)939-1398
E-mail: email@theplan.com
URL: www.theplan.com
Founded: 1980. **Staff:** 12. Activities: Provides strategic and operational planning as well as proactive crisis management consulting, risk and disaster management services. Serves private industries as well as government agencies.

ALGOMOD TECHNOLOGIES CORP.
116 John St.
New York, NY 10038
Diya Obeid, President
PH: (212)306-0100
TF: (877)711-8700
FX: (212)306-0191
E-mail: info@algomod.com
URL: www.algomod.com

Founded: 1977. **Staff:** 125. Activities: Active in the programming and development of commercial application software. Areas of specialty include client/server applications, PowerBuilder, Motif, Visual Basic, Visual C++, INFORMIX, SYBASE, ORACLE, System Administration, Database Administration, UNIX, C, C++, MS-Windows, DB2, CICS, OS/2, COBOL, PL1, and LOTUS Notes. Industries served: communications, telephone, banking, insurance, brokerage, and pharmaceutical in the eastern U.S.

ALLEGIANCE TECHNOLOGIES
1100 Corporate Pky., Ste. 204
Birmingham, AL 35242
Mike Dickinson, Vice President
PH: (205)981-0440
TF: (800)382-8857
FX: (205)981-0444
E-mail: recruiting@allegiancetechnologies.com
URL: www.allegiancetechnologies.com
Founded: 1992. **Staff:** 35. Activities: Offers software development and consulting services. Provides legacy system and client/server development. Consultants are specialists in research and development projects. Specialists in Peoplesoft Implementation and benefits administration.

ALLIED COMPUTER SERVICES
255 W. 98th St., 3D
New York, NY 10025
Philip Brotman, President
PH: (212)222-5665
E-mail: a.catink.net
Founded: 1979. **Staff:** 12. Activities: Microcomputer, minicomputer, and networking consultant for CPA management, law practice management, telemarketing, and productivity systems. Installs microcomputer, networking, and multi-user systems for office management. Additional experience in bar code reader/handheld computer system for field repair and service. Industries served: legal departments, field sales and service agencies, as well as government agencies in the U.S.

ALLMEDIA INC.
17060 Dallas Pky., Ste. 105
Dallas, TX 75248
Laura McClendon, President
PH: (818)612-4060
FX: (818)612-4061
E-mail: lmcclendon@allmediainc.com
URL: www.allmediainc.com
Founded: 1981. **Staff:** 28. Activities: Provides direct mail list brokerage and management, computer services, marketing planning, and mail plan analysis to direct mailers in the U.S. and worldwide. Industries served: business and consumer magazines, catalogs, financial services, and retailers.

ALTAIR CONSULTING GROUP, INC.
A-2 Brier Hill Ct.
East Brunswick, NJ 08816
Michael DiGiovanni, Pres.
PH: (732)432-0300
FX: (732)238-4715
E-mail: altair@altairgroup.com
URL: www.altairgroup.com
Founded: 1984. **Staff:** 70. Activities: Provides computer consulting services to the IT industry.

ALTAIR SYSTEMS DESIGN LTD.
600 N. McClurg, 3rd Fl.
Chicago, IL 60611
Diane Cielak, President
PH: (773)775-4141
FX: (773)775-4242
E-mail: jknerem_altair@csi.com
URL: www.altairsystems.com
Founded: 1992. **Staff:** 25. Activities: A Systems Integrator and Value Added Reseller offering a complete range of consulting and sup-

port services specializing in providing client/server solutions offering both turnkey and custom application solutions with total implementation strategies. Altair is also a FileNet partner offering Panagon, SAROS, Ensemble, Report Manager, FAXSys and other products.

ALTEK CO.
PO Box 1128
Torrington, CT 06790
Stephen Altschuler, President
PH: (860)482-7626
FX: (860)496-7113
Founded: 1972. **Staff:** 80. Activities: Designs and develops quality control computer software for beverage processing concerns. Also provides laboratory and testing equipment, including container lid, crush, and closure testers, and container test data communicators.

ALTMAN WEIL, INC.
2 Campus Blvd.
Newtown Square, PA 19073
Daniel J. DiLucchio
PH: (610)359-9900
FX: (610)359-0467
URL: www.altmanweil.com
Founded: 1970. **Staff:** 43. Activities: Offers services in strategic planning, process engineering, benchmarking, organizational development, profitability marketing and planning, micro-economic forecasting, marketing planning, compensation systems, law firm mergers and acquisitions, attorney and staff training, human resources management, quality management programs, financial management, client surveys, and automation technology.

ALTSCHULER MELVOIN & GLASSER
30 S. Wacker Dr., Ste. 2600
Chicago, IL 60606-7494
Howard L. Stone, Managing Partner
PH: (312)207-2800
FX: (312)207-2954
Founded: 1923. **Staff:** 435. Activities: Assists in strategic planning; actuarial benefits and compensation; mergers, acquisitions, and divestitures; activity-based costing; information systems management; and succession and estate planning. Industries served: real estate, manufacturing, distribution, construction, nonprofit, legal, advertising, printing, and automotive aftermarket in the United States and worldwide through affiliates.

AMDAHL EDUCATION-AMDAHL CORP.
1250 E. Arques Ave.
Sunnyvale, CA 94088-3470
PH: (408)746-6000
FX: (408)738-1051
URL: www.amdahl.com
Founded: 1970. **Staff:** 5552. Activities: Offers an extensive series of training programs on computer technology, communications systems, and management development. Firm will develop customized, on-site training and will conduct needs assessment studies upon request.

AMERICAN DATA MANAGEMENT, INC.
1920 Old Middlefield Way
Mountain View, CA 94043
Douglas Winslow, President
PH: (415)968-5800
TF: (800)829-5800
FX: (415)968-9870
URL: wwwamericandata.com
Founded: 1985. **Staff:** 13. Activities: Offers computer services and direct mail services to political campaigns and private industry. Specifically variable text laser-printed computer letters, mailing labels, walking lists, and phone lists. Serves private companies as well as government agencies.

AMERICAN MANAGEMENT SYSTEMS INC.
4050 Legato Rd.
Fairfax, VA 22033
Charles O. Rossotti, Chairman of the Board
PH: (703)267-5000
FX: (703)267-5067
E-mail: corp_mktg_comm@mail.amsinc.com
URL: www.amsinc.com
Founded: 1970. **Staff:** 8000. Activities: Firm's business is to partner with clients to achieve breakthrough performance through the intelligent use of information technology. As a business and information technology consulting firm, AMS provides business reengineering, change management, system integration, and systems development and implementation services. Headquartered in Fairfax, Virginia, firm's offices throughout North America and Europe number 57. For addresses and phone/fax information for affiliates contact headquarters.

AMERICAN TECHNICAL RESOURCES INC.
1651 Old Meadow Rd., 6th Fl.
McLean, VA 22102
Charles F. Phillips, President
PH: (703)917-7800
FX: (703)917-1616
Founded: 1985. **Staff:** 475. Activities: Firm provides computer software and hardware professionals, technicians, technical writers, and communication experts to scientific, engineering, and general business customers. Serves private industries as well as government agencies.

AMERICAN TRAFFIC INFORMATION (ATI)
1877 Clove Rd.
Staten Island, NY 10304
Dan Talmor
PH: (718)447-5161
FX: (718)447-7995
E-mail: atidata@aol.com
Founded: 1986. **Staff:** 18. Activities: Firm provides extensive knowledge in traffic data collection and processing. Highways and street surveys; pedestrians counting and interviews; bus surveys; data processing and presentation.

ANALYSTS INTERNATIONAL CORP.
7615 Metro Blvd.
Minneapolis, MN 55439-3050
F.W. Lang, Chairman/CEO
PH: (612)835-5900
TF: (800)8005044
FX: (612)897-4555
URL: www.analysts.com
Founded: 1966. **Staff:** 4300. Activities: Provides contract programming, consulting, and systems design for computer users in business, government, and industry; and special software systems, consulting, design and implementation for computer manufacturers, industry and government. Industries served: all major categories of industry including manufacturing, distribution, insurance, banking, transportation, and the financial marketplace. Projects have been accomplished for most of the major computer manufacturers, many of the Fortune 1000 companies, and a variety of small to medium sized businesses in the U.S.

ANNAPOLIS MICRO SYSTEMS
190 Admiral Cochrane Dr.
Annapolis, MD 21401
Jane S. Donaldson, President
PH: (410)841-2514
FX: (410)841-2518
E-mail: annapmicro@aol.com
URL: www.annapmicro.com
Founded: 1982. **Staff:** 35. Activities: Provides custom hardware, software and systems design.

ANSTEC, INC.
1410 Spring Hill Rd., Ste 500
McLean, VA 22102
Sumeet Shrivastana, Exec. Vice President
PH: (703)848-7200
FX: (703)848-7601
URL: www.anstec.com
Founded: 1982. **Staff:** 560. Activities: Computer systems design consultants specializing in C, Unix/Xenix, Informix, and data communications on microcomputers in multi-user environments, Ada language and software engineering, C3I software, systems engineering support and training, computer facilities management, telecommunication networks, LAN, WAN, and systems integration. Serves private industries as well as government agencies.

MICHAEL ANTHONY ASSOCIATES, INC.
42 Washington St., Ste. 310
Wellesley, MA 02181-1803
Justin Fulman, Account Executive
PH: (617)237-4950
TF: (800)337-4950
FX: (617)237-6811
E-mail: maainc@world.std.com
Founded: 1982. **Staff:** 40. Activities: Applications development, systems programming, communications, and database specialists servicing the IBM mainframe, midrange, and PC marketplace. Provides technical expertise of conversions, system software installation and upgrades, performance and tuning, capacity planning, and data communications. In addition to contract services also provide retained search and contingency placement of computer professionals ranging from senior staff to senior management. Also act as brokers for independent consultants and small consulting firms requiring the services of marketing specialists. Industries served: banking, financial services, hospitals, HMO's, manufacturers, software development, universities, defense, and consulting firms.

D. APPLETON CO., INC.
1840 Michael Faraday Dr., Ste. 300
Reston, VA 20190-5338
Mark Smith, Senior Vice President
PH: (703)709-3682
TF: (800)556-8886
FX: (703)709-3640
Founded: 1979. **Staff:** 60. Activities: A major business engineering consulting firm focused on issues of improving business performance, productivity, and time-to-market through business process improvements. Emphasis is on resolving problems in information technology, processes, people, and understanding. Industries served: corporations, systems integrators, government, the information processing industry, manufacturing industry, and executive management personnel.

APPLICATION PROGRAMMING & DEVELOPMENT, INC.
6805 Cool Ridge Dr., 2nd Fl.
Camp Springs, MD 20748
Mark Burnett
PH: (301)449-1400
TF: (800)785-2734
FX: (301)449-1224
URL: www.apdi.net
Founded: 1991. **Staff:** 15. Activities: Firm is one of the largest service bureaus and provides online service bureau, Internet connection, X.25, Worldwide Web, BBS, and custom online services throughout the U.S.

APPLIED SOLUTIONS, INC.
1730 Madison Rd.
Cincinnati, OH 45206-1865
H. Breneman Blaine, President
PH: (513)751-9800
FX: (513)751-4115
E-mail: appliedsol@fuse.net
Founded: 1979. **Staff:** 15. Activities: Offers computer consulting and software. Experienced in manufacturing, distribution, freight,

medical/hospitals, retailing, education, construction, and general service organizations.

APPWORX CORP.
2475 140th NE
Bellevue, WA 98005-1820
William A. Wrenn, President
PH: (425)644-2121
TF: (877)277-9679
FX: (425)644-2266
URL: www.appworx.com
Founded: 1992. **Staff:** 40. Activities: Firm offers computer technology counseling, with particular expertise in the development of batch software.

ARCCA INC.
2288 Second St. Pike
Penns Park, PA 18943
Alan Cantor, President
PH: (215)322-8396
FX: (215)598-9751
Founded: 1987. **Staff:** 27. Activities: Technical consulting firm specializing in seat belts, child restraints and occupant crash dynamics for both automobiles and aircraft. Performs accident analysis, hardware and material failure analysis, occupant crash protection and consultation, safety research, testing and expert testimony. Performs analysis for both plaintiff and defense attorneys, insurance companies, manufacturers, and the federal government.

ARIEL PERFORMANCE CENTERED SYSTEM CORP.
1350 Pear Ave., Ste. B
Mountain View, CA 94043
Barry Raybould, President
PH: (650)694-7880
FX: (650)694-7865
URL: www.aries.pcs.com
Founded: 1991. **Staff:** 15. Activities: Develops Electronic Performance Support Systems (EPSS) that provide employees with immediate information, advice, training and tools to perform a job with a minimum of support by other people. EPSSs improve profitability by reducing training costs and improving performance on-the-job. Ariel uses standardized development methodologies and automated development tools to develop quality EPSSs at the lowest cost possible. Platform capabilities include: Microsoft Windows, OS/2, UNIX, Macintosh and IBM mainframes. Ariel's consulting division provides management consulting services to Fortune 500 companies on how to successfully design, develop, and implement EPSS technologies to improve profitability. Industries served: banking, finance, manufacturing, computer software, service industries, and government agencies.

ARIS ASSOCIATES - SUBSIDIARY OF I.I. SOLOMON ASSOCIATES INC.
85 East End Ave., Ste. 3E 64
New York, NY 10028-8026
Irving I. Solomon, President
PH: (212)772-7858
FX: (212)772-7858
Founded: 1976. **Staff:** 14. Activities: Offers consulting services on the turnkey applications and design of security systems for data processing hardware, software, and facilities. Also designs computer equipment for medical offices and has developed specialized retail point of sale devices. Industries served: retail, medical clinics, small colleges and government agencies.

ARKANSAS SYSTEMS, INC.
17500 Chenal Pky.
Little Rock, AR 72211
Ron Ferguson, President
PH: (501)218-7300
FX: (501)218-7302
URL: www.arksys.com
Founded: 1975. **Staff:** 180. Activities: Provides computer oriented services to organizations who need or utilize computers in their daily

environments. Also assists clients in long-range planning, organizing, and control for their computer operation. Specializes in communications and distributed processing applications for financial institutions, processors, and other industries. Specific services include design, development, and installation of software systems; and customizing software obtained from other sources for a client's operation. After installation, the firm will assist clients' systems with operations support and software modifications to meet their changing business needs. Also specializes in financial networks, remittance processing, ATMs, teller-terminal, card processing, and financial electronic funds (EFT). Serves private industries as well as government agencies.

ASPEN TECHNOLOGY, INC., MANUFACTURING SYSTEMS DIVISION
14701 St. Mary's Ln.
Houston, TX 77079-2995
David Mushin, Senior Vice President
PH: (281)584-1000
FX: (281)584-4329
E-mail: msdinfo@aspentech.com
Founded: 1981. **Staff:** 250. Activities: Provides software and services for the analysis, design, and automation of process manufacturing plants in industries such as chemical, petrochemical, pharmaceuticals, electric power, pulp and paper, and metals.

ASPIRE SYSTEMS
28550 SW Ashland Dr., Ste. 64
Wilsonville, OR 97070
PH: (503)570-1003
TF: (877)8-ASPIRE
FX: (503)682-9579
E-mail: info@aspiresys.com
URL: www.aspiresys.com
Founded: 1995. **Staff:** 30. Activities: A computer consulting company which offers services in the areas of intranet and extranet applications development, client/server applications development, turnkey web presence management, simulation, layout and scheduling solutions, and enterprise planning solutions. Software products help companies model new manufacturing facilities. Assists businesses realize goals through technology.

ASSOCIATED BUSINESS CONSULTANTS, INC.
105 S. 5th St., Ste. 1850
Minneapolis, MN 55402-1249
Patrick Messerich, President
PH: (612)375-0234
FX: (612)342-2043
E-mail: LandATC@visi.com
Founded: 1989. **Staff:** 60. Activities: Offers computer software education and training.

ASU CONSULTING
3333 Bowers Ave., Ste. 160
Santa Clara, CA 95054
Eli Rothbart
PH: (408)654-7810
FX: (408)654-7820
URL: www.asucon.com
Founded: 1989. **Staff:** 20. Activities: Computer technology consulting firm.

ATLANTIC CONSULTING CONSORTIUM, INC.
PO Box 5304
Virginia Beach, VA 23455
Raymond White, Director
PH: (804)671-9154
FX: (804)460-4695
Founded: 1993. **Staff:** 13. Activities: An organization of independent consultants and business professionals providing expertise to industry and government in business areas critical to their success. Expertise includes accounting, advertising, business law, computer/data processing, curriculum development, executive development, marketing, media relations, new product introduction, mergers and ac-

quisitions, new venture development, opinion polls, strategic planning, political campaigning, public relations, quality control/ management, sales training, commercial real estate, sports marketing, tax planning, training programs, and venture capital. Industries served: healthcare, retail, wholesale, manufacturing, government agencies, food, communications, education, sports, political and electronics.

AURA TECHNOLOGY CORP.
441 Central Ave.
Scarsdale, NY 10583-9367
Richard A. Sandell
PH: (914)834-2322
TF: (800)878-3703
FX: (914)833-0930
E-mail: info@aura1.com
URL: www.aura1.com
Founded: 1974. **Staff:** 93. Activities: Provides comprehensive operational audits for large and medium-size firms in the metalworking, aluminum smelting and fabricating, and steel foundry and manufacturing industries. Offers expertise in management reorganization processes for all large and medium industries in countries with mixed economies. Conducts economic impact and market assessment studies for firms operating in developing countries of the western hemisphere. Supplies management of privatization processes, restructuring and personnel reassignment for large and medium scale industries in developing countries. Oversees international trade and contracts negotiation, between firms in the U.S. and those located in the Caribbean Basin and Latin America. Industries served: international energy market, oil industry, construction, industrial machinery, metal fabrication, aluminum smelting, and others.

AUTOMATED BUSINESS SYSTEMS
1555 NW Gage
PO Box 750080
Topeka Industrial/Business Park
Topeka, KS 66675
John E. Willett, President
PH: (785)232-9325
TF: (800)821-0275
FX: (785)232-9628
Founded: 1976. **Staff:** 16. Activities: Business imaging systems consulting firm. Industries served: healthcare, financial, insurance, manufacturing, distribution, educational, and government agencies.

AUTOMATED CONCEPTS INC.
1500 Broadway
New York, NY 10036
Frederick B. Harris, President
PH: (212)391-2100
FX: (212)391-1720
URL: www.autocon.com
Founded: 1966. **Staff:** 400. Activities: Offers computer services including training and information systems development/management. Serves clients in private sector industries and government agencies in the U.S.

AUTOMATED MEDIA INC.
12171 Beech Daly
Livonia, MI 48154
Gerald Gentile, President
PH: (313)937-5000
FX: (313)937-5008
E-mail: ggentile@wwnet.net
URL: auto-med.com
Founded: 1999. **Staff:** 30. Activities: Unix specialists offer expertise in the 4GL database. EDI integration, manufacturing ERP software.

AUTOMATION COUNSELORS, INC.
PO Box 3917
Frederick, MD 21705
Ross Benitez, President

PH: (301)663-3700
TF: (800)966-6725
FX: (301)663-6692
Founded: 1970. **Staff:** 20. Activities: Furnishes data processing consulting, encompassing the following specialty areas: biomedical systems design and design of government financial systems. Industries served: primarily government.

AXIAN, INC.
4800 SW Griffith Dr., Ste. 202
Beaverton, OR 97005
Larry G. Rogers, VP, Sales
PH: (503)644-6106
FX: (503)643-8425
E-mail: info@axian.com
URL: www.axian.com
Founded: 1991. **Staff:** 30. Activities: Provides expertise and support to developers and end-users. Axian's staff includes engineers with backgrounds ranging from computer programming to systems and network design.

AZS ASSOCIATES, INC.
309 Yoakum Pkwy, Ste. 507
Alexandria, VA 22304
Sam Dalil
PH: (703)751-4501
FX: (703)751-1757
E-mail: sdalil@azs-inc.com
URL: www.azs-inc.com
Founded: 1985. **Staff:** 25. Activities: Data processing consulting firm experienced with main-frame computers, mini-computers, and personal computers. Services cover design, code and conversion of various business and financial applications. Specialized in PC LAN and networking; GUI based applications and object orient programming WEB and Internet development.

B-K DYNAMICS, INC.
3204 Tower Oaks Blvd.
Rockville, MD 20852
Edward Smith, President
PH: (301)984-7300
FX: (301)984-3199
Founded: 1963. **Staff:** 90. Activities: Offers research and development consulting services in areas of data processing, engineering, information retrieval, operations research, technology transfer and advanced technology analysis. Serves private industries as well as government agencies.

BABBAGE SIMMEL & ASSOCIATES INC.
5131 Post Rd., Ste 100. 185
Dublin, OH 43017-1367
Louis Maani
PH: (614)764-8777
FX: (614)764-9049
URL: www.babsim.com
Staff: 16. Activities: Computer technology consulting firm.

RB BALCH & ASSOCIATES, INC.
PO Box 10007
Glendale, AZ 85318-0007
Rochelle Balch, Pres.
PH: (623)561-9366
TF: (800)922-5249
FX: (623)561-0012
E-mail: rb@rbbalch.com
URL: www.rbbalch.com
Founded: 1993. **Staff:** 30. Activities: Computer Consulting Services for personal, mid-range, and mainframe environments, including systems analysis and design, programming, training. Contract programming PC Office Support. Databases, E-mail, Internet, Networks, Upgrades. Industries served: finance, retail, manufacturing, construction, government, general business. Internet and client/ server development.

THE BARANTI GROUP INC.
210 Cochrane Dr., Unit 6
Markham, Canada L3R 8E6
PH: (905)479-0148
FX: (905)479-0149
E-mail: sales@baranti.com
URL: www.baranti.com
Founded: 1990. **Staff:** 14. Activities: Contract electronics and software design and manufacturing for companies in Canada and the U.S. The firm specializes in design for manufacture of commercial, industrial, and consumer products. Particular expertise in the area of professional video, audio, picture film, and multimedia products. Related design work encompasses a broad spectrum of products including telecom, energy management, small appliances, embedded microprocessor systems (hardware and firmware), and instrumentation. Industries served: manufacturers of electronic products or products containing electronic subsystems.

BARCUS BRITT CONSULTING
Parkway Towers, Ste. 1500
Nashville, TN 37219
Sam W. Barcus, III
PH: (615)256-4100
FX: (615)256-6493
E-mail: sbarcus@tmsnet.com
Founded: 1985. **Staff:** 13. Activities: Computer consultants with strong accounting and business background. Firm will take on the design, implementation, and evaluation of systems in the financial and operational areas and work with staff to establish accounting, inventory, forecasting, and tracking systems ideally suited to client needs. Offers four broad services to help organizations effectively choose, implement and use information technology: system diagnosis and improvement, information and operational planning, design and development, and system project management and software implementation. These services encompass feasibility studies, needs analysis and software design, software/hardware review, long range data processing planning, system network configuration and installation, and executive and staff training. Serves private industries as well as government agencies.

BARRON SYSTEMS GROUP, LTD.
Empire State Bldg., Ste. 5116, 51st Fl
New York, NY 10118-4854
Irving Stummer
PH: (212)643-1111
FX: (212)643-9798
E-mail: hr@barronsys.com
URL: www.barronsys.com
Founded: 1979. **Staff:** 143. Activities: Computer technology group offers specialized expertise with information systems development.

BARSA CONSULTING, LLC
2900 Westchester Ave.
Purchase, NY 10577
Albert S. Barsa, Jr., President
PH: (914)251-1234
FX: (914)251-9406
URL: www.barsaconsulting.com
Founded: 1982. **Staff:** 13. Activities: Offers AS/400 computer selection, optimization, and software support services to businesses primarily in the northeastern United States.

THE BASEX GROUP, INC.
15 E. 26th St., 14th Fl.
New York, NY 10010
Jonathan B. Spira, Senior Managing Director
PH: (212)725-2600
FX: (212)532-5406
E-mail: info@basex.com
URL: www.basex.com
Founded: 1983. **Staff:** 12. Activities: Management consulting firm which helps clients effect change through the introduction and deployment of new and innovative technologies. Provides consulting services which emphasize the importance of organizing and

disseminating information which can then be used as a strategic corporate asset. Serves healthcare, financial, professional services, and legal industries.

ERIC C. BAUM & ASSOCIATES
27134A Paseo Espada, Ste. 321A
San Juan Capistrano, CA 92675
Larry D. Hinterman, VP, Sales
PH: (714)489-9424
TF: (800)366-2570
FX: (714)489-9436
Founded: 1955. **Staff:** 15. Activities: Provides a full range of industrial engineering and management consulting with emphasis on improving productivity. The firm has developed and implemented successful programs utilizing engineered performance standards applied with computers. Serves clients in manufacturing and distribution facilities.

BAY COMPUTER ASSOCIATES, INC.
95 Hathaway Center Ste. 1
Providence, RI 02907
PH: (401)461-1484
FX: (401)461-1218
URL: www.baycomp.com
Founded: 1989. **Staff:** 15. Activities: Consultants in computer hardware design, software design, and systems design; systems maintenance, implementation, and documentation; FDA design process; FCC compliance; Windows software; and medical product development. Industries served: medical products, scientific lab products, computer software, embedded computer products, and government agencies.

BAY ENGINEERING, INC.
253 N. First Ave.
Sturgeon Bay, WI 54235
J.P. Fischer, President
PH: (920)743-8282
FX: (920)743-9543
E-mail: jfische1@mail.wiscnet.net
Founded: 1996. **Staff:** 21. Activities: Offers design in naval architecture (hull/vessel design, ship outfitting), and marine engineering (piping, machinery, electrical/electronics), and related computer services. Other services include surveys for hull and machinery condition.

BDM INTERNATIONAL INC.
7915 Jones Branch Dr.
McLean, VA 22102
Phillip Odeen, CEO
PH: (703)848-5000
FX: (703)848-5391
URL: www.bdm.com
Staff: 1200. Activities: Specializes in designing computer systems for both government and commercial clients.

BEAM TECHNOLOGIES INC.
110 N. Cayuga St.
Ithaca, NY 14850-4331
Gal Berkooz, President
PH: (607)273-4367
FX: (607)275-9527
E-mail: gb@beamtech.com
Founded: 1993. **Staff:** 11. Activities: Develops models to solve problems of fluid flows in aerospace, industry, and the environment. Specializes in control of flows and problems that cannot be solved with off-the-shelf Computational Fluid Dynamics (CFD) programs. Industries served: manufacturing, automotive, aerospace, and environmental.

BEDFORD ASSOCIATES INC., SUBSIDIARY OF BRITISH AIRWAYS
101 Merritt 7
Norwalk, CT 06851
PH: (203)846-0230
FX: (203)846-1487
URL: www.bedford.com
Staff: 40. Activities: Offers expertise in the area of computer information systems design and management, including LotusNotes, UNIX, C and C++ programming, and TPF.

BENCHMARK COMPUTER LEARNING, INC.
4510 W. 77th St., Ste. 300
Minneapolis, MN 55435-5123
Scott Schwefel, President
PH: (612)896-6800
TF: (800)869-1325
FX: (612)896-9728
Founded: 1973. **Staff:** 23. Activities: Computer network consulting and training firm..

BENSON & MCLAUGHLIN P.S.
1400 Blanchard Plz.
22061 6th Ave.
Seattle, WA 98121-1810
Steven B. Bishop, CPA
PH: (206)441-3500
FX: (206)441-1551
Founded: 1949. **Staff:** 50. Activities: The firm offers profit enhancement services which is an established program to install a systematic process to identify, measure and implement profit improvement. Additional benefits of the program are improved communication, efficiency, and morale, plus lower stress. Other services include litigation support, construction systems and management, alternate dispute resolution (arbitration and mediation), skills system for attorneys, insurance claim adjustment, public sector management, and productivity reviews. Industries served: construction, distribution, manufacturing, professional services, import/export, public sector/government agencies, and general office automation.

BERKLEY INFORMATION SERVICES
10 Roundwind Rd.
Luverne, MN 56156
PH: (507)283-9195
FX: (507)283-2627
E-mail: bisadmin@wrbc.com
URL: bis.wrbc.com
Founded: 1989. **Staff:** 100. Activities: An information technology provider for the insurance industry. Provides insurance management software, as well as consulting services. Experienced in such areas as system analysis, programming, technical and customer documentation, testing of computerized applications, and customer training.

BEZ SYSTEMS, INC.
570 Lake Cook Rd., Ste. 407
Deerfield, IL 60015
Boris E. Zibitsker
PH: (847)940-1010
FX: (847)940-1559
E-mail: bezplus@bez.com
Founded: 1984. **Staff:** 35. Activities: BEZ offers a full range of consulting services for DB2, ORACLE and Teradata, DBC/1012, AT&TGIS 3600, 3555, 3700, including strategic planning; enterprise prototyping, modeling; performance prediction; database design and administration; application design and development; performance management and capacity planning; and planning for distributed databases. Industries served: insurance, financial, manufacturing, retail, government, and transportation.

THE BGM GROUP
3700 Steeles Ave. W., Ste. 204
Woodbridge, Canada L4L 8K8
Gilles Belanger, CEO
PH: (905)850-8780
FX: (905)850-8781
URL: www.bgw.ca/bgw/
Founded: 1985. **Staff:** 90. Activities: Provides logistics and distribution strategies and design, projects implementation, manufactur-

ing improvements, warehouse management systems integration, and multimedia training software development.

BIBLIOGRAPHICAL CENTER FOR RESEARCH
14394 E. Evans Ave.
Aurora, CO 80014-1478
David Brunell, Executive Director
PH: (303)751-6277
TF: (800)397-1552
FX: (303)751-9787
E-mail: admin@bcr.org
URL: www.bcr.org
Founded: 1935. **Staff:** 27. Activities: Provides OCLC services, technical support, consulting, training, cataloging retrospective conversion, Internet services, microcomputer products and online- and CD-ROM-based databases.

BINAR GRAPHICS, INC.
2880 Junction Ave.
San Jose, CA 95134-1922
Scott Vouri, President
PH: (415)491-1565
FX: (415)491-1164
E-mail: binar@crl.com
URL: www.binar.com
Founded: 1989. **Staff:** 22. Activities: Computer graphics software consulting/contracting firm specializing in the development of graphics software, graphics display device drivers, and demonstration programs. Industries served: PC computer.

BNK INFORMATICS CANADA, INC. IDI
789 Don Mills Rd., Ste. 606
Toronto, Canada M3C 1T5
Dr. S.M. Sweid, Senior Consultant - Technology
PH: (416)467-8138
FX: (416)467-0273
E-mail: bnkinfo@bnkinfo.ca
URL: www.bnkinfo.ca
Founded: 1990. **Staff:** 12. Activities: Specialists in information technology assessment, systems and networks design, ICT policies and strategies, information resources, planning and management.

BONNER & MOORE ASSOCIATES, INC.
2727 Allen Pky.
Houston, TX 77019
Joe F. Moore, President & CEO
PH: (713)522-6800
TF: (800)367-4621
FX: (713)522-1134
E-mail: bonmorck@bonnermoore.com
URL: www.bonnermoore.com
Founded: 1956. **Staff:** 150. Activities: Provides consulting in two major areas: corporate/plant operations and integrated maintenance management. Corporate/plant operations work includes corporate merger/acquisition economic feasibility studies; corporate planning and plant operations in the energy, petrochemical and petroleum fields; and corporate and plant computer usage, production optimization and expert testimony on energy related matters. Applied management science using quantitative analysis through mathematical models are the foundation of consulting practices. Services in the area of integrated maintenance management involve the development of plant maintenance strategies improving production quality and effectiveness; operational research and management science analysis applied to organizational, technical support, inventory control, purchasing and preventive/predictive maintenance issues; and quantitative and qualitative consulting using mathematical models. Industries served: mining, construction, manufacturing, transportation, public utilities, public administration, energy, petrochemical, and petroleum.

BORN INFORMATION SERVICES INC.
294 E. Grove Ln.
Wayzata, MN 55391-1670
Rick Born, President
PH: (612)404-4000
FX: (612)404-4444
URL: www.born.com
Founded: 1990. **Staff:** 1000. Activities: Provides a broad portfolio of services, including open client/server, object-oriented, Internet, networking, desktop and AS/400 solutions. In addition, two of the company's business practices have evolved into national strategic partnerships with Forte and J.D. Edwards.

BOSTON SYSTEMS GROUP, INC.
145 South St.
Boston, MA 02111
Theodore Klein, President
PH: (617)423-1670
FX: (617)423-7538
Founded: 1982. **Staff:** 18. Activities: Management consultants offering expertise in systems integration and distributed computing. Specialty is downsizing mainframe applications onto LAN-based and work station-based technologies. Industries served: mainly Fortune 500 firms, but also serves government agencies.

THE BRADY GROUP
3304 Bandolino, Ste. 200
Plano, TX 75023
James T. Brady
PH: (214)612-0992
FX: (214)596-1336
Founded: 1974. **Staff:** 19. Activities: Consulting firm offers services in the fields of customer service, strategies, processes, and technology design and implementation management.

BRANCH, RICHARDS & CO.
2201 6th Ave., Ste. 1009
Seattle, WA 98121-1899
Andrew L. Branch, President
PH: (206)624-4723
FX: (206)626-0377
Founded: 1972. **Staff:** 16. Activities: Provides full CPA services including, accounting, tax, auditing, and contract/construction auditing of public projects. Clients include government entities, state agencies, quasi-public bodies, and numerous businesses in the private sector. The firm qualifies as a small business as codified in the small business regulations, is a minority-owned business (MBE).

BROUGHTON SYSTEMS INC.
7325 Beaufont Springs Dr., Ste. 110
Richmond, VA 23225
Dan Garfi, President
PH: (804)270-5999
FX: (804)270-6555
E-mail: info@broughton-sys.com
URL: www.broughton-sys.com
Founded: 1981. **Staff:** 400. Activities: Computer technology and management consulting firm specializes in contract programming, client-server projects, management consulting, turnkey development, telecommunications, network solutions and training. Also provides expertise in mid-range systems consulting, PC systems development, JD Edwards and other software packages, government contracts and developmental outsourcing. Industries served: Fortune 500 companies and mid-sized companies in all industries, and local, state and federal government departments and agencies throughout the U.S.

PAUL L. BROUSSARD & ASSOCIATES, INC.
501 Crawford St., Ste. 401
Houston, TX 77002
Paul L. Broussard, President
PH: (713)227-9735
FX: (713)227-3102
URL: www.broussardtrans.com
Founded: 1978. **Staff:** 14. Activities: Provides freight transportation consulting services for business and industry, including freight bill auditing, payment and computerized management reporting. Also provides contract rate/discount negotiations, carrier selection and

evaluation, transportation regulatory advice, freight rate quotations, and analysis of distribution systems and shipping patterns.

BSG
11 Greenway Plaza, Ste. 900
Houston, TX 77046
Jeffrey J. Weiner
PH: (713)965-9000
FX: (713)993-9249
URL: www.bsginc.com
Founded: 1987. **Staff:** 500. Activities: Provides services for technology-enabled change, including systems integration, consulting, technology transfer, and education.

BUSINESS LOGIC INC.
853 Broadway, Ste. 1406
New York, NY 10003
Howard P. Zien, President
PH: (212)505-9323
FX: (212)505-8891
E-mail: blogic@blogicnyc.aol.org
Founded: 1980. **Staff:** 20. Activities: Data processing/automation consultants experienced in all phases of automation, including workflow analysis and the design, development and implementation of turnkey systems using relational database technology. Emphasis is on the design and installation of automated solutions which optimize effective work flow and efficient use of computer capabilities. Systems experience includes: hardware and associated systems (PCs, UNIX, XENIX, VAX UMS, MVS, VM/CMS) and programming languages (C, C Plus Plus, ORACLE, INFORMIX, SYBASE, INGRES, DBZ, RDMS, FOX, CLIPPER, PARADOX, COBOL, PASCAL, FORTRAN and ASSEMBLER). Has served large corporate and government clients as well as the small businessman. Industries served: banking, brokerage, nonprofit, entertainment, healthcare, legal, chemical, insurance, and accounting.

BUSINESS TECHNOLOGY GROUP
14044 W. Petronella, Ste. 2
Libertyville, IL 60048
Rick Duris, President
PH: (847)367-1310
FX: (847)367-1349
E-mail: info@btgi.com
URL: btgi.com
Founded: 1982. **Staff:** 20. Activities: Systems integrations offering expertise in the development of business information systems. All phases of software development life cycle are addressed. Major emphasis is on requirements definition and management consulting relating to information systems. Also emphasize use and implementation of systems.

CACI INTERNATIONAL INC.
1100 N. Glebe Rd.
Arlington, VA 22201
Dr. J.P. London, Chairman
PH: (703)841-7801
TF: (800)235-5915
FX: (703)528-4196
E-mail: jbrown@hq.caci.com
URL: www.caci.com
Founded: 1962. **Staff:** 4200. Activities: Specializes in developing and integrating systems, software, and simulation products and providing information assurance services to government agencies and commercial enterprises worldwide. Delivers client solutions for systems integration, year 2000 conversion, information assurance/ security, reengineering, electronic commerce, intelligent document management, product data management, software development and reuse, telecommunications and network services, and market analysis.

CAI/SISCO
886 W. Diamond Ave., Ste. 301
Gaithersburg, MD 20878
Anthony C. Constable, President

PH: (301)840-5959
FX: (301)840-1859
E-mail: caisisco@clark.net
URL: www.caisisco.com
Founded: 1975. **Staff:** 16. Activities: Suppliers of opportunity-exclusive business development support services for information technology systems and services providers. Offers integrator clients team building, solution development, product sourcing, proposal development, bid pricing, business development training, and other support services.

CAMM INC.
10 Executive Dr.
Farmington, CT 06032-2837
Richard Baker
PH: (860)674-2600
FX: (860)674-2619
URL: www.camminc.com
Founded: 1985. **Staff:** 25. Activities: Consulting firm provides computer software development services.

CAMPBELL SOFTWARE, INC.
161 N. Clark St., Ste. 3700
Chicago, IL 60601-3290
Michael H. Campbell, President
PH: (312)425-0200
FX: (312)425-0205
E-mail: sales_info.campbellsoft.com
URL: www.campbellsoft.com
Founded: 1989. **Staff:** 80. Activities: Software firm specializes in the development of labor scheduling, forecasting, and time and attendance products.

CAMPOS MARKET RESEARCH
216 Boulevard of the Allies
Pittsburgh, PA 15222
PH: (412)471-8484
FX: (412)471-8497
E-mail: campos@campos.com
Founded: 1986. **Staff:** 15. Activities: Provides data processing, analysis, and quantitative and qualitative research. Maintains two focus group suites, test kitchen, and high quality moderating.

CANDLE CORP.
2425 Olympic Blvd.
Santa Monica, CA 90404
Aubrey Chernick, Chairman and CEO
PH: (310)829-5800
FX: (310)582-4287
URL: www.candle.com
Founded: 1976. **Staff:** 1400. Activities: An independent developer and provider of integrated availability, performance, systems and database management solutions for mainframe and client/server systems.

CANNON & CO.
2160 Country Club Rd.
Winston-Salem, NC 27104
William Rose
PH: (910)725-0635
FX: (910)725-0630
Founded: 1940. **Staff:** 40. Activities: Management consulting firm provides the following services: procedure development, policy development, feasibility studies, design, contract negotiating, human resources, organizational design, work flow control and implementation of financial and operational manual and computer-based systems. Office automation and organizational design are primary areas of expertise. Industries served: nonprofit organizations, shopping malls, land development, construction, real estate, healthcare (including nursing homes, hospitals and retirement homes), insurance, attorney firms, accounting firms, manufacturing and distribution, and government agencies.

CAP GEMINI AMERICA, INC.
1114 Avenue of the Americas, 29th Fl.
New York, NY 10036
Michel Berty, President and CEO
PH: (212)768-2066
FX: (212)768-9797
URL: www.capgemini.com
Founded: 1967. **Staff:** 3000. Activities: The Cap Gemini Group works to escort its customers through the implementation of profound change in business practices, mobilizing all of a company's resources in formulating its strategy for change, adapting its structures and processes, evolving its skills and products. Gemini Consulting is one of the world leaders in strategic and management consulting, specializing in: strategy formulation and implementation; management of change; business process improvement and redesign; organizational effectiveness; mobilization and renewal of the organization's people; information management; and implementation of automated systems and applications.

CARDINAL NETWORK USA CORP.
620 Moorefield Park Dr.
Richmond, VA 23236-3655
Peter Bursidge
PH: (804)320-3313
FX: (804)320-7667
E-mail: simpson3@ix.netcom.com
Founded: 1989. **Staff:** 450. Activities: Consulting firm offers expertise in computer technology and high level technical analysis of most Unisys architecture/operating environments; specializing in LINC on A-Series, Unix, 2200, V-Series, and System 80.

CARMEL INTERNET, L.L.C.
200 Clocktower Pl., Ste. B-205
Carmel, CA 93923-8723
Brian D. Steckler, President/CEO
PH: (408)622-5000
FX: (408)622-5010
E-mail: brian@carmelnet.com
URL: www.universal-net.com
Founded: 1995. **Staff:** 12. Activities: World Wide Web publishing, merchandising, marketing, sales, Internet Service Provider, Inter-net and Intra-net consulting, Internet guidance and training, network consulting, hardware/software integration. Serves private industry as well as government agencies worldwide.

CB TECHNOLOGIES, INC.
Glenloch Corporate Campus
1487 Dunwoody Dr.
West Chester, PA 19380
PH: (610)889-7300
FX: (610)993-8405
E-mail: sales@cbtech.com
URL: www.cbtech.com
Staff: 130. Activities: Delivers custom software development, e-Business solutions, and consulting services to Fortune 500 and other leading companies. Our clients gain strategic advantage through our leading-edge technology solutions and our understanding of their business processes.

C.C. PACE SYSTEMS, INC.
12450 Fair Lakes Cir., Ste. 450
Fairfax, VA 22033-3810
Michael Gordon, President
PH: (703)631-6600
FX: (703)378-1589
URL: www.ccpace.con
Founded: 1980. **Staff:** 100. Activities: Provides a full range of computer services from strategic MIS plans and software package evaluations and installations to customized system design, development, and implementation. Industries served: financial and telecommunications media.

CCC INFORMATION SERVICES, INC.
444 Merchandise Mart
Chicago, IL 60654
PH: (312)222-4636
FX: (312)527-2298
Founded: 1980. **Staff:** 1000. Activities: Firm provides state-of-the-art computerized information services to the automotive industry.

CCC LOGISTICS COMPANY LTD.
3390 S. Service Rd.
Burlington, Canada L7N 3L6
Robert J. Pearce, President
PH: (905)639-1271
FX: (905)639-1441
E-mail: ccc@.customsconsultants.on.ca
URL: www.customsconsultants.on.ca
Founded: 1976. **Staff:** 35. Activities: Provides expertise in audits and recoveries for customs duties, drawbacks, sales tax. Also performs freight audits and transportation studies. Additional services include installation of computerized broker programs, pre-audit and pay freight bills.

CDA, INC.
8301 Greensboro Dr., Ste. 350
McLean, VA 22102
Paul E. Moyer, President
PH: (703)821-1858
FX: (703)821-9859
E-mail: cda@cda1.com
URL: www.cda1.com
Founded: 1988. **Staff:** 65. Activities: Provides software, network, and quality assurance engineering. Specializes in developing and testing real-time embedded applications, network management solutions, device drives and firmware, GUI (graphical user interface), APIs, protocols, and heterogeneous networks.

CEC CONTROLS CO. INC.
14555 Barber
Warren, MI 48093
Gilbert E. Bates, CEO
PH: (810)779-0222
FX: (810)779-0266
URL: www.ceccontrols.com
Founded: 1989. **Staff:** 90. Activities: Firm consults on the design of electrical controls and monitoring systems. Services include planning, building, and start-up of systems.

THE CENTECH GROUP, INC.
4200 Wilson Blvd., Ste. 700
Arlington, VA 22203
Fernando V. Galaviz, CEO
PH: (703)525-4444
FX: (703)525-2349
E-mail: fgalaviz@centechgroup.com
Founded: 1988. **Staff:** 200. Activities: Firm provides a variety of computer and information systems services. Work involves program management support; computer systems analysis and integration; software engineering and development; network services; imaging, document conversion, manufacturing and engineering, LAN/WAN; workflow; and document management and data warehousing; including analysis, design, and implementation; information systems modernization and integration; and information engineering. Also provides conference management.

CFC, INC. - CATALYST FOR CHANGE
211 S. Main St., Ste. 300
Dayton, OH 45402
Larry E. Shpiner, President
PH: (937)461-9201
FX: (937)222-8280
Founded: 1974. **Staff:** 15. Activities: Develops and implements manufacturing strategic plans to train and motivate the workforce, improve the delivery of systems information, optimize the factory/inventory flow, develop a quality supplier base, and transfer technol-

ogy effectively. Offers not only manufacturing strategic planning, but also specific assistance in the areas of Total Quality Management, ISO9000 certification, systems integration, logistics and materials management, simulation modeling, and technology transfer. Training includes extensive media support. Firm will also assist clients in meeting criteria for participation in the Department of Defense Industrial Modernization Incentives Program. Industries served: aerospace, automotive, banking, casting, electronic, forging, government, machine tool, materials, processing, and transportation.

CGI SYSTEMS, INC., AN IBM CO.
300 Berwyn Park, Ste. 100
Berwyn, PA 19312
Gianfranco Moi
PH: (610)695-8100
TF: (800)366-3244
FX: (610)695-8585
Founded: 1980. **Staff:** 400. Activities: Client/server and I.S. counseling in the following: local area network, system development methodology, expert system development, system development (project management, analysis, design, implementation), technology training (methodology technique tools), CASE and systems integration. Industries served: financial services, insurance, manufacturing, retail, government, and Fortune 1000.

CHARLES RIVER COMPUTERS
575 Lexington Ave. 4th Fl
New York, NY 10022-6102
Joshua Wurzburger
PH: (212)906-1000
FX: (212)906-9500
Founded: 1978. **Staff:** 67. Activities: A leading firm in data center facilities management and technology consulting.

CHARTER PROFESSIONAL SERVICES
7001 Peachtree Industrial Blvd., Ste. 405
Norcross, GA 30092
Murli N. Reddy
PH: (770)326-9933
FX: (770)326-9922
E-mail: cps.@charter.com
URL: www.charterpro.com
Founded: 1994. **Staff:** 12. Activities: Offers consulting and programming services in mainframe applications, y2k solutions, custom client server applications, object oriented design and implementation, project management and database administration. CPS also specializes in the GIS, CAD/CAM industry.

CHESAPEAKE DECISION SCIENCES INC.
200 South St.
New Providence, NJ 07974-2151
Dr. Thomas E. Baker, President/Dir. R&D
PH: (908)464-8300
FX: (908)464-4134
URL: www.chesapeake.com
Founded: 1982. **Staff:** 45. Activities: Computer technology consultants specializing in software management solutions for production planning and scheduling, and supply chain optimization. Industries served: chemical, pulp and paper, petroleum companies in the process industries, food and beverage, electronics, semiconductor, pharmaceuticals, and repetitive manufacturing.

CHILSON'S MANAGEMENT CONTROLS, INC.
9645 Arrow Rt., Ste. L
Rancho Cucamonga, CA 91730
Richard L. Chilson, President
PH: (909)980-5338
FX: (909)987-3154
E-mail: chilson@chilson.com
URL: www.chilson.com
Founded: 1973. **Staff:** 22. Activities: Active in egg production, processing, and marketing management consulting. Provides turnkey computer systems for the poultry industry and agribusiness, including hardware, software, installation, training, and continuing sup-

port. Software includes flock records, egg processing, perishable distribution, feed mill, and all accounting packages (20 systems). Industries served: poultry, feed, and perishable distribution.

CIBER INC.
5251 DTC Pky., Ste. 1400
Englewood, CO 80111
Bob Stevenson, Chairman
PH: (303)220-0100
TF: (800)242-3799
FX: (303)220-7100
URL: www.ciber.com
Founded: 1974. **Staff:** 5700. Activities: Provides strategic information technology consulting, multi-line ERP/EAS consulting, professional staff supplemental services including computer network services for our clients information technology needs.

CIMQUEST, INC.
262 Chapman Rd., Ste. 105
Newark, DE 19702
Franklin A. Kurtz, President/CEO
PH: (302)738-1900
TF: (800)283-2667
FX: (302)737-1914
E-mail: cimquest@cimquest.com
URL: www.cimquest.com
Founded: 1986. **Staff:** 55. Activities: Computer technology consulting firm.

CLAREMONT TECHNOLOGY GROUP, INC.
1600 NW Compton Dr., Ste. 210
Beaverton, OR 97006-6905
Steve Darrow, President
PH: (503)690-4000
FX: (503)690-4004
URL: www.CLRMNT.com
Founded: 1989. **Staff:** 147. Activities: Computer technology consulting firm serving commercial concerns in the U.S. and Canada.

CLARK SCHAEFER HACKETT AND CO.
105 E. Fourth St., 16th Fl.
Cincinnati, OH 45202
Neil J. O'Connor, President
PH: (513)241-3111
FX: (513)241-1212
E-mail: noconnor@chsco.com
URL: www.cshco.com
Founded: 1938. **Staff:** 165. Activities: Offers network consulting, business directional and software development, and accounting and tax software support.

CLARKSTON * POTOMAC
2605 Meridian Pky., Ste. 100
Durham, NC 27713-2297
Tom Finegan, Principal
PH: (800)652-4274
FX: (919)484-4450
E-mail: info@clarkstonp.com
URL: www.clarkstonpotomac.com/
Founded: 1991. **Staff:** 100. Activities: A full-service consulting firm that provides a range of information technology consulting services. Specializes in strategic enterprise-wide packaged software implementations, by offering objective insights. Helps companies improve their performance in areas such as continuous flow manufacturing; process flows and system design of workstations; routings and bill of materials; pipeline transfers; outbound logistics including bulk material handling via rail, tank trucks, and ISO containers; capacity planning; work scheduling; active ingredient pricing; EDI; consignment inventory; seasonal planning, scheduling, and forecasting; third-party manufacturing; warehousing of bulk and packaged products; and export/import.

CLIENT SERVER ASSOCIATES
312 Plum St., Ste. 1110
Cincinnati, OH 45202
John Bostick, President
PH: (513)241-5949
FX: (513)241-6731
Staff: 25. Activities: Business directional and software specialization consultants offering software development, training, and data warehousing. Possess expertise in Sybase and PowerBuilder.

CMR TECHNOLOGIES INC.
136 Central Ave.
Island Heights, NJ 08732
John E. Olejack, President
PH: (908)270-9300
FX: (908)506-6786
Founded: 1976. **Staff:** 22. Activities: Engineering consulting firm specializing in electronics, computers, and testing equipment. Serves commercial clients and the government in the U.S.

CO-DEVELOPMENT INTERNATIONAL
16615 Lark Ave., Ste. 100
Los Gatos, CA 95030
John B. Christensen, Principal
PH: (408)358-5233
FX: (408)358-5236
URL: www.codevelop.com
Founded: 1986. **Staff:** 20. Activities: Provides integrated change management consulting that supports strategic planning, strategic sourcing, process re-engineering and alliance building by developing the competence of the organization. Services include executive development, team building, and the Co-Development Learning Alliance that supplements human resource and training departments. Capabilities include management consulting: strategy development; breakthrough solutions facilitation; marketplace assessments; strategic vision — implementation planning; enterprise development planning; rapid cycle strategy development departmental transformation; best practices implementation; acting turnaround leadership; outsourcing strategies; new technology introduction; reorganization process reengineering; reengineering design and execution; reengineering change management; continuous improvement/quality program development; process simplification and "work-out" sessions; benchmarking/"best practices" strategic sourcing/partnering; supply management redesign; enterprise wide purchasing reduction; partnering/alliance team development; vendor selection and quality programs; outsourcing analysis and negotiation technology solutions; information systems consulting; interactive multimedia systems; facilitation software and services; customized solutions major capital projects; definition of philosophy and goals; owner contractor alliances; project phase transition planning; project team building; communication and diversity strategies; development of permanent organizations organization development: leadership coaching; executive coaching; project leader coaching; transition planning; assessments; individual developmental plans team development; management, functional and project team building; team conflict resolution; process consultation; outdoor challenge programs; new team "start-up" custom training; high impact design and delivery; emphasis on integration with business strategy; innovative methodologies; expertise in many areas change management; change workshop design and facilitation; change leadership and support teams; change implementation management; communication planning; performance management diversity applications; cross cultural team building; cross cultural marketing and management; and global enterprise development training and awareness programs.

COGNETICS CORP.
PO Box 386
Princeton Junction, NJ 08550-0386
Charles B. Kreitzberg, President
PH: (609)799-5005
TF: (800)229-8437
FX: (609)799-8555
E-mail: info@cognetics.com
URL: www.cognetics.com

Founded: 1982. **Staff:** 22. Activities: Specialists in usability engineering, human centered software design: games, education, training, exhibits, optical disk, and CD-ROM. The firm can support all phases of product development from initial conception through implementation and launch. Offers a full range of services including technical, programming, human factors, content, graphics, and writing. Industries served: publishing, pharmaceutical, financial, chemical, and communications.

COLEMAN RESEARCH CORP.
9891 Broken Land Parkway, Ste. 200
Columbia, MD 21046
Thomas G. Lightner
PH: (301)621-8600
FX: (410)312-5600
URL: www.colemanresearch.com
Founded: 1980. **Staff:** 40. Activities: Performs engineering, geophysical, statistical, and software analyses related to strategic, aerospace, industrial, and software systems. Multi-disciplinary staff of aerospace, electrical, and mechanical engineers, mathematicians, physicists, geophysicists, computer scientists, and DBMS specialists who can combine and focus skills in a variety of systems studies.

COMBINED RESOURCE TECHNOLOGY INC.
PO Box 3242
Baton Rouge, LA 70821
Chris B. Moran, President
PH: (504)927-0176
TF: (800)962-0177
FX: (504)927-0177
Founded: 1986. **Staff:** 14. Activities: Offers overhead cost reduction services and related software product development to all industries in the United States and Canada.

COMMERCIAL BUSINESS SYSTEMS
614 E. 4th St.
Marion, IN 46952
Mike McCarty, President
PH: (765)662-9851
FX: (765)668-3270
E-mail: wswcbc@comek.com
URL: www.IConTECK.COM/~WSWCBS/WATERSOFT.WARE/MAIN.HTML
Founded: 1975. **Staff:** 12. Activities: Custom design and programming consultants specialize in Unix, networks and PCs. Other areas of expertise include: accounting and data processing, document image storage and retrieval, and complete hardware and software service.

COMMUNICATION PLANNING CORP.
4160 Southside Blvd., Ste. 3
Jacksonville, FL 32216-5470
Frank Bisbee
PH: (904)645-9077
FX: (904)645-9058
E-mail: acp@wireville.com
URL: www.wireville.com
Founded: 1980. **Staff:** 25. Activities: Computer and telecommunications technology consulting firm. Specializing in cabling.

COMMUNICATIONS TECHNOLOGY GROUP INC.
7855 Gross Point Rd., Ste. H-1
Skokie, IL 60077
Alan G. Kraus, President
PH: (847)675-7800
FX: (847)675-2635
E-mail: marketing@ctg.comcal.compuserve.com
Founded: 1983. **Staff:** 20. Activities: Established to provide in-depth engineering and integration services to the growing high performance enterprise network market. CTG has the ability to turnkey design, install, test, and maintain large scale data communications networks of fiber, coax, twisted pair, and wireless media. Experience and expertise in all aspects of multi-product local area networking integration and installation. Projects have included the complete de-

sign, installation and certification of major facility networks for large manufacturing, educational, and office facilities.

COMPASS COMPUTER SERVICES, INC.
3110 Fairview Park Dr., Ste. 1050
Falls Church, VA 22042
Daniel R. Burk, President
PH: (703)876-5577
FX: (703)876-5588
E-mail: dburk@compasscomputer.com
URL: www.compasscomputer.com
Founded: 1987. **Staff:** 13. Activities: Computer consulting firm specializing in law office and association automation. Firm provides a variety of technical consulting services including system acquisition, establishment of standard automation procedures, troubleshooting, and software design and development. Will assist with office moves, word processing conversion, training, planning and budgeting. Services encompass numerous applications such as accounting, attorney recruiting, cite checking, debt collection, estate tax planning, expense tracking, forms preparation and management, law library management, legislation tracking, litigation support, patent and trademark docketing, and real estate settlements. Industries served: legal.

COMPASS INTERNATIONAL RESEARCH
1301 Corporate Center Dr., Ste. 113
St. Paul, MN 55124
George Zirnhelt, President
PH: (612)454-0147
FX: (612)686-9981
Founded: 1962. **Staff:** 21. Activities: Firm specializes in marketing research and analysis and statistical services. Industries served: advertising, agriculture and forestry, employee benefits, banking, finance and insurance, consumer products, data processing and computer, education, energy industries, food and beverage, healthcare, manufacturing, publishing and broadcasting, and utilities.

COMPETITIVE COMPUTER SYSTEMS
2839 Boardwalk
Ann Arbor, MI 48104
Jemmie Wang, CEO
TF: (800)442-2748
FX: (313)747-8516
E-mail: info@ccsys.com
URL: www.ccsys.com
Founded: 1991. **Staff:** 20. Activities: Firm specializes in servicing networks, computer assembly, and troubleshooting activities.

COMPLETE BUSINESS SOLUTIONS INC.
32605 W. 12 Mile Rd., Ste. 250
Farmington Hills, MI 48334-3337
Raj Vatikuti, President
PH: (248)488-2088
FX: (248)488-2089
Founded: 1985. **Staff:** 700. Activities: Computer technology specialists offering expertise in turnkey vending and prepackaged software development.

COMPREHENSIVE DATA PROCESSING INC.
24700 Northwestern Hwy., Ste. 350
Southfield, MI 48075
Jerome W. Sheppard, President
PH: (248)353-6800
FX: (248)353-2825
E-mail: cdp@cdpsys.com
URL: www.cdpsys.com
Founded: 1978. **Staff:** 150. Activities: CDP is an Information Technology Staffing firm that services a wide range of technical requirements including but not limited to mainframe, client server, web development, systems administration, networking, project management, and trainers.

COMPSET SYSTEMS CONSULTANTS INC.
521 Fellowship Rd., Ste. 160
Mount Laurel, NJ 08054-2224
Robert J. Maier, President
PH: (609)727-5080
FX: (609)727-5250
Founded: 1970. **Staff:** 15. Activities: Offers computer technology consulting including typesetting, and database and desktop publishing.

COMPUBAHN, INC.
851 Burlway Rd., Ste. 625
Burlingame, CA 94010
Rajeev K. Aggarwal, President
PH: (650)696-8500
FX: (650)696-8515
E-mail: aggarwal@compubahn.com
URL: www.compubahn.com
Founded: 1990. **Staff:** 48. Activities: Software design and development services offered include: Windows NT and Unix development; shifts from mainframe operations to client/server platforms; Oracle applications; Visual Basic, Visual C++, and Powerbuilder applications; Intranet and workflow design; and PC LAN protocols.

COMPUTEC INTERNATIONAL RESOURCES INC.
801 North Branc Blvd., 6th Fl.
Glendale, CA 91203
Alicia Lancashire, CEO
PH: (818)500-3921
FX: (818)500-3924
E-mail: 76622.1671@compuserve.com
Founded: 1988. **Staff:** 100. Activities: An international data processing consulting firm specializing in rare skills resourcing.

COMPUTECH INC.
7735 Old Georgetown Rd., 12th Fl.
Bethesda, MD 20814-2930
J.D. Murphy, Jr.
PH: (301)656-4030
FX: (301)656-7060
URL: www.computechinc.com
Founded: 1979. **Staff:** 40. Activities: Computer consulting firm.

COMPUTER BASED SYSTEMS INC.
2750 Prosperity Ave.
Fairfax, VA 22031-4312
PH: (703)849-8080
FX: (703)849-1763
URL: www.cbsi.com
Founded: 1978. **Staff:** 550. Activities: A premier provider of Information Technology services and products to Federal, State, and commercial clients. Services include: Internet and Intranet Development; Database/Systems Administration; Client/Server Development; Network Design and Management; LAN/WAN Support; Mainframe Programming and Support; Customer Service and Help Desks; Imaging Systems.

COMPUTER CONSULTANTS INTERNATIONAL INC.
700 Larkspur Landing Circ., Ste. 235
Larkspur, CA 94939-1710
Robert Jones
PH: (415)461-8989
FX: (415)461-4601
E-mail: staff@cciusa.com
URL: www.cciusa.com
Founded: 1985. **Staff:** 64. Activities: Computer consulting firm.

COMPUTER CONSULTING ASSOCIATES INTERNATIONAL INC.
30 Jelliff Ln., Ste. 202
Southport, CT 06490
Kenton J. Clarke

PH: (203)255-8966
FX: (203)255-8501
E-mail: cca@ccaii.com
URL: www.ccaii.com
Founded: 1980. **Staff:** 80. Activities: Information services consulting firm providing system integration and programming services.

COMPUTER DATA SYSTEMS, INC.
1 Curie Ct.
Rockville, MD 20850
Clifford M. Kendall, Chairman
PH: (301)921-7000
FX: (301)948-9328
URL: www.cdsi.com
Founded: 1968. **Staff:** 2800. Activities: A professional and processing services firm which provides consulting and data processing services to the federal government, nonprofit institutions, and commercial clients. The services and support provided by CDSI include evaluation, design, programming, conversion, and implementation of EDP systems in the areas of management information, accounting and financial systems, communications, mailing, fulfillment, electronic composition, and facilities management.

COMPUTER ESSENTIALS INC.
3490 Piedmont Rd. NE, Ste. 520
Atlanta, GA 30305-4808
Sandy Murray, President
PH: (404)816-2482
TF: (800)582-3462
FX: (404)816-4737
E-mail: mgoins@propoint.com
Founded: 1983. **Staff:** 15. Activities: Provides software development for databases, systems integration, and training services. Serves private industries as well as government agencies.

COMPUTER GRAPHICS SYSTEMS DEVELOPMENT CORP.
2483 Old Middlefield Way, Ste. 140
Mountain View, CA 94043-2330
Roy W. Latham, President
PH: (415)903-4920
FX: (415)967-5252
URL: www.cgsd.com
Founded: 1990. **Staff:** 16. Activities: Designs and integrates real-time systems for virtual reality applications, simulation training, and high-end electronic entertainment attractions. Services include system specifications preparation and custom software development. Performs graphics systems research and development, including new algorithms and system architectures development. Analyzes real-time graphics systems market and evaluates client products. Prepares client patents and government and commercial proposals. Industries served: aerospace, electronic entertainment, computer, computer graphics, and virtual reality worldwide.

COMPUTER GROUP INC.
1230 St. Andrews Rd.
Columbia, SC 29210-5822
Michael Anderer
PH: (803)798-3424
FX: (803)731-3826
Founded: 1985. **Staff:** 230. Activities: Hardware and software computer consultants.

COMPUTER HARDWARE SERVICE CO.
Jacksonville Park, 11 Vincent Cir.
Ivyland, PA 18974
Joseph F. Colyar, President
PH: (215)443-9220
FX: (215)443-9024
E-mail: chs11@juno.com
Founded: 1974. **Staff:** 28. Activities: Provides computer services including hardware evaluation and insurance claims.

COMPUTER HORIZONS CORP.
4555 Lake Forest Dr., Ste. 396
Cincinnati, OH 45242
Terry Quinn, Senior Vice President
PH: (513)769-3355
TF: (800)227-3550
FX: (513)769-3371
URL: www.chccorp.com
Staff: 4000. Activities: Firm specializes in network consulting, business directional and software development, training and education, conversions/migrations, and document management implementation.

COMPUTER MANAGEMENT TECHNOLOGIES INC.
731 Gratiot Ave.
Saginaw, MI 48602-2109
William Loeffler
PH: (517)791-4860
FX: (517)791-4928
URL: www.cmtonline.com
Founded: 1984. **Staff:** 25. Activities: Offers computer technology expertise.

COMPUTER-PEOPLE CONSULTING SERVICES
8790 Governor's Hill Dr., Ste. 204
Cincinnati, OH 45249
Douglas Dockery, Branch Manager
PH: (513)683-4000
FX: (513)583-4933
E-mail: www.cp-consulting.com
Staff: 1200. Activities: Business consultants specializing in network and software development, training, information systems project management, and client/server migration consulting.

COMPUTER PEOPLE, INC.
1960 Grand Ave., Ste. 555
El Segundo, CA 90245
Anthony Vickers, President/CEO
TF: (800)444-3572
FX: (310)335-4820
Founded: 1972. **Staff:** 750. Activities: Provides professional services in information technology. Experienced with wide variety of machines such as IBM, DEC, Honeywell, UNISYS, and Hewlett Packard, and operating environments including IMS DB/DC, CICS, DB2, IDMS, ADS/0, ADABAS, DATACOM, TOTAL, etc. Industries served: banking, insurance, shopping, manufacturing, financial services, pharmaceutical, and automobile.

COMPUTER PLANNING AND ANALYSIS, INC.
17000 Freedom Way
Rockville, MD 20853-1123
Norma J. Errera, President
PH: (301)924-2208
FX: (301)774-1358
Founded: 1981. **Staff:** 27. Activities: Performs capacity management for government agencies including functional requirements analysis, workload projection, short and long-term growth requirements, profile of current and future ADP usage, future hardware configuration and sizing, and software support requirements. Installs company developed capacity management and fee-for-service software.

COMPUTER SCIENCE CORP.
3170 Fairview Park Dr.
Falls Church, VA 22042
E.T. Jones, President
PH: (703)876-1000
FX: (703)849-1003
URL: www.csc.com
Founded: 1953. **Staff:** 2400. Activities: As part of Atlantic Research Corporation, the Group specializes in applications of advanced science and technology to government and industry. Services include systems engineering and integration; software engineering, development and maintenance; operational and administrative support services; training systems development; integrated logistics sys-

tems support; shop and combat systems engineering; computer systems and management support services; and command, control, communications, and intelligence (C31).

COMPUTER SOLUTIONS & DEVELOPMENT INC.
CS&D Marketing Dept.
1105 B. Spring St.
Silver Spring, MD 20910
Robert D. Clasen, President
PH: (301)565-4711
FX: (301)565-4720
E-mail: bclasen@CSD-memex.com
URL: www.csd-memex.com
Founded: 1985. **Staff:** 11. Activities: Developed software package for association management (MemEx for Windows). Also market and support these programs as well as consult on all phases of association management. Industries served: associations and other membership and event management groups.

COMPUTER SUPPORT CENTRES, INC.
1920 Thoreau Dr., Ste. 150
Schaumburg, IL 60173-4749
Keith Cook
PH: (847)397-8000
FX: (847)397-8032
E-mail: keithc@ctrain.com
URL: www.csctrain.com
Founded: 1988. **Staff:** 20. Activities: Computer training and consulting firm specializing in: Classroom training on all popular desktop applications; Database design and development; Network installation; Software transition; Mac/Windows transition; Mobile computing; Macro design and customization; Web page design and development; Data conversion.

COMPUTER SUPPORT TECHNOLOGY INC.
1409 Allen Dr., Ste. G
Troy, MI 48083-4003
Roger Geelhood, P.E., President & Secretary
PH: (248)616-9200
FX: (248)616-8980
E-mail: kanderson@cst-pcg.com
Founded: 1973. **Staff:** 14. Activities: Firm specializes in providing computer room support services, air/power conditioning, UPS, distribution, command bridge control and LAN storage modules, and Tate Access Flooring.

COMPUTER SYNERGETICS, INC.
109 W. Front St.
Tyler, TX 75711
Robert M. Franks, President
PH: (903)597-5311
FX: (903)597-0467
Founded: 1981. **Staff:** 14. Activities: Offers professional and technical data processing consulting services including cable television computerization, professional office computerization, feasibility studies and implementation, data communications implementation, and end user education and training. Industries served: distribution and retail.

COMPUTER SYSTEMS SOLUTIONS INC.
3133 Dundee Rd.
Northbrook, IL 60062
Avi Azoulay
PH: (847)498-0061
FX: (847)498-0046
Founded: 1986. **Staff:** 17. Activities: Computer systems consulting firm.

COMPUTER TASK GROUP, INC.
800 Delaware Ave.
Buffalo, NY 14209-2094
Joseph G. Makowski, V.P., General Counsel & Secretary

PH: (716)882-8000
TF: (800)992-5350
FX: (716)887-7464
URL: www.ctg.com
Founded: 1966. **Staff:** 4600. Activities: International information technology consulting, professional services and systems integration firm. Services cover all phases of the systems development life cycle, such as: management consulting, information systems planning, hardware/software evaluation, systems integration, project management, systems analysis and design, systems development, systems maintenance, and software product customization. Specialty services include the following: voice and data communications, documentation services, database consulting, information engineering, and migration services. Industries served: manufacturing, utilities, transportation, wholesale/retail, banking, insurance, health services, business services, and state/local government.

COMPUTERIZED MANAGEMENT OF VEHICLES, INC.
100 S. Marion Rd.
Sioux Falls, SD 57107-0544
J.E. Mitchell, President
PH: (605)338-6645
TF: (800)888-1649
FX: (605)334-8521
E-mail: cmovinc@aol.com
URL: www.cmov.com
Founded: 1978. **Staff:** 15. Activities: Offers analysis of business needs as well as problem solving. Directs most services toward data processing but also offers management consulting to help streamline an operation or prepare it for computerization at a later time. Industries served: trucking, distribution, livestock marketing, banking, and forestry services.

COMPUTERIZED MANAGEMENT SYSTEMS INC.
404 Reisterstown Rd.
Baltimore, MD 21208-5321
Henry Tyrangiel
PH: (410)653-3394
FX: (410)358-8068
URL: www.cmsincmd.com
Founded: 1982. **Staff:** 30. Activities: Offers computer systems technology, network integration and support, and Lotus Notes implementation.

COMPUTERPEOPLE
1231 Delaware Ave.
Buffalo, NY 14209
Frank Codella, President
PH: (716)883-0771
FX: (716)883-0776
E-mail: consult@cpstaffing.com
URL: cpstaffing.com
Founded: 1970. **Staff:** 42. Activities: Provides a full range of consulting services to computer users. Offers recommendation to first time users, provides upgrade systems solutions to existing (those systems in use now) accounts, and assists customers with the need for additional personnel at peak load intervals. Serves private industries as well as government agencies.

COMRISE TECHNOLOGY, INC.
1301 Concord Center, Hwy. 36
Hazlet, NJ 07730-1663
Gwo Ching Liou, President
PH: (732)739-2330
TF: (800)862-2330
FX: (732)739-1996
E-mail: recruiter@mail.comrise.com
URL: www.comrise.com
Founded: 1984. **Staff:** 120. Activities: Provides computer, data communications, and telecommunications consulting and project development.

COMSHARE
555 Briarwood Cir.
Ann Arbor, MI 48108
PH: (313)994-4800
FX: (313)769-6943
E-mail: info@comshare.com
URL: www.comshare.com
Founded: 1966. **Staff:** 750. Activities: An international software and services company specializing in planning, analysis and reporting applications. Services include business problems analysis, design, and implementation of computerized decision support.

COMSYS TECHNICAL SERVICES, INC.
4 Research Pl., 3rd Fl.
Rockville, MD 20850
Frederick M. Shulman, President
PH: (301)921-3600
FX: (301)921-3670
URL: www.comsysinc.com
Founded: 1979. **Staff:** 550. Activities: Provides programmers, systems analysts, hardware design engineers, software architects, technical writers, electrical engineers, technicians, and other computer project support personnel to high-tech clients. Such personnel are available for short or long-term projects on an hourly or fixed-price basis. Expertise on all computer makes/models and software. Specializes in systems design and development.

ARTHUR L. CONN & ASSOCIATES, LTD.
1469 E. Park Pl.
Chicago, IL 60637
Arthur L. Conn, President
PH: (773)667-1828
Founded: 1978. **Staff:** 29. Activities: Provides independent technological assessments and planning assistance in the areas of new energy technologies, management of research and development, and the application of new technologies to information management. Energy-related work includes petroleum refining; biotechnology; coal production, gasification and liquefaction; fluidized combustion, flue gas scrubbing, shale oil and tar sands extraction. Information management includes technologies involved in the organization, availability and transmittal of data; and new computer technologies, word processors and telecommunications.

CONNECTING POINT COMPUTER CENTER
324 E. Fourth
Hutchinson, KS 67501
Steven B. Harper, President
PH: (316)669-0797
TF: (800)638-7767
FX: (316)669-8302
URL: www.nmgi.com
Founded: 1992. **Staff:** 26. Activities: Computer connectivity including Local Area Networks (LANs), Wide Area Networks (WANs), and host communication in the IBM mainframe or minicomputer environment. Year 2000, accounting and other business management services. Training seminars on many topics also provided. Industries served: CPAs, legal, medical, insurance, banking, and fast food.

THE CONSORTIUM
1156 Avenue of the Americas, 4th Fl.
New York, NY 10036
Martin Blaire, Executive Vice President
PH: (212)221-1544
FX: (212)764-6848
E-mail: avalck@mail.rcmt.com
Founded: 1975. **Staff:** 825. Activities: Computer specialists provide services for large mainframes, help desk, Unix, and PC's. Maintain strong capabilities in application development and maintenance for financial service, law firms, real estate, communications, manufacturing companies, and government agencies. Firm has heavy involvement in on-line, database, fourth generation languages and systems internals. Also offers executive search services.

CONSULTEC
112 South St.
Boston, MA 02111
Chuck Dickinson
PH: (617)695-9779
FX: (617)695-9844
E-mail: contec@trac.net
URL: www.consultec-Boston.com
Founded: 1986. **Staff:** 15. Activities: Firm helps organizations improve job performance through the effective use of customized learning and support resources. Specialty is equipping employees with the tools to help them increase their productivity. Consultants are skilled in project management, instructional design, graphic design, technical writing, training delivery, and needs analysis. Firm will design, develop, and implement a variety of learning and support services, including technology-based and interactive multimedia programs, computer-based reference, online help, instructor-led courses, print documentation, and job aids. Industries served: financial services, utilities, retail, high tech, hospitality, insurance, and human services.

CONVERGENT GROUP
6200 S. Syracuse Way, Ste. 200
Englewood, CO 80111
Glenn E. Montgomery, CEO
PH: (303)741-8400
FX: (303)741-8401
Founded: 1985. **Staff:** 120. Activities: A technical and management consulting firm specializing in the identification of functional requirements for Geographic Information Systems (GIS) projects and the development and implementation of system integration plans to satisfy those requirements. The firm has an established reputation in North America as a leading independent GIS consulting firm with extensive experience in building agreement on GIS technical and management issues. Strong emphasis on end-user requirements. Industries served: city, county, and state; electric, gas, water/ wastewater utilities; telephone companies; and government agencies.

CORDIANT SOFTWARE
1810 Embarcadero Rd.
Palo Alto, CA 94303-3308
Carol Realini, President and CEO
PH: (415)493-3800
FX: (415)493-2215
URL: www.chordiant.com
Founded: 1985. **Staff:** 55. Activities: Assists clients in transition to enterprise-wide client/server systems by providing initial strategy, needs analysis, strategic architecture, technology assessment, infrastructure implementation, client/server development, and staff retraining. Industries served: telecommunications, finance, computer technology, and agriculture.

CORPORATE DIVERSIFIED SERVICES, SUBSIDIARY OF DIVERSIFIED MATERIAL
575 E. Big Beaver Rd.
Troy, MI 48083
Jack Troyanovich, Ph.D., President
PH: (248)680-2147
FX: (248)680-2152
Founded: 1991. **Staff:** 31. Activities: Specializes in foreign acquisition and joint-venture facilitation; foreign culture sensitivity training and multicultural teambuilding; productivity improvements through international system integration; translation and interpretation services in German, Czech-Slovak, Polish, Spanish, and Portuguese. Services are provided primarily for automobile manufacturers and their suppliers, others upon request.

CORPORATE SOLUTIONS INC.
2 Broadway
New York, NY 10004-2207
Jonathan Strizower, President
PH: (212)742-8100
FX: (212)742-8218
Founded: 1986. **Staff:** 14. Activities: Computer technology firm.

COTC COMPUTER CONSULTING
44 E. Spaulding Ave. #12
Pueblo West, CO 81007
Tom Renz, CEO, CIO
PH: (719)547-0938
TF: (888)547-0938
FX: (719)547-7714
E-mail: info@cotc-consulting.com
URL: www.cotc-consulting.com
Founded: 1996. **Staff:** 15. Activities: Provides software consulting services to organizations who require assistance with their HP3000 Computer System. Provides systems analysis, programming, operations support, system management and performance specialists. Also provides PC software and hardware support and consulting. Additionally, they provide various training for the HP3000 computer system. Industries served: healthcare, aerospace procurement, aerospace proposal activities, HP3000 computer systems.

CRAWFORD & ASSOCIATES INC.
6133 N. River Rd., Ste. 120E
Rosemont, IL 60018-4247
Sally Crawford, President
PH: (847)698-6670
FX: (847)698-6992
URL: www.Netcai.com
Founded: 1982. **Staff:** 36. Activities: Offers end-user training on ERP applications such as SAP, Baan, Oracle and proprietary systems.

CRC INFORMATION SYSTEMS, INC.
3100 47th Ave.
Long Island City, NY 11101
Joseph E. Rafael, President
PH: (718)937-2727
FX: (718)729-2444
Founded: 1976. **Staff:** 60. Activities: Operate complete data processing centers with services including CATI interviewing, coding, data entry, tabulations, table reformatting, PC programs and statistical analysis. A powerful on-line system is also available on a time-sharing basis for complete in-house capabilities. Provides expert assistance in statistical techniques. Industries served: market research and telemarketing.

CROWE, CHIZEK AND CO. LLP
330 E. Jefferson Blvd.
South Bend, IN 46624-0007
Mark L. Hildebrand, CEO
PH: (219)232-3992
FX: (219)236-8692
URL: www.crowechizek.com
Founded: 1942. **Staff:** 1350. Activities: Offers accounting and non-traditional services for the automotive, agricultural, commercial, construction, financial, government, healthcare, manufacturing, and transportation industries. Also specializes in system integration, software, human resources and litigation.

CTC COMPUTER-TECH CONSULTANTS LTD.
2420-101 6th Ave. SW
Calgary, Canada T2P 3P4
PH: (403)233-7233
FX: (403)233-7343
E-mail: resumes@ctctech.com
URL: www.ctctech.com/
Founded: 1985. **Staff:** 120. Activities: A contract resource provider within Western Canada. Provides technical professionals in virtually all IT related field. The company's database contains skill sets covering Programmers/Developers, Software/Hardware Engineers, Project Managers, Senior Managers, Network/Technical Support Representatives, Systems Engineers and Sales and Marketing Representatives. Provides clients with the flexibility of employees who start on a sub-contract basis with the option to become as permanent staff members.

CURRENT TECHNOLOGY, INC.
97 Madbury Rd.
Durham, NH 03824
D.C. Current, President
PH: (603)868-2270
FX: (603)868-1352
E-mail: dcc@curtech.com
URL: www.curtech.com
Founded: 1988. **Staff:** 20. Activities: Software and hardware systems design, implementation, and integration. Industries served: data communication, telecommunications, imaging technologies, and miscellaneous. Integration of data acquisition modules into UNIX VME-based systems and SBus systems also available.

CURRIER MCCABE & ASSOCIATES INC.
14 Wade Rd.
Latham, NY 12110-2609
Kay McCabe, President
PH: (518)783-9003
FX: (518)783-5093
Founded: 1984. **Staff:** 90. Activities: Computer technology consulting firm.

CUSTOM SOFTWARE SERVICES, INC.
1120 E. Long Lake Rd., Ste. 204
Troy, MI 48098
Amanda Schneider, President
PH: (248)528-1980
FX: (248)528-2243
E-mail: css@custsoft.com
URL: www.custsoft.com
Founded: 1981. **Staff:** 65. Activities: Offers wide range of computer services on IBM midrange, PC, client/server, and LAN platforms: contract programming and software design, project management, training, and permanent placements. Also provides help desk services and end user technical support. Industries served: manufacturing, distribution, retail, advertising, government, healthcare, transportation, and environmental management.

CUSTOM SOFTWARE SERVICES, INC.
10900 NE 4th St., Ste. 900
Bellevue, WA 98004
Franklin L. Orth, President
PH: (425)455-3507
FX: (425)646-9582
E-mail: sales@csspro.com
URL: www.csspro.com
Founded: 1979. **Staff:** 61. Activities: General business consultants offering economic analysis and research services, marketing research and analysis, management, office automation studies, and related data processing services. Industries served: legal market, corporate legal departments, and government agencies.

CUTLER-WILLIAMS, INC.
4000 McEwen S, Ste. 200
Dallas, TX 75244
Ed Burns, Vice President
PH: (972)960-7053
TF: (800)282-7413
FX: (972)991-9021
Founded: 1969. **Staff:** 630. Activities: Data processing/computer technology consultants offering information and systems integration services as well as consulting contract programming. Industries served: utilities, energy, transportation, communications, finance, retail, banking, manufacturing, and government agencies.

CYBER RESOURCES CORP.
1101 Bristol Rd.
Mountainside, NJ 07092
Timothy J. McEvoy, President
TF: (800)395-9700
FX: (908)789-3000
URL: cyberresource.net
Founded: 1975. **Staff:** 12. Activities: Provides consulting services

regarding computer software and/or computer hardware; markets a turnkey collection and recovery system. Industries served: hospital labs, industrial process control, banking, and government.

CYBERDATA CORP.
2555 Garden Rd.
Monterey, CA 93940-5337
Charles J. Lembo, President
PH: (408)373-2601
FX: (408)373-4093
Founded: 1974. **Staff:** 14. Activities: Computer technology consulting firm.

CYBERGATE, INC.
1301 W. Newport Ctr. Dr.
Deerfield Beach, FL 33442
Thomas R. Benham, CEO
PH: (954)429-8000
TF: (800)NET-GATE
FX: (954)429-8001
E-mail: sales@gate.net
URL: www.gate.net
Founded: 1993. **Staff:** 75. Activities: Specialize in Dedicated data lines with Internet services and the utilization of the global Internet Industry. We can show businesses and organizations how to benefit from Internet access and marketing capabilities such as World Wide Web services. Complete network engineering and configuration capabilities.

DALY & WOLCOTT INC.
1 Hospital Trust Plaza 21st fl.
Providence, RI 02903
Terrance Daly, President
PH: (401)823-8400
FX: (401)351-2690
E-mail: www.dalywolcott.com
Founded: 1978. **Staff:** 100. Activities: Computer systems consulting firm.

DANIELS ASSOCIATES INC.
225 S. East St., Ste. 244
Indianapolis, IN 46202-4042
Peter F. Daniels, President
PH: (317)692-8830
FX: (317)692-8833
Founded: 1979. **Staff:** 45. Activities: Informations systems consultancy.

DAPRU INC.
27 Maiden Ln., Ste. 300
San Francisco, CA 94108-5415
David Killingsworth, President
PH: (415)544-9260
FX: (415)788-2592
Founded: 1988. **Staff:** 120. Activities: Computer technology consulting firm.

DATA IMAGINATION, INC.
11423 Moorpark St.
Studio City, CA 91602
Mike P. Shulem, President
PH: (818)985-6100
TF: (800)422-5222
FX: (818)985-6160
Founded: 1982. **Staff:** 15. Activities: Computer services firm offers expertise with campaign and legislative software. Experienced with database development and generation of campaign materials. Consultants have developed the Vote-Tech campaign software and Monarch Legislative software.

DATA ARTS & SCIENCES, INC.
8 Strathmore Rd.
Natick, MA 01760
John Travers, President

PH: (508)651-8200
FX: (508)651-2936
E-mail: dasi@cotl.com
URL: www.cotl.com
Founded: 1975. **Staff:** 200. Activities: Provides consulting services to companies requiring analysis, design and development of computer software either for internal business applications or software engineering applications.

DATA CAPTURE TECHNOLOGIES, INC.
4328 Farragut St.
Hyattsville, MD 20781
Philip L. Gray, President
PH: (301)864-3196
FX: (301)864-0246
Founded: 1985. **Staff:** 19. Activities: Data processing consultants providing data entry/verification, application programming, data telecommunication, coding and data preparations, data entry facilities management, temporary services, office automation, systems analysis, and word processing. Serves federal, state and local governments as well as the private sector.

DATA CORE SYSTEMS, INC.
3700 Science Center
Philadelphia, PA 19104-3147
Sadhan C. Dutt, Pres.
PH: (215)243-1990
FX: (215)243-1978
Founded: 1988. **Staff:** 300. Activities: Specializes in marketing services and developing financial software.

DATA MANAGEMENT CONSULTANTS, INC.
18 N. Howell
Hillsdale, MI 49242
David L. Cleveland, Founder and President
PH: (517)437-7349
TF: (800)639-DMCI
FX: (517)437-2338
E-mail: internet.sales@dmci.net
URL: www.dmci.net
Founded: 1987. **Staff:** 25. Activities: Full-service provider of computers and computer-related services, including computer hardware, computer software, and networking. Teaches software applications. Provides LAN instruction.

DATA RESOURCES, INC.
24 Hartwell Ave.
Lexington, MA 02173
Kevin Mulvaney, President
PH: (617)863-5100
TF: (800)933-3DRI
FX: (617)860-6332
E-mail: client_services@dri.mgh.com
URL: www.dri.mcgraw-hill.com
Founded: 1968. **Staff:** 500. Activities: Provides economic forecasting and consulting services to business and government clients in countries throughout the world. Provides market planning, risk assessment, competitive analysis, financial management and government policy analysis. Provides these advisory service across business units, functional lines and throughout clients' global operations. Also maintains one of the world's largest private collections of information, including economic, financial, industry, and regional data. Data services feature global coverage of worldwide markets, extensive history, and regular data updates. Provides several convenient ways of accessing DRI data, and a variety of software tools for data analysis, graphing and reporting. Industries served: numerous industries including automotive, banking and finance, telecommunications, transportation, energy, environmental, manufacturing, and government agencies.

DATA SECURITIES INTERNATIONAL
21 Terry Ave.
Burlington, MA 01803-2504
John Noekr, Chairman of the Board

PH: (617)273-5432
TF: (800)962-0652
FX: (617)273-5633
URL: www.dsiescrow.com
Founded: 1982. **Staff:** 35. Activities: Offers software and technology escrow services for protection of technology licenses. Provides trade secret and proprietary technology protection programs that strengthen rights.

DATA STUDY INC.
119 Cherry Hill Rd.
Parsippany, NJ 07054-1114
Michael Gulban
PH: (973)402-7802
TF: (877)402-7804
FX: (973)316-0181
E-mail: rcalcagno@datastudyinc.com
URL: www.datastudy.com
Founded: 1984. **Staff:** 320. Activities: Provider of evaluation and rapid implementation of financial and human resource software. The company offers a wide range of services including business re-engineering, project management, customization, upgrade support and efficiency tuning.

DATA TRANSFORMATION CORP.
8300 Colesville Rd., Ste. 600
Silver Spring, MD 20910-3243
Andrew Thrash, President
PH: (301)587-4580
FX: (301)587-8058
Staff: 60. Activities: Offers computer consulting and systems analysis, primarily to government agencies.

DATABASE DESIGN SOLUTIONS, INC.
40 Morristown Rd., Ste. 1A
Bernardsville, NJ 07924
Adrienne Tannenbaum, President
PH: (908)204-0900
FX: (908)204-0606
E-mail: info@dbdsolutions.com
URL: www.dbdsolutions.com
Founded: 1989. **Staff:** 24. Activities: Offers consulting on the revitalization of corporate databases including: data warehouse development, database design and re-design, data modeling/enterprise data modeling, client/server architecture planning and implementation, database downsizing, repository implementation, consolidation/ integration of corporate databases, application and database re-engineering, application of artificial intelligence products to existing systems, and technical course development and instruction. Industries served: major corporate enterprises including pharmaceutical, insurance, telecommunications, financial, research, and manufacturing organizations.

DATALOGIX INTERNATIONAL, INC.
100 Summit Lake Dr.
Valhalla, NY 10595
Richard C. Giordanella, CEO and Pres.
PH: (914)747-2900
FX: (914)747-2987
E-mail: crweb@us.oracle.com
URL: www.crwebus.oracle.com
Staff: 200. Activities: Provides process manufacturing and financial software to Fortune 500 clients worldwide.

DATAMETRICS SYSTEMS CORP.
12150 E Monument Dr., Ste. 300
Fairfax, VA 22033
John Kelly, President
PH: (703)385-7700
FX: (703)385-7700
URL: www.datametrics.com
Founded: 1979. **Staff:** 42. Activities: Computer technology consulting firm.

DATASKILL
12520 High Bluff Dr., Ste. 300
San Diego, CA 92130-2064
Nigel Hook, President and CTO
PH: (619)755-3800
FX: (619)755-3282
E-mail: inform@dataskill.com
URL: www.dataskill.com
Founded: 1981. **Staff:** 68. Activities: Computer technology consultants providing total information systems solutions through systems integration, contract personnel, and management consulting. Clients include large corporations and small businesses.

DATATEL, INC.
4375 Fair Lakes Ct.
Fairfax, VA 22033
Russ Griffith, President and CEO
PH: (703)968-9000
TF: (800)DAT-ATEL
URL: www.datatel.com
Founded: 1968. **Staff:** 300. Activities: Provides software solutions and services to institutions of higher education.

W.R. DAVIS ENGINEERING LTD.
1260 Old Innes Rd.
Ottawa, Canada K1B 3V3
W.R. Davis, President
PH: (613)748-5500
FX: (613)748-3972
URL: www.davis-eng.on.ca
Founded: 1975. **Staff:** 55. Activities: Offers research and development in electronics and mechanical engineering for specialized studies, designs, and prototype fabrication. Also provides testing and tabulation. General areas include machine design and drafting, system integration, software development, and documentation. Clients include shipyards, marine consultants, and others.

D.B. TECHNOLOGY INC.
100 Wood Ave., S., Ste. 119
Iselin, NJ 08830
David Wecholer, Pres.
PH: (732)603-8300
URL: www.dbtech.com
Founded: 1983. **Staff:** 20. Activities: Offers expertise in PC and LAN technology to regional businesses and industrial concerns.

DECISION AIDS, INC.
1720 Parkhaven Dr.
Champaign, IL 61820
Stuart S. Nagel, President
PH: (217)359-8541
FX: (217)352-3037
E-mail: s-nagel@uiuc.edu
URL: www.staff.uiuc.edu/~s-nagel/
Founded: 1985. **Staff:** 20. Activities: Specializes in the analysis of public policy issues through the use of microcomputers. Microcomputer capabilities assist in the processing of a set of goals to be achieved, alternatives for achieving them, and relations between goals and alternatives in order to choose the best alternative or combination for maximizing benefits minus costs. Also utilizes microcomputers for predicting decisions, facilitating negotiation, allocating scarce resources, evaluating alternative public policies, and related matters.

DECISION SCIENCES CORP.
Box 28848
St. Louis, MO 63123
Kevin M. Curran, Vice President
PH: (314)739-2662
FX: (314)536-1001
URL: www.uncertain.com
Founded: 1968. **Staff:** 16. Activities: Specializes in application of probabilistic computer simulation to problems of profit planning and budgetary control, capital investments, new products, and acquisi-

tions. Developed concept known as "Bracket Budgeting" and a specialized version called "Range Estimating" for the engineering, construction, and allied industries for use in planning, bidding on, and managing construction projects. Developed Risk Established Value (REV) for probabilistic valuation of companies and business expansion plans. Also plans and manages relocations of large and critical data centers. Clients include manufacturing, construction, engineering, insurance, government agencies, and other service industries.

DECISION SYSTEMS TECHNOLOGIES, INC.
1700 Research Blvd.
Rockville, MD 20850
Joy Koshy, President
PH: (301)315-9200
FX: (301)315-9688
E-mail: webmaster@dsti.com
URL: www.dsti.com
Founded: 1986. **Staff:** 550. Activities: Professional services consulting firm with extensive experience in government and private sectors, providing information technology, engineering, and technical services. Offers a complete spectrum of cutting-edge technologies. Competencies include: client/server, software engineering, SIV&V, video teleconferencing, information systems management, facilities management, and computer-based engineering.

DEL TECHNOLOGY INTERNATIONAL INC.
7404 E. Via Estrella, Ste. 10
Scottsdale, AZ 85258
David Donahoe, Vice President
PH: (602)483-7588
FX: (602)483-7533
Founded: 1990. **Staff:** 12. Activities: Provides services in three areas: management consulting, information technology, and micro business. Focuses on organizational assessment, business process re-engineering, quality assurance program development, hardware/software evaluation and acquisition, applications software development, systems integration, LAN support, and new technology training. Industries served: all.

THE DELPHI GROUP INC.
100 City Hall Plaza
Boston, MA 02108-2106
Thomas M. Koulopoulos, President
PH: (617)247-1511
FX: (617)247-4957
E-mail: client_services@delphigroup.com
URL: www.delphigroup.com
Founded: 1989. **Staff:** 25. Activities: Provides consulting, market research, seminars and publications on the subjects of workflow, internet/intranets, document management, text retrieval, imaging, and business process redesign. Provides the knowledge foundation upon which over 10,000 professionals have based their IT strategies. Delphi's consulting services span business and technology requirements analysis, to recommendations, and RFP development/review.

DEMETRIUS & CO.
145 State Hwy., Rte. 46
Wayne, NJ 07470-6830
John A. Demetrius, Managing Partner
PH: (973)812-0100
FX: (973)812-0750
Founded: 1985. **Staff:** 20. Activities: Management consulting firm offering expertise in business services such as accounting, computer systems, and mergers.

THE DESCARTES SYSTEMS GROUP INC.
120 Randall Dr.
Waterloo, Canada N2V 1C6
Peter J. Schwartz
PH: (519)746-8110
TF: (800)419-8495
FX: (519)747-0082
URL: www.descartes.com

Founded: 1981. **Staff:** 80. Activities: Designs and develops routing and scheduling computer software and systems.

DESIGN AUTOMATION
905 W. Eisenhower Cir., Ste. 102
Ann Arbor, MI 48108
Carl Rose
PH: (734)761-1686
FX: (734)761-9705
E-mail: sales@da.com
URL: www.da.com
Founded: 1985. **Staff:** 29. Activities: Firm serves as a AutoCAD reseller and consultancy.

DESIGN CONTINUUM
1220 Washington St.
West Newton, MA 02165
PH: (617)969-5400
FX: (617)969-5400
E-mail: main@dcontinuum.com
URL: www.dcontinuum.com
Founded: 1983. **Staff:** 100. Activities: Provides complete product planning, design and engineering, software, electronics, technology development, and graphic design of clinical, medical, and surgical products. Development focuses on integrating user needs and technology for superior design solutions resulting in market differentiation for leading corporations.

DESIGN SYSTEMS, INC.
170 Township Line Rd.
Belle Mead, NJ 08502
James Dowd, President
PH: (908)874-4030
FX: (908)874-8050
E-mail: jsnyder@designsystemsinc.com
URL: www.designsystemsinc.com
Founded: 1970. **Staff:** 32. Activities: Provides general support for PCs, mid-range, and mini-computer systems. Offers expertise in hardware/software evaluation and installation; client/server architecture; IBM AS/400 and PC applications development tools and graphical user interfaces (e.g. PowerBuilder, Access, and Visual Basic); and CASE (computer-aided software engineering) tools.

DEVON CONSULTING
950 West Valley Rd., Ste. 2602
Wayne, PA 19087-1824
Ned Frey, President
PH: (610)964-2700
FX: (610)964-2708
E-mail: devoncnsul@aol.com
Founded: 1982. **Staff:** 258. Activities: Provides data processing technical personnel to organizations in Pennsylvania, Delaware, and New Jersey. Referrals include programmers, systems analysts, systems programmers, database administrators, and data processing project leaders. Serves data processing departments in all industries and government agencies.

/DHARMA SYSTEMS, INC.
15 Trafalgar Sq.
Nashua, NH 03063
J. Sasidhar, President
PH: (603)886-1400
FX: (603)883-6904
E-mail: info@dharmas.com
Founded: 1987. **Staff:** 48. Activities: Software firm providing SQL interfacing technology for proprietary (non-SQL) database management systems.

DIAMOND MANAGEMENT SYSTEMS INC.
101 Greenwood Ave., Ste. 600
Jenkintown, PA 19046-2627
Douglas L. Diamond, President

PH: (215)887-2515
FX: (215)572-9908
URL: www.dms.net.com
Founded: 1969. **Staff:** 55. Activities: Computer management and information systems consulting firm providing data conversion and training support to clients in the U.S.

DIAQUEST/GENERAL ELECTRONICS SYSTEMS, INC.
1440 San Pablo Ave.
Berkeley, CA 94702
Dan Lindheim, President
PH: (510)526-7167
FX: (510)526-7073
E-mail: sales@diaquest.com
Founded: 1953. **Staff:** 25. Activities: Video and computer graphics systems specialists provide expertise in animation, scientific visualization, point of purchase/information displays, custom software and hardware design and manufacture. Industries served: computer graphics, video animation, and government agencies.

DIGITAL CONSULTING INC.
204 Andover St.
Andover, MA 01810
George Schussel, CEO
PH: (508)470-3880
FX: (508)470-0526
URL: www.dci.com
Founded: 1982. **Staff:** 130. Activities: Assists companies in solving technology management and applications development problems. Specializes in helping companies select the right application and software tools for their computer environment and business objectives through conferences, expositions, and seminars targeting the IS professional. Serves private industry and government agencies worldwide.

DIGITAL PROCESSING CORP.
180 Newport Center Dr., Ste. 180
Newport Beach, CA 92660-6915
Richard A. Finn, President
PH: (949)759-9244
FX: (949)759-0455
Founded: 1972. **Staff:** 14. Activities: Engineering and computer software development consulting firm specializing in services to the oil, coal, and gasoline industries worldwide.

DIGITAL SOFTWARE CORP.
1010 S. Jolite St., Ste. 200
Aurora, CO 80012
Richard E. Stansberry, Chairman
PH: (303)367-1225
FX: (303)367-2010
E-mail: personnel@digital-software.com
Founded: 1982. **Staff:** 65. Activities: Provides software and engineering services including software design and management, applications software implementation, test and verification/validation, operating systems development, and systems design to the aerospace and defense industry. Specializes in design and development of complex ground and airborne computer systems, communication, radar warning receivers, and nuclear radiation monitoring systems. Serves private industries as well as government agencies.

DIRECTIONS IN RESEARCH, INC.
8593 Aero Dr.
San Diego, CA 92123
David Phife, President
PH: (619)299-5883
TF: (800)676-5883
FX: (619)299-5888
URL: DIResearch.com
Founded: 1985. **Staff:** 200. Activities: Specializes in market research and analysis for U.S. businesses.

DISTRIBUTOR DYNAMICS INC.
11944 N. 54th St.
Grand Junction, MI 49056
David C. Loggins, Mgr.
PH: (616)434-6970
Founded: 1980. **Staff:** 20. Activities: Computer technology and telecommunications firm serving business and the general public in the Chicago region and Michigan.

DIVERSIFIED SYSTEMS RESOURCES LTD.
TRW Bldg., Ste. 312
401 SE Dewey Ave.
Bartlesville, OK 74003
John H. Bond
PH: (918)336-6900
FX: (918)336-6922
E-mail: usnbptup@ibmmail.com
URL: dsrglobal.com
Founded: 1982. **Staff:** 30. Activities: Computer technology consulting firm providing systems analysis and design services, and computer programming for business and industry clients. EDI and communications expertise providing software, training, and technical support/help desk services.

DOCTOR DESIGN
10505 Sorrento Valley Road, #1
San Diego, CA 92121
Marco J. Thompson, President
PH: (619)457-4545
FX: (619)457-1168
URL: www.doctord.com
Founded: 1983. **Staff:** 25. Activities: Provides electronic engineering design services from concept to prototype to production for custom hardware and software projects and integrated circuit design. Specialists in microprocessor applications, graphics, high-speed logic, VME, multibus boards, DSP, Unix, all programming languages, firmware, diagnostics, and design reviews. Industries served include graphics and communications as well as many others.

DOMUS SOFTWARE LTD.
309 Cooper St., Ste. 500
Ottawa, Canada K2P 0G5
R. Moxley, President
PH: (613)230-6285
FX: (613)230-3274
E-mail: info@domus.com
URL: www.domus.com
Founded: 1983. **Staff:** 100. Activities: Information Technology (IT) services and software products firm providing solutions to the international customer base. DOMUS provides a broad range of IT consulting services, including security, quality, network engineering, and system development.

DRT SYSTEMS INTERNATIONAL
160 Bloor St. E, Ste. 920
Toronto, Canada M4W 1B9
Mel Steinke, President
PH: (416)920-5777
FX: (416)920-3532
Founded: 1980. **Staff:** 750. Activities: Established to help major organizations effectively apply computer technology in addressing critical business applications. To achieve this, Polaris provides a full range of information technology consulting services. The company is strategically focused in four areas: (1) management consulting encompasses project management, strategic systems planning, technology evaluations and feasibility studies; (2) specialized consulting concentrates on providing expertise in highly complex data base and fourth generation areas, information resource management and methodologies; (3) professional services provide qualified application development personnel such as systems analysts, programmer/analysts and programmers to help support the client with the implementation of strategic systems; and (4) the technology conversion group helps companies through the difficult challenge of migrating

from aging technologies to newer, more cost effective ones. Serves private industries as well as government agencies.

DST BELVEDERE FINANCIAL SYSTEMS, INC.
470 Atlantic Ave.
Boston, MA 02210-2209
PH: (617)482-8800
FX: (617)482-8878
E-mail: belvedere@belv.com
URL: www.dstbelvedere.com
Founded: 1983. **Staff:** 75. **Activities:** Software development firm specializing in financial information systems.

DTI TECHNOLOGIES, INC.
10 Commerce Park North, Unit 10
Bedford, NH 03110
Dustin H. Smith, VP
PH: (603)626-7799
TF: (800)370-2670
FX: (603)626-7981
Founded: 1981. **Staff:** 50. **Activities:** Data processing and CAD consultancy provides total concept consulting services from initial selection of hardware and software through installation, implementation, and recurrent training.

DUCOM INC.
850 Sligo Ave., Ste. 700
Silver Spring, MD 20910-4703
Duke C. Chung, President
PH: (301)585-0900
FX: (301)585-5950
E-mail: ducominc@clark.net
Founded: 1985. **Staff:** 31. **Activities:** Computer technology consulting firm.

KEVIN DUFFY
c/o Accountmate/The Linden Group
39-49 48th St., Ste. 201
Long Island City, NY 11104
PH: (718)672-3773
FX: (718)672-1101
Founded: 1985. **Staff:** 11. **Activities:** Computer systems and software consultant experienced with nonprofit groups, social service agencies, foundations, governments, libraries, unions, and health and welfare groups.

DUNN SYSTEMS, INC.
5550 W. Touhy Ave.
Skokie, IL 60077
William Dunn, President
PH: (847)673-0900
TF: (800)486-DUNN
FX: (847)673-0904
E-mail: dave@dunnsys.com
Founded: 1988. **Staff:** 70. **Activities:** Computer consulting firm focusing mainly on microcomputer systems. Assists clients in all aspects of development and decision making, including hardware and software specifications, custom programming, and multi-user installations. Company provides professional services to the data processing community on Windows and Internet platforms. Works primarily with Intel based platforms but also offers services on the NCR Tower, DG Avion, Macintosh, UNISYS 6000, IBM RS6000 and the AT&T 3B2. Industries served: wholesale distribution, manufacturing, accounting, education, medical, and corporate business.

DYNAMIC COMMUNICATIONS, INC.
8625 SW Cascade Blvd.
Beaverton, OR 97008
Robert Larson, Chairman of the Board
PH: (503)626-3081
FX: (503)641-6012
E-mail: dci@pacinter.net
Founded: 1984. **Staff:** 16. **Activities:** Engineering consulting firm specializing in leading edge software development and systems de-

sign. Experience and skills include protected mode programming, DOS and OS/2 internals and device drivers, Microsoft Windows and Presentation Manager, and LAN drivers and protocol implementation. Intel microprocessors and OSI network standards are particular specialities. Also work in Apple Macintosh and a variety of mini-computer environments. The firm has a Graphics Division that handles most aspects of graphics programming and driver development for a wide variety of hardware and software products. Particular expertise in T134010 Assembly, DGIS and GSS-CGI. Industries served: telecommunications.

DYNAMIC SEARCH SYSTEMS, INC.
3800 N. Wilke Rd., Ste. 485
Arlington Heights, IL 60004
Michael J. Brindise, President
PH: (847)259-3444
FX: (847)259-3480
E-mail: dynamsys@aol.com
URL: dssjobs.com
Founded: 1983. **Staff:** 15. **Activities:** Provides executive and professional search services to the IT community. Firm specializes in the placement of developers, programmers, programmer analysts, systems analysts, project leaders, project managers, systems programmers, data processing consultants, IT directors, and other information technology related candidates. Industries served: all.

DYNAX RESOURCES INC.
6800 Jericho 204 W.
Syosset, NY 11791
Daniel Bivona, Secretary/Vice President
PH: (516)932-9080
TF: (800)345-8902
FX: (516)932-3152
E-mail: postmstr@dynax.com
URL: www.dynax.com
Founded: 1969. **Staff:** 40. **Activities:** Offers computer services to commercial and industrial clients in the metropolitan New York area, New Jersey, Connecticut, and Florida. Provides web pages, lotus domino, AS/400 hardware and software services.

EARTHINFO INC.
5541 Central Ave.
Boulder, CO 80301
John B. Edwards, President
PH: (303)938-1788
FX: (303)938-8183
E-mail: earthinfo@CSN.net
URL: www.Earthinfo.com/Earthinfo
Founded: 1986. **Staff:** 12. **Activities:** The company publishes, and annually updates, a broad spectrum of government agency datasets along with firm's proprietary access interface, CD2-an easy-to-use, yet powerful interface. Customers use the firm's CD's to access the U.S. Geological Survey's hydrology files, Environment Canada's water and sediment files, the National Climatic Center's climatology files, EPA's water quality files, the Global Historical Climatology Network's Global Climate database, and the SCS's soils files.

ECHO ASSOCIATES INC.
8500 Leesburg Pike
Vienna, VA 22182-2409
Edward C. Okunak
PH: (703)448-0633
FX: (703)734-7980
E-mail: callecho@ix.netcom.com
URL: www.callecho.com
Founded: 1981. **Staff:** 65. **Activities:** Computer technology consulting firm serving business clients worldwide.

ECHO CONSULTING SERVICES, INC.
1620 E. Main St.
Center Conway, NH 03813
Joseph Braga, CEO

PH: (603)447-5453
TF: (800)635-8209
FX: (603)447-2037
E-mail: sales@echoman.com
URL: www.echoman.com
Founded: 1980. **Staff:** 70. Activities: JCAHO and COA accreditation assessment and preparation, organization assessment, organization development and quality management services for behavioral healthcare, social service and nonprofit organizations in the US and Canada.

ECONOMIC DEVELOPMENT COUNCIL
1151 Oak St.
Pittston, PA 18640
Howard Grossman
PH: (717)655-5581
FX: (717)654-5137
E-mail: edcnp@microserve.net
URL: www.microserve.net/edcnp
Founded: 1964. **Staff:** 28. Activities: Conducts specialized regional market analysis (demographic and census studies, economic indicator analysis, financial feasibility studies); research and analysis (grant and loan packaging, economic impact studies, transportation and historical research); and seminar and workshop coordination (logistical planning, mailing lists, displays). Extensive experience with land planning (waste management studies, environmental impact studies); mapping and graphics (customized maps/displays, graphic designs); business development and management (financial packaging, market surveys, procurement assistance); and planning and forecasting (economic and employment). Will also assist with computer services (information and retrieval for special projects, training); data directory (economic/demographic material, community profiles, mapping); mass transit operations research, transportation planning, impact fees, and transportation mapping, zoning ordinance and mapping, benefit assessments and tax increment financing. Industries served: private sector businesses, local governments, nonprofit organizations, financial institutions, consultants requiring specialized support, developers, professionals, human and social service agencies.

EDITORIAL CODE AND DATA, INC.
Onyx Plaza
29777 Telegraph Rd., Ste. 2250
Southfield, MI 48034
Arsen Darnay, President
PH: (248)356-6990
TF: (800)883-6072
FX: (248)356-6426
E-mail: ecdi@ixnetcom.com
URL: www.statrom.com
Founded: 1990. **Staff:** 13. Activities: Firm provides data and computer services primarily to the publishing industry, with specialization in statistical data drawn from government sources. Services include data acquisition, analysis, formatting, and typesetting; archiving of computer data on CD-ROM; custom data display, search, and printing software; information brokering services; and related services such as design, writing, and data processing design. Industries served: publishing, in-house printing, non-profit organizations, government agencies, utilities, and manufacturing.

EDUCATION LOGISTICS INC.
3000 Palmer St.
Missoula, MT 59802-1671
Hien Nguyen
PH: (406)728-0893
FX: (406)728-8754
URL: www.montana.com/edulog
Founded: 1977. **Staff:** 150. Activities: Computer technology firm offers expertise in computer technology to school districts in the U.S.

EDUCATIONAL INFORMATION AND RESOURCE CENTER
606 Delsea Dr.
Sewell, NJ 08080
Arthur Rainear
PH: (609)582-7000
FX: (609)582-4206
E-mail: info.eirc.org
URL: www.eirc.org
Founded: 1968. **Staff:** 60. Activities: Provides programs and consulting services for schools, communities, public agencies and nonprofit organizations. Programs are available on many topics from locating proven teaching techniques, to comprehensive in-service teacher training; from international exchange programs for educators to critical and creative thinking; from leadership programs such as Model Congress to technical assistance for school-age child care and special needs child care programs; from printing newsletters and brochures to communications seminars for nonprofit agencies. Also offers hands-on computer training on major PC application programs such as Word-Perfect, Lotus 1-2-3 and dbase III, as well as specialized consultation and training services including data analysis, applications development and on-site assistance.

EDUTECH INC.
11211 Katy Fwy., Ste. 604
Houston, TX 77079-2125
Mark Ramert
PH: (713)827-1314
FX: (713)464-9411
Founded: 1987. **Staff:** 85. Activities: Computer technology consulting firm offering training in computer-based education programs to businesses worldwide.

EDUTRENDS, INC.
25 Clifton Rd.
Oak Ridge, NJ 07438-9120
Ronnie Colfin, President
PH: (973)697-7007
TF: (800)253-8379
FX: (973)697-7638
E-mail: edutrend@bellatlantic.net
URL: www.edutrends.com
Founded: 1983. **Staff:** 11. Activities: Specializes in development of customized, computer-based training and multimedia products. Serves all industries in the U.S. and Canada.

EFG
1390 Timberlake Manor Pky., Ste. 200
Chesterfield, MO 63017
William Levin, President
PH: (314)537-0044
TF: (800)277-4456
FX: (314)530-0017
E-mail: efg@stl.com
URL: www.efgstl.com
Founded: 1984. **Staff:** 80. Activities: Computer consulting firm.

EJR COMPUTER ASSOCIATES INC.
5 Marine View Plaza
Hoboken, NJ 07030-5722
Elliot J. Rosenzweit
PH: (201)795-3601
FX: (201)795-5355
Founded: 1979. **Staff:** 150. Activities: Computer technology consulting firm serving business clients in New Jersey and the New York metropolitan area.

ELECTION DATA SERVICES, INC.
1401 K St., NW, Ste. 500
Washington 20005-3417
Kimball William Brace, P

PH: (202)789-2004
FX: (202)789-2007
E-mail: kbrace@aol.com
URL: www.electiondataservices.com
Founded: 1977. **Staff:** 12. Activities: Strategic advice and litigation support for congressional, state legislative, and local government redistricting. Feasibility studies, needs assessments and systems requirements analyses on voting equipment and voter registration systems for election administration.

ELECTRONIC WARFARE ASSOCIATES, INC.
13873 Park Center Rd., Ste. 500
Herndon, VA 20171
Carl N. Guerreri, President
PH: (703)904-5700
FX: (703)904-5779
URL: www.ewn.com
Founded: 1977. **Staff:** 150. Activities: A technical services firm offering consulting in electronic warfare, communication, C3, and threat analysis and design. Recent experience in software development, minicomputer and microprocessor applications, and development of automated test equipment systems.

ELIASSEN GROUP, INC.
Lakeside Office Park
591 North Ave., 5B
Wakefield, MA 01880
Mona Eliassen, Chairman and Founder
PH: (617)246-1600
TF: (800)428-9073
FX: (617)245-6537
E-mail: wc@eliassen.com
URL: www.eliassev.com
Founded: 1989. **Staff:** 121. Activities: Offers computer consulting services focusing on the critical "high-end" software engineering skills required in numerous industries. Focus is on the recent and continuing advances in all aspects of "state-of-the-art" computing, especially in the software and hardware associated with microcomputing, networking and information technology. Expertise includes distributed computing architectures and client/server-based applications, and mirrors industry trends including GUI, relational database development, and 00 Programming. Industries served: financial, communications, computer, government, multimedia, healthcare, and utilities.

ELITE ENGINEERING CORP.
667 Rancho Conejo Blvd.
Newbury Park, CA 91320
Pat Kay
PH: (805)480-1161
FX: (805)480-9141
E-mail: patkay@eliteeng.com
URL: www.eliteeng.com
Founded: 1988. **Staff:** 30. Activities: Product development, electronic design, and software engineering. Product prototyping, customized test equipment, and manufacturing for electronic systems. Specializing in solving problems to get products to market on time, in cost, to spec. Services include: technology verification for electronic-based systems, engineering, design verification, project reviews, and prototyping of electronic assemblies.

ELM SERVICES, INC.
11600 Nebel St., Ste. 201
Rockville, MD 20852
Lee E. Mortenson, President/CEO
PH: (301)984-1242
FX: (301)770-1949
E-mail: elmconsulting@worldnet.att.net
Founded: 1976. **Staff:** 30. Activities: For the past 20 years, ELM Services, Inc., has been the leader in guiding, advising, and supporting the practice and delivery of oncology nationwide. ELM has influence the art, business, and science of this industry as it continues to undergo radical change and transformation. ELM, oncology's premier consulting firm, is assisting hospitals, physicians, health care

systems, and academic/university programs in the development of whole new approaches to cancer program management.

EMA SERVICES, INC.
1970 Oakcrest Ave.
St. Paul, MN 55113-2624
Alan W. Manning, CEO
PH: (612)639-5600
FX: (612)639-5730
E-mail: info@ema-inc.com
URL: www.ema-inc.com
Founded: 1975. **Staff:** 180. Activities: EMA helps clients develop and implement operational strategies for improving work practices, addressing organizational development, and leveraging technology. Focuses on services which maximize productivity and improve long-term performance. Industries served: public and private utilities and manufacturing.

EMERALD INFORMATION SYSTEMS INC.
1750 S. Mesa Dr., Ste. 100
Mesa, AZ 85210-6226
Clarke Stephan
PH: (602)464-1802
Founded: 1989. **Staff:** 15. Activities: Computer technology firm specializes in business and financial information systems.

ENABLE SOFTWARE, INC.
313 Ushers Rd.
Northway 10 Executive Park
Ballston Lake, NY 12019-1519
Curtis Noel, C.E.O. & President
PH: (518)877-8600
FX: (518)877-5225
Staff: 140. Activities: Firm is a leading developer of integrated office automation, group productivity, and e-mail software for microcomputers.

ENCORE ASSOCIATES INC.
3851 S. Sherwood Forest Blvd., Ste. 500
Baton Rouge, LA 70816-4476
J.H. Linden
PH: (504)291-7080
FX: (504)291-7392
E-mail: teckers@encore21.com
URL: www.encore21.com
Founded: 1984. **Staff:** 26. Activities: Firm provides software development services for medical practices.

ENCOTECH ENGINEERING, P.C.
207 State St.
PO Box 714
Schenectady, NY 12301
Fred H. Kindl, Chairman of the Board
PH: (518)374-0924
TF: (888)362-6832
FX: (518)374-1665
E-mail: 76041.3555@compuserve.com
URL: www.encotech.com
Founded: 1973. **Staff:** 15. Activities: Technical consultants to the power generation industry. Services in failure analysis, vibration monitoring and diagnostics, design, cogeneration planning, conversions, modifications and upgrades, and machinery performance improvement. Industries served: electric utilities, pulp and paper mills, and insurance companies.

ENERTECH CONSULTANTS
300 Orchard City Dr., Ste. 132
Campbell, CA 95008
J. Michael Silva, Founder
PH: (408)866-7266
FX: (408)866-7279
E-mail: etcsales@enertech.net
URL: www.enertech.net
Founded: 1982. **Staff:** 25. Activities: Provides engineering consult-

ing services, performs applied research, and develops and markets software and instrumentation systems to serve clients. Projects and services include electric and magnetic field (EMF) characterization; field measurements and applied research; computer modeling of electric and magnetic fields; EMF modeling for transportation; industrial and commercial facilities; EMF evaluation of residences; schools; and other locations; development; calibration; testing and marketing of instrumentation; and design and development of computer software, seminars, technical support, training, publication of technical reports.

ENGINEERING MANAGEMENT CONCEPTS
295 Willis Ave., Ste. B
Camarillo, CA 93010-8585
Joseph C. Hall
PH: (805)484-9082
FX: (805)484-4607
Founded: 1982. Staff: 75. Activities: Consulting firm provides software design and engineering services to business and U.S. military agencies.

ENGINEERING SERVICES INC.
5 King's College Rd.
Toronto, Canada M5S 3G8
PH: (416)595-5519
FX: (416)595-9994
URL: www.esit.com
Founded: 1982. Staff: 15. Activities: Offers a wide variety of engineering consulting services with emphasis on prototyping for industrial automation through robotics. Also develops software and control systems for automation projects.

ENGINEERING TECHNOLOGY ASSOCIATES, INC. (ETA)
1100 E. Mandoline Rd., Ste. B
Madison Heights, MI 48071
Abe Keisoglou, President
PH: (248)588-9010
FX: (248)588-9014
E-mail: akers@eta.com
URL: www.eta.com
Founded: 1983. Staff: 80. Activities: Structural analysis and scientific/engineering software development specialists whose offerings include: computer processing alternatives, computer facilities, structural analysis services and Variation Simulation Analysis Software (VSAS). Experienced in crashworthiness software. Currently developing metal-forming software for use in the automotive industry.

ENHANCE SYSTEMS
999 8th St. SW, Ste. 406
Calgary, Canada T2R 1J5
Len Johnson, President
PH: (403)228-8103
FX: (403)245-1577
URL: www.enhance.com
Founded: 1982. Staff: 40. Activities: Provides consulting services in the areas of enterprise systems management, consolidated service desk, and storage management.

ENTEC RPD
9555 James Ave. S., Ste. 245
Bloomington, MN 55431
David Keller, CEO
PH: (612)884-9339
FX: (612)884-9370
E-mail: info@art2part.com
URL: www.art2part.com
Founded: 1989. Staff: 30. Activities: An engineering resource company focused on rapid product development through the application of advanced Computer-Aided Engineering (CAE). Technical consulting services offered include the use of state-of-the-art CAE tools for structural analysis, heat transfer, material selection, noise and vibration, and modal analysis. Additional services offered include rapid prototyping with SLA, reverse engineering and computer-aided verification through 3-D laser digitizing, rapid molding, and indus-

trial design. Industries served include aerospace and defense, automotive, biomedical, electronics, and consumer products.

ENVIRO DYNAMICS INC.
7923 Jones Branch Dr., Ste. 201
McLean, VA 22102-3304
William J. Keane, President
PH: (703)760-0023
TF: (800)887-3341
FX: (703)760-9382
E-mail: kliam@aol.com
Founded: 1984. Staff: 18. Activities: Occupational and environmental health consultants offering the following services: industrial hygiene programs, indoor air quality studies, and hazardous materials management, involving asbestos, lead, PCB's, pesticides, radon, etc. Environmental consulting includes environmental assessments, environmental impact statements, and wetlands studies. Also provides software development, information management systems, and Auto CAD support. Industries served: private and government sector, and public utilities.

ENVIRONMENTAL SYSTEMS & TECHNOLOGIES, INC. (ES&T)
2608 Sheffield Dr.
Blacksburg, VA 24060-8270
Dr. Jack C. Parker
PH: (540)552-0685
FX: (703)951-5307
E-mail: admin@esnt.com
URL: www.esnt.com
Founded: 1988. Staff: 35. Activities: An internationally recognized provider of environmental computer models for the assessment and remediation of soil, groundwater, and air pollutants. Specializes in subsurface hydrocarbon and solvent release problems. Integrates field characterization, data management, modeling, and data visualization to minimize cost. Also provides litigation support services including forensic site investigations and expert testimony. Industries served: oil, chemical, engineering, energy, legal, and government.

ENVISIONEERING, INC.
3594 Byron St. NW
Silverdale, WA 98383
James S. Kuga, President
PH: (360)692-2602
FX: (360)692-5917
URL: www.ering.com
Founded: 1984. Staff: 60. Activities: Provides a wide range of engineering computer, communications, and information technology management and professional services to government and commercial users of computer-based technology. The company has been conducting ongoing research and design studies for automating and integrating technical documentation systems with printing and publication activities. These studies include the use of computer assisted retrieval, networking, and laser disk technology. Also provides solutions for the conversion of hardcopy graphics to electronic media; this includes a wide variety of CAD and technical publishing system formats. Industries served: government, A/E firms, construction, and environmental. Also provide environmental compliance documentation to government activities.

ERBE & ASSOCIATES
8929 S. Sepulveda Blvd., Ste. 201
Los Angeles, CA 90045
Robert H. Erbe, Sr., Chairman
PH: (310)417-9740
FX: (310)417-8249
E-mail: asmith@erbe.com
URL: www.erbe.com
Founded: 1979. Staff: 12. Activities: Computer consulting firm offering expertise in electronic communications, computer installation management, automatic test equipment, microprocessor and microprogramming, operating systems, and real time systems. Performs studies and assists firms in the selection of hardware and software. Experienced with business, financial, law, manufacturing, and medi-

cal applications. Familiar with Apple II, DEC VAX/VMS, Digital Equipment Corp., Hewlett Packard, IBM, Radio Shack, and Wang equipment, as well as BASIC, COBOL, CP/M, PASCAL, PDP-11, and UNIX languages and operating systems.

ESA INC.
300 Thompson Park Dr., Ste. 311
Cranberry Township, PA 16066
Andrew J. Kalnas, III, President
PH: (412)776-2870
FX: (412)776-4452
Founded: 1988. **Staff:** 71. Activities: Software engineering consultants with expertise in process control and systems control. Serves business clients in the Pennsylvania region.

ESS CONNECT
64 E. Broadway Rd., Ste. 220
Tempe, AZ 85282
Kipp Diesron, AutoCAD Specialist
PH: (602)784-4900
TF: (800)530-4475
FX: (602)921-0892
URL: www.essconnect.com
Founded: 1985. **Staff:** 35. Activities: Provides the AEC client with an enterprise-wide IS strategy encompassing workflow automation, CAD workstations, LAN development and support, Internet solutions, visualization services, and electronic communication and e-mail to architectural, engineering and mechanical design professionals, from one-person offices to multi-office companies.

ESSENSE SYSTEMS INC.
Two Corporation Way, Ste. 260
Peabody, MA 01960
PH: (508)977-9800
FX: (508)977-3130
Founded: 1991. **Staff:** 50. Activities: Computer technology firm specializing in human resources software and enterprise self-service.

ETES CORP.
PO Box 8259
Chicago, IL 60680
Rod J. Oancea, President
PH: (312)332-1067
FX: (219)923-4812
E-mail: rjo@etes.com
Founded: 1974. **Staff:** 15. Activities: Offers services in engineering, construction management, security, data processing and office automation, energy conservation and management, and microsystems integration and related software to commercial and industrial clients.

EUREKA SOFTWARE SOLUTIONS, INC.
3305 Northland Dr., No. 305
Austin, TX 78731
Kevin Rhodes, Director of Business Development
PH: (512)459-9292
FX: (512)459-6244
E-mail: info@eurekasoft.com
URL: www.eurekasoft.com
Founded: 1986. **Staff:** 32. Activities: Provides turnkey custom application/system software design development, QA services, and for Windows/95/NT and other platforms: client server; GUI; object oriented, e-commerce, net-enabled applications, databases, data acquisition, embedded, imaging, and other services.

EVEREST DATA RESEARCH, INC.
140 Dorchester Square
Westerville, OH 43081
Margaret Fenton, President
PH: (614)794-9910
FX: (614)794-9210
E-mail: mfenton@netwalk.com
Founded: 1988. **Staff:** 16. Activities: A consulting company spe-

cializing in technical services, database consultants and communication. Serves all industries and Fortune 500 companies in the U.S.

EVOLVING SYSTEMS
9777 Mt. Pyramid Ct.
Englewood, CO 80112
George Hallenbeck, CEO, President
PH: (303)802-1000
TF: (800)360-9923
FX: (303)802-1400
E-mail: webmaster@evolving.com
URL: www.evolving.com
Founded: 1985. **Staff:** 300. Activities: Telecommunications Consulting Specialists in the area of local number portability, voiceover IP, Network and Service Provisioning and wireless data, utilizing strategic and business process modeling techniques.

EVOTECH MICROENGINEERING CONSULTANTS, INC.
875 Cowan Rd., Ste. B-203
Burlingame, CA 94010
Basilio Chen, President
PH: (650)697-3861
FX: (650)697-6598
E-mail: info@evotech.com
Founded: 1984. **Staff:** 20. Activities: Offers product development services in software, digital hardware, telecommunications, and embedded firmware from requirement specifications to design and programming. Services include analysis, development, maintenance, and enhancement in hardware, and software for ISDN (integrated services digital network), ATM, ADSL, SNMP, real-time, scientific applications, and telecommunication systems (voice & data). Serves private industries and government agencies.

EXCEL MANAGEMENT SYSTEMS, INC.
691 N. High St.
Columbus, OH 43201-1550
Robert Radigan, Vice President
PH: (614)224-4007
TF: (800)886-4925
FX: (614)244-4857
E-mail: excel@emsi.com
Founded: 1989. **Staff:** 100. Activities: Specializes in computer information systems development, testing, documentation, and training. Focuses resources on document imaging and reengineering. Provides support for most computer hardware environments, client/server databases, and tools. Also designs and implements telecommunications networks. Industries served: government, insurance, construction, banking, manufacturing, and office automation in the United States.

EXCELL DATA CORP.
1756 114th Ave. SE., Ste. 220
Bellevue, WA 98004-6931
Leonard J. Pacheco, President
PH: (425)974-2000
FX: (425)974-2001
URL: www.excell.com
Founded: 1991. **Staff:** 90. Activities: A consultancy with expertise in computer technology-systems integration and software development-serving major corporations in the Northwest.

EXECU-FLOW SYSTEMS, INC.
1 Ethel Rd., No. 106
Edison, NJ 08817
Michael J. Custode, President
PH: (908)287-9191
FX: (908)287-2329
Founded: 1981. **Staff:** 75. Activities: Provides computerized healthcare systems, with special expertise in hardware and physicians' practice management software.

EXPERT CHOICE INC.
5001 Baum Blvd., Ste. 650
Pittsburgh, PA 15213-2807
Mark Cirucci, General Mgr.
PH: (412)682-3844
TF: (800)447-0506
FX: (412)682-7008
E-mail: info@expertchoice.com
URL: www.expertchoice.com
Founded: 1983. **Staff:** 12. Activities: Computer technology consultants with expertise in decision support software, and group decision making and facilitation.

EXPERTEC CORP.
340 N. Main St., Ste. 304
Plymouth, MI 48170-1249
William T. Downs, President
PH: (313)451-2272
FX: (313)451-9515
Founded: 1989. **Staff:** 26. Activities: Computer technology management firm.

EXPRESS STAR SYSTEMS INC.
1101 S. Capital of Texas Hwy., Bldg I
Austin, TX 78746-6437
Trent Smith, President
PH: (512)479-8053
FX: (512)479-6659
Founded: 1988. **Staff:** 25. Activities: Computer systems consulting firm.

FACILITY ROBOTICS, INC.
400 Market Place
Roswell, GA 30075
Vic Villalobos
PH: (770)640-0071
FX: (770)640-7224
Founded: 1986. **Staff:** 35. Activities: Systems integrator for commercial and industrial facilities using direct digital controls such as Teletrol and Echelon. Serves the southeast U.S.

SYLVAIN FAUST INTERNATIONAL
880 Blvd. De La Carriere, Ste. 130
Hull, Canada J8Y 6T5
Sylvain Faust, President & CEO
PH: (819)778-5045
TF: (800)567-9127
FX: (819)778-7943
E-mail: info@sfi-software.com
URL: www.sfi-software.com
Founded: 1988. **Staff:** 25. Activities: Offers consulting services to integrate and support its product suite designed for Oracle, Microsoft, and Sybase SQL Server RDBMS computing environments.

FCG ENTERPRISES INC.
111 W. Ocean Blvd., 4th Fl.
PO Box 22676
Long Beach, CA 90801-5686
Tom Reep, Vice President
PH: (562)624-5200
TF: (800)251-8005
FX: (562)432-5774
URL: www.fcgnet.com
Founded: 1976. **Staff:** 310. Activities: Offers healthcare organizations computer and telecommunications support, including planning and implementation services.

FEDERAL SOURCES INC.
8400 Westpark Dr., 4th Fl.
McLean, VA 22102
Tom Hewitt
PH: (703)610-8700
FX: (703)883-0362

Founded: 1984. **Staff:** 50. Activities: Computer technology consulting firm.

C. H. FENSTERMAKER & ASSOCIATES INC.
135 Regency Square
Lafayette, LA 70508
PH: (318)237-2200
FX: (318)232-3299
Founded: 1950. **Staff:** 75. Activities: Environmental consulting firm offers computer technology expertise to clients in the oil industry and government agencies in the U.S.

FINANCIAL COMPUTER SUPPORT, INC.
14 Commerce Dr.
Oakland, MD 21550
Dusty Huxford
PH: (301)553-1900
FX: (301)334-1896
E-mail: info@dbcams.com
URL: www.dbcams.com
Founded: 1981. **Staff:** 55. Activities: Independent user group which provides computer and administrative support for financial planners, money managers, and insurance agents. Developed and supports the practice management software, dbCAMS+ (Client Asset Management System). Serves the finance and insurance industries in the U.S., Canada, Australia, and other English-speaking countries.

FINANCIAL CONTROL SYSTEMS, INC.
200 Chadds Ford Professional Center, Ste. 214
Chadds Ford, PA 19317
Roger Cerasoli, President
PH: (610)358-2400
FX: (610)358-4850
Founded: 1974. **Staff:** 15. Activities: FCS' global investment accounting software provides record keeping and reporting capabilities to both public and corporate pension plans. Services include transaction processing, monthly asset valuations, accrual accounting, verification of income and tax reclaims, capital entitlement verification, and general ledger capabilities. A full range of both detailed and summary level reporting is available. The system serves as the book of record for many of our clients. Computer time sharing arrangements over FCS' Wide Area Network provide computer access to clients nationwide.

FIND/SVP INC.
625 Avenue of the Americas
New York, NY 10011
Andrew P. Garvin, Chairman, President
PH: (212)645-4500
TF: (800)346-3787
FX: (212)645-7681
E-mail: postmaster@findsvp.com
Founded: 1969. **Staff:** 220. Activities: Offers expertise in computer management information services, market analysis and research, and making better business decisions through firm's Quick Consulting and Research Service. Gathers data for clients from in-house company files, periodicals, online databases, CD-ROMS, directories, and reference works. Supported by staff of 100 U.S. consultants and 1,000 researchers worldwide. Serves libraries, brokerage firms, advertising agencies, financial institutions, research houses, and other commercial concerns in the United States.

FIRST CHOICE PERSONNEL, INC.
723 Main St., Ste. 518
Houston, TX 77002
Clifford E. Day, President/Treasurer
PH: (713)956-7464
FX: (713)688-5999
E-mail: fchoice@swbell.net
Founded: 1980. **Staff:** 26. Activities: Provides computer software support to banking, manufacturing, oil, and gas industries in the U.S.

FIRST CLASS SOLUTIONS, INC.
2060 Concourse Dr.
St. Louis, MO 63146
Raymond Dunn, President
PH: (314)997-8998
TF: (800)274-1214
FX: (314)997-0400
E-mail: info@firstclasssolutions.com
URL: www.firstclasssolutions.com
Founded: 1988. **Staff:** 29. Activities: First Class Solutions, Inc. is a diversified computer and healthcare consulting firm, serving clients throughout the United States. Computer consulting services include: complete internet services, website design and host, network design, installation services and sales, software installation, hardware sales, system design and application programming. Healthcare consulting services include: interim management and operational assessments of medical records, and business office management, quality assurance and utilization review services, JCAHO and preparation, recruitment, temporary staffing for coding activities, transcription assessments, coding proficiency and DRG validation studies, and HMO/PPO provider network development. Industries served: all industries, with emphasis on hospitals, physicians, insurance companies, and clinics.

ROBERT J. FLEMING
c/o Clark Nuber P.S.
10900 NE 4th St., Ste. 1700
Bellevue, WA 98004
Robert J. Fleming
PH: (425)454-4919
TF: (800)504-8747
FX: (425)454-4620
E-mail: rfleming@cnuber.com
URL: www.cnuber.com
Founded: 1952. **Staff:** 95. Activities: Offers financial consulting expertise in the following areas: computer systems and programming, taxes, fundraising and development, and strategic planning. Industries served: government, nonprofit, distribution, professional firms, and construction.

FLEX-PLAN SERVICES, INC.
PO Box 70366
Bellevue, WA 98007
James C. Aitken
PH: (425)562-9259
TF: (800)669-3539
FX: (425)747-2604
E-mail: stan@flex-plan.com
URL: www.flex-plan.com
Founded: 1989. **Staff:** 20. Activities: Flexible benefit plan design and administration for cafeteria-type plans, form 5500 preparation, and employee benefit statements. Also assists with the design and administration of retirement plans. Offers customized Windows-based software systems that allow employers to communicate with and to enroll employees electronically for all employee benefit plans. Provides employee self service via internet and/or intranet. Industries served: all.

FMR SYSTEMS, INC.
855 Sterling Ave., Ste. 150
Palatine, IL 60067
Jack Liess, Managing Director
PH: (847)934-5566
FX: (847)934-6815
E-mail: sales@fmr-systems.com
URL: www.fmr-systems.com
Founded: 1994. **Staff:** 12. Activities: Developers of the Relationship Management System (RMS). Browser-based banking focused solutions for Client Relationship Management (CRM), Contact Management, Product & Service Implementation Setup Workflow, and Customer Service. A leader in providing client/server and internet based solutions, legacy system & desktop software integration, and support to financial services industry. Produces object-oriented,

platform independent, and database independent solutions for the enterprise.

FRANKEL AND TOPCHE, P.C.
111 Northfield Ave.
West Orange, NJ 07052
Gary R. Topche, CPA, Director
PH: (973)669-9600
FX: (973)669-0440
E-mail: ftcpa@aol.com
Founded: 1990. **Staff:** 14. Activities: Offers financial consulting for closely held businesses. Assists in mergers and acquisitions, tax planning, strategic business planning, family succession planning, accounting, auditing, and obtaining financing. It also helps in the computerization of small businesses. The firm serves small businesses in the service, retail, wholesale, and manufacturing industries. Specializes in real estate, lumber and building materials, and service businesses.

FRANKLIN COVEY
2200 W. Parkway Blvd.
Salt Lake City, UT 84119
Richard L. Shipley, President/CEO
PH: (801)956-1301
TF: (800)343-0009
FX: (801)299-4705
Founded: 1972. **Staff:** 200. Activities: Provides communication counseling, training, and products that enable companies and individuals to improve production and performance through effective written and verbal communication. Serves business and government agencies worldwide.

FSC INTERNET CORP.
The FSC Bldg.
188 Davenport Rd.
Toronto, Canada M5R 1J2
Carolyn L. Burke, President
PH: (416)921-4280
FX: (416)966-2451
E-mail: fsc@fscinternet.com
Founded: 1984. **Staff:** 15. Activities: Provides broad range of e-commerce and internet security related services to clients throughout Canada and the northern United States. Provides Internet connectivity; data security services; Internet publishing, advertising, and marketing services using the World Wide Web; and interfacing of WWW applications to legacy information systems for applications such as on-line order-entry and inventory access. Industries served: legal, financial, manufacturing, publishing, entertainment, advertising, and government.

FUTURE STRATEGY INTERNATIONAL INC.
1635 Sherbrooke St. W, Ste. 405
Montreal, Canada H3H 1E2
Doug Squarek, President
PH: (514)932-3295
TF: (877)932-3295
FX: (514)932-4639
E-mail: info@futurestrategy.com
URL: www.futurestrategy.com
Founded: 1981. **Staff:** 30. Activities: A strategic planning company specializing in the conception, development, and implementation of enterprise strategic-planning software solutions.

FYI SYSTEMS, INC.
160 Littleton Rd.
Parsippany, NJ 07054
Mindy Johnston, President
PH: (201)331-9050
FX: (201)331-9055
E-mail: fyi@fyi-systems.com
URL: www.fyi-systems.com
Founded: 1984. **Staff:** 80. Activities: An information resource consulting firm specializing in supporting businesses using Internet/ Intranet, midrange and mainframe technologies, in both centralized

and distributed environments. Industries served: automobile, broker-age, communications, education, financial, manufacturing, publishing, banking, chemicals, electronics, insurance, pharmaceuticals.

GANCOM-DIVISION OF GANNETT FLEMING, INC.
PO Box 67100
Harrisburg, PA 17106-7100
William C. Ehresman
PH: (717)763-7226
TF: (800)446-9236
FX: (717)763-8150
Founded: 1973. **Staff:** 90. Activities: Offers mainframe, mini, and micro data processing services in time sharing; data entry; system design and programming; and batch processing for government, manufacturing, healthcare, and engineering. Provides high-speed laser printing and direct mail/mailing list support. Also offers printing, engineering reproduction, phototypesetting, graphic (CADD) services, and Xerographic services for all types of clientele.

GARBER BUSINESS SYSTEMS
670 Yalesville Rd.
Cheshire, CT 06410-2930
Jack Garber, Owner
PH: (203)272-3620
FX: (203)272-8546
Founded: 1981. **Staff:** 15. Activities: Offers computer technology services on the northeastern seaboard.

GBS CORP.
1020 N. University Parks Dr.
Waco, TX 76707
David Bethea, C.O.O.
PH: (254)756-6181
TF: (800)583-6181
FX: (254)745-2566
Founded: 1962. **Staff:** 55. Activities: Firm provides financial management, business counseling, and tax-related products and services to business owners and professionals. Additional services include proper record-keeping systems, accurate tax return preparation, computer software services, and financial planning services. Initial and continuous training is available to franchisees in all areas: business and tax counseling, client acquisition and business operations. Training provided at headquarters in Waco, Texas and in the field. Ongoing managerial and technical support from field support managers and national office. Manuals, sales aids, advertising materials, tax services, product development and media relations training are also included.

GE CAPITAL CONSULTING, INC.
2550 University Ave. W., Ste. 180 S.
St. Paul, MN 55114
PH: (612)642-2100
TF: (800)695-5854
FX: (612)642-2101
Founded: 1984. **Staff:** 300. Activities: Wholly owned subsidiary of GE Capital that provides professional business and information systems consulting services. Services include strategic information systems planning, business performance improvement, facilitation, architecture design and support, application solutions and support, testing, and project management.

GEAC COMPUTERS
9 Technology Dr.
Westborough, MA 01581
William G. Nelson, Chairman of the Board/CEO
PH: (508)871-6800
TF: (800)825-2574
FX: (508)871-6850
E-mail: info@geac.com
URL: www.geac.com
Founded: 1971. **Staff:** 175. Activities: Consultants in the field of library automation and the building of automated databases for libraries. Supplies both hardware and software.

GENERAL SYSTEMS GROUP INC.
5 Manor Pky.
Salem, NH 03079-2842
Ugo O. Gagliardi, President
PH: (603)893-1000
FX: (603)893-9838
E-mail: mbh@gsb.com
Founded: 1974. **Staff:** 16. Activities: Offers services in the areas of computer technology and software development to businesses worldwide.

GENICOM CONSULTANTS INC.
3400 Blvd. Maisonneuve West
Montreal, Canada H3Z 3B8
Robert Carrier, Gen. Manager
PH: (514)931-3000
FX: (514)931-2118
E-mail: info@safework.com
URL: www.safework.com
Founded: 1984. **Staff:** 13. Activities: The firm specializes in advanced ergonomic design consulting.

GEO DECISIONS INC.
301 N. Science Park Rd.
State College, PA 16803
Barry M. Evans, President
PH: (814)234-8625
FX: (814)234-8086
Founded: 1986. **Staff:** 13. Activities: Computer mapping consultant. Serves private industries as well as government agencies.

GEOGRAPHIC RESOURCE SOLUTIONS
1125 16th St., Ste. 213
Arcata, CA 95521-5580
John Koltun
PH: (707)822-8005
TF: (888)477-5460
FX: (707)822-2864
E-mail: grs@northcoast.com
URL: www.grsgis.com/~grs
Founded: 1989. **Staff:** 14. Activities: Computer technology consultants offer expertise with Geographic Information Systems and image processing.

GEOTECH, INC.
4900 Cascade Rd. SE
Grand Rapids, MI 49546-3788
George J. Orphan, President
PH: (616)949-3340
FX: (616)949-8238
E-mail: yorg@voyager.net
Founded: 1971. **Staff:** 25. Activities: Telecommunications specialists offer expertise in the following: telephone outside plant, telephone central office switches, PBX switches, PBX distribution plant, microwave systems, video systems, data transmission systems, standby power systems, and uninterruptable power systems. Additional expertise available in cable television systems, central office buildings, grounding systems, lightning protection systems, casualty investigations, continuing property records, expert testimony, computer mapping, and electrical/mechanical design. Industries served: telephone industry, manufacturing industry, commercial business, hospitals, healthcare, governmental, and educational.

GEOTRAIN
171 Carlos Dr.
San Rafael, CA 94903
Jim Bensman, CEO
PH: (415)491-8950
TF: (800)268-7737
FX: (415)491-8955
E-mail: register@geotrain.com
URL: www.geotrain.com
Founded: 1985. **Staff:** 150. Activities: Offers interrelated network integration, distributed systems implementation, wan & lan audits,

skills gap & technology analysis consulting and education. Industries served: telecommunication, government agencies, consumer products, ISPS, finance, service, and defense.

GESTALT SYSTEMS, INC.
2070 Chain Bridge Rd.
Vienna, VA 22182
Harry Alton Lee, President
PH: (703)748-1817
FX: (703)748-1553
Founded: 1986. **Staff:** 17. **Activities:** Computer systems consulting firm provides expertise in Macs and PC networking, fourth dimension development, and DTP, multimedia, and training. Serves commercial businesses, individuals, and government in the U.S.

GIFFELS ASSOCIATES LTD.
30 International Blvd.
Rexdale, Canada M9W 5P3
J. Shufelt
PH: (416)675-5950
FX: (416)675-4620
E-mail: geninfok@giffels.com
URL: www.giffels.com
Founded: 1949. **Staff:** 250. **Activities:** Offers multidiscipline architectural and engineering design services related to planning, design, construction, and project management of major capital projects for industry, institutions and government. Projects include buildings, industrial plant facilities, highways, roads, bridges, and transit systems. Also provides expertise in CADD computer systems and applications, generates software under contract or via license, and offers technical training in these areas. Industries served: architecture, construction services, engineering, plant layout/interior design/space planning, traffic and parking, transportation - highway, computer technology, industrial process engineering, environmental engineering, and government agencies.

GIGA INFORMATION GROUP
1 Longwater Cir.
Norwell, MA 02061
John Struck, CEO
PH: (781)982-9500
FX: (781)878-6650
Founded: 1979. **Staff:** 300. **Activities:** A worldwide organization of industry analysts providing research, consulting services, and strategic advice to companies that produce and use information technology. Specializes in the fields of information processing, telecommunications, and electronic imaging technology, working with business leaders to analyze new products, technologies, markets, and opportunities. Emphasis is on integrating advanced technology with business strategies for technology vendors and users. Custom research projects for primary markets focus on market analysis, market structure, vendor image and reputation, corporate strategy, and industry strategy.

GIRO INC.
75 Port Royal E, Ste. 500
Montreal, Canada H3L 3T1
Jean-Yves Blais, President
PH: (514)383-0404
FX: (514)383-4971
E-mail: info@giro.ca
URL: www.giro.ca
Founded: 1979. **Staff:** 120. **Activities:** Transportation software and consulting firm in rail, bus and subway systems. Experienced in the application of advanced mathematical optimization techniques to the problems of the transportation industry. Other services include vehicle and manpower scheduling, paratransit management and scheduling systems, passenger information systems for transit authorities, routing/scheduling systems for postal authorities, municipalities and waste management firms. Serves private industries as well as government agencies.

GLASGAL COMMUNICATIONS, INC.
20C Commerce Way
Totowa, NJ 07512
Ralph Glasgal, President & Chairman of the Board
PH: (973)890-4800
TF: (800)LAN-WAN1
FX: (973)890-2888
URL: www.datatec.com
Founded: 1975. **Staff:** 160. **Activities:** Offers computer expertise in the design and specification of computer networks for enterprise wide systems. Services include providing plans and estimates for file servers, network operating systems, building wiring, groupware, video and voice integration, wide area network hardware and software, carrier facilities, power backup, automatic backup and recovery systems and network management services. Industries served: brokerage, publishing, hospitals, government, military, education, banking, legal, and pharmaceutical.

GLOBAL DYNAMICS INTERNATIONAL INC.
325 E. Eisenhower Pky., Ste. 107
Ann Arbor, MI 48108-3307
Bhushan Kulkarni, President & CEO
PH: (734)913-0214
TF: (800)608-7682
FX: (734)913-0764
E-mail: arnold@gdii.com
URL: www.gdii.com
Founded: 1993. **Staff:** 100. **Activities:** Specializes in computer systems, development, and implementation. Provides knowledge in client/server systems, AS400 and IBM mainframe applications development, project management, and turnkey solutions.

GLOBAL TECHNOLOGY CORP.
11160 Viers Mill Rd.
Wheaton, MD 20902-2538
Gerald T. Charles, President
PH: (301)949-5723
FX: (301)949-6140
Founded: 1982. **Staff:** 48. **Activities:** Provides design and development of training materials in a variety of media: computer-aided instruction, correspondence courses, video and cinema, and platform. Also offers computer system and office automation consulting work. Serves private industries as well as government agencies.

GOLD SYSTEMS, INC.
4865 Riverbend Rd.
Boulder, CO 80301
G. Terry Gold, President
PH: (303)447-2837
FX: (303)447-0814
URL: www.goldsys.com
Founded: 1991. **Staff:** 34. **Activities:** Offers consulting in the telecommunications field, specifically in voice-response and PBX-to-host applications. Provides feasibility studies, requirements generation, and also develops custom applications software. Industries served: communications, banking, and telemarketing.

GORDIAN
20361 Irvine Ave.
Santa Ana, CA 92707
Gregory A. Bone, President
PH: (714)850-0205
FX: (714)850-0533
E-mail: info@gordian.com
URL: www.gordian.com
Founded: 1986. **Staff:** 25. **Activities:** Firm specializes in contract research, design, and prototype development, applying leading edge technologies to the creation of new products. Offers expertise in computer networking and peripherals, telecommunications, operating systems, optical technology and imaging, and raster graphics processing.

GRASS ROOTS SYSTEMS, INC.
7315 Wisconsin Ave., Ste. 200W
Bethesda, MD 20814
John Convy, President
PH: (301)951-3600
FX: (301)951-4148
Founded: 1985. **Staff:** 15. Activities: Computer services firm specializes in campaign management computer systems and the development of prepackaged software.

GRC INTERNATIONAL, INC.
1900 Gallows Rd.
Vienna, VA 22182
Jim Roth, President/CEO
PH: (703)506-5000
FX: (703)356-4289
URL: www.grci.com
Founded: 1961. **Staff:** 1300. Activities: Technical services consulting firm specializing in computer integrated systems design, engineering, and technical support.

GTS DURATEK
10100 Old Columbia Rd.
Columbia, MD 21046
Robert E. Prince, President
PH: (301)621-8222
TF: (800)338-4GTS
FX: (410)290-9070
URL: www.gtsduratek.com
Founded: 1982. **Staff:** 90. Activities: Firm of data processing/ information management consultants serving the following industries: agriculture, aerospace, banking, construction, data processing, education, electronics, energy, government, insurance, and publishing. Provides training for data processing software and techniques as well as project management for individuals and companies.

HAESTAD METHODS, INC.
37 Brookside Rd.
Waterbury, CT 06708
John R. Haestad, President
PH: (203)755-1666
TF: (800)727-6555
FX: (203)597-1488
E-mail: info@haestad.com
URL: www.haestad.com
Founded: 1979. **Staff:** 50. Activities: Group of civil engineers, hydrologists and computer experts dedicated to providing high quality hydrologic/hydraulic models for PCs. Also provides a wider range of consulting services, such as free user support on the firm's models, technical advice on hardware and software, and work in the field of computing. Industries served: engineering, CAD, hydrology and hydraulics, government agencies, and municipalities for storm water management, sanitary sewers, and water supply.

E.P. HAMILTON & ASSOCIATES, INC.
1406 Three Points Rd., Ste. B-9
Pflugerville, TX 78660
E.P. Hamilton, III, President
PH: (512)251-4279
FX: (512)251-4705
E-mail: epha@io.com
URL: www.io.com
Founded: 1981. **Staff:** 12. Activities: Offers engineering and consulting services in the following areas: commercial electrical design and evaluation, research and development, quality control, government contracts assistance in q/a and q/c, electrical accidents and failure analysis (analysis, field investigation, expert witness), fires and explosions, product liability, industrial psychology and human factors, rail transportation including rail facilities design, intermodal mass transit (analysis and facilities design), coal transportation, custom software, financial auditing and analysis, and economics. Industries served: government agencies, transportation companies, construction and development, utilities, manufacturers, computer and electronics-related industries, insurance, and legal firms.

HANOVER COMPUTER CENTER
600 Carlisle St.
Hanover, PA 17331-5101
Richard C. Hamilton
PH: (717)633-6767
FX: (717)633-5143
E-mail: btc@pa.net
Founded: 1987. **Staff:** 16. Activities: Active in the design of single user, Novell, DOS, and Mac business systems, mostly accounting oriented using CYMA and Great Plains software. Provides training and in-house service after the sale.

HATCH ASSOCIATES
2800 Speakman Dr.
Mississauga, Canada L5K 2R7
R.R. Nolan, President/CEO
PH: (905)855-7600
FX: (905)855-8270
E-mail: tomreid@hatch.ca
URL: www.hatch.ca
Founded: 1955. **Staff:** 2300. Activities: Offers comprehensive engineering, (ISO 9001-94 registered), procurement, project and construction management services in the following fields: iron and steel, nonferrous metals and minerals, information technology, energy, petrochemical, pulp and paper, rapid transit and tunneling, pharmaceuticals and industrial/manufacturing. Specific services include feasibility studies, assistance with project financing, technology transfer, process development, systems development, environmental assessment studies and pollution control. Industries served: chemical, energy, iron and steel, pulp and paper, manufacturing, mining, transportation, base metals and minerals, transit and tunneling, utilities, and government agencies.

HAUSHAHN SYSTEMS & ENGINEERS
5460 Corporate Grove Blvd., SE
Grand Rapids, MI 49512-5500
Kenneth W. Lewis, President CEO
PH: (616)285-3311
FX: (616)285-3312
E-mail: hse@haushahn.com
URL: www.haushahn.com
Founded: 1988. **Staff:** 150. Activities: A leading global provider of supply chain execution software. In addition to developing and selling their software product suite, Haushahn provides installation and implementation support through their 6-step project implementation methodology.

HAYNES AND ASSOCIATES, INC.
8300 Colesville Rd., Ste. 700
Silver Spring, MD 20910
Floyd N. Haynes, President
PH: (301)495-1500
TF: (800)827-9378
FX: (301)495-9776
Founded: 1990. **Staff:** 60. Activities: Expertise and experience is in three major areas: Accounting and Financial Analysis, Management Consulting, and Information Technology. Firm is a certified 8(a) minority business under the terms of Public Law 95-507. This 8(a) certification provides customers with a timely procurement vehicle, while assuring products and services are obtained at reasonable cost to the government. This provides a flexible contracting tool for the program manager to meet specific program requirements. Industries Served: Federal military and civilian agencies.

HBA MANAGEMENT SERVICES GROUP, INC.
1450 Mercantile Ln., Ste. 201
Upper Marlboro, MD 20774
M. Harrison Boyd, CEO, President
PH: (301)218-0900
Staff: 45. Activities: Firm specializes in helping businesses develop the most cost-effective way to enhance their operational performance. Specific objectives focus on cost containment, quality initiatives, diversity appreciation, management development, systems efficiency, and strategic planning. Facility support services include

LAN installation, help desk/facilities management, word processing, data entry, and technical writing and editing.

HEALTH EQUIPMENT LOGISTICS & PLANNING INC.
850 Central Pky. E., Ste. 260
Plano, TX 75074
Larry Hampton, President/CEO
PH: (972)985-1313
FX: (972)423-2398
E-mail: eghampton@mindspring.com
Founded: 1983. **Staff:** 23. Activities: Medical equipment consultants and planners. Industries served: healthcare.

A. FOSTER HIGGINS & CO., INC.
125 Broad St., 4th Fl.
New York, NY 10004
John Feldtmose, President
PH: (212)574-9000
FX: (212)574-8719
E-mail: poe-s@fosterhiggins.com
Founded: 1922. **Staff:** 700. Activities: Nationwide and international human resources and employee benefit consulting firm offering employers a full range of professional skills to assist in developing and managing benefit programs. Firm provides services in five major areas: health and welfare, which includes healthcare cost containment, retiree healthcare, and flexible compensation; retirement, which includes defined contribution planning; employee communication; outsourcing and business process reengineering; and healthcare counseling. Serves private industries as well as government agencies. affiliated companies.

HOLLANDER ASSOCIATES
PO Box 2276
Fullerton, CA 92837
Gerhard L. Hollander, President
PH: (714)879-9000
Founded: 1961. **Staff:** 20. Activities: Engineering consulting and research assignments on computers and systems-related problems. Over half of the activities are in original research supported by companies and government. Approximately 70 percent of the work is of an engineering nature, 20 percent mathematical analysis and ten percent management control systems.

HONEYWELL HI-SPEC SOLUTIONS
343 Dundas St., Ste. 500
London, Canada N6B 1V5
Jim Sergeant
PH: (519)679-6570
FX: (519)679-3977
URL: www.honeywell.com
Founded: 1973. **Staff:** 105. Activities: Firm provides process simulation modeling services for engineering design and operator training. Will also build dedicated models based on customer's specific industrial processes. Consulting services are based on MASSBAL 2.0 steady state simulation and MASSBAL 3.0 dynamic simulation software which are used to build process models and then calculate heat and mass balances. Industries served: pulp and paper, petrochemical, chemical, mineralogical, food and beverage, oil and gas worldwide.

HORNBY ZELLER ASSOCIATES
256 Broadway
Troy, NY 12180
Dennis Zeller, President
PH: (518)273-1614
FX: (518)273-0431
E-mail: hzatroy@aol.com
URL: www.hsa-inc.com
Founded: 1988. **Staff:** 15. Activities: Specializes in management consulting to government agencies in human and social services fields; program evaluations; business process reengineering; computer mapping, data entry; development of case management systems; and development of quality assurance systems. Capabilities include proficiency in German.

HOWARD SYSTEMS INTERNATIONAL INC.
One Canterbury Green
Stamford, CT 06901
Howard Persky, President
PH: (203)324-4600
FX: (203)324-7722
E-mail: corporate@howardsystems.com
URL: www.howardsystems.com
Founded: 1975. **Staff:** 800. Activities: Provides a broad range of services through its network of 12 branch offices. The successful delivery of business solutions across all industry sectors include: Management Consulting, Project Management, Full Project Life Cycle; Year 2000 Assessment; Staff Supplementation; Outsourcing; Feasibility/Requirements Definition, Network Implementation, Education and Training and Support Services.

HTL TELEMANAGEMENT LTD.
3901 National Dr., Ste. 270
Burtonsville, MD 20866
Michael T. Hills, President
PH: (301)236-0780
TF: (800)CAL-LHTL
FX: (301)421-9513
E-mail: sales@htlt.com
URL: www.htlt.com
Founded: 1980. **Staff:** 15. Activities: Software development consulting firm specializing in voice traffic engineering software for least-cost routing. Also active in the design and management of voice and data networks for corporations and resellers. Industries served: Fortune 500 companies, interexchange (long distance) carriers, interconnect companies, national and regional operating companies, and government agencies.

HUNTER BUSINESS DIRECT
4650 N. Port Washington Rd.
Milwaukee, WI 53212
PH: (414)332-8050
FX: (414)332-7377
Founded: 1981. **Staff:** 78. Activities: Direct marketing consultants (business-to-business) offering marketing programs to improve the marketing and sales productivity of companies. Includes market identification, planning, and implementation.

THE HUNTER GROUP
100 E. Pratt St., Ste. 1600
Baltimore, MD 21202
Terry Hunter, President/CEO
PH: (410)576-1515
FX: (410)752-2879
E-mail: info@hunter-group.com
URL: www.hunter-group.com
Founded: 1981. **Staff:** 350. Activities: Offers information management consulting services that support enterprise-wide application solutions from leading software providers. Concept-to-Completion (tm) services provide organizations with advice and assistance with visioning and strategy development, needs assessment, vendor selection, business process (re)engineering, workflow automation, systems implementation and end-user training.

IBM LIFEPRO SOLUTION
9465 Counselors Row
Indianapolis, IN 46240
PH: (317)844-7750
FX: (317)575-6099
Founded: 1984. **Staff:** 83. Activities: Computer consultants specializing in network integration and rightsizing. Areas of expertise include: system design, global networking strategies, imaging, enterprise cabling systems design, fiber specialists, network support and Novell Authorized Education Center.

IDC CONSULTING
5 Speen St.
Framingham, MA 01701
Pat McGovern, Chairman

PH: (508)872-8200
TF: (800)343-4935
FX: (508)935-4015
E-mail: mault@idcreserch.com
URL: www.idcreserch.com
Founded: 1964. **Staff:** 600. Activities: Separate operating division of International Data Corporation that provides custom work for clients who require an analysis not specifically provided by IDC's published materials. Typical assignments include the following: For vendors-identifying markets; evaluating product/market fit; assessing competitive positioning; supporting strategic planning activities; understanding distribution channel requirements; developing diversification/acquisition programs. For users-systems planning; competitive advantage assessment; disaster recovery planning; user needs assessment; CIM (Computer Integrated Manufacturing) strategy development; technical and software support program development; other MIS, communications, and office automation advisory services; measuring end-user satisfaction; assessing suppliers' potential long-term strengths; and supporting software product spin-off efforts. For investors-planning major corporate diversification programs; evaluating new technologies; and assessing potential investment/acquisition candidates. Industries served: primarily serves information technology industry; others include manufacturing, distribution, business services, healthcare, insurance, banking, nonprofit organizations, trade organizations, government agencies, technology consortiums, and publishing.

IEEE CONSULTANTS' NETWORK
255 Bear Hill Rd.
Waltham, MA 02154-1017
James Littlefield
PH: (617)890-5294
FX: (617)890-5290
Founded: 1989. **Staff:** 70. Activities: Multidisciplined engineering group offers the following expertise: analog hardware design, microwave systems engineering, digital hardware design, chemical engineering, reliability engineering, regulatory compliance, ULSI design, mechanical engineering, software engineering (PC's through mainframes), firmware and real-time systems development, business plan development, marketing surveys, technical publications, and optics. Industries served: medical, industrial process control and measurement, academic computing and laboratory instrumentation, military systems, telecommunications, air and space systems, and government agencies.

IMMAD ECVS
3235 14th Ave.
Markham, Canada L3R 0H3
Stephen F. Pumple, Chairman & CEO
PH: (905)470-2545
FX: (905)470-2559
E-mail: info@immad.com
URL: www.immad.com
Founded: 1975. **Staff:** 50. Activities: Involved in design and construction of broadcast, satellite and telecommunications systems in the United States, South America, Africa, the Middle East, and Canada. Also offers project management software and systems analysis. Industries served: television broadcast networks, TV stations, post production cable television, and corporate A/V, including government agencies.

INFOGAIN
10670 N. Tantau Ave.
Cupertino, CA 95014
Kapil Nanda
PH: (408)366-0900
FX: (408)366-1329
URL: www.infogain.com
Founded: 1990. **Staff:** 60. Activities: Computer technology consulting firm serving major software and systems companies in the U.S., with a special focus on California.

INFORMATION ALTERNATIVES
1313 E. Kemper Rd., Ste. 220
Cincinnati, OH 45246
Mark Fullerton, President
PH: (513)671-1644
FX: (513)346-4707
Founded: 1985. **Staff:** 33. Activities: Network and software specialization consulting and training.

INFORMATION BUILDERS INC.
1250 Broadway
New York, NY 10001-3701
Gerald Cohen, President
PH: (212)736-4433
FX: (212)967-6406
Founded: 1975. **Staff:** 1500. Activities: Computer technology firm offers expertise in information system design, computer software/hardware, systems analysis, licensing and legal services to clients in the U.S., western Europe, Canada, Africa, the Middle East, and South America.

INFORMATION IMPACT INTERNATIONAL, INC.
871 Nialta Ln.
Brentwood, TN 37027
Larry P. English, President
PH: (615)377-7770
FX: (615)377-7789
E-mail: lenglish@infoimpact.com
URL: www.infoimpact.com
Founded: 1986. **Staff:** 12. Activities: Provides management and technical consulting and training in all areas of information resource management and database technology, including data quality; data warehousing; strategic information planning; information technology evaluation (including C/S DBMS and Object DBMS); data resource management and modeling; client/server and distributed data modeling and management; object-oriented analysis; data and object modeling workshops; information management in cyberspace value-centric application development methods; project management; and business process reengineering.

INFORMATION MANAGEMENT CONSULTANTS & ASSOCIATES, INC.
PO Box 5963
Metairie, LA 70009
Jerry Neumeyer, President
PH: (504)832-3186
FX: (504)832-3921
Founded: 1973. **Staff:** 12. Activities: Custom software consultation offered on the IBM System/36, Series/I, and personal computers. Provides installation support on commercial application software packages and communication systems.

INFORMATION RESOURCE GROUP
35200 Dequindre
Sterling Heights, MI 48310-4857
Terry L. Olson, President
PH: (810)978-3000
TF: (800)843-8338
FX: (810)978-3029
URL: www.irgweb.com
Founded: 1982. **Staff:** 100. Activities: Offers expertise to businesses in the computer hardware, software, and communications industries who are seeking increased responses in all aspects of their direct marketing and sales activities.

INFORMATION RETRIEVAL COMPANIES INC.
225 West Wacker St., Ste. 2260
Chicago, IL 60606-1721
Valerie Hernon, Vice President, Consulting
PH: (312)726-7587
FX: (312)726-1607
Founded: 1983. **Staff:** 50. Activities: Computer consulting firm with expertise in mainframe and client/server technology; I/S man-

agement process consulting and education. Industries served: major corporations and manufacturers worldwide.

INFORMATION SYSTEMS CONSULTANTS INC.
9707 Elrod Rd.
Kensington, MD 20895-3413
Richard W. Boss, Managing Partner
PH: (301)946-2240
FX: (301)946-6505
E-mail: dickboss@erols.com
Founded: 1978. **Staff:** 22. Activities: Provides needs assessments, RFP development, bid evaluation and contract negotiation for automated systems and other information technologies. Also provides services on the impact of technologies on space planning.

INFORMATION TECHNOLOGY INTERNATIONAL
6701 Democracy Blvd., Ste. 700
Bethesda, MD 20817-1572
Lawrence Novotney
PH: (301)564-4200
FX: (301)564-3005
Founded: 1988. **Staff:** 20. Activities: Consulting firm offering expertise in Management Information Systems and computer technology to business and government agencies at all levels in the U.S.

INFOSYS CONSULTING INC.
101 S. Hough St., Ste. 5
Barrington, IL 60010
Tedd M. Gagen, President
PH: (847)524-5242
FX: (847)524-5249
E-mail: mailbox@insyscon.com
URL: www.insyscon.com
Founded: 1993. **Staff:** 43. Activities: Serves as a contract agency for computer consultants.

INFOSYSTEMS TECHNOLOGY INC.
6411 Ivy Ln.
Greenbelt, MD 20770-1405
J. Testa, Ph.D., President
PH: (301)345-7800
FX: (301)982-9847
Founded: 1976. **Staff:** 18. Activities: Computer technology consulting firm specializing in systems and security. Industries served: government, banks and financial institutions worldwide.

INFOTECH ENTERPRISES, INC.
600 Anton Blvd., Ste. 1230
Costa Mesa, CA 92626
Gianni Manucci
PH: (714)546-4851
FX: (714)546-4853
E-mail: sales@infotechent.com
URL: www.infotechent.com
Founded: 1987. **Staff:** 16. Activities: Provides development and implementation of strategies for companies. Analyzes current business operations and corporate structure. Experienced in architectural, engineering, construction, and computer aide facilities management. Offers a suite of hardware and software products.

INNOSYS INC.
3095 Richmond Pky., Ste. 207
Richmond, CA 94806-1900
Dale Sekijima, President
PH: (510)769-7717
FX: (510)222-0323
Founded: 1973. **Staff:** 13. Activities: Develops terminal and protocol conversion products for airline and travel industry communications. Industries served: transportation and travel.

INNOVATIVE BUSINESS SYSTEMS, INC. (IBS)
6501 Watts Rd.
Madison, WI 53719
John C. Klein, President/Treasurer

PH: (608)271-2010
TF: (800)345-8861
FX: (608)271-6921
E-mail: jklein@ibs-madison.com
URL: www.ibs-madison.com
Founded: 1978. **Staff:** 11. Activities: Data processing consultants offering programming and software packages for retail and wholesale firms, manufacturing firms, and engineering firms. Also IBM remarketers for AS/400.

INNOVATIVE COMMUNICATIONS TECHNOLOGIES INC.
352-C Christopher Ave.
Gaithersburg, MD 20879-3660
PH: (301)948-4841
FX: (301)948-4843
Founded: 1989. **Staff:** 20. Activities: Computer technology firm emphasizing telecommunications and systems integration (satellite, cellular, and PCs).

INOTECH OF VIRGINIA
3701 Pender Dr.
Fairfax, VA 22030
Eric Jacobs, President
PH: (703)995-1710
FX: (703)995-1725
Founded: 1982. **Staff:** 15. Activities: Technical support services consultancy specializing in UNIX systems and network integration as well as PowerBuilder. Range of services includes: downsizing through modernization; technology assessment and management; application conversion, migration and reengineering; client/server and distributed computing implementation; database engineering and development; enterprise communications; and imaging systems. As a professional firm serving the government and private sectors, InoTech develops, implements and supports information systems across mainframe, mini and microcomputer environments. Offers clients a full range of technical services including: feasibility and requirements analysis; systems analysis and engineering; database engineering, development, implementation and management; software engineering, development and deployment; project management and control; and systems support and documentation. Has developed proficiency in distinct application areas - developing systems for financial information, membership, engineering, simulation and modeling, health benefits and integrated hospital management.

INPUT
1881 Landings Dr.
Mountain View, CA 94043-0848
Peter A. Cunningham, President
PH: (415)961-3300
FX: (415)961-3966
URL: www.input.com
Founded: 1974. **Staff:** 65. Activities: An international market research and strategic planning firm serving the computer services and telecommunications industries. Areas of expertise include electronic data interchange, systems integration, software, federal government computer services markets, hardware maintenance, and information systems planning.

INSIGHT BUSINESS CONSULTANTS, INC.
East Tower, Ste. 300
Toronto, Canada M8X 2Z1
Peter J. Hamilton, CEO
PH: (416)236-5282
FX: (905)625-1653
Founded: 1985. **Staff:** 60. Activities: Provides systems and management services as well as the sale and support of IBM AS/400, PageNet, Mimix, Sales Tracker, and other business application software in Canada. Activities include software applications design and documentation; implementation of application systems in distribution, finance, manufacturing, and warehousing; systems conversion; software/hardware evaluation and selection; software development management; inventory and materials management; organizational development; operations management; workflow and document retrieval planning; high availability and disaster prevention planning;

facilities planning; and communications network design. Also offers expertise in education services for JDEdwards software, LANSA Application Development and Client/Server tools, Lotus Notes, AS/400, and PC desktop products.

INSTITUTE FOR MANAGEMENT DEVELOPMENT
Westgate, Ste. 11A
New York, NY 10025
William R. Dorsey
PH: (212)222-0308
FX: (212)222-0308
E-mail: jean@managementmatters.org
URL: www.managementmatters.org
Founded: 1977. **Staff:** 14. Activities: Management and marketing consultants with expertise in the development and review of business plans incorporating a variety of computer based technologies. Also serve as information systems specialists skilled in the development and presentation of technology transfer programs for all levels of staff, especially the non-traditional user profiles. Available to conduct systems requirements reviews. Significant public and private sector experience. Serves as resource for development and evaluation of Requests for Proposals (RFPs) in all areas of office automation.

INSTRUCTION SET, INC.
16 Tech Cir., 2nd Fl.
Natick, MA 01760
Beran Peter, CEO
PH: (508)651-9085
TF: (800)874-6738
FX: (508)651-9084
E-mail: sales@instructionset.com
URL: www.instructionset.com
Founded: 1984. **Staff:** 180. Activities: Independent supplier of consulting and training in object-oriented technologies, programming languages, operating systems, networking and relational databases and specializes in designing, delivering and managing skills enhancement programs for companies that are migrating to new technologies. Industries served: telecommunications, finance, government, and manufacturing.

INSTRUMENTATION TECHNOLOGY ASSOCIATES INC.
35 E. Uwchlan Ave., Ste. 300
Exton, PA 19341-1259
Michael Bem, Director for International Operations
PH: (610)363-8343
FX: (610)363-8569
E-mail: itaincusa@aol.com
Founded: 1978. **Staff:** 15. Activities: ITA, a commercial space equipment and services company, specializes in providing turnkey commercial service for users to fly experiments in the microgravity environment of space using ITA's flight-proven space processing hardware on a pay-to-fly basis. ITA has commercial flight agreements for Space Shuttle, MIR, and orbital re-entry vehicle missions.

INTEGRATED DOCUMENT SOLUTIONS
19031 33rd Ave. W, Ste. 100
Lynnwood, WA 98036
Cres Francisco, General Manager
PH: (425)776-0900
FX: (425)670-6791
Founded: 1956. **Staff:** 80. Activities: Specialists in the design and implementation of record and micrographic systems. Experience extends to the aerospace, banking and finance, education, healthcare, insurance, legal, manufacturing, utility and service industries.

INTEGRATED LOGISTICS SYSTEMS, INC.
630 Johnson Ave., Ste. 105
Bohemia, NY 11716
Kenneth L. Miller, President/CEO
PH: (516)563-2000
FX: (516)563-3099
URL: www.tadmis.com
Founded: 1981. **Staff:** 21. Activities: Systems design and software

development with primary services geared to the management of logistics and all associated activities. Applications cover a broad range of industry type and size and include on-line, real-time access to its comprehensive database to assist management in the decision process regarding such areas as site selection, distribution modeling, cash management, payment controls, commissions payables, inventory and warehouse management, labor forecasting, and JIT. Addresses the need to identify areas of opportunity and provide integrated solutions. Serves private industries as well as government agencies. international.

INTEGRATED MANAGEMENT ENTERPRISES, LTD.
230 Park Ave., Ste. 951
New York, NY 10169
Frank Bacchus, President
PH: (908)741-3101
FX: (908)842-7319
Founded: 1975. **Staff:** 27. Activities: Involved in human resources and management information systems consulting. Recent experience with LAN management and training evaluation, client/server application and contact programming. Serves private industries as well as government agencies.

INTEGRATED SYSTEMS DEVELOPMENT INC.
400 N. 136th Ave., Bldg. 100
Holland, MI 49424-2903
Mike McHanna
PH: (616)396-0880
FX: (616)396-0542
URL: www.isdwhq.com
Founded: 1985. **Staff:** 60. Activities: Computer technology consulting firm specializing in services to education engineers, and the retail sector in the U.S.

INTELL MART INC.
5800 Foxridge Dr., Ste. 400
Mission, KS 66202
Wendell Maness, President
PH: (913)722-1611
Founded: 1990. **Staff:** 37. Activities: Provides information and computer technology expertise to businesses and government agencies in the U.S. and Canada.

INTELLIGENT ELECTRONICS, INC.
411 Eagleview Blvd.
Exton, PA 19341
Richard D. Sanford, CEO, Chairman
PH: (610)458-5500
FX: (610)458-8454
URL: www.inel.com
Founded: 1982. **Staff:** 809. Activities: Supplies wholesale microcomputers, peripherals, and software.

INTERACTIVE BUSINESS SYSTEMS, INC.
2625 Butterfield Rd., Ste. 114W
Oak Brook, IL 60523
Daniel T. Williams, President
PH: (847)571-9100
TF: (800)555-5IBS
FX: (847)571-9110
Founded: 1981. **Staff:** 800. Activities: Data processing firm offering expertise with mainframe computers, PC/networking systems, DEC systems, and custom software development.

INTERACTIVE SOFTWARE ENGINEERING INC.
270 Storke Rd.
Goleta, CA 93117
Bertrand Meyer, President
PH: (805)685-1006
FX: (805)685-6869
E-mail: info@eiffel.com
URL: www.eiffel.com
Founded: 1985. **Staff:** 32. Activities: Training in object oriented software development. Provides complete service from analysis and

design to programming and implementation of O-O systems. Also offers strategic planning for organizations addressing problems such as: switching to object-oriented technology, choosing the right tools, and training and educating key personnel. Industries served: banking, telecommunications, information systems, document systems, data acquisition and transfer, and scientific software.

INTERAMERICA TECHNOLOGIES INC.
8150 Leesburg Pike, Ste. 1400
Vienna, VA 22182
Juan J. Gutierrez, President
PH: (703)893-3514
FX: (703)893-1741
URL: www.interamerica.com
Founded: 1972. **Staff:** 90. Activities: Consultants in computer software correspondence management document management and imaging. Serves private industries as well as federal, state, and local government agencies.

INTERCOM INC.
3 Grogan's Park Dr., Ste. 200
The Woodlands, TX 77380
C.E. Hahne, Marketing
PH: (281)298-1010
TF: (800)298-7070
FX: (281)364-7032
E-mail: intercom@intercom-interactive.com
URL: www.intercom-interactive.com
Founded: 1978. **Staff:** 25. Activities: InterCom's services help companies in all industries make their entry into multimedia or computer-based training more efficient by providing a source of experienced advice. Firm can assist by: helping present CBT to management when discussing the CBT benefits; studying training needs and evaluating the appropriateness of CBT to meet them; and providing information on authoring systems and helping select one to match the needs. InterCom has the staff and equipment to design, develop and program custom computer-based training on PC's, networks, or intranets, using many programming languages and authoring systems. Also provides off-the-shelf CD-ROM-based training on writing, telephone skills, customer service, and management skills.

INTERCONNECT NETWORK CONSULTING GROUP INC.
3420 Ocean Park Blvd.
Santa Monica, CA 90405-3304
Dan Sarto, Pres.
PH: (310)392-2800
FX: (310)392-6913
Founded: 1987. **Staff:** 20. Activities: Provides management information services, network support, and training. Has expertise in Novell and Lotus. Industries served: U.S. businesses.

INTERDISCIPLINE CONSULTANTS, INC.
400 W. Main St.
Wyckoff, NJ 07481
Joel L. Levine, President
PH: (201)848-8500
FX: (201)848-9127
URL: www.idcinc.org
Founded: 1982. **Staff:** 15. Activities: A full service computer systems firm providing hands-on support in assisting clients with business and financial solutions such as: accounting/financial, sales and marketing analysis, manufacturing inventory control, and office automation systems. Services include: business approach in analyzing hardware and software which meet client needs, custom programming applications, integrating hardware and software as a package, testing to ensure hardware and software work together, training client staff, and on-going user and systems support. Clients are companies in the manufacturing and distribution industries.

INTERIM TECHNOLOGY
630 Third Ave., 12th Fl.
New York, NY 10017
Ray Marchy, CEO
PH: (212)986-7600
FX: (212)986-9649
E-mail: intrmnyc@sprynet.com
Founded: 1968. **Staff:** 2000. Activities: Provides a full range of data processing consulting services including strategic planning, systems integration, professional and technical resources, education and training, software maintenance services, network and operations management, and software testing. Serves private industry as well as government agencies.

INTERIM TECHNOLOGY, INC.
9 Polito Ave., 9th Fl.
Lyndhurst, NJ 07071
Ira B. Brown, President/CEO
PH: (201)392-0800
FX: (201)842-0989
URL: www.interim.com
Founded: 1968. **Staff:** 250. Activities: Provides computer operations technical support and management consulting services. Capabilities include evaluating existing software and hardware, and the development of total EDP plans to meet changing business needs of clients. Active in outsourcing data centers, setting up PC help desks and training in open systems technology. Industries served: financial, insurance, telecommunications, retail, manufacturing, medical, distribution, general business, and government.

INTERLEAF
9 Hillside Ave.
Waltham, MA 02154
Michael Shanker, VP, Doc. Mgmt. Consulting Group
PH: (617)290-0710
FX: (617)290-4955
Founded: 1980. **Staff:** 90. Activities: Information technology management consulting firm assists customers with solving complex document management problems through software development, project management, and various technical architecture and data architecture solutions.

INTERNATIONAL BUSINESS & TECHNICAL CONSULTANTS INC. (IBTCI)
8614 Westwood Center Dr., Ste. 400
Vienna, VA 22182
Jayant Kalotra, President
PH: (703)749-0100
TF: (800)589-1905
FX: (703)749-0110
E-mail: ibtci@ibtci.com
URL: www.ibtci.com
Founded: 1969. **Staff:** 25. Activities: Management consultants providing expertise in privatization, restructuring, private sector development, healthcare sectors, banking, finance, capital markets, and public awareness and environmental programs.

INTERNATIONAL MANAGEMENT SERVICES, INC.
363 E. Central St.
Franklin, MA 02038
Raymond P. Wenig, President
PH: (508)520-1555
FX: (508)520-1558
E-mail: rpwenig@aol.com
Founded: 1973. **Staff:** 18. Activities: Offers computer systems planning, minicomputer systems consulting, business reengineering, information strategies, and graphical user interface design, advice on microprocessor selection and evaluation, small computer feasibility studies, and operational planning and procedures. Serves private industries as well as government agencies.

INTERNATIONAL MANAGEMENT SYSTEMS CORP.
4640 Admiralty Way, Ste. 1101
Marina del Rey, CA 90292
G.N. Plier, CEO

PH: (310)822-2022
FX: (310)305-8683
E-mail: imsadmin@dmssus.com
URL: www.iussvs.com
Founded: 1973. **Staff:** 85. Activities: Provides a broad range of computer consulting services, including strategic planning year 2000 conversion, software development, technical services and project management. Also offers technical support for IBM's DB2/CSP/QMF database products as well as IBM's AS/400 technology.

THE INTERNET GROUP
305 S Craig St., Ste. 200
Pittsburgh, PA 15232
Michael Baver, President
PH: (412)688-9696
FX: (412)688-9697
Founded: 1993. **Staff:** 12. Activities: Firm assists in creating an Internet presence for all industries worldwide.

INTERSOLV INC.
1800 Perimeter Park Dr., Ste. 210
Morrisville, NC 27560
Kevin Burns, CEO
PH: (919)461-4200
TF: (800)876-3101
FX: (919)461-4526
Founded: 1986. **Staff:** 100. Activities: Provides full range of consulting, contract programming, and performance tuning for the Oracle RDBMS. Also provides consulting and software development services under the Microsoft Windows and QS/2 Presentation Manager environments. Further consulting provided using C, Unix, Informix, and Ingres. Serves private and government organizations worldwide.

INTRACOMP GROUP
Georgetown Atrium, 52303 Emmons Rd.
South Bend, IN 46637-4288
PH: (219)272-9800
FX: (219)272-9810
URL: www.intracomgroup.com
Founded: 1985. **Staff:** 75. Activities: Specialists in large-scale computer systems: Honeywell/Bull (GCOS) and IBM (MVS). Services include application development and/or package installation, data base design, systems software, hardware and software evaluation, and conversions. Specialty is oracle, IDMS, DB 2, and Honeywell/Bull to IBM conversion. Serves private industries as well as government agencies.

IPT CORP.
1076 E. Meadow Cir.
Palo Alto, CA 94303
C. Stephen Carr, Ph.D., President
PH: (415)494-7500
TF: (800)656-8876
FX: (415)494-2758
E-mail: steve@iptcorp.com
URL: www.IPTWeb.com
Founded: 1974. **Staff:** 35. Activities: Fully integrated contract product development and manufacturing company specializing in medical, diagnostic and biotechnology products. Firm is active in electronic product design, design and manufacture of medical instruments, UNIX and CI programming, and microprocessor systems design. Serves private industries as well as government agencies.

IT DESIGN USA, INC.
10430 S. De Anza Blvd., Ste. 130
Cupertino, CA 95014
Tom Wilson, President
PH: (408)342-0435
TF: (800)437-7339
FX: (408)252-8705
E-mail: info@itdesign.com
URL: www.itdesign.com
Founded: 1994. **Staff:** 20. Activities: Offers software engineering

for large business. Specializes in the development of complex software application for Windows, Macintosh and UNIX. Focuses on object-oriented design techniques. Skills include C++, C, Visual Basic, Oracle, Windows NT, Macintosh, TCP/IP, CORBA, Orbix, and OpenDoc.

JACKSON AND TULL CHARTERED ENGINEERS
2705 Bladensburg Rd. NE
Washington 20018
Knox W. Tull, Jr., President
PH: (202)333-9100
FX: (202)526-2876
Founded: 1974. **Staff:** 342. Activities: Offers civil and structural design engineering services, including storm water management; water supply and treatment; highway, bridge, and railroad design, mass transportation, dam inspection, and construction inspection and management. Also provides expertise in aerospace engineering.

JMI SOFTWARE CONSULTANTS, INC.
904 Sheble Ln.
Spring House, PA 19477-0481
Kevin J. Brennan
PH: (215)628-0840
FX: (215)628-0353
E-mail: info@jmisoftware.com
URL: ourworld.compuserve.com/homepages/jmi/
Founded: 1980. **Staff:** 18. Activities: Provides contract C/C++ software development services for PC, Macintosh, and Unix platforms. Specialties include device drivers, input devices, real-time communications and control, semiconductor manufacturing, and industrial automation. Direct systems experience includes DOS, Windows, Macintosh, OS/2, OS-9, QNX, VxWorks, and others.

BERNARD JOHNSON INC.
3000 Wilcrest
Houston, TX 77042-3390
Gregg W. Young, CEO
PH: (713)977-7411
FX: (713)977-4781
E-mail: dallas.morris@houston.bjy.com
Founded: 1947. **Staff:** 120. Activities: Provides consulting services in the fields of engineering, architecture planning, and systems. Has designed hospitals, research, federal and educational facilities, office buildings, airport terminals, maintenance facilities, industrial plants and municipal buildings. Civil engineering experience includes design of water supply and treatment systems, highways and bridges, drainage, railroads, waste collection and treatment systems, docks, industrial parks and subdivisions. Other projects include: environmental engineering and related technical services, command and control systems, and building modernization systems. Industries served: government agencies, transportation, port and airport authorities, private commercial industry, oil/energy companies, educational and research institutions, hospitals, pharmaceuticals, airlines, real estate developers, and hotels worldwide. Also has branches in Austin, Dallas, Frankfort, Houston, San Diego, and Washington, D.C.

KEANE, INC.
Ten City Sq.
Boston, MA 02129
PH: (617)241-9200
TF: (800)36KEANE
FX: (617)241-9507
URL: www.keane.com
Founded: 1965. **Staff:** 10000. Activities: Helps clients gain greater business value from Information Technology through its end-to-end solutions in planning, building, and managing application software.

KELTIC TECHNOLOGIES GROUP
1809 Barrington St., Ste. 900
Halifax, Canada B3J 3K8
PH: (902)429-9911
FX: (902)423-5316
URL: www.keltic.ca
Founded: 1963. **Staff:** 120. Activities: Services include professional

management and network consulting, technical services, and hardware and software solutions. Helps clients design and build networks. Experts in Internet technologies and the World Wide Web.

KEMPER-MASTERSON, INC.
375 Concord Ave.
Belmont, MA 02178
Dr. Clarence Kemper, Chairman of the Board
PH: (617)484-9920
TF: (800)458-9920
FX: (617)484-9068
E-mail: lester@KMInc.com
Founded: 1989. **Staff:** 100. Activities: Firm of engineering professionals and former FDA investigators provide validation and compliance services to pharmaceuticals, biotech, and medical device clients worldwide. Has expertise in process, process control, and IS/IT. Services include training, consulting, and full validation implementation for projects ranging from unit operations and expansion projects to complete new facilities.

KESSLER-HANCOCK INFORMATION SERVICES INC.
203 F St., Ste. E
Davis, CA 95616-4514
Brian Hancock, President
PH: (916)756-4636
FX: (916)756-6943
E-mail: khinfo@class.org
Founded: 1989. **Staff:** 31. Activities: Firm offers Internet consulting; document delivery automation consulting; hardware/software installation and training, configuration, and custom Unix shells. Industries served: most high-tech fields, with a specialty in library clients.

KEY DATA SYSTEMS
111 Military
Dodge City, KS 67801-4932
Peggy Powers, VP
PH: (316)227-2101
TF: (800)658-1660
FX: (316)227-6216
E-mail: keyoffice1@aol.com
Founded: 1976. **Staff:** 20. Activities: Offers services in data processing, specifically in system hardware and maintenance, warranty support programs and facility management systems.

KORTEK SYSTEMS, LLC
14500 Edgewater Dr.
Gregory, MI 48137
Donald Koretz, President
PH: (248)471-1141
FX: (248)471-4447
E-mail: sales@kortek.com
URL: www.kortek.com
Founded: 1988. **Staff:** 12. Activities: Provides Internet and computer systems development, consulting, and support services. Develops and maintains Internet applications for banking and other industries. Skilled in interface design for software systems, information products, and web sites. Designs, configures, installs, and maintains computer networks (LAN and WAN), including Windows NT, Novell, and Macintosh. Develops computer-based training programs on CD-ROM and Internet.

KUPFERBERG, GOLDBERG & NEIMARK, L.L.C.
111 E. Wacker Dr., Ste. 1400
Chicago, IL 60601
Stephen Levin, Managing Member
PH: (312)819-4300
TF: (800)467-3504
FX: (312)819-4343
E-mail: kgn@kgn.com
URL: www.kgn.com
Founded: 1976. **Staff:** 95. Activities: CPA/computer consulting firm providing services in accounting applications, network design

and installation, custom software development, network and software training. Also offers financial consulting services.

LAKES ENVIRONMENTAL CONSULTANTS INC.
465 Phillips St., Ste. 4
Waterloo, Canada N2L 6C7
Jesse C. The, Ph.D.
PH: (519)746-5995
FX: (519)746-0793
E-mail: info@lakes-environmental.com
URL: www.lakes-environmental.com
Founded: 1995. **Staff:** 11. Activities: Air quality modeling and risk assessment software, training, and services.

LANAR SYSTEMS INC.
135 William St., 6th Fl.
New York, NY 10038
Robert Narcisco, President
PH: (212)619-2271
FX: (212)619-0276
Founded: 1982. **Staff:** 30. Activities: Services include database administration, programming, applications and system software development, business analysis, communications, technical support, and project management. Industries served: banking, brokerage, manufacturing, software development, public utilities, communications, government agencies, etc.

THE LANDIS GROUP, INC.
1551 Forum Pl., Ste. 500 A
West Palm Beach, FL 33401
Steve Landis, President
PH: (561)684-3636
FX: (561)478-4457
Founded: 1972. **Staff:** 15. Activities: Worldwide research and consulting. Offers clients a "Window on the Future". Analytical/ decision-making tools define, prioritize, validate brand equality/ business growth strategies with unparalleled accuracy. MATRIX (tm) software integrates and visualizes the linkage of consumer needs, product image, attitudes, and behavior.

LANDRUM & BROWN
11279 Cornell Park Dr.
Cincinnati, OH 45242
Jeffrey N. Thomas, President
PH: (513)530-5333
FX: (513)530-1278
E-mail: marketing@landrum-brown.com
URL: www.landrum-brown.com
Founded: 1949. **Staff:** 98. Activities: Provides planning and development services for airports and allied industries. The consulting services are of six broad categories: facilities planning and development, environmental planning, financial management, management strategies, computer services, market development and terminal planning services.

LANTE CORP.
161 N. Clark, Ste. 4900
Chicago, IL 60601
Mark Tebbe, President
PH: (312)696-5000
FX: (312)696-0060
E-mail: info@lante.com
URL: www.lante.com
Founded: 1984. **Staff:** 85. Activities: Specializes in the design and implementation of PC-based information systems. Emphasis is on the strategic use of networks in reengineering of client companies.

LAYNE GEOSCIENCES, INC.
1900 Shawnee Mission Pky.
Shawnee Mission, KS 66205
Michael J. Lally, Pres., General Manager
PH: (913)362-9906
FX: (913)362-2359
E-mail: mjlallv@laynechristensen.com

Founded: 1985. **Staff:** 22. Activities: Provides borehole geophysical logging services and consulting services involving the exploration, development, protection and management of groundwater resources. Also provides environmental consulting services.

LDA SYSTEMS INC.
1 Financial Way, Ste. 306
Cincinnati, OH 45242
PH: (513)984-1634
FX: (513)984-1619
Staff: 140. Activities: Specialists in network and software development, integration, and information systems strategies.

LEGAL ANALYSIS, INC.
1720 Parkhaven
Champaign, IL 61821
Stuart Nagel
PH: (217)352-7700
FX: (217)352-4401
E-mail: s-nagel@uiuc.edu
Founded: 1987. **Staff:** 30. Activities: Conducts research, training, and publishing relevant to systematic legal analysis of law as an instrument for improving society and individual interaction. Industries served: legal profession, including practicing lawyers, judges, legislators, law professors, law students, and government agencies.

I. LEVY & ASSOCIATES, INC.
1630 Des Peres Rd., Ste. 300
St. Louis, MO 63131
Irving Levy, President
PH: (314)822-0810
FX: (314)822-0309
E-mail: ilasales@ilevy.com
URL: www.ilevy.com
Founded: 1975. **Staff:** 33. Activities: Specialists in image-based solutions for government, insurance, banking and Fortune 1000 companies. Provide open system packaged solutions in document management, workflow and COM (Computer Output Microform) replacement in addition to comprehensive support services. Gupta and Informix database specialist.

LEXINGTON GROUP INTERNATIONAL, INC.
10300 North Central Expressway, Ste. 330
Dallas, TX 75231
Norman A. Ofstad, President
PH: (214)750-9090
FX: (214)750-9393
E-mail: lgi_dallas@noval.net
Founded: 1991. **Staff:** 20. Activities: Offers Process Safety Management (PSM), environmental and process engineering services, and computer software development and sales. Specializes in sour gas process sector including sulfur recovery units, amine units, and tail gas treating units. Also has expertise in gas plant processing units; environmental planning; permitting; industrial hygiene; with all services including fugitive emissions tied into the LGI proprietary software system Site Manager. Industries served: general industrial, chemical, construction management, refinery, power, hospital, semiconductor, computer software, and gas processing in the U.S.

PHILIP LIEBERMAN & ASSOCIATES INC.
1010 S. Weinbach Ave.
Evansville, IN 47714
Philip Lieberman, President
PH: (812)479-5064
FX: (812)479-8295
E-mail: info@plainc.com
Founded: 1977. **Staff:** 13. Activities: Provides consulting and advocacy services in the management information systems processing area to various organizations in the Midwest. In addition to these services, the company conducts seminars, assists in decision making processes, and provides crisis management for firms with severe management problems. Past and present clients include large government agencies, mental health centers, construction companies, associations, and small and medium sized private companies.

LIGHTING TECHNOLOGIES
5171 ElDorado Springs Dr.
Boulder, CO 80303
Michael Smith, President
PH: (303)499-1822
FX: (303)499-1832
URL: www.lighting-technologies.com
Founded: 1982. **Staff:** 13. Activities: Complete custom and commercial software solutions for the lighting industry; includes luminaire design and analysis, and indoor/outdoor lighting design and analysis software.

L.M.S. TECHNICAL SERVICES, INC.
21 Grand Ave.
Farmingdale, NY 11735
Larry Shulman, President
PH: (516)694-2034
FX: (516)694-2315
Founded: 1979. **Staff:** 26. Activities: Specializes in power systems design and development for computer systems, and computer maintenance and repair. Also offers network design and installation (including Novell), and communication interfaces. Serves private and government agencies.

LOGICAL SERVICES, INC.
3235 Kifer Rd., Ste. 210
Santa Clara, CA 95051
Robert W. Ulrickson, President
PH: (408)739-2600
FX: (408)739-6364
URL: www.logicalservices.com
Founded: 1973. **Staff:** 30. Activities: Full-service contract engineering, software development, industrial design, mechanical engineering, and turnkey-manufacturing including electronic assembly, materials management, plastic tooling and molding, sheet metal fabrication, and system assembly and test. Special emphasis on medical devices and wireless telecommunications. More than 300 ideas converted to products in control systems, analytical instrumentation, computing and networking. Proprietary Product Introduction Process takes new product ideas and market requirements, adds design teams led by program managers and its development laboratory to provide prototype designs, documentation, and pilot production of new products. Logical takes responsibility for program management and product qualification projects that require FDA QSR (510K & PMA), UL, FCC, CE and other agency approvals. Through strategic alliances, fulfills client needs for synchronized, engineering-driven manufacturing.

LRP PUBLICATIONS DIV.
747 Dresher Rd., PO Box 980
Horsham, PA 19044-0908
Ken Kahn, President
PH: (215)784-0860
TF: (800)341-7874
FX: (215)784-9639
Founded: 1977. **Staff:** 300. Activities: Legal publisher of loose-leaf publications, books, videos, software, and newsletters on various topics: employment, education, elder care, federal sector employment, bankruptcy, health, workers' compensation, disability, and family and personal injury. Privately owned, the company has expanded into various other media such as conferences, commercial printing, and magazine publishing.

M/A/R/C INC.
7850 N. Belt Line Rd.
Irving, TX 75063-6098
Cecil B. Phillips, Chairman
PH: (972)506-3400
FX: (972)506-3505
URL: www.marcgroup.com
Founded: 1984. **Staff:** 900. Activities: Offers services in custom marketing research, database marketing and promotion, syndicated research, and software licensing and facilities management. Primari-

ly serves consumer packaged goods and services companies and business-to-business marketers.

M C SQUARED CONSULTING
120 Dennis Dr., Ste. 3
Lexington, KY 40503
Sam C. McIntosh, Managing Partner
PH: (606)278-9299
TF: (800)370-6071
FX: (606)276-3824
E-mail: mc2debbie@mindspring.com
URL: www.mc2con.com
Founded: 1987. **Staff:** 20. **Activities:** Provides comprehensive quantitative market research and analysis services, encompassing telephone interviewing, focus group studies, field service, customer intercepts, and studies in cannibalization and traffic flow. Also designs television and radio advertisements, custom and specialized lists, custom software applications, and mass market and targeted literature distribution. Produces true RDD (Random Digit Dialing) telephone samples using Waksberg method. Industries served: advertising, public relations, publishing, politics, equine, banking, healthcare, and government worldwide.

CHARLES H. MACK & ASSOCIATES, INC.
11311 Cornell Park Dr., Ste. 114
Cincinnati, OH 45242
PH: (513)530-5800
FX: (513)530-5858
URL: www.chamck.com
Staff: 20. **Activities:** Computer network consultants specializing in business directional and software development and customization.

MICHAEL F. MACLEOD
1800 Diagonal Rd., Ste. 400
Alexandria, VA 22314
PH: (703)683-9500
FX: (703)683-9537
Founded: 1987. **Staff:** 75. **Activities:** Independent computer software and programming for nonprofit groups.

MACOLA SOFTWARE
333 E. Center St.
Marion, OH 43302
Bruce A. Hollinger, President
PH: (614)382-5999
TF: (800)468-0834
FX: (614)382-0239
Founded: 1971. **Staff:** 200. **Activities:** Provides services in the following areas: (1) writing and marketing a business management software package which consists of a modular, yet fully integrated accounting/distribution system with vertical links to manufacturing, retail, sales management, shipping, and professional services. PC-based, it can be run as a single user system or on a multi-user LAN; and (2) writing and marketing wastewater and water treatment plant software designed to aid in their effective management. Industries served: printing and publishing, rubber and plastic, instrumentation, aerospace, automotive, chemicals and pharmaceuticals, electronic and computer equipment, fabricated metal products, food processing, furniture, industrial machinery, and textiles.

MACRO CORP.
700 Business Center Dr.
Horsham, PA 19044
W.B. Schultz, Chairman
PH: (215)674-2000
TF: (800)622-7621
FX: (215)674-3464
E-mail: rwb@macro.ccmail.compuserve.com
Founded: 1968. **Staff:** 75. **Activities:** Provides systems engineering and custom systems development services for the application of digital technology and associated communication components to the industrial and utility markets. Services include planning studies, specifications, evaluations, project management, functional definition, system design, implementation, training, and startup. Also provides audits, mid-term assessments, and system integration services. Applications include EMS, Process Control, SCADA, Lab Automation, and Factory and Manufacturing Support Systems. Industries served: electric, gas, and water utilities; pipeline; steel; pharmaceuticals; electronics; automotive; and government.

MAGNETIC MEDIA INFORMATION SERVICES, CHICAGO OFFICE
655 W. Irving Park, Ste. 5516
Chicago, IL 60613
Laurence B. Lueck, President
PH: (312)266-2624
FX: (312)348-2542
Founded: 1965. **Staff:** 42. **Activities:** Provides consulting for magnetic and optical recording industries on pre-recorded software of all types, and commodities and materials used in production of recorded and recordable media. Industries served: magnetic recording hardware, software, media producers; optical and semiconductor storage system manufacturers; polyester film and magnetic pigment producers; and consumer electronics manufacturers.

MAGNUM COMMUNICATIONS, LTD.
280 Interstate North Pky., Ste. 520
Atlanta, GA 30339
Carl Eikhoff, CEO
PH: (770)952-4940
FX: (770)952-9534
E-mail: info@magnum.net
URL: www.magnum.net
Founded: 1976. **Staff:** 65. **Activities:** Provides solutions in credit management and data communications. Offers consulting in risk management, custom design, bureau communications, operational review, database access, and data communications.

MAJESCO COMPUTER RESOURCES
1420 Jamike Ln., Ste. 7
Erlanger, KY 41018
Mark A. Seifried, General Manager
PH: (606)283-6777
FX: (606)283-6770
E-mail: info@majesco.net
URL: www.majesconet.net
Founded: 1992. **Staff:** 20. **Activities:** Business consultants specializing in network, business directional and software development, group and individual training, Internet access and home page design, accounting systems sales and installation, and custom database design.

MAN MACHINE INTERFACE, INC.
24419 Hilliard Blvd.
Westlake, OH 44145
Carl A. Zander, President
PH: (216)871-6496
FX: (216)871-6496
Founded: 1979. **Staff:** 13. **Activities:** Provides comprehensive computer hardware, computer software, and systems consulting services.

MANAGEMENT ACTION CORP.
7040 Westchester Dr.
Manassas, VA 20112-4154
David L. McChrystal, Principal
PH: (703)330-1368
FX: (703)330-8189
E-mail: maxtools.com
URL: www.maxtools.com
Founded: 1988. **Staff:** 16. **Activities:** Logistics engineering consulting firm serving the U.S. Department of Defense. Also offers expertise in software development.

MANAGEMENT SERVICES GROUP, INC.
129 Sierra Vista Ln.
Valley Cottage, NY 10989
Joseph C. Scordato, President

PH: (914)358-0070
FX: (914)358-9035
E-mail: jscordato@aol.com
Founded: 1977. **Staff:** 16. Activities: An information management consulting firm offering a broad spectrum of professional support, technical assistance and turnkey systems packages for business. Provides a full range of business consulting in systems analysis and design, information systems management, systems integration and telecommunications. Firm has performed systems planning and feasibility studies, established functional and technical requirements for the purchase of hardware and/or software, prepared disaster recovery and contingency plans, conducted operational and management audits, delivered and installed customized turnkey computer systems and trained client personnel. Industries served: banking, insurance, importing, government agencies, manufacturing, distribution, professional services, transportation and publishing industries.

MANHATTAN GRAPHICS CORP.
62 Candlewood Rd.
Scarsdale, NY 10583-6040
Martin Rosenberg, President
PH: (914)725-2048
FX: (914)725-2450
E-mail: rsgtech@aol.com
Founded: 1984. **Staff:** 17. Activities: Experts in computerized typesetting and developers of "Ready, Set, Go!," desktop publishing software.

CREIGHTON MANNING INC.
500 Kenwood Ave.
Delmar, NY 12054-1822
Barbara C. Manning, Chair
PH: (518)439-4991
TF: (800)433-5530
FX: (518)439-5995
URL: www.cmisoft.com
Founded: 1965. **Staff:** 21. Activities: Prepares school bus transportation plans for school districts and social service agencies, including installation and training for major software packages.

MARATHON SYSTEM SERVICES, INC.
3400 Industrial Ln., Unit 1
Broomfield, CO 80020-1650
Gary Glasscock, President
PH: (303)469-3700
FX: (303)469-3737
URL: www.marasyssys.com
Founded: 1979. **Staff:** 30. Activities: Data processing consultants specializing in service to the construction industry. Consults on obtaining and using automated management information in construction companies.

RANDY MARUSYK/MBM & CO.
PO Box 809, Station B
Ottawa, Canada K1P 5P9
Randall Marusyk, Senior Partner
PH: (613)567-0762
FX: (613)563-7671
E-mail: mbm@mbm-law.com
URL: www.mbm-law.com
Founded: 1994. **Staff:** 14. Activities: Firm provides intellectual property services, patents/trademarks development, positioning of companies regarding their intellectual property portfolio, and assisting in commercialization of technology. Specializes in biotechnology and computer technology and serves biotechnology, pharmaceutical, and computer technology industries mainly in the G-7 countries.

MATRIX CONSULTING LTD.
12 Sunbeam Ave.
Downsview, Canada M3H 1W7
H. Markus, President
PH: (416)635-9336
Founded: 1976. **Staff:** 15. Activities: Electronic data processing software consultant specializes in design and programming. Expert

on Mark IV and Hogan Application Systems. Serves private industries as well as government agencies.

MBG ASSOCIATES LTD.
370 Lexington Ave., 23rd Fl.
New York, NY 10017
Michael Greenspan, President
PH: (212)822-4400
FX: (212)822-4499
Founded: 1977. **Staff:** 15. Activities: Telecommunications software consulting firm provides customized billing/telecommunications software, billing applications, software accommodated to the clients needs. Experience in many computer languages. Software runs on many computer environments. Offer the following software packages: T-MIS (Telecommunications Management Information Software) which allows all users to effectively utilize the call detail data for improved network management, customized billing software for call accounting, CDR, SMDR, and telemanagement systems, and SDN and most important tariff 12 VTNS billing and audit software. In addition, firm provides all these systems as a service bureau. Has developed a tariff 12 update service to provide an in-depth analysis and consulting for the entire marketplace. Industries served: brokerage, financial, interexchange carriers, hotels, automobiles, airlines, retailing, videotex, and all Fortune 100, 500 and 1000 companies.

MCCAFFERY & WHITENER, INC.
3143 Mt. Vernon Ave.
Alexandria, VA 22305-2640
Thomas McCaffery, President
PH: (703)684-6900
FX: (703)684-6900
Founded: 1991. **Staff:** 16. Activities: Transportation consultants offer expertise in Paradox systems analysis and systems design for transportation industry and related challenges.

OMAR MCCALL AND ASSOCIATES, INC.
11325 Maryland Ave., Ste. A
Beltsville, MD 20705
Omar McCall, CEO
PH: (301)937-7717
FX: (301)937-3342
Founded: 1978. **Staff:** 70. Activities: An engineering and professional services company specializing in systems engineering, computer related technologies, technical publications and marine systems. Serves private industries as well as government agencies.

MCGLADREY & PULLEN, LLP
1699 E. Woodfield Rd., Ste. 200
Schaumburg, IL 60173
Larry L. Dowell, Managing Partner of Consulting
PH: (847)517-7070
TF: (800)365-8353
FX: (847)517-7095
URL: www.mcgladrey.com
Founded: 1926. **Staff:** 3000. Activities: Provides a wide range of consulting services in the following broad areas: financial management consulting (including financial planning, valuations and financial feasibility analysis); business and strategic planning services (including succession planning and family business counseling); data processing and systems consulting (including all levels of systems—micro, mini and mainframe); human resources consulting (including personnel search, compensation planning, organization planning, outplacement, etc.); office automation and telecommunication consulting; operational consulting (including inventory and production control systems, operational reviews and productivity improvement); and marketing consulting. Industries served: banking, manufacturing, apparel and textiles, construction, education, government, healthcare, hospitality, insurance, legal, printing/publishing, broadcasting, retail/wholesale, and service.

MCHUGH SOFTWARE INTERNATIONAL
20700 Swenson Dr.
Waukesha, WI 53186

PH: (414)317-2000
TF: (888)624-8448
FX: (414)317-2001
URL: www.mchugh.com
Founded: 1975. **Staff:** 400. Activities: Software development consultants specializing in programming for inventory control, warehousing, and distribution. Develops training programs to accompany installation of computerized systems for client companies.

MECHANICAL TECHNOLOGY INC.
968 Albany-Shaker Rd.
Latham, NY 12110
George C. McNamee, CEO
PH: (518)785-2211
TF: (800)828-8210
FX: (518)785-2127
URL: www.mechtech.com
Founded: 1961. **Staff:** 300. Activities: Offers counsel, research and development to industry and government in fields of mechanical engineering, instrumentation, automation, rotor dynamics, computer programming and data processing, tribology, energy, and quality control. Serves private industries as well as government agencies.

MEDICAL MANAGER INC.
503 Grasslands Rd.
Valhalla, NY 10595-1503
Michael Sherman
PH: (914)592-2525
FX: (914)592-4784
Founded: 1983. **Staff:** 70. Activities: Computer technology consultants serving healthcare clients.

MEDICUS SYSTEMS CORP.
1 Rotary Center, Ste. 1111
Evanston, IL 60201
Jim Alland, Vice President
PH: (847)570-7500
TF: (800)257-2805
FX: (847)570-7597
URL: www.medicus.com
Founded: 1969. **Staff:** 280. Activities: Offers consulting services to healthcare providers in the U.S. and Canada. Areas of expertise include case management, clinical pathway automation/management, computer information systems management, cost containment, fiscal management, flexible budgeting, patient care workload measurement, patient care productivity management, and nurse staffing/scheduling.

THE MEDSTAT GROUP, INC.
777 E. Eisenhower Pky., Ste. 500
Ann Arbor, MI 48108
David Chinsky, Executive VP
PH: (313)996-1180
FX: (734)913-3500
URL: www.medstat.com
Founded: 1981. **Staff:** 97. Activities: Builds and maintains computerized medical cost databases and provides on-line analytical computing services to corporations and insurance companies. Services include data management, off-line management reports, consulting studies, and technical training and customer support. Also helps insurance managers and benefit professionals monitor and control employee medical benefit costs and redesign medical benefit programs. Also offers Decision Support Systems and contrast management programs for hospitals, integrated delivery systems, and managed care organizations. Consultation support is also available to these healthcare organizations. Industries served: no limits.

MEGADYNE INFORMATION SYSTEMS
2800 28th St., Ste. 205
Santa Monica, CA 90405-2934
Robert A. Chapman, President

PH: (310)452-1677
TF: (888)452-1677
FX: (310)452-7039
E-mail: magadmin@mrgeyneinfo.com
URL: www.megadyneinfo.com
Founded: 1981. **Staff:** 15. Activities: Provides automated information systems for transit services; as well as software and consulting to insurance/healthcare, and customized system development and integration. Also serves government agencies.

MEI SOFTWARE SYSTEMS, INC.
11720 Sunrise Valley Dr., Ste. 400
Reston, VA 20191
Hank Firey, President, CEO
PH: (703)620-9600
TF: (888)288-4634
FX: (703)620-4858
E-mail: marketing@meisoft.com
URL: www.neisoft.com
Founded: 1975. **Staff:** 131. Activities: Provides consulting and systems analysis on present and new computer systems and software. Serves associations, and other nonprofit organizations.

META GROUP, INC.
208 Harbor Dr.
PO Box 120061
Stamford, CT 06912-0061
Joe Gottlieb, Exec. Vice President Sales & Marketing
PH: (203)973-6700
FX: (203)359-8066
URL: www.metagroup.com
Founded: 1989. **Staff:** 200. Activities: Consulting firm specializing in assessment of information technology markets. Industries served: all Global 2000 companies.

METEOROLOGICAL EVALUATION SERVICES CO., INC.
165 Broadway
Amityville, NY 11701
Patrick T. Brennan, President
PH: (516)691-3395
TF: (800)952-2052
FX: (516)691-3550
Founded: 1968. **Staff:** 13. Activities: Provides air quality and meteorological consulting services to utilities, industries, businesses, governments, and attorneys nationwide. Specialty is developing environmental information for clients to enable them to fulfill legal and regulatory requirements in the most timely and cost-efficient manner. Experienced in the collection, organization and effective presentation of weather and air quality information. The following capabilities illustrate the nature of the firm's services: air pollution dispersion modeling studies; design of meteorological and pollutant field monitoring programs, with subsequent processing and analysis of measured data; weather investigations for legal and insurance firms; expert testimony in legal proceedings and public hearings; development of custom environmental software to meet unique industrial needs; and editing and preparation of conference proceedings and other technical publications.

METRO INFORMATION SERVICES, INC.
PO Box 8888
Virginia Beach, VA 23450
John H. Fain, President
PH: (757)486-1900
FX: (757)306-0816
Staff: 1300. Activities: Information technology consulting services company which offers a wide range of "people" services ranging from management assistance to all areas of computer-related services to technical training. Examples of these services are: project management, analysis and requirements definition, systems design, applications programming, systems programming, software package and hardware evaluation, conversion planning and assistance, systems installation, user and technical documentation, user training, and technical education.

MHM ASSOCIATES INC.
1920 Ridgedale Rd.
South Bend, IN 46614
Jerry H. Mohajeri, President
PH: (219)291-4793
FX: (219)291-4800
E-mail: mhmassoc@aol.com
Founded: 1974. **Staff:** 12. Activities: A multi-service civil engineering firm specializing in development of computerized pavement maintenance management programs, pavement evaluation techniques and instrumentation for collection of pavement distress data through video image processing applications. Primarily engaged in providing the necessary technology and equipment in the design, investigation and development of pavement maintenance management systems to most effectively serve government and industry.

MIACO CORP.
6300 S. Syracuse Way, Ste. 415
Englewood, CO 80111-6720
Shari Leigh, Pres.
PH: (303)741-0381
FX: (303)741-5901
URL: www.miaco.com
Founded: 1985. **Staff:** 55. Activities: Provides computer software support, specializing in relational databases for government and business concerns worldwide.

MICRO ANALYSIS & DESIGN, INC.
4900 Pearl East Cir., Ste. 201E
Boulder, CO 80301-6108
Catherine Barnes, Marketing Dir.
PH: (303)442-6947
FX: (303)442-8274
E-mail: sales@maad.com
URL: www.maad.com
Founded: 1982. **Staff:** 30. Activities: Firms products and services includes simulation software; computer simulation consulting; human factors engineering, ergonomics, and graphical user interface design; software development.

MICRO TECHNOLOGY CONSULTANTS, INC.
132 Osigian Blvd.
Warner Robins, GA 31088
Randy Smith, President
PH: (912)953-1921
FX: (912)953-7994
E-mail: Webmaster@mtc-support.com
URL: www.mtc-support.com
Founded: 1990. **Staff:** 18. Activities: Provides computer, cable and consulting services.

MICROMEGA SYSTEMS INC.
2 Fifer Ave., Ste. 120
Corte Madera, CA 94925
Charles J. "Chick" Bornheim, President
PH: (415)924-4700
FX: (415)945-3301
E-mail: consult@micromegasystems.com
URL: www.micromegasystems.com
Founded: 1979. **Staff:** 12. Activities: Data processing consultants in downsizing business DBMS applications. Services include strategic planning, consulting, requirements definition, design, programming, hardware and software search, RFP preparation, installation, and support and training. Provides several kinds of software: custom systems; vertical market packages developed for sales support, telemarketing, customer service, competitor tracking, office communication, workflow management, budget control, and financial reporting. Specialize in Microsoft database environments including FoxPro Visual FoxPro, Access, MS SQL Server and Visual Basic. Industries served: banking, finance, insurance, healthcare, securities, venture capital, computer and data processing, and government agencies.

MICROSTRATEGY
8000 Towers Crescent Dr., Ste. 1400
Vienna, VA 22182
Michael J. Saylor, President and CEO
PH: (703)848-8600
TF: (800)264-3205
FX: (703)848-8610
E-mail: info@strategy.com
URL: www.strategy.com/
Founded: 1989. **Staff:** 312. Activities: Firm is involved in Decision Support Systems (DSS) and Data Warehousing Relational OLAP (ROLAP) software.

MINDBANK CONSULTING GROUP
8500 Leesburg Pike, Ste. 602
Vienna, VA 22182
Dr. Neal Grunstra, Pres.
PH: (703)893-4700
TF: (800)444-2234
FX: (703)761-3038
URL: www.mindbank.com
Founded: 1986. **Staff:** 45. Activities: Mindbank consulting group is a software contracting consulting firm offering professional services consulting to major firms.

MININGHAM & OELLERICH, INC.
225 Broadway
New York, NY 10007-3002
Robert Miningham
PH: (212)349-4410
FX: (212)693-2765
Founded: 1966. **Staff:** 35. Activities: Data processing/programming consultants specializing in the development of financial accounting systems and other computerized information processing systems. Areas of expertise are brokerage, banking, manufacturing and cross industry financial applications.

MINNETRONIX, INC.
2610 University Ave., Ste. 400
St. Paul, MN 55114
Jonathan D. Pierce
PH: (651)917-4060
FX: (651)917-4066
E-mail: info@minnetronix.com
URL: www.minnetronix.com
Founded: 1996. **Staff:** 18. Activities: Develops state-of-the-art electronic and software solutions in partnership with medical and industrial companies.

M.I.S. CONSULTANTS
20 Holly St., Ste. 200
Toronto, Canada M4S 3B1
Eric Liberi, President
PH: (416)489-4334
TF: (800)311-2828
FX: (416)489-0918
E-mail: jobs@misconsult.com
URL: www.misconsult.com
Founded: 1978. **Staff:** 28. Activities: Specializes in contracting, consulting and recruitment in the information technology industry. Main focus is in the mainframe, mini and PC market, which includes database, case tool technology development, client/server, object oriented programming, 'RDB's, 4thGLs and software/technical support.

MIS TECHNOLOGY INC.
10335 W. Oklahoma Ave.
Milwaukee, WI 53227
David E. Capel, President
PH: (414)327-7318
FX: (414)327-5618
Founded: 1970. **Staff:** 20. Activities: Offers counsel on the development of complete computer installations. Developer of "CMI Profit" and "Profit-IV(tm)" application programs for manufacturing,

distribution, and accounting. Specializes in IBM RS/6000 SCO, UNIX, and PC-network machines. Industries served: manufacturing, job shops, and distribution worldwide.

MISI CO., LTD.
350 Park Ave., 4th Fl.
New York, NY 10022
Y. Tanaka, President
PH: (212)355-5585
FX: (212)751-5964
Founded: 1978. **Staff:** 150. **Activities:** Computer technology specialists offer expertise in the following application programming - IBM (mainframe, mid-range, PC), VAX, and Wang; systems programming; technical support/communications; package software for manufacturing distribution and international banking; hardware sales IBM midrange; PC networking; and bar code and data collection systems. Industries served: manufacturing, distribution, banking, insurance, brokerage, government, communications, and pharmaceutical.

MONICUS CORP.
1025 Bask Dr.
Tampa, FL 33603
Kevin Fitzgerald, President
PH: (813)238-2254
FX: (813)239-1339
URL: www.monicus.com
Founded: 1990. **Staff:** 15. **Activities:** Computer consultants providing software support for all types of computers, from mainframe through PCs. Specializes in database and communications programming services, as well as site planning. Serves private industries as well as government agencies.

MORE SYSTEMS, INC.
Westwood Business Center
690 Canton St., Ste. 290
Westwood, MA 02090
Joseph P. Doherty
PH: (617)251-9217
FX: (617)251-9218
URL: www.moresys.com
Founded: 1988. **Staff:** 21. **Activities:** Software development and consulting firm serving computers, commercial concerns, utilities, and educational institutes in the U.S. and Canada.

MORGAN PARKER & JOHNSON, INC.
45 Wall St., Penthouse
New York, NY 10005
M. K. Morgan, President and CEO
PH: (212)968-1100
TF: (888)968-1169
FX: (212)968-8702
E-mail: Piercep@mpj.com
Founded: 1986. **Staff:** 35. **Activities:** A New York-based corporation which serves the needs of banks, brokerage firms and other financial concerns by providing consultants and consultant teams to solve challenges in "computer and people systems" technology. Assists in the design and use of technology which serves users. Specializes in the areas of Enterprise Computing (both data driven and process control driver), Methodologies/Tools and Object and Neural Technology. Expertise also includes object-oriented program development and client server systems.

A DIVISION OF MOSAIC MEDIA, INC.
2055 Army Trail Rd., Dept. GR598, Ste. 100
Addison, IL 60101
Lee McFadden, President
PH: (630)628-0500
TF: (800)424-8668
FX: (630)628-0550
E-mail: oneonone@pincom.com
URL: www.oootraining.com
Founded: 1976. **Staff:** 45. **Activities:** Firm offers expertise in setting up comprehensive computer training programs.

MOSKOWITZ & CO. INC.
1 Insurance Center Pl.
St. Louis, MO 63141
Daniel B. Moskowitz, President
PH: (314)878-7780
Founded: 1980. **Staff:** 40. **Activities:** Consultants in the development of computerized financial systems for banking, savings and loan, brokerage, manufacturing, and insurance companies. Provides on-site assistance and software package installation with custom modification (HOGAN specialists), and teller/platform automation systems.

B I MOYLE ASSOCIATES, INC.
5788 Lincoln Dr.
Minneapolis, MN 55436
Bennett I. Moyle
PH: (612)933-2885
FX: (612)933-7764
E-mail: bmoyle@bimoyle.com
URL: www.bimoyle.com
Founded: 1978. **Staff:** 20. **Activities:** Offers IBM mainframe systems programming consulting and system implementation.

MSI CONSULTING GROUP
4700 42nd Ave. SW, Ste. 440
Seattle, WA 98116
Allan Adler, CEO
PH: (206)933-0330
FX: (206)937-6130
E-mail: aadler@msicri.com
URL: www.msiconsulting.com
Staff: 40. **Activities:** Offers marketing and sales strategy expertise to the computer industry through in-house research and service groups. Focuses on distribution channels, encompassing hardware, software, and telecommunications products on an international basis.

M.S.I. INDUSTRIES, INC.
1808 Baltimore Blvd.
Westminster, MD 21157
F.W. Meyers, CEO and President
PH: (410)857-4466
FX: (410)751-9067
Founded: 1978. **Staff:** 23. **Activities:** Offers maintenance, engineering, and consultation experience in real-time computer applications, nuclear power plant military training simulator maintenance and modification, training simulator specification writing, training simulator verification and validation, graphics systems, and computer upgrade and replacement for Gould (Encore) and Charles River Data System (CRDS). Serves private industries as well as government agencies.

MULLER MEDIA CONVERSIONS
32 Broadway, Ste. 1600
New York, NY 10004
Chris Muller, President
PH: (212)344-0474
FX: (212)968-0789
E-mail: mmco@compuserve.com
URL: www.mullermedia.com
Founded: 1978. **Staff:** 12. **Activities:** Offers consulting and programming for these applications: media conversion, document conversion, document managers, publishing, word processing, DEC minicomputers, PCDOS and UNIX micros, and telecommunications. Specialty is installations which involve massive amounts of information. Firm is an IBM business partner as well as a registered third-party developer with Wang, DEC, Microsoft, Lotus, and WordPerfect. Industries served: any large volume office automation users, including government agencies and legal and pharmaceutical industries worldwide.

MULTISYSTEMS, INC.
10 Fawcett St.
Cambridge, MA 02138
John P. Attanucci, President

PH: (617)864-5810
FX: (617)864-3521
E-mail: kdossin@multisystems.com
URL: www.multisystems.com
Founded: 1966. **Staff:** 120. Activities: Firm has expertise in the transit and paratransit industries, offering a full complement of specialized application software products, planning and policy analysis counseling services and, through its TMSI subsidiary, operations and management services. Also designs, develops, and markets a complete family of transit operations support software for bid processing/dispatch control/timekeeping, fixed route vehicle operator scheduling and runcutting, management, paratransit scheduling and dispatch, customer information, GIS, data collection and analysis, and financial accounting.

MVC CORP.
49 Sherwood Terr., Ste. W
Lake Bluff, IL 60044
Don Cran, President
PH: (847)283-9000
FX: (847)283-9023
Founded: 1981. **Staff:** 40. Activities: Specializes in client/server applications development and support and consulting services for a variety of languages. Serves private industry and government agencies primarily in the Chicago and Milwaukee areas.

NATIONAL CAD SERVICES
30100 Telegraph Rd., Ste. 377
Bingham Farms, MI 48025-4517
Darrel Ashby
PH: (248)647-6777
TF: (800)775-DRAW
FX: (248)647-6776
E-mail: info@nationalcad.com
URL: www.nationalcad.com
Founded: 1992. **Staff:** 20. Activities: Firm offers CAD drafting services, as well as plotting services. Specializing in construction trades and facilities, field surveys, and CAD transfers, construction documentation.

NATIONAL COMPUTER SYSTEMS, INC.
PO Box 9365
Minneapolis, MN 55440
Russell A. Gullotti, Chairman and CEO
PH: (612)829-3000
FX: (612)829-3186
URL: www.ncs.com
Founded: 1962. **Staff:** 2750. Activities: Provides systems solutions to the financial services/asset management marketplace. Provides automated information management products and services to collect and analyze data.

NATIONAL EDUCATION TRAINING GROUP
1751 W. Diehl Rd., Ste. 200
Naperville, IL 60563-9099
Robert T. Soto, President
PH: (630)369-3000
FX: (630)983-4800
URL: www.netg.com
Founded: 1981. **Staff:** 450. Activities: Firm develops software productivity tools and human resources education and training programs for businesses and government agencies worldwide.

NATIVE AMERICAN CONSULTANTS, INC.
725 2nd St. NE
Washington 20002
A. Patrick Hanes, CEO
PH: (202)547-0576
TF: (800)347-0576
FX: (202)547-0589
Founded: 1975. **Staff:** 85. Activities: Data processing and information services consultants primarily serving the government, Federal Aviation Association (FAA), Navy, State Department, and Treasury Department and DLA. Offers computer design, programming, and

systems operation. Also provides expertise in general logistics and support. Assists with seminar organization.

NDC/FEDERAL SYSTEMS INC.
1300 Piccard Dr.
Rockville, MD 20850
Ronald Trusty, President
PH: (301)590-7700
Founded: 1980. **Staff:** 193. Activities: Data processing consultants offering services in time sharing, facility management and maintenance, and computer analysis, programming, operating and documentation to various federal and state government agencies as well as private industry clients.

NETWORK CALIFORNIA CORP.
30 East San Carlos St., No. 222
San Jose, CA 95113
Allan Baumgartner
PH: (408)298-6300
FX: (408)298-6430
Founded: 1986. **Staff:** 11. Activities: Business management firm consults on accounting and business as well as computer and communications support and integration. Provides total business system support. Installs and supports accounting software network and communication systems, and upgrades, modifies and maintains computer systems and networks. Industries served: all.

NETWORK DESIGN ENGINEERS INC.
11300 Executive Center Dr.
Little Rock, AR 72211
D. Leo Turnbow, Vice President
PH: (501)219-0911
TF: (800)221-0911
FX: (501)219-2145
Founded: 1989. **Staff:** 40. Activities: Designs networks for communications businesses and municipalities worldwide.

NEW ENGLAND COMPUTER SERVICES, INC.
Prestige Park, Units 6 & 7
168 Boston Post Rd.
Madison, CT 06443-2402
Christopher Anatra, President
PH: (203)245-3999
TF: (800)766-6327
FX: (203)245-4513
E-mail: office@necs.com
URL: www.necs.com
Founded: 1987. **Staff:** 11. Activities: Makes hardware and software recommendations for needs of food distributing business. Has computerized more than 800 food distributorships throughout the United States.

NICHOLS RESEARCH
10260 Old Columbia Rd.
Columbia, MD 21046
D. Bruce McIndoe, President
PH: (410)290-9500
FX: (410)290-2012
Founded: 1982. **Staff:** 32. Activities: Offers consulting, systems engineering, and computer programming on a broad range of computer applications. These services include: proposal development; product specification and development; project planning and management; requirements analysis; system specification; interface definition; trade-off analysis; functional specification; hardware and software design, implementation, test, integration, and documentation; data communications; device driver development; data management; diagnostics development; system integration and test; V&V; QA; and training. Serves private industries as well as government agencies.

NICKEL GROUP
6360 I 55 N., Ste. 300
Jackson, MS 39211
John A. Conway, Jr., President

PH: (601)957-7400
FX: (601)957-9492
URL: www.nickels.com
Founded: 1978. Staff: 65. Activities: Computer technology consultants and software development firm specializing in systems design, integration, and reengineering.

NIELSEN-PM ASSOCIATES, INC.
19 Lent Ave.
Le Roy, NY 14482
James N. Nielsen, President
PH: (716)768-2282
TF: (800)836-0072
FX: (716)768-6852
E-mail: sales@npma.com
Founded: 1982. Staff: 12. Activities: Maintenance management specialists providing computer systems and consulting support to industrial, hospital, governmental, and commercial organizations. The PM-MMS ProTek is an interactive Maintenance Management system (CMMS) solution for the year 2000 and beyond. It adapts to customers' envrionment and supports tracking required by ISO 9000, JCAHO, FDA, and OSHA. It is a highly effective tool for maintenance functions tin commercial, health care and manufacturing. Client/server and single user versions are available.

THE NOBLE GROUP, LTD.
Foster City, CA 94404
Dean Noble
PH: (415)570-5399
TF: (800)640-5959
FX: (415)573-1924
E-mail: 73427.224@compuserve.com
URL: www.noblegroup.com
Founded: 1984. Staff: 23. Activities: An information technologies company and Microsoft Solution Provider, firm specializes in networks, software and systems integration, and the Internet, including client/server solutions, RAD (Rapid Applications Development), Windows, Visual Basic, Multimedia, Windows-NT, and Intranet.

NOBLITT & RUELAND
5405 Alton Pky., Ste. A530
Irvine, CA 92604
Dennis Rubenacker
PH: (714)258-4646
FX: (714)528-3990
E-mail: info@noblitt-rueland.com
URL: www.noblitt-rueland.com
Founded: 1989. Staff: 15. Activities: Provides software development, software quality assurance, software compliance assessments, independent verification and validation, testing, engineering, reverse engineering, and hazard analysis. Also provides 510 (k), IDE, and PMA submissions. In-house training seminars are offered on FDA/ISO software SQA (design and manufacturing), new GMP, design control, risk and hazard analysis, and CE mark.

NORTHWEST SOFTWARE, INC.
PO Box 91396
Portland, OR 97291-0396
Sonal Shah, President
PH: (503)629-5947
FX: (503)645-5892
E-mail: nsi@nwsi.com
Founded: 1988. Staff: 65. Activities: Provides structured software development, quality assurance, documentation, and training services. NSI's large and diverse local staff provides a quick response in a variety of specialties, including scientific, engineering, and business data-processing applications. Off-shore development staff provide a quality and cost-effective alternative. Offers a full spectrum of business terms, including hourly (time and materials), fixed price, and in some cases strategic alliances. Specialties include: software development and quality assurance; on-site or off-site services; UNIX, MS-Windows, DOS, and other environments; high level and assembly languages; database design and implementation; data communications; graphical user interfaces; and data processing on

mainframes and minicomputers. Industries served: scientific, engineering, and data processing, as well as government agencies.

NOT-FOR-PROFIT SOFTWARE
91 Lukens Dr.
New Castle, DE 19720
Barbara L. Hines, President
PH: (302)652-3370
FX: (302)652-4591
URL: www.sscel.com
Founded: 1981. Staff: 16. Activities: Computer systems and software consultancy extends assistance to not-for-profit organizations and agencies. Industries served: nonprofit organizations and businesses.

NUMBER SIX SOFTWARE, INC.
1101 30th St. NW, Ste. 500
Washington 20007
Robert Daly, President
PH: (202)625-4364
TF: (888)292-6862
FX: (202)338-8539
E-mail: info@numbersix.com
URL: www.numbersix.com/
Founded: 1994. Staff: 12. Activities: Software consulting and development firm. An object-oriented software services company, specializing in technology insertion.

NURSING TECHNOMICS
814 Sunset Hollow Rd.
West Chester, PA 19380
Joan I. McCrea, President
PH: (610)436-4551
FX: (610)436-0255
E-mail: jimccrea@bellatlantic.net
Founded: 1983. Staff: 17. Activities: Administrative nursing consultants offer expertise in the design and implementation of customized software applications for departments of nursing, organizational design and implementation, and executive nurse search. Also specializes in department staffing, scheduling and nurse recruitment. Serves private industries as well as government agencies.

OAK ENTERPRISES DATA SERVICES INC.
800 Roosevelt Rd., Bldg. E
Glen Ellyn, IL 60137-5839
Timothy Waterloo, President
PH: (630)858-4443
FX: (630)858-4594
E-mail: staffing@oakent.com
URL: www.oakenterprises.com
Founded: 1984. Staff: 60. Activities: Provides quality computer consultants to discriminating clients. Consultants are highly skilled on a variety of computer platforms, including IBM mainframes, midrange and microcomputers; UNIX systems; and Tandem systems. Specialties include client/server systems, GUI, RDBMs and emerging technologies. Industries served: distribution, healthcare, pharmaceutical, telecommunications, investments, and insurance.

OBJECT ORIENTED DESIGN GROUP, INC.
3716 159th Dr., SE
Snohomish, WA 98290-9339
Robert P. Folline
PH: (425)334-8889
FX: (425)335-5101
E-mail: Bobf@eskimo.com
Founded: 1988. Staff: 31. Activities: Services include turnkey engineering, telecommunications/datacom system design, hardware design and layout from specification through product release, and software systems design from conceptual through product life. Industries served: military, datacom, telecom, and government agencies.

OCCUPATIONAL HEALTH RESEARCH
28 Research Dr.
PO Box 900
Skowhegan, ME 04976
Michael Keller, President
PH: (207)474-8432
TF: (800)660-0818
FX: (207)474-6398
E-mail: webmaster@systoc.com
URL: www.systoc.com
Founded: 1985. **Staff:** 56. Activities: OHR offers a cost effective approach to occupational health program development, product enhancement and operational improvement. Our consulting associates provide a broad range of services to help health care organizations establish high quality, competitive occupational health programs tailored to their market areas. Each project is unique and our consultants always create client-specific solutions. No assessment or report is ever produced using standardized forms, templates, or methods.

ODR INC.
2900 Chamblee-Tucker Rd., Bldg. 16
Atlanta, GA 30341
Daryl R. Conner, Founder/CEO
PH: (770)455-7145
TF: (800)CHANGE U
FX: (770)455-8974
E-mail: mdc@odrinc.com
URL: www.odrinc.com
Founded: 1974. **Staff:** 30. Activities: Provides clients with a disciplined methodology for implementing the human aspects of major organizational change. Methodology includes structured approaches for the planning, decision-making, and execution phases of change implementation. Consulting services assist management in determining how such projects can be installed with minimal disruption to the work force while maximizing employee support and commitment to the change. Industries served: financial services, healthcare, business services, manufacturing, high-tech, telecommunications, and transportation.

OLEEN HEALTHCARE INFORMATION MANAGEMENT, INC.
7979 Old Georgetown Rd., Ste. 500
Bethesda, MD 20814
PH: (301)907-4760
TF: (800)466-4760
FX: (301)718-1809
Founded: 1988. **Staff:** 66. Activities: A managed healthcare consulting firm that develops software and supports management information systems for local or national HMO's.

OMNEX MANAGEMENT AND ENGINEERING CONSULTANTS, LLC
3025 Boardwalk, Ste. 110
Ann Arbor, MI 48108
David Watkins, President
PH: (734)668-1000
FX: (734)668-9414
E-mail: omec@omecconsultants.com
Founded: 1984. **Staff:** 12. Activities: OMEC is a quality and management systems consulting firm that specializes in ISO/QS-9000, QOS and APQP Implementation. Performance enhancement using BOS, Kaizen, Theory of Constraints, new product development and launch, and continuous improvement techniques are used to implement Best-in-Class systems. Industries Served: Manufacturing and Service, Automotive Logistics, Engineering, Architecture and Testing.

ON-LINE FINANCIAL SERVICES, INC.
900 Commerce Dr., Ste. 203
Oak Brook, IL 60523
Robert T. Stokes, C.E.O. & President
PH: (847)571-7900
FX: (847)571-7971

Staff: 150. Activities: Data processing firm offers expertise to banks, savings banks, and other financial institutions in the Midwest.

OPTIMUM SERVICES & SYSTEMS INC.
4500 Forbes Blvd., Ste. 210
Lanham, MD 20706
Carlton Joseph, President/Treasurer
PH: (301)459-9100
FX: (301)731-6285
Founded: 1977. **Staff:** 110. Activities: Offers professional services in the areas of computer software applications, programming and analysis, data entry, publications and graphics, ADP facilities management, data collection and analysis, maintenance and operations, training and documentation. Serves private industries as well as government agencies.

ORACLE CONSULTING
222 Berkeley St., Ste. 1200
Boston, MA 02116
FX: (617)424-5290
Staff: 1000. Activities: Consulting division of Oracle Corporation, a major supplier of database software and services. Firm provides assistance in such areas as strategic information system planning, business process re-engineering, system integration, packaged application implementation, software development, and education.

ORCHARD HILTZ & MCCLIMENT INC.
34935 Schoolcraft Rd.
Livonia, MI 48150-1322
David L. Mariner, P.E., President
PH: (734)522-6711
FX: (734)522-6427
Founded: 1962. **Staff:** 130. Activities: Orchard, Hiltz & McCliment, Inc. (OHM), is a consulting engineering firm that specializes in providing municipal engineering and geographic information system services. Municipal engineering services include transportation, structural and utility design, hydraulics/hydrology, surveying, right-of-way, construction and inspection, and site development. Geographic & Information Services, Inc., a division of OHM, provides needs assessment, systems implementation, custom programming, data conversion, scanning, digitizing, GPS surveys, and technical assistance.

ORIGIN INTERNATIONAL INC.
6509 A Mississauga Rd.
Mississauga, Canada L5N 1A6
Murray J. Desnoyer, CEO
PH: (905)821-1820
FX: (905)821-0216
URL: www.origin.com
Founded: 1975. **Staff:** 15. Activities: Offers custom software products for coordinate measuring machines and provides math data output. Industries served: automotive, machine tool, aerospace, and government agencies.

ORIGIN TECHNOLOGY IN BUSINESS INC.
8044 Montgomery Rd., Ste. 200 W
Cincinnati, OH 45236
Ann Wurster, Managing Director
PH: (513)793-4334
FX: (513)793-5062
Staff: 5600. Activities: Computer consultancy specializing in project management, network, software and systems design/ development/implementation/documentation, training, SAP, and business analysis.

ORION GROUP SOFTWARE ENGINEERS, INC.
5770 Nimtz Pky.
South Bend, IN 46628
Matt Street, CEO

PH: (219)233-3401
TF: (800)59-ORION
FX: (219)239-3348
E-mail: sales@ogse.com
URL: www.ogse.com
Founded: 1986. **Staff:** 32. Activities: Computer technology firm specializes in networking, accounting, wholesale distribution, and computerized manufacturing systems. Also provides complete web site development, including electronic commerce, database and firewall implementation.

ORTHSTAR INC.

Airport Corporate Prk.
PO Box 459
Big Flats, NY 14814-0459
James Orsillo, CEO
PH: (607)562-2100
FX: (607)562-2110
E-mail: orsillo@orthstar.com
URL: www.orthstar.com
Founded: 1974. **Staff:** 70. Activities: High-technology systems engineering group which provides systems design, software integration, and computer consulting ranging from systems studies, to preparation and presentation of final systems design, to integrated solutions to information and computer-oriented problems. As a division of ORTHSTAR Inc., the software engineering group has access to the in-house computers (DEC, SGI's, HP, SUN, IBM), robot and machine vision lab, microelectronic prototype lab, and support and word processing facilities. Industries served: aerospace, military, transportation, railroads, automation, simulation, and power utilities.

OUELLETTE & ASSOCIATES CONSULTING, INC.

40 S. River Rd., Ste. 66
Bedford, NH 03110
L. Paul Ouellette, CEO
PH: (603)623-7373
FX: (603)623-4052
E-mail: kkeller@ouellette-online.com
URL: ouellette-online.com
Founded: 1984. **Staff:** 12. Activities: An international information systems (IS) management consulting and professional development firm. The consulting group focuses on various information systems issues. These include strategic planning, organizational structures, managing change, professional development, service orientation, and enhancing quality improvement. Firm is experienced in supporting clients through short, medium, and long term initiatives from planning through implementation. Team members are professionals from information systems organizations and understand the theoretical and the day-to-day issues of information organizations. In addition, they are published authors, keynote speakers, and corporate team facilitators. Serves private industries as well as government agencies.

P/K ASSOCIATES INC.

3006 Gregory St.
Madison, WI 53711
Judi K. Turkel, President
PH: (608)231-1003
FX: (608)231-1446
E-mail: cpacomputerreport@execpc.com
URL: www.accounting.org/computer; www.cpacomputerreport.com
Founded: 1977. **Staff:** 11. Activities: Evaluates microcomputer networks and software, and does extensive evaluations of larger systems. Based on this knowledge, aids clients in selecting, installing, and training for computer use. Advises computer industry on marketing, public relations, and advertising worldwide.

PACIFIC COMPUTING

133 Mission St., Ste. 103
Santa Cruz, CA 95060
Steven P. DeLaney

PH: (408)427-4280
FX: (408)427-4282
E-mail: info@pacific_computing.com
URL: www.pacific_computing.com
Founded: 1991. **Staff:** 15. Activities: Designs and implements software for real-time, video, control, and client/server applications. Includes embedded microprocessor firmware, GUI, and database programming.

PACIFIC SCIENCE & ENGINEERING GROUP INC.

6310 Greenwich Dr., Ste. 200
San Diego, CA 92122
James Callan, President
PH: (619)535-1661
FX: (619)535-1665
E-mail: pseg@aol.com
Founded: 1984. **Staff:** 25. Activities: Human factors consulting firm specializes in software development. Industries served: defense, medical, transportation, and computer.

PANAMETRICS, INC., AUTOMATED SYSTEMS DIVISION

102 Langmuir Lab
Ithaca, NY 14850
Thomas E. Michaels
PH: (607)257-5501
FX: (607)257-8228
Founded: 1988. **Staff:** 21. Activities: Offers consulting services in technology and systems designed for nondestructive testing applications, with capabilities in the areas of ultrasonic testing, video methods, electronics, software, and mechanics. Services range from problem definition studies to building complete computer-based testing systems. Products include scanning equipment, ultrasonic instrumentation, high resolution video cameras, data acquisition systems, and integrated software packages.

PANETH, HABER & ZIMMERMAN

600 3rd Ave.
New York, NY 10016
PH: (212)503-8800
FX: (212)370-3759
Founded: 1966. **Staff:** 50. Activities: Computer technology consultants provide the following services: operations appraisals, diagnostic studies, definition of system requirements, system design, application software selection, computer feasibility studies, assistance in implementation, clerical procedure manuals, and data processing management audits. Industries served: no limits.

THE PARK GROUP, INC.

443 Park Ave. S, Ste. 1006
New York, NY 10016
Jerry W. Eastep, President/CEO
PH: (212)679-9609
FX: (212)679-9604
Founded: 1984. **Staff:** 16. Activities: The Park Group is a team of transportation specialists offering comprehensive consultation and information services for transportation companies, government, and financial institutions. The firm's product line includes a group of interrelated activities and software offerings designed to bring large carrier information and management system sophistication to both domestic and overseas clients. Industries served: airlines, hotel companies, car rental firms, government, and financial institutions.

PATEL CONSULTANTS CORP.

1525 Morris Ave.
Union, NJ 07083
Mac Patel, President
PH: (908)964-7575
FX: (908)964-3176
E-mail: patel@castle.net
URL: www.patelcorp.com
Founded: 1973. **Staff:** 90. Activities: Provides contract services of highly skilled and experienced technical personnel in the data processing and engineering field, including programmers, analysts, sys-

tems programmers/analysts, project managers, computer operators, engineers, designers, and technicians.

PB FARRADYNE INC.
3200 Tower Oaks Blvd.
Rockville, MD 20852
Walter H. Kraft, Senior Vice President
PH: (301)468-5568
FX: (301)816-1884
E-mail: jobs@pbworld.com
URL: www.pbfi.com
Founded: 1984. **Staff:** 110. Activities: Provides transportation planning and engineering software development and systems integration services for intelligent transportation system applications. Also offers telecommunications systems planning and design for data and voice communications; and LAN (local area network) design and implementation. Focuses on computer systems interoperability. Serves government agencies, transportation, and defense industries in the United States.

PERENNIAL
4699 Old Ironsides Dr., Ste. 210
Santa Clara, CA 95054
Barry E. Hedquist, President
PH: (408)727-2255
FX: (408)748-2909
Founded: 1986. **Staff:** 14. Activities: Provides software engineering for micro, mini and super mini computers. Specializes in software development for real-time command and control, industrial applications, UNIX and IBM PC/AT applications.

PERFORMANCE DEVELOPMENT CORP.
707 Alexander Rd., Ste. 208
Princeton, NJ 08540-6331
Arvind D. Shah
PH: (609)419-4411
TF: (800)554-9131
FX: (609)514-1420
E-mail: perfdev@ix.netcom.com
URL: www.perfdev.com
Founded: 1971. **Staff:** 23. Activities: Offers consulting and educational services in the areas of change management business analysis and business reengineering, IS strategic planning, methodologies and CASE tools, data administration, database administration, and relational database support (DB2, Oracle, Sybase). Other services include IS organization planning and restructuring and IT implementation services. Industries served: aerospace, banking and finance, government, healthcare, insurance, manufacturing, pharmaceuticals, retail/wholesale, and utilities.

PERIPHERAL SYSTEMS, INC.
PO Box 258
Oley, PA 19547
Cora Williams, President
PH: (610)987-3421
FX: (610)987-9871
Founded: 1978. **Staff:** 20. Activities: An information management company offering business systems consulting including management and engineering consulting, methods analysis, facilities management, and equipment selection. Also offers services in data processing including hardware design, systems analysis, programming, and customized software; technical training, technical writing and manual preparation; word processing; records management; micrographic; and reprographic, also CAD/CAM design drafting and desktop publishing. Specializes in service to small businesses and support services for professionals. Also active with government agencies.

PEROT SYSTEMS
12377 Merit Dr., Ste. 1100
Dallas, TX 75251
Ross Perot, President, CEO & Chairman
PH: (972)788-3000
TF: (800)688-4333
E-mail: corp.comm@ps.net
URL: www.ps.net
Founded: 1988. **Staff:** 6000. Activities: Works with our customers to develop business strategies, including evaluating and designing organizational structures, managing major change events, and redesigning business processes. These services include assisting clients with strategic decisions regarding platforms, networks and delivery media, developing overall architecture platform, technology or application to another.

PFEIFFER ENGINEERING COMPANY
2701 Lindsay Ave.
Louisville, KY 40206-2222
John C. Pfeiffer, President
PH: (502)897-1630
FX: (502)895-3894
URL: www.pfeiffereng.com
Founded: 1981. **Staff:** 19. Activities: Offers industrial control systems design, construction supervision, and start-up assistance. Also furnishes engineering services and hardware/software design. Industries served include: chemical, food processing, packaging, tobacco, explosives, automotive, and metal forming. Serves private industries as well as government agencies.

PHILLIPS INFOTECH
1111 Marlkress
Cherry Hill, NJ 08003-5062
Lawrence Feidelman, President
PH: (609)424-1100
TF: (800)678-4642
FX: (609)424-1999
URL: www.phillips.com
Founded: 1971. **Staff:** 27. Activities: International information service organization offering assistance with evaluations of computer software, communications and office system products. Services also include user surveys and market research. Serves private industries as well as government agencies.

PILLER NATALE & OH MANAGEMENT CONSULTANTS INC.
1 Yonge St., 19th Fl.
Toronto, Canada M5E 1N4
Ralph Piller, President
PH: (416)361-6252
FX: (416)361-6291
E-mail: pno@io.org
URL: www.io.org/~pno/
Founded: 1990. **Staff:** 30. Activities: Offers full spectrum of reengineering and technology services, including reengineering team facilitation and process design; reengineering implementation and training; enterprise wide software selection; and world-class manufacturing technologies. Developed ReMAP, a comprehensive methodology which includes tools and job aids proven critical to success of reengineering projects.

PIONEER TECHNOLOGY
4824 W. Coon Rd.
Howell, MI 48843
Antonio Robinson, Pres.
PH: (517)546-2855
TF: (800)849-9067
FX: (517)546-5310
E-mail: pioneer_technology@compuserve.com
Founded: 1987. **Staff:** 12. Activities: Specializes in system integration services and engineering and computer services, including manufacturing automation, factory automation, test machines development, special machine development, new product development, embedded controller development, software development, Year 2000 conversion.

PITTIGLIO RABIN TODD & MCGRATH
1050 Winter St.
Waltham, MA 02451-1297
Michael McGrath
PH: (781)647-2800
FX: (781)647-2804
URL: www.prtm.com
Founded: 1976. **Staff:** 300. **Activities:** Focuses on technology-based industry, helping high-tech companies integrate their business strategy into world-class management processes. Focus on the following industry sectors: Aerospace and Defense; Automotive and Industrial Products; Chemical and Advanced Materials; Computers; Electronic Equipment; Software; Semiconductors; Telecommunications; Pharmaceuticals; and Medical Devices.

PORT-TO-PORT CONSULTING
1317 N. Pennsylvania St.
Indianapolis, IN 46202
Damon Richards, President
PH: (317)624-9380
FX: (317)624-9390
E-mail: info@port-to-port.com
URL: www.port-to-port.com
Founded: 1991. **Staff:** 12. **Activities:** Computer consultants specializing in information resource management and business process reengineering. Assists in strategic planning and implementation of technology that improves information flow and impacts the bottom line.

POTOMAC CONSULTING GROUP, INC.
1600 Wilson Blvd., Ste. 1060
Arlington, VA 22209-2505
Chris Maas
PH: (703)527-1260
FX: (703)527-2527
E-mail: potomac@cais.com
URL: www.potomac.com
Founded: 1989. **Staff:** 24. **Activities:** Computer consultancy offers expertise in the following areas: dBase, FoxPro, Microsoft, Windows, Access, Lotus Notes, C, and Paradox. Industries served: legal firms associations.

PREFERRED MEDICAL MARKETING CORP.
7400 Carmel Executive Pk., Ste. 240
Charlotte, NC 28226
Roger L. Shaul, Jr., President
PH: (704)543-8103
FX: (704)543-8106
URL: www.pmmconline.com
Founded: 1987. **Staff:** 20. **Activities:** Health care consultants.

PROFESSIONAL CONSULTING SERVICES OF GEORGIA
3025 Aiken Cir.
Dallas, GA 30132
Krishna V. Srinivasa, President
PH: (770)443-4300
FX: (770)445-6600
Founded: 1980. **Staff:** 58. **Activities:** Provides programming, project management, system analysis and design, data base implementation, and data processing help to clients on most available hardware including micro-computers.

PROJECT MANAGEMENT SERVICES, INC.
PO Box 4113
Rockville, MD 20849
Douglas N. Mitten
PH: (301)340-0527
FX: (301)424-3660
E-mail: pmsimail@aol.com
URL: www.libra.wcupa.edu/Valu/Link/pmsindex.html
Founded: 1987. **Staff:** 12. **Activities:** Independent construction cost estimating, scheduling and value engineering services. Provides risk analyses, cost analyses, range estimating, surety value analysis(sm) facility security (CPTED) studies, and asbestos cost estimating. Provides master, preconstruction, and construction scheduling. Value engineering workshops and program studies are by certified value specialists. Claims review and expert witness services provided as well. Develops software in related fields.

PURVIS SYSTEMS INC.
7001 Brush Hollow Rd.
Westbury, NY 11590-1743
Walter E. Landauer, President
PH: (516)952-3030
TF: (800)645-7234
FX: (516)952-3466
Founded: 1973. **Staff:** 150. **Activities:** Specializes in custom electronic and computer-based systems, hardware and software products, and engineering support services for complex weapons systems and computer-based military and commercial systems. Also offers custom systems support tactical system development, T&E, strategic communications and other special purpose applications. Products include electronic mail and office information systems, NTDS interfaces to commercial computers, switching systems, interfaces between HP computers and IDM database machines. Engineering support includes system engineering, system and equipment maintenance, training, software support, ILS, exercise planning and reconstruction for DoD. Industries served: communications, data processing and computer electronics, and government agencies.

PYRAMID SOLUTIONS INC.
100 W. Big Beaver Rd., Ste. 345
Troy, MI 48084
Daniel R. Kosmalski, CEO
PH: (248)524-3890
FX: (248)524-3899
Founded: 1990. **Staff:** 34. **Activities:** Firm provides computer and document management services, including imaging, to clients in the Detroit metropolitan area.

Q-M CONSULTING GROUP, INC.
141 Fifth Ave.
New York, NY 10010
Elizabeth Quinn, President
PH: (212)995-5287
FX: (212)995-5415
URL: www.qmgroup.com
Founded: 1981. **Staff:** 18. **Activities:** Focuses on software development in client/server environment, emphasizing Microsoft database development products, especially Visual BASIC and Access. Provides specific business automation services - from a thorough review of requirements to total support and training after installation. Provides expertise in microcomputers, office automation, and networking. Has developed sophisticated, easy-to-use systems for large and small businesses. Serves private and government organizations in United States.

QA TECHNOLOGIES, INC.
222 S. 72nd St., Ste. 301
Omaha, NE 68114
Ken Bass, Partner
PH: (402)391-9200
FX: (402)391-1175
E-mail: qat@qat.com
URL: www.qat.com
Founded: 1995. **Staff:** 15. **Activities:** Provides information systems consulting and software development and product services. Offers analysis, planning, implementation, and support of computer systems. Experienced in Client/server and Legacy Mainframe Systems.

QUADRANT CONSULTING
11811 N. Tatum, Ste. 3031
Phoenix, AZ 85028
Jeff Colon, Principal
PH: (602)953-7838
FX: (602)953-7839
Founded: 1994. **Staff:** 15. **Activities:** Firm is a business process reengineering specialist providing clients with expertise on how to

build and sustain successful solutions to strategic planning, organizational design, information technology, and human resource issues. Services include fully customized planning, design, and implementation of work processes. Clients include the healthcare and manufacturing industries, public utilities, and government agencies in the U.S.

QUANTEC AMERICA INC.
599 Lexington Ave., Ste. 2300
New York, NY 10022
Robert Spearpoint
PH: (212)571-2620
FX: (212)836-4873
Founded: 1980. **Staff:** 25. **Activities:** Firm provides investment technology and proprietary consulting services to fund managers and plan sponsors around the world. The firm's PC-based tools are used by both traditional and quantitative active managers to design portfolios and to manage portfolio risk, and are also used to run index funds. Systematic return forecasting models are also available which enable the user to construct and test different investment strategies, significantly reducing the time and cost involved in multi-factor model development. Industries served: investment management, including corporate plans, public plans, insurance companies, international money managers, and consulting actuaries.

QUANTITATIVE TECHNOLOGY CORP.
8625 SW Cascade Blvd.
Beaverton, OR 97005
Larry Sullivan, CEO
PH: (503)626-3081
FX: (503)641-6012
Founded: 1981. **Staff:** 50. **Activities:** Provides standard software, custom software and consultation on high performance computer architectures including array processors, vector processors and parallel computers. Specialties include application conversion, optimization, application development tools, programmer training, and device drivers. Industries served: petrochemical, oil and gas exploration, semiconductors, systems integrators, signal processing applications, and government agencies.

QUANTRA
13760 Noel Rd., Ste. 930
Dallas, TX 75240
James E. Melson, CEO
PH: (972)521-9600
FX: (972)774-1982
E-mail: Quantra@.com
Founded: 1984. **Staff:** 90. **Activities:** Firm specializes in real estate information management systems. Has created relational databases for loan management, asset management, appraisal review and tracking, real estate marketing, facilities management and investment yield analysis, and accounting software for property level accounting and consolidations of portfolio activity. Consultants also develop policies and procedures manuals for real estate accounting, loan management, asset management, appraisal review and tracking and property management. Sub-systems integration services include interfacing loan servicing systems, accounting systems and analysis software to the relational databases. Artists and word processing specialists produce marketing materials and procedures manuals with state-of-the-art publishing software and color copying equipment. Industries served: banks, thrifts, insurance, real estate advisors, corporations and governmental entities involved in large-scale real estate activities.

QUANTUM COMPUTER CONSULTANTS LTD.
21415 Civic Center Dr., Ste. 300
Southfield, MI 48076-3954
Joseph Salzman, President
PH: (248)353-7030
FX: (248)350-8393
E-mail: quantumcomputerconsultants@compuserve.com
URL: www.qccltd.com
Founded: 1989. **Staff:** 90. **Activities:** Firm has experience in contract programming, contract/hire, outsourcing, project management, mainframes, midranges, and PCs.

QUANTUM RESEARCH CORP.
7315 Wisconsin Ave., Ste. 400w
Bethesda, MD 20814
George J. Nozicka, President
PH: (301)657-3070
FX: (301)657-3862
E-mail: dabraham@qrc.com
Founded: 1982. **Staff:** 85. **Activities:** Computer technology firm specializing in software development, for analytical systems, analytical support services, survey research and data collection services; also World Wide Web services including development of custom Web pages, database search capabilities, links of Web pages to client/server databases; other capabilities are in the area of feasibility studies, foreign trade zone applications, and expert testimony. Industries served: federal and state governments, electric and gas utilities, pharmaceutical, steel, automotive, railroads, trucking, and water transport.

RADEX, INC.
3 Preston Ct.
Bedford, MA 01730
K.H. Bhavnani, President
PH: (781)275-6767
FX: (781)275-3303
E-mail: bhavnani@ziggy.radex.plh.as.net
Founded: 1976. **Staff:** 20. **Activities:** Provides software development and other research and development support for the aerospace industry. Serves government agencies also.

RAMCO CONSULTING SERVICES, INC.
8619 29th St., Ct. E.
Edgewood, WA 98371
PH: (253)841-8998
TF: (800)821-1359
FX: (253)848-3166
E-mail: ramco@-training.com
URL: www.ramco-training.com
Founded: 1983. **Staff:** 35. **Activities:** Software training firm offers one-on-one consulting, public class training, as well as group training. Classes are available at client's site or at training centers. Develops and markets courseware for PC applications and the Internet.

RAYMOND, CHABOT, MARTIN, PARE, & CIE
Tour De La Banque Nationale
Rm. 600
Montreal, Canada H3B 4L8
Serge Saucier, President/CEO
PH: (514)878-2691
FX: (514)878-2127
Founded: 1948. **Staff:** 160. **Activities:** Management consultants offering a wide range of services: management information systems and management process redesign; data processing study and implementation of data processing systems, computer communications and office automation, and accounting software for microcomputers; human resources organization development and compensation, advice on employee relations, psychological testing, executive search, outplacement and coaching; financing - business valuation, mergers, and acquisitions, corporate financing, forensic accounting; organization productivity improvement, training, total quality implementation; real estate - appraisals, financing, brokerage; strategic planning; and marketing - socioeconomic analyses and marketing plans. Services for small and medium-sized businesses include export assistance and international financing, setting up boards of directors, public financing, and corporate planning. Consulting assignments are undertaken at the local, national and international level, benefiting from wide network of agents, contacts, offices and affiliates in the developed world.

THE RAYMOND CORP.
South Canal St.
PO Box 130
Greene, NY 13778
James J. Maluaso, CEO and President
PH: (607)656-2311
TF: (800)235-7200
FX: (607)656-9005
Founded: 1922. **Staff:** 1700. Activities: Offers services to U.S. manufacturers in the areas of facilities planning, shelf space management, equipment cost analysis software, and equipment leasing.

RCG INFORMATION TECHNOLOGY
2900 N. Loop W, Ste. 1300
Houston, TX 77092
David R. Cassell
PH: (713)548-1200
TF: (800)877-5383
FX: (713)548-1400
Founded: 1982. **Staff:** 1200. Activities: Offers technical services to organizations. Leads in applications development and support, database design, case development, AS/400 implementation/support and mainframe/micro application programming.

REAL
600 Hunter Dr., Ste. 100
Oak Brook, IL 60523
Ken Baker
PH: (630)571-6600
FX: (630)571-6613
Founded: 1969. **Staff:** 95. Activities: Computer software consultants.

REED TECHNOLOGY & INFORMATION SERVICES
1 Progress Dr.
Horsham, PA 19044
Mark Beyland, President
PH: (215)641-6000
TF: (800)872-2828
FX: (215)382-5082
URL: www.ReedTech.com
Founded: 1965. **Staff:** 1000. Activities: Provides consulting services to the communications industry specializing in the printing/ publishing/telephone fields: system consultation, hardware and software configurations and support directed toward electronic composition production, administrative and financial systems, and directory assistance systems, all of which are derived from proper utilization of a "Universal Data Base System."

REGIONAL ECONOMIC RESEARCH, INC.
11236 El Camino Real, Ste. A
San Diego, CA 92130-2650
Frederick D. Sebold, President
PH: (619)481-0081
TF: (800)755-9585
FX: (619)481-7550
E-mail: info@rer.com
URL: www.rer.com
Founded: 1979. **Staff:** 30. Activities: RER offers expertise in end-use data development, analysis and forecasting; energy analysis software; DSM potential analysis; DSM program design and evaluation; resource bidding support, competitive analysis,; forecasting non-utility supplies; and environmental externalities. Industries served: include utilities, regulatory agencies, private industry and government agencies throughout the U.S. and Canada.

THE REGISTRY, INC.
11235 Davenport St., Ste. 109
Omaha, NE 68154
Don Peterson, President
PH: (402)333-8060
FX: (402)697-5621
E-mail: scrcisar@mcimail.com
URL: www.srock.com

Staff: 325. Activities: . Services include information technology consulting, architectural review and design, training software planning, and methodology consulting. Helps clients plan, design and execute business applications using Web-based technology. Provides expertise to help clients create graphical user interfaces.

RELIANCE SYSTEMS, INC.
40 Washington St.
Wellesley, MA 02181-1802
John B. Hepburn, III, President, Treasurer
PH: (617)237-3002
FX: (617)237-0740
Founded: 1984. **Staff:** 30. Activities: Firm offers computer programming and data processing expertise to commercial accounts.

RELIANT TECH, INC.
5 Warrenton Ln.
Colts Neck, NJ 07722
Subhash Kothari
PH: (908)946-2303
FX: (908)946-1240
Founded: 1985. **Staff:** 20. Activities: Computer technology firm offering expertise in UNIX, data communications, databases, OLTP systems, LAN networks, and network management. Provides UNIX, NT, DB, Networking and SAP consultants.

RESEARCH & DATA SYSTEMS CORP.
7833 Walker Dr., Ste. 550
Greenbelt, MD 20770
K.S. Vasan, President
PH: (301)982-3700
FX: (301)982-3749
E-mail: mailbag@rdchp1.rdsc.com
Founded: 1978. **Staff:** 120. Activities: A professional service corporation specializing in scientific and engineering data analysis. Extensive capabilities in the following areas: atmospheric sciences and remote sensing, geophysical sciences and satellite technology, telecommunications, and environmental technology and information systems. Active with both government agencies and private industry.

RESEARCH & MANAGEMENT TECHNICIANS, INC.
955 A Russell Ave.
Gaithersburg, MD 20879
John A. Belding, President
PH: (301)840-9660
FX: (301)670-6860
Founded: 1982. **Staff:** 33. Activities: Provides computer and engineering services and product consultation expertise particularly in commercial and custom software engineering. Also specializes in slide and graphics presentations engineering. Conducts extensive training for hardware and software. Industries served: armed forces, space planning and architectural, mechanical and engineering publications industry, and government agencies.

RESOURCE INFORMATION MANAGEMENT SYSTEMS, INC.
500 Technology Dr.
PO Box 3094
Naperville, IL 60566-7094
Judy Pearson, Director of Human Resources
PH: (630)369-5300
FX: (630)369-5168
E-mail: marketing@rims.com
URL: www.rims.com
Founded: 1981. **Staff:** 250. Activities: RIMS's QicClaim/2 Health and Managed Care Administration software applies advanced technology to claims adjudication and managed care processing, accommodating indemnity to point-of-service plans, risk-based capitated payment and package pricing programs. RIMS also provides health information products to transform data into valuable information.

RESPONSE MANAGEMENT TECHNOLOGIES, INC.
2550 9th St., Ste. 103
Berkeley, CA 94710
Mal Warick, Chairman
PH: (510)843-8180
FX: (510)843-8020
Founded: 1987. **Staff:** 12. Activities: Offers a wide range of donor management services, including gift processing, donor acknowledgment, list maintenance, and data processing. Industries served: non-profit fundraisers.

THE REVERE GROUP
1751 Lake Cook Road, Ste. 600
Deerfield, IL 60015
Michael Parks, CEO
PH: (847)790-9800
FX: (847)790-2100
URL: www.reveregroup.com
Founded: 1991. **Staff:** 375. Activities: System integrators and information technology consultants.

RMP CONSULTING PARTNERS LLC
421 W. Lawson Rd., #57
Dallas, TX 75253
Robert M. Pritchett, President
PH: (972)557-6583
FX: (972)557-6583
E-mail: rmpcp@pobox.com
URL: pobox.com/~rmpcp
Founded: 1987. **Staff:** 12. Activities: Custom software development, system analysis and design, conversions.

ROBOCOM SYSTEMS INTERNATIONAL
511 Ocean Ave.
Massapequa, NY 11758
Irwin Balaban, President
PH: (516)795-5100
TF: (800)795-5100
FX: (516)795-6933
E-mail: info@robocom.com
URL: www.robocom.com
Founded: 1982. **Staff:** 65. Activities: Systems development engineering firm specializing in the design and development of factory and warehouse automation projects. Serves a wide variety of industries and government facilities. Offers services ranging from engineering studies to complete turnkey projects. Projects usually involve automated material handling equipment.

THE ROOT GROUP, INC.
4700 Walnut St., Ste. 110
Boulder, CO 80303
William Pachoud, President
PH: (303)447-8093
FX: (303)447-0197
URL: www.rootgroup.com
Founded: 1989. **Staff:** 12. Activities: Total computer networking services include on-site diagnostics, application environment rationalization, the use of network management tools, and training system administrators to work in the UNIX environment. Especially strong in Ethernet networks. Industries served: all.

ROSENTHAL ENGINEERING PC. DIOG-NOSTIC
    UTILITIES
PO Box 1650
San Luis Obispo, CA 93406-1650
Doren Rosenthal
PH: (805)541-0910
URL: slonet.org/~doren/
Founded: 1978. **Staff:** 15. Activities: Provides technical consulting electronic engineering throughout California in analog, digital and microprocessor applications from prototype development through production and test. Strong experience in software, hardware and system design. In-house development systems with full support of most microprocessors. Facilities include well equipped office and

shop with test equipment, computer-aided drafting and printed circuit board artwork design system, technical library and complete prototyping facilities, software/firmware - assembly through high level languages.

RTMS, INC.
N16 W23250 Stone Ridge Dr.
Waukesha, WI 53188
Timothy J. Keane, President & CEO
PH: (414)650-8228
FX: (414)650-8275
E-mail: info@rtms.com
URL: www.rtms.com
Founded: 1989. **Staff:** 55. Activities: The firm works with retailers and catalogers, providing them with the systems and consulting services necessary to implement database driven marketing programs that are based on the actual purchase behavior of their customers in their stores.

RUHL & ASSOCIATES - FORENSIC, INC.
1906 Fox Dr.
Champaign, IL 61820
Roland L. Ruhl, President
PH: (217)355-7800
TF: (800)355-7800
FX: (217)355-7900
E-mail: ruhl@net66.com
Founded: 1977. **Staff:** 32. Activities: Firm of multidisciplined engineering consultants with several specialty areas. Forensic engineering services include: accident and heavy vehicle investigation and reconstruction, vehicle dynamics, product liability, machine safety, and biomedical and biomechanical testifying. Clients are attorneys and insurance companies. Second area of expertise is engineering systems support for industry. Specialists on staff for OSHA, fire, electrical, biomechanical. Performs structural analysis and finite element analysis. Designs custom real-time microcomputer programs for the controls industry.

THE RUST CONSULTING GROUP, INC.
205 Van Buren St., Ste. 180
Herndon, VA 20170-5336
Ronald A. Rust, Chairman
PH: (703)437-4200
TF: (800)826-3035
FX: (703)689-4965
Founded: 1976. **Staff:** 145. Activities: Consultants in the area of litigation support for law firms, corporate legal departments and governmental units. The firm has direct experience (over 500 cases) with many database management and retrieval systems used for litigation projects. The firm has built full-text databases, fielded databases, imaged databases and applications containing all three. To help attorneys develop the full potential of their systems, the firm offers decision-making assistance in the following areas: feasibility studies, computer software and hardware analysis, vendor analysis review, coding and management of documents and system design.

RYAN MCFARLAND, A DIVISION OF LIANT
8911 Capital of Texas Hwy. N
Austin, TX 78759
John Hatcher, General Manager
PH: (512)343-1010
TF: (800)762-6265
FX: (512)343-9487
E-mail: info@liant.com
URL: www.liant.com
Founded: 1970. **Staff:** 100. Activities: Data processing consultants who design systems software including language processors, assemblers, operating systems, interactive timesharing systems, and complete software development factories for computer manufacturers and large end-users. Also develops and markets proprietary portable systems software packages for microsystems. Serves private industries as well as government agencies.

　　　　　　　　　　　　　　　　　D&B/Gale Industry Handbook

RYDER/ATE, INC.
705 Central Ave., Ste. 500
Cincinnati, OH 45202
James Davis, Mgr., Technical Svcs./Bus. Development
PH: (513)241-2200
FX: (513)381-0149
URL: www.ryder.com
Founded: 1969. **Staff:** 2500. Activities: Offers management consulting in every aspect of transportation. Services offered include: advisory services; transit bus, rail, paratransit and school bus management consulting; bus quality assurance inspections; and maintenance and transportation productivity analyses.

S & S COMPUTER SERVICES, INC.
434 W. Downer
Aurora, IL 60506
David L. Sweeney, President
PH: (630)892-7222
FX: (630)892-7466
Founded: 1970. **Staff:** 40. Activities: Provides computer services to magazine publishers, book publishers, associations, direct mail users, and firms that sell products/services through the mail.

SACHS GROUP
1800 Sherman Ave., Ste. 609
Evanston, IL 60201-3790
Michael Sachs, Chairman
PH: (847)475-7526
TF: (800)366-7526
FX: (847)475-7830
E-mail: info@sachs.com
URL: www.sachs.com
Founded: 1984. **Staff:** 100. Activities: Develops computer software for the healthcare industry in the U.S.

KALMAN SAFFRAN ASSOCIATES, INC.
1841 Commonwealth Ave.
Newton, MA 02466
Kalman Saffran, President
PH: (617)527-2000
FX: (617)244-3879
E-mail: info@ksa1.com
URL: www.ksa1.com
Founded: 1978. **Staff:** 110. Activities: KSA rapidly develops state of the art products for leaders in data communications and telecommunications. KSA decreases time to market and reduces cost and risk. Technology available for licensing includes SONET, CompactPCI Hot Swap, MPEG-2, and ATM. KSA offers technical consulting in information systems, electronics engineering, software engineering, and mechanical engineering.

SAI SOFTWARE CONSULTANTS, INC.
2313 Timber Shadows, Ste. 200
Kingwood, TX 77339
TF: (800)929-1850
FX: (713)358-8953
URL: www.saisoft.com
Staff: 300. Activities: Software consulting for business and industry.

SAVILLE & HOLDSWORTH
575 Boylston St.
Boston, MA 02116
Chuck Boyle, CEO
PH: (617)236-1550
TF: (800)899-7451
FX: (617)236-2092
E-mail: Tim.Anderson@shlgroup.com
URL: www.shlusa.com
Founded: 1977. **Staff:** 600. Activities: A leading developer of assessment tools for human resource decision making. Products include personality questionnaires, ability tests, assessment center exercises and job analysis software. Consulting services are designed to develop assessment solutions and decision systems for the human resource areas of selection, development and compensation

for all levels of an organization. Philosophy is to train human resource professionals in the use of techniques, tools and software so that an internal expertise is developed and reliance on consulting services is reduced. Industries served: all.

SCANTRON-SERVICE GROUP
2020 S. 156th Cir.
Omaha, NE 68130
David E. Conway, Executive Vice President
PH: (402)697-3000
FX: (402)697-3350
E-mail: palewis@scantrom.com
URL: www.scantron.com
Founded: 1981. **Staff:** 315. Activities: A computer maintenance and installation services organization . Services include maintaining data management system, custom maintenance agreements, and network implementation services. Offers specialized service options for depot customers, national and major accounts, educational institutions, state and local government agencies, the federal government, commercial businesses and resellers of Scantron products.

SCHICK & AFFILIATES, INC.
320 E. 45th, Ste. 100
Indianapolis, IN 46205-1752
Curt M. Huff, VP
PH: (202)338-1048
FX: (317)283-2262
Founded: 1984. **Staff:** 13. Activities: Firm provides general management consulting services to the healthcare industry. Areas of specialized knowledge include systems for quantification of nursing care requirements in a variety of settings. Microcomputer based software supports results of projects.

SCIENCE APPLICATIONS INTERNATIONAL CORP.
10260 Campus Point Dr.
San Diego, CA 92121
J. Robert Beyster, CEO & Chairman of the Board
PH: (619)546-6000
FX: (619)535-7191
URL: www.saic.com
Founded: 1969. **Staff:** 13242. Activities: An employee-owned, diversified, high-technology, research and engineering company, focusing principally in the market areas of national security, space, energy, health, environment, transportation, and high-technology support and products for both government and industry. Principal business involves technology development and analysis, systems development and integration, technical support services, and manufactured and software products. SAIC applies its scientific expertise, together with computer and systems technology, to solve complex technical problems. Industries served: national security, space, energy, health, environment, transportation, and utilities.

SCIENTECH
PO Box 50736
Idaho Falls, ID 83405
Darrell G. Eisenhut, Pres.
PH: (208)529-1000
FX: (208)524-9282
Founded: 1960. **Staff:** 2500. Activities: Provides real-time computer systems for nuclear and fossil power plants, proprietary computer software for utility and industrial plant management and performance improvement applications, a number of computer programs for the nuclear industry, minicomputer hardware/software systems, and special electrical/electronic instrumentation and control systems and panels. Serves private industries and government agencies worldwide.

SCOTT SOFTWARE, CONTRACT CONSULTANT
10511 Decatur Cir.
Bloomington, MN 55438
James S. Scott, President/CEO

PH: (612)943-1555
FX: (612)943-1555
E-mail: jscott@infogoal.com
URL: www.infogoal.com
Founded: 1980. Staff: 25. Activities: Computer consultants providing software selection and application advice, feasibility studies, management assistance, and hardware evaluation. Serves all enterprises.

SEARCH TECHNOLOGY INC.
4898 S. Old Peachtree Rd., Ste. 200
Norcross, GA 30071-4707
Ruston M. Hunt, President
PH: (770)441-1457
FX: (770)263-0802
Founded: 1980. Staff: 20. Activities: Specialists in the design and evaluation of human-machine systems with emphasis on the interfaces between human users and hardware/software. Ensures that system productivity goals are met by considering user capabilities and limitations in the design process. Clients include aircraft manufacturers, electronics manufacturers, package delivery companies, government agencies, and other industries where human operators of equipment must be accommodated in the design of new equipment or the evaluation of existing systems. Also provides expert witness services.

S.E.I., INC.
De Diego 472 OF. A-2
San Juan, PR 00923
Fernando B. Muniz, President
PH: (809)751-1045
FX: (809)751-7811
E-mail: 71102.2105@compuserve.com
Staff: 12. Activities: Firm's services focus on integrating human systems with computers hardware and software (systems engineering). Consultants advise, exercise and implement methodology on aspects that are critical to information systems as: strategic planning, information systems administration, project management, data management, translate technical information to upper management language, bilingual Spanish-English (speaking, writing, reading), and information quality procedures. Experienced on work flow analysis; task flow analysis; computerized applications analysis, design and programming; imaging systems integration; and voice response systems integration. Industries served: telecommunications and telephony, banking, utilities, universities, and government agencies.

SEI INFORMATION TECHNOLOGY
212 E. Ohio St., 2nd Fl.
Chicago, IL 60611-3203
Fidelis N. Umeh, President
PH: (312)440-8300
FX: (312)440-8373
URL: www.sei_it.com
Founded: 1969. Staff: 300. Activities: Performs analysis, design, development, and enhancement of information intensive systems with emphasis on online systems, data base systems, communications networks, microprocessor-based product development, industrial automation, office automation, financial systems, fulfillment systems, system and network configuration, training, document preparation, and systems integration. Also provides feasibility studies, information system planning studies, and market analyses for computer-based products. Primary client base is large (Fortune 500) corporations, financial and service institutions, and local and federal government agencies.

SELECTEC CORP.
22000 Springbrook Ave., Ste. 106
Farmington Hills, MI 48336-4375
PH: (248)477-3322
FX: (248)477-3232
Founded: 1994. Staff: 50. Activities: Firm specializes in data processing, consulting, and direct placement.

SEMIOTICA CORP.
25935 Detroit Rd., Ste. 241
Westlake, OH 44145-2426
John H. Whitehouse, Jr., Ph.D, C.C.P., President
PH: (216)356-8738
FX: (216)835-9201
E-mail: consultx@ix.netcom.com
URL: www.webcom.com/~semiotic
Founded: 1991. Staff: 20. Activities: Consultant and value-added reseller. Firm offers consulting, installation, configuration, customization, integration, programming, and training. Industries served: focus and heaviest experience are in wholesale, medical/dental, manufacturing, and small- to mid-size firms.

SES, INC.
4301 Westbank Dr., Bldg. A
Austin, TX 78746-6546
Charles L. Rees, President
PH: (512)328-5544
TF: (800)759-6333
FX: (512)327-6646
E-mail: info@sec.com
URL: www.ses.com/
Founded: 1989. Staff: 85. Activities: A technical software development consulting firm offering on-site seminars and demonstrations, on-site product evaluations, training classes, custom programming, system design, system migration, technical support, and turn-key applications.

SES STAFFING SOLUTIONS
104 Church Ln., Ste. 100
Pikesville, MD 21208-3734
Ronnie E. Silverstein, President
PH: (410)486-4330
Founded: 1986. Staff: 34. Activities: Temporary placement firm specializing in the light industrial, technical, and clerical fields. Industries served: light industrial and technical, government agencies, manufacturing and production, distribution, transportation, food service, and administrative business sector.

SHERPA CORP.
1325 McCandless Dr.
Milpitas, CA 95035
John C. Moore, President/CEO
PH: (408)941-4600
TF: (800)736-9778
FX: (408)941-4622
URL: www.sherpa.com
Founded: 1985. Staff: 220. Activities: Provides enterprise software solutions (PDM - product data management) for concurrent engineering to Fortune 500 and 1000 manufacturing and engineering companies worldwide.

SIGNATRON TECHNOLOGY CORP.
29 Domino Dr.
Concord, MA 01742-2845
Edward H. Getchell, CEO
PH: (978)371-0550
FX: (978)371-7414
E-mail: sig@world.std.com
URL: www.signatron.com
Founded: 1962. Staff: 18. Activities: Offers consulting and hardware for communication systems, specializing in TROPO, HF/VH digital data transmission. Activities include system evaluation, prototype development, performance prediction, error rate analysis, and cost effectiveness tradeoffs.

THE SIMS CONSULTING GROUP, INC.
111 N. Broad St.
PO Box 968
Lancaster, OH 43130-0968
Edward J. Phillips, President

PH: (740)654-1091
TF: (800)797-4670
FX: (740)654-2323
E-mail: scg@simsconsult.com
URL: www.simsconsult.com
Founded: 1958. **Staff:** 38. Activities: Consultants in industrial engineering and management of manufacturing processes, distribution services, and logistics. Provides counsel on physical distribution management, manufacturing plant design, material handling and storage systems, warehouse design, manufacturing engineering, facilities layout and design, facilities diversification and development, plant and systems evaluation, automation and information systems, systems integration, custom software development, industrial architecture and retrofitting, strategic planning, and growth strategy. Serves private industries as well as government agencies.

SMART COMMUNICATIONS, INC.
885 Third Ave., 29th Fl.
PO Box 963, FDR Sta.
New York, NY 10022
John M. Smart, President
PH: (212)486-1894
FX: (212)826-9775
E-mail: info@smartny.com
URL: www.smartny.com
Founded: 1976. **Staff:** 30. Activities: Develops artificial intelligence software for electronic publishing and information networks in AECMA Simplified, English, French, Spanish, Greek, Italian, Japanese, Portuguese, Mandarin Chinese, and other controlled languages. Specializes in computer-assisted language translation software and desktop publishing.

SMITH, BUCKLIN & ASSOCIATES
401 N. Michigan Ave.
Chicago, IL 60611-4267
PH: (312)644-6610
FX: (312)321-6869
E-mail: Chicago@sba.com
URL: www.sba.com
Founded: 1949. **Staff:** 700. Activities: A full-service association management firm with services in the areas of accounting and financial management, administrative services, conferences and meeting management, conference evaluations and member surveys, general consulting, executive management, government affairs, graphic design, industry statistical research, information services, marketing and public relations, print services, registration and travel, trade show management, and web design and management.

SMITH-MCCANN COMPUTER RESOURCE
7502 Holmes Island Rd. SE
Olympia, WA 98503-4027
Susette McCann, President
PH: (360)923-9544
FX: (360)923-9544
Founded: 1991. **Staff:** 13. Activities: Offers computer application development consulting that includes project management, systems analysis, technical design, and programming support for large and medium sized on-line DBMS projects. Serves private industries as well as government agencies.

THE SOFTA GROUP, INC.
707 Skokie Blvd., 7th Fl.
Northbrook, IL 60062
Joseph Vito, Director of Human Resources
PH: (847)291-4000
FX: (847)291-4022
Founded: 1982. **Staff:** 83. Activities: Firm is a provider of network-based, personal computer software solutions for commercial, residential, and retail property management.

SOFTEACH
85 Wells Ave.
Newton, MA 02459-3215
Elizabeth W. Brown, President

PH: (617)244-0037
TF: (800)815-5424
FX: (617)332-0533
E-mail: sales@softeachusa.com
URL: www.softeachusa.com
Founded: 1984. **Staff:** 22. Activities: Computer software consultant specializing in Internet training, software training/DOS, Windows, and Mac applications. Industries served: legal, medical, retail, distributors, manufacturers, nonprofits and others. Woman owned firm.

SOFTECH, INC.
3260 Eagle Park Dr. NE
Grand Rapids, MI 49505-4569
Douglas T. Ross, Chairman
PH: (616)890-6900
FX: (616)890-6055
Founded: 1969. **Staff:** 550. Activities: Strives to increase the effectiveness of computers by the use of software engineering principles and techniques; to introduce innovative systems analysis methods; to extend the use of automated techniques in the production of computer languages and programs; to extend the availability of software factory techniques for the production of application programs for minicomputers; to increase the industry's ability to transfer programs easily from one make of computer to another.

SOFTEX, INC.
PO Box 7892
Lancaster, PA 17604
James R. Brooks
PH: (717)397-8875
TF: (800)798-7102
FX: (717)397-2368
E-mail: softex@redrose.net
Founded: 1983. **Staff:** 22. Activities: Designs, develops and publishes standard and custom computer software for sensory evaluation, market research and manufacturing applications, including quality control. Onsite training services for the Sensorex(r) Automated Data Entry System.

SOFTMED SYSTEMS, INC.
6610 Rockledge Dr., Ste. 500
Bethesda, MD 20817
Don Segal, President
PH: (301)897-3400
FX: (301)897-3409
Founded: 1983. **Staff:** 100. Activities: Software company offers various areas of computer expertise particularly with regard to document management and medical record field. Serves healthcare industry.

SOFTOUCH SOFTWARE INC., SUBSIDIARY OF
    MEDICODE, INC.
5225 Wiley Post Way
Salt Lake City, UT 84116-2889
Ken Lame, President
PH: (801)536-1000
FX: (801)536-1009
URL: www.medicode.com
Founded: 1984. **Staff:** 14. Activities: Computer software consultants.

SOFTWARE DEVELOPMENT AND MAINTENANCE,
    INTERNATIONAL
134 Spring Ave.
PO Box 579
Duncan, NC 27526-0579
P. Eugene Truelove, CEO
PH: (919)552-1100
FX: (919)552-6116
URL: www.sdm-international.com
Founded: 1980. **Staff:** 50. Activities: Provides comprehensive consulting services to assist in the development, systems integration, and customization of software solutions for electronic funds transfer (EFT), point-of-sale (POS), and electronic data interchange (EDI).

Offers product lines that serve as foundations for developing software solutions to meet each customer's unique requirements. Has extensive experience building systems that manage high-speed transmission and routing of large volumes of messages and transactions.

SOFTWARE ENGINEERING SOLUTIONS, INC.
914 N. Rengstorff Ave.
Mountain View, CA 94043
David G. Stroebe, Dir. of Marketing
PH: (415)969-0141
TF: (800)737-0141
FX: (415)969-0177
E-mail: resume@sesinc.com
Founded: 1982. **Staff:** 38. Activities: Specialize in fixed price projects, consulting, and contract programmers related to Sun Microsystems, Client/Server, and Systems Integration Services. Industries served: computer, telecommunications, utilities, petroleum and chemical, biotechnology, manufacturing, banking, and financial.

SOFTWARE PROFESSIONALS INC.
1200 Walnut Hill Ln., Ste. 1300
Irving, TX 75038
Ms. Reena Batra
PH: (972)518-0198
FX: (972)518-0334
E-mail: spi@ix.netcom.com
URL: www.software-professionals.com
Founded: 1992. **Staff:** 35. Activities: A Dallas based consulting company that provides contract programming services nationwide. Provides full life cycle system engineering support and management to companies and government agencies. Experienced in complex information engineering techniques, structured methodologies, case tools, graphical user interfaces, fourth generation languages, and telecommunications. Offers training services and facility management services.

SOFTWARE SEARCH
2163 Northlake Pkwy., Ste. 100
Tucker, GA 30084
Paul Nymark, President
PH: (770)934-5138
FX: (770)939-6410
E-mail: jobs@softwaresearch.com
Founded: 1966. **Staff:** 15. Activities: Data processing consulting firm.

SOFTWARE SETT CORP.
233 Oak Meadow Dr.
Los Gatos, CA 95032
Claudia Dencker, President
PH: (408)395-9376
FX: (408)354-6477
E-mail: cdencker@softsett.com
URL: www.softsett.com
Founded: 1987. **Staff:** 20. Activities: Systems evaluation, testing and training. Industries served: Computer hardware manufacturers, vertical market software publishers, embedded systems, and medical device manufacturers.

SOFTWARE SYNERGY INC.
2416 Hermosa Ave.
Hermosa Beach, CA 90254
Roy A. Judd, President
PH: (310)379-3914
Founded: 1983. **Staff:** 140. Activities: Data processing consultants specializing in conversions: hardware and software, including operating systems, languages, and databases. Offers the following: database selection, installation and support. Particular expertise in security: physical and communications. Serves private industries as well as government agencies.

SOFTWRITE COMPUTER SYSTEMS, INC.
Welsh Commons
1364 Welsh Rd.
North Wales, PA 19454
Mark S. Talaba, CEO
PH: (215)540-8048
TF: (800)538-9081
FX: (215)542-8898
E-mail: mailbox@softwrite.com
URL: www.softwrite.com
Founded: 1990. **Staff:** 24. Activities: An information technology consulting firm providing custom e-business solutions. Our mission is to assist clients in gaining a competitive edge, reducing operating costs, improving customer satisfaction and/or improving overall operations through the use of strategic technologies.

SOLUTECH CONSULTING SERVICES, INC.
951 Forest Ln.
PO Box 1039
Alamo, CA 94507
Christa Schenk, President
PH: (510)831-3405
FX: (510)831-3406
E-mail: hq@solutech.com
URL: www.solutech.com
Founded: 1994. **Staff:** 20. Activities: Provides software consulting services for customers using relational database products, such as Oracle and Sybase.

SOLUTION CONSULTANTS, INC.
20863 Stevens Creek Blvd., Ste. 330
Cupertino, CA 95014-2187
Jess A. Pawlak, President
PH: (408)446-5118
FX: (408)973-1046
Founded: 1984. **Staff:** 30. Activities: A systems consulting and project development company specializing in the development, implementation, testing and certification, and support of information systems, networks, and software. Services cover all phases of project and program management - analysis, development, implementation, documentation, training, and support. Industries served: biotechnology, telecommunications, computers, real estate and financial services.

SOLUTION TECHNOLOGIES, INC.
702 Lisburn Rd.
Camp Hill, PA 17011-7423
Larry A. Putt, President
PH: (717)763-5611
FX: (717)763-4387
E-mail: sti@sti.net
URL: www.sti.net
Founded: 1987. **Staff:** 250. Activities: Computer and data processing consulting firm specializing in development and support of client application systems.

SOLVERIS, INC.
19119 N. Creek Pky., Ste. 105
Bothell, WA 98011-8023
Dave Senestraro, President
PH: (425)485-4357
TF: (800)999-4829
FX: (425)481-7633
E-mail: info@solveris.com
URL: www.solveris.com
Founded: 1986. **Staff:** 15. Activities: Offers expertise in information systems design and implementation. VAX/VMS network and systems specialists. Can assist companies with all facets of information systems management. Industries served: manufacturing, telecommunications, service, banking, education, ecumenical, and government.

SOUTHERN COMPUTER SYSTEMS
2732 7th Ave. S
Birmingham, AL 35233
Stephen Freeman, President
PH: (205)251-2985
TF: (800)533-6879
FX: (205)322-4851
URL: www.scsinc.com
Founded: 1979. **Staff:** 40. Activities: Provides consulting services in distributed processing, cooperative processing, image-based data entry, large scale LAN design and deployment, downsizing systems analysis, and systems integration. For systems integration, firm provides clients with a total solution that includes every aspect of a distributed system from beginning to end: initial design and analysis, installation, configuration, conversion, training, application design and development, integration, and on-going support. Recent experience in the development of turnkey systems for high-volume production image-assisted data input applications. Industries served: all. international.

SPECTRUM TECHNOLOGIES UTILITY SERVICES (USA) INC.
133 Wall St.
Schenectady, NY 12305
Brij M. Bhartey, President
PH: (518)382-0056
FX: (518)382-0283
E-mail: spectrum@global1.net
URL: www.ypweblink.com/company/spectrum.shtml
Founded: 1986. **Staff:** 25. Activities: Nuclear safety consultants offering expertise in qualification programs, plant life extension programs for nuclear/fossil plants, spare parts, power system coordination studies, quality assurance programs, computer systems, class IE qualified computer systems, verification validation of software and expert testimony. Industries served: nuclear plants in USA, Taiwan, Mexico; fossil plants in U.S. and India.

SPIKE TECHNOLOGIES, INC.
500 E. Calaveras Blvd., Ste. 333
Milpitas, CA 95035
Nikhil Modi, Pres.
PH: (408)945-0354
FX: (408)945-0293
E-mail: webmaster@spiketech.com
URL: www.spiketech.com/spike
Founded: 1994. **Staff:** 31. Activities: Consulting firm offers the following services: EDA Services, including UNIX programming; X windows; GUI; development of EDA tool kits, utilities, validation, evaluations, and porting; and development of GUI tool kits. Circuit Design, including CMOS cell development and verification; spice runs; and library development. ASIC Services, including ASIC/FPGA design and verification; re-targeting; test insertion and test vector generation; die-size reduction; system validation; and megafunctions and megacell development. HDL Modeling, including the development of Verilog Models; VHDL models; and C models. Industries served: semiconductor companies; CAD companies; computer systems companies.

SPO AMERICA INC.
650 Worcester Rd.
Framingham, MA 01701
Michael Adolphs, President & CEO
PH: (508)875-9900
TF: (800)SPO-4454
FX: (508)875-5177
E-mail: web@spo-us.com
URL: www.spo-us.com/
Founded: 1993. **Staff:** 100. Activities: Consulting firm specializing in SAP implementation, implementation tools.

SPS INFORMATION TECHNOLOGY
187 Lyon St., Ste. 100
Ottawa, Canada K1R 7Y4
PH: (613)238-1700
FX: (613)238-6770
E-mail: ottawa@sps-it.com
URL: www.sps-it.com
Founded: 1969. **Staff:** 100. Activities: Offers computer hardware and software contract support services to all industries in Canada and worldwide.

SRI INTERNATIONAL
333 Ravenswood Ave.
Menlo Park, CA 94025
William P. Sommers, CEO
PH: (415)326-6200
FX: (415)326-5512
Founded: 1946. **Staff:** 2170. Activities: Performs basic and applied research and consulting under contract for clients in business, industry, and government, on a worldwide basis. Staff includes over 1,900 researchers and consultants in over 100 disciplines. Major disciplines include: Technology Management; Economic Policy Division; Executive Programs; Business Intelligence Center; Health and Social Policy Division; Process Industries Division; Manufacturing and Service Industries Division; Environmental Management; Life Sciences Division; Physical Sciences Division; Information, Telecommunications, and Automation Division; Advanced Development Division; Systems Development Division; System Technology Division; and Computing and Engineering Sciences Division.

STATISTICA, INC.
800 S. Frederick Ave., Ste. 204
Gaithersburg, MD 20877
Jerry Ashworth, President/CEO
PH: (301)926-9000
FX: (301)926-8819
URL: www.statistica.com
Founded: 1977. **Staff:** 325. Activities: A high-technology, research and development firm that offers a wide range of software engineering and systems integration services. Areas of expertise include Ada software engineering, digital image information systems, instructional systems development, computer-based training, facilities management, and database management systems. Serves private industries as well as government agencies.

STN COMPUTER SYSTEMS
5113 Leesburg Pike, Ste. 810
Falls Church, VA 22041
James Fleming, Treasurer
PH: (703)379-9700
TF: (800)321-1969
FX: (703)824-0699
E-mail: james@stn.com
URL: www.stn.com
Founded: 1981. **Staff:** 12. Activities: Computer systems consultants specializing in custom software for multi-user computers. All work based on the UNIX environment, with "C" language and database management system expertise on staff. Serves private industry and government agencies worldwide.

STOCKTON BATES
42 S. 15th St., Ste. 600
Philadelphia, PA 19102
James W. Smith
PH: (215)241-7500
FX: (215)567-3813
Founded: 1900. **Staff:** 65. Activities: Business consultants whose wide-ranging services include operational audits, mergers and acquisitions expertise, litigation support, and computer hardware and software consulting. Industries served: manufacturing, construction, services, banking, retail and wholesale, and government agencies.

STORY BUSINESS SYSTEMS, INC.
15007 Shore Acres Dr.
Cleveland, OH 44110-1239
Carlton V. Story, President

PH: (216)531-0126
TF: (800)STO-RYDP
FX: (216)786-7937
Founded: 1984. **Staff:** 12. **Activities:** Provides professional information systems development services for business, government and service organizations. These services include, but are not limited to providing or identifying project managers, systems analysts, designers, programmers, and/or documentors as an extension to client's in-house staff; solutions to specific business systems needs, including fully tested and documented software systems, based upon a proven system design methodology and experience; analysis of client firm's information requirements, resulting in systems definition and the preparation of an action plan; and consulting on equipment/software selection, performance evaluation, business systems planning, selected application and technical areas.

STRATEGIC STAFFING SOLUTIONS INC.
600 Woodbridge St., Ste. 1-B
Detroit, MI 48226-4302
Cynthia J. Pasky, President
PH: (313)393-2876
TF: (800)585-8326
FX: (313)858-8326
E-mail: s3detroit@strategicstaff.com
URL: www.strategicstaff.com
Founded: 1982. **Staff:** 220. **Activities:** Provides staffing for customized systems development, contract programming, customer specific training programs, and alternate staffing options. Industries served: banking, retail, healthcare, manufacturing, telecommunications, and automotive.

STRUCTURED LOGIC CO., INC.
330 7th Ave., 15th Fl.
New York, NY 10001-5010
Gene Lerner, President
PH: (212)947-7510
FX: (212)947-9338
Founded: 1981. **Staff:** 300. **Activities:** Computer consultants for commercial industries in the United States.

SUNDBERG, CARLSON AND ASSOCIATES
510 Mather Ave.
Ishpeming, MI 49849
Darryll L. Sundberg, P.E., President
PH: (906)486-3272
TF: (800)336-1109
FX: (906)486-5523
E-mail: profconsulting@sundcarl.com
URL: www.sundcarl.com
Founded: 1980. **Staff:** 115. **Activities:** Architectural/engineering consulting firm offering architectural, civil, structural, mechanical, electrical engineering, land surveying, planning, environmental, and computer services to municipalities, industrial, commercial, residential, and healthcare facilities.

SUNGARD DATA SYSTEMS, INC.
1285 Drummers Ln., Ste. 300
Wayne, PA 19087-1572
Bruce Battjer, President
PH: (610)341-8700
TF: (800)523-4970
FX: (610)341-8739
Staff: 50. **Activities:** Offers services in disaster recovery/business resumption planning for computer systems for all industries. Serves private industries as well as government agencies.

SYGENEX INC.
15446 Bel-Red Rd., Ste. 450
Redmond, WA 98052
Donna Roberts, CEO/President
PH: (425)881-5500
FX: (425)869-2837
E-mail: sygenex@ix.netcom.com
Founded: 1984. **Staff:** 15. **Activities:** Computer technology consult-

ing firm offering system concepts definition, systems engineering, systems design, and trade studies. Develops decision support software. Industries served: aerospace, military, and business.

SYNAXOS CORP.
145 Rosemary St., Ste. H
Needham Heights, MA 02194-3259
Leonard Heier
PH: (617)449-5837
FX: (617)449-1125
URL: www.synaxix.com
Staff: 30. **Activities:** Computer software consultants.

SYNECTICS CORP.
10400 Eaton Pl., Ste. 200
Fairfax, VA 22030
James W. Altman, Chairman/President
PH: (703)385-0190
FX: (703)385-1987
URL: www.syncorp.com
Founded: 1969. **Staff:** 145. **Activities:** Uses interdisciplinary capabilities in generating practical solutions to complex data programs. The solutions capitalize on the creative design of various forms of analytic aids. Technology developed by firm facilitates routine knowledge production and supports system research and design processes. Services to clients are provided at all stages of system life cycle and all knowledge processing. Major areas of R&D application include tactical intelligence sensor exploitation; C3I; cartographic systems; national and strategic intelligence; information representation and display; perceptive systems; and human performance. Particular effort has been devoted to the development and application of systems integration methods and tools.

SYSCOM CONSULTING INC.
Ste. 1000-1090 West Georgia St.
Vancouver, Canada V6E 3V7
John Roberts, President
PH: (604)684-5344
FX: (604)684-5322
E-mail: jroberts@sci.syscom.com
URL: www.sci-syscom.com/
Founded: 1989. **Staff:** 40. **Activities:** Provides computer consulting and technical support services, with emphasis on technical support services for PC hardware and software products, local and wide area networks, and data communications infrastructure; and application software development and support; data center operations and management; technology consulting and planning; and training and education.

SYSTEM MODELING CORP.
The Park Building
504 Beaver St.
Sewickley, PA 15143-1755
C. Dennis Pegden, President
PH: (412)741-3727
FX: (412)741-5635
E-mail: smcorp@sm.com
URL: www.sm.com
Founded: 1982. **Staff:** 50. **Activities:** Production Scheduling Specialists. Industries served: metals, automotive, manufacturing, pharmaceuticals, plastics, chemicals, electronics, textiles, and more.

SYSTEM SOLVERS, LTD.
30685 Barrington Ave., Ste. 100
Madison Heights, MI 48071-5133
Randy Merrifield, President
PH: (248)588-7400
TF: (888)TEAM-SSL
FX: (248)588-7170
E-mail: solvers@sslinfo.com
URL: www.sslinfo.com
Founded: 1986. **Staff:** 26. **Activities:** Offers information management services, including systems assessments/needs, application design and development, real-time database system implementation,

platform migration planning, EDI, bar coding, Internet database connectivity, materials handling, and ISO/QS9000 systems certification assistance. Industries served: manufacturing and distribution in the Midwestern U.S. and Canada.

SYSTEM TECHNOLOGY INSTITUTE, INC.
PO Box 6907
Malibu, CA 90264-6907
Michael B. Sanson, Director
PH: (310)457-0851
TF: (888)299-9071
FX: (310)457-0951
E-mail: STIclass@aol.com
URL: www.STItraining.com
Founded: 1984. **Staff:** 25. Activities: Offers consulting in development, management and assurance of software systems. Industries served: aerospace, utilities, chemical, and others, including government agencies, medical, telecommunications and business systems.

SYSTEMS CONSULTANTS, INC.
121 Hunter Ave., Ste. 100
St. Louis, MO 63124
John A. Sharp, Ph.D., CEO
PH: (314)863-0262
FX: (314)863-0264
URL: www.sci-gateway.com/
Founded: 1983. **Staff:** 90. Activities: Provides application software and services to the public sector. In depth knowledge of Budgetary (encumbrance) accounting, payroll/human resources, and property-based applications such as utilities, geographic database, property taxes, permits and inspections, etc.

SYSTEMS GROUP, INC.
50 S. Beretania St., Ste. C119B
Honolulu, HI 96813
Gordon S. Young, Vice President
PH: (808)526-1551
FX: (808)599-5098
URL: sgi-hi.com
Founded: 1972. **Staff:** 15. Activities: Specialists in data communications: network design installation and performance measurement; in telecommunications: network planning and voice data integration; and in fiber optic communications systems design and installation. Serves private industries as well as government agencies.

SYSTEMS RESEARCH AND APPLICATIONS CORP.
2000 15th St. N
Arlington, VA 22201
William K. Brehm, Chairman
PH: (703)558-4700
FX: (703)558-4723
Founded: 1978. **Staff:** 730. Activities: Information processing/ communications consultants active in strategic planning and requirements analysis, systems development, and systems integration with applications to computer, logistic, command and control, and telecommunications systems; defense analyses of weapon systems, operations, and personnel; resource management; and crisis management and national emergency programs. Applies expert system technology to build artificial intelligence systems that use a natural-language interface. Consultation services include computer-aided logistic support of earth-based systems, and top-level support to and evaluations of major exercises for the Joint Chiefs of Staff, the Army, and the Federal Emergency Management Agency. Services also are provided to the Air Force, the Navy, and other Department of Defense organizations, as well as civil federal government agencies and commercial firms.

SYSTEMS SERVICE ENTERPRISES INC.
795 Office Pkwy., Ste. 101
St. Louis, MO 63141
Susan S. Elliott, Chairman and CEO

PH: (314)997-4700
FX: (314)997-5426
E-mail: sales@sseinc.com
URL: www.sseinc.com
Founded: 1966. **Staff:** 131. Activities: Client/server networking, customs application development, strategic planning, Internet/ Intranet, CPB, custom courseware, multimedia development, year 2000, project management, technical writing and training, and IT staffing.

TA ENGINEERING CO., INC.
1150 Moraga Way
Moraga, CA 94556
T.A. Lu, President
PH: (510)376-8500
FX: (510)376-4977
URL: www.ta-eng.com
Founded: 1984. **Staff:** 15. Activities: Specializes in design of software interfacing with industrial digital controllers and program logic controllers.

TAJ TECHNOLOGIES INC.
1168 Northland Dr.
Mendota Heights, MN 55120
PH: (651)688-2801
FX: (651)688-8321
E-mail: webmaster@tajtech.com
URL: www.tajtech.com
Founded: 1987. **Staff:** 150. Activities: A minority owned software consulting firm. Provides services in software development, project management, systems integration, network implementation and support, and management consulting, Internet/Intranet development and e-commerce.

TAMAROFF ASSOCIATES INC.
106 S. Columbus St.
Alexandria, VA 22314-5000
Judith Ross
PH: (703)683-1422
FX: (703)683-0194
URL: www.propoint.com
Founded: 1983. **Staff:** 25. Activities: Consults in the computer field on software training and on-site training programs.

TASK FORCE INC.
636 Broadway, Ste. 1010
New York, NY 10012-2623
John Sullivan, President
PH: (212)777-4280
FX: (212)777-3879
Founded: 1988. **Staff:** 17. Activities: Task Force specialists work in consulting teams whose primary job is the application of technology to business problems. Provide unbiased evaluations of microcomputer programs and hardware platforms. Offers a wide variety of hardware and software solutions for clients, including: integrated word processing and document management system using Microsoft Word for Windows, Excel and Saros' Mezzanine on a Novel NetWare network for a financial publishing group; worldwide software migration plan from Lotus 1-2-3 to Microsoft Excel for a financial services organization; and client-server project management system using Microsoft Excel and the SQL Server database engine on a Novell Network for a worldwide management consulting group. Customized training is provided both onsite and at Task Force. In each case a senior instructor consults with the client to determine the specific goal of training and examines examples of the client's current and future work.

TATA CONSULTANCY SERVICES
3010 LBJ Fwy., Ste. 715
Dallas, TX 75234
F.C. Kohli

PH: (972)484-6465
FX: (972)484-0450
E-mail: rkdawar@gte.net
URL: www.tcs.com
Founded: 1968. **Staff:** 9600. Activities: Information processing specialists offer expertise in custom software, product development, case tools, conversions/migrations, quality assurance support, and facilities management and training. Industries served: finance, insurance, manufacturing, banking, distribution, and healthcare.

TEC-ED TECHNICAL COMMUNICATION AND GRAPHICS SERVICES, INC.
PO Box 1905
Ann Arbor, MI 48106
Stephanie Rosenbaum, President
PH: (313)995-1010
FX: (313)995-1025
E-mail: tec-ed.com
Founded: 1967. **Staff:** 11. Activities: Specializes in serving computer industry clients, especially software product developers and microprocessor-based product manufacturers with documentation, training, usability testing and user interfaces. Leader in CD-ROM documentation, networking products, task-based user manuals, and usability testing. Serves private industries as well as government agencies.

TECH HACKERS INC.
50 Broad St.
New York, NY 10004
Atul Jain, President
PH: (212)344-9500
FX: (212)344-9519
Founded: 1986. **Staff:** 25. Activities: Practice focuses on the design and implementation of information systems using state-of-the-art computer technologies. The firm has expertise in an array of technologies including software architecture, user interface paradigms and window systems, rule-based expert systems, object-oriented programming, distributed computing, and database design. Industries served: all, including government agencies.

TECHNICAL MANAGEMENT SYSTEMS, INC.
PO Box 50610
New Orleans, LA 70150
Earl N. Pressler, President
PH: (504)624-8288
FX: (504)624-8565
E-mail: techman@communique.net
Founded: 1987. **Staff:** 15. Activities: Offers computer systems integration specializing in local area networks and bar code systems. Provides expertise in production and inventory control systems design and procedures. Develops custom computer programming on PC based systems. Additionally offers PC production scheduling and project management. Industries served: shipbuilding, manufacturing, chemical and refining, textile, distribution, and government agencies.

TECHNICAL SUPPORT GROUP, INC.
35 East Wacker Dr., No. 2120
Chicago, IL 60601
Neal Rubin
PH: (312)704-5100
FX: (312)704-5101
E-mail: nrubin@tsgrp.com
Founded: 1982. **Staff:** 67. Activities: Project-oriented data processing consulting firm offering expertise with systems programming, application development in CICS, UNIX, ADABAS, client server environments, NATURAL, and local area networks.

TECHNOLOGY CONSULTING CORP.
Two Mid America Plaza, Ste. 110
Oakbrook Terrace, IL 60181
Karen A. Wilson, Branch Manager
PH: (630)368-1111
FX: (630)368-1120

Founded: 1979. **Staff:** 165. Activities: Offers full range of services in client/server, mainframe and mid-range computers, and networking. IBM Business Partner, Microsoft Solution Provider Partner. Also has expertise in GUPTA, Oracle, and Magic Affiliations.

TECHNOLOGY SOLUTIONS CO.
205 N. Michigan Ave., Ste. 1500
Chicago, IL 60601
William H. Waltrip, Chairman
PH: (312)228-4500
TF: (800)819-2250
FX: (312)228-4501
URL: www.TechSol.com
Founded: 1988. **Staff:** 1572. Activities: A systems integration and management consulting firm that brings technology and business sections together through the design, development, and implementation of complex computer systems that help Fortune 1000 clients achieve clearly defined business benefits. Well defined practice areas in financial services, call centers, managed healthcare, products and manufacturing, and packaged software implementation and training.

TECMARK ASSOCIATES INC.
PO Box 545
Port Washington, NY 11050
Donald P. Valentine
PH: (516)883-6336
E-mail: info@tecmark.com
URL: www.tecmark.com
Founded: 1968. **Staff:** 43. Activities: Serves only the electronics and computer industries through counseling corporate clients in the recruiting, selection, testing and evaluation of executives and scientific/engineering personnel. Functional spectrum includes upper management, sales, marketing, engineering, research manufacturing, production, and control. Industries served: high technology industry only. i.e. semiconductors, electronic design automation (EDA/CAE); automatic test equipment (ATE), data communications, production equipment for semiconductor and printed circuit process and manufacturing.

TECO GROUP INC.
5983 S. Transit Rd.
Lockport, NY 14094-6305
David McNulty, VP
PH: (716)433-2605
FX: (716)434-0541
Founded: 1984. **Staff:** 30. Activities: Training consultants specializing in the development of multimedia and web-based instruction for adult learners. focus on technical skills training—machine operation, maintenance and industrial safety.

TEKEDGE CORP.
333 W. El Camino Real, Ste. 270
Sunnyvale, CA 94087
Girish Gaitonde, President
PH: (408)732-2739
FX: (408)732-5701
Founded: 1989. **Staff:** 200. Activities: Provides turnkey software development, as well as on-site and off-site contract programming. Industries served: computer, telecommunications, commercial, and government agencies.

TELERIDESAGE LTD.
156 Front St. W, 5th Fl.
Toronto, Canada M5J 2L6
Josef Kates, Chairman
PH: (416)596-1940
FX: (416)595-5653
E-mail: info@teleride.on.ca
Founded: 1977. **Staff:** 60. Activities: Offers comprehensive computer information, communications and control systems consulting for the transit industry. Activities include computer scheduling, traffic timekeeping, operator bidding, payroll, vehicle maintenance, materials management, financial systems, management support tools,

computerized telephone information to the transit user, automatic vehicle location and communications systems, and related consulting and computer services.

TENERA
1500 Cherry St., Ste. C
Louisville, CO 80027
Michael D. Thomas, Chairman, CEO
PH: (303)664-9310
FX: (303)664-9309
E-mail: tenerallc@worldnet.att.net
URL: www.tenera-11c.com
Staff: 140. Activities: Provides management, specialty engineering, and technical support services to the commercial nuclear power industry and to DOE and DOE contractors. Includes strategic business planning; environmental, safety, health, and quality program development and implementation; business process analysis and reengineering; risk analysis and management; regulatory management and compliance; project and environmental engineering; and project management.

THOROUGHBRED SOFTWARE
19 Schoolhouse Rd.
Somerset, NJ 08875
Carmen Randazzo, President
PH: (732)560-1377
TF: (800)524-0430
FX: (732)560-1594
E-mail: tbred@tbred.com
URL: www.tbred.com
Founded: 1982. Staff: 120. Activities: Develops and internationally markets Thoroughbred systems and software product lines aimed at the small to medium business systems marketplace. All Thoroughbred software and system products are available through authorized Thoroughbred distributors and dealers based domestically and in 32 foreign countries.

THURIDION
269 Mt. Hermon Rd., Ste. 200
Scotts Valley, CA 95066-4029
Tonee Picard, Director of Marketing and Sales
PH: (408)439-9800
FX: (408)439-6963
E-mail: tonee@thuridion.com
URL: www.thuridion.com/
Founded: 1990. Staff: 50. Activities: Company specializes in Microsoft Windows development and provides web-centric groupware products and services.

TORREY PINES RESEARCH
6359 Paseo Del Lago
Carlsbad, CA 92009
William J. Hanson, President
PH: (760)929-4800
FX: (760)931-1671
URL: www.tpr.com
Founded: 1986. Staff: 55. Activities: Independent engineering and development group specializing in non-impact printing technology. Firm has the capability in house to design "laser" and other non-impact printers from scratch. Also maintains top-notch controller design and software development capability. Industries served: printer manufacturers and distributors.

TOTAL SOLUTIONS
22 Saw Mill River Rd.
Hawthorne, NY 10532
W.P. Hegan, Chairman
PH: (914)592-1060
FX: (914)592-3625
Founded: 1964. Staff: 18. Activities: Consulting specialists in the appraisal and sale of used IBM computers.

TOUCHSTONE RESEARCH LABORATORY, LTD.
The Millennium Centre
Triadelphia, WV 26059
Elizabeth Kraftician, Chief Executive Officer
PH: (304)547-5800
FX: (304)547-5764
E-mail: jkm@gold.trl.com
URL: www.trl.com
Founded: 1980. Staff: 26. Activities: A leading industrial problem-solving and applied research company. The firm operates in the fields of materials science, metallurgy, industrial problem solving, technology transfer, failure analysis, environmental sciences and microbiology. Staff includes: metallurgical, mechanical, aerospace, electrical and chemical engineers; materials scientists; chemists; physicists; computer scientists and microbiologists. Services include manufacturing process development, product evaluation, reverse engineering, on-site engineering consultation, non-standards testing development, quality control program development, chemical analysis, qualification and characterization of materials, corrosion testing, composite interfacial property evaluation, custom test equipment development, video production, tensile and compression testing, fatigue and thermomechanical fatigue testing, water testing, computer modeling, software development, and expert testimony.

THE TRATTNER NETWORK
170 State, Ste. 240
Los Altos, CA 94022
James H. Trattner, Chairman/CEO
PH: (415)949-9555
FX: (415)949-1026
E-mail: TTN@tratnet.com
URL: www.dice.dlinc.com/trattner
Staff: 240. Activities: Provides services in the areas of client server design and development, system and network administration, software engineering and programming, project management, software quality assurance and testing, and multimedia, World Wide Web and Internet design.

TRC ENVIRONMENTAL CORP.
Five Waterside Crossing
Windsor, CT 06095-1561
PH: (860)289-8631
TF: (800)TRC-5601
FX: (860)298-6399
Founded: 1970. Staff: 550.

TRIAD SYSTEMS CORP.
3055 Triad Dr.
Livermore, CA 94550
James R. Porter, CEO, Pres.
PH: (510)449-0606
FX: (510)455-6917
Founded: 1972. Staff: 1391. Activities: Offers computer services, including custom CD-ROM databases for automotive industry.

TRILOGY CONSULTING CORP.
850 S. Greenbay Rd.
Waukegan, IL 60085
William J. Phillips, President
PH: (708)244-9520
TF: (800)323-7528
FX: (847)244-9335
Founded: 1982. Staff: 250. Activities: Trilogy provides technical professionals on a time and materials basis primarily to large companies. The firm's staff supports micro, mini and mainframe environments, in the areas of systems analysis and design; programming; systems programming; software engineering; communications; micro consulting, design and programming; database; and statistics. Industries served: pharmaceutical manufacturing, healthcare, food processors, chemical manufacturing, packaged consumer goods, agriculture/animal health, manufacturing, financial, communications, distribution, transportation, and government agencies.

TRIPLE-I, SUBSIDIARY OF INFORMATION INDUSTRIES
510 Research Rd.
Richmond, VA 23236-3047
Michael Chambers, Pres.
PH: (804)794-0371
FX: (804)794-3371
Founded: 1989. **Staff:** 14. Activities: Offers information technology services, including data processing and software development.

TRUSTED INFORMATION SYSTEMS, INC.
3060 Washington Rd.
Glenwood, MD 21738
Stephen T. Walker, President/CEO
PH: (301)854-6889
FX: (301)854-5363
E-mail: hrdept@tis.com
URL: www.tis.com
Founded: 1983. **Staff:** 250. Activities: Provider of comprehensive security solutions for protection of computer networks, including global Internet-based systems, internal networks, and individual workstations and laptops. Firm will develop, market, license, and support the Gauntlet(r) family of firewall products and other network security products. Supports both civilian and military agencies with: security analysis, threat and vulnerability studies, policy development, security modeling, system security designs, system security design reviews, certification and accreditation support. Industries served: healthcare, financial, pharmaceutical, universities, state, local, and federal government agencies, international organizations, and military organizations.

TUCKER & ASSOCIATES, INC.
616 Girod St.
New Orleans, LA 70130
Janee Tucker, President
PH: (504)522-4627
FX: (504)523-7184
Founded: 1978. **Staff:** 150. Activities: Provides a wide range of services to federal and state government agencies, as well as private sector organizations. Services include: automated data processing (ADP) systems design and implementation, facilities operations/management, data base management, applications systems and software development; project management including quality control, verification and validation services; records, construction and energy management; technical writing and clerical services; urban planning and related environmental impact studies; cost estimating; training and curriculum development; mathematical modeling and operations research; and marketing and public relations.

TUSTIN TECHNICAL INSTITUTE
22 E. Los Olivos St.
Santa Barbara, CA 93105
Colin M. Stephens, President
PH: (805)682-7171
FX: (805)687-6949
E-mail: training@ttiedu.com
URL: www.ttiedu.com
Founded: 1961. **Staff:** 30. Activities: Presents continuing education short courses on various engineering subjects, both on an "open" basis and "on-site" for specific clients. Subject areas include vibration related topics, computer software and hardware quality, and utilities-related topics (power, gas, communications, water). Industries served: high-tech related manufacturers, software developers, power companies, automobile manufacturers, medical, and aerospace.

UBIQUINET, INC.
18 Crow Canyon Ct., Ste. 250
San Ramon, CA 94583
Richard A. Johnson, President
PH: (510)820-1510
TF: (800)800UNET
FX: (510)831-4994
Founded: 1989. **Staff:** 14. Activities: Telecommunications services include planning, engineering, and consulting. Computer systems software consulting includes inventory management, vehicle route management, dispatching operations, field service operations, network management design and implementation, as well as large and small systems integration. Expertise in Supervisory Control and Data Acquisition (SCADA) systems and cellular radio systems design. Industries served: utilities, telephone companies, cable TV, telecommunications equipment vendors, interconnects, large industrial, transportation, and public safety.

UNITEL TELECOM INDUSTRIES
8450 Westfield Blvd.
Indianapolis, IN 46240
D. Peter Raw, Vice President Sales & Marketing
PH: (317)574-1000
FX: (317)574-1020
Founded: 1990. **Staff:** 103. Activities: Computer technology firm consults on network and systems design, PCs, Mac, Unix systems networking, and computer and telephone systems integration.

USA SOFTWARE
924 Professional Pl.
Chesapeake, VA 23320
Tom Henry, President
PH: (757)548-1010
FX: (757)549-1661
E-mail: usasoft@usasoft.com
URL: www.usasoft.com/
Founded: 1991. **Staff:** 15. Activities: Provides design, duplication, packaging, and publishing of computer software. Online marketing, electronic publishing, digital text, scanning.

VALINOR
7 Perimeter Rd.
Manchester, NH 03103
PH: (603)668-1776
FX: (603)641-5352
E-mail: gguarhlo@valinor.com
Founded: 1980. **Staff:** 90. Activities: Firm provides computer consulting, system engineering, programming and training expertise (Microsoft ATEC, high density and Microsoft certification). Technical experience includes Windows 95, NT Server and Workstation, Microsoft Office, Microsoft BackOffice, SQL Server, System Management Server, SNA Server, Mail/Exchange, VB, Ethernet, Token Ring, TCP/IP, and languages such as C++ and Visual. Serves large and medium-sized clients worldwide.

J.G. VANDYKE AND ASSOCIATES
6550 Rock Spring Dr., Ste. 360
Bethesda, MD 20817
J. Gary O. VanDyke, President
PH: (301)897-8970
FX: (301)897-5389
URL: www.jgvandyke.com
Founded: 1978. **Staff:** 195. Activities: Offers consulting services in the design, development, and application of data processing, data communications and networking technologies, specializing in critical response systems and environments (defense and intelligence communities)Products offered include PC based network security software and secure messaging capability.

VANGUARD RESEARCH
1508 John F. Kennedy Dr.
Bellevue, NE 68005-3642
Mel Chaskin, President/CEO
PH: (402)291-3475
FX: (402)291-3695
Founded: 1984. **Staff:** 105. Activities: Provides technical support services to the government and commercial customers. Services include engineering and technical services, innovative systems research, applied modeling, technical analysis, and medical and hazardous waste processing.

VANSTAR
199 Wells Ave.
Newton, MA 02159-3321

PH: (617)890-0009
FX: (617)890-6143
URL: www.vanstar.com
Founded: 1982. Staff: 11. Activities: Company specializes in computer based training courses custom-tailored to meet client's needs. Areas covered include personal computer operating systems, word processing, spreadsheets, and information management. Also does network consulting, programming and applications development. Typical clients are employees of business and government.

VASCO CORP.
1901 S. Meyers Rd., Ste. 210
Oakbrook Terrace, IL 60181
Michael Wiggen, CFO
PH: (630)495-0755
TF: (800)486-0755
FX: (630)495-0279
URL: www.vasco.com
Founded: 1984. Staff: 53. Activities: Provides high-level counsel and training to Fortune 1000 clients in strategic computer automation to improve productivity, profitability, and competitiveness. Assists in major sales force automation; instructional design and methodologies. Also distributes computer-based adult literacy training. Industries served: all in North America.

VECTOR RESEARCH, INC.
PO Box 1506
Ann Arbor, MI 48106
Seth Bonder, President
PH: (313)973-9210
FX: (313)973-7845
Founded: 1969. Staff: 107. Activities: Broad-based operations research and data-processing effort with sharp focus on solving complex healthcare planning and delivery problems for private industry and government, including Department of Defense, Veterans Administration and Public Health Service. Consulting experience spans large-scale computer modeling of healthcare demand and demographics of physician supply, automated quality-of-care monitoring, medical database management and information quality engineering, site-specific economic analyses, software development for integrated hospital information systems, and graduate medical education.

VENTURE DEVELOPMENT CORP.
1 Apple Hill
Natick, MA 01760
Lewis I. Solomon, President
PH: (508)653-9000
FX: (508)653-9836
E-mail: msr@vdc-corp.com
URL: www.vdc-corp.com
Founded: 1971. Staff: 35. Activities: VDC serves the electronics industry in the areas of management consulting, strategic planning, financial analysis, market research, and merger and acquisitions. Publishes industry reports, multiclient studies, and annual business planning services dealing with: computers and computer peripherals, electronic instrumentation, industrial measurement and process control, consumer electronics, electronic components and semiconductors, data communications and telecommunications, office equipment, power conversion and control, automatic identification, sensors and transducers, and retail automation.. Industries served: all industries/vertical markets where products under investigation are sold.

VERITAAQ TECHNOLOGY HOUSE LTD.
2430 Don Reid Dr.
Ottawa, Canada K1H 1E1
Jean Genier
PH: (613)736-6120
FX: (613)736-6123
E-mail: veritaaq@compuserve.com
Founded: 1983. Staff: 70. Activities: Offers expertise in programming services, systems analysis, LAN design and support, project management, and management counseling services.

ANIL VERMA ASSOCIATES, INC.
911 Wilshire Blvd., Ste. 1700
Los Angeles, CA 90017
Anil Verma, President
PH: (213)624-6908
FX: (213)624-1188
E-mail: anilverma@aol.com
Founded: 1985. Staff: 23. Activities: Firm offers special knowledge in architecture, engineering, construction management, project management, planning, landscape architecture, GIS, mapping, and computer drafting services.

VIGYAN, INC.
30 Research Dr.
Hampton, VA 23666-1325
Richard White, Vice President
PH: (757)865-1400
TF: (800)288-3998
FX: (757)865-8177
URL: www.vigyan.com
Founded: 1979. Staff: 45. Activities: Offers scientific and engineering research services in aerodynamics, structural analysis, control system, computer programming data analysis, environmental systems, and mathematical modeling as related to aeronautical and aerospace engineering. Current areas of investigation include computational fluid dynamics (both internal and external flows), turbomachinery, aircraft control surface evaluation, aircraft stability and controls, atmospheric science, experimental aerodynamics (in firm's own subsonic test facilities), high speed rarefied flow aerodynamics, adaptive control laws for use in robotic systems, computer graphics, relational databases, and structural analysis. Serves private industries as well as government agencies.

VILA DEL CORRAL & CO.
PO Box 10528
San Juan, PR 00922-0528
Rodrigo G. Morell
PH: (787)751-6164
FX: (787)759-7479
URL: www.vdc-pr.com
Founded: 1977. Staff: 78. Activities: Computer consultants providing assistance in the definition of information requirements and the implementation of systems. Primary area of service is manufacturing, distribution and healthcare. Serves private industries as well as government agencies.

VIRTUALOGIC
6707 Democracy Blvd., Ste. 202
Bethesda, MD 20817
Peter C. Johnson, President
PH: (301)571-5100
FX: (301)571-8530
URL: www.virtualogic.com/
Founded: 1993. Staff: 85. Activities: Offers computer consulting services to Fortune-1000 clients using technologies from Microsoft, Powersoft, Sybase, Informix, Sun, Hewlett Packard, Oracle, and others.

VITAL RESEARCH, LLC
8380 Melrose Ave., Ste. 309
Los Angeles, CA 90069
Gwen C. Uman, R.N., Ph.D.
PH: (323)653-7441
TF: (888)848-2555
FX: (323)653-0123
E-mail: hurman@vitalresearch.com
Founded: 1982. Staff: 12. Activities: Applied research and evaluation specializing in research design, survey development and statistical analysis. Expert in inferential statistics and multivariate analysis. Studies focus on customer satisfaction, service quality, and program evaluation. Industries served: education, healthcare, financial services, utilities, and information technology.

VOELKER, CASTILLA & KOPCZYNSKI, INC.
4106 Office Pky.
Dallas, TX 75204
Richard J. Voelker, Chairman of the Board
PH: (214)823-1202
FX: (214)821-1454
Founded: 1991. **Staff:** 16. Activities: Corporate facilities engineering firm specializes in construction management, software and relocation consulting services. Also offers expertise in institutional property services including consulting, leasing and property management. Industries served: electronics, energy, and education.

VOLT TECHNICAL SERVICES
1212 Avenue of the Americas, 9th Fl.
New York, NY 10036
William Shaw, President & Chairman of the Board
PH: (212)719-7800
TF: (800)975-8658
FX: (212)719-7850
E-mail: usjobs@volt.com
URL: www.volt.com
Founded: 1950. **Staff:** 35000. Activities: A supplier of contract personnel in the areas of information technology and business process consulting. Provides specialists in software development, hardware configuration and maintenance, ERP, business re-engineering, telecommunications, and wireless technology.

VOTER CONTACT SERVICES
PO Box 43
Amherst, MA 01004-0043
Mike Hannahan, Vice President
PH: (413)256-8884
TF: (800)823-4537
FX: (413)256-8766
E-mail: mihann@crocker.com
Founded: 1972. **Staff:** 50. Activities: Data processing consultants assisting in political campaigns. Provides fundraising, targeting, polling, direct mail, door-to-door, election analysis, canvassing, phone banks, and random sampling.

VR SYSTEMS INC.
1 Executive Dr.
Ste. 215
Somerset, NJ 08873
Radha Visweswar
PH: (732)469-1212
FX: (732)469-3566
E-mail: webadmin@vrsys.com
URL: www.vrsys.com
Founded: 1994. **Staff:** 40. Activities: A systems integrator and solutions provider that specializes in full life cycle application development, testing, maintenance and project management. Main focus on internet, client server and object technologies. Experienced in TC/IPO, Visual C++, JAVA, CORBA, COM/DCOM, Oracle, Sybase, DBZ, Informix, MS-SQL, Server on all UNIX and Window NT Platforms. Windows, HTML, JAVA, various UNIX platforms, and many other areas of technology.

W & J PARTNERSHIP
18876 Edwin Markham Dr.
Castro Valley, CA 94552
William A. Morgan, Managing Partner
PH: (510)583-7751
FX: (510)583-7645
E-mail: warmorgan@wjpartnership.com
URL: www.wjpartnership.com
Founded: 1982. **Staff:** 13. Activities: Areas of expertise include: communications and computing, fiber optics, campus wiring, local and wide area networks, wireless networks, satellite communications, command and control, data communications, microwave and video applications, PBXs and key telephone systems, artificial intelligence, cellular communications, network management, disaster recovery for corporate data centers, ATM, frame relay, SMDS, and ISDN. Services provided include: communications systems design

and specification, communications vendor proposal review, usage and needs studies, computing systems consulting, software development, and management consulting.

WAID & ASSOCIATES
14205 Burnet Rd., Ste. 500
Austin, TX 78728-6533
Patrick Murin, P.E., President
PH: (512)255-9999
FX: (512)255-8780
E-mail: waid@waid.com
URL: www.waid.com
Founded: 1978. **Staff:** 50. Activities: Environmental consulting firm with experience in related software programs. Specific services include: general air quality consulting, facility permitting; air pollutant dispersion modeling; compliance audits and support; emission inventory preparation; regulation analysis, expert testimony; solid/hazardous waste management and permitting; wastewater permitting; pollution prevention; and waste minimization. Industries served: oil and gas production and processing, printing (lithography), lead-acid battery production, petroleum refining, petrochemicals, inorganic and organic chemicals, foundries, electric utilities, natural gas transmission, and bulk storage terminals.

WALLACH ASSOCIATES, INC.
6101 Executive Blvd., Ste. 380
Rockville, MD 20852-3907
Donald M. Wallach, President/Treasurer
PH: (301)231-9000
FX: (301)770-9015
E-mail: jobs@wallach.org
URL: www.wallach.org
Founded: 1965. **Staff:** 11. Activities: Specialists in recruitment of professional personnel, primarily in electronic systems, energy research and development, management consulting, operations research, computers, defense systems, and programmers. Specializes in Internet and software engineer for intelligence community (DOD, NSA, CIA, DIA, etc.).

WARD ASSOCIATES
145 Wellington St. W, Ste. 210
Toronto, Canada M5J 1H8
Peter Ward, President
PH: (416)593-1660
TF: (800)668-8215
FX: (416)593-1661
URL: www.ward-associates.com
Founded: 1978. **Staff:** 33. Activities: Placement service provides careers and contract positions and professionals specifically related to the computing field. Providing personnel from operations to senior management within the information systems world. Industries served: various industries from government to small business; including banking, service, retail, distribution, manufacturing that use central, distributed or network computing facilities.

J.F. WARD ASSOCIATES
5512 Merlyn Dr.
Salt Lake City, UT 84117
J.F. Ward, Chairman and CEO
PH: (801)942-5020
FX: (801)272-5218
Founded: 1956. **Staff:** 16. Activities: Offers consulting in the following areas: (1) space planning, work flow, space utilization, and materials handling for warehouses, factories, and retail stores; (2) strategic planning; (3) financial planning and turn around management; and (4) computer planning.

WARDROP ENGINEERING INC.
400 386 Broadway
Winnipeg, Canada R3C 4M8
E.C. Card, Vice Chairman and CEO

PH: (204)956-0980
FX: (204)957-5389
E-mail: winnipeg@wardrop.com
URL: www.wardrop.com
Founded: 1955. Staff: 150. Activities: Engineering consultants offering services in aerospace, chemical, civil, electrical, instrumentation, environmental, mechanical, and nuclear engineering; land use planning; pollution control; and technology transfer. Specialists in the application of finite element computer codes to provide industry with accurate, cost-effective engineering analysis for design optimization, failure diagnosis, viability of new designs, and prototype development. Industries served: aerospace, nuclear, food processing, pulp and paper, mining, manufacturing, public works, transportation, and defense/military agencies.

THE WARNER GROUP
5950 Canoga Ave., Ste. 600
Woodland Hills, CA 91367
William R. Kumagai
PH: (818)710-8855
FX: (818)710-1467
E-mail: twg@warnergroup.com
URL: www.warnergroup.com
Founded: 1980. Staff: 70. Activities: Provides consulting services nationwide to government and industry. Serves clients in three broad areas: information technology, communications policy and planning, and performance improvement. Recognized as one of the nation's leading public safety (police, sheriff, fire and EMS) consulting firms having assisted more than 250 agencies in their technology and management planning.

JERVIS B. WEBB CO.
34375 W. Twelve Mile Rd.
Farmington Hills, MI 48331-5624
Paul Hopersberger, Dir of Mktg
PH: (248)553-1220
FX: (248)553-1228
URL: www.jervisbwebb.com
Founded: 1919. Staff: 2100. Activities: Designs and fabricates conveyor systems, automated storage/retrieval systems, automatic guided vehicle systems, and computer software for manufacturing concerns. Also provides shelf space management and warehousing services.

WELLMAN CORP.
10300 Eaton Pl., Ste. 320
Fairfax, VA 22030
Mike Wellman
PH: (703)352-9066
FX: (703)352-3418
E-mail: wellman@wellmancorp.com
URL: www.wellmancorp.com
Founded: 1988. Staff: 12. Activities: Consulting firm comprised of PC, Mac and database experts, provides database systems analysis, design, and development for PCs and Macs, FoxPro, dBase, Oracle, Paradox, Novell and Lans.

WESTAT, INC.
1650 Research Blvd.
Rockville, MD 20850
Joseph Waksburg, Chairman
PH: (301)251-1500
FX: (301)294-2040
URL: www.westat.com
Founded: 1961. Staff: 600. Activities: Social science and survey research firm offering counsel in the following areas: survey research design and statistical process control; sample design and selection; field, telephone, and mail surveys; statistical analysis; census data application; social program evaluation; data editing, coding, and processing. Study areas include health/epidemiology; job training and manpower; education; environmental protection; energy; social services; and organizational studies.

WESTERN MANAGEMENT CONSULTANTS
1188 W. Georgia St., Ste. 2000
Vancouver, Canada V6E 4A2
Richard Savage, Financial Director
PH: (604)687-0391
FX: (604)687-2315
E-mail: western@westernmgmt.com
Founded: 1975. Staff: 60. Activities: Offers a full range of management consulting services and related human resource development expertise. One of the largest national consulting organizations in Canada.

WESTLAKE SOLUTIONS INC.
4445 Wisconsin Ave. NW
Washington 20016-2141
Greg Eoyang, Pres./Dir. of Web Development
PH: (202)237-6600
TF: (800)357-2320
FX: (202)237-8649
URL: www.westlake.com
Founded: 1994. Staff: 12. Activities: WestLake Solutions offers a complete range of service for Internet and Intranet Website development, including page design and construction; CGI script, JavaScript and Java authoring; Web-to-database and Web-to-fax integration; on-site Internet/Web server setup and maintenance, and Internet market analysis and site promotion.

WESTOVER CORP. AND ASSOCIATES
4860 N. Hopkins St.
Milwaukee, WI 53209
Jeff A. Westover, Chairman/Treasurer
PH: (414)461-1960
Founded: 1930. Staff: 14. Activities: Offers counsel in the following areas: process and method evaluations; facilities design and construction management; design of pollution control systems; design of custom equipment and controls; develop work measurement standards, formulas, and cost conversion factors for incentive payroll systems and product costing; provide data processing systems for manufacturing and accounting. Industries served: foundries and metalworking companies.

WHAT'S UP INTERACTIVE
1200 Ashwood Pky., Ste. 135
Atlanta, GA 30338
Lynn LeBreter
PH: (770)671-0200
TF: (888)WHATSUP
FX: (770)671-0110
E-mail: sales@whatsup.com
URL: www.whatsup.com
Founded: 1990. Staff: 11. Activities: Web site and application development.

WHITTMAN-HART L.P.
311 S. Wacker Dr., Ste. 3500
Chicago, IL 60606
Robert Bernard, CEO, Chairman
PH: (312)922-9200
TF: (800)426-7767
FX: (312)913-3020
URL: www.whittman-hart.com
Founded: 1984. Staff: 2300. Activities: Offers information technology services focused on client/server, open systems, AS/400, and mainframe computing.

WINNERTECH CORP.
75 W. Front St.
Red Bank, NJ 07701
Drew Morris, President
PH: (732)758-9500
FX: (732)758-9503
E-mail: recruiters@winnertech.com
Founded: 1983. Staff: 30. Activities: Consultants specializing in making businesses more successful. Services include management

training, computer systems analysis, design and development and communications. Industries served: communications, pharmaceuticals, insurance and consumer products.

WIRE SPEED COMMUNICATIONS
4825 University Sq., Ste. 2
Huntsville, AL 35806
PH: (205)837-3838
FX: (205)837-3839
E-mail: solutions@wirespeed.com
URL: www.wirespeed.com
Founded: 1995. **Staff:** 13. Activities: Writes device drivers for networking products, creates programs for embedded systems and port applications to new environments. Experts in UNIX and Windows 3.X/95/NT environments and have developed drivers for Token-Ring, ATM, FDDI, and Ethemet products. In addition, has experience with X.25, Token-Ring, Fibre Channel, and HIPPI devices.

WORLD COM
800 Ridge Lake Blvd.
Memphis, TN 38120
Charlie Johnson, President/CEO
PH: (901)761-1177
TF: (800)637-7170
FX: (901)766-0229
Founded: 1976. **Staff:** 100. Activities: A data communications network service offering consulting services for companies who need to build a network of computers and terminals over a wide geographic area. Industries served: transportation, banking, manufacturing, service companies, insurance and finance.

XTEND COMMUNICATIONS
171 Madison Ave.
New York, NY 10016
William I. Schwartz, President
PH: (212)951-7600
TF: (800)231-2556
FX: (212)951-7683
Founded: 1967. **Staff:** 75. Activities: Computer/ telecommunications consultants offering communications, automation, and microcomputer to PBX integration. Specializes in integration of facilities and services. Industries served: healthcare, financial, legal, publishing, advertising, education, and government in the U.S. and Canada.

YORK & ASSOCIATES, INC.
2010 Centerpoint Dr.
St. Paul, MN 55120
Richard J. York, President
PH: (612)905-7370
FX: (612)905-7301
Founded: 1980. **Staff:** 45. Activities: Management systems and data processing consultants offering services in the following areas: systems planning, development and implementation in manufacturing, sales/marketing and electronic data interchange.

ZINTECH CORP.
Atrium 3
Reston, VA 20190-5202
Raffael Liuzzi, President
PH: (703)478-6641
FX: (703)478-6649
Founded: 1985. **Staff:** 14. Activities: A software specialty consultancy concentrating in communications and connectivity. Tandem computers are an integral part of integration solutions. Areas of expertise include the problem of interspersing access to different databases on different vendor mainframes, migrating applications from one vendor mainframe to another, and making maximum use of current systems and applications while developing or installing new ones. Serves private industries as well as government agencies.

TRADE INFORMATION SOURCES

Adapted from Gale's *Encyclopedia of Business Information Sources* (*EBIS*), the entries featured in this chapter show trade journals and other published sources, including web sites and databases. Entries list the title of the work, the name of the author (where available), name and address of the publisher, frequency or year of publication, prices or fees, and Internet address (in many cases).

3D DESIGN
Miller Freeman, Inc.
425 Market St.
San Francisco, CA 94105
PH: (800)227-4675
FX: (415)278-5343
URL: http://www.mfi.com
Computer Animation. See also: Virtual Reality. Monthly. $50.00 per year. Edited for computer graphics and multimedia professionals. Special features include "Animation Mania" and "Interactive 3D."

ACM GUIDE TO COMPUTING LITERATURE
Association for Computing Machinery
1515 Broadway, 17th Fl.
New York, NY 10036-5701
PH: (212)869-7440
FX: (212)944-1318
Computers. Annual. Free to members; non-members, $190.00 per year. A comprehensive guide to each year's computer literature (books, proceedings, journals, etc.), with an emphasis on technical material. Indexed by author, keyword, category, proper noun, reviewer, and source.

ACM TRANSACTIONS ON GRAPHICS
Association for Computing Machinery
1515 Broadway, 17th Fl.
New York, NY 10036-5701
PH: (212)869-7440
FX: (212)944-1318
Computer Graphics Computer-Aided Design and Manufacturing (CAD/CAM). Quarterly. Free to members; non-members, $110.00 per year.

ADVANCED IMAGING
Cygnus Publishing
445 Broad Hollow Rd.
Melville, NY 11747-4722
PH: (516)845-2700
FX: (516)845-2797
Electronic Publishing. Monthly. Free to qualified personnel. Covers document-based imaging technologies, products, systems, and services. Coverage is also devoted to multimedia and electronic printing and publishing.

ADVANCED MANUFACTURING TECHNOLOGY: MONTHLY REPORT
Technical Insights, Inc.
32 N. Dean St.
Englewood, NJ 07631-2807
PH: (201)568-4744
FX: (201)568-8247
E-mail: htminfo@insights.com
URL: http://www.insights.com
Computer Graphics. Monthly. $630.00 per year. Newsletter. Covers technological developments relating to robotics, computer graphics, automation, computer-integrated manufacturing, and machining.

ALMANAC OF BUSINESS AND INDUSTRIAL FINANCIAL RATIOS
Prentice Hall
One Lake St.
Upper Saddle River, NJ 07458
PH: (800)223-1360
FX: (800)445-6991
URL: http://www.prenhall.com
Leo Troy. Annual. $99.95. Contains financial ratios derived from federal tax returns. Ratios for each of about 200 industries are arranged according to company asset size.

ANDREW SEYBOLD'S OUTLOOK
Pinecrest Press, Inc.
P.O. Box 917
Brookdale, CA 95007

PH: (408)338-7701
FX: (408)338-7806
URL: http://www.outlook.com
Microcomputers and Minicomputers. Monthly. $395.00 per year. Newsletter. Provides analysis of the computer industry to corporate buyers and to end users. Reports on hardware, software trends and future products. Formerly Andrew Seybold's Outlook on Communications and Computing.

ANNUAL REVIEW OF INFORMATION SCIENCE AND TECHNOLOGY
Information Today, Inc.
143 Old Marlton Pike
Medford, NJ 08055-8750
PH: (800)300-9868
FX: (609)654-4309
E-mail: custserv@infotoday.com
URL: http://www.infotoday.com
Information Industry. Martha E. Williams, editor. Irregular. $95.00. Published on behalf of the American Society for Information Science (ASIS). Covers trends in planning, basic techniques, applications, and the information profession in general.

THE ART OF 3-D COMPUTER ANIMATION AND IMAGING
Van Nostrand Reinhold
115 Fifth Ave.
New York, NY 10003
PH: (800)842-3636
FX: (212)254-9499
E-mail: info@vnr.com
URL: http://www.vnr.com
Computer Animation See also: Virtual Reality. Isaac V. Kerlow. 1996. $49.95. Covers special effects, hypermedia formats, video output, the post-production process, etc. Includes full-color illustrations and step-by-step examples.

ARTIFICIAL INTELLIGENCE AND SOFTWARE ENGINEERING
Fitzroy Dearborn Publishers
70 East Walton Street
Chicago, IL 60611
PH: (800)850-8102
FX: (312)587-1049
URL: http://www.fitzroydearborn.com
Computer Software Industry. Darek Partridge. 1998. $55.00. Includes applications of artificial intelligence software to banking and financial services.

ASLIB PROCEEDINGS
Available from Information Today, Inc.
143 Old Marlton Pike
Medford, NJ 08055-8750
PH: (800)300-9868
FX: (609)654-4309
Online Information Systems Information Industry. Ten times a year. $230.00 per year. Published in London by Aslib: The Associationfor Information Management. Covers a wide variety of information industry and library management topics.

ASSOCIATION FOR INTERACTIVE MEDIA
1019 19th St., N. W.
Washington, DC 20036
PH: (202)408-0008
FX: (202)408-0111
E-mail: info@interactivehg.org
URL: http://www.interactivehg.org
Computer Communications Internet. Members are companies engaged in various interactive enterprises, utilizing the Internet, interactive television, computer communications, and multimedia.

AUTOMATION
Available from U. S. Government Printing Office.
Washington, DC 20402

PH: (202)512-1800
FX: (202)512-2250
Computers. Annual. Free. Issued by the Superintendent of Documents. A list of government publications on automation, computers, and related topics. Formerly Computers and Data Processing. (Subject Bibliography No. 51.)

BANKING AND FINANCE ON THE INTERNET
Van Nostrand Reinhold
115 Fifth Ave.
New York, NY 10003
PH: (800)842-3636
FX: (212)254-9499
E-mail: info@vnr.com
URL: http://www.vnr.com
Internet. Mary J. Cronin, editor. 1997. $39.95. Contains articles on Internet services, written by bankers, money mangers, investment analysts, and stockbrokers. Emphasis is on operations management. (Communications Series).

BASIC INTERNET FOR BUSY LIBRARIANS: A QUICK COURSE FOR CATCHING UP
American Library Association
50 East Huron St.
Chicago, IL 60611
PH: (800)545-2433
FX: (312)944-2641
URL: http://www.ala.org
Internet. Laura K. Murray. 1997. $26.00. A "practical crash-course primer" for learning how to effectively navigate the Internet and the World Wide Web.

BATTELLE MEMORIAL INSTITUTE
505 King Ave.
Columbus, OH 43201-2693
PH: (614)424-6424
FX: (614)424-3260
E-mail: solutions@battelle.org
URL: http://www.battelle.org
Microcomputers and Minicomputers Computer Peripherals and Accessories. Multidisciplinary research facilities at various locations include: Microcomputer Applications and Technology Center; Battelle Industrial Technology Center; Technology and Society Research Center; Office of Transportation Systems and Planning; Office of Waste Technology Development; Materials Information Center; Office of Nuclear Waste Isolation.

BEST BET INTERNET: REFERENCE AND RESEARCH WHEN YOU DON'T HAVE TIME TO MESS AROUND
American Library Association
50 East Huron St.
Chicago, IL 60611
PH: (800)545-2433
FX: (312)944-2641
E-mail: bseged@ala.org
URL: http://www.ala.org
Internet Online Information Systems. Shirley D. Kennedy. 1997. $35.00. Provides advice for librarians and others on the effective use of World Wide Web information sources.

BETTER BUYS FOR BUSINESS: THE INDEPENDENT CONSUMER GUIDE TO OFFICE EQUIPMENT
American Library
Post Office Box 22857
Association
Santa Barbara, CA 93121-2857
PH: (800)247-2185
FX: (805)963-3740
E-mail: orders@betterbuys.com
URL: http://www.betterbuys.com
Computer Peripherals and Accessories. 10 times a year. $134.00 per year. Each issue is on a particular office product, with detailed evaluation of specific models: 1. Low-Volume Copier Guide, 2. Mid-Volume Copier Guide, 3. High-Volume Copier Guide, 4. Plain

Paper Fax and Low-Volume Multifunctional Guide, 5. Mid/High-Volume Multifunctional Guide, 6. Laser Printer Guide, 7. Color Printer and Color Copier Guide, 8. Scan-to-File Guide, 9. Business Phone Systems Guide, 10. Postage Meter Guide, with a Short Guide to Shredders.

BIBLIOGRAPHICAL CENTER FOR RESEARCH, INC., ROCKY MOUNTAIN REGION
14394 East Evans Ave.
Aurora, CO 80014-1478
PH: (800)932-1552
FX: (303)751-9780
E-mail: bcradmin@ibrc.org
URL: http://www.ber.org
Internet Online Information Systems. Fields of research include information retrieval systems, Internet technology, CD-ROM technology, document delivery, and library automation.

BOARDWATCH MAGAZINE: GUIDE TO THE INTERNET, WORLD WIDE WEB, AND BBS
Boardwatch Magazine Publisher
8500 West Bowles Ave., Suite 210
Littleton, CO 80123
PH: (800)933-6038
FX: (303)973-3731
E-mail: subscriptions@boardwatch.com
URL: http://www.boardwatch.com
Internet Computer Communications. Monthly. $36.00 per year. Covers World Wide Web publishing, Internet technology, educational aspects of online communication, Internet legalities, and other computer communication topics.

BOOKS AND PERIODICALS ONLINE: THE GUIDE TO BUSINESS AND LEGAL INFORMATION ON DATABASES AND CD-ROMS
Library Alliance
PO Box 77232
Washington, DC 20013-8232
Online Information Systems. Nuchine Nobari, editor. Annual. $325.00 per year. 87,000 periodicals available as part of online and CD-ROM databases; international coverage.

BROADBAND NETWORKING
Datapro Information Services Group
600 Delran Parkway
Delran, NJ 08075
PH: (800)328-2776
FX: (609)764-2814
URL: http://www.datapro.com/products
Optics Industry. One looseleaf volume. Monthly updates. New subscriptions, $621.00 per year; renewals, $580.00 per year. Includes information about microwave, satellite, fiber optics, infrared, CATV, FM subcarrier, and other modern methods of communication. Formerly Datapro Reports on Communications Alternatives.

BUILDING THE SERVICE-BASED LIBRARY WEB SITE: A STEP-BY-STEP GUIDE TO DESIGN AND OPTIONS
American Library Association
50 East Huron St.
Chicago, IL 60611-2795
PH: (800)545-2433
FX: (312)944-2641
E-mail: bseged@ala.org
URL: http://www.ala.org
Internet. Kristen L. Garlock and Sherry Piontek. 1996. $25.00. Provides practical information for libraries planning a World Wide Web home page.

BUSINESS CONSUMER GUIDE
Beacon Research Group
125 Walnut St.
Watertown, MA 02172-4043

PH: (800)938-0088
FX: (617)924-0055
E-mail: custserv@buyerszone.com
URL: http://www.buyerszone.com
Microcomputers and Minicomputers Computer Peripherals and Accessories Portable Computers. Monthly. $119.00 per year. Looseleaf. Provides recommendations of specific brands and models of office equipment.

BUSINESS DICTIONARY OF COMPUTERS
John Wiley and Sons, Inc.
605 Third Ave.
New York, NY 10158-0012
PH: (800)225-5945
FX: (212)850-6088
Computers Microcomputers and Minicomputers. Jerry M. Rosenberg. 1993. $14.95. Third edition. Provides concise definitions of over 7,500 computer terms, including slang terms, abbreviations, acronyms, and technical jargon.

BUSINESS INDEX
Gale Group
27500 Drake Rd.
Farmington Hills, MI 48331
PH: (800)227-8431
FX: (650)378-5369
Electronic Publishing Online Information Systems Information Industry. Monthly. $3,500.00 per year. Provides comprehensive CD-ROM indexing of more than 800 business and trade journals and selective indexing of 3,000 other magazines and newspapers. Covers the current four years.

BUSINESS INFORMATION MARKETS: THE STRATEGIC OUTLOOK
SIMBA Information, Inc.
Post Office Box 4234
Stamford, CT 06907-0234
PH: (800)307-2529
FX: (203)358-5824
E-mail: info@simbanet.com
URL: http://www.simbanet.com
Electronic Publishing Online Information Systems Information Industry. Biennial. $2500.00. Provides five years of data relating to a wide variety of business information markets and providers of business information.

BUSINESS INTERNET AND INTRANETS: A MANAGER'S GUIDE TO KEY TERMS AND CONCEPTS
Harvard Business School Publishing
60 Harvard Way
Boston, MA 02163
PH: (800)545-7685
FX: (617)495-6985
E-mail: custserv@cchbspub.harvard.edu
URL: http://www.hbsp.harvard.edu
Internet. Peter G. W. Keen and others. 1998. $39.95. Defines more than 100 words and phrases relating to the Internet or corporate intranets.

BUSINESS ORGANIZATIONS, AGENCIES, AND PUBLICATIONS DIRECTORY
Gale Group
27500 Drake Rd.
Farmington Hills, MI 48331
PH: (800)877-GALE
FX: (248) 699-4253
E-mail: galeord@gale.com
URL: http://www.gale.com
Online Information Systems. 1996. $390.00. Eighth edition. Over 30,000 entries describing 39 types of business information sources. Classified by type of organization, publication, or service. Includes state, national, and international agencies and organizations. Master index to names and keywords.

BUSINESS-PROFESSIONAL ONLINE SERVICES: REVIEW, TRENDS, AND FORECAST
SIMBA Information, Inc.
Post Office Box 4234
Stamford, CT 06907-0234
PH: (800)307-2529
FX: (203)358-5824
E-mail: info@simbanet.com
URL: http://www.simbanet.com
Online Information Systems. Annual. $1,295.00 Provides a review of current conditions in the online information industry. Profiles of major database producers and online services are included. Formerly Online Services: Review, Trends and Forecast.

BYTE
McGraw-Hill Companies Byte Publications
One Phoenix Mill Lane
Peterborough, NH 03458
PH: (800)722-4726
FX: (603)924-2550
Microcomputers and Minicomputers. Monthly. $29.95 per year. A broad based microcomputer magazine for business professional users emphasizing technical information, applications and products.

CD-ROMS IN PRINT
Gale Group
27500 Drake Rd.
Farmington Hills, MI 48331
PH: (800)877-GALE
FX: (800)414-5043
E-mail: galeord@gale.com
URL: http://www.gale.com
Electronic Publishing. Annual. $150.00. Describes more than 11,500 currrently available reference and multimedia CD-ROM titles and provides contact information for about 4,000 CD-ROM publishing and distribution companies. Includes several indexes.

COMMLINE
Numeridex, Inc.
P.O. Box 11000
Wheeling, IL 60090
PH: (312)541-8840
Computer-Aided Design and Manufacturing (CAD/CAM). Bimonthly. Free to qualified personnel; others, $20.00 per year. Emphasizes NC/CNC (numerically controlled and computer numerically controlled machinery).

COMPUMATH CITATION INDEX
Institute for Scientific Information
3501 Market St.
Philadelphia, PA 19104
PH: (800)336-4474
FX: (215)386-2991
Portable Computers Computers. Three times a year. $1,090.00 per year. Provides citations to the worldwide literature of computer science and mathematics.

COMPUSERVE INTERNET TOUR GUIDE
Ventana Communications Group, Inc.
Post Office Box 13964
Research Triangle Park, NC 27709-3964
PH: (800)743-5369
E-mail: feedback@vmedia.com
URL: http://www.vmedia.com
Computer Communications Internet Online Information Systems. Richard Wagner. 1996. $34.95. A detailed guide to accessing various features of the Internet by way of the Compuserve online service.

COMPUTER
Institute of Electrical and Electronic
10662 Los Vaqueros Circle
Engineers, Inc.
Los Alamitos, CA 90720-1264

PH: (800)678-4333
FX: (714)821-4641
E-mail: csinfo@computer.org
URL: http://www.computer.org
Computers Semiconductor Industry. IEEE Computer Society Press. Monthly. Free to members; non-members, $455.00 per year. Edited for computer technology professionals.

COMPUTER BOOK REVIEW
Microcomputers and Minicomputers Online Information Systems
P.O. Box 61067
Honolulu, HI 96839
E-mail: char@pixi.com
URL: http://www.bookwire.com/cbr
Computer Graphics Computer Communications Computer Software Industry Bimonthly. $30.00 per year. Includes annual index. Reviews new computer books. Back issues available.

COMPUTER BUYER'S GUIDE AND HANDBOOK
Bedford Communications, Inc.
150 Fifth Ave.
New York, NY 10011
PH: (212)807-8220
FX: (212)807-1098
Microcomputers and Minicomputers Computer Peripherals and Accessories. Monthly. $36.00 per year. Includes six issues of the bimonthly Computer Buyer's Guide and Handbook and six issues of the bimonthly Laptop Buyer's Guide and Handbook. Includes equipment reviews, articles, comparison charts, and "Street Price Guide" (discounted prices with names, addresses, and telephone numbers of dealers).

COMPUTER DEALERS DIRECTORY
American Business Information, Inc.
5711 S. 86th Circle
Omaha, NE 68127
PH: (800)555-6124
FX: (402)331-5481
E-mail: directory@abii.com
URL: http://www.abii.com
Computer Retailing. Annual. Price on application. Lists over 30,847 computer dealers. Brand names are indicated. Compiled from telephone company yellow pages. Regional editions and franchise editions available.

COMPUTER ECONOMICS REPORT: STRATEGIC ADVICE FOR ENTERPRISE IT EXECUTIVES
Computer Economics, Inc.
5841 Edison Place
Carlsbad, CA 92008
PH: (800)326-8100
FX: (760)431-1126
E-mail: info@compecon.com
URL: http://www.computereconomics.com
Computers. Monthly. $595.00 per year. Newsletter on lease/ purchase decisions, prices, discounts, residual value forecasts, personnel allocation, cost control, and other corporate computer topics. Edited for information technology (IT) executives.

COMPUTER INDUSTRY ALMANAC
Available from Hoover's, Inc.
1033 La Posada Drive, Suite 250
Austin, TX 78752
PH: (800)486-8666
FX: (512)374-4501
E-mail: orders@hoovers.com
URL: http://www.hoovers.com
Computers Computer Software Industry Microcomputers and Minicomputers. Karen Juliussen and Egil Juliussen. Annual. $70.00. Published by Computer Industry Almanac, Inc. Analyzes recent trends in various segments of the computer industry, with forecasts, employment data and industry salary information. Includes directories of computer companies, industry organizations, and publications.

COMPUTER INDUSTRY FORECASTS: THE SOURCE FOR MARKET INFORMATION ON COMPUTERS, PERIPHERALS & SOFTWARE
Data Analysis Group
P.O. Box 128
Cloverdale, CA 95425
PH: (707)539-3009
FX: (707)486-5618
URL: http://www.cifi.com
Microcomputers and Minicomputers Desktop Publishing Computer Crime and Security Computer Peripherals and Accessories Local Area Networks Computers Computer Communications Computer Software Industry Quarterly. $365.00 per year. Summarizes market data from computer industry periodicals.

COMPUTER PARTS AND SUPPLIES
American Business Information, Inc.
5711 S. 86th Circle
Omaha, NE 68127
PH: (800)555-6124
FX: (402)331-5481
E-mail: directory@abii.com
URL: http://www.abii.com
Computer Peripherals and Accessories. Annual. Price on application. Lists 8,476 companies. Compiled from telephone company yellow pages.

COMPUTER PRICE GUIDE: THE BLUE BOOK OF USED IBM COMPUTER PRICES
Computer Economics, Inc.
5841 Edison Place
Carlsbad, CA 92008
PH: (800)326-8100
FX: (760)431-1126
E-mail: info@compecon.com
URL: http://www.computereconomics.com
Computers Microcomputers and Minicomputers. Quarterly. $125.00 per year. Provides average prices of used IBM computer equipment, including "complete lists of obsolete IBM equipment." Includes a newsletter on trends in the used computer market. Edited for dealers, leasing firms, and business computer buyers.

COMPUTER PUBLISHING MARKET FORECAST
SIMBA Information, Inc.
Post Office Box 4234
Stamford, CT 06907-0234
PH: (800)307-2529
FX: (203)358-5824
E-mail: info@simbanet.com
URL: http://www.simbanet.com
Computers. Annual. $1,795.00. Provides market data on computer-related books, magazines, newsletters, and other publications. Includes profiles of major publishers of computer-related material.

COMPUTER RESELLER NEWS: THE NEWSPAPER FOR MICROCOMPUTER RESELLING
CMP Publications, Inc.
600 Community Dr.
Manhasset, NY 11030
PH: (800)829-0421
FX: (516)733-6916
URL: http://www.crn.com
Local Area Networks Computer Retailing Computers. Weekly. $189.00 per year. Includes bimonthly supplement. Incorporates Computer Reseller Sources and Macintosh News. Formerly Computer Retailer News.

COMPUTER SELECT
Gale Group
27500 Drake Rd.
Farmington Hills, MI 48331
PH: (248)699-4253
FX: (800)414-5043
URL: http://www.gale.com

Computer Animation See also: Virtual Reality Computer Software Industry Computers Microcomputers and Minicomputers Virtual Reality See also: Computer Animation Electronic Publishing Internet Desktop Publishing Online Information Systems Information Industry. Monthly. $1,250.00 per year. Provides one year of full-text on CD-ROM for 120 leading computer-related publications. Also includes 70,000 product specifications and brief profiles of 13,000 computer product vendors and manufacturers. (Formerly produced by Ziff Communications Co.)

COMPUTER SOFTWARE: PROTECTION, LIABILITY, FORMS
Clark Boardman Callaghan
155 Pfingsten Rd.
Deerfield, IL 60015
PH: (800)328-4880
FX: (847)948-8955
URL: http://www.westgroup.com
Computer Software Industry Computer Law. L. J. Kutten. Two looseleaf volumes. $350.00. Periodic supplementation. Covers copyright law, patents, trade secrets, licensing, publishing contracts, and other legal topics related to computer software.

COMPUTER SYSTEMS SERIES
Datapro Information Services Group
600 Delran Parkway
Delran, NJ 08075-1252
PH: (800)328-2776
FX: (609)764-2812
URL: http://www.datapro.com/products
Computers Computer Software Industry Computer Peripherals and Accessories. Monthly. New subscriptions, $1,746.00 per year; renewals, $1,564.00 per year. Four looseleaf volumes: 1) Overviews, 2) Systems, 3) Peripherals, 4) Software. Intended for MIS personnel making purchasing decisions for midrange and main frame computers. Peripherals volume includes storage devices, printers, plotters, disk drives, tape drives, scanners, and displays. "Computer System Reports" and "Computer User Ratings" are provided.

CONSUMER INTERNET REPORT
Jupiter Communications Co.
627 Broadway, 2nd Floor
New York, NY 10012
PH: (800)488-4345
FX: (212)780-6075
E-mail: jupiter@jup.com
URL: http://www.jup.com
Computer Software Industry Internet. Annual. $995.00. Market research report. Provides data and forecasts relating to various hardware and software elements of the Internet, including browsers, provision of service, telephone line modems, cable modems, wireless access devices, online advertising, programming languages, and Internet chips. Includes company profiles.

CONSUMER ONLINE SERVICES REPORT
Jupiter Communications Co.
627 Broadway, 2nd Floor
New York, NY 10012
PH: (800)488-4345
FX: (212)780-6075
E-mail: jupiter@jup.com
URL: http://www.jup.com
Electronic Publishing Internet Online Information Systems. Annual. $1,895.00. Market research report. Provides analysis of trends in the online information industry, with projections of growth in future years (five-year forecasts). Contains profiles of electronic media companies.

CONTROL ENGINEERING PC HARDWARE AND SOFTWARE GUIDE
Cahners Publishing Co.
P. O. Box 5080
Des Plaines, IL 60017-5080

PH: (800)662-7776
FX: (847)390-2618
E-mail: marketaccess@cahners.com
URL: http://www.cahners.com
Computer Peripherals and Accessories Microcomputers and Minicomputers. Annual. $45.00. Contains specifications, prices, and manufacturers' listings for computer hardware and software, as related to control engineering.

CSA ENGINEERING
Cambridge Scientific Abstracts
7200 Wisconsin Ave., Suite 601
Bethesda, MD 20814
PH: (800)843-7751
FX: (301)961-6720
Portable Computers Computers Electronics Industry Semiconductor Industry Superconductors. Provides the online version of Computer and Information Systems Abstracts, Electronics and Communications Abstracts, Health and Safety Science Abstracts, ISMEC: Mechanical Engineering Abstracts (Information Service in Mechanical Engineering)and Solid State and Superconductivity Abstracts. Time period is 1981 to date, with monthly updates. Inquire as to online cost and availability.

CURRENT CONTENTS: ENGINEERING, COMPUTING AND TECHNOLOGY
Institute for Scientific Information
3501 Market St.
Philadelphia, PA 19104
PH: (800)336-4474
FX: (215)386-2991
Portable Computers. Weekly. $730.00 per year. Reproductions of contents pages of technical journals. Formerly Current Contents: Engineering, Technology and Applied Sciences.

CYBERSPACE LEXICON: AN ILLUSTRATED DICTIONARY OF TERMS FROM MULTIMEDIA TO VIRTUAL REALITY
Available from Chronicle Books.
275 Fifth St.
San Francisco, CA 94103
PH: (800)722-6657
FX: (415)777-2289
Electronic Publishing Internet Online Information Systems. Bob Cotton and Richard Oliver. 1994. $29.95. Published by Phaidon Press. Defines more than 800 terms, with many illustrations. Includes a bibliography.

CYBERSPEAK: AN ONLINE DICTIONARY
201 East 50th St.
New York, NY 10022
PH: (800)726-0600
FX: (800)659-2436
URL: http://www.randomhouse.com
Computer Animation See also: Virtual Reality Computer Software Industry Computers Microcomputers and Minicomputers Virtual Reality See also: Computer Animation Electronic Publishing Internet. Andy Ihnatko. Random House, Inc. 1996. $12.95. An informal guide to the language of computers, multimedia, and the Internet.

DATA NETWORKING
Datapro Information Services Group
600 Delran Parkway
Delran, NJ 08075
PH: (800)328-2776
FX: (609)764-2812
Computer Communications. Monthly. $1,400.00 per year. Four looseleaf volumes. Provides broad coverage of data communications and networks, including product evaluation (hardware and software).

DATA SOURCES: THE COMPREHENSIVE GUIDE TO THE DATA PROCESSING INDUSTRY; HARDWARE,DATA COMMUNICATIONS PRODUCTS, SOFTWARE, COMPANY PROFILES
Gale Group
27500 Drake Rd.
Farmington Hills, MI 48331
PH: (248)699-4253
FX: (800)414-5043
Computer Peripherals and Accessories Computer Software Industry Computers Desktop Publishing Microcomputers and Minicomputers Portable Computers Local Area Networks Information Industry Electronic Publishing. Semiannual. $495.00 per year. Published in two volumes containing 1) hardware and 2) software products for all computer operating systems, including prices and technical details. Covers a total of over 75,000 products from about 14,000 manufacturers and suppliers. Software applications are included for a wide variety of industries.

DATAMATION: THE EMERGING TECHNOLOGIES MAGAZINE FOR TODAY'S IS
275 Washington St.
Newton, MA 02158-1630
PH: (800)662-7776
FX: (617)558-4506
E-mail: marketaccess@cahners.com
URL: http://www.cahners.com
Microcomputers and Minicomputers. Cahners Publishing Co., Inc. Monthly. Free to qualified personnel; others, $75.00 per year. Technical, semi-technical and general news covering EDP topics.

DATAPRO DIRECTORY OF MICROCOMPUTER SOFTWARE
Datapro Information Services Group
600 Delran Parkway
Delran, NJ 08075
PH: (800)328-2776
FX: (609)764-2812
URL: http://www.dataprom.com/products
Computer Software Industry Computer Peripherals and Accessories Microcomputers and Minicomputers Computer Communications Desktop Publishing. Three looseleaf volumes. Monthly updates. $860.00 per year. Detailed information about personal computer software applications and software companies.

DATAPRO DIRECTORY OF SOFTWARE
Datapro Information Services Group
600 Delran Parkway
Delran, NJ 08075
PH: (800)328-2776
FX: (609)764-2812
URL: http://www.dataprom.com/products
Computer Software Industry. Monthly. $949.00 per year. Three looseleaf volumes. Includes a wide variety of software programs for mainframe and other computers, arranged by area of application. Provides detailed descriptions.

DATAPRO MANAGEMENT OF APPLICATIONS SOFTWARE
Datapro Information Services Group
600 Delran Parkway
Delran, NJ 08075
PH: (800)328-2776
FX: (609)764-2812
URL: http://www.datapro.com/products
Computer Software Industry. Monthly. Two looseleaf volumes. New subscriptions, $937.00 per year; renewals, $897.00 per year. A guide for data processing managers. Covers planning, design, selection, costs, testing, maintenance, and other topics relating to applications software management.

DATAPRO MANAGING DATA NETWORKS
Datapro Information Services
600 Delran Parkway
Group
Delran, NJ 08075
PH: (800)328-2776
FX: (609)764-2812
URL: http://www.datapro.com/products
Local Area Networks Computer Communications. Monthly. $964.00 per year. Two looseleaf volumes. Covers the management aspects of communications networks, including equipment selection, operational details, personnel, and security.

DATAPRO MANAGING LANS
Datapro Information Services Group
600 Delran Parkway
Delran, NJ 08075
PH: (800)328-2776
FX: (609)764-2812
URL: http://www.datapro.com/products
Local Area Networks. Monthly. $783.00 per year. Two looseleaf volumes. Covers the general management aspects of local area networks, including planning, staffing, and security.

DATAPRO REPORTS ON BANKING AUTOMATION
Datapro Information Services
600 Delran Parkway
Group
Delran, NJ 08075
PH: (800)328-2776
FX: (609)764-2812
URL: http://www.datapro.com/products
Electronic Funds Transfer Systems (EFTS). Monthly. New subscriptions, $1,066.00; per year; renewals, $926.00 per year. Looseleaf. Evaluates bank automation equipment, such as automated teller machines, computer imaging systems, electronic funds transfer (EFT) installations, and check processing equipment.

DATAPRO REPORTS ON INFORMATION SECURITY
Datapro Information Services Group
600 Delran Parkway
Delran, NJ 08075
PH: (800)328-2776
FX: (609)764-2812
URL: http://www.datapro.com/products
Computer Crime and Security. Monthly. New subscriptions, $1,264.00 per year; renewals, $1,141 per year. Three looseleaf volumes. Provides detailed information on all aspects of security for computer operations, including virus control, software shielding, and physical site protection.

DATAPRO SOFTWARE FINDER
Datapro Information Services Group
600 Delran Parkway
Delran, NJ 08075
PH: (800)328-2776
FX: (609)764-2812
Computer Software Industry. Quarterly. $1,770.00 per year. On CD-ROM, provides detailed information on more than 18,000 software products for a wide variety of computers, personal to mainframe. Covers software for 130 types of business, finance, and industry. (Editions limited to either microcomputer or mainframe software are available at $995.00 per year.)

DATAPRO WORKGROUP COMPUTING SERIES
Datapro Information Services
600 Delran Parkway
Group
Delran, NJ 08075
PH: (800)328-2776
FX: (609)764-2812
URL: http://www.datapro.com/products
Microcomputers and Minicomputers Local Area Networks Computer Peripherals and Accessories Computer Communications. Month-

ly. $3,380.00 per year. Ten looseleaf volumes. A comprehensive service covering all aspects of microcomputer software and hardware for business use. Includes detailed product evaluations and specifications.

DATAWORLD
Faulkner Information Services, Inc.
7905 Browning Rd.
114 Cooper Center
Pennsauken, NJ 08109-4319
PH: (609)662-2070
FX: (609)662-3380
Microcomputers and Minicomputers Desktop Publishing Computer Crime and Security Computer Peripherals and Accessories Local Area Networks Computer Software Industry Computers. Four looseleaf volumes, with monthly supplements. $1395.00 per year. Describes and evaluates both hardware and software relating to midrange, micro, and mainframe computers. Available on CD-ROM.

DICTIONARY OF PC HARDWARE AND DATA COMMUNICATIONS TERMS
O'Reilly &
90 Sherman St.
Associates, Inc.
Cambridge, MA 02140
PH: (800)775-7731
FX: (800)775-7731
E-mail: cs@ora.com
URL: http://www.ora.com
Microcomputers and Minicomputers Computer Communications Local Area Networks Computer Peripherals and Accessories. Mitchell Shnier. 1996. $19.95. (Online updates to print version available at http://www.ora.com/reference/dictionary.)

DIRECTORY OF COMPUTER RETAILERS, DEALERS AND DISTRIBUTORS
Chain Store Guide
3922 Coconut Palm Dr.
Information Services
Tampa, FL 33619
PH: (800)927-9292
FX: (813)664-6682
E-mail: valkelly@sprynet.com
URL: http://www.d-net.com/csgis
Computer Retailing Computer Software Industry. Annual. $290.00. Detailed information about companies operating computer and/or computer software stores. Formerly Directory of Computer and Software Retailers.

DIRECTORY OF MULTIMEDIA SYSTEMS AND SOFTWARE
International
363 East Central St.
Management Services, Inc.
Franklin, MA 02038-1300
PH: (508)520-1555
FX: (508)520-1558
Computer Software Industry. Raymond Wenig, editor. Annual. $135.00 per year. Listing of software sources for minicomputer applications. Partially supersedes *Minicomputer Software Directory.*

DIRECTORY OF VALUE ADDED RESELLERS (COMPUTER EQUIPMENT)
Chain
3922 Coconut Palm Drive
Store Guide Information Services
Tampa, FL 33619
PH: (800)927-9292
FX: (813)664-6882
E-mail: valkelly@sprynet.com
URL: http://www.d-net.com/csgis
Computers Computer Retailing Computer Peripherals and Accessories. Annual. $290.00. Provides information on computer companies that modify, enhance, or customize hardware or software. Includes

systems houses, systems integrators, turnkey systems specialists, original equipment manufacturers, and value added retailers.

DIRECTORY OF VIDEO, COMPUTER, AND AUDIO-VISUAL PRODUCTS
International Communications Industries Association
11242 Waples Mill Rd., Suite 200
Fairfax, VA 22030-6079
PH: (800)764-7469
FX: (703)278-8082
Computer Graphics. Annual. $65.00. Contains detailed descriptions and photographs of specific items of equipment. Includes video cameras, overhead projectors, LCD panels, computer projection systems, film recording equipment, etc. A "Glossary of Terms" is also provided.

DR. DOBB'S JOURNAL: SOFTWARE TOOLS FOR THE PROFESSIONAL PROGRAMMER
Miller Freeman, Inc.
600 Harrison St.
San Francisco, CA 94107
PH: (800)227-4675
FX: (415)905-2239
Computer Software Industry. Monthly. $34.95 per year. A technical publication covering software development, languages, operating systems, and applications.

EDP WEEKLY: THE LEADING WEEKLY COMPUTER NEWS SUMMARY
Computer Age and E D P News Services
714 Church St.
Alexandria, VA 22314-4202
PH: (703)739-8500
FX: (703)739-8505
Microcomputers and Minicomputers Desktop Publishing Computer Crime and Security Computer Peripherals and Accessories Local Area Networks. Weekly. $495.00 per year. Newsletter. Summarizes news from all areas of the computer and microcomputer industries.

ELECTRONIC BUSINESS TODAY
Cahners Publishing Co.
275 Washington St.
Newton, MA 02158-1630
PH: (800)662-7776
FX: (617)558-4470
E-mail: marketaccess@cahners.com
URL: http://www.cahners.com
Electronics Industry. Monthly. $65.00 per year. For the non-technical manager and executive in the electronics industry. Offers news, trends, figures and forecasts.

ELECTRONIC FRONTIER FOUNDATION
1550 Bryant St., Ste. 725
San Francisco, CA 94103
PH: (415)668-7171
FX: (415)436-9993
E-mail: EFF@EFF.ORG
Computer Communications Internet Online Information Systems. Members are individuals with an interest in computer-based communications. Promotes electronic communication civil liberties and First Amendment rights.

ELECTRONIC INFORMATION REPORT: EMPOWERING INFORMATION INDUSTRY DECISION MAKERS SINCE 1979
SIMBA Information, Inc.
Post Office Box 4234
Stamford, CT 06907-0234
PH: (800)307-2529
FX: (203)358-5824
E-mail: info@simbanet.com
URL: http://www.simbanet.com
Information Industry Online Information Systems Electronic Publishing. Weekly. $499.00 per year. Newsletter. Provides business

and financial news and trends for online services, electronic publishing, storage media, multimedia, and voice services. Includes information on relevant IPOs (initial public offerings) and mergers. Formerly *IDP Report*.

ELECTRONIC SELLING: TWENTY-THREE STEPS TO E-SELLING PROFITS
McGraw-Hill
1221 Ave. of the Americas
New York, NY 10020
PH: (800)722-4726
FX: (212)512-2821
E-mail: customer.service@mcgraw-hill.com
URL: http://www.mcgraw-hill.com
Internet. Brian Jamison and others. 1997. $24.95. Covers selling on the World Wide Web, including security and payment issues. Provides a glossary and directory information. The authors are consultants specializing in Web site production.

ENCYCLOPEDIA OF COMPUTER SCIENCE AND TECHNOLOGY
Marcel Dekker, Inc.
270 Madison Ave.
New York, NY 10016
PH: (800)228-1160
FX: (212)685-4540
Computers. Allen Kent and James G. Williams, editors. Various dates, volumes, and prices (information on request). Contains scholarly articles written by computer experts. Includes bibliographies.

ENCYCLOPEDIA OF MICROCOMPUTERS
Marcel Dekker, Inc.
270 Madison Ave.
New York, NY 10016
PH: (800)228-1160
FX: (212)685-4540
Microcomputers and Minicomputers. Allen Kent and James G. Williams, editors. 16 volumes. Contains scholarly articles written by microcomputer experts. Includes bibliographies.

FAULKNER TECHNICAL REPORTS
Faulkner Information Services, Inc.
7905 Browning Rd.
Pennsauken, NJ 08109-4319
PH: (609)662-2070
FX: (609)662-3380
Microcomputers and Minicomputers Desktop Publishing Computer Crime and Security Computer Peripherals and Accessories Local Area Networks. Looseleaf. Monthly updates. Many titles and volumes, covering virtually all aspects of computer software and hardware. Gives descriptions and technical data for specific products, including producers' names and addresses. Prices and details on request. Formerly The Auerbach Series.

FAULKNER'S ENTERPRISE NETWORKING
Faulkner Information Services, Inc.
7905 Browning Rd.
114 Cooper Center
Pennsauken, NJ 08109-4319
PH: (609)622-2070
FX: (609)662-3380
Computer Communications. Three looseleaf volumes, with monthly supplements. $1275.00 per year. Contains product reports and management articles relating to computer communications and networking. Available on CD-ROM. Quarterly updates. Formerly Data Communications Reports.

FAULKNER'S LOCAL AREA NETWORKING
Faulkner Information
7905 Browning Rd.
114 Cooper Center
Services, Inc.
Pennsauken, NJ 08109-4319

PH: (609)662-2070
FX: (609)662-3380
Local Area Networks Computer Crime and Security. Looseleaf, with monthly supplements. $715.00 per year. Contains product reports and other information relating to PC networking, including security, gateways/bridges, and emerging standards. Formerly Faulkner Report on Microcomputer and Software.

THE FEDERAL INTERNET SOURCE: A GUIDE TO NEARLY 800 OF FEDERAL, STATE AND POLITICAL INTERNET SITES, AND HOW TO FIND AND USE THEM
National Journal, Inc.
1501 M St., N. W., Suite 300
Washington, DC 20005
PH: (800)356-4838
FX: (202)833-8069
Internet. Annual. $44.95 per year. Provides descriptions, addresses, and home page information for more than 500 governmental Internet sources.

GALE DIRECTORY OF DATABASES
Gale Group
27500 Drake Rd.
Farmington Hills, MI 48331
PH: (248)699-4253
FX: (800)414-5043
Online Information Systems Information Industry. 1999. $370.00. Two volumes. Volume 1: Online Databases and Volume 2: CD-ROM, Diskette, Magnetic Tape, Handheld, and Batch Access Database Products. Volumes are also available individually at $249.00 for Volume 1 and $165.00 for Volume 2.

GALE DIRECTORY OF DATABASES [ONLINE]
Gale Group
27500 Drake Rd.
Farmington Hills, MI 48331
PH: (248)699-4253
FX: (800)414-5043
Online Information Systems Information Industry. Presents the online version of the printed Gale Directory of Databases, Volume 1: Online Databases and Gale Directory of Databases, Volume 2: CD-ROM, Diskette, Magnetic Tape, Handheld, and Batch Access Database Products. Semiannual updates. Inquire as to online cost and availability.

GALENET
Gale Group
27500 Drake Rd.
Farmington Hills, MI 48331
PH: (248)699-4253
FX: (800)414-5043
Online Information Systems. Web site provides a wide variety of full-text information from Gale databases, Taft, and other sources. Covers associations, biography, business directories, education, the information industry, literature, publishing, and science. Fee-based subscriptions are available for individual databases (free demonstration). Includes Boolean search features and the BRS/Search user interface.

THE GEEK'S GUIDE TO INTERNET BUSINESS SUCCESS
Van Nostrand Reinhold
115 Fifth Ave.
New York, NY 10003-1004
PH: (800)842-3636
FX: (212)254-9499
E-mail: info@vnr.com
URL: http://www.vnr.com
Internet. Bob Schmidt. 1997. $22.95. Written for beginning Internet entrepreneurs, especially those with technical expertise but little or no business experience. Covers fee or rate setting, developing new business, product mix, budgeting, partnerships, personnel, and planning. Includes checklists and worksheets.

GLOBALBASE
Gale Group
27500 Drake Rd.
Farmington Hills, MI 48331
PH: (248)699-4253
FX: (800)414-5043
Optoelectronics Computer-Aided Design and Manufacturing (CAD/CAM) Computer Communications Microcomputers and Minicomputers. Formerly produced by Information Access Co. Provides more than one million online summaries of business, industrial, and economic news reports from more than 1,000 publications worldwide. Covers a wide range of material appearing in international trade journals, professional magazines, and newspapers. Time period is 1984 to date, with weekly updates. Inquire as to online cost and availability.

GOVERNMENT INFORMATION ON THE INTERNET
Bernan Associates
4611-F Assembly Drive
Lanham, MD 20706-4391
PH: (800)274-4447
FX: (800)865-3450
E-mail: info@bernan.com
URL: http://www.bernan.com
Internet. Greg R. Notess. 1997. $24.00. A directory of publicly-accessible Internet sites maintained by the U. S. Government. Also includes selected foreign government sites, state sites, and non-government sites containing government-provided data.

HOOVER'S GUIDE TO COMPUTER COMPANIES
Hoover's, Inc.
1033 La Posada Drive, Suite 250
Austin, TX 78752
PH: (800)486-8666
FX: (512)374-4501
E-mail: orders@hoovers.com
URL: http://www.hoovers.com
Computers Computer Software Industry Microcomputers and Minicomputers. Annual. $34.95. Published in association with Upside magazine. Contains profiles of about 1,400 computer hardware and software companies.

IEEE COMPUTER SOCIETY
1730 Massachusetts Ave., N. W.
Washington, DC 20036
PH: (202)371-0101
FX: (202)728-9614
E-mail: csinfo@computer.org
Computer Communications Computer Graphics Computer-Aided Design and Manufacturing (CAD/CAM) Microcomputers and Minicomputers Computer Crime and Security Computer Software Industry. A society of the Institute of Electrical and Electronics Engineers said to be the world's largest organization of computer professionals. Some of the specific committees are: Computer Communications; Computer Graphics; Computers in Education; Design Automation; Office Automation; Personal Computing; Robotics; Security and Privacy; Software Engineering.

IEEE LASERS AND ELECTRO-OPTICS SOCIETY
Institute of Electrical and Electronics Engineers
PO Box 1331
Piscataway, NJ 08855
PH: (732)562-3892
FX: (732)981-1769
Fiber Optics Industry Optoelectronics. A society of the Institute of Electrical and Electronics Engineers. Fields of interest include lasers, fiber optics, optoelectronics, and photonics.

IEEE MICRO
Institute of
10662 Los Vaqueros Circle
Electrical and Electronics Engineers, Inc.
Los Alamitos, CA 90720-1264

PH: (800)678-4333
FX: (714)821-4010
Microcomputers and Minicomputers Semiconductor Industry. IEEE Computer Society Press. Bimonthly. Free to members; non members, $270.00 per year.

IEEE SOFTWARE
Institute of Electrical and Electronic
10662 Los Vacqueros Circle
Engineers, Inc.
Los Alamitos, CA 90720-1264
PH: (800)678-4333
FX: (714)821-4010
E-mail: csinfo@computer.org
URL: http://www.computer.org
Computer Software Industry. IEEE Computer Society Press. Bimonthly. Free to members; non-members, $310.00 per year. Covers software engineering, technology, and development. Affiliated with the Institute of Electrical and Electronics Engineers.

INFOALERT: YOUR EXPERT GUIDE TO ONLINE BUSINESS INFORMATION
Economics Press, Inc.
12 Daniel Rd.
Fairfield, NJ 07004-2565
PH: (800)526-2554
FX: (201)227-9742
E-mail: info@epinc.com
URL: http://www.epinc.com
Internet Online Information Systems. Monthly. $129.00 per year. Newsletter. Provides information on recommended World Wide Web sites in various business, marketing, industrial, and financial areas.

INFORMATION BROKER
Entrepreneur, Inc.
2392 Morse Ave.
Irvine, CA 92714
PH: (800)421-2300
FX: (714)851-9088
Information Industry. Looseleaf. $59.50. A practical guide to starting an information retrieval business. Covers profit potential, start-up costs, market size evaluation, pricing, accounting, advertising, promotion, etc. (Start-Up Business Guide No. E1237.)

INFORMATION INDUSTRY DIRECTORY
Gale Group
27500 Drake Rd.
Farmington Hills, MI 48331
PH: (248)699-4253
FX: (800)414-5043
Information Industry Online Information Systems. 1997. $580.00. 18th edition. Two volumes. Lists nearly 4,600 producers and vendors of electronic information and related services. Subject, geographic, and master indexes are provided. Supplement available, $390.00. Formerly Encyclopedia of Information Systems and Services.

INFORMATION INDUSTRY FACTBOOK: THE INFORMATION INDUSTRY'S ANNUAL REPORT
Digital Information Group
PO Box 110235
Stamford, CT 06911-0235
PH: (203)348-2751
FX: (203)977-8310
Information Industry Online Information Systems. Irregular. $195.00. Includes market forecasts, directory information, financial ratios, executive compensation data, statistical tables, charts, company profiles, etc.

INFORMATION AND INTERACTIVE SERVICES REPORT: THE BIWEEKLY NEWSLETTER FOR THE INFORMATION INDUSTRY
Telecommunications Reports International
1333 H St., N. W., No. 100-E
Washington, DC 20005
PH: (800)822-6338
FX: (202)842-3047
E-mail: customerservice@tr.com
Information Industry. Biweekly. $495.00 per year. Newsletter. Incorporates the former *International Videotex Teletext News* and *Information Industry Alert.*

INFORMATION MANAGEMENT AND WORKFLOW: PREPARING FOR THE GLOBAL INFORMATION SUPERHIGHWAY
Datapro Information Services Group
600 Delran Parkway
Delran, NJ 08075-1252
PH: (800)328-2776
FX: (609)764-2812
URL: http://www.datapro.com/products
Information Industry Computer Communications Computer Crime and Security Computer Law Internet. Monthly. $2,000.00 per year. Three looseleaf volumes. Includes case studies, user surveys, emerging technologies, legal issues, security, standards, communications issues, and other topics related to various forms of information. Data, text, graphics, and voice transmissions are covered. An "International Vendor Directory" is provided.

INFORMATION OUTLOOK: THE MONTHLY MAGAZINE OF THE SPECIAL LIBRARIES ASSOCIATION
1700 18th St., N. W.
Washington, DC 20009-2514
PH: (202)234-4700
FX: (202)265-9317
URL: http://www.sla.org
Information Industry Internet Online Information Systems. Special Libraries Association. Monthly. $65.00 per year. Topics include information technology, the Internet, copyright, research techniques, library management, and professional development. Replaces *Special Libraries* and *SpeciaList.*

INFORMATION SCIENCE ABSTRACTS [ONLINE]
IFI/Plenum Data Corp.
102 Eastwood Rd., Suite D-6-F
Wilmington, NC 28405
PH: (800)368-3093
FX: (910)392-0240
Information Industry Online Information Systems Internet. Provides indexing and abstracting of the international literature of information science, including library science, from 1966 to date. Monthly updates. Inquire as to online cost and availability.

INFORMATION SCIENCE ABSTRACTS PLUS
IFI/Plenum Data Corp.
102 Eastwood Rd., Suite D-6-F
Wilmington, NC 28405
PH: (800)368-3093
FX: (919)392-0240
Information Industry Online Information Systems. Quarterly. $1,095.00 per year. Presents CD-ROM abstracts of worldwide information science and library science literature from 1966 to date.

INFORMATION STANDARDS QUARTERLY: NEWS ABOUT LIBRARY, INFORMATION SCIENCES, AND PUBLISHING STANDARDS
National Information Standards Organization (NISO)
4733 Bethesda Ave.
Bethesda, MD 20814
PH: (301)654-2512
FX: (301)654-1721
E-mail: nisohq@cnl.org
URL: http://www.niso.org

Internet Information Industry. Quarterly. $75.00 per year. Newsletter. Reports on activities of the National Information Standards Organization.

INFORMATION SYSTEMS SPENDING
Computer Economics, Inc.
5841 Edison Place
Carlsbad, CA 92008
PH: (800)326-8100
FX: (760)431-1126
E-mail: info@compecon.com
URL: http://www.computereconomics.com
Computers Information Industry. Annual. $1,595.00. Three volumes. Based on "in-depth surveys of public and private companies amd government organizations." Provides detailed data on management information systems spending, budgeting, and benchmarks. Includes charts, graphs, and analysis.

INFORMATION TECHNOLOGY ASSOCIATION OF AMERICA
1616 N. Fort Myer Dr., Suite 1300
Arlington, VA 22209
PH: (703)522-5055
FX: (703)525-2279
E-mail: hmiller@itaa.org
URL: http://wwwlitaa.org
Computer Software Industry Computers Microcomputers and Minicomputers. Members are computer software and services companies. Maintains an Information Systems Integration Services Section. Formerly ADAPSO: The Computer Software and Services Industry Association.

INFORMATION TECHNOLOGY OUTLOOK
Organization for Economic Cooperation and Development
2001 L St., N. W., Suite 650
OECD Washington Center
Washington, DC 20036-4922
PH: (800)456-6323
FX: (202)785-0350
E-mail: washcont@oecd.org
URL: http://www.oecd.org
Computers Information Industry Microcomputers and Minicomputers. Annual. $43.00. A review of recent developments in international markets for computer hardware, software, and services. Also examines current legal provisions for information systems security and privacy in OECD countries.

INFOWORLD: THE VOICE OF PERSONAL COMPUTING IN THE ENTERPRISE
InfoWorld Publishing, Inc.
155 Bovet Rd., Suite 800
San Mateo, CA 94402
PH: (800)227-8365
FX: (415)358-1269
URL: http://www.192.216.48.63
Microcomputers and Minicomputers Information Industry Computer Software Industry. Weekly. $145.00 per year. For personal computing professionals.

INSTITUTE OF ADVANCED MANUFACTURING SCIENCES
1111 Edison Dr.
Cincinnati, OH 45216
PH: (513)948-2000
FX: (513)948-2109
E-mail: conley@iams.org
URL: http://www.iams.org
Computer-Aided Design and Manufacturing (CAD/CAM). Fields of research include quality improvement, computer-aided design, artificial intelligence, and employee training.

INTER-NOT: ONLINE & INTERNET STATISTICS REALITY CHECK

New Networks Institute
26 Broadway, Suite 400
New York, NY 10004
PH: (212)837-7687
E-mail: internot@interport.net
URL: http://www.newnetworks.com
Internet Online Information Systems. Bruce Kushnick. Annual. $495.00. Compares, analyzes, and criticizes statistics issued by Nielsen Media, Forrester Research, FIND/SVP, Yankelovich Partners and many others relating to online and Internet activities. For example, estimates of the number of Internet users have ranged from about 40 million down to six million. Topics include "Adjusting for the Puffery" and "The Most Plausible Statistics."

INTER-NOT: THE TERRIBLE TWOS—ONLINE INDUSTRY'S LEARNING CURVE

New Networks Institute
26 Broadway, Suite 400
New York, NY 10004
PH: (212)837-7687
E-mail: internot@interport.net
URL: http://www.newnetworks.com
Internet Online Information Systems. Bruce Kushnick. 1996. $495.00. Second edition. A market research report discussing the growing pains of the online industry, especially with regard to the Internet. The importance of market segmentation and customer service is emphasized.

INTERACTIVE ADVERTISING SOURCE

SRDS
1700 Higgins Rd.
Des Plaines, IL 60018
PH: (800)851-7737
FX: (847)375-5001
URL: http://www.srds.com
Internet Online Information Systems. Quarterly. $249.00 per year. Provides descriptive profiles, rates, audience, personnel, etc., for producers of various forms of interactive or multimedia advertising: online/Internet, CD-ROM, interactive TV, interactive cable, interactive telephone, interactive kiosk, and others.

INTERACTIVE AGE: CONTENT, TECHNOLOGY, AND COMMUNICATIONS FOR THE INFORMATION HIGHWAY

CMP Publications, Inc.
600 Community Drive
Manhasset, NY 11030
PH: (800)829-0421
FX: (516)562-5474
E-mail: interact@interact.cmp.com
Computer Communications Information Industry Internet. Biweekly. Free to qualified personnel; others, $79.00 per year. Provides "coverage of developments across the interactive spectrum," including computer communications, telecommunications, the cable industry, and the "entertainment/information/media industry."

INTERACTIVE CONSUMERS

FIND/SVP, Inc.
625 Ave. of the Americas
New York, NY 10011-2002
PH: (800)346-3787
FX: (212)807-2716
E-mail: catalog@findsvp.com
URL: http://www.findsvp.com
Internet. Monthly. $395.00 per year. Newsletter. Covers the emerging markets for digital content, products, and services. Includes market information on telecommuting, online services, the Internet, online investing, and other areas of electronic commerce.

INTERACTIVE DIGITAL SOFTWARE ASSOCIATION

1130 Connecticut Ave., Suite 710
Washington, DC 20036
PH: (202)833-4372
FX: (202)833-4431
E-mail: info@idsa.com
Computer Software Industry. Members are interactive entertainment software publishers concerned with rating systems, software piracy, government relations, and other industry issues.

INTERACTIVE MULTIMEDIA ASSOCIATION

48 Maryland Ave., Suite 202
Annapolis, MD 21401-8011
PH: (410)626-1380
FX: (410)263-0590
E-mail: info@ima.org
URL: http://www.ima.org
Computer Peripherals and Accessories. Members are companies, organizations, and institutions that produce interactive multimedia hardware and software.

INTERACTIVE SERVICES ASSOCIATION

8403 Colesville Rd., Suite 865
Silver Spring, MD 20910-3366
PH: (301)495-4955
FX: (301)495-4959
E-mail: isa@isa.net
Online Information Systems Computer Communications. Members are business firms that furnish electronic interactive services in the areas of online information, communication, entertainment, business transactions, and videotex. Formerly Videotex Industry Association.

INTERACTIVE SOURCE BOOK

North American Publishing Co.
401 N. Broad St.
Philadelphia, PA 19108-9958
PH: (215)238-5300
FX: (215)238-5099
URL: http://www.napco.com
Internet. Annual. $545.00. Lists companies providing interactive media products and services in the following areas: television, the Internet, wireless cable, and satellite systems.

INTERACTIVITY: TOOLS AND TECHNIQUES FOR INTERACTIVE MEDIA DEVELOPERS

Miller Freeman, Inc.
411 Borel Ave.
San Mateo, CA 94402
PH: (888)776-7002
FX: (650)655-4360
E-mail: interactivity@mfi.com
URL: http://www.mfi.com
Computer Animation See also: Virtual Reality. Monthly. $59.95 per year. Edited for professional interactive media developers. Includes a special issue on computer animation.

INTERNATIONAL ANIMATED FILM SOCIETY

725 South Victory Blvd.
Burbank, CA 91502
PH: (818)842-8330
FX: (818)842-5645
E-mail: asifa@earthlink.net
Computer Animation See also: Virtual Reality. Members are professional animation artists, fans, and students. Promotes advancements in the art of animation.

INTERNATIONAL SEMICONDUCTOR DIRECTORY: D.A.T.A. DIGEST MASTER TYPE LOCATER

D.A.T.A. Business Publishing
Post Office Box 6510
Englewood, CO 80155-6510
PH: (800)447-4666
FX: (303)799-0381
Semiconductor Industry. D.A.T.A. Digest. Semiannual. $150.00 per year. Lists semiconductor devices and indicates their manufacturers. Addresses and telephone numbers given for about 900 manufacturers. Formerly *International Semiconductor Directory ICS and*

INTERNET COMPUTING
IEEE Computer Society Press
10662 Los Vacqueros Circle
Los Alamitos, CA 90720-1264
PH: (800)678-4333
FX: (714)821-4010
E-mail: csinfo@computer.org
URL: http://www.computer.org
Computers Internet. Institute of Electrical and Electronic Engineers, Inc. Bimonthly. Price on application. Covers technology, standards, research, and engineering for the Internet and the World Wide Web. Affiliated with the Institute of Electrical and Electronics Engineers.

INTERNET REFERENCE SERVICES QUARTERLY: A JOURNAL OF INNOVATIVE INFORMATION PRACTICE, TECHNOLOGIES, AND RESOURCES
Haworth Press, Inc.
10 Alice St.
Binghamton, NY 13904-1580
PH: (800)429-6784
FX: (800)895-0582
E-mail: getinfo@haworth.com
URL: http://www.haworth.com
Internet Online Information Systems. Quarterly. Libraries, $48.00 per year. Individuals, $36.00 per year. Covers both theoretical research and practical applications.

INTERNETWEEK
CMP Media, Inc.
600 Community Drive
Manhasset, NY 11030
PH: (516)562-5549
FX: (516)562-5913
URL: http://www.internetwk.com
Internet. Weekly. $65.00 per year. Edited for professionals involved with the Internet, intranets, and extranets. Formerly *Communications Week*.

INTERNETWORKING
Datapro Information Services Group
600 Delran Parkway
Delran, NJ 08075
PH: (800)328-2776
FX: (609)764-2812
URL: http://www.datapro.com/products
Local Area Networks. Monthly. $1,144.00 per year. Three looseleaf volumes. Provides detailed evaluations of hardware and software for local area networks. Formerly *Datapro Local Area Networks, with LAN Internet working*.

INTEROPERABILITY
Miller Freeman, Inc.
600 Harrison St.
San Francisco, CA 94107
PH: (800)227-4675
FX: (415)905-2239
Computer Communications. Quarterly. Price on application. Covers the operation of wide-area networks, including UNIX systems.

INTRANET AND NETWORKING STRATEGIES REPORT: ADVISING IT DECISION MAKERS ON BEST PRACTICES AND CURRENT TRENDS
Computer Economics, Inc.
5841 Edison Place
Carlsbad, CA 92008
PH: (800)326-8100
FX: (760)431-1126
E-mail: info@compecon.com
URL: http://www.computereconomics.com
Computers Local Area Networks. Monthly. $395.00 per year. Newsletter. Edited for information technology managers. Covers news and trends relating to a variety of corporate computer network and management information systems topics. Emphasis is on costs.

IWORLD: INTERNET NEWS AND RESOURCES
Mecklermedia Corp.
PH: (800)632-5537
FX: (203)454-5840
E-mail: info@mecklermedia.com
URL: http://www.iworld.com
Internet Online Information Systems Virtual Reality See also: Computer Animation. Web site provides news and information about the Internet, online information sources, and electronic media. Includes daily news, weekly features, directories, and content from *Internet World*, *Web Week*, and *Web Developer* magazines. Fees: Free.

KEY ABSTRACTS: COMPUTER COMMUNICATIONS AND STORAGE
INSPEC/IEEE Operations Center
PO Box 1331
Piscataway, NJ 08855-1331
PH: (800)678-4333
FX: (908)562-8737
Computer Communications Local Area Networks Internet. Monthly. $200.00 per year. Provides international coverage of journal and proceedings literature, including material on optical disks and networks. Published in England by the Institution of Electrical Engineers (IEE).

KEY ABSTRACTS: COMPUTING IN ELECTRONICS AND POWER
INSPEC/IEEE Operations Center
PO Box 1331
Piscataway, NJ 08855-1331
PH: (800)678-4333
FX: (908)562-8737
Electronics Industry. $200.00 per year. Provides international coverage of journal and proceedings literature. Published in England by the Institution of Electrical Engineers (IEE).

KEY ABSTRACTS: HIGH TEMPERATURE SUPERCONDUCTORS
INSPEC/IEEE Operations Center
PO Box 1331
Piscataway, NJ 08855-1331
PH: (800)678-4333
FX: (908)562-8737
Superconductors. Monthly. $200.00 per year. Provides international coverage of journal and proceedings literature. Published in England by the Institution of Electrical Engineers (IEE).

KEY ABSTRACTS: OPTOELECTRONICS
INSPEC/IEEE Operations Service Center
PO Box 1331
Piscataway, NJ 08854-1331
PH: (800)678-4333
FX: (908)562-8737
Fiber Optics Industry Optoelectronics. Monthly. $200.00 per year. Provides international coverage of journal and proceedings literature relating to fiber optics, lasers, and optoelectronics in general. Published in England by the Institution of Electrical Engineers (IEE).

KEY ABSTRACTS: SEMICONDUCTOR DEVICES
INSPEC/IEEE Operations Center
PO Box 1331
Piscataway, NJ 08855-1331
PH: (800)678-4333
FX: (908)562-8737
Semiconductor Industry. Monthly. $200.00 per year. Provides international coverage of journal and proceedings literature. Published in England by the Institution of Electrical Engineers (IEE).

KEY ABSTRACTS: SOFTWARE ENGINEERING
INSPEC/IEEE Operations Center
PO Box 1331
Piscataway, NJ 08855-1331
PH: (800)678-4333
FX: (908)562-8737

Computer Software Industry. Monthly. $200.00 per year. Provides international coverage of journal and proceedings literature. Published in England by the Institution of Electrical Engineers (IEE).

LABORATORY FOR COMPUTER SCIENCE
Massachusetts Institute of Technology
545 Technology Square
Cambridge, MA 02139
PH: (617)253-5851
FX: (617)258-8682
E-mail: (ncsa)mld@hq.lcs.mit.edu
URL: http://web.mit.edu
Computers Online Information Systems. Research is in four areas: Intelligent Systems; Parallel Systems; Systems, Languages, and Networks; and Theory. Emphasis is on the application of online computing.

LABORATORY FOR INFORMATION AND DECISION SYSTEMS
Massachusetts Institute of Technology
Bldg. 35, Room 308
Cambridge, MA 02139
PH: (617)253-2160
FX: (617)253-3578
E-mail: mitter@lids.mit.edu
URL: http://www.web.mit.edu
Fiber Optics Industry Computer Communications Local Area Networks. Research areas include data communication networks and fiber optic networks.

LAMP (LITERATURE ANALYSIS OF MICROCOMPUTER PUBLICATIONS)
200 Route 17
Mahwah, NJ 07430
PH: (201)529-1440
Computer Graphics Computer Communications Computer Software Industry Microcomputers and Minicomputers. Soft Images. Bimonthly. $89.95 per year. Annual cumulation.

LAPTOP BUYER'S GUIDE AND HANDBOOK
Bedford Communications, Inc.
150 Fifth Ave.
New York, NY 10011
PH: (212)807-8220
FX: (212)807-1098
Portable Computers. Subscription at $36.00 per year includes six issues of the bimonthly *Laptop Buyer's Guide and Handbook* and six issues of the bimonthly *Computer Buyer's Guide and Handbook*. Includes equipment reviews, articles, comparison charts, and "Street Price Guide" (discounted prices with names, addresses, and telephone numbers of dealers).

LASER FOCUS WORLD BUYERS GUIDE
PennWell Publishing Co.
10 Tara Blvd., 5th Fl.
Nashua, NH 03062-2801
PH: (800)331-4463
FX: (603)891-0574
URL: http://www.pennwell.com
Fiber Optics Industry Optoelectronics. Annual. $125.00. Lists more than 2,000 suppliers of optoelectronic and laser products and services.

LASER FOCUS WORLD: THE MAGAZINE OF ELECTRO-OPTICS TECHNOLOGY
PennWell Publishing Co.
20 Ames St., E-15
Massachusetts Institute of Technology
10 Tara Blvd., 5th Fl.
Cambridge, MA 02139
PH: (617)253-0338
FX: (617)258-6164
E-mail: casr@media.mit.edu
URL: http://www.media.mit.edu

Fiber Optics Industry Optoelectronics. Monthly. $156.00 per year. Covers business and technical aspects of electro-optics, including lasers and fiberoptics. Media Laboratory Electronic Publishing. Research areas include electronic publishing, spatial imaging, human-machine interface, computer vision, and advanced television.

MOBILE OFFICE
Cowles Business Media.
21800 Oxnard St., Suite 250
Warner Plaza
Woodland Hills, CA 91367-3633
PH: (800)795-5445
FX: (818)593-6153
URL: http://www.mediacentral.com
Portable Computers. Monthly. $23.90 per year. Covers cellular phones, notebook computers, and other portable electronic items. New products are featured.

MULTI-MEDIA SCHOOLS: A PRACTICAL JOURNAL OF MULTIMEDIA, CD-ROM, ONLINE AND INTERNET IN K-12
Online, Inc.
462 Danbury Rd.
Wilton, CT 06897-2126
PH: (800)248-8466
FX: (203)761-1444
E-mail: booksales@onlineinc.com
URL: http://www.onlineinc.com
Internet. Five times a year. $38.00 per year. Covers the use of multimedia in elementary and secondary education, including applications for CD-ROM and the Internet.

MULTIMEDIA ENTERTAINMENT AND TECHNOLOGY REPORT
SIMBA Information, Inc.
Post Office Box 4234
Stamford, CT 06907-0234
PH: (800)307-2529
FX: (203)358-5824
E-mail: info@simbanet.com
URL: http://www.simbanet.com
Online Information Systems. Biweekly. $549.00 per year. Newsletter. Covers new technology, joint ventures, licensing, marketing, finance, and other topics relating to multimedia products. Formerly *Multimedia Business Report*.

MULTIMEDIA SCHOOLS: A PRACTICAL JOURNAL OF MULTIMEDIA
Information Today, Inc.
143 Old Marlton Pike
Medford, NJ 08055-8750
PH: (800)300-9868
FX: (609)654-4309
E-mail: custserv@infotoday.com
URL: http://www.infotoday.com
Internet Online Information Systems. Bimonthly. $38.00 per year. Edited for school librarians, media center directors, computer coordinators, and others concerned with educational multimedia. Coverage includes the use of CD-ROM sources, the Internet, online services, and library technology.

NETWORK WORLD: THE NEWSWEEKLY OF ENTERPRISE NETWORK COMPUTING
Network World Inc.
161 Worcester Rd., 5th Fl.
Framingham, MA 01701
PH: (508)875-6400
FX: (508)879-3167
URL: http://www.nwfusion
Internet Computer Communications Local Area Networks. Weekly. $129.00 per year. Includes special feature issues on enterprise Internets, network operating systems, network management, high-speed modems, LAN management systems, and Internet access providers.

NEW MEDIA: THE MAGAZINE FOR CREATORS OF THE DIGITAL FUTURE
HyperMedia Communications,Inc.
901 Mariner's Island Blvd., Suite 365
San Mateo, CA 94404
PH: (800)253-6641
FX: (415)573-5131
E-mail: publisher@newmedia.com
URL: http://www.hyperstand.com
Computer Animation See also: Virtual Reality. 16 times a year. $52.00 per year. Edited for multimedia professionals, with emphasis on digital video and Internet graphics, including animation. Contains reviews of new products.

NEW TELECOM QUARTERLY—THE FUTURE OF TELECOMMUNICATIONS
Technology Futures, Inc.
13740 Research Blvd., Ste. C-1
Austin, TX 78750-1859
PH: (800)835-3887
FX: (512)258-0087
E-mail: info@tfi.com
URL: http://www.tfi.com
Computer Communications Fiber Optics Industry. Quarterly. $120.00 per year. Includes articles on trends in wireless telecommunications, fiber optics technology, interactive multimedia, online information systems, telephone systems, and telecommunications in general.

NFAIS YEARBOOK OF THE INFORMATION INDUSTRY
Information Today, Inc.
143 Old Marlton Pike
Medford, NJ 08055-8750
PH: (800)300-9868
FX: (609)654-4309
Information Industry. Arthur W. Elias. Annual. $50.00. Compiled by the National Federation of Abstracting and Information Services (NFAIS). Summarizes and analyzes the impacts of each year's events on information, abstracting, and indexing activities.

NTIS ALERTS: COMPUTERS, CONTROL & INFORMATION THEORY
National Technical Information Service
5285 Port Royal Rd.
Technology Administration
U. S. Department of Commerce
Springfield, VA 22161
PH: (800)553-6847
FX: (703)321-8547
Computers. Semimonthly. $180.00 per year. Formerly *Abstract Newsletter*. Provides descriptions of government-sponsored research reports and software, with ordering information. Covers computer hardware, software, control systems, pattern recognition, image processing, and related subjects.

ONLINE AND CD NOTES
Available from Information Today, Inc.
143 Old Marlton Pike
Medford, NJ 08055-8750
PH: (800)300-9868
FX: (609)654-4309
Online Information Systems. 10 times a year. Free to members; non-members, $140.00 per year. Published in London by Aslib: The Association for Information Management. Contains news and reviews of the online information industry. Formerly *Online and CD-ROM Notes.*

ONLINE MARKETPLACE
Jupiter Communications Co.
627 Broadway, 2nd Floor
New York, NY 10012
PH: (800)488-4345
FX: (212)780-6075
E-mail: jupiter@jup.com
URL: http://www.jup.com
Internet. Monthly. $545.00 per year. Newsletter on the collection of electronic payments ("e-money") for goods and services offered through the Internet. Covers trends in retailing, banking, travel, and other areas.

ONLINE NEWSLETTER
Information Intelligence, Inc.
Post Office Box 31098
Phoenix, AZ 85046
PH: (602)996-2283
E-mail: order@infointelligence.com
URL: http://www.infointelligence.com
Information Industry Online Information Systems. 10 times a year. Individuals, $43.75 per year; institutions, $62.50 per year; students, $25.00 per year. $62.50 per year. Covers the online and CD-ROM information industries, including news of mergers, acquisitions, personnel, meetings, new products, and new technology.

PLUNKETT'S ENTERTAINMENT & MEDIA INDUSTRY ALMANAC
Available from Hoover's, Inc.
1033 La Posada Drive, Suite 250
Austin, TX 78752
PH: (800)486-8666
FX: (512)374-4501
E-mail: orders@hoovers.com
URL: http://www.hoovers.com
Online Information Systems. Annual. $149.95. Published by Plunkett Research. Provides profiles of leading firms in online information, films, radio, television, cable, multimedia, magazines, and book publishing. Includes World Wide Web sites, where available, plus information on careers and industry trends.

PLUNKETT'S INFOTECH INDUSTRY ALMANAC
Available from Hoover's, Inc.
1033 La Posada Dr., Suite 250
Austin, TX 78752
PH: (800)486-8666
FX: (512)374-4501
E-mail: orders@hoovers.com
URL: http://www.hoovers.com
Computers Computer Communications Information Industry Internet. Annual. $131.50. Published by Plunkett Research. Five hundred major information companies are profiled, with corporate culture aspects. Discusses major trends in various sectors of the computer and information industry, including data on careers and job growth. Includes several indexes.

SECURITY MANAGEMENT
American Society for Industrial Security
1655 N. Fort Myer Dr., Suite 1200
Mary Alice Crawford Publishers
Arlington, VA 22209-3198
PH: (703)522-5800
FX: (703)522-5226
Computer Crime and Security. Monthly. $48.00 per year. Articles cover the protection of corporate assets, including personnel property and information security.

SECURITY: PRODUCT SERVICE SUPPLIERS GUIDE
Cahners Publishing Co., Inc.
Post Office Box 5080
Des Plains, IL 60017-5080
PH: (800)662-7776
FX: (847)390-2690
E-mail: marketaccess@cahners.com
URL: http://www.cahners.com
Computer Crime and Security. Annual. $50.00 Includes computer and information protection products. Formerly *Security - Directory of Products and Services.*

STUDIO FOR CREATIVE INQUIRY
Carnegie Mellon University
College of Fine Arts
Pittsburgh, PA 15213
PH: (412)268-3454
FX: (412)268-2829
E-mail: brogers@atscmu.edu
Virtual Reality See also: Computer Animation. Research areas include artificial intelligence, virtual reality, hypermedia, multimedia, and telecommunications, in relation to the arts.

SURVEY OF ADVANCED TECHNOLOGY
Computer Economics, Inc.
5841 Edison Place
Carlsbad, CA 92008
PH: (800)326-8100
FX: (760)431-1126
E-mail: info@compecon.com
URL: http://www.computereconomics.com
Computers. Annual. $795.00. Surveys the corporate use (or neglect) of advanced computer technology. Topics include major technology trends and emerging technologies.

TELECOM PERSPECTIVES
Northern Business Information
1221 Ave. of the Americas
New York, NY 10020-1001
PH: (212)512-2898
FX: (212)512-2859
Computer Communications. Monthly. $995.00 per year. Newsletter. Emphasis is on the "market opportunities" that exist within various segments of the telecommunications industry. Provides detailed analysis of both emerging and obsolescing market segments.

TELECOMMUNICATIONS DIRECTORY
Gale Group
27500 Drake Rd
Farmington Hills, MI 48331-3535
PH: (800)877-GALE
FX: (800)414-5043
E-mail: galeord@galegroup.com
URL: http://www.galegroup.com
Computer Communications. National and international voice, data, facsimile, and video communications services. Formerly *Telecommunications Systems and Services Directory.*

U. S. INDUSTRY AND TRADE OUTLOOK
McGraw-Hill
1221 Ave. of the Americas
New York, NY 10020
PH: (800)722-4726
FX: (212)512-2821
E-mail: customer.service@mcgraw-hill.com
URL: http://www.mcgraw-hill.com
Computer Communications. Annual. $69.95. Produced by the International Trade Administration, U. S. Department of Commerce, in a "public-private" partnership with DRI/McGraw-Hill and Standard & Poor's. Provides basic data, outlook for the current year, and "Long-Term Prospects" (five-year projections) for a wide variety of products and services. Includes high technology industries. Formerly *U. S. Industrial Outlook.*

U. S. LAN SERVER MARKETS
Available from FIND/SVP, Inc.
625 Ave. of the Americas
New York, NY 10011-2002
PH: (800)346-3787
FX: (212)807-2716
E-mail: catalog@findsvp.com
URL: http://www.findsvp.com
Local Area Networks Internet. $2,450.00. Market research report published by Frost & Sullivan. Covers local area network server markets relative to groupware, the Internet, intranets, and remote access. Includes company profiles.

THE U. S. MARKET FOR PAYMENT SYSTEMS
Available from FIND/SVP, Inc.
625 Ave. of the Americas
New York, NY 10011-2002
PH: (800)346-3787
FX: (212)807-2716
E-mail: catalog@findsvp.com
URL: http://www.findsvp.com
Electronic Funds Transfer Systems (EFTS). $2,500.00. Market research report published by Packaged Facts. Covers credit cards, charge cards, debit cards, and smart cards. Provides profiles of Visa, Mastercard, American Express, Discover, Diners Club, and others.

WEB WEEK
Mecklermedia Corp.
20 Ketchum St.
Westport, CT 06880
PH: (800)632-5537
FX: (203)454-5840
E-mail: info@mecklermedia.com
URL: http://www.iworld.com
Internet. Weekly. Controlled circulation. Provides news of Internet and World Wide Web commercial and technical developments. Includes product reviews and technical reports.

WEFA INDUSTRIAL MONITOR
John Wiley and Sons, Inc.
605 Third Ave.
New York, NY 10158-0012
PH: (800)225-5945
FX: (212)850-6088
E-mail: business@jwiley.
URL: http://www.wiley.com
Computers Electronics Industry. Annual. $59.95. Prepared by industry analysts at WEFA, an economic forecasting and consulting firm (originally Wharton Econometric Forecasting Associates). Contains discussions of the outlook for major U. S. industries, with many 10-year forecasts (WEFA Web site is http://www.wefa.com).

WHO'S WHO IN TECHNOLOGY
Gale Group
27500 Drake Rd
Farmington Hills, MI 48331-3535
PH: (800)877-GALE
FX: (800)414-5043
E-mail: galeord@galegroup.com
URL: http://www.galegroup.com
Computer Communications Information Industry Microcomputers and Minicomputers Semiconductor Industry. Covers the fields of electronics, computer science, physics, optics, chemistry, biotechnology, mechanics, energy, and earth science.

WILSONDISC: APPLIED SCIENCE AND TECHNOLOGY
  ABSTRACTS
H. W. Wilson Co.
950 University Ave.
Bronx, NY 10452
PH: (800)367-6770
FX: (718)590-1617
Fiber Optics Industry. Monthly. $1,495.00 per year, including unlimited access to the online version of *Applied Science and Technology Abstracts* through WILSONLINE. Provides CD-ROM indexing and abstracting of 400 prominent scientific, technical, engineering, and industrial periodicals. Indexing coverage is provided from 1983 to date and abstracting from 1993 to date.

WILSONLINE: APPLIED SCIENCE AND TECHNOLOGY
  ABSTRACTS
H. W. Wilson Co.
950 University Ave.
Bronx, NY 10452

PH: (800)367-6770
FX: (718)590-1617
E-mail: hwwmsg@info.hwwilson.com
URL: http://www.hwwilson.com
Fiber Optics Industry Computer Peripherals and Accessories Superconductors. Provides online indexing and abstracting of 400 major scientific, technical, industrial, and engineering periodicals. Time period is 1983 to date for indexing and 1993 to date for abstracting, with updating twice a week. Inquire as to online cost and availability.

WIRED

Wired Ventures Ltd.
520 Third St., 4th Fl.
San Francisco, CA 94107-1815
PH: (800)769-4733
FX: (415)222-6209
E-mail: editor@wired.com
Internet Computer Communications Online Information Systems Information Industry Electronic Publishing. Monthly. $39.95 per year. Edited for creators and managers in various areas of electronic information and entertainment, including multimedia, the Internet, and video. Often considered to be the primary publication of the "digital generation."

WIRELESS DATA NETWORKS

Warren Publishing, Inc., Telecom Publishing Group.
2115 Ward Court, N. W.
Washington, DC 20037-1209
PH: (202)872-9200
FX: (202)293-3435
E-mail: info@telecommunications.com
URL: http://www.telecommunications.com
Computer Communications. 1998. $1,995.00. Fourth edition. Presents market research information relating to cellular data networks, paging networks, packet radio networks, satellite systems, and other areas of wireless communication. Contains "summaries of recent developments and trends in wireless markets."

WIRELESS DATA NEWS

Phillips Business Information, Inc.
1201 Seven Locks Rd., Suite 300
Potomac, MD 20854
PH: (800)777-5006
FX: (301)309-3847
Computer Communications Local Area Networks. Biweekly. $597.00 per year. Newsletter. Covers the wireless data communications industry, including wireless LANs.

WORLDWIDE FIBEROPTIC SUPPLIERS DIRECTORY

Kessler Marketing Intelligence.
America's Cup Ave. at 31 Bridge St.
Newport, RI 02840
PH: (401)849-6771
FX: (401)847-5866
E-mail: kmi@ids.net
Fiber Optics Industry. Annual. $65.00. A directory of over 1,350 manufacturers and suppliers of fiber optics components and systems.

TRADE SHOWS

Information presented in this chapter is adapted from Gale's *Trade Shows Worldwide* (*TSW*). Entries present information needed for all those planning to visit or to participate in trade shows for the Computers & Software sector. *TSW* entries include U.S. and Canadian shows and exhibitions.

Entries are arranged in alphabetical order by the name of the event and include the exhibition management company with full contact information, frequency of the event, audience, and principal exhibits.

THE 3D DESIGN AND CONFERENCE EXHIBITION
525 Market St., Ste. 500
San Francisco, CA 94105
PH: (415)278-5300
FX: (415)278-5341
Frequency: Annual. **Principal Exhibits:** Equipment, supplies, and services for the 3D design industry.

ACCOUNTING MANAGEMENT
Rotebuhlstrasse 83-85
D-70178 Stuttgart, Germany
PH: 49 11 619460
FX: 49 11 6194698
E-mail: buss@mesago.de
URL: http://www.mesago.de
Principal Exhibits: Management systems and software.

AE ASIA/AUTOMAT ASIA/LOGISTIK MALAYSIA
Level 21, 19A-21-2, UOA Centre
19 Jalan Pinang
50450 Kuala Lumpur, Malaysia
PH: 60 3 264 5663
FX: 60 2 264 5660
Frequency: Biennial.

AIE - ASIAN INDUSTRIAL EXPO
Unit 1223, 12/F, Hong Kong International Trade & Exhibition
1 Trademart Dr.
Kowloon Bay, Hong Kong
PH: 852 2865 2633
FX: 852 2866 1770
Principal Exhibits: Industrial equipment, supplies, and services.

ALLIANCE SUD - THE SUBCONTRACTING AND DESIGN ENGINEERING EXPOSITION
Parc des Expositions bp 55
33030 Bordeaux Lac, France
PH: 33 56 11 99 00
FX: 33 56 11 99 99
URL: http://www.bordeaux-expo.com
Frequency: Annual. **Principal Exhibits:** Subcontracting exhibits, including sheet iron works, boiler engineering, press operations, foundries, thermal and surface treatments, plastics transformation technology, electronics automation, and robotics.

AMERICAN COLLEGE OF MEDICAL QUALITY
PO Box 34493
Bethesda, MD 20827-0493
PH: (301)365-3570
TF: (800)924-2149
FX: (301)365-3202
E-mail: acma@aol.com
URL: http://www.acmq.org
Frequency: Annual. **Audience:** Physicians, nurses, and other healthcare professionals interested in medical quality assurance and utilization review and risk management. **Principal Exhibits:** Computer hardware and software, pharmaceuticals, medical publications, and related equipment, supplies, and services. **Formerly:** Managed Care and Care Managers Focusing on Clinical Quality.

AMERICAN PSYCHIATRIC ASSOCIATION ANNUAL MEETING
1400 K St., NW
Washington, DC 20005
PH: (202)682-6100
FX: (202)682-6132
URL: http://www.psych.org
Frequency: Annual. **Audience:** Psychiatrists, mental health professionals, and general public. **Principal Exhibits:** Pharmaceuticals, data processing hardware & software, biofeedback instrumentation; furnishings; information from private psychiatric hospitals and state mental health agencies; and related publications.

AMERICAN TRADESHOW OF COMPUTERIZED AUTOMATION SERVICES
22106 Knollwood Dr.
Brownstown, MI 48134
Frequency: Annual. **Principal Exhibits:** Computer automation technology.

ANNUAL INTERACTIVE SERVICE ASSOCIATION CONFERENCE
8403 Colesville Rd., Ste. 865
Silver Spring, MD 20910
PH: (301)495-4955
FX: (301)495-4959
URL: http://www.isa.net
Frequency: Annual. **Audience:** Corporate executives concerned with delivering and incentive electronic services to mass markets. **Principal Exhibits:** Computer hardware and software; interactive electronics systems and services for home, office, and public use.

AUTOMAN - EUROPEAN ADVANCED MANUFACTURING SYSTEMS EXHIBITION AND CONFERENCE
383 Main Ave.
PO Box 6059
Norwalk, CT 06851
PH: (203)840-5358
FX: (203)840-4804
E-mail: inquiry@nepcon.reedexpo.com
Frequency: Annual. **Audience:** Persons involved in purchasing of advanced manufacturing equipment. **Principal Exhibits:** Automated manufacturing equipment, supplies, and services.

AUTOMATE AUSTRALIA - AUSTRALIAN INTERNATIONAL ROBOTICS AND INDUSTRIAL AUTOMATION EXHIBITION
Illoura Plaza
424 St. Kilda Rd.
Melbourne, VIC 3004, Australia
PH: 61 3 92614500
FX: 61 3 92614545
E-mail: shows@ausexhibit.com.au
URL: http://www.ausexhibit.com.au
Frequency: Annual. **Audience:** Senior and manufacturing management; production, design, senior, and consulting engineers. **Principal Exhibits:** Automated technology equipment, supplies, and services, including robotics computers in manufacturing, process control, automation and materials handling equipment.

AUTOMATED MANUFACTURING EXHIBITION AND CONFERENCE
111 Executive Center Dr.
Columbia, SC 29210
PH: (803)737-9352
TF: (800)553-7702
FX: (803)737-9343
Frequency: Biennial. **Audience:** Managers and engineers interested in the manufacturing environment. **Principal Exhibits:** Computer and automation applications: robotics, AGV's, laser inspection and counting equipment, vision systems, quality control, and instrumentation.

AUTOMATION EUROPE - EVENT FOR DESIGNERS AND USERS OF AUTOMATIC DEVICES, PROCESS AND INDUSTRIAL DATA PROCESSING
1 rue du Parc
F-92593 Levallois Perret, France
PH: 331 49685100
FX: 331 47377438
E-mail: simd@cepexposium.fr
URL: http://www.simd.fr
Frequency: Annual. **Principal Exhibits:** Equipment, supplies, and services for automatic users and designers.

BALTECOLOGIA
5 Laisves Ave.
2600 Vilnius, Lithuania
PH: 3702 454500
FX: 3702 454511
E-mail: info@litexpo.lt
Frequency: Annual. **Principal Exhibits:** Software, hardware, computers and electronics, telecommunication facilities, informational systems, security systems.

BANKING SHANGHAI - SHANGHAI INTERNATIONAL EXHIBITION ON BANKING AND FINANCIAL EQUIPMENT, COMPUTER AND OFFICE AUTOMATION
4/F Stanhope House
734 King's Rd.
North Point, Hong Kong
PH: 852 2811 8897
FX: 852 2516 5024
E-mail: aes@adsaleexh.com
URL: http://www.adsaleexh.com
Frequency: Biennial. **Audience:** Trade professionals. **Principal Exhibits:** Various machines and equipment for banking services, computer systems and peripherals for banking, communication systems and equipment, and office equipment.

BASIL WORLD CFD USER DAYS WORLD CONFERENCE IN APPLIED COMPUTATIONAL FLUID DYNAMICS WITH EXHIBITION
Frequency: Biennial. **Audience:** Those engaged in the actual application process in CFD. **Principal Exhibits:** Software, hardware, applications, and services in CFD.

BETT - BRITISH EDUCATION AND TRAINING TECHNOLOGY EXHIBITION
Maclaren House
19 Scarbrook Rd.
Croydon CR9 1QM, England
PH: 44 181 277 5000
FX: 44 181 277 5125
Frequency: Annual. **Audience:** Head teachers, deputy heads, department heads, IT coordinators, teachers, and advisors. **Principal Exhibits:** Computer hardware, software, peripherals, multimedia, CD ROM, interactive video, books, and stationery.

BIPA EXPO - MULTIMEDIA EXHIBITION FOR PICTURE, SOUND, AND LIGHT
Center Blvd.
DK-2300 Copenhagen S, Denmark
PH: 45 32 52 88 11
FX: 45 32 51 96 36
E-mail: bc@bella.dk
URL: http://www.bellacenter.dk
Frequency: Biennial. **Principal Exhibits:** Multimedia equipment, supplies, and services.

BITS & FUN - INFORMATION AND SALES EXHIBITION FOR COMPUTERS AND CONSUMER ELECTRONICS
Messegelande
Postfach 121009
D-80034 Munich, Germany
PH: 49 89 5107143
FX: 49 89 5107177
E-mail: info@messe-muenchen.de
URL: http://www.messe.muenchen.de
Frequency: Annual. **Principal Exhibits:** PCs, laptops, palmtops; monitors, printers, scanners, disk drives, software; graphic, sound, and video cards; telephones, handies, and mobile communications; modems, mail systems, telefaxes, multifunctional communications equipment; networks and accessories; online services and solutions, accessories; CD-ROMs, multimedia programs; games software, games consoles; learning programs, infotainment; consumer electronics, CD-I, video technology, and entertainment accessories.

BUSINESS SHOW TOKYO
3-11-8 Sendagaya
Shibuya-ku
Tokyo 151, Japan
PH: 3 3403 1331
FX: 3 3403 5716
URL: http://www.noma-businessshow.or.jp
Frequency: Annual. **Audience:** Trade professionals. **Principal Exhibits:** Computers, peripherals, data processing equipment, data communication equipment, office equipment, stationery, office furniture, and software. **Formerly:** IBS - International Business Show.

C-TECH - EXHIBITION FOR COMPUTING IN INDUSTRY AND TECHNOLOGY
383 Main Ave.
PO Box 6059
Norwalk, CT 06851
PH: (203)840-5358
FX: (203)840-4804
E-mail: inquiry@nepcon.reedexpo.com
Frequency: Biennial. **Audience:** Decision makers and senior management. **Principal Exhibits:** Research and development, handling and assembly equipment, manipulators, robotics and industrial IT technologies.

CABLING SYSTEMS TELECOMS EXPO
1 rue du Parc
F-92593 Levallois Perret, France
PH: 331 49685100
FX: 331 47377438
E-mail: simd@cepexposium.fr
URL: http://www.simd.fr
Frequency: Annual. **Principal Exhibits:** Design integration and installation, test & validation of all wired networks.

CAD/CAM - COMPUTER AIDED DESIGN-MANUFACTURING SYSTEMS AND GRAPHICS EXHIBITION
PO Box 2460
Germantown, MD 20875-2460
PH: (301)515-0012
FX: (301)515-0016
E-mail: glahe@glahe.com
Frequency: Biennial. **Audience:** Professional trade buyers. **Principal Exhibits:** Computer-aided design-manufacturing and graphic equipment, supplies, and services.

CAD/CAM - COMPUTER SHOW/LONDON
12 Bedford Row
London WC1R 4DU, England
PH: 71 4044844
FX: 71 4040747
Frequency: Annual. **Audience:** Engineering, manufacturing, electronics, construction, and architecture professionals. **Principal Exhibits:** Computer integrated technology for design and manufacturing automation, including hardware, software, and peripherals.

CAD/CAM - INTERNATIONAL TRADE FAIR FOR COMPUTER AIDED DESIGN AND MANUFACTURING
Doorniksesteenweg 216
B-8500 Kortrijk, Belgium
PH: 56 24 11 11
FX: 56 21 79 30
E-mail: info@hallen.be
URL: http://www.hallen.be/
Frequency: Annual. **Audience:** Trade professionals. **Principal Exhibits:** Computer-aided design and manufacturing equipment, supplies, and services.

CAD/CAM SYSTEMS SHOW
1-28-5, Kanda-Jimbo-cho
Chiyoda-ku
Tokyo 101, Japan

PH: 3 2736181
FX: 3 2414999
Frequency: Annual. **Audience:** Mechanical, electronic, and architectural engineers. **Principal Exhibits:** CAE, CAD, CAM, CAT, and CG related systems and equipments; AI systems-related software and equipment; and EWS.

CANADIAN CONSTRUCTION SHOW
20 Butterick Rd.
Toronto, ON, Canada M8W 3Z8
PH: (416)252-7791
FX: (416)252-9848
Frequency: Annual. **Audience:** Trade professionals, including buyers. **Principal Exhibits:** Heavy equipment and supporting products used in building projects and road and public works construction, including cranes, bulldozers, front-end loaders, trucks, trailers, survey equipment, paving equipment, safety equipment and training programs, and heating and roofing products.

CAPITAL INDUSTRIAL SHOW
1794 The Alameda
San Jose, CA 95126
PH: (408)286-8834
FX: (408)286-8836
Frequency: Annual. **Principal Exhibits:** Industrial Equipment, supplies, and services.

CAROLINA'S INDUSTRIAL SHOW
111 Executive Center Dr.
Columbia, SC 29210
TF: (800)553-7702
FX: (803)737-7440
Frequency: Annual. **Audience:** buyers & specifiers of industrial equipment and products, communications systems and handling equipment. **Principal Exhibits:** Industrial supplies, including coatings and maintenance, material handling & packaging, computer hardware, software and peripherals for design, data collection, inventory control, process control and manufacturing. Instrumentation for testing and quality control, environmental products.

CAT ENGINEERING - COMPUTER-AIDED TECHNOLOGIES -INTERNATIONAL TRADE FAIR FOR INNOVATIVE PRODUCT DEVELOPMENT AND ENGINEERING
Am Kochenhof 16
Postfach 103252
D-70028 Stuttgart, Germany
PH: 711 2589 0
FX: 711 2589 440
URL: http://www.messe-stuttgart.de
Frequency: Annual. **Principal Exhibits:** CAD/CAM and manufacturing systems.

CATT - COMPUTER AIDED TECHNOLOGIES EXHIBIT
41 Lertpanya Bldg., Ste. 801
Khet Rajathewee
Kwaeng Thanon Phyathai
8th Fl., Soi Lertpanya
Bangkok 10400, Thailand
PH: 662 6426911
FX: 662 6426919
Frequency: Annual. **Audience:** Chief executive and managing directors, government executives, directors & managers of design and production, system managers, project managers. **Principal Exhibits:** Mechanical engineering design and manufacturing - (CAD), electronic engineering - (CAM), computer integrated manufacturing (CIM), architecture engineering and construction (AEC), geographic information systems (GIS).

CDES - CANADIAN DESIGN ENGINEERING SHOW
800 Dennison St., Unit 7
Markham, ON, Canada L3R 5M9
PH: (416)479-3939
FX: (416)479-5144

Frequency: Biennial. **Audience:** Executive and production management, engineering design, MIS, research and development, and related OEM professionals. **Principal Exhibits:** Computer-aided design and manufacturing equipment, supplies, and services; robotics equipment, supplies, and services; automated material handling systems; CAD/CAM, CAE, CIM, CNC, and factory automation. **Dates and Locations:**2000 Oct; Toronto, ON. **Held in conjunction with:** Canadian Manufacturing Week.

CEBIT HOME ELECTRONICS- INTERNATIONAL TRADE FAIR FOR HOME AND CONSUMER ELECTRONICS
Messegelande
D-30521 Hannover, Germany
PH: 511 89 32116
FX: 511 893 3126
URL: http://www.messe.de
Frequency: Biennial. **Audience:** Trade professionals and general public. **Principal Exhibits:** Home and consumer electronic products and services in the areas of information technology, network computing, software and online services, telecommunications, consumer electronics, media, and home automation and security.

CENTRAL PENNSYLVANIA INDUSTRIAL AND CONSTRUCTION SHOW
164 Lake Front Dr.
Cockeysville, MD 21030-2215
PH: (410)252-1167
TF: (800)638-6396
FX: (410)560-0477
E-mail: info@isoa.com
URL: http://www.isoa.com
Frequency: Annual. **Principal Exhibits:** Industrial and construction equipment, supplies, and services.

CHINAPHOTO
100 Beach Rd.
26-00 Shaw Towers
Singapore 189702, Singapore
PH: 65 294 3366
FX: 65 299 9782
E-mail: exnet@singnet.com.sg
Frequency: Annual. **Principal Exhibits:** Manufacturers and suppliers of photographic, imaging and video equipment and supplies.

CHINAPLASTICS
100 Beach Rd.
26-00 Shaw Towers
Singapore 189702, Singapore
PH: 65 294 3366
FX: 65 299 9782
E-mail: exnet@singnet.com.sg
Frequency: Annual. **Principal Exhibits:** Mould and die equipment and technology, plastic packaging materials and technology, laminating equipment, heat sealing and stamping equipment, measuring and testing equipment, and water reprocessing equipment.

CIM JAPAN - COMPUTER INTEGRATED MANUFACTURING SYSTEMS EXHIBITION AND CONFERENCE
383 Main Ave.
PO Box 6059
Norwalk, CT 06851
PH: (203)840-5358
FX: (203)840-4804
E-mail: inquiry@nepcon.reedexpo.com
Frequency: Annual. **Audience:** Senior management; managers of manufacturing, planning, and control systems; production managers; inventory control managers. **Principal Exhibits:** Computing technology, manufacturing planning and control systems group technology, CAD, automated materials handling, CAM, and robotics.

**CIMEX - COMPUTERIZED INTEGRATED
   MANUFACTURING EXHIBITION**
Parc des Expositions
Place de Belgique
B-1020 Brussels, Belgium
PH: 32 2 474 8447
FX: 32 2 474 8540
URL: http://www.bitf.be
Audience: Trade professionals. **Principal Exhibits:** Computerized
manufacturing. **Held in conjunction with:** EUROPLASTICA;
EUROSUPPLY; EUROTECH; HYDROPNEUMA; INTERREGIO.

CINCINNATI INDUSTRIAL EXPO
431 Ohio Pike, Ste. 104 S.
Cincinnati, OH 45255
PH: (704)331-9095
FX: (704)344-0504
Frequency: Annual. **Principal Exhibits:** Industrial equipment, sup-
plies, and services.

CINCINNATI SYSTEMS EXPO
431 Ohio Pike, Ste. 104 S.
Cincinnati, OH 45255
PH: (704)331-9095
FX: (704)344-0504
Principal Exhibits: Computers, peripherals, and software.

CIPHEX/WEST
295 The West Mall, Ste. 330
Toronto, ON, Canada M9C 4Z4
PH: (416)695-0447
TF: (800)NEX-CIPH
FX: (416)695-0450
E-mail: ciph@ican.net
URL: http://www.ciph.com
Frequency: Biennial. **Audience:** Trade professionals. **Principal
Exhibits:** Plumbing, heating, refrigeration, ventilating and air-condi-
tioning trades equipment, supplies, and services. **Dates and Loca-
tions:** 1998. **Formerly:** CEPHRA - Canadian Exposition of Plumb-
ing, Heating, Refrigeration, and Air Conditioning.

**COMDEX/ASIA AT SINGAPORE INFORMATICS -
   INTERNATIONAL INFORMATION TECHNOLOGY
   EXHIBITION**
300 1st Ave.
Needham, MA 02194-2722
PH: (617)449-6600
FX: (617)444-7722
E-mail: compuserve: 74667, 3241
URL: http://www.comdex.com
Frequency: Annual. **Audience:** Information technicians, bankers,
financiers, builders, defense contractors; general public. **Principal
Exhibits:** Information technology products and services. **Formerly:**
(96) SINGAPORE INFORMATICS - International Information
Technology Exhibition.

**COMDEX/ASIA AT SINGAPORE INFORMATICS -
   INTERNATIONAL INFORMATION TECHNOLOGY
   EXHIBITION**
300 1st Ave.
Needham, MA 02194-2722
PH: (617)449-6600
FX: (617)444-7722
E-mail: compuserve: 74667, 3241
URL: http://www.comdex.com
Frequency: Annual. **Audience:** Information technicians, bankers,
financiers, builders, defense contractors; general public. **Principal
Exhibits:** Information technology products and services. **Formerly:**
(96) SINGAPORE INFORMATICS - International Information
Technology Exhibition.

COMDEX/FALL
300 1st Ave.
Needham, MA 02194-2722

PH: (617)449-6600
FX: (617)444-7722
E-mail: compuserve: 74667, 3241
URL: http://www.comdex.com
Frequency: Annual. **Audience:** Volume resellers and value-adders
of small computers and related items. **Principal Exhibits:** Small
computer systems, related peripherals, software, accessories, servi-
ces, and supplies.

COMDEX/IT FRANCE
21 rue Pasteur
92300 Levallois-Perret, France
PH: 33 1 41 27 21 50
FX: 33 1 47 37 52 77
Frequency: Annual. **Principal Exhibits:** Manufacturers and suppliers of hardware, software and peripherals for computers.

COMDEX/MEXICO
Col. Juarez
PO Box 6-628
06600 Mexico City, Mexico
PH: 52 6391750
FX: 52 6395945
Frequency: Annual. **Audience:** Corporate buyers, specifiers and
resellers of software, electronics, and communication equipment.
Principal Exhibits: Computers, software, and communications
equipment, supplies, and services.

COMDEX/PACRIM
300 1st Ave.
Needham, MA 02194-2722
PH: (617)449-6600
FX: (617)444-7722
E-mail: compuserve: 74667, 3241
URL: http://www.comdex.com
Frequency: Annual. **Audience:** Computer professionals, and vol-
ume buyers of PC/desktop computer solutions. **Principal Exhibits:**
PC systems, peripherals, and computers with emphasis on desktop
products and related peripherals; applications, systems and utility
software, and related courseware; information and communications
services.

COMDEX/SPRING
300 1st Ave.
Needham, MA 02194-2722
PH: (617)449-6600
FX: (617)444-7722
E-mail: compuserve: 74667, 3241
URL: http://www.comdex.com
Frequency: Annual. **Audience:** Resellers and value-adders of small
computers and related accessories. **Principal Exhibits:** Small com-
puter systems and related peripherals, software, accessories, servi-
ces, and supplies. **Held in conjunction with:** Windows World;
CES Spring.

**COMDEX SUCESU-SP - INFORMATICS AND
   TELECOMMUNICATION INTERNATIONAL FAIR WITH
   CONGRESS**
Al. Rio Negro, 433
Predio I
3 andar
06454-904 Barueri, SP, Brazil
PH: 55 11 7291 0440
FX: 55 11 7291 0660
E-mail: guafair@guazzelli.com.br
URL: http://www.guazzelli.com.br
Frequency: Annual. **Audience:** Corporate decision makers,
resellers, and MIS professionals. **Principal Exhibits:** Computer and
communications products and services.

COMPOTEK - COMPUTER FAIR
PO Box 67067
Parque Ferial Juan Carlos I
28067 Madrid, Spain

PH: 34 1 722 5000
FX: 34 1 722 5788
URL: http://www.arco.sei.es.
Frequency: Annual. **Principal Exhibits:** Computer systems, computer software and hardware, printers computer plotter, scanner, computer terminals, telecommunication systems, computerized manufacturing systems, office automation, computer usage in research, computer materials, disks, and related publications.

COMPUTAX - INTERNATIONAL COMPUTER TECHNOLOGY SHOW AND BAR CODE EXHIBITION
12 Tverski St.
67210 Tel Aviv, Israel
PH: 972 3 5626090
FX: 972 3 5615463
E-mail: expo@stier.co.il
URL: http://www.stier.co.il
Frequency: Annual. **Audience:** Buyers, business managers, research and development staff. **Principal Exhibits:** PC & AAC systems, peripheral equipment, bar code, software and communications, multi-media and Internet tools. **Held in conjunction with:** BAR CODE; COM/LAN; COM/UNIX; GRAFIX; MULTIMEDIA.

COMPUTER & BURO LINZ - TRADE FAIR FOR COMPUTER, HARD-AND SOFTWARE, OFFICE FURNITURE, AND SUPPLIES
Postfach 285
Am Messezentrum
A-5021 Salzburg, Austria
PH: 43 662 4477 0
FX: 662 4477 161
E-mail: info@reedexpo.at
URL: http://www.reedexpo.at
Frequency: Annual. **Principal Exhibits:** Computer hardware and software, particularly that for commercial and administrative branches and for desktop publishing; office equipment, including furniture and telecommunications products.

COMPUTER - EXHIBITION OF INFORMATICS EQUIPMENT, OFFICE SUPPLIES, HOME COMPUTING, AND MULTIMEDIA
CP 89
CH-1000 Lausanne, Switzerland
PH: 6432111
FX: 6433711
E-mail: beaulieu@comptoir.ch
URL: http://www.beaulieu.comptoir.ch
Frequency: Annual. **Audience:** Trade professionals and general public. **Principal Exhibits:** Management information technology, security/data protection, telecommunications, CAD/CAM/CIM, office high-tech equipment, information technology in construction, and training materials.

COMPUTER - INTERNATIONAL COMPUTER EXPO
Unit 1223, 12/F, Hong Kong International Trade & Exhibition
1 Trademart Dr.
Kowloon Bay, Hong Kong
PH: 852 2865 2633
FX: 852 2866 1770
Frequency: Annual. **Audience:** EDP professionals, end-users, and related trade professionals; general public. **Principal Exhibits:** Main frames, mini-and micro-computers, personal computers, data communication equipment, software packages, CAD/CAM systems, Auto-ID and Bar Code equipment, peripherals, computer furniture and supplies, and related supplies and services.

COMPUTER SHOPPER SHOW - SPRING
630 Chiswick High Rd.
London W4 5BG, England
PH: 44 181 742 2828
FX: 44 181 747 3856
URL: http://www.mf-exhibitions.co.uk
Frequency: Annual. **Audience:** General public. **Principal Exhi-**

bits: Personal computers; hardware, software, and peripherals for home and business use.

COMPUTEX ABU DHABI - INTERNATIONAL COMPUTER AND OFFICE TECHNOLOGY EXHIBITION
PO Box 2460
Germantown, MD 20875-2460
PH: (301)515-0012
FX: (301)515-0016
E-mail: glahe@glahe.com
Frequency: Biennial. **Principal Exhibits:** Computers, office technology, processors, software and related components.

CONSTRUCT I.T.
39 Moreland St.
London EC1 8BB, England
PH: 44 181 953 7572
Frequency: Annual. **Principal Exhibits:** Software and hardware computer products for the construction industry.

CONSUMER/INDUSTRIAL APPLIANCES
Tung Wai Commercial Bldg., Rm. 1703
109 Gloucester Rd.
Wanchai, Hong Kong
PH: 852 2 511 7427
FX: 852 2 511 9692
E-mail: cpexhbit@hk.super.net
URL: http://www.hk.super.net/~cpexhbit
Frequency: Annual. **Audience:** Trade professionals. **Principal Exhibits:** Consumer and industrial appliances equipment, supplies, and services.

CZECH CONTRACT
Rotebuhlstrasse 83-85
D-70178 Stuttgart, Germany
PH: 49 11 619460
FX: 49 11 6194698
E-mail: buss@mesago.de
URL: http://www.mesago.de
Principal Exhibits: Industry and technology fair for: subcontracting and industrial supply; manufacturing and quality assurance; assembly, handling, and industrial robotics; drives and fluid technology; and electronics, sensors, and optoelectronics.

DAYTON INDUSTRIAL EXHIBITION
325 Essjay Rd., Ste. 100
Williamsville, NY 14221-8280
PH: (716)631-2266
TF: (800)274-6948
FX: (716)631-2425
URL: http://www.southex.com
Frequency: Annual. **Audience:** Buyers and buying decision makers involved in the manufacturing industries. **Principal Exhibits:** Machine tools, weighing instruments, die makers, CAD/CAM systems, robotics equipment, and related industrial equipment, supplies, and services.

DELMARVA INDUSTRIAL SHOW
164 Lake Front Dr.
Cockeysville, MD 21030-2215
PH: (410)252-1167
TF: (800)638-6396
FX: (410)560-0477
E-mail: info@isoa.com
URL: http://www.isoa.com
Frequency: Biennial. **Audience:** Trade professionals. **Principal Exhibits:** Industrial equipment, supplies, and services.

DEMONSTRATION OF MANUFACTURING MACHINES
Av. Reina Maria Cristina, s/n
E-08004 Barcelona, Spain
PH: 93 804 0102
FX: 93 805 4802

Frequency: Triennial. **Principal Exhibits:** Pressing and finishing equipment; folding and bag-packing equipment; accessories.

DESIGN AUTOMATION CONFERENCE
5305 Spine Rd., Ste. A
Boulder, CO 80301
PH: (303)530-4333
TF: (800)321-4573
FX: (303)530-4334
E-mail: mpa@dac.com
URL: http://www.dac.com
Frequency: Annual. **Audience:** Electrical and software engineers, trade professionals. **Principal Exhibits:** EDA/CAD/CAE tools. **Dates and Locations:** 2000 Jun 05-09; San Diego, CA • 2001 Jun 04-07; San Francisco, CA.

DEVELOP!
630 Chiswick High Rd.
London W4 5BG, England
PH: 44 181 742 2828
FX: 44 181 747 3856
URL: http://www.mf-exhibitions.co.uk
Frequency: Annual. **Principal Exhibits:** Software development and publishing tools.

DIE & MOULD/ASIA
Frequency: Biennial. **Principal Exhibits:** Dies and moulds, measurement/inspection/testing, and services.

DIE AND MOULD/CHINA - INTERNATIONAL EXHIBITION ON DIE AND MOULD TECHNOLOGY
28 Jinling Xi Lu
Shanghai 200021, People's Republic of China
PH: 86 21 6387 2828
FX: 86 21 6512 4191
E-mail: siec@stn.sh.com
URL: http://www.siec-ccpit.com
Frequency: Biennial. **Audience:** Trade professionals. **Principal Exhibits:** Die casting equipment, supplies, and services and related technology.

DIGITAL CONTENT CREATION (DCC) CONFERENCE AND EXPOSITION
363 Reef Rd.
PO Box 915
Fairfield, CT 06430-0915
PH: (203)256-4700
FX: (203)256-4730
E-mail: ecv@expocon.com
URL: http://www.expocon.com
Principal Exhibits: Equipment, supplies, and services for the digital content creation marketplace with emphasis on expanding reseller channels and education end users, including: digital video, hardware systems, software, production studios, support services, and content labs.

THE DIGITAL VIDEO CONFERENCE AND EXPOSITION
525 Market St., Ste. 500
San Francisco, CA 94105
PH: (415)278-5300
FX: (415)278-5341
Frequency: Annual. **Principal Exhibits:** Digital technology hardware, software, tools and services.

DMS - DESIGN ENGINEERING & MANUFACTURING SOLUTION EXPO & CONFERENCE
2F Ginza-Eiwa Bldg.
8-18-7 Ginza Chuo-Ku
Tokyo 104, Japan
PH: 81 3 5565 0861
FX: 81 3 5565 0860
Frequency: Annual. **Audience:** Company owners; managing directors; financial directors; managers of manufacturing, planning, quality control, and information/computer systems. **Principal Exhibits:**
Computing technology; manufacturing, planning, and control systems group technology; CAD, CAM, CAE, ERP, and rapid prototyping systems; automated materials handling.

DOCUMENT
630 Chiswick High Rd.
London W4 5BG, England
PH: 44 181 742 2828
FX: 44 181 747 3856
URL: http://www.mf-exhibitions.co.uk
Frequency: Annual. **Principal Exhibits:** Hardware, software, application vendors and systems integrators.

E3 - ELECTRONIC ENTERTAINMENT EXPO
1130 Connecticut Ave. NW, Ste. 710
Washington, DC 20036-3904
PH: (202)833-4372
FX: (202)833-4431
Frequency: Annual. **Principal Exhibits:** Interactive entertainment equipment, supplies, and services.

ELECTRIX & INSTRUMENTATION
383 Main Ave.
PO Box 6059
Norwalk, CT 06851
PH: (203)840-5358
FX: (203)840-4804
E-mail: inquiry@nepcon.reedexpo.com
Frequency: Biennial. **Principal Exhibits:** Equipment, supplies, and services for manufacturing.

ELECTRONICS: INDUSTRIAL ELECTRONICS TRADE FAIR
Europaplein 8
PO Box 77777
1070 MS Amsterdam, Netherlands
PH: 20 5491212
FX: 20 6464469
E-mail: mail@rai.nl
Frequency: Biennial. **Principal Exhibits:** Parts, semi-conductors, integrated circuits and electron tubes, custom made IC's, components (standard and to measure); electronic measuring and test equipment; electro-acoustic equipment for industrial and scientific use; materials for telecommunication installations and electronic audio-visual equipment for professional purposes; computer hardware and software for the development of electronics; mechanical aids; supplies and tools for service and production purposes.

EMBEDDED SYSTEMS CONFERENCE
600 Harrison St.
San Francisco, CA 94107
PH: (415)905-2200
TF: (800)227-4675
FX: (415)905-2232
URL: http://www.mfi.com
Frequency: Annual. **Audience:** Embedded systems programmers and software engineers. **Principal Exhibits:** Existing, new, and emerging technologies for software and hardware designers in the embedded systems industry, including microprocessors, microcontrollers, DSPs, development tools, real-time operating systems, emulators, and single board computer manufacturers.

EMV KARLSRUHE - INTERNATIONAL EXHIBITION AND CONFERENCE ON ELECTROMAGNETIC COMPATIBILITY
Rotebuhlstrasse 83-85
D-70178 Stuttgart, Germany
PH: 49 11 619460
FX: 49 11 6194698
E-mail: buss@mesago.de
URL: http://www.mesago.de
Frequency: Biennial. **Audience:** Decision-makers of industry and science; directors, technical managers, developers and designers, and production engineers. **Principal Exhibits:** Car manufacturing sys-

tems; mechanical, electronic/electrical, and precision engineering; space/aerospace systems; and defense technology.

EUROPEAN COATINGS SHOW - FORMULATION- PRODUCTION-APPLICATION

Schiffgraben 41
Postfach 6247
D-30175 Hannover, Germany
PH: 511 9110 272
FX: 511 9910 279
Frequency: Biennial. **Audience:** Industrial users and manufacturers of paints and coatings and process and production technology. **Principal Exhibits:** Raw materials, process and production engineering, measuring and testing, pretreatment, application, coating materials, waste disposal, environmental protection services, surface mount technology, process automation, coating materials, application.

EXPO VIETNAM - THE REGIONAL TRADE AND INDUSTRIAL LINKAGE EXHIBITION FOR VIETNAM

Unit 1223, 12/F, Hong Kong International Trade & Exhibition
1 Trademart Dr.
Kowloon Bay, Hong Kong
PH: 852 2865 2633
FX: 852 2866 1770
Frequency: Annual. **Principal Exhibits:** Industrial equipment, supplies, and services.

EXPORT MANUFACTURING THAILAND

41 Lertpanya Bldg., Ste. 801
Khet Rajathewee
Kwaeng Thanon Phyathai
8th Fl., Soi Lertpanya
Bangkok 10400, Thailand
PH: 662 6426911
FX: 662 6426919
Frequency: Annual. **Principal Exhibits:** Manufacturing technology exhibition for the export industries.

FENASOFT - INTERNATIONAL SOFTWARE, HARDWARE, AND INFORMATICS SERVICES FAIR

Av. Faria Lima 1993
01452-001 Sao Paulo, SP, Brazil
PH: 55 11 815 4011
FX: 55 11 816 2447
E-mail: fenasoft@fenasoft.com.br
URL: http://www.fenasoft.com.br

FOSE - AMERICA'S INTEGRATED INFORMATION TECHNOLOGY EXPOSITION

383 Main Ave.
PO Box 6059
Norwalk, CT 06851
PH: (203)840-5358
FX: (203)840-4804
E-mail: inquiry@nepcon.reedexpo.com
Frequency: Annual. **Audience:** Government professionals, suppliers to government and systems integrators. **Principal Exhibits:** Computer systems and services, image management equipment, networks, communications and office systems and services. **Formerly:** FOSE - Federal Government's Information Systems Conference and Exposition **Held in conjunction with:** FOSE Computer Graphics; FOSE Software.

FUTURSHOW - MULTIMEDIA INFORMATION TECHNOLOGY TELEMATICS, TV, AND PHOTOTECHNOLOGY FAIR

Via Bruno Buozzi, 25
I-40057 Cadriano, Italy
PH: 51 765056
FX: 51 766133
Frequency: Annual. **Principal Exhibits:** Hardware and hardware components; software and software components; video games; Internet networks; databases; television and radio broadcasting technology; audio and video technology.

GASTRO

Helsinki Fair Centre
PO Box 21
Messuaukio 1
FIN-00521 Helsinki, Finland
PH: 358 9 150 91
FX: 358 9 142 358
E-mail: info@finnexpo.fi
URL: http://www.finnexpo.fi
Frequency: Biennial. **Principal Exhibits:** Food and related equipment, supplies, and services.

GIS - GEOGRAPHICAL INFORMATION SYSTEMS, VANCOUVER

1102 Homer St., Ste. 207
Vancouver, BC, Canada V6B 2X6
PH: (604)688-0188
FX: (604)688-1573
Frequency: Annual. **Audience:** Trade professionals. **Principal Exhibits:** Geographical information systems and related equipment, supplies, and services including computer hardware, software, and peripherals.

GREAT LAKES INDUSTRIAL SHOW

33 Rutherford Ave.
Charlestown, MA 02129
PH: (617)242-6092
TF: (800)225-1577
FX: (617)242-1817
Frequency: Annual. **Audience:** Buyers and officers from maintenance, material handling, engineering, production, purchasing, management, shipping and related professionals. **Principal Exhibits:** Industrial products, machine tools, hand tools, pneumatics, hydraulics, plant engineering, and maintenance, paper and packaging, plastics, rubber products, material handling equipment, and dies and stampings.

HITEC

PO Box 163
FIN-33201 Tampere, Finland
PH: 358 3 2516 111
FX: 358 3 2123 888
E-mail: helpdesk@tampereenmessut.fi
URL: http://www.tampereenmessut.fi
Principal Exhibits: CAD/CAM, data communications, and software technology.

IA SWITZERLAND - TRADE FAIR FOR DATA PROCESSING SYSTEMS FOR INDUSTRIAL AUTOMATION

Gustav-Werner-Strasse 6
D-72636 Frickenhausen-Linsenhofen, Germany
PH: 70 25 92 06 0
FX: 70 25 92 06 20
E-mail: info@schall-messen.de
URL: http://www.schall-messen.de
Frequency: Semiannual. **Audience:** Trade professionals. **Principal Exhibits:** Computers; software; data processing systems; and related equipment, supplies, and services for industry automation.

ICA - INTERNATIONAL EXHIBITION OF COMPUTERS AND APPLICATIONS FOR CHINA

Unit 1223, 12/F, Hong Kong International Trade & Exhibition
1 Trademart Dr.
Kowloon Bay, Hong Kong
PH: 852 2865 2633
FX: 852 2866 1770
Frequency: Annual. **Principal Exhibits:** Computer related products, equipment and related services including: Auto-ID and Bar Code technology.

IFABO PRAGUE - INTERNATIONAL TRADE FAIR FOR OFFICE ORGANIZATION AND COMMUNICATION TECHNOLOGY
Messeplatz 1
Postfach 124, 284
1071 Vienna, Austria
PH: 1 521 200
FX: 1 521 20290
Frequency: Annual. **Audience:** General public. **Principal Exhibits:** Office communication equipment, supplies, and services. **Formerly:** (96) IFABO PRAGUE - International Trade Fair for Office and Communications Engineering, with the Software Fair PROGRAMMA.

IIRA WORLD CONGRESS
c/o LEGREL
International Labour Office
CH-1211 Geneva, Switzerland
PH: 41 22 7996841
FX: 41 22 7884709
E-mail: mennie@ilo.org
Frequency: Triennial. **Principal Exhibits:** Exhibits relating to the study of industrial relations worldwide.

IMAC
41 Lertpanya Bldg., Ste. 801
Khet Rajathewee
Kwaeng Thanon Phyathai
8th Fl., Soi Lertpanya
Bangkok 10400, Thailand
PH: 662 6426911
FX: 662 6426919
Frequency: Annual. **Principal Exhibits:** Manufacturers and distributors of industrial instruments, measurement, analyzers and control equipment and technology.

IN-TECH - THE INDUSTRIAL PRODUCT, SERVICE AND TECHNICAL EXPO FOR CENTRAL NEW YORK
3494 Delaware Ave.
Buffalo, NY 14217
PH: (716)871-1125
TF: (800)222-4465
FX: (716)871-9638
E-mail: ppminc@buffnet.net
Frequency: Annual. **Audience:** Trade. **Principal Exhibits:** Industrial products. **Formerly:** Rochester Industrial Product Exhibit.

IN-TECH - THE INDUSTRY & TECHNOLOGY EXPO-BUFFALO
3494 Delaware Ave.
Buffalo, NY 14217
PH: (716)871-1125
TF: (800)222-4465
FX: (716)871-9638
E-mail: ppminc@buffnet.net
Frequency: Annual. **Audience:** Industrial buyers. **Principal Exhibits:** Industrial equipment, supplies, and services. **Formerly:** Buffalo Industrial Product Exhibit.

INDUSTRIAL EQUIPMENT
Parc des Expositions
Place de Belgique
B-1020 Brussels, Belgium
PH: 32 2 474 8447
FX: 32 2 474 8540
URL: http://www.bitf.be
Audience: Trade professionals. **Principal Exhibits:** Industrial equipment, supplies, and services. **Held in conjunction with:** EUROTECH.

INDUSTRY & TECHNOLOGY EXHIBITION
Parc des Expositions
Place de Belgique
B-1020 Brussels, Belgium
PH: 32 2 474 8447
FX: 32 2 474 8540
URL: http://www.bitf.be
Principal Exhibits: Industrial equipment, supplies, and services.

INFO-GRYF - INTERNATIONAL FAIR OF ELECTRONIC, TELECOMMUNICATION AND COMPUTER TECHNOLOGY
ul. Struga 6-8
70-777 Szczecin, Poland
PH: 091 64 44 01
FX: 091 64 44 02
Frequency: Annual. **Principal Exhibits:** Computers, peripherals, system and application software, telecommunication in administration, data bases text processing, and cellular phones.

INFO/TECH MANAGEMENT CONFERENCE AND EXPOSITION
505 Busse Hwy.
Park Ridge, IL 60068-3191
PH: (708)825-8124
FX: (708)825-1693
Frequency: Annual. **Audience:** Information systems professionals. **Principal Exhibits:** Computer equipment, supplies, and services.

INFOBASE - INTERNATIONAL TRADE FAIR FOR INFORMATION AND COMMUNICATION
Postfach 150210
Ludwig-Erhard-Anlage 1
D-60062 Frankfurt am Main, Germany
PH: 69 7575 6452
FX: 69 7575 6433
E-mail: overseas-exhibitions@messefrankfurt.de
URL: http://www.messefrankfurt.de/
Frequency: Annual. **Audience:** Database customers. **Principal Exhibits:** Information processing software and hardware, data processing software, new information systems, and databases. **Formerly:** INFOBASE - International Trade Fair for Information.

INFOMAN - INTERNATIONAL INFORMATION MANAGEMENT FAIR
ul. Beniowskiego 5
80-382 Gdansk, Poland
PH: 0 58 5 52 36 00
FX: 0 58 5 52 21 68
E-mail: sekretariat@mtgsa.com.pl
Frequency: Annual. **Principal Exhibits:** Systems, hardware and software for the collection and management of data for the administrative, banking, capital markets, and insurance.

INFOSYSTEM - INTERNATIONAL FAIR OF ELECTRONICS, TELECOMMUNICATION, AND COMPUTER ENGINEERING
Glogowska 14
PL-60-734 Poznan, Poland
PH: 61 692592
FX: 61 665827
E-mail: MTP@POL.PL
URL: http://www.mtp.pol.pl
Frequency: Annual. **Audience:** Trade and general public. **Principal Exhibits:** Installations, equipment, systems, and technologies for the electronic industry, including software, electronic subunits, teletransmission and telecommunications equipment, and computer hardware. **Held in conjunction with:** POLYGRAFIA - International Exhibition of Printing Machines.

INFOTECHASIA - ASIAN INTERNATIONAL COMPUTER COMMUNICATIONS AND INFORMATION SYSTEMS SHOW AND CONFERENCE
2 Handy Rd.
15-09 Cathay Bldg.
Singapore 229233, Singapore

PH: 65 3384747
FX: 65 3395651
E-mail: info@sesmontnet.com
URL: http://www.sesmontnet.com
Frequency: Biennial. **Audience:** Managers, administrative personnel, business trade, office communications trade, and computer trade. **Principal Exhibits:** Office automation equipment; computer hardware and software; data communication systems and equipment. **Held in conjunction with:** CommunicAsia - Asian International Electronic Communications Show and Conference.

INTERNATIONAL AGRICULTURAL FAIR - FOOD, AGRICULTURE AND EQUIPMENT
7847 Convoy Ct., Ste. 105
San Diego, CA 92111-1220
PH: (619)277-5580
FX: (619)277-9411
E-mail: vniic@aol.com
Frequency: Annual. **Principal Exhibits:** Agricultural equipment, supplies, and services.

INTERNATIONAL DIE CASTING CONGRESS AND EXPOSITION
Frequency: Biennial. **Audience:** Die casting executives and engineers; parts specifiers; purchasing managers; industry suppliers; academicians. **Principal Exhibits:** Die casting machines and ancillary equipment.

INTERNATIONAL INDUSTRIAL BODY-WORKS EXHIBITION
55, quai Alphonse Le Gallo
BP 317
92107 Boulogne, France
PH: 33 1 49 09 60 00
FX: 33 1 49 09 60 03
E-mail: info@comite-expo-paris.asso.fr
URL: http://www.comite-expo-paris.asso.fr
Frequency: Biennial. **Principal Exhibits:** Industrial body works.

INTERNATIONAL SPECTRUM - THE BUSINESS PERSON'S COMPUTER SHOW
10675 Treena St., Ste. 103
San Diego, CA 92131
PH: (619)578-3152
TF: (800)767-SHOW
FX: (619)271-1032
E-mail: spectrum50@aol.com
Frequency: Annual. **Audience:** End users, vendors, consultants, computer software houses, dealers, related professionals, and general public. **Principal Exhibits:** Computer hardware, software, and peripherals for business people.

INTERNATIONAL TEST CONFERENCE (ITC)
7357 Alicante Rd.
Carlsbad, CA 92009
PH: (760)603-0110
FX: (760)603-0119
Frequency: Annual. **Audience:** Test engineers, managers, and test software professionals; design, manufacturing and product engineering; marketing, sales, and corporate managers. **Principal Exhibits:** Manufacturing companies producing test equipment for automated semiconductor industry, including: equipment for testing, handlers, probers, and computer software.

INTERTECH BODENSEE - INTERNATIONAL TECHNOLOGY FAIR
Splugenstrasse 12
Postfach
CH-9008 St. Gallen, Switzerland
PH: 71 242 0101
FX: 71 242 0103
E-mail: olma-messen@bluewin.ch
URL: http://www.olma-messen.ch

Frequency: Triennial. **Principal Exhibits:** Automation, plastics technology, mechanical, and implement engineering.

INTERTRONIC - ELECTRONICS INDUSTRY SHOW
70 rue Rivay
F-92532 Levallois-Perret, France
PH: 33 1 47 56 50 00
FX: 33 1 47 56 91 86
E-mail: mffrance@unmf.fr
URL: http://www.unmf.fr
Frequency: Annual. **Principal Exhibits:** Manufacturers and suppliers of electronic components. **Formerly:** Pronic.

INTOOLEX QUALITY SWITZERLAND - EXHIBITION FOR PRODUCTION TOOLING, PRODUCT ON MEASUREMENT, AND QUALITY CONTROL
383 Main Ave.
PO Box 6059
Norwalk, CT 06851
PH: (203)840-5358
FX: (203)840-4804
E-mail: inquiry@nepcon.reedexpo.com
Frequency: Biennial. **Audience:** Trade professionals, including buyers and engineers. **Principal Exhibits:** Cutting tools; industrial hand tools; mould making, stamping, punching, and metal forming tools; tool maintenance and care; materials; accessories; surface treatment lubricants/coolants; CAD/CAM/CAE computers and tooling; research, development, consulting; training, teaching and materials; specialized literature; and professional associations and organizations information.

IT FORUM
600 Harrison St.
San Francisco, CA 94107-1387
TF: (800)232-3976
Frequency: Annual. **Audience:** Corporate volume buyers, trade resellers, and systems integrators of UNIX products and services. **Principal Exhibits:** IT technologies, including applications, systems, networking, and Internet/Intranet solutions. **Incorporating:** DB/Expo New York; I2 - Internet/Intranet Expo; Unix plus Windows NT Expo.

KNITS - KWAZULU NATAL INDUSTRIAL TRADE SHOW
PO Box 182
Pinegowrie 2123, Republic of South Africa
PH: 11 886 3734
FX: 11 789 6497
Frequency: Biennial. **Principal Exhibits:** Industrial equipment, supplies, and services.

KOFA - INTERNATIONAL FACTORY AUTOMATION SYSTEM EXHIBITION/KOREA
383 Main Ave.
PO Box 6059
Norwalk, CT 06851
PH: (203)840-5358
FX: (203)840-4804
E-mail: inquiry@nepcon.reedexpo.com
Frequency: Annual. **Audience:** Management, purchasers, accountants, marketing personnel, and other manufacturing professionals interested in factory automation. **Principal Exhibits:** Computer integrated manufacturing (CIM) systems; software and systems. **Held in conjunction with:** ENTEC.

KOTI & INTERNET
PO Box 163
FIN-33201 Tampere, Finland
PH: 358 3 2516 111
FX: 358 3 2123 888
E-mail: helpdesk@tampereenmessut.fi
URL: http://www.tampereenmessut.fi
Principal Exhibits: Home electronics, games, and computers.

**LATIN DIGITAL IMAGING & DOCUMENT
  MANAGEMENT SHOW**
8000 Victor Pittsford Rd.
Victor, NY 14564-1050
PH: (716)383-8330
FX: (716)383-8442
Frequency: 3/yr. **Principal Exhibits:** PC digital imaging electronic
document management, groupware & workflow systems, micrographics, electronic print-on-demand, WWW publishing, all imaging
systems & solutions.

LEHIGH VALLEY INDUSTRIAL SHOW
164 Lake Front Dr.
Cockeysville, MD 21030-2215
PH: (410)252-1167
TF: (800)638-6396
FX: (410)560-0477
E-mail: info@isoa.com
URL: http://www.isoa.com
Frequency: Annual. **Audience:** Trade professionals. **Principal Exhibits:** Industrial equipment, supplies, and services.

**LOGISMAT - ASIA PACIFIC LOGISTIC, DISTRIBUTION
  AND MATERIAL HANDLING**

EXHIBITION
c/o Miller Freeman Pte Ltd.
Shaw Towers
100 Beach Rd., No. 26-00
Singapore 189702, Singapore
PH: 294 3366
FX: 299 9782
Frequency: Biennial. **Principal Exhibits:** Automated and handling
equipment.

LOGISTICS CHINA
Unit D, 10/F, Eton Bldg.
288 Des Voeux Rd. Central
Hong Kong, Hong Kong
PH: 852 2850 7311
FX: 852 2850 7727
Frequency: Semiannual. **Principal Exhibits:** Heavy and serial lifting equipment, industrial trucks, passenger escalators, and storage
supplies and methods.

MACWORLD EXPOSITION/NEW YORK
1400 Providence Hwy.
PO Box 9127
Norwood, MA 02062-9127
PH: (617)551-9800
FX: (617)440-0351
Frequency: Annual. **Principal Exhibits:** MacIntosh equipment,
supplies, and services. **Formerly:** MacWorld, Boston.

MACWORLD EXPOSITION/SAN FRANCISCO
1400 Providence Hwy.
PO Box 9127
Norwood, MA 02062-9127
PH: (617)551-9800
FX: (617)440-0351
Frequency: Annual. **Principal Exhibits:** MacIntosh-related equipment, supplies, and services.

MACWORLD EXPOSITION/TOKYO
1-28-5, Kanda-Jimbo-cho
Chiyoda-ku
Tokyo 101, Japan
PH: 3 2736181
FX: 3 2414999
Frequency: Annual. **Principal Exhibits:** MacIntosh computers and
related equipment, supplies, and services, including software.

MAINE INDUSTRIAL SHOW
333 Trapelo Rd.
Belmont, MA 02178
PH: (617)489-2302
TF: (800)543-5259
FX: (617)489-5534
Frequency: Biennial. **Audience:** Pulp and paper and plant maintenance trade. **Principal Exhibits:** Industrial equipment and supplies,
including compressors, pumps, PTE, material handling equipment,
and pneumatics.

**MANUFACTURING CHINA - INTERNATIONAL
  MANUFACTURING MACHINERY, PRODUCTION
  TECHNOLOGY & SUPPORT SERVICES EXHIBITION**
Room A803
No. 318-322 Xian Xia Rd.
Singular Mansion
Shanghai 200335, People's Republic of China
PH: 86 21 62095209
FX: 86 21 62095210
E-mail: tmnchina@uninet.com.cn
Frequency: Biennial. **Principal Exhibits:** Equipment, supplies, and
services for manufacturing machinery.

**MANUFACTURING WEEK - INTERNATIONAL
  MANUFACTURING TECHNOLOGY EXHIBITION**
Oriel House
26 The Quadrant
Richmond, Surrey TW9 1DL, England
PH: 181 910 7825
FX: 181 910 7926
E-mail: info@reedexpo.co.uk
URL: http://www.reedexpo.com
Frequency: Annual. **Principal Exhibits:** Manufacturing equipment,
supplies, and services for the automotive aerospace, packaging, plastic and rubber, food and drink, industrial machinery, mechanical engineering, electronic engineering, and process industries. **Formerly:**
UK Manufacturing Week **Held in conjunction with:** Automan;
CAMMS; Design Engineering Show; Plant Engineering.

MEDICAL DESIGN & MANUFACTURING MINNEAPOLIS
3340 Ocean Park Blvd., Ste. 1000
Santa Monica, CA 90405
PH: (310)392-5509
FX: (310)392-1557
E-mail: feedback@cancom.com
URL: http://www.cancom.com
Frequency: Annual. **Audience:** Trade professionals. **Principal Exhibits:** Suppliers to medical OEM's of adhesives, laboratory equipment and supplies, raw materials, computer hardware, thermoforming plastics, CAD-CAM and computer software.

MICAD
17 avenue ledru rollin
75012 Paris, France
PH: 33 1 53 17 11 40
FX: 33 1 53 17 11 45
URL: http://www.birp.com
Frequency: Annual. **Principal Exhibits:** Cad/Cam, computer graphics and computer technologies.

MICROBANKER
PO Box 708
Lake George, NY 12845-0708
PH: (518)745-7071
FX: (518)745-7009
Frequency: Annual. **Audience:** Controllers, credit officers, end-user financial executives, operations officers, trust executives, and
related professionals. **Principal Exhibits:** Microcomputer software,
hardware, and services for banking, savings and loans, and credit unions.

MICROELECTRONICS THAILAND

323 Bond St., Office Villa
Chaengwattana
Muang Thong Thani
Nonthaburi 11120, Thailand
PH: 2503 2199
FX: 2503 4100
E-mail: rtdxbkk@ksc5.th.com
Frequency: Biennial. **Audience:** Manufacturers electronic sub-contracting and PCB assembly personnel, and related professionals. **Principal Exhibits:** Equipment, supplies, and services PLB, semiconductor, and microelectronic design, production, processing, packaging and test technology.

MID-SOUTH INDUSTRIAL AND MACHINE TOOL SHOW

164 Lake Front Dr.
Cockeysville, MD 21030-2215
PH: (410)252-1167
TF: (800)638-6396
FX: (410)560-0477
E-mail: info@isoa.com
URL: http://www.isoa.com
Frequency: Annual. **Audience:** Trade professionals. **Principal Exhibits:** Industrial equipment, supplies, and services. **Formerly:** Mid-South Industrial Show; Mississippi Valley Industrial Show.

MIDDLE EAST MANUFACTURING - THE INTERNATIONAL EXHIBITION FOR INDUSTRIAL MACHINERY, EQUIPMENT, TECHNOLOGY AND RAW MATERIALS

PO Box 28943
Dubai, United Arab Emirates
PH: 9714 365161
FX: 9714 360137
E-mail: iirx@emirates.net.ae
Frequency: Biennial. **Principal Exhibits:** Industrial machinery and equipment, technology, machine tools, metalworking, material handling, woodworking, plastics and raw materials.

MODERN LANGUAGE ASSOCIATION ANNUAL CONVENTION

10 Astor Pl., 5th Fl.
New York, NY 10003
PH: (212)614-6386
FX: (212)477-9863
Frequency: Annual. **Audience:** Teachers and scholars of humanities. **Principal Exhibits:** College-level texts, products, and services concerned with language and literature; software for humanities scholarship, foreign language teaching, or writing labs.

MOSFOOD AND DRINK

Byron House
112A Shirland Rd.
London W9 EQ, England
PH: 44 171 286 9720
FX: 44 171 266 1126
E-mail: healthcare@ITE-Group.com
Frequency: Annual. **Principal Exhibits:** Food and drink manufacturers, wholesalers and distributors.

MTM - MALMO TECHNICAL FAIR

Box 468 (V. Varvsgatan 10)
201 24 Malmo, Sweden
PH: 46 40 690 85 00
FX: 46 40 690 85 01
E-mail: info@millerfreeman.se
URL: http://www.millerfreeman.se
Frequency: Annual. **Principal Exhibits:** Fair for the mechanical and technical industry.

MTQ - TRADE FAIR FOR QUALITY ASSURANCE SYSTEMS

Rheinlanddamm 200
Postfach 104444
D-44139 Dortmund, Germany
PH: 231 1204521
FX: 231 1204678
Frequency: Biennial. **Audience:** Trade professionals. **Principal Exhibits:** Computers and related equipment.

NATIONAL ASSOCIATION OF INDUSTRIAL TECHNOLOGY ANNUAL CONVENTION

3300 Washtenaw Ave., Ste. 220
Ann Arbor, MI 48104-4200
PH: (734)677-0720
FX: (734)677-2407
URL: http://www.nait.org
Frequency: Annual. **Principal Exhibits:** Textbooks and equipment related to the business industry and education.

NETWORKS DATA & TELECOM

International House
Central Blvd. 5
DK-2300 Copenhagen, Denmark
PH: 45 32 47 33 22
FX: 45 32 52 35 66
Frequency: Annual. **Principal Exhibits:** Manufacturers of computer networking hardware, software and services.

THE NEW ANIMATION TECHNOLOGY EXPOSITION

525 Market St., Ste. 500
San Francisco, CA 94105
PH: (415)278-5300
FX: (415)278-5341
Frequency: Annual. **Principal Exhibits:** Digital animation tools and technology.

NEW HAMPSHIRE INDUSTRIAL SHOW

333 Trapelo Rd.
Belmont, MA 02178
PH: (617)489-2302
TF: (800)543-5259
FX: (617)489-5534
Frequency: Annual. **Audience:** Machine shop and plant maintenance trade. **Principal Exhibits:** Machine tools, power tools, compressors, plumbing supplies, and industrial supplies.

NEW JERSEY INDUSTRIAL SHOW

164 Lake Front Dr.
Cockeysville, MD 21030-2215
PH: (410)252-1167
TF: (800)638-6396
FX: (410)560-0477
E-mail: info@isoa.com
URL: http://www.isoa.com
Frequency: Annual. **Audience:** Trade professionals. **Principal Exhibits:** Industrial equipment, supplies, and services.

NMW - NATIONAL MANUFACTURING WEEK

383 Main Ave.
PO Box 6059
Norwalk, CT 06851
PH: (203)840-5358
FX: (203)840-4804
E-mail: inquiry@nepcon.reedexpo.com
Frequency: Annual. **Audience:** Trade Professionals. **Principal Exhibits:** Product design, control engineering, plant engineering, maintenance, electrical equipment for industrial/commercial use, and control technology for manufacturing facilities. **Incorporating:** National Industrial Automation; National Industrial Enterprise IT; National Plant Engineering & Management; National Design Engineering.

**NOR-SHOP - TRADE FAIR FOR SHOP EQUIPMENT,
DISPLAY, AND MERCHANDISING CONFERENCE**
Drammensveien 154
PO Box 130 Skoyen
N-0212 Oslo, Norway
PH: 47 22 439100
FX: 47 22 431914
E-mail: nv@messe.no
URL: http://www.messe.no
Audience: Shop-equipment retail trade, including proprietors, managers, and employees. **Principal Exhibits:** Shop equipment; display and sales material.

NORBIT
Drammensveien 154
PO Box 130 Skoyen
N-0212 Oslo, Norway
PH: 47 22 439100
FX: 47 22 431914
E-mail: nv@messe.no
URL: http://www.messe.no
Frequency: Biennial. **Audience:** Trade professionals, general public, and government. **Principal Exhibits:** Software, CAD/CAM/CIM, Multimedia, Virtual Reality, Hardware, Network/ Communication, Peripherals, Security, and Telecom. **Formerly:** Data IT Uken.

NORTH CAROLINA INDUSTRIAL SHOW
2 Centerview Dr., Ste. 35
Greensboro, NC 27407-3708
PH: (910)294-3080
FX: (910)854-8949
Frequency: Biennial. **Audience:** Trade professionals. **Principal Exhibits:** Industrial equipment; machine tools; business services; hand tools; related equipment, supplies, and services.

**NORTHEAST PENNSYLVANIA INDUSTRIAL AND
CONSTRUCTION SHOW**
164 Lake Front Dr.
Cockeysville, MD 21030-2215
PH: (410)252-1167
TF: (800)638-6396
FX: (410)560-0477
E-mail: info@isoa.com
URL: http://www.isoa.com
Frequency: Biennial. **Audience:** Trade. **Principal Exhibits:** Industrial equipment, machine tools, business services, hand tools, and related equipment, supplies, and services.

NORTHERN ALABAMA INDUSTRIAL SHOW
164 Lake Front Dr.
Cockeysville, MD 21030-2215
PH: (410)252-1167
TF: (800)638-6396
FX: (410)560-0477
E-mail: info@isoa.com
URL: http://www.isoa.com
Frequency: Annual. **Principal Exhibits:** Industrial equipment, supplies, and services.

NWMT - NORTHWEST MACHINE TOOL SHOW
47361 Bayside Pkwy.
Fremont, CA 94538
PH: (510)354-3131
TF: (800)548-1407
FX: (510)354-3159
E-mail: showinfo@proshows.com
Frequency: Annual. **Principal Exhibits:** Plant operations equipment, supplies, and services. bd*Held in conjunction with: NWPE - Northwest Plant Engineering & Maintenance Show.*

OITF - OSAKA INTERNATIONAL TRADE FAIR
5-102 Nanko-kita, 1-Chome
Suminoe-ku
Osaka 559-0034, Japan
PH: 81 6 6123773
FX: 81 6 6128585
URL: http://www.oitfc.fair.or.jp/
Frequency: Biennial. **Audience:** General public. **Principal Exhibits:** General fair consisting of seven shows covering the following industries: Import/export, home remodeling and construction, electric and electronic products, industrial technology, home furnishings, outdoor sporting and leisure goods, and audio-visual equipment. **Held in conjunction with:** AV Show; Eletech Fair; Import Fair; Industrial Technology Fair; Japan Domestic Industry Fair.

OKLAHOMA INDUSTRIAL SHOW
164 Lake Front Dr.
Cockeysville, MD 21030-2215
PH: (410)252-1167
TF: (800)638-6396
FX: (410)560-0477
E-mail: info@isoa.com
URL: http://www.isoa.com
Frequency: Annual. **Audience:** Trade. **Principal Exhibits:** Industrial equipment, supplies, and services.

**ORGANIZATION FOR BLACK DESIGNERS ANNUAL
CONFERENCE**
300 M St. SW, Ste. N110
Washington, DC 20024
PH: (202)659-3918
FX: (202)488-3838
E-mail: OBDesign@aol.com
URL: http://www.core77.com/OBD
Frequency: Annual. **Principal Exhibits:** Exhibits of interest to African American designers holding college degrees who are practicing graphic, industrial, fashion, textile, and interior design.

THE PARTNERS' CONFERENCE AND EXHIBITION
PO Box 4440
369 Lexington Ave.
New York, NY 10017
PH: (212)286-0333
FX: (212)286-0086
Frequency: Annual. **Principal Exhibits:** Information and technology, Internet/Intranet, financial management systems, computer accounting systems, software, tax preparation, business systems, CD-ROM systems, and industry web sites.

PC EXPO IN NEW YORK
1 Penn Plaza
New York, NY 10119-0002
PH: (212)714-1300
TF: (800)829-3976
FX: (212)643-4803
Frequency: Annual. **Audience:** Volume buyers and resellers. **Principal Exhibits:** Networking, graphics, CAD/CAM, portables, windows products, multimedia, workstations, desktop publishing, CASE, mobile computing pen-based, and palm tops.

PC MELBOURNE - PERSONAL COMPUTER SHOW
Illoura Plaza
424 St. Kilda Rd.
Melbourne, VIC 3004, Australia
PH: 61 3 92614500
FX: 61 3 92614545
E-mail: shows@ausexhibit.com.au
URL: http://www.ausexhibit.com.au
Frequency: Annual. **Audience:** Small/medium/large business professionals; corporations; professional users; and education, manufacturing, trade, and finance professionals. **Principal Exhibits:** Computer hardware, software, peripherals, services, publications, multimedia, in the areas of Cad, Networking, Training & Education,

Communications and Office Systems. **Formerly:** Communications and Office Technology.

PIEDMONT INDUSTRIAL SHOW
164 Lake Front Dr.
Cockeysville, MD 21030-2215
PH: (410)252-1167
TF: (800)638-6396
FX: (410)560-0477
E-mail: info@isoa.com
URL: http://www.isoa.com
Frequency: Annual. **Audience:** Trade professionals. **Principal Exhibits:** Industrial equipment, supplies, and services.

PLANT ENGINEERING CHINA
383 Main Ave.
PO Box 6059
Norwalk, CT 06851
PH: (203)840-5358
FX: (203)840-4804
E-mail: inquiry@nepcon.reedexpo.com
Frequency: Biennial. **Audience:** Manufacturers. **Principal Exhibits:** Products for the manufacturing industry.

PRINTED CIRCUIT BOARD DESIGN CONFERENCE EAST
525 Market St., Ste. 500
San Francisco, CA 94105
PH: (415)278-5300
FX: (415)278-5341
Frequency: Annual. **Principal Exhibits:** Equipment, supplies, and services for the printed circuit design industry.

PRINTED CIRCUIT BOARD DESIGN CONFERENCE WEST
525 Market St., Ste. 500
San Francisco, CA 94105
PH: (415)278-5300
FX: (415)278-5341
Frequency: Annual. **Principal Exhibits:** Equipment, supplies, and services for the printed circuit design industry.

PROCESS EQUIPMENT - TECHNOLOGICAL EXHIBITION ON PUMPS & VALVES EXHIBITION
Autolei 337
B-2160 Wommelgem, Belgium
PH: 3 3540880
FX: 3 3540810
Frequency: Biennial. **Principal Exhibits:** Pumps, valves, and related industrial products and systems.

PROSPECTORS AND DEVELOPERS ASSOCIATION OF CANADA ANNUAL MEETING AND CONVENTION
34 King St. E., 9th Fl.
Toronto, ON, Canada M5C 2X8
PH: (416)362-1969
FX: (416)362-0101
E-mail: info@pdac.ca
Frequency: Annual. **Audience:** Geologists, prospectors, developers, geochemists, and geophysicists. **Principal Exhibits:** Exploration services, computer software, and field supplies.

RICHMOND INDUSTRIAL AND CONSTRUCTION SHOW
164 Lake Front Dr.
Cockeysville, MD 21030-2215
PH: (410)252-1167
TF: (800)638-6396
FX: (410)560-0477
E-mail: info@isoa.com
URL: http://www.isoa.com
Frequency: Annual. **Audience:** Trade professionals. **Principal Exhibits:** Industrial equipment, supplies, and services.

RINEC
PO Box 19
191040 St. Petersburg, Russia

PH: 812 164 7043
FX: 812 1122348
E-mail: root@restec.spb.su
URL: http://www.restec.ru/
Frequency: Annual. **Principal Exhibits:** Personal computers and computer software.

ROBERT MORRIS ASSOCIATES' ANNUAL FALL CONFERENCE
1650 Market St., Ste. 2300
Philadelphia, PA 19103
PH: (215)446-4122
FX: (215)446-4101
URL: http://www.rmahq.org
Frequency: Annual. **Principal Exhibits:** Software manufacturers, information services providers, appraisers, consultants, and publishers serving the commercial lending and credit industry. **Dates and Locations:** 2000 Nov 11-14; Nashville, TN.

SAUDICOMPUTER - COMPUTER AND COMPUTER GRAPHICS SHOW
PO Box 56010
Riyadh 11554, Saudi Arabia
PH: 966 1 454 1448
FX: 966 1 454 4846
E-mail: recsa@midleast.net
Frequency: Annual. **Principal Exhibits:** Equipment, supplies, and services for the computer industry. **Held in conjunction with:** SaudiBusiness - Office Technology Show; SaudiEducation - Education and Training Show.

SOFT CIM
383 Main Ave.
PO Box 6059
Norwalk, CT 06851
PH: (203)840-5358
FX: (203)840-4804
E-mail: inquiry@nepcon.reedexpo.com
Frequency: Biennial. **Audience:** Trade professionals. **Principal Exhibits:** Software and technology in computer integrated manufacturing. **Held in conjunction with:** Industrial Handling.

SOFTARG SOFTWARE INTERNATIONAL FAIR
ul. Bytkowska 1b
40-955 Katowice, Poland
PH: 032 59 83 12
FX: 03 154 02 27
E-mail: mtk@silesia.ternet.pl
Frequency: Annual. **Principal Exhibits:** Software, data teletransmission, and structural cable systems.

SOFTEX IN ACCOUNTING AND FINANCE, ATLANTA
2560 Embarcadero Rd., Ste. 101
Palo Alto, CA 94303
PH: (650)847-4100
FX: (415)847-4100
URL: http://www.softinfo.com
Principal Exhibits: Software for integrated accounting systems and best-of-breed solutions; OLAP and executive information systems; ABC/ABM, fund accounting, and project accounting.

SOFTEX IN ACCOUNTING AND FINANCE, DALLAS
2560 Embarcadero Rd., Ste. 101
Palo Alto, CA 94303
PH: (650)847-4100
FX: (415)847-4100
URL: http://www.softinfo.com
Frequency: Annual. **Principal Exhibits:** Software for integrated accounting systems; A/P and A/R; general ledgers; fixed assets; purchase order management; billing and invoicing; financial analysis; reporting and consolidation; OLAP and executive information systems; ABC/ABM, fund accounting, and project accounting.

SOFTEX IN ACCOUNTING AND FINANCE, NEW YORK
2560 Embarcadero Rd., Ste. 101
Palo Alto, CA 94303
PH: (650)847-4100
FX: (415)847-4100
URL: http://www.softinfo.com
Frequency: Annual. **Principal Exhibits:** Software for integrated accounting systems; A/P and A/R; general ledgers; fixed assets; purchase order management; billing and invoicing; financial analysis; reporting and consolidation; OLAP and executive information systems; ABC/ABM, fund accounting, and project accounting.

SOFTEX IN HUMAN RESOURCES & PAYROLL WEST
2560 Embarcadero Rd., Ste. 101
Palo Alto, CA 94303
PH: (650)847-4100
FX: (415)847-4100
URL: http://www.softinfo.com
Principal Exhibits: Software for integrated HRIS/HRMS, payroll, employee self-service systems, time and attendance tracking, employment management, and HR administration.

SOFTEX IN MANUFACTURING & DISTRIBUTION
2560 Embarcadero Rd., Ste. 101
Palo Alto, CA 94303
PH: (650)847-4100
FX: (415)847-4100
URL: http://www.softinfo.com
Principal Exhibits: Software for ERP, MRP/MRP II, and MES; supply chain management; advanced planning and scheduling; warehouse management systems; and distribution resource planning.

SOFTEX IN SALES AUTOMATION, SAN FRANCISCO
2560 Embarcadero Rd., Ste. 101
Palo Alto, CA 94303
PH: (650)847-4100
FX: (415)847-4100
URL: http://www.softinfo.com
Principal Exhibits: Software for integrated sales force automation, forecasting, sales opportunity, field sales management, quotation, lead and sales tracking and analysis, database marketing, enterprise customer management, help-desk, call-center and CTI, and SFA using the Internet and Intranet.

**SOFTEX TAIPEI - INTERNATIONAL COMPUTER
  SOFTWARE SHOW**
CETRA Exhibition Dept.
5 Hsinyi Rd., Sec. 5
Taipei World Trade Center Exhibition Hall
Taipei 110, Taiwan
PH: 886 2 2725 1111
FX: 886 2 2725 1314
E-mail: cetra@cetra.org.tw
URL: http://www.taipeitradeshows.org.tw
Frequency: Annual. **Audience:** Trade professionals. **Principal Exhibits:** Computer software and related equipment, supplies, and services.

**SOFTWARE AUTOMATION - TRADE FAIR FOR SYSTEMS
  SOFTWARE**
Doorniksesteenweg 216
B-8500 Kortrijk, Belgium
PH: 56 24 11 11
FX: 56 21 79 30
E-mail: info@hallen.be
URL: http://www.hallen.be/
Frequency: Annual. **Audience:** Trade professionals. **Principal Exhibits:** Information science systems software.

SOFTWARE DEVELOPMENT
630 Chiswick High Rd.
London W4 5BG, England

PH: 44 181 742 2828
FX: 44 181 747 3856
URL: http://www.mf-exhibitions.co.uk
Frequency: Annual. **Principal Exhibits:** Software tools and systems development products and services.

SOFTWARE DEVELOPMENT ASIA
Level 21, 19A-21-2, UOA Centre
19 Jalan Pinang
50450 Kuala Lumpur, Malaysia
PH: 60 3 264 5663
FX: 60 2 264 5660
Frequency: Annual. **Principal Exhibits:** Software development tools, systems, and accessories.

**SOFTWARE DEVELOPMENT EAST CONFERENCE &
  EXPO**
600 Harrison St.
San Francisco, CA 94107
PH: (415)905-2200
TF: (800)227-4675
FX: (415)905-2232
URL: http://www.mfi.com
Frequency: Annual. **Audience:** Corporate end-users, trade professionals and consultants. **Principal Exhibits:** Graphical applications; develop client server applications; develop database applications; develop RAD, CASE, CAST; testing & debugging 4GL's, GUI builders, object oriented programming & systems, compilers, reverse engineering.

SOFTWARE DEVELOPMENT WEST
600 Harrison St.
San Francisco, CA 94107
PH: (415)905-2200
TF: (800)227-4675
FX: (415)905-2232
URL: http://www.mfi.com
Frequency: Annual. **Principal Exhibits:** Equipment, supplies, and services for the software development industry.

**SOFTWARE PUBLISHERS ASSOCIATION CONFERENCE
  AND SYMPOSIUM**
1730 M St. NW, Ste. 700
Washington, DC 20036-4510
PH: (202)452-1600
FX: (202)223-8756
Frequency: Semiannual. **Audience:** Trade professionals. **Principal Exhibits:** Computer software and related products and services. **Dates and Locations:** 1998 Mar 21-25; San Jose, CA.

SOUTH CAROLINA INDUSTRIAL SHOW
164 Lake Front Dr.
Cockeysville, MD 21030-2215
PH: (410)252-1167
TF: (800)638-6396
FX: (410)560-0477
E-mail: info@isoa.com
URL: http://www.isoa.com
Frequency: Annual. **Audience:** Trade professionals. **Principal Exhibits:** Industrial equipment, supplies, and services.

SOUTH TEXAS INDUSTRIAL SHOW
164 Lake Front Dr.
Cockeysville, MD 21030-2215
PH: (410)252-1167
TF: (800)638-6396
FX: (410)560-0477
E-mail: info@isoa.com
URL: http://www.isoa.com
Frequency: Annual. **Audience:** Trade professionals. **Principal Exhibits:** Industrial equipment, machine tools, hand tools, business services and related equipment, supplies, and services.

SPS - INTERNATIONAL EXHIBITION AND CONFERENCE ON PROGRAMMABLE CONTROLLERS

Rotebuhlstrasse 83-85
D-70178 Stuttgart, Germany
PH: 49 11 619460
FX: 49 11 6194698
E-mail: buss@mesago.de
URL: http://www.mesago.de
Frequency: Annual. **Audience:** Corporate owners and presidents; construction and application engineers; production managers; consultants; scientists; and instructors. **Principal Exhibits:** Programmable controllers, computers, components, and assemblies.

SQE - INTERNATIONAL CONFERENCE ON SOFTWARE QUALITY ENGINEERING

Conference Secretariat
Ashurst
Ashurst Lodge
Southampton SO40 7AA, England
PH: 44 0 1703 293 223
FX: 44 0 1703 292 853
E-mail: wit@wessex.ac.uk
URL: http://www.wessex.ac.uk/
Principal Exhibits: Academic and industrial research and applications relating to a scientific approach to software quality engineering.

SUMMER COMPUTER SIMULATION CONFERENCE

4838 Romsom Ct., Ste. L
PO Box 17900
San Diego, CA 92117
PH: (619)277-3888
FX: (619)277-3930
Frequency: Annual. **Audience:** Computer scientists, engineers, university professors, and students. **Principal Exhibits:** Simulation software and hardware, publications, and books.

SUPERGAMES MOSCOW

Byron House
112A Shirland Rd.
London W9 EQ, England
PH: 44 171 286 9720
FX: 44 171 266 1126
E-mail: healthcare@ITE-Group.com
Frequency: Annual. **Principal Exhibits:** Casino supply companies, manufacturers and distributors of hardware and software for education and entertainment.

SYSTEMS - INTERNATIONAL TRADE FAIR FOR INFORMATION TECHNOLOGY AND TELECOMMUNICATIONS

Messegelande
Postfach 121009
D-80034 Munich, Germany
PH: 49 89 5107143
FX: 49 89 5107177
E-mail: info@messe-muenchen.de
URL: http://www.messe.muenchen.de
Frequency: Annual. **Audience:** Professionals interested in the uses and applications of computers and communication systems; general public. **Principal Exhibits:** Computers and computer peripherals, computer-aided design and manufacturing systems, office equipment maintenance products, communication systems, and software. **Formerly:** Systec; Systems Computers and Communications Exhibition; SYSTEMS - Computers, Peripherals, and Software Communications International Trade Fair.

TAIPEI INTERNATIONAL AUTOMATION & PRECISION MACHINERY SHOW

CETRA Exhibition Dept.
5 Hsinyi Rd., Sec. 5
Taipei World Trade Center Exhibition Hall
Taipei 110, Taiwan

PH: 886 2 2725 1111
FX: 886 2 2725 1314
E-mail: cetra@cetra.org.tw
URL: http://www.taipeitradeshows.org.tw
Frequency: Biennial. **Audience:** Trade professionals. **Principal Exhibits:** Machinery for metal working, CNC, plastics processing, woodworking, shoe making, electronics processing, packing and material handling; automation machinery, computer systems, and measuring and testing equipment.

TEKNIK & DATA - SPECIAL FAIR AND CONFERENCE FOR TECHNICAL DATA PROCESSING AND CAD/CAM/CIM

Falkoner Alle 90
DK-2000 Frederiksberg, Denmark
PH: 45 35 363700
FX: 45 35 363799
E-mail: df@df-jm.dk
URL: http://www.df-jm.dk
Frequency: Annual. **Audience:** Trade Professionals. **Principal Exhibits:** Equipment, supplies, and services for the technical data processing industry.

TELNETS

9200 S. Dadeland Blvd., Ste. 309
Miami, FL 33156
PH: (305)670-9444
FX: (305)670-9459
Principal Exhibits: Computer hardware and software.

TENNESSEE INDUSTRIAL SHOW/NASHVILLE

164 Lake Front Dr.
Cockeysville, MD 21030-2215
PH: (410)252-1167
TF: (800)638-6396
FX: (410)560-0477
E-mail: info@isoa.com
URL: http://www.isoa.com
Frequency: Annual. **Audience:** Trade professionals. **Principal Exhibits:** Industrial equipment, machine tools, hand tools, business services, and related equipment, supplies, and services.

TRADE FAIR/LEPER

Westhoek Expo-Industrielaan
B-8900 Leper, Belgium
PH: 57 219190
FX: 57 219390
Frequency: Annual. **Audience:** General public. **Principal Exhibits:** Industrial products.

TRANSINFO - INTERNATIONAL TRANSPORT AND LOGISTICS EXHIBITION

Av. Reina Maria Cristina, s/n
E-08004 Barcelona, Spain
PH: 93 804 0102
FX: 93 805 4802
Frequency: Biennial. **Audience:** Trade professionals. **Principal Exhibits:** Logistics service suppliers, carriers, hirers, EDI, telecommunications, computing companies, infrastructures, manufacturers and distributors of storage and packaging material, handling material and equipment, containers and swap bodies, professional organizations, communication and press.

TRI-CITIES INDUSTRIAL SHOW

164 Lakefront Dr.
Huntvalley, MD 21030
TF: (800)638-6396
E-mail: shwbusines@aol.com
Frequency: Annual. **Audience:** Trade professionals. **Principal Exhibits:** Industrial equipment, supplies, and services.

UNIX EXPO
Fort Lee Executive Park
1 Executive Dr.
Fort Lee, NJ 07024
PH: (201)546-1400
FX: (201)750-8568
Frequency: Annual. **Principal Exhibits:** Application development tools, business application software, client/server solutions, computer hardware and systems, enterprise computing solutions, networking/system hardware and software, vertical market software and peripherals.

USA/MEXICO INDUSTRIAL EXPO
164 Lake Front Dr.
Cockeysville, MD 21030-2215
PH: (410)252-1167
TF: (800)638-6396
FX: (410)560-0477
E-mail: info@isoa.com
URL: http://www.isoa.com
Frequency: Annual. **Principal Exhibits:** Industrial equipment, supplies, and services.

VIDEO SOFTWARE DEALERS ASSOCIATION CONVENTION
16530 Ventura Blvd., Ste. 400
Encino, CA 91436-4551
PH: (818)385-1500
FX: (818)385-0567
Frequency: Annual. **Audience:** Video retailers. **Principal Exhibits:** Pre-recorded video software, computer software for video retailers, accessory products for retailers and manufacturers, and trade publications.

VIE - VANCOUVER INDUSTRIAL EXHIBITION
383 Main Ave.
PO Box 6059
Norwalk, CT 06851
PH: (203)840-5358
FX: (203)840-4804
E-mail: inquiry@nepcon.reedexpo.com
Frequency: Biennial. **Audience:** Industrial purchasing management. **Principal Exhibits:** Equipment ranging from the latest CNC machine tools, tooling and accessories, quality control and inspection equipment, plant engineering and maintenance hardware and software, pollution control and energy efficiency products and industrial supplies, and offshore technology supplies and equipment. **Dates and Locations:** 2000 Jun; Abbotsford, BC.

VIRGINIA INDUSTRIAL SHOW
164 Lake Front Dr.
Cockeysville, MD 21030-2215
PH: (410)252-1167
TF: (800)638-6396
FX: (410)560-0477
E-mail: info@isoa.com
URL: http://www.isoa.com
Frequency: Annual. **Principal Exhibits:** Industrial equipment, supplies, and services.

WEB DESIGN & DEVELOPMENT EAST
600 Harrison St.
San Francisco, CA 94107
PH: (415)905-2200
TF: (800)227-4675
FX: (415)905-2232
URL: http://www.mfi.com
Frequency: Annual. **Principal Exhibits:** Equipment, supplies, and services for the development of Web-based applications and sites.

WEB DESIGN & DEVELOPMENT WEST
600 Harrison St.
San Francisco, CA 94107
PH: (415)905-2200
TF: (800)227-4675
FX: (415)905-2232
URL: http://www.mfi.com
Frequency: Annual. **Principal Exhibits:** Equipment, supplies, and services for the development of Web-based applications and sites.

WEC: WELD EXPO CANADA
383 Main Ave.
PO Box 6059
Norwalk, CT 06851
PH: (203)840-5358
FX: (203)840-4804
E-mail: inquiry@nepcon.reedexpo.com
Frequency: Biennial. **Audience:** Production managers, plant engineers, welding technicians, welding engineers, and other plant personnel. **Principal Exhibits:** Metal forming, cutting, rolling, and bending equipment; punch presses machinery; finishing products and supplies; pollution controls; liquid air and liquid oxygen; welding torch and supplies; safety products and supplies; environmental supplies; air compression. **Dates and Locations:** 2000 Oct; Toronto, ON. **Held in conjunction with:** Plant Maintenance and Engineering Show/CeTech.

WEST VIRGINIA INDUSTRIAL & MINING SHOW
164 Lake Front Dr.
Cockeysville, MD 21030-2215
PH: (410)252-1167
TF: (800)638-6396
FX: (410)560-0477
E-mail: info@isoa.com
URL: http://www.isoa.com
Frequency: Biennial. **Audience:** Trade professionals. **Principal Exhibits:** Industrial equipment, supplies, and services.

WHICH COMPUTER? SHOW
383 Main Ave.
PO Box 6059
Norwalk, CT 06851
PH: (203)840-5358
FX: (203)840-4804
E-mail: inquiry@nepcon.reedexpo.com
Frequency: Annual. **Audience:** Business and corporate end users of computers and related services. **Principal Exhibits:** Business computer hardware, software, and related equipment, supplies, and services, including mainframes, minis, micro computers, peripherals, consumables, and networking.

WINDOWS EXPO SIBERIA - THE INTERNATIONAL WINDOWS SOFTWARE EXHIBITION
16 Gorky St.
6300099 Novosibirsk, Russia
PH: 7 3832 102674
FX: 7 3832 236335
E-mail: siberian.fair@sovcust.sprint.com
Frequency: Biennial. **Principal Exhibits:** Manufacturers, distributors, importers of hardware and software.

WINDOWS WORLD/UNITED STATES
300 1st Ave.
Needham, MA 02194-2722
PH: (617)449-6600
FX: (617)444-7722
E-mail: compuserve: 74667, 3241
URL: http://www.comdex.com
Frequency: Annual. **Audience:** End users, developers, integrators, dealers, value-adders, distributors. **Principal Exhibits:** Windows compatible software, tools, memory and machine upgrades, networking hardware/software products and services.

PART II
BROADCASTING & TELECOMMUNICATIONS

"INTERESTING TIMES": CONVERGENCE AND FUTURE DIRECTIONS IN BROADCASTING AND TELECOMMUNICATIONS

Nigel David Allen
Allen Telecommunications
Policy Consultants

As broadcasting and telecommunications technology becomes better and cheaper, telecommunications carriers are turning new technology into new services, and many of their customers will use these new services to enhance their profitability. An explosive growth in demand for bandwidth is changing the way telecommunications companies design their networks. But the growth of the telecommunications sector threatens to leave some less-profitable customers behind.

Regulatory and Public Policy Issues

To understand how broadcasting and telecommunications technology develops in a competitive environment, it helps to look at how the environment developed.

Many people once believed that telephone service was a "natural monopoly," where the most efficient way to provide service was to have a single, regulated supplier in any given area, which is normally the case for water utilities and fire-fighting services. But proponents of competition in telecommunications argue that monopolies are inherently inefficient and don't have the same incentive to innovate that companies do in a competitive environment.

In the United States and Canada, telephone companies developed a shared understanding with public officials of basic policy goals for telecommunications: universal service and value-of-service pricing. Universal service meant that local residential service was priced below what it cost the telephone companies to provide it, and that long distance and other optional services such as extension telephones were priced well above cost to compensate for low basic telephone rates. Value-of-service pricing meant that telecommunications services were priced on the basis of what they were worth, rather than on how much they cost. For example, monthly telephone rates in some areas were set on the basis of the number of how many telephone numbers were in a user's local calling area, so that people in a large city would pay more than those in a small town. These pricing principles have been replaced by a general commitment to base prices on cost, with subsidies for low-income or rural users, as well as for schools and libraries, made explicit rather than buried in other costs. This has led to sharply higher rates for local telephone service, with monthly rates in smaller communities rising to levels close to those of larger cities, while long distance rates have dropped.

Deregulation also meant that telephone companies were no longer the only supplier of telecommunications equipment, and customers were free to buy equipment from any supplier, as long as it was certified not work with the telephone network. As telephone companies lost market share through competition and automated some functions formerly done by hand, many jobs were eliminated. At the same time, new jobs were created at companies that provided equipment and services in competition with the telephone companies.

Traditionally, prices charged by telephone companies were set by regulatory commissions, such as the Federal Communications Commission and the public utilities commissions of individual states. Prices were usually set so that a company's investors could expect to receive a return on their investment that was considered fair and appropriate to the level of risk involved in their investment, within the framework of universal service and value-of-service pricing. In most jurisdictions, this has changed substantially. Services for which there is well-established competition are regulated lightly or not at all; services provided on a monopoly basis are regulated on the basis of price rather than of profitability, which has generally led to significant increases in telephone company profits.

While much of the decision-making involving the telecommunications industry took place before regulatory commissions, the courts and legislatures also had roles to play. Competitors and government agencies launched lawsuits against the former Bell System (that is, AT&T and its local telephone company subsidiaries) which claimed that the telephone companies were behaving illegally. These lawsuits led to the break-up of the Bell System in 1984: the Bell System was split into seven regional Bell holding companies, which provided local telephone service, and AT&T, which retained manufacturing and long distance operations. Several years later, the manufacturing arm, renamed Lucent Technologies, became a separate company. Legislation passed in state legislatures, the U.S. Congress and national parliaments in other countries has removed much of the monopoly power of telecommunications carriers and many of the restrictions on them, although the regional Bell companies have not yet been allowed to offer national long-distance services.

Safety and technical standards for telecommunications equipment used to be set by the telephone companies themselves, with large companies like AT&T leading the way and others copying their standards. To avoid the possibility of telephone companies writing standards that would give an unfair advantage to equipment supplied by the telephone companies, regulators assigned responsibility for writing telecommunications industry standards to independent standards-writing committees with representation from manufacturers, carriers and end-users. These standards-writing bodies include Committee T1 in the United States, sponsored by the Alliance for Telecommunications Industry Solutions, and the Telecommunications Standards Advisory Council of Canada (TSACC). Much standards work is done by the International Telecommunication Union (ITU), an intergovernmental organization based in Switzerland.

Other countries have regulatory structures that reflect local priorities. In the United Kingdom, which privatized the former government-owned carrier British Telecom many years ago, government offices that deal with telecommunications include the Office of Telecommunications (Oftel), a regulatory body that establishes the framework for pricing and assigning telephone numbers, and the Department of Trade and Industry. A private body, the British Approvals Board for Telecommunications (BABT) deals with standards issues. Other British government agencies that handle telecommunications include the Central Computer and Telecommunications Agency, which operates telecommunications and computer networks throughout the government; the Government Communications Headquarters, which monitors telecommunications signals for national security purposes; the signals and communications units of the army, navy and air force; and the courts, which are often called upon to deal with litigation involving telecommunications carriers.

In some other countries, telecommunications services are provided by a government agency. Even where a national government chooses to keep the dominant telecommunications carrier under government ownership, the trend is to convert the telecommunications carrier from a department of government to a government-owned corporation (in the same way, for exam-

ple, that the U.S. Post Office Department was replaced by the U.S. Postal Service). At the same time that a country's government turns its telecommunications carrier into a government-owned corporation, it may also set up a separate regulatory tribunal to set prices and hear complaints about the telecommunications carrier.

Many telecommunications regulators have established quality-of-service standards which carriers are required to meet. These standards typically deal with delays in installation and repair of telephone lines and speed and reliability of other services, including directory assistance, operator services and the telephone company's business office. When telecommunications companies have reduced staff levels to the point where quality-of-service standards were not being met, regulators have ordered the carriers to make rebates to the customers who did not receive the correct level of service.

Another regulatory responsibility is spectrum management: deciding which radio frequencies will be available for mobile telephone and other users. Radio and television stations have traditionally received an allocation of frequency for free because they were considered to be serving the public interest, but other spectrum users have not been so lucky. The U.S. government has chosen to auction off the right to use the higher-frequency bands used by mobile telephone service, selling a license to the highest bidder. Frequency management is an issue elsewhere as well: the introduction of cellular service in Russia was delayed because a band of frequencies that was used for cellular phones elsewhere could not be used for cellular phones in Russia because the band was used by the Russian military.

Taxation of Broadcasting and Telecommunications

In many jurisdictions, telecommunications carriers are required to pay a tax based on their total revenues (a "gross receipts tax") that non-telecommunications companies are not subject to. These taxes have been imposed as payment for the carriers' use of public space for their cables. Taxes apply as well on telecommunications services, sometimes at a higher rate than a jurisdiction's sales tax for other goods and services.

But some items on a bill for telecommunications service that look like taxes are payments to an industry fund or to other telecommunications carriers rather than a tax paid to government. For example, in the United States, service in rural and remote areas is subsidized by a fund that some carriers pay into and others receive funding from. Subsidized telecommunications access for schools and libraries (the "E-rate") is paid for through a surcharge on telecommunications carriers. There has been opposition to the E-rate, but the idea of an earmarked fee is more palatable to some individuals than direct government grants for telecommunications services.

Reliability and Security

Telecommunications networks have to be built to withstand the risk of accident and disaster. In most cases, they are; if the electrical power in a home goes out during a thunderstorm, the phones will probably still work. Networks are often designed as a loop, with two cables on separate routes connecting telephone switching buildings so that if one cable is damaged, the other cable will able to handle most of the displaced traffic. Burying telephone cable, while more expensive than hanging it from telephone poles, reduces the risk of damage from bad weather or accident.

Other measures to reduce the risk of include building telecommunications switching buildings on high ground, to reduce the risk of flooding, avoiding geological fault lines, ensuring that electrical generators are available to take over when commercial power fails, and providing emergency backup switching equipment in a trailer that can be transported to a site where the telephone switch has been destroyed by a disaster. Telecommunications carriers cooperate with other utility companies to let contractors know the location of buried telecommunications cables so that the contractor doesn't damage them during excavation work. Even so, damage caused by excavation equipment—nicknamed "backhoe fade"—continues to be a concern for all broadcast and telecommunications companies.

Like telecommunications carriers, corporate and institutional telecommunications managers have a responsibility to design their broadcast and telecommunications systems to withstand natural disasters. Many corporate communications users are connected to more than one telephone central office, in case their main communication link fails. They have to be security-conscious and keep unauthorized individuals from tampering with their equipment.

Telecommunications carriers and users can become victims of fraud. Poorly-designed telephone and voice mail systems can allow an intruder to break in and make thousands of dollars worth of international telephone calls at the user's expense before the fraud is detected. Computers connected to the Internet without adequate security can be broken into and valuable data taken or destroyed. Telecommunications managers should monitor and investigate odd calling patterns, such as a sudden large volume of international calls outside working hours.

Telephone credit cards, now called calling cards, also raise security concerns. A dishonest person can observe the numbers on a user's calling card while the user is making a long-distance call from a payphone, or the card may be sometimes stolen in the mail. Users should be careful not to allow their calling card number to be seen by anyone else.

Another form of fraud is dishonest marketing of telecommunications services. Users can find their long distance service switched to another carrier without their authorization. This is referred to as "slamming". In other cases, a small telecommunications carrier may pretend to be a well-known one. The problem is not restricted to small carriers; outside sales firms working for large carriers are sometimes guilty of dishonestly switching a user's long distance service.

Premium and International Audiotex Pay-per-call

Pay-per-call numbers (in the 900 area code or with a distinctive local prefix such as 976) can be used, for example, to provide premium levels of support for computer software, to allow individuals to make a donation to a charity, or, in the case of Canada's Environment Department, to allow people, for $2 a minute, to talk to a government weather forecaster. (The 900/976 industry is sometimes referred to as "audiotex"). But the bulk of 900 numbers are for more questionable and sometimes fraudulent purposes: information about jobs that do not exist or results of giveaways where the possible prize is worth less than the cost of the phone call, advice from psychics and various forms of "adult entertainment." Because the public has learned to be cynical about 976 and 900, many legitimate companies may find their use of these numbers viewed with suspicion. Companies concerned about their employees calling these numbers may want to have their telephone equipment block calls to some or all 900 and 976 numbers. Telecommunications users may be able to request that their telecommunications carrier block all calls from their line to pay-per-call numbers.

Because 900 and 976 numbers cannot be dialed from some phone lines, some audiotex companies provide their programs through international phone numbers, perhaps to the Caribbean which shares an area code system with Canada and the United States so that the call seems to be a domestic one. In these situations, the call is charged for at regular international rates and the telephone company in the distant country, or some telecommunications carrier, rebates a portion of the cost of the call to the company owning the phone number. Telecommunications users should not phone an area code they do not recognize without checking its location in a telephone directory or with a long distance operator.

Privacy Issues in Voice, Telephony and on the Internet

Many consumers do not realize their e-mail is no more secure than a postcard. Virtually anybody can read email messages without encryption. As for voice communication, if you use a call center, there's a chance that your call will be monitored by the call center's manager.

On the Internet, criminals are interested in stealing credit card numbers, names and other forms of identification they need to make fraudulent credit card purchases. These are not likely to be intercepted on the Internet, as merchants who accept credit card purchases arrange for order forms containing a credit card number to be encrypted so that the card number remains secure. But the danger in making a purchase over the Internet is that the merchant, or an employee of the merchant, may be dishonest and either fail to deliver the material ordered or make fraudulent use of the credit card number.

Another area of Internet-related fraud is bulk e-mail messages and Internet discussion groups' messages promoting fraudulent or over-priced business opportunities, merchandise offerings or corporate stocks.

An encrypted message sent through the Internet is reasonably secure if it is encoded using PGP (Pretty Good Privacy) or Secure Sockets Layer (SSL) encryption, although the encryption licensed for export by the U.S. government is less secure than that available to U.S. citizens. Breaking modern codes requires a substantial investment in code-breaking computational power, the kind normally only possessed by such bodies as the National Security Agency in the United States, or its counterparts in other countries, like Canada's Communications Security Establishment, although there have been some reports of users at universities breaking the less difficult levels of encryption.

Communications Satellites

One of the greatest influences on telecommunications today are communications satellites. They promise to play an increasingly important role in telecommunications and broadcasting.

The earliest satellite receiving stations were huge. But as new satellites were designed, operating with more power on higher frequencies, smaller and cheaper earth stations became more available. But launching a satellite remains a risky venture: even with the most painstaking precautions, launches sometimes fail, and satellites once in place can mysteriously shut down in the face of higher-than-average solar radiation, meteorite storms, or simple bad luck. In May 1998, PanAmSat's Galaxy IV communications satellite mysteriously failed, probably because of a component problem. Recognizing these risks, companies that own satellites buy insurance and make contingency plans to switch traffic to other satellites in case a satellite fails.

Many communications satellites are in geosynchronous orbits, which means they orbit the earth once a day so they are always in a fixed position above the same point on the equator at all times. Geosynchronous satellites are well-suited for "one-to-many" trans-missions, such as television broadcasts and nationwide paging, where a single paging message is transmitted to many different paging transmitters. They can also be used for point-to-point communications applications where communications cables are not available, such as in providing telephone, data and fax service to isolated communities in the Arctic and elsewhere, areas damaged by war or natural disaster, and ships at sea. Some satellites are domestic and provide service primarily within one country, while others carry mostly international traffic. New satellites use digital transmission for television signals, which makes more efficient use of bandwidth and can be encrypted to prevent unauthorized people from watching the signal. Increasingly, communications satellites are using frequencies in the Ku band, which requires only a four-foot antenna for television reception, rather than the older C band which usually requires a twelve-foot satellite dish for television.

Other satellites operate in lower orbits which do not maintain a fixed position above the earth, usually as part of a group or "constellation" of several other identical satellites. These low-earth-orbit satellite constellations include the U.S. military's Global Positioning System, which allows military and civilian users to measure their location within a few hundred feet anywhere in the world, and two rival networks of communications satellites, Iridium and Globalstar, which are likely to play a greater role in providing satellite communication services in rural and remote areas. These low-earth-orbit satellites, introduced the late 1990s, cost significantly less than existing technology because they are cheaper to build and launch than geosynchronous satellites and use receivers that are smaller and more affordable than existing satellite receivers. They promise to bring telecommunications services to rural and remote areas that have not had them before.

Satellite service to ships at sea and some aircraft is provided by Inmarsat, the International Mobile Satellite Organization. Satellite service for ships and aircraft has proven to be more reliable, with a wider range of data options than high-frequency radio, used previously by ships at sea to communicate with ship owners and port officials. Similarly, rural and remote areas could communicate by radio before satellite service was available, but this form of transmission was slow and expensive and offered little privacy.

Submarine and Transcontinental Fiber-optic Cables

As prices for trans-Atlantic and trans-Pacific telephone calls drop and demand for Internet bandwidth increases, more communications cables (called "submarine cables") are laid on the ocean floor between countries. Submarine cables are often designed in self-healing loops, so that if a cable breaks, traffic can be rerouted to another cable. New cables are designed to handle data efficiently, rather than being designed with the assumption that most of the traffic will be voice calls. Traditionally, submarine cables were owned by consortia of national telecommunications carriers, but some are now being built by new companies not owned by existing telecommunications carriers, and some submarine cable owners are planning to build cable networks on land to connect with their submarine cables.

On land as well, long-distance communications networks continue to grow, responding to the insatiable demand for more Internet bandwidth, as well as growing voice and fax traffic. Some fiber-optic cables are being installed in disused oil pipelines, while others are installed along railroad rights-of-way and highways, in some cases with the railroad or highway administration as part-owner of the cable. Many new cables are designed to take advantage of frame relay and asynchronous transfer mode, which are technologies designed to handle large amounts of data well.

The transportation industry has been among the heaviest users of broadcast and telecommunications services, because better telecommunications allows transportation companies to control their equipment and employees more efficiently. For this reason, railroad companies are interested in sharing fiber-optic cables with telecommunications carriers and investing in equipment that lets them locate their trains more reliably.

Cellular and Other Mobile Services

Demand for mobile telephone service continues to grow, both from communications-intensive businesses such as courier companies and from individual consumers. New mobile telephone technology such as PCS (Personal Communications System) and GSM allow text messages to be sent to mobile telephone handsets, so that a mobile telephone is no longer just for voice. Data transmissions over mobile telephone networks will continue to grow. Even in the area of private radio systems used for dispatching taxicabs and transit vehicles, text-based terminals in individual vehicles have proven faster and more efficient in many places than voice conversations with a dispatcher.

While the new mobile technology works well, some companies that submitted high bids to the government for a license to provide PCS services have been unable to pay the full amount of their bid. These financial uncertainties may delay acceptance of PCS in some areas.

Users of mobile telephone service can often use their handsets in locations outside the area served by the carrier they usually deal with. This is called "roaming", and the cellular industry has agreements in place that generally allow a customer of one cellular company in the United States or Canada to place calls elsewhere, but at a higher price than calls made in their home communities. Similar agreements are being negotiated among PCS carriers.

Monthly mobile telephone bills can be unexpectedly high, which is why some mobile telephone companies are offering pre-paid service that doesn't require a contract or credit check. Instead, a customers pays in advance for a certain amount of service. Once this pre-paid amount is used up, the customer cannot make any further calls without buying additional service.

Pagers continue to be an important part of mobile communications in cases where the user needs to be reachable but does not want the expense of a mobile phone.

Competition in the Local Exchange

Local telephone companies are facing competition in many areas from competitive local exchange carriers (CLECs), which provide a full range of telecommunications services, primarily to large business users. In the United Kingdom, cable television companies have for several years offered telephone service over the cable television network to homes and businesses at lower prices than British Telecom, the dominant carrier. In the United States and Canada, there has been less interest in telephone service from cable television companies, partly because of the perception that the quality of service of cable television is less than that of the incumbent telephone companies. However, some North American cable television companies are successfully providing Internet access over their cable networks. (In response, some telephone companies are offering pay television service in competition with existing cable television companies, either through newly-constructed networks or by investing in direct-to-home satellite services.)

Multi-tenant commercial buildings are being built with Internet access in place, so that a tenant who needs high-speed Internet access only has to have the existing wiring activated rather than waiting for a connection to be designed and built. Increasingly, new buildings are designed with conduit in place that makes it fast and easy to install new telecommunications cabling, perhaps from a CLEC or an Internet service provider.

Deregulation of pay telephone service has led to higher prices for local calls from pay telephones, but also more sophisticated pay phones that in some cases offer the convenience of being able to pay for pay phone calls with a pre-paid card rather than with coins.

Phone companies—now sometimes referred to as incumbent local exchange carriers (ILECs)—are vulnerable to competition because traditionally they had the same prices for every company for the same type of service within a particular area. This meant that serving densely-populated office complexes was fairly profitable. It also meant that a new entrant, if it were legally permitted to, could make a profit at prices less than charged by the regular phone company, the incumbent local exchange carrier. Phone companies are now trying to de-average costs, so that they can set prices on a customer-by-customer basis, which would enable them to offer lower prices to large institutional users to keep the customer from switching to a CLEC or building their own systems.

Voice over Internet, Fax Traffic over the Internet

The Internet was designed to distribute data. It can also be used to transmit faxes, voice and other sounds, but not as effectively, because of the way information is transmitted over the Internet. Rather than setting up a physical circuit like a telephone call between two computers, an Internet connection breaks data (which could be sound or voice) into a series of small "packets" which are reassembled on the receiving end. This has its problems: sometimes packets don't successfully get transmitted from one end to another, so that the lost packet has to be re-transmitted or lost. In the case of voice over the Internet, these losses and delays lead to sound quality that is often noticeably worse than a regular telephone call, particularly when the user's access to the Internet is through a comparatively slow modem. (In the same way, a radio station's program broadcast over the Internet usually does not sound as good as the same program heard on a radio receiver.)

If both parties on a conversation have a fast connection to the Internet, as would be the case with a corporate or institutional workplace, the sound quality can be acceptable. Voice over the Internet requires compatible software at both ends of the connection, as well as a speaker and microphone. Videoconferencing over the Internet is also possible, but the image quality is less than broadcast television. Similarly, faxes can be transmitted over the Internet, so that a customer can avoid long-distance charges for a fax by sending the fax to a fax server in the recipient's city which delivers the fax as a local phone call.

Voice, video, fax and other multimedia technology will contribute to demands for more Internet bandwidth, which may lead some Internet service providers to try to charge for Internet access by the byte, rather than by the hour or by the month.

Military and Government Telecommunications

The U.S. military makes extensive use of telecommunications and computers to manage its operations. Its equipment has to be more resistant to damage than consumer-grade equipment, so that "mil-spec" (military specification) equipment is often more expensive than its civilian counterpart, and is designed to be secure from enemy monitoring. The military has its own communications satellites, and fixed and mobile telephone networks. Both the military and the National Aeronautics and Space Administration (NASA) have developed broadcast and telecommunications technologies that later became widely used by the population at large. For example, the walkie-talkie, the "radio on a backpack," was developed to fit a military need in the World War II.

And we all know that the Advanced Research Projects Agency of the U.S. Department of Defense funded the creation of the Internet by asking for a computer network that would survive a nuclear war. Other pioneering military telecommunications initiatives included Autovon, an electronic telephone network which incorporated different levels of priority for phone calls, using a fourth column of buttons on the telephone keypad, and scrambler (encrypted) telephones and fax machines.

Civilian government agencies have also driven developments in the telecommunications industry. Research laboratories operated by the U.S. Department of Energy, along with universities, were early Internet users. Government laboratories, including the Communications Research Centre in Canada, have carried out much important research with satellites in other areas of telecommunications.

Governments, particularly government labs conducting high energy and telecommunications research have done a lot of interesting things. The payoffs in a business context of setting up a call center rather than having individual offices answer in different cities, makes sense for government because keeping customers happy has some impact on profitability for the public sector. Where governments are delivering services in a social services context, however, there is less concern about keeping the clients happy and more on cost control. And in that environment, innovations in telecommunications and working with call centers can flounder, because the concern is not doing things better, but doing things more cheaply.

Marketing Issues

Bundling means that the telephone company is selling services that it provides directly, and is also acting as reseller of other firms' services. Typically these services are owned by the same corporate family—but not necessarily. The package of services may include local and long distance services and mobile services such as cellular and paging services, voice mail, Internet access and telecommunications equipment. Including different services on a single monthly invoice means that a user only has to write a single check and may be less likely to switch providers.

When cellular services were first introduced, two cellular companies were licensed in each market: one owned by one or more of the local telephone companies (the wireline carrier), and one not (the non-wireline) carrier. Regulators put policies in place that would keep telephone companies from discriminating against the non-wireline carrier, but recent policy changes make it easier for telephone companies to promote the services of the wireline cellular company and of the paging provider with which they are affiliated.

The trend of small Internet service providers being acquired by large communication carriers is likely to continue because smaller firms will have difficulty financing the equipment they need to accommodate growth and the marketing expenditures they need to complete directly with the larger firms and the Internet service units of the major local and long distance telecommunications carriers. This consolidation of the Internet service provider industry will result in more consistent and uniform service, but at the price of losing some services offered only by local carriers, such as shell access (timesharing on a Unix server that is convenient for users who only have text-based terminal or who are experienced programmers).

Among long-distance companies, the smaller carriers may be able to survive by promoting their unique features and catering to a niche market such as an ethnic group by selling services to these groups in their own languages, in their own media, and in their own neigh-

borhoods. Ethnic communities are an important market: Recent immigrants will phone back to their home countries a great deal, and may be more likely to use pre-paid long distance card or storefront locations where they make an international phone call and pay the attendant for the call in cash. Even less recent immigrants still maintain the home country ties and will represent a valuable market. Serving these communities may imply a greater need for face-to-face sales as distinct from calling into a call center.

Serving the Needs of Vulnerable Groups

It is expensive to provide service in rural and remote areas, although once service is established, phone companies can derive a great deal of income from these locations through long-distance revenue. Service in these communities can often only be delivered there with a subsidy of some kind, whether from the government or from a universal service fund. In situations where subsidies are not available, phone companies will provide new lines for service only if the user pays for some part of the cost of construction and installation, which is not affordable for many consumers.

Service in rural areas has traditionally been provided through party lines, on which modems and fax machines cannot usually be used because the phone line is shared with other users, and tying up a party line with a modem transmission might keep another user on the party line from making an emergency call. Individual lines, which allow modems and other customer-provided equipment to be attached are gradually replacing party lines, but some customers are reluctant to pay construction charges imposed by the telephone company for the upgrade in service.

Telemedicine—transmitting an X-ray from a nursing station or doctor's office in a small community to a radiologist in a large hospital, for example—can provide a better quality of care to rural residents and save the cost of an ambulance trip from the small community to the large hospital. Medical imaging such as X-rays requires a high-bandwidth connection, but other forms of telemedicine, such as continuing education courses for health professionals, can be delivered over a regular telephone line.

Cellular phones and two-way radios have been used in some rural communities as a substitute for basic telephone service. Users of mobile telephones may be able to use them to transit data or faxes but the mobile services can be expensive and slow. In developing countries, radio-based and satellite-based systems are used as basic telephone service in areas which the national telephone number does not reach.

In response to increases in the cost of basic local telephone service in the United States, subsidized "lifeline" service has been made available to some low-income consumers, including recipients of food stamps or welfare payments. Individuals who qualify receive a lower rate for local telephone service and may be exempt from their long distance company's minimum monthly charge. Despite the lifeline program, many needy individuals do not have telephone service because they cannot afford to pay installation charges or a previous long distance bill they may have incurred.

Telecommunications users with a disability have special needs. Hearing-aid users have reported that PCS wireless telephones interfere with the sound provided by their hearing aids, and that some telephones do not activate their hearing aids properly. Wheelchair users need pay phones located at a height they can reach. Deaf users need a telecommunications device for the deaf (TDD or TTY), a keyboard that uses regular phone lines to communicate with similar terminals, and a voice relay service to reach companies and individuals who do not have a TDD. Blind people and others with a visual disability need to be able to access telephone directory information when they are unable to use the directory itself. This issue has traditionally been dealt with by providing people who cannot see well with free access to the telephone company's directory assistance service. Blind and low-vision people can access the Internet with text-reader and speech-synthesizer software, but Web designers need to design text-reader-friendly pages that can be accessed by people with a vision disability.

Employment Trends among Carriers and Manufacturers

Telecommunications companies will be continue to hire many university graduates in engineering, computer science and commerce with good communication

and interpersonal skills. On the non-management side, there may be growth in call center personnel who sell telecommunications services, but traditional areas of employment like operator services and installation work will decline.

Corporate and government users of communications services will need expert staff to purchase and manage telecommunications products and services for their own needs. If a company thinks that telecommunications is an important key to its success, it will want to attract and retain superior telecommunications staff. If it considers telecommunications only as an expense to be kept to a minimum, it may have difficulty keeping a good telecommunications manager. An employer considering hiring a telecommunications manager will look for expertise that is normally only obtained either from working for a telecommunications carrier, or studying at a community college or university telecommunications program.

Companies will continue to provide some on the job training, but will prefer to hire already trained staff. Rather than invest in on-the-job training, a potential employer may ask an educational institution to offer a course to meet the employer's needs in the expectation that the employer would hire some graduates of the course.

New businesses will continue to hire well-trained staff away from industry leaders. Computer and telecommunications start-ups often find it valuable to hire employees who have gained experience with a well-established company in their field.

Continuing education will remain important for all telecommunications industry personnel, particularly those who are in danger of losing their jobs if they don't upgrade their skills. Many telecommunications carriers provide tuition subsidies to their employees, which makes taking evening or weekend courses to upgrade one's skills more attractive. A directory assistance operator who takes courses in sales and business administration may find a better-paying job within the telephone company and avoid the risk that the directory assistance function might be contracted out to an external supplier.

Another growth area in telecommunications employment is the call center, which receives inbound calls to place orders or request information, makes outbound calls to sell goods and services or conduct surveys. In locations where an inexpensive labor force, reliable telecommunications facilities and exemptions from some taxes are available, calls centers are likely to be established. The province of New Brunswick in Canada, with many bilingual workers, has had considerable success in attracting call centers. A single large call center can be managed more easily than several smaller ones; which is why smaller courier dispatch centers and airline reservations centers are being replaced with a few larger ones. Some reputable telemarketing firms belong to trade associations which have established voluntary codes of ethics, but other telemarketers are clearly dishonest.

Despite working conditions that cause heavy turnover of staff (stress and erratic working hours), call centers may provide a way of introducing new jobs into the economy of high-unemployment areas.

Labor Unions and Telecommunications Industry Employees

Collective bargaining in the telecommunications industry will continue to be a bitter process as hourly-paid staff continue to experience job losses, jobs are contracted out or eliminated by automation, and older manufacturing facilities in high-cost areas are replaced by newer facilities in lower-cost areas.

Employees at most recently-created telecommunications businesses do not have unions, particularly if the workplace is located in an area of high unemployment, where local legislation makes it difficult to organize a union. Longer-established workplaces are more likely to be unionized, but live under the threat that the employer will close the facility and transfer production to an outside contractor or a location where labor is less expensive and health and safety requirements are less strict.

High-technology companies and the research-based universities often attract other high-technology companies to the same area, and this phenomenon has led to the growth of high-technology employment in the Silicon Valley area of California and the Ottawa-Carleton and Waterloo areas in Canada.

Conclusion

Broadcast and telecommunications will continue to offer much opportunity, allowing business and institutions to make more effective use of human and capital resources. This progress will create both jobs and wealth. At the same time, other jobs will be lost. It is important for public officials to ensure that consumers and small business are protected in the midst of anticipated change.

—Nigel David Allen

Nigel David Allen is president of Allen Telecommunications Policy Consultants, a Toronto-based firm which specializes in Canadian telecommunications regulatory issues and Internet policy issues. He develops Web sites, which are designed to be accessible to people with disabilities and to be indexable by search engines. As well, he worked with Canadian University Press (CUP), an association of student newspapers, to represent CUP's concerns about telecommunications rates before the Canadian Radio-television and Telecommunications Commission.

CHAPTER 1 - PART II

INDUSTRY OVERVIEW

This chapter presents a comprehensive overview of the Broadcasting & Telecommunications industry. Major topics covered include an Industry Snapshot, Organization and Structure, Background and Development, Pioneers in the Industry, Current Conditions and Future Projections, Industry Leaders, Work Force, and North America and the World. A suggested list for further reading, including web sites to visit, completes the chapter. Additional company information is presented in Chapter 6 - Mergers & Acquisitions.

The broadcast and telecommunications industry is in the midst of a revolution. Technological innovation and governmental deregulation have laid the groundwork for a flurry of exciting changes. Closely linked with the computer industry, break-throughs in telecommunications technology are occurring at a pace comparable with that of computers. A number of innovations are related to the Internet, which impacts and is a product of both industries. Fiber optics allow telephone and cable companies to serve customers more efficiently and to offer an array of new services. Wireless communication is becoming commonplace in the U.S., and emerging as an alternative to wireline services in developing countries. Television stations will soon debut digital transmission, promising to provide viewers with sharper reception.

Perhaps even more profound is recent deregulation of telecommunications, opening up a world of new opportunities, literally. In early 1998, member countries of the World Trade Organization terminated their state-run telecommunications monopolies by opening their markets to foreign and domestic competition. Within the U.S., the Telecommunications Act of 1996 broke the barriers between local telephone, long-distance telephone, and cable markets by allowing those companies to operate in each other's arenas. Not only are these players capitalizing on their strengths to develop new technology, many also have plans to offer a combination of services to customers, providing them with "one-stop shopping" for all of their telecommunications needs.

Telecommunications is defined as the transmission of data over wire, fiber optics, optical wireless, or radio wave systems. Specifically, it is comprised of 12 SICs (standard industrial codes): **3651: Household Audio and Video Equipment**, electronic audio and video equipment for the home, such as radios, televisions, and VCRs; **3661: Telephone and Telegraph Apparatus**, including wireline telephones, fax machines, modems, and answering machines; **3663: Radio and Television Broadcasting and Communications Equipment**, like cable television equipment, cellular telephones and mobile communication equipment, pagers, radio and television transmitting antennas, and satellites; **3669: Communications Equipment, Not Elsewhere Classified**, such as burglar and fire alarms

and electronic intercommunications equipment; **3679: Electronic Components, Not Elsewhere Classified**, like satellite and other receiving antennas, amplifiers, and electronic switches; **4812: Radiotelephone Communications**, including paging and cellular telephone services; **4813: Telephone Communications, Except Radiotelephone**, including local and long-distance services; **4822: Telegraph and Other Message Communications**, such as cablegram, fax, telegram, and telegraph services; **4832: Radio Broadcasting Stations**; **4833: Television Broadcasting Stations**; **4841: Cable and Other Pay Television Services**, including direct broadcast satellite (DBS) services; and **4899: Communications Services, Not Elsewhere Classified**, such as satellite earth stations.

Organization and Structure

The Telecommunications Act of 1996 broke the boundaries between local telephone, long-distance telephone, and cable television companies by permitting them to conduct business in each other's markets. It also made provisions affecting broadcast media, relaxing the rules of television, radio, and cable system ownership, and deregulating cable service rates. In similar fashion, the 69 member countries of the World Trade Organization voted in February 1997 to open their telecommunications markets to both domestic and foreign competition, thereby ending their state-run monopolies. Effective February 1998, its passage opened a wealth of new markets for U.S. companies, increasing their incentive to expand business lines.

As a result of the opportunities created by these deregulatory policies, some telecommunication companies plan to expand into one or two new markets, while others aim to offer "bundled" services, packages of local, long-distance, and wireless telephone services, as well as Internet, paging, and cable television services.

To overcome the hurdles of efficiently entering a new industry, businesses may seek to acquire or merge with an existing company in the target market. An example is AT&T's $43 billion purchase of Tele-Communications, Inc. in June 1998, providing the long-distance telephone company direct access to residences through the cable operator's wiring.

The Federal Communications Commission (FCC) is responsible for regulating and implementing interstate and U.S.-based international telecommunications laws passed by Congress and the President. At the state level, public utility commissions (PUC) or public service commissions (PSC) regulate and implement state telecommunications legislation.

Radio

Radio stations operate by broadcasting sound waves from transmitting towers for reception by a consumer-owned device. Amplitude-modulated (AM) radio is the older type of radio broadcast, and has a lower frequency band than that of frequency-modulated (FM) signals. Stations receive revenue primarily from advertising. A station's sales staff is usually responsible for local and regional sales, while a national representative firm negotiates national advertising.

Television

Like radio, television signals are transmitted from station towers. Commercial television broadcasting in the U.S. operates on channels 2 through 69. Channels 2 through 13 are VHF (very high frequency), and usually enjoy better reception than UHF (ultra high frequency) channels, 14 through 69. However, the advent of cable has improved the reception of all channels, thereby increasing the advertising value of the UHF band.

The FCC requires that a television channel broadcast at least two hours per day and 28 hours per week to obtain and maintain a network license. In August 1998, seven networks existed: ABC, CBS, NBC, Fox, UPN, WB, and Pax TV. A commercial TV station may be affiliated with one of the networks, which provide affiliates with a certain amount of broadcasting per week in exchange for the right to sell the commercial spots airing during those programs. Stations unaffiliated with any network are known as independents.

In addition to network programming (or instead of such programming, in the case of independents), all stations receive independent programming, usually in the form of syndicated programs or feature films. Syndication companies, while retaining the rights, sell these programs either by licensing the program to a

station for a fee; waiving this fee while retaining the advertising time to sell to a third party; or a combination of the two, known as a cash-plus-barter deal.

Television stations derive revenues from advertising and network affiliate compensation. As with radio, a representative sales operation handles national advertising, while an in-house staff sells local and regional advertising.

Cable Television

Cable operators receive broadcast signals from antennas, microwave relay systems, fiber-optics cables, or satellite receivers. They distribute them to subscribers through a network of cable, either coaxial or fiber-optic.

Coaxial cable is the more popular of the two, but it is far from perfect: the number of signals transmitted is limited, and the signal quality degrades over distance, necessitating costly amplifiers. Fiber-optic cable quickly and efficiently transmits data in digital form with pulses of light. Despite coaxial's drawbacks, however, most cable operators are reluctant to incur the enormous expense of replacing their entire network with fiber optics. Instead, some are working toward a "fiber to the curb" system, wherein fiber optics are installed throughout the network to the point of residential curbs, from where copper wire or coaxial cable is extended into the home.

An alternative to fiber optics is digital compression, which works over coaxial cable by compressing analog signals into digital signals, thereby permitting more than one signal to be transmitted at a given time. This technology provides an alternative solution for operators seeking to delay conversion to fiber optics.

There are two types of cable networks: advertiser-based, which comprises "basic" cable programming, and pay-TV, premium channels that are subject to additional subscriber fees. Like the television industry, cable networks provide programming to affiliates, in this case, affiliated cable systems. The networks generate revenue through advertising and carriage fees from affiliates in the form of a monthly fee per subscriber or a percentage of gross receipts. As more networks compete for the limited space available on cable systems, more networks either waive this carriage fee or pay a fee themselves to the affiliate.

Subscriber fees generate 65-70% of cable operators' revenues. Other sources include installation charges, equipment rental fees, pay-per-view fees, commissions from home-shopping channels, and the sale of commercial time on advertiser-supported programs.

The Cable Communications Act of 1984 deregulated the industry, overturning regulation granted to the FCC in 1965. This Act abolished rate and rate increase limitations, and operators quickly responded by enacting significant rate hikes. Acting upon public protest to those hikes, Congress passed the Cable Television Consumer Protection and Competition Act of 1992, which included three main points: local municipalities can regulate subscription, installation, and equipment rental rates; cable operators may carry no more than 40% of its programming from channels in which it owns more than a 5% interest; and television broadcasters can insist that their signals be carried by cable operators in their market or, conversely, they can demand that their signals not be carried without prior consent.

Direct broadcast satellite (DBS) systems bypass cable operators by providing consumers, for a subscription, access to programs transmitted via satellite to a receiving dish, which is purchased, installed, and maintained by the subscriber. Its drawbacks include the inability to receive local broadcasts and the susceptibility to interference by weather conditions.

Wireline Telephone

Local exchange carriers (LEC) own and operate telephone lines linking their central office switches to consumers. Local access and transport areas (LATA) are 164 geographic areas in which local carriers can offer long-distance service. Calls that extend into another LATA are handled by any of the national long-distance companies, creating intense competition in that industry. Local companies charge long-distance providers a fee for access to the customer, typically 40% of each long-distance charge.

The regional holding companies (RHC), or "Baby Bells," may begin to offer in-region long-distance service only after opening their local markets to com-

petition. To facilitate the meeting of this requirement, RHCs implement a resale system similar to the long-distance arrangement, whereas they sell local capacity to competitors for resale to consumers. Upon regulatory approval by the FCC, these RHCs may then purchase out-of-region capacity from long-distance operators and resell it to customers.

Direct access into consumers' homes give local telephone and cable system operators a leading edge over long-distance carriers in the expansion to other business lines. Just as the cable industry is experimenting with offering telephone services over its cable network, local telephone systems are looking to provide cable services over existing phone lines. Other options for offering bundled service is to install a separate cable network, offer wireless cable (which would allow only basic cable), and offer DBS.

Internet access is available through local telephone lines via digital subscriber lines (DSL), which increases the bandwidth, or amount of data that can be transmitted, of conventional copper wiring.

Wireless Telephone

A wireless telephone transmits low energy radio waves to a local antenna, which connects the caller with the destination. The service area of cellular companies is divided into "cells," each with a base station. As a user crosses a cell boundary, the call is transferred to the corresponding cell's base station for transmission surveillance.

The two main divisions of the wireless industry are cellular wireless and broadband personal communications service (PCS). The first category is divided into cellular (or analog) and wireless (or digital). The older of the two is analog, which uses radio waves to transmit data. It is susceptible to electrical interference, requires repeaters and amplifiers every few thousand feet, and, as it permits only one call per channel, is relatively slow. Digital technology converts analog signals into binary data that are transmitted quickly and then reassembled at their destination, and it allows multiple-use of a channel.

PCS is a type of digital wireless technology that provides various services—including paging, phone, caller ID, e-mail, and fax—from a single handheld device. It operates at a higher frequency than digital wireless, and is therefore more efficient.

The U.S. has several competing standards of digital technology: time division multiple access (TDMA), code division multiple access (CDMA), frequency division multiple access (FDMA), and global system for mobile communication (GSM). These standards are incompatible, and when a user enters into a cell having a different standard, the signal is automatically converted into analog. This conversion, while imperceptible in most cases, renders PCS inoperable.

In 1981, the FCC granted two wireless licenses to each of the 305 metropolitan statistical areas (MSA), one to its local wireline carrier and another to the winner of a lottery. The 1996 Telecommunications Act expanded this limit to a maximum of nine wireless companies per MSA. This Act also requires wireless carriers to pinpoint a caller's location in the case of a 911 emergency, and to contribute to wireline service maintenance expenses, which previously had been the sole responsibility of local carriers.

Information Retrieval

Information retrieval services provide consumers online access to one or more databases. They do not typically produce the database; they merely link customers to them by connections through telephone or telecommunications networks. The customer pays for such access either on a contract or fee basis.

Background and Development

Long-distance communication has been possible for centuries, first through the media of smoke, drums, and reflected sunlight signals, then by more systematic means. In 1791, the semaphore signaling system, developed in France, utilized pairs of movable arms whose angular positions represented letters and numbers. A similar system, introduced in England in 1795, consisted of six shutters that were opened and closed in various combinations to convey characters.

The discovery and harnessing of electricity set forth an avalanche of new communications systems. The year 1837 is particularly significant in this respect. Charles Wheatstone received a patent for an electric telegraph,

and founded The Cooke and Wheatstone Electric Telegraph Company, the first electric telegraph system. Samuel F. B. Morse received a patent that year for the electromagnetic telegraph, and then demonstrated his telegraph code seven years later, on a transmission from Washington, DC to Baltimore, Maryland. The following year, in 1845, the New York-based General Oceanic Telegraph Company is founded to establish a telegraphic link from Europe and North America.

1851—Work commences on the first commercial submarine telegraph cable service, linking France with England; and Frederick Blakewell demonstrates a new means of communication at the World's Fair in London—the first facsimile (fax) transmission.

1856—Western Union Telegraph Company, America's top telegraph company, is founded. Five years later, it completes the first transcontinental telegraph line, linking San Francisco to the Midwest, and then to the East Coast. In 1866, it completes the first transatlantic cable installation, joining the United Kingdom and Canada.

1863—Fiovanni Caselli introduces the first commercial fax system.

1875—Elisha Gray and Alexander Graham Bell independently invent devices for the electric transmission of speech. Neither is yet capable of transmitting speech, though Gray's device transmits tones and Bell's transmits "speech-like" sounds. On March 7 of the following year, Bell patents the telephone, narrowly beating Gray's patent application intent for a similar device. Three days later, Bell makes the first successful transmission of speech with his famous statement, "Mr. Watson, come here. I want you."

1877—Bell and a group of investors form the Bell Telephone Company; installation of the telephone for the E. T. Holmes burglar alarm company marks the first commercial application of the telephone.

1880—The world's first pay phone, staffed by an attendant to collect money, is introduced in New York City.

1881—The first long-distance telephone line, joining Massachusetts and Rhode Island, comes into service, followed a few months later by the first international phone line, linking Michigan with Canada.

1885—The National Bell Telephone Corporation establishes American Telephone and Telegraph Company (AT&T) to operate as its long-distance subsidiary.

1886—Thomas Alva Edison invents the carbon transmitter, which remains the telephone industry standard until the 1970s.

1892—The General Electric Company (GE) is formed through the merger of Edison General Electric Company and Thomson-Houston Company.

1895—Guglielmo Marconi transmits the first wireless signal.

1896—The world's first dial telephone is installed.

1901—Marconi transmits the first transatlantic wireless signal, the same year that Reginald Fessenden successfully transmits voice signals.

1906—The first U.S. radio program, featuring music and readings, is broadcast by Fessenden, and is received by ship wireless operators several hundred miles away.

1917—The U.S. Navy assumes control over all domestic wireless stations and equipment, both commercial and amateur, after the U.S. declares war on Germany. Federal financing and an immediate crisis provide the groundwork for rapid technological evolution. After World War I, the Navy's request for permanent control of U.S. radio is refused by Congress, and it seeks instead a private monopoly. So the government requests GE to organize a U.S. radio operation, and in October 1919, GE forms Radio Corporation of America (RCA) from the Marconi Wireless Telegraph Company of America.

1920—Westinghouse receives the first commercial radio broadcasting license, for station KDKA. This Pittsburgh station airs on November 2 with a broadcast of the returns of the Harding-Cox presidential election.

1922—The concept of using long-distance telephone lines for radio broadcast is introduced by connecting New York and Chicago radio stations for coverage of

a football game. Columbia Pictures Inc. is formed as C.B.C. Film Sales Corporation, changing its name to Columbia Pictures Corp. in 1924 upon incorporation. The British Broadcasting Company, Ltd. is established as a private company; in 1927, it is liquidated and replaced by the government-controlled British Broadcasting Corporation (BBC).

1923—Warner Brothers Pictures, Inc. is formed; and AT&T transmits the world's first network radio broadcast over station WEAF.

1924—AT&T introduces a fax system to run over telephone lines, and RCA transmits the first radio photograph; Zenith Radio Corporation develops the first portable radio; and Metro Picture Corporation, Louis B. Mayer Pictures, and Goldwyn Picture Corporation merge to form Metro-Goldwyn-Mayer (MGM), Inc.

1926—J. Baird demonstrates television in the United Kingdom; the National Broadcasting Company (NBC) is formed by GE, Westinghouse, and RCA; and Warner Brothers' *Don Juan* is the first feature film to incorporate synchronized orchestral accompaniment.

1927—The first commercial transatlantic telephone service commences; Philo T. Farnsworth transmits the first television broadcast—a dollar sign; the Radio Act of 1927 establishes the Federal Radio Commission (FRC) to assign radio wavelengths to broadcasters; the success of *The Jazz Singer*, which features recorded dialogue and original songs in addition to the orchestral score, paves the way for the movie industry's conversion to sound; Columbia Phonograph Broadcasting System, which later becomes CBS, is formed; and NBC operates two networks: the Red and the Blue.

1929—Bell Telephone Laboratories demonstrates the first color television signal, simultaneously broadcasting three colors and Walt Disney Productions is incorporated.

1930—Three years after his application, Farnsworth receives a patent for an electronic television system.

1932—Technicolor Corporation introduces a three-color system that becomes the industry standard for the next twenty-five years.

1933—Edwin H. Armstrong develops the frequency modulation (FM) system, which eliminates the problem of interference plaguing AM transmissions; Karl Jansky detects radio signals originating in the Milky Way, pioneering the field of radio astronomy, and President Franklin D. Roosevelt inaugurates the Fireside Chats radio program.

1934—The Communications Act of **1934** replaces the FRC with the Federal Communications Commission (FCC) and adds the telephone to its jurisdiction.

1936—The BBC introduces the first black-and-white television service. It also adopts a 405-line television scanning standard; the world's first high-definition television service, it perseveres until 1962, when it is succeeded by a 625-line standard.

1938—The "War of the Worlds" radio broadcast creates widespread panic when much of America's listening public believes that the broadcast describes an actual alien invasion.

1939—The first American demonstration of television takes place at the New York World's Fair by NBC and RCA. Within months, station W9XZV, the first all-electronic television station, goes on the air.

1943—Upon U.S. Supreme Court decree, NBC sells its Blue network, which is renamed the American Broadcasting Company (ABC).

1946—The U.S. Army Signal Corps makes the first extraterrestrial communication by bouncing radar signals off of the moon and receiving them back on Earth, demonstrating the possibility of radio transmission through the Earth's atmosphere.

1947—Bell Labs invents the transistor, a device used to amplify and switch signals, thereby replacing the cumbersome vacuum tube technology.

1948—Cable television is introduced to give remote television viewers better reception. Cable system operators install antennas in communities with good reception and then transmit the signals to viewers for a fee.

1956—The *Trans-Atlantic Telephone Cable Number 1* (TAT1) satellite service establishes service between the U.K. and Canada, setting off a string of satellite launches. The Union of the Soviet Socialist Republics (U.S.S.R.) launches *SPUTNIK*, the first communications satellite, in 1957, followed the next year by the U.S. launch of the *Explorer*. The *Explorer 2*, launched in 1959, provides the first satellite television transmission. The following year, the U.S. launches the *Echo* satellite, the first self-powered communications satellite, and the *Courier 1*, the first solar-celled satellite.

1962—AT&T introduces the nation's first commercially available modem. Bell Labs launches *Telstar*, the first commercial orbiting international communications satellite. It relays television signals between Maine, England, and France. Reception is limited to only 15 minutes, the amount of time that the satellite can be reached by all three terrestrial points. This problem is solved in 1964 by the launch of a "stationary," or synchronous communications, satellite, which revolves at an equal rate as the Earth, thereby permitting continuous international transmission.

1963—The world's first car stereo is developed by Pioneer Electronic Corporation; and Communications Satellite Corporation (COMSAT) is incorporated as the first step in building a satellite network to provide communications services between spacecraft and ground control. The following year, the International Telecommunications Satellite Consortium (INTELSAT) is formed by the U.S., Canada, Japan, The Netherlands, Spain, the United Kingdom, and the Vatican to establish a global commercial satellite system.

1964—BBN Corporation develops the first telephone line-based computer modem; and Bell Labs introduces the first touch-tone telephone, succeeding the rotary dial.

1965—ABC is the first U.S. company to seek approval from the FCC to launch a domestic satellite system.

1966—FCC begins regulating cable television.

1967—The Corporation for Public Broadcasting (CPB) is established.

1969—The U.S. Department of Defense's Advanced Research Project Agency (ARPA) creates ARPANET, the forerunner of the Internet, to allow scientists to share information with geographically dispersed colleagues.

1970—CPB forms the Public Broadcasting Service (PBS) and National Public Radio (NPR) to produce and broadcast educational television and radio programming.

1971—Cigarette commercials are banned from U.S. television.

1972—Home Box Office (HBO) is founded by Time Inc. to offer the first pay-TV cable television services.

1974—MCI and the U.S. Department of Justice file antitrust suits against AT&T, claiming non-competitive practices in the telecommunications industry; and the Furukawa Electric Company, Ltd. introduces the world's first fiber-optic cable.

1981—In the largest merger between communication companies in U.S. history to date, Westinghouse Broadcasting expands its cable television operations by acquiring Teleprompter Corporation.

1982—AT&T settles its 1974 antitrust suit, agreeing to divest itself of its regional operating companies, which are to become unregulated, competing businesses. While AT&T retains its long-distance, international, equipment manufacturing, and retail sales businesses, its 22 Bell operating companies are consolidated and reorganized into seven regional holding companies (RHCs) that are spun off to shareholders. These "Baby Bells"—BellSouth, Bell Atlantic, NYNEX, American Information Technologies, Southwestern Bell, U S West, and Pacific Telesis—hold AT&T's former local telephone, directory publishing, and cellular telephone operations.

1983—Ameritech Mobile Communications, Inc. offers the first cellular telephone service in North America.

1985—For the first time since the early part of the century, independent studios release more films than do the major producers, in response to the growing demands of the cable and home-video markets.

1986—Fox Broadcasting Company, the first new U.S. network in 40 years, debuts.

1988—The installation of the first transatlantic fiber-optic cable is completed, and in the largest network launch in cable history, TNT is introduced in 17 million homes.

1995—United Paramount Network (UPN) and Warner Brothers Television Network (WB) premiere.

1996—The Telecommunications Act of 1996 permits local telephone, long-distance telephone, and cable television companies to enter into each other's markets.

1997—The 69 member countries of the World Trade Organization vote to open their markets to both domestic and foreign competition, thereby ending their state-run monopolies; and WorldCom Inc. purchases MCI Communications for $51 billion—the largest deal in the industry's history.

1998—In June, AT&T announces its $43 billion acquisition of Tele-Communications Inc., and in August, the Pax TV network debuts.

Pioneers and Newsmakers in the Industry

Alexander Graham Bell

Alexander Graham Bell's impact on the broadcast and telecommunications industry is profound and well known. On March 10, 1876, history was made when Bell's utterance, "Mr. Watson, come here. I want you," was the first telephonic voice transmission. Three days earlier, he had secured a patent for the telephone, and the following year, the Bell Telephone Company was founded, when Bell was only 30 years old.

The man behind the telephone, however, did not start out interested in telecommunications. Born in Edinburgh, Scotland, on March 3, 1847, Bell continued in his family's tradition as a teacher of elocution, applying his father's system of "Visible Speech" to teaching the deaf to speak. In 1864, he received a post at Elgin's Western House Academy, where he began the study of sound.

In 1871, the Bell family moved to Ontario, Canada, from where young Bell moved to Boston the following

year. That year, he opened a training school for teachers of the deaf, and in 1873 he became a professor at
Boston University.

Bell invented the photophone, which transmits sound
on rays of light, in 1880. Pursuing an interest in medical research, he invented the induction balance, which
located metal objects in a human body, in 1881. Five
years later, he introduced the graphophone, a sound recording device employing an engraving stylus and wax
cylinders and disks, which would lead to the development of the phonograph.

In 1898, Bell became president of the National Geographic Society, and developed its publication into a
worldwide educational journal. At this time, Bell's primary interest was aeronautics, and in 1907, he invented a large, one-passenger kite, followed by innovations for airplane wings and landing gear. Applying
aeronautical principles to marine propulsion, in 1917
he invented the hydrodome, a hydrofoil boat capable
of reaching speeds of 70 mph.

Bell died at his summer home in Nova Scotia, Canada,
on August 2, 1922. As testimony to his many diverse
achievements and interests, he held 30 patents for devices that would prove to shape the world to come.

Guglielmo Marconi

On December 12, 1901, Guglielmo Marconi, listening
intently from a small shelter in Newfoundland, re-
moves and passes a telephone receiver to his assistant,
calmly asking, "Do you hear anything, Mr. Kemp?"
After a moment, Kemp responds with a smile and a
nod. An unremarkable reaction to such a remarkable e-
vent—the signal heard was Morse code for the letter
"s," and, having been originated in England, marked
the first transatlantic radio communication.

Marconi was born on April 25, 1874, in Bologna,
Italy, to a successful businessman and Irish-born
mother. Fascinated by physics, he often closed himself
off in his room, reading and experimenting. At the age
of 20, he focused on the works of Heinrich Hertz, in-
ventor of a method of transmitting energy through
space by producing an electrical discharge that was detected a few feet away. Marconi was able to increase
the intensity of the spark and, using a vertical aerial,

the receiving distance, until that distance reached one
mile in 1895.

Seeing the potential for transmitting information via
electric waves, he offered his apparatus to the Italian
Ministry of Posts & Telegraphs. They rejected him,
but directed him to England's maritime industry. Continuing to achieve improvements in the receiving distance, he filed for his first patent in 1896, and formed
the Wireless Telegraph and Signal Co., Ltd. the following year.

Though the commercial market continued unimpres-
sed, the scientific community began to take notice. To
hold onto his lead in the face of emerging competition,
Marconi needed to develop an innovation. He did so
by solving the problem of interference—shared frequencies drowning out competing signals—by developing and patenting technology allowing transmitters
and receivers to be tuned to the same frequency, thereby isolated from foreign signals.

To the disbelief of scientists, Marconi's signals were
breaking the known laws of physics by following the
curvature of the Earth's surface instead of disappear-
ing into the atmosphere just over the horizon. To test
the limits of his results, Marconi proposed a transmission across the Atlantic. The success of this 1901 ex-
periment lead to new study into the laws of the propagation of radiowaves.

The year 1899 was significant to his fame in the U.S.
That autumn, he transmitted coverage of the America's
Cup yacht race, enabling the New York *Herald* to
scoop the competition. Marconi then incorporated the
Marconi Wireless Telegraph Company of America. By
1919, this company controlled nearly all of America's
radio communication. The U.S. government was un-
easy with allowing the subsidiary of a foreign company to control such a valuable national resource. Thus
in 1919, the subsidiary was bought by General Electric
and transformed into the Radio Corporation of America (RCA).

Before his death on July 30, 1937, Marconi developed
the shortwave communication system that is the basis
for modern radio communication, and proved that radio begins with the letter "s."

David Sarnoff

David Sarnoff was born on February 27, 1891, in Minsk, Russia. In 1906, with his family now settled in New York, he got a job with a telegraph company, followed by a position as a radio operator for the Marconi Wireless Telegraph Company of America. On April 14, 1912, he was the first to pick up the distress signal of the *Titanic*, and for 72 hours, he monitored the signals and broadcast details to an anxious public.

In 1916 he proposed the first commercially available radio receiver, the "radio music box." The proposal sat idle until July 2, 1921, when Sarnoff, now general manager of the Radio Corporation of America (RCA), won acceptance by broadcasting a boxing match between Jack Dempsey and Georges Carpentier, which was picked up by 300,000 amateur wireless operators. Three years later RCA had sold $80 million worth of radio receivers.

Sarnoff founded the National Broadcasting Company (NBC) in 1926. Two years later, he established a television station and, on April 20, 1939, broadcast the first coverage of a news event—the New York World's Fair. His speech that day was entitled the "Birth of an Industry" and foretold the emergence of television as an important entertainment medium.

During World War II, Sarnoff served as a communications consultant to General Dwight D. Eisenhower, achieved the rank of brigadier general, and received the Legion of Merit. President of RCA since 1930, he was named its chairman of the board in 1947. On December 12, 1971, one year after retiring from RCA, Sarnoff died in New York, leaving behind a legacy in both radio and television broadcasting.

Ted Turner

Robert Edward Turner III, the man credited with fueling the growth of the cable television industry, was born in Cincinnati, Ohio on November 19, 1938. Nine years later, his family moved to Atlanta, Georgia, where his father formed a billboard advertising company. Plagued by business problems, his father committed suicide in 1963. Young Ted Turner assumed control of the company, and turned it into a profitable business.

Turner ventured into broadcasting by purchasing a small UHF television station in Atlanta in 1970. In 1975, having renamed the station WTBS (or TBS, for Turner Broadcasting System), he introduced it to cable television by using a communications satellite to reach a nationwide audience. Expanding on the success of his cable venture, he formed the Cable News Network (CNN) in 1980. This 24-hour all-news channel boasted the ability to broadcast live coverage of any event worldwide, a fact that was clearly appreciated by an alert American public during the Persian Gulf War.
He continued to build on his empire by forming new cable channels: Turner Network Television (TNT), 1988; the Cartoon Network, 1992; CNN International, 1993; and Turner Classic Movies (TCM), 1994.

Aside from his cable ventures, Turner also has a hand in the movie industry. In 1986 he purchased the MGM/UA Entertainment Company, acquiring its movie library of more than 4,000 titles. A sore point with the film industry, he proceeded to "colorize" many black-and-white classics. The year 1993 marked his expansion into film production with his acquisition of two movie studios: Castle Rock Entertainment and New Line Cinema. Having gone into debt in order to acquire MGM, Turner sold 82% of Turner Broadcasting to Time-Warner Inc. in 1996, stepping down as chairman of Turner to become vice-chairman of Time-Warner.

Turner's notoriety outside the boardroom has also garnered him a fair share of media attention. Since his marriage to Jane Fonda in December 1991, this twice-divorced father of five has struck a balance between business and relaxation. An environmentalist, he is also an avid hunter and fisher, and owns ranches in Montana and New Mexico, as well as property in South Carolina, Florida, Nebraska, California, and Argentina. His interest in sports is apparent: he won the America's Cup in 1977, owns two professional sports teams (the Atlanta Braves and the Atlanta Hawks), and founded the Goodwill Games in 1986. He is also a record-breaking philanthropist. In 1997 he made the largest single charitable contribution in history by donating $1 billion, nearly one-third of his worth, to the United Nations Association.

With so many interests, both personal and professional, it may seem unlikely that Turner will be able to maintain such a breakneck pace. Yet this pace is in keeping with his philosophy, in which, as was quoted in *Ted Turner: It Ain't as Easy as It Looks,* "The worst sin, the ultimate sin for me, is to be bored."

Current Conditions, Future Projections

Wireline Telephone

Local and long-distance telephone companies comprise the U.S. wireline industry. The major local carriers in 1997 were the four remaining Bell regional holding companies (RHCs): Ameritech, Bell Atlantic, BellSouth, and U S West. These five companies account for 75% of the nation's total 170 million local access lines, while the remaining 25% are served by some 1,000 independent companies. The largest independent is GTE Corp., operating 20 million lines.

Two companies dominate the long-distance segment. AT&T has the largest market share, 54%, followed by MCI WorldCom which will possess 32% of the market share, should their proposed merger with Sprint pass regulatory scrunity. Long-distance companies traditionally have not operated access lines, since they did not directly extend into residences or businesses. However, with the local market now open to them, some are installing local lines of their own. Other long-distance companies opt to gain direct access not by establishing a new network of lines, but by acquiring or merging with companies that already maintain such a network, either local telephone or cable operators. Another option for long-distance carriers is to purchase network capacity wholesale from the local carrier and then resell it to the customer.

Wireless Communication

Wireless communication accounts for only five percent of the world's telephone traffic in 1997. Of the $27.5 billion wireless market, cellular services accounted for 95%, with personal communications systems (PCS) contributing the remainder. The 55.3 million U.S. customers generated revenues of $27.5 billion, and industry experts estimate its annual growth rate to be 20%.

Although wireline communication accounts for 95% of telephone traffic, the gap between wireless and wire-

line is shrinking. As digital technology improves the quality of wireless voice clarity, the main distinction between the two will be price. Wireless calls cost approximately twice as much as wireline, but these higher prices are expected to drop as the industry attracts more consumers. PCS offers numerous services, including telephone, fax, paging, and e-mail, through a single handset. Although a growth area, these services are currently available in limited areas and at a relatively high price.

The Personal Communications Industry Association reports that wireless communication in 1997 had penetrated 41% of U.S. households, or 50 million subscribers. A trend toward multiple wireless devices is apparent, as the average number in those households reached 1.7 devices.

Bundling

As telecommunications companies venture into new markets and begin offering multiple services, they are called upon by customers to "bundle" those services, that is, issue a single invoice reflecting all charges. On the surface, this may appear to be a fairly simple task; behind the scenes, however, it is proving to be a challenge. Organizational issues abound, as bundling requires not only integrated billing systems, but also cohesive customer service and sales departments, forcing the company to coordinate inter-departmental communication systems, training and educational programs, and computer technology.

In selecting a company from which to order bundled service, customers' first choices are long-distance telephone companies, followed by local carriers. As far as the top consumer choices of services to be bundled, companies are discovering that there is no clear-cut winning combination. According to *Telephony* magazine, a June 1998 survey revealed that long-distance and local telephone services were the most sought-after components of a bundle, with 94% and 92% of votes, respectively. After them, preferences declined, and the next three services vary by only a handful of percentage points: cellular/PCS, with 71%; Internet, with 67%, and cable television, with 65%. Paging services ranked last, with 41%. Of these six services, only cable decreased in popularity since November 1996, when it received a 75% vote.

Television

In 1997, the number of U.S. television households was 98 million, and the number of cable or satellite households was 68 million, or 70% of those households. The U.S. broadcast television audience of the Big Four networks—ABC, CBS, Fox, and NBC—continued its steady decline, reaching 22.6 million, or a 44.7% market share, in mid-1998. At the same time, cable's steady annual market share increase of seven percent brought it to 43.9%, or an audience of 22.2 million.

The decline in broadcast viewership is partially attributable to the increasing popularity of cable's ever-growing selection of channels. *Business Week* reports that an average of 75 channels were available to cable subscribers in 1997; by the year 2010, that number will have increased to more than 1,000, thanks to digital compression of signals. Broadcast television's audience is increasingly turning to other pastimes, such as viewing videos and utilizing the Internet. Americans spend an average of 9.5 hours per day in leisure pursuits, and with only so many daily hours available, an increase in one activity usually calls for a decrease in another.

Direct broadcast satellite (DBS) is a growing competitor of both broadcast and cable television. In 1994, DBS had 600,000 subscribers; by late 1997, its subscriber base jumped to 5.8 million. Its main attraction is signal clarity and a multitude of available channels, while its drawbacks include the inability to receive local programming and its susceptibility to signal interference.

DTV

November 1, 1998 was the voluntary deadline for the first U.S. commercial launch of digital television (DTV), at which time 24 stations in various locations agreed to begin digital transmission. By late July 1998, only three stations had expressed doubt about meeting the deadline, two due to tower problems and the third, a Detroit station, due to Canadian signal interference. The other stations were confident about their transmission capabilities, but were concerned about possible consumer reception problems.

The only formal reception test was performed in 1994, and it focused solely on outdoor antenna sets; indoor antennas have not been formally tested. Experts agree that not only may outdoor antennas be necessary for reception, it is likely that they must also conform to specific requirements: they must be tall, capable of rotation, and designed specifically for the set's geographic location. Precision is extremely important, because with digital signals there's no such thing as a bad picture—either reception is perfect or it is non-existent.

Industry Leaders

ABC Inc.

In order to reduce the possibility of an NBC monopoly of the broadcasting industry, the FCC directed the company in 1941 to divest itself of one of its two networks. Two years later, NBC sold its Blue network to Edward J. Noble, who renamed it the American Broadcasting Company (ABC).

In 1953, ABC merged with United Paramount Theatres, Paramount Picture's movie theater division, to form American Broadcast-Paramount Theatres. The merger gave ABC access to capital, and it loaned the Walt Disney Company $4.5 million for the construction of Disneyland in exchange for a Disney television show. In 1955 *The Mickey Mouse Club* debuted on ABC.

The network became a major player in sports broadcasting, and it introduced the "instant replay" during a 1961 Thanksgiving football game. In 1968, it was comprised of three divisions: entertainment, sports, and news. Barbara Walters, the first full-time female new anchor in history, was hired in 1975. In 1979, ABC divested itself of its record business, which it had begun in 1955, replacing it with a video division.

Capital Cities Communications, Inc. acquired ABC Companies for $3.5 billion in 1985, and the newly combined company was renamed Capital Cities/ABC Inc. Ten years later, on July 31, 1995, the company was acquired by Walt Disney Company for $19 billion, creating the largest media and entertainment enterprise in the world. These two companies consolidated their international television operations as Disney/ABC International Television in 1996, the same year that Capital Cities/ABC Inc. changed its name to ABC Inc.

Fiscal 1997 figures indicated a 6% increase both in overall profits and revenue, reaching $1.7 billion and $6.5 billion, respectively. Cable and international operations generated the most profit, $650 million, although that segment's revenue of $1.9 billion is significantly lower than the television network business, which had $3.1 billion in revenues while producing profits of $480 million. Of the two remaining operating divisions, network-owned television stations were the next highest earners, with $460 million profit on $975 million in revenues. Radio operations ranked last, earning $135 million on revenues of $450 million.

Alcatel

The Compagnie Générale d'Electricité (CGE) was formed by the 1898 merger of a light bulb manufacturer and two electricity-generating companies. By 1939, CGE had become a diversified manufacturer of electronics equipment, a primary supplier to utilities, and a major distributor of electricity. Recognized as a valuable national asset, it was consequently taken over by the French government for protection against the Nazi regime. At the end of the war, the government maintained control of the utilities operations while returning CGE's other businesses to the private sector.

Having diversified into the manufacture of home appliances, telephone equipment, and industrial electronics, CGE acquired Société Générale d'Enterprises, a large communications company, in 1966. Under national decree in 1969, CGE traded its data processing and appliance businesses to Thomson-Brandt in exchange for that company's Alsthom subsidiary, a manufacturer of power generating equipment. The following year, it acquired the communications company Alcatel and combined it with its CIT telecommunications subsidiary to form CIT Alcatel. In 1983, Thomson-Brandt's telecommunication operations were transferred to CGE, making it the world's fifth-largest telephone equipment manufacturer. CGE made one of France's largest initial public offerings when it was privatized in 1986. That year, it acquired a majority interest in the European telephone equipment operations of International Telephone and Telegraph Corp. (ITT), consolidating them with CIT Alcatel to form Alcatel

NV, the world's second-largest telecommunications company.

In 1989, its Alsthom subsidiary merged with the power system division of General Electric Company (GEC) to form GEC Alsthom NV, of which CGE held a majority interest. The following year, the Alcatel division usurped AT&T as the world's largest telecommunication equipment manufacturer.

On January 1, 1991, CGE changed its name to Alcatel Alsthom Companie Générale d'Electricité. Later that year, it acquired America's third-largest telephone equipment supplier, the telephone transmission equipment division of Rockwell International, for $625 million. It closed the year as the world's seventh-largest electric equipment manufacturer; three years later it became the world's largest manufacturer of telecommunications equipment, systems, and cables.

Net income for 1997 grew to FF4.7 billion on revenues that increased to FF185.9 billion. By operating unit, the Telecom segment accounted for the most sales, FF83 billion, followed by Cable & Components, GEC Alsthom, and finally Engineering & Systems, with FF28 billion.

In September 1998, the company shortened its name to Alcatel. It also acquired DSC Communications Corp. to form the Alcatel USA, Inc. subsidiary, thereby doubling its U.S. business and making the U.S. its largest telecommunications market, accounting for 21% of total sales.

AT&T

Bell Telephone Company was formed in 1877 by Alexander Graham Bell to develop the market potential of the newly invented telephone. In 1881, it acquired Western Electric Manufacturing Co., the main supplier of telegraph equipment for Western Union, as the exclusive manufacturer of its equipment. After several acquisitions of competing telephone companies, including Western Union's telephone network, the company, now called National Bell Telephone Company, created the American Telephone and Telegraph Company (AT&T) in 1885. This long-distance subsidiary was charged with creating a national telephone network.

National Bell's nearly monopolistic control of the U.S. telephone market came to an end in 1893 as Bell's telephone patent expired, allowing many small independent companies to arise and flourish. It immediately began a campaign of suing these independents; a decade later it changed its competitive tactic to lowering prices and acquiring competitors.

Company engineers continued to make technological advancements, including the development of the vacuum tube amplifier in 1912, and the completion of the first transcontinental telephone line, from New York City to San Francisco, in 1915. In 1922 it expanded into the commercial radio business by transmitting the world's first radio broadcast; this industry expansion was short-lived, however, as the company exited broadcasting three years later.

By 1939, AT&T controlled 83% of U.S. telephones and 98% of long-distance cables, with Western Electric manufacturing 90% of the nation's telephone equipment. In 1946, it re-entered the broadcasting business by transmitting the first long-distance television signal using coaxial cable. Two years later, Bell Telephone Laboratories, formed as the research and development division in 1925, invented the transmitter, thereby replacing vacuum tube technology and revolutionizing electronics. Telstar, the first orbiting international communications satellite, was launched by AT&T in 1962, the same year that the company formed Comsat to manage U.S. satellite communications.

The latter half of the century brought important changes to AT&T's role in the telecommunications industry. In 1956, the U.S. Attorney General settled its 1949 antitrust suit against the company, limiting AT&T to providing common carrier service and Western Electric to supplying equipment to its parent company. In 1968, the FCC ruled that competitors of AT&T were free to use that company's long-distance network, paving the way for increased competition in the industry.

Serious legal troubles began in 1974, when MCI and the U.S. Department of Justice filed antitrust suits against AT&T, charging monopoly of the telecommunications industry. The suits were settled in 1982, and in 1984, while retaining its long-distance, international, equipment manufacturing, and retail sales businesses, AT&T's 22 Bell operating companies were consolidated and reorganized into seven regional holding companies (RHCs) that were spun off to shareholders. These "Baby Bells"—BellSouth, Bell Atlantic, NYNEX, American Information Technologies, Southwestern Bell, U S West, and Pacific Telesis—held AT&T's former local telephone, directory publishing, and cellular telephone operations.

The Telecommunications Act of 1996 permitted local telephone, long-distance telephone, and cable television companies to enter into each other's markets. Taking advantage of the markets now open to it, AT&T (the company's official name since 1994) made an aggressive move into the cable industry with its 1998 acquisition of Tele-Communications Inc. for $48 billion. Other acquisitions occurred during the decade, namely that of NCR Corp., a computer manufacturer, in 1991; McCaw Cellular Communications Inc., a provider of cellular telephone service, in 1994; and Teleport Communications Group in July 1998.

Fiscal 1997 net income reached $4.6 billion on revenues of $51.3 billion. With 90 million customers on more than 250 countries, AT&T was the operator of the world's largest long-distance network and the largest digital wireless network in North America.

Bell Atlantic Corp.

Bell Atlantic was established in January 1984 as one of the seven regional holding companies (RHCs) formed by the break-up of AT&T. Its territory included Washington DC and six northeastern states, making it the nation's third-largest provider of local telephone services. At the end of its first year, Bell earned $973 million on revenues of $8 billion.

The new company quickly expanded domestically and internationally by establishing new services and subsidiaries, forging joint ventures, and acquiring a variety of companies. One such acquisition, that of Sorbus Inc., the second-largest computer services firm in the U.S., was completed in 1985. This company became the world's largest computer services enterprise five years later, and changed its name to Bell Atlantic Business Systems Services.

The Telecommunications Act of 1996 allowed RHCs to immediately begin offering cellular and out-of-area long-distance service. They may offer in-area long-distance services only after complying with a 14-point checklist proving that their local markets have been opened to competition. Bell was the first RHC to enter this long-distance business, gaining approval that same year to pursue customers in Florida, Illinois, North Carolina, South Carolina, and Texas.

On August 14, 1997, Bell merged with NYNEX Corp., another RHC. The newly-formed company retained the Bell Atlantic name and, with a network of 41 million access lines, was the nation's second-largest telecommunications company. Fiscal 1997 closed with net income of $2.4 billion on revenues of $30.2 billion. At that time, Bell Atlantic had three operating divisions: Telecom, wireline services reaching 22 million customers from Maine to Virginia; Global Wireless, operating in 25 states and Latin America, Europe, and the Pacific Rim; and International, communications operations in Europe and the Pacific Rim.

On July 28, 1998, Bell announced its proposed merger with GTE Corp. The new company has an international presence encompassing more than 30 countries. It is also the largest cellular service provider in the U.S., the nation's largest local exchange carrier (with 63 million access lines in 38 states), and the world's largest telephone directory publisher.

CBS, Inc.

United Independent Broadcasters, Inc. was founded in January 1927 as a radio broadcaster for the promotion of classical music. Several months later, the struggling company was purchased by Columbia Phonograph and renamed the Columbia Phonograph Broadcasting System. The following year, it was sold back, and its name shortened to Columbia Broadcasting System (CBS). In order to attract the large audience needed to draw increased advertising revenues, the young radio network offered free programming to its affiliates in exchange for airing the network's sponsored broadcasts; this arrangement was unique, as NBC charged its affiliates for programming. In 1933, the network formed the Columbia News Service as the first step in carving out a niche in the news and public affairs arena, leaving entertainment broadcasting to NBC. By 1936, CBS was the nation's largest radio network.

In 1938, it purchased the American Recording Corp. Ten years later, this company, now known as Colum-

bia Records, introduced the first long-playing (LP) record. Expansion into television broadcasting began in 1945, and it set about luring such stars as Jack Benny and George Burns from NBC. It competed with RCA to introduce a color television broadcasting system, and although the FCC selected CBS's version in 1950, it reversed this decision three years later. Throughout the 1960s, CBS acquired many diverse companies, including publications, musical instruments, and toys.

The debut of *60 Minutes* took place in 1968. In 1970, upon the FCC ruling that prohibited television networks from owning cable television companies, CBS begins divesting itself of cable holdings. Later in the decade, it expanded its divestiture program to include most of the eclectic mix of companies that it acquired over the previous decade, focusing now on television and radio broadcasting.

The 1980s marked its entry in the movie and video industries. In 1982, it formed the videocassette distributor CBS/Fox with Twentieth Century Fox-Video. The following year, it acquired MGM/UA Entertainment, and formed Tri-Star Pictures as a joint venture with Columbia Pictures and Home Box Office. In a criticized move, it sold the highly profitable CBS Records to Sony Corp. for $2 billion in 1988. On August 1, 1995, Westinghouse Electric Corporation acquired CBS for $5.4 billion. In 1996, CBS acquired Infinity Broadcasting, as well as the cable channels The Nashville Network and Country Music Television.

For fiscal 1997, overall profits jumped 41% to $648 million on a 29% increase in revenues of $5.4 billion. Radio was its leading segment, earning profits of $390 million on revenues of $1.5 billion, a 142% and 266% increase, respectively. Network-owned television stations was the next profitable group, earning $325 million on revenues of $836 million, while cable operations profits jumped 300% to $40 million on a 158% increase in revenues of $302 million. Its television network business, although the segment with the highest revenues, $2.8 billion, reported a $107 million loss.

Lucent Technologies, Inc.

In preparation for the enactment of The Telecommunications Act of 1996, AT&T incorporated Lucent Technologies on November 29, 1995 as an independent company for the design, development, and manufacture of communications systems, software, and products. On February 1, 1996, AT&T began spinning off its systems and technology units, including Bell Laboratories, into Lucent. Two months later, Lucent achieved the largest initial public offering in American history by raising over $3 billion on 112 million shares. At the close of its first fiscal year that September, Lucent's net income was $1 billion on sales of $23.2 billion.

Independence from AT&T served to increase business, as competitors of the long-distance giant now felt free to become Lucent's customers. Acquisitions, too, played a role in the young company's development. In October 1996, it acquired Agile Networks, Inc., a provider of switches, and it paid $1.8 billion in September 1997 to acquire Octel Communications Corp., a voice, fax, and electronic messaging equipment provider. The following December, it made two significant acquisitions: Livingston Enterprises, Inc., provider of remote-access network products, for $610 million, and Prominent Corp., LAN switching equipment provider, for $200 million. In May 1998, it purchased Yurie Systems, Inc., supplier of ATM access technology.

In October 1997, the company entered into a joint venture with Philips Electronics N.V. to form Philips Consumer Communications, L.P. as a provider of a range of personal communications products such as telephones and answering machines. Revenue for fiscal 1997 was $26.4 billion, and Lucent's worldwide employees numbered 130,000 by the end of that calendar year.

National Broadcasting Company, Inc.

In 1926, the Radio Corporation of America (RCA), General Electric Corp., and Westinghouse Electric Corp. jointly purchased radio station WEAF and organized the National Broadcasting Co. (NBC). Station WEAF became the anchor station of NBC's Red Network while station WJZ served that role for the Blue Network.

In 1932, NBC became a wholly-owned subsidiary of RCA, the same year that it established a television station. By 1938, the Red Network broadcast 75% of NBC's programming. Five years later, NBC sold the Blue Network, which became the American Broadcasting Company (ABC).

In the late 1940s, NBC's ratings suffered when CBS lured away top performers, such as Jack Benny, George Burns and Gracie Allen, and Red Skelton. In 1951, however, it reestablished its success by launching national television service and debuting the *Today* show. The mid-1950s saw innovation in television broadcasting as NBC pioneered the first nationwide color television transmission, followed by the first recorded show. As its television business boomed, its radio operations declined, and in 1988 it sold the last of its radio stations.

For fiscal 1997, although registering a slight decrease in overall revenue of $5.2 billion, NBC posted a 20% increase in profits, to $1 billion. Network-owned television stations was the most profitable segment, netting $550 million on revenues of $1 billion; its television network profited $475 million on revenues of $3.8 billion; and although its cable and international businesses posted profits of only $50 million and revenues of $350 million, these figures represent 400% and 24% increases, respectively.

Sony Corp.

Tokyo Tsushin Kogyo (TTK), or Tokyo Telecommunications Engineering Corp., was founded in 1946 by Ibuka Masaru and Morita Akio. Dedicated to the production of home appliances, TTK's first offering was a rice cooker. Its commercial failure prompted the company to focus instead on electronic goods, and it introduced an audio tape recorder designed after an American model in 1947. This product was so successful that the company was forced to relocate to a larger factory.

In 1954, after acquiring a patent license from Western Electric, TTK introduced a transistor radio that was called Sony, after the Latin word for sound, "sonus." Following overseas expansion, it changed the company's name in 1958 to Sony Kabushiki Kaisha Corp. in reflection of the popularity of its product.

Continuous innovation occurred regularly, with Sony's introduction of the first pocket-sized transistor radio in 1957, an eight-inch transistorized television in 1960, the Trinitron color television in 1968, an industrial-use color VCR in 1971, and the Betamax, its first VCR for the consumer market, in 1975. Matsushita Electric introduced a competing VCR format, the VHS (video home system) in 1977, and despite Sony's determination to produce only Betamax products, a severe decrease in market share forced it to relent in 1987.

In 1979, Sony introduced the Walkman, and the following year it collaborated with Philips to develop the compact disc. In 1988 it acquired CBS Records, the world's largest record company, for $2 billion. The next year, it purchased Columbia Pictures Entertainment Group from Coca-Cola for $3.4 billion, renaming it Sony Pictures. In addition to its electronics and entertainment product lines, Sony participated in joint ventures in such diverse markets as battery production, life insurance, sporting goods, and computers.

At fiscal 1998 year-end, Sony's net income was ¥222 billion on revenues of ¥6.76 trillion, a growth of 59% and 19%, respectively. The Columbia TriStar Motion Picture Group grossed $1.27 billion in the U.S. and $2.3 billion worldwide. Total employees numbered 173,000, of which 25,300 were located in the U.S.

Tele-Communications Inc.

Bob Magness entered the cable television business in the 1950s, and throughout the decade he founded several cable systems in Texas. In the 1960s, he partnered with other cable pioneers to offer service in Colorado, and by 1965 the partnership reached more than 12,000 customers through the operation of six systems. Three years later, Tele-Communications Inc. (TCI) was formed.

By 1970, as the country's largest cable system operator, TCI was forced to go public to pay off debt incurred from its swift expansion program. In 1982, it maintained its rank as the largest system, now serving two million customers. After the FCC deregulated cable in 1984, TCI expanded into larger metropolitan markets. Throughout the late 1980s, it made several significant acquisitions, including United Artists Entertainment, Heritage Communications Inc., Viacom Cable, and TeleCable Corp.

In 1996, TCI launched the @Home Internet service, and the following year it employed limited digital cable service, providing digital access to 20 million residences by year-end. At the end of 1997, TCI employed 32,000 worldwide and reached 14.4 million customers.

The Telecommunications Act of 1996 permitted local telephone, long-distance telephone, and cable television companies to enter each other's markets. Taking advantage of this deregulation, in June 1998, AT&T announced its $48 billion acquisition of TCI, and outlined plans to consolidate AT&T's consumer telecommunications services with TCI's businesses, forming AT&T Consumer Services.

By 1998, TCI was comprised of three operating units. TCI Group, the company's domestic cable and Internet services, had $6.4 billion in revenues in fiscal 1997. Liberty Media Group held its cable and satellite broadcasting investments, including holdings in Time Warner Inc., Discovery Communications, Inc., Encore Media Group, QVC Inc., USA Networks, Inc., Fox/Liberty Networks, and DMX Inc.; Liberty had 1997 revenues of $75 million. TCI Ventures Group, its non-cable, non-programming, and international assets, reported 1997 revenues of $969 million.

Walt Disney Co.

Walt Elias Disney, a twenty-one-year old aspiring cartoonist, left Chicago in 1923 and headed for Hollywood, California, where he and his brother Roy established the Disney Brothers Cartoon Studio. In 1928, it released the first film featuring Mickey Mouse, *Plane Crazy*, followed later in the year by *Steamboat Willie*, the industry's first film to incorporate fully synchronized sound. The company's name became Walt Disney Productions the following year, and over the next several years it began marketing Mickey Mouse merchandise, such as a comic strip, the *Mickey Mouse Book*, and watches. This character's popularity spawned the creation of other well-known characters, including Minnie Mouse, Donald Duck, and Goofy.

Among Disney's releases during the 1930s was the 1937 debut of the industry's first full-length feature film, *Snow White and the Seven Dwarfs*. Disney suspended commercial production for the duration of World War II in favor of the production of military films. Increased labor costs during the late 1940s prompted the company to expand into live-action productions.

The *Disneyland* television series premiered in 1954, and proved to be the longest-running prime-time series in history, broadcasting for 29 years; in 1997, it was reborn on ABC as the *Wonderful World of Disney*. In 1955, the Disneyland park opened in Anaheim, California, and the Mickey Mouse Club debuted on ABC. Walt Disney World opened in Orlando, Florida, in 1971, as did Tokyo Disneyland in 1983, the same year that the Disney Channel premiered on cable television. It founded Touchstone Pictures in 1984 for the production of more adult entertainment than standard Disney fare, releasing its first film, *Splash*.

Over the past four decades, Disney established several companies, including Walt Disney Music Co. in 1949; WED Enterprises (later known as Walt Disney Imagineering) in 1952; Buena Vista Distribution Co., Ltd., in 1953; Walt Disney Educational Materials Co., in 1969; and Hollywood Records, in 1989.

In 1986 the company's name was shortened to The Walt Disney Company, and the following year it opened the first Disney store. In 1988, Disney/MGM Studios completed its first filming project. In 1992 it opened EuroDisney in France. The following year, it acquired Miramax Films, and in 1996 it acquired Capital Cities/ABC Inc. Net income grew 23% in 1997 to $1.9 billion, while revenue jumped 20% to $22.5 billion.

Work Force

Increased competition created by the deregulation of the telecommunications industry in 1996 has prompted companies to reduce expenditures, including employment levels. As another cost-cutting measure, company-sponsored training programs are being slashed, holding employees responsible for their own training, when such training is required. Telecommunications training programs are available at community colleges and vocational schools, and are beginning to surface on the World Wide Web, such as those offered by Bellcore Learning Service and the International Engineering Consortium.

Line installers and cable splicers are employed by telephone and cable companies for the construction, maintenance, and repair of wire and cable networks. The need for swifter networks that can handle two-way communication has spurred the replacement of worn or obsolete copper cables with the more efficient fiber optic cable, the nature of which puts more training and

experience pressure on the technician. Despite that fact, most training is provided on-the-job, and a high school diploma is usually considered sufficient for entry-level placement. Employment in this occupation is expected to undergo average growth through the year 2006. In 1996, about 309,000 people were employed as line installers and cable splicers, and more than half worked for telephone and cable companies (the remainder worked for utility and construction companies). In 1996, their median weekly wage was $703.

Electronic equipment repair professions are expected to experience below-average growth through 2006. The need for repairs will diminish as product reliability increases, while equipment and replacement costs decrease. Formal training in electronics, offered as one-to-two year programs by vocational and technical institutes, is usually required for entry-level job applicants. Voluntary certification programs, which may allow a potential employee to negotiate higher wages, are offered through organizations such as the Society of Cable Telecommunications Engineers, the International Society of Certified Electronics Technicians, and the Electronics Technicians Association. The telecommunications industry employs three types of repair professionals: communications equipment mechanics, electronic home entertainment equipment repairers, and telephone installers and repairers.

In 1996, about 116,000 communications equipment mechanics worked for telephone, radio, and cable companies, earning a median weekly wage of $602. While some are employed by cable television and radio broadcasters to diagnose and repair transmission systems, most were employed by telephone companies for the installation and repair of switching and transmission systems. This field is expected to experience only a four-percent growth through 2006, since the telephone industry has embarked on a transformation from an electromechanical system to an entirely electronic system, thus requiring fewer mechanics.

Electronic home entertainment equipment repairers face a 19% drop in the job market through 2006. These professionals repair such equipment as audio systems, televisions, and home security systems. As these products become more reliable and cheaper to replace, fewer consumers will go to the effort and delay of getting them repaired. Still, employees who advance to higher-paying jobs will create an employment gap in this field.

Telephone installation and repair is expected to experience a sharp decline in job growth, down 74%, by 2006. These professionals work on the customer's property, installing, servicing, and repairing telephone systems, and earned a median weekly wage in 1996 of $717. In 1996, this occupation employed 37,000 people, but technological improvements in the diagnosis and repair of equipment, combined with the falling prices for equipment replacement, will require the need for fewer professionals in the future.

North America and the World

U.S. Trade

In 1997, U.S. exports of telecommunications equipment were valued at $19.76 billion while imports were $14.68 billion, creating a trade surplus of over $5 billion, its fifth consecutive year for a surplus. According to U.S. Office of Telecommunications reports, exports increased 25.6% over 1996, and imports increased 9.9% over the same period. Canada topped both lists, as the United States' largest import source as well as export destination.

The U.S. imported $2.84 billion worth of Canadian telecommunications equipment, a 19% increase over 1996. Canada was followed by Japan, with $2.36 billion; Mexico, with $2.08 billion; and China, with $1.59 billion. The leading export destinations were Canada, receiving $2.69 billion worth of U.S. equipment, a 14% increase over the previous year. Japan followed, receiving $2.07 billion; Mexico, with $1.44 billion; and Brazil, with $1.26 billion.

World Market

Members of the World Trade Organization voted in February 1997 to allow foreign companies into their previously state-owned telecommunications monopolies by offering local, long-distance, and international services. The 69 countries that adopted this agreement represented 90% of the world's telecommunications revenues. The agreement, which became effective on January 1, 1998, provides tremendous opportunity for U.S. companies, both for direct activity and for invest-

ments, particularly since the U.S. telecommunications industry had recently undergone deregulation itself, permitting various types of companies—local telephone, long-distance telephone, and cable—to expand their business lines.

The agreement is comprised of three general issues: market access—52 countries agreed to permit international access to facilities and services; telecommunications ownership—44 countries will allow foreign ownership of telecom business; and regulation—35 countries voted to allow international competition in areas that were formerly closed to them.

U.S. services and equipment manufacturers should realize the greatest revenue potential in areas where demand far exceeds supply. India, for example, has 1.5 telephone lines per 100 people, a "teledensity" far below the average of 60 lines per 100 people in more developed countries. Wireless local loop (WLL) technology has a particularly large market potential in such areas. WLL works by transmitting voice data over radio waves to stationary telephone receivers. Because these systems can become operational in less time and with less expense than establishing a traditional wireline service, some areas are bypassing wireline systems altogether in favor of WLL systems.

European Mobile Standards

In February 1998, the European Telecommunications Standards Institute (ETSI) met with cellular equipment manufacturers to decide upon a standard third-generation mobile communications system. The current system, GSM (global system for mobile communications), was introduced in the 1980s and accounted for 81% of worldwide cellular subscribers in 1997. New technologies are making GSM obsolete, but the decision of selecting a successor is difficult, as the new systems are incompatible, that is, their signals cannot be transmitted by other systems.

Code division multiple access (CDMA) is a system that sends encrypted transmissions based on the unique signal of the handset, thereby allowing more traffic on the same frequency band. The two rival successors are based on CDMA technology: wideband CDMA (W-CDMA) and time division CDMA (TD-CDMA).

ETSI members voted twice but arrived at no decision, and instead agreed to a compromise—the third-generation system will encompass both technologies. Since this requires that all handsets be compatible with both standards, as well as the current GSM standard, they are likely to be expensive. The ETSI will resume its quest for a seamless technology with a fourth-generation system.

Research and Technology

Broadcast and telecommunications technology is advancing at lightning speed, and will continue to do so in the foreseeable future. More people, in more locations, will have more contact with each other, and have more options available for doing so.

The foundation for much, if not most, of the progress is bandwidth, or the amount of data that a channel can carry. Fiber optic and digital compression technology have effectively increased bandwidth, yet elevated traffic levels fuel a constant demand for even more. Several technologies on the horizon could address this ever-present need. Dense wavelength division multiplexing (DWDM) creates additional room on a line by transmitting optical signals on multiple wavelengths over the same line. A driving force behind DWDM is erbium doped fiber amplifiers (EDFA). This technology will forge DWDM's expansion into new markets, such as local access. Another solution is multi-layer ultrafast routing and switching, which allows for increased data speeds over the Internet with fewer routers and switches by analyzing and prioritizing a signal's destination and content.

Local multipoint distribution service (LMDS) is wireless, two-way communications technology. Operating without a single wire or cable, LMDS is expected to become a viable method for long-distance carriers to directly access the consumer—especially when entering local, cable, and Internet markets. At the same time, it will provide cable and local telephone carriers two-way transmission capability without having to modify existing cables or install new lines. Although LMDS is wireless, it is not mobile, and can connect users only at fixed locations.

The Internet is central to the future of telecommunications. Internet traffic doubles every 3.5 months, and by the year 2004, 99% of the world's telecommunications traffic will be Internet-based, according to *Network World*. The relationship between computer and telecommunications technology is circular, such that computer technology fuels telecommunications technology, which attracts more consumers and data traffic, creating further demand for technological innovation. It is no surprise, therefore, that a number of emerging telecommunications technologies are Internet-related.

Web-enabled call centers will allow World Wide Web users to click on a company's Web page to speak directly with a representative from its call center for product inquiries, sales, and complaints. Another Web-based emerging technology is XML, or eXtensible Markup Language. XML will improve upon HTML by providing more accurate and intelligent search capabilities.

Several new technologies are related to the workplace. The Internet VPN (virtual private network) enables a business to create a private, work-related data communications network by using the backbone of the Internet. Desktop videoconferencing systems (DVCS) use a monitor-mounted camera and a microphone to simulate face-to-face communication. Although similar systems have been available for several years, only recently has this technology become available in user-friendly formats and at a cost-effective price, typically less than $1,000 per workstation.

Further Reading

The 1997 PCIA Wireless Market Monitor. September 1998. Available from http://www.pcia.com/wireres/monitor.htm.

1998-99 Occupational Outlook Handbook. Bureau of Labor Statistics: January 1998.

AT&T 1997 Annual Report. September 1998. Available from http://www.att.com/ar-1997.

Barnouw, Erik. *Tube of Plenty: The Evolution of American Television.* New York: Oxford University Press, 1975.

Bell Atlantic Corp. 1997 Annual Report. September 1998. Available from http://www.bellatlantic.com/ invest/financial/annual97/index.htm.

Bibb, Porter. *Ted Turner: It Ain't as Easy as It Looks.* Boulder, Colo.: Johnson Books, 1993. Reprint, *It Ain't as Easy as It Looks,* New York: Crown, 1993.

Dickson, Glen. "Counting Down to DTV." *Broadcasting & Cable.* 20 July 1998.

"Financial Highlights." *Sony Corp. 1998 Annual Report.* July 1998. Available from http://www.sony.co.jp/soj/CorporateInfo/AnnualReport98.

"Financial Highlights." *Walt Disney Co. 1997 Annual Report.* July 1998. Available from http://www.disney.com/investors/annual97/index.htm.

Flanagan, Patrick. "This Year's 10 Hottest Technologies in Telecommunications." *Telecommunications.* May 1998.

"Guglielmo Marconi." *Britannica CD 98 Multimedia Edition, 1994-1998.* Encyclopedia Britannica, Inc.

Hunt, Kimberly N., and AnnaMarie L. Sheldon, eds. *Notable Corporate Chronologies.* 2nd ed. Detroit: Gale Research, 1999.

"Internet Access: Cable TV Positioned to Dominate Internet-on-TV Service Market Long Term." *EDGE: On & about AT&T.* 10 August 1998.

Leinwoll, Stanley. *From Spark to Satellite: A History of Radio Communication.* Edited by Fred Shunaman. New York: Charles Scribner's Sons, 1979.

Lucent Fast Facts September 1998. Available from http://www.lucent.com.

McClellan, Steve. "Nets are Big 4's Weakest Link." *Broadcasting & Cable.* 2 March 1998.

Powell, Johanna. "Web TV's Remote Control." *The Financial Post.* 18 July 1998.

Rees, David W. E. *Satellite Communications: The First Quarter Century of Service.* New York: John Wiley & Sons, 1990.

Schmelling, Sarah. "Bundling Takes on New Meaning." *Telephony. 13 July 1998.*

Shankar, Bhawani. "3rd Generation, 4th Dimension." *Telecommunications.* June 1998.

Sidgmore, John. "The Golden Age of Telecommunications." *Network World.* 10 August 1998.

Slide, Anthony. *The American Film Industry: A Historical Dictionary.* Westport, Conn.: Greenwood Press, 1986.

Standard & Poor's Industry Surveys. New York: Standard & Poor's, 1998.

Stevens, Elizabeth Lesly, and Ronald Grover. "The Entertainment Glut." *Business Week.* 16 February 1998.

Tele-Communications Inc. 1997 Annual Report. September 1998. Available from http://www.tci.com/annualreports/reportsframe.html.

"Top 25 TV Groups." *Broadcasting & Cable.* 6 April 1998.

"Top 200 Operators." *CableVision.* 4 May 1998.

Tyco International Ltd. 1997 Annual Report. September 1998. Available from http://www.tycoint.com/finainfo/97ar.asp.

U.S. Telecommunications Equipment Trade in 1997. The Office of Telecommunications. September 1998. Available from http://infoserv2.ita.doc.gov/ot/home.nsf.

Workman, Will. "The Ratings Equinox." *CableVision.* 23 February 1998.

—Deborah J. Untener is freelance writer and editor based in Broomfield, Colorado.

INDUSTRY STATISTICS & PERFORMANCE INDICATORS

This chapter presents statistical information on the Broadcasting & Telecommunications industry. This view of the industry is through the lens of federal statistics. All the data shown are drawn from government sources, including the 100 percent surveys of the Economic Census and the partial surveys of manufacturing, services, and other industries conducted annually by the U.S. Department of Commerce.

Tables for the Manufacturing sector begin with a graphic charting the value of industry shipments. Thereafter, general statistics, indices of change, and selected ratios are presented.

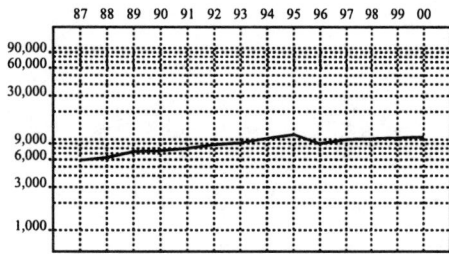

87 88 89 90 91 92 93 94 95 96 97 98 99 00

Revenues ($ millions)

SIC 3651 HOUSEHOLD AUDIO AND VIDEO EQUIPMENT: GENERAL STATISTICS

Year	Estab-lish-ments	Employment			Compensation		Production ($ mil.)		
		Total (000)	Production		Payroll ($ mil.)	Wages ($/hr)	Cost of Materials	Value of Shipments	Capital Inves.
			Workers (000)	Hours (mil.)					
1987	378	30.9	23.6	45.2	583.9	8.02	4,247.8	5,911.2	124.9
1988	368	31.6	24.2	47.1	659.2	8.54	4,709.3	6,326.8	127.7
1989	376	34.0	24.9	50.1	704.1	8.54	5,532.1	7,360.2	139.0
1990	395	33.7	22.5	45.2	704.3	9.00	5,592.9	7,520.5	255.7
1991	401	31.1	21.7	41.9	732.4	9.36	5,893.8	7,993.6	277.5
1992	427	31.2	22.3	44.3	736.6	9.52	6,444.2	8,769.3	252.9
1993	439	31.2	22.6	45.0	774.8	9.60	6,596.7	9,159.3	211.5
1994	454	30.5	23.3	46.6	798.2	9.64	7,617.4	10,285.6	225.8
1995	477	30.5	22.5	43.7	847.1	10.38	9,208.9	11,278.0	270.3
1996	434[1]	31.0	23.3	43.4	839.9	10.17	6,769.9	8,988.1	276.0
1997	438[1]	25.3[1]	18.5[1]	36.6[1]	719.1[1]	9.85[1]	7,516.3[1]	9,979.0[1]	263.7[1]
1998	441[1]	23.9[1]	17.4[1]	34.7[1]	706.3[1]	9.91[1]	7,684.4[1]	10,202.3[1]	269.9[1]
1999	444[1]	22.5[1]	16.4[1]	32.7[1]	693.5[1]	9.97[1]	7,852.5[1]	10,425.5[1]	276.0[1]
2000	448[1]	21.1[1]	15.3[1]	30.8[1]	680.8[1]	10.02[1]	8,020.7[1]	10,648.7[1]	282.2[1]

Source: 1987 and 1992 Economic Census; *Annual Survey of Manufactures,* 88-91, 93-96. Establishment counts for non-Census years are from *County Business Patterns.* Extracted from *Manufacturing USA,* 6th Edition, Gale, 1998. Note: 1. Projections by the editors.

SIC 3651 HOUSEHOLD AUDIO AND VIDEO EQUIPMENT: INDICES OF CHANGE

Year	Estab-lish-ments	Employment			Compensation		Production ($ mil.)		
		Total (000)	Production		Payroll ($ mil.)	Wages ($/hr)	Cost of Materials	Value of Shipments	Capital Inves.
			Workers (000)	Hours (mil.)					
1987	89	99	106	102	79	84	66	67	49
1988	86	101	109	106	89	90	73	72	50
1989	88	109	112	113	96	90	86	84	55
1990	93	108	101	102	96	95	87	86	101
1991	94	100	97	95	99	98	91	91	110
1992	100	100	100	100	100	100	100	100	100
1993	103	100	101	102	105	101	102	104	84
1994	106	98	104	105	108	101	118	117	89
1995	112	98	101	99	115	109	143	129	107
1996	102[1]	99	104	98	114	107	105	102	109
1997	103[1]	81[1]	83[1]	83[1]	98[1]	104[1]	117[1]	114[1]	104[1]
1998	103[1]	77[1]	78[1]	78[1]	96[1]	104[1]	119[1]	116[1]	107[1]
1999	104[1]	72[1]	73[1]	74[1]	94[1]	105[1]	122[1]	119[1]	109[1]
2000	105[1]	68[1]	69[1]	70[1]	92[1]	105[1]	124[1]	121[1]	112[1]

Source: Same as General Statistics. Values reflect change from the base year, 1992. Values above 100 mean greater than 1992, values below 100 mean less than 1992, and a value of 100 in the 1982-91 or 1993-2000 period means same as 1992. Note: 1. Projections by the editors.

SIC 3651 HOUSEHOLD AUDIO AND VIDEO EQUIPMENT: SELECTED RATIOS

For 1996	Average of All Manufacturing	Analyzed Industry	Index
Employees per Establishment	49	71	147
Payroll per Establishment	1,574,035	1,933,589	123
Payroll per Employee	32,350	27,094	84
Production Workers per Establishment	34	54	157
Wages per Establishment	890,687	1,016,125	114
Wages per Production Worker	26,064	18,943	73
Hours per Production Worker	2,055	1,863	91
Wages per Hour	12.68	10.17	80
Value Added per Establishment	4,932,584	4,670,864	95
Value Added per Employee	101,376	65,448	65
Value Added per Production Worker	144,340	87,077	60
Cost per Establishment	5,569,059	15,585,431	280
Cost per Employee	114,457	218,384	191
Cost per Production Worker	162,965	290,554	178
Shipments per Establishment	10,422,474	20,692,094	199
Shipments per Employee	214,207	289,939	135
Shipments per Production Worker	304,989	385,755	126
Investment per Establishment	394,953	635,398	161
Investment per Employee	8,117	8,903	110
Investment per Production Worker	11,557	11,845	102

Source: Same as General Statistics. The 'Average of All Manufacturing' column represents the average of all manufacturing industries reported for the most recent complete year available. The Index shows the relationship between the Average and the Analyzed Industry. For example, 100 means that they are equal; 500 that the Analyzed Industry is five times the average; 50 means that the Analyzed Industry is half the national average. The abbreviation 'na' is used to show that data are 'not available'.

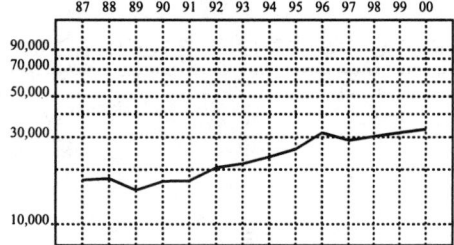

Revenues ($ millions)

SIC 3661 TELEPHONE AND TELEGRAPH APPARATUS: GENERAL STATISTICS

Year	Estab-lish-ments	Employment			Compensation		Production ($ mil.)		
		Total (000)	Production		Payroll ($ mil.)	Wages ($/hr)	Cost of Materials	Value of Shipments	Capital Inves.
			Workers (000)	Hours (mil.)					
1987	469	112.3	58.6	109.4	3,178.4	12.82	7,956.3	17,582.5	552.0
1988	448	111.7	57.2	107.5	3,458.4	13.37	8,756.7	17,901.1	625.1
1989	449	101.7	49.0	93.9	3,312.6	14.51	6,975.0	15,467.0	573.1
1990	433	94.0	46.5	91.8	3,421.2	14.48	7,606.3	17,297.3	592.7
1991	468	94.1	46.9	89.7	3,468.1	14.47	7,838.7	17,424.9	458.7
1992	544	91.0	44.7	87.4	3,741.4	14.95	8,153.5	20,498.3	614.8
1993	532	84.9	38.5	75.1	3,731.1	15.34	8,002.8	21,539.8	594.6
1994	528	86.1	41.2	78.6	3,576.6	15.46	9,638.6	23,471.8	781.3
1995	509	88.1	40.0	75.1	3,835.8	16.79	11,426.1	25,858.6	739.9
1996	543[1]	93.6	38.1	77.0	4,468.7	16.57	12,859.9	31,726.5	730.8
1997	554[1]	81.0[1]	33.7[1]	67.0[1]	4,178.5[1]	17.06[1]	11,688.9[1]	28,837.6[1]	746.8[1]
1998	566[1]	78.3[1]	31.5[1]	63.1[1]	4,280.2[1]	17.46[1]	12,275.6[1]	30,285.0[1]	768.7[1]
1999	577[1]	75.7[1]	29.2[1]	59.1[1]	4,381.8[1]	17.85[1]	12,862.3[1]	31,732.4[1]	790.6[1]
2000	588[1]	73.0[1]	27.0[1]	55.2[1]	4,483.5[1]	18.25[1]	13,449.0[1]	33,179.8[1]	812.6[1]

Source: 1987 and 1992 Economic Census; *Annual Survey of Manufactures*, 88-91, 93-96. Establishment counts for non-Census years are from *County Business Patterns*. Extracted from *Manufacturing USA*, 6th Edition, Gale, 1998. Note: 1. Projections by the editors.

SIC 3661 TELEPHONE AND TELEGRAPH APPARATUS: INDICES OF CHANGE

Year	Estab-lish-ments	Employment			Compensation		Production ($ mil.)		
		Total (000)	Production		Payroll ($ mil.)	Wages ($/hr)	Cost of Materials	Value of Shipments	Capital Inves.
			Workers (000)	Hours (mil.)					
1987	86	123	131	125	85	86	98	86	90
1988	82	123	128	123	92	89	107	87	102
1989	83	112	110	107	89	97	86	75	93
1990	80	103	104	105	91	97	93	84	96
1991	86	103	105	103	93	97	96	85	75
1992	100	100	100	100	100	100	100	100	100
1993	98	93	86	86	100	103	98	105	97
1994	97	95	92	90	96	103	118	115	127
1995	94	97	89	86	103	112	140	126	120
1996	100[1]	103	85	88	119	111	158	155	119
1997	102[1]	89[1]	75[1]	77[1]	112[1]	114[1]	143[1]	141[1]	121[1]
1998	104[1]	86[1]	70[1]	72[1]	114[1]	117[1]	151[1]	148[1]	125[1]
1999	106[1]	83[1]	65[1]	68[1]	117[1]	119[1]	158[1]	155[1]	129[1]
2000	108[1]	80[1]	60[1]	63[1]	120[1]	122[1]	165[1]	162[1]	132[1]

Source: Same as General Statistics. Values reflect change from the base year, 1992. Values above 100 mean greater than 1992, values below 100 mean less than 1992, and a value of 100 in the 1982-91 or 1993-2000 period means same as 1992. Note: 1. Projections by the editors.

SIC 3661 TELEPHONE AND TELEGRAPH APPARATUS: SELECTED RATIOS

For 1996	Average of All Manufacturing	Analyzed Industry	Index
Employees per Establishment	49	172	354
Payroll per Establishment	1,574,035	8,228,387	523
Payroll per Employee	32,350	47,743	148
Production Workers per Establishment	34	70	205
Wages per Establishment	890,687	2,349,345	264
Wages per Production Worker	26,064	33,488	128
Hours per Production Worker	2,055	2,021	98
Wages per Hour	12.68	16.57	131
Value Added per Establishment	4,932,584	34,653,429	703
Value Added per Employee	101,376	201,065	198
Value Added per Production Worker	144,340	493,955	342
Cost per Establishment	5,569,059	23,679,423	425
Cost per Employee	114,457	137,392	120
Cost per Production Worker	162,965	337,530	207
Shipments per Establishment	10,422,474	58,419,211	561
Shipments per Employee	214,207	338,958	158
Shipments per Production Worker	304,989	832,717	273
Investment per Establishment	394,953	1,345,650	341
Investment per Employee	8,117	7,808	96
Investment per Production Worker	11,557	19,181	166

Source: Same as General Statistics. The 'Average of All Manufacturing' column represents the average of all manufacturing industries reported for the most recent complete year available. The Index shows the relationship between the Average and the Analyzed Industry. For example, 100 means that they are equal; 500 that the Analyzed Industry is five times the average; 50 means that the Analyzed Industry is half the national average. The abbreviation 'na' is used to show that data are 'not available'.

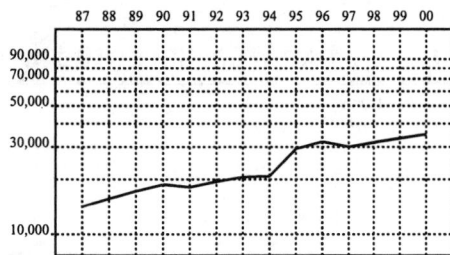

Revenues ($ millions)

SIC 3663 RADIO & TV COMMUNICATIONS EQUIPMENT: GENERAL STATISTICS

Year	Estab-lish-ments	Employment			Compensation		Production ($ mil.)		
		Total (000)	Production		Payroll ($ mil.)	Wages ($/hr)	Cost of Materials	Value of Shipments	Capital Inves.
			Workers (000)	Hours (mil.)					
1987	655	126.0	58.5	115.2	3,775.6	11.17	5,265.0	14,228.6	622.7
1988	605	129.4	58.5	115.3	4,080.4	11.55	6,052.1	15,693.1	704.5
1989	657	135.8	62.1	125.2	4,624.4	12.10	6,434.4	17,286.5	697.5
1990	657	129.2	62.4	125.0	4,651.9	11.90	7,840.0	18,759.3	751.8
1991	681	123.4	53.7	110.4		12.51	7,638.7	18,164.9	592.4
1992	948	124.4	58.3	115.1	4,700.8	13.81	7,311.6	19,472.3	700.3
1993	907	122.6	56.0	108.4	4,630.4	13.66	9,186.0	20,649.9	850.6
1994	920	120.2	54.5	111.1	4,836.7	13.91	8,892.4	20,877.2	799.5
1995	915	128.3	60.2	118.5	5,265.9	14.49	9,960.7	29,360.3	1,212.3
1996	1,003[1]	140.0	68.9	132.4	6,201.5	16.18	14,972.6	32,080.1	1,357.2
1997	1,049[1]	128.6[1]	61.1[1]	119.7[1]		15.84[1]	14,017.1[1]	30,032.8[1]	1,198.2[1]
1998	1,096[1]	128.8[1]	61.4[1]	120.1[1]		16.33[1]	14,812.7[1]	31,737.4[1]	1,265.3[1]
1999	1,142[1]	128.9[1]	61.7[1]	120.5[1]		16.82[1]	15,608.3[1]	33,442.1[1]	1,332.5[1]
2000	1,188[1]	129.0[1]	62.0[1]	120.8[1]		17.32[1]	16,403.9[1]	35,146.7[1]	1,399.6[1]

Source: 1987 and 1992 Economic Census; *Annual Survey of Manufactures*, 88-91, 93-96. Establishment counts for non-Census years are from *County Business Patterns*. Extracted from *Manufacturing USA*, 6th Edition, Gale, 1998. Note: 1. Projections by the editors.

SIC 3663 RADIO & TV COMMUNICATIONS EQUIPMENT: INDICES OF CHANGE

Year	Estab-lish-ments	Employment			Compensation		Production ($ mil.)		
		Total (000)	Production		Payroll ($ mil.)	Wages ($/hr)	Cost of Materials	Value of Shipments	Capital Inves.
			Workers (000)	Hours (mil.)					
1987	69	101	100	100	80	81	72	73	89
1988	64	104	100	100	87	84	83	81	101
1989	69	109	107	109	98	88	88	89	100
1990	69	104	107	109	99	86	107	96	107
1991	72	99	92	96		91	104	93	85
1992	100	100	100	100	100	100	100	100	100
1993	96	99	96	94	99	99	126	106	121
1994	97	97	93	97	103	101	122	107	114
1995	97	103	103	103	112	105	136	151	173
1996	106[1]	113	118	115	132	117	205	165	194
1997	111[1]	103[1]	105[1]	104[1]		115[1]	192[1]	154[1]	171[1]
1998	116[1]	104[1]	105[1]	104[1]		118[1]	203[1]	163[1]	181[1]
1999	120[1]	104[1]	106[1]	105[1]		122[1]	213[1]	172[1]	190[1]
2000	125[1]	104[1]	106[1]	105[1]		125[1]	224[1]	180[1]	200[1]

Source: Same as General Statistics. Values reflect change from the base year, 1992. Values above 100 mean greater than 1992, values below 100 mean less than 1992, and a value of 100 in the 1982-91 or 1993-2000 period means same as 1992. Note: 1. Projections by the editors.

SIC 3663 RADIO & TV COMMUNICATIONS EQUIPMENT: SELECTED RATIOS

For 1996	Average of All Manufacturing	Analyzed Industry	Index
Employees per Establishment	49	140	287
Payroll per Establishment	1,574,035	6,182,951	393
Payroll per Employee	32,350	44,296	137
Production Workers per Establishment	34	69	201
Wages per Establishment	890,687	2,135,825	240
Wages per Production Worker	26,064	31,092	119
Hours per Production Worker	2,055	1,922	93
Wages per Hour	12.68	16.18	128
Value Added per Establishment	4,932,584	17,167,797	348
Value Added per Employee	101,376	122,995	121
Value Added per Production Worker	144,340	249,917	173
Cost per Establishment	5,569,059	14,927,817	268
Cost per Employee	114,457	106,947	93
Cost per Production Worker	162,965	217,309	133
Shipments per Establishment	10,422,474	31,984,148	307
Shipments per Employee	214,207	229,144	107
Shipments per Production Worker	304,989	465,604	153
Investment per Establishment	394,953	1,353,141	343
Investment per Employee	8,117	9,694	119
Investment per Production Worker	11,557	19,698	170

Source: Same as General Statistics. The 'Average of All Manufacturing' column represents the average of all manufacturing industries reported for the most recent complete year available. The Index shows the relationship between the Average and the Analyzed Industry. For example, 100 means that they are equal; 500 that the Analyzed Industry is five times the average; 50 means that the Analyzed Industry is half the national average. The abbreviation 'na' is used to show that data are 'not available'.

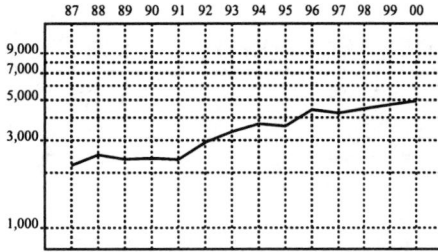

Revenues ($ millions)

SIC 3669 COMMUNICATIONS EQUIPMENT, NEC: GENERAL STATISTICS

Year	Estab-lish-ments	Employment			Compensation		Production ($ mil.)		
		Total (000)	Production		Payroll ($ mil.)	Wages ($/hr)	Cost of Materials	Value of Shipments	Capital Inves.
			Workers (000)	Hours (mil.)					
1987	382	21.9	11.1	21.5	533.0	9.21	870.9	2,189.6	64.1
1988	403	25.4	12.3	24.4	647.9	9.19	999.0	2,498.5	58.7
1989	411	24.4	10.6	20.7	566.2	9.41	942.4	2,364.1	69.6
1990	402	24.2	10.5	21.7	587.9	9.30	945.0	2,395.1	71.6
1991	421	20.0	8.8	18.2	530.7	9.72	926.2	2,356.1	63.3
1992	517	22.5	10.8	21.3	650.2	10.36	1,167.5	2,923.9	65.0
1993	523	23.7	11.7	22.6	698.4	10.19	1,412.5	3,349.7	83.8
1994	510	23.9	12.3	23.0	745.3	10.44	1,492.8	3,703.4	99.6
1995	488	23.7	12.0	23.1	762.0	10.34	1,425.4	3,595.6	124.9
1996	541[1]	24.8	12.4	24.3	851.4	10.73	1,758.7	4,425.3	179.5
1997	559[1]	23.9[1]	12.0[1]	23.2[1]	824.3[1]	10.90[1]	1,686.8[1]	4,244.4[1]	144.4[1]
1998	577[1]	24.0[1]	12.2[1]	23.4[1]	854.7[1]	11.08[1]	1,778.2[1]	4,474.3[1]	154.6[1]
1999	595[1]	24.0[1]	12.3[1]	23.6[1]	885.1[1]	11.26[1]	1,869.5[1]	4,704.2[1]	164.8[1]
2000	613[1]	24.1[1]	12.5[1]	23.8[1]	915.4[1]	11.44[1]	1,960.9[1]	4,934.1[1]	175.1[1]

Source: 1987 and 1992 Economic Census; *Annual Survey of Manufactures*, 88-91, 93-96. Establishment counts for non-Census years are from *County Business Patterns*. Extracted from *Manufacturing USA*, 6th Edition, Gale, 1998. Note: 1. Projections by the editors.

SIC 3669 COMMUNICATIONS EQUIPMENT, NEC: INDICES OF CHANGE

Year	Estab-lish-ments	Employment			Compensation		Production ($ mil.)		
		Total (000)	Production		Payroll ($ mil.)	Wages ($/hr)	Cost of Materials	Value of Shipments	Capital Inves.
			Workers (000)	Hours (mil.)					
1987	74	97	103	101	82	89	75	75	99
1988	78	113	114	115	100	89	86	85	90
1989	79	108	98	97	87	91	81	81	107
1990	78	108	97	102	90	90	81	82	110
1991	81	89	81	85	82	94	79	81	97
1992	100	100	100	100	100	100	100	100	100
1993	101	105	108	106	107	98	121	115	129
1994	99	106	114	108	115	101	128	127	153
1995	94	105	111	108	117	100	122	123	192
1996	105[1]	110	115	114	131	104	151	151	276
1997	108[1]	106[1]	111[1]	109[1]	127[1]	105[1]	144[1]	145[1]	222[1]
1998	112[1]	106[1]	113[1]	110[1]	131[1]	107[1]	152[1]	153[1]	238[1]
1999	115[1]	107[1]	114[1]	111[1]	136[1]	109[1]	160[1]	161[1]	254[1]
2000	119[1]	107[1]	115[1]	112[1]	141[1]	110[1]	168[1]	169[1]	269[1]

Source: Same as General Statistics. Values reflect change from the base year, 1992. Values above 100 mean greater than 1992, values below 100 mean less than 1992, and a value of 100 in the 1982-91 or 1993-2000 period means same as 1992. Note: 1. Projections by the editors.

SIC 3669 COMMUNICATIONS EQUIPMENT, NEC: SELECTED RATIOS

For 1996	Average of All Manufacturing	Analyzed Industry	Index
Employees per Establishment	49	46	94
Payroll per Establishment	1,574,035	1,573,429	100
Payroll per Employee	32,350	34,331	106
Production Workers per Establishment	34	23	67
Wages per Establishment	890,687	481,859	54
Wages per Production Worker	26,064	21,027	81
Hours per Production Worker	2,055	1,960	95
Wages per Hour	12.68	10.73	85
Value Added per Establishment	4,932,584	4,927,454	100
Value Added per Employee	101,376	107,512	106
Value Added per Production Worker	144,340	215,024	149
Cost per Establishment	5,569,059	3,250,164	58
Cost per Employee	114,457	70,915	62
Cost per Production Worker	162,965	141,831	87
Shipments per Establishment	10,422,474	8,178,172	78
Shipments per Employee	214,207	178,440	83
Shipments per Production Worker	304,989	356,879	117
Investment per Establishment	394,953	331,725	84
Investment per Employee	8,117	7,238	89
Investment per Production Worker	11,557	14,476	125

Source: Same as General Statistics. The 'Average of All Manufacturing' column represents the average of all manufacturing industries reported for the most recent complete year available. The Index shows the relationship between the Average and the Analyzed Industry. For example, 100 means that they are equal; 500 that the Analyzed Industry is five times the average; 50 means that the Analyzed Industry is half the national average. The abbreviation 'na' is used to show that data are 'not available'.

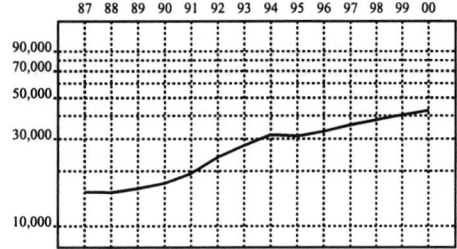

Revenues ($ millions)

SIC 3679 ELECTRONIC COMPONENTS, NEC: GENERAL STATISTICS

Year	Estab-lish-ments	Employment Total (000)	Production Workers (000)	Production Hours (mil.)	Compensation Payroll ($ mil.)	Compensation Wages ($/hr)	Production ($ mil.) Cost of Materials	Production ($ mil.) Value of Shipments	Production ($ mil.) Capital Inves.
1987	2,900	162.6	97.3	187.9	3,890.7	8.93	7,285.2	15,438.5	533.3
1988	2,846	157.6	99.9	196.9	3,738.1	8.98	7,139.2	15,299.4	448.1
1989	2,499	166.8	103.3	202.9	4,013.8	8.94	8,403.6	16,122.5	539.4
1990	2,441	161.0	101.1	203.2	4,107.6	9.06	8,380.0	17,222.4	485.0
1991	2,503	165.4	101.6	219.5	4,530.5	8.99	9,875.8	19,450.3	540.3
1992	3,295	182.4	109.2	238.8	5,180.5	9.32	11,842.4	23,869.9	740.8
1993	2,995	195.2	115.5	257.2	5,857.6	9.27	16,051.6	27,687.1	991.9
1994	3,024	196.5	118.9	261.6	5,964.7	9.33	16,872.5	31,609.5	990.6
1995	3,006	204.3	126.4	267.5	6,171.6	9.66	18,452.2	31,070.6	992.3
1996	3,068[1]	205.8	129.2	277.4	6,265.0	9.99	18,960.4	32,969.0	1,082.4
1997	3,115[1]	212.6[1]	130.3[1]	290.4[1]	6,773.9[1]	9.82[1]	20,581.6[1]	35,788.0[1]	1,158.7[1]
1998	3,161[1]	218.5[1]	133.9[1]	301.2[1]	7,101.6[1]	9.92[1]	21,911.0[1]	38,099.6[1]	1,235.8[1]
1999	3,208[1]	224.5[1]	137.6[1]	311.9[1]	7,429.2[1]	10.03[1]	23,240.4[1]	40,411.3[1]	1,313.0[1]
2000	3,255[1]	230.4[1]	141.2[1]	322.7[1]	7,756.8[1]	10.13[1]	24,569.9[1]	42,722.9[1]	1,390.1[1]

Source: 1987 and 1992 Economic Census; *Annual Survey of Manufactures*, 88-91, 93-96. Establishment counts for non-Census years are from *County Business Patterns*. Extracted from *Manufacturing USA*, 6th Edition, Gale, 1998. Note: 1. Projections by the editors.

SIC 3679 ELECTRONIC COMPONENTS, NEC: INDICES OF CHANGE

Year	Estab-lish-ments	Employment Total (000)	Production Workers (000)	Production Hours (mil.)	Compensation Payroll ($ mil.)	Compensation Wages ($/hr)	Production ($ mil.) Cost of Materials	Production ($ mil.) Value of Shipments	Production ($ mil.) Capital Inves.
1987	88	89	89	79	75	96	62	65	72
1988	86	86	91	82	72	96	60	64	60
1989	76	91	95	85	77	96	71	68	73
1990	74	88	93	85	79	97	71	72	65
1991	76	91	93	92	87	96	83	81	73
1992	100	100	100	100	100	100	100	100	100
1993	91	107	106	108	113	99	136	116	134
1994	92	108	109	110	115	100	142	132	134
1995	91	112	116	112	119	104	156	130	134
1996	93[1]	113	118	116	121	107	160	138	146
1997	95[1]	117[1]	119[1]	122[1]	131[1]	105[1]	174[1]	150[1]	156[1]
1998	96[1]	120[1]	123[1]	126[1]	137[1]	106[1]	185[1]	160[1]	167[1]
1999	97[1]	123[1]	126[1]	131[1]	143[1]	108[1]	196[1]	169[1]	177[1]
2000	99[1]	126[1]	129[1]	135[1]	150[1]	109[1]	207[1]	179[1]	188[1]

Source: Same as General Statistics. Values reflect change from the base year, 1992. Values above 100 mean greater than 1992, values below 100 mean less than 1992, and a value of 100 in the 1982-91 or 1993-2000 period means same as 1992. Note: 1. Projections by the editors.

SIC 3679 ELECTRONIC COMPONENTS, NEC: SELECTED RATIOS

For 1996	Average of All Manufacturing	Analyzed Industry	Index
Employees per Establishment	49	67	138
Payroll per Establishment	1,574,035	2,042,047	130
Payroll per Employee	32,350	30,442	94
Production Workers per Establishment	34	42	123
Wages per Establishment	890,687	903,268	101
Wages per Production Worker	26,064	21,449	82
Hours per Production Worker	2,055	2,147	104
Wages per Hour	12.68	9.99	79
Value Added per Establishment	4,932,584	4,604,074	93
Value Added per Employee	101,376	68,636	68
Value Added per Production Worker	144,340	109,329	76
Cost per Establishment	5,569,059	6,180,052	111
Cost per Employee	114,457	92,130	80
Cost per Production Worker	162,965	146,752	90
Shipments per Establishment	10,422,474	10,746,089	103
Shipments per Employee	214,207	160,199	75
Shipments per Production Worker	304,989	255,178	84
Investment per Establishment	394,953	352,803	89
Investment per Employee	8,117	5,259	65
Investment per Production Worker	11,557	8,378	72

Source: Same as General Statistics. The 'Average of All Manufacturing' column represents the average of all manufacturing industries reported for the most recent complete year available. The Index shows the relationship between the Average and the Analyzed Industry. For example, 100 means that they are equal; 500 that the Analyzed Industry is five times the average; 50 means that the Analyzed Industry is half the national average. The abbreviation 'na' is used to show that data are 'not available'.

SIC 4812 - RADIOTELEPHONE COMMUNICATIONS: GENERAL STATISTICS

Year	Estab- lish- ments	Employment		Payroll		Revenues	
		Total (number)	Per estab.	Total ($ mil.)	Per estab. ($)	Total ($ mil.)	Per estab. ($)
1987	-	-	-	-	-	-	-
1988	1,167	23,924	21	647.1	554,512	-	-
1989	1,370	28,043	20	818.3	597,318	-	-
1990	1,583	37,055	23	1,036.9	655,006	-	-
1991	2,464	49,035	20	1,561.4	633,699	-	-
1992	3,063	61,077	20	2,091.4	682,784	12,269.7	4,005,790
1993	3,462	70,425	20	2,481.6	716,806	-	-
1994	3,810	83,734	22	2,894.0	759,588	-	-
1995	4,359[1]	91,644[1]	21[1]	3,236.1[1]	742,412[1]	-	-
1996	4,844[1]	101,938[1]	21[1]	3,633.3[1]	750,007[1]	-	-
1997	5,330[1]	112,231[1]	21[1]	4,030.5[1]	756,218[1]	-	-
1998	5,815[1]	122,524[1]	21[1]	4,427.7[1]	761,392[1]	-	-

Source: Economic Census of the United States, 1987 and 1992. Establishment counts, employment, and payroll are from *County Business Patterns* for non-Census years. Data are the most recent available at this level of detail. Extracted from *Transportation and Public Utilities USA*, Gale, 1998. Note: 1. Projections made by the editor.

SIC 4812 - RADIOTELEPHONE COMMUNICATIONS: INDICES OF CHANGE

Year	Estab- lish- ments	Employment		Payroll		Revenues	
		Total (number)	Per estab.	Total ($ mil.)	Per estab. ($)	Total ($ mil.)	Per estab. ($)
1987	-	-	-	-	-	-	-
1988	38.1	39.2	102.8	30.9	81.2	-	-
1989	44.7	45.9	102.7	39.1	87.5	-	-
1990	51.7	60.7	117.4	49.6	95.9	-	-
1991	80.4	80.3	99.8	74.7	92.8	-	-
1992	100.0	100.0	100.0	100.0	100.0	100.0	100.0
1993	113.0	115.3	102.0	118.7	105.0	-	-
1994	124.4	137.1	110.2	138.4	111.2	-	-
1995	142.3[1]	150.0[1]	105.4[1]	154.7[1]	108.7[1]	-	-
1996	158.2[1]	166.9[1]	105.5[1]	173.7[1]	109.8[1]	-	-
1997	174.0[1]	183.8[1]	105.6[1]	192.7[1]	110.8[1]	-	-
1998	189.9[1]	200.6[1]	105.7[1]	211.7[1]	111.5[1]	-	-

Source: Same as General Statistics. The values shown reflect change from the base year, 1992. Values above 100 mean greater than 1992, values below 100 mean less than 1992, and a value of 100 in the 1987-91 or 1993-98 period means same as 1992. Data are the most recent available at this level of detail. Note: 1. Index based on a projected value.

SIC 4812 - RADIOTELEPHONE COMMUNICATIONS: SELECTED RATIOS

For 1992	Average of All Trans/Util.	Analyzed Industry	Index
Payroll as % of Revenues	20	17	83
Payroll per Establishment	595,843	682,784	115
Payroll per Employee	32,055	34,241	107
Employees per Establishment	19	20	105
Revenues per Establishment	3,112,739	4,005,790	129
Revenues per Employee	156,168	200,890	129

Source: Sources: Same as General Statistics. The 'Average of Sector' column represents the average of all transportation, communications, and utilities industries reported for the most recent complete year available. Establishment ratios only include those portions of the sector for which establishment data were reported. The Index shows the relationship between the Average and the Analyzed Industry. For example, 100 means that they are equal; 500 that the Analyzed Industry is five times the average; 50 means that the Analyzed Industry is half the national average. The abbreviation 'na' is used to show that data are 'not available'.

SIC 4813 - TELEPHONE COMMUNICATIONS, EXCEPT RADIO: GENERAL STATISTICS

Year	Estab-lish-ments	Employment		Payroll		Revenues	
		Total (number)	Per estab.	Total ($ mil.)	Per estab. ($)	Total ($ mil.)	Per estab. ($)
1987	-	-	-	-	-	-	-
1988	15,432	799,299	52	26,782.2	1,735,496	-	-
1989	16,566	818,703	49	26,741.3	1,614,228	-	-
1990	16,576	819,297	49	28,316.4	1,708,278	-	-
1991	21,198	908,596	43	34,110.0	1,609,114	-	-
1992	21,667	867,168	40	33,809.2	1,560,401	159,310.4	7,352,673
1993	21,520	842,038	39	33,972.5	1,578,650	-	-
1994	22,273	824,345	37	34,551.7	1,551,280	-	-
1995	24,393[1]	864,161[1]	35[1]	37,363.9[1]	1,531,718[1]	-	-
1996	25,662[1]	870,221[1]	34[1]	38,909.0[1]	1,516,206[1]	-	-
1997	26,931[1]	876,281[1]	33[1]	40,454.1[1]	1,502,156[1]	-	-
1998	28,199[1]	882,341[1]	31[1]	41,999.3[1]	1,489,370[1]	-	-

Source: Economic Census of the United States, 1987 and 1992. Establishment counts, employment, and payroll are from *County Business Patterns* for non-Census years. Data are the most recent available at this level of detail. Extracted from *Transportation and Public Utilities USA*, Gale, 1998. Note: 1. Projections made by the editor.

SIC 4813 - TELEPHONE COMMUNICATIONS, EXCEPT RADIO: INDICES OF CHANGE

Year	Estab-lish-ments	Employment		Payroll		Revenues	
		Total (number)	Per estab.	Total ($ mil.)	Per estab. ($)	Total ($ mil.)	Per estab. ($)
1987	-	-	-	-	-	-	-
1988	71.2	92.2	129.4	79.2	111.2	-	-
1989	76.5	94.4	123.5	79.1	103.4	-	-
1990	76.5	94.5	123.5	83.8	109.5	-	-
1991	97.8	104.8	107.1	100.9	103.1	-	-
1992	100.0	100.0	100.0	100.0	100.0	100.0	100.0
1993	99.3	97.1	97.8	100.5	101.2	-	-
1994	102.8	95.1	92.5	102.2	99.4	-	-
1995	112.6[1]	99.7[1]	88.5[1]	110.5[1]	98.2[1]	-	-
1996	118.4[1]	100.4[1]	84.7[1]	115.1[1]	97.2[1]	-	-
1997	124.3[1]	101.1[1]	81.3[1]	119.7[1]	96.3[1]	-	-
1998	130.1[1]	101.7[1]	78.2[1]	124.2[1]	95.4[1]	-	-

Source: Same as General Statistics. The values shown reflect change from the base year, 1992. Values above 100 mean greater than 1992, values below 100 mean less than 1992, and a value of 100 in the 1987-91 or 1993-98 period means same as 1992. Data are the most recent available at this level of detail. Note: 1. Index based on a projected value.

SIC 4813 - TELEPHONE COMMUNICATIONS, EXCEPT RADIO: SELECTED RATIOS

For 1992	Average of All Trans/Util.	Analyzed Industry	Index
Payroll as % of Revenues	20	21	104
Payroll per Establishment	595,843	1,560,401	262
Payroll per Employee	32,055	38,988	122
Employees per Establishment	19	40	211
Revenues per Establishment	3,112,739	7,352,673	236
Revenues per Employee	156,168	183,713	118

Source: Sources: Same as General Statistics. The 'Average of Sector' column represents the average of all transportation, communications, and utilities industries reported for the most recent complete year available. Establishment ratios only include those portions of the sector for which establishment data were reported. The Index shows the relationship between the Average and the Analyzed Industry. For example, 100 means that they are equal; 500 that the Analyzed Industry is five times the average; 50 means that the Analyzed Industry is half the national average. The abbreviation 'na' is used to show that data are 'not available'.

SIC 4820 - TELEGRAPH AND OTHER COMMUNICATIONS: GENERAL STATISTICS

Year	Estab-lish-ments	Employment		Payroll		Revenues	
		Total (number)	Per estab.	Total ($ mil.)	Per estab. ($)	Total ($ mil.)	Per estab. ($)
1987	883	10,512	12	323.7	366,636	-	-
1988	1,146	17,839	16	501.3	437,422	-	-
1989	967	15,741	16	503.1	520,300	-	-
1990	576	12,788	22	481.4	835,752	-	-
1991	512	8,948	17	291.2	568,785	-	-
1992	489	5,536	11	217.8	445,399	988.1	2,020,740
1993	526	5,742	11	226.3	430,319	-	-
1994	564	5,800	10	234.7	416,124	-	-
1995	342[1]	3,510[1]	10[1]	184.4[1]	539,207[1]	-	-
1996	261[1]	1,987[1]	8[1]	148.1[1]	568,403[1]	-	-
1997	179[1]	464[1]	3[1]	111.9[1]	624,087[1]	-	-
1998	98[1]	-	-	75.6[1]	772,216[1]	-	-

Source: Economic Census of the United States, 1987 and 1992. Establishment counts, employment, and payroll are from *County Business Patterns* for non-Census years. Data are the most recent available at this level of detail. Extracted from *Transportation and Public Utilities USA*, Gale, 1998. Note: 1. Projections made by the editor.

SIC 4820 - TELEGRAPH AND OTHER COMMUNICATIONS: INDICES OF CHANGE

Year	Estab-lish-ments	Employment		Payroll		Revenues	
		Total (number)	Per estab.	Total ($ mil.)	Per estab. ($)	Total ($ mil.)	Per estab. ($)
1987	180.6	189.9	105.2	148.6	82.3	-	-
1988	234.4	322.2	137.5	230.2	98.2	-	-
1989	197.8	284.3	143.8	231.0	116.8	-	-
1990	117.8	231.0	196.1	221.0	187.6	-	-
1991	104.7	161.6	154.4	133.7	127.7	-	-
1992	100.0	100.0	100.0	100.0	100.0	100.0	100.0
1993	107.6	103.7	96.4	103.9	96.6	-	-
1994	115.3	104.8	90.8	107.8	93.4	-	-
1995	69.9[1]	63.4[1]	90.7[1]	84.7[1]	121.1[1]	-	-
1996	53.3[1]	35.9[1]	67.4[1]	68.0[1]	127.6[1]	-	-
1997	36.7[1]	8.4[1]	22.9[1]	51.4[1]	140.1[1]	-	-
1998	20.0[1]	-	-	34.7[1]	173.4[1]	-	-

Source: Same as General Statistics. The values shown reflect change from the base year, 1992. Values above 100 mean greater than 1992, values below 100 mean less than 1992, and a value of 100 in the 1987-91 or 1993-98 period means same as 1992. Data are the most recent available at this level of detail. Note: 1. Index based on a projected value.

SIC 4820 - TELEGRAPH AND OTHER COMMUNICATIONS: SELECTED RATIOS

For 1992	Average of All Trans/Util.	Analyzed Industry	Index
Payroll as % of Revenues	20	22	108
Payroll per Establishment	595,843	445,399	75
Payroll per Employee	32,055	39,342	123
Employees per Establishment	19	11	60
Revenues per Establishment	3,112,739	2,020,740	65
Revenues per Employee	156,168	178,494	114

Source: Sources: Same as General Statistics. The 'Average of Sector' column represents the average of all transportation, communications, and utilities industries reported for the most recent complete year available. Establishment ratios only include those portions of the sector for which establishment data were reported. The Index shows the relationship between the Average and the Analyzed Industry. For example, 100 means that they are equal; 500 that the Analyzed Industry is five times the average; 50 means that the Analyzed Industry is half the national average. The abbreviation 'na' is used to show that data are 'not available'.

SIC 483-4 - BROADCASTING AND CABLE SERVICES, RADIO AND TV: GENERAL STATISTICS

Year	Estab-lish-ments	Employment		Payroll		Revenues	
		Total (number)	Per estab.	Total ($ mil.)	Per estab. ($)	Total ($ mil.)	Per estab. ($)
1987	-	-	-	-	-	-	-
1988	-	-	-	-	-	-	-
1989	-	-	-	-	-	-	-
1990	-	-	-	-	-	-	-
1991	-	-	-	-	-	-	-
1992	13,017	350,718	27	10,535.1	809,331	55,741.0	4,282,173
1993	-	-	-	-	-	-	-
1994	-	-	-	-	-	-	-
1995	-	-	-	-	-	-	-
1996	-	-	-	-	-	-	-
1997	-	-	-	-	-	-	-
1998	-	-	-	-	-	-	-

Source: Economic Census of the United States, 1987 and 1992. Establishment counts, employment, and payroll are from *County Business Patterns* for non-Census years. Data are the most recent available at this level of detail. Extracted from *Transportation and Public Utilities USA*, Gale, 1998. Note: 1. Projections made by the editor.

SIC 483-4 - BROADCASTING AND CABLE SERVICES, RADIO AND TV: INDICES OF CHANGE

Year	Estab-lish-ments	Employment		Payroll		Revenues	
		Total (number)	Per estab.	Total ($ mil.)	Per estab. ($)	Total ($ mil.)	Per estab. ($)
1987	-	-	-	-	-	-	-
1988	-	-	-	-	-	-	-
1989	-	-	-	-	-	-	-
1990	-	-	-	-	-	-	-
1991	-	-	-	-	-	-	-
1992	100.0	100.0	100.0	100.0	100.0	100.0	100.0
1993	-	-	-	-	-	-	-
1994	-	-	-	-	-	-	-
1995	-	-	-	-	-	-	-
1996	-	-	-	-	-	-	-
1997	-	-	-	-	-	-	-
1998	-	-	-	-	-	-	-

Source: Same as General Statistics. The values shown reflect change from the base year, 1992. Values above 100 mean greater than 1992, values below 100 mean less than 1992, and a value of 100 in the 1987-91 or 1993-98 period means same as 1992. Data are the most recent available at this level of detail. Note: 1. Index based on a projected value.

SIC 483-4 - BROADCASTING AND CABLE SERVICES, RADIO AND TV: SELECTED RATIOS

For 1992	Average of All Trans/Util.	Analyzed Industry	Index
Payroll as % of Revenues	20	19	92
Payroll per Establishment	595,843	809,331	136
Payroll per Employee	32,055	30,039	94
Employees per Establishment	19	27	142
Revenues per Establishment	3,112,739	4,282,173	138
Revenues per Employee	156,168	158,934	102

Source: Sources: Same as General Statistics. The 'Average of Sector' column represents the average of all transportation, communications, and utilities industries reported for the most recent complete year available. Establishment ratios only include those portions of the sector for which establishment data were reported. The Index shows the relationship between the Average and the Analyzed Industry. For example, 100 means that they are equal; 500 that the Analyzed Industry is five times the average; 50 means that the Analyzed Industry is half the national average. The abbreviation 'na' is used to show that data are 'not available'.

SIC 4830 - RADIO AND TV BROADCASTING: GENERAL STATISTICS

Year	Estab-lish-ments	Employment		Payroll		Revenues	
		Total (number)	Per estab.	Total ($ mil.)	Per estab. ($)	Total ($ mil.)	Per estab. ($)
1987	7,822	226,298	29	6,002.7	767,414	-	-
1988	7,590	225,912	30	6,179.0	814,097	-	-
1989	7,704	236,476	31	6,677.4	866,748	-	-
1990	7,899	236,313	30	7,029.6	889,940	-	-
1991	8,156	235,480	29	7,037.3	862,835	-	-
1992	8,549	221,755	26	6,976.4	816,046	28,228.9	3,302,017
1993	8,754	229,680	26	7,434.6	849,277	-	-
1994	8,760	244,271	28	7,888.6	900,523	-	-
1995	8,967[1]	237,362[1]	26[1]	7,995.2[1]	891,586[1]	-	-
1996	9,148[1]	238,548[1]	26[1]	8,237.8[1]	900,501[1]	-	-
1997	9,329[1]	239,735[1]	26[1]	8,480.5[1]	909,071[1]	-	-
1998	9,509[1]	240,921[1]	25[1]	8,723.1[1]	917,316[1]	-	-

Source: Economic Census of the United States, 1987 and 1992. Establishment counts, employment, and payroll are from *County Business Patterns* for non-Census years. Data are the most recent available at this level of detail. Extracted from *Transportation and Public Utilities USA*, Gale, 1998. Note: 1. Projections made by the editor.

SIC 4830 - RADIO AND TV BROADCASTING: INDICES OF CHANGE

Year	Estab-lish-ments	Employment		Payroll		Revenues	
		Total (number)	Per estab.	Total ($ mil.)	Per estab. ($)	Total ($ mil.)	Per estab. ($)
1987	91.5	102.0	111.5	86.0	94.0	-	-
1988	88.8	101.9	114.7	88.6	99.8	-	-
1989	90.1	106.6	118.3	95.7	106.2	-	-
1990	92.4	106.6	115.3	100.8	109.1	-	-
1991	95.4	106.2	111.3	100.9	105.7	-	-
1992	100.0	100.0	100.0	100.0	100.0	100.0	100.0
1993	102.4	103.6	101.1	106.6	104.1	-	-
1994	102.5	110.2	107.5	113.1	110.4	-	-
1995	104.9[1]	107.0[1]	102.0[1]	114.6[1]	109.3[1]	-	-
1996	107.0[1]	107.6[1]	100.5[1]	118.1[1]	110.3[1]	-	-
1997	109.1[1]	108.1[1]	99.1[1]	121.6[1]	111.4[1]	-	-
1998	111.2[1]	108.6[1]	97.7[1]	125.0[1]	112.4[1]	-	-

Source: Same as General Statistics. The values shown reflect change from the base year, 1992. Values above 100 mean greater than 1992, values below 100 mean less than 1992, and a value of 100 in the 1987-91 or 1993-98 period means same as 1992. Data are the most recent available at this level of detail. Note: 1. Index based on a projected value.

SIC 4830 - RADIO AND TV BROADCASTING: SELECTED RATIOS

For 1992	Average of All Trans/Util.	Analyzed Industry	Index
Payroll as % of Revenues	20	25	121
Payroll per Establishment	595,843	816,046	137
Payroll per Employee	32,055	31,460	98
Employees per Establishment	19	26	137
Revenues per Establishment	3,112,739	3,302,017	106
Revenues per Employee	156,168	127,298	82

Source: Sources: Same as General Statistics. The 'Average of Sector' column represents the average of all transportation, communications, and utilities industries reported for the most recent complete year available. Establishment ratios only include those portions of the sector for which establishment data were reported. The Index shows the relationship between the Average and the Analyzed Industry. For example, 100 means that they are equal; 500 that the Analyzed Industry is five times the average; 50 means that the Analyzed Industry is half the national average. The abbreviation 'na' is used to show that data are 'not available'.

SIC 4832 - RADIO BROADCASTING STATIONS: GENERAL STATISTICS

Year	Estab-lish-ments	Employment		Payroll		Revenues	
		Total (number)	Per estab.	Total ($ mil.)	Per estab. ($)	Total ($ mil.)	Per estab. ($)
1987	-	-	-	-	-	-	-
1988	-	-	-	-	-	-	-
1989	-	-	-	-	-	-	-
1990	-	-	-	-	-	-	-
1991	-	-	-	-	-	-	-
1992	6,956	112,385	16	2,547.7	366,259	6,865.4	986,978
1993	-	-	-	-	-	-	-
1994	-	-	-	-	-	-	-
1995	-	-	-	-	-	-	-
1996	-	-	-	-	-	-	-
1997	-	-	-	-	-	-	-
1998	-	-	-	-	-	-	-

Source: Economic Census of the United States, 1987 and 1992. Establishment counts, employment, and payroll are from *County Business Patterns* for non-Census years. Data are the most recent available at this level of detail. Extracted from *Transportation and Public Utilities USA*, Gale, 1998. Note: 1. Projections made by the editor.

SIC 4832 - RADIO BROADCASTING STATIONS: INDICES OF CHANGE

Year	Estab-lish-ments	Employment		Payroll		Revenues	
		Total (number)	Per estab.	Total ($ mil.)	Per estab. ($)	Total ($ mil.)	Per estab. ($)
1987	-	-	-	-	-	-	-
1988	-	-	-	-	-	-	-
1989	-	-	-	-	-	-	-
1990	-	-	-	-	-	-	-
1991	-	-	-	-	-	-	-
1992	100.0	100.0	100.0	100.0	100.0	100.0	100.0
1993	-	-	-	-	-	-	-
1994	-	-	-	-	-	-	-
1995	-	-	-	-	-	-	-
1996	-	-	-	-	-	-	-
1997	-	-	-	-	-	-	-
1998	-	-	-	-	-	-	-

Source: Same as General Statistics. The values shown reflect change from the base year, 1992. Values above 100 mean greater than 1992, values below 100 mean less than 1992, and a value of 100 in the 1987-91 or 1993-98 period means same as 1992. Data are the most recent available at this level of detail. Note: 1. Index based on a projected value.

SIC 4832 - RADIO BROADCASTING STATIONS: SELECTED RATIOS

For 1992	Average of All Trans/Util.	Analyzed Industry	Index
Payroll as % of Revenues	20	37	181
Payroll per Establishment	595,843	366,259	61
Payroll per Employee	32,055	22,669	71
Employees per Establishment	19	16	85
Revenues per Establishment	3,112,739	986,978	32
Revenues per Employee	156,168	61,088	39

Source: Sources: Same as General Statistics. The 'Average of Sector' column represents the average of all transportation, communications, and utilities industries reported for the most recent complete year available. Establishment ratios only include those portions of the sector for which establishment data were reported. The Index shows the relationship between the Average and the Analyzed Industry. For example, 100 means that they are equal; 500 that the Analyzed Industry is five times the average; 50 means that the Analyzed Industry is half the national average. The abbreviation 'na' is used to show that data are 'not available'.

SIC 4833 - TELEVISION BROADCASTING STATIONS: GENERAL STATISTICS

Year	Estab-lish-ments	Employment		Payroll		Revenues	
		Total (number)	Per estab.	Total ($ mil.)	Per estab. ($)	Total ($ mil.)	Per estab. ($)
1987	-	-	-	-	-	-	-
1988	-	-	-	-	-	-	-
1989	-	-	-	-	-	-	-
1990	-	-	-	-	-	-	-
1991	-	-	-	-	-	-	-
1992	1,593	109,370	69	4,428.7	2,780,085	21,363.5	13,410,874
1993	-	-	-	-	-	-	-
1994	-	-	-	-	-	-	-
1995	-	-	-	-	-	-	-
1996	-	-	-	-	-	-	-
1997	-	-	-	-	-	-	-
1998	-	-	-	-	-	-	-

Source: Economic Census of the United States, 1987 and 1992. Establishment counts, employment, and payroll are from *County Business Patterns* for non-Census years. Data are the most recent available at this level of detail. Extracted from *Transportation and Public Utilities USA*, Gale, 1998. Note: 1. Projections made by the editor.

SIC 4833 - TELEVISION BROADCASTING STATIONS: INDICES OF CHANGE

Year	Estab-lish-ments	Employment		Payroll		Revenues	
		Total (number)	Per estab.	Total ($ mil.)	Per estab. ($)	Total ($ mil.)	Per estab. ($)
1987	-	-	-	-	-	-	-
1988	-	-	-	-	-	-	-
1989	-	-	-	-	-	-	-
1990	-	-	-	-	-	-	-
1991	-	-	-	-	-	-	-
1992	100.0	100.0	100.0	100.0	100.0	100.0	100.0
1993	-	-	-	-	-	-	-
1994	-	-	-	-	-	-	-
1995	-	-	-	-	-	-	-
1996	-	-	-	-	-	-	-
1997	-	-	-	-	-	-	-
1998	-	-	-	-	-	-	-

Source: Same as General Statistics. The values shown reflect change from the base year, 1992. Values above 100 mean greater than 1992, values below 100 mean less than 1992, and a value of 100 in the 1987-91 or 1993-98 period means same as 1992. Data are the most recent available at this level of detail. Note: 1. Index based on a projected value.

SIC 4833 - TELEVISION BROADCASTING STATIONS: SELECTED RATIOS

For 1992	Average of All Trans/Util.	Analyzed Industry	Index
Payroll as % of Revenues	20	21	101
Payroll per Establishment	595,843	2,780,085	467
Payroll per Employee	32,055	40,493	126
Employees per Establishment	19	69	361
Revenues per Establishment	3,112,739	13,410,874	431
Revenues per Employee	156,168	195,333	125

Source: Sources: Same as General Statistics. The 'Average of Sector' column represents the average of all transportation, communications, and utilities industries reported for the most recent complete year available. Establishment ratios only include those portions of the sector for which establishment data were reported. The Index shows the relationship between the Average and the Analyzed Industry. For example, 100 means that they are equal; 500 that the Analyzed Industry is five times the average; 50 means that the Analyzed Industry is half the national average. The abbreviation 'na' is used to show that data are 'not available'.

SIC 4840 - CABLE AND OTHER PAY TV: GENERAL STATISTICS

Year	Estab-lish-ments	Employment		Payroll		Revenues	
		Total (number)	Per estab.	Total ($ mil.)	Per estab. ($)	Total ($ mil.)	Per estab. ($)
1987	-	-	-	-	-	-	-
1988	3,595	104,614	29	2,282.1	634,797	-	-
1989	3,480	111,967	32	2,657.2	763,558	-	-
1990	3,478	120,212	35	3,125.3	898,593	-	-
1991	4,157	123,770	30	3,360.2	808,332	-	-
1992	4,468	128,963	29	3,558.7	796,484	27,512.1	6,157,587
1993	4,475	135,503	30	3,720.7	831,448	-	-
1994	4,545	134,299	30	3,949.7	869,029	-	-
1995	4,861[1]	143,458[1]	30[1]	4,316.8[1]	888,015[1]	-	-
1996	5,069[1]	148,632[1]	29[1]	4,586.9[1]	904,827[1]	-	-
1997	5,278[1]	153,806[1]	29[1]	4,857.0[1]	920,312[1]	-	-
1998	5,486[1]	158,981[1]	29[1]	5,127.1[1]	934,621[1]	-	-

Source: Economic Census of the United States, 1987 and 1992. Establishment counts, employment, and payroll are from *County Business Patterns* for non-Census years. Data are the most recent available at this level of detail. Extracted from *Transportation and Public Utilities USA*, Gale, 1998. Note: 1. Projections made by the editor.

SIC 4840 - CABLE AND OTHER PAY TV: INDICES OF CHANGE

Year	Estab-lish-ments	Employment		Payroll		Revenues	
		Total (number)	Per estab.	Total ($ mil.)	Per estab. ($)	Total ($ mil.)	Per estab. ($)
1987	-	-	-	-	-	-	-
1988	80.5	81.1	100.8	64.1	79.7	-	-
1989	77.9	86.8	111.5	74.7	95.9	-	-
1990	77.8	93.2	119.7	87.8	112.8	-	-
1991	93.0	96.0	103.2	94.4	101.5	-	-
1992	100.0	100.0	100.0	100.0	100.0	100.0	100.0
1993	100.2	105.1	104.9	104.6	104.4	-	-
1994	101.7	104.1	102.4	111.0	109.1	-	-
1995	108.8[1]	111.2[1]	102.2[1]	121.3[1]	111.5[1]	-	-
1996	113.5[1]	115.3[1]	101.6[1]	128.9[1]	113.6[1]	-	-
1997	118.1[1]	119.3[1]	101.0[1]	136.5[1]	115.5[1]	-	-
1998	122.8[1]	123.3[1]	100.4[1]	144.1[1]	117.3[1]	-	-

Source: Same as General Statistics. The values shown reflect change from the base year, 1992. Values above 100 mean greater than 1992, values below 100 mean less than 1992, and a value of 100 in the 1987-91 or 1993-98 period means same as 1992. Data are the most recent available at this level of detail. Note: 1. Index based on a projected value.

SIC 4840 - CABLE AND OTHER PAY TV: SELECTED RATIOS

For 1992	Average of All Trans/Util.	Analyzed Industry	Index
Payroll as % of Revenues	20	13	63
Payroll per Establishment	595,843	796,484	134
Payroll per Employee	32,055	27,595	86
Employees per Establishment	19	29	152
Revenues per Establishment	3,112,739	6,157,587	198
Revenues per Employee	156,168	213,333	137

Source: Sources: Same as General Statistics. The 'Average of Sector' column represents the average of all transportation, communications, and utilities industries reported for the most recent complete year available. Establishment ratios only include those portions of the sector for which establishment data were reported. The Index shows the relationship between the Average and the Analyzed Industry. For example, 100 means that they are equal; 500 that the Analyzed Industry is five times the average; 50 means that the Analyzed Industry is half the national average. The abbreviation 'na' is used to show that data are 'not available'.

SIC 4890 - COMMUNICATIONS SERVICES, NEC: GENERAL STATISTICS

Year	Estab-lish-ments	Employment		Payroll		Revenues	
		Total (number)	Per estab.	Total ($ mil.)	Per estab. ($)	Total ($ mil.)	Per estab. ($)
1987	5,400	150,357	28	3,788.6	701,601	-	-
1988	949	32,476	34	981.4	1,034,166	-	-
1989	1,125	30,856	27	1,024.8	910,970	-	-
1990	1,201	34,609	29	1,098.2	914,440	-	-
1991	1,320	24,983	19	1,011.5	766,266	-	-
1992	1,008	9,737	10	404.5	401,288	2,357.9	2,339,175
1993	1,105	15,259	14	605.1	547,632	-	-
1994	1,034	13,063	13	576.2	557,234	-	-
1995	-	-	-	-	-	-	-
1996	-	-	-	-	-	-	-
1997	-	-	-	-	-	-	-
1998	-	-	-	-	-	-	-

Source: Economic Census of the United States, 1987 and 1992. Establishment counts, employment, and payroll are from *County Business Patterns* for non-Census years. Data are the most recent available at this level of detail. Extracted from *Transportation and Public Utilities USA*, Gale, 1998. Note: 1. Projections made by the editor.

SIC 4890 - COMMUNICATIONS SERVICES, NEC: INDICES OF CHANGE

Year	Estab-lish-ments	Employment		Payroll		Revenues	
		Total (number)	Per estab.	Total ($ mil.)	Per estab. ($)	Total ($ mil.)	Per estab. ($)
1987	535.7	1,544.2	288.2	936.6	174.8	-	-
1988	94.1	333.5	354.3	242.6	257.7	-	-
1989	111.6	316.9	283.9	253.4	227.0	-	-
1990	119.1	355.4	298.3	271.5	227.9	-	-
1991	131.0	256.6	195.9	250.1	191.0	-	-
1992	100.0	100.0	100.0	100.0	100.0	100.0	100.0
1993	109.6	156.7	143.0	149.6	136.5	-	-
1994	102.6	134.2	130.8	142.4	138.9	-	-
1995	-	-	-	-	-	-	-
1996	-	-	-	-	-	-	-
1997	-	-	-	-	-	-	-
1998	-	-	-	-	-	-	-

Source: Same as General Statistics. The values shown reflect change from the base year, 1992. Values above 100 mean greater than 1992, values below 100 mean less than 1992, and a value of 100 in the 1987-91 or 1993-98 period means same as 1992. Data are the most recent available at this level of detail. Note: 1. Index based on a projected value.

SIC 4890 - COMMUNICATIONS SERVICES, NEC: SELECTED RATIOS

For 1992	Average of All Trans/Util.	Analyzed Industry	Index
Payroll as % of Revenues	20	17	84
Payroll per Establishment	595,843	401,288	67
Payroll per Employee	32,055	41,542	130
Employees per Establishment	19	10	51
Revenues per Establishment	3,112,739	2,339,175	75
Revenues per Employee	156,168	242,158	155

Source: Sources: Same as General Statistics. The 'Average of Sector' column represents the average of all transportation, communications, and utilities industries reported for the most recent complete year available. Establishment ratios only include those portions of the sector for which establishment data were reported. The Index shows the relationship between the Average and the Analyzed Industry. For example, 100 means that they are equal; 500 that the Analyzed Industry is five times the average; 50 means that the Analyzed Industry is half the national average. The abbreviation 'na' is used to show that data are 'not available'.

FINANCIAL NORMS AND RATIOS

Industry-specific financial norms and ratios are shown in this chapter for twelve industries in the Broadcasting & Telecommunications sector. For each industry, balance sheets are presented for the years 1996 through 1998, with the most recent year shown first. As part of each balance sheet, additional financial averages for net sales, gross profits, net profits after tax, and working capital are shown. The number of establishments used to calculate the averages are shown for each year.

The second table in each display shows D&B Key Business Ratios for the SIC-denominated industry. These data, again, are for the years 1996 through 1998. Ratios measuring solvency (e.g., Quick ratio), efficiency (e.g., Collection period, in days), and profitability (e.g. % return on sales) are shown. A total of 14 ratios are featured. Ratios are shown for the upper quartile, median, and lowest quartile of the D&B sample.

This product includes proprietary data of Dun & Bradstreet Inc.

D&B INDUSTRY NORMS: SIC 3651 - HOUSEHOLD AUDIO AND VIDEO EQUIPMENT

	1998 (66) Estab.		1997 (95) Estab.		1996 (75) Estab.	
	$	%	$	%	$	%
Cash	266,254	10.7	248,171	13.4	344,875	11.3
Accounts Receivable	676,832	27.2	468,561	25.3	784,362	25.7
Notes Receivable	9,953	.4	9,260	.5	21,364	.7
Inventory	933,132	37.5	622,279	33.6	1,086,510	35.6
Other Current Assets	121,929	4.9	101,861	5.5	167,860	5.5
Total Current Assets	2,008,100	80.7	1,450,132	78.3	2,404,971	78.8
Fixed Assets	318,509	12.8	275,951	14.9	439,487	14.4
Other Non-current Assets	161,743	6.5	125,937	6.8	207,536	6.8
Total Assets	2,488,352	100.0	1,852,020	100.0	3,051,994	100.0
Accounts Payable	358,323	14.4	264,839	14.3	402,863	13.2
Bank Loans	2,488	.1	7,408	.4	-	-
Notes Payable	106,999	4.3	64,821	3.5	112,924	3.7
Other Current Liabilities	482,740	19.4	287,063	15.5	567,671	18.6
Total Current Liabilities	950,550	38.2	624,131	33.7	1,083,458	35.5
Other Long Term	335,928	13.5	259,283	14.0	552,411	18.1
Deferred Credits	2,488	.1	1,852	.1	3,052	.1
Net Worth	1,199,386	48.2	966,755	52.2	1,413,073	46.3
Total Liabilities & Net Worth	2,488,352	100.0	1,852,021	100.0	3,051,994	100.0
Net Sales	7,584,379	100.0	7,798,967	100.0	15,567,507	100.0
Gross Profits	2,419,417	31.9	2,409,881	30.9	4,981,602	32.0
Net Profit After Tax	182,025	2.4	233,969	3.0	467,025	3.0
Working Capital	1,057,550	-	826,001	-	1,321,512	-

Source: Dun & Bradstreet. Data in this table are copyright (c) 1999 of Dun & Bradstreet. Reprinted by special arrangement with D&B. *Notes:* Values in parentheses above columns indicate the number of establishments in the sample. Data shown are for all companies.

D&B KEY BUSINESS RATIOS: SIC 3651

	1998			1997			1996		
	UQ	MED	LQ	UQ	MED	LQ	UQ	MED	LQ
Solvency									
Quick ratio	1.6	1.0	.6	3.1	1.3	.7	1.7	1.1	.7
Current ratio	3.2	2.2	1.6	5.5	3.0	1.6	4.4	2.5	1.4
Current liabilities/Net worth (%)	49.3	70.0	134.4	18.6	42.0	133.5	30.5	67.8	148.3
Current liabilities/Inventory (%)	59.6	94.3	138.8	47.8	85.8	148.8	41.3	93.7	151.9
Total liabilities/Net worth (%)	58.0	105.7	254.3	29.7	68.2	208.3	37.8	103.0	179.5
Fixed assets/Net worth (%)	9.2	19.3	35.7	11.4	20.5	42.7	9.2	27.0	55.4
Efficiency									
Collection period (days)	31.8	50.4	71.2	30.9	43.6	64.5	34.7	44.2	65.0
Sales to Inventory	8.6	4.9	3.3	8.0	5.7	4.0	7.9	6.6	4.5
Assets/Sales (%)	35.0	58.0	76.2	32.6	47.3	66.6	34.7	51.0	64.2
Sales/Net Working Capital	8.8	5.9	3.1	9.9	5.5	3.5	9.6	5.0	3.3
Accounts payable/Sales (%)	4.8	7.6	11.4	2.9	4.9	8.2	3.3	5.1	8.0
Profitability									
Return - Sales (%)	7.8	2.5	.3	8.6	3.6	.2	6.2	3.1	.3
Return - Assets (%)	21.3	4.9	.9	15.1	8.0	.5	12.6	5.2	.9
Return - Net Worth (%)	44.2	11.8	3.6	25.7	12.6	1.4	31.0	13.8	2.7

Source: Dun & Bradstreet. Data in this table are copyright (c) 1999 of Dun & Bradstreet. Reprinted by special arrangement with D&B. *Note:* UQ stands for "Upper Quartile" and represents the top 25 percent of sample; MED stands for "Median"; and LQ stands for "Lower Quartile" and represents the lowest 25 percent.

D&B INDUSTRY NORMS: SIC 3661 - TELEPHONE AND TELEGRAPH APPARATUS

	1998 (182) Estab.		1997 (156) Estab.		1996 (128) Estab.	
	$	%	$	%	$	%
Cash	3,379,529	20.8	1,673,676	18.4	2,370,364	19.2
Accounts Receivable	4,110,677	25.3	2,546,898	28.0	3,197,522	25.9
Notes Receivable	32,495	.2	18,192	.2	37,037	.3
Inventory	3,574,502	22.0	2,001,134	22.0	2,604,931	21.1
Other Current Assets	1,592,278	9.8	736,781	8.1	1,209,873	9.8
Total Current Assets	12,689,481	78.1	6,976,681	76.7	9,419,727	76.3
Fixed Assets	2,242,187	13.8	1,309,833	14.4	1,839,501	14.9
Other Non-current Assets	1,316,067	8.1	809,550	8.9	1,086,417	8.8
Total Assets	16,247,735	100.0	9,096,064	100.0	12,345,645	100.0
Accounts Payable	2,095,958	12.9	1,127,912	12.4	1,481,477	12.0
Bank Loans	-	-	-	-	-	-
Notes Payable	276,211	1.7	263,786	2.9	296,295	2.4
Other Current Liabilities	2,307,178	14.2	1,300,737	14.3	2,012,340	16.3
Total Current Liabilities	4,679,347	28.8	2,692,435	29.6	3,790,112	30.7
Other Long Term	1,608,526	9.9	864,126	9.5	999,997	8.1
Deferred Credits	-	-	27,288	.3	24,691	.2
Net Worth	9,959,862	61.3	5,512,215	60.6	7,530,843	61.0
Total Liabilities & Net Worth	16,247,735	100.0	9,096,064	100.0	12,345,643	100.0
Net Sales	31,282,623	100.0	22,905,884	100.0	23,083,321	100.0
Gross Profits	11,762,266	37.6	9,139,448	39.9	9,441,078	40.9
Net Profit After Tax	563,087	1.8	1,007,859	4.4	1,292,666	5.6
Working Capital	8,010,133	-	4,284,247	-	5,629,613	-

Source: Dun & Bradstreet. Data in this table are copyright (c) 1999 of Dun & Bradstreet. Reprinted by special arrangement with D&B. *Notes:* Values in parentheses above columns indicate the number of establishments in the sample. Data shown are for all companies.

D&B KEY BUSINESS RATIOS: SIC 3661

	1998			1997			1996		
	UQ	MED	LQ	UQ	MED	LQ	UQ	MED	LQ
Solvency									
Quick ratio	3.0	1.9	1.0	2.7	1.7	1.0	2.8	1.6	.9
Current ratio	5.2	3.3	1.8	5.4	3.0	1.9	4.7	3.2	1.7
Current liabilities/Net worth (%)	18.5	35.9	79.7	17.5	39.0	93.3	18.0	37.6	81.8
Current liabilities/Inventory (%)	67.8	128.7	200.8	60.7	125.3	180.4	74.7	143.4	227.5
Total liabilities/Net worth (%)	22.0	41.0	127.1	19.8	47.4	114.2	22.5	41.4	97.2
Fixed assets/Net worth (%)	10.4	17.1	34.1	10.9	21.2	38.2	10.0	18.8	35.4
Efficiency									
Collection period (days)	48.6	61.7	78.0	45.3	56.2	71.9	43.8	56.6	73.0
Sales to Inventory	10.0	7.0	4.8	12.4	8.3	5.7	11.1	7.9	5.5
Assets/Sales (%)	50.7	75.3	96.7	41.4	64.8	91.6	43.5	65.7	88.2
Sales/Net Working Capital	6.0	2.7	1.8	6.7	3.5	2.0	6.4	3.4	1.9
Accounts payable/Sales (%)	4.5	7.3	12.1	3.7	6.0	9.5	4.1	5.5	8.5
Profitability									
Return - Sales (%)	10.5	2.4	-3.2	9.9	5.1	1.1	11.1	6.2	1.1
Return - Assets (%)	15.0	7.4	-1.7	15.8	8.6	1.4	16.6	9.2	1.0
Return - Net Worth (%)	24.1	10.5	-2.1	28.1	13.1	1.5	25.3	15.9	5.4

Source: Dun & Bradstreet. Data in this table are copyright (c) 1999 of Dun & Bradstreet. Reprinted by special arrangement with D&B. *Note:* UQ stands for "Upper Quartile" and represents the top 25 percent of sample; MED stands for "Median"; and LQ stands for "Lower Quartile" and represents the lowest 25 percent.

D&B INDUSTRY NORMS: SIC 3663 - RADIO & TV COMMUNICATIONS EQUIPMENT

	1998 (225) Estab.		1997 (236) Estab.		1996 (214) Estab.	
	$	%	$	%	$	%
Cash	1,116,363	16.6	429,962	14.5	377,942	16.2
Accounts Receivable	1,640,919	24.4	756,141	25.5	608,906	26.1
Notes Receivable	13,450	.2	5,931	.2	6,999	.3
Inventory	1,661,094	24.7	830,272	28.0	590,243	25.3
Other Current Assets	490,931	7.3	201,637	6.8	167,974	7.2
Total Current Assets	4,922,757	73.2	2,223,943	75.0	1,752,064	75.1
Fixed Assets	1,129,813	16.8	438,858	14.8	408,271	17.5
Other Non-current Assets	672,508	10.0	302,456	10.2	172,640	7.4
Total Assets	6,725,078	100.0	2,965,257	100.0	2,332,975	100.0
Accounts Payable	847,360	12.6	403,275	13.6	286,956	12.3
Bank Loans	26,900	.4	-	-	-	-
Notes Payable	147,952	2.2	88,958	3.0	69,989	3.0
Other Current Liabilities	1,049,112	15.6	459,615	15.5	356,945	15.3
Total Current Liabilities	2,071,324	30.8	951,848	32.1	713,890	30.6
Other Long Term	827,184	12.3	308,387	10.4	240,296	10.3
Deferred Credits	6,725	.1	5,931	.2	4,666	.2
Net Worth	3,819,844	56.8	1,699,092	57.3	1,374,122	58.9
Total Liabilities & Net Worth	6,725,077	100.0	2,965,258	100.0	2,332,974	100.0
Net Sales	10,081,516	100.0	3,409,725	100.0	4,678,261	100.0
Gross Profits	3,347,063	33.2	1,244,550	36.5	1,688,852	36.1
Net Profit After Tax	-30,245	-	37,507	1.1	154,383	3.3
Working Capital	2,851,432	-	1,272,096	-	1,038,174	-

Source: Dun & Bradstreet. Data in this table are copyright (c) 1999 of Dun & Bradstreet. Reprinted by special arrangement with D&B. *Notes:* Values in parentheses above columns indicate the number of establishments in the sample. Data shown are for all companies.

D&B KEY BUSINESS RATIOS: SIC 3663

	1998			1997			1996		
	UQ	MED	LQ	UQ	MED	LQ	UQ	MED	LQ
Solvency									
Quick ratio	2.6	1.4	.8	2.4	1.2	.7	2.4	1.5	.8
Current ratio	4.1	2.7	1.8	4.1	2.7	1.6	4.3	2.7	1.7
Current liabilities/Net worth (%)	23.0	41.3	79.2	25.8	46.0	82.4	25.0	43.4	84.2
Current liabilities/Inventory (%)	67.9	112.6	189.4	60.2	98.9	169.4	61.5	110.6	180.5
Total liabilities/Net worth (%)	30.2	56.3	112.4	32.8	66.1	138.3	31.4	62.4	109.3
Fixed assets/Net worth (%)	13.3	24.2	50.4	12.1	22.2	41.2	11.5	23.7	46.2
Efficiency									
Collection period (days)	40.4	61.0	87.3	37.1	53.3	81.4	38.4	55.7	84.5
Sales to Inventory	9.3	6.4	3.6	9.0	5.6	3.8	9.3	6.6	4.3
Assets/Sales (%)	45.7	70.0	104.4	40.1	62.7	87.5	37.7	58.5	84.7
Sales/Net Working Capital	5.9	3.2	2.0	6.4	3.6	2.4	6.7	3.7	2.5
Accounts payable/Sales (%)	4.2	7.4	11.3	3.6	7.2	11.6	3.9	6.5	10.9
Profitability									
Return - Sales (%)	6.8	2.2	-5.2	6.9	3.2	.1	7.2	3.1	.1
Return - Assets (%)	11.1	3.5	-4.8	12.6	4.6	.1	13.9	5.3	-.3
Return - Net Worth (%)	19.9	7.8	-9.2	23.7	10.5	-.1	25.5	8.9	.4

Source: Dun & Bradstreet. Data in this table are copyright (c) 1999 of Dun & Bradstreet. Reprinted by special arrangement with D&B. *Note:* UQ stands for "Upper Quartile" and represents the top 25 percent of sample; MED stands for "Median"; and LQ stands for "Lower Quartile" and represents the lowest 25 percent.

D&B INDUSTRY NORMS: SIC 3669 - COMMUNICATIONS EQUIPMENT, NEC

	1998 (64) Estab.		1997 (81) Estab.		1996 (59) Estab.	
	$	%	$	%	$	%
Cash	367,469	13.5	169,034	12.0	116,659	11.4
Accounts Receivable	794,822	29.2	414,134	29.4	316,207	30.9
Notes Receivable	-	-	5,634	.4	1,023	.1
Inventory	645,112	23.7	339,477	24.1	284,484	27.8
Other Current Assets	272,199	10.0	139,453	9.9	55,259	5.4
Total Current Assets	2,079,602	76.4	1,067,732	75.8	773,632	75.6
Fixed Assets	443,685	16.3	229,605	16.3	149,405	14.6
Other Non-current Assets	198,705	7.3	111,281	7.9	100,286	9.8
Total Assets	2,721,992	100.0	1,408,618	100.0	1,023,323	100.0
Accounts Payable	362,025	13.3	185,938	13.2	190,338	18.6
Bank Loans	-	-	-	-	-	-
Notes Payable	114,324	4.2	74,657	5.3	35,816	3.5
Other Current Liabilities	381,079	14.0	245,100	17.4	181,128	17.7
Total Current Liabilities	857,428	31.5	505,695	35.9	407,282	39.8
Other Long Term	253,145	9.3	167,626	11.9	114,612	11.2
Deferred Credits	16,332	.6	2,817	.2	3,070	.3
Net Worth	1,595,088	58.6	732,482	52.0	498,359	48.7
Total Liabilities & Net Worth	2,721,993	100.0	1,408,620	100.0	1,023,323	100.0
Net Sales	5,084,232	100.0	3,009,349	100.0	3,391,761	100.0
Gross Profits	2,038,777	40.1	1,278,973	42.5	1,295,653	38.2
Net Profit After Tax	213,538	4.2	141,439	4.7	122,103	3.6
Working Capital	1,222,175	-	562,039	-	366,350	-

Source: Dun & Bradstreet. Data in this table are copyright (c) 1999 of Dun & Bradstreet. Reprinted by special arrangement with D&B. *Notes:* Values in parentheses above columns indicate the number of establishments in the sample. Data shown are for all companies.

D&B KEY BUSINESS RATIOS: SIC 3669

	1998			1997			1996		
	UQ	MED	LQ	UQ	MED	LQ	UQ	MED	LQ
Solvency									
Quick ratio	2.2	1.4	.9	2.2	1.3	.7	2.0	1.0	.7
Current ratio	4.9	2.4	1.7	3.9	2.4	1.4	3.8	1.8	1.2
Current liabilities/Net worth (%)	23.6	55.0	95.8	27.5	51.6	139.7	20.9	56.8	143.9
Current liabilities/Inventory (%)	66.7	128.4	234.0	66.1	144.4	213.0	64.2	127.6	246.4
Total liabilities/Net worth (%)	26.8	81.4	132.3	35.4	83.3	193.0	31.7	70.5	184.0
Fixed assets/Net worth (%)	11.6	28.0	43.6	10.7	21.2	47.2	9.2	17.1	52.6
Efficiency									
Collection period (days)	39.7	50.0	80.8	39.5	56.4	75.7	36.5	56.9	69.0
Sales to Inventory	10.1	7.7	4.9	11.1	6.6	4.7	12.9	7.6	5.0
Assets/Sales (%)	41.0	59.8	73.2	35.5	48.2	70.5	34.4	49.5	62.8
Sales/Net Working Capital	6.8	4.2	2.8	11.5	4.7	2.7	16.4	5.1	3.1
Accounts payable/Sales (%)	4.4	6.5	10.5	3.5	5.7	9.3	3.5	5.8	9.3
Profitability									
Return - Sales (%)	7.5	3.8	1.4	9.7	3.7	.5	8.1	5.3	.6
Return - Assets (%)	12.7	6.1	2.4	20.9	7.8	1.3	19.3	6.8	1.9
Return - Net Worth (%)	23.8	11.0	5.5	40.3	16.4	5.8	34.6	16.7	5.6

Source: Dun & Bradstreet. Data in this table are copyright (c) 1999 of Dun & Bradstreet. Reprinted by special arrangement with D&B. *Note:* UQ stands for "Upper Quartile" and represents the top 25 percent of sample; MED stands for "Median"; and LQ stands for "Lower Quartile" and represents the lowest 25 percent.

D&B INDUSTRY NORMS: SIC 3679 - ELECTRONIC COMPONENTS, NEC

	1998 (371) Estab.		1997 (427) Estab.		1996 (377) Estab.	
	$	%	$	%	$	%
Cash	227,792	14.2	196,487	15.4	168,622	15.9
Accounts Receivable	455,585	28.4	372,559	29.2	291,641	27.5
Notes Receivable	8,021	.5	6,379	.5	3,182	.3
Inventory	401,043	25.0	331,731	26.0	272,552	25.7
Other Current Assets	88,229	5.5	63,794	5.0	60,449	5.7
Total Current Assets	1,180,670	73.6	970,950	76.1	796,446	75.1
Fixed Assets	322,438	20.1	237,315	18.6	201,497	19.0
Other Non-current Assets	101,063	6.3	67,622	5.3	62,570	5.9
Total Assets	1,604,171	100.0	1,275,887	100.0	1,060,513	100.0
Accounts Payable	218,167	13.6	187,556	14.7	148,472	14.0
Bank Loans	1,604	.1	2,552	.2	-	-
Notes Payable	59,354	3.7	43,380	3.4	47,723	4.5
Other Current Liabilities	243,834	15.2	188,831	14.8	161,198	15.2
Total Current Liabilities	522,959	32.6	422,319	33.1	357,393	33.7
Other Long Term	205,334	12.8	167,141	13.1	133,625	12.6
Deferred Credits	3,208	.2	1,276	.1	2,121	.2
Net Worth	872,669	54.4	685,152	53.7	567,374	53.5
Total Liabilities & Net Worth	1,604,170	100.0	1,275,888	100.0	1,060,513	100.0
Net Sales	3,814,489	100.0	3,100,627	100.0	3,085,364	100.0
Gross Profits	1,323,628	34.7	1,072,817	34.6	1,113,816	36.1
Net Profit After Tax	217,426	5.7	145,729	4.7	169,695	5.5
Working Capital	657,710	-	548,632	-	439,052	-

Source: Dun & Bradstreet. Data in this table are copyright (c) 1999 of Dun & Bradstreet. Reprinted by special arrangement with D&B. *Notes:* Values in parentheses above columns indicate the number of establishments in the sample. Data shown are for all companies.

D&B KEY BUSINESS RATIOS: SIC 3679

	1998			1997			1996		
	UQ	MED	LQ	UQ	MED	LQ	UQ	MED	LQ
Solvency									
Quick ratio	2.4	1.4	.8	2.7	1.5	.9	2.4	1.4	.8
Current ratio	4.2	2.4	1.6	4.6	2.6	1.6	4.1	2.4	1.6
Current liabilities/Net worth (%)	21.8	49.9	106.9	21.6	48.2	121.9	23.0	54.4	129.6
Current liabilities/Inventory (%)	65.0	113.8	197.7	64.5	110.9	177.6	63.3	116.2	186.8
Total liabilities/Net worth (%)	30.9	77.3	159.6	31.1	75.6	166.8	28.1	84.3	177.6
Fixed assets/Net worth (%)	14.2	33.3	61.8	13.0	28.6	56.6	14.1	30.7	62.2
Efficiency									
Collection period (days)	35.4	47.5	62.3	33.6	46.0	60.6	30.3	45.3	58.4
Sales to Inventory	13.5	8.2	4.7	16.9	8.6	5.2	15.5	8.6	5.2
Assets/Sales (%)	33.1	47.7	70.4	33.0	44.1	64.6	32.1	43.2	62.8
Sales/Net Working Capital	8.6	4.9	2.7	9.0	5.4	3.1	9.7	5.4	3.3
Accounts payable/Sales (%)	3.2	5.4	9.0	2.9	5.3	8.5	3.2	4.9	8.4
Profitability									
Return - Sales (%)	10.7	5.0	1.9	9.1	4.5	1.2	8.7	4.8	1.9
Return - Assets (%)	20.2	9.2	2.7	18.8	7.9	2.6	19.6	11.1	4.0
Return - Net Worth (%)	39.5	18.5	6.2	34.1	17.7	6.3	46.2	22.1	8.8

Source: Dun & Bradstreet. Data in this table are copyright (c) 1999 of Dun & Bradstreet. Reprinted by special arrangement with D&B. *Note:* UQ stands for "Upper Quartile" and represents the top 25 percent of sample; MED stands for "Median"; and LQ stands for "Lower Quartile" and represents the lowest 25 percent.

D&B INDUSTRY NORMS: SIC 4812 - RADIOTELEPHONE COMMUNICATIONS

	1998 (177) Estab.		1997 (205) Estab.		1996 (154) Estab.	
	$	%	$	%	$	%
Cash	209,908	16.4	155,543	11.7	144,848	12.7
Accounts Receivable	236,786	18.5	255,250	19.2	229,248	20.1
Notes Receivable	2,560	.2	7,977	.6	6,843	.6
Inventory	121,593	9.5	116,989	8.8	125,459	11.0
Other Current Assets	56,317	4.4	53,177	4.0	33,076	2.9
Total Current Assets	627,164	49.0	588,936	44.3	539,474	47.3
Fixed Assets	444,134	34.7	502,523	37.8	435,686	38.2
Other Non-current Assets	208,628	16.3	237,967	17.9	165,378	14.5
Total Assets	1,279,926	100.0	1,329,426	100.0	1,140,538	100.0
Accounts Payable	133,112	10.4	143,578	10.8	122,038	10.7
Bank Loans	2,560	.2	-	-	-	-
Notes Payable	21,759	1.7	38,553	2.9	31,935	2.8
Other Current Liabilities	156,151	12.2	186,120	14.0	133,443	11.7
Total Current Liabilities	313,582	24.5	368,251	27.7	287,416	25.2
Other Long Term	309,742	24.2	345,651	26.0	286,275	25.1
Deferred Credits	7,680	.6	2,659	.2	3,422	.3
Net Worth	648,922	50.7	612,865	46.1	563,426	49.4
Total Liabilities & Net Worth	1,279,926	100.0	1,329,426	100.0	1,140,539	100.0
Net Sales	1,776,572	100.0	2,361,514	100.0	2,204,183	100.0
Gross Profits	955,796	53.8	1,294,110	54.8	1,192,463	54.1
Net Profit After Tax	97,711	5.5	127,522	5.4	116,822	5.3
Working Capital	313,581	-	220,684	-	252,059	-

Source: Dun & Bradstreet. Data in this table are copyright (c) 1999 of Dun & Bradstreet. Reprinted by special arrangement with D&B. *Notes:* Values in parentheses above columns indicate the number of establishments in the sample. Data shown are for all companies.

D&B KEY BUSINESS RATIOS: SIC 4812

	1998			1997			1996		
	UQ	MED	LQ	UQ	MED	LQ	UQ	MED	LQ
Solvency									
Quick ratio	3.6	1.3	.7	2.2	1.0	.5	3.2	1.3	.6
Current ratio	4.7	1.8	1.1	3.6	1.5	.9	4.7	1.7	1.0
Current liabilities/Net worth (%)	10.7	34.0	84.3	13.1	31.0	118.5	12.1	30.2	94.7
Current liabilities/Inventory (%)	82.2	236.7	445.2	93.3	256.6	459.4	79.0	200.0	454.5
Total liabilities/Net worth (%)	18.5	74.8	196.9	20.4	76.7	216.5	20.9	69.1	150.9
Fixed assets/Net worth (%)	29.3	66.6	122.8	37.0	75.0	153.3	35.2	69.2	124.5
Efficiency									
Collection period (days)	22.7	41.3	60.1	27.7	38.0	54.5	30.1	42.5	60.0
Sales to Inventory	43.7	25.3	13.7	49.0	25.3	14.5	45.4	20.8	12.3
Assets/Sales (%)	33.3	69.9	181.1	32.3	67.6	160.8	40.7	80.6	174.0
Sales/Net Working Capital	14.6	7.3	4.1	15.7	8.2	4.6	12.1	6.4	2.9
Accounts payable/Sales (%)	2.9	5.7	11.9	3.0	5.5	9.9	3.0	5.3	10.6
Profitability									
Return - Sales (%)	17.7	8.1	-.7	13.7	6.2	.1	14.9	7.2	-.5
Return - Assets (%)	22.4	6.3	-1.2	17.9	6.2	-1.1	22.0	9.8	-.4
Return - Net Worth (%)	39.4	21.6	-.9	40.7	19.3	1.6	56.3	19.1	.7

Source: Dun & Bradstreet. Data in this table are copyright (c) 1999 of Dun & Bradstreet. Reprinted by special arrangement with D&B. *Note:* UQ stands for "Upper Quartile" and represents the top 25 percent of sample; MED stands for "Median"; and LQ stands for "Lower Quartile" and represents the lowest 25 percent.

D&B INDUSTRY NORMS: SIC 4813 - TELEPHONE COMMUNICATIONS, EXCEPT RADIOTELEPHONE

	1998 (934) Estab.		1997 (1050) Estab.		1996 (839) Estab.	
	$	%	$	%	$	%
Cash	1,372,190	15.0	1,067,504	13.7	1,099,029	12.6
Accounts Receivable	1,372,190	15.0	989,584	12.7	1,133,919	13.0
Notes Receivable	54,888	.6	31,168	.4	52,335	.6
Inventory	155,515	1.7	148,048	1.9	174,449	2.0
Other Current Assets	521,432	5.7	467,520	6.0	558,237	6.4
Total Current Assets	3,476,215	38.0	2,703,824	34.7	3,017,969	34.6
Fixed Assets	4,244,640	46.4	3,841,456	49.3	4,282,726	49.1
Other Non-current Assets	1,427,077	15.6	1,246,720	16.0	1,421,760	16.3
Total Assets	9,147,932	100.0	7,792,000	100.0	8,722,455	100.0
Accounts Payable	832,462	9.1	631,152	8.1	689,074	7.9
Bank Loans	-	-	-	-	-	-
Notes Payable	146,367	1.6	116,880	1.5	104,669	1.2
Other Current Liabilities	969,681	10.6	763,616	9.8	837,356	9.6
Total Current Liabilities	1,948,510	21.3	1,511,648	19.4	1,631,099	18.7
Other Long Term	2,323,574	25.4	2,096,048	26.9	2,302,728	26.4
Deferred Credits	182,959	2.0	163,632	2.1	235,506	2.7
Net Worth	4,692,889	51.3	4,020,672	51.6	4,553,122	52.2
Total Liabilities & Net Worth	9,147,932	100.0	7,792,000	100.0	8,722,455	100.0
Net Sales	4,319,590	100.0	3,644,572	100.0	3,783,534	100.0
Gross Profits	1,753,754	40.6	1,516,142	41.6	1,600,435	42.3
Net Profit After Tax	548,588	12.7	492,017	13.5	529,695	14.0
Working Capital	1,527,705	-	1,192,176	-	1,386,871	-

Source: Dun & Bradstreet. Data in this table are copyright (c) 1999 of Dun & Bradstreet. Reprinted by special arrangement with D&B. *Notes:* Values in parentheses above columns indicate the number of establishments in the sample. Data shown are for all companies.

D&B KEY BUSINESS RATIOS: SIC 4813

	1998			1997			1996		
	UQ	MED	LQ	UQ	MED	LQ	UQ	MED	LQ
Solvency									
Quick ratio	3.1	1.3	.8	3.2	1.4	.8	3.2	1.5	.8
Current ratio	4.3	1.9	1.0	4.7	2.0	1.1	4.6	2.3	1.1
Current liabilities/Net worth (%)	10.6	24.0	65.8	10.0	20.9	50.8	10.4	20.1	46.5
Current liabilities/Inventory (%)	249.9	450.2	674.6	242.2	435.0	633.0	255.3	447.8	648.4
Total liabilities/Net worth (%)	39.0	94.0	195.2	41.1	93.6	174.5	41.0	89.7	172.2
Fixed assets/Net worth (%)	56.7	98.4	164.6	60.4	102.9	167.4	60.5	101.2	163.1
Efficiency									
Collection period (days)	35.4	52.6	72.6	36.9	52.2	69.8	39.8	54.8	70.8
Sales to Inventory	66.7	38.1	20.5	65.7	37.3	21.4	60.2	36.2	19.8
Assets/Sales (%)	69.1	209.2	323.9	80.6	226.7	334.5	121.4	240.1	337.6
Sales/Net Working Capital	12.0	4.0	1.6	10.6	4.1	1.8	9.5	3.3	1.4
Accounts payable/Sales (%)	4.5	7.9	12.6	4.1	7.7	12.9	4.7	8.2	12.8
Profitability									
Return - Sales (%)	22.7	13.9	5.4	22.7	14.5	6.6	24.2	15.6	5.8
Return - Assets (%)	11.1	6.9	3.5	10.6	6.7	3.4	10.4	6.6	3.7
Return - Net Worth (%)	23.7	13.4	8.0	21.0	13.1	7.9	20.2	14.0	8.7

Source: Dun & Bradstreet. Data in this table are copyright (c) 1999 of Dun & Bradstreet. Reprinted by special arrangement with D&B. *Note:* UQ stands for "Upper Quartile" and represents the top 25 percent of sample; MED stands for "Median"; and LQ stands for "Lower Quartile" and represents the lowest 25 percent.

D&B INDUSTRY NORMS: SIC 4822 - TELEGRAPH & OTHER COMMUNICATIONS

	1998 (15) Estab.		1997 (19) Estab.		1996 (17) Estab.	
	$	%	$	%	$	%
Cash	166,567	22.9	55,009	19.9	108,875	26.2
Accounts Receivable	150,565	20.7	91,222	33.0	94,746	22.8
Notes Receivable	-	-	-	-	-	-
Inventory	8,728	1.2	3,317	1.2	28,258	6.8
Other Current Assets	10,183	1.4	-	-	29,504	7.1
Total Current Assets	336,043	46.2	149,548	54.1	261,383	62.9
Fixed Assets	331,680	45.6	97,027	35.1	101,810	24.5
Other Non-current Assets	59,644	8.2	29,854	10.8	52,360	12.6
Total Assets	727,367	100.0	276,429	100.0	415,553	100.0
Accounts Payable	74,192	10.2	39,253	14.2	84,773	20.4
Bank Loans	-	-	-	-	-	-
Notes Payable	32,004	4.4	15,756	5.7	12,882	3.1
Other Current Liabilities	112,742	15.5	34,277	12.4	55,684	13.4
Total Current Liabilities	218,938	30.1	89,286	32.3	153,339	36.9
Other Long Term	116,379	16.0	39,253	14.2	80,202	19.3
Deferred Credits	-	-	276	.1	-	-
Net Worth	392,051	53.9	147,613	53.4	182,012	43.8
Total Liabilities & Net Worth	727,368	100.0	276,428	100.0	415,553	100.0
Net Sales	1,802,015	100.0	772,262	100.0	2,499,093	100.0
Gross Profits	882,987	49.0	250,985	32.5	864,686	34.6
Net Profit After Tax	176,597	9.8	-	-	219,920	8.8
Working Capital	117,106	-	60,261	-	108,044	-

Source: Dun & Bradstreet. Data in this table are copyright (c) 1999 of Dun & Bradstreet. Reprinted by special arrangement with D&B. *Notes:* Values in parentheses above columns indicate the number of establishments in the sample. Data shown are for all companies.

D&B KEY BUSINESS RATIOS: SIC 4822

	1998			1997			1996		
	UQ	MED	LQ	UQ	MED	LQ	UQ	MED	LQ
Solvency									
Quick ratio	1.4	1.2	1.0	4.6	1.4	1.1	4.1	1.6	.7
Current ratio	1.5	1.3	1.0	4.8	1.5	1.0	4.2	2.1	1.2
Current liabilities/Net worth (%)	39.7	58.0	82.6	7.4	31.3	99.5	14.7	26.4	46.7
Current liabilities/Inventory (%)	365.9	460.5	570.6	635.3	836.4	886.9	135.1	426.2	713.6
Total liabilities/Net worth (%)	40.7	110.4	182.1	15.4	55.0	145.7	14.7	46.5	65.4
Fixed assets/Net worth (%)	54.0	96.2	176.1	26.5	49.1	83.9	18.8	32.4	84.6
Efficiency									
Collection period (days)	19.0	30.3	40.5	19.1	50.6	82.4	13.5	23.0	41.6
Sales to Inventory	69.6	63.2	56.7	56.4	50.2	43.9	77.1	41.7	22.3
Assets/Sales (%)	27.7	32.8	38.4	20.1	34.8	44.3	24.4	36.6	135.6
Sales/Net Working Capital	82.7	26.6	17.9	19.6	11.9	3.4	18.5	3.9	1.2
Accounts payable/Sales (%)	3.1	4.4	5.9	2.6	7.6	22.8	.4	.8	13.3
Profitability									
Return - Sales (%)	12.6	11.0	9.9	5.1	1.0	-.9	24.3	11.2	2.9
Return - Assets (%)	38.4	22.2	17.6	2.4	1.3	-26.9	13.6	7.2	4.0
Return - Net Worth (%)	130.5	50.3	30.8	6.0	3.5	-85.0	23.1	15.4	12.8

Source: Dun & Bradstreet. Data in this table are copyright (c) 1999 of Dun & Bradstreet. Reprinted by special arrangement with D&B. *Note:* UQ stands for "Upper Quartile" and represents the top 25 percent of sample; MED stands for "Median"; and LQ stands for "Lower Quartile" and represents the lowest 25 percent.

D&B INDUSTRY NORMS: SIC 4832 - RADIO BROADCASTING STATIONS

	1998 (107) Estab.		1997 (164) Estab.		1996 (165) Estab.	
	$	%	$	%	$	%
Cash	265,562	14.2	205,619	15.8	153,995	15.6
Accounts Receivable	254,341	13.6	178,290	13.7	145,111	14.7
Notes Receivable	1,870	.1	3,904	.3	4,936	.5
Inventory	1,870	.1	10,411	.8	4,936	.5
Other Current Assets	127,170	6.8	92,398	7.1	80,946	8.2
Total Current Assets	650,813	34.8	490,622	37.7	389,924	39.5
Fixed Assets	682,605	36.5	438,567	33.7	353,399	35.8
Other Non-current Assets	536,734	28.7	372,197	28.6	243,825	24.7
Total Assets	1,870,152	100.0	1,301,386	100.0	987,148	100.0
Accounts Payable	56,105	3.0	58,562	4.5	53,306	5.4
Bank Loans	-	-	-	-	987	.1
Notes Payable	72,936	3.9	39,042	3.0	22,704	2.3
Other Current Liabilities	187,015	10.0	145,755	11.2	108,586	11.0
Total Current Liabilities	316,056	16.9	243,359	18.7	185,583	18.8
Other Long Term	527,383	28.2	307,127	23.6	230,992	23.4
Deferred Credits	7,481	.4	3,904	.3	4,936	.5
Net Worth	1,019,233	54.5	746,996	57.4	565,635	57.3
Total Liabilities & Net Worth	1,870,153	100.0	1,301,386	100.0	987,146	100.0
Net Sales	1,727,858	100.0	1,353,249	100.0	1,037,194	100.0
Gross Profits	974,512	56.4	834,955	61.7	798,639	77.0
Net Profit After Tax	60,475	3.5	100,140	7.4	70,529	6.8
Working Capital	334,757	-	247,264	-	204,339	-

Source: Dun & Bradstreet. Data in this table are copyright (c) 1999 of Dun & Bradstreet. Reprinted by special arrangement with D&B. *Notes:* Values in parentheses above columns indicate the number of establishments in the sample. Data shown are for all companies.

D&B KEY BUSINESS RATIOS: SIC 4832

	1998			1997			1996		
	UQ	MED	LQ	UQ	MED	LQ	UQ	MED	LQ
Solvency									
Quick ratio	4.2	1.9	1.0	4.2	1.8	1.0	5.4	2.2	.8
Current ratio	6.3	2.4	1.2	5.8	2.3	1.2	6.8	2.6	1.3
Current liabilities/Net worth (%)	7.9	18.6	53.7	5.9	18.9	58.1	7.9	22.3	68.1
Current liabilities/Inventory (%)	351.1	461.7	600.3	109.6	185.7	483.1	72.9	155.2	305.1
Total liabilities/Net worth (%)	15.8	76.1	159.9	7.7	39.4	114.9	10.6	53.1	146.1
Fixed assets/Net worth (%)	35.3	58.5	106.3	27.5	53.1	91.7	30.7	62.6	102.4
Efficiency									
Collection period (days)	35.3	54.2	80.3	18.1	51.9	72.9	17.3	54.4	71.2
Sales to Inventory	319.7	185.1	67.9	123.6	53.9	21.7	62.4	28.5	22.5
Assets/Sales (%)	74.5	103.6	153.7	65.1	110.7	149.6	60.6	95.0	154.1
Sales/Net Working Capital	9.0	5.3	2.9	8.5	4.9	3.2	8.8	4.6	3.0
Accounts payable/Sales (%)	1.1	2.1	5.7	1.5	3.0	6.9	1.4	2.6	6.6
Profitability									
Return - Sales (%)	9.6	4.5	-2.6	15.9	6.9	-.7	13.8	9.4	2.2
Return - Assets (%)	9.7	4.8	-.1	14.7	6.3	-.4	19.3	7.1	.9
Return - Net Worth (%)	19.9	7.9	.1	26.7	9.9	-.4	36.7	18.3	1.1

Source: Dun & Bradstreet. Data in this table are copyright (c) 1999 of Dun & Bradstreet. Reprinted by special arrangement with D&B. *Note:* UQ stands for "Upper Quartile" and represents the top 25 percent of sample; MED stands for "Median"; and LQ stands for "Lower Quartile" and represents the lowest 25 percent.

D&B INDUSTRY NORMS: SIC 4833 - TELEVISION BROADCASTING STATIONS

	1998 (86) Estab.		1997 (152) Estab.		1996 (129) Estab.	
	$	%	$	%	$	%
Cash	1,305,835	9.3	740,115	10.7	657,975	11.7
Accounts Receivable	1,839,402	13.1	843,870	12.2	691,717	12.3
Notes Receivable	42,124	.3	27,668	.4	39,366	.7
Inventory	42,124	.3	48,419	.7	33,742	.6
Other Current Assets	1,684,949	12.0	906,122	13.1	669,222	11.9
Total Current Assets	4,914,434	35.0	2,566,194	37.1	2,092,022	37.2
Fixed Assets	4,802,103	34.2	2,739,118	39.6	2,457,565	43.7
Other Non-current Assets	4,324,701	30.8	1,611,653	23.3	1,074,130	19.1
Total Assets	14,041,238	100.0	6,916,965	100.0	5,623,717	100.0
Accounts Payable	758,227	5.4	373,516	5.4	331,799	5.9
Bank Loans	-	-	6,917	.1	-	-
Notes Payable	154,454	1.1	41,502	.6	112,474	2.0
Other Current Liabilities	1,474,330	10.5	878,454	12.7	725,460	12.9
Total Current Liabilities	2,387,011	17.0	1,300,389	18.8	1,169,733	20.8
Other Long Term	3,777,093	26.9	1,224,303	17.7	972,903	17.3
Deferred Credits	154,454	1.1	34,585	.5	22,495	.4
Net Worth	7,722,681	55.0	4,357,687	63.0	3,458,587	61.5
Total Liabilities & Net Worth	14,041,239	100.0	6,916,964	100.0	5,623,718	100.0
Net Sales	8,839,656	100.0	6,813,890	100.0	6,151,310	100.0
Gross Profits	5,339,152	60.4	4,415,401	64.8	2,288,287	37.2
Net Profit After Tax	441,983	5.0	490,600	7.2	221,447	3.6
Working Capital	2,527,423	-	1,265,805	-	922,290	-

Source: Dun & Bradstreet. Data in this table are copyright (c) 1999 of Dun & Bradstreet. Reprinted by special arrangement with D&B. *Notes:* Values in parentheses above columns indicate the number of establishments in the sample. Data shown are for all companies.

D&B KEY BUSINESS RATIOS: SIC 4833

	1998			1997			1996		
	UQ	MED	LQ	UQ	MED	LQ	UQ	MED	LQ
Solvency									
Quick ratio	2.1	1.2	.7	2.7	1.2	.7	2.4	1.2	.7
Current ratio	3.4	1.9	1.3	4.5	2.2	1.2	3.8	2.0	1.1
Current liabilities/Net worth (%)	12.5	24.6	44.6	9.1	18.5	43.3	10.4	23.5	59.0
Current liabilities/Inventory (%)	389.5	507.0	585.2	241.9	412.4	518.5	259.0	414.7	536.2
Total liabilities/Net worth (%)	22.5	52.9	147.3	13.9	32.0	86.3	14.9	37.6	83.2
Fixed assets/Net worth (%)	23.2	57.4	101.0	39.4	66.3	94.2	37.5	70.4	101.2
Efficiency									
Collection period (days)	21.0	58.0	74.5	14.8	38.3	64.3	15.0	41.3	63.7
Sales to Inventory	175.0	105.7	43.5	156.4	57.1	33.6	121.0	73.3	26.3
Assets/Sales (%)	76.0	136.7	300.2	82.8	111.6	189.4	74.4	115.4	150.2
Sales/Net Working Capital	10.8	5.8	2.4	13.9	5.3	2.4	16.4	5.6	3.1
Accounts payable/Sales (%)	2.7	5.3	9.6	2.3	3.5	7.9	2.4	4.4	7.4
Profitability									
Return - Sales (%)	13.0	4.6	-2.7	15.0	5.3	-1.1	9.6	2.8	-1.2
Return - Assets (%)	11.7	4.2	-.3	9.8	4.4	-1.7	10.0	2.5	-1.2
Return - Net Worth (%)	16.8	6.4	-.4	16.4	6.7	-.3	15.5	4.4	-2.7

Source: Dun & Bradstreet. Data in this table are copyright (c) 1999 of Dun & Bradstreet. Reprinted by special arrangement with D&B. *Note:* UQ stands for "Upper Quartile" and represents the top 25 percent of sample; MED stands for "Median"; and LQ stands for "Lower Quartile" and represents the lowest 25 percent.

D&B INDUSTRY NORMS: SIC 4841 - CABLE AND OTHER PAY TV SERVICES

	1998 (134) Estab.		1997 (172) Estab.		1996 (136) Estab.	
	$	%	$	%	$	%
Cash	797,029	15.2	455,502	15.0	267,831	15.4
Accounts Receivable	776,055	14.8	349,218	11.5	168,699	9.7
Notes Receivable	31,462	.6	3,037	.1	6,957	.4
Inventory	110,116	2.1	78,954	2.6	53,914	3.1
Other Current Assets	388,027	7.4	279,374	9.2	95,654	5.5
Total Current Assets	2,102,689	40.1	1,166,085	38.4	593,055	34.1
Fixed Assets	1,982,086	37.8	1,242,001	40.9	808,710	46.5
Other Non-current Assets	1,158,839	22.1	628,592	20.7	337,397	19.4
Total Assets	5,243,614	100.0	3,036,678	100.0	1,739,162	100.0
Accounts Payable	351,322	6.7	242,934	8.0	109,567	6.3
Bank Loans	-	-	3,037	.1	-	-
Notes Payable	120,603	2.3	63,770	2.1	45,218	2.6
Other Current Liabilities	838,978	16.0	455,502	15.0	292,179	16.8
Total Current Liabilities	1,310,903	25.0	765,243	25.2	446,964	25.7
Other Long Term	1,405,289	26.8	844,196	27.8	495,661	28.5
Deferred Credits	31,462	.6	30,367	1.0	40,001	2.3
Net Worth	2,495,960	47.6	1,396,872	46.0	756,535	43.5
Total Liabilities & Net Worth	5,243,614	100.0	3,036,678	100.0	1,739,161	100.0
Net Sales	5,168,585	100.0	3,284,816	100.0	1,521,635	100.0
Gross Profits	2,336,200	45.2	1,566,857	47.7	747,123	49.1
Net Profit After Tax	62,023	1.2	9,854	.3	76,082	5.0
Working Capital	791,785	-	400,841	-	146,090	-

Source: Dun & Bradstreet. Data in this table are copyright (c) 1999 of Dun & Bradstreet. Reprinted by special arrangement with D&B. *Notes:* Values in parentheses above columns indicate the number of establishments in the sample. Data shown are for all companies.

D&B KEY BUSINESS RATIOS: SIC 4841

	1998			1997			1996		
	UQ	MED	LQ	UQ	MED	LQ	UQ	MED	LQ
Solvency									
Quick ratio	2.1	1.0	.6	2.2	.8	.3	1.7	.8	.4
Current ratio	3.5	1.3	.9	3.5	1.3	.6	3.1	1.3	.5
Current liabilities/Net worth (%)	13.1	33.3	82.1	10.6	36.9	85.0	14.9	39.1	111.7
Current liabilities/Inventory (%)	119.0	281.6	540.5	118.0	265.3	435.6	130.7	288.8	460.9
Total liabilities/Net worth (%)	28.0	84.7	211.4	26.5	71.3	212.2	24.1	102.3	206.6
Fixed assets/Net worth (%)	24.1	64.4	156.9	26.9	78.0	160.5	40.7	82.5	188.6
Efficiency									
Collection period (days)	15.5	34.0	60.1	15.0	23.4	40.9	17.9	31.3	53.6
Sales to Inventory	52.0	19.4	8.5	47.4	19.9	9.6	45.1	26.4	12.9
Assets/Sales (%)	85.1	179.5	301.3	46.6	144.5	254.5	66.0	149.6	253.2
Sales/Net Working Capital	16.2	5.5	1.9	23.8	8.3	2.3	13.3	5.3	1.5
Accounts payable/Sales (%)	2.9	5.6	12.4	2.3	6.6	11.9	1.9	5.0	8.7
Profitability									
Return - Sales (%)	11.5	1.7	-9.5	10.5	2.1	-9.0	11.6	4.5	-2.1
Return - Assets (%)	9.7	2.8	-2.6	9.5	2.0	-3.3	10.4	2.9	-2.6
Return - Net Worth (%)	24.1	5.9	-3.1	30.8	3.3	-9.9	24.3	5.4	-4.3

Source: Dun & Bradstreet. Data in this table are copyright (c) 1999 of Dun & Bradstreet. Reprinted by special arrangement with D&B. *Note:* UQ stands for "Upper Quartile" and represents the top 25 percent of sample; MED stands for "Median"; and LQ stands for "Lower Quartile" and represents the lowest 25 percent.

D&B INDUSTRY NORMS: SIC 4899 - COMMUNICATIONS SERVICES, NEC

	1998 (63) Estab.		1997 (63) Estab.		1996 (60) Estab.	
	$	%	$	%	$	%
Cash	453,066	20.1	309,095	14.1	239,196	18.0
Accounts Receivable	599,579	26.6	653,265	29.8	336,203	25.3
Notes Receivable	9,016	.4	8,769	.4	2,658	.2
Inventory	99,179	4.4	59,188	2.7	54,483	4.1
Other Current Assets	151,022	6.7	227,985	10.4	93,021	7.0
Total Current Assets	1,311,862	58.2	1,258,302	57.4	725,561	54.6
Fixed Assets	689,742	30.6	734,375	33.5	471,747	35.5
Other Non-current Assets	252,454	11.2	199,487	9.1	131,558	9.9
Total Assets	2,254,058	100.0	2,192,164	100.0	1,328,866	100.0
Accounts Payable	265,979	11.8	326,632	14.9	172,752	13.0
Bank Loans	-	-	-	-	-	-
Notes Payable	42,827	1.9	89,879	4.1	67,772	5.1
Other Current Liabilities	295,282	13.1	374,860	17.1	252,484	19.0
Total Current Liabilities	604,088	26.8	791,371	36.1	493,008	37.1
Other Long Term	459,828	20.4	344,170	15.7	215,276	16.2
Deferred Credits	13,524	.6	15,345	.7	1,329	.1
Net Worth	1,176,618	52.2	1,041,278	47.5	619,251	46.6
Total Liabilities & Net Worth	2,254,058	100.0	2,192,164	100.0	1,328,864	100.0
Net Sales	3,321,541	100.0	3,227,191	100.0	3,111,331	100.0
Gross Profits	1,179,147	35.5	1,197,288	37.1	1,029,851	33.1
Net Profit After Tax	222,543	6.7	338,855	10.5	40,447	1.3
Working Capital	707,774	-	466,931	-	232,551	-

Source: Dun & Bradstreet. Data in this table are copyright (c) 1999 of Dun & Bradstreet. Reprinted by special arrangement with D&B. *Notes:* Values in parentheses above columns indicate the number of establishments in the sample. Data shown are for all companies.

D&B KEY BUSINESS RATIOS: SIC 4899

	1998			1997			1996		
	UQ	MED	LQ	UQ	MED	LQ	UQ	MED	LQ
Solvency									
Quick ratio	5.3	1.4	.8	2.4	1.3	.7	2.2	1.3	.5
Current ratio	5.8	2.2	1.1	3.1	1.7	1.0	2.4	1.6	.9
Current liabilities/Net worth (%)	12.8	34.3	103.7	14.2	47.9	120.0	20.2	62.2	105.1
Current liabilities/Inventory (%)	99.9	170.3	260.2	310.2	679.1	714.3	189.5	263.2	498.8
Total liabilities/Net worth (%)	34.2	83.4	165.1	18.5	88.8	168.2	25.3	90.0	179.4
Fixed assets/Net worth (%)	16.2	40.5	127.2	27.6	50.6	97.9	29.8	51.5	140.5
Efficiency									
Collection period (days)	30.7	53.3	84.0	34.3	57.1	81.0	32.7	46.8	66.8
Sales to Inventory	141.6	47.6	16.7	114.1	36.6	21.8	55.7	23.7	15.6
Assets/Sales (%)	30.8	41.4	88.9	31.1	51.3	96.7	31.0	47.8	73.3
Sales/Net Working Capital	16.2	6.8	4.0	13.4	8.2	3.7	12.6	8.7	5.0
Accounts payable/Sales (%)	2.5	5.4	13.3	4.0	7.8	12.8	2.8	5.1	11.9
Profitability									
Return - Sales (%)	16.3	6.5	1.2	19.2	5.3	1.6	10.0	3.7	.7
Return - Assets (%)	31.9	11.4	1.7	16.6	10.4	3.6	11.6	7.7	.2
Return - Net Worth (%)	71.4	23.8	3.6	36.3	18.3	11.5	48.0	20.0	-2.9

Source: Dun & Bradstreet. Data in this table are copyright (c) 1999 of Dun & Bradstreet. Reprinted by special arrangement with D&B. *Note:* UQ stands for "Upper Quartile" and represents the top 25 percent of sample; MED stands for "Median"; and LQ stands for "Lower Quartile" and represents the lowest 25 percent.

COMPANY DIRECTORY

This chapter presents brief profiles of 1064 companies in the Broadcasting & Telecommunications sector. Companies are public, private, and elements of public companies ("public family members").

Each entry features the *D-U-N-S* access number for the company, the company name, its parent (if applicable), address, telephone, sales, employees, the company's primary SIC classification, a brief description of the company's business activity, and the name and title of its chairman, president, or other high-ranking officer. If the company is an exporter, importer, or both, the fact is indicated by the abbreviations EXP, IMP, and IMP EXP shown facing the *D-U-N-S* number.

Rankings of these companies are shown in Chapter 5. Additional financial data—on an aggregated, industry level—are shown in Chapter 3.

This product includes proprietary data of Dun & Bradstreet, Inc.

D-U-N-S 80-274-5240
1-800-RECONEX, INC.
2500 Industrial Ave, Hubbard, OR 97032
Phone: (503) 982-8000
Sales: $48,100,000   *Employees:* 125
Company Type: Private   *Employees here:* 92
SIC: 4813
   Telephone communications service
Todd Meislahn, President

D-U-N-S 60-587-0682
360 COMMUNICATIONS COMPANY
   (Parent: Alltel Corporation)
8725 W Higgins Rd, Chicago, IL 60631
Phone: (773) 399-2500
Sales: $305,600,000   *Employees:* 4,400
Company Type: Public Family Member   *Employees here:* 325
SIC: 4812
   Cellular telephone service
Dennis E Foster, President

D-U-N-S 13-192-3328
A & E TELEVISION NETWORKS
235 E 45th St, New York, NY 10017
Phone: (212) 210-1400
Sales: $46,500,000   *Employees:* 350
Company Type: Private   *Employees here:* 290
SIC: 4841
   Cable television service
Nickolas Davatzes, President

D-U-N-S 00-100-4670
A-R CABLE SERVICES INC.
   (Parent: CSC Holdings Inc)
420 Crossways Park Dr, Woodbury, NY 11797
Phone: (516) 364-8450
Sales: $120,355,000   *Employees:* 563
Company Type: Public Family Member   *Employees here:* 55
SIC: 4841
   Cable television service
Charles F Dolan, Chairman of the Board

D-U-N-S 00-257-6817   EXP
AAVID THERMAL PRODUCTS, INC.
   (Parent: Aavid Thermal Technologies)
1 Kool Path Oshea Indust, Laconia, NH 03246
Phone: (603) 528-3400
Sales: $134,619,000   *Employees:* 1,088
Company Type: Public   *Employees here:* 1,088
SIC: 3679
   Mfg thermal electronic components
Ronald F Borelli, President

D-U-N-S 00-787-5560
ABC INC
   (Parent: Walt Disney Company Inc)
77 W 66th St Rm 100, New York, NY 10023
Phone: (212) 456-7777
Sales: $2,554,200,000   *Employees:* 22,200
Company Type: Public Family Member   *Employees here:* 34
SIC: 4833
   TV & radio broadcasting produces cable TV programs
      publishes newspapers magazines trade journals shopping
      guides
John Iger, Chief Executive Officer

D-U-N-S 00-262-2434
ABC MONEY TRANSACTIONS, INC.
3538 W Walnut St, Garland, TX 75042
Phone: (972) 272-2253

Sales: $40,000,000   *Employees:* 30
Company Type: Private   *Employees here:* 6
SIC: 4822
   Telegraph communications
John T Vu, President

D-U-N-S 79-793-7232
ABRACON CORPORATION
125 Columbia, Aliso Viejo, CA 92656
Phone: (949) 448-7070
Sales: $50,000,000   *Employees:* 75
Company Type: Private   *Employees here:* 75
SIC: 3679
   Mfg crystals oscillators & inductors
Christophe Polley, Managing Partner

D-U-N-S 18-481-1545
ACC LONG DISTANCE CORP
   (Parent: ACC Corp)
400 West Ave, Rochester, NY 14611
Phone: (716) 987-3000
Sales: $308,767,000   *Employees:* 250
Company Type: Public Family Member   *Employees here:* 162
SIC: 4813
   Telecommunications company
Alex Volta, President

D-U-N-S 14-475-4959
ACCESS COMMUNICATIONS INC.
215 S State St Ste 1000, Salt Lake City, UT 84111
Phone: (801) 363-9600
Sales: $85,900,000   *Employees:* 300
Company Type: Private   *Employees here:* 150
SIC: 4813
   Telephone long distance service
James R Greenbaum Jr, Chairman of the Board

D-U-N-S 96-789-1789
ACI COMMUNICATIONS INC.
1060 8th Ave Ste 209, San Diego, CA 92101
Phone: (619) 233-5719
Sales: $48,800,000   *Employees:* 385
Company Type: Private   *Employees here:* 300
SIC: 4813
   Telephone communications
Christophe G Bucci, President

D-U-N-S 18-339-4626   EXP
ACT NETWORKS INC.
188 Camino Ruiz, Camarillo, CA 93012
Phone: (805) 388-2474
Sales: $54,964,000   *Employees:* 242
Company Type: Public   *Employees here:* 110
SIC: 3661
   Mfg communications equipment
Martin Woll, Chief Financial Officer

D-U-N-S 15-381-6491   EXP
ACTIVE VOICE CORPORATION
2901 3rd Ave Ste 500, Seattle, WA 98121
Phone: (206) 441-4700
Sales: $53,151,000   *Employees:* 336
Company Type: Public   *Employees here:* 278
SIC: 3661
   Mfg & develops call processing systems
Frank Costa, President

D-U-N-S 15-415-2904   EXP
ADC BROADBAND COMMUNICATIONS
   (Parent: ADC Telecommunications Inc)
999 Research Pkwy, Meriden, CT 06450
Phone: (203) 630-5700

Sales: $37,300,000   *Employees:* 390
Company Type: Public Family Member   *Employees here:* 370
SIC: 3661
    Mfg telephone/telegraph dvcs
Vivek Ragavan, President

D-U-N-S 00-624-9312   EXP
ADC TELECOMMUNICATIONS, INC.
12501 Whitewater Dr, Hopkins, MN 55343
Phone: (612) 938-8080
Sales: $1,379,678,000   *Employees:* 8,000
Company Type: Public   *Employees here:* 2,300
SIC: 3661
    Mfg transmission networking & broadband connectivity
     products
Vivek Ragavan, President

D-U-N-S 06-365-2341
ADELPHIA COMMUNICATIONS CORP
Main At Water St, Coudersport, PA 16915
Phone: (814) 274-9830
Sales: $528,442,000   *Employees:* 3,895
Company Type: Public   *Employees here:* 350
SIC: 4841
    Cable television system
Timothy J Rigas, Chief Financial Officer

D-U-N-S 80-528-9451
ADFLEX SOLUTIONS, INC.
2001 W Chandler Blvd, Chandler, AZ 85224
Phone: (602) 963-4584
Sales: $213,878,000   *Employees:* 5,254
Company Type: Public   *Employees here:* 709
SIC: 3679
    Mfg electronic interconnection products
Rolando C Esteverena, Chairman of the Board

D-U-N-S 14-787-1412   EXP
ADTRAN INC.
901 Explorer Blvd NW, Huntsville, AL 35806
Phone: (256) 971-8000
Sales: $265,335,000   *Employees:* 1,008
Company Type: Public   *Employees here:* 969
SIC: 3661
    Mfg digital telephone transmission equipment
Mark C Smith, Chairman of the Board

D-U-N-S 08-125-5788   EXP
ADVANCED CIRCUIT TECHNOLOGY
   (Parent: Amphenol Corporation)
100 Northeastern Blvd, Nashua, NH 03062
Phone: (603) 880-6000
Sales: $30,000,000   *Employees:* 270
Company Type: Public Family Member   *Employees here:* 270
SIC: 3679
    Mfg sculptured & flexible printed circuits
Joseph A Roberts, Chief Executive Officer

D-U-N-S 00-926-4271
ADVANCED COMMUNICATIONS GROUP
390 S Woods Mill Rd, Chesterfield, MO 63017
Phone: (314) 205-8668
Sales: $73,900,000   *Employees:* 580
Company Type: Private   *Employees here:* 175
SIC: 4813
    Telephone communications
Richard O Neal, Acting Ceo

D-U-N-S 18-117-5597
ADVANCED COMMUNICATIONS SYSTEMS
10089 Lee Hwy, Fairfax, VA 22030
Phone: (703) 934-8130

Sales: $107,752,000   *Employees:* 1,850
Company Type: Public   *Employees here:* 200
SIC: 4899
    Communication systems information technology system
     integration and products
George Robinson, President

D-U-N-S 02-119-2422   EXP
ADVANCED ENERGY INDUSTRIES
1625 Sharp Point Dr, Fort Collins, CO 80525
Phone: (970) 407-4670
Sales: $141,923,000   *Employees:* 1,059
Company Type: Public   *Employees here:* 900
SIC: 3679
    Mfg electronic power supplies & controls
Douglas A Schatz, Chairman of the Board

D-U-N-S 78-901-9106   EXP
ADVANCED FIBRE COMMUNICATIONS
1 Willowbrook Ct, Petaluma, CA 94954
Phone: (707) 794-7700
Sales: $267,858,000   *Employees:* 800
Company Type: Public   *Employees here:* 750
SIC: 3661
    Mfg telecommunication systems
Donald Green, Chairman of the Board

D-U-N-S 07-191-4048
ADVENTIST MEDIA CENTER, INC.
101 W Cochran St, Simi Valley, CA 93065
Phone: (805) 373-7777
Sales: $42,619,000   *Employees:* 150
Company Type: Private   *Employees here:* 140
SIC: 4833
    Television and radio production
Glenn Aufderhar, President

D-U-N-S 92-922-8351
AERIAL COMMUNICATIONS INC.
   (Parent: Telephone and Data Systems)
8410 W Bryn Mawr Ave, Chicago, IL 60631
Phone: (773) 399-4200
Sales: $55,952,000   *Employees:* 500
Company Type: Public   *Employees here:* 300
SIC: 4812
    Telephone & communications services
Don Warkentin, President

D-U-N-S 15-557-5095
AEROFLEX LABORATORIES INC.
   (Parent: Aeroflex Inc)
35 S Service Rd, Plainview, NY 11803
Phone: (516) 694-6700
Sales: $54,371,000   *Employees:* 425
Company Type: Public Family Member   *Employees here:* 425
SIC: 3679
    Manufactures infrared scanning devices electric motors
     microcircuits synthesizers microprocessors & multichip
     modules
Leonard Borow, President

D-U-N-S 00-342-1310
AERONAUTICAL RADIO INC.
   (Parent: Arinc Incorporated)
2551 Riva Rd, Annapolis, MD 21401
Phone: (410) 266-4000
Sales: $63,000,000   *Employees:* 632
Company Type: Private   *Employees here:* 421
SIC: 4812
    Owns & operates essential air/ground voice & data
     communication networks
James L Pierce, Chairman of the Board

D-U-N-S 14-716-2069
AFFILIATED REGIONAL COMM
1440 S Sepulveda Blvd, Los Angeles, CA 90025
Phone: (310) 444-8123
Sales: $115,041,000   *Employees:* 225
Company Type: Private   *Employees here:* 25
SIC: 4841
   Sports cable network
Andy Hubsch, Treasurer

D-U-N-S 36-183-2637   EXP
AG COMMUNICATION SYSTEMS CORP
   (Parent: Lucent Technologies Inc)
2500 W Utopia Rd, Phoenix, AZ 85027
Phone: (602) 582-7000
Sales: $442,346,000   *Employees:* 2,400
Company Type: Public Family Member   *Employees here:* 1,400
SIC: 3661
   Develops mfgs & markets advanced digital central-office
     switching sys for telephone companies private networks &
     gov agencies
Jeffrey W Siegel, President

D-U-N-S 10-872-5003
AIRTOUCH CELLULAR
   (Parent: Airtouch Communications)
2999 Oak Rd Ste 700, Walnut Creek, CA 94596
Phone: (925) 210-3900
Sales: $187,700,000   *Employees:* 2,700
Company Type: Public Family Member   *Employees here:* 200
SIC: 4812
   Cellular telephone services
C L Cox, President

D-U-N-S 19-620-7930
AIRTOUCH COMMUNICATIONS
1 California St, San Francisco, CA 94111
Phone: (415) 658-2000
Sales: $3,594,000,000   *Employees:* 8,800
Company Type: Public   *Employees here:* 100
SIC: 4812
   Wireless communications services
Sam Ginn, Chairman of the Board

D-U-N-S 61-715-5809
AIRTOUCH PAGING OF TEXAS
   (Parent: Airtouch Communications)
12221 Merit Dr Ste 800, Dallas, TX 75251
Phone: (972) 860-3210
Sales: $86,000,000   *Employees:* 1,234
Company Type: Public Family Member   *Employees here:* 55
SIC: 4812
   Paging services & ret pagers
Charlie E Jackson, President

D-U-N-S 04-459-3515
ALASCOM INC.
   (Parent: AT&T Corp)
210 E Bluff Dr, Anchorage, AK 99501
Phone: (907) 264-7000
Sales: $265,087,000   *Employees:* 624
Company Type: Public Family Member   *Employees here:* 500
SIC: 4813
   Telephone communication services
Gerald De Fransisco, President

D-U-N-S 16-098-9919   EXP
ALCATEL DATA NETWORKS, INC.
44983 Knoll Sq, Ashburn, VA 20147
Phone: (703) 724-2000

Sales: $145,000,000   *Employees:* 385
Company Type: Private   *Employees here:* 285
SIC: 3663
   Mfg & services data communication equipment
Jacques Dunogue, Chairman of the Board

D-U-N-S 78-235-2793   EXP
ALCATEL NETWORK SYSTEMS, INC.
   (Parent: Alcatel USA Corp)
1225 Alma Rd, Richardson, TX 75081
Phone: (214) 996-5000
Sales: $1,500,000,000   *Employees:* 5,000
Company Type: Private   *Employees here:* 2,500
SIC: 3661
   Mfg & develops communication equipment
Krish Prabhu, Chief Executive Officer

D-U-N-S 08-365-4947   EXP
ALCATEL USA, INC.
1000 Coit Rd, Plano, TX 75075
Phone: (972) 519-3000
Sales: $639,900,000   *Employees:* 6,681
Company Type: Private   *Employees here:* 4,500
SIC: 3661
   Mfg & installation of telephone switching systems &
     transmission equipment
Krish Prabu, President

D-U-N-S 96-488-3557
ALERT MARKETING INC.
258 Promenade Cir, Lake Mary, FL 32746
Phone: (407) 333-2112
Sales: $108,000,000   *Employees:* 7
Company Type: Private   *Employees here:* 7
SIC: 4813
   Telecommunications product marketing
Michael Battistelli, President

D-U-N-S 13-050-4384   EXP
ALESIS STUDIO ELECTRONICS
1633 26th St, Santa Monica, CA 90404
Phone: (310) 255-3400
Sales: $84,730,000   *Employees:* 230
Company Type: Private   *Employees here:* 230
SIC: 3651
   Mfg sound equipment
Keith Barr, Chairman of the Board

D-U-N-S 00-696-9752
ALIANT COMMUNICATIONS CO.
   (Parent: Aliant Communications Inc)
1440 M St, Lincoln, NE 68508
Phone: (402) 474-2211
Sales: $194,606,000   *Employees:* 1,104
Company Type: Public Family Member   *Employees here:* 400
SIC: 4813
   Telephone utility
Frank H Hilsabeck, President

D-U-N-S 06-673-7990
ALIANT SYSTEMS INC.
   (Parent: Aliant Communications Inc)
2201 Winthrop Rd, Lincoln, NE 68502
Phone: (402) 486-7200
Sales: $34,000,000   *Employees:* 165
Company Type: Public Family Member   *Employees here:* 105
SIC: 4813
   Provides long distance service
Richard Mc Laughlin, President

D-U-N-S 05-861-0890
ALLBRITTON COMMUNICATIONS CO.
  (Parent: Perpetual Corporation)
808 17th St NW Ste 300, Washington, DC 20006
Phone: (202) 789-2130
Sales: $155,573,000
Company Type: Private   *Employees:* 770
SIC: 4833   *Employees here:* 16
  Television broadcasting and production
Robert L Allbritton, President

D-U-N-S 04-252-3316
ALLEN TELECOM INC.
25101 Chagrin Blvd, Cleveland, OH 44122
Phone: (216) 765-5800
Sales: $432,508,000   *Employees:* 3,300
Company Type: Public   *Employees here:* 20
SIC: 3663
  Manufactures mobile communications equipment & truck
  products
Robert G Paul, President

D-U-N-S 04-101-4242
ALLIEDSIGNAL TECHNICAL SVCS
  (Parent: Alliedsignal Inc)
1 Bendix Rd, Columbia, MD 21045
Phone: (410) 964-7000
Sales: $852,200,000   *Employees:* 7,000
Company Type: Public Family Member   *Employees here:* 600
SIC: 4899
  Installs operates & maintains satellite & shuttle tracking
  stations & provides field engineering services
Ivan Stern, Chairman of the Board

D-U-N-S 10-281-5537
ALLSUP ENTERPRISES, INC.
2112 Thornton St, Clovis, NM 88101
Phone: (505) 769-2311
Sales: $102,000,000   *Employees:* 1,238
Company Type: Private   *Employees here:* 4
SIC: 4832
  Stock holding company
Lonnie Allsup, President

D-U-N-S 13-974-2134
ALLTEL COMMUNICATIONS, INC.
  (Parent: Alltel Corporation)
1 Allied Dr, Little Rock, AR 72202
Phone: (501) 661-8100
Sales: $540,000,000   *Employees:* 1,060
Company Type: Public Family Member   *Employees here:* 191
SIC: 4812
  Cellular mobile phone & paging service
Michael T Flynn, President

D-U-N-S 00-790-2802
ALLTEL CORPORATION
1 Allied Dr, Little Rock, AR 72202
Phone: (501) 905-8000
Sales: $5,194,008,000   *Employees:* 20,000
Company Type: Public   *Employees here:* 500
SIC: 4813
  Telephone utility & whol communications equipment and
  other
Joe T Ford, Chairman of the Board

D-U-N-S 00-985-9059
ALLTEL NEW YORK INC.
  (Parent: Alltel Corporation)
201 E 4th St, Jamestown, NY 14701
Phone: (716) 661-5689

Sales: $49,881,000   *Employees:* 297
Company Type: Public Family Member   *Employees here:* 219
SIC: 4813
  Telephone communications
J M Johnson, President

D-U-N-S 00-791-1985
ALLTEL PENNSYLVANIA, INC.
  (Parent: Alltel Corporation)
1 Allied Dr, Little Rock, AR 72202
Phone: (501) 661-8000
Sales: $64,400,000   *Employees:* 506
Company Type: Public Family Member   *Employees here:* 138
SIC: 4813
  Local & long distance telephone utility
George Page, President

D-U-N-S 00-103-0311
ALPHA INDUSTRIES INC.
20 Sylvan Rd, Woburn, MA 01801
Phone: (781) 935-5150
Sales: $116,881,000   *Employees:* 801
Company Type: Public   *Employees here:* 565
SIC: 3679
  Mfg microwave devices & components
George S Kariotis, Chairman of the Board

D-U-N-S 15-450-3411
ALPINE ELECTRONICS MANUFACTURING OF AMERICA
  (Parent: Alpine Electronics of America)
421 N Emerson Ave, Greenwood, IN 46143
Phone: (317) 881-7700
Sales: $146,976,000   *Employees:* 1,100
Company Type: Private   *Employees here:* 250
SIC: 3651
  Mfg car stereos & assembly of electronic components
Bernard Pierce, President

D-U-N-S 62-333-8357   EXP
ALSTOM SIGNALING INC.
150 Sawgrass Dr, Rochester, NY 14620
Phone: (716) 783-2000
Sales: $120,000,000   *Employees:* 560
Company Type: Private   *Employees here:* 370
SIC: 3669
  Mfg communications equipment
William Darling, President

D-U-N-S 94-894-8930   EXP
ALTEON NETWORKS INC.
50 Great Oaks Blvd, San Jose, CA 95119
Phone: (408) 574-5500
Sales: $30,000,000   *Employees:* 125
Company Type: Private   *Employees here:* 100
SIC: 3663
  Mfg gigabit ethernet products
Dominic Orr, President

D-U-N-S 14-722-1006
AMERICA ONLINE INC.
22000 Aol Way, Sterling, VA 20166
Phone: (703) 448-8700
Sales: $2,600,000,000   *Employees:* 8,500
Company Type: Public   *Employees here:* 500
SIC: 4813
  Computer communication services
Stephen M Case, Chairman of the Board

D-U-N-S 00-697-9819
AMERICAN BROADCASTING COMPANIES
  (Parent: ABC Holding Company Inc)
77 W 66th St, New York, NY 10023
Phone: (212) 456-7777

Sales: $4,142,000,000
Company Type: Public Family Member
SIC: 4833
   Tv network broadcasting
David Westin, President

Employees: 8,000
Employees here: 1,000

D-U-N-S 09-745-3419
AMERICAN CABLESYSTEMS OF MASS
   (*Parent:* MediaOne of Delaware Inc)
180 Greenleaf Ave, Portsmouth, NH 03801
Phone: (603) 683-5500
Sales: $107,300,000
Company Type: Public Family Member
SIC: 4841
   Cable television service
Amos B Hostetter, Chief Executive Officer

Employees: 800
Employees here: 50

D-U-N-S 18-681-8241
AMERICAN CELLULAR COMMUNICATIONS CORP
   (*Parent:* Bellsouth Cellular Corp)
1100 Peachtree St Ne, Atlanta, GA 30309
Phone: (404) 249-4000
Sales: $42,000,000
Company Type: Public Family Member
SIC: 4812
   Cellular telephone services
Robert J Frame, Chief Executive Officer

Employees: 600
Employees here: 50

D-U-N-S 78-140-1849
AMERICAN CELLULAR CORPORATION
1375 E Woodfield Rd, Schaumburg, IL 60173
Phone: (847) 843-9081
Sales: $181,000,000
Company Type: Public
SIC: 4812
   Cellular telephone service
Steven Price, President

Employees: 700
Employees here: 20

D-U-N-S 79-785-9832
AMERICAN COMMUNICATIONS NETWORK
100 W Big Beaver Rd, Troy, MI 48084
Phone: (248) 528-2500
Sales: $98,072,000
Company Type: Private
SIC: 4813
   Long distance telecommunications paging service & internet
    services
David J Thomas, Chief Executive Officer

Employees: 250
Employees here: 200

D-U-N-S 01-444-3449
AMERICAN GATEWAY TELECOM
5151 San Felipe St, Houston, TX 77056
Phone: (713) 621-5255
Sales: $50,000,000
Company Type: Private
SIC: 4813
   Long distance telecommunications
Arnold Salinas, President

Employees: 3
Employees here: 3

D-U-N-S 01-021-2207
AMERICAN HOLDINGS LP
1717 E Buckeye Ave, Spokane, WA 99207
Phone: (509) 484-4931
Sales: $38,025,000
Company Type: Private
SIC: 4841
   Cable television
Ken Watts, General Manager

Employees: 150
Employees here: 150

D-U-N-S 15-729-2327
AMERICAN LONG LINES INC.
410 Horsham Rd, Horsham, PA 19044
Phone: (215) 784-0900

Sales: $40,000,000
Company Type: Private
SIC: 4813
   Long distance telephone co
Alan Widra, President

Employees: 40
Employees here: 30

D-U-N-S 60-678-2928
AMERICAN MOBILE SATELLITE CORP
10802 Parkridge Blvd, Reston, VA 20191
Phone: (703) 758-6000
Sales: $44,214,000
Company Type: Public
SIC: 4899
   Communication services
Gary Parsons, Chairman of the Board

Employees: 300
Employees here: 250

D-U-N-S 19-368-7241
AMERICAN MOVIE CLASSICS CO.
150 Crossways Park Dr W, Woodbury, NY 11797
Phone: (516) 364-2222
Sales: $139,203,000
Company Type: Private
SIC: 4841
   Non-commercial cable television service
Katie Mcenroe, President

Employees: 195
Employees here: 68

D-U-N-S 17-762-3998
AMERICAN NETWORK EXCHANGE INC.
   (*Parent:* Amnex Inc)
100 W Lucerne Cir Ste 500, Orlando, FL 32801
Phone: (407) 246-1234
Sales: $75,909,000
Company Type: Public Family Member
SIC: 4813
   Telecommunication service providing long distance &
    operator service
Peter Izzo, President

Employees: 224
Employees here: 66

D-U-N-S 60-262-8166
AMERICAN TELECASTING, INC.
5575 Tech Center Dr, Colorado Springs, CO 80919
Phone: (719) 260-5533
Sales: $59,031,000
Company Type: Public
SIC: 4841
   Cable & subscription television services
Robert D Hostetler, President

Employees: 448
Employees here: 85

D-U-N-S 92-639-6870
AMERICAN TOWER CORP
116 Huntington Ave, Boston, MA 02116
Phone: (617) 375-7500
Sales: $61,000,000
Company Type: Public
SIC: 4899
   Owner/operator of radio & television towers
Steven Dodge, Chairman of the Board

Employees: 500
Employees here: 10

D-U-N-S 10-898-9690
AMERICOM GROUP
1300 Bellona Ave, Lutherville Timonium, MD 21093
Phone: (410) 823-1300
Sales: $44,000,000
Company Type: Private
SIC: 4812
   Outsourcing vendor to wireless telecommunications carriers
    & distributor of wireless products
R M Gill, President

Employees: 325
Employees here: 60

D-U-N-S 10-333-0684
AMERITECH CORPORATION
30 S Wacker Dr Fl 34, Chicago, IL 60606
Phone: (312) 750-5000

Sales: $15,998,000,000 *Employees:* 74,359
Company Type: Public *Employees here:* 370
SIC: 4813
   Telephone service publishes directories markets
   telecommunication equipment finance leasing & cellular
   mobile service & other
Neil E Cox, President

D-U-N-S 10-400-6085
AMERITECH MOBILE COMMUNICATIONS
   (Parent: Ameritech Corporation)
2000 W Ameritech Center D, Hoffman Estates, IL 60195
Phone: (847) 706-7600
Sales: $200,000,000 *Employees:* 4,400
Company Type: Public Family Member *Employees here:* 500
SIC: 4812
   Cellular radio telephone communications & paging services
Herb Hribar, President

D-U-N-S 62-408-6203
AMERIVISION COMMUNICATIONS
5900 Mosteller Dr, Oklahoma City, OK 73112
Phone: (405) 600-3800
Sales: $130,000,000 *Employees:* 750
Company Type: Private *Employees here:* 750
SIC: 4813
   Long distance telephone service provider
Stephen D Halliday, President

D-U-N-S 78-279-2659
AMERIX ELECTRONIC INC.
431 E Grand Ave, El Segundo, CA 90245
Phone: (310) 322-2600
Sales: $38,437,000 *Employees:* 8
Company Type: Private *Employees here:* 8
SIC: 3679
   Mfg satellite video receivers and circuit debuggers and whol
   electronic components
Soon O Kim, President

D-U-N-S 14-750-2306
AMNEX INC.
145 Huguenot St Ste 401, New Rochelle, NY 10801
Phone: (914) 235-1003
Sales: $116,498,000 *Employees:* 344
Company Type: Public *Employees here:* 6
SIC: 4813
   Telecommunication services & wholesales voice response
   telecommunication systems
Alan J Rossi, Chairman of the Board

D-U-N-S 19-704-7665
AMPHENOL INTERCONNECT PRODUCTS
   (Parent: Amphenol Corporation)
358 Hall Ave, Wallingford, CT 06492
Phone: (203) 265-8900
Sales: $55,000,000 *Employees:* 500
Company Type: Public Family Member *Employees here:* 5
SIC: 3679
   Manufactures electronic interconnect assemblies
Martin H Loeffler, President

D-U-N-S 78-667-3947
ANABA AUDIO INTERNATIONAL INC.
3116 E Via Mondo, Compton, CA 90221
Phone: (310) 223-0400
Sales: $42,000,000 *Employees:* 30
Company Type: Private *Employees here:* 30
SIC: 3651
   Mfg car audio equipment
Sameer Aboabdo, President

D-U-N-S 04-235-2922 EXP
ANAREN MICROWAVE INC.
6635 Kirkville Rd, East Syracuse, NY 13057
Phone: (315) 432-8909
Sales: $37,449,000 *Employees:* 285
Company Type: Public *Employees here:* 285
SIC: 3679
   Mfg electronic microwave components
Hugh A Hair, Chairman

D-U-N-S 00-517-7084
ANDREW CORPORATION
10500 W 153rd St, Orland Park, IL 60462
Phone: (708) 349-3300
Sales: $852,915,000 *Employees:* 3,261
Company Type: Public *Employees here:* 1,306
SIC: 3663
   Mfg communication systems equipment
Thomas E Charlton, President

D-U-N-S 80-719-6852 EXP
ANTEC CORPORATION (DEL)
5720 Peachtree Pkwy, Norcross, GA 30092
Phone: (770) 441-0007
Sales: $480,078,000 *Employees:* 1,893
Company Type: Public *Employees here:* 100
SIC: 3663
   Manufactures and wholesales cable television equipment and
   supplies
John M Egan, Chairman of the Board

D-U-N-S 02-609-8640 IMP EXP
ANTRONIX INC.
440 Forsgate Dr, Cranbury, NJ 08512
Phone: (609) 395-1390
Sales: $36,000,000 *Employees:* 600
Company Type: Private *Employees here:* 30
SIC: 3663
   Mfg & whol cable television equipment including electronic
   converters & amplifiers
Daniel Tang, President

D-U-N-S 10-162-9988
APPLIED INNOVATION INC.
5800 Innovation Dr, Dublin, OH 43016
Phone: (614) 798-2000
Sales: $46,661,000 *Employees:* 240
Company Type: Public *Employees here:* 200
SIC: 3661
   Mfg data switching systems & electronic communications
   equipment
Gerard B Moersdorf Jr, President

D-U-N-S 00-834-2198 EXP
APPLIED MAGNETICS CORPORATION
75 Robin Hill Rd, Goleta, CA 93117
Phone: (805) 683-5353
Sales: $183,597,000 *Employees:* 4,700
Company Type: Public *Employees here:* 1,000
SIC: 3679
   Mfg computer disk drive components
Craig Crisman, Chairman of the Board

D-U-N-S 17-482-9663
APPLIED SCIENCE & TECHNOLOGY
35 Cabot Rd, Woburn, MA 01801
Phone: (781) 933-5560
Sales: $83,436,000 *Employees:* 355
Company Type: Public *Employees here:* 105
SIC: 3679
   Mfg microwave components
Dr Richard S Post, President

D-U-N-S 13-163-3125
APPLIED SIGNAL TECHNOLOGY INC.
400 W California Ave, Sunnyvale, CA 94086
Phone: (408) 749-1888
Sales: $110,087,000   *Employees:* 617
Company Type: Public   *Employees here:* 572
SIC: 3663
  Mfg signal processing equipment
Gary L Yancey, Chairman of the Board

D-U-N-S 79-301-7328
APUNET
833 E Arapaho Rd, Richardson, TX 75081
Phone: (972) 234-0055
Sales: $51,000,000   *Employees:* 4
Company Type: Private   *Employees here:* 4
SIC: 4813
  Long distance telephone service
Michael Clifford, Owner

D-U-N-S 15-519-5951
ARCH COMMUNICATIONS GROUP INC.
1800 W Park Dr Ste 250, Westborough, MA 01581
Phone: (508) 898-0962
Sales: $396,841,000   *Employees:* 2,800
Company Type: Public   *Employees here:* 52
SIC: 4812
  Paging service & retails pagers
C E Baker Jr, Chairman of the Board

D-U-N-S 04-148-1417
ARKANSAS DEMOCRAT GAZETTE
  (Parent: Camden News Publishing Co)
115 E Capital & Scott Sts, Little Rock, AR 72201
Phone: (501) 378-3400
Sales: $39,800,000   *Employees:* 300
Company Type: Private   *Employees here:* 10
SIC: 4841
  Cable television system & radio stations
Walter E Hussman Jr, Chairman of the Board

D-U-N-S 10-850-0810   EXP
ARTESYN NORTH AMERICA INC.
  (Parent: Artesyn Technologies Inc)
7575 Market Place Dr, Eden Prairie, MN 55344
Phone: (612) 941-1100
Sales: $228,168,000   *Employees:* 2,848
Company Type: Public Family Member *Employees here:* 102
SIC: 3679
  Mfg electronic components electrical repair
Lou Debartelo, Chairman of the Board

D-U-N-S 04-493-0139   EXP
ARTESYN TECHNOLOGIES INC.
7900 Glades Rd Ste 500, Boca Raton, FL 33434
Phone: (561) 451-1000
Sales: $527,236,000   *Employees:* 6,900
Company Type: Public   *Employees here:* 16
SIC: 3679
  Mfg power conversion products
Joseph M O Donnell, Chairman of the Board

D-U-N-S 13-924-5831
ARVIG TELCOM INC.
  (Parent: TDS Telecommunication Corp)
301 S Westfield Rd, Madison, WI 53717
Phone: (608) 845-4000
Sales: $40,000,000   *Employees:* 75
Company Type: Public Family Member   *Employees here:* 3
SIC: 4813
  Telephone company
Vince Reed, President

D-U-N-S 19-706-4066
ASANTE TECHNOLOGIES, INC.
821 Fox Ln, San Jose, CA 95131
Phone: (408) 435-8388
Sales: $51,433,000   *Employees:* 190
Company Type: Public   *Employees here:* 170
SIC: 3661
  Mfg local area network products
Wilson Wong, President

D-U-N-S 93-248-5030
ASCENT ENTERTAINMENT GROUP
1200 17th St Ste 2800, Denver, CO 80202
Phone: (303) 626-7000
Sales: $428,500,000   *Employees:* 1,021
Company Type: Public   *Employees here:* 20
SIC: 4841
  On-demand in-room entertainment satellite support svcs
    professional sports franchises & motion picture/television
    production
Charles Lyons, Chairman of the Board

D-U-N-S 60-543-8423
ASTEC AMERICA INC.
5810 Van Allen Way, Carlsbad, CA 92008
Phone: (760) 757-1880
Sales: $357,000,000   *Employees:* 2,000
Company Type: Private   *Employees here:* 110
SIC: 3679
  Mfg electronic equipment
Jay L Geldmacher, President

D-U-N-S 14-993-2188
AT&T COMMUNICATIONS OF NJ
  (Parent: AT&T Corp)
295 N Maple Ave, Basking Ridge, NJ 07920
Phone: (908) 221-2000
Sales: $514,000,000   *Employees:* 4,004
Company Type: Public Family Member *Employees here:* 4,000
SIC: 4813
  Long-distance telephone communications
Robert E Allen, President

D-U-N-S 00-698-0080
AT&T CORP
32 Avenue Of The Americas, New York, NY 10013
Phone: (212) 387-5400
Sales: $53,223,000,000   *Employees:* 118,900
Company Type: Public   *Employees here:* 1,500
SIC: 4813
  Telecommunications services
C M Armstrong, Chairman of the Board

D-U-N-S 13-059-8238
AT&T WIRELESS SERVICES INC.
  (Parent: AT&T Corp)
5400 Carillon Pt, Kirkland, WA 98033
Phone: (425) 827-4500
Sales: $4,330,000,000   *Employees:* 13,000
Company Type: Public Family Member *Employees here:* 600
SIC: 4812
  Cellular telephone & messaging services
Daniel Hesse, President

D-U-N-S 94-302-3135
AT HOME CORP
425 Broadway St, Redwood City, CA 94063
Phone: (650) 569-5000
Sales: $48,045,000   *Employees:* 329
Company Type: Public   *Employees here:* 329
SIC: 4813
  Internet service provider
Kenneth A Goldman, Chief Financial Officer

D-U-N-S 93-771-3725
ATG INTERNATIONAL INC.
1260 S Simpson Cir, Anaheim, CA 92806
Phone: (714) 991-9080
Sales: $60,000,000
Company Type: Private
SIC: 4813   *Employees:* 15
Telephone communications   *Employees here:* 15
Michael Banyan, President

D-U-N-S 61-506-5802
ATLANTIC CELLULAR COMPANY L P
15 Westminster St Ste 830, Providence, RI 02903
Phone: (401) 458-1900
Sales: $45,087,000
Company Type: Private   *Employees:* 160
SIC: 4812   *Employees here:* 18
Cellular phone carriers
Charles C Townsend III, Chairman of the Board

D-U-N-S 18-356-5613
ATLANTIC TELE-NETWORK INC.
Chase Fincl Ctr Fl 2, Christiansted, VI 00821
Phone: (340) 777-8000
Sales: $235,230,000
Company Type: Public   *Employees:* NA
SIC: 4813   *Employees here:* NA
Telephone communications
Cornelius P Prior, Chairman of the Board

D-U-N-S 00-691-9484
ATLANTIC-WASHINGTON BELL DC
(Parent: Bell Atlantic Corporation)
1710 H St NW, Washington, DC 20006
Phone: (202) 392-1234
Sales: $611,222,000
Company Type: Public Family Member *Employees:* 1,500
SIC: 4813   *Employees here:* 867
Telephone service
Judith H Mopsik, Executive Director

D-U-N-S 01-678-3347
ATU TELECOMMUNICATIONS
(Parent: Anchorage Municipality Of)
600 Telephone Ave, Anchorage, AK 99503
Phone: (907) 564-1414
Sales: $110,000,000
Company Type: Private   *Employees:* 620
SIC: 4813   *Employees here:* 620
Telecommunication services
Thomas C Edrington, Chief Executive Officer

D-U-N-S 07-664-6785   EXP
AUGAT COMMUNICATION PRODUCTS
(Parent: Thomas & Betts International)
23315 66th Ave S, Kent, WA 98032
Phone: (253) 854-9802
Sales: $64,457,000
Company Type: Public Family Member *Employees:* 325
SIC: 3663   *Employees here:* 270
Mfg telecommunication equipment
Larry Bostwick, Vice-President

D-U-N-S 61-064-1219   EXP
AUTO CLUB CELLULAR CORPORATION
828 Newtown Yardley Rd, Newtown, PA 18940
Phone: (215) 579-4985
Sales: $43,057,000
Company Type: Private   *Employees:* 242
SIC: 4812   *Employees here:* 239
Cellular telephone services
James J Shields, President

D-U-N-S 10-334-7886   EXP
AVT CORPORATION
11410 Ne 122nd Way, Kirkland, WA 98034
Phone: (425) 820-6000
Sales: $81,126,000
Company Type: Public   *Employees:* 325
SIC: 3661   *Employees here:* 130
Mfg call processing and unified message products
Tim Wudi, President

D-U-N-S 86-140-0315
AXIOM INC.
4000 Midlantic Dr, Mount Laurel, NJ 08054
Phone: (609) 866-1000
Sales: $33,007,000
Company Type: Public   *Employees:* 196
SIC: 3669   *Employees here:* 146
Mfg of billing data collection & traffic management solutions
for the telecommunications industry
C T Faulders III, Chairman of the Board

D-U-N-S 04-357-0142   EXP
AYDIN CORPORATION
700 Dresher Rd, Horsham, PA 19044
Phone: (215) 657-7510
Sales: $115,371,000
Company Type: Public   *Employees:* 1,200
SIC: 3663   *Employees here:* 10
Mfg telecommunication equipment & systems computer
equipment & systems & electronic warfare components
James Henderson, President

D-U-N-S 00-895-6807
BAHAKEL COMMUNICATIONS LTD
1 Television Pl, Charlotte, NC 28205
Phone: (704) 372-4434
Sales: $55,300,000
Company Type: Private   *Employees:* 500
SIC: 4833   *Employees here:* 60
Radio & television stations
Cy N Bahakel, President

D-U-N-S 78-595-3605
BBS HOLDINGS, INC.
(Parent: Bellsouth Telecommunications)
1800 Century Blvd Ne, Atlanta, GA 30345
Phone: (404) 235-3700
Sales: $673,600,000
Company Type: Public Family Member *Employees:* 5,246
SIC: 4813   *Employees here:* 3
Operates as a holding company
Roderick D Odom, Chief Executive Officer

D-U-N-S 60-206-5120
BEE TRONICS INC.
3960 Carmel Springs Way, San Diego, CA 92130
Phone: (619) 594-6063
Sales: $34,100,000
Company Type: Private   *Employees:* 400
SIC: 3663   *Employees here:* 400
Mfg radio/TV communication equipment management
consulting services radio/television repair
Bayard Rehkopf, President

D-U-N-S 79-972-2327
BEI SENSORS & SYSTEMS COMPANY
(Parent: BEI Technologies Inc)
13100 Telfair Ave, Sylmar, CA 91342
Phone: (818) 362-7151

Sales: $150,000,000
Employees: 977
Company Type: Public Family Member
Employees here: 150
SIC: 3679
   Mfg sensors other electronic components
Dr Asad Madni, President

D-U-N-S 17-759-9784
                          EXP
BEI TECHNOLOGIES INC.
1 Post St Ste 2500, San Francisco, CA 94104
Phone: (415) 956-4477
Sales: $101,539,000
Employees: 977
Company Type: Public
Employees here: 10
SIC: 3679
   Mfg advanced electronic products to control and drive the
     motion of machinery & equipment
Gary D Wrench, Chief Financial Officer

D-U-N-S 00-132-1389
BEL FUSE INC.
198 Van Vorst St 200, Jersey City, NJ 07302
Phone: (201) 432-0463
Sales: $73,531,000
Employees: 707
Company Type: Public
Employees here: 47
SIC: 3679
   Mfg electronic components electric fuses coils &
     transformers
Elliot Bernstein, Chairman of the Board

D-U-N-S 10-721-2169
BELL ATLANTIC CORPORATION
1095 Avenue Of The Americ, New York, NY 10036
Phone: (212) 395-2121
Sales: $30,193,900,000
Employees: 141,000
Company Type: Public
Employees here: 400
SIC: 4813
   Telecommunications services
Ivan G Seidenberg, President

D-U-N-S 12-267-9749
BELL ATLANTIC ENTERPRISES INTL
   (Parent: Bell Atlantic Investments Inc)
1717 Arch St Fl 29, Philadelphia, PA 19103
Phone: (215) 963-6700
Sales: $834,800,000
Employees: 6,500
Company Type: Public Family Member
Employees here: 67
SIC: 4813
   International telecommunications software whol cellular
     mobile telephone & paging services & computer
     maintenance
Lawrence Babbio Jr, Chairman of the Board

D-U-N-S 00-694-9895
BELL ATLANTIC-MARYLAND, INC.
   (Parent: Bell Atlantic Corporation)
1 E Pratt St Ste 8, Baltimore, MD 21202
Phone: (410) 539-9900
Sales: $2,047,900,000
Employees: 7,000
Company Type: Public Family Member
Employees here: 1,200
SIC: 4813
   Telephone network communication
Sherry F Bellamy, President

D-U-N-S 10-673-4213
BELL ATLANTIC NETWORK SERVICES
   (Parent: Bell Atlantic Corporation)
1310 N Courthouse Rd, Arlington, VA 22201
Phone: (703) 974-3000
Sales: $2,000,000,000
Employees: 8,539
Company Type: Public Family Member
Employees here: 1,800
SIC: 4813
   Telephone services
William Tomlinson, Asst Vice Pres

D-U-N-S 00-697-3762
BELL ATLANTIC-NEW JERSEY, INC.
   (Parent: Bell Atlantic Corporation)
540 Broad St, Newark, NJ 07102
Phone: (973) 649-9900
Sales: $3,753,900,000
Employees: 12,500
Company Type: Public Family Member
Employees here: 1,400
SIC: 4813
   Telecommunications svcs
William M Freeman, President

D-U-N-S 00-791-3171
BELL ATLANTIC-PENNSYLVANIA
   (Parent: Bell Atlantic Corporation)
1 Parkway, Philadelphia, PA 19102
Phone: (215) 466-9900
Sales: $3,320,500,000
Employees: 12,500
Company Type: Public Family Member
Employees here: 1,000
SIC: 4813
   Telephone communication service
Daniel Whelan, President

D-U-N-S 00-794-1081
BELL ATLANTIC-VIRGINIA, INC.
   (Parent: Bell Atlantic Corporation)
600 E Main St Ste 1000, Richmond, VA 23219
Phone: (804) 225-6300
Sales: $2,071,100,000
Employees: 6,500
Company Type: Public Family Member
Employees here: 440
SIC: 4813
   Telephone service
Edwin F Hall, Controller

D-U-N-S 78-265-7209
BELLSOUTH CELLULAR CORP
   (Parent: Bellsouth Mobile Systems Inc)
1100 W Peachtree St NW, Atlanta, GA 30309
Phone: (404) 847-3600
Sales: $805,300,000
Employees: 11,604
Company Type: Public Family Member
Employees here: 283
SIC: 4812
   Radiotelephone communications
C S Hamm, President

D-U-N-S 10-667-8006
BELLSOUTH CORPORATION
1155 Peachtree St Ne, Atlanta, GA 30309
Phone: (404) 249-2000
Sales: $23,123,000,000
Employees: 81,000
Company Type: Public
Employees here: 982
SIC: 4813
   Telecommunications services
Duane Ackerman, President

D-U-N-S 10-202-6754
BELLSOUTH MOBILITY INC.
   (Parent: Bellsouth Enterprises Inc)
5600 Glenridge Dr Ne, Atlanta, GA 30342
Phone: (404) 250-1123
Sales: $208,500,000
Employees: 3,000
Company Type: Public Family Member
Employees here: 10
SIC: 4812
   Cellular mobile telephone service
Mark Feidler, President

D-U-N-S 80-703-6041
BELLSOUTH PER COMMUNICATIONS
   (Parent: Bellsouth Enterprises Inc)
3353 Peachtree Rd Ne, Atlanta, GA 30326
Phone: (404) 841-2000

Sales: $150,000,000   *Employees:* 1,150
Company Type: Public Family Member   *Employees here:* 150
SIC: 4813
   Wireless telephone communications
Stephen A Brake, Chief Financial Officer

D-U-N-S 00-692-5333
BELLSOUTH TELECOMMUNICATIONS
   (Parent: Bellsouth Corporation)
675 West Peachtree St NW, Atlanta, GA 30308
Phone: (404) 529-8611
Sales: $16,622,000,000   *Employees:* 59,100
Company Type: Public Family Member   *Employees here:* 4,000
SIC: 4813
   Telecommunication
Mark L Feidler, President

D-U-N-S 78-418-3238
BEN M JACOBY
13 Woodlake Sq Ste 130, Houston, TX 77063
Phone: (713) 978-7361
Sales: $32,800,000   *Employees:* 260
Company Type: Private   *Employees here:* 260
SIC: 4813
   Communication resalers and rebuilders
Ben Jacoby, Owner

D-U-N-S 04-587-5218
BENEDEK BROADCASTING CORP.
   (Parent: Benedek Cmmunications Corp Del)
100 Park Ave, Rockford, IL 61101
Phone: (815) 987-5350
Sales: $127,073,000   *Employees:* 1,272
Company Type: Private   *Employees here:* 14
SIC: 4833
   Owner/operator of television stations
A R Benedek, Chairman of the Board

D-U-N-S 83-608-5779
BEST INTERNET INC.
   (Parent: Verio Inc)
5050 Blue Lake Dr Ste 100, Boca Raton, FL 33431
Phone: (561) 912-2402
Sales: $31,200,000   *Employees:* 248
Company Type: Public Family Member   *Employees here:* 140
SIC: 4813
   Internet service provider & world wide web hosting
Art Cahoon, Chief Executive Officer

D-U-N-S 78-279-9241
BET HOLDINGS INC.
1 Bates St NW, Washington, DC 20001
Phone: (202) 608-2000
Sales: $115,222,000   *Employees:* 435
Company Type: Public   *Employees here:* 300
SIC: 4841
   Cable television network
Robert L Johnson, Chairman of the Board

D-U-N-S 78-023-3409
BHC COMMUNICATIONS, INC.
   (Parent: Chris-Craft Industries Inc)
767 5th Ave Fl 46, New York, NY 10153
Phone: (212) 421-0200
Sales: $443,499,000   *Employees:* 1,055
Company Type: Public   *Employees here:* 9
SIC: 4833
   Television broadcasting
Herbert J Siegel, Chairman of the Board

D-U-N-S 09-869-8269
BLACK ENTERTAINMENT TELEVISION
   (Parent: Bet Holdings Inc)
1 Bates St NW, Washington, DC 20001
Phone: (202) 608-2000
Sales: $85,300,000   *Employees:* 350
Company Type: Public Family Member   *Employees here:* 20
SIC: 4841
   Cable television service
Robert L Johnson, Chairman of the Board

D-U-N-S 94-145-4456
BLACKSTONE CALLING CARD, INC.
7900 NW 36th St, Miami, FL 33166
Phone: (305) 639-9590
Sales: $61,000,000   *Employees:* 51
Company Type: Private   *Employees here:* 51
SIC: 4813
   Ret prepaid telephone calling cards
Luis Arias, President

D-U-N-S 00-213-6265   EXP
BLONDER-TONGUE LABORATORIES
1 Jake Brown Rd Ste 1, Old Bridge, NJ 08857
Phone: (732) 679-4000
Sales: $62,057,000   *Employees:* 587
Company Type: Public   *Employees here:* 582
SIC: 3663
   Mfg television and satellite distribution equipment
James Luksch, Chairman of the Board

D-U-N-S 13-178-8879   EXP
BOCA RESEARCH INC.
1377 Clint Moore Rd Ste 4, Boca Raton, FL 33487
Phone: (561) 997-6227
Sales: $70,207,000   *Employees:* 304
Company Type: Public   *Employees here:* 290
SIC: 3661
   Mfr modems & computer enhancement products
Anthony Zalenski, President

D-U-N-S 17-779-4450
BOEING CORINTH COMPANY
   (Parent: The Boeing Company)
7801 S Stemmons Fwy, Lake Dallas, TX 75065
Phone: (940) 497-7600
Sales: $121,900,000   *Employees:* 2,100
Company Type: Public Family Member   *Employees here:* 2,100
SIC: 3679
   Mfg electronic components
J B Self, General Manager

D-U-N-S 94-879-2031
BOGEN COMMUNICATIONS INTL
50 Spring St, Ramsey, NJ 07446
Phone: (201) 934-8500
Sales: $49,779,000   *Employees:* 196
Company Type: Private   *Employees here:* 107
SIC: 3661
   Develops manufactures and markets digital voice processing
      telecommunications peripherals and sound processing
      systems
Jonathan Guss, Chief Executive Officer

D-U-N-S 00-485-7660
BONNEVILLE INTERNATIONAL CORP
   (Parent: Deseret Management Corporation)
55 N 300 W Ste 800, Salt Lake City, UT 84180
Phone: (801) 575-7500

Sales: $90,500,000   *Employees:* 1,100
Company Type: Private   *Employees here:* 600
SIC: 4832
   Radio television broadcasting stations and television program production
Bruce T Reese, President

D-U-N-S 00-890-0102
BOOTH AMERICAN COMPANY
333 W Fort St Ste 1230, Detroit, MI 48226
Phone: (313) 202-3360
Sales: $79,700,000   *Employees:* 970
Company Type: Private   *Employees here:* 118
SIC: 4832
   Radio broadcasting & cable TV
John L Booth, Chairman of the Board

D-U-N-S 00-257-9431
BOSE CORPORATION
The Mountain, Framingham, MA 01701
Phone: (508) 879-7330
Sales: $850,000,000   *Employees:* 4,000
Company Type: Private   *Employees here:* 1,500
SIC: 3651
   Mfg high-fidelity stereo systems loudspeakers & automotive speaker systems
Dr Amar G Bose, Chairman of the Board

D-U-N-S 09-628-9657   EXP
BOSTON ACOUSTICS INC.
300 Jubilee Dr, Peabody, MA 01960
Phone: (978) 538-5000
Sales: $82,399,000   *Employees:* 260
Company Type: Public   *Employees here:* 230
SIC: 3651
   Mfg hi-fidelity speaker systems
Andrew Kotsatos, Chairman of the Board

D-U-N-S 12-228-5620
BRESNAN COMMUNICATIONS LP
709 Westchester Ave, White Plains, NY 10604
Phone: (914) 997-5656
Sales: $46,500,000   *Employees:* 350
Company Type: Private   *Employees here:* 11
SIC: 4841
   Cable television service
William J Bresnan, President

D-U-N-S 15-409-1961
BRITE VOICE SYSTEMS INC.
250 International Pkwy, Lake Mary, FL 32746
Phone: (407) 357-1000
Sales: $119,849,000   *Employees:* 681
Company Type: Public   *Employees here:* 119
SIC: 3661
   Mfg voice response & voice mail systems and services
Stanley Brannan, Chairman of the Board

D-U-N-S 92-789-6977
BRITTAN COMMUNICATIONS INTL
600 Jefferson St Ste 500, Houston, TX 77002
Phone: (713) 659-8700
Sales: $48,000,000   *Employees:* 150
Company Type: Private   *Employees here:* 150
SIC: 4813
   Long distance reseller
Jim G Edwards, President

D-U-N-S 79-331-7173
BRK BRANDS, INC.
   (Parent: First Alert Inc (del))
3920 Enterprise Ct, Aurora, IL 60504
Phone: (630) 851-7330

Sales: $186,941,000   *Employees:* 2,125
Company Type: Public Family Member   *Employees here:* 180
SIC: 3669
   Mfg home safety and security products
Malcolm Candlish, Chairman of the Board

D-U-N-S 10-914-6019
BTI TELECOM CORP
4300 Six Forks Rd Ste 500, Raleigh, NC 27609
Phone: (919) 510-7000
Sales: $194,949,000   *Employees:* 550
Company Type: Private   *Employees here:* 275
SIC: 4813
   Long distance telephone service
Peter T Loftin, President

D-U-N-S 05-416-5857
BUCKEYE CABLE VISION INC.
   (Parent: Blade Communications Inc)
5566 Southwyck Blvd, Toledo, OH 43614
Phone: (419) 866-5802
Sales: $50,000,000   *Employees:* 376
Company Type: Private   *Employees here:* 165
SIC: 4841
   Cable television service
David Huey, President

D-U-N-S 00-377-1573
BUFORD TELEVISION INC.
13850 Paluxy Dr, Tyler, TX 75703
Phone: (903) 581-2121
Sales: $58,136,000   *Employees:* 370
Company Type: Private   *Employees here:* 150
SIC: 4841
   Cable television service
Robert P Buford, Chairman of the Board

D-U-N-S 00-100-9901
C & K COMPONENTS INC.
57 Stanley Ave, Watertown, MA 02472
Phone: (617) 926-6400
Sales: $225,000,000   *Employees:* 1,000
Company Type: Private   *Employees here:* 400
SIC: 3679
   Mfg electronic switches
Charles A Coolidge Jr, Chairman of the Board

D-U-N-S 05-330-8375
C & K SYSTEMS INC.
   (Parent: C & K Components Inc)
625 Coolidge Dr, Folsom, CA 95630
Phone: (916) 351-1131
Sales: $126,000,000   *Employees:* 2,000
Company Type: Private   *Employees here:* 125
SIC: 3669
   Mfg electronic sensory alarms & controls
Richard Johnson, President

D-U-N-S 00-300-5527   EXP
C-COR ELECTRONICS INC.
60 Decibel Rd, State College, PA 16801
Phone: (814) 238-2461
Sales: $152,144,000   *Employees:* 1,200
Company Type: Public   *Employees here:* 450
SIC: 3663
   Mfg electronic communication equipment
David A Woodle, President

D-U-N-S 80-853-9506
C-NET, INC.
150 Chestnut St, San Francisco, CA 94111
Phone: (415) 395-7800

Sales: $33,640,000   *Employees:* 581
Company Type: Public   *Employees here:* 105
SIC: 4841
    Cable network selling advertising producing television
      programs & websites on the internet
Halsey Minor, President

D-U-N-S 02-029-5663
CABLE & WIRELESS, INC.
    (Parent: Cable & Wireless Holdings Inc)
8219 Leesburg Pike, Vienna, VA 22182
Phone: (703) 790-5300
Sales: $948,600,000   *Employees:* 2,300
Company Type: Private   *Employees here:* 1,300
SIC: 4813
    Long distance telephone service and dedicated transmission
      services
Carl Grivener, Chief Executive Officer

D-U-N-S 92-956-0076
CABLE NETWORK SERVICES LLC
281 Tresser Blvd, Stamford, CT 06901
Phone: (203) 406-2500
Sales: $66,800,000   *Employees:* NA
Company Type: Private   *Employees here:* NA
SIC: 4841
    Cable television network
Roger Werner, President

D-U-N-S 09-857-8669
CABLE NEWS NETWORK INC.
    (Parent: Turner Broadcasting System)
1 CNN Ctr NW, Atlanta, GA 30303
Phone: (404) 827-1700
Sales: $296,400,000   *Employees:* 2,200
Company Type: Public Family Member   *Employees here:* 1,750
SIC: 4841
    Cable/pay television service
W T Johnson Jr, Chief Executive Officer

D-U-N-S 15-595-5644
CABLE ONE, INC.
    (Parent: The Washington Post Company)
1314 N 3rd St Fl 3, Phoenix, AZ 85004
Phone: (602) 364-6000
Sales: $257,732,000   *Employees:* 1,139
Company Type: Public Family Member   *Employees here:* 71
SIC: 4841
    Cable television multiple systems operator
Thomas O Might, President

D-U-N-S 84-900-1466
CABLE SYSTEMS INTL INC.
    (Parent: Cable Systems Holding Company)
505 N 51st Ave, Phoenix, AZ 85043
Phone: (602) 233-5000
Sales: $400,000,000   *Employees:* 1,800
Company Type: Private   *Employees here:* 1,790
SIC: 3661
    Mfg copper cable connectorized wire cords and cable
      assemblies
Peter A Woog, President

D-U-N-S 19-631-3811
CABLEVISION CONNECTICUT CORP
    (Parent: CSC Holdings Inc)
28 Cross St Ste 1, Norwalk, CT 06851
Phone: (203) 750-5600
Sales: $55,076,000   *Employees:* 503
Company Type: Public Family Member   *Employees here:* 291
SIC: 4841
    Cable television system
Charles F Dolan, Chairman of the Board

D-U-N-S 80-003-1320
CABLEVISION LIGHTPATH INC.
    (Parent: CSC Holdings Inc)
111 New South Rd, Hicksville, NY 11801
Phone: (516) 733-3434
Sales: $38,000,000   *Employees:* 100
Company Type: Public Family Member   *Employees here:* 100
SIC: 4841
    Commercial telecommunications service
Charles F Dolan, Chairman of the Board

D-U-N-S 87-677-4712
CABLEVISION OF MONMOUTH INC.
    (Parent: Cablevision Mfr Inc)
1501 18th Ave, Belmar, NJ 07719
Phone: (732) 681-8222
Sales: $123,103,000   *Employees:* 180
Company Type: Private   *Employees here:* 145
SIC: 4841
    Cable television service
Steven Randell, Principal

D-U-N-S 01-400-0363
CABLEVISION SYSTEMS CORP
1111 Stewart Ave, Bethpage, NY 11714
Phone: (516) 803-2300
Sales: $1,075,600,000   *Employees:* 7,969
Company Type: Private   *Employees here:* 20
SIC: 4841
    Cable television service
Joseph Azznara, President

D-U-N-S 04-452-6671   EXP
CALIFORNIA AMPLIFIER INC.
460 Calle San Pablo, Camarillo, CA 93012
Phone: (805) 987-9000
Sales: $46,933,000   *Employees:* 348
Company Type: Public   *Employees here:* 317
SIC: 3663
    Mfg radio/tv communication equipment
Fred Sturm, Chief Executive Officer

D-U-N-S 04-372-3717   EXP
CALIFORNIA MICROWAVE INC.
1143 Borregas Ave, Sunnyvale, CA 94089
Phone: (408) 732-4000
Sales: $269,189,000   *Employees:* 1,528
Company Type: Public   *Employees here:* 40
SIC: 3663
    Manufactures electronic equipment for communications
Donald V Anderson, President

D-U-N-S 15-038-8569
CALLTASK, INCORPORATED
    (Parent: Norrell Corporation)
3535 Piedmont Rd Ne, Atlanta, GA 30309
Phone: (404) 240-3000
Sales: $31,500,000   *Employees:* 250
Company Type: Public Family Member   *Employees here:* 250
SIC: 4813
    Telephone call center
C D Miller, President

D-U-N-S 18-696-0241
CAMBRIDGE SOUNDWORKS INC.
311 Needham St, Newton, MA 02464
Phone: (617) 332-5936
Sales: $30,400,000   *Employees:* 280
Company Type: Private   *Employees here:* 130
SIC: 3651
    Mfg & direct sale stereo speakers & components
Wayne P Garrett, Chief Financial Officer

D-U-N-S 87-990-4019
CAPROCK COMMUNICATIONS CORP
13455 Noel Rd Ste 1925, Dallas, TX 75240
Phone: (972) 788-4800
Sales: $48,500,000   *Employees:* 327
Company Type: Private   *Employees here:* 150
SIC: 4813
    Telecommunication services
Jere W Thompson Jr, President

D-U-N-S 02-357-7211
CAPSTAR BROADCASTING CORP
600 Congress Ave Ste 1400, Austin, TX 78701
Phone: (512) 340-7800
Sales: $351,993,000   *Employees:* 4,000
Company Type: Public   *Employees here:* 100
SIC: 4832
    Radio broadcasting
R S Hicks, President

D-U-N-S 04-646-6231
CASIO PHONEMATE INC.
20665 Manhattan Pl, Torrance, CA 90501
Phone: (310) 618-9910
Sales: $100,000,000   *Employees:* 175
Company Type: Private   *Employees here:* 160
SIC: 3661
    Mfg telephone answering machines
Stephen B Knuth, President

D-U-N-S 00-131-7056
CBS BROADCASTING INC.
    (Parent: CBS Corporation)
51 W 52nd St, New York, NY 10019
Phone: (212) 975-4321
Sales: $734,700,000   *Employees:* 6,400
Company Type: Public Family Member   *Employees here:* 1,800
SIC: 4833
    TV & radio broadcasting TV films
Mel Karmazin, President

D-U-N-S 00-134-3953   EXP
CBS CORPORATION
11 Stanwix St, Pittsburgh, PA 15222
Phone: (412) 244-2000
Sales: $5,363,000,000   *Employees:* 51,444
Company Type: Public   *Employees here:* 800
SIC: 4833
    TV & radio svcs broadcasting & production mfr power plant
    turbine-generators process control systems
Michael H Jordan, Chief Executive Officer

D-U-N-S 13-163-5765
CELERITEK INC.
3236 Scott Boulvard, Santa Clara, CA 95054
Phone: (408) 986-5060
Sales: $56,317,000   *Employees:* 325
Company Type: Public   *Employees here:* 325
SIC: 3663
    Mfg high frequency radio products
Tamer Husseini, Chairman of the Board

D-U-N-S 14-433-4943
CELLNET COMMUNICATIONS INC.
31075 John R Rd, Madison Heights, MI 48071
Phone: (248) 588-3894
Sales: $55,195,000   *Employees:* 75
Company Type: Private   *Employees here:* 75
SIC: 4812
    Provides cellular air time service
Richard A Goldsmith, President

D-U-N-S 85-849-6490
CELLULAR COMMUNICATIONS INTL
110 E 59th St, New York, NY 10022
Phone: (212) 906-8440
Sales: $105,000,000   *Employees:* 10
Company Type: Public   *Employees here:* 10
SIC: 4812
    Provides cellular telephone service
William B Ginsberg, Chairman of the Board

D-U-N-S 12-251-4268
CELLULAR TELEPHONE COMPANY
    (Parent: AT&T Wireless Services Inc)
15 E Midland Ave, Paramus, NJ 07652
Phone: (201) 967-3000
Sales: $97,500,000   *Employees:* 1,400
Company Type: Public Family Member   *Employees here:* 1,000
SIC: 4812
    Wireless communication services
Dennis O Connell, President

D-U-N-S 00-696-9869
CENTEL CORPORATION
    (Parent: Sprint Corporation)
2330 Shawnee Mission Pkwy, Shawnee Mission, KS 66205
Phone: (913) 624-3000
Sales: $1,194,600,000   *Employees:* 9,300
Company Type: Public Family Member   *Employees here:* 5
SIC: 4813
    Telephone utilities & cellular communications systems
William T Esrey, President

D-U-N-S 78-247-7996
CENTENNIAL CELLULAR CORP
    (Parent: Century Communications Corp)
1305 Campus Pkwy, Neptune, NJ 07753
Phone: (732) 919-1000
Sales: $237,501,000   *Employees:* 1,632
Company Type: Public   *Employees here:* 65
SIC: 4812
    Cellular phone services
Rudy Graf, President

D-U-N-S 08-700-6714   EXP
CENTIGRAM COMMUNICATIONS CORP
91 E Tasman Dr, San Jose, CA 95134
Phone: (408) 944-0250
Sales: $77,587,000   *Employees:* 325
Company Type: Public   *Employees here:* 250
SIC: 3661
    Mfg audio information processing systems
Robert L Puette, President

D-U-N-S 82-556-9528
CENTRAL KENTUCKY CELLULAR
    (Parent: American Cellular Corporation)
301 Highland Park Dr, Richmond, KY 40475
Phone: (888) 844-6985
Sales: $44,000,000   *Employees:* 145
Company Type: Public Family Member   *Employees here:* 59
SIC: 4812
    Cellular telephone services
Steve Lochmuller, General Manager

D-U-N-S 00-696-9760
CENTRAL TELEPHONE CO OF ILLINOIS
    (Parent: Centel Corporation)
900 Springmill St, Mansfield, OH 44906
Phone: (419) 755-8711

Sales: $280,600,000

Company Type: Public Family Member   *Employees:* 2,188

SIC: 4813   *Employees here:* 330

   Long distance telephone communications

William T Esrey, Chairman of the Board

D-U-N-S 06-707-0524

CENTURY COMMUNICATIONS CORP

50 Locust Ave, New Canaan, CT 06840

Phone: (203) 966-8746

Sales: $484,736,000   *Employees:* 4,211

Company Type: Public   *Employees here:* 126

SIC: 4841

   Operates cable television cellular telephone paging & two-way mobile radio systems

Leonard Tow, Chief Executive Officer

D-U-N-S 05-091-1668

CENTURY TELEPHONE ENTERPRISES

100 Century Park Dr, Monroe, LA 71203

Phone: (318) 388-9000

Sales: $901,521,000   *Employees:* 7,000

Company Type: Public   *Employees here:* 1,500

SIC: 4813

   Telecommunications & cellular services

Glen F Post III, President

D-U-N-S 05-605-4687

CENTURY TELEPHONE OF WASHINGTON

   (Parent: Pacific Telecom Inc)

805 Broadway St, Vancouver, WA 98660

Phone: (360) 696-0983

Sales: $73,582,000   *Employees:* 415

Company Type: Public Family Member   *Employees here:* 7

SIC: 4813

   Telephone communications

Glen Post, Chairman of the Board

D-U-N-S 06-476-6777

CENTURY TELEPHONE OF WISCONSIN

   (Parent: Century Telephone Enterprises)

5th & Jay Sts, La Crosse, WI 54601

Phone: (608) 782-9980

Sales: $33,773,000   *Employees:* 180

Company Type: Public Family Member   *Employees here:* 100

SIC: 4813

   Telephone communication services

Clark M Williams Sr, Chairman of the Board

D-U-N-S 14-703-9820

CERBERUS HOLDINGS INC.

3411 Silverside Rd, Wilmington, DE 19810

Phone: (302) 478-6160

Sales: $87,800,000   *Employees:* 1,000

Company Type: Private   *Employees here:* 3

SIC: 3669

   Holding company mfg distributes & services life safety & fire systems

Karl Bollmann, President

D-U-N-S 00-836-5215   EXP

CERWIN-VEGA INC.

555 E Easy St, Simi Valley, CA 93065

Phone: (805) 584-9332

Sales: $42,114,000   *Employees:* 420

Company Type: Private   *Employees here:* 400

SIC: 3651

   Mfg electronic speakers & sound systems

Eugene Czerwinski, Chief Executive Officer

D-U-N-S 19-688-6592

CFW COMMUNICATIONS COMPANY

401 Spring Ln Ste 300, Waynesboro, VA 22980

Phone: (540) 946-3500

Sales: $59,010,000   *Employees:* 492

Company Type: Public   *Employees here:* 40

SIC: 4813

   Holding company

James S Quarforth, President

D-U-N-S 10-795-8845

CHAMBERS COMMUNICATIONS CORP

2975 Chad Dr, Eugene, OR 97408

Phone: (541) 485-5611

Sales: $39,800,000   *Employees:* 300

Company Type: Private   *Employees here:* 120

SIC: 4841

   Cable television services & television broadcasting

Carolyn S Chambers, Chairman of the Board

D-U-N-S 19-592-9872

CHANCELLOR MEDIA CORPORATION

300 Crescent Ct Ste 600, Dallas, TX 75201

Phone: (214) 922-8700

Sales: $582,078,000   *Employees:* 4,300

Company Type: Public   *Employees here:* 10

SIC: 4832

   Broadcast radio stations

Scott K Ginsburg, President

D-U-N-S 80-980-1269

CHANNEL MASTER LLC

1315 Industrial Park Dr, Smithfield, NC 27577

Phone: (919) 934-9711

Sales: $166,000,000   *Employees:* 850

Company Type: Private   *Employees here:* 850

SIC: 3679

   Mfg receiving antennas

Harold E Mills, President

D-U-N-S 82-507-9619

CHARTER COMMUNICATIONS, INC.

12444 Pwrscurt Dr Ste 400, Saint Louis, MO 63131

Phone: (314) 965-0555

Sales: $363,900,000   *Employees:* 2,700

Company Type: Private   *Employees here:* 100

SIC: 4841

   Cable/pay television service

Jerald L Kent, President

D-U-N-S 79-344-7160

CHAUNCEY COMMUNICATIONS CORP

   (Parent: Adelphia Communications Corp)

5 W 3rd St, Coudersport, PA 16915

Phone: (814) 274-9830

Sales: $112,000,000   *Employees:* 50

Company Type: Public Family Member   *Employees here:* 1

SIC: 4841

   Cable/pay television service

John J Rigas, President

D-U-N-S 09-915-6259

CHEROKEE INTERNATIONAL LLC

2841 Dow Ave, Tustin, CA 92780

Phone: (714) 544-6665

Sales: $77,022,000   *Employees:* 868

Company Type: Private   *Employees here:* 389

SIC: 3679

   Mfg electronic power supplies & other electronic components

Ganpat Patel, President

D-U-N-S 07-734-5494

CHEROKEE NATION

4 1/2 Mi So On Hwy 62, Tahlequah, OK 74464

Phone: (918) 456-0671

Sales: $42,733,000   *Employees:* 1,800
Company Type: Private   *Employees here:* 800
SIC: 3679
   Mfg cable harness assemblies & legislative body
Joe Byrd, Chief

D-U-N-S 00-699-8991
THE CHILLICOTHE TELEPHONE CO.
   (Parent: Horizon Telecom Inc)
68 E Main St, Chillicothe, OH 45601
Phone: (740) 772-8200
Sales: $35,106,000   *Employees:* 175
Company Type: Private   *Employees here:* 165
SIC: 4813
   Telephone communications
Thomas McKell, President

D-U-N-S 96-583-1985
CHOCTAW COMMUNICATIONS, INC.
   (Parent: Vartec Telecom Inc)
8400 S Gessner Dr, Houston, TX 77074
Phone: (713) 779-0692
Sales: $36,000,000   *Employees:* 100
Company Type: Private   *Employees here:* 100
SIC: 4813
   Local telephone communication
Glenn Massey, President

D-U-N-S 17-660-6184
CHORUS COMMUNICATIONS GROUP
1912 Parmenter St, Middleton, WI 53562
Phone: (608) 831-1000
Sales: $36,337,000   *Employees:* 240
Company Type: Private   *Employees here:* 95
SIC: 4813
   Local telephone communications
Dean E Voeks, President

D-U-N-S 04-542-2433
CHRIS-CRAFT INDUSTRIES INC.
767 5th Ave Fl 46, New York, NY 10153
Phone: (212) 421-0200
Sales: $464,646,000   *Employees:* 1,169
Company Type: Public   *Employees here:* 10
SIC: 4833
   Television broadcasting mfg plastic film products & other
Herbert J Siegel, Chairman of the Board

D-U-N-S 04-617-2946   EXP
CHYRON CORPORATION
5 Hub Dr Ste 3, Melville, NY 11747
Phone: (516) 845-2000
Sales: $86,774,000   *Employees:* 406
Company Type: Public   *Employees here:* 196
SIC: 3663
   Manufactures electronic television equipment
Edward Grebow, President

D-U-N-S 61-195-2078   EXP
CIDCO INCORPORATED
220 Cochrane Cir, Morgan Hill, CA 95037
Phone: (408) 779-1162
Sales: $257,033,000   *Employees:* 422
Company Type: Public   *Employees here:* 422
SIC: 3661
   Mfg telecommunications equipment
Paul Locklin, Chairman of the Board

D-U-N-S 80-666-9768
CIENA CORPORATION
920 Elkridge Landing Rd, Linthicum Heights, MD 21090
Phone: (410) 865-8500

Sales: $508,087,000   *Employees:* 1,382
Company Type: Public   *Employees here:* 150
SIC: 3661
   Mfg high capacity fiber optic transmission systems
Joseph R Chinnici, Chief Financial Officer

D-U-N-S 10-149-6735
CINCINNATI BELL INC.
201 E 4th St 102-700, Cincinnati, OH 45202
Phone: (513) 397-9900
Sales: $1,756,800,000   *Employees:* 20,800
Company Type: Public   *Employees here:* 100
SIC: 4813
   Telephone communication services (see operation section for
     other lines of business)
John T Lamaccia, President

D-U-N-S 11-288-2816
CINCINNATI BELL LONG DISTANCE
   (Parent: Cincinnati Bell Inc)
36 E 7th St Ste 2200, Cincinnati, OH 45202
Phone: (513) 369-2100
Sales: $37,900,000   *Employees:* 300
Company Type: Public Family Member   *Employees here:* 160
SIC: 4813
   Communication service
Barry L Nelson, President

D-U-N-S 00-699-9239
CINCINNATI BELL TELEPHONE CO.
   (Parent: Cincinnati Bell Inc)
201 E 4th St Ste 1-13, Cincinnati, OH 45202
Phone: (513) 397-9900
Sales: $670,100,000   *Employees:* 3,500
Company Type: Public Family Member   *Employees here:* 900
SIC: 4813
   Telephone communication services
Richard G Ellenberger, President

D-U-N-S 05-910-6484
CINCINNATI ELECTRONICS CORP
   (Parent: Canadian Marconi Company)
7500 Innovation Way, Mason, OH 45040
Phone: (513) 573-6100
Sales: $46,800,000   *Employees:* 317
Company Type: Private   *Employees here:* 317
SIC: 3663
   Mfr satellite communications equipment infra-red scan &
     detection systems
James T Wimmers Phd, Chairman of the Board

D-U-N-S 17-760-4626
CITADEL BROADCASTING COMPANY
   (Parent: Citadel Communications Corp)
140 S Ash Ave, Tempe, AZ 85281
Phone: (602) 731-5222
Sales: $115,500,000   *Employees:* 1,400
Company Type: Public Family Member   *Employees here:* 9
SIC: 4832
   Radio stations
D R Proffitt, President

D-U-N-S 83-469-3871
CITIZENS COMMUNICATIONS
   (Parent: Citizens Utilities Company)
High Ridge Park Bldg 3, Stamford, CT 06905
Phone: (203) 329-8800
Sales: $320,700,000   *Employees:* 2,500
Company Type: Public Family Member   *Employees here:* 2,050
SIC: 4813
   Telecommunication services
Leonard Tow, Chairman of the Board

D-U-N-S 84-849-6105
CITIZENS TELECOM CO OF NY
(*Parent:* Citizens Utilities Company)
3 High Ridge Park, Stamford, CT 06905
Phone: (203) 329-8800
Sales: $194,553,000   *Employees:* 408
Company Type: Public Family Member   *Employees here:* 1
SIC: 4813
  Local & long distance telephone communications service
Daryl A Ferguson, President

D-U-N-S 00-691-8296
CITIZENS UTILITIES COMPANY
3 High Ridge Park Ste 2, Stamford, CT 06905
Phone: (203) 329-8800
Sales: $1,393,619,000   *Employees:* 5,400
Company Type: Public   *Employees here:* 150
SIC: 4813
  Telecommunications natural gas & electric utility services
Leonard Tow, Chairman of the Board

D-U-N-S 15-068-0999   EXP
CLARION MANUFACTURING CORP AMERICA
(*Parent:* Clarion Corporation America)
237 Beaver Rd, Walton, KY 41094
Phone: (606) 485-6600
Sales: $82,897,000   *Employees:* 228
Company Type: Private   *Employees here:* 228
SIC: 3651
  Mfr car radios stereos & amplifiers
Larry H Maxey, President

D-U-N-S 00-112-8537   EXP
CLARK DAVID COMPANY INC.
360 Franklin St, Worcester, MA 01604
Phone: (508) 756-6216
Sales: $45,214,000   *Employees:* 360
Company Type: Private   *Employees here:* 350
SIC: 3663
  Mfg communication equipment medical surgical appliances/
    supplies & personal protective equipment
Robert A Vincent, President

D-U-N-S 15-761-1005
CLASSIC CABLE INC.
(*Parent:* Classic Communications Inc)
515 Congress Ave Ste 2626, Austin, TX 78701
Phone: (512) 476-9095
Sales: $65,000,000   *Employees:* 350
Company Type: Private   *Employees here:* 9
SIC: 4841
  Cable/pay television service
J M Belisle, Chief Executive Officer

D-U-N-S 06-945-6655
CLEAR CHANNEL COMMUNICATIONS
200 Concord Plz Ste 600, San Antonio, TX 78216
Phone: (210) 822-2828
Sales: $697,068,000   *Employees:* 5,400
Company Type: Public   *Employees here:* 19
SIC: 4832
  Radio & television broadcasting & outdoor advertising
L L Mays, Chairman of the Board

D-U-N-S 61-856-8315   EXP
CMC INDUSTRIES INC.
4950 Patrick Henry Dr, Santa Clara, CA 95054
Phone: (408) 982-9999

Sales: $301,955,000   *Employees:* 1,205
Company Type: Public   *Employees here:* 3
SIC: 3661
  Mfg telecommunications equipment computer peripherals
    and printed circuit boards
Matthew G Landa, President

D-U-N-S 88-473-3874
CMT PARTNERS
651 Gateway Blvd Ste 1500, South San Francisco, CA 94080
Phone: (650) 871-9500
Sales: $88,200,000   *Employees:* 1,266
Company Type: Private   *Employees here:* 745
SIC: 4812
  Cellular communications systems
Sam Ginn, Principal

D-U-N-S 19-865-3990
CNBC, INC.
(*Parent:* National Broadcasting Co Inc)
2200 Fletcher Ave, Fort Lee, NJ 07024
Phone: (201) 585-2622
Sales: $38,000,000   *Employees:* 350
Company Type: Public Family Member   *Employees here:* 260
SIC: 4833
  Cable television station
William Bolster, President

D-U-N-S 18-970-6674   EXP
CNET TECHNOLOGY CORP
1455 Mccandless Dr, Milpitas, CA 95035
Phone: (408) 934-0800
Sales: $47,000,000   *Employees:* 250
Company Type: Private   *Employees here:* 35
SIC: 3661
  Mfg communications equipment
Simon J Chang, President

D-U-N-S 86-696-2020
COHESIVE TECHNOLOGY SOLUTIONS
2465 E Bayshore Rd, Palo Alto, CA 94303
Phone: (650) 855-1700
Sales: $37,900,000   *Employees:* 300
Company Type: Private   *Employees here:* 8
SIC: 4813
  Provides access to internet
Dr Dennis Rohan, Chairman of the Board

D-U-N-S 05-150-9594
COLONY COMMUNICATIONS, INC.
(*Parent:* MediaOne of Delaware Inc)
75 Fountain St, Providence, RI 02902
Phone: (617) 742-9500
Sales: $120,800,000   *Employees:* 602
Company Type: Public Family Member   *Employees here:* 7
SIC: 4841
  Cable television services
Amos B Hostetter Jr, Chairman of the Board

D-U-N-S 12-630-9996
COLORADO SPRINGS CABLEVISION
(*Parent:* Century Communications Corp)
213 N Union Blvd, Colorado Springs, CO 80909
Phone: (719) 633-6616
Sales: $30,300,000   *Employees:* 230
Company Type: Public Family Member   *Employees here:* 150
SIC: 4841
  Provides cable television service
Leonard Tow, Chairman of the Board

D-U-N-S 84-799-9745
COM TECH INTERNATIONAL CORP
  (Parent: Circle International Comm)
6001 Broken Sound Pkwy, Boca Raton, FL 33487
Phone: (561) 989-8300
Sales: $110,000,000
Company Type: Private
SIC: 4813
  Long distance telephone communications
Lawrence Ferk, Chief Executive Officer

Employees: 42
Employees here: 35

D-U-N-S 87-638-4926
COM21 INC.
750 Tasman Dr, Milpitas, CA 95035
Phone: (408) 953-9100
Sales: $48,114,000
Company Type: Public
SIC: 3663
  Mfg telecommunications equipment
Peter Fenner, President

Employees: 131
Employees here: 129

D-U-N-S 09-998-6077
COMCAST CABLEVISION OF MERCER COUNTY
  (Parent: Comcast Corporation)
1500 Market St, Philadelphia, PA 19102
Phone: (215) 665-1700
Sales: $134,300,000
Company Type: Public Family Member
SIC: 4841
  Cable television system
Thomas Baxter, President

Employees: 1,000
Employees here: 700

D-U-N-S 06-428-7006
COMCAST CABLEVISION OF NJ
  (Parent: Comcast Corporation)
800 Rahway Ave, Union, NJ 07083
Phone: (732) 602-7400
Sales: $129,828,000
Company Type: Public Family Member
SIC: 4841
  Cable & pay television service electrical contractor
Buck Dopp, President

Employees: 400
Employees here: 400

D-U-N-S 09-564-9208   EXP
COMDIAL CORPORATION
1180 Seminole Trl, Charlottesville, VA 22901
Phone: (804) 978-2200
Sales: $118,561,000
Company Type: Public
SIC: 3661
  Mfg telecommunications products & systems
William G Mustain, President

Employees: 865
Employees here: 810

D-U-N-S 09-066-6314
COMINEX LLC
1409 Cantillon Blvd, Mays Landing, NJ 08330
Phone: (609) 625-2100
Sales: $100,000,000
Company Type: Private
SIC: 4813
  Telecommunication services
Ethan Rosen, Partner

Employees: 20
Employees here: 20

D-U-N-S 88-402-9067
COMM SOUTH COMPANIES, INC.
6830 Walling Ln, Dallas, TX 75231
Phone: (972) 690-9955
Sales: $130,000,000
Company Type: Private
SIC: 4813
  Reseller of residential telephone land lines
Jim Graham, President

Employees: 301
Employees here: 289

D-U-N-S 15-105-1166
COMMNET CELLULAR INC.
8350 E Crescent Pkwy, Englewood, CO 80111
Phone: (303) 694-3234
Sales: $150,867,000
Company Type: Public
SIC: 4812
  Cellular telephone services
Arnold C Pohs, Chief Executive Officer

Employees: 374
Employees here: 280

D-U-N-S 00-791-0441
COMMONWEALTH TELEPHONE CO.
  (Parent: Commonwealth Telephone Entps)
100 Lake St, Dallas, PA 18612
Phone: (570) 675-1121
Sales: $87,000,000
Company Type: Public Family Member
SIC: 4813
  Telephone communication service
David C McCourt, Chairman of the Board

Employees: 682
Employees here: 114

D-U-N-S 79-545-5112
COMMUNICATIONS CONCEPTS INVESTMENTS
1334 N State Road 7, Pompano Beach, FL 33063
Phone: (954) 968-4887
Sales: $50,000,000
Company Type: Private
SIC: 4813
  Local and long distance telephone communication
Jordan Levinson, President

Employees: 21
Employees here: 21

D-U-N-S 09-921-6798   EXP
COMMUNICATIONS INSTRUMENTS
  (Parent: Code Hennessy & Simmons Lp)
1396 Charlotte Hwy, Fairview, NC 28730
Phone: (828) 628-1711
Sales: $89,436,000
Company Type: Private
SIC: 3679
  Mfg electro-mechanical stepping switches and solenoids and
    electronic relays
Ramzi A Dabbagh, Chief Executive Officer

Employees: 1,200
Employees here: 400

D-U-N-S 05-273-3714   EXP
COMMUNICATIONS SYSTEMS, INC.
213 Main St N, Hector, MN 55342
Phone: (320) 848-6231
Sales: $75,732,000
Company Type: Public
SIC: 3661
  Mfg telephone station apparatus & equipment contract
    manufacturing of related electronic assemblies
Curtis A Sampson, Chairman of the Board

Employees: 1,135
Employees here: 20

D-U-N-S 78-137-1133
COMMUNICATIONS TELESYSTEMS INTL
9999 Willow Creek Rd, San Diego, CA 92131
Phone: (619) 547-5700
Sales: $43,000,000
Company Type: Private
SIC: 4813
  Long distance telephone carrier
Roger B Abbott, Chief Executive Officer

Employees: 340
Employees here: 75

D-U-N-S 10-208-5750
COMMUNIGROUP INC.
  (Parent: Telephone Electronics Corp)
236 E Capitol St Ste 500, Jackson, MS 39201
Phone: (601) 354-9066

Sales: $869,623,000   *Employees:* 870
Company Type: Private   *Employees here:* 3
SIC: 4813
   Telephone service
Robert F Chafin, President

D-U-N-S 13-293-1692
COMMUNIGROUP OF KC, INC.
6950 W 56th St, Shawnee Mission, KS 66202
Phone: (913) 722-6005
Sales: $40,000,000   *Employees:* 115
Company Type: Private   *Employees here:* 85
SIC: 4813
   Telecommunication service
David L Jones, Chairman of the Board

D-U-N-S 00-678-1348
COMMUNITY TV OF SOUTHERN CALIFORNIA
4401 W Sunset Blvd, Los Angeles, CA 90027
Phone: (323) 666-6500
Sales: $48,466,000   *Employees:* 300
Company Type: Private   *Employees here:* 300
SIC: 4833
   Television station
Al Jerome, President

D-U-N-S 62-609-5756
COMPUTER SCIENCE RAYTHEON
1201 Minuteman St, Cocoa, FL 32922
Phone: (407) 494-5272
Sales: $100,000,000   *Employees:* 1,500
Company Type: Private   *Employees here:* 1,500
SIC: 4899
   Engineering technology services
Pat Walsh, Chief Financial Officer

D-U-N-S 00-325-7979   EXP
COMSAT CORPORATION
6560 Rock Spring Dr, Bethesda, MD 20817
Phone: (301) 214-3000
Sales: $562,651,000   *Employees:* 2,732
Company Type: Public   *Employees here:* 500
SIC: 4899
   Satellite communications services
Betty C Alewine, President

D-U-N-S 12-171-5809
COMSTREAM CORPORATION
   (Parent: Spar Aerospace Limited)
6350 Sequence Dr, San Diego, CA 92121
Phone: (619) 458-1800
Sales: $55,923,000   *Employees:* 200
Company Type: Private   *Employees here:* 180
SIC: 3663
   Mfg satellite data communications equipment
Robert Clasen, President

D-U-N-S 15-519-4954
COMVERSE NETWORK SYSTEMS INC.
   (Parent: Comverse Technology Inc)
100 Quannapowitt Pkwy, Wakefield, MA 01880
Phone: (781) 246-9000
Sales: $86,200,000   *Employees:* 900
Company Type: Public Family Member   *Employees here:* 370
SIC: 3661
   Mfg telephone interconnect equipment
Francis E Girard, President

D-U-N-S 78-935-7407
CONCENTRIC NETWORK CORPORATION
1400 Parkmoor Ave, San Jose, CA 95126
Phone: (408) 342-2800

Sales: $82,807,000   *Employees:* 387
Company Type: Public   *Employees here:* 250
SIC: 4813
   Network services
Henry R Nothhaft, Chairman of the Board

D-U-N-S 78-486-8986
CONCERT MANAGEMENT SERVICES
11921 Freedom Dr, Reston, VA 20190
Phone: (703) 707-4000
Sales: $85,300,000   *Employees:* 700
Company Type: Private   *Employees here:* 300
SIC: 4899
   International communication services
Peter Manning, President

D-U-N-S 60-857-2517
CONESTOGA ENTERPRISES INC.
202 E 1st St, Birdsboro, PA 19508
Phone: (610) 582-8711
Sales: $56,185,000   *Employees:* 272
Company Type: Public   *Employees here:* 6
SIC: 4813
   Holding company through subsidiary operates a local & long
      distance telephone communication and paging services
John R Bentz, Chairman of the Board

D-U-N-S 02-541-6025   EXP
CONEXANT SYSTEMS, INC.
4311 Jamboree Rd, Newport Beach, CA 92660
Phone: (949) 221-4600
Sales: $76,600,000   *Employees:* 800
Company Type: Private   *Employees here:* 600
SIC: 3661
   Mfg telephone and telecommunication equipment
Dwight W Decker, President

D-U-N-S 07-140-9460   EXP
CONFEDERATED SLISH KTNAI TRIBES
Hwy 93, Pablo, MT 59855
Phone: (406) 675-2700
Sales: $61,975,000   *Employees:* 800
Company Type: Private   *Employees here:* 550
SIC: 3679
   Tribal management mfg electronic circuits & harness
      assemblies & information technical services & document
      scanning
Vern Clairmont, Executive

D-U-N-S 60-736-1540
CONQUEST TELECOM SVCS
   (Parent: Smartalk Teleservices Inc)
5500 Frantz Rd Ste 125, Dublin, OH 43017
Phone: (614) 764-2933
Sales: $37,400,000   *Employees:* 296
Company Type: Public Family Member   *Employees here:* 75
SIC: 4813
   Long distance operator assisted service
James E Sobwick, President

D-U-N-S 11-747-8529
CONSOLIDATED COMMUNICATION
   (Parent: Mcleod USA Incorporated)
121 S 17th St, Mattoon, IL 61938
Phone: (217) 235-3311
Sales: $192,100,000   *Employees:* 1,500
Company Type: Public Family Member   *Employees here:* 7
SIC: 4813
   Telephone holding company
Clark Mcleod, Chairman

D-U-N-S 11-468-5548
CONTEL FEDERAL SYSTEMS INC.
(Parent: GTE Corporation)
77 A St, Needham, MA 02494
Phone: (781) 449-2000
Sales: $1,200,000,000   *Employees:* 7,000
Company Type: Public Family Member   *Employees here:* 1,500
SIC: 3661
   Mfg telecommunications equipment & telephone utility
Armen Dermarderosian, President

D-U-N-S 00-691-4584
CONTEL OF CALIFORNIA INC.
(Parent: GTE Corporation)
600 Hidden Rdg, Irving, TX 75038
Phone: (000) 000-0000
Sales: $156,000,000   *Employees:* 1,219
Company Type: Public Family Member   *Employees here:* 750
SIC: 4813
   Telephone communication services
James F Miles, President

D-U-N-S 09-636-1530
CONTEL OF NEW YORK, INC.
(Parent: GTE Corporation)
600 Hidden Rdg, Irving, TX 75038
Phone: (972) 718-5000
Sales: $125,500,000   *Employees:* 982
Company Type: Public Family Member   *Employees here:* 6
SIC: 4813
   Local & long distance telephone services
Earl A Goode, President

D-U-N-S 62-026-3145   EXP
CONTINENTAL ELECTRONICS CORP
(Parent: Tech-Sym Corporation)
4212 S Buckner Blvd, Dallas, TX 75227
Phone: (214) 381-7161
Sales: $34,100,000   *Employees:* 300
Company Type: Public Family Member   *Employees here:* 103
SIC: 3663
   Mfg radio & military communication equipment
David F Burkey, President

D-U-N-S 03-112-7637
CONVERGENT COMMUNICATIONS SVCS
(Parent: Convergent Communications Inc)
67 Inverness Dr E, Englewood, CO 80112
Phone: (303) 749-3000
Sales: $106,500,000   *Employees:* 917
Company Type: Private   *Employees here:* 303
SIC: 4813
   Computer integration services
John Evans, Chief Executive Officer

D-U-N-S 79-805-6347   EXP
CONVERGENT MEDIA SYSTEMS CORP
3490 Piedmont Rd Ne, Atlanta, GA 30305
Phone: (404) 262-1555
Sales: $30,900,000   *Employees:* 288
Company Type: Private   *Employees here:* 118
SIC: 4833
   Intra communications/ business television
Jeffrey L Freemyer, Chief Executive Officer

D-U-N-S 55-609-1551
COOPERATIVE COMMUNICATIONS
412 Washington Ave, Belleville, NJ 07109
Phone: (973) 759-8100

Sales: $50,000,000   *Employees:* 100
Company Type: Private   *Employees here:* 100
SIC: 4813
   Telephone communications
Louis Lombardi Sr, President

D-U-N-S 10-116-2808   EXP
COPLEY CONTROLS CORP
410 University Ave, Westwood, MA 02090
Phone: (781) 329-8200
Sales: $45,000,000   *Employees:* 200
Company Type: Private   *Employees here:* 197
SIC: 3679
   Mfg power amplifiers
Matthew Lorber, President

D-U-N-S 79-092-4054
CORDILLERA COMMUNICATIONS INC.
(Parent: Evening Post Publishing Co)
134 Columbus St, Charleston, SC 29403
Phone: (843) 577-7111
Sales: $50,700,000   *Employees:* 460
Company Type: Private   *Employees here:* 2
SIC: 4833
   Television broadcasting
Paul Cassidy, President

D-U-N-S 87-794-3803
CORSAIR COMMUNICATIONS INC.
3408 Hillview Ave, Palo Alto, CA 94304
Phone: (650) 856-2677
Sales: $47,838,000   *Employees:* 132
Company Type: Public   *Employees here:* 57
SIC: 3663
   Mfg cellular fraud control system
Mary A Byrnes, President

D-U-N-S 00-791-9715
COSMOS BROADCASTING CORP
(Parent: Liberty Corporation)
2000 Wade Hampton Blvd, Greenville, SC 29615
Phone: (864) 609-4370
Sales: $119,000,000   *Employees:* 932
Company Type: Public Family Member   *Employees here:* 11
SIC: 4833
   Television stations
James M Keelor, President

D-U-N-S 04-390-5707
COURTROOM TV NETWORK LLC
600 3rd Ave, New York, NY 10016
Phone: (212) 973-3200
Sales: $32,300,000   *Employees:* 300
Company Type: Private   *Employees here:* 300
SIC: 4833
   Televised courtroom cases
Henry Chleiff, Managing Member

D-U-N-S 78-911-1374
COX COMMUNICATIONS INC.
(Parent: Cox Enterprises Inc)
1400 Lake Hearn Dr Ne, Atlanta, GA 30319
Phone: (404) 843-5000
Sales: $1,460,285,000   *Employees:* 7,200
Company Type: Public   *Employees here:* 1,000
SIC: 4841
   Cable television operator
James O Robbins, President

D-U-N-S 10-719-5786
COX COMMUNICATIONS NEW ORLEANS
(Parent: Cox Enterprises Inc)
2120 Canal St, New Orleans, LA 70112

Phone: (504) 734-7345
Sales: $110,985,000
Company Type: Private   *Employees:* 600
SIC: 4841   *Employees here:* 300
   Cable television services
C R Nagin, Vice-President

D-U-N-S 04-365-8160
COX COMMUNICATIONS SAN DIEGO INC.
   (Parent: Cox Communications Inc)
5159 Federal Blvd, San Diego, CA 92105
Phone: (619) 263-9251
Sales: $1,610,364,000
Company Type: Public Family Member   *Employees:* 750
SIC: 4841   *Employees here:* 680
   Cable television service
Bill Geppert, Senior Vice-President

D-U-N-S 13-088-4570
CSC HOLDINGS, INC.
   (Parent: Cablevision Systems Corp)
1 Media Crossways, Woodbury, NY 11797
Phone: (516) 364-8450
Sales: $1,949,358,000
Company Type: Public   *Employees:* 7,969
SIC: 4841   *Employees here:* 500
   Cable television service
Charles F Dolan, Chairman of the Board

D-U-N-S 84-045-1777
CT COMMUNICATIONS INC.
68 Cabarrus Ave E, Concord, NC 28025
Phone: (704) 722-2500
Sales: $78,484,000
Company Type: Public   *Employees:* 410
SIC: 4813   *Employees here:* 283
   Telephone utility
Michael R Coltrane, President

D-U-N-S 05-876-7641   EXP
CUMING CORP
230 Bodwell St, Avon, MA 02322
Phone: (508) 580-2660
Sales: $30,000,000
Company Type: Private   *Employees:* 110
SIC: 3679   *Employees here:* 110
   Mfg microwave materials free space absorber & floatation
     materials
William R Cuming, President

D-U-N-S 11-109-1286
CUMULUS BROADCASTING INC.
875 N Michigan Ave, Chicago, IL 60611
Phone: (312) 867-0091
Sales: $54,665,000
Company Type: Private   *Employees:* 250
SIC: 4832   *Employees here:* 3
   Radio broadcast station
William M Bungeroth, President

D-U-N-S 11-414-8190
CURRENT ELECTRONICS INC.
   (Parent: EFTC Corporation)
125 Elliott Rd, Newberg, OR 97132
Phone: (503) 538-0626
Sales: $55,000,000
Company Type: Public Family Member   *Employees:* 390
SIC: 3679   *Employees here:* 370
   Mfg electronic circuitry
Greg Hewitson, President

D-U-N-S 17-777-7794   EXP
CUSTOMTRACKS CORPORATION
1 Galleria Tower, Dallas, TX 75240

Phone: (972) 702-7055
Sales: $117,706,000
Company Type: Public   *Employees:* 800
SIC: 3663   *Employees here:* 280
   Mfg radio frequency (wireless) electronic systems
David P Cook, Chairman of the Board

D-U-N-S 04-381-8983
CYBERFONE
999 Old Eagle School Rd, Wayne, PA 19087
Phone: (610) 989-9330
Sales: $70,000,000
Company Type: Private   *Employees:* 20
SIC: 3661   *Employees here:* 20
   System/telecomm developer
Joe Martino, Chief Executive Officer

D-U-N-S 12-136-6280   EXP
CYLINK CORPORATION
910 Hermosa Ct, Sunnyvale, CA 94086
Phone: (408) 735-5800
Sales: $49,333,000
Company Type: Public   *Employees:* 432
SIC: 3663   *Employees here:* 335
   Mfg network security products
William P Crowell, Chairman of the Board

D-U-N-S 03-342-9528
DATEK ONLINE HOLDING COMPANY
100 Wood Ave, Iselin, NJ 08830
Phone: (732) 549-3600
Sales: $50,700,000
Company Type: Private   *Employees:* 400
SIC: 4813   *Employees here:* 20
   On line trading
Jeff Citron, President

D-U-N-S 17-816-0560   EXP
DATEL INC.
   (Parent: Datel Holding Corp)
11 Cabot Blvd, Mansfield, MA 02048
Phone: (508) 339-3000
Sales: $35,000,000
Company Type: Private   *Employees:* 450
SIC: 3679   *Employees here:* 400
   Mfg electronic components & boards modular dc/dc
     connectors & miniature digital volt meters
Nicholas G Tagaris, President

D-U-N-S 61-790-5401   EXP
DATRON/TRANSCO, INC.
   (Parent: Datron Systems Incorporated)
200 W Los Angeles Ave, Simi Valley, CA 93065
Phone: (805) 584-1717
Sales: $45,000,000
Company Type: Public Family Member   *Employees:* 200
SIC: 3663   *Employees here:* 200
   Mfg satellite antenna communication systems & remote
     sensing systems
John J Digioia, President

D-U-N-S 06-761-9114   EXP
DATRON WORLD COMMUNICATIONS
   (Parent: Datron Systems Incorporated)
304 Enterprise St, Escondido, CA 92029
Phone: (760) 747-1079
Sales: $54,628,000
Company Type: Public Family Member   *Employees:* 140
SIC: 3663   *Employees here:* 140
   Mfg communication equipment specializing in transceivers
Rick Hyde, President

D-U-N-S 05-445-8922
DAVEL COMMUNICATIONS GROUP
1429 Massaro Blvd, Tampa, FL 33619
Phone: (813) 620-0713
Sales: $48,166,000   *Employees:* 226
Company Type: Public   *Employees here:* 70
SIC: 4813
  Pay telephone services
Robert D Hill, President

D-U-N-S 00-760-0489
DBT ONLINE, INC.
5550 W Flamingo Rd Ste B5, Las Vegas, NV 89103
Phone: (702) 257-1102
Sales: $37,546,000   *Employees:* 98
Company Type: Public   *Employees here:* 6
SIC: 4813
  Holding company
Hank Asher, President

D-U-N-S 00-121-0186   EXP
DEL GLOBAL TECHNOLOGIES CORP
1 Commerce Park, Valhalla, NY 10595
Phone: (914) 686-3600
Sales: $62,305,000   *Employees:* 466
Company Type: Public   *Employees here:* 68
SIC: 3679
  Mfg power supplies electronic filters power transformers
    capacitors & radiographic & mammography equipment
Leonard A Trugman, Chairman of the Board

D-U-N-S 18-504-6869   EXP
DELTA PRODUCTS CORPORATION
  (Parent: Delta America Ltd)
1650 W Calle Plata, Nogales, AZ 85621
Phone: (520) 294-8400
Sales: $52,200,000   *Employees:* 900
Company Type: Private   *Employees here:* 9
SIC: 3679
  Mfg electronic parts and peripherals
Bruce C Cheng, President

D-U-N-S 15-367-3595
DELTEC ELECTRONICS CORPORATION
  (Parent: Exide Electronics Group Inc)
2727 Kurtz St, San Diego, CA 92110
Phone: (619) 291-4211
Sales: $145,000,000   *Employees:* 1,300
Company Type: Private   *Employees here:* 250
SIC: 3679
  Mfg electronic circuits and power supplies
Raymond E Meyer, President

D-U-N-S 07-295-8770
DESERET MANAGEMENT CORPORATION
  (Parent: President of Latter Day Saints)
60 E South Temple Ste 575, Salt Lake City, UT 84111
Phone: (801) 538-0651
Sales: $186,200,000   *Employees:* 2,248
Company Type: Private   *Employees here:* 25
SIC: 4832
  Radio and television broadcasting ret books real estate
    operators investment and management and insurance
    agents
Rodney H Brady, Chief Executive Officer

D-U-N-S 88-314-2424   EXP
DESTIA COMMUNICATIONS, INC.
95 Route 17 S, Paramus, NJ 07652
Phone: (201) 226-4500

Sales: $83,003,000   *Employees:* 408
Company Type: Private   *Employees here:* 60
SIC: 4813
  Long distance telephone communications service
Alfred West, Chairman of the Board

D-U-N-S 10-653-9174
DIALIGHT CORP
  (Parent: Roxboro Holdings Inc)
1913 Atlantic Ave, Manasquan, NJ 08736
Phone: (732) 223-9400
Sales: $70,000,000   *Employees:* 430
Company Type: Private   *Employees here:* 80
SIC: 3679
  Mfg electronic components and optoelectronics
Michael J Kirchoff, Chief Executive Officer

D-U-N-S 11-887-9667   EXP
DIALOGIC CORPORATION
1515 Route 10, Parsippany, NJ 07054
Phone: (973) 993-3000
Sales: $261,310,000   *Employees:* 994
Company Type: Public   *Employees here:* 535
SIC: 3661
  Mfr hardware and software signal computing components
Howard G Bubb, President

D-U-N-S 79-727-3489
DIGEX, INCORPORATED
  (Parent: Intermedia Communications Inc)
1 Digex Plz, Beltsville, MD 20705
Phone: (301) 847-5000
Sales: $50,700,000   *Employees:* 400
Company Type: Public Family Member   *Employees here:* 390
SIC: 4813
  Online service and internet connectivity services
Chris Mc Cleary, President

D-U-N-S 13-160-7822
DIGITAL LINK CORPORATION
217 Humboldt Ct, Sunnyvale, CA 94089
Phone: (408) 745-6200
Sales: $54,627,000   *Employees:* 281
Company Type: Public   *Employees here:* 240
SIC: 3661
  Mfg electronic data communication equipment
Vinita Gupta, Chairman of the Board

D-U-N-S 11-329-9986   EXP
DIGITAL MICROWAVE CORPORATION
170 Rose Orchard Way, San Jose, CA 95134
Phone: (408) 943-0777
Sales: $310,490,000   *Employees:* 1,147
Company Type: Public   *Employees here:* 450
SIC: 3663
  Mfr microwave radios and equipment & fiber optic
    communication products
Charles D Kissner, Chairman of the Board

D-U-N-S 92-980-3716
DIGITEC 2000 INC.
8 W 38th St, New York, NY 10018
Phone: (212) 944-8888
Sales: $35,033,000   *Employees:* 75
Company Type: Private   *Employees here:* 75
SIC: 4813
  Markets & distributes pre-paid telephone cards & other
    telecommunications products & services
Frank Magliato, President

D-U-N-S 80-480-0266   EXP
DII GROUP, INC.
6273 Monarch Park Pl, Longmont, CO 80503

Phone: (303) 652-2221
Sales: $779,603,000
Company Type: Public
SIC: 3679
    Employees: 6,350
    Employees here: 8
   Contract electronics manufacturer mfr printed circuit boards
     software development mfr electronic test equip
Ronald R Budacz, Chairman of the Board

D-U-N-S 14-855-3662
DIRECTED ELECTRONICS INC.
2560 Progress St, Vista, CA 92083
Phone: (760) 598-6200
Sales: $74,161,000
Company Type: Private
SIC: 3669
    Employees: 95
    Employees here: 95
   Mfg automobile security alarms
Darrell E Issa, President

D-U-N-S 82-501-6934
DIRECTV, INC.
   (Parent: DirecTV Enterprises Inc)
2230 E Imperial Hwy, El Segundo, CA 90245
Phone: (310) 535-5000
Sales: $1,000,000,000
Company Type: Public Family Member
SIC: 4841
    Employees: 900
    Employees here: 650
   Direct home satellite tv services
Eddy W Hartenstein, President

D-U-N-S 84-105-0537
DISCOUNT LONG DISTANCE INC.
3100 S Harbor Blvd, Santa Ana, CA 92704
Phone: (714) 445-3900
Sales: $34,000,000
Company Type: Private
SIC: 4813
    Employees: 270
    Employees here: 270
   Telecommunications carrier
Mike Mancuso, President

D-U-N-S 12-154-5180
DISCOVERY COMMUNICATIONS INC.
7700 Wisconsin Ave, Bethesda, MD 20814
Phone: (301) 986-0444
Sales: $201,800,000
Company Type: Private
SIC: 4841
    Employees: 1,500
    Employees here: 125
   Cable television programming service
John S Hendricks, Chairman of the Board

D-U-N-S 17-605-1605
DISH, LTD
   (Parent: Echostar DBS Corporation)
90 Inverness Cir E, Englewood, CO 80112
Phone: (303) 799-8222
Sales: $475,902,000
Company Type: Public Family Member
SIC: 4841
    Employees: 150
    Employees here: 150
   Direct satellite broadcast service
Charles Ergen, President

D-U-N-S 10-307-1247
DISNEY CHANNEL INC.
   (Parent: Disney Enterprises Inc)
3800 W Alameda Ave, Burbank, CA 91505
Phone: (818) 569-7500
Sales: $46,500,000
Company Type: Public Family Member
SIC: 4841
    Employees: 350
    Employees here: 200
   Cable television service
John F Cooke, President

D-U-N-S 83-443-4532
DISPLAY TECHNOLOGIES INC.
9300 Hall Rd, Downey, CA 90241

Phone: (562) 923-9600
Sales: $55,000,000
Company Type: Private
SIC: 3669
    Employees: 275
    Employees here: 275
   Mfg traffic control devices
Ron Turcotte, President

D-U-N-S 82-489-5981   EXP
DISTANCE LONG INTERNATIONAL
888 S Andrews Ave Ste 205, Fort Lauderdale, FL 33316
Phone: (954) 522-3300
Sales: $40,116,000
Company Type: Private
SIC: 4813
    Employees: 279
    Employees here: 171
   Telecommunication services
David Hess, Chief Executive Officer

D-U-N-S 05-571-6039
DIVERSIFIED COMMUNICATIONS
121 Free St, Portland, ME 04101
Phone: (207) 842-5400
Sales: $49,496,000
Company Type: Private
SIC: 4833
    Employees: 476
    Employees here: 158
   Television broadcasting & cable television operator
David H Lowell, President

D-U-N-S 06-185-9815
DIVERSIFIED DATA PROCESSING CONSULTING
10811 Nort End, Ferndale, MI 48220
Phone: (248) 399-0715
Sales: $45,000,000
Company Type: Private
SIC: 4822
    Employees: 200
    Employees here: 60
   Electronic mail
Jon C Whiteman, President

D-U-N-S 96-643-5190
DOBSON COMMUNICATION CORP
13439 N Broadway Ext, Oklahoma City, OK 73114
Phone: (405) 391-8500
Sales: $85,169,000
Company Type: Private
SIC: 4812
    Employees: 330
    Employees here: 60
   Cellular telephone wireline telephone & fiber optic
     telecommunications services
Everett Dobson, Chairman of the Board

D-U-N-S 08-385-7383   EXP
DOLBY LABORATORIES INC.
100 Potrero Ave, San Francisco, CA 94103
Phone: (415) 558-0200
Sales: $98,573,000
Company Type: Private
SIC: 3663
    Employees: 445
    Employees here: 322
   Mfg audio electronic systems & patent licensing
Ray Dolby, Chairman of the Board

D-U-N-S 62-706-6269
DOVATRON INTERNATIONAL, INC.
   (Parent: DII Group Inc)
5405 Spine Rd, Boulder, CO 80301
Phone: (303) 581-1400
Sales: $274,651,000
Company Type: Public Family Member
SIC: 3679
    Employees: 900
    Employees here: 10
   Contract electronics manufacturer
Ronald R Budacz, Chairman of the Board

D-U-N-S 14-860-6767   EXP
DOVER TECHNOLOGIES INTL
   (Parent: Delaware Capital Holdings Inc)
1 Marine Midland Plz, Binghamton, NY 13901
Phone: (607) 773-2290

Sales: $435,400,000   *Employees:* 7,500
Company Type: Public Family Member   *Employees here:* 6
SIC: 3679
   Holding company (see operations)
John Pomeroy, President

D-U-N-S 00-514-5560   EXP
DUKANE CORPORATION
2900 Dukane Dr, Saint Charles, IL 60174
Phone: (630) 584-2300
Sales: $87,863,000   *Employees:* 642
Company Type: Private   *Employees here:* 560
SIC: 3663
   Mfg communication audio-visual and ultrasonic welding
     equipment and underwater location beacons
John M Stone Jr, Chairman of the Board

D-U-N-S 10-188-2157   EXP
E C I TELECOM INC.
927 Fern St, Altamonte Springs, FL 32701
Phone: (407) 331-5500
Sales: $176,000,000   *Employees:* 110
Company Type: Private   *Employees here:* 105
SIC: 3661
   Mfg telecommunications equipment
J R Kennedy, President

D-U-N-S 00-984-8524
E N M R TELEPHONE COOP
7111 N Prince St, Clovis, NM 88101
Phone: (505) 389-5100
Sales: $59,950,000   *Employees:* 220
Company Type: Private   *Employees here:* 150
SIC: 4813
   Telephone cooperative
Jeff Harlow, Marketing Manager

D-U-N-S 07-085-6372   EXP
EAGLE COMTRONICS INC.
4562 Waterhouse Rd, Clay, NY 13041
Phone: (315) 622-3402
Sales: $49,000,000   *Employees:* 890
Company Type: Private   *Employees here:* 80
SIC: 3663
   Mfg cable television security equipment
Alan Devendorf, Chairman of the Board

D-U-N-S 00-278-0898
EAST ASCENSION TELEPHONE CO.
   (*Parent:* Eatelcorp Inc)
913 S Burnside Ave, Gonzales, LA 70737
Phone: (225) 621-4200
Sales: $30,007,000   *Employees:* 150
Company Type: Private   *Employees here:* 104
SIC: 4813
   Telephone system
A G Scanlan II, Chief Executive Officer

D-U-N-S 09-485-1755   EXP
EASTERN ACOUSTIC WORKS, INC.
1 Main St, Whitinsville, MA 01588
Phone: (508) 234-6158
Sales: $35,305,000   *Employees:* 212
Company Type: Private   *Employees here:* 212
SIC: 3651
   Mfg loud speakers
Kenneth Berger, President

D-U-N-S 96-382-3786
EBAY, INC.
2005 Hamilton Ave Ste 350, San Jose, CA 95125
Phone: (408) 369-4830

Sales: $47,352,000   *Employees:* 76
Company Type: Public   *Employees here:* 76
SIC: 4813
   Internet trading service
Pierre M Omidyar, Chairman of the Board

D-U-N-S 18-769-7131   EXP
ECHELON CORPORATION
4015 Miranda Ave, Palo Alto, CA 94304
Phone: (650) 855-7400
Sales: $32,201,000   *Employees:* 150
Company Type: Public   *Employees here:* 112
SIC: 3663
   Mfg electronics
M K Oshman, Chairman of the Board

D-U-N-S 82-702-8143
ECHOSTAR COMMUNICATIONS CORP
5701 S Santa Fe Dr, Littleton, CO 80120
Phone: (303) 723-1000
Sales: $477,418,000   *Employees:* 2,000
Company Type: Public   *Employees here:* 150
SIC: 4841
   Direct broadcast satellite service and mfg satellite television
     equipment
Charles W Ergen, Chairman of the Board

D-U-N-S 08-416-2577
ECONOLITE CONTROL PRODUCTS
3360 E La Palma Ave, Anaheim, CA 92806
Phone: (714) 630-3700
Sales: $42,000,000   *Employees:* 200
Company Type: Private   *Employees here:* 150
SIC: 3669
   Mfg traffic control equipment
Michael C Doyle, Chief Executive Officer

D-U-N-S 00-805-3204
EDCO LLC
148 East Ave, Norwalk, CT 06851
Phone: (203) 855-8088
Sales: $93,000,000   *Employees:* 18
Company Type: Private   *Employees here:* 7
SIC: 4813
   International telecommunications
Edward Fantegrossi, President

D-U-N-S 16-185-4914   EXP
EDS PERSONAL COMMUNICATIONS CORP
   (*Parent:* Electronic Data Systems Corp)
1601 Trapelo Rd Ste 4, Waltham, MA 02451
Phone: (781) 890-1000
Sales: $35,100,000   *Employees:* 500
Company Type: Public Family Member   *Employees here:* 500
SIC: 4812
   Cellular telephone communication services
Charles H Ansley, Chief Executive Officer

D-U-N-S 00-393-3595
EDUCATIONAL BROADCASTING CORP
356 W 58th St, New York, NY 10019
Phone: (212) 560-2000
Sales: $123,498,000   *Employees:* 427
Company Type: Private   *Employees here:* 427
SIC: 4833
   Television broadcasting
William F Baker, President

D-U-N-S 14-457-5396   EXP
EFDATA CORP.
   (*Parent:* California Microwave Inc)
2105 W 5th Pl, Tempe, AZ 85281
Phone: (602) 968-0447

Sales: $90,000,000
Company Type: Public Family Member   *Employees:* 623
SIC: 3663   *Employees here:* 623
    Mfg satellite & microwave communication equipment
Donald V Anderson Jr, President

D-U-N-S 80-908-1490
EGLOBE INC.
4260 E Evans Ave, Denver, CO 80222
Phone: (303) 758-8461
Sales: $33,123,000   *Employees:* 166
Company Type: Public   *Employees here:* 166
SIC: 4813
    Long distance telephone communications
Christophe Vizas, Chairman of the Board

D-U-N-S 05-604-5974   EXP
EIS INTERNATIONAL INC.
555 Herndon Pkwy, Herndon, VA 20170
Phone: (703) 478-9808
Sales: $85,630,000   *Employees:* 389
Company Type: Public   *Employees here:* 140
SIC: 3661
    Mfg call processing systems data backup and retrieval
      develops computer software & finance leases computer
      equipment
James E Mcgowan, President

D-U-N-S 55-591-4779
ELCOM, INC.
    (Parent: Yazaki North America Inc)
20 Butterfield Trail Blvd, El Paso, TX 79906
Phone: (915) 779-0077
Sales: $32,200,000   *Employees:* 555
Company Type: Private   *Employees here:* 555
SIC: 3679
    Mfg electronic components
T Nagahashi, President

D-U-N-S 14-810-2015   EXP
ELCOTEL INC.
6428 Parkland Dr, Sarasota, FL 34243
Phone: (941) 758-0389
Sales: $46,250,000   *Employees:* 360
Company Type: Public   *Employees here:* 120
SIC: 3661
    Mfg telecommunication apparatus
Tracey L Gray, President

D-U-N-S 17-858-5113
ELECTRIC LIGHTWAVE INC.
    (Parent: Cu Capitalcorp)
4400 Ne 77th Ave, Vancouver, WA 98662
Phone: (360) 892-1000
Sales: $61,084,000   *Employees:* 573
Company Type: Public   *Employees here:* 300
SIC: 4813
    Telephone network supplier
David B Sharkey, President

D-U-N-S 04-794-9979   EXP
ELECTROMAGNETIC SCIENCES, INC.
660 Engineering Dr, Norcross, GA 30092
Phone: (770) 263-9200
Sales: $171,230,000   *Employees:* 1,200
Company Type: Public   *Employees here:* 600
SIC: 3663
    Mfg advanced communications & signal-processing
      equipment systems integration services
Dr Thomas E Sharon, Chairman of the Board

D-U-N-S 00-969-2351
ELGAR ELECTRONICS CORPORATION
    (Parent: Elgar Holdings Inc)
9250 Brown Deer Rd, San Diego, CA 92121
Phone: (619) 450-0085
Sales: $62,500,000   *Employees:* 433
Company Type: Private   *Employees here:* 290
SIC: 3679
    Mfg precision power supplies
Kenneth Kilpatrick, President

D-U-N-S 00-651-6835
EMINENCE SPEAKER CORPORATION
838 Mulberry Pike, Eminence, KY 40019
Phone: (502) 845-5622
Sales: $37,000,000   *Employees:* 225
Company Type: Private   *Employees here:* 225
SIC: 3651
    Mfg musical instrument speakers & radio loudspeakers
Robert A Gault, Chief Executive Officer

D-U-N-S 92-781-5746
EMKAY COMMUNICATIONS INC.
590 Madison Ave 18d, New York, NY 10022
Phone: (212) 583-1333
Sales: $40,000,000   *Employees:* 12
Company Type: Private   *Employees here:* 12
SIC: 4813
    Wholesales telecommunications
Mel Cooper, President

D-U-N-S 02-666-2379
EMMIS COMMUNICATIONS CORP
1 Emmis Plz, Indianapolis, IN 46204
Phone: (317) 266-0100
Sales: $125,855,000   *Employees:* 663
Company Type: Public   *Employees here:* 90
SIC: 4832
    Radio broadcasting station
Jeffrey H Smulyan, Chairman of the Board

D-U-N-S 62-249-1173
ENCORE MEDIA CORPORATION
    (Parent: Liberty Media Corporation)
5445 Dtc Pkwy Ste 600, Englewood, CO 80111
Phone: (303) 771-7700
Sales: $35,000,000   *Employees:* 265
Company Type: Public Family Member   *Employees here:* 140
SIC: 4841
    Cable television programming
John J Sie, President

D-U-N-S 05-899-4237
ENTERCOM COMMUNICATIONS CORP
401 E City Line Ave, Bala Cynwyd, PA 19004
Phone: (610) 660-5610
Sales: $132,998,000   *Employees:* 700
Company Type: Public   *Employees here:* 14
SIC: 4832
    Radio broadcasting station
Joseph M Field, President

D-U-N-S 17-622-4459
ENTERTAINMENT INC.
1 Commercial Plz, Hartford, CT 06103
Phone: (860) 549-1674
Sales: $38,138,000   *Employees:* 864
Company Type: Public   *Employees here:* 3
SIC: 4841
    Holding company
Francisco Gebauer, Investor Relation-Us Contact

D-U-N-S 13-955-7425   EXP
ERICSSON INC.
   (Parent: Ericsson Holding II Inc)
740 E Campbell Rd, Richardson, TX 75081
Phone: (972) 583-0000
Sales: $3,038,400,000   *Employees:* 8,000
Company Type: Private   *Employees here:* 2,600
SIC: 3663
   Mfg radio communications systems
Bo Hedfors, President

D-U-N-S 79-819-5251
E.SPIRE COMMUNICATIONS INC.
131 National Business Pkw, Annapolis Junction, MD 20701
Phone: (301) 617-4200
Sales: $59,000,000   *Employees:* 550
Company Type: Public   *Employees here:* 10
SIC: 4813
   Operates fiber optic networks
Anthony J Pompliano, Chairman of the Board

D-U-N-S 09-207-7171
ESPN INC.
   (Parent: ESPN Holding Company Inc)
935 Middle St Ste 2, Bristol, CT 06010
Phone: (860) 585-2000
Sales: $202,600,000   *Employees:* 1,506
Company Type: Public Family Member   *Employees here:* 1,000
SIC: 4841
   Cable television services
George Bodenheimer, President

D-U-N-S 05-070-0467   EXP
ETO INC.
   (Parent: Applied Science & Technology)
4975 N 30th St, Colorado Springs, CO 80919
Phone: (719) 260-1191
Sales: $30,000,000   *Employees:* 160
Company Type: Public Family Member *Employees here:* 160
SIC: 3663
   Mfg radio frequency amplifying & generating equipment
Tim Coutts, President

D-U-N-S 04-844-9862
EUROTHERM DRIVES INC.
   (Parent: Eurotherm International Inc)
9225 Forsyth Park Dr, Charlotte, NC 28273
Phone: (704) 588-3246
Sales: $37,000,000   *Employees:* 106
Company Type: Private   *Employees here:* 99
SIC: 3679
   Mfg electronic drive systems for motors
Dan Barnhouse, President

D-U-N-S 00-619-1613
EVENING TELEGRAM CO INC.
1226 Ogden Ave, Superior, WI 54880
Phone: (715) 394-4411
Sales: $43,800,000   *Employees:* 400
Company Type: Private   *Employees here:* 5
SIC: 4833
   Television broadcasting
John B Murphy, President

D-U-N-S 96-572-7498
EVERCOM, INC.
8201 Tristar Dr, Irving, TX 75063
Phone: (972) 988-3737
Sales: $42,900,000   *Employees:* 339
Company Type: Private   *Employees here:* 37
SIC: 4813
   Pay phone service
Todd Follmer, Chairman of the Board

D-U-N-S 60-615-5133
EXCEL COMMUNICATIONS, INC.
8750 N Central Expy, Dallas, TX 75231
Phone: (214) 863-8000
Sales: $1,454,352,000   *Employees:* 3,000
Company Type: Public   *Employees here:* 500
SIC: 4813
   Telecommunications services including residential &
   commercial service paging service dial-around service and
   calling cards
Kenny A Troutt, Chairman of the Board

D-U-N-S 19-860-4811   EXP
EXCEL SWITCHING CORPORATION
255 Independence Dr, Hyannis, MA 02601
Phone: (508) 862-3000
Sales: $88,727,000   *Employees:* 190
Company Type: Public   *Employees here:* 186
SIC: 3661
   Mfg switching platforms
Robert Madonna, President

D-U-N-S 86-119-0080
EXCITE INC.
555 Broadway St, Redwood City, CA 94063
Phone: (650) 568-6000
Sales: $154,105,000   *Employees:* 470
Company Type: Public   *Employees here:* 250
SIC: 4813
   World wide web search company
George Bell, Chief Executive Officer

D-U-N-S 10-281-3961
EXECUTONE INFORMATION SYSTEMS
478 Wheelers Farms Rd, Milford, CT 06460
Phone: (203) 876-7600
Sales: $156,396,000   *Employees:* 650
Company Type: Public   *Employees here:* 350
SIC: 3661
   Computer telephony & healthcare communications
Stanley J Kabala, Chairman of the Board

D-U-N-S 80-230-4923
EXODUS COMMUNICATIONS, INC.
2650 San Tomas Expy, Santa Clara, CA 95051
Phone: (408) 486-5000
Sales: $35,000,000   *Employees:* 345
Company Type: Public   *Employees here:* 186
SIC: 4813
   Managed internet services
Ellen M Hancock, Chief Executive Officer

D-U-N-S 11-628-6048
EXPRESS MANUFACTURING, INC.
3115 W Warner Ave, Santa Ana, CA 92704
Phone: (714) 556-1878
Sales: $34,200,000   *Employees:* 590
Company Type: Private   *Employees here:* 590
SIC: 3679
   Manufacturers through contract assembly electronic
   components and printed circuit boards
C P Chin, President

D-U-N-S 07-041-3489   EXP
F E L CORPORATION
& Central Ave Rr 547, Farmingdale, NJ 07727
Phone: (732) 938-9000
Sales: $68,800,000   *Employees:* 806
Company Type: Private   *Employees here:* 200
SIC: 3663
   Manufactures communications equipment countermeasures
   and shipboard environmental processing
William D Hurley, Chairman of the Board

D-U-N-S 92-686-2939   EXP
FACILICOM INTERNATIONAL LLC
1401 New York Ave NW, Washington, DC 20005
Phone: (202) 496-1100
Sales: $117,146,000   *Employees:* 240
Company Type: Private   *Employees here:* 100
SIC: 4813
    Long distance telecommunication services
Walter Burmeister, President

D-U-N-S 00-202-6953   EXP
FAIR-RITE PRODUCTS CORP
1 Commercial Row, Wallkill, NY 12589
Phone: (914) 895-2055
Sales: $42,164,000   *Employees:* 500
Company Type: Private   *Employees here:* 235
SIC: 3679
    Mfg electronic cores & emi suppression products
Richard Parker, Chairman of the Board

D-U-N-S 83-457-9195
FALCON HOLDING GROUP LP
10900 Wilshire Blvd, Los Angeles, CA 90024
Phone: (310) 824-9990
Sales: $255,886,000   *Employees:* 967
Company Type: Private   *Employees here:* 536
SIC: 4841
    Cable television service
Marc B Nathanson, Managing Partner

D-U-N-S 79-806-7864   EXP
FARGO ASSEMBLY OF PA INC.
800 W Washington St, Norristown, PA 19401
Phone: (610) 272-6850
Sales: $31,000,000   *Employees:* 430
Company Type: Private   *Employees here:* 105
SIC: 3679
    Mfg electrical specialty wire harnesses
Ron Bergan, Chairman of the Board

D-U-N-S 00-978-7623
FARMERS TELEPHONE COOPERATIVE
1101 E Main St, Kingstree, SC 29556
Phone: (843) 382-2333
Sales: $37,603,000   *Employees:* 270
Company Type: Private   *Employees here:* 150
SIC: 4813
    Telephone communication, except radio
John L Mcdaniel, Executive Vice-President

D-U-N-S 15-528-1413
FEDERAL BROADCASTING COMPANY
    (Parent: Raycom Media Inc)
201 Monroe St Ste 710, Montgomery, AL 36104
Phone: (334) 206-1400
Sales: $55,300,000   *Employees:* 500
Company Type: Private   *Employees here:* 7
SIC: 4833
    Operates television stations
Dale Rands, Chairman of the Board

D-U-N-S 80-014-3497   EXP
FILTRONIC COMTEK INC.
31901 Comteck Ln, Salisbury, MD 21804
Phone: (410) 546-7700
Sales: $73,159,000   *Employees:* 509
Company Type: Private   *Employees here:* 307
SIC: 3679
    Manufactures commercial uhf vhf & microwave components
      & sub systems
Thomas A Lambalot, President

D-U-N-S 00-117-6544   EXP
FIRE-LITE ALARMS, INC.
    (Parent: Pittway Corporation)
12 Clintonville Rd, Northford, CT 06472
Phone: (203) 484-7161
Sales: $30,700,000   *Employees:* 350
Company Type: Public Family Member   *Employees here:* 320
SIC: 3669
    Mfg fire detection systems
Mark Levy, President

D-U-N-S 79-695-4634   EXP
FIRST ALERT INC.
    (Parent: Sunbeam Corporation)
3901 Liberty Street Rd, Aurora, IL 60504
Phone: (630) 851-7330
Sales: $186,941,000   *Employees:* 3,142
Company Type: Public Family Member   *Employees here:* 6
SIC: 3669
    Mfg home safety and security products
B J Messner, President

D-U-N-S 00-794-2659
FISHER BROADCASTING INC.
    (Parent: Fisher Companies Inc)
100 4th Ave N, Seattle, WA 98109
Phone: (206) 443-4000
Sales: $84,100,000   *Employees:* 750
Company Type: Public Family Member   *Employees here:* 315
SIC: 4833
    Television & radio broadcasting stations
Patrick Scott, President

D-U-N-S 01-568-1414
FIVE RIVERS ELECTRONIC INNOV
1915 Snapps Ferry Rd, Greeneville, TN 37745
Phone: (423) 636-5260
Sales: $400,000,000   *Employees:* 1,200
Company Type: Private   *Employees here:* 1,200
SIC: 3651
    Electronics manufacturing
George B Taylor, Chief Executive Officer

D-U-N-S 86-947-2647
FLORIDA RSA 8 INC.
    (Parent: United States Cellular Corp)
8410 W Bryn Mawr Ave, Chicago, IL 60631
Phone: (773) 399-8900
Sales: $35,100,000   *Employees:* 500
Company Type: Public Family Member   *Employees here:* 500
SIC: 4812
    Cellular wireless communications
Donald Nelson, President

D-U-N-S 60-670-9988   EXP
FNET CORP
    (Parent: Franklin Telecommunications)
733 Lakefield Rd, Thousand Oaks, CA 91361
Phone: (805) 373-8688
Sales: $210,000,000   *Employees:* 15
Company Type: Public Family Member   *Employees here:* 5
SIC: 4813
    Internet services
James L Magruder, Chief Executive Officer

D-U-N-S 96-208-4174
FOSTER NORTH AMERICA INC.
1000 E State Pkwy Ste G, Schaumburg, IL 60173
Phone: (847) 310-8200

Sales: $89,400,000   *Employees:* 900
Company Type: Private   *Employees here:* 25
SIC: 3651
    Whol audio electronic components & mfg speakers and
    speaker systems
Mitsugu Takada, President

D-U-N-S 16-160-6314
FOX BROADCASTING COMPANY
    (Parent: Fox Entertainment Group Inc)
10201 W Pico Blvd, Los Angeles, CA 90064
Phone: (310) 277-2211
Sales: $1,456,530,000   *Employees:* 300
Company Type: Public Family Member   *Employees here:* 200
SIC: 4833
    Television broadcasting
Larry Jacobsen, Chief Financial Officer

D-U-N-S 14-859-0383
FOX TELEVISION STATIONS INC.
    (Parent: Fox Entertainment Group Inc)
1999 S Bundy Dr, Los Angeles, CA 90025
Phone: (310) 584-2000
Sales: $1,133,141,000   *Employees:* 1,350
Company Type: Public Family Member   *Employees here:* 200
SIC: 4833
    Television broadcasting
Les Hinton, Chairman of the Board

D-U-N-S 14-980-7000
FPL GROUP CAPITAL INC.
    (Parent: FPL Group Inc)
700 Universe Blvd, North Palm Beach, FL 33408
Phone: (561) 694-4000
Sales: $66,800,000   *Employees:* 500
Company Type: Public Family Member   *Employees here:* 1
SIC: 4841
    Holding company through subsidiaries operates in real estate
    agriculture consulting non utility energy projects & cable
    TV
James Broadhead, President

D-U-N-S 00-699-4065
FRONTIER CORPORATION
180 S Clinton Ave, Rochester, NY 14646
Phone: (716) 777-1000
Sales: $2,352,886,000   *Employees:* 7,444
Company Type: Public   *Employees here:* 750
SIC: 4813
    Telephone communications & wireless communications
Joseph P Clayton, President

D-U-N-S 78-694-5451   EXP
FUJITSU NETWORK COMMUNICATIONS
    (Parent: Fujitsu America Inc)
2801 Telecom Pkwy, Richardson, TX 75082
Phone: (972) 690-6000
Sales: $1,017,486,000   *Employees:* 2,100
Company Type: Private   *Employees here:* 1,285
SIC: 3661
    Mfg fiber optic communication equip cellular phones &
    accessories
Shigeki Saito, Chief Financial Officer

D-U-N-S 08-198-0286
G E AMERICAN COMMUNICATIONS
    (Parent: General Electric Company)
4 Research Way, Princeton, NJ 08540
Phone: (609) 987-4000

Sales: $67,100,000   *Employees:* 550
Company Type: Public Family Member   *Employees here:* 225
SIC: 4899
    Domestic satellite communications
John F Connelly, Chairman of the Board

D-U-N-S 80-014-7837
G E CAPITAL COMM SVCS CORP
    (Parent: General Electric Capital Corp)
6540 Powers Ferry Rd NW, Atlanta, GA 30339
Phone: (770) 644-7600
Sales: $49,110,000   *Employees:* 200
Company Type: Public Family Member   *Employees here:* 200
SIC: 4813
    Resale of long distance telephone services
Gregg L Haddad, President

D-U-N-S 17-737-2224
G S COMMUNICATIONS INC.
    (Parent: Great Southern Prtg & Mfg Co)
442 W Patrick St, Frederick, MD 21701
Phone: (301) 662-6419
Sales: $45,000,000   *Employees:* 221
Company Type: Private   *Employees here:* 146
SIC: 4841
    Cable television service & installation
George B Delaplaine Jr, Chief Executive Officer

D-U-N-S 86-118-5627
G S T TELECOM, INC.
    (Parent: GST USA Inc)
4001 Main St, Vancouver, WA 98663
Phone: (350) 906-7100
Sales: $140,700,000   *Employees:* 1,100
Company Type: Public Family Member   *Employees here:* 400
SIC: 4813
    Telecommunications
John Warta, Chairman of the Board

D-U-N-S 16-140-9123
GABRIEL INC.
1500 Executive Dr, Elgin, IL 60123
Phone: (847) 888-7259
Sales: $70,051,000   *Employees:* 300
Company Type: Private   *Employees here:* 10
SIC: 3663
    Mfg CB radio antennas and radios switches auto OEM
    electro-mechanical components radar detectors & laser
    defusers
James P Liautaud, Chairman of the Board

D-U-N-S 00-232-4473   EXP
GAI-TRONICS CORPORATION
    (Parent: Salient 3 Communications Inc)
400 E Wyomissing Ave, Mohnton, PA 19540
Phone: (610) 777-1374
Sales: $59,790,000   *Employees:* 619
Company Type: Public Family Member   *Employees here:* 280
SIC: 3661
    Mfg telephone equipment & parts
G E Smith, President

D-U-N-S 83-882-5263
GALAXY TELECOM, L P
1220 N Main St, Sikeston, MO 63801
Phone: (573) 472-8200
Sales: $68,808,000   *Employees:* 500
Company Type: Private   *Employees here:* 55
SIC: 4841
    Cable/pay television service
Jimmy Gleason, Chief Operating Officer

D-U-N-S 17-403-4553
GANNETT TENNESSEE LTD PARTNR
(*Parent:* Gannett Co Inc De)
1513 Hutchison Ave, Knoxville, TN 37917
Phone: (423) 637-1010
Sales: $30,000,000   *Employees:* 130
Company Type: Public Family Member   *Employees here:* 130
SIC: 4833
   Television station
Jeffrey Lee, President

D-U-N-S 61-476-1385
GARDEN STATE CABLE VISION, LP
1250 Haddonfield Berlin R, Cherry Hill, NJ 08034
Phone: (609) 354-1880
Sales: $109,126,000   *Employees:* 300
Company Type: Private   *Employees here:* 280
SIC: 4841
   Cable television systems
Patrick Mc Call, Vice-President

D-U-N-S 09-240-4961   EXP
GARDINER COMMUNICATIONS CORP
3605 Security St, Garland, TX 75042
Phone: (214) 348-4747
Sales: $35,000,000   *Employees:* 200
Company Type: Private   *Employees here:* 200
SIC: 3663
   Manufactures satellite and television reception low noise
      block down converters
James M Harris, President

D-U-N-S 83-704-6630   EXP
GE-HARRIS RAILWAY ELECTRIC LLC
407 N John Rodes Blvd, Melbourne, FL 32934
Phone: (407) 242-4000
Sales: $114,200,000   *Employees:* 394
Company Type: Private   *Employees here:* 324
SIC: 3669
   Mfg electronic systems
Greg Lucier, President

D-U-N-S 00-252-1359   EXP
GEMINI INDUSTRIES INC.
(*Parent:* Gemini Holdings Inc)
215 Entin Rd, Clifton, NJ 07014
Phone: (973) 471-9050
Sales: $159,100,000   *Employees:* 450
Company Type: Private   *Employees here:* 441
SIC: 3663
   Mfrs tv antennas and wholesales imported video and audio
      equipment accessories computer and telephone accessories
George Nebel, Chairman of the Board

D-U-N-S 06-828-9610   EXP
GEMINI SOUND PRODUCTS CORP
8 Germak Dr, Carteret, NJ 07008
Phone: (732) 969-9000
Sales: $44,000,000   *Employees:* 100
Company Type: Private   *Employees here:* 85
SIC: 3651
   Manufactures audio equipment speaker systems and carrying
      cases
Isaac Cabasso, Chairman of the Board

D-U-N-S 93-794-1615
GEMSTAR INTL GROUP LTD
135 N Los Robles Ave, Pasadena, CA 91101
Phone: (626) 792-5700

Sales: $126,552,000   *Employees:* 150
Company Type: Public   *Employees here:* 50
SIC: 4841
   Provider of on-screen interactive television guide and vcr
      control service and licensing services
Thomas L Lau, Chairman of the Board

D-U-N-S 01-119-9767   EXP
GENERAL COMMUNICATION, INC.
2550 Denali St Ste 1000, Anchorage, AK 99503
Phone: (907) 265-5600
Sales: $223,809,000   *Employees:* 1,000
Company Type: Public   *Employees here:* 400
SIC: 4813
   Telephone company & whol satellite communication
      equipment
Ronald A Duncan, President

D-U-N-S 62-387-7461
GENERAL DATACOMM INC.
(*Parent:* General Datacomm Industries)
1579 Straits Tpke, Middlebury, CT 06762
Phone: (203) 574-1118
Sales: $162,800,000   *Employees:* 1,700
Company Type: Public Family Member   *Employees here:* 1,500
SIC: 3661
   Mfg telecommunications equipment & installs & services
      multi media networks
Charles P Johnson, Chairman of the Board

D-U-N-S 00-218-3333   EXP
GENERAL INSTRUMENT CORPORATION
101 Tournament Dr, Horsham, PA 19044
Phone: (215) 323-1000
Sales: $1,764,088,000   *Employees:* 7,350
Company Type: Public   *Employees here:* 60
SIC: 3663
   Mfg communication equipment
Edward D Breen, Chairman of the Board

D-U-N-S 11-995-8049
GENERAL SEMICONDUCTOR INC.
10 Melville Park Rd, Melville, NY 11747
Phone: (516) 847-3000
Sales: $361,891,000   *Employees:* 3,000
Company Type: Public   *Employees here:* 123
SIC: 3679
   Mfg rectifiers & transient voltage suppression components
Ronald A Ostertag, Chairman of the Board

D-U-N-S 00-780-9783
GEORGIA ALLTEL INC.
(*Parent:* Alltel Corporation)
906 Vista Dr, Dalton, GA 30721
Phone: (706) 279-7600
Sales: $3,192,418,000   *Employees:* 450
Company Type: Public Family Member   *Employees here:* 127
SIC: 4813
   Telephone utility
J S Chesbro, President

D-U-N-S 80-847-4100
GEORGIA PUBLIC TELECOM COMM
260 14th St NW, Atlanta, GA 30318
Phone: (404) 685-2400
Sales: $31,465,000   *Employees:* 145
Company Type: Private   *Employees here:* 125
SIC: 4832
   Radio and television brodcast company
Dr Werner Rogers, Director

D-U-N-S 19-895-5015   EXP
GEOTEK COMMUNICATIONS, INC.
102 Chestnut Ridge Rd, Montvale, NJ 07645
Phone: (201) 930-9305
Sales: $65,510,000   *Employees:* 685
Company Type: Public   *Employees here:* 240
SIC: 4812
  Wireless telecommunications
Stephen G Pearse, President

D-U-N-S 11-125-8539
G.I.K TECHNOLOGY, INC.
436 14th St Ste 1005, Oakland, CA 94612
Phone: (415) 381-5581
Sales: $50,000,000   *Employees:* 4
Company Type: Private   *Employees here:* 4
SIC: 4813
  Multi media services
Michael Ledbetter, President

D-U-N-S 80-386-4149
GLENAYRE TECHNOLOGIES INC.
5935 Carnegie Blvd, Charlotte, NC 28209
Phone: (704) 553-0038
Sales: $451,679,000   *Employees:* 1,900
Company Type: Public   *Employees here:* 15
SIC: 3663
  Mfg electronic paging voice messaging message management
    mobile data systems transit and radio telephone systems
Ramon D Ardizzone, Chairman of the Board

D-U-N-S 80-996-0156
GLOBAL COMMERCE & MEDIA NETWORK
430 Park Ave Fl 19, New York, NY 10022
Phone: (212) 754-1616
Sales: $100,000,000   *Employees:* 25
Company Type: Private   *Employees here:* 25
SIC: 4813
  Long distance telecommunications service investment service
    and television wire cable & satellite distribution service
Al Mason, President

D-U-N-S 78-579-9362
GLOBAL ONE COMMUNICATIONS LLC
  (*Parent:* Utelcom Inc)
12490 Sunrise Valley Dr, Reston, VA 20191
Phone: (703) 689-6000
Sales: $365,300,000   *Employees:* 3,000
Company Type: Public Family Member   *Employees here:* 2,474
SIC: 4899
  Holding company
Viesturs Vucins, Chief Executive Officer

D-U-N-S 80-889-9587
GLOBAL TELESYSTEMS GROUP INC.
1751 Pinnacle Dr, Mc Lean, VA 22102
Phone: (703) 918-4500
Sales: $47,098,000   *Employees:* 2,000
Company Type: Public   *Employees here:* 100
SIC: 4813
  Holding company which through subsidiaries provides
    telecommunication services
Gerald Thames, President

D-U-N-S 83-911-1606
GLOBALSTAR, L. P.
3200 Zanker Rd, San Jose, CA 95134
Phone: (408) 933-4000
Sales: $31,500,000   *Employees:* 250
Company Type: Private   *Employees here:* 200
SIC: 4813
  Telephone communication, except radio
Fuad A Executive, N/A

D-U-N-S 17-794-5870
GLOBECAST NORTH AMERICA INC.
7291 NW 74th St, Miami, FL 33166
Phone: (305) 887-1600
Sales: $120,000,000   *Employees:* 250
Company Type: Private   *Employees here:* 125
SIC: 4841
  Satellite systems
Robert Behar, President

D-U-N-S 15-726-9697
GN NETCOM INC.
77 Northeastern Blvd, Nashua, NH 03062
Phone: (603) 598-1100
Sales: $45,000,000   *Employees:* 200
Company Type: Private   *Employees here:* 190
SIC: 3661
  Mfg telephone headsets
P M Fairweather, President

D-U-N-S 13-114-6698   EXP
GO-VIDEO, INC.
7835 E Mcclain Dr, Scottsdale, AZ 85260
Phone: (602) 998-3400
Sales: $48,898,000   *Employees:* 76
Company Type: Public   *Employees here:* 50
SIC: 3651
  Mfg video cassette recorders and video surveillance products
Douglas P Klein, Chief Financial Officer

D-U-N-S 96-847-3223
GOLDEN SKY SYSTEMS, INC.
605 W 47th St Ste 300, Kansas City, MO 64112
Phone: (816) 753-5544
Sales: $60,000,000   *Employees:* 450
Company Type: Private   *Employees here:* 25
SIC: 4841
  Direct broadcast satellite services (dbs)
Rodney Weary, President

D-U-N-S 79-954-1099
GOLDENLINE NETWORK SERVICE
501 Santa Monica Blvd, Santa Monica, CA 90401
Phone: (310) 656-5267
Sales: $50,000,000   *Employees:* 100
Company Type: Private   *Employees here:* 8
SIC: 4813
  Telephone communications
Jeffrey Sudikoff, Chairman

D-U-N-S 16-649-7057
GRANITE BROADCASTING CORP
767 3rd Ave Fl 34, New York, NY 10017
Phone: (212) 826-2530
Sales: $153,512,000   *Employees:* 1,160
Company Type: Public   *Employees here:* 8
SIC: 4833
  Television broadcasting
W D Cornwell, Chairman of the Board

D-U-N-S 07-272-1111   EXP
GRAPHNET INC.
  (*Parent:* Q Net Inc)
329 Alfred Ave, Teaneck, NJ 07666
Phone: (201) 837-5100
Sales: $50,000,000   *Employees:* 250
Company Type: Private   *Employees here:* 100
SIC: 4822
  Data record carrier providing computer based messaging
    services
Yaakov Elkon, President

D-U-N-S 04-297-3875
GRAY COMMUNICATIONS SYSTEMS
126 N Washington St, Albany, GA 31701
Phone: (912) 888-9390
Sales: $103,548,000　　　　　　　　　　*Employees:* 1,200
Company Type: Public　　　　　　　　　*Employees here:* 200
SIC: 4833
　Television broadcasting and newspaper publishing
J M Robinson, President

D-U-N-S 82-599-7059
GREAT UNIVERSAL INCORPORATED
　(*Parent:* MIC-USA Inc (de Corp))
153 E 53rd St Ste 5900, New York, NY 10022
Phone: (212) 355-3440
Sales: $144,368,000　　　　　　　　　*Employees:* 1,300
Company Type: Private　　　　　　　　*Employees here:* 50
SIC: 4812
　Cellular radio telephone & communication services
William Mustard, President

D-U-N-S 00-585-4849
GREATER WASHINGTON EDUCATIONAL TELECOM ASSN
2775 S Quincy St, Arlington, VA 22206
Phone: (703) 998-2600
Sales: $58,380,000　　　　　　　　　*Employees:* 305
Company Type: Private　　　　　　　　*Employees here:* 230
SIC: 4833
　Television broadcasting
Sharon Rockefeller, President

D-U-N-S 60-312-0296
GROUP LONG DISTANCE INC.
1451 W Cypress Ave, Fort Lauderdale, FL 33309
Phone: (954) 771-9696
Sales: $54,341,000　　　　　　　　　*Employees:* 7
Company Type: Public　　　　　　　　*Employees here:* 7
SIC: 4813
　Telephone communication service
Gerald M Dunne Jr, President

D-U-N-S 93-186-7402
GST TELECOMMUNICATIONS INC.
4001 Main Streer, Vancouver, WA 98663
Phone: (360) 906-7100
Sales: $194,700,000　　　　　　　　*Employees:* 1,520
Company Type: Public　　　　　　　　*Employees here:* 3
SIC: 4813
　Telecommunications
Joseph Basile Jr, Chief Executive Officer

D-U-N-S 05-984-5990
GTE AIRFONE INCORPORATED (DEL)
　(*Parent:* GTE Mobile Communications Inc)
2809 Butterfield Rd, Oak Brook, IL 60523
Phone: (630) 572-1800
Sales: $100,000,000　　　　　　　　*Employees:* 210
Company Type: Public Family Member　*Employees here:* 100
SIC: 4812
　Telephone communication
Kathy Harless, President

D-U-N-S 00-129-3950
GTE CORPORATION
1255 Corporate Dr, Irving, TX 75038
Phone: (972) 507-5000
Sales: $23,260,000,000　　　　　　*Employees:* 114,000
Company Type: Public　　　　　　　*Employees here:* 650
SIC: 4813
　Telephone communication telecommunication products and
　services
Charles R Lee, Chairman of the Board

D-U-N-S 96-429-7782
GTE CYBERTRUST SOLUTIONS INC.
　(*Parent:* GTE Government Systems Corp)
77 A St, Needham, MA 02494
Phone: (781) 449-2000
Sales: $63,600,000　　　　　　　　　*Employees:* 500
Company Type: Public Family Member　*Employees here:* 500
SIC: 4813
　Operates as a security system via the internet
Peter Hussey, President

D-U-N-S 11-618-7758
GTE GOVERNMENT SYSTEMS CORP
　(*Parent:* Contel Federal Systems Inc)
77 A St, Needham, MA 02494
Phone: (781) 449-2000
Sales: $1,300,000,000　　　　　　　*Employees:* 7,000
Company Type: Public Family Member　*Employees here:* 1,200
SIC: 3661
　Mfg telecommunications information & technologies systems
　& solutions
Armen D Marderosian, President

D-U-N-S 19-557-7333
GTE INTELLIGENT NETWORK SVCS INC.
　(*Parent:* GTE Corporation)
5525 N Macarthur Blvd, Irving, TX 75038
Phone: (972) 751-3900
Sales: $44,300,000　　　　　　　　　*Employees:* 350
Company Type: Public Family Member　*Employees here:* 350
SIC: 4813
　Internet provider
Alex Coleman, General Manager

D-U-N-S 86-132-0992
GTE MIDWEST INCORPORATED
　(*Parent:* GTE Corporation)
1000 Gte Dr, Wentzville, MO 63385
Phone: (314) 332-7300
Sales: $576,022,000　　　　　　　　*Employees:* NA
Company Type: Public Family Member　*Employees here:* NA
SIC: 4813
　Telephone service
M M Foster, President

D-U-N-S 61-446-4964
GTE MOBILE COMMUNICATIONS INC.
　(*Parent:* GTE Corporation)
245 Perimeter Center Pkwy, Atlanta, GA 30346
Phone: (770) 391-8000
Sales: $2,549,000,000　　　　　　　*Employees:* 9,000
Company Type: Public Family Member　*Employees here:* 1,000
SIC: 4812
　Through subsidiaries operates as a mobile telephone service
　paging service and ret cellular telephones and equipment
Mark Feighner, President

D-U-N-S 62-777-3328
GTE MOBILNET HAWAII INC.
　(*Parent:* GTE Wireless Incorporated)
733 Bishop St Ste 1900, Honolulu, HI 96813
Phone: (808) 536-4848
Sales: $56,000,000　　　　　　　　　*Employees:* 175
Company Type: Public Family Member　*Employees here:* 100
SIC: 4812
　Cellular telephone services
Ronald Grawert, Chief Executive Officer

D-U-N-S 11-539-6525
GTE MOBILNET TAMPA INC.
　(*Parent:* GTE Wireless Incorporated)
600 N West Shore Blvd, Tampa, FL 33609
Phone: (813) 282-6000

Sales: $55,900,000
Company Type: Public Family Member
SIC: 4812
   Cellular radio services
Byron W Smith, President

Employees: 800
Employees here: 250

D-U-N-S 00-143-2210
GTE SERVICE CORPORATION
   (Parent: GTE Corporation)
700 Hidden Rdg, Irving, TX 75038
Phone: (972) 718-5000
Sales: $83,500,000
Company Type: Public Family Member
SIC: 4813
   Telephone service
Philip W Matzke, President

Employees: 890
Employees here: 3

D-U-N-S 00-279-8957
GTE WEST COAST INCORPORATED
   (Parent: GTE Northwest Incorporated)
1800 41st St, Everett, WA 98201
Phone: (425) 261-5321
Sales: $66,400,000
Company Type: Public Family Member
SIC: 4813
   Local & long distance telephone service
Eilene Oneill-Odum, President

Employees: 522
Employees here: 13

D-U-N-S 62-777-3567
GTE WIRELESS OF MIDWEST INC.
   (Parent: GTE Wireless Incorporated)
17500 Rockside Rd, Cleveland, OH 44146
Phone: (219) 927-3000
Sales: $111,400,000
Company Type: Public Family Member
SIC: 4812
   Cellular telephone service
Michael Ritter, President

Employees: 1,600
Employees here: 600

D-U-N-S 60-507-1703
G.T.E. WORLD HEADQUARTERS
600 Hidden Rdg, Irving, TX 75038
Phone: (972) 718-5000
Sales: $125,700,000
Company Type: Private
SIC: 4813
   Marketing of business systems
Mark Feigher, President

Employees: 983
Employees here: 983

D-U-N-S 00-118-8218
GTI CORPORATION
   (Parent: Technitrol Inc)
9715 Businesspark Ave, San Diego, CA 92131
Phone: (619) 537-2500
Sales: $82,591,000
Company Type: Public Family Member
SIC: 3679
   Mfg electronic components
Albert J Hugo-Martinez, President

Employees: 6,280
Employees here: 140

D-U-N-S 79-227-1652
GULF COAST SERVICES INC.
100 W Laurel Ave, Foley, AL 36535
Phone: (334) 952-5100
Sales: $49,559,000
Company Type: Private
SIC: 4813
   Telephone communications
Marjorie Snook, President

Employees: 365
Employees here: 31

D-U-N-S 00-484-7851
GULF TELEPHONE COMPANY, INC.
   (Parent: Gulf Coast Services Inc)
116 N Alston St, Foley, AL 36535
Phone: (334) 952-5100
Sales: $42,606,000
Company Type: Private
SIC: 4813
   Telephone communications
Marjorie Snook, President

Employees: 373
Employees here: 50

D-U-N-S 78-595-2862
H C CROWN CORP
2501 Mcgee St, Kansas City, MO 64108
Phone: (816) 274-5111
Sales: $112,900,000
Company Type: Private
SIC: 4833
   Operates television stations
Don Hall, President

Employees: 1,000
Employees here: 1,000

D-U-N-S 08-267-2197
HARBOR ELECTRONICS INC.
   (Parent: Berg Electronics Group Inc)
825 Old Trail Rd, Etters, PA 17319
Phone: (717) 938-7200
Sales: $57,000,000
Company Type: Private
SIC: 3679
   Mfg electronic cable harness assemblies
Timothy Conlon, President

Employees: 720
Employees here: 20

D-U-N-S 04-765-3555   EXP
HARMAN INTERNATIONAL INDUSTRIES INC.
1101 Penn Ave NW Ste 1010, Washington, DC 20004
Phone: (202) 393-1101
Sales: $1,513,255,000
Company Type: Public
SIC: 3651
   Mfg audio and video electronic components
Bernard A Girod, President

Employees: 10,010
Employees here: 5

D-U-N-S 01-925-5041   EXP
HARMAN-MOTIVE INC.
   (Parent: Harman International Inds Inc)
1201 S Ohio St, Martinsville, IN 46151
Phone: (765) 342-5551
Sales: $131,600,000
Company Type: Public Family Member
SIC: 3651
   Mfg amplifiers & automotive speakers
Gregory P Stapleton, President

Employees: 1,172
Employees here: 1,000

D-U-N-S 02-092-4197   EXP
HARMAN MUSIC GROUP INC.
   (Parent: Harman International Inds Inc)
8760 Sandy Pkwy, Sandy, UT 84070
Phone: (801) 566-8800
Sales: $49,700,000
Company Type: Public Family Member
SIC: 3651
   Mfg electronic audio sound reproduction equipment
Wayne Morris, President

Employees: 450
Employees here: 450

D-U-N-S 16-110-2256
HARMAN PRO NORTH AMERICA, INC.
   (Parent: Harman International Inds Inc)
1449 Donaldson Pike, Nashville, TN 37217
Phone: (615) 399-2199

Sales: $40,000,000　　　　　　　　　　　　　　*Employees:* 42
Company Type: Public Family Member　　　　　*Employees here:* 40
SIC: 3651
　　Distributor of audio equipment
Brian Dever, Credit Manager

D-U-N-S 00-715-1327　　　　　　　　　　　　　　　　　EXP
HARMON INDUSTRIES INC.
1600 Ne Coronado, Blue Springs, MO 64014
Phone: (816) 229-3345
Sales: $213,530,000　　　　　　　　　　　　*Employees:* 1,504
Company Type: Public　　　　　　　　　　　*Employees here:* 44
SIC: 3669
　　Mfg electronic equipment for the railroad industry
Bjorn E Olsson, President

D-U-N-S 60-278-8580　　　　　　　　　　　　　　　　　EXP
HARMONIC LIGHTWAVES INC.
549 Baltic Way, Sunnyvale, CA 94089
Phone: (408) 542-2500
Sales: $83,857,000　　　　　　　　　　　　　*Employees:* 215
Company Type: Public　　　　　　　　　　　*Employees here:* 175
SIC: 3663
　　Designs mfg and markets optical transmitters nodes receivers
　　digital video compression and modulation equipment and
　　elements
Anthony J Ley, Chairman of the Board

D-U-N-S 00-420-3337
HARRIS CORPORATION
1025 W Nasa Blvd, Melbourne, FL 32919
Phone: (407) 727-9100
Sales: $3,890,200,000　　　　　　　　　　　*Employees:* 28,500
Company Type: Public　　　　　　　　　　　*Employees here:* 269
SIC: 3663
　　Mfg electronic systems semiconductors communications and
　　office equipment
Phillip W Farmer, Chairman of the Board

D-U-N-S 00-378-7231
HARRON COMMUNICATIONS CORP
70 Lancaster Ave, Malvern, PA 19355
Phone: (610) 644-7500
Sales: $66,800,000　　　　　　　　　　　　　*Employees:* 500
Company Type: Private　　　　　　　　　　　*Employees here:* 50
SIC: 4841
　　Cable television services & operates television stations
Paul F Harron Jr, President

D-U-N-S 10-395-4525
HARTFORD TELEVISION, INC.
　　(Parent: Tribune Company)
1 Corporate Ctr, Hartford, CT 06103
Phone: (860) 527-6161
Sales: $40,000,000　　　　　　　　　　　　　*Employees:* 110
Company Type: Public Family Member　　　　*Employees here:* 110
SIC: 4833
　　Television broadcasting station
Jerome Martin, General Manager

D-U-N-S 86-930-5961
HARVARD CUSTOM MANUFACTURING
　　(Parent: Harvard Custom Mfg Llc)
600 Glen Ave, Salisbury, MD 21804
Phone: (410) 548-7800
Sales: $43,000,000　　　　　　　　　　　　　*Employees:* 425
Company Type: Private　　　　　　　　　　　*Employees here:* 230
SIC: 3679
　　Mfg electronic cables harnesses and electric boxes
Gregg Moffitt, President

D-U-N-S 15-124-2435
HAUSER COMMUNICATIONS INC.
712 5th Ave, New York, NY 10019
Phone: (212) 956-5665
Sales: $100,500,000　　　　　　　　　　　　*Employees:* 750
Company Type: Private　　　　　　　　　　　*Employees here:* 750
SIC: 4841
　　Cable television systems
Gustave M Hauser, Chairman of the Board

D-U-N-S 96-139-0762
HAYES CORPORATION
5835 Peachtree Cors E, Norcross, GA 30092
Phone: (770) 840-9200
Sales: $199,612,000　　　　　　　　　　　　*Employees:* 768
Company Type: Public　　　　　　　　　　　*Employees here:* 600
SIC: 3661
　　Mfg remote access products
Ronald A Howard, Chairman of the Board

D-U-N-S 05-644-4060　　　　　　　　　　　　　　　　　EXP
H.C.C. INDUSTRIES INC.
　　(Parent: Windward Capital Partners L P)
4232 Temple City Blvd, Rosemead, CA 91770
Phone: (626) 443-8933
Sales: $46,400,000　　　　　　　　　　　　　*Employees:* 800
Company Type: Private　　　　　　　　　　　*Employees here:* 15
SIC: 3679
　　Mfg electronic connectors and hermetic seals
Andrew Goldfarb, President

D-U-N-S 87-774-9861
HEARST-ARGYLE TELEVISION INC.
　　(Parent: Hearst Corporation)
888 7th Ave Ste 801, New York, NY 10106
Phone: (212) 649-2300
Sales: $128,512,000　　　　　　　　　　　　*Employees:* 3,200
Company Type: Public　　　　　　　　　　　*Employees here:* 17
SIC: 4833
　　Network-affiliated television stations production of
　　programming for cable networks & broadcast stations
　　management services
Bob Marbut, Chairman of the Board

D-U-N-S 84-850-8073
HEARTLAND WIRELESS COMMUNICATIONS
200 Chisholm Pl Ste 200, Plano, TX 75075
Phone: (972) 423-9494
Sales: $78,792,000　　　　　　　　　　　　　*Employees:* 790
Company Type: Public　　　　　　　　　　　*Employees here:* 10
SIC: 4841
　　Own & operate wireless cable television systems
Carroll D Mchenry, President

D-U-N-S 78-624-9797
HEFTEL BROADCASTING CORP
3102 Oak Lawn Ave Ste 215, Dallas, TX 75219
Phone: (214) 855-8882
Sales: $154,869,000　　　　　　　　　　　　*Employees:* 609
Company Type: Public　　　　　　　　　　　*Employees here:* 90
SIC: 4832
　　Radio stations
Mchenry T Tichenor Jr, Chairman of the Board

D-U-N-S 86-939-5194
HELICON GROUP, L.P.
630 E Palisade Ave, Englewood Cliffs, NJ 07632
Phone: (201) 568-7720
Sales: $42,946,000　　　　　　　　　　　　　*Employees:* 180
Company Type: Private　　　　　　　　　　　*Employees here:* 30
SIC: 4841
　　Cable television service
Baum Investments, General Partner

D-U-N-S 06-522-1475
HERITAGE CABLEVISION, (IA)
 (*Parent:* Heritage Communications Inc)
2205 Ingersoll Ave, Des Moines, IA 50312
Phone: (515) 246-1890
Sales: $269,400,000
Company Type: Public Family Member
SIC: 4841
 Cable television service
Douglas Nix, General Manager

Employees: 2,000
Employees here: 300

D-U-N-S 04-234-5363
HERITAGE CABLEVISION OF CAL
1900 S 10th St, San Jose, CA 95112
Phone: (408) 452-9100
Sales: $82,228,000
Company Type: Public Family Member
SIC: 4841
 Cable television service
Barry Marshall, President

Employees: 276
Employees here: 245

D-U-N-S 05-792-0977
HERITAGE COMMUNICATIONS INC.
 (*Parent:* TCI Communications Inc)
5619 Dtc Pkwy, Englewood, CO 80111
Phone: (303) 267-5000
Sales: $426,725,000
Company Type: Public Family Member
SIC: 4841
 Cable & pay television services
John C Malone, President

Employees: 2,000
Employees here: 5

D-U-N-S 14-758-7554
HICKORY TECH CORPORATION
221 E Hickory St, Mankato, MN 56001
Phone: (507) 387-1151
Sales: $76,462,000
Company Type: Public
SIC: 4813
 Local telephone communications whol and mfg
  telecommunications equipment data processing
Robert D Alton, Chairman of the Board

Employees: 500
Employees here: 35

D-U-N-S 87-633-6983
HIGHWAYMASTER COMMUNICATIONS
1155 Kas Dr Ste 100, Richardson, TX 75081
Phone: (972) 301-2000
Sales: $33,416,000
Company Type: Private
SIC: 4812
 Wireless enhanced network service which provides integrated
  mobile voice data tracking & fleet management information
  services
Jana Bell, President

Employees: 425
Employees here: 137

D-U-N-S 79-298-4031   EXP
HIGHWAYMASTER CORPORATION
 (*Parent:* Highwaymaster Communications)
1155 Kas Dr, Richardson, TX 75081
Phone: (972) 301-2000
Sales: $54,632,000
Company Type: Public
SIC: 4812
 Wireless enhanced services network providing integrated
  mobile voice data tracking & fleet management information
  services
Jana Bell, President

Employees: 295
Employees here: 150

D-U-N-S 60-289-8991
HITACHI TELECOM USA INC.
 (*Parent:* Hitachi America Ltd)
3617 Parkway Ln, Norcross, GA 30092
Phone: (770) 446-8820

Sales: $200,000,000
Company Type: Private
SIC: 3661
 Mfg telephone switching equipment
M Toyia, President

Employees: 300
Employees here: 230

D-U-N-S 15-113-0713
HONOLULU CELLULAR TELEPHONE CO.
500 Kahelu Ave, Mililani, HI 96789
Phone: (808) 625-8646
Sales: $57,400,000
Company Type: Private
SIC: 4812
 Cellular telephone services
Gil Mendelson, General Manager

Employees: 290
Employees here: 100

D-U-N-S 93-358-1456
HORIZON TELECOM INC.
68 E Main St, Chillicothe, OH 45601
Phone: (740) 772-8200
Sales: $36,985,000
Company Type: Private
SIC: 4813
 Holding company
Thomas Mc Kell, President

Employees: 517
Employees here: 262

D-U-N-S 00-978-8811
HORRY TELEPHONE COOPERATIVE
3480 Highway 701 N, Conway, SC 29526
Phone: (843) 365-2151
Sales: $47,470,000
Company Type: Private
SIC: 4813
 Telephone cooperative
Curley Huggins, General Manager

Employees: 420
Employees here: 420

D-U-N-S 13-754-4599
HOUSTON CELLULAR TELEPHONE CO.
1 West Loop S Ste 300, Houston, TX 77027
Phone: (713) 850-9933
Sales: $35,100,000
Company Type: Private
SIC: 4812
 Cellular telephone company
Donald Kovalevich, President

Employees: 500
Employees here: 300

D-U-N-S 00-192-3481
HRB SYSTEMS, INC.
 (*Parent:* Raytheon E-Systems Inc)
300 S Science Park Rd, State College, PA 16801
Phone: (814) 238-5668
Sales: $125,000,000
Company Type: Public Family Member
SIC: 3669
 Mfg tactical & strategic electronic systems
David Woodle, Vice-President

Employees: 1,200
Employees here: 950

D-U-N-S 05-562-6063
HUB FABRICATING COMPANY
100 Gibraltar Rd, Reading, PA 19606
Phone: (610) 779-2200
Sales: $50,000,000
Company Type: Private
SIC: 3661
 Mfg telecommunication equipment
Thomas W Martell, President

Employees: 420
Employees here: 340

D-U-N-S 15-531-7522   EXP
HUBER + SUHNER INC.
 (*Parent:* Huber & Suhner North Amer Corp)
19 Thompson Dr, Essex Junction, VT 05452
Phone: (802) 878-0555

Sales: $60,000,000   *Employees:* 160
Company Type: Private   *Employees here:* 140
SIC: 3679
   Mfg & whol r f and microwave components as well as sub
   systems
George Powch, President

D-U-N-S 04-037-6824
HUGHES COMMUNICATIONS INC.
   (Parent: Hughes Telecom & Space Co)
1500 Hughes Way Bldg A1, Long Beach, CA 90810
Phone: (310) 525-5000
Sales: $70,700,000   *Employees:* 580
Company Type: Public Family Member   *Employees here:* 390
SIC: 4899
   Satellite communications
Frank A Taormina, President

D-U-N-S 05-518-5102
HUGHES ELECTRONICS CORPORATION
   (Parent: General Motors Corporation)
200 N Sepulveda Blvd, Los Angeles, CA 90049
Phone: (310) 364-6000
Sales: $5,128,300,000   *Employees:* 14,000
Company Type: Public Family Member   *Employees here:* 17
SIC: 3663
   Satellite construction communication and direct-to-home
   satellite television services
Michael T Smith, Chairman of the Board

D-U-N-S 92-898-9730   EXP
HUGHES SPACE COMMUNICATIONS CO.
   (Parent: Hughes Telecom & Space Co)
2260 E Imperial Hwy, El Segundo, CA 90245
Phone: (310) 568-7200
Sales: $640,800,000   *Employees:* 7,500
Company Type: Public Family Member   *Employees here:* 7,500
SIC: 3663
   Mfg communications satellites
Tig H Krekel, President

D-U-N-S 95-912-0924
HUSKO INC.
100 S Milpitas Blvd, Milpitas, CA 95035
Phone: (408) 956-7100
Sales: $219,177,000   *Employees:* 49
Company Type: Private   *Employees here:* 19
SIC: 3679
   Mfg magnetic recording heads
Wai H Ng, President

D-U-N-S 00-645-6768   EXP
HUTCHINSON TECHNOLOGY INC.
40 W Highland Park Dr Ne, Hutchinson, MN 55350
Phone: (320) 587-3797
Sales: $407,616,000   *Employees:* 8,293
Company Type: Public   *Employees here:* 3,891
SIC: 3679
   Mfg disk drive electronic components
Wayne M Fortun, President

D-U-N-S 82-777-3342
ICG COMMUNICATIONS INC.
161 Inverness Dr W, Englewood, CO 80112
Phone: (303) 414-5000
Sales: $381,100,000   *Employees:* 2,970
Company Type: Public   *Employees here:* 850
SIC: 4813
   Integrated communications provider
J S Bryan, President

D-U-N-S 16-136-6075
ICG HOLDINGS, INC.
   (Parent: ICG Holdings (Canada) Inc)
161 Inverness Dr, Englewood, CO 80112
Phone: (303) 414-5000
Sales: $395,000,000   *Employees:* 2,219
Company Type: Public Family Member   *Employees here:* 850
SIC: 4813
   Integrated communications provider
J S Bryan, Chairman of the Board

D-U-N-S 62-080-3320
ICG TELECOM GROUP INC.
   (Parent: ICG Holdings Inc)
9605 S Maroon Cir, Englewood, CO 80112
Phone: (303) 414-5000
Sales: $217,800,000   *Employees:* 1,700
Company Type: Public Family Member   *Employees here:* 26
SIC: 4813
   Local exchange carrier
Falk Douglas I, President

D-U-N-S 80-903-9910
IDT CORPORATION
294 State St, Hackensack, NJ 07601
Phone: (201) 928-1000
Sales: $335,373,000   *Employees:* 712
Company Type: Public   *Employees here:* 50
SIC: 4813
   Telecommunications services
Howard S Balter, Vice-Chairman

D-U-N-S 96-020-0657
ILD TELECOMMUNICATIONS INC.
14651 Dallas Pkwy Ste 905, Dallas, TX 75240
Phone: (972) 503-8700
Sales: $54,000,000   *Employees:* 425
Company Type: Private   *Employees here:* 3
SIC: 4813
   Reseller of long distance telephone and operator services
Michael F Lewis, Chairman of the Board

D-U-N-S 00-693-0655
ILLINOIS BELL TELEPHONE CO.
   (Parent: Ameritech Corporation)
225 W Randolph St, Chicago, IL 60606
Phone: (312) 727-9411
Sales: $3,808,200,000   *Employees:* 14,929
Company Type: Public Family Member   *Employees here:* 3,000
SIC: 4813
   Telephone communication service
Douglas L Whitley, President

D-U-N-S 07-959-6490
INCOMNET, INC.
2801 Main St, Irvine, CA 92614
Phone: (949) 887-3400
Sales: $125,144,000   *Employees:* 350
Company Type: Public   *Employees here:* 10
SIC: 4813
   Long distance telephone communications
Denis Richard, President

D-U-N-S 11-850-1170
INDEPENDENT TELEVISION NETWORK
747 3rd Ave, New York, NY 10017
Phone: (212) 572-9200
Sales: $150,000,000   *Employees:* 80
Company Type: Private   *Employees here:* 55
SIC: 4833
   Independent television network
Timothy J Connors Jr, Chief Executive Officer

D-U-N-S 00-693-8187
INDIANA BELL TELEPHONE CO INC.
  (*Parent:* Ameritech Corporation)
240 N Meridian St, Indianapolis, IN 46204
Phone: (317) 265-2266
Sales: $1,299,900,000
Company Type: Public Family Member
SIC: 4813
  Telecommunication
Kent A Lebherz, President

Employees: 4,002
Employees here: 2,000

D-U-N-S 00-907-2773
INFINITY BROADCASTING CORP CAL DEL
  (*Parent:* CBS Broadcasting Inc)
5901 Venice Blvd, Los Angeles, CA 90034
Phone: (323) 937-5230
Sales: $40,000,000
Company Type: Public Family Member
SIC: 4832
  Radio broadcasting station
Mel Karmazin, President

Employees: 80
Employees here: 80

D-U-N-S 05-989-8486
INFINITY BROADCASTING CORP DEL
  (*Parent:* CBS Corporation)
40 W 57th St, New York, NY 10019
Phone: (212) 314-9230
Sales: $65,700,000
Company Type: Public
SIC: 4832
  Radio broadcasting
Mel Karmazin, Chairman of the Board

Employees: 803
Employees here: 20

D-U-N-S 01-546-9133
INFINITY WIRELESS PRODUCTS
  (*Parent:* Elexa Consumer Prod Inc)
2013 W Division St, Chicago, IL 60622
Phone: (773) 395-3200
Sales: $37,000,000
Company Type: Private
SIC: 3661
  Mfg & import cellular accessories
Larry Beger, President

Employees: 350
Employees here: 350

D-U-N-S 80-936-0076
INFOSEEK CORPORATION
1399 Moffett Park Dr, Sunnyvale, CA 94089
Phone: (408) 543-6000
Sales: $34,603,000
Company Type: Public
SIC: 4813
  Online services
Steve Kirsch, Chairman of the Board

Employees: 180
Employees here: 150

D-U-N-S 61-081-6381   EXP
INNOVA CORPORATION
3325 S 116th St, Seattle, WA 98168
Phone: (206) 439-9121
Sales: $36,100,000
Company Type: Public
SIC: 3679
  Mfg antennas & microwave radios
J F Grenon, Chief Executive Officer

Employees: 138
Employees here: 138

D-U-N-S 05-709-3734
INNOVEX PRECISION COMPONENTS
  (*Parent:* Innovex Inc)
530 11th Ave S, Hopkins, MN 55343
Phone: (612) 938-4155

Sales: $133,436,000
Company Type: Public Family Member
SIC: 3679
  Mfg electronic components
Thomas W Haley, Chief Executive Officer

Employees: 600
Employees here: 2

D-U-N-S 08-438-2365   EXP
INRANGE TECHNOLOGIES CORP
  (*Parent:* General Signal Holdings Co)
13000 Midlantic Dr, Mount Laurel, NJ 08054
Phone: (609) 234-7900
Sales: $218,971,000
Company Type: Public Family Member
SIC: 3663
  Design & mfg channel extension network management
    switching cable management diagnostic & test products
Robert Coackley, President

Employees: 942
Employees here: 270

D-U-N-S 14-799-8280
INSIGHT COMMUNICATIONS CO LP
126 E 56th St Fl 33, New York, NY 10022
Phone: (212) 371-2266
Sales: $68,476,000
Company Type: Private
SIC: 4841
  Cable television services
Michael S Willner, President

Employees: 276
Employees here: 30

D-U-N-S 09-681-1229   IMP EXP
INTECOM INC.
  (*Parent:* Matra Communication USA Inc)
5057 Keller Springs Rd, Dallas, TX 75248
Phone: (972) 855-8000
Sales: $71,300,000
Company Type: Private
SIC: 3661
  Mfg multimedia network switching platforms providing
    integrated voice data text graphics & video
George C Platt, President

Employees: 558
Employees here: 300

D-U-N-S 06-567-8252
INTEK GLOBAL CORPORATION
99 Park Ave, New York, NY 10016
Phone: (212) 949-4200
Sales: $35,654,000
Company Type: Public
SIC: 3663
  Through subsidiary develops wireless communication
    networks
Robert J Shiver, Chairman of the Board

Employees: 375
Employees here: 6

D-U-N-S 03-751-0500   EXP
INTELIDATA TECHNOLOGIES CORP
13100 Worldgate Dr, Herndon, VA 20170
Phone: (703) 834-8311
Sales: $60,309,000
Company Type: Public
SIC: 3661
  Design and market telecommunications equipment
Al Dominick, President

Employees: 300
Employees here: 100

D-U-N-S 12-235-1315
INTELLICALL INC.
2155 Chenault Dr Ste 410, Carrollton, TX 75006
Phone: (972) 416-0022
Sales: $116,986,000
Company Type: Public
SIC: 4813
  Telecommunications service
William O Hunt, Chairman of the Board

Employees: 166
Employees here: 160

D-U-N-S 92-952-6879
INTELNET INTERNATIONAL CORP
432 Kelly Dr, West Berlin, NJ 08091
Phone: (609) 768-2201
Sales: $58,396,000   *Employees:* 60
Company Type: Private   *Employees here:* 60
SIC: 4813
  Communications
Dominic Dalia, Chairman of the Board

D-U-N-S 04-838-4143   EXP
INTER-TEL INCORPORATED
120 N 44th St Ste 200, Phoenix, AZ 85034
Phone: (602) 302-8900
Sales: $223,569,000   *Employees:* 1,248
Company Type: Public   *Employees here:* 68
SIC: 3661
  Mfg installs & services electronic pabx/key telephone systems
Steven Mihaylo, Chairman of the Board

D-U-N-S 17-507-1398
INTERMEDIA COMMUNICATIONS INC.
3625 Queen Palm Dr, Tampa, FL 33619
Phone: (813) 829-0011
Sales: $247,899,000   *Employees:* 2,575
Company Type: Public   *Employees here:* 225
SIC: 4813
  Telephone communications
Vincent D Orazio, Cio

D-U-N-S 93-376-7451
INTERMEDIA MANAGEMENT INC.
424 Church St Ste 1600, Nashville, TN 37219
Phone: (615) 244-2300
Sales: $169,000,000   *Employees:* 1,257
Company Type: Private   *Employees here:* 1,200
SIC: 4841
  Cable/pay television service
Leo Hindery Jr, President

D-U-N-S 19-172-9904
INTERMEDIA PARTNERS
235 Montgomery St Ste 420, San Francisco, CA 94104
Phone: (415) 397-4121
Sales: $107,300,000   *Employees:* 800
Company Type: Private   *Employees here:* 84
SIC: 4841
  Acquires & manages cable television systems
Derek Chang, Assistant Treasurer

D-U-N-S 60-679-5698
INTERNATIONAL FAMILY ENTERTAINMENT
  (Parent: Fox Kids Wordwide Inc)
2877 Guardian Ln, Virginia Beach, VA 23452
Phone: (757) 459-6000
Sales: $112,300,000   *Employees:* 837
Company Type: Private   *Employees here:* 150
SIC: 4841
  Cable television and entertainment services
Timothy B Robertson, President

D-U-N-S 96-166-3143
INTERNATIONAL JENSEN INC.
25 Tri State Intl Ste 400, Lincolnshire, IL 60069
Phone: (847) 317-3700
Sales: $134,800,000   *Employees:* 1,200
Company Type: Private   *Employees here:* 15
SIC: 3651
  Mfg speakers & speaker components
Robert G Shaw, President

D-U-N-S 80-265-3253   EXP
INTERNATIONAL TELCOM LTD
100 W Harrison St Fl 2, Seattle, WA 98119
Phone: (206) 286-5280
Sales: $68,000,000   *Employees:* 210
Company Type: Private   *Employees here:* 60
SIC: 4813
  Telephone long distance service provider
A J Eisenberg, President

D-U-N-S 87-646-8257
INTERNATIONAL TELECOM GROUP LTD
5550 Topanga Canyon Blvd, Woodland Hills, CA 91367
Phone: (818) 888-7600
Sales: $300,000,000   *Employees:* 150
Company Type: Private   *Employees here:* 50
SIC: 4813
  International telecommunications carrier
Charles Piluso, President

D-U-N-S 06-485-7527   EXP
INTERNATIONAL TELECOMM SATELLITE ORG
3400 Intl Dr NW, Washington, DC 20008
Phone: (202) 944-6800
Sales: $961,619,000   *Employees:* 700
Company Type: Private   *Employees here:* 600
SIC: 4899
  Satellite telecommunications services
Irving Goldstein, Chief Executive Officer

D-U-N-S 03-323-1171
INTEROUTE TELECOMMUNICATIONS
230 Park Ave Rm 1000, New York, NY 10169
Phone: (212) 808-6520
Sales: $100,000,000   *Employees:* 300
Company Type: Private   *Employees here:* 12
SIC: 4813
  Comuunication services
Nicholas Razey, Chief Executive Officer

D-U-N-S 11-743-9273   EXP
INTERVOICE INC.
17811 Waterview Pkwy, Dallas, TX 75252
Phone: (972) 454-8000
Sales: $102,308,000   *Employees:* 700
Company Type: Public   *Employees here:* 400
SIC: 3661
  Mfg telephone equipment
Daniel D Hammond, Chairman of the Board

D-U-N-S 18-682-5956
IOWA NETWORK SERVICES INC.
4201 Corporate Dr, West Des Moines, IA 50266
Phone: (515) 830-0110
Sales: $38,765,000   *Employees:* 114
Company Type: Private   *Employees here:* 35
SIC: 4813
  Long distance carrier and internet service
W N Harvey, Chairman of the Board

D-U-N-S 07-771-4061   EXP
IPC INFORMATION SYSTEMS INC.
88 Pine St 6th&14, New York, NY 10005
Phone: (212) 825-9060
Sales: $270,323,000   *Employees:* 1,088
Company Type: Public   *Employees here:* 450
SIC: 3661
  Mfg telecommunication equipment & technical support
Peter A Woog, Chairman of the Board

D-U-N-S 01-099-2084
ISLANDLIFE LLC
4 Columbus Cir, New York, NY 10019

Phone: (212) 506-5800
Sales: $63,600,000
Company Type: Private
SIC: 4813

Employees: 500
Employees here: 20

Christopher Blackwell, President

D-U-N-S 61-347-0236
ITC HOLDING COMPANY, INC.
1239 O G Skinner Dr, West Point, GA 31833
Phone: (706) 645-1011
Sales: $320,700,000
Company Type: Private
SIC: 4813

Employees: 2,500
Employees here: 13

Through interest of subsidiary telephone communications
Campbell B Lanier III, Chairman of the Board

D-U-N-S 10-691-6554
ITCDELTACOM, INC.
1241 O G Skinner Dr, West Point, GA 31833
Phone: (706) 645-3880
Sales: $114,590,000
Company Type: Public
SIC: 4813

Employees: 220
Employees here: 60

Long distance telephone company
Campbell B Lanier III, Chairman of the Board

D-U-N-S 09-364-9895   EXP
ITRON INC.
2818 N Sullivan Rd, Spokane, WA 99216
Phone: (509) 924-9900
Sales: $216,117,000
Company Type: Public
SIC: 3663

Employees: 1,167
Employees here: 569

Mfg remote data collection & data management systems &
software
Johnny M Humphreys, President

D-U-N-S 80-103-9371
ITT DEFENSE & ELECTRONICS
(Parent: ITT Industries Inc)
1650 Tysons Blvd, Mc Lean, VA 22102
Phone: (703) 790-6300
Sales: $812,900,000
Company Type: Public Family Member
SIC: 3679

Employees: 14,000
Employees here: 50

Mfg electronic components
Louis J Giuliano, President

D-U-N-S 00-697-4133   EXP
ITT FEDERAL SERVICES CORP
(Parent: ITT Industries Inc)
1 Gateway Plz, Colorado Springs, CO 80910
Phone: (719) 591-3600
Sales: $293,414,000
Company Type: Public Family Member
SIC: 4899

Employees: 4,800
Employees here: 150

Operation & maintenance of radar systems &
intercommunication & electronic equipment & base
services & job training
John R Spearing, President

D-U-N-S 86-930-1754   EXP
IXC COMMUNICATIONS, INC.
1122 S Capital Of Texas H, Austin, TX 78746
Phone: (512) 231-5100
Sales: $203,731,000
Company Type: Public
SIC: 4813

Employees: 1,290
Employees here: 600

Provides telecommunications services
Benjamin Scott, Chairman of the Board

D-U-N-S 95-802-0877
IXC, INC.
20354 Monteverdi Cir, Boca Raton, FL 33498
Phone: (561) 477-8238
Sales: $40,000,000
Company Type: Private
SIC: 4813

Employees: 2
Employees here: 2

Telecommunications specializing in wholesaling international
long distance carrier terminating services
Bob Brogdon, President

D-U-N-S 06-340-4230
JACOR BROADCASTING OF TAMPA BAY
(Parent: Jacor Communications Inc)
4002 W Gandy Blvd, Tampa, FL 33611
Phone: (813) 839-9393
Sales: $35,000,000
Company Type: Public Family Member
SIC: 4832

Employees: 380
Employees here: 320

Radio broadcasting
David Reinhart, Vice-President

D-U-N-S 04-848-4356
JACOR COMMUNICATIONS INC.
50 E Rivercenter Blvd, Covington, KY 41011
Phone: (606) 655-2267
Sales: $530,574,000
Company Type: Public
SIC: 4832

Employees: 4,300
Employees here: 13

Radio broadcasting
Randy Michaels, Chief Executive Officer

D-U-N-S 00-837-4605
JBL INCORPORATED
(Parent: Harman International Inds Inc)
1101 Pennsylvania Ave NW, Washington, DC 20004
Phone: (202) 393-1101
Sales: $123,500,000
Company Type: Public Family Member
SIC: 3651

Employees: 1,100
Employees here: 1,090

Mfg speakers & speaker systems
Sidney Harman, Chairman of the Board

D-U-N-S 00-699-6144
JEFFERSON-PLOT COMMUNICATIONS CO.
(Parent: Jefferson-Pilot Corporation)
100 N Greene St, Greensboro, NC 27401
Phone: (336) 691-3000
Sales: $195,575,000
Company Type: Public Family Member
SIC: 4833

Employees: 1,100
Employees here: 8

Television & radio broadcasting program syndication
Terry Stone, President

D-U-N-S 96-590-3784
JMR COMMUNICATION CORPORATION
4104 Cole Ave Apt 109, Dallas, TX 75204
Phone: (214) 526-6631
Sales: $75,000,000
Company Type: Private
SIC: 4812

Employees: 3
Employees here: 3

Whol long distance
Robert Mallory, President

D-U-N-S 00-296-8246   EXP
JOHN MEZZALINGUA ASSOCIATES
6176 E Molloy Rd, East Syracuse, NY 13057
Phone: (315) 431-7200
Sales: $70,000,000
Company Type: Private
SIC: 3663

Employees: 200
Employees here: 150

Mfg cable television related products
John Mezzalingua, Chairman of the Board

D-U-N-S 95-895-1212
JONES COMMUNICATIONS
4601 Forbes Blvd Fl 3, Lanham, MD 20706
Phone: (301) 918-0910
Sales: $134,300,000   *Employees:* 1,000
Company Type: Private   *Employees here:* 1,000
SIC: 4841
   Cable/pay television service
Jim O Brien, President

D-U-N-S 82-479-7393
JONES GLOBAL GROUP, INC.
   (Parent: Jones International Ltd)
9697 E Mineral Ave, Englewood, CO 80112
Phone: (303) 792-3111
Sales: $80,300,000   *Employees:* NA
Company Type: Private   *Employees here:* NA
SIC: 4841
   Cable television services
Lorri Ellies, President

D-U-N-S 07-339-1740
JONES INTERCABLE INC.
9697 E Mineral Ave, Englewood, CO 80112
Phone: (303) 792-3111
Sales: $460,729,000   *Employees:* 3,060
Company Type: Public   *Employees here:* 254
SIC: 4841
   Cable television systems
Glenn R Jones, Chairman of the Board

D-U-N-S 07-340-9864
JONES INTERNATIONAL LTD
9697 E Mineral Ave, Englewood, CO 80112
Phone: (303) 792-3111
Sales: $43,800,000   *Employees:* 330
Company Type: Private   *Employees here:* 225
SIC: 4841
   Cable television
Glenn R Jones, Chairman of the Board

D-U-N-S 06-351-1216
JOURNAL BROADCAST GROUP INC.
   (Parent: Journal Communications Inc)
720 E Capitol Dr, Milwaukee, WI 53212
Phone: (414) 332-9611
Sales: $64,500,000   *Employees:* 580
Company Type: Private   *Employees here:* 300
SIC: 4833
   Television & radio stations
Douglas G Kiel, President

D-U-N-S 00-301-6342   EXP
JPM COMPANY (INC)
155 N 15th St, Lewisburg, PA 17837
Phone: (570) 524-8225
Sales: $128,351,000   *Employees:* 2,800
Company Type: Public   *Employees here:* 15
SIC: 3679
   Mfg wire & cable harness assemblies
John H Mathias, Chairman of the Board

D-U-N-S 80-478-2514
JUSTICE TECHNOLOGY CORPORATION
6700 S Centinela Ave, Culver City, CA 90230
Phone: (310) 526-2000
Sales: $59,000,000   *Employees:* 125
Company Type: Private   *Employees here:* 100
SIC: 4813
   International long distance services
David Glickman, President

D-U-N-S 05-393-7421   EXP
K & L MICROWAVE INC.
   (Parent: Dover Technologies Intl)
408 Coles Cir, Salisbury, MD 21804
Phone: (410) 749-2424
Sales: $37,000,000   *Employees:* 500
Company Type: Public Family Member   *Employees here:* 500
SIC: 3679
   Mfg radio frequency & microwave filters
Charles J Schaub, President

D-U-N-S 08-013-9223   EXP
K SYSTEMS INC.
950 Tower Ln Ste 800, Foster City, CA 94404
Phone: (650) 349-7400
Sales: $259,191,000   *Employees:* 1,600
Company Type: Private   *Employees here:* 5
SIC: 3679
   Mfg electronic components nose cones & guided missile
      engine parts
Dr Harold J Smead, Chairman of the Board

D-U-N-S 10-267-3100
K-TEC ELECTRONICS CORPORATION
   (Parent: Kent Electronics Corporation)
1111 Gillingham Ln, Sugar Land, TX 77478
Phone: (281) 243-5000
Sales: $30,700,000   *Employees:* 529
Company Type: Public Family Member   *Employees here:* 329
SIC: 3679
   Fabricator of industrial electronic components
Morrie K Abramson, Chairman of the Board

D-U-N-S 12-664-2529
KANSAS CITY CABLE PARTNERS, LP
6550 Winchester Ave, Kansas City, MO 64133
Phone: (816) 358-5360
Sales: $76,200,000   *Employees:* 570
Company Type: Private   *Employees here:* 200
SIC: 4841
   Cable television
Robert Niles, President

D-U-N-S 00-826-7262   EXP
KAVLICO CORPORATION
14501 E Los Angeles Ave, Moorpark, CA 93021
Phone: (805) 523-2000
Sales: $75,400,000   *Employees:* 1,300
Company Type: Private   *Employees here:* 1,293
SIC: 3679
   Mfg electronic components
Fred Kavli, Chairman of the Board

D-U-N-S 86-729-2567
KBL PORTLAND CABLESYSTEMS LP
3075 Ne Sandy Blvd, Portland, OR 97232
Phone: (503) 230-2099
Sales: $36,400,000   *Employees:* 275
Company Type: Private   *Employees here:* 225
SIC: 4841
   Cable television services
Kevin Kidd, President

D-U-N-S 80-010-8219
KCAL TV, INC.
   (Parent: Young Broadcasting Inc)
5515 Melrose Ave, Los Angeles, CA 90038
Phone: (323) 467-9999
Sales: $120,000,000   *Employees:* 250
Company Type: Public Family Member   *Employees here:* 250
SIC: 4833
   Television broadcasting
Don Corsini, President

D-U-N-S 04-319-0198   IMP EXP
KEARNEY-NATIONAL INC.
(*Parent:* The Dyson-Kissner-Moran)
108 Corporate Park Dr, White Plains, NY 10604
Phone: (914) 694-6700
Sales: $200,000,000   *Employees:* 1,780
Company Type: Private   *Employees here:* 10
SIC: 3679
   Mfg sensors electronic & electrical systems
Robert R Dyson, Chairman

D-U-N-S 00-691-1069
KELLY BROADCASTING CO A LTD PARTNR
3 Television Cir, Sacramento, CA 95814
Phone: (916) 325-3322
Sales: $50,000,000   *Employees:* 250
Company Type: Private   *Employees here:* 210
SIC: 4833
   Television station
Jon S Kelly, Manager

D-U-N-S 06-878-5104   EXP
KENTROX INDUSTRIES INC.
(*Parent:* ADC Telecommunications Inc)
14375 NW Science Park Dr, Portland, OR 97229
Phone: (503) 643-1681
Sales: $150,000,000   *Employees:* 500
Company Type: Public Family Member   *Employees here:* 450
SIC: 3661
   Mfg telephone central office high speed interface equipment
Richard S Gilbert, President

D-U-N-S 11-262-2907
KEPTEL INC.
(*Parent:* Antec Corporation (del))
56 Park Rd, Eatontown, NJ 07724
Phone: (732) 389-8800
Sales: $80,000,000   *Employees:* 900
Company Type: Public Family Member   *Employees here:* 110
SIC: 3661
   Mfg telecommunication & telephone testing equipment
David Stehlin, President

D-U-N-S 10-267-2284
KHOU-TV, INC.
(*Parent:* A H Belo Corporation)
1945 Allen Pkwy, Houston, TX 77019
Phone: (713) 526-1111
Sales: $60,000,000   *Employees:* 220
Company Type: Public Family Member   *Employees here:* 220
SIC: 4833
   Television station
Peter Diaz, President

D-U-N-S 19-974-4715
KIDDE-FENWAL INC.
(*Parent:* Williams Fire Protection Inc)
400 Main St, Ashland, MA 01721
Phone: (508) 881-2000
Sales: $48,200,000   *Employees:* 550
Company Type: Private   *Employees here:* 420
SIC: 3669
   Mfg fire detection systems & industrial temperature
      instruments
Richard H Demarle, President

D-U-N-S 00-634-2505   EXP
KLIPSCH, LLC
8900 Kystne Crssing 120, Indianapolis, IN 46240
Phone: (317) 574-3866

Sales: $55,800,000   *Employees:* 504
Company Type: Private   *Employees here:* 25
SIC: 3651
   Mfg home audio & home theatre equipment
Fred S Klipsch, Chairman of the Board

D-U-N-S 00-511-5902   EXP
KNOWLES ELECTRONICS DEL
1151 Maplewood Dr, Itasca, IL 60143
Phone: (630) 250-5100
Sales: $100,000,000   *Employees:* 641
Company Type: Private   *Employees here:* 204
SIC: 3679
   Mfg acoustic transducers and solenoid switches
Reginald G Garratt, Chairman of the Board

D-U-N-S 00-790-8841
KOIN-TV INC.
(*Parent:* Lee Enterprises Incorporated)
222 Sw Columbia St, Portland, OR 97201
Phone: (503) 464-0600
Sales: $32,000,000   *Employees:* 205
Company Type: Public Family Member   *Employees here:* 205
SIC: 4833
   TV broadcasting station film video tape production & mobile
      video services
Peter Maroney, General Manager

D-U-N-S 04-129-7623
KOPLAR COMMUNICATIONS INC.
(*Parent:* Acme Television Holdings Llc)
4935 Lindell Blvd, Saint Louis, MO 63108
Phone: (314) 367-7211
Sales: $30,000,000   *Employees:* 100
Company Type: Private   *Employees here:* 100
SIC: 4833
   Television broadcasting station
Edward J Koplar, President

D-U-N-S 00-128-6020
KOSS CORPORATION
4129 N Port Washington Rd, Milwaukee, WI 53212
Phone: (414) 964-5000
Sales: $40,639,000   *Employees:* 350
Company Type: Public   *Employees here:* 350
SIC: 3651
   Mfg stereo headphones & loudspeaker systems
Michael J Koss, President

D-U-N-S 00-477-0921
KQED INC.
2601 Mariposa St, San Francisco, CA 94110
Phone: (415) 864-2000
Sales: $36,046,000   *Employees:* 170
Company Type: Private   *Employees here:* 170
SIC: 4833
   Television broadcasting
Mary G Bitterman, President

D-U-N-S 06-339-3698   EXP
KRAUTKRAMER BRANSON INC.
(*Parent:* Emerson Electric Co)
50 Industrial Park Rd, Lewistown, PA 17044
Phone: (717) 242-0327
Sales: $40,000,000   *Employees:* 252
Company Type: Public Family Member   *Employees here:* 240
SIC: 3679
   Mfg electronic components & measuring & controlling
      devices
Peter Strong, President

D-U-N-S 15-361-1926   EXP
KRONE INC.
(Parent: Krone USA Inc)
6950 S Tucson Way Ste R, Englewood, CO 80112
Phone: (303) 790-2619
Sales: $34,667,000   *Employees:* 140
Company Type: Private   *Employees here:* 100
SIC: 3661
  Mfg telecommunications equipment
Klaus Remy, Vice-President

D-U-N-S 06-515-0732
KTLA INC.
(Parent: Tribune Broadcasting Company)
5800 W Sunset Blvd, Los Angeles, CA 90028
Phone: (323) 460-5500
Sales: $190,000,000   *Employees:* 250
Company Type: Public Family Member   *Employees here:* 248
SIC: 4833
  Television broadcasting station
Vince Giannini, Treasurer

D-U-N-S 78-624-9987
KTNQ/KLVE, INC (NOT INC)
(Parent: Heftel Broadcasting Corp)
1645 Vine St, Los Angeles, CA 90028
Phone: (323) 465-3171
Sales: $35,000,000   *Employees:* 100
Company Type: Public Family Member   *Employees here:* 100
SIC: 4832
  Radio broadcast station
Randall Mays, Chairman of the Board

D-U-N-S 78-559-3906
KYUSHU MATSUSHITA ELC CORP AMERICA
2602 Hoover Ave Ste B, National City, CA 91950
Phone: (619) 474-7980
Sales: $155,000,000   *Employees:* 2,600
Company Type: Private   *Employees here:* 30
SIC: 3663
  Mfg TV communication equipment mfg telephones
Takehiro Semba, President

D-U-N-S 00-889-8884
L-3 COMMUNICATIONS CORPORATION
(Parent: L-3 Communications Holding Inc)
600 3rd Ave Fl 35, New York, NY 10016
Phone: (212) 697-1111
Sales: $705,398,000   *Employees:* 6,100
Company Type: Public Family Member   *Employees here:* 30
SIC: 3663
  Manufacturer of electronic equipment communications
  equipment and defense electronics
Frank Lanza, Chairman of the Board

D-U-N-S 80-598-1073
LAMBDA HOLDINGS INC.
515 Broadhollow Rd, Melville, NY 11747
Phone: (516) 694-4200
Sales: $87,100,000   *Employees:* 1,500
Company Type: Private   *Employees here:* 200
SIC: 3679
  Manufactures electronic power supplies
Joshua A Hauser, President

D-U-N-S 06-353-8375   EXP
LARSCOM INCORPORATED
(Parent: Axel Johnson Inc)
1845 Mccandless Dr, Milpitas, CA 95035
Phone: (408) 941-4000

Sales: $75,955,000   *Employees:* 291
Company Type: Public   *Employees here:* 190
SIC: 3661
  Mfg telecommunication systems
George Donohoe, Acting Ceo

D-U-N-S 60-296-9123
LCI INTERNATIONAL INC.
(Parent: Qwest Communications Intl)
4250 Fairfax Dr, Arlington, VA 22203
Phone: (703) 363-0220
Sales: $500,600,000   *Employees:* 3,900
Company Type: Public Family Member   *Employees here:* 200
SIC: 4813
  Telecommunications service
H B Thompson, Chairman of the Board

D-U-N-S 01-240-5395
LENFEST COMMUNICATIONS INC.
200 Cresson Blvd, Oaks, PA 19456
Phone: (610) 650-3000
Sales: $62,784,000   *Employees:* 1,800
Company Type: Private   *Employees here:* 200
SIC: 4841
  Cable television systems
H F Lenfest, President

D-U-N-S 00-697-0263
LEVEL 3 COMMUNICATIONS, INC.
7581 W 103rd Ave, Broomfield, CO 80021
Phone: (303) 635-9200
Sales: $332,000,000   *Employees:* 3,600
Company Type: Private   *Employees here:* 500
SIC: 4813
  Telecommunications information services and mining
Walter Scott Jr, Chairman of the Board

D-U-N-S 80-389-9400
LEVEL 3 TELECOM HOLDINGS, INC.
(Parent: Level 3 Holdings Inc)
100 Peter Kiewit Plz, Omaha, NE 68131
Phone: (402) 342-2052
Sales: $50,700,000   *Employees:* 400
Company Type: Private   *Employees here:* 1
SIC: 4813
  Telephone communications & cable television service
David C Mccourt, President

D-U-N-S 02-904-9590   EXP
LG ELECTRONICS ALABAMA, INC.
201 James Record Rd Sw, Huntsville, AL 35824
Phone: (256) 772-0623
Sales: $398,541,000   *Employees:* 1,500
Company Type: Private   *Employees here:* 200
SIC: 3651
  Mfg color television sets
Kevin J Kim, President

D-U-N-S 61-346-0104
LIBERTY CELLULAR, INC.
621 Westport Blvd, Salina, KS 67401
Phone: (785) 823-5049
Sales: $70,427,000   *Employees:* 140
Company Type: Private   *Employees here:* 80
SIC: 4812
  Cellular telephone service & ret phone centers
Jesse R Gailey, President

D-U-N-S 04-493-5542
LIBERTY CORPORATION
2000 Wade Hampton Blvd, Greenville, SC 29615
Phone: (864) 609-8111

Sales: $107,354,000   *Employees:* 3,100
Company Type: Public   *Employees here:* 55
SIC: 4833
    Life accident & health insurance carriers & television
      broadcasting
W H Hipp, Chairman of the Board

D-U-N-S 87-481-9428
LIBERTY MEDIA CORPORATION
    (Parent: Tele-Communications Inc)
8101 E Prentice Ave, Englewood, CO 80111
Phone: (303) 721-5400
Sales: $374,223,000   *Employees:* NA
Company Type: Public Family Member   *Employees here:* NA
SIC: 4841
    Cable television programming
Peter Barton, President

D-U-N-S 08-003-0042   EXP
LIFELINE SYSTEMS INC.
640 Memorial Dr Ste 2e, Cambridge, MA 02139
Phone: (617) 679-1000
Sales: $56,964,000   *Employees:* 350
Company Type: Public   *Employees here:* 275
SIC: 3669
    Mfg emergency alarms
Ronald Feinstein, President

D-U-N-S 10-330-5082
LIFETIME ENTERTAINMENT SVCS
309 W 49th St, New York, NY 10019
Phone: (212) 424-7000
Sales: $53,300,000   *Employees:* 400
Company Type: Private   *Employees here:* 350
SIC: 4841
    Cable television network
Carole Black, President

D-U-N-S 00-238-2849
LIGHT TECHNOLOGIES LLC
422 W Riverside Ave, Spokane, WA 99201
Phone: (509) 444-1590
Sales: $46,000,000   *Employees:* 264
Company Type: Private   *Employees here:* 264
SIC: 4813
    Internet science applications
Dallas Crockett, Member

D-U-N-S 79-143-1067
LIN TELEVISION CORPORATION
    (Parent: Lin Holdings)
4 Richmond Sq, Providence, RI 02906
Phone: (401) 454-2880
Sales: $300,000,000   *Employees:* 134
Company Type: Public   *Employees here:* 5
SIC: 4833
    Television broadcasting stations
Gary R Chapman, President

D-U-N-S 92-789-4402
LIN TELEVISION OF TEXAS, L P
908 W Martin Luther, Austin, TX 78701
Phone: (512) 478-5400
Sales: $55,300,000   *Employees:* 500
Company Type: Private   *Employees here:* 120
SIC: 4833
    Television broadcasting
Anne F Peterson, Business Manager

D-U-N-S 04-391-5896
LLOYD DANIELS DEV GROUP
10925 Reed Hartman Hwy, Cincinnati, OH 45242
Phone: (513) 784-9743

Sales: $90,000,000   *Employees:* 22
Company Type: Private   *Employees here:* 22
SIC: 4822
    Communications services
Wanda Lloyd, Chairman of the Board

D-U-N-S 19-532-8133
LOCKHEED MARTIN TECH OPER
    (Parent: Lockheed Martin Corporation)
1309 Moffett Park Dr, Sunnyvale, CA 94089
Phone: (408) 756-8340
Sales: $300,000,000   *Employees:* 3,300
Company Type: Public Family Member   *Employees here:* 700
SIC: 4899
    Satellite command & control operations
Richard W Dessling, President

D-U-N-S 10-229-2851   EXP
LODGENET ENTERTAINMENT CORP
3900 W Innovation St, Sioux Falls, SD 57107
Phone: (605) 988-1000
Sales: $166,351,000   *Employees:* 763
Company Type: Public   *Employees here:* 509
SIC: 4841
    Provider of pay television services
Tim Flynn, Chairman of the Board

D-U-N-S 04-893-0218   EXP
LOJACK CORPORATION
333 Elm St Ste 5, Dedham, MA 02026
Phone: (781) 326-4700
Sales: $74,502,000   *Employees:* 405
Company Type: Public   *Employees here:* 105
SIC: 3663
    Mfg micro computer detection devices
C M Daley, Chairman of the Board

D-U-N-S 01-340-7135
LONG DISTANCE SAVERS INC.
3009 Desoto St, Monroe, LA 71201
Phone: (318) 323-8600
Sales: $47,500,000   *Employees:* 375
Company Type: Private   *Employees here:* 100
SIC: 4813
    Long distance telephone services
Freddy Nolan, President

D-U-N-S 07-745-9709   EXP
LORAL ORION NETWORK SYSTEMS
    (Parent: Loral Space & Communications)
2440 Research Blvd, Rockville, MD 20850
Phone: (301) 258-8101
Sales: $72,000,000   *Employees:* 400
Company Type: Public   *Employees here:* 200
SIC: 4899
    Provides satellite services & facilities
Neil Bauer, President

D-U-N-S 94-681-6212
LORAL SPACE & COMMUNICATIONS
600 3rd Ave, New York, NY 10016
Phone: (212) 697-1105
Sales: $1,312,591,000   *Employees:* 3,300
Company Type: Public   *Employees here:* 60
SIC: 3663
    Mfg communications & weather satellites & provides
      satellite-based telecommunications services
Bernard L Schwartz, Chairman of the Board

D-U-N-S 11-502-4598
LOS ANGELES CELLULAR TELE CO.
17785 Center Court Dr N, Cerritos, CA 90703
Phone: (562) 924-0000

Sales: $198,600,000　　　　　　　*Employees:* 1,550
Company Type: Private　　　　　　*Employees here:* 500
SIC: 4813
　Telephone communications
John H Bonde, President

D-U-N-S 15-427-2587
LOS ANGELES SMSA LTD PARTNER
3 Park Plz, Irvine, CA 92614
Phone: (949) 222-7000
Sales: $69,700,000　　　　　　　*Employees:* 1,000
Company Type: Private　　　　　　*Employees here:* 1,000
SIC: 4812
　Mobile telephone communication
Brian Jones, Executive Vice-President

D-U-N-S 10-792-0258
LOW COUNTRY TELEPHONE COMPANY
　(Parent: Hargray Holding Corp)
856 William Hilton Pkwy, Hilton Head Island, SC 29928
Phone: (843) 785-2166
Sales: $60,000,000　　　　　　　*Employees:* 200
Company Type: Private　　　　　　*Employees here:* 4
SIC: 4813
　Local telephone communications
Gloria Taggart, President

D-U-N-S 93-350-3385
LUCENT TECHNOLOGIES INC.
600 Mountain Ave, New Providence, NJ 07974
Phone: (908) 582-8500
Sales: $30,147,000,000　　　　　*Employees:* 141,600
Company Type: Public　　　　　　*Employees here:* 1,300
SIC: 3661
　Manufactures telecommunications systems software &
　products
Richard A Mcginn, Chairman of the Board

D-U-N-S 05-718-6181
LUFKIN-CONROE COMMUNICATIONS CO.
　(Parent: Texas Utilities Company)
321 N 1st St, Lufkin, TX 75901
Phone: (409) 634-8861
Sales: $104,825,000　　　　　　　*Employees:* 751
Company Type: Public Family Member　*Employees here:* 250
SIC: 4813
　Telephone communication
Ross G I, Chairman of the Board

D-U-N-S 62-283-0933
LXE INC.
　(Parent: Electromagnetic Sciences Inc)
125 Technology Pkwy, Norcross, GA 30092
Phone: (770) 447-4224
Sales: $90,000,000　　　　　　　*Employees:* 400
Company Type: Public Family Member　*Employees here:* 350
SIC: 3663
　Mfg radio/TV communication equipment
Thomas E Sharon, Chairman of the Board

D-U-N-S 05-783-1729　　　　　　　　　　　　　　EXP
M C L, INC.
501 Woodcreek Dr, Bolingbrook, IL 60440
Phone: (630) 759-9500
Sales: $36,000,000　　　　　　　*Employees:* 165
Company Type: Private　　　　　　*Employees here:* 165
SIC: 3663
　Mfg satellite communication equipment
Frank P Morgan, Chief Executive Officer

D-U-N-S 04-447-0680
M P D TECHNOLOGIES, INC.
　(Parent: Microwave Power Devices Inc)
49 Wireless Blvd, Hauppauge, NY 11788
Phone: (516) 231-1400
Sales: $52,000,000　　　　　　　*Employees:* 335
Company Type: Public Family Member　*Employees here:* 335
SIC: 3663
　Manufactures microwave communication equipment
Edward J Shubel, President

D-U-N-S 00-778-5116
MAC AMERICA COMMUNICATIONS INC.
5555 N 7th Ave, Phoenix, AZ 85013
Phone: (602) 207-3333
Sales: $70,000,000　　　　　　　*Employees:* 350
Company Type: Private　　　　　　*Employees here:* 200
SIC: 4833
　Television broadcasting
Delbert R Lewis, President

D-U-N-S 93-203-8961
MACDERMID INC.
　(Parent: MacDermid Incorporated)
1 Norman Dr, Wilmington, DE 19808
Phone: (302) 995-3563
Sales: $80,500,000　　　　　　　*Employees:* 152
Company Type: Public Family Member　*Employees here:* 67
SIC: 3679
　Design
Patricia Janssen, President

D-U-N-S 19-464-0272　　　　　　　　　　　　　　EXP
MACKIE DESIGNS INC.
16220 Wood Red Rd, Woodinville, WA 98072
Phone: (425) 487-4333
Sales: $74,889,000　　　　　　　*Employees:* 585
Company Type: Public　　　　　　*Employees here:* 585
SIC: 3651
　Mfg audio mixers amplifiers and loudspeakers
Roy D Wemyss, Chief Operating Officer

D-U-N-S 06-172-5032
MALRITE COMMUNICATIONS GROUP
1660 W 2nd St Ste 800, Cleveland, OH 44113
Phone: (216) 781-3010
Sales: $78,300,000　　　　　　　*Employees:* 700
Company Type: Private　　　　　　*Employees here:* 13
SIC: 4833
　Television broadcasting stations
Milton Maltz, Chairman of the Board

D-U-N-S 14-834-6653　　　　　　　　　　　　　　EXP
MAPLE CHASE COMPANY
　(Parent: Ranco Incorporated)
2820 Thatcher Rd, Downers Grove, IL 60515
Phone: (630) 963-1550
Sales: $100,000,000　　　　　　　*Employees:* 1,000
Company Type: Private　　　　　　*Employees here:* 125
SIC: 3669
　Mfg smoke detectors and thermostats
Patrick McEvoy, President

D-U-N-S 80-858-2191
MARCUS CABLE COMPANY LLC
2911 Turtle Creek Blvd, Dallas, TX 75219
Phone: (214) 521-7898
Sales: $479,315,000　　　　　　　*Employees:* 1,801
Company Type: Private　　　　　　*Employees here:* 17
SIC: 4841
　Cable television systems
Jeffrey A Marcus, President

D-U-N-S 05-017-5843
MATANUSKA TELEPHONE ASSN.
1740 S Chugach St, Palmer, AK 99645
Phone: (907) 745-3211
Sales: $49,914,000   *Employees:* 300
Company Type: Private   *Employees here:* 50
SIC: 4813
   Local telephone service
Scott Smith, Chief Executive Officer

D-U-N-S 79-660-6911
MATRA COMMUNICATION USA INC.
1633 Broadway Fl 45, New York, NY 10019
Phone: (212) 767-6754
Sales: $81,792,000   *Employees:* 545
Company Type: Private   *Employees here:* 3
SIC: 3661
   Mfg telecommunication switching systems
Jacques Payer, President

D-U-N-S 78-290-8446   EXP
MATSUS ELECTRIC COMP ON CORP AME
5105 National Dr, Knoxville, TN 37914
Phone: (423) 673-0700
Sales: $165,416,000   *Employees:* 2,180
Company Type: Private   *Employees here:* 538
SIC: 3651
   Mfg home audio/video equipment mfg aluminum sheet/foil
      mfg electronic capacitors
Naoki Kono, President

D-U-N-S 18-146-0239
MATSUSHITA COMM INDUS CORP US
776 Highway 74 S, Peachtree City, GA 30269
Phone: (770) 487-3356
Sales: $250,000,000   *Employees:* 1,400
Company Type: Private   *Employees here:* 900
SIC: 3663
   Maufactures car audios and digital business telephone
      systems
Toshiyuki Imazu, President

D-U-N-S 15-401-8436
MATSUSHITA KOTOBUKI ELECTRONIC
2001 Kotobuki Way, Vancouver, WA 98660
Phone: (360) 695-1338
Sales: $160,950,000   *Employees:* 320
Company Type: Private   *Employees here:* 280
SIC: 3651
   Mfg television/VCRs
Kenzo Hayashi, President

D-U-N-S 60-701-7449   EXP
MATTHEY JOHNSON ELECTRONICS
   (Parent: Matthey Johnson Investments)
15128 E Euclid Ave, Spokane, WA 99216
Phone: (509) 924-2200
Sales: $130,000,000   *Employees:* 1,100
Company Type: Private   *Employees here:* 1,000
SIC: 3679
   Mfg electronic components
Dr Michael Cleare, President

D-U-N-S 18-312-5970
MC CAIN TRAFFIC SUPPLY INC.
2575 Pioneer Ave, Vista, CA 92083
Phone: (760) 727-8100
Sales: $35,000,000   *Employees:* 350
Company Type: Private   *Employees here:* 150
SIC: 3669
   Mfg traffic signals & controllers
Jeffrey L Mc Cain, President

D-U-N-S 36-192-1745
MC LIQUIDATING CORPORATION
26899 Northwestern Hwy, Southfield, MI 48034
Phone: (248) 304-1780
Sales: $98,283,000   *Employees:* NA
Company Type: Private   *Employees here:* NA
SIC: 4813
   Facsimile broadcast services & conference call services
William H Oberlin, President

D-U-N-S 93-364-4510
MCE COMPANIES, INC.
310 Depot St, Ann Arbor, MI 48104
Phone: (734) 761-8191
Sales: $81,000,000   *Employees:* 660
Company Type: Private   *Employees here:* 5
SIC: 3679
   Holding company
John L Smucker, President

D-U-N-S 05-829-6054
MCGRAW-HILL BROADCASTING CO.
   (Parent: McGraw-Hill Companies Inc)
1221 Avenue Of The Americ, New York, NY 10020
Phone: (212) 512-2000
Sales: $63,900,000   *Employees:* 575
Company Type: Public Family Member   *Employees here:* 3
SIC: 4833
   Television broadcasting stations
Edward J Quinn, President

D-U-N-S 04-476-0643
MCI COMMUNICATIONS CORPORATION
   (Parent: MCI Worldcom Inc)
1801 Pennsylvania Ave NW, Washington, DC 20006
Phone: (202) 872-1600
Sales: $7,711,000,000   *Employees:* 60,000
Company Type: Public Family Member *Employees here:* 600
SIC: 4813
   Telecommunications and related services
Gerald H Taylor, Chief Executive Officer

D-U-N-S 10-137-9501
MCI INTERNATIONAL INC.
   (Parent: MCI Communications Corporation)
2 International Dr, Port Chester, NY 10573
Phone: (914) 937-3444
Sales: $205,000,000   *Employees:* 1,600
Company Type: Public Family Member *Employees here:* 330
SIC: 4813
   International telephone & telegraph communications
Seth D Blumenfeld, President

D-U-N-S 13-088-6823
MCI WIRELESS, INC.
   (Parent: MCI Communications Corporation)
901 Stewart Ave, Garden City, NY 11530
Phone: (516) 745-0600
Sales: $52,400,000   *Employees:* 750
Company Type: Public Family Member *Employees here:* 185
SIC: 4812
   Resells cellular telephone service and retails and wholesales
      cellular telephone equipment
Edward D Seidenberg, Chief Financial Officer

D-U-N-S 15-203-5432
MCI WORLDCOM INC.
515 E Amite St, Jackson, MS 39201
Phone: (601) 360-8600

Sales: $30,000,000,000   *Employees:* 75,000
Company Type: Public   *Employees here:* 150
SIC: 4813
   Telecommunications company
Bernard J Ebbers, President

D-U-N-S 80-886-2957
MCLEOD USA INCORPORATED
6400 C St Sw, Cedar Rapids, IA 52404
Phone: (319) 364-0000
Sales: $267,886,000   *Employees:* 4,941
Company Type: Public   *Employees here:* 1,200
SIC: 4813
   Holding company for maintenance of fiber optic network and
     communication telemanagement services
Clark Mccleod, Chairman of the Board

D-U-N-S 80-895-0117
MCLEOD USA TELECOMMUNICATIONS
   (Parent: Mcleod USA Incorporated)
6400 C St Sw, Cedar Rapids, IA 52404
Phone: (319) 364-0000
Sales: $307,800,000   *Employees:* 2,400
Company Type: Public Family Member   *Employees here:* 1,800
SIC: 4813
   Communication telemanagement services
Clark Mcleod, Chairman of the Board

D-U-N-S 07-117-2589
MEDIA GEN CABLE OF FAIRFAX CNTY
   (Parent: Media General Inc)
14650 Old Lee Rd, Chantilly, VA 20151
Phone: (703) 378-8400
Sales: $143,006,000   *Employees:* 616
Company Type: Public Family Member   *Employees here:* 338
SIC: 4841
   Cable television service
Thomas E Waldrop, Chairman of the Board

D-U-N-S 00-830-3807
MEDIACOM SOUTHEAST LLC
100 Crystal Run Rd, Middletown, NY 10941
Phone: (914) 695-2600
Sales: $102,000,000   *Employees:* 540
Company Type: Private   *Employees here:* 1
SIC: 4841
   Cable television & internet service
Mediacom Llc, Member

D-U-N-S 01-960-1553
MEDIAONE GROUP, INC.
188 Inverness Dr W Fl 2, Englewood, CO 80112
Phone: (303) 858-5800
Sales: $2,419,000,000   *Employees:* 16,350
Company Type: Public   *Employees here:* 100
SIC: 4841
   Cable television and telecommunications services
Charles M Lillis, Chairman of the Board

D-U-N-S 03-851-0764
MEDIAONE NORTHERN ILLINOIS INC.
   (Parent: MediaOne of Delaware Inc)
688 Industrial Dr, Elmhurst, IL 60126
Phone: (630) 716-2000
Sales: $120,800,000   *Employees:* 900
Company Type: Public Family Member   *Employees here:* 850
SIC: 4841
   Cable television services
William Schleyer, President

D-U-N-S 78-764-5019
MEDIAONE OF FRESNO
   (Parent: MediaOne of Sierra Valleys)
1945 N Helm Ave, Fresno, CA 93727
Phone: (559) 252-8210
Sales: $70,000,000   *Employees:* 305
Company Type: Public Family Member   *Employees here:* 305
SIC: 4841
   Cable television services
Jan Peters, Chief Executive Officer

D-U-N-S 09-165-8591
MEDIAONE OF GREATER FLORIDA
   (Parent: MediaOne of Delaware Inc)
5934 Richard St, Jacksonville, FL 32216
Phone: (904) 731-8810
Sales: $73,500,000   *Employees:* NA
Company Type: Public Family Member   *Employees here:* NA
SIC: 4841
   Cablevision service
Janice Peters, President

D-U-N-S 03-706-6743
MEDIAONE OF LOS ANGELES, INC.
   (Parent: MediaOne of Delaware Inc)
550 Continental Blvd, El Segundo, CA 90245
Phone: (310) 647-3000
Sales: $309,900,000   *Employees:* 2,300
Company Type: Public Family Member   *Employees here:* 125
SIC: 4841
   Provides cable television telephone & high speed data
     transmission services
Amos B Hostetter Jr, Chairman of the Board

D-U-N-S 05-599-1442
MEDIAONE OF NEW ENGLAND INC.
   (Parent: MediaOne of Delaware Inc)
River Bend Business Park, Andover, MA 01810
Phone: (978) 683-5500
Sales: $53,300,000   *Employees:* 400
Company Type: Public Family Member   *Employees here:* 25
SIC: 4841
   Cable television service
Amos B Hostetter, Chief Executive Officer

D-U-N-S 04-270-6721
MEDIAONE OF OHIO INC.
   (Parent: MediaOne of Delaware Inc)
211 W Main Cross St, Findlay, OH 45840
Phone: (419) 423-8282
Sales: $90,300,000   *Employees:* 674
Company Type: Public Family Member   *Employees here:* 45
SIC: 4841
   Cable television service
Jan Peters, President

D-U-N-S 78-968-3950
MEDIAONE OF SIERRA VALLEYS
   (Parent: MediaOne of Delaware Inc)
3443 Deer Park Dr, Stockton, CA 95219
Phone: (209) 474-1747
Sales: $51,200,000   *Employees:* 385
Company Type: Public Family Member   *Employees here:* 25
SIC: 4841
   Cable television service
Jan Peters, Chief Executive Officer

D-U-N-S 09-442-6244
MEDIAONE OF VIRGINIA, INC.
   (Parent: MediaOne of Delaware Inc)
5401 Staples Mill Rd, Richmond, VA 23228
Phone: (804) 915-5400

Sales: $39,800,000   *Employees:* 300
Company Type: Public Family Member   *Employees here:* 22
SIC: 4841
   Cable television service
Janice C Peters, Chief Executive Officer

D-U-N-S 00-527-9138
MEREDITH CORPORATION
1716 Locust St, Des Moines, IA 50309
Phone: (515) 284-3000
Sales: $1,009,927,000   *Employees:* 2,559
Company Type: Public   *Employees here:* 268
SIC: 4833
   Publish & print magazines book publishing TV broadcasting
John P Loughlin, President

D-U-N-S 88-440-8550
MERIDIAN TELECOM CORP
141 S Central Ave Ste 300, Hartsdale, NY 10530
Phone: (404) 869-6550
Sales: $50,000,000   *Employees:* 22
Company Type: Private   *Employees here:* 4
SIC: 4813
   International exchange carrier for long distance local and
     enhanced communication
Steve Scheerer, President

D-U-N-S 15-089-5977
METATEC CORP
7001 Metatec Blvd, Dublin, OH 43017
Phone: (614) 766-3139
Sales: $43,900,000   *Employees:* 756
Company Type: Private   *Employees here:* 483
SIC: 3679
   Mfg
Jeffrey M Wilkins, Chairman of the Board

D-U-N-S 13-962-4829
METROCALL, INC.
6677 Richmond Hwy, Alexandria, VA 22306
Phone: (703) 660-9343
Sales: $289,364,000   *Employees:* 2,261
Company Type: Public   *Employees here:* 102
SIC: 4812
   Wireless communications paging services
William L Collins III, President

D-U-N-S 00-451-3461   IMP EXP
METROMEDIA INTL GROUP INC.
1 Meadowlands Plz, East Rutherford, NJ 07073
Phone: (201) 531-8000
Sales: $204,328,000   *Employees:* 1,300
Company Type: Private   *Employees here:* 11
SIC: 4841
   Telecommunications company and mfg lawn & garden equip
Stuart Subotnick, Vice-Chairman

D-U-N-S 19-410-1309
MFS TELECOM, INC. (DEL)
   (Parent: MFS Network Technologies Inc)
1 Tower Ln Ste 1600, Villa Park, IL 60181
Phone: (630) 203-7000
Sales: $57,200,000   *Employees:* 450
Company Type: Public Family Member   *Employees here:* 133
SIC: 4813
   Telecommunication services
Mark L Gershien, President

D-U-N-S 00-695-8524
MICHIGAN BELL TELEPHONE CO.
   (Parent: Ameritech Corporation)
444 Michigan Ave, Detroit, MI 48226
Phone: (313) 223-9900

Sales: $3,384,800,000   *Employees:* 12,249
Company Type: Public   *Employees here:* 2,200
SIC: 4813
   Telephone company
James E Wilkes, President

D-U-N-S 00-149-8260   EXP
MICROCOM INC.
   (Parent: Compaq Computer Corporation)
500 River Ridge Dr, Norwood, MA 02062
Phone: (781) 551-1000
Sales: $31,100,000   *Employees:* 325
Company Type: Public Family Member   *Employees here:* 325
SIC: 3661
   Mfg data communications equipment
Lewis A Bergins, President

D-U-N-S 80-987-3722   EXP
MICROELECTRONIC MODULES CORP
2601 S Moorland Rd, New Berlin, WI 53151
Phone: (414) 785-6506
Sales: $35,000,000   *Employees:* 320
Company Type: Private   *Employees here:* 316
SIC: 3679
   Mfg electronic circuit assemblies
Kenneth A Hammer, President

D-U-N-S 00-904-7614   EXP
MICROFLECT CO INC.
   (Parent: Valmont Industries Inc)
3575 25th St Se, Salem, OR 97302
Phone: (503) 363-9267
Sales: $56,000,000   *Employees:* 272
Company Type: Public Family Member   *Employees here:* 197
SIC: 3663
   Mfg microwave communication equipment
James R Callaway, President

D-U-N-S 05-607-4784
MIDCONTINENT CABLE CO.
   (Parent: Midcontinent Media Inc)
24 1st Ave Ne, Aberdeen, SD 57401
Phone: (605) 229-1775
Sales: $48,100,000   *Employees:* 362
Company Type: Private   *Employees here:* 44
SIC: 4841
   Cable television services
N L Bentson, Chairman of the Board

D-U-N-S 00-792-0457
MIDCONTINENT MEDIA, INC.
7900 Xerxes Ave S, Minneapolis, MN 55431
Phone: (612) 844-2600
Sales: $66,000,000   *Employees:* 494
Company Type: Private   *Employees here:* 20
SIC: 4841
   Cable tv radio satellite earth station & long distance wats
N L Bentson, Chairman of the Board

D-U-N-S 96-571-1096
MIDWEST WIRELESS COMMUNICATIONS LLC
12 Civic Center Plz, Mankato, MN 56001
Phone: (507) 345-5660
Sales: $48,000,000   *Employees:* 130
Company Type: Private   *Employees here:* 20
SIC: 4812
   Cellular telephone service
Dennis Miller, President

D-U-N-S 00-411-8006
MILGO SOLUTIONS
   (Parent: Platinum Equity Holdings)
1601 Harrison Pkwy, Fort Lauderdale, FL 33323

Phone: (954) 846-1601
Sales: $157,700,000   *Employees:* 1,647
Company Type: Private   *Employees here:* 1,212
SIC: 3661
    Mfg sales & service data communications equipment
George K Webster, President

D-U-N-S 62-110-1823
MINNESOTA EQUAL ACCESS
10300 6th Ave N, Minneapolis, MN 55441
Phone: (612) 230-4100
Sales: $34,738,000   *Employees:* 145
Company Type: Private   *Employees here:* 110
SIC: 4813
    Telephone communications services
David H Kelley, President

D-U-N-S 07-764-6446
MISSISSIPPI BAND CHOCTAW INDIANS
Hwy 16 W, Philadelphia, MS 39350
Phone: (601) 656-5251
Sales: $261,300,000   *Employees:* 4,500
Company Type: Private   *Employees here:* 2,000
SIC: 3679
    Mfg wiring harnesses car speakers and computer component
      boards and leases commercial real estate
Phillip Martin, Chief

D-U-N-S 10-684-2545   EXP
MITEK CORPORATION
4545 E Baseline Rd, Phoenix, AZ 85040
Phone: (602) 438-4545
Sales: $38,300,000   *Employees:* 350
Company Type: Private   *Employees here:* 100
SIC: 3651
    Mfg loudspeakers speaker systems wood stereo cabinets &
      amplifiers
Loyd L Ivey, Chief Executive Officer

D-U-N-S 03-869-7942
MITEL INC.
    (Parent: Mitel Corporation)
205 Van Buren St Ste 400, Herndon, VA 20170
Phone: (703) 318-7020
Sales: $200,000,000   *Employees:* 720
Company Type: Private   *Employees here:* 91
SIC: 3661
    Mfg telecommunications equip including switchboards pabx
      equip telephone system leasing installation & systems
      integration
Kirk Mandy, President

D-U-N-S 02-178-9045
MITSUBISHI DIGITAL ELECTRIC AMERICA
    (Parent: Mitsubishi Electric America)
9351 Jeronimo Rd, Irvine, CA 92618
Phone: (949) 445-3000
Sales: $500,000,000   *Employees:* 1,200
Company Type: Private   *Employees here:* 600
SIC: 3651
    Mfg television sets
Suketaka Tachibana, Chairman of the Board

D-U-N-S 86-816-3775
MJD COMMUNICATIONS, INC.
521 E Morehead St Ste 250, Charlotte, NC 28202
Phone: (704) 344-8150
Sales: $42,972,000   *Employees:* 700
Company Type: Private   *Employees here:* 14
SIC: 4813
    Local telephone exchange carrier
Pam Clark, Assistant Treasurer

D-U-N-S 16-163-2278
ML MEDIA PARTNERS, L.P.
350 Park Ave, New York, NY 10022
Phone: (212) 980-7110
Sales: $60,280,000   *Employees:* 570
Company Type: Private   *Employees here:* 2
SIC: 4841
    Cable television services and radio and television
      broadcasting stations
Martin Pompadur I, Chief Executive Officer

D-U-N-S 06-952-3090
MOBILE COMMUNICATIONS CORP. OF AMERICA
    (Parent: Mobilemedia Communications Inc)
1 Executive Dr Ste 500, Fort Lee, NJ 07024
Phone: (201) 224-9200
Sales: $88,500,000   *Employees:* 1,271
Company Type: Public Family Member   *Employees here:* 158
SIC: 4812
    Cellular telephone & radio paging communications service
Ronald Grawert, Chief Executive Officer

D-U-N-S 60-197-4199
MOBILEMEDIA COMMUNICATIONS INC.
    (Parent: Mobilemedia Corporation)
65 Challenger Rd, Ridgefield Park, NJ 07660
Phone: (201) 440-8400
Sales: $640,710,000   *Employees:* 1,345
Company Type: Public Family Member   *Employees here:* 135
SIC: 4812
    Paging services
Ronald Grawert, Chief Executive Officer

D-U-N-S 82-490-3710
MOBILEMEDIA CORPORATION
1 Executive Dr Ste 500, Fort Lee, NJ 07024
Phone: (201) 224-9200
Sales: $240,000,000   *Employees:* 3,455
Company Type: Public   *Employees here:* 200
SIC: 4812
    Paging services
Ronald Grawert, Chief Executive Officer

D-U-N-S 08-421-0228   EXP
MOD-TAP CORP
    (Parent: Molex Incorporated)
285 Ayer Rd, Harvard, MA 01451
Phone: (978) 772-5630
Sales: $69,000,000   *Employees:* 296
Company Type: Public Family Member   *Employees here:* 60
SIC: 3669
    Mfg communication systems
David C Bundy, President

D-U-N-S 13-012-8036   EXP
MOSAIX INC.
6464 185th Ave Ne, Redmond, WA 98052
Phone: (425) 881-7544
Sales: $121,144,000   *Employees:* 625
Company Type: Public   *Employees here:* 292
SIC: 3661
    Mfg telephone call processing systems
Nicholas Tiliacos, President

D-U-N-S 62-026-7922
MOTOROLA CELLULAR SERVICE INC.
    (Parent: Motorola Inc)
2441 Commerce Dr, Libertyville, IL 60048
Phone: (847) 632-5000

Sales: $72,050,000   *Employees:* 3,000
Company Type: Public Family Member   *Employees here:* 2,950
SIC: 4812
     Reseller of cellular air time
Ed Staiano, President

D-U-N-S 00-132-5463   EXP
MOTOROLA INC.
1303 E Algonquin Rd, Schaumburg, IL 60196
Phone: (847) 576-5000
Sales: $29,794,000,000   *Employees:* 149,800
Company Type: Public   *Employees here:* 225
SIC: 3663
     Mfg communication equipment semiconductor products
     computer equipment automotive and other electronic
     products
Christophe Galvin-Ceo, N/A

D-U-N-S 02-969-0059
MOTOROLA MESSAGING INFO MEDIA
     (Parent: Motorola Inc)
1500 Gateway Blvd, Boynton Beach, FL 33426
Phone: (561) 739-2000
Sales: $341,700,000   *Employees:* 4,000
Company Type: Public Family Member   *Employees here:* 4,000
SIC: 3663
     Mfg radio & communication equipment

D-U-N-S 05-274-7987
MULTI-TECH SYSTEMS INC.
2205 Woodale Dr, Saint Paul, MN 55112
Phone: (612) 785-3500
Sales: $109,813,000   *Employees:* 340
Company Type: Private   *Employees here:* 340
SIC: 3661
     Mfg data communications equipment
Raghu N Sharma, Chairman of the Board

D-U-N-S 17-403-4611
MULTIMEDIA CABLEVISION, INC.
     (Parent: Gannett Co Inc De)
701 E Douglas Ave, Wichita, KS 67202
Phone: (316) 262-4270
Sales: $107,300,000   *Employees:* 800
Company Type: Public Family Member   *Employees here:* 350
SIC: 4841
     Cable television service
Michael C Burrus, President

D-U-N-S 17-403-4546
MULTIMEDIA KSDK INC.
     (Parent: Gannett Co Inc De)
1000 Market St, Saint Louis, MO 63101
Phone: (314) 421-5055
Sales: $40,000,000   *Employees:* 220
Company Type: Public Family Member   *Employees here:* 220
SIC: 4833
     Television station
Lynn Beall, President

D-U-N-S 96-483-2778
MUSICBOX NETWORK
6114 Lasalle Ave Ste 125, Oakland, CA 94611
Phone: (510) 531-9090
Sales: $60,000,000   *Employees:* 9
Company Type: Private   *Employees here:* 9
SIC: 4833
     Television programming network
Jon Korchin, Chairman of the Board

D-U-N-S 83-634-2006
N I C E SYSTEMS INC (DE CORP)
200 Plaza Dr Ste 4, Secaucus, NJ 07094

Phone: (201) 617-8800
Sales: $69,270,000   *Employees:* 50
Company Type: Private   *Employees here:* 35
SIC: 4813
     Digital voice recording service & computer software servicing
Ted Mooney, Vice-President

D-U-N-S 83-982-4992
NASSAU BROADCASTING PARTNERS LP
619 Alexander Rd, Princeton, NJ 08540
Phone: (609) 924-1515
Sales: $33,000,000   *Employees:* 295
Company Type: Private   *Employees here:* 295
SIC: 4832
     Radio broadcast station
Louis F Mercatanti Jr, Chairman of the Board

D-U-N-S 00-698-8034
NATIONAL BROADCASTING CO INC.
     (Parent: National Broadcasting Co Holdg)
30 Rockefeller Plz, New York, NY 10112
Phone: (212) 664-4444
Sales: $5,153,000,000   *Employees:* 5,000
Company Type: Public Family Member   *Employees here:* 2,600
SIC: 4833
     Television broadcasting & motion picture production
Robert C Wright, President

D-U-N-S 03-776-3653
NATIONAL CABLE SATELLITE CORP
400 N Capitol St NW, Washington, DC 20001
Phone: (202) 737-3220
Sales: $40,828,000   *Employees:* 260
Company Type: Private   *Employees here:* 260
SIC: 4841
     Cable subscription television
Brian P Lamb, Chairman of the Board

D-U-N-S 62-578-7791   EXP
NATIONAL DISPATCH CENTER INC.
8911 Balboa Ave, San Diego, CA 92123
Phone: (619) 654-9000
Sales: $33,537,000   *Employees:* 1,000
Company Type: Private   *Employees here:* 300
SIC: 4813
     Telecommunication services
John Macleod, Chairman of the Board

D-U-N-S 78-722-3486
NATIONAL MOBILE TELEVISION INC.
     (Parent: Oaktree Capital Management Llc)
12698 Gateway Dr, Seattle, WA 98168
Phone: (206) 242-0642
Sales: $50,000,000   *Employees:* 203
Company Type: Private   *Employees here:* 23
SIC: 4833
     Television remote broadcasting
Steve Clifford, Chairman of the Board

D-U-N-S 62-647-8077
NATIONAL TELE & COMMUNICATIONS
     (Parent: Incomnet Inc)
2801 Main St, Irvine, CA 92614
Phone: (949) 251-8000
Sales: $125,000,000   *Employees:* 250
Company Type: Public Family Member   *Employees here:* 250
SIC: 4813
     Long distance telephone reseller
Denis Richard, Chief Executive Officer

D-U-N-S 00-183-6014   EXP
NEC AMERICA INC.
     (Parent: NEC USA Inc)
8 Corporate Center Dr, Melville, NY 11747

Phone: (516) 753-7000
Sales: $928,199,000   *Employees:* 2,500
Company Type: Private   *Employees here:* 150
SIC: 3661
  Mfg office switching equip fiber optic & digital microwave
    comm equip satellite comm systems digital key equip pbx
    systems
Kaoru Yano, President

D-U-N-S 55-584-3192   EXP
NETCOM SYSTEMS INC.
20550 Nordhoff St, Chatsworth, CA 91311
Phone: (818) 700-5100
Sales: $56,000,000   *Employees:* 150
Company Type: Private   *Employees here:* 150
SIC: 3663
  Mfg network communication products
Barry Phelps, President

D-U-N-S 15-070-6968   EXP
NETRIX CORPORATION
13595 Dulles Technology D, Herndon, VA 20171
Phone: (703) 742-6000
Sales: $43,635,000   *Employees:* 250
Company Type: Public   *Employees here:* 200
SIC: 3679
  Mfg electronic network switching products
Lynn Chapman, Chairman of the Board

D-U-N-S 03-535-7768
NETSELECT, INC.
5655 Lindero Canyon Rd, Westlake Village, CA 91362
Phone: (818) 879-5800
Sales: $41,100,000   *Employees:* 325
Company Type: Private   *Employees here:* 3
SIC: 4813
  Multiple listing service internet web site host software
    development
Stuart Wolff, Chief Executive Officer

D-U-N-S 94-911-7659
NETSOURCE COMMUNICATIONS INC.
1304 Sthpint Blvd Ste 100, Petaluma, CA 94954
Phone: (707) 762-9600
Sales: $100,000,000   *Employees:* 120
Company Type: Private   *Employees here:* 100
SIC: 4813
  Telecommunications & internet services
Charlie Schoenhoeft, President

D-U-N-S 10-277-6481   EXP
NETWORK EQUIPMENT TECHNOLOGIES
6500 Paseo Padre Pkwy, Fremont, CA 94555
Phone: (510) 713-7300
Sales: $308,721,000   *Employees:* 1,414
Company Type: Public   *Employees here:* 900
SIC: 3661
  Manufacturer of telecommunications & other data
    communications
Joseph J Francesconi, President

D-U-N-S 19-692-6836
NETWORK OPERATOR SERVICES
119 W Tyler St Ste 260, Longview, TX 75601
Phone: (903) 758-9350
Sales: $75,000,000   *Employees:* 350
Company Type: Private   *Employees here:* 350
SIC: 4813
  Telephone operator & long distance service
Tim Martin, President

D-U-N-S 61-170-3356
NETWORK PLUS INC.
234 Copeland St, Quincy, MA 02169

Phone: (617) 786-8400
Sales: $98,209,000   *Employees:* 420
Company Type: Private   *Employees here:* 200
SIC: 4813
  Broker resells telephone services
Robert T Hale Sr, Chairman of the Board

D-U-N-S 00-697-0925
NEVADA BELL
  (Parent: Southwestern Bell Tele Co)
645 E Plumb Ln B128, Reno, NV 89502
Phone: (775) 333-3124
Sales: $190,397,000   *Employees:* 860
Company Type: Public Family Member   *Employees here:* 400
SIC: 4813
  Telephone communications
Lora Watts, President

D-U-N-S 00-695-2899
NEW ENGLAND TELE & TELEGRAPH CO.
  (Parent: Nynex Corporation)
125 High St Ste P3, Boston, MA 02110
Phone: (617) 743-9800
Sales: $4,565,700,000   *Employees:* 18,500
Company Type: Public Family Member   *Employees here:* 1,800
SIC: 4813
  Telephone communications
Ivan G Seidenberg, President

D-U-N-S 79-055-2749
NEW PAR
5175 Emerald Pkwy, Dublin, OH 43017
Phone: (614) 560-2000
Sales: $243,100,000   *Employees:* 3,500
Company Type: Private   *Employees here:* 500
SIC: 4812
  Cellular telephone service & ret cellular telephones
Terry A Tindel, Executive Vice-President

D-U-N-S 00-699-2242
NEW VALLEY CORPORATION
100 Se 2nd St, Miami, FL 33131
Phone: (305) 579-8000
Sales: $114,568,000   *Employees:* 438
Company Type: Public   *Employees here:* 50
SIC: 4822
  Operations through subsidiaries are investing reinvesting
    owning holding trading in securities and real estate
    development
Bennet S Lebow, Chairman of the Board

D-U-N-S 00-698-8349
NEW YORK TELEPHONE COMPANY
  (Parent: Nynex Corporation)
1095 Avenue Of The Americ, New York, NY 10036
Phone: (212) 395-2121
Sales: $7,957,300,000   *Employees:* 38,600
Company Type: Public Family Member   *Employees here:* 4,000
SIC: 4813
  Telephone communication service and leasing of
    underground conduits
Ivan G Seidenberg, President

D-U-N-S 17-336-9091   EXP
NEWBRIDGE NETWORKS INC.
  (Parent: Newbridge Networks Corporation)
593 Herndon Pkwy Ste 200, Herndon, VA 20170
Phone: (703) 834-3600
Sales: $276,620,000   *Employees:* 1,650
Company Type: Private   *Employees here:* 450
SIC: 3661
  Mfg digital communication equipment
Michael Pascoe, President

D-U-N-S 17-821-9796
NEXTEL COMMUNICATIONS, INC.
1505 Farm Credit Dr, Mc Lean, VA 22102
Phone: (703) 394-3000
Sales: $738,897,000   *Employees:* 7,000
Company Type: Public   *Employees here:* 200
SIC: 4812
    Wireless communication services
Daniel Akerson, Chairman of the Board

D-U-N-S 01-442-3052
THE NEXTEL COMMUNICATIONS OF
    (Parent: Nextel Finance Company)
10700 Parkridge Blvd, Reston, VA 20191
Phone: (703) 390-5100
Sales: $57,400,000   *Employees:* 822
Company Type: Public Family Member   *Employees here:* 821
SIC: 4812
    Wireless communication services
Lodewijk A Van Gemert, President

D-U-N-S 79-064-5188
NEXTEL OF CALIFORNIA INC.
    (Parent: Nextel Finance Company)
475 14th St Ste 200, Oakland, CA 94612
Phone: (510) 645-1400
Sales: $67,400,000   *Employees:* 966
Company Type: Public Family Member   *Employees here:* 1
SIC: 4812
    Wireless communication services
Steven P Dussek, President

D-U-N-S 80-940-8545
NEXTEL OF NEW YORK, INC.
    (Parent: Nextel Finance Company)
1 N Broadway Ste 11, White Plains, NY 10601
Phone: (914) 421-2800
Sales: $72,000,000   *Employees:* 450
Company Type: Public Family Member   *Employees here:* 450
SIC: 4812
    Wireless communication service
Lodewijk A Van Gemert, President

D-U-N-S 05-187-3040
NEXTEL OF TEXAS INC.
    (Parent: Nextel Finance Company)
111 Congress Ave, Austin, TX 78701
Phone: (512) 342-3800
Sales: $42,100,000   *Employees:* 601
Company Type: Public Family Member   *Employees here:* 601
SIC: 4812
    Wireless communication services
Richard W Orchard, President

D-U-N-S 82-484-2520
NEXTEL SOUTH CORP
    (Parent: Nextel Finance Company)
6575 The Corners Pkwy, Norcross, GA 30092
Phone: (770) 825-9111
Sales: $108,200,000   *Employees:* 1,555
Company Type: Public Family Member   *Employees here:* 1
SIC: 4812
    Wireless communication services
Richard W Orchard, President

D-U-N-S 60-886-2546
NEXTEL WEST CORP
    (Parent: Nextel Finance Company)
320 108th Ave Ne Ste 200, Bellevue, WA 98004
Phone: (425) 452-7400

Sales: $181,800,000   *Employees:* 2,616
Company Type: Public Family Member   *Employees here:* 1
SIC: 4812
    Wireless communication services
Steven P Dussek, President

D-U-N-S 87-704-3612
NEXTLINK COMMUNICATIONS, INC.
500 108th Ave Ne Ste 2200, Bellevue, WA 98004
Phone: (425) 519-8900
Sales: $57,579,000   *Employees:* 1,500
Company Type: Public   *Employees here:* 130
SIC: 4813
    Local & long distance telephone services
George Tronsrue, President

D-U-N-S 87-943-2086
NEXTLINK PENNSYLVANIA LP
925 Berkshire Blvd, Reading, PA 19610
Phone: (610) 375-3400
Sales: $30,000,000   *Employees:* 190
Company Type: Private   *Employees here:* 170
SIC: 4813
    Telecommunications provider
Gary A Rawding, General Partner

D-U-N-S 10-664-8322   EXP
NOKIA INC.
2300 Valley View Ln, Irving, TX 75062
Phone: (972) 257-9800
Sales: $111,000,000   *Employees:* 1,300
Company Type: Private   *Employees here:* 110
SIC: 3663
    Mfg & whol cellular telephones
Ilkka Teras, VP Finance

D-U-N-S 82-574-2406
NOKIA MOBILE PHONES INC.
    (Parent: Nokia Inc)
5650 Alliance Gateway Fwy, Fort Worth, TX 76178
Phone: (817) 491-7800
Sales: $1,000,000,000   *Employees:* 1,200
Company Type: Private   *Employees here:* 1,100
SIC: 3663
    Mfg cellular telephones
K P Wilska, President

D-U-N-S 83-727-7672
NOKIA TELECOMMUNICATIONS INC.
    (Parent: Nokia Inc)
6000 Connection Dr, Irving, TX 75039
Phone: (972) 894-5000
Sales: $69,700,000   *Employees:* 1,000
Company Type: Private   *Employees here:* 790
SIC: 4812
    Telecommunications
Olli-Pekka Kallasvuo, Chairman of the Board

D-U-N-S 93-186-1330
NORLIGHT TELECOMMUNICATIONS
    (Parent: Journal Communications Inc)
275 N Corporate Dr, Brookfield, WI 53045
Phone: (414) 792-9700
Sales: $60,751,000   *Employees:* 180
Company Type: Private   *Employees here:* 80
SIC: 4813
    Telecommunications carrier & service
Robert A Kahlor, Chairman of the Board

D-U-N-S 01-042-9728   EXP
NORTECH SYSTEMS INCORPORATED
4050 Norris Ct NW, Bemidji, MN 56601
Phone: (218) 751-0110

Sales: $36,434,000   *Employees:* 537
Company Type: Public   *Employees here:* 150
SIC: 3679
   Mfg wire harnesses cables & electromechanical assemblies &
   mfg high resolution video monitors
Quintin E Finkelson, Chairman of the Board

D-U-N-S 60-333-5373
NORTELL NORTHERN TELECOM CORP
   (Parent: Northern Telecom Limited)
4100 Guardian St, Simi Valley, CA 93063
Phone: (805) 583-8600
Sales: $34,400,000   *Employees:* 393
Company Type: Private   *Employees here:* 393
SIC: 3669
   Mfg data communications equipment
Warren B Phelps III, Chairman of the Board

D-U-N-S 18-506-7949
NORTH AMERICAN LONG DISTANCE CORP
5124 5th Ave, Pittsburgh, PA 15232
Phone: (412) 621-9280
Sales: $44,300,000   *Employees:* 350
Company Type: Private   *Employees here:* 350
SIC: 4813
   Telephone communications
Avery Abrams, President

D-U-N-S 14-818-6844
NORTH PITTSBURGH SYSTEMS, INC.
4008 Gibsonia Rd, Gibsonia, PA 15044
Phone: (724) 443-9600
Sales: $66,207,000   *Employees:* 276
Company Type: Public   *Employees here:* 9
SIC: 4813
   Telephone communications
Harry R Brown, President

D-U-N-S 03-323-1916
NORTH STATE TELECOMMUNICATIONS
111 N Main St, High Point, NC 27260
Phone: (336) 886-3600
Sales: $72,867,000   *Employees:* 396
Company Type: Private   *Employees here:* 100
SIC: 4813
   Holding company
Royster M Tucker Jr, Chairman of the Board

D-U-N-S 05-781-2224   EXP
NORTHERN TELECOM INC DEL
   (Parent: Northern Telecom Limited)
200 Athens Way, Nashville, TN 37228
Phone: (615) 734-4000
Sales: $2,011,200,000   *Employees:* 21,000
Company Type: Private   *Employees here:* 20,000
SIC: 3661
   R & D design mfg mkting sales financing install svc &
   support of switching enterprise wireless & broadband
   networks
Donald J Schuenke, Chairman of the Board

D-U-N-S 15-147-0317
NORTHLAND TELECOM CORP
1201 3rd Ave Ste 3600, Seattle, WA 98101
Phone: (206) 621-1351
Sales: $37,831,000   *Employees:* 456
Company Type: Private   *Employees here:* 140
SIC: 4841
   Cable television services & develops computer software
John S Whetzell, Chairman of the Board

D-U-N-S 62-308-6725
NOS COMMUNICATIONS, INC.
4380 Boulder Hwy, Las Vegas, NV 89121
Phone: (702) 547-8000
Sales: $195,000,000   *Employees:* 1,050
Company Type: Private   *Employees here:* 350
SIC: 4813
   Long distance telephone communication services
Michael Arnau, Chief Executive Officer

D-U-N-S 96-046-0400
NPG HOLDINGS, INC.
   (Parent: News-Press & Gazette Company)
825 Edmond St, Saint Joseph, MO 64501
Phone: (816) 271-8500
Sales: $70,000,000   *Employees:* 550
Company Type: Private   *Employees here:* 275
SIC: 4841
   Cable television broadcast television and newspaper
Henry H Bradley, Chairman

D-U-N-S 82-487-7625
NTL INCORPORATED
110 E 59th St Fl 26, New York, NY 10022
Phone: (212) 319-7015
Sales: $491,775,000   *Employees:* 650
Company Type: Public   *Employees here:* 20
SIC: 4841
   Cable television telephone and telecommunications services
George Blumenthal, Chairman of the Board

D-U-N-S 94-619-0980   EXP
NTX, INC.
   (Parent: Verio Inc)
5 Financial Plz Ste 210, Napa, CA 94558
Phone: (707) 256-1999
Sales: $35,000,000   *Employees:* 90
Company Type: Public Family Member   *Employees here:* 90
SIC: 4813
   Internet host service and domain name registration
Kenneth Leonard, President

D-U-N-S 94-571-7163
NUERA COMMUNICATIONS, INC.
10445 Pacific Center Ct, San Diego, CA 92121
Phone: (619) 625-2400
Sales: $30,798,000   *Employees:* 144
Company Type: Private   *Employees here:* 131
SIC: 3661
   Mfg telephone/telegraph apparatus
William Ingram, President

D-U-N-S 10-115-2403
NYNEX CORPORATION
   (Parent: Bell Atlantic Corporation)
1095 Avenue Of The Americ, New York, NY 10036
Phone: (212) 395-2121
Sales: $8,752,100,000   *Employees:* 68,100
Company Type: Public Family Member   *Employees here:* 100
SIC: 4813
   Telephone communications services publishes telephone
   directories & other
Ivan Seidenberg, President

D-U-N-S 06-652-0404   EXP
OCTEL COMMUNICATIONS CORP
   (Parent: Lucent Technologies Inc)
1001 Murphy Ranch Rd, Milpitas, CA 95035
Phone: (408) 321-2000

Sales: $277,700,000
Company Type: Public Family Member
SIC: 3661

Employees: 2,900
Employees here: 1,200

Mfg voice processing systems
Robert Cohn, President

D-U-N-S 04-876-5937   EXP
ODETICS, INC.
1515 S Manchester Ave, Anaheim, CA 92802
Phone: (714) 774-5000
Sales: $89,836,000
Company Type: Public
SIC: 3663

Employees: 554
Employees here: 475

Mfg radio & TV broadcasting & communications equip time-lapse VCRs & digital recorders
Joel Slutzky, Chairman of the Board

D-U-N-S 00-902-4233
OECO CORPORATION
4607 Se International Way, Milwaukie, OR 97222
Phone: (503) 659-5999
Sales: $83,356,000
Company Type: Private
SIC: 3679

Employees: 865
Employees here: 865

Mfg electronic components
John F Lillicrop, President

D-U-N-S 00-790-1093
THE OHIO BELL TELEPHONE CO.
(*Parent:* Ameritech Corporation)
45 Erieview Plz, Cleveland, OH 44114
Phone: (216) 822-9700
Sales: $2,339,900,000
Company Type: Public Family Member
SIC: 4813

Employees: 8,419
Employees here: 1,500

Telephone service
Jacqueline F Woods, President

D-U-N-S 04-659-8855
OKI TELECOM, INC.
70 Crestridge Dr Ste 150, Suwanee, GA 30024
Phone: (678) 482-9640
Sales: $59,700,000
Company Type: Private
SIC: 3663

Employees: 700
Employees here: 700

Mfg cellular phones& equipment
Tetsuji Banno, Chief Executive Officer

D-U-N-S 61-680-9943
OLYMPUS COMMUNICATIONS, L P
Main At Water St, Coudersport, PA 16915
Phone: (814) 274-9830
Sales: $120,968,000
Company Type: Private
SIC: 4841

Employees: 539
Employees here: 539

Cable/pay television service
John J Rigas, Chief Executive Officer

D-U-N-S 87-978-6945
OMNES
5599 San Felipe St, Houston, TX 77056
Phone: (713) 513-3000
Sales: $30,800,000
Company Type: Private
SIC: 4813

Employees: 245
Employees here: 180

Wireless communication
Jean Chevallier, President

D-U-N-S 07-654-8353
OMNIPOINT CORPORATION
3 Bethesda Metro Ctr, Bethesda, MD 20814
Phone: (301) 951-2500

Sales: $51,950,000
Company Type: Public
SIC: 4812

Employees: 1,423
Employees here: 30

Wireless communications service manufacturer of telecommunications equipment
Douglas G Smith, Chairman of the Board

D-U-N-S 18-107-4345
ON COMMAND CORPORATION
(*Parent:* Ascent Entertainment Group)
6331 San Ignacio Ave, San Jose, CA 95119
Phone: (408) 360-4500
Sales: $222,103,000
Company Type: Public
SIC: 4841

Employees: 773
Employees here: 300

Pay television services
Brian Steel, President

D-U-N-S 79-101-8179
ONCOR COMMUNICATIONS, INC.
3530 Forest Ln Ste 195, Dallas, TX 75234
Phone: (214) 350-5060
Sales: $127,900,000
Company Type: Private
SIC: 4813

Employees: 1,000
Employees here: 250

Provides long distance telephone services
Ronald J Haan, Chief Executive Officer

D-U-N-S 10-212-0847
ONE CALL COMMUNICATIONS INC.
801 Congressional Blvd, Carmel, IN 46032
Phone: (317) 843-1300
Sales: $52,000,000
Company Type: Private
SIC: 4813

Employees: 410
Employees here: 386

Long distance telephone communications and operator assistance services
Larry Dunigan, Chief Executive Officer

D-U-N-S 04-740-8823
ONEMAIN.COM, INC (DE)
50 Hawthorne Rd, Southampton, NY 11968
Phone: (516) 287-4084
Sales: $76,400,000
Company Type: Private
SIC: 4813

Employees: 600
Employees here: 600

Internet connectivity services
Stephen E Smith, Chairman of the Board

D-U-N-S 61-420-4733   EXP
ONEWORLD SYSTEMS INC.
1144 E Arques Ave, Sunnyvale, CA 94086
Phone: (408) 523-1000
Sales: $61,468,000
Company Type: Public
SIC: 3661

Employees: 70
Employees here: 50

Mfg communications products for personal computers
Leonard A Lehmann, Chairman of the Board

D-U-N-S 19-180-4640   EXP
ONKYO AMERICA INC.
3030 Barker Dr, Columbus, IN 47201
Phone: (812) 342-0332
Sales: $58,066,000
Company Type: Private
SIC: 3651

Employees: 475
Employees here: 475

Mfg stereo loudspeakers
Charles Limburg, President

D-U-N-S 17-778-3222
OPERATOR SERVICE COMPANY
5302 Avenue Q Ste 6, Lubbock, TX 79412
Phone: (806) 747-2474

Sales: $30,237,000   *Employees:* 350
Company Type: Private   *Employees here:* 346
SIC: 4813
    Long distance telephone communication service
Michael R Smith, Chairman of the Board

D-U-N-S 80-660-5200
OPTEL, INC.
    (Parent: VPC Corporation)
1111 W Mockingbird Ln, Dallas, TX 75247
Phone: (214) 634-3800
Sales: $64,963,000   *Employees:* 706
Company Type: Private   *Employees here:* 150
SIC: 4841
    Cable television and telephone services
Louis Brunel, President

D-U-N-S 82-484-2249
ORBITAL IMAGING CORPORATION
    (Parent: Orbital Sciences Corporation)
21700 Atlantic Blvd, Sterling, VA 20166
Phone: (703) 406-5000
Sales: $39,800,000   *Employees:* 300
Company Type: Public Family Member   *Employees here:* 300
SIC: 4841
    Cable/pay television service
Gilbert D Rye, President

D-U-N-S 17-629-2043
ORIX GLOBAL COMMUNICATIONS
1771 E Flamingo Rd Ste B, Las Vegas, NV 89119
Phone: (702) 795-2500
Sales: $120,000,000   *Employees:* 25
Company Type: Private   *Employees here:* 15
SIC: 4813
    Data communications telecommunications provider
Steven R Logisci, President

D-U-N-S 03-807-1643   EXP
ORTEL CORPORATION
2015 Chestnut St, Alhambra, CA 91803
Phone: (626) 281-3636
Sales: $76,870,000   *Employees:* 507
Company Type: Public   *Employees here:* 459
SIC: 3663
    Mfg linear fiberoptic communications products
Wim H Selders, President

D-U-N-S 15-123-3194
OSBORN COMMUNICATIONS CORP
    (Parent: Capstar Broadcasting Partners)
4754 N Royal Atlanta Dr, Tucker, GA 30084
Phone: (770) 414-9555
Sales: $37,200,000   *Employees:* 543
Company Type: Public Family Member   *Employees here:* 12
SIC: 4832
    Radio & television broadcasting stations
Frank D Osborn, President

D-U-N-S 05-492-6308   EXP
OSICOM TECHNOLOGIES INC.
2800 28th St Ste 100, Santa Monica, CA 90405
Phone: (310) 828-7496
Sales: $119,049,000   *Employees:* 1,677
Company Type: Public   *Employees here:* 18
SIC: 3661
    Mfg telecommunications equipment
Parvinder S Chadha, Chairman of the Board

D-U-N-S 16-199-8331
OUTLET COMMUNICATIONS INC.
    (Parent: National Broadcasting Co Inc)
23 Kenney Dr, Cranston, RI 02920

Phone: (401) 455-9200
Sales: $37,400,000   *Employees:* 345
Company Type: Public Family Member   *Employees here:* 345
SIC: 4833
    Television broadcasting
James G Babb, Chairman of the Board

D-U-N-S 78-870-3643   EXP
P-COM INC.
3175 Winchester Blvd, Campbell, CA 95008
Phone: (408) 866-3666
Sales: $220,702,000   *Employees:* 754
Company Type: Public   *Employees here:* 170
SIC: 3661
    Mfg short haul millimeter wave radio systems
George P Roberts, Chairman of the Board

D-U-N-S 10-340-1618
PACIFIC BELL
    (Parent: Pacific Telesis Group)
140 New Montgomery St, San Francisco, CA 94105
Phone: (415) 542-9000
Sales: $9,938,000,000   *Employees:* 50,030
Company Type: Public Family Member   *Employees here:* 2,000
SIC: 4813
    Telephone communications services & directory publishing
Edward A Mueller, President

D-U-N-S 80-938-2559
PACIFIC BELL INFORMATION SERVICES
    (Parent: Pacific Bell)
3401 Crow Canyon Rd, San Ramon, CA 94583
Phone: (925) 806-4227
Sales: $200,000,000   *Employees:* 250
Company Type: Public Family Member   *Employees here:* 250
SIC: 4813
    Provides voice mail to residents & businesses
Linda Standen, President

D-U-N-S 87-875-5032
PACIFIC BELL VIDEO SERVICES
5000 Executive Pkwy, San Ramon, CA 94583
Phone: (925) 328-4200
Sales: $39,800,000   *Employees:* 300
Company Type: Private   *Employees here:* 80
SIC: 4841
    Wireless & cable pay television services
Mark Greenberg, President

D-U-N-S 87-688-2978
PACIFIC BELL WIRELESS
    (Parent: SBC Communications Inc)
4420 Rosewood Dr, Pleasanton, CA 94588
Phone: (925) 227-3000
Sales: $94,200,000   *Employees:* 1,352
Company Type: Public Family Member   *Employees here:* 1,146
SIC: 4812
    Radiotelephone communication
Bob Shaner, President

D-U-N-S 78-693-9694
PACIFIC GATEWAY EXCHANGE, INC.
533 Airport Blvd Ste 505, Burlingame, CA 94010
Phone: (650) 375-6700
Sales: $298,609,000   *Employees:* 120
Company Type: Public   *Employees here:* 20
SIC: 4813
    Long distance telephone communications
Howard A Neckowitz, Chairman of the Board

D-U-N-S 06-715-9855
PACIFIC TELECOM INC.
    (Parent: Century Telephone Enterprises)
100 Century Park Dr, Monroe, LA 71203

Phone: (318) 388-9000
Sales: $280,400,000   *Employees:* NA
Company Type: Public Family Member   *Employees here:* NA
SIC: 4813
    Telephone utility
Glen F Post III, President

D-U-N-S 10-346-0846
PACIFIC TELESIS GROUP
    (Parent: SBC Communications Inc)
175 East Houston, San Antonio, TX 78205
Phone: (210) 821-4105
Sales: $6,438,600,000   *Employees:* 50,100
Company Type: Public Family Member   *Employees here:* 2,000
SIC: 4813
    Telecommunication services
Edward E Whitacre, Chairman of the Board

D-U-N-S 13-197-4297
PACIFICORP HOLDINGS, INC.
    (Parent: Pacificorp)
700 Ne Multnomah St, Portland, OR 97232
Phone: (503) 731-2000
Sales: $1,332,973,000   *Employees:* 4,160
Company Type: Public Family Member   *Employees here:* 8
SIC: 4813
    Telecommunications financial services & energy services
Michael C Henderson, President

D-U-N-S 80-534-5337
PACKARD-HUGHES INTERCONNECT CO.
    (Parent: General Motors Corporation)
17150 Von Karman Ave, Irvine, CA 92614
Phone: (949) 660-5701
Sales: $98,700,000   *Employees:* 1,700
Company Type: Public Family Member   *Employees here:* 400
SIC: 3679
    Mfg & assembles electronic components & provides
    engineering services
David Schramm, President

D-U-N-S 12-873-7350
PACKARD-HUGHES INTRCNCT WR SYS
    (Parent: Packard-Hghes Interconnect Co)
17195 Us Highway 98, Foley, AL 36535
Phone: (334) 943-1623
Sales: $75,000,000   *Employees:* 600
Company Type: Public Family Member   *Employees here:* 400
SIC: 3679
    Mfg electronic components
David J Schramm, President

D-U-N-S 95-802-7203
PAGEMART WIRELESS, INC.
3333 Lee Pkwy Ste 100, Dallas, TX 75219
Phone: (214) 765-4000
Sales: $277,778,000   *Employees:* 2,335
Company Type: Public   *Employees here:* 1,633
SIC: 4812
    Wireless telecommunications
John D Beletic, Chairman of the Board

D-U-N-S 01-192-5401
PAGING NETWORK INC.
14911 Quorum Dr, Dallas, TX 75240
Phone: (972) 801-8000
Sales: $960,976,000   *Employees:* 4,500
Company Type: Public   *Employees here:* 125
SIC: 4812
    Paging services
John P Frazee Jr, Chairman of the Board

D-U-N-S 60-263-6821
PAIRGAIN TECHNOLOGIES, INC.
14402 Franklin Ave, Tustin, CA 92780
Phone: (714) 832-9922
Sales: $282,325,000   *Employees:* 640
Company Type: Public   *Employees here:* 270
SIC: 3661
    Mfg telecommunications products
Michael Pascoe, President

D-U-N-S 95-721-6146
PAMPLIN COMMUNICATIONS CORP
10209 Se Division St, Portland, OR 97266
Phone: (503) 251-1579
Sales: $61,000,000   *Employees:* 500
Company Type: Private   *Employees here:* 8
SIC: 4899
    Communication services
R B Pamplin, Chief Executive Officer

D-U-N-S 83-980-9159
PANAMSAT CORPORATION
    (Parent: Hughes Communications Inc)
1 Pickwick Plz Ste 270, Greenwich, CT 06830
Phone: (203) 622-6664
Sales: $726,800,000   *Employees:* 500
Company Type: Public   *Employees here:* 100
SIC: 4899
    Provides global telecommunications services via satellite
R D Kahn, Chief Executive Officer

D-U-N-S 05-349-7517   EXP
PARADYNE CORPORATION
    (Parent: Texas Pacific Group Inc)
8545 126th Ave, Largo, FL 33773
Phone: (727) 530-2000
Sales: $81,400,000   *Employees:* 850
Company Type: Private   *Employees here:* 750
SIC: 3661
    Mfg telecommunications equipment & systems
Thomas E Epley, Chairman of the Board

D-U-N-S 04-350-2715
PARAMOUNT STATIONS GROUP, INC.
    (Parent: Viacom Inc)
5555 Melrose Ave, Los Angeles, CA 90038
Phone: (323) 956-5000
Sales: $450,000,000   *Employees:* 1,000
Company Type: Public Family Member   *Employees here:* 30
SIC: 4833
    Television broadcasting stations
Anthony Cassara, President

D-U-N-S 14-423-4127
PARAMUNT STNS GROUP OF DETROIT
    (Parent: Viacom Inc)
26905 W 11 Mile Rd, Southfield, MI 48034
Phone: (248) 350-5050
Sales: $60,000,000   *Employees:* 185
Company Type: Public Family Member   *Employees here:* 185
SIC: 4833
    Television broadcasting station
Sumner Redstone, President

D-U-N-S 11-534-3113
PARCEL CONSULTANTS INC.
150 Commerce Rd, Cedar Grove, NJ 07009
Phone: (973) 857-4200
Sales: $193,425,000   *Employees:* 500
Company Type: Private   *Employees here:* 400
SIC: 4813
    Telecommunications & traffic consulting firm
Thomas Salzano, President

D-U-N-S 88-453-0197
PAXSON COMMUNICATION OF NEW LND
   (Parent: Paxson Communications Corp)
3 Shaws Cv Ste 226, New London, CT 06320
Phone: (860) 444-2626
Sales: $88,421,000   *Employees:* 20
Company Type: Public Family Member   *Employees here:* 16
SIC: 4833
   Tv station
Lowell W Paxson, Chairman of the Board

D-U-N-S 55-687-4980
PAXSON COMMUNICATIONS CORP
601 Clearwater Park Rd, West Palm Beach, FL 33401
Phone: (561) 659-4122
Sales: $134,196,000   *Employees:* 1,270
Company Type: Public   *Employees here:* 200
SIC: 4833
   Television broadcasting
Lowell W Paxson, Chairman of the Board

D-U-N-S 02-620-7428
PAYLEXX UTILITIES & TELECOMMUN
1091 Jackson Ave, Long Island City, NY 11101
Phone: (718) 729-2525
Sales: $40,000,000   *Employees:* 7
Company Type: Private   *Employees here:* 7
SIC: 4813
   Long distance telephone services
Peter Fontanes, President

D-U-N-S 61-207-1456
PCS TRITON INC.
   (Parent: Triton Pcs Holdings Inc)
375 Technology Dr, Malvern, PA 19355
Phone: (610) 651-5900
Sales: $118,300,000   *Employees:* 400
Company Type: Private   *Employees here:* 18
SIC: 4812
   Cellular communications
Michael Kalogris, Chairman of the Board

D-U-N-S 03-339-4602   EXP
PEAVEY ELECTRONICS CORPORATION
711 A St, Meridian, MS 39301
Phone: (601) 483-5365
Sales: $271,000,000   *Employees:* 2,400
Company Type: Private   *Employees here:* 1,500
SIC: 3651
   Mfg audio electronic equipment
Hartley D Peavey, Chairman of the Board

D-U-N-S 19-687-4507
PECO II INC.
1376 State Route 598, Galion, OH 44833   .
Phone: (419) 468-7600
Sales: $48,261,000   *Employees:* 500
Company Type: Private   *Employees here:* 370
SIC: 3661
   Mfg power conversion equipment for the telephone &
     communication industry
Matthew P Smith, President

D-U-N-S 61-032-4089
PEEK CORPORATION
   (Parent: Thermo Power Corporation)
3000 Commonwealth Blvd, Tallahassee, FL 32303
Phone: (850) 562-2253
Sales: $80,000,000   *Employees:* 350
Company Type: Public Family Member   *Employees here:* 160
SIC: 3669
   Mfg traffic control systems
Tim Corcoran, President

D-U-N-S 95-911-4182
PEGASUS COMMUNICATIONS CORP
5 Radnor Corporate Ctr, Radnor, PA 19087
Phone: (610) 341-1801
Sales: $86,818,000   *Employees:* 877
Company Type: Private   *Employees here:* 28
SIC: 4833
   Media & communications holding co
Marshall W Pagon, President

D-U-N-S 84-791-4660
PEGASUS MEDIA & COMMUNICATIONS
   (Parent: Pegasus Communications Corp)
5 Radnor Corp Ctr Ste 454, Radnor, PA 19087
Phone: (610) 341-1801
Sales: $66,404,000   *Employees:* 459
Company Type: Public   *Employees here:* 25
SIC: 4833
   Broadcast television & cable management & ownership
Marshall W Pagon, President

D-U-N-S 60-905-2584
PENT PRODUCTS INC.
6928 N 400 E, Kendallville, IN 46755
Phone: (219) 347-5828
Sales: $47,000,000   *Employees:* 365
Company Type: Private   *Employees here:* 40
SIC: 3679
   Mfg electric wiring harnesses & wiring devices
Rick Nowels, President

D-U-N-S 15-773-4294   EXP
PERIPHONICS CORPORATION
4000 Veterans Memorial Hw, Bohemia, NY 11716
Phone: (516) 468-9000
Sales: $117,299,000   *Employees:* 866
Company Type: Public   *Employees here:* 500
SIC: 3661
   Manufactures interactive voice response systems application
     software
Peter J Cohen, Chairman of the Board

D-U-N-S 10-392-8438
PERPETUAL CORPORATION
808 17th St NW Ste 300, Washington, DC 20006
Phone: (202) 789-2130
Sales: $89,800,000   *Employees:* 800
Company Type: Private   *Employees here:* 16
SIC: 4833
   Holding company through its subsidiaries provides television
     broadcasting and cable programming services
Joe L Allbritton, Chairman of the Board

D-U-N-S 04-810-0747
PHILIPS BROADBAND NETWORKS
   (Parent: Philips Electronics North Amer)
100 Fairgrounds Dr, Manlius, NY 13104
Phone: (315) 682-9105
Sales: $50,000,000   *Employees:* 1,000
Company Type: Private   *Employees here:* 900
SIC: 3663
   Mfg cable television equipment
Dieter Brauer, President

D-U-N-S 00-129-1111
PHILIPS ELECTRONICS NORTH AMERICA
   (Parent: Philips Holding USA Inc)
1251 Avenue Of The Americ, New York, NY 10020
Phone: (212) 536-0500

Sales: $7,495,000,000   *Employees:* 21,000
Company Type: Private   *Employees here:* 200
SIC: 3651
    Mfr consumer electronics professional equipment electrical
    & electronic components electrical consumer products &
    other
Michael P Moakley, President

D-U-N-S 94-310-2368
PHILIPS HOLDING U.S.A., INC.
100 E 42nd St, New York, NY 10017
Phone: (212) 850-5000
Sales: $2,268,700,000   *Employees:* 20,000
Company Type: Private   *Employees here:* 4
SIC: 3651
    Mfr consumer electronics professional equipment electrical
    & electronic components electrical consumer products &
    other
W De Kleuver, Chairman of the Board

D-U-N-S 01-808-0379
PHONE EXCHANGE INC.
4685 Macarthur Ct, Newport Beach, CA 92660
Phone: (949) 794-8880
Sales: $62,000,000   *Employees:* 22
Company Type: Private   *Employees here:* 22
SIC: 4813
    Long distance telecommunications
David Chadwick, President

D-U-N-S 13-046-9539
PHONETEL TECHNOLOGIES INC.
1001 Lakeside Ave, Cleveland, OH 44114
Phone: (216) 623-2589
Sales: $109,644,000   *Employees:* 500
Company Type: Public   *Employees here:* 110
SIC: 4813
    Manages and operates pay telephones
Peter G Graf, Chairman of the Board

D-U-N-S 11-524-1424   EXP
PICTURETEL CORPORATION
100 Minuteman Rd, Andover, MA 01810
Phone: (978) 292-5000
Sales: $466,425,000   *Employees:* 1,450
Company Type: Public   *Employees here:* 800
SIC: 3669
    Mfg videoconferencing equipment
Bruce R Bond, Chairman of the Board

D-U-N-S 15-510-2361
PINNACLE SYSTEMS INC.
280 Bernardo Ave, Mountain View, CA 94043
Phone: (650) 526-1600
Sales: $105,296,000   *Employees:* 323
Company Type: Public   *Employees here:* 225
SIC: 3663
    Mfg video post-production products
Mark Sanders, President

D-U-N-S 60-997-5925
PIONEER SPEAKERS INC.
212 W 24th St Ste D, National City, CA 91950
Phone: (619) 477-2146
Sales: $115,000,000   *Employees:* 1,300
Company Type: Private   *Employees here:* 16
SIC: 3651
    Mfg speaker systems
Soichi Ishijima, Chairman of the Board

D-U-N-S 00-720-9976
PIONEER TELEPHONE COOP INC.
108 E Robberts Ave, Kingfisher, OK 73750

Phone: (405) 375-4111
Sales: $54,928,000   *Employees:* 600
Company Type: Private   *Employees here:* 250
SIC: 4813
    Telephone service
Johnnie R Ruhl, Chief Executive Officer

D-U-N-S 14-859-6315
PIONEER VIDEO MANUFACTURING
    (Parent: Pioneer North America Inc)
1041 E 230th St, Carson, CA 90745
Phone: (310) 518-0710
Sales: $49,700,000   *Employees:* 450
Company Type: Private   *Employees here:* 450
SIC: 3651
    Mfg laser video disks
Junichi Kurata, President

D-U-N-S 00-699-0683   EXP
PITTWAY CORPORATION
200 S Wacker Dr, Chicago, IL 60606
Phone: (312) 831-1070
Sales: $1,348,703,000   *Employees:* 7,800
Company Type: Public   *Employees here:* 32
SIC: 3669
    Mfr burglar & fire alarms/fire detectrs & extinguish/secur
    lights/publshr/prtg/mktg svcs & organ/consultng svc/
    software design
King Harris, President

D-U-N-S 15-231-2922
PITTWAY INTERNATIONAL LTD
    (Parent: Pittway Corporation)
200 S Wacker Dr Ste 700, Chicago, IL 60606
Phone: (312) 831-1070
Sales: $38,900,000   *Employees:* 444
Company Type: Public Family Member   *Employees here:* 27
SIC: 3669
    International holding company
King Harris, President

D-U-N-S 36-441-1603
PLANAR STANDISH
    (Parent: Planar Systems Inc)
W7514 Highway V, Lake Mills, WI 53551
Phone: (920) 648-1000
Sales: $33,800,000   *Employees:* 316
Company Type: Public Family Member   *Employees here:* 285
SIC: 3679
    Mfg liquid crystal displays
Charles P Hoke, General Manager

D-U-N-S 04-605-7246   EXP
PLANT EQUIPMENT INC.
42505 Rio Nedo, Temecula, CA 92590
Phone: (909) 676-4802
Sales: $30,000,000   *Employees:* 250
Company Type: Private   *Employees here:* 180
SIC: 3661
    Mfg telephone station equipment and parts
John H Fuller, Chairman of the Board

D-U-N-S 00-918-0902
PLANTRONICS INC.
337 Encinal St, Santa Cruz, CA 95060
Phone: (831) 426-6060
Sales: $236,112,000   *Employees:* 1,817
Company Type: Public   *Employees here:* 283
SIC: 3661
    Mfg telephone equipment & apparatus
Robert S Cecil, Chairman of the Board

D-U-N-S 62-036-0479
PLATEAU CELLULAR NETWORK INC.
(Parent: Telecommunications Holdings E)
7111 N Prince St, Clovis, NM 88101
Phone: (505) 389-3333
Sales: $59,950,000   *Employees:* 45
Company Type: Private   *Employees here:* 35
SIC: 4812
     Cellular telephone service
Tom M Phelps, Ex Vice Pres

D-U-N-S 11-075-9982
PLD TELEKOM, INC.
505 Park Ave Fl 21, New York, NY 10022
Phone: (212) 527-3800
Sales: $114,424,000   *Employees:* 1,000
Company Type: Private   *Employees here:* 7
SIC: 4813
     Telecommunications
James Hatt, Chief Executive Officer

D-U-N-S 05-917-0373
POLK AUDIO INC.
5601 Metro Dr, Baltimore, MD 21215
Phone: (410) 358-3600
Sales: $54,153,000   *Employees:* 150
Company Type: Public   *Employees here:* 100
SIC: 3651
     Mfg speaker systems
James M Herd, President

D-U-N-S 62-344-8073   EXP
POLYCOM, INC.
2584 Junction Ave, San Jose, CA 95134
Phone: (408) 526-9000
Sales: $111,696,000   *Employees:* 175
Company Type: Public   *Employees here:* 130
SIC: 3661
     Mfg audio & dataconferencing equipment & products
Brian L Hinman, Chairman of the Board

D-U-N-S 78-806-7007
POSITIVE COMMUNICATIONS INC.
5753 W Las Positas Blvd, Pleasanton, CA 94588
Phone: (925) 416-8686
Sales: $41,400,000   *Employees:* 270
Company Type: Private   *Employees here:* 270
SIC: 4812
     Radiotelephone communication & paging services
Rick Martin, Chairman of the Board

D-U-N-S 04-954-2848
POST-NEWSWEEK STATIONS FLA INC.
3 Constitution Plz, Hartford, CT 06103
Phone: (860) 728-3333
Sales: $35,700,000   *Employees:* 330
Company Type: Private   *Employees here:* 5
SIC: 4833
     Television broadcasting station operators
G W Ryan, President

D-U-N-S 04-549-4663
POST-NEWSWEEK STATIONS INC.
(Parent: The Washington Post Company)
3 Constitution Plz, Hartford, CT 06103
Phone: (860) 493-6530
Sales: $69,700,000   *Employees:* 625
Company Type: Public Family Member   *Employees here:* 5
SIC: 4833
     Television broadcasting stations
G W Ryan, President

D-U-N-S 06-458-5565   EXP
POWER-ONE INC.
740 Calle Plano, Camarillo, CA 93012
Phone: (805) 987-8741
Sales: $91,583,000   *Employees:* 1,704
Company Type: Public   *Employees here:* 194
SIC: 3679
     Mfg direct current power supplies
Steven J Goldman, Chairman of the Board

D-U-N-S 78-297-7813
POWERTEL, INC.
1233 O G Skinner Dr, West Point, GA 31833
Phone: (706) 645-2000
Sales: $78,916,000   *Employees:* 1,000
Company Type: Public   *Employees here:* 150
SIC: 4812
     Pcs & cellular communications
Campbell B Lanier III, Chairman of the Board

D-U-N-S 13-959-5268   EXP
POWERWAVE TECHNOLOGIES, INC.
2026 Mcgaw Ave, Irvine, CA 92614
Phone: (949) 757-0530
Sales: $100,231,000   *Employees:* 461
Company Type: Public   *Employees here:* 461
SIC: 3663
     Mfg ultra-linear radio frequency power amplifiers
Bruce Edwards, President

D-U-N-S 79-054-6998
PREFERRED NETWORKS INC.
850 Center Way, Norcross, GA 30071
Phone: (770) 582-3500
Sales: $35,982,000   *Employees:* 373
Company Type: Public   *Employees here:* 70
SIC: 4812
     Radio paging service
Mark H Dunaway, Chairman of the Board

D-U-N-S 79-282-7669
PREMIERE TECHNOLOGIES, INC.
3399 Peachtree Rd Ne, Atlanta, GA 30326
Phone: (404) 262-8400
Sales: $395,505,000   *Employees:* 2,200
Company Type: Public   *Employees here:* 75
SIC: 4813
     Telecommunication and information services provider
Boland T Jones, Chairman of the Board

D-U-N-S 61-895-4945   EXP
PREMISYS COMMUNICATIONS INC.
48664 Milmont Dr, Fremont, CA 94538
Phone: (510) 353-7600
Sales: $102,298,000   *Employees:* 331
Company Type: Public   *Employees here:* 200
SIC: 3661
     Mfg integrated access equipment
Nicholas J Williams, President

D-U-N-S 06-698-6324
PRESTIGE CABLE TV INC.
406 Old Mill Rd, Cartersville, GA 30120
Phone: (770) 382-0531
Sales: $70,000,000   *Employees:* 350
Company Type: Private   *Employees here:* 150
SIC: 4841
     Cable television service
Jon Oscher, Chief Executive Officer

D-U-N-S 61-465-9639
PREVUE NETWORKS, INC.
    (Parent: U V Satellite Group Corp)
7140 S Lewis Ave, Tulsa, OK 74136
Phone: (918) 488-4000
Sales: $65,000,000   *Employees:* 400
Company Type: Public Family Member   *Employees here:* 400
SIC: 4833
    Television broadcasting company
Gary Howard, Chairman of the Board

D-U-N-S 05-080-9011
PRICE COMMUNICATIONS CORP
45 Rockefeller Plz, New York, NY 10111
Phone: (212) 757-5600
Sales: $43,713,000   *Employees:* 169
Company Type: Public   *Employees here:* 8
SIC: 4832
    Radio & television broadcasting newspaper & book
      publishing & cellular telephone system
Robert Price, President

D-U-N-S 83-650-3144
PRIME/MATRIX INC.
26635 Agoura Rd Ste 250, Calabasas, CA 91302
Phone: (818) 880-8700
Sales: $47,703,000   *Employees:* 150
Company Type: Private   *Employees here:* 100
SIC: 4812
    Cellular telephone billing service and retails cellular
      equipment
Steven Cogswell, Chief Operating Officer

D-U-N-S 82-488-4506
PRIME SPORTS CHANNEL NETWORK LP
3 Crossways Park Dr, Woodbury, NY 11797
Phone: (516) 364-2222
Sales: $36,287,000   *Employees:* 266
Company Type: Private   *Employees here:* 266
SIC: 4841
    Cable television network specializing in national sports
Joshua Sapan, President

D-U-N-S 88-348-6748
PRIMECO PER COMMUNICATIONS LP
6 Campus Cir, Roanoke, TX 76262
Phone: (817) 258-1000
Sales: $243,100,000   *Employees:* 3,500
Company Type: Private   *Employees here:* 862
SIC: 4812
    Telephone communications
Lowell Mcadam, President

D-U-N-S 17-430-4238
PRIMETIME 24 JOINT VENTURE
153 E 53rd St Fl 59, New York, NY 10022
Phone: (212) 754-3320
Sales: $50,689,000   *Employees:* 22
Company Type: Private   *Employees here:* 22
SIC: 4899
    Communication service
Sid Amirao, Chairman of the Board

D-U-N-S 06-948-4509   EXP
PRIMO MICROPHONES INC.
1805 Couch Dr, Mc Kinney, TX 75069
Phone: (972) 548-9807
Sales: $48,000,000   *Employees:* 120
Company Type: Private   *Employees here:* 118
SIC: 3651
    Mfg microphones telephones & other audio-related devices
Minoru Nomura, President

D-U-N-S 87-432-3868   EXP
PRIMUS TELECOM GROUP
1700 Old Meadow Dr, Mc Lean, VA 22102
Phone: (703) 902-2800
Sales: $280,197,000   *Employees:* 600
Company Type: Public   *Employees here:* 200
SIC: 4813
    Global long distance telephone communications
K P Singh, Chairman of the Board

D-U-N-S 17-355-9147   EXP
PRODELIN CORPORATION
    (Parent: TBG Industries Inc)
1700 Cable Dr, Conover, NC 28613
Phone: (828) 464-4141
Sales: $50,000,000   *Employees:* 265
Company Type: Private   *Employees here:* 165
SIC: 3663
    Mfg satellite antenna systems
Larry Bowman, President

D-U-N-S 02-356-4888
PRODELIN HOLDING CORPORATION
    (Parent: TBG Industries Inc)
1700 Cable Dr 368, Conover, NC 28613
Phone: (828) 464-4141
Sales: $128,100,000   *Employees:* 1,500
Company Type: Private   *Employees here:* 2
SIC: 3663
    Holding company
Larry Bowman, President

D-U-N-S 11-279-0977
PRODIGY COMMUNICATIONS INC.
44 S Broadway, White Plains, NY 10601
Phone: (914) 448-8000
Sales: $134,192,000   *Employees:* 355
Company Type: Public   *Employees here:* 300
SIC: 4813
    Internet service provider
Pillar Russell I, Vice-Chairman

D-U-N-S 93-831-6817
PROMINET CORPORATION
    (Parent: Lucent Technologies Inc)
300 Baker Ave, Concord, MA 01742
Phone: (978) 287-9000
Sales: $125,000,000   *Employees:* 100
Company Type: Public Family Member   *Employees here:* 100
SIC: 3663
    Mfg communication equipment
Menachem Abraham, President

D-U-N-S 15-392-4972
PROXIM INC.
295 Bernardo Ave, Mountain View, CA 94043
Phone: (650) 960-1630
Sales: $42,951,000   *Employees:* 176
Company Type: Public   *Employees here:* 170
SIC: 3663
    Mfg wireless networking products
David C King, Chairman of the Board

D-U-N-S 06-410-0076
PROXIMA CORPORATION
9440 Carroll Park Dr, San Diego, CA 92121
Phone: (619) 457-5500
Sales: $154,665,000   *Employees:* 444
Company Type: Private   *Employees here:* 246
SIC: 3679
    Mfg liquid crystal display products
Kenneth E Olsen, Chairman of the Board

D-U-N-S 07-482-9417
PUBLIC BROADCASTING SERVICE
1320 Braddock Pl, Alexandria, VA 22314
Phone: (703) 739-5000
Sales: $444,112,000   *Employees:* 530
Company Type: Private   *Employees here:* 510
SIC: 4833
   Television broadcasting service
Ervin S Duggan, President

D-U-N-S 06-055-4169
PULITZER BROADCASTING COMPANY
   (Parent: Pulitzer Publishing Company)
101 S Hanley Rd Ste 1250, Saint Louis, MO 63105
Phone: (314) 721-7335
Sales: $156,100,000   *Employees:* 1,375
Company Type: Public Family Member   *Employees here:* 9
SIC: 4833
   Television broadcasting stations & radio broadcasting
     stations
Ken J Elkins, President

D-U-N-S 11-807-6561
PULSAR DATA SYSTEMS, INC.
4500 Forbes Blvd, Lanham, MD 20706
Phone: (301) 459-2650
Sales: $160,000,000   *Employees:* 145
Company Type: Private   *Employees here:* 125
SIC: 4813
   Whol & mfg computers & accessories systems integration
     services
William W Davis Sr, President

D-U-N-S 60-276-1421   EXP
Q NET INC.
329 Alfred Ave, Teaneck, NJ 07666
Phone: (201) 837-5100
Sales: $42,000,000   *Employees:* 200
Company Type: Private   *Employees here:* 30
SIC: 4822
   Data record carrier providing computer based messaging
     services
Yaakov Elkon, President

D-U-N-S 14-435-6508
QUALCOMM, INCORPORATED
6455 Lusk Blvd, San Diego, CA 92121
Phone: (619) 587-1121
Sales: $3,347,870,000   *Employees:* 11,600
Company Type: Public   *Employees here:* 1,200
SIC: 3663
   Mfg advanced communication systems and equipment
Irwin M Jacobs, Chairman of the Board

D-U-N-S 87-688-0816
QUALCOMM PER ELECTRIC A CAL PARTNR
10300 Campus Point Dr, San Diego, CA 92121
Phone: (619) 651-8700
Sales: $150,000,000   *Employees:* 550
Company Type: Private   *Employees here:* 550
SIC: 3661
   Mfg phones
Derek R May, President

D-U-N-S 00-629-6719
QUINCY NEWSPAPERS INC.
130 S 5th St 38, Quincy, IL 62301
Phone: (217) 223-5100
Sales: $45,000,000   *Employees:* 450
Company Type: Private   *Employees here:* 135
SIC: 4833
   Television & radio station & newspaper publishing
Thomas Oakley, President

D-U-N-S 14-872-1178
QWEST COMMUNICATIONS INTL
   (Parent: Anschutz Company)
555 17th St 700, Denver, CO 80202
Phone: (303) 992-1400
Sales: $696,703,000   *Employees:* 6,900
Company Type: Public   *Employees here:* 1,000
SIC: 4813
   Long distance telecommunications service & fiber optic
     telephone and communication line construction
Joseph P Nacchio, Chairman of the Board

D-U-N-S 03-168-4095
R & E ASSOCIATES, LLC
251 W Central St, Natick, MA 01760
Phone: (508) 655-0200
Sales: $45,000,000   *Employees:* 12
Company Type: Private   *Employees here:* 12
SIC: 3663
   Television broadcasting manufacturers rep and liquidation
     company
Michael Antino, Finance

D-U-N-S 09-681-7002   EXP
R F MONOLITHICS INC.
4347 Sigma Rd, Dallas, TX 75244
Phone: (972) 448-3700
Sales: $55,172,000   *Employees:* 600
Company Type: Public   *Employees here:* 524
SIC: 3679
   Mfg radio frequency transmitting components
Sam L Densmore, President

D-U-N-S 05-473-9313   EXP
R F POWER PRODUCTS, INC.
1007 Laurel Oak Rd, Voorhees, NJ 08043
Phone: (609) 627-6100
Sales: $33,834,000   *Employees:* 160
Company Type: Public   *Employees here:* 140
SIC: 3679
   Mfg radio frequency power delivery systems
Dr Joseph Stach, President

D-U-N-S 83-619-3102
R S L COMMUNICATIONS INC.
767 5th Ave Ste 4300, New York, NY 10153
Phone: (212) 572-6964
Sales: $300,796,000   *Employees:* 350
Company Type: Private   *Employees here:* 15
SIC: 4813
   International telecommunications carrier
Itzhak Fisher, President

D-U-N-S 10-193-9122
RACAL CORPORATION
1601 Harrison Pkwy, Fort Lauderdale, FL 33323
Phone: (954) 846-1601
Sales: $502,988,000   *Employees:* 700
Company Type: Private   *Employees here:* 50
SIC: 3661
   Holding company
David C Elsbury, Executive

D-U-N-S 17-536-2508   EXP
RADIO FREQUENCY SYSTEMS INC.
   (Parent: Alcatel NA Cable Systems Inc)
39 2nd St NW, Hickory, NC 28601
Phone: (828) 323-1120

Sales: $98,200,000   *Employees:* 1,150
Company Type: Private   *Employees here:* 20
SIC: 3663
   Mfg mobile antennas line of sight microwave antennas &
     wave guide cable & associated equipment
Oliver Houssin, Chairman of the Board

D-U-N-S 03-880-1346
RADIO ONE INC.
5900 Princess Garden Pkwy, Lanham, MD 20706
Phone: (301) 306-1111
Sales: $36,955,000   *Employees:* 250
Company Type: Private   *Employees here:* 100
SIC: 4832
   Radio broadcasting stations
Alfred C Liggins III, President

D-U-N-S 11-812-7729   EXP
RALTRON ELECTRONICS CORP
10651 NW 19th St, Miami, FL 33172
Phone: (305) 593-6033
Sales: $75,000,000   *Employees:* 275
Company Type: Private   *Employees here:* 210
SIC: 3679
   Manufacturer and supplier of passive electronic components
Alexander Wolloch, President

D-U-N-S 80-666-9396
RAYCOM AMERICA, INC.
   (Parent: Raycom Media Inc)
201 Monroe St Ste 710, Montgomery, AL 36104
Phone: (334) 206-1555
Sales: $57,200,000   *Employees:* 700
Company Type: Private   *Employees here:* 10
SIC: 4832
   Television and radio broadcasting stations and sports
     production
John Hayes, President

D-U-N-S 94-869-4641
RAYCOM MEDIA INC.
201 Monroe St Fl 20, Montgomery, AL 36104
Phone: (334) 206-1400
Sales: $330,000,000   *Employees:* 2,000
Company Type: Private   *Employees here:* 27
SIC: 4833
   Television broadcasting stations
John Hayes, President

D-U-N-S 04-559-1104   EXP
RAYTHEON E-SYSTEMS, INC.
   (Parent: Raytheon Company)
501 S Jupiter Rd, Garland, TX 75042
Phone: (972) 661-1000
Sales: $1,401,400,000   *Employees:* 16,400
Company Type: Public Family Member   *Employees here:* 100
SIC: 3663
   Mfg defense electronics command control & communication
     systems & aircraft maintenance & modifications other pdts
     & services
A L Lawson, Chairman of the Board

D-U-N-S 05-680-2275
RCN CABLE SYSTEMS INC.
   (Parent: Commonwealth Telephone Entps)
100 Lake St, Dallas, PA 18612
Phone: (570) 674-1969
Sales: $170,000,000   *Employees:* 416
Company Type: Public Family Member   *Employees here:* 40
SIC: 4841
   Cable television service
David C Mccourt, Chairman of the Board

D-U-N-S 00-173-2007
RCN TELECOM SERVICES OF PA
   (Parent: Rcn Corporation)
5508 Nor Bath Blvd, Northampton, PA 18067
Phone: (610) 366-2000
Sales: $53,900,000   *Employees:* 405
Company Type: Public Family Member   *Employees here:* 135
SIC: 4841
   Community subscription television service
George Duffy, General Manager

D-U-N-S 10-276-2192   EXP
READ-RITE CORPORATION
345 Los Coches St, Milpitas, CA 95035
Phone: (408) 262-6700
Sales: $808,622,000   *Employees:* 18,000
Company Type: Public   *Employees here:* 1,500
SIC: 3679
   Mfg thin film magnetic recording heads
Cyril J Yansouni, Chairman of the Board

D-U-N-S 00-521-1701   EXP
RECOTON AUDIO CORPORATION
   (Parent: Recoton Corp)
2950 Lake Emma Rd, Lake Mary, FL 32746
Phone: (407) 333-8900
Sales: $32,700,000   *Employees:* 300
Company Type: Public Family Member   *Employees here:* 123
SIC: 3651
   Mfg & dist audio electronic equipment
James Braun, Vice-President

D-U-N-S 00-151-8323   EXP
RECOTON CORP
2950 Lake Emma Rd, Lake Mary, FL 32746
Phone: (407) 333-8900
Sales: $502,048,000   *Employees:* 2,500
Company Type: Public   *Employees here:* 600
SIC: 3651
   Mfg consumer electronic accessory products
Robert L Borchardt, Chairman of the Board

D-U-N-S 83-586-6062
RELIANCE COMTECH
2100 Reliance Pkwy, Bedford, TX 76021
Phone: (817) 267-3141
Sales: $127,900,000   *Employees:* 1,000
Company Type: Private   *Employees here:* 1,000
SIC: 4813
   Telephone communications

D-U-N-S 00-641-8933   EXP
RELM COMMUNICATIONS INC.
   (Parent: Relm Wireless Corporation)
7505 Technology Dr, Melbourne, FL 32904
Phone: (407) 984-1414
Sales: $45,376,000   *Employees:* 229
Company Type: Public Family Member   *Employees here:* 224
SIC: 3663
   Mfg electronic communications equipment
Donald F Goebert, Chairman of the Board

D-U-N-S 60-236-3301   EXP
RELTEC COMMUNICATIONS INC.
   (Parent: Reltec Corporation)
5900 Landerbrook Dr, Cleveland, OH 44124
Phone: (440) 460-3600
Sales: $887,200,000   *Employees:* 5,200
Company Type: Public Family Member   *Employees here:* 50
SIC: 3661
   Mfg service and install telecommunications equipment
Dudley Sheffler, President

D-U-N-S 36-257-1432
RENAISSANCE COMMUNICATIONS
(Parent: Tribune Company)
435 N Michigan Ave, Chicago, IL 60611
Phone: (312) 222-9100
Sales: $52,500,000   *Employees:* 476
Company Type: Public Family Member   *Employees here:* 10
SIC: 4833
    Television station owner and operator

D-U-N-S 00-959-5992
RETLAW ENTERPRISES INC.
12716 Riverside Dr, North Hollywood, CA 91607
Phone: (818) 985-2171
Sales: $47,800,000   *Employees:* 435
Company Type: Private   *Employees here:* 90
SIC: 4833
    Operates tv station
Christophe Miller, President

D-U-N-S 14-868-3360
ROBIN MEDIA GROUP INC.
(Parent: Robin Cable Systems II Inc)
235 Montgomery St Ste 420, San Francisco, CA 94104
Phone: (415) 616-4600
Sales: $34,100,000   *Employees:* 200
Company Type: Private   *Employees here:* 80
SIC: 4841
    Cable/pay television service
Frank Washington, Chief Executive Officer

D-U-N-S 00-986-2665
ROCK HILL TELEPHONE COMPANY
330 E Black St, Rock Hill, SC 29730
Phone: (803) 324-6007
Sales: $33,699,000   *Employees:* 302
Company Type: Private   *Employees here:* 302
SIC: 4813
    Telephone company
Frank S Barnes Jr, President

D-U-N-S 02-506-9303   EXP
ROSCOR CORPORATION
1061 Feehanville Dr, Mount Prospect, IL 60056
Phone: (847) 299-8080
Sales: $45,000,000   *Employees:* 120
Company Type: Private   *Employees here:* 90
SIC: 3663
    Mfg distribute lease & service mobile communications
       equipment studio equipment satellites video & television
       equipment
Paul Roston, President

D-U-N-S 01-526-1936
ROSEVILLE COMMUNICATIONS CO.
200 Vernon St, Roseville, CA 95678
Phone: (916) 786-6141
Sales: $114,888,000   *Employees:* 565
Company Type: Private   *Employees here:* 1
SIC: 4899
    Communication services
Brian H Strom, President

D-U-N-S 04-290-2916   EXP
ROWE INTERNATIONAL INC.
(Parent: Ri Holdings Inc)
1500 Union Ave Se, Grand Rapids, MI 49507
Phone: (616) 243-3633
Sales: $85,000,000   *Employees:* 450
Company Type: Public Family Member   *Employees here:* 400
SIC: 3651
    Mfg jukeboxes & bill changers & vending machines
David G Sadler, Chairman of the Board

D-U-N-S 94-681-2963
RRV ENTERPRISES INC.
5120 Woodway Dr Ste 7007, Houston, TX 77056
Phone: (713) 626-1661
Sales: $42,470,000   *Employees:* 100
Company Type: Private   *Employees here:* 100
SIC: 4813
    Reseller of long distance
Scott Moster, President

D-U-N-S 00-324-5834
RSI, INC.
(Parent: Prodelin Holding Corporation)
1501 Moran Rd, Sterling, VA 20166
Phone: (703) 450-5680
Sales: $190,000,000   *Employees:* 1,200
Company Type: Private   *Employees here:* 250
SIC: 3663
    Mfg communication systems and antennas
Bruce L Crockett, Chairman of the Board

D-U-N-S 62-285-2267
RSL COM U.S.A., INC.
(Parent: Interntonal Telecom Group Ltd)
5550 Topanga Canyon Blvd, Woodland Hills, CA 91367
Phone: (818) 888-7600
Sales: $300,000,000   *Employees:* 260
Company Type: Private   *Employees here:* 130
SIC: 4813
    International telecommunications carrier
Edmond Thomas, President

D-U-N-S 79-472-4054
RURAL CELLULAR CORPORATION
3905 Dakota St, Alexandria, MN 56308
Phone: (320) 762-2000
Sales: $53,903,000   *Employees:* 358
Company Type: Public   *Employees here:* 150
SIC: 4812
    Wireless communcations
Richard Eckstrand, President

D-U-N-S 78-662-3249
SA TELECOMMUNICATIONS, INC.
1600 Promenade Ctr Fl 15, Richardson, TX 75080
Phone: (972) 690-5888
Sales: $39,841,000   *Employees:* 285
Company Type: Public   *Employees here:* 64
SIC: 4813
    Telecommunications services
Howard F Curd, Chairman of the Board

D-U-N-S 05-681-9642
SAFETRAN SYSTEMS CORPORATION
(Parent: H S Investments Inc)
4650 Main St Ne, Minneapolis, MN 55421
Phone: (612) 572-1400
Sales: $65,800,000   *Employees:* 750
Company Type: Private   *Employees here:* 230
SIC: 3669
    Mfg railroad signalling equipment
George L Kline, President

D-U-N-S 79-807-3136
SAGA COMMUNICATIONS INC.
73 Kercheval Ave, Detroit, MI 48236
Phone: (313) 886-7070
Sales: $56,240,000   *Employees:* 445
Company Type: Public   *Employees here:* 6
SIC: 4832
    Radio stations
Edward K Christian, Chairman of the Board

D-U-N-S 00-632-6292   EXP
ST LOUIS MUSIC INC.
1400 Ferguson Ave, Saint Louis, MO 63133
Phone: (314) 727-4512
Sales: $60,000,000   *Employees:* 400
Company Type: Private   *Employees here:* 75
SIC: 3651
   Mfg amplifiers & whol musical instruments
Eugene Kornblum, President

D-U-N-S 10-307-5636
SALEM COMMUNICATION CORP
4880 Santa Rosa Rd, Camarillo, CA 93012
Phone: (805) 987-0400
Sales: $67,912,000   *Employees:* 600
Company Type: Private   *Employees here:* 35
SIC: 4832
   Radio broadcasting
Stuart Epperson, Chairman of the Board

D-U-N-S 07-077-1282   EXP
SANYO MANUFACTURING CORP
3333 Sanyo Rd, Forrest City, AR 72335
Phone: (870) 633-5030
Sales: $500,978,000   *Employees:* 600
Company Type: Private   *Employees here:* 550
SIC: 3651
   Mfg tabletop color television receivers
Naoki Nakamura, President

D-U-N-S 18-118-4060
SATELLINK COMMUNICATIONS INC.
1125 Northmeadow Pkwy, Roswell, GA 30076
Phone: (770) 625-2599
Sales: $39,661,000   *Employees:* 57
Company Type: Private   *Employees here:* 57
SIC: 4813
   Voice mail & paging service company
Jerry W Mayfield, President

D-U-N-S 06-125-8232
SATELLITE SERVICES, INC.
   (Parent: TCI Holdings Inc)
5619 Dtc Pkwy, Englewood, CO 80111
Phone: (303) 267-5500
Sales: $1,177,235,000   *Employees:* 25
Company Type: Public Family Member   *Employees here:* 11
SIC: 4841
   Cable television purchasing service
Brendan R Clouston, Chairman of the Board

D-U-N-S 10-802-4050
SBC COMMUNICATIONS INC.
175 E Houston St, San Antonio, TX 78205
Phone: (210) 821-4105
Sales: $24,856,000,000   *Employees:* 118,340
Company Type: Public   *Employees here:* 590
SIC: 4813
   Telephone service directory publishing whol
     telecommunication equipment & other
Edward E Whitacre Jr, Chairman of the Board

D-U-N-S 10-393-3230
SBC MEDIA VENTURES INC.
   (Parent: SBC Communications Inc)
20 W Gude Dr, Rockville, MD 20850
Phone: (301) 294-7600
Sales: $64,600,000   *Employees:* 484
Company Type: Public Family Member   *Employees here:* 84
SIC: 4841
   Cable television operators
Steve Dimmitt, President

D-U-N-S 00-326-5022   EXP
SCIENTIFIC-ATLANTA INC.
1 Technology Pkwy S, Norcross, GA 30092
Phone: (770) 903-5000
Sales: $1,181,404,000   *Employees:* 5,736
Company Type: Public   *Employees here:* 75
SIC: 3663
   Mfg communications equipment & electronic instruments
Wallace Haislip, Chief Financial Officer

D-U-N-S 00-699-9817
SCRIPPS HOWARD BROADCASTING CO.
   (Parent: The E W Scripps Company)
312 Walnut St Ste 2800, Cincinnati, OH 45202
Phone: (513) 977-3000
Sales: $500,000,000   *Employees:* 1,800
Company Type: Public Family Member   *Employees here:* 10
SIC: 4833
   Television broadcasting and cable television services
William A Burleigh, President

D-U-N-S 00-132-5869
SDI TECHNOLOGIES INC.
1299 Main St, Rahway, NJ 07065
Phone: (732) 574-9000
Sales: $50,000,000   *Employees:* 138
Company Type: Private   *Employees here:* 74
SIC: 3651
   Manufactures audio electronic systems
Ely E Ashkenazi, Chairman of the Board

D-U-N-S 80-749-9595
SEACHANGE INTERNATIONAL, INC.
124 Acton St, Maynard, MA 01754
Phone: (978) 897-0100
Sales: $67,887,000   *Employees:* 280
Company Type: Public   *Employees here:* 175
SIC: 3663
   Provides advanced digital video systems for the television
     industry
Bill Styslinger, Chief Executive Officer

D-U-N-S 12-098-5577
SENIOR SYSTEMS TECHNOLOGY INC.
600 Technology Dr, Palmdale, CA 93551
Phone: (661) 575-8500
Sales: $50,000,000   *Employees:* 350
Company Type: Private   *Employees here:* 350
SIC: 3679
   Mfg electronic components
Joseph Candella, President

D-U-N-S 00-791-2330
SERVICE ELECTRIC TELEVISION
201 W Centre St, Mahanoy City, PA 17948
Phone: (570) 773-2585
Sales: $101,607,000   *Employees:* 489
Company Type: Private   *Employees here:* 41
SIC: 4841
   Cable/pay television service
John Walson Jr, President

D-U-N-S 18-074-8642
SHARED COMMUNICATIONS SERVICES
3723 Fairview Industrial, Salem, OR 97302
Phone: (503) 399-7000
Sales: $42,051,000   *Employees:* 155
Company Type: Private   *Employees here:* 52
SIC: 4813
   Long distance telephone carrier
Charles F Columbus, Chief Executive Officer

D-U-N-S 17-623-5463
SHARED TECH COMMUNICATIONS LLC
100 Constitution Plz, Hartford, CT 06103
Phone: (860) 240-9600
Sales: $30,000,000   *Employees:* 100
Company Type: Private   *Employees here:* 100
SIC: 4813
   Telephone communications
Paul C Barry, President

D-U-N-S 14-492-8694
SHARED TECHNOLOGIES FAIRCHILD
   (*Parent:* Intermedia Communications Inc)
3625 Queen Palm Dr, Tampa, FL 33619
Phone: (813) 829-0011
Sales: $157,241,000   *Employees:* 744
Company Type: Public Family Member   *Employees here:* 37
SIC: 4813
   Data local long distance & voice telecommunications ret
   central office tele equip ret & installs tele equip & systems
James D Rivette, President

D-U-N-S 60-608-4770
SIEMENS INFO & COMM NETWORK INC.
   (*Parent:* Siemens Corporation)
900 Broken Sound Pkwy, Boca Raton, FL 33487
Phone: (561) 955-5000
Sales: $565,100,000   *Employees:* 5,900
Company Type: Private   *Employees here:* 1,800
SIC: 3661
   Mfg install & service office communications equipment
Karl Geng, President

D-U-N-S 16-158-5260   EXP
SIGCOM INC.
4413 W Market St, Greensboro, NC 27407
Phone: (336) 547-9700
Sales: $41,824,000   *Employees:* 135
Company Type: Private   *Employees here:* 65
SIC: 4813
   Systems integration & engineering
John Kim, Chief Executive Officer

D-U-N-S 07-838-8451
SIGNAL TECHNOLOGY CORPORATION
222 Rosewood Dr, Danvers, MA 01923
Phone: (978) 774-2281
Sales: $102,279,000   *Employees:* 820
Company Type: Public   *Employees here:* 175
SIC: 3679
   Mfg electronic components & subsystems
George Lombard, President

D-U-N-S 94-725-9735
SINCLAIR COMMUNICATIONS, INC.
   (*Parent:* Sinclair Broadcast Group Inc)
2000 W 41st St, Baltimore, MD 21211
Phone: (410) 467-5005
Sales: $378,000,000   *Employees:* 75
Company Type: Public Family Member   *Employees here:* 4
SIC: 4833
   Broadcasting company
Michael Fileck, Vice-President

D-U-N-S 94-949-1344
SINCLAIR PROPERTIES L.L.C.
2000 W 4th St, Baltimore, MD 21211
Phone: (410) 467-4545
Sales: $55,300,000   *Employees:* 500
Company Type: Private   *Employees here:* 4
SIC: 4833
   Television and radio stations
David H Smith, Principal

D-U-N-S 10-401-6027
SJI INC.
112 W 10th St, Cut Off, LA 70345
Phone: (504) 693-4567
Sales: $89,093,000   *Employees:* 512
Company Type: Private   *Employees here:* 130
SIC: 4813
   Telephone & communications services & mfg electronic
      automation systems
John A Brady Jr, President

D-U-N-S 19-674-3942   EXP
SKYTEL COMMUNICATIONS INC.
200 S Lamar St Ste 400, Jackson, MS 39201
Phone: (601) 944-1300
Sales: $407,968,000   *Employees:* 2,300
Company Type: Public   *Employees here:* 250
SIC: 4812
   Nationwide paging & nationwide voice messaging
John T Stupka, President

D-U-N-S 80-867-7843
SLC TECHNOLOGIES INC.
   (*Parent:* Berwind Industries Inc)
12345 Sw Leveton Dr, Tualatin, OR 97062
Phone: (503) 692-4052
Sales: $105,300,000   *Employees:* 1,800
Company Type: Private   *Employees here:* 1,240
SIC: 3669
   Mfg communications equipment whol electrical equipment
Kenneth L Boyda, President

D-U-N-S 87-944-3844
SMARTALK TELESERVICES, INC.
5080 Tuttle Crossing Blvd, Dublin, OH 43016
Phone: (614) 789-8500
Sales: $71,862,000   *Employees:* 565
Company Type: Public   *Employees here:* 250
SIC: 4813
   Telecommunication services
Erich Spangenberg, Chief Executive Officer

D-U-N-S 93-326-5340
SMS TECHNOLOGIES INC.
   (*Parent:* Spectragraphics Corporation)
9877 Waples St, San Diego, CA 92121
Phone: (619) 587-6900
Sales: $41,000,000   *Employees:* 197
Company Type: Private   *Employees here:* 197
SIC: 3679
   Electronic contract manufacturer
Robert Blumberg, Chief Executive Officer

D-U-N-S 04-341-6945
SNAP LLC
1 Beach St, San Francisco, CA 94133
Phone: (415) 875-7900
Sales: $35,000,000   *Employees:* 200
Company Type: Private   *Employees here:* 200
SIC: 4813
   Internet host services
Halsey Minor, Chief Executive Officer

D-U-N-S 19-558-1061
SNET MOBILITY INC.
   (*Parent:* Southern Neng Telecom Corp)
500 Enterprise Dr Ste 6, Rocky Hill, CT 06067
Phone: (860) 513-7600
Sales: $227,000,000   *Employees:* 130
Company Type: Private   *Employees here:* 129
SIC: 4812
   Resells cellular communication & paging services
Ronald M Serrano, President

D-U-N-S 96-589-7994
SOLECTRON MASSACHUSETTS CORP
(*Parent:* Solectron Corporation)
1 Solectron Dr, Westborough, MA 01581
Phone: (508) 616-6000
Sales: $75,000,000   *Employees:* 300
Company Type: Public Family Member   *Employees here:* 300
SIC: 3679
   Printed circuit board assembly electrical engineering services
       computer equip maintenance packaging & labeling services
Walter Wilson, President

D-U-N-S 00-590-2150
SONY ELECTRONICS INC.
(*Parent:* Sony Corporation of America)
1 Sony Dr, Park Ridge, NJ 07656
Phone: (201) 930-1000
Sales: $2,949,700,000   *Employees:* 26,000
Company Type: Private   *Employees here:* 1,000
SIC: 3651
   Mfr & distributor of video and audio equipment televisions
       monitors semiconductors computers and other
Dr Teruaki Aoki, President

D-U-N-S 60-318-4565
SONY TRANS COM INC.
(*Parent:* Sony Corporation of America)
1833 Alton Pkwy, Irvine, CA 92606
Phone: (949) 252-0600
Sales: $42,600,000   *Employees:* 500
Company Type: Private   *Employees here:* 450
SIC: 3663
   Mfg on board airline audio & visual entertainment systems
J D Cline, President

D-U-N-S 00-785-2320
SOURIS RIVER TELECOM COOP
3615 N Broadway, Minot, ND 58703
Phone: (701) 858-1200
Sales: $31,571,000   *Employees:* 200
Company Type: Private   *Employees here:* 200
SIC: 4813
   Telephone communications cable/pay television service
Warren Hight, Purchasing

D-U-N-S 07-805-1026
SOUTH CAROLINA EDUCATIONAL TV COMM
1101 George Rogers Blvd, Columbia, SC 29201
Phone: (803) 737-3240
Sales: $41,032,000   *Employees:* 337
Company Type: Private   *Employees here:* 263
SIC: 4833
   Educational television broadcasting station
Paul R Amos, President

D-U-N-S 00-691-7926
THE SOUTHERN NENG TELE CO.
(*Parent:* Southern Neng Telecom Corp)
227 Church St, New Haven, CT 06510
Phone: (203) 771-5200
Sales: $872,200,000   *Employees:* 6,791
Company Type: Private   *Employees here:* 5,000
SIC: 4813
   Telephone service
Daniel J Miglio, Chairman of the Board

D-U-N-S 15-118-0593
SOUTHERN NENG TELECOM CORP
310 Orange St, New Haven, CT 06510
Phone: (203) 771-2801

Sales: $1,264,200,000   *Employees:* 9,841
Company Type: Private   *Employees here:* 300
SIC: 4813
   Telephone service
Daniel J Miglio, Chairman of the Board

D-U-N-S 93-785-7910
SOUTHWEST CO WIRELESS, INC.
(*Parent:* Bell Atlantic Corporation)
11333 N Scottsdale Rd, Scottsdale, AZ 85254
Phone: (602) 948-8543
Sales: $42,700,000   *Employees:* 610
Company Type: Public Family Member   *Employees here:* 100
SIC: 4812
   Cellular phone services
Greg Klimek, President

D-U-N-S 12-145-2809
SOUTHWESTERN BELL MOBILE SYSTEMS
(*Parent:* SBC Communications Inc)
17330 Preston Rd S100a, Dallas, TX 75252
Phone: (972) 733-2000
Sales: $334,000,000   *Employees:* 4,810
Company Type: Public Family Member   *Employees here:* 300
SIC: 4812
   Cellular mobile telephone service
John T Stupka, President

D-U-N-S 00-696-8523
SOUTHWESTERN BELL TELE CO.
(*Parent:* SBC Communications Inc)
1 Bell Ctr, Saint Louis, MO 63101
Phone: (314) 235-9800
Sales: $10,313,000,000   *Employees:* 50,500
Company Type: Public Family Member   *Employees here:* 10,000
SIC: 4813
   Telephone communication
John H Atterbury III, President

D-U-N-S 00-227-9123
SPACE SYSTEMS/LORAL INC.
(*Parent:* Loral Space & Communications)
3825 Fabian Way, Palo Alto, CA 94303
Phone: (650) 852-4000
Sales: $1,442,600,000   *Employees:* 3,000
Company Type: Public Family Member   *Employees here:* 2,500
SIC: 3663
   Mfg communication satellites & weather satellites
Bernard L Schwartz, Chairman of the Board

D-U-N-S 10-112-9252
SPANISH BROADCASTING SYSTEM
(*Parent:* Spanish Brdcstg Sys Inc De)
26 W 56th St, New York, NY 10019
Phone: (212) 541-9200
Sales: $76,143,000   *Employees:* 96
Company Type: Private   *Employees here:* 40
SIC: 4832
   Radio station
Raul Alarcon Sr, Chairman of the Board

D-U-N-S 11-329-6545   EXP
SPECTRIAN CORPORATION
350 W Java Dr, Sunnyvale, CA 94089
Phone: (408) 745-5400
Sales: $168,798,000   *Employees:* 688
Company Type: Public   *Employees here:* 688
SIC: 3663
   Mfr radio frequency power amplifiers
Garrett A Garrettson, President

D-U-N-S 60-951-6083
SPECTRONICS CORP
3190 Northeast Expy Ne, Atlanta, GA 30341
Phone: (770) 455-9750
Sales: $30,700,000   *Employees:* 244
Company Type: Private   *Employees here:* 182
SIC: 4813
    Telecommunications & data networks contractor
Dorothy D Rollins, President

D-U-N-S 15-782-3535
SPLITROCK SERVICES INC.
8665 New Trails Dr, The Woodlands, TX 77381
Phone: (281) 465-1200
Sales: $70,000,000   *Employees:* 110
Company Type: Private   *Employees here:* 110
SIC: 4899
    Provides network data communication services
William R Wilson, President

D-U-N-S 94-758-5436
SPORT SOUTH NETWORK, LTD
1175 Peachtree St Ne, Atlanta, GA 30361
Phone: (404) 230-7300
Sales: $51,839,000   *Employees:* 26
Company Type: Private   *Employees here:* 26
SIC: 4841
    Cable television service
Hunter Nickell, General Manager

D-U-N-S 10-122-3378
SPORTSCHANNEL ASSOCIATES
200 Crossways Park Dr, Woodbury, NY 11797
Phone: (516) 364-2222
Sales: $62,044,000   *Employees:* 47
Company Type: Private   *Employees here:* 47
SIC: 4841
    Cable television broadcasting
Jim Bates, General Manager

D-U-N-S 13-971-0685
SPORTSCHANNEL CHICAGO ASSOC
300 N Orleans, Chicago, IL 60654
Phone: (312) 396-9800
Sales: $55,023,000   *Employees:* 74
Company Type: Private   *Employees here:* 74
SIC: 4841
    Regional sports cable network
James Corno, Vice-President

D-U-N-S 15-422-9660
SPRINT COMMUNICATIONS CO LP
8140 Ward Pkwy, Kansas City, MO 64114
Phone: (913) 624-6000
Sales: $9,000,000,000   *Employees:* 18,000
Company Type: Private   *Employees here:* 3,500
SIC: 4813
    Long distance telephone system
William Esrey, Chairman of the Board

D-U-N-S 00-694-2395
SPRINT CORPORATION
2330 Shawnee Mission Pkwy, Shawnee Mission, KS 66205
Phone: (913) 624-3000
Sales: $14,873,900,000   *Employees:* 51,000
Company Type: Public   *Employees here:* 700
SIC: 4813
    Telecommunications company
William T Esrey, Chairman of the Board

D-U-N-S 00-692-1092
SPRINT-FLORIDA, INCORPORATED
   (Parent: Central Telephone Company)
555 Lake Border Dr, Apopka, FL 32703
Phone: (407) 889-6000
Sales: $1,241,327,000   *Employees:* 5,300
Company Type: Public Family Member   *Employees here:* 700
SIC: 4813
    Telecommunication service
Michael B Fuller, President

D-U-N-S 94-702-0087
SPRINT TELECENTERS INC.
   (Parent: Florida Telephone Corporation)
2301 Lucien Way Ste 400, Maitland, FL 32751
Phone: (407) 661-0201
Sales: $31,500,000   *Employees:* 250
Company Type: Public Family Member   *Employees here:* 250
SIC: 4813
    Telephone communications
David Matheson, President

D-U-N-S 15-077-5591
SSE TELECOM INC.
47823 Westinghouse Dr, Fremont, CA 94539
Phone: (510) 657-7552
Sales: $36,739,000   *Employees:* 460
Company Type: Public   *Employees here:* 200
SIC: 3663
    Mfg radio/tv communication equipment
Leon F Blachowicz, President

D-U-N-S 18-697-8524
STANDARD GROUP INC.
   (Parent: Alltel Corporation)
2000 Industrial Blvd, Cornelia, GA 30531
Phone: (706) 778-2201
Sales: $121,000,000   *Employees:* 400
Company Type: Public Family Member   *Employees here:* 70
SIC: 4813
    Local and toll telephone service
Howard M Stewart Jr, Chairman of the Board

D-U-N-S 00-389-9291
STANDARD TELEPHONE COMPANY
   (Parent: Standard Group Inc)
2000 Communications Blvd, Cornelia, GA 30531
Phone: (706) 778-2201
Sales: $39,200,000   *Employees:* 310
Company Type: Public Family Member   *Employees here:* 75
SIC: 4813
    Telephone company
Howard M Stewart Jr, Chairman of the Board

D-U-N-S 06-354-7475   EXP
STANFORD TELECOMMUNICATIONS
1221 Crossman Ave, Sunnyvale, CA 94089
Phone: (408) 745-0818
Sales: $153,260,000   *Employees:* 1,025
Company Type: Public   *Employees here:* 316
SIC: 3663
    Mfg & operates communication & electronic systems for
      aerospace
Dr James J Spilker Jr, Chairman of the Board

D-U-N-S 87-907-4755   EXP
STAR TELECOMMUNICATIONS, INC.
223 E De La Guerra St, Santa Barbara, CA 93101
Phone: (805) 899-1962

Sales: $376,198,000   *Employees:* 116
Company Type: Public   *Employees here:* 110
SIC: 4813
    Long distance international service provider
Christophe E Edgecomb, Chairman of the Board

D-U-N-S 04-233-8819
STARPOWER COMMUNICATIONS LLC
1130 Connecticut Ave NW, Washington, DC 20036
Phone: (202) 955-7960
Sales: $65,000,000   *Employees:* 40
Company Type: Private   *Employees here:* 4
SIC: 4813
    Telecommunication independent services providing local &
      long distance services
Dean Shepard, Finance

D-U-N-S 03-049-0445
STAVELEY INC.
    (Parent: Staveley Investments Inc)
50 Main St, White Plains, NY 10606
Phone: (914) 682-6830
Sales: $91,000,000   *Employees:* 1,568
Company Type: Private   *Employees here:* 15
SIC: 3679
    Mfg ultrasonic transducers & test equip industrial weighing
      machines & sales distributor of parts for coal crushing
      machines
Sal Busciolano, Principal

D-U-N-S 79-945-0473
STELLEX MICROWAVE SYSTEMS
    (Parent: Stellex Industries Inc)
3333 Hillview Ave, Palo Alto, CA 94304
Phone: (650) 813-2000
Sales: $89,000,000   *Employees:* 504
Company Type: Private   *Employees here:* 504
SIC: 3679
    Mfg electronic components
Keith Gilbert, President

D-U-N-S 11-281-4835   EXP
STM WIRELESS INC.
1 Mauchly, Irvine, CA 92618
Phone: (949) 753-7864
Sales: $52,148,000   *Employees:* 140
Company Type: Public   *Employees here:* 125
SIC: 3663
    Provides software & hardware for wireless communications
Emil Youssefzadeh, President

D-U-N-S 60-628-0873   EXP
STONERIDGE, INC.
9400 E Market St, Warren, OH 44484
Phone: (330) 856-2443
Sales: $449,506,000   *Employees:* 4,400
Company Type: Public   *Employees here:* 7
SIC: 3679
    Mfr vehicle elec power & distribution systems electron & elec
      switch pdts elec instrumentation & info display pdts
David M Draime, Chairman

D-U-N-S 80-096-9552
STRATOS MOBILE NETWORKS USA LLC
6903 Rockledge Dr Ste 500, Bethesda, MD 20817
Phone: (301) 214-8800
Sales: $50,000,000   *Employees:* 59
Company Type: Private   *Employees here:* 9
SIC: 4899
    Satellite communications services
Derrick Rowe, President

D-U-N-S 09-370-8568
SUBURBAN CABLE TV CO INC.
    (Parent: Lenfest Communications Inc)
200 Cresson Blvd, Oaks, PA 19456
Phone: (610) 650-1000
Sales: $354,561,000   *Employees:* 400
Company Type: Private   *Employees here:* 50
SIC: 4841
    Cable television services
Harold F Lenfest, Chairman of the Board

D-U-N-S 00-594-8625
SUGAR LAND TELEPHONE COMPANY
    (Parent: Alltel Corporation)
1 Sugar Creek Center Blvd, Sugar Land, TX 77478
Phone: (281) 494-2121
Sales: $37,900,000   *Employees:* 300
Company Type: Public Family Member   *Employees here:* 40
SIC: 4813
    Telephone communication
R C Brown III, President

D-U-N-S 17-524-9424
SULLIVAN BROADCASTING COMPANY
    (Parent: Sullivan Broadcast Holdings)
18 Newbury St, Boston, MA 02116
Phone: (617) 369-7755
Sales: $137,774,000   *Employees:* 450
Company Type: Private   *Employees here:* 3
SIC: 4833
    Television broadcasting
J D Sullivan, President

D-U-N-S 00-377-5418
SUNBEAM TELEVISION CORP
1401 79th Street Cswy, Miami, FL 33141
Phone: (305) 751-6692
Sales: $201,000,000   *Employees:* 475
Company Type: Private   *Employees here:* 250
SIC: 4833
    Television station
Edmund Ansin, President

D-U-N-S 18-216-4707
SUNBELT COMMUNICATIONS COMPANY
1500 Foremaster Ln, Las Vegas, NV 89101
Phone: (702) 642-3333
Sales: $55,000,000   *Employees:* 450
Company Type: Private   *Employees here:* 15
SIC: 4833
    Television stations
James E Rogers, Chairman of the Board

D-U-N-S 79-297-9627
SUPERIOR MODULAR PRODUCTS INC.
    (Parent: Preformed Line Products Co)
33 Superior Way, Swannanoa, NC 28778
Phone: (828) 298-2260
Sales: $32,000,000   *Employees:* 325
Company Type: Private   *Employees here:* 300
SIC: 3663
    Mfg plastic insulated communication equipment
Dr Kenneth Brownell, President

D-U-N-S 55-695-4535
SUPERSTATION INC.
    (Parent: Turner Entrmt Networks Inc)
1050 Techwood Dr NW, Atlanta, GA 30318
Phone: (404) 827-1700

Sales: $89,800,000
Company Type: Public Family Member
SIC: 4833
   Television station
Terry McGuirk, President

Employees: 800
Employees here: NA

D-U-N-S 78-449-4080
SYGNET WIRELESS INC.
6550b Seville Dr, Canfield, OH 44406
Phone: (330) 565-1000
Sales: $85,634,000
Company Type: Private
SIC: 4812
   Cellular phone communication
Albert Pharis, President

Employees: 415
Employees here: 22

D-U-N-S 00-824-8593
SYMMETRICOM INC.
2300 Orchard Pkwy, San Jose, CA 95131
Phone: (408) 943-9403
Sales: $120,581,000
Company Type: Public
SIC: 3661
   Mfg telecommunications equipment & integrated circuits
Roger A Strauch, Chief Executive Officer

EXP

Employees: 642
Employees here: 153

D-U-N-S 62-681-9510
T-NETIX, INC.
67 Inverness Dr E 100, Englewood, CO 80112
Phone: (303) 790-9111
Sales: $38,213,000
Company Type: Public
SIC: 4813
   Telephone call processing services
Alvyn A Schopp, Chief Executive Officer

Employees: 198
Employees here: 185

D-U-N-S 78-214-4661
TAL FINANCIAL CORPORATION
   (Parent: TCA Cable TV Inc)
3015 S Southeast Loop 323, Tyler, TX 75701
Phone: (903) 595-3701
Sales: $32,263,000
Company Type: Public Family Member
SIC: 4841
   Holding company
Fred Nichols, President

Employees: 900
Employees here: 95

D-U-N-S 60-545-6979
TALLA-COM TALLAHASSEE COMM IND
   (Parent: Tadiran Electronic Industries)
1720 W Paul Dirac Dr, Tallahassee, FL 32310
Phone: (850) 580-0200
Sales: $68,413,000
Company Type: Private
SIC: 3669
   Mfg electronic communications
Yehuda Peress, President

Employees: 235
Employees here: 235

D-U-N-S 16-949-1032
TAYLOR UNIVERSITY BROADCASTING
   (Parent: Taylor University)
1025 W Rudisill Blvd, Fort Wayne, IN 46807
Phone: (219) 745-0576
Sales: $53,379,000
Company Type: Private
SIC: 4832
   Radio broadcast station advertising representative
Char Binkley, Manager

Employees: 25
Employees here: 25

D-U-N-S 06-278-4905
TCA CABLE TV INC.
3015 S Southeast Loop 323, Tyler, TX 75701
Phone: (903) 595-3701

Sales: $385,737,000
Company Type: Public
SIC: 4841
   Cable television service
Jimmie F Taylor, Chief Financial Officer

Employees: 1,900
Employees here: 80

D-U-N-S 78-583-6396
TCI CABLE INVESTMENTS INC.
   (Parent: Tele-Communications Inc)
8101 E Prentice Ave Ste 5, Englewood, CO 80111
Phone: (303) 721-5400
Sales: $674,600,000
Company Type: Public Family Member
SIC: 4841
   Cable television services
Brendan R Clouston, President

Employees: NA
Employees here: NA

D-U-N-S 60-460-0098
TCI CABLEVISION OF ALABAMA
   (Parent: TCI Southeast Inc)
3443 Lorna Ln, Birmingham, AL 35216
Phone: (205) 822-3699
Sales: $134,300,000
Company Type: Public Family Member
SIC: 4841
   Cable television service
John Anglin, Manager

Employees: 1,000
Employees here: 6

D-U-N-S 12-084-7736
TCI CABLEVISION OF CALIFORNIA
   (Parent: TCI West Inc)
1722 Orange Tree Ln, Redlands, CA 92374
Phone: (909) 798-3588
Sales: $32,000,000
Company Type: Public Family Member
SIC: 4841
   Cable television service
John Kopchik, President

Employees: 200
Employees here: 160

D-U-N-S 19-559-9634
TCI CABLEVISION OF MISSOURI
   (Parent: TCI North Central Inc)
4160 Old Mill Pkwy, Saint Peters, MO 63376
Phone: (314) 441-7737
Sales: $90,988,000
Company Type: Public Family Member
SIC: 4841
   Cable television service
William Forrest, General Manager

Employees: 350
Employees here: 5

D-U-N-S 07-894-1739
TCI CABLEVISION OF WISCONSIN
   (Parent: TCI North Central Inc)
5618 Odana Rd, Madison, WI 53719
Phone: (608) 274-3822
Sales: $38,000,000
Company Type: Public Family Member
SIC: 4841
   Cable television service
Stephen Bryan, President

Employees: 250
Employees here: 230

D-U-N-S 19-602-3725
TCI CENTRAL, INC.
   (Parent: TCI Communications Inc)
4700 S Syracuse St, Denver, CO 80237
Phone: (303) 267-4200
Sales: $469,478,000
Company Type: Public Family Member
SIC: 4841
   Cable television service
Richard E Franklin, President

Employees: 96
Employees here: 16

D-U-N-S 04-629-0706
TCI COMMUNICATIONS, INC.
(Parent: Tele-Communications Inc)
5619 Dtc Pkwy, Englewood, CO 80111
Phone: (303) 267-5500
Sales: $6,166,711,000
Company Type: Public
SIC: 4841
   Cable television
John C Malone, President
Employees: 36,000
Employees here: 500

D-U-N-S 61-726-3363
TCI GREAT LAKES, INC.
(Parent: TCI Communications Inc)
111 S Pfingsten Rd, Deerfield, IL 60015
Phone: (847) 480-9292
Sales: $57,012,000
Company Type: Public Family Member
SIC: 4841
   Cable television services
Allan Goodson, President
Employees: NA
Employees here: NA

D-U-N-S 18-060-6659
TCI HOLDINGS, INC.
(Parent: TCI Communications Inc)
5619 Dtc Pkwy, Englewood, CO 80111
Phone: (303) 267-5500
Sales: $1,496,864,000
Company Type: Public Family Member
SIC: 4841
   Cable television service
Brendon R Clouston, President
Employees: 2,000
Employees here: 4

D-U-N-S 09-976-7030
TCI OF LEXINGTON, INC.
(Parent: TCI Holdings Inc)
2544 Palumbo Dr, Lexington, KY 40509
Phone: (606) 268-1123
Sales: $31,000,000
Company Type: Public Family Member
SIC: 4841
   Cable television service
Bill Mitchell, President
Employees: 160
Employees here: 146

D-U-N-S 05-289-7378
TCI OF OVERLAND PARK, INC.
(Parent: TCI Holdings Inc)
8221 W 119th St, Shawnee Mission, KS 66213
Phone: (913) 451-5858
Sales: $35,000,000
Company Type: Public Family Member
SIC: 4841
   Cable television service
Leo Hindery, Chief Executive Officer
Employees: 179
Employees here: 179

D-U-N-S 19-604-2659
TCI OF PENNSYLVANIA, INC.
(Parent: TCI Communications Inc)
300 Corliss St, Pittsburgh, PA 15220
Phone: (412) 771-8100
Sales: $80,300,000
Company Type: Public Family Member
SIC: 4841
   Cable/pay television service
Leo Hindery, President
Employees: 600
Employees here: 600

D-U-N-S 60-535-1618
TCI SOUTHEAST INC.
(Parent: TCI Holdings Inc)
2204 Lakeshore Dr Ste 325, Birmingham, AL 35209
Phone: (205) 871-0044

Sales: $188,300,000
Company Type: Public Family Member
SIC: 4841
   Cable television service
Tom Barberini, Chief Operating Officer
Employees: 1,400
Employees here: 35

D-U-N-S 09-804-9471
TCI TKR CABLE I INC.
(Parent: TCI Communications Inc)
18601 NW 2nd Ave, Miami, FL 33169
Phone: (305) 653-5541
Sales: $43,100,000
Company Type: Public Family Member
SIC: 4841
   Cable television services
J C Spark, Chairman of the Board
Employees: 325
Employees here: 195

D-U-N-S 86-959-3558
TCI TKR OF SOUTH FLORIDA, INC.
(Parent: TCI TKR Cable I Inc)
18601 NW 2nd Ave, Miami, FL 33169
Phone: (305) 652-9900
Sales: $34,400,000
Company Type: Private
SIC: 4841
   Cable/pay television service
Anthony Pope, General Manager
Employees: 260
Employees here: 260

D-U-N-S 15-108-6089
TCI WEST, INC.
(Parent: TCI Communications Inc)
2233 112th Ave Ne, Bellevue, WA 98004
Phone: (425) 462-2620
Sales: $827,082,000
Company Type: Public Family Member
SIC: 4841
   Cable television service
Barry Marshall, President
Employees: 4,250
Employees here: 60

D-U-N-S 00-808-8403   EXP
TECH-SYM CORPORATION
10500 Wstffice Dr Ste 200, Houston, TX 77042
Phone: (713) 785-7790
Sales: $294,100,000
Company Type: Public
SIC: 3663
   Mfg electronic equipment
J M Camp, President
Employees: 2,398
Employees here: 8

D-U-N-S 08-413-0400
TECHDYNE INC.
(Parent: Medicore Inc)
2230 W 77th St, Hialeah, FL 33016
Phone: (305) 556-9210
Sales: $33,169,000
Company Type: Public
SIC: 3679
   Mfg electronic circuits & printed circuit boards
Thomas K Langbein, Chairman of the Board
Employees: 470
Employees here: 109

D-U-N-S 00-230-0556   EXP
TECHNITROL INC.
1210 Northbrook Dr, Langhorne, PA 19053
Phone: (215) 355-2900
Sales: $397,067,000
Company Type: Public
SIC: 3679
   Mfg electronic components & modules electrical contacts
      laminating metal pdts
James M Papada III, Chief Executive Officer
Employees: 14,400
Employees here: 10

D-U-N-S 92-952-5046   EXP
TECHNOLOGY CONTROL SERVICES
   (Parent: Hemisphere Investments Inc)
200 E Broward Blvd, Fort Lauderdale, FL 33301
Phone: (954) 712-0500
Sales: $50,000,000   *Employees:* 80
Company Type: Private   *Employees here:* 35
SIC: 4813
   Provider of telecommunication services
Ben Holzemer, Chief Executive Officer

D-U-N-S 05-590-6002   EXP
TECHSONIC INDUSTRIES INC.
   (Parent: Teleflex Incorporated)
5 Humminbird Ln, Eufaula, AL 36027
Phone: (334) 687-6613
Sales: $52,000,000   *Employees:* 285
Company Type: Public Family Member   *Employees here:* 255
SIC: 3679
   Mfg marine information systems
Steven Duvall, N/A

D-U-N-S 09-944-9076   EXP
TEKELEC
26580 Agoura Rd, Calabasas, CA 91302
Phone: (818) 880-5656
Sales: $125,140,000   *Employees:* 450
Company Type: Public   *Employees here:* 150
SIC: 3661
   Mfg network switching solutions & diagnostic systems for the
      communications marketplace
Michael L Margolis, President

D-U-N-S 60-814-0281
TEL-SAVE INC.
   (Parent: Tel-Savecom Inc)
6805 Route 202, New Hope, PA 18938
Phone: (215) 862-1500
Sales: $460,000,000   *Employees:* 400
Company Type: Public Family Member   *Employees here:* 150
SIC: 4813
   Whol telephone long distance services & ret long distance
      services through AOL
Daniel Borislow, Chief Executive Officer

D-U-N-S 83-025-0163
TELCO COMMUNICATIONS GROUP
   (Parent: Excel Communications Inc)
3900 Skyhawk Dr, Chantilly, VA 20151
Phone: (703) 631-5600
Sales: $192,100,000   *Employees:* 1,500
Company Type: Public Family Member   *Employees here:* 200
SIC: 4813
   Long distance telephone communications
Kenny A Troutt, Chairman of the Board

D-U-N-S 86-739-8794
TELE-COMMUNICATIONS, INC.
5619 Dtc Pkwy, Englewood, CO 80111
Phone: (303) 267-5500
Sales: $7,570,000,000   *Employees:* 32,000
Company Type: Public   *Employees here:* 1,400
SIC: 4841
   Cable television and programming
John C Malone, Chairman of the Board

D-U-N-S 17-427-1460
TELE-FIBERNET CORPORATION
   (Parent: MCI Worldcom Inc)
515 E Amite St, Jackson, MS 39201
Phone: (601) 360-8600

Sales: $89,300,000   *Employees:* 700
Company Type: Public Family Member   *Employees here:* 500
SIC: 4813
   Long distance telephone company
Bernard Ebbers, President

D-U-N-S 83-596-0154
TELECARD DISPENSING CORP
1909 Tyler St Fl 35, Hollywood, FL 33020
Phone: (954) 929-6111
Sales: $79,498,000   *Employees:* 50
Company Type: Private   *Employees here:* 50
SIC: 4813
   Sells prepaid calling cards and machines that dispense them
Harris M Cohen, President

D-U-N-S 06-274-1368   EXP
TELECT, INC.
N2111 Molter Rd, Liberty Lake, WA 99019
Phone: (509) 926-6000
Sales: $121,000,000   *Employees:* 847
Company Type: Private   *Employees here:* 754
SIC: 3661
   Mfg telephone communications equipment & low voltage
      controls
Bill Williams Jr, Chairman of the Board

D-U-N-S 79-870-4698
TELEDATA INTERNATIONAL INC.
   (Parent: Teledata World Services Inc)
1000 Circle 75 Pkwy Se, Atlanta, GA 30339
Phone: (770) 850-0005
Sales: $80,000,000   *Employees:* 40
Company Type: Private   *Employees here:* 40
SIC: 4813
   Telecommunication services
Alec Mclarty, President

D-U-N-S 83-629-8323
TELEGLOBE INTERNATIONAL CORP
   (Parent: Teleglobe Inc)
11480 Commerce Park Dr, Reston, VA 20191
Phone: (703) 755-2000
Sales: $278,656,000   *Employees:* 250
Company Type: Private   *Employees here:* 244
SIC: 4813
   Long-distance telephone service
Paolo Guidi, President

D-U-N-S 61-119-2527
TELEGROUP INC.
2098 Nutmeg Ave, Fairfield, IA 52556
Phone: (515) 472-5000
Sales: $337,432,000   *Employees:* 500
Company Type: Public   *Employees here:* 250
SIC: 4813
   Facilities based and reseller of long distance telephone
      communications services
Fred Gratzon, Chairman of the Board

D-U-N-S 15-718-0951
TELEMEDIA INTERNATIONAL USA
1 Evertrust Plz Fl 4, Jersey City, NJ 07302
Phone: (201) 536-5000
Sales: $36,370,000   *Employees:* 150
Company Type: Private   *Employees here:* 70
SIC: 4813
   Reseller of enhanced telecommunications services
Claudio Albanese, Chairman of the Board

D-U-N-S 04-525-9215
TELEMUNDO GROUP INC.
(*Parent:* Telemundo Holdings Inc)
2290 W 8th Ave, Hialeah, FL 33010
Phone: (305) 884-8200
Sales: $89,800,000   *Employees:* 800
Company Type: Private   *Employees here:* 70
SIC: 4833
    Tv station owner & operator & advertising sales
Roland A Hernandez, Chairman of the Board

D-U-N-S 04-897-9558
TELENOTICIAS LLC
2470 W 8th Ave, Hialeah, FL 33010
Phone: (305) 889-7200
Sales: $30,400,000   *Employees:* 200
Company Type: Private   *Employees here:* 100
SIC: 4841
    Cable television
Maneul Abud, President

D-U-N-S 05-057-5695
TELEPHONE AND DATA SYSTEMS
30 N Lasalle St Ste 4000, Chicago, IL 60602
Phone: (312) 630-1900
Sales: $1,471,533,000   *Employees:* 9,685
Company Type: Public   *Employees here:* 43
SIC: 4812
    Telephone & communications services
Le R Carlson Jr, President

D-U-N-S 08-437-2432
TELEPHONE ELECTRONICS CORP
236 E Capitol St Ste 500, Jackson, MS 39201
Phone: (601) 354-9066
Sales: $1,001,266,000   *Employees:* 900
Company Type: Private   *Employees here:* 30
SIC: 4813
    Local telephone exchange
Joseph D Fail, Chairman of the Board

D-U-N-S 08-150-9218
TELEPHONICS CORPORATION
(*Parent:* Griffon Corporation)
815 Broadhollow Rd, Farmingdale, NY 11735
Phone: (516) 755-7000
Sales: $156,864,000   *Employees:* 1,000
Company Type: Public Family Member   *Employees here:* 600
SIC: 3669
    Designs builds integrates & installs select information &
      communication systems
Joseph J Battaglia, President

D-U-N-S 07-256-3638
TELETOUCH COMMUNICATIONS, INC.
110 N College Ave Ste 200, Tyler, TX 75702
Phone: (903) 595-8800
Sales: $35,834,000   *Employees:* 337
Company Type: Public   *Employees here:* 25
SIC: 4812
    Leases communication equipment services and installs
      equipment and ret communication equipment
R J McMurrey, Chairman of the Board

D-U-N-S 06-653-4611
TELEX COMMUNICATIONS INC.
(*Parent:* Telex Communication Group)
9600 Aldrich Ave S, Minneapolis, MN 55420
Phone: (612) 884-4051

Sales: $355,000,000   *Employees:* 3,300
Company Type: Public Family Member   *Employees here:* 200
SIC: 3663
    Mfg audio visual and multimedia communications equipment
      and hearing aids
Ned C Jackson, Chief Executive Officer

D-U-N-S 07-441-0333   EXP
TELLABS INC.
4951 Indiana Ave, Lisle, IL 60532
Phone: (630) 378-8800
Sales: $1,203,546,000   *Employees:* 4,087
Company Type: Public   *Employees here:* 20
SIC: 3661
    Mfg telecommunications equipment
Michael J Birck, President

D-U-N-S 78-583-8954
TELSCAPE INTERNATIONAL INC.
2700 Post Oak Blvd, Houston, TX 77056
Phone: (713) 968-0968
Sales: $36,154,000   *Employees:* 400
Company Type: Public   *Employees here:* 159
SIC: 4813
    Services
E S Crist, President

D-U-N-S 09-898-5898   EXP
TELTREND INC.
620 Stetson Ave, Saint Charles, IL 60174
Phone: (630) 377-1700
Sales: $96,762,000   *Employees:* 519
Company Type: Public   *Employees here:* 450
SIC: 3661
    Mfg telecommunication equipment
Howard L Kirby Jr, Chairman of the Board

D-U-N-S 19-820-5619   EXP
TELTRONICS INC.
2150 Whitfield Industrial, Sarasota, FL 34243
Phone: (941) 753-5000
Sales: $34,673,000   *Employees:* 210
Company Type: Public   *Employees here:* 190
SIC: 3661
    Mfg equip & application software for the telecommunications
      industry
Mark Scott, Treasurer

D-U-N-S 80-998-8595
TELULAR CORPORATION (DEL)
647 Lakeview Pkwy, Vernon Hills, IL 60061
Phone: (847) 247-9400
Sales: $40,436,000   *Employees:* 665
Company Type: Public   *Employees here:* 95
SIC: 3663
    Mfg wireless telecommunications equipment
Kenneth E Millard, President

D-U-N-S 00-780-4404
TEXAS TELEVISION INC.
4750 S Padre Island Dr, Corpus Christi, TX 78411
Phone: (361) 854-4733
Sales: $40,000,000   *Employees:* 84
Company Type: Private   *Employees here:* 4
SIC: 4833
    Television station
Mike Mckinnon, President

D-U-N-S 79-447-0724
TGC INC
7580 Commerce Dr, Orlando, FL 32819
Phone: (407) 363-4653

Sales: $33,000,000   *Employees:* 250
Company Type: Private   *Employees here:* 250
SIC: 4841
   Cable/pay television service
Joseph E Gibbs, President

D-U-N-S 04-199-3668   EXP
THERMO VOLTEK CORP
   (Parent: TMD Securities Corporation)
470 Wildwood Ave, Woburn, MA 01801
Phone: (781) 938-3786
Sales: $44,648,000   *Employees:* 275
Company Type: Public   *Employees here:* 1
SIC: 3679
   Mfr electronic power surge testing equipment & high voltage
     power supply systems & components
John W Wood Jr, Chairman of the Board

D-U-N-S 78-747-4949
TIME WARNER CABLE PROGRAMMING
   (Parent: Time Warner Companies Inc)
290 Harbor Dr, Stamford, CT 06902
Phone: (203) 328-0600
Sales: $33,400,000   *Employees:* 192
Company Type: Public Family Member   *Employees here:* 150
SIC: 4841
   Cable television services
Thayer Bigelow, President

D-U-N-S 83-635-1197
TIME WARNER ENTERTAINMENT
300 First Stamford Pl, Stamford, CT 06902
Phone: (203) 328-0600
Sales: $133,200,000   *Employees:* 992
Company Type: Private   *Employees here:* 1
SIC: 4841
   Cable television service
Gerald M Levin, Chairman of the Board

D-U-N-S 01-950-6133
TIME WARNER TELECOM LLC
5700 S Quebec St, Englewood, CO 80111
Phone: (303) 566-1000
Sales: $55,401,000   *Employees:* 898
Company Type: Private   *Employees here:* 420
SIC: 4813
   Telephone communication, except radio
Larissa Herda, President

D-U-N-S 06-134-2705   EXP
TIMEPLEX INC.
400 Chestnut Ridge Rd, Woodcliff Lake, NJ 07675
Phone: (201) 391-1111
Sales: $176,867,000   *Employees:* 1,000
Company Type: Private   *Employees here:* 250
SIC: 3661
   Design mfg implementation & support of multinational wide-
     area networking systems & services
Jacques De Labry, President

D-U-N-S 04-834-1838   EXP
TITAN CORPORATION
3033 Science Park Rd, San Diego, CA 92121
Phone: (619) 552-9500
Sales: $171,186,000   *Employees:* 1,500
Company Type: Public   *Employees here:* 600
SIC: 3663
   Provides state-of-the-art information technology & electronic
     systems & services
Gene W Ray, President

D-U-N-S 01-114-7928
TITAN TECH & INFO SYSTEMS CORP
   (Parent: Titan Corporation)
1900 Campus Commons Dr, Reston, VA 20191
Phone: (703) 758-5600
Sales: $220,000,000   *Employees:* 1,100
Company Type: Public Family Member   *Employees here:* 250
SIC: 3663
   Provides technology and information solutions to defense-
     related government customers
John L Slack, President

D-U-N-S 08-290-0689   EXP
TIW SYSTEMS, INC.
   (Parent: Vertex Communications Corp)
2211 Lawson Ln, Santa Clara, CA 95054
Phone: (408) 734-3900
Sales: $45,000,000   *Employees:* 250
Company Type: Public Family Member   *Employees here:* 175
SIC: 3669
   Satellite communications equipment
Dr Rein Luik, President

D-U-N-S 92-843-7482
TMR SALES, INC.
1263 Oakmead Pkwy Ste 100, Sunnyvale, CA 94086
Phone: (408) 245-7700
Sales: $40,000,000   *Employees:* 14
Company Type: Private   *Employees here:* 14
SIC: 3679
   Represents electronic manufactures
Michael Johnson, President

D-U-N-S 04-447-7784
TODD PRODUCTS CORP
50 Emjay Blvd Ste 7, Brentwood, NY 11717
Phone: (516) 231-3366
Sales: $31,395,000   *Employees:* 500
Company Type: Private   *Employees here:* 290
SIC: 3679
   Mfg electronic components
Kathy Todd, Chairman of the Board

D-U-N-S 18-584-6953
TOLLGRADE COMMUNICATIONS, INC.
493 Nixon Rd, Cheswick, PA 15024
Phone: (724) 274-2156
Sales: $45,421,000   *Employees:* 205
Company Type: Public   *Employees here:* 200
SIC: 3661
   Mfg communication equipment & components
Christian L Allison, Chairman of the Board

D-U-N-S 60-645-6119
TOSHIBA AMERICA ELECTRONIC COMPONENTS
   (Parent: Toshiba America Inc)
9775 Toledo Way, Irvine, CA 92618
Phone: (949) 455-2000
Sales: $116,100,000   *Employees:* 2,000
Company Type: Private   *Employees here:* 300
SIC: 3679
   Mfg and whol electronic components
Hideo Ito, Chairman of the Board

D-U-N-S 06-499-3082
TOSHIBA AMERICA INC.
1251 Ave Of Americas, New York, NY 10020
Phone: (212) 596-0600

Sales: $6,095,697,000
Company Type: Private
SIC: 3651
    Mfg & imports consumer pdts industrial electronics
        electronic components & medical systems
Takeshi Okatomi, Chairman of the Board

Employees: 7,500
Employees here: 28

D-U-N-S 00-194-0840
TOTAL-TEL USA COMMUNICATIONS INC.
150 Clove Rd Ste 8, Little Falls, NJ 07424
Phone: (973) 812-1100
Sales: $123,286,000
Company Type: Public
SIC: 4813
    Provides long distance telephone service
Dennis Spina, President

Employees: 270
Employees here: 200

D-U-N-S 87-815-9797
TOUCH 1 COMMUNICATIONS INC.
100 Brookwood Dr, Atmore, AL 36502
Phone: (334) 368-8600
Sales: $35,664,000
Company Type: Private
SIC: 4813
    Long distance telephone communications
Kathy Hawkins, President

Employees: 415
Employees here: 415

D-U-N-S 79-902-0896
TRANS NATIONAL COMMUNICATIONS
133 Federal St, Boston, MA 02110
Phone: (617) 369-1000
Sales: $63,082,000
Company Type: Private
SIC: 4813
    Direct marketing reseller of switchless long distance phone
        services and independent affinity long distance carrier
Bruce Rogoff, Chief Executive Officer

Employees: 150
Employees here: 150

D-U-N-S 00-397-2080
TRANS WORLD RADIO
300 Gregson Dr, Cary, NC 27511
Phone: (919) 460-3700
Sales: $33,660,000
Company Type: Private
SIC: 4832
    Radio broadcasting
Thomas J Lowell, President

Employees: 100
Employees here: 100

D-U-N-S 62-386-2562
TRANSACTION NETWORK SERVICES
1939 Roland Clarke Pl, Reston, VA 20191
Phone: (703) 453-8300
Sales: $63,344,000
Company Type: Public
SIC: 4813
    Data communications including credit card authorization
John J McDonnell Jr, President

Employees: 112
Employees here: 90

D-U-N-S 78-329-8201
TRANSAMERICA BUS TECH CORPORATIONS
    (*Parent:* Transamerica Corporation)
1149 S Broadway Ste 1021, Los Angeles, CA 90015
Phone: (213) 742-4484
Sales: $50,000,000
Company Type: Public Family Member
SIC: 4813
    Telecommunications service
Maureen Breakiron-Evans, President

Employees: 160
Employees here: 160

D-U-N-S 05-627-1489
TRANSCALL AMERICA INC.
    (*Parent:* MCI Worldcom Inc)
515 E Amite St, Jackson, MS 39201

Phone: (601) 360-8600
Sales: $37,900,000
Company Type: Public Family Member
SIC: 4813
    Telephone communications company
John A Porter, Chairman

Employees: 300
Employees here: 300

D-U-N-S 10-231-7096   EXP
TRANSCRYPT INTERNATIONAL, INC.
4800 NW 1st St, Lincoln, NE 68521
Phone: (402) 474-4800
Sales: $62,041,000
Company Type: Public
SIC: 3663
    Mfg voice and data privacy devices signaling technology &
        land mobile radios
R A Massey, N/A

Employees: 494
Employees here: 130

D-U-N-S 82-473-2218   EXP
TRESCOM INTERNATIONAL, INC.
200 E Broward Blvd, Fort Lauderdale, FL 33301
Phone: (954) 763-4000
Sales: $157,641,000
Company Type: Public
SIC: 4813
    International long distance service
Wesley T O Brien, President

Employees: 250
Employees here: 100

D-U-N-S 78-760-2887
TRIATHLON BROADCASTING COMPANY
750 B St Ste 1920, San Diego, CA 92101
Phone: (619) 239-4242
Sales: $40,000,000
Company Type: Public
SIC: 4832
    Radio broadcasting stations
Bill Thompson, Chief Financial Officer

Employees: 289
Employees here: 4

D-U-N-S 61-416-7856
TRIAX USA ASSOCIATES, LP
100 Fillmore St Ste 600, Denver, CO 80206
Phone: (303) 333-2424
Sales: $80,300,000
Company Type: Private
SIC: 4841
    Cable & pay TV
Jay Busch, Partner

Employees: 600
Employees here: 600

D-U-N-S 01-628-1073
TRIBUNE BROADCASTING COMPANY
    (*Parent:* Tribune Company)
435 N Michigan Ave, Chicago, IL 60611
Phone: (312) 222-3333
Sales: $877,000,000
Company Type: Public Family Member
SIC: 4833
    Television & radio broadcasting & produces & syndicates
        television shows
James C Dowdle, President

Employees: 1,700
Employees here: 20

D-U-N-S 00-509-4099   EXP
TRIPPE MANUFACTURING COMPANY
1111 W 35th St, Chicago, IL 60609
Phone: (312) 755-5400
Sales: $125,000,000
Company Type: Private
SIC: 3679
    Mfg electronic power supplies
Elbert Howell, Chief Executive Officer

Employees: 400
Employees here: 398

D-U-N-S 02-366-4027
TRITON CELLULAR PARTNERS LP
375 Technology Dr, Malvern, PA 19355
Phone: (610) 651-5900

Sales: $118,000,000
Company Type: Private
SIC: 4812
    Cellular communications
James W Akerhielm, President

Employees: 300
Employees here: 12

D-U-N-S 18-270-9253
TSR WIRELESS LLC
400 Kelby St, Fort Lee, NJ 07024
Phone: (201) 947-5300
Sales: $220,000,000
Company Type: Private
SIC: 4812
    Paging services
Leonard Di Savino, Chairman

Employees: 1,500
Employees here: 75

D-U-N-S 04-018-2198
TULALIP TRIBES INC.
6700 Totem Beach Rd, Marysville, WA 98271
Phone: (360) 651-4000
Sales: $161,300,000
Company Type: Private
SIC: 4841
    Tribal council organization
Stanley G Jones Sr, Chairman of the Board

Employees: 1,200
Employees here: 350

D-U-N-S 05-808-0433
TULSA CABLE TELEVISION, INC.
    (Parent: Tele-Communications Inc)
8421 E 61st St Ste U, Tulsa, OK 74133
Phone: (918) 459-3500
Sales: $44,100,000
Company Type: Public Family Member
SIC: 4841
    Cable television service
Rick Comfort, General Manager

Employees: 332
Employees here: 327

D-U-N-S 00-331-9068
TURNER BROADCASTING SYSTEM
    (Parent: Time Warner Inc)
1 CNN Ctr NW, Atlanta, GA 30303
Phone: (404) 827-1700
Sales: $803,800,000
Company Type: Public Family Member
SIC: 4833
    Information & entertainment
Terence F McGuirk, Chief Executive Officer

Employees: 7,000
Employees here: 2,750

D-U-N-S 09-598-2245
TURNER ORIGINAL PRODUCTIONS INC.
    (Parent: Superstation Inc)
1 CNN Ctr NW, Atlanta, GA 30303
Phone: (404) 827-1700
Sales: $89,800,000
Company Type: Public Family Member
SIC: 4833
    Television station
Wayne Pace, Manager

Employees: 800
Employees here: 90

D-U-N-S 00-284-3159
TURNER-VISION, INC.
S View Mall, Bluefield, WV 24701
Phone: (304) 589-7400
Sales: $53,300,000
Company Type: Private
SIC: 4841
    Subscription television service
William Turner, President

Employees: 400
Employees here: 400

D-U-N-S 78-282-3926
TWC CABLE PARTNERS LP
100 Cable Way, Staten Island, NY 10303
Phone: (718) 447-7000

Sales: $30,300,000
Company Type: Private
SIC: 4841
    Cable/pay television service
Steven Payand, General Manager

Employees: 230
Employees here: 160

D-U-N-S 61-503-8775
TWENTIETH CENTURY-FOX TV INTL
    (Parent: Twentieth Cntury Fox Film Corp)
10201 W Pico Blvd, Los Angeles, CA 90064
Phone: (310) 277-2211
Sales: $170,400,000
Company Type: Private
SIC: 4833
    Television broadcasting service
K R Murdoch, Chairman of the Board

Employees: 1,500
Employees here: 1,000

D-U-N-S 06-054-8104
TWI CABLE INC.
    (Parent: Time Warner Companies Inc)
75 Rockefeller Plz, New York, NY 10019
Phone: (212) 484-8000
Sales: $910,288,000
Company Type: Public Family Member
SIC: 4841
    Cable television service
David O'Hayre, Branch Manager

Employees: 1,900
Employees here: 2

D-U-N-S 00-901-0484
U S DIGITEL INC.
1909 Tyler St Fl 8, Hollywood, FL 33020
Phone: (954) 927-7770
Sales: $40,000,000
Company Type: Private
SIC: 4813
    Whol prepaid telephone card
David Griffee, President

Employees: 5
Employees here: 5

D-U-N-S 80-446-9385
U S MEDIA HOLDINGS, INC.
115 W 18th St, New York, NY 10011
Phone: (212) 519-1252
Sales: $45,000,000
Company Type: Private
SIC: 4833
    Media company
Charles Fischer, Vice-President

Employees: 85
Employees here: 65

D-U-N-S 87-652-3556
U S WEST COMMUNICATIONS GROUP
    (Parent: U S West Inc)
1801 California St, Denver, CO 80202
Phone: (303) 784-2900
Sales: $10,319,000,000
Company Type: Private
SIC: 4812
    Telephone communications
Sol Trujillo, President

Employees: 50,000
Employees here: 1

D-U-N-S 18-476-5444
U S WEST COMMUNICATIONS, INC.
    (Parent: U S West Communications Group)
1801 California St, Denver, CO 80202
Phone: (303) 896-3099
Sales: $10,083,000,000
Company Type: Private
SIC: 4813
    Telephone communications
Sol Trujillo, President

Employees: 45,000
Employees here: 15

D-U-N-S 10-256-2451
U S WEST INC.
1801 California St, Denver, CO 80202

Phone: (303) 896-1111
Sales: $12,378,000,000
Company Type: Private
SIC: 4813
   Telephone communication directory publishing
Solomon D Trujillo, President

Employees: 54,483
Employees here: 150

D-U-N-S 12-275-2793
UACC MIDWEST, INC.
   (Parent: United Artsts Cblesystems Corp)
3500 Patterson Ave Se, Grand Rapids, MI 49512
Phone: (616) 977-2200
Sales: $93,800,000
Company Type: Public Family Member
SIC: 4841
   Cable television service
Tom Tidd, Operations-Production-Mfg

Employees: 700
Employees here: 250

D-U-N-S 03-915-3242   EXP
ULTRAK INC.
1301 Waters Ridge Dr, Lewisville, TX 75057
Phone: (972) 353-6500
Sales: $188,741,000
Company Type: Public
SIC: 3663
   Mfr video closed circuit television (CCTV) products
George K Broady, Chairman of the Board

Employees: 672
Employees here: 220

D-U-N-S 80-754-6916
UNIDIAL INCORPORATED
9931 Corporate Campus Dr, Louisville, KY 40223
Phone: (502) 394-0789
Sales: $112,315,000
Company Type: Private
SIC: 4813
   Long distance telephone service reseller
J S Henderson III, President

Employees: 350
Employees here: 330

D-U-N-S 62-480-1577
UNIFI COMMUNICATIONS INC.
900 Chelmsford St Ste 312, Lowell, MA 01851
Phone: (978) 551-7501
Sales: $43,857,000
Company Type: Private
SIC: 4822
   International telecommunications carrier
Douglas J Ranalli, President

Employees: 615
Employees here: 364

D-U-N-S 79-022-1188
UNIPHASE TELECOM PRODUCTS
   (Parent: Uniphase Corporation)
1289 Blue Hills Ave, Bloomfield, CT 06002
Phone: (860) 769-3010
Sales: $80,000,000
Company Type: Public Family Member
SIC: 3661
   Mfr fiber optic communications equipment
Robert C Harris, President

Employees: 340
Employees here: 200

D-U-N-S 60-206-7621
UNITED ARTISTS ENTERTAINMENT CO.
   (Parent: TCI Communications Inc)
9110 E Nichols Ave, Englewood, CO 80112
Phone: (303) 792-3600
Sales: $1,177,828,000
Company Type: Public Family Member
SIC: 4841
   Operates cable television systems
Fred Vierra, President

Employees: 16,000
Employees here: 300

D-U-N-S 61-119-6411
UNITED ARTISTS HOLDINGS, INC.
   (Parent: United Artists Entrmt Co)
5619 Dtc Pkwy, Englewood, CO 80111

Phone: (303) 843-8600
Sales: $1,173,762,000
Company Type: Public Family Member
SIC: 4841
   Cable television service
Brendan R Clouston, President

Employees: NA
Employees here: NA

D-U-N-S 18-460-2514
UNITED CABLE TELEVISION
2525 Kirk Ave, Baltimore, MD 21218
Phone: (410) 649-9000
Sales: $33,000,000
Company Type: Private
SIC: 4841
   Cable/pay television service
Coles Ruff, Manager

Employees: 250
Employees here: 250

D-U-N-S 60-545-0485
UNITED INTERNATIONAL HOLDING
4643 S Ulster St Ste 1300, Denver, CO 80237
Phone: (303) 770-4001
Sales: $98,622,000
Company Type: Public
SIC: 4841
   Cable systems
Gene Schneider, Chairman of the Board

Employees: 130
Employees here: 40

D-U-N-S 11-823-9292
UNITED STATES CELLULAR CORP
   (Parent: Telephone and Data Systems)
8410 W Bryn Mawr Ave, Chicago, IL 60631
Phone: (773) 399-8900
Sales: $876,965,000
Company Type: Public
SIC: 4812
   Operator of cellular telephone services and financial investor
Leroy T Carlson Jr, Chairman of the Board

Employees: 1,675
Employees here: 200

D-U-N-S 10-224-6196
UNITED STATES SATELLITE BROADCASTING
   (Parent: Hubbard Broadcasting Inc)
3415 University Ave W, Saint Paul, MN 55114
Phone: (651) 645-4500
Sales: $456,619,000
Company Type: Public
SIC: 4899
   Satellite broadcasting
Stanley S Hubbard, Chairman of the Board

Employees: 142
Employees here: 35

D-U-N-S 00-697-4018
UNITED TELEPHONE CO NJ INC.
   (Parent: Sprint Corporation)
160 Center St, Clinton, NJ 08809
Phone: (908) 730-7171
Sales: $59,100,000
Company Type: Public Family Member
SIC: 4813
   Telephone utility
Dale L Cross, President

Employees: 465
Employees here: 465

D-U-N-S 00-694-0241
UNITED TELEPHONE CO OF INDIANA
   (Parent: Sprint Corporation)
665 Lexington Ave, Mansfield, OH 44907
Phone: (419) 755-8011
Sales: $180,483,000
Company Type: Public Family Member
SIC: 4813
   Telephone utility
Randy Osler, President

Employees: 3,159
Employees here: 2,499

D-U-N-S 00-790-3495
UNITED TELEPHONE CO OF OHIO
(Parent: Sprint Corporation)
665 Lexington Ave, Mansfield, OH 44907
Phone: (419) 755-8011
Sales: $469,614,000   *Employees:* 2,407
Company Type: Public Family Member   *Employees here:* 500
SIC: 4813
    Telephone communications
Randy Osler, President

D-U-N-S 00-791-0128
UNITED TELEPHONE CO OF PA INC.
(Parent: Sprint Corporation)
1201 Walnut Bottom Rd, Carlisle, PA 17013
Phone: (717) 245-6312
Sales: $259,393,000   *Employees:* 1,683
Company Type: Public Family Member   *Employees here:* 605
SIC: 4813
    Telephone utility
Dale L Cross, President

D-U-N-S 00-694-2387
UNITED TELEPHONE COMPANY OF KANSAS
(Parent: Sprint Corporation)
5454 W 110th St, Shawnee Mission, KS 66211
Phone: (913) 345-6000
Sales: $74,872,000   *Employees:* 1,900
Company Type: Public Family Member   *Employees here:* 896
SIC: 4813
    Telephone communications
M B Fuller, President

D-U-N-S 00-793-7386
UNITED TELEPHONE COMPANY OF TEXAS
(Parent: Sprint Corporation)
5454 W 110th St, Shawnee Mission, KS 66211
Phone: (913) 345-6000
Sales: $128,186,000   *Employees:* 683
Company Type: Public Family Member   *Employees here:* 683
SIC: 4813
    Local telephone company
M B Fuller, Chairman of the Board

D-U-N-S 04-114-9899
UNITED TELEPHONE-SOUTHEAST
(Parent: Sprint Corporation)
14111 Capital Blvd, Wake Forest, NC 27587
Phone: (919) 554-7900
Sales: $110,100,000   *Employees:* 862
Company Type: Public Family Member   *Employees here:* 600
SIC: 4813
    Telephone service
William McDonald, President

D-U-N-S 00-885-8177
UNITED TELEVISION INC.
(Parent: BHC Communications Inc)
132 S Rodeo Dr Fl 4, Beverly Hills, CA 90212
Phone: (310) 281-4844
Sales: $170,963,000   *Employees:* 559
Company Type: Public   *Employees here:* 6
SIC: 4833
    Television broadcasting
Evan C Thompson, President

D-U-N-S 06-162-7006   EXP
UNITED VIDEO SATELLITE GROUP
7140 S Lewis Ave, Tulsa, OK 74136
Phone: (918) 488-4000

Sales: $507,598,000   *Employees:* 1,500
Company Type: Public   *Employees here:* 1,100
SIC: 4841
    Satellite distribution
Gary S Howard, Chairman of the Board

D-U-N-S 94-431-3899
UNITY MOTION, INC.
2310 Millpark Dr, Maryland Heights, MO 63043
Phone: (314) 592-9700
Sales: $350,000,000   *Employees:* 45
Company Type: Private   *Employees here:* 45
SIC: 4841
    Broadcasts high definiton programing
Larry Miller, Chief Executive Officer

D-U-N-S 60-205-2169   EXP
UNIVERSAL ELECTRONICS INC.
6101 Gateway Dr, Cypress, CA 90630
Phone: (714) 820-1000
Sales: $114,338,000   *Employees:* 264
Company Type: Public   *Employees here:* 200
SIC: 3651
    Mfr infrared universal remote controls
Camille Jayne, Chairman of the Board

D-U-N-S 78-854-7164
UNIVERSAL LOGIC TECHNOLOGIES
556 Lexington Ave, Mansfield, OH 44907
Phone: (888) 287-2589
Sales: $43,000,000   *Employees:* 200
Company Type: Private   *Employees here:* 43
SIC: 4813
    Telephone communication, except radio
Larry S Waddell, President

D-U-N-S 00-952-2694
UNIVISION COMMUNICATIONS, INC.
1999 Avenue Of The Stars, Los Angeles, CA 90067
Phone: (310) 556-7676
Sales: $459,741,000   *Employees:* 1,500
Company Type: Public   *Employees here:* 200
SIC: 4833
    Television broadcasting/television translator station
A J Perenchio, Chairman of the Board

D-U-N-S 60-483-4234
UNIVISION TELEVISION GROUP
(Parent: Univision Communications Inc)
500 Frank W Burr Blvd, Teaneck, NJ 07666
Phone: (201) 287-4200
Sales: $412,442,000   *Employees:* 1,136
Company Type: Public Family Member   *Employees here:* 165
SIC: 4833
    Television broadcasting stations
Thomas Arnost, Co-President

D-U-N-S 01-251-7181
US TELECOM INC.
(Parent: Sprint Corporation)
2330 Shawnee Mission Pkwy, Shawnee Mission, KS 66205
Phone: (913) 624-3000
Sales: $2,827,000,000   *Employees:* 22,000
Company Type: Public Family Member   *Employees here:* 17
SIC: 4813
    Voice video and data long distance service
Arthur B Krause, Chief Financial Officer

D-U-N-S 11-849-0085
US UNWIRED INC.
1 Lakeshore Dr Ste 1900, Lake Charles, LA 70629
Phone: (318) 433-6298

Sales: $61,893,000
Employees: 619
Company Type: Private
Employees here: 400
SIC: 4813
   Provides telephone communication service and related
      services and retails cellular telephone
Robert Piper, President

D-U-N-S 60-822-9704
US WATS INC.
3331 Street Rd Ste 275, Bensalem, PA 19020
Phone: (215) 633-9400
Sales: $56,467,000
Employees: 69
Company Type: Public
Employees here: 64
SIC: 4813
   Telephone communication services
David H Int, Chief Executive Officer

D-U-N-S 03-824-6922
USA NETWORKS
1230 Avenue Of The Americ, New York, NY 10020
Phone: (212) 408-9100
Sales: $700,000,000
Employees: 550
Company Type: Private
Employees here: 330
SIC: 4841
   All entertainment cable & sci-fi networks
Stephen Brenner, President-Operations

D-U-N-S 18-120-2508
USLD COMMUNICATIONS CORP
   (Parent: LCI International Inc)
4250 Fairfax Dr, Arlington, VA 22203
Phone: (703) 363-0220
Sales: $83,900,000
Employees: 658
Company Type: Private
Employees here: 160
SIC: 4813
   Direct dial long distance services & operator services
H B Thompson, Chairman of the Board

D-U-N-S 82-486-9309
USN COMMUNICATIONS MIDWEST
   (Parent: USN Communications Inc)
10 S Rverside Plz Ste 401, Chicago, IL 60606
Phone: (312) 906-3600
Sales: $59,200,000
Employees: 466
Company Type: Public Family Member
Employees here: 150
SIC: 4813
   Provider of integrated local & long distance
      telecommunications services
J T Elliott, President

D-U-N-S 93-359-5837
USWEB CORPORATION
2880 Lakeside Dr Ste 350, Santa Clara, CA 95054
Phone: (408) 987-3200
Sales: $100,000,000
Employees: 1,000
Company Type: Public
Employees here: 125
SIC: 4813
   Single source provider of web solutions for business
Robert Shaw, Chief Executive Officer

D-U-N-S 78-908-4092   EXP
UTSTARCOM, INC.
1275 Harbor Bay Pkwy, Alameda, CA 94502
Phone: (510) 864-8800
Sales: $100,117,000
Employees: 788
Company Type: Private
Employees here: 35
SIC: 3661
   Mfg/sales of telecommunications and paging systems
Hong L Lu, President

D-U-N-S 19-733-3123
UUNET WORLDCOM, INC.
   (Parent: MCI Worldcom Inc)
3060 Williams Dr, Fairfax, VA 22031
Phone: (703) 206-5600
Sales: $38,700,000
Employees: 306
Company Type: Public Family Member
Employees here: 306
SIC: 4813
   Provider of internet access options
John W Sidgmore, Chief Executive Officer

D-U-N-S 01-861-5146
VAI CORPORATION
1941 Ringwood Ave, San Jose, CA 95131
Phone: (408) 452-7811
Sales: $53,000,000
Employees: 90
Company Type: Private
Employees here: 70
SIC: 3661
   Mfg (assembly) of telecommunication equipment & whol
      multimedia equip & software
Pudong Weng, President

D-U-N-S 94-451-6152
VALUE TEL
220 Montgomery St, San Francisco, CA 94104
Phone: (415) 951-1922
Sales: $41,100,000
Employees: 325
Company Type: Private
Employees here: 325
SIC: 4813
   Telephone communications
David Strut, Owner

D-U-N-S 14-420-3452
VANGUARD CELLULAR SYSTEMS INC.
2002 Pisgah Church Rd, Greensboro, NC 27455
Phone: (336) 282-3690
Sales: $374,518,000
Employees: 2,000
Company Type: Public
Employees here: 420
SIC: 4812
   Cellular telephone service
Haynes G Griffin, Chairman of the Board

D-U-N-S 60-361-3605
VARTEC TELECOM, INC.
   (Parent: Telephone Electronics Corp)
3200 W Pleasant Run Rd, Lancaster, TX 75146
Phone: (972) 230-7200
Sales: $105,600,000
Employees: 827
Company Type: Private
Employees here: 670
SIC: 4813
   Long distance telephone service
A J Mitchell Jr, President

D-U-N-S 01-562-5890   EXP
VECTRON TECHNOLOGIES INC.
   (Parent: Dover Technologies Intl)
267 Lowell Rd, Hudson, NH 03051
Phone: (603) 598-0070
Sales: $60,000,000
Employees: 225
Company Type: Public Family Member
Employees here: 225
SIC: 3679
   Mfg electronic components
Terence Ede, President

D-U-N-S 10-290-4406   EXP
VERILINK CORPORATION
145 Baytech Dr, San Jose, CA 95134
Phone: (408) 945-1199
Sales: $50,915,000
Employees: 250
Company Type: Public
Employees here: 145
SIC: 3661
   Mfg digital electronic telecommunication equipment
Leigh S Belden, President

D-U-N-S 11-744-5338   EXP
VERTEX COMMUNICATIONS CORP
2600 N Longview St, Kilgore, TX 75662
Phone: (903) 984-0555
Sales: $130,017,000   *Employees:* 927
Company Type: Public   *Employees here:* 450
SIC: 3663
   Mfg satellite communications earth station antennas
J R Vardeman, Chairman of the Board

D-U-N-S 15-428-7825
VIACOM INC.
   (Parent: National Amusements Inc)
1515 Broadway, New York, NY 10036
Phone: (212) 258-6000
Sales: $13,206,100,000   *Employees:* 116,700
Company Type: Public   *Employees here:* 1,700
SIC: 4841
   Entertainment & publishing
George S Smith, Chief Financial Officer

D-U-N-S 83-632-5100
VIATEL, INC (DE CORP)
800 3rd Ave Fl 18, New York, NY 10022
Phone: (212) 935-6800
Sales: $73,018,000   *Employees:* 290
Company Type: Public   *Employees here:* 20
SIC: 4813
   International voice & data telecommunications services
Michael J Mahoney, President

D-U-N-S 04-383-7947   EXP
VICON INDUSTRIES INC.
89 Arkay Dr, Hauppauge, NY 11788
Phone: (516) 952-2288
Sales: $63,310,000   *Employees:* 217
Company Type: Public   *Employees here:* 160
SIC: 3663
   Manufactures closed circuit tv components & accessories
Donald N Horn, Chairman of the Board

D-U-N-S 09-000-0266
VIRGIN ISLAND TELEPHONE CORP
   (Parent: Atlantic Tele-Network Inc)
First Floor Spencely Bldg, Charlotte Amalie, VI 00801
Phone: (340) 776-5555
Sales: $64,734,000   *Employees:* 421
Company Type: Public Family Member   *Employees here:* 421
SIC: 4813
   Telephone communications
Jeffrey Prosser, President

D-U-N-S 96-852-3720
VISTA INFORMATION TECHNOLOGIES
2195 Fox Mill Rd, Herndon, VA 20171
Phone: (703) 561-4000
Sales: $30,000,000   *Employees:* 1,300
Company Type: Private   *Employees here:* 8
SIC: 4813
   Holding company
James H Duggan, President

D-U-N-S 06-198-8127
VISTA-UNITED TELECOM
3100 Bonnet Creek Rd, Lake Buena Vista, FL 32830
Phone: (407) 827-2000
Sales: $63,568,000   *Employees:* 550
Company Type: Private   *Employees here:* 412
SIC: 4813
   Telecommunications
Richard L Astleford, General Manager

D-U-N-S 87-286-7155
VODAVI TECHNOLOGY, INC.
8300 E Raintree Dr, Scottsdale, AZ 85260
Phone: (602) 443-6000
Sales: $47,675,000   *Employees:* 173
Company Type: Public   *Employees here:* 34
SIC: 3661
   Mfr telephone systems and products
Gregory K Roeper, President

D-U-N-S 14-713-4548
VTEL CORPORATION
108 Wild Basin Rd S, Austin, TX 78746
Phone: (512) 314-2700
Sales: $179,684,000   *Employees:* 740
Company Type: Public   *Employees here:* 300
SIC: 3669
   Mfg video conferencing systems
Jerry S Benson Jr, President

D-U-N-S 92-637-4943
VXI ELECTRONICS, INC.
4607 SE International Way, Milwaukie, OR 97222
Phone: (503) 659-7920
Sales: $50,000,000   *Employees:* 220
Company Type: Private   *Employees here:* 220
SIC: 3679
   Design & mfg power supplies
Doug Mcilvoy, President

D-U-N-S 93-152-4508
VYVX, INC.
   (Parent: Williams Communications Group)
Tulsa Union Depot 111 E 1, Tulsa, OK 74103
Phone: (918) 588-2000
Sales: $66,000,000   *Employees:* 541
Company Type: Public Family Member   *Employees here:* 250
SIC: 4899
   Communication services
Delwin Bothof, President

D-U-N-S 00-206-5910   EXP
WARD PRODUCTS CORP
633 Nassau St, North Brunswick, NJ 08902
Phone: (732) 873-2200
Sales: $39,000,000   *Employees:* 365
Company Type: Private   *Employees here:* 75
SIC: 3679
   Manufactures automobile antennas and wire cable assemblies
Eleanor Milazzo, President

D-U-N-S 05-976-5743
WARNER CABLE COMMUNICATION
   (Parent: Time Warner Entrmt Co Lp)
1610 N 2nd St, Milwaukee, WI 53212
Phone: (414) 277-4000
Sales: $53,300,000   *Employees:* 400
Company Type: Private   *Employees here:* 250
SIC: 4841
   Cable/pay television service
Tom Sharrard, President

D-U-N-S 02-463-8835
WEATHER CHANNEL INC.
   (Parent: Landmark Communications Inc)
300 Interstate North Pkwy, Atlanta, GA 30339
Phone: (770) 226-0000
Sales: $47,900,000   *Employees:* 360
Company Type: Private   *Employees here:* 300
SIC: 4841
   Cable television service specializing in weather news
John O Wynne, Chairman of the Board

D-U-N-S 00-510-6042   EXP
WELLS-GARDNER ELECTRONICS CORP
2701 N Kildare Ave, Chicago, IL 60639
Phone: (773) 252-8220
Sales: $42,989,000   *Employees:* 190
Company Type: Public   *Employees here:* 190
SIC: 3663
    Designs and mfg color and monochrome video monitors
Anthony Spier, Chairman of the Board

D-U-N-S 18-819-2280
WESTEC SECURITY GROUP INC.
100 Bayview Cir Ste 1000, Newport Beach, CA 92660
Phone: (949) 725-6600
Sales: $263,500,000   *Employees:* 3,000
Company Type: Private   *Employees here:* 100
SIC: 3669
    Installs and services security alarms
Michael S Kaye, Chief Executive Officer

D-U-N-S 03-963-8226
WESTELL, INC.
   (Parent: Westell Technologies Inc)
750 N Commons Dr, Aurora, IL 60504
Phone: (630) 898-2500
Sales: $73,000,000   *Employees:* 602
Company Type: Public Family Member   *Employees here:* 602
SIC: 3661
    Mfg telecommunications equipment
Marc J Zionts, Chief Executive Officer

D-U-N-S 85-917-1134   EXP
WESTELL TECHNOLOGIES INC.
101 Kendall Point Dr, Oswego, IL 60543
Phone: (630) 898-2500
Sales: $86,351,000   *Employees:* 649
Company Type: Public   *Employees here:* 400
SIC: 3661
    Mfg telecommunication products
Richard P Riviere, President

D-U-N-S 00-790-3149
WESTERN RESERVE TELE CO INC.
   (Parent: Alltel Corporation)
245 N Main St, Hudson, OH 44236
Phone: (330) 650-8000
Sales: $47,100,000   *Employees:* 372
Company Type: Public Family Member   *Employees here:* 150
SIC: 4813
    Telephone communications
Dennis Mc Giles, Vice-President

D-U-N-S 00-186-4016
WESTERN UNION INTERNATIONAL
   (Parent: MCI International Inc)
201 Centennial Ave, Piscataway, NJ 08854
Phone: (732) 885-4000
Sales: $32,700,000   *Employees:* 638
Company Type: Public Family Member   *Employees here:* 552
SIC: 4822
    Telegraphic communication service
Seth D Blumenfeld, President

D-U-N-S 86-101-5782
WESTERN WIRELESS CORPORATION
2001 NW Sammamish Rd, Issaquah, WA 98027
Phone: (425) 313-5200
Sales: $380,578,000   *Employees:* 3,210
Company Type: Public   *Employees here:* 300
SIC: 4812
    Wireless communications services
John W Stanton, Chairman of the Board

D-U-N-S 19-005-4759
WFAA-TV INC.
   (Parent: A H Belo Corporation)
606 Young St, Dallas, TX 75202
Phone: (214) 748-9631
Sales: $30,300,000   *Employees:* 283
Company Type: Public Family Member   *Employees here:* 273
SIC: 4833
    Television broadcasting station
Kathy Clements-Hill, President

D-U-N-S 13-702-1663
WGNX INC.
   (Parent: Tribune Broadcasting Company)
1810 Briarcliff Rd Ne, Atlanta, GA 30329
Phone: (404) 325-4646
Sales: $39,000,000   *Employees:* 132
Company Type: Public Family Member   *Employees here:* 132
SIC: 4833
    Television station
Dennis Fitzsimmons, President

D-U-N-S 05-069-6871
WHDH, TV, INC.
   (Parent: Sunbeam Television Corp)
7 Bulfinch Pl, Boston, MA 02114
Phone: (617) 725-0777
Sales: $32,300,000   *Employees:* 300
Company Type: Private   *Employees here:* 300
SIC: 4833
    Television station
Edmund N Ansin, President

D-U-N-S 00-217-0702   EXP
WHEELOCK INC.
273 Branchport Ave, Long Branch, NJ 07740
Phone: (732) 222-6880
Sales: $37,777,000   *Employees:* 350
Company Type: Private   *Employees here:* 350
SIC: 3669
    Mfg electronic communication signaling equipment and
     telephone pagers
Peter Tarlton, President

D-U-N-S 95-983-7931
WHITE OAK SEMICONDUCTOR
6000 Technology Blvd, Sandston, VA 23150
Phone: (804) 952-6000
Sales: $46,400,000   *Employees:* 800
Company Type: Private   *Employees here:* 800
SIC: 3679
    Mfg integrated circuits
Wayne Nesbit, President

D-U-N-S 19-846-0511   EXP
WILLIAMS CONTROLS INC.
14100 Sw 72nd Ave, Portland, OR 97224
Phone: (503) 684-8600
Sales: $57,646,000   *Employees:* 511
Company Type: Public   *Employees here:* 175
SIC: 3679
    Mfg heavy vehicle agricultural equipment and electrical
     products
Gerard A Herlihy, Chief Financial Officer

D-U-N-S 62-757-8016
WILLIAMS FIRE PROTECTION INC.
1105 N Market St Ste 1014, Wilmington, DE 19801
Phone: (302) 427-9352

Sales: $237,100,000
Company Type: Private   *Employees:* 2,700
SIC: 3669   *Employees here:* 1
   Through subsidiaries mfg fire detection & suppression
     systems & industrial temperature instruments
Martin O Brien, President

D-U-N-S 83-601-5263
WILLIAMS INTERNATIONAL CO.
   (Parent: Williams Holdings of Delaware)
1 Williams Ctr, Tulsa, OK 74172
Phone: (918) 588-2000
Sales: $642,000,000
Company Type: Public Family Member   *Employees:* 5,000
SIC: 4813   *Employees here:* 2,000
   Telephone communications
Keith E Bailey, Controller

D-U-N-S 00-692-9186
WINDOW TO THE WORLD COMMUNICATIONS
5400 N Saint Louis Ave, Chicago, IL 60625
Phone: (773) 583-5000
Sales: $43,000,000
Company Type: Private   *Employees:* 300
SIC: 4833   *Employees here:* 300
   Television & radio broadcast production
William J Mc Carter, President

D-U-N-S 62-389-6503   EXP
WINSTAR COMMUNICATIONS INC.
230 Park Ave, New York, NY 10169
Phone: (212) 687-7577
Sales: $79,631,000
Company Type: Public   *Employees:* 2,100
SIC: 4813   *Employees here:* 35
   Telecommunications & information services mfg bath & hair
     products
William J Rouhana Jr, Chairman of the Board

D-U-N-S 82-465-2382
WIRELESS ONE, INC.
2506 Lakeland Dr Ste 600, Jackson, MS 39208
Phone: (601) 936-1515
Sales: $34,580,000
Company Type: Public   *Employees:* 500
SIC: 4841   *Employees here:* 100
   Wireless subscription television services
Henry M Burkhalter, President

D-U-N-S 18-119-3392
WIRELESS ONE NETWORK, L.P.
2100 Electronics Ln, Fort Myers, FL 33912
Phone: (941) 489-1600
Sales: $100,000,000
Company Type: Private   *Employees:* 400
SIC: 4812   *Employees here:* 50
   Cellular telephone service
James A Dwyer, President

D-U-N-S 87-920-2133
WIRETECH, LTD
1889 Preston White Dr, Reston, VA 20191
Phone: (703) 391-0200
Sales: $54,112,000
Company Type: Private   *Employees:* 550
SIC: 4812   *Employees here:* 20
   Cellular telecommunications
Joseph F Gatt, Chairman of the Board

D-U-N-S 00-794-7443
WISCONSIN BELL INC.
   (Parent: Ameritech Corporation)
722 N Broadway, Milwaukee, WI 53202

Phone: (414) 549-7102
Sales: $1,220,500,000
Company Type: Public Family Member   *Employees:* 4,080
SIC: 4813   *Employees here:* 600
   Telephone communication service
Ellen M Gardner, President

D-U-N-S 87-918-9470
WISCONSIN EDUCATIONAL COMMUNICATIONS BD
3319 W Beltline Hwy, Madison, WI 53713
Phone: (608) 264-9600
Sales: $31,300,000
Company Type: Private   *Employees:* 390
SIC: 4832   *Employees here:* 110
   State public radio & television
Kate Wede, Executive Director

D-U-N-S 94-288-6656
WLVI, INC.
   (Parent: Tribune Broadcasting Company)
75 Morrissey Blvd, Boston, MA 02125
Phone: (617) 265-5656
Sales: $40,000,000
Company Type: Public Family Member   *Employees:* 125
SIC: 4833   *Employees here:* 125
   Television station
Dennis Fitzsimons, President

D-U-N-S 80-115-5409
WORKING ASSETS FUNDING SERVICE
701 Montgomery St Ste 400, San Francisco, CA 94111
Phone: (415) 788-0777
Sales: $104,408,000
Company Type: Private   *Employees:* 120
SIC: 4813   *Employees here:* 40
   Reseller of long distance telecommunications
Laura Scher, Chief Executive Officer

D-U-N-S 11-432-8180   EXP
WORLD ACCESS INC.
945 E Paces Ferry Rd Ne, Atlanta, GA 30326
Phone: (404) 231-2025
Sales: $92,984,000
Company Type: Public   *Employees:* 510
SIC: 3661   *Employees here:* 10
   Mfg telecommunication products
John D Phillips, President

D-U-N-S 18-538-0409
WORLDCOM INC.
   (Parent: MCI Worldcom Inc)
4001 Carmichael Rd, Montgomery, AL 36106
Phone: (334) 244-5680
Sales: $37,900,000
Company Type: Public Family Member   *Employees:* 300
SIC: 4813   *Employees here:* 300
   Telephone communication
Kathy Griffin, Principal

D-U-N-S 11-537-3169
WORLDCOM WIRELESS, INC.
   (Parent: MCI Worldcom Inc)
3928 Point Eden Way, Hayward, CA 94545
Phone: (510) 732-1100
Sales: $31,500,000
Company Type: Public Family Member   *Employees:* 250
SIC: 4813   *Employees here:* 80
   Cellular telephone service & whol telecommunication equip
Berneard J Ebbers, President

D-U-N-S 60-553-9022
WPGH, INC.
   (Parent: Sinclair Broadcast Group Inc)
750 Ivory Ave, Pittsburgh, PA 15214

Phone: (412) 931-5300
Sales: $35,000,000   *Employees:* 100
Company Type: Public Family Member   *Employees here:* 100
SIC: 4833
  Television station
David Smith, President

D-U-N-S 00-985-3946
WPIX, INC.
  (Parent: Tribune Broadcasting Company)
220 E 42nd St Fl 10, New York, NY 10017
Phone: (212) 949-1100
Sales: $173,000,000   *Employees:* 275
Company Type: Public Family Member   *Employees here:* 275
SIC: 4833
  Television broadcasting station
Michael Eigner, Executive Vice-President

D-U-N-S 36-144-8400
XPEDITE SYSTEMS INC.
  (Parent: Premiere Technologies Inc)
1 Industrial Way W Bldg D, Eatontown, NJ 07724
Phone: (732) 389-3900
Sales: $36,900,000   *Employees:* 720
Company Type: Public Family Member   *Employees here:* 220
SIC: 4822
  Enhanced fax services
Roy B Anderson Jr, President

D-U-N-S 88-436-4530
YAHOO INC.
3400 Central Expy 201, Santa Clara, CA 95051
Phone: (408) 731-3300
Sales: $203,270,000   *Employees:* 155
Company Type: Public   *Employees here:* 135
SIC: 4813
  Internet navigational services
Timothy Koogle, Chairman of the Board

D-U-N-S 18-317-4127
YOUNG BROADCASTING INC.
599 Lexington Ave, New York, NY 10022
Phone: (212) 754-7070
Sales: $263,535,000   *Employees:* 1,300
Company Type: Public   *Employees here:* 7
SIC: 4833
  Television broadcasting stations
Vincent J Young, Chairman of the Board

D-U-N-S 93-358-6257
ZEKKO CORPORATION
170 Hwy A1a N, Ponte Vedra Beach, FL 32082
Phone: (904) 280-1450
Sales: $100,000,000   *Employees:* 10
Company Type: Private   *Employees here:* 10
SIC: 4899
  Telecommunications processor & bandwidth technology
R E Turner IV, President

D-U-N-S 00-512-0704   EXP
ZENITH ELECTRONICS CORPORATION
1000 Milwaukee Ave, Glenview, IL 60025
Phone: (847) 391-7000
Sales: $1,173,100,000   *Employees:* 11,400
Company Type: Public   *Employees here:* 700
SIC: 3651
  Mfg consumer electronic products
Jeffrey P Gannon, President

D-U-N-S 08-421-6316   EXP
ZOOM TELEPHONICS CANADIAN CORP
207 South St Fl 5, Boston, MA 02111
Phone: (617) 423-1072

Sales: $61,364,000   *Employees:* 342
Company Type: Public   *Employees here:* 87
SIC: 3661
  Manufactures computer faxmodems
Robert A Crist, Chief Financial Officer

RANKINGS AND COMPANIES

The companies presented in Chapter 4 - Company Directory are arranged in this chapter in rank order based first on sales and next on employment. Each company's name, rank, location, type, sales, employment, and primary SIC are shown. Only companies with reported sales data are included in the "rankings by sales" table; similarly, only companies that report employment are ranked in the "rankings by employment" table.

Company type is either Public, Private, or Public Family Member. The last category is used to label corporate entities that belong to a group of companies, the relationship being that of a subsidiary or element of a parent. The parents of Public Family Member companies can be reviewed in the directory presented in Chapter 4.

This product includes proprietary data of Dun & Bradstreet, Inc.

D&B COMPANY RANKINGS BY SALES

Company	Rank	Location	Type	Sales ($ mil.)	Employ- ment	Primary SIC
AT&T Corp	1	New York, NY	Public	53,223.0	118,900	4813
Bell Atlantic Corporation	2	New York, NY	Public	30,193.9	141,000	4813
Lucent Technologies Inc.	3	New Providence, NJ	Public	30,147.0	141,600	3661
MCI Worldcom Inc.	4	Jackson, MS	Public	30,000.0	75,000	4813
Motorola Inc.	5	Schaumburg, IL	Public	29,794.0	149,800	3663
SBC Communications Inc.	6	San Antonio, TX	Public	24,856.0	118,340	4813
GTE Corporation	7	Irving, TX	Public	23,260.0	114,000	4813
BellSouth Corporation	8	Atlanta, GA	Public	23,123.0	81,000	4813
BellSouth Telecommunications	9	Atlanta, GA	Public Family Member	16,622.0	59,100	4813
Ameritech Corporation	10	Chicago, IL	Public	15,998.0	74,359	4813
Sprint Corporation	11	Shawnee Mission, KS	Public	14,873.9	51,000	4813
Viacom Inc.	12	New York, NY	Public	13,206.1	116,700	4841
U S West Inc.	13	Denver, CO	Private	12,378.0	54,483	4813
U S West Communications Group	14	Denver, CO	Private	10,319.0	50,000	4812
Southwestern Bell Tele Co.	15	Saint Louis, MO	Public Family Member	10,313.0	50,500	4813
U S West Communications, Inc.	16	Denver, CO	Private	10,083.0	45,000	4813
Pacific Bell	17	San Francisco, CA	Public Family Member	9,938.0	50,030	4813
Sprint Communications Co LP	18	Kansas City, MO	Private	9,000.0	18,000	4813
NYNEX Corporation	19	New York, NY	Public Family Member	8,752.1	68,100	4813
New York Telephone Company	20	New York, NY	Public Family Member	7,957.3	38,600	4813
MCI Communications Corporation	21	Washington, DC	Public Family Member	7,711.0	60,000	4813
Tele-Communications, Inc.	22	Englewood, CO	Public	7,570.0	32,000	4841
Philips Electronics North America	23	New York, NY	Private	7,495.0	21,000	3651
Pacific Telesis Group	24	San Antonio, TX	Public Family Member	6,438.6	50,100	4813
TCI Communications, Inc.	25	Englewood, CO	Public	6,166.7	36,000	4841
Toshiba America Inc.	26	New York, NY	Private	6,095.7	7,500	3651
CBS Corporation	27	Pittsburgh, PA	Public	5,363.0	51,444	4833
Alltel Corporation	28	Little Rock, AR	Public	5,194.0	20,000	4813
National Broadcasting Co Inc.	29	New York, NY	Public Family Member	5,153.0	5,000	4833
Hughes Electronics Corporation	30	Los Angeles, CA	Public Family Member	5,128.3	14,000	3663
New England Tele & Telegraph Co.	31	Boston, MA	Public Family Member	4,565.7	18,500	4813
AT&T Wireless Services Inc.	32	Kirkland, WA	Public Family Member	4,330.0	13,000	4812
American Broadcasting Companies	33	New York, NY	Public Family Member	4,142.0	8,000	4833
Harris Corporation	34	Melbourne, FL	Public	3,890.2	28,500	3663
Illinois Bell Telephone Co.	35	Chicago, IL	Public Family Member	3,808.2	14,929	4813
Bell Atlantic-New Jersey, Inc.	36	Newark, NJ	Public Family Member	3,753.9	12,500	4813
Airtouch Communications	37	San Francisco, CA	Public	3,594.0	8,800	4812
Michigan Bell Telephone Co.	38	Detroit, MI	Public	3,384.8	12,249	4813
Qualcomm, Incorporated	39	San Diego, CA	Public	3,347.9	11,600	3663
Bell Atlantic-Pennsylvania	40	Philadelphia, PA	Public Family Member	3,320.5	12,500	4813
Georgia Alltel Inc.	41	Dalton, GA	Public Family Member	3,192.4	450	4813
Ericsson Inc.	42	Richardson, TX	Private	3,038.4	8,000	3663
Sony Electronics Inc.	43	Park Ridge, NJ	Private	2,949.7	26,000	3651
US Telecom Inc.	44	Shawnee Mission, KS	Public Family Member	2,827.0	22,000	4813
America Online Inc.	45	Sterling, VA	Public	2,600.0	8,500	4813
ABC Inc	46	New York, NY	Public Family Member	2,554.2	22,200	4833
GTE Mobile Communications Inc.	47	Atlanta, GA	Public Family Member	2,549.0	9,000	4812
Mediaone Group, Inc.	48	Englewood, CO	Public	2,419.0	16,350	4841
Frontier Corporation	49	Rochester, NY	Public	2,352.9	7,444	4813
The Ohio Bell Telephone Co.	50	Cleveland, OH	Public Family Member	2,339.9	8,419	4813
Philips Holding U.S.A., Inc.	51	New York, NY	Private	2,268.7	20,000	3651
Bell Atlantic-Virginia, Inc.	52	Richmond, VA	Public Family Member	2,071.1	6,500	4813
Bell Atlantic-Maryland, Inc.	53	Baltimore, MD	Public Family Member	2,047.9	7,000	4813
Northern Telecom Inc Del	54	Nashville, TN	Private	2,011.2	21,000	3661
Bell Atlantic Network Services	55	Arlington, VA	Public Family Member	2,000.0	8,539	4813
CSC Holdings, Inc.	56	Woodbury, NY	Public	1,949.4	7,969	4841
General Instrument Corporation	57	Horsham, PA	Public	1,764.1	7,350	3663
Cincinnati Bell Inc.	58	Cincinnati, OH	Public	1,756.8	20,800	4813
Cox Communications San Diego Inc.	59	San Diego, CA	Public Family Member	1,610.4	750	4841
Harman International Industries Inc.	60	Washington, DC	Public	1,513.3	10,010	3651
Alcatel Network Systems, Inc.	61	Richardson, TX	Private	1,500.0	5,000	3661
TCI Holdings, Inc.	62	Englewood, CO	Public Family Member	1,496.9	2,000	4841
Telephone And Data Systems	63	Chicago, IL	Public	1,471.5	9,685	4812
Cox Communications Inc.	64	Atlanta, GA	Public	1,460.3	7,200	4841
Fox Broadcasting Company	65	Los Angeles, CA	Public Family Member	1,456.5	300	4833
Excel Communications, Inc.	66	Dallas, TX	Public	1,454.4	3,000	4813
Space Systems/Loral Inc.	67	Palo Alto, CA	Public Family Member	1,442.6	3,000	3663
Raytheon E-Systems, Inc.	68	Garland, TX	Public Family Member	1,401.4	16,400	3663
Citizens Utilities Company	69	Stamford, CT	Public	1,393.6	5,400	4813
ADC Telecommunications, Inc.	70	Hopkins, MN	Public	1,379.7	8,000	3661

D&B COMPANY RANKINGS BY SALES

Company	Rank	Location	Type	Sales ($ mil.)	Employ-ment	Primary SIC
Pittway Corporation	71	Chicago, IL	Public	1,348.7	7,800	3669
Pacificorp Holdings, Inc.	72	Portland, OR	Public Family Member	1,333.0	4,160	4813
Loral Space & Communications	73	New York, NY	Public	1,312.6	3,300	3663
GTE Government Systems Corp	74	Needham, MA	Public Family Member	1,300.0	7,000	3661
Indiana Bell Telephone Co Inc.	75	Indianapolis, IN	Public Family Member	1,299.9	4,002	4813
Southern Neng Telecom Corp	76	New Haven, CT	Private	1,264.2	9,841	4813
Sprint-Florida, Incorporated	77	Apopka, FL	Public Family Member	1,241.3	5,300	4813
Wisconsin Bell Inc.	78	Milwaukee, WI	Public Family Member	1,220.5	4,080	4813
Tellabs Inc.	79	Lisle, IL	Public	1,203.5	4,087	3661
Contel Federal Systems Inc.	80	Needham, MA	Public Family Member	1,200.0	7,000	3661
Centel Corporation	81	Shawnee Mission, KS	Public Family Member	1,194.6	9,300	4813
Scientific-Atlanta Inc.	82	Norcross, GA	Public	1,181.4	5,736	3663
United Artists Entertainment Co.	83	Englewood, CO	Public Family Member	1,177.8	16,000	4841
Satellite Services, Inc.	84	Englewood, CO	Public Family Member	1,177.2	25	4841
United Artists Holdings, Inc.	85	Englewood, CO	Public Family Member	1,173.8	NA	4841
Zenith Electronics Corporation	86	Glenview, IL	Public	1,173.1	11,400	3651
Fox Television Stations Inc.	87	Los Angeles, CA	Public Family Member	1,133.1	1,350	4833
Cablevision Systems Corp	88	Bethpage, NY	Private	1,075.6	7,969	4841
Fujitsu Network Communications	89	Richardson, TX	Private	1,017.5	2,100	3661
Meredith Corporation	90	Des Moines, IA	Public	1,009.9	2,559	4833
Telephone Electronics Corp	91	Jackson, MS	Private	1,001.3	900	4813
DirecTV, Inc.	92	El Segundo, CA	Public Family Member	1,000.0	900	4841
Nokia Mobile Phones Inc.	93	Fort Worth, TX	Private	1,000.0	1,200	3663
International Telecomm Satellite Org	94	Washington, DC	Private	961.6	700	4899
Paging Network Inc.	95	Dallas, TX	Public	961.0	4,500	4812
Cable & Wireless, Inc.	96	Vienna, VA	Private	948.6	2,300	4813
NEC America Inc.	97	Melville, NY	Private	928.2	2,500	3661
TWI Cable Inc.	98	New York, NY	Public Family Member	910.3	1,900	4841
Century Telephone Enterprises	99	Monroe, LA	Public	901.5	7,000	4813
Reltec Communications Inc.	100	Cleveland, OH	Public Family Member	887.2	5,200	3661
Tribune Broadcasting Company	101	Chicago, IL	Public Family Member	877.0	1,700	4833
United States Cellular Corp	102	Chicago, IL	Public	877.0	1,675	4812
The Southern Neng Tele Co.	103	New Haven, CT	Private	872.2	6,791	4813
Communigroup Inc.	104	Jackson, MS	Private	869.6	870	4813
Andrew Corporation	105	Orland Park, IL	Public	852.9	3,261	3663
AlliedSignal Technical Svcs	106	Columbia, MD	Public Family Member	852.2	7,000	4899
Bose Corporation	107	Framingham, MA	Private	850.0	4,000	3651
Bell Atlantic Enterprises Intl	108	Philadelphia, PA	Public Family Member	834.8	6,500	4813
TCI West, Inc.	109	Bellevue, WA	Public Family Member	827.1	4,250	4841
ITT Defense & Electronics	110	Mc Lean, VA	Public Family Member	812.9	14,000	3679
Read-Rite Corporation	111	Milpitas, CA	Public	808.6	18,000	3679
BellSouth Cellular Corp	112	Atlanta, GA	Public Family Member	805.3	11,604	4812
Turner Broadcasting System	113	Atlanta, GA	Public Family Member	803.8	7,000	4833
DII Group, Inc.	114	Longmont, CO	Public	779.6	6,350	3679
Nextel Communications, Inc.	115	Mc Lean, VA	Public	738.9	7,000	4812
CBS Broadcasting Inc.	116	New York, NY	Public Family Member	734.7	6,400	4833
Panamsat Corporation	117	Greenwich, CT	Public	726.8	500	4899
L-3 Communications Corporation	118	New York, NY	Public Family Member	705.4	6,100	3663
USA Networks	119	New York, NY	Private	700.0	550	4841
Clear Channel Communications	120	San Antonio, TX	Public	697.1	5,400	4832
Qwest Communications Intl	121	Denver, CO	Public	696.7	6,900	4813
TCI Cable Investments Inc.	122	Englewood, CO	Public Family Member	674.6	NA	4841
BBS Holdings, Inc.	123	Atlanta, GA	Public Family Member	673.6	5,246	4813
Cincinnati Bell Telephone Co.	124	Cincinnati, OH	Public Family Member	671.0	3,500	4813
Williams International Co.	125	Tulsa, OK	Public Family Member	642.0	5,000	4813
Hughes Space Communications Co.	126	El Segundo, CA	Public Family Member	640.8	7,500	3663
Mobilemedia Communications Inc.	127	Ridgefield Park, NJ	Public Family Member	640.7	1,345	4812
Alcatel USA, Inc.	128	Plano, TX	Private	639.9	6,681	3661
Atlantic-Washington Bell DC	129	Washington, DC	Public Family Member	611.2	1,500	4813
Chancellor Media Corporation	130	Dallas, TX	Public	582.1	4,300	4832
GTE Midwest Incorporated	131	Wentzville, MO	Public Family Member	576.0	NA	4813
Siemens Info & Comm Network Inc.	132	Boca Raton, FL	Private	565.1	5,900	3661
Comsat Corporation	133	Bethesda, MD	Public	562.7	2,732	4899
Alltel Communications, Inc.	134	Little Rock, AR	Public Family Member	540.0	1,060	4812
Jacor Communications Inc.	135	Covington, KY	Public	530.6	4,300	4832
Adelphia Communications Corp	136	Coudersport, PA	Public	528.4	3,895	4841
Artesyn Technologies Inc.	137	Boca Raton, FL	Public	527.2	6,900	3679
AT&T Communications Of NJ	138	Basking Ridge, NJ	Public Family Member	514.0	4,004	4813
Ciena Corporation	139	Linthicum Heights, MD	Public	508.1	1,382	3661
United Video Satellite Group	140	Tulsa, OK	Public	507.6	1,500	4841

D&B COMPANY RANKINGS BY SALES

Company	Rank	Location	Type	Sales ($ mil.)	Employ-ment	Primary SIC
Racal Corporation	141	Fort Lauderdale, FL	Private	503.0	700	3661
Recoton Corp	142	Lake Mary, FL	Public	502.0	2,500	3651
Sanyo Manufacturing Corp	143	Forrest City, AR	Private	501.0	600	3651
LCI International Inc.	144	Arlington, VA	Public Family Member	500.6	3,900	4813
Mitsubishi Digital Electric America	145	Irvine, CA	Private	500.0	1,200	3651
Scripps Howard Broadcasting Co.	146	Cincinnati, OH	Public Family Member	500.0	1,800	4833
NTL Incorporated	147	New York, NY	Public	491.8	650	4841
Century Communications Corp	148	New Canaan, CT	Public	484.7	4,211	4841
Antec Corporation (Del)	149	Norcross, GA	Public	480.1	1,893	3663
Marcus Cable Company LLC	150	Dallas, TX	Private	479.3	1,801	4841
Echostar Communications Corp	151	Littleton, CO	Public	477.4	2,000	4841
Dish, LTD	152	Englewood, CO	Public Family Member	475.9	150	4841
United Telephone Co Of Ohio	153	Mansfield, OH	Public Family Member	469.6	2,407	4813
TCI Central, Inc.	154	Denver, CO	Public Family Member	469.5	96	4841
Picturetel Corporation	155	Andover, MA	Public	466.4	1,450	3669
Chris-Craft Industries Inc.	156	New York, NY	Public	464.6	1,169	4833
Jones Intercable Inc.	157	Englewood, CO	Public	460.7	3,060	4841
Tel-Save Inc.	158	New Hope, PA	Public Family Member	460.0	400	4813
Univision Communications, Inc.	159	Los Angeles, CA	Public	459.7	1,500	4833
United States Satellite Broadcasting	160	Saint Paul, MN	Public	456.6	142	4899
Glenayre Technologies Inc.	161	Charlotte, NC	Public	451.7	1,900	3663
Paramount Stations Group, Inc.	162	Los Angeles, CA	Public Family Member	450.0	1,000	4833
Stoneridge, Inc.	163	Warren, OH	Public	449.5	4,400	3679
Public Broadcasting Service	164	Alexandria, VA	Private	444.1	530	4833
BHC Communications, Inc.	165	New York, NY	Public	443.5	1,055	4833
AG Communication Systems Corp	166	Phoenix, AZ	Public Family Member	442.3	2,400	3661
Dover Technologies Intl	167	Binghamton, NY	Public Family Member	435.4	7,500	3679
Allen Telecom Inc.	168	Cleveland, OH	Public	432.5	3,300	3663
Ascent Entertainment Group	169	Denver, CO	Public	428.5	1,021	4841
Heritage Communications Inc.	170	Englewood, CO	Public Family Member	426.7	2,000	4841
Univision Television Group	171	Teaneck, NJ	Public Family Member	412.4	1,136	4833
Skytel Communications Inc.	172	Jackson, MS	Public	408.0	2,300	4812
Hutchinson Technology Inc.	173	Hutchinson, MN	Public	407.6	8,293	3679
Cable Systems Intl Inc.	174	Phoenix, AZ	Private	400.0	1,800	3661
Five Rivers Electronic Innov	175	Greeneville, TN	Private	400.0	1,200	3651
LG Electronics Alabama, Inc.	176	Huntsville, AL	Private	398.5	1,500	3651
Technitrol Inc.	177	Langhorne, PA	Public	397.1	14,400	3679
Arch Communications Group Inc.	178	Westborough, MA	Public	396.8	2,800	4812
Premiere Technologies, Inc.	179	Atlanta, GA	Public	395.5	2,200	4813
ICG Holdings, Inc.	180	Englewood, CO	Public Family Member	395.0	2,219	4813
TCA Cable TV Inc.	181	Tyler, TX	Public	385.7	1,900	4841
ICG Communications Inc.	182	Englewood, CO	Public	381.1	2,970	4813
Western Wireless Corporation	183	Issaquah, WA	Public	380.6	3,210	4812
Sinclair Communications, Inc.	184	Baltimore, MD	Public Family Member	378.0	75	4833
Star Telecommunications, Inc.	185	Santa Barbara, CA	Public	376.2	116	4813
Vanguard Cellular Systems Inc.	186	Greensboro, NC	Public	374.5	2,000	4812
Liberty Media Corporation	187	Englewood, CO	Public Family Member	374.2	NA	4841
Global One Communications LLC	188	Reston, VA	Public Family Member	365.3	3,000	4899
Charter Communications, Inc.	189	Saint Louis, MO	Private	363.9	2,700	4841
General Semiconductor Inc.	190	Melville, NY	Public	361.9	3,000	3679
Astec America Inc.	191	Carlsbad, CA	Private	357.0	2,000	3679
Telex Communications Inc.	192	Minneapolis, MN	Public Family Member	355.0	3,300	3663
Suburban Cable TV Co Inc.	193	Oaks, PA	Private	354.6	400	4841
Capstar Broadcasting Corp	194	Austin, TX	Public	352.0	4,000	4832
Unity Motion, Inc.	195	Maryland Heights, MO	Private	350.0	45	4841
Motorola Messaging Info Media	196	Boynton Beach, FL	Public Family Member	341.7	4,000	3663
Telegroup Inc.	197	Fairfield, IA	Public	337.4	500	4813
IDT Corporation	198	Hackensack, NJ	Public	335.4	712	4813
Southwestern Bell Mobile Systems	199	Dallas, TX	Public Family Member	334.0	4,810	4812
Level 3 Communications, Inc.	200	Broomfield, CO	Private	332.0	3,600	4813
Raycom Media Inc.	201	Montgomery, AL	Private	330.0	2,000	4833
Citizens Communications	202	Stamford, CT	Public Family Member	320.7	2,500	4813
ITC Holding Company, Inc.	203	West Point, GA	Private	320.7	2,500	4813
Digital Microwave Corporation	204	San Jose, CA	Public	310.5	1,147	3663
Mediaone Of Los Angeles, Inc.	205	El Segundo, CA	Public Family Member	309.9	2,300	4841
ACC Long Distance Corp	206	Rochester, NY	Public Family Member	308.8	250	4813
Network Equipment Technologies	207	Fremont, CA	Public	308.7	1,414	3661
McLeod USA Telecommunications	208	Cedar Rapids, IA	Public Family Member	307.8	2,400	4813
360 Communications Company	209	Chicago, IL	Public Family Member	305.6	4,400	4812
CMC Industries Inc.	210	Santa Clara, CA	Public	302.0	1,205	3661

D&B COMPANY RANKINGS BY SALES

Company	Rank	Location	Type	Sales ($ mil.)	Employ-ment	Primary SIC
R S L Communications Inc.	211	New York, NY	Private	300.8	350	4813
International Telecom Group LTD	212	Woodland Hills, CA	Private	300.0	150	4813
LIN Television Corporation	213	Providence, RI	Public	300.0	134	4833
Lockheed Martin Tech Oper	214	Sunnyvale, CA	Public Family Member	300.0	3,300	4899
RSL Com U.S.A., Inc.	215	Woodland Hills, CA	Private	300.0	260	4813
Pacific Gateway Exchange, Inc.	216	Burlingame, CA	Public	298.6	120	4813
Cable News Network Inc.	217	Atlanta, GA	Public Family Member	296.4	2,200	4841
Tech-Sym Corporation	218	Houston, TX	Public	294.1	2,398	3663
ITT Federal Services Corp	219	Colorado Springs, CO	Public Family Member	293.4	4,800	4899
Metrocall, Inc.	220	Alexandria, VA	Public	289.4	2,261	4812
Pairgain Technologies, Inc.	221	Tustin, CA	Public	282.3	640	3661
Central Telephone Co Of Illinois	222	Mansfield, OH	Public Family Member	280.6	2,188	4813
Pacific Telecom Inc.	223	Monroe, LA	Public Family Member	280.4	NA	4813
Primus Telecom Group	224	Mc Lean, VA	Public	280.2	600	4813
Teleglobe International Corp	225	Reston, VA	Private	278.7	250	4813
Pagemart Wireless, Inc.	226	Dallas, TX	Public	277.8	2,335	4812
Octel Communications Corp	227	Milpitas, CA	Public Family Member	277.7	2,900	3661
Newbridge Networks Inc.	228	Herndon, VA	Private	276.6	1,650	3661
Dovatron International, Inc.	229	Boulder, CO	Public Family Member	274.7	900	3679
Peavey Electronics Corporation	230	Meridian, MS	Private	271.0	2,400	3651
IPC Information Systems Inc.	231	New York, NY	Public	270.3	1,088	3661
Heritage Cablevision, (Ia)	232	Des Moines, IA	Public Family Member	269.4	2,000	4841
California Microwave Inc.	233	Sunnyvale, CA	Public	269.2	1,528	3663
McLeod USA Incorporated	234	Cedar Rapids, IA	Public	267.9	4,941	4813
Advanced Fibre Communications	235	Petaluma, CA	Public	267.9	800	3661
Adtran Inc.	236	Huntsville, AL	Public	265.3	1,008	3661
Alascom Inc.	237	Anchorage, AK	Public Family Member	265.1	624	4813
Young Broadcasting Inc.	238	New York, NY	Public	263.5	1,300	4833
Westec Security Group Inc.	239	Newport Beach, CA	Private	263.5	3,000	3669
Dialogic Corporation	240	Parsippany, NJ	Public	261.3	994	3661
Mississippi Band Choctaw Indians	241	Philadelphia, MS	Private	261.3	4,500	3679
United Telephone Co Of PA Inc.	242	Carlisle, PA	Public Family Member	259.4	1,683	4813
K Systems Inc.	243	Foster City, CA	Private	259.2	1,600	3679
Cable One, Inc.	244	Phoenix, AZ	Public Family Member	257.7	1,139	4841
Cidco Incorporated	245	Morgan Hill, CA	Public	257.0	422	3661
Falcon Holding Group LP	246	Los Angeles, CA	Private	255.9	967	4841
Matsushita Comm Indus Corp Us	247	Peachtree City, GA	Private	250.0	1,400	3663
Intermedia Communications Inc.	248	Tampa, FL	Public	247.9	2,575	4813
New Par	249	Dublin, OH	Private	243.1	3,500	4812
Primeco Per Communications LP	250	Roanoke, TX	Private	243.1	3,500	4812
Mobilemedia Corporation	251	Fort Lee, NJ	Public	240.0	3,455	4812
Centennial Cellular Corp	252	Neptune, NJ	Public	237.5	1,632	4812
Williams Fire Protection Inc.	253	Wilmington, DE	Private	237.1	2,700	3669
Plantronics Inc.	254	Santa Cruz, CA	Public	236.1	1,817	3661
Atlantic Tele-Network Inc.	255	Christiansted, VI	Public	235.2	NA	4813
Artesyn North America Inc.	256	Eden Prairie, MN	Public Family Member	228.2	2,848	3679
Snet Mobility Inc.	257	Rocky Hill, CT	Private	227.0	130	4812
C & K Components Inc.	258	Watertown, MA	Private	225.0	1,000	3679
General Communication, Inc.	259	Anchorage, AK	Public	223.8	1,000	4813
Inter-Tel Incorporated	260	Phoenix, AZ	Public	223.6	1,248	3661
On Command Corporation	261	San Jose, CA	Public	222.1	773	4841
P-Com Inc.	262	Campbell, CA	Public	220.7	754	3661
Titan Tech & Info Systems Corp	263	Reston, VA	Public Family Member	220.0	1,100	3663
TSR Wireless LLC	264	Fort Lee, NJ	Private	220.0	1,500	4812
Husko Inc.	265	Milpitas, CA	Private	219.2	49	3679
Inrange Technologies Corp	266	Mount Laurel, NJ	Public Family Member	219.0	942	3663
ICG Telecom Group Inc.	267	Englewood, CO	Public Family Member	217.8	1,700	4813
Itron Inc.	268	Spokane, WA	Public	216.1	1,167	3663
Adflex Solutions, Inc.	269	Chandler, AZ	Public	213.9	5,254	3679
Harmon Industries Inc.	270	Blue Springs, MO	Public	213.5	1,504	3669
Fnet Corp	271	Thousand Oaks, CA	Public Family Member	210.0	15	4813
BellSouth Mobility Inc.	272	Atlanta, GA	Public Family Member	208.5	3,000	4812
MCI International Inc.	273	Port Chester, NY	Public Family Member	205.0	1,600	4813
Metromedia Intl Group Inc.	274	East Rutherford, NJ	Private	204.3	1,300	4841
IXC Communications, Inc.	275	Austin, TX	Public	203.7	1,290	4813
Yahoo Inc.	276	Santa Clara, CA	Public	203.3	155	4813
ESPN Inc.	277	Bristol, CT	Public Family Member	202.6	1,506	4841
Discovery Communications Inc.	278	Bethesda, MD	Private	201.8	1,500	4841
Sunbeam Television Corp	279	Miami, FL	Private	201.0	475	4833
Ameritech Mobile Communications	280	Hoffman Estates, IL	Public Family Member	200.0	4,400	4812

D&B COMPANY RANKINGS BY SALES

Company	Rank	Location	Type	Sales ($ mil.)	Employ-ment	Primary SIC
Hitachi Telecom USA Inc.	281	Norcross, GA	Private	200.0	300	3661
Kearney-National Inc.	282	White Plains, NY	Private	200.0	1,780	3679
Mitel Inc.	283	Herndon, VA	Private	200.0	720	3661
Pacific Bell Information Services	284	San Ramon, CA	Public Family Member	200.0	250	4813
Hayes Corporation	285	Norcross, GA	Public	199.6	768	3661
Los Angeles Cellular Tele Co.	286	Cerritos, CA	Private	198.6	1,550	4813
Jefferson-Plot Communications Co.	287	Greensboro, NC	Public Family Member	195.6	1,100	4833
NOS Communications, Inc.	288	Las Vegas, NV	Private	195.0	1,050	4813
BTI Telecom Corp	289	Raleigh, NC	Private	194.9	550	4813
GST Telecommunications Inc.	290	Vancouver, WA	Public	194.7	1,520	4813
Aliant Communications Co.	291	Lincoln, NE	Public Family Member	194.6	1,104	4813
Citizens Telecom Co Of NY	292	Stamford, CT	Public Family Member	194.6	408	4813
Parcel Consultants Inc.	293	Cedar Grove, NJ	Private	193.4	500	4813
Consolidated Communication	294	Mattoon, IL	Public Family Member	192.1	1,500	4813
Telco Communications Group	295	Chantilly, VA	Public Family Member	192.1	1,500	4813
Nevada Bell	296	Reno, NV	Public Family Member	190.4	860	4813
KTLA Inc.	297	Los Angeles, CA	Public Family Member	190.0	250	4833
RSI, Inc.	298	Sterling, VA	Private	190.0	1,200	3663
Ultrak Inc.	299	Lewisville, TX	Public	188.7	672	3663
TCI Southeast Inc.	300	Birmingham, AL	Public Family Member	188.3	1,400	4841
Airtouch Cellular	301	Walnut Creek, CA	Public Family Member	187.7	2,700	4812
BRK Brands, Inc.	302	Aurora, IL	Public Family Member	186.9	2,125	3669
First Alert Inc.	303	Aurora, IL	Public Family Member	186.9	3,142	3669
Deseret Management Corporation	304	Salt Lake City, UT	Private	186.2	2,248	4832
Applied Magnetics Corporation	305	Goleta, CA	Public	183.6	4,700	3679
Nextel West Corp	306	Bellevue, WA	Public Family Member	181.8	2,616	4812
American Cellular Corporation	307	Schaumburg, IL	Public	181.0	700	4812
United Telephone Co Of Indiana	308	Mansfield, OH	Public Family Member	180.5	3,159	4813
Vtel Corporation	309	Austin, TX	Public	179.7	740	3669
Timeplex Inc.	310	Woodcliff Lake, NJ	Private	176.9	1,000	3661
E C I Telecom Inc.	311	Altamonte Springs, FL	Private	176.0	110	3661
WPIX, Inc.	312	New York, NY	Public Family Member	173.0	275	4833
Electromagnetic Sciences, Inc.	313	Norcross, GA	Public	171.2	1,200	3663
Titan Corporation	314	San Diego, CA	Public	171.2	1,500	3663
United Television Inc.	315	Beverly Hills, CA	Public	171.0	559	4833
Twentieth Century-Fox TV Intl	316	Los Angeles, CA	Private	170.4	1,500	4833
RCN Cable Systems Inc.	317	Dallas, PA	Public Family Member	170.0	416	4841
Intermedia Management Inc.	318	Nashville, TN	Private	169.0	1,257	4841
Spectrian Corporation	319	Sunnyvale, CA	Public	168.8	688	3663
Lodgenet Entertainment Corp	320	Sioux Falls, SD	Public	166.4	763	4841
Channel Master LLC	321	Smithfield, NC	Private	166.0	850	3679
Matsus Electric Comp On Corp Ame	322	Knoxville, TN	Private	165.4	2,180	3651
General Datacomm Inc.	323	Middlebury, CT	Public Family Member	162.8	1,700	3661
Tulalip Tribes Inc.	324	Marysville, WA	Private	161.3	1,200	4841
Matsushita Kotobuki Electronic	325	Vancouver, WA	Private	160.9	320	3651
Pulsar Data Systems, Inc.	326	Lanham, MD	Private	160.0	145	4813
Gemini Industries Inc.	327	Clifton, NJ	Private	159.1	450	3663
Milgo Solutions	328	Fort Lauderdale, FL	Private	157.7	1,647	3661
Trescom International, Inc.	329	Fort Lauderdale, FL	Public	157.6	250	4813
Shared Technologies Fairchild	330	Tampa, FL	Public Family Member	157.2	744	4813
Telephonics Corporation	331	Farmingdale, NY	Public Family Member	156.9	1,000	3669
Executone Information Systems	332	Milford, CT	Public	156.4	650	3661
Pulitzer Broadcasting Company	333	Saint Louis, MO	Public Family Member	156.1	1,375	4833
Contel Of California Inc.	334	Irving, TX	Public Family Member	156.0	1,219	4813
Allbritton Communications Co.	335	Washington, DC	Private	155.6	770	4833
Kyushu Matsushita Elc Corp Am	336	National City, CA	Private	155.0	2,600	3663
Heftel Broadcasting Corp	337	Dallas, TX	Public	154.9	609	4832
Proxima Corporation	338	San Diego, CA	Private	154.7	444	3679
Excite Inc.	339	Redwood City, CA	Public	154.1	470	4813
Granite Broadcasting Corp	340	New York, NY	Public	153.5	1,160	4833
Stanford Telecommunications	341	Sunnyvale, CA	Public	153.3	1,025	3663
C-Cor Electronics Inc.	342	State College, PA	Public	152.1	1,200	3663
Commnet Cellular Inc.	343	Englewood, CO	Public	150.9	374	4812
BEI Sensors & Systems Company	344	Sylmar, CA	Public Family Member	150.0	977	3679
BellSouth Per Communications	345	Atlanta, GA	Public Family Member	150.0	1,150	4813
Independent Television Network	346	New York, NY	Private	150.0	80	4833
Kentrox Industries Inc.	347	Portland, OR	Public Family Member	150.0	500	3661
Qualcomm Per Electric A Cal Partnr	348	San Diego, CA	Private	150.0	550	3661
Alpine Electronics Man. Of America	349	Greenwood, IN	Private	147.0	1,100	3651
Alcatel Data Networks, Inc.	350	Ashburn, VA	Private	145.0	385	3663

D&B COMPANY RANKINGS BY SALES

Company	Rank	Location	Type	Sales ($ mil.)	Employ-ment	Primary SIC
Deltec Electronics Corporation	351	San Diego, CA	Private	145.0	1,300	3679
Great Universal Incorporated	352	New York, NY	Private	144.4	1,300	4812
Media Gen Cable Of Fairfax Cnty	353	Chantilly, VA	Public Family Member	143.0	616	4841
Advanced Energy Industries	354	Fort Collins, CO	Public	141.9	1,059	3679
G S T Telecom, Inc.	355	Vancouver, WA	Public Family Member	140.7	1,100	4813
American Movie Classics Co.	356	Woodbury, NY	Private	139.2	195	4841
Sullivan Broadcasting Company	357	Boston, MA	Private	137.8	450	4833
International Jensen Inc.	358	Lincolnshire, IL	Private	134.8	1,200	3651
Aavid Thermal Products, Inc.	359	Laconia, NH	Public	134.6	1,088	3679
Comcast Cablvision Of Mercer Cnty	360	Philadelphia, PA	Public Family Member	134.3	1,000	4841
Jones Communications	361	Lanham, MD	Private	134.3	1,000	4841
TCI Cablevision Of Alabama	362	Birmingham, AL	Public Family Member	134.3	1,000	4841
Paxson Communications Corp	363	West Palm Beach, FL	Public	134.2	1,270	4833
Prodigy Communications Inc.	364	White Plains, NY	Public	134.2	355	4813
Innovex Precision Components	365	Hopkins, MN	Public Family Member	133.4	600	3679
Time Warner Entertainment	366	Stamford, CT	Private	133.2	992	4841
Entercom Communications Corp	367	Bala Cynwyd, PA	Public	133.0	700	4832
Harman-Motive Inc.	368	Martinsville, IN	Public Family Member	131.6	1,172	3651
Vertex Communications Corp	369	Kilgore, TX	Public	130.0	927	3663
Amerivision Communications	370	Oklahoma City, OK	Private	130.0	750	4813
Comm South Companies, Inc.	371	Dallas, TX	Private	130.0	301	4813
Matthey Johnson Electronics	372	Spokane, WA	Private	130.0	1,100	3679
Comcast Cablevision Of NJ	373	Union, NJ	Public Family Member	129.8	400	4841
Hearst-Argyle Television Inc.	374	New York, NY	Public	128.5	3,200	4833
JPM Company (Inc)	375	Lewisburg, PA	Public	128.4	2,800	3679
United Telephone Co Of Texas	376	Shawnee Mission, KS	Public Family Member	128.2	683	4813
Prodelin Holding Corporation	377	Conover, NC	Private	128.1	1,500	3663
Oncor Communications, Inc.	378	Dallas, TX	Private	127.9	1,000	4813
Reliance Comtech	379	Bedford, TX	Private	127.9	1,000	4813
Benedek Broadcasting Corp.	380	Rockford, IL	Private	127.1	1,272	4833
Gemstar Intl Group LTD	381	Pasadena, CA	Public	126.6	150	4841
C & K Systems Inc.	382	Folsom, CA	Private	126.0	2,000	3669
Emmis Communications Corp	383	Indianapolis, IN	Public	125.9	663	4832
G.T.E. World Headquarters	384	Irving, TX	Private	125.7	983	4813
Contel Of New York, Inc.	385	Irving, TX	Public Family Member	125.5	982	4813
Incomnet, Inc.	386	Irvine, CA	Public	125.1	350	4813
Tekelec	387	Calabasas, CA	Public	125.1	450	3661
HRB Systems, Inc.	388	State College, PA	Public Family Member	125.0	1,200	3669
National Tele & Communications	389	Irvine, CA	Public Family Member	125.0	250	4813
Prominet Corporation	390	Concord, MA	Public Family Member	125.0	100	3663
Trippe Manufacturing Company	391	Chicago, IL	Private	125.0	400	3679
JBL Incorporated	392	Washington, DC	Public Family Member	123.5	1,100	3651
Educational Broadcasting Corp	393	New York, NY	Private	123.5	427	4833
Total-Tel USA Communications Inc.	394	Little Falls, NJ	Public	123.3	270	4813
Cablevision Of Monmouth Inc.	395	Belmar, NJ	Private	123.1	180	4841
Boeing Corinth Company	396	Lake Dallas, TX	Public Family Member	121.9	2,100	3679
Mosaix Inc.	397	Redmond, WA	Public	121.1	625	3661
Standard Group Inc.	398	Cornelia, GA	Public Family Member	121.0	400	4813
Telect, Inc.	399	Liberty Lake, WA	Private	121.0	847	3661
Olympus Communications, L P	400	Coudersport, PA	Private	121.0	539	4841
Colony Communications, Inc.	401	Providence, RI	Public Family Member	120.8	602	4841
Mediaone Northern Illinois Inc.	402	Elmhurst, IL	Public Family Member	120.8	900	4841
Symmetricom Inc.	403	San Jose, CA	Public	120.6	642	3661
A-R Cable Services Inc.	404	Woodbury, NY	Public Family Member	120.4	563	4841
Alstom Signaling Inc.	405	Rochester, NY	Private	120.0	560	3669
Globecast North America Inc.	406	Miami, FL	Private	120.0	250	4841
Kcal TV, Inc.	407	Los Angeles, CA	Public Family Member	120.0	250	4833
Orix Global Communications	408	Las Vegas, NV	Private	120.0	25	4813
Brite Voice Systems Inc.	409	Lake Mary, FL	Public	119.8	681	3661
Osicom Technologies Inc.	410	Santa Monica, CA	Public	119.0	1,677	3661
Cosmos Broadcasting Corp	411	Greenville, SC	Public Family Member	119.0	932	4833
Comdial Corporation	412	Charlottesville, VA	Public	118.6	865	3661
PCS Triton Inc.	413	Malvern, PA	Private	118.3	400	4812
Triton Cellular Partners LP	414	Malvern, PA	Private	118.0	300	4812
Customtracks Corporation	415	Dallas, TX	Public	117.7	800	3663
Periphonics Corporation	416	Bohemia, NY	Public	117.3	866	3661
Facilicom International LLC	417	Washington, DC	Private	117.1	240	4813
Intellicall Inc.	418	Carrollton, TX	Public	117.0	166	4813
Alpha Industries Inc.	419	Woburn, MA	Public	116.9	801	3679
Amnex Inc.	420	New Rochelle, NY	Public	116.5	344	4813

D&B COMPANY RANKINGS BY SALES

Company	Rank	Location	Type	Sales ($ mil.)	Employ-ment	Primary SIC
Toshiba America Electronic Comp.	421	Irvine, CA	Private	116.1	2,000	3679
Citadel Broadcasting Company	422	Tempe, AZ	Public Family Member	115.5	1,400	4832
Aydin Corporation	423	Horsham, PA	Public	115.4	1,200	3663
BET Holdings Inc.	424	Washington, DC	Public	115.2	435	4841
Affiliated Regional Comm	425	Los Angeles, CA	Private	115.0	225	4841
Pioneer Speakers Inc.	426	National City, CA	Private	115.0	1,300	3651
Roseville Communications Co.	427	Roseville, CA	Private	114.9	565	4899
ITCdeltacom, Inc.	428	West Point, GA	Public	114.6	220	4813
New Valley Corporation	429	Miami, FL	Public	114.6	438	4822
PLD Telekom, Inc.	430	New York, NY	Private	114.4	1,000	4813
Universal Electronics Inc.	431	Cypress, CA	Public	114.3	264	3651
GE-Harris Railway Electric LLC	432	Melbourne, FL	Private	114.2	394	3669
H C Crown Corp	433	Kansas City, MO	Private	112.9	1,000	4833
Unidial Incorporated	434	Louisville, KY	Private	112.3	350	4813
International Family Entertainment	435	Virginia Beach, VA	Private	112.3	837	4841
Chauncey Communications Corp	436	Coudersport, PA	Public Family Member	112.0	50	4841
Polycom, Inc.	437	San Jose, CA	Public	111.7	175	3661
GTE Wireless Of Midwest Inc.	438	Cleveland, OH	Public Family Member	111.4	1,600	4812
Nokia Inc.	439	Irving, TX	Private	111.0	1,300	3663
Cox Communications New Orleans	440	New Orleans, LA	Private	111.0	600	4841
United Telephone-Southeast	441	Wake Forest, NC	Public Family Member	110.1	862	4813
Applied Signal Technology Inc.	442	Sunnyvale, CA	Public	110.1	617	3663
ATU Telecommunications	443	Anchorage, AK	Private	110.0	620	4813
Com Tech International Corp	444	Boca Raton, FL	Private	110.0	42	4813
Multi-Tech Systems Inc.	445	Saint Paul, MN	Private	109.8	340	3661
Phonetel Technologies Inc.	446	Cleveland, OH	Public	109.6	500	4813
Garden State Cable Vision, LP	447	Cherry Hill, NJ	Private	109.1	300	4841
Nextel South Corp	448	Norcross, GA	Public Family Member	108.2	1,555	4812
Alert Marketing Inc.	449	Lake Mary, FL	Private	108.0	7	4813
Advanced Communications Systems	450	Fairfax, VA	Public	107.8	1,850	4899
Liberty Corporation	451	Greenville, SC	Public	107.4	3,100	4833
American CableSystems Of Mass	452	Portsmouth, NH	Public Family Member	107.3	800	4841
Intermedia Partners	453	San Francisco, CA	Private	107.3	800	4841
Multimedia Cablevision, Inc.	454	Wichita, KS	Public Family Member	107.3	800	4841
Convergent Communications Svcs	455	Englewood, CO	Private	106.5	917	4813
Vartec Telecom, Inc.	456	Lancaster, TX	Private	105.6	827	4813
SLC Technologies Inc.	457	Tualatin, OR	Private	105.3	1,800	3669
Pinnacle Systems Inc.	458	Mountain View, CA	Public	105.3	323	3663
Cellular Communications Intl	459	New York, NY	Public	105.0	10	4812
Lufkin-Conroe Communications Co.	460	Lufkin, TX	Public Family Member	104.8	751	4813
Working Assets Funding Service	461	San Francisco, CA	Private	104.4	120	4813
Gray Communications Systems	462	Albany, GA	Public	103.5	1,200	4833
Intervoice Inc.	463	Dallas, TX	Public	102.3	700	3661
Premisys Communications Inc.	464	Fremont, CA	Public	102.3	331	3661
Signal Technology Corporation	465	Danvers, MA	Public	102.3	820	3679
Allsup Enterprises, Inc.	466	Clovis, NM	Private	102.0	1,238	4832
Mediacom Southeast LLC	467	Middletown, NY	Private	102.0	540	4841
Service Electric Television	468	Mahanoy City, PA	Private	101.6	489	4841
BEI Technologies Inc.	469	San Francisco, CA	Public	101.5	977	3679
Hauser Communications Inc.	470	New York, NY	Private	100.5	750	4841
Powerwave Technologies, Inc.	471	Irvine, CA	Public	100.2	461	3663
UTstarcom, Inc.	472	Alameda, CA	Private	100.1	788	3661
Casio Phonemate Inc.	473	Torrance, CA	Private	100.0	175	3661
Cominex LLC	474	Mays Landing, NJ	Private	100.0	20	4813
Computer Science Raytheon	475	Cocoa, FL	Private	100.0	1,500	4899
Global Commerce & Media Network	476	New York, NY	Private	100.0	25	4813
GTE Airfone Incorporated (Del)	477	Oak Brook, IL	Public Family Member	100.0	210	4812
Interoute Telecommunications	478	New York, NY	Private	100.0	300	4813
Knowles Electronics Del	479	Itasca, IL	Private	100.0	641	3679
Maple Chase Company	480	Downers Grove, IL	Private	100.0	1,000	3669
Netsource Communications Inc.	481	Petaluma, CA	Private	100.0	120	4813
USWeb Corporation	482	Santa Clara, CA	Public	100.0	1,000	4813
Wireless One Network, L.P.	483	Fort Myers, FL	Private	100.0	400	4812
Zekko Corporation	484	Ponte Vedra Beach, FL	Private	100.0	10	4899
Packard-Hughes Interconnect Co.	485	Irvine, CA	Public Family Member	98.7	1,700	3679
United International Holding	486	Denver, CO	Public	98.6	130	4841
Dolby Laboratories Inc.	487	San Francisco, CA	Private	98.6	445	3663
MC Liquidating Corporation	488	Southfield, MI	Private	98.3	NA	4813
Network Plus Inc.	489	Quincy, MA	Private	98.2	420	4813
Radio Frequency Systems Inc.	490	Hickory, NC	Private	98.2	1,150	3663

D&B COMPANY RANKINGS BY SALES

Company	Rank	Location	Type	Sales ($ mil.)	Employ-ment	Primary SIC
American Communications Network	491	Troy, MI	Private	98.1	250	4813
Cellular Telephone Company	492	Paramus, NJ	Public Family Member	97.5	1,400	4812
Teltrend Inc.	493	Saint Charles, IL	Public	96.8	519	3661
Pacific Bell Wireless	494	Pleasanton, CA	Public Family Member	94.2	1,352	4812
UACC Midwest, Inc.	495	Grand Rapids, MI	Public Family Member	93.8	700	4841
EDCO LLC	496	Norwalk, CT	Private	93.0	18	4813
World Access Inc.	497	Atlanta, GA	Public	93.0	510	3661
Power-One Inc.	498	Camarillo, CA	Public	91.6	1,704	3679
Staveley Inc.	499	White Plains, NY	Private	91.0	1,568	3679
TCI Cablevision Of Missouri	500	Saint Peters, MO	Public Family Member	91.0	350	4841
Bonneville International Corp	501	Salt Lake City, UT	Private	90.5	1,100	4832
MediaOne Of Ohio Inc.	502	Findlay, OH	Public Family Member	90.3	674	4841
Efdata Corp.	503	Tempe, AZ	Public Family Member	90.0	623	3663
Lloyd Daniels Dev Group	504	Cincinnati, OH	Private	90.0	22	4822
LXE Inc.	505	Norcross, GA	Public Family Member	90.0	400	3663
Odetics, Inc.	506	Anaheim, CA	Public	89.8	554	3663
Perpetual Corporation	507	Washington, DC	Private	89.8	800	4833
Superstation Inc.	508	Atlanta, GA	Public Family Member	89.8	800	4833
Telemundo Group Inc.	509	Hialeah, FL	Private	89.8	800	4833
Turner Original Productions Inc.	510	Atlanta, GA	Public Family Member	89.8	800	4833
Communications Instruments	511	Fairview, NC	Private	89.4	1,200	3679
Foster North America Inc.	512	Schaumburg, IL	Private	89.4	900	3651
Tele-Fibernet Corporation	513	Jackson, MS	Public Family Member	89.3	700	4813
SJI Inc.	514	Cut Off, LA	Private	89.1	512	4813
Stellex Microwave Systems	515	Palo Alto, CA	Private	89.0	504	3679
Excel Switching Corporation	516	Hyannis, MA	Public	88.7	190	3661
Mobile Comm. Corp. of America	517	Fort Lee, NJ	Public Family Member	88.5	1,271	4812
Paxson Communication Of New Lnd	518	New London, CT	Public Family Member	88.4	20	4833
CMT Partners	519	South San Francisco, CA	Private	88.2	1,266	4812
Dukane Corporation	520	Saint Charles, IL	Private	87.9	642	3663
Cerberus Holdings Inc.	521	Wilmington, DE	Private	87.8	1,000	3669
Lambda Holdings Inc.	522	Melville, NY	Private	87.1	1,500	3679
Commonwealth Telephone Co.	523	Dallas, PA	Public Family Member	87.0	682	4813
Pegasus Communications Corp	524	Radnor, PA	Private	86.8	877	4833
Chyron Corporation	525	Melville, NY	Public	86.8	406	3663
Westell Technologies Inc.	526	Oswego, IL	Public	86.4	649	3661
Comverse Network Systems Inc.	527	Wakefield, MA	Public Family Member	86.2	900	3661
Airtouch Paging Of Texas	528	Dallas, TX	Public Family Member	86.0	1,234	4812
Access Communications Inc.	529	Salt Lake City, UT	Private	85.9	300	4813
Sygnet Wireless Inc.	530	Canfield, OH	Private	85.6	415	4812
EIS International Inc.	531	Herndon, VA	Public	85.6	389	3661
Black Entertainment Television	532	Washington, DC	Public Family Member	85.3	350	4841
Concert Management Services	533	Reston, VA	Private	85.3	700	4899
Dobson Communication Corp	534	Oklahoma City, OK	Private	85.2	330	4812
Rowe International Inc.	535	Grand Rapids, MI	Public Family Member	85.0	450	3651
Alesis Studio Electronics	536	Santa Monica, CA	Private	84.7	230	3651
Fisher Broadcasting Inc.	537	Seattle, WA	Public Family Member	84.1	750	4833
USLD Communications Corp	538	Arlington, VA	Private	83.9	658	4813
Harmonic Lightwaves Inc.	539	Sunnyvale, CA	Public	83.9	215	3663
GTE Service Corporation	540	Irving, TX	Public Family Member	83.5	890	4813
Applied Science & Technology	541	Woburn, MA	Public	83.4	355	3679
OECO Corporation	542	Milwaukie, OR	Private	83.4	865	3679
Destia Communications, Inc.	543	Paramus, NJ	Private	83.0	408	4813
Clarion Manufacturing Corp America	544	Walton, KY	Private	82.9	228	3651
Concentric Network Corporation	545	San Jose, CA	Public	82.8	387	4813
GTI Corporation	546	San Diego, CA	Public Family Member	82.6	6,280	3679
Boston Acoustics Inc.	547	Peabody, MA	Public	82.4	260	3651
Heritage Cablevision Of Cal	548	San Jose, CA	Public Family Member	82.2	276	4841
Matra Communication USA Inc.	549	New York, NY	Private	81.8	545	3661
Paradyne Corporation	550	Largo, FL	Private	81.4	850	3661
AVT Corporation	551	Kirkland, WA	Public	81.1	325	3661
MCE Companies, Inc.	552	Ann Arbor, MI	Private	81.0	660	3679
MacDermid Inc.	553	Wilmington, DE	Public Family Member	80.5	152	3679
Jones Global Group, Inc.	554	Englewood, CO	Private	80.3	NA	4841
TCI Of Pennsylvania, Inc.	555	Pittsburgh, PA	Public Family Member	80.3	600	4841
Triax USA Associates, LP	556	Denver, CO	Private	80.3	600	4841
Keptel Inc.	557	Eatontown, NJ	Public Family Member	80.0	900	3661
Peek Corporation	558	Tallahassee, FL	Public Family Member	80.0	350	3669
Teledata International Inc.	559	Atlanta, GA	Private	80.0	40	4813
Uniphase Telecom Products	560	Bloomfield, CT	Public Family Member	80.0	340	3661

D&B COMPANY RANKINGS BY SALES

Company	Rank	Location	Type	Sales ($ mil.)	Employ-ment	Primary SIC
Booth American Company	561	Detroit, MI	Private	79.7	970	4832
Winstar Communications Inc.	562	New York, NY	Public	79.6	2,100	4813
Telecard Dispensing Corp	563	Hollywood, FL	Private	79.5	50	4813
Powertel, Inc.	564	West Point, GA	Public	78.9	1,000	4812
Heartland Wireless Communications	565	Plano, TX	Public	78.8	790	4841
CT Communications Inc.	566	Concord, NC	Public	78.5	410	4813
Malrite Communications Group	567	Cleveland, OH	Private	78.3	700	4833
Centigram Communications Corp	568	San Jose, CA	Public	77.6	325	3661
Cherokee International LLC	569	Tustin, CA	Private	77.0	868	3679
Ortel Corporation	570	Alhambra, CA	Public	76.9	507	3663
Conexant Systems, Inc.	571	Newport Beach, CA	Private	76.6	800	3661
Hickory Tech Corporation	572	Mankato, MN	Public	76.5	500	4813
Onemain.Com, Inc (De)	573	Southampton, NY	Private	76.4	600	4813
Kansas City Cable Partners, LP	574	Kansas City, MO	Private	76.2	570	4841
Spanish Broadcasting System	575	New York, NY	Private	76.1	96	4832
Larscom Incorporated	576	Milpitas, CA	Public	76.0	291	3661
American Network Exchange Inc.	577	Orlando, FL	Public Family Member	75.9	224	4813
Communications Systems, Inc.	578	Hector, MN	Public	75.7	1,135	3661
Kavlico Corporation	579	Moorpark, CA	Private	75.4	1,300	3679
JMR Communication Corporation	580	Dallas, TX	Private	75.0	3	4812
Network Operator Services	581	Longview, TX	Private	75.0	350	4813
Packard-Hughes Intrcnct Wr Sys	582	Foley, AL	Public Family Member	75.0	600	3679
Raltron Electronics Corp	583	Miami, FL	Private	75.0	275	3679
Solectron Massachusetts Corp	584	Westborough, MA	Public Family Member	75.0	300	3679
Mackie Designs Inc.	585	Woodinville, WA	Public	74.9	585	3651
United Telephone Co Of Kansas	586	Shawnee Mission, KS	Public Family Member	74.9	1,900	4813
Lojack Corporation	587	Dedham, MA	Public	74.5	405	3663
Directed Electronics Inc.	588	Vista, CA	Private	74.2	95	3669
Advanced Communications Group	589	Chesterfield, MO	Private	73.9	580	4813
Century Telephone Of Washington	590	Vancouver, WA	Public Family Member	73.6	415	4813
Bel Fuse Inc.	591	Jersey City, NJ	Public	73.5	707	3679
Mediaone Of Greater Florida	592	Jacksonville, FL	Public Family Member	73.5	NA	4841
Filtronic Comtek Inc.	593	Salisbury, MD	Private	73.2	509	3679
Viatel, Inc (De Corp)	594	New York, NY	Public	73.0	290	4813
Westell, Inc.	595	Aurora, IL	Public Family Member	73.0	602	3661
North State Telecommunications	596	High Point, NC	Private	72.9	396	4813
Motorola Cellular Service Inc.	597	Libertyville, IL	Public Family Member	72.1	3,000	4812
Loral Orion Network Systems	598	Rockville, MD	Public	72.0	400	4899
Nextel Of New York, Inc.	599	White Plains, NY	Public Family Member	72.0	450	4812
Smartalk Teleservices, Inc.	600	Dublin, OH	Public	71.9	565	4813
Intecom Inc.	601	Dallas, TX	Private	71.3	558	3661
Hughes Communications Inc.	602	Long Beach, CA	Public Family Member	70.7	580	4899
Liberty Cellular, Inc.	603	Salina, KS	Private	70.4	140	4812
Boca Research Inc.	604	Boca Raton, FL	Public	70.2	304	3661
Gabriel Inc.	605	Elgin, IL	Private	70.1	300	3663
Cyberfone	606	Wayne, PA	Private	70.0	20	3661
Dialight Corp	607	Manasquan, NJ	Private	70.0	430	3679
John Mezzalingua Associates	608	East Syracuse, NY	Private	70.0	200	3663
Mac America Communications Inc.	609	Phoenix, AZ	Private	70.0	350	4833
Mediaone Of Fresno	610	Fresno, CA	Public Family Member	70.0	305	4841
NPG Holdings, Inc.	611	Saint Joseph, MO	Private	70.0	550	4841
Prestige Cable TV Inc.	612	Cartersville, GA	Private	70.0	350	4841
Splitrock Services Inc.	613	The Woodlands, TX	Private	70.0	110	4899
Los Angeles SMSA LTD Partner	614	Irvine, CA	Private	69.7	1,000	4812
Nokia Telecommunications Inc.	615	Irving, TX	Private	69.7	1,000	4812
Post-Newsweek Stations Inc.	616	Hartford, CT	Public Family Member	69.7	625	4833
N I C E Systems Inc (De Corp)	617	Secaucus, NJ	Private	69.3	50	4813
Mod-Tap Corp	618	Harvard, MA	Public Family Member	69.0	296	3669
Galaxy Telecom, L P	619	Sikeston, MO	Private	68.8	500	4841
F E L Corporation	620	Farmingdale, NJ	Private	68.8	806	3663
Insight Communications Co LP	621	New York, NY	Private	68.5	276	4841
Talla-Com Tallahassee Comm Ind	622	Tallahassee, FL	Private	68.4	235	3669
International Telcom LTD	623	Seattle, WA	Private	68.0	210	4813
Salem Communication Corp	624	Camarillo, CA	Private	67.9	600	4832
Seachange International, Inc.	625	Maynard, MA	Public	67.9	280	3663
Nextel Of California Inc.	626	Oakland, CA	Public Family Member	67.4	966	4812
G E American Communications	627	Princeton, NJ	Public Family Member	67.1	550	4899
Cable Network Services LLC	628	Stamford, CT	Private	66.8	NA	4841
FPL Group Capital Inc.	629	North Palm Beach, FL	Public Family Member	66.8	500	4841
Harron Communications Corp	630	Malvern, PA	Private	66.8	500	4841

D&B COMPANY RANKINGS BY SALES

Company	Rank	Location	Type	Sales ($ mil.)	Employ-ment	Primary SIC
Pegasus Media & Communications	631	Radnor, PA	Public	66.4	459	4833
GTE West Coast Incorporated	632	Everett, WA	Public Family Member	66.4	522	4813
North Pittsburgh Systems, Inc.	633	Gibsonia, PA	Public	66.2	276	4813
Midcontinent Media, Inc.	634	Minneapolis, MN	Private	66.0	494	4841
VYVX, Inc.	635	Tulsa, OK	Public Family Member	66.0	541	4899
Safetran Systems Corporation	636	Minneapolis, MN	Private	65.8	750	3669
Infinity Broadcasting Corp Del	637	New York, NY	Public	65.7	803	4832
Geotek Communications, Inc.	638	Montvale, NJ	Public	65.5	685	4812
Classic Cable Inc.	639	Austin, TX	Private	65.0	350	4841
Prevue Networks, Inc.	640	Tulsa, OK	Public Family Member	65.0	400	4833
Starpower Communications LLC	641	Washington, DC	Private	65.0	40	4813
Optel, Inc.	642	Dallas, TX	Private	65.0	706	4841
Virgin Island Telephone Corp	643	Charlotte Amalie, VI	Public Family Member	64.7	421	4813
SBC Media Ventures Inc.	644	Rockville, MD	Public Family Member	64.6	484	4841
Journal Broadcast Group Inc.	645	Milwaukee, WI	Private	64.5	580	4833
Augat Communication Products	646	Kent, WA	Public Family Member	64.5	325	3663
Alltel Pennsylvania, Inc.	647	Little Rock, AR	Public Family Member	64.4	506	4813
McGraw-Hill Broadcasting Co.	648	New York, NY	Public Family Member	63.9	575	4833
GTE Cybertrust Solutions Inc.	649	Needham, MA	Public Family Member	63.6	500	4813
Islandlife LLC	650	New York, NY	Private	63.6	500	4813
Vista-United Telecom	651	Lake Buena Vista, FL	Private	63.6	550	4813
Transaction Network Services	652	Reston, VA	Public	63.3	112	4813
Vicon Industries Inc.	653	Hauppauge, NY	Public	63.3	217	3663
Trans National Communications	654	Boston, MA	Private	63.1	150	4813
Aeronautical Radio Inc.	655	Annapolis, MD	Private	63.0	632	4812
Lenfest Communications Inc.	656	Oaks, PA	Private	62.8	1,800	4841
Elgar Electronics Corporation	657	San Diego, CA	Private	62.5	433	3679
Del Global Technologies Corp	658	Valhalla, NY	Public	62.3	466	3679
Blonder-Tongue Laboratories	659	Old Bridge, NJ	Public	62.1	587	3663
Sportschannel Associates	660	Woodbury, NY	Private	62.0	47	4841
Transcrypt International, Inc.	661	Lincoln, NE	Public	62.0	494	3663
Phone Exchange Inc.	662	Newport Beach, CA	Private	62.0	22	4813
Confederated Slish Ktnai Tribes	663	Pablo, MT	Private	62.0	800	3679
US Unwired Inc.	664	Lake Charles, LA	Private	61.9	619	4813
Oneworld Systems Inc.	665	Sunnyvale, CA	Public	61.5	70	3661
Zoom Telephonics Canadian Corp	666	Boston, MA	Public	61.4	342	3661
Electric Lightwave Inc.	667	Vancouver, WA	Public	61.1	573	4813
American Tower Corp	668	Boston, MA	Public	61.0	500	4899
Blackstone Calling Card, Inc.	669	Miami, FL	Private	61.0	51	4813
Pamplin Communications Corp	670	Portland, OR	Private	61.0	500	4899
Norlight Telecommunications	671	Brookfield, WI	Private	60.8	180	4813
Intelidata Technologies Corp	672	Herndon, VA	Public	60.3	300	3661
Ml Media Partners, L.P.	673	New York, NY	Private	60.3	570	4841
ATG International Inc.	674	Anaheim, CA	Private	60.0	15	4813
Golden Sky Systems, Inc.	675	Kansas City, MO	Private	60.0	450	4841
Huber + Suhner Inc.	676	Essex Junction, VT	Private	60.0	160	3679
KHOU-TV, Inc.	677	Houston, TX	Public Family Member	60.0	220	4833
Low Country Telephone Company	678	Hilton Head Island, SC	Private	60.0	200	4813
Musicbox Network	679	Oakland, CA	Private	60.0	9	4833
Paramunt Stns Group Of Detroit	680	Southfield, MI	Public Family Member	60.0	185	4833
St Louis Music Inc.	681	Saint Louis, MO	Private	60.0	400	3651
Vectron Technologies Inc.	682	Hudson, NH	Public Family Member	60.0	225	3679
E N M R Telephone Coop	683	Clovis, NM	Private	60.0	220	4813
Plateau Cellular Network Inc.	684	Clovis, NM	Private	60.0	45	4812
Gai-Tronics Corporation	685	Mohnton, PA	Public Family Member	59.8	619	3661
Oki Telecom, Inc.	686	Suwanee, GA	Private	59.7	700	3663
USN Communications Midwest	687	Chicago, IL	Public Family Member	59.2	466	4813
United Telephone Co NJ Inc.	688	Clinton, NJ	Public Family Member	59.1	465	4813
American Telecasting, Inc.	689	Colorado Springs, CO	Public	59.0	448	4841
CFW Communications Company	690	Waynesboro, VA	Public	59.0	492	4813
E.Spire Communications Inc.	691	Annapolis Junction, MD	Public	59.0	550	4813
Justice Technology Corporation	692	Culver City, CA	Private	59.0	125	4813
Intelnet International Corp	693	West Berlin, NJ	Private	58.4	60	4813
Gr. Wash. Educational Telecom Assn	694	Arlington, VA	Private	58.4	305	4833
Buford Television Inc.	695	Tyler, TX	Private	58.1	370	4841
Onkyo America Inc.	696	Columbus, IN	Private	58.1	475	3651
Williams Controls Inc.	697	Portland, OR	Public	57.6	511	3679
Nextlink Communications, Inc.	698	Bellevue, WA	Public	57.6	1,500	4813
Honolulu Cellular Telephone Co.	699	Mililani, HI	Private	57.4	290	4812
The Nextel Communications	700	Reston, VA	Public Family Member	57.4	822	4812

D&B COMPANY RANKINGS BY SALES

Company	Rank	Location	Type	Sales ($ mil.)	Employ-ment	Primary SIC
MFS Telecom, Inc. (Del)	701	Villa Park, IL	Public Family Member	57.2	450	4813
Raycom America, Inc.	702	Montgomery, AL	Private	57.2	700	4832
TCI Great Lakes, Inc.	703	Deerfield, IL	Public Family Member	57.0	NA	4841
Harbor Electronics Inc.	704	Etters, PA	Private	57.0	720	3679
Lifeline Systems Inc.	705	Cambridge, MA	Public	57.0	350	3669
US Wats Inc.	706	Bensalem, PA	Public	56.5	69	4813
Celeritek Inc.	707	Santa Clara, CA	Public	56.3	325	3663
Saga Communications Inc.	708	Detroit, MI	Public	56.2	445	4832
Conestoga Enterprises Inc.	709	Birdsboro, PA	Public	56.2	272	4813
GTE Mobilnet Hawaii Inc.	710	Honolulu, HI	Public Family Member	56.0	175	4812
Microflect Co Inc.	711	Salem, OR	Public Family Member	56.0	272	3663
Netcom Systems Inc.	712	Chatsworth, CA	Private	56.0	150	3663
Aerial Communications Inc.	713	Chicago, IL	Public	56.0	500	4812
Comstream Corporation	714	San Diego, CA	Private	55.9	200	3663
GTE Mobilnet Tampa Inc.	715	Tampa, FL	Public Family Member	55.9	800	4812
Klipsch, LLC	716	Indianapolis, IN	Private	55.8	504	3651
Time Warner Telecom LLC	717	Englewood, CO	Private	55.4	898	4813
Bahakel Communications LTD	718	Charlotte, NC	Private	55.3	500	4833
Federal Broadcasting Company	719	Montgomery, AL	Private	55.3	500	4833
LIN Television Of Texas, L P	720	Austin, TX	Private	55.3	500	4833
Sinclair Properties L.L.C.	721	Baltimore, MD	Private	55.3	500	4833
Cellnet Communications Inc.	722	Madison Heights, MI	Private	55.2	75	4812
R F Monolithics Inc.	723	Dallas, TX	Public	55.2	600	3679
Cablevision Connecticut Corp	724	Norwalk, CT	Public Family Member	55.1	503	4841
Sportschannel Chicago Assoc	725	Chicago, IL	Private	55.0	74	4841
Amphenol Interconnect Products	726	Wallingford, CT	Public Family Member	55.0	500	3679
Current Electronics Inc.	727	Newberg, OR	Public Family Member	55.0	390	3679
Display Technologies Inc.	728	Downey, CA	Private	55.0	275	3669
Sunbelt Communications Company	729	Las Vegas, NV	Private	55.0	450	4833
ACT Networks Inc.	730	Camarillo, CA	Public	55.0	242	3661
Pioneer Telephone Coop Inc.	731	Kingfisher, OK	Private	54.9	600	4813
Cumulus Broadcasting Inc.	732	Chicago, IL	Private	54.7	250	4832
Highwaymaster Corporation	733	Richardson, TX	Public	54.6	295	4812
Datron World Communications	734	Escondido, CA	Public Family Member	54.6	140	3663
Digital Link Corporation	735	Sunnyvale, CA	Public	54.6	281	3661
Aeroflex Laboratories Inc.	736	Plainview, NY	Public Family Member	54.4	425	3679
Group Long Distance Inc.	737	Fort Lauderdale, FL	Public	54.3	7	4813
Polk Audio Inc.	738	Baltimore, MD	Public	54.2	150	3651
Wiretech, LTD	739	Reston, VA	Private	54.1	550	4812
ILD Telecommunications Inc.	740	Dallas, TX	Private	54.0	425	4813
Rural Cellular Corporation	741	Alexandria, MN	Public	53.9	358	4812
RCN Telecom Services Of Pa	742	Northampton, PA	Public Family Member	53.9	405	4841
Taylor University Broadcasting	743	Fort Wayne, IN	Private	53.4	25	4832
Lifetime Entertainment Svcs	744	New York, NY	Private	53.3	400	4841
Mediaone Of New England Inc.	745	Andover, MA	Public Family Member	53.3	400	4841
Turner-Vision, Inc.	746	Bluefield, WV	Private	53.3	400	4841
Warner Cable Communication	747	Milwaukee, WI	Private	53.3	400	4841
Active Voice Corporation	748	Seattle, WA	Public	53.2	336	3661
VAI Corporation	749	San Jose, CA	Private	53.0	90	3661
Renaissance Communications	750	Chicago, IL	Public Family Member	52.5	476	4833
MCI Wireless, Inc.	751	Garden City, NY	Public Family Member	52.4	750	4812
Delta Products Corporation	752	Nogales, AZ	Private	52.2	900	3679
STM Wireless Inc.	753	Irvine, CA	Public	52.1	140	3663
M P D Technologies, Inc.	754	Hauppauge, NY	Public Family Member	52.0	335	3663
One Call Communications Inc.	755	Carmel, IN	Private	52.0	410	4813
Techsonic Industries Inc.	756	Eufaula, AL	Public Family Member	52.0	285	3679
Omnipoint Corporation	757	Bethesda, MD	Public	51.9	1,423	4812
Sport South Network, LTD	758	Atlanta, GA	Private	51.8	26	4841
Asante Technologies, Inc.	759	San Jose, CA	Public	51.4	190	3661
Mediaone Of Sierra Valleys	760	Stockton, CA	Public Family Member	51.2	385	4841
Apunet	761	Richardson, TX	Private	51.0	4	4813
Verilink Corporation	762	San Jose, CA	Public	50.9	250	3661
Cordillera Communications Inc.	763	Charleston, SC	Private	50.7	460	4833
Datek Online Holding Company	764	Iselin, NJ	Private	50.7	400	4813
Digex, Incorporated	765	Beltsville, MD	Public Family Member	50.7	400	4813
Level 3 Telecom Holdings, Inc.	766	Omaha, NE	Private	50.7	400	4813
Primetime 24 Joint Venture	767	New York, NY	Private	50.7	22	4899
Abracon Corporation	768	Aliso Viejo, CA	Private	50.0	75	3679
American Gateway Telecom	769	Houston, TX	Private	50.0	3	4813
Buckeye Cable Vision Inc.	770	Toledo, OH	Private	50.0	376	4841

D&B COMPANY RANKINGS BY SALES

Company	Rank	Location	Type	Sales ($ mil.)	Employment	Primary SIC
Communications Concepts Invest.	771	Pompano Beach, FL	Private	50.0	21	4813
Cooperative Communications	772	Belleville, NJ	Private	50.0	100	4813
G.I.K Technology, Inc.	773	Oakland, CA	Private	50.0	4	4813
Goldenline Network Service	774	Santa Monica, CA	Private	50.0	100	4813
Graphnet Inc.	775	Teaneck, NJ	Private	50.0	250	4822
Hub Fabricating Company	776	Reading, PA	Private	50.0	420	3661
Kelly Broadcasting Co A LTD Partnr	777	Sacramento, CA	Private	50.0	250	4833
Meridian Telecom Corp	778	Hartsdale, NY	Private	50.0	22	4813
National Mobile Television Inc.	779	Seattle, WA	Private	50.0	203	4833
Philips Broadband Networks	780	Manlius, NY	Private	50.0	1,000	3663
Prodelin Corporation	781	Conover, NC	Private	50.0	265	3663
SDI Technologies Inc.	782	Rahway, NJ	Private	50.0	138	3651
Senior Systems Technology Inc.	783	Palmdale, CA	Private	50.0	350	3679
Stratos Mobile Networks USA LLC	784	Bethesda, MD	Private	50.0	59	4899
Technology Control Services	785	Fort Lauderdale, FL	Private	50.0	80	4813
Transamerica Bus Tech Corporations	786	Los Angeles, CA	Public Family Member	50.0	160	4813
VXI Electronics, Inc.	787	Milwaukie, OR	Private	50.0	220	3679
Matanuska Telephone Assn.	788	Palmer, AK	Private	49.9	300	4813
Alltel New York Inc.	789	Jamestown, NY	Public Family Member	49.9	297	4813
Bogen Communications Intl	790	Ramsey, NJ	Private	49.8	196	3661
Harman Music Group Inc.	791	Sandy, UT	Public Family Member	49.7	450	3651
Pioneer Video Manufacturing	792	Carson, CA	Private	49.7	450	3651
Gulf Coast Services Inc.	793	Foley, AL	Private	49.6	365	4813
Diversified Communications	794	Portland, ME	Private	49.5	476	4833
Cylink Corporation	795	Sunnyvale, CA	Public	49.3	432	3663
G E Capital Comm Svcs Corp	796	Atlanta, GA	Public Family Member	49.1	200	4813
Eagle Comtronics Inc.	797	Clay, NY	Private	49.0	890	3663
Go-Video, Inc.	798	Scottsdale, AZ	Public	48.9	76	3651
ACI Communications Inc.	799	San Diego, CA	Private	48.8	385	4813
Caprock Communications Corp	800	Dallas, TX	Private	48.5	327	4813
Community TV Of S. California	801	Los Angeles, CA	Private	48.5	300	4833
Peco Ii Inc.	802	Galion, OH	Private	48.3	500	3661
Kidde-Fenwal Inc.	803	Ashland, MA	Private	48.2	550	3669
Davel Communications Group	804	Tampa, FL	Public	48.2	226	4813
Com21 Inc.	805	Milpitas, CA	Public	48.1	131	3663
1-800-Reconex, Inc.	806	Hubbard, OR	Private	48.1	125	4813
Midcontinent Cable Co.	807	Aberdeen, SD	Private	48.1	362	4841
At Home Corp	808	Redwood City, CA	Public	48.0	329	4813
Brittan Communications Intl	809	Houston, TX	Private	48.0	150	4813
Midwest Wireless Comm. LLC	810	Mankato, MN	Private	48.0	130	4812
Primo Microphones Inc.	811	Mc Kinney, TX	Private	48.0	120	3651
Weather Channel Inc.	812	Atlanta, GA	Private	47.9	360	4841
Corsair Communications Inc.	813	Palo Alto, CA	Public	47.8	132	3663
Retlaw Enterprises Inc.	814	North Hollywood, CA	Private	47.8	435	4833
Prime/Matrix Inc.	815	Calabasas, CA	Private	47.7	150	4812
Vodavi Technology, Inc.	816	Scottsdale, AZ	Public	47.7	173	3661
Long Distance Savers Inc.	817	Monroe, LA	Private	47.5	375	4813
Horry Telephone Cooperative	818	Conway, SC	Private	47.5	420	4813
Ebay, Inc.	819	San Jose, CA	Public	47.4	76	4813
Western Reserve Tele Co Inc.	820	Hudson, OH	Public Family Member	47.1	372	4813
Global Telesystems Group Inc.	821	Mc Lean, VA	Public	47.1	2,000	4813
Cnet Technology Corp	822	Milpitas, CA	Private	47.0	250	3661
Pent Products Inc.	823	Kendallville, IN	Private	47.0	365	3679
California Amplifier Inc.	824	Camarillo, CA	Public	46.9	348	3663
Cincinnati Electronics Corp	825	Mason, OH	Private	46.8	317	3663
Applied Innovation Inc.	826	Dublin, OH	Public	46.7	240	3661
Bresnan Communications LP	827	White Plains, NY	Private	46.5	350	4841
Disney Channel Inc.	828	Burbank, CA	Public Family Member	46.5	350	4841
H.C.C. Industries Inc.	829	Rosemead, CA	Private	46.4	800	3679
White Oak Semiconductor	830	Sandston, VA	Private	46.4	800	3679
Elcotel Inc.	831	Sarasota, FL	Public	46.3	360	3661
Light Technologies LLC	832	Spokane, WA	Private	46.0	264	4813
Tollgrade Communications, Inc.	833	Cheswick, PA	Public	45.4	205	3661
Relm Communications Inc.	834	Melbourne, FL	Public Family Member	45.4	229	3663
Clark David Company Inc.	835	Worcester, MA	Private	45.2	360	3663
Atlantic Cellular Company L P	836	Providence, RI	Private	45.1	160	4812
Copley Controls Corp	837	Westwood, MA	Private	45.0	200	3679
Datron/Transco, Inc.	838	Simi Valley, CA	Public Family Member	45.0	200	3663
Diversified Data Process. Consult.	839	Ferndale, MI	Private	45.0	200	4822
G S Communications Inc.	840	Frederick, MD	Private	45.0	221	4841

D&B COMPANY RANKINGS BY SALES

Company	Rank	Location	Type	Sales ($ mil.)	Employ-ment	Primary SIC
GN Netcom Inc.	841	Nashua, NH	Private	45.0	200	3661
Quincy Newspapers Inc.	842	Quincy, IL	Private	45.0	450	4833
R & E Associates, LLC	843	Natick, MA	Private	45.0	12	3663
Roscor Corporation	844	Mount Prospect, IL	Private	45.0	120	3663
TIW Systems, Inc.	845	Santa Clara, CA	Public Family Member	45.0	250	3669
U S Media Holdings, Inc.	846	New York, NY	Private	45.0	85	4833
Thermo Voltek Corp	847	Woburn, MA	Public	44.6	275	3679
GTE Intelligent Network Svcs Inc.	848	Irving, TX	Public Family Member	44.3	350	4813
North American Long Distance Corp	849	Pittsburgh, PA	Private	44.3	350	4813
American Mobile Satellite Corp	850	Reston, VA	Public	44.2	300	4899
Tulsa Cable Television, Inc.	851	Tulsa, OK	Public Family Member	44.1	332	4841
Americom Group	852	Luthrvil Timnium, MD	Private	44.0	325	4812
Central Kentucky Cellular	853	Richmond, KY	Public Family Member	44.0	145	4812
Gemini Sound Products Corp	854	Carteret, NJ	Private	44.0	100	3651
Metatec Corp	855	Dublin, OH	Private	43.9	756	3679
Unifi Communications Inc.	856	Lowell, MA	Private	43.9	615	4822
Evening Telegram Co Inc.	857	Superior, WI	Private	43.8	400	4833
Jones International LTD	858	Englewood, CO	Private	43.8	330	4841
Price Communications Corp	859	New York, NY	Public	43.7	169	4832
Netrix Corporation	860	Herndon, VA	Public	43.6	250	3679
TCI TKR Cable I Inc.	861	Miami, FL	Public Family Member	43.1	325	4841
Auto Club Cellular Corporation	862	Newtown, PA	Private	43.1	242	4812
Communications Telesystems Intl	863	San Diego, CA	Private	43.0	340	4813
Harvard Custom Manufacturing	864	Salisbury, MD	Private	43.0	425	3679
Universal Logic Technologies	865	Mansfield, OH	Private	43.0	200	4813
Window To The World Comm.	866	Chicago, IL	Private	43.0	300	4833
Wells-Gardner Electronics Corp	867	Chicago, IL	Public	43.0	190	3663
MJD Communications, Inc.	868	Charlotte, NC	Private	43.0	700	4813
Proxim Inc.	869	Mountain View, CA	Public	43.0	176	3663
Helicon Group, L.P.	870	Englewood Cliffs, NJ	Private	42.9	180	4841
Evercom, Inc.	871	Irving, TX	Private	42.9	339	4813
Cherokee Nation	872	Tahlequah, OK	Private	42.7	1,800	3679
Southwest Co Wireless, Inc.	873	Scottsdale, AZ	Public Family Member	42.7	610	4812
Adventist Media Center, Inc.	874	Simi Valley, CA	Private	42.6	150	4833
Gulf Telephone Company, Inc.	875	Foley, AL	Private	42.6	373	4813
Sony Trans Com Inc.	876	Irvine, CA	Private	42.6	500	3663
RRV Enterprises Inc.	877	Houston, TX	Private	42.5	100	4813
Fair-Rite Products Corp	878	Wallkill, NY	Private	42.2	500	3679
Cerwin-Vega Inc.	879	Simi Valley, CA	Private	42.1	420	3651
Nextel Of Texas Inc.	880	Austin, TX	Public Family Member	42.1	601	4812
Shared Communications Services	881	Salem, OR	Private	42.1	155	4813
American Cellular Comm. Corp	882	Atlanta, GA	Public Family Member	42.0	600	4812
Anaba Audio International Inc.	883	Compton, CA	Private	42.0	30	3651
Econolite Control Products	884	Anaheim, CA	Private	42.0	200	3669
Q Net Inc.	885	Teaneck, NJ	Private	42.0	200	4822
Sigcom Inc.	886	Greensboro, NC	Private	41.8	135	4813
Positive Communications Inc.	887	Pleasanton, CA	Private	41.4	270	4812
Netselect, Inc.	888	Westlake Village, CA	Private	41.1	325	4813
Value Tel	889	San Francisco, CA	Private	41.1	325	4813
S. Carolina Educational TV Comm	890	Columbia, SC	Private	41.0	337	4833
SMS Technologies Inc.	891	San Diego, CA	Private	41.0	197	3679
National Cable Satellite Corp	892	Washington, DC	Private	40.8	260	4841
Koss Corporation	893	Milwaukee, WI	Public	40.6	350	3651
Telular Corporation (Del)	894	Vernon Hills, IL	Public	40.4	665	3663
Distance Long International	895	Fort Lauderdale, FL	Private	40.1	279	4813
ABC Money Transactions, Inc.	896	Garland, TX	Private	40.0	30	4822
American Long Lines Inc.	897	Horsham, PA	Private	40.0	40	4813
Arvig Telcom Inc.	898	Madison, WI	Public Family Member	40.0	75	4813
Communigroup Of KC, Inc.	899	Shawnee Mission, KS	Private	40.0	115	4813
Emkay Communications Inc.	900	New York, NY	Private	40.0	12	4813
Harman Pro North America, Inc.	901	Nashville, TN	Public Family Member	40.0	42	3651
Hartford Television Inc.	902	Hartford, CT	Public Family Member	40.0	110	4833
Infinity Broadcasting Corp Cal Del	903	Los Angeles, CA	Public Family Member	40.0	80	4832
IXC, Inc.	904	Boca Raton, FL	Private	40.0	2	4813
Krautkramer Branson Inc.	905	Lewistown, PA	Public Family Member	40.0	252	3679
Multimedia KSDK Inc.	906	Saint Louis, MO	Public Family Member	40.0	220	4833
Paylexx Utilities & Telecommun	907	Long Island City, NY	Private	40.0	7	4813
Texas Television Inc.	908	Corpus Christi, TX	Private	40.0	84	4833
TMR Sales, Inc.	909	Sunnyvale, CA	Private	40.0	14	3679
Triathlon Broadcasting Company	910	San Diego, CA	Public	40.0	289	4832

D&B COMPANY RANKINGS BY SALES

Company	Rank	Location	Type	Sales ($ mil.)	Employ-ment	Primary SIC
U S Digitel Inc.	911	Hollywood, FL	Private	40.0	5	4813
WLVI, Inc.	912	Boston, MA	Public Family Member	40.0	125	4833
Sa Telecommunications, Inc.	913	Richardson, TX	Public	39.8	285	4813
Arkansas Democrat Gazette	914	Little Rock, AR	Private	39.8	300	4841
Chambers Communications Corp	915	Eugene, OR	Private	39.8	300	4841
Mediaone Of Virginia, Inc.	916	Richmond, VA	Public Family Member	39.8	300	4841
Orbital Imaging Corporation	917	Sterling, VA	Public Family Member	39.8	300	4841
Pacific Bell Video Services	918	San Ramon, CA	Private	39.8	300	4841
Satellink Communications Inc.	919	Roswell, GA	Private	39.7	57	4813
Standard Telephone Company	920	Cornelia, GA	Public Family Member	39.2	310	4813
Ward Products Corp	921	North Brunswick, NJ	Private	39.0	365	3679
WGNX Inc.	922	Atlanta, GA	Public Family Member	39.0	132	4833
Pittway International LTD	923	Chicago, IL	Public Family Member	38.9	444	3669
Iowa Network Services Inc.	924	West Des Moines, IA	Private	38.8	114	4813
Uunet Worldcom, Inc.	925	Fairfax, VA	Public Family Member	38.7	306	4813
Amerix Electronic Inc.	926	El Segundo, CA	Private	38.4	8	3679
Mitek Corporation	927	Phoenix, AZ	Private	38.3	350	3651
T-Netix, Inc.	928	Englewood, CO	Public	38.2	198	4813
Entertainment Inc.	929	Hartford, CT	Public	38.1	864	4841
American Holdings LP	930	Spokane, WA	Private	38.0	150	4841
Cablevision Lightpath Inc.	931	Hicksville, NY	Public Family Member	38.0	100	4841
CNBC, Inc.	932	Fort Lee, NJ	Public Family Member	38.0	350	4833
TCI Cablevision Of Wisconsin	933	Madison, WI	Public Family Member	38.0	250	4841
Cincinnati Bell Long Distance	934	Cincinnati, OH	Public Family Member	37.9	300	4813
Cohesive Technology Solutions	935	Palo Alto, CA	Private	37.9	300	4813
Sugar Land Telephone Company	936	Sugar Land, TX	Public Family Member	37.9	300	4813
Transcall America Inc.	937	Jackson, MS	Public Family Member	37.9	300	4813
Worldcom Inc.	938	Montgomery, AL	Public Family Member	37.9	300	4813
Northland Telecom Corp	939	Seattle, WA	Private	37.8	456	4841
Wheelock Inc.	940	Long Branch, NJ	Private	37.8	350	3669
Farmers Telephone Cooperative	941	Kingstree, SC	Private	37.6	270	4813
DBT Online, Inc.	942	Las Vegas, NV	Public	37.5	98	4813
Anaren Microwave Inc.	943	East Syracuse, NY	Public	37.4	285	3679
Conquest Telecom Svcs	944	Dublin, OH	Public Family Member	37.4	296	4813
Outlet Communications Inc.	945	Cranston, RI	Public Family Member	37.4	345	4833
ADC Broadband Communications	946	Meriden, CT	Public Family Member	37.3	390	3661
Osborn Communications Corp	947	Tucker, GA	Public Family Member	37.2	543	4832
Eminence Speaker Corporation	948	Eminence, KY	Private	37.0	225	3651
Eurotherm Drives Inc.	949	Charlotte, NC	Private	37.0	106	3679
Infinity Wireless Products	950	Chicago, IL	Private	37.0	350	3661
K & L Microwave Inc.	951	Salisbury, MD	Public Family Member	37.0	500	3679
Horizon Telecom Inc.	952	Chillicothe, OH	Private	37.0	517	4813
Radio One Inc.	953	Lanham, MD	Private	37.0	250	4832
Xpedite Systems Inc.	954	Eatontown, NJ	Public Family Member	36.9	720	4822
SSE Telecom Inc.	955	Fremont, CA	Public	36.7	460	3663
Nortech Systems Incorporated	956	Bemidji, MN	Public	36.4	537	3679
KBL Portland Cablesystems LP	957	Portland, OR	Private	36.4	275	4841
Telemedia International USA	958	Jersey City, NJ	Private	36.4	150	4813
Chorus Communications Group	959	Middleton, WI	Private	36.3	240	4813
Prime Sports Channel Network LP	960	Woodbury, NY	Private	36.3	266	4841
Telscape International Inc.	961	Houston, TX	Public	36.2	400	4813
Innova Corporation	962	Seattle, WA	Public	36.1	138	3679
KQED Inc.	963	San Francisco, CA	Private	36.0	170	4833
Antronix Inc.	964	Cranbury, NJ	Private	36.0	600	3663
Choctaw Communications, Inc.	965	Houston, TX	Private	36.0	100	4813
M C L, Inc.	966	Bolingbrook, IL	Private	36.0	165	3663
Preferred Networks Inc.	967	Norcross, GA	Public	36.0	373	4812
Teletouch Communications, Inc.	968	Tyler, TX	Public	35.8	337	4812
Post-Newsweek Stations FLA Inc.	969	Hartford, CT	Private	35.7	330	4833
Touch 1 Communications Inc.	970	Atmore, AL	Private	35.7	415	4813
Intek Global Corporation	971	New York, NY	Public	35.7	375	3663
Eastern Acoustic Works, Inc.	972	Whitinsville, MA	Private	35.3	212	3651
The Chillicothe Telephone Co.	973	Chillicothe, OH	Private	35.1	175	4813
EDS Personal Communications Corp	974	Waltham, MA	Public Family Member	35.1	500	4812
Florida RSA 8 Inc.	975	Chicago, IL	Public Family Member	35.1	500	4812
Houston Cellular Telephone Co.	976	Houston, TX	Private	35.1	500	4812
Digitec 2000 Inc.	977	New York, NY	Private	35.0	75	4813
Datel Inc.	978	Mansfield, MA	Private	35.0	450	3679
Encore Media Corporation	979	Englewood, CO	Public Family Member	35.0	265	4841
Exodus Communications, Inc.	980	Santa Clara, CA	Public	35.0	345	4813

D&B COMPANY RANKINGS BY SALES

Company	Rank	Location	Type	Sales ($ mil.)	Employ-ment	Primary SIC
Gardiner Communications Corp	981	Garland, TX	Private	35.0	200	3663
Jacor Broadcasting Of Tampa Bay	982	Tampa, FL	Public Family Member	35.0	380	4832
KTNQ/KLVE, Inc (Not Inc)	983	Los Angeles, CA	Public Family Member	35.0	100	4832
Mc Cain Traffic Supply Inc.	984	Vista, CA	Private	35.0	350	3669
Microelectronic Modules Corp	985	New Berlin, WI	Private	35.0	320	3679
NTX, Inc.	986	Napa, CA	Public Family Member	35.0	90	4813
Snap LLC	987	San Francisco, CA	Private	35.0	200	4813
TCI Of Overland Park, Inc.	988	Shawnee Mission, KS	Public Family Member	35.0	179	4841
WPGH, Inc.	989	Pittsburgh, PA	Public Family Member	35.0	100	4833
Minnesota Equal Access	990	Minneapolis, MN	Private	34.7	145	4813
Teltronics Inc.	991	Sarasota, FL	Public	34.7	210	3661
Krone Inc.	992	Englewood, CO	Private	34.7	140	3661
Infoseek Corporation	993	Sunnyvale, CA	Public	34.6	180	4813
Wireless One, Inc.	994	Jackson, MS	Public	34.6	500	4841
Nortell Northern Telecom Corp	995	Simi Valley, CA	Private	34.4	393	3669
TCI TKR Of South Florida, Inc.	996	Miami, FL	Private	34.4	260	4841
Express Manufacturing, Inc.	997	Santa Ana, CA	Private	34.2	590	3679
Bee Tronics Inc.	998	San Diego, CA	Private	34.1	400	3663
Continental Electronics Corp	999	Dallas, TX	Public Family Member	34.1	300	3663
Robin Media Group Inc.	1000	San Francisco, CA	Private	34.1	200	4841
Aliant Systems Inc.	1001	Lincoln, NE	Public Family Member	34.0	165	4813
Discount Long Distance Inc.	1002	Santa Ana, CA	Private	34.0	270	4813
R F Power Products, Inc.	1003	Voorhees, NJ	Public	33.8	160	3679
Planar Standish	1004	Lake Mills, WI	Public Family Member	33.8	316	3679
Century Telephone Of Wisconsin	1005	La Crosse, WI	Public Family Member	33.8	180	4813
Rock Hill Telephone Company	1006	Rock Hill, SC	Private	33.7	302	4813
Trans World Radio	1007	Cary, NC	Private	33.7	100	4832
C-Net, Inc.	1008	San Francisco, CA	Public	33.6	581	4841
National Dispatch Center Inc.	1009	San Diego, CA	Private	33.5	1,000	4813
Highwaymaster Communications	1010	Richardson, TX	Private	33.4	425	4812
Time Warner Cable Programming	1011	Stamford, CT	Public Family Member	33.4	192	4841
Techdyne Inc.	1012	Hialeah, FL	Public	33.2	470	3679
Eglobe Inc.	1013	Denver, CO	Public	33.1	166	4813
Axiom Inc.	1014	Mount Laurel, NJ	Public	33.0	196	3669
Nassau Broadcasting Partners LP	1015	Princeton, NJ	Private	33.0	295	4832
TGC Inc	1016	Orlando, FL	Private	33.0	250	4841
United Cable Television	1017	Baltimore, MD	Private	33.0	250	4841
Ben M Jacoby	1018	Houston, TX	Private	32.8	260	4813
Recoton Audio Corporation	1019	Lake Mary, FL	Public Family Member	32.7	300	3651
Western Union International	1020	Piscataway, NJ	Public Family Member	32.7	638	4822
Courtroom TV Network LLC	1021	New York, NY	Private	32.3	300	4833
WHDH, TV, Inc.	1022	Boston, MA	Private	32.3	300	4833
TAL Financial Corporation	1023	Tyler, TX	Public Family Member	32.3	900	4841
Echelon Corporation	1024	Palo Alto, CA	Public	32.2	150	3663
Elcom, Inc.	1025	El Paso, TX	Private	32.2	555	3679
KOIN-TV Inc.	1026	Portland, OR	Public Family Member	32.0	205	4833
Superior Modular Products Inc.	1027	Swannanoa, NC	Private	32.0	325	3663
TCI Cablevision Of California	1028	Redlands, CA	Public Family Member	32.0	200	4841
Souris River Telecom Coop	1029	Minot, ND	Private	31.6	200	4813
Calltask, Incorporated	1030	Atlanta, GA	Public Family Member	31.5	250	4813
Globalstar, L. P.	1031	San Jose, CA	Private	31.5	250	4813
Sprint Telecenters Inc.	1032	Maitland, FL	Public Family Member	31.5	250	4813
Worldcom Wireless, Inc.	1033	Hayward, CA	Public Family Member	31.5	250	4813
Georgia Public Telecom Comm	1034	Atlanta, GA	Private	31.5	145	4832
Todd Products Corp	1035	Brentwood, NY	Private	31.4	500	3679
Wisconsin Educational Comm Bd	1036	Madison, WI	Private	31.3	390	4832
Best Internet Inc.	1037	Boca Raton, FL	Public Family Member	31.2	248	4813
Microcom Inc.	1038	Norwood, MA	Public Family Member	31.1	325	3661
Fargo Assembly Of PA Inc.	1039	Norristown, PA	Private	31.0	430	3679
TCI Of Lexington, Inc.	1040	Lexington, KY	Public Family Member	31.0	160	4841
Convergent Media Systems Corp	1041	Atlanta, GA	Private	30.9	288	4833
Omnes	1042	Houston, TX	Private	30.8	245	4813
Nuera Communications, Inc.	1043	San Diego, CA	Private	30.8	144	3661
Fire-Lite Alarms, Inc.	1044	Northford, CT	Public Family Member	30.7	350	3669
K-Tec Electronics Corporation	1045	Sugar Land, TX	Public Family Member	30.7	529	3679
Spectronics Corp	1046	Atlanta, GA	Private	30.7	244	4813
Cambridge Soundworks Inc.	1047	Newton, MA	Private	30.4	280	3651
Telenoticias LLC	1048	Hialeah, FL	Private	30.4	200	4841
Colorado Springs Cablevision	1049	Colorado Springs, CO	Public Family Member	30.3	230	4841
TWC Cable Partners LP	1050	Staten Island, NY	Private	30.3	230	4841

D&B COMPANY RANKINGS BY SALES

Company	Rank	Location	Type	Sales ($ mil.)	Employ-ment	Primary SIC
WFAA-TV Inc.	1051	Dallas, TX	Public Family Member	30.3	283	4833
Operator Service Company	1052	Lubbock, TX	Private	30.2	350	4813
East Ascension Telephone Co.	1053	Gonzales, LA	Private	30.0	150	4813
Advanced Circuit Technology	1054	Nashua, NH	Public Family Member	30.0	270	3679
Alteon Networks Inc.	1055	San Jose, CA	Private	30.0	125	3663
Cuming Corp	1056	Avon, MA	Private	30.0	110	3679
ETO Inc.	1057	Colorado Springs, CO	Public Family Member	30.0	160	3663
Gannett Tennessee LTD Partnr	1058	Knoxville, TN	Public Family Member	30.0	130	4833
Koplar Communications Inc.	1059	Saint Louis, MO	Private	30.0	100	4833
Nextlink Pennsylvania LP	1060	Reading, PA	Private	30.0	190	4813
Plant Equipment Inc.	1061	Temecula, CA	Private	30.0	250	3661
Shared Tech Communications LLC	1062	Hartford, CT	Private	30.0	100	4813
Vista Information Technologies	1063	Herndon, VA	Private	30.0	1,300	4813

D&B COMPANY RANKINGS BY EMPLOYMENT

Company	Rank	Location	Type	Sales ($ mil.)	Employ-ment	Primary SIC
Motorola Inc.	1	Schaumburg, IL	Public	29,794.0	149,800	3663
Lucent Technologies Inc.	2	New Providence, NJ	Public	30,147.0	141,600	3661
Bell Atlantic Corporation	3	New York, NY	Public	30,193.9	141,000	4813
AT&T Corp	4	New York, NY	Public	53,223.0	118,900	4813
SBC Communications Inc.	5	San Antonio, TX	Public	24,856.0	118,340	4813
Viacom Inc.	6	New York, NY	Public	13,206.1	116,700	4841
GTE Corporation	7	Irving, TX	Public	23,260.0	114,000	4813
BellSouth Corporation	8	Atlanta, GA	Public	23,123.0	81,000	4813
MCI Worldcom Inc.	9	Jackson, MS	Public	30,000.0	75,000	4813
Ameritech Corporation	10	Chicago, IL	Public	15,998.0	74,359	4813
NYNEX Corporation	11	New York, NY	Public Family Member	8,752.1	68,100	4813
MCI Communications Corporation	12	Washington, DC	Public Family Member	7,711.0	60,000	4813
BellSouth Telecommunications	13	Atlanta, GA	Public Family Member	16,622.0	59,100	4813
U S West Inc.	14	Denver, CO	Private	12,378.0	54,483	4813
CBS Corporation	15	Pittsburgh, PA	Public	5,363.0	51,444	4833
Sprint Corporation	16	Shawnee Mission, KS	Public	14,873.9	51,000	4813
Southwestern Bell Tele Co.	17	Saint Louis, MO	Public Family Member	10,313.0	50,500	4813
Pacific Telesis Group	18	San Antonio, TX	Public Family Member	6,438.6	50,100	4813
Pacific Bell	19	San Francisco, CA	Public Family Member	9,938.0	50,030	4813
U S West Communications Group	20	Denver, CO	Private	10,319.0	50,000	4812
U S West Communications, Inc.	21	Denver, CO	Private	10,083.0	45,000	4813
New York Telephone Company	22	New York, NY	Public Family Member	7,957.3	38,600	4813
TCI Communications, Inc.	23	Englewood, CO	Public	6,166.7	36,000	4841
Tele-Communications, Inc.	24	Englewood, CO	Public	7,570.0	32,000	4841
Harris Corporation	25	Melbourne, FL	Public	3,890.2	28,500	3663
Sony Electronics Inc.	26	Park Ridge, NJ	Private	2,949.7	26,000	3651
ABC Inc	27	New York, NY	Public Family Member	2,554.2	22,200	4833
US Telecom Inc.	28	Shawnee Mission, KS	Public Family Member	2,827.0	22,000	4813
Northern Telecom Inc Del	29	Nashville, TN	Private	2,011.2	21,000	3661
Philips Electronics North America	30	New York, NY	Private	7,495.0	21,000	3651
Cincinnati Bell Inc.	31	Cincinnati, OH	Public	1,756.8	20,800	4813
Alltel Corporation	32	Little Rock, AR	Public	5,194.0	20,000	4813
Philips Holding U.S.A., Inc.	33	New York, NY	Private	2,268.7	20,000	3651
New England Tele & Telegraph Co.	34	Boston, MA	Public Family Member	4,565.7	18,500	4813
Read-Rite Corporation	35	Milpitas, CA	Public	808.6	18,000	3679
Sprint Communications Co LP	36	Kansas City, MO	Private	9,000.0	18,000	4813
Raytheon E-Systems, Inc.	37	Garland, TX	Public Family Member	1,401.4	16,400	3663
Mediaone Group, Inc.	38	Englewood, CO	Public	2,419.0	16,350	4841
United Artists Entertainment Co.	39	Englewood, CO	Public Family Member	1,177.8	16,000	4841
Illinois Bell Telephone Co.	40	Chicago, IL	Public Family Member	3,808.2	14,929	4813
Technitrol Inc.	41	Langhorne, PA	Public	397.1	14,400	3679
Hughes Electronics Corporation	42	Los Angeles, CA	Public Family Member	5,128.3	14,000	3663
ITT Defense & Electronics	43	Mc Lean, VA	Public Family Member	812.9	14,000	3679
AT&T Wireless Services Inc.	44	Kirkland, WA	Public Family Member	4,330.0	13,000	4812
Bell Atlantic-New Jersey, Inc.	45	Newark, NJ	Public Family Member	3,753.9	12,500	4813
Bell Atlantic-Pennsylvania	46	Philadelphia, PA	Public Family Member	3,320.5	12,500	4813
Michigan Bell Telephone Co.	47	Detroit, MI	Public	3,384.8	12,249	4813
BellSouth Cellular Corp	48	Atlanta, GA	Public Family Member	805.3	11,604	4812
Qualcomm, Incorporated	49	San Diego, CA	Public	3,347.9	11,600	3663
Zenith Electronics Corporation	50	Glenview, IL	Public	1,173.1	11,400	3651
Harman International Industries Inc.	51	Washington, DC	Public	1,513.3	10,010	3651
Southern Neng Telecom Corp	52	New Haven, CT	Private	1,264.2	9,841	4813
Telephone And Data Systems	53	Chicago, IL	Public	1,471.5	9,685	4812
Centel Corporation	54	Shawnee Mission, KS	Public Family Member	1,194.6	9,300	4813
GTE Mobile Communications Inc.	55	Atlanta, GA	Public Family Member	2,549.0	9,000	4812
Airtouch Communications	56	San Francisco, CA	Public	3,594.0	8,800	4812
Bell Atlantic Network Services	57	Arlington, VA	Public Family Member	2,000.0	8,539	4813
America Online Inc.	58	Sterling, VA	Public	2,600.0	8,500	4813
The Ohio Bell Telephone Co.	59	Cleveland, OH	Public Family Member	2,339.9	8,419	4813
Hutchinson Technology Inc.	60	Hutchinson, MN	Public	407.6	8,293	3679
ADC Telecommunications, Inc.	61	Hopkins, MN	Public	1,379.7	8,000	3661
American Broadcasting Companies	62	New York, NY	Public Family Member	4,142.0	8,000	4833
Ericsson Inc.	63	Richardson, TX	Private	3,038.4	8,000	3663
Cablevision Systems Corp	64	Bethpage, NY	Private	1,075.6	7,969	4841
CSC Holdings, Inc.	65	Woodbury, NY	Public	1,949.4	7,969	4841
Pittway Corporation	66	Chicago, IL	Public	1,348.7	7,800	3669
Dover Technologies Intl	67	Binghamton, NY	Public Family Member	435.4	7,500	3679
Hughes Space Communications Co.	68	El Segundo, CA	Public Family Member	640.8	7,500	3663
Toshiba America Inc.	69	New York, NY	Private	6,095.7	7,500	3651
Frontier Corporation	70	Rochester, NY	Public	2,352.9	7,444	4813

D&B COMPANY RANKINGS BY EMPLOYMENT

Company	Rank	Location	Type	Sales ($ mil.)	Employ-ment	Primary SIC
General Instrument Corporation	71	Horsham, PA	Public	1,764.1	7,350	3663
Cox Communications Inc.	72	Atlanta, GA	Public	1,460.3	7,200	4841
AlliedSignal Technical Svcs	73	Columbia, MD	Public Family Member	852.2	7,000	4899
Bell Atlantic-Maryland, Inc.	74	Baltimore, MD	Public Family Member	2,047.9	7,000	4813
Century Telephone Enterprises	75	Monroe, LA	Public	901.5	7,000	4813
Contel Federal Systems Inc.	76	Needham, MA	Public Family Member	1,200.0	7,000	3661
GTE Government Systems Corp	77	Needham, MA	Public Family Member	1,300.0	7,000	3661
Nextel Communications, Inc.	78	Mc Lean, VA	Public	738.9	7,000	4812
Turner Broadcasting System	79	Atlanta, GA	Public Family Member	803.8	7,000	4833
Artesyn Technologies Inc.	80	Boca Raton, FL	Public	527.2	6,900	3679
Qwest Communications Intl	81	Denver, CO	Public	696.7	6,900	4813
The Southern Neng Tele Co.	82	New Haven, CT	Private	872.2	6,791	4813
Alcatel USA, Inc.	83	Plano, TX	Private	639.9	6,681	3661
Bell Atlantic Enterprises Intl	84	Philadelphia, PA	Public Family Member	834.8	6,500	4813
Bell Atlantic-Virginia, Inc.	85	Richmond, VA	Public Family Member	2,071.1	6,500	4813
CBS Broadcasting Inc.	86	New York, NY	Public Family Member	734.7	6,400	4833
DII Group, Inc.	87	Longmont, CO	Public	779.6	6,350	3679
GTI Corporation	88	San Diego, CA	Public Family Member	82.6	6,280	3679
L-3 Communications Corporation	89	New York, NY	Public Family Member	705.4	6,100	3663
Siemens Info & Comm Network Inc.	90	Boca Raton, FL	Private	565.1	5,900	3661
Scientific-Atlanta Inc.	91	Norcross, GA	Public	1,181.4	5,736	3663
Citizens Utilities Company	92	Stamford, CT	Public	1,393.6	5,400	4813
Clear Channel Communications	93	San Antonio, TX	Public	697.1	5,400	4832
Sprint-Florida, Incorporated	94	Apopka, FL	Public Family Member	1,241.3	5,300	4813
Adflex Solutions, Inc.	95	Chandler, AZ	Public	213.9	5,254	3679
BBS Holdings, Inc.	96	Atlanta, GA	Public Family Member	673.6	5,246	4813
Reltec Communications Inc.	97	Cleveland, OH	Public Family Member	887.2	5,200	3661
Alcatel Network Systems, Inc.	98	Richardson, TX	Private	1,500.0	5,000	3661
National Broadcasting Co Inc.	99	New York, NY	Public Family Member	5,153.0	5,000	4833
Williams International Co.	100	Tulsa, OK	Public Family Member	642.0	5,000	4813
McLeod USA Incorporated	101	Cedar Rapids, IA	Public	267.9	4,941	4813
Southwestern Bell Mobile Systems	102	Dallas, TX	Public Family Member	334.0	4,810	4812
ITT Federal Services Corp	103	Colorado Springs, CO	Public Family Member	293.4	4,800	4899
Applied Magnetics Corporation	104	Goleta, CA	Public	183.6	4,700	3679
Mississippi Band Choctaw Indians	105	Philadelphia, MS	Private	261.3	4,500	3679
Paging Network Inc.	106	Dallas, TX	Public	961.0	4,500	4812
360 Communications Company	107	Chicago, IL	Public Family Member	305.6	4,400	4812
Ameritech Mobile Communications	108	Hoffman Estates, IL	Public Family Member	200.0	4,400	4812
Stoneridge, Inc.	109	Warren, OH	Public	449.5	4,400	3679
Chancellor Media Corporation	110	Dallas, TX	Public	582.1	4,300	4832
Jacor Communications Inc.	111	Covington, KY	Public	530.6	4,300	4832
TCI West, Inc.	112	Bellevue, WA	Public Family Member	827.1	4,250	4841
Century Communications Corp	113	New Canaan, CT	Public	484.7	4,211	4841
Pacificorp Holdings, Inc.	114	Portland, OR	Public Family Member	1,333.0	4,160	4813
Tellabs Inc.	115	Lisle, IL	Public	1,203.5	4,087	3661
Wisconsin Bell Inc.	116	Milwaukee, WI	Public Family Member	1,220.5	4,080	4813
AT&T Communications Of NJ	117	Basking Ridge, NJ	Public Family Member	514.0	4,004	4813
Indiana Bell Telephone Co Inc.	118	Indianapolis, IN	Public Family Member	1,299.9	4,002	4813
Bose Corporation	119	Framingham, MA	Private	850.0	4,000	3651
Capstar Broadcasting Corp	120	Austin, TX	Public	352.0	4,000	4832
Motorola Messaging Info Media	121	Boynton Beach, FL	Public Family Member	341.7	4,000	3663
LCI International Inc.	122	Arlington, VA	Public Family Member	500.6	3,900	4813
Adelphia Communications Corp	123	Coudersport, PA	Public	528.4	3,895	4841
Level 3 Communications, Inc.	124	Broomfield, CO	Private	332.0	3,600	4813
Cincinnati Bell Telephone Co.	125	Cincinnati, OH	Public Family Member	670.1	3,500	4813
New Par	126	Dublin, OH	Private	243.1	3,500	4812
Primeco Per Communications LP	127	Roanoke, TX	Private	243.1	3,500	4812
Mobilemedia Corporation	128	Fort Lee, NJ	Public	240.0	3,455	4812
Allen Telecom Inc.	129	Cleveland, OH	Public	432.5	3,300	3663
Lockheed Martin Tech Oper	130	Sunnyvale, CA	Public Family Member	300.0	3,300	4899
Loral Space & Communications	131	New York, NY	Public	1,312.6	3,300	3663
Telex Communications Inc.	132	Minneapolis, MN	Public Family Member	355.0	3,300	3663
Andrew Corporation	133	Orland Park, IL	Public	852.9	3,261	3663
Western Wireless Corporation	134	Issaquah, WA	Public	380.6	3,210	4812
Hearst-Argyle Television Inc.	135	New York, NY	Public	128.5	3,200	4833
United Telephone Co Of Indiana	136	Mansfield, OH	Public Family Member	180.5	3,159	4813
First Alert Inc.	137	Aurora, IL	Public Family Member	186.9	3,142	3669
Liberty Corporation	138	Greenville, SC	Public	107.4	3,100	4833
Jones Intercable Inc.	139	Englewood, CO	Public	460.7	3,060	4841
BellSouth Mobility Inc.	140	Atlanta, GA	Public Family Member	208.5	3,000	4812

D&B COMPANY RANKINGS BY EMPLOYMENT

Company	Rank	Location	Type	Sales ($ mil.)	Employ- ment	Primary SIC
Excel Communications, Inc.	141	Dallas, TX	Public	1,454.4	3,000	4813
General Semiconductor Inc.	142	Melville, NY	Public	361.9	3,000	3679
Global One Communications LLC	143	Reston, VA	Public Family Member	365.3	3,000	4899
Motorola Cellular Service Inc.	144	Libertyville, IL	Public Family Member	72.1	3,000	4812
Space Systems/Loral Inc.	145	Palo Alto, CA	Public Family Member	1,442.6	3,000	3663
Westec Security Group Inc.	146	Newport Beach, CA	Private	263.5	3,000	3669
ICG Communications Inc.	147	Englewood, CO	Public	381.1	2,970	4813
Octel Communications Corp	148	Milpitas, CA	Public Family Member	277.7	2,900	3661
Artesyn North America Inc.	149	Eden Prairie, MN	Public Family Member	228.2	2,848	3679
Arch Communications Group Inc.	150	Westborough, MA	Public	396.8	2,800	4812
JPM Company (Inc)	151	Lewisburg, PA	Public	128.4	2,800	3679
Comsat Corporation	152	Bethesda, MD	Public	562.7	2,732	4899
Airtouch Cellular	153	Walnut Creek, CA	Public Family Member	187.7	2,700	4812
Charter Communications, Inc.	154	Saint Louis, MO	Private	363.9	2,700	4841
Williams Fire Protection Inc.	155	Wilmington, DE	Private	237.1	2,700	3669
Nextel West Corp	156	Bellevue, WA	Public Family Member	181.8	2,616	4812
Kyushu Matsushita Elc Corp Am	157	National City, CA	Private	155.0	2,600	3663
Intermedia Communications Inc.	158	Tampa, FL	Public	247.9	2,575	4813
Meredith Corporation	159	Des Moines, IA	Public	1,009.9	2,559	4833
Citizens Communications	160	Stamford, CT	Public Family Member	320.7	2,500	4813
ITC Holding Company, Inc.	161	West Point, GA	Private	320.7	2,500	4813
NEC America Inc.	162	Melville, NY	Private	928.2	2,500	3661
Recoton Corp	163	Lake Mary, FL	Public	502.0	2,500	3651
United Telephone Co Of Ohio	164	Mansfield, OH	Public Family Member	469.6	2,407	4813
AG Communication Systems Corp	165	Phoenix, AZ	Public Family Member	442.3	2,400	3661
McLeod USA Telecommunications	166	Cedar Rapids, IA	Public Family Member	307.8	2,400	4813
Peavey Electronics Corporation	167	Meridian, MS	Private	271.0	2,400	3651
Tech-Sym Corporation	168	Houston, TX	Public	294.1	2,398	3663
Pagemart Wireless, Inc.	169	Dallas, TX	Public	277.8	2,335	4812
Cable & Wireless, Inc.	170	Vienna, VA	Private	948.6	2,300	4813
Mediaone Of Los Angeles, Inc.	171	El Segundo, CA	Public Family Member	309.9	2,300	4841
Skytel Communications Inc.	172	Jackson, MS	Public	408.0	2,300	4812
Metrocall, Inc.	173	Alexandria, VA	Public	289.4	2,261	4812
Deseret Management Corporation	174	Salt Lake City, UT	Private	186.2	2,248	4832
ICG Holdings, Inc.	175	Englewood, CO	Public Family Member	395.0	2,219	4813
Cable News Network Inc.	176	Atlanta, GA	Public Family Member	296.4	2,200	4841
Premiere Technologies, Inc.	177	Atlanta, GA	Public	395.5	2,200	4813
Central Telephone Co Of Illinois	178	Mansfield, OH	Public Family Member	280.6	2,188	4813
Matsus Electric Comp On Corp Ame	179	Knoxville, TN	Private	165.4	2,180	3651
BRK Brands, Inc.	180	Aurora, IL	Public Family Member	186.9	2,125	3669
Boeing Corinth Company	181	Lake Dallas, TX	Public Family Member	121.9	2,100	3679
Fujitsu Network Communications	182	Richardson, TX	Private	1,017.5	2,100	3661
Winstar Communications Inc.	183	New York, NY	Public	79.6	2,100	4813
Astec America Inc.	184	Carlsbad, CA	Private	357.0	2,000	3679
C & K Systems Inc.	185	Folsom, CA	Private	126.0	2,000	3669
Echostar Communications Corp	186	Littleton, CO	Public	477.4	2,000	4841
Global Telesystems Group Inc.	187	Mc Lean, VA	Public	47.1	2,000	4813
Heritage Cablevision, (Ia)	188	Des Moines, IA	Public Family Member	269.4	2,000	4841
Heritage Communications Inc.	189	Englewood, CO	Public Family Member	426.7	2,000	4841
Raycom Media Inc.	190	Montgomery, AL	Private	330.0	2,000	4833
TCI Holdings, Inc.	191	Englewood, CO	Public Family Member	1,496.9	2,000	4841
Toshiba America Electronic Comp.	192	Irvine, CA	Private	116.1	2,000	3679
Vanguard Cellular Systems Inc.	193	Greensboro, NC	Public	374.5	2,000	4812
Glenayre Technologies Inc.	194	Charlotte, NC	Public	451.7	1,900	3663
TCA Cable TV Inc.	195	Tyler, TX	Public	385.7	1,900	4841
TWI Cable Inc.	196	New York, NY	Public Family Member	910.3	1,900	4841
United Telephone Co Of Kansas	197	Shawnee Mission, KS	Public Family Member	74.9	1,900	4813
Antec Corporation (Del)	198	Norcross, GA	Public	480.1	1,893	3663
Advanced Communications Systems	199	Fairfax, VA	Public	107.8	1,850	4899
Plantronics Inc.	200	Santa Cruz, CA	Public	236.1	1,817	3661
Marcus Cable Company LLC	201	Dallas, TX	Private	479.3	1,801	4841
Cable Systems Intl Inc.	202	Phoenix, AZ	Private	400.0	1,800	3661
Cherokee Nation	203	Tahlequah, OK	Private	42.7	1,800	3679
Lenfest Communications Inc.	204	Oaks, PA	Private	62.8	1,800	4841
Scripps Howard Broadcasting Co.	205	Cincinnati, OH	Public Family Member	500.0	1,800	4833
SLC Technologies Inc.	206	Tualatin, OR	Private	105.3	1,800	3669
Kearney-National Inc.	207	White Plains, NY	Private	200.0	1,780	3679
Power-One Inc.	208	Camarillo, CA	Public	91.6	1,704	3679
General Datacomm Inc.	209	Middlebury, CT	Public Family Member	162.8	1,700	3661
ICG Telecom Group Inc.	210	Englewood, CO	Public Family Member	217.8	1,700	4813

D&B COMPANY RANKINGS BY EMPLOYMENT

Company	Rank	Location	Type	Sales ($ mil.)	Employ-ment	Primary SIC
Packard-Hughes Interconnect Co.	211	Irvine, CA	Public Family Member	98.7	1,700	3679
Tribune Broadcasting Company	212	Chicago, IL	Public Family Member	877.0	1,700	4833
United Telephone Co Of PA Inc.	213	Carlisle, PA	Public Family Member	259.4	1,683	4813
Osicom Technologies Inc.	214	Santa Monica, CA	Public	119.0	1,677	3661
United States Cellular Corp	215	Chicago, IL	Public	877.0	1,675	4812
Newbridge Networks Inc.	216	Herndon, VA	Private	276.6	1,650	3661
Milgo Solutions	217	Fort Lauderdale, FL	Private	157.7	1,647	3661
Centennial Cellular Corp	218	Neptune, NJ	Public	237.5	1,632	4812
GTE Wireless Of Midwest Inc.	219	Cleveland, OH	Public Family Member	111.4	1,600	4812
K Systems Inc.	220	Foster City, CA	Private	259.2	1,600	3679
MCI International Inc.	221	Port Chester, NY	Public Family Member	205.0	1,600	4813
Staveley Inc.	222	White Plains, NY	Private	91.0	1,568	3679
Nextel South Corp	223	Norcross, GA	Public Family Member	108.2	1,555	4812
Los Angeles Cellular Tele Co.	224	Cerritos, CA	Private	198.6	1,550	4813
California Microwave Inc.	225	Sunnyvale, CA	Public	269.2	1,528	3663
GST Telecommunications Inc.	226	Vancouver, WA	Public	194.7	1,520	4813
ESPN Inc.	227	Bristol, CT	Public Family Member	202.6	1,506	4841
Harmon Industries Inc.	228	Blue Springs, MO	Public	213.5	1,504	3669
Atlantic-Washington Bell DC	229	Washington, DC	Public Family Member	611.2	1,500	4813
Computer Science Raytheon	230	Cocoa, FL	Private	100.0	1,500	4899
Consolidated Communication	231	Mattoon, IL	Public Family Member	192.1	1,500	4813
Discovery Communications Inc.	232	Bethesda, MD	Private	201.8	1,500	4841
Lambda Holdings Inc.	233	Melville, NY	Private	87.1	1,500	3679
LG Electronics Alabama, Inc.	234	Huntsville, AL	Private	398.5	1,500	3651
Nextlink Communications, Inc.	235	Bellevue, WA	Public	57.6	1,500	4813
Prodelin Holding Corporation	236	Conover, NC	Private	128.1	1,500	3663
Telco Communications Group	237	Chantilly, VA	Public Family Member	192.1	1,500	4813
Titan Corporation	238	San Diego, CA	Public	171.2	1,500	3663
TSR Wireless LLC	239	Fort Lee, NJ	Private	220.0	1,500	4812
Twentieth Century-Fox TV Intl	240	Los Angeles, CA	Private	170.4	1,500	4833
United Video Satellite Group	241	Tulsa, OK	Public	507.6	1,500	4841
Univision Communications, Inc.	242	Los Angeles, CA	Public	459.7	1,500	4833
Picturetel Corporation	243	Andover, MA	Public	466.4	1,450	3669
Omnipoint Corporation	244	Bethesda, MD	Public	51.9	1,423	4812
Network Equipment Technologies	245	Fremont, CA	Public	308.7	1,414	3661
Cellular Telephone Company	246	Paramus, NJ	Public Family Member	97.5	1,400	4812
Citadel Broadcasting Company	247	Tempe, AZ	Public Family Member	115.5	1,400	4832
Matsushita Comm Indus Corp Us	248	Peachtree City, GA	Private	250.0	1,400	3663
TCI Southeast Inc.	249	Birmingham, AL	Public Family Member	188.3	1,400	4841
Ciena Corporation	250	Linthicum Heights, MD	Public	508.1	1,382	3661
Pulitzer Broadcasting Company	251	Saint Louis, MO	Public Family Member	156.1	1,375	4833
Pacific Bell Wireless	252	Pleasanton, CA	Public Family Member	94.2	1,352	4812
Fox Television Stations Inc.	253	Los Angeles, CA	Public Family Member	1,133.1	1,350	4833
Mobilemedia Communications Inc.	254	Ridgefield Park, NJ	Public Family Member	640.7	1,345	4812
Deltec Electronics Corporation	255	San Diego, CA	Private	145.0	1,300	3679
Great Universal Incorporated	256	New York, NY	Private	144.4	1,300	4812
Kavlico Corporation	257	Moorpark, CA	Private	75.4	1,300	3679
Metromedia Intl Group Inc.	258	East Rutherford, NJ	Private	204.3	1,300	4841
Nokia Inc.	259	Irving, TX	Private	111.0	1,300	3663
Pioneer Speakers Inc.	260	National City, CA	Private	115.0	1,300	3651
Vista Information Technologies	261	Herndon, VA	Private	30.0	1,300	4813
Young Broadcasting Inc.	262	New York, NY	Public	263.5	1,300	4833
IXC Communications, Inc.	263	Austin, TX	Public	203.7	1,290	4813
Benedek Broadcasting Corp.	264	Rockford, IL	Private	127.1	1,272	4833
Mobile Comm. Corp. of America	265	Fort Lee, NJ	Public Family Member	88.5	1,271	4812
Paxson Communications Corp	266	West Palm Beach, FL	Public	134.2	1,270	4833
CMT Partners	267	South San Francisco, CA	Private	88.2	1,266	4812
Intermedia Management Inc.	268	Nashville, TN	Private	169.0	1,257	4841
Inter-Tel Incorporated	269	Phoenix, AZ	Public	223.6	1,248	3661
Allsup Enterprises, Inc.	270	Clovis, NM	Private	102.0	1,238	4832
Airtouch Paging Of Texas	271	Dallas, TX	Public Family Member	86.0	1,234	4812
Contel Of California Inc.	272	Irving, TX	Public Family Member	156.0	1,219	4813
CMC Industries Inc.	273	Santa Clara, CA	Public	302.0	1,205	3661
Aydin Corporation	274	Horsham, PA	Public	115.4	1,200	3663
C-Cor Electronics Inc.	275	State College, PA	Public	152.1	1,200	3663
Communications Instruments	276	Fairview, NC	Private	89.4	1,200	3679
Electromagnetic Sciences, Inc.	277	Norcross, GA	Public	171.2	1,200	3663
Five Rivers Electronic Innov	278	Greeneville, TN	Private	400.0	1,200	3651
Gray Communications Systems	279	Albany, GA	Public	103.5	1,200	4833
HRB Systems, Inc.	280	State College, PA	Public Family Member	125.0	1,200	3669

D&B COMPANY RANKINGS BY EMPLOYMENT

Company	Rank	Location	Type	Sales ($ mil.)	Employ-ment	Primary SIC
International Jensen Inc.	281	Lincolnshire, IL	Private	134.8	1,200	3651
Mitsubishi Digital Electric America	282	Irvine, CA	Private	500.0	1,200	3651
Nokia Mobile Phones Inc.	283	Fort Worth, TX	Private	1,000.0	1,200	3663
RSI, Inc.	284	Sterling, VA	Private	190.0	1,200	3663
Tulalip Tribes Inc.	285	Marysville, WA	Private	161.3	1,200	4841
Harman-Motive Inc.	286	Martinsville, IN	Public Family Member	131.6	1,172	3651
Chris-Craft Industries Inc.	287	New York, NY	Public	464.6	1,169	4833
Itron Inc.	288	Spokane, WA	Public	216.1	1,167	3663
Granite Broadcasting Corp	289	New York, NY	Public	153.5	1,160	4833
BellSouth Per Communications	290	Atlanta, GA	Public Family Member	150.0	1,150	4813
Radio Frequency Systems Inc.	291	Hickory, NC	Private	98.2	1,150	3663
Digital Microwave Corporation	292	San Jose, CA	Public	310.5	1,147	3663
Cable One, Inc.	293	Phoenix, AZ	Public Family Member	257.7	1,139	4841
Univision Television Group	294	Teaneck, NJ	Public Family Member	412.4	1,136	4833
Communications Systems, Inc.	295	Hector, MN	Public	75.7	1,135	3661
Aliant Communications Co.	296	Lincoln, NE	Public Family Member	194.6	1,104	4813
Alpine Electronics Man. Of America	297	Greenwood, IN	Private	147.0	1,100	3651
Bonneville International Corp	298	Salt Lake City, UT	Private	90.5	1,100	4832
G S T Telecom, Inc.	299	Vancouver, WA	Public Family Member	140.7	1,100	4813
JBL Incorporated	300	Washington, DC	Public Family Member	123.5	1,100	3651
Jefferson-Plot Communications Co.	301	Greensboro, NC	Public Family Member	195.6	1,100	4833
Matthey Johnson Electronics	302	Spokane, WA	Private	130.0	1,100	3679
Titan Tech & Info Systems Corp	303	Reston, VA	Public Family Member	220.0	1,100	3663
Aavid Thermal Products, Inc.	304	Laconia, NH	Public	134.6	1,088	3679
IPC Information Systems Inc.	305	New York, NY	Public	270.3	1,088	3661
Alltel Communications, Inc.	306	Little Rock, AR	Public Family Member	540.0	1,060	4812
Advanced Energy Industries	307	Fort Collins, CO	Public	141.9	1,059	3679
BHC Communications, Inc.	308	New York, NY	Public	443.5	1,055	4833
NOS Communications, Inc.	309	Las Vegas, NV	Private	195.0	1,050	4813
Stanford Telecommunications	310	Sunnyvale, CA	Public	153.3	1,025	3663
Ascent Entertainment Group	311	Denver, CO	Public	428.5	1,021	4841
Adtran Inc.	312	Huntsville, AL	Public	265.3	1,008	3661
C & K Components Inc.	313	Watertown, MA	Private	225.0	1,000	3679
Cerberus Holdings Inc.	314	Wilmington, DE	Private	87.8	1,000	3669
Comcast Cablvision Of Mercer Cnty	315	Philadelphia, PA	Public Family Member	134.3	1,000	4841
General Communication, Inc.	316	Anchorage, AK	Public	223.8	1,000	4813
H C Crown Corp	317	Kansas City, MO	Private	112.9	1,000	4833
Jones Communications	318	Lanham, MD	Private	134.3	1,000	4841
Los Angeles SMSA LTD Partner	319	Irvine, CA	Private	69.7	1,000	4812
Maple Chase Company	320	Downers Grove, IL	Private	100.0	1,000	3669
National Dispatch Center Inc.	321	San Diego, CA	Private	33.5	1,000	4813
Nokia Telecommunications Inc.	322	Irving, TX	Private	69.7	1,000	4812
Oncor Communications, Inc.	323	Dallas, TX	Private	127.9	1,000	4813
Paramount Stations Group, Inc.	324	Los Angeles, CA	Public Family Member	450.0	1,000	4833
Philips Broadband Networks	325	Manlius, NY	Private	50.0	1,000	3663
PLD Telekom, Inc.	326	New York, NY	Private	114.4	1,000	4813
Powertel, Inc.	327	West Point, GA	Public	78.9	1,000	4812
Reliance Comtech	328	Bedford, TX	Private	127.9	1,000	4813
TCI Cablevision Of Alabama	329	Birmingham, AL	Public Family Member	134.3	1,000	4841
Telephonics Corporation	330	Farmingdale, NY	Public Family Member	156.9	1,000	3669
Timeplex Inc.	331	Woodcliff Lake, NJ	Private	176.9	1,000	3661
USWeb Corporation	332	Santa Clara, CA	Public	100.0	1,000	4813
Dialogic Corporation	333	Parsippany, NJ	Public	261.3	994	3661
Time Warner Entertainment	334	Stamford, CT	Private	133.2	992	4841
G.T.E. World Headquarters	335	Irving, TX	Private	125.7	983	4813
Contel Of New York, Inc.	336	Irving, TX	Public Family Member	125.5	982	4813
BEI Sensors & Systems Company	337	Sylmar, CA	Public Family Member	150.0	977	3679
BEI Technologies Inc.	338	San Francisco, CA	Public	101.5	977	3679
Booth American Company	339	Detroit, MI	Private	79.7	970	4832
Falcon Holding Group LP	340	Los Angeles, CA	Private	255.9	967	4841
Nextel Of California Inc.	341	Oakland, CA	Public Family Member	67.4	966	4812
Inrange Technologies Corp	342	Mount Laurel, NJ	Public Family Member	219.0	942	3663
Cosmos Broadcasting Corp	343	Greenville, SC	Public Family Member	119.0	932	4833
Vertex Communications Corp	344	Kilgore, TX	Public	130.0	927	3663
Convergent Communications Svcs	345	Englewood, CO	Private	106.5	917	4813
Comverse Network Systems Inc.	346	Wakefield, MA	Public Family Member	86.2	900	3661
Delta Products Corporation	347	Nogales, AZ	Private	52.2	900	3679
DirecTV, Inc.	348	El Segundo, CA	Public Family Member	1,000.0	900	4841
Dovatron International, Inc.	349	Boulder, CO	Public Family Member	274.7	900	3679
Foster North America Inc.	350	Schaumburg, IL	Private	89.4	900	3651

D&B COMPANY RANKINGS BY EMPLOYMENT

Company	Rank	Location	Type	Sales ($ mil.)	Employ-ment	Primary SIC
Keptel Inc.	351	Eatontown, NJ	Public Family Member	80.0	900	3661
Mediaone Northern Illinois Inc.	352	Elmhurst, IL	Public Family Member	120.8	900	4841
TAL Financial Corporation	353	Tyler, TX	Public Family Member	32.3	900	4841
Telephone Electronics Corp	354	Jackson, MS	Private	1,001.3	900	4813
Time Warner Telecom LLC	355	Englewood, CO	Private	55.4	898	4813
Eagle Comtronics Inc.	356	Clay, NY	Private	49.0	890	3663
GTE Service Corporation	357	Irving, TX	Public Family Member	83.5	890	4813
Pegasus Communications Corp	358	Radnor, PA	Private	86.8	877	4833
Communigroup Inc.	359	Jackson, MS	Private	869.6	870	4813
Cherokee International LLC	360	Tustin, CA	Private	77.0	868	3679
Periphonics Corporation	361	Bohemia, NY	Public	117.3	866	3661
Comdial Corporation	362	Charlottesville, VA	Public	118.6	865	3661
OECO Corporation	363	Milwaukie, OR	Private	83.4	865	3679
Entertainment Inc.	364	Hartford, CT	Public	38.1	864	4841
United Telephone-Southeast	365	Wake Forest, NC	Public Family Member	110.1	862	4813
Nevada Bell	366	Reno, NV	Public Family Member	190.4	860	4813
Channel Master LLC	367	Smithfield, NC	Private	166.0	850	3679
Paradyne Corporation	368	Largo, FL	Private	81.4	850	3661
Telect, Inc.	369	Liberty Lake, WA	Private	121.0	847	3661
International Family Entertainment	370	Virginia Beach, VA	Private	112.3	837	4841
Vartec Telecom, Inc.	371	Lancaster, TX	Private	105.6	827	4813
The Nextel Communications	372	Reston, VA	Public Family Member	57.4	822	4812
Signal Technology Corporation	373	Danvers, MA	Public	102.3	820	3679
F E L Corporation	374	Farmingdale, NJ	Private	68.8	806	3663
Infinity Broadcasting Corp Del	375	New York, NY	Public	65.7	803	4832
Alpha Industries Inc.	376	Woburn, MA	Public	116.9	801	3679
Advanced Fibre Communications	377	Petaluma, CA	Public	267.9	800	3661
American CableSystems Of Mass	378	Portsmouth, NH	Public Family Member	107.3	800	4841
Conexant Systems, Inc.	379	Newport Beach, CA	Private	76.6	800	3661
Confederated Slish Ktnai Tribes	380	Pablo, MT	Private	62.0	800	3679
Customtracks Corporation	381	Dallas, TX	Public	117.7	800	3663
GTE Mobilnet Tampa Inc.	382	Tampa, FL	Public Family Member	55.9	800	4812
H.C.C. Industries Inc.	383	Rosemead, CA	Private	46.4	800	3679
Intermedia Partners	384	San Francisco, CA	Private	107.3	800	4841
Multimedia Cablevision, Inc.	385	Wichita, KS	Public Family Member	107.3	800	4841
Perpetual Corporation	386	Washington, DC	Private	89.8	800	4833
Superstation Inc.	387	Atlanta, GA	Public Family Member	89.8	800	4833
Telemundo Group Inc.	388	Hialeah, FL	Private	89.8	800	4833
Turner Original Productions Inc.	389	Atlanta, GA	Public Family Member	89.8	800	4833
White Oak Semiconductor	390	Sandston, VA	Private	46.4	800	3679
Heartland Wireless Communications	391	Plano, TX	Public	78.8	790	4841
UTstarcom, Inc.	392	Alameda, CA	Private	100.1	788	3661
On Command Corporation	393	San Jose, CA	Public	222.1	773	4841
Allbritton Communications Co.	394	Washington, DC	Private	155.6	770	4833
Hayes Corporation	395	Norcross, GA	Public	199.6	768	3661
Lodgenet Entertainment Corp	396	Sioux Falls, SD	Public	166.4	763	4841
Metatec Corp	397	Dublin, OH	Private	43.9	756	3679
P-Com Inc.	398	Campbell, CA	Public	220.7	754	3661
Lufkin-Conroe Communications Co.	399	Lufkin, TX	Public Family Member	104.8	751	4813
Amerivision Communications	400	Oklahoma City, OK	Private	130.0	750	4813
Cox Communications San Diego Inc.	401	San Diego, CA	Public Family Member	1,610.4	750	4841
Fisher Broadcasting Inc.	402	Seattle, WA	Public Family Member	84.1	750	4833
Hauser Communications Inc.	403	New York, NY	Private	100.5	750	4841
MCI Wireless, Inc.	404	Garden City, NY	Public Family Member	52.4	750	4812
Safetran Systems Corporation	405	Minneapolis, MN	Private	65.8	750	3669
Shared Technologies Fairchild	406	Tampa, FL	Public Family Member	157.2	744	4813
Vtel Corporation	407	Austin, TX	Public	179.7	740	3669
Harbor Electronics Inc.	408	Etters, PA	Private	57.0	720	3679
Mitel Inc.	409	Herndon, VA	Private	200.0	720	3661
Xpedite Systems Inc.	410	Eatontown, NJ	Public Family Member	36.9	720	4822
IDT Corporation	411	Hackensack, NJ	Public	335.4	712	4813
Bel Fuse Inc.	412	Jersey City, NJ	Public	73.5	707	3679
Optel, Inc.	413	Dallas, TX	Private	65.0	706	4841
American Cellular Corporation	414	Schaumburg, IL	Public	181.0	700	4812
Concert Management Services	415	Reston, VA	Private	85.3	700	4899
Entercom Communications Corp	416	Bala Cynwyd, PA	Public	133.0	700	4832
International Telecomm Satellite Org	417	Washington, DC	Private	961.6	700	4899
Intervoice Inc.	418	Dallas, TX	Public	102.3	700	3661
Malrite Communications Group	419	Cleveland, OH	Private	78.3	700	4833
MJD Communications, Inc.	420	Charlotte, NC	Private	43.0	700	4813

D&B COMPANY RANKINGS BY EMPLOYMENT

Company	Rank	Location	Type	Sales ($ mil.)	Employ-ment	Primary SIC
Oki Telecom, Inc.	421	Suwanee, GA	Private	59.7	700	3663
Racal Corporation	422	Fort Lauderdale, FL	Private	503.0	700	3661
Raycom America, Inc.	423	Montgomery, AL	Private	57.2	700	4832
Tele-Fibernet Corporation	424	Jackson, MS	Public Family Member	89.3	700	4813
UACC Midwest, Inc.	425	Grand Rapids, MI	Public Family Member	93.8	700	4841
Spectrian Corporation	426	Sunnyvale, CA	Public	168.8	688	3663
Geotek Communications, Inc.	427	Montvale, NJ	Public	65.5	685	4812
United Telephone Co Of Texas	428	Shawnee Mission, KS	Public Family Member	128.2	683	4813
Commonwealth Telephone Co.	429	Dallas, PA	Public Family Member	87.0	682	4813
Brite Voice Systems Inc.	430	Lake Mary, FL	Public	119.8	681	3661
MediaOne Of Ohio Inc.	431	Findlay, OH	Public Family Member	90.3	674	4841
Ultrak Inc.	432	Lewisville, TX	Public	188.7	672	3663
Telular Corporation (Del)	433	Vernon Hills, IL	Public	40.4	665	3663
Emmis Communications Corp	434	Indianapolis, IN	Public	125.9	663	4832
MCE Companies, Inc.	435	Ann Arbor, MI	Private	81.0	660	3679
USLD Communications Corp	436	Arlington, VA	Private	83.9	658	4813
Executone Information Systems	437	Milford, CT	Public	156.4	650	3661
NTL Incorporated	438	New York, NY	Public	491.8	650	4841
Westell Technologies Inc.	439	Oswego, IL	Public	86.4	649	3661
Dukane Corporation	440	Saint Charles, IL	Private	87.9	642	3663
Symmetricom Inc.	441	San Jose, CA	Public	120.6	642	3661
Knowles Electronics Del	442	Itasca, IL	Private	100.0	641	3679
Pairgain Technologies, Inc.	443	Tustin, CA	Public	282.3	640	3661
Western Union International	444	Piscataway, NJ	Public Family Member	32.7	638	4822
Aeronautical Radio Inc.	445	Annapolis, MD	Private	63.0	632	4812
Mosaix Inc.	446	Redmond, WA	Public	121.1	625	3661
Post-Newsweek Stations Inc.	447	Hartford, CT	Public Family Member	69.7	625	4833
Alascom Inc.	448	Anchorage, AK	Public Family Member	265.1	624	4813
Efdata Corp.	449	Tempe, AZ	Public Family Member	90.0	623	3663
ATU Telecommunications	450	Anchorage, AK	Private	110.0	620	4813
Gai-Tronics Corporation	451	Mohnton, PA	Public Family Member	59.8	619	3661
US Unwired Inc.	452	Lake Charles, LA	Private	61.9	619	4813
Applied Signal Technology Inc.	453	Sunnyvale, CA	Public	110.1	617	3663
Media Gen Cable Of Fairfax Cnty	454	Chantilly, VA	Public Family Member	143.0	616	4841
Unifi Communications Inc.	455	Lowell, MA	Private	43.9	615	4822
Southwest Co Wireless, Inc.	456	Scottsdale, AZ	Public Family Member	42.7	610	4812
Heftel Broadcasting Corp	457	Dallas, TX	Public	154.9	609	4832
Colony Communications, Inc.	458	Providence, RI	Public Family Member	120.8	602	4841
Westell, Inc.	459	Aurora, IL	Public Family Member	73.0	602	3661
Nextel Of Texas Inc.	460	Austin, TX	Public Family Member	42.1	601	4812
American Cellular Comm. Corp	461	Atlanta, GA	Public Family Member	42.0	600	4812
Antronix Inc.	462	Cranbury, NJ	Private	36.0	600	3663
Cox Communications New Orleans	463	New Orleans, LA	Private	111.0	600	4841
Innovex Precision Components	464	Hopkins, MN	Public Family Member	133.4	600	3679
Onemain.Com, Inc (De)	465	Southampton, NY	Private	76.4	600	4813
Packard-Hughes Intrcnct Wr Sys	466	Foley, AL	Public Family Member	75.0	600	3679
Pioneer Telephone Coop Inc.	467	Kingfisher, OK	Private	54.9	600	4813
Primus Telecom Group	468	Mc Lean, VA	Public	280.2	600	4813
R F Monolithics Inc.	469	Dallas, TX	Public	55.2	600	3679
Salem Communication Corp	470	Camarillo, CA	Private	67.9	600	4832
Sanyo Manufacturing Corp	471	Forrest City, AR	Private	501.0	600	3651
TCI Of Pennsylvania, Inc.	472	Pittsburgh, PA	Public Family Member	80.3	600	4841
Triax USA Associates, LP	473	Denver, CO	Private	80.3	600	4841
Express Manufacturing, Inc.	474	Santa Ana, CA	Private	34.2	590	3679
Blonder-Tongue Laboratories	475	Old Bridge, NJ	Public	62.1	587	3663
Mackie Designs Inc.	476	Woodinville, WA	Public	74.9	585	3651
C-Net, Inc.	477	San Francisco, CA	Public	33.6	581	4841
Advanced Communications Group	478	Chesterfield, MO	Private	73.9	580	4813
Hughes Communications Inc.	479	Long Beach, CA	Public Family Member	70.7	580	4899
Journal Broadcast Group Inc.	480	Milwaukee, WI	Private	64.5	580	4833
McGraw-Hill Broadcasting Co.	481	New York, NY	Public Family Member	63.9	575	4833
Electric Lightwave Inc.	482	Vancouver, WA	Public	61.1	573	4813
Kansas City Cable Partners, LP	483	Kansas City, MO	Private	76.2	570	4841
Ml Media Partners, L.P.	484	New York, NY	Private	60.3	570	4841
Roseville Communications Co.	485	Roseville, CA	Private	114.9	565	4899
Smartalk Teleservices, Inc.	486	Dublin, OH	Public	71.9	565	4813
A-R Cable Services Inc.	487	Woodbury, NY	Public Family Member	120.4	563	4841
Alstom Signaling Inc.	488	Rochester, NY	Private	120.0	560	3669
United Television Inc.	489	Beverly Hills, CA	Public	171.0	559	4833
Intecom Inc.	490	Dallas, TX	Private	71.3	558	3661

D&B COMPANY RANKINGS BY EMPLOYMENT

Company	Rank	Location	Type	Sales ($ mil.)	Employ-ment	Primary SIC
Elcom, Inc.	491	El Paso, TX	Private	32.2	555	3679
Odetics, Inc.	492	Anaheim, CA	Public	89.8	554	3663
BTI Telecom Corp	493	Raleigh, NC	Private	194.9	550	4813
E.Spire Communications Inc.	494	Annapolis Junction, MD	Public	59.0	550	4813
G E American Communications	495	Princeton, NJ	Public Family Member	67.1	550	4899
Kidde-Fenwal Inc.	496	Ashland, MA	Private	48.2	550	3669
NPG Holdings, Inc.	497	Saint Joseph, MO	Private	70.0	550	4841
Qualcomm Per Electric A Cal Partnr	498	San Diego, CA	Private	150.0	550	3661
USA Networks	499	New York, NY	Private	700.0	550	4841
Vista-United Telecom	500	Lake Buena Vista, FL	Private	63.6	550	4813
Wiretech, LTD	501	Reston, VA	Private	54.1	550	4812
Matra Communication USA Inc.	502	New York, NY	Private	81.8	545	3661
Osborn Communications Corp	503	Tucker, GA	Public Family Member	37.2	543	4832
VYVX, Inc.	504	Tulsa, OK	Public Family Member	66.0	541	4899
Mediacom Southeast LLC	505	Middletown, NY	Private	102.0	540	4841
Olympus Communications, L P	506	Coudersport, PA	Private	121.0	539	4841
Nortech Systems Incorporated	507	Bemidji, MN	Public	36.4	537	3679
Public Broadcasting Service	508	Alexandria, VA	Private	444.1	530	4833
K-Tec Electronics Corporation	509	Sugar Land, TX	Public Family Member	30.7	529	3679
GTE West Coast Incorporated	510	Everett, WA	Public Family Member	66.4	522	4813
Teltrend Inc.	511	Saint Charles, IL	Public	96.8	519	3661
Horizon Telecom Inc.	512	Chillicothe, OH	Private	37.0	517	4813
SJI Inc.	513	Cut Off, LA	Private	89.1	512	4813
Williams Controls Inc.	514	Portland, OR	Public	57.6	511	3679
World Access Inc.	515	Atlanta, GA	Public	93.0	510	3661
Filtronic Comtek Inc.	516	Salisbury, MD	Private	73.2	509	3679
Ortel Corporation	517	Alhambra, CA	Public	76.9	507	3663
Alltel Pennsylvania, Inc.	518	Little Rock, AR	Public Family Member	64.4	506	4813
Klipsch, LLC	519	Indianapolis, IN	Private	55.8	504	3651
Stellex Microwave Systems	520	Palo Alto, CA	Private	89.0	504	3679
Cablevision Connecticut Corp	521	Norwalk, CT	Public Family Member	55.1	503	4841
Aerial Communications Inc.	522	Chicago, IL	Public	56.0	500	4812
American Tower Corp	523	Boston, MA	Public	61.0	500	4899
Amphenol Interconnect Products	524	Wallingford, CT	Public Family Member	55.0	500	3679
Bahakel Communications LTD	525	Charlotte, NC	Private	55.3	500	4833
EDS Personal Communications Corp	526	Waltham, MA	Public Family Member	35.1	500	4812
Fair-Rite Products Corp	527	Wallkill, NY	Private	42.2	500	3679
Federal Broadcasting Company	528	Montgomery, AL	Private	55.3	500	4833
Florida RSA 8 Inc.	529	Chicago, IL	Public Family Member	35.1	500	4812
FPL Group Capital Inc.	530	North Palm Beach, FL	Public Family Member	66.8	500	4841
Galaxy Telecom, L P	531	Sikeston, MO	Private	68.8	500	4841
GTE Cybertrust Solutions Inc.	532	Needham, MA	Public Family Member	63.6	500	4813
Harron Communications Corp	533	Malvern, PA	Private	66.8	500	4841
Hickory Tech Corporation	534	Mankato, MN	Public	76.5	500	4813
Houston Cellular Telephone Co.	535	Houston, TX	Private	35.1	500	4812
Islandlife LLC	536	New York, NY	Private	63.6	500	4813
K & L Microwave Inc.	537	Salisbury, MD	Public Family Member	37.0	500	3679
Kentrox Industries Inc.	538	Portland, OR	Public Family Member	150.0	500	3661
LIN Television Of Texas, L P	539	Austin, TX	Private	55.3	500	4833
Pamplin Communications Corp	540	Portland, OR	Private	61.0	500	4899
Panamsat Corporation	541	Greenwich, CT	Public	726.8	500	4899
Parcel Consultants Inc.	542	Cedar Grove, NJ	Private	193.4	500	4813
Peco Ii Inc.	543	Galion, OH	Private	48.3	500	3661
Phonetel Technologies Inc.	544	Cleveland, OH	Public	109.6	500	4813
Sinclair Properties L.L.C.	545	Baltimore, MD	Private	55.3	500	4833
Sony Trans Com Inc.	546	Irvine, CA	Private	42.6	500	3663
Telegroup Inc.	547	Fairfield, IA	Public	337.4	500	4813
Todd Products Corp	548	Brentwood, NY	Private	31.4	500	3679
Wireless One, Inc.	549	Jackson, MS	Public	34.6	500	4841
Midcontinent Media, Inc.	550	Minneapolis, MN	Private	66.0	494	4841
Transcrypt International, Inc.	551	Lincoln, NE	Public	62.0	494	3663
CFW Communications Company	552	Waynesboro, VA	Public	59.0	492	4813
Service Electric Television	553	Mahanoy City, PA	Private	101.6	489	4841
SBC Media Ventures Inc.	554	Rockville, MD	Public Family Member	64.6	484	4841
Diversified Communications	555	Portland, ME	Private	49.5	476	4833
Renaissance Communications	556	Chicago, IL	Public Family Member	52.5	476	4833
Onkyo America Inc.	557	Columbus, IN	Private	58.1	475	3651
Sunbeam Television Corp	558	Miami, FL	Private	201.0	475	4833
Excite Inc.	559	Redwood City, CA	Public	154.1	470	4813
Techdyne Inc.	560	Hialeah, FL	Public	33.2	470	3679

D&B COMPANY RANKINGS BY EMPLOYMENT

Company	Rank	Location	Type	Sales ($ mil.)	Employ-ment	Primary SIC
Del Global Technologies Corp	561	Valhalla, NY	Public	62.3	466	3679
USN Communications Midwest	562	Chicago, IL	Public Family Member	59.2	466	4813
United Telephone Co NJ Inc.	563	Clinton, NJ	Public Family Member	59.1	465	4813
Powerwave Technologies, Inc.	564	Irvine, CA	Public	100.2	461	3663
Cordillera Communications Inc.	565	Charleston, SC	Private	50.7	460	4833
SSE Telecom Inc.	566	Fremont, CA	Public	36.7	460	3663
Pegasus Media & Communications	567	Radnor, PA	Public	66.4	459	4833
Northland Telecom Corp	568	Seattle, WA	Private	37.8	456	4841
Datel Inc.	569	Mansfield, MA	Private	35.0	450	3679
Gemini Industries Inc.	570	Clifton, NJ	Private	159.1	450	3663
Georgia Alltel Inc.	571	Dalton, GA	Public Family Member	3,192.4	450	4813
Golden Sky Systems, Inc.	572	Kansas City, MO	Private	60.0	450	4841
Harman Music Group Inc.	573	Sandy, UT	Public Family Member	49.7	450	3651
MFS Telecom, Inc. (Del)	574	Villa Park, IL	Public Family Member	57.2	450	4813
Nextel Of New York, Inc.	575	White Plains, NY	Public Family Member	72.0	450	4812
Pioneer Video Manufacturing	576	Carson, CA	Private	49.7	450	3651
Quincy Newspapers Inc.	577	Quincy, IL	Private	45.0	450	4833
Rowe International Inc.	578	Grand Rapids, MI	Public Family Member	85.0	450	3651
Sullivan Broadcasting Company	579	Boston, MA	Private	137.8	450	4833
Sunbelt Communications Company	580	Las Vegas, NV	Private	55.0	450	4833
Tekelec	581	Calabasas, CA	Public	125.1	450	3661
American Telecasting, Inc.	582	Colorado Springs, CO	Public	59.0	448	4841
Dolby Laboratories Inc.	583	San Francisco, CA	Private	98.6	445	3663
Saga Communications Inc.	584	Detroit, MI	Public	56.2	445	4832
Pittway International LTD	585	Chicago, IL	Public Family Member	38.9	444	3669
Proxima Corporation	586	San Diego, CA	Private	154.7	444	3679
New Valley Corporation	587	Miami, FL	Public	114.6	438	4822
BET Holdings Inc.	588	Washington, DC	Public	115.2	435	4841
Retlaw Enterprises Inc.	589	North Hollywood, CA	Private	47.8	435	4833
Elgar Electronics Corporation	590	San Diego, CA	Private	62.5	433	3679
Cylink Corporation	591	Sunnyvale, CA	Public	49.3	432	3663
Dialight Corp	592	Manasquan, NJ	Private	70.0	430	3679
Fargo Assembly Of PA Inc.	593	Norristown, PA	Private	31.0	430	3679
Educational Broadcasting Corp	594	New York, NY	Private	123.5	427	4833
Aeroflex Laboratories Inc.	595	Plainview, NY	Public Family Member	54.4	425	3679
Harvard Custom Manufacturing	596	Salisbury, MD	Private	43.0	425	3679
Highwaymaster Communications	597	Richardson, TX	Private	33.4	425	4812
ILD Telecommunications Inc.	598	Dallas, TX	Private	54.0	425	4813
Cidco Incorporated	599	Morgan Hill, CA	Public	257.0	422	3661
Virgin Island Telephone Corp	600	Charlotte Amalie, VI	Public Family Member	64.7	421	4813
Cerwin-Vega Inc.	601	Simi Valley, CA	Private	42.1	420	3651
Horry Telephone Cooperative	602	Conway, SC	Private	47.5	420	4813
Hub Fabricating Company	603	Reading, PA	Private	50.0	420	3661
Network Plus Inc.	604	Quincy, MA	Private	98.2	420	4813
RCN Cable Systems Inc.	605	Dallas, PA	Public Family Member	170.0	416	4841
Century Telephone Of Washington	606	Vancouver, WA	Public Family Member	73.6	415	4813
Sygnet Wireless Inc.	607	Canfield, OH	Private	85.6	415	4812
Touch 1 Communications Inc.	608	Atmore, AL	Private	35.7	415	4813
CT Communications Inc.	609	Concord, NC	Public	78.5	410	4813
One Call Communications Inc.	610	Carmel, IN	Private	52.0	410	4813
Citizens Telecom Co Of NY	611	Stamford, CT	Public Family Member	194.6	408	4813
Destia Communications, Inc.	612	Paramus, NJ	Private	83.0	408	4813
Chyron Corporation	613	Melville, NY	Public	86.8	406	3663
Lojack Corporation	614	Dedham, MA	Public	74.5	405	3663
RCN Telecom Services Of Pa	615	Northampton, PA	Public Family Member	53.9	405	4841
Bee Tronics Inc.	616	San Diego, CA	Private	34.1	400	3663
Comcast Cablevision Of NJ	617	Union, NJ	Public Family Member	129.8	400	4841
Datek Online Holding Company	618	Iselin, NJ	Private	50.7	400	4813
Digex, Incorporated	619	Beltsville, MD	Public Family Member	50.7	400	4813
Evening Telegram Co Inc.	620	Superior, WI	Private	43.8	400	4833
Level 3 Telecom Holdings, Inc.	621	Omaha, NE	Private	50.7	400	4813
Lifetime Entertainment Svcs	622	New York, NY	Private	53.3	400	4841
Loral Orion Network Systems	623	Rockville, MD	Public	72.0	400	4899
LXE Inc.	624	Norcross, GA	Public Family Member	90.0	400	3663
Mediaone Of New England Inc.	625	Andover, MA	Public Family Member	53.3	400	4841
PCS Triton Inc.	626	Malvern, PA	Private	118.3	400	4812
Prevue Networks, Inc.	627	Tulsa, OK	Public Family Member	65.0	400	4833
St Louis Music Inc.	628	Saint Louis, MO	Private	60.0	400	3651
Standard Group Inc.	629	Cornelia, GA	Public Family Member	121.0	400	4813
Suburban Cable TV Co Inc.	630	Oaks, PA	Private	354.6	400	4841

D&B COMPANY RANKINGS BY EMPLOYMENT

Company	Rank	Location	Type	Sales ($ mil.)	Employ-ment	Primary SIC
Tel-Save Inc.	631	New Hope, PA	Public Family Member	460.0	400	4813
Telscape International Inc.	632	Houston, TX	Public	36.2	400	4813
Trippe Manufacturing Company	633	Chicago, IL	Private	125.0	400	3679
Turner-Vision, Inc.	634	Bluefield, WV	Private	53.3	400	4841
Warner Cable Communication	635	Milwaukee, WI	Private	53.3	400	4841
Wireless One Network, L.P.	636	Fort Myers, FL	Private	100.0	400	4812
North State Telecommunications	637	High Point, NC	Private	72.9	396	4813
GE-Harris Railway Electric LLC	638	Melbourne, FL	Private	114.2	394	3669
Nortell Northern Telecom Corp	639	Simi Valley, CA	Private	34.4	393	3669
ADC Broadband Communications	640	Meriden, CT	Public Family Member	37.3	390	3661
Current Electronics Inc.	641	Newberg, OR	Public Family Member	55.0	390	3679
Wisconsin Educational Comm Bd	642	Madison, WI	Private	31.3	390	4832
EIS International Inc.	643	Herndon, VA	Public	85.6	389	3661
Concentric Network Corporation	644	San Jose, CA	Public	82.8	387	4813
ACI Communications Inc.	645	San Diego, CA	Private	48.8	385	4813
Alcatel Data Networks, Inc.	646	Ashburn, VA	Private	145.0	385	3663
Mediaone Of Sierra Valleys	647	Stockton, CA	Public Family Member	51.2	385	4841
Jacor Broadcasting Of Tampa Bay	648	Tampa, FL	Public Family Member	35.0	380	4832
Buckeye Cable Vision Inc.	649	Toledo, OH	Private	50.0	376	4841
Intek Global Corporation	650	New York, NY	Public	35.7	375	3663
Long Distance Savers Inc.	651	Monroe, LA	Private	47.5	375	4813
Commnet Cellular Inc.	652	Englewood, CO	Public	150.9	374	4812
Gulf Telephone Company, Inc.	653	Foley, AL	Private	42.6	373	4813
Preferred Networks Inc.	654	Norcross, GA	Public	36.0	373	4812
Western Reserve Tele Co Inc.	655	Hudson, OH	Public Family Member	47.1	372	4813
Buford Television Inc.	656	Tyler, TX	Private	58.1	370	4841
Gulf Coast Services Inc.	657	Foley, AL	Private	49.6	365	4813
Pent Products Inc.	658	Kendallville, IN	Private	47.0	365	3679
Ward Products Corp	659	North Brunswick, NJ	Private	39.0	365	3679
Midcontinent Cable Co.	660	Aberdeen, SD	Private	48.1	362	4841
Clark David Company Inc.	661	Worcester, MA	Private	45.2	360	3663
Elcotel Inc.	662	Sarasota, FL	Public	46.3	360	3661
Weather Channel Inc.	663	Atlanta, GA	Private	47.9	360	4841
Rural Cellular Corporation	664	Alexandria, MN	Public	53.9	358	4812
Applied Science & Technology	665	Woburn, MA	Public	83.4	355	3679
Prodigy Communications Inc.	666	White Plains, NY	Public	134.2	355	4813
Black Entertainment Television	667	Washington, DC	Public Family Member	85.3	350	4841
Bresnan Communications LP	668	White Plains, NY	Private	46.5	350	4841
Classic Cable Inc.	669	Austin, TX	Private	65.0	350	4841
CNBC, Inc.	670	Fort Lee, NJ	Public Family Member	38.0	350	4833
Disney Channel Inc.	671	Burbank, CA	Public Family Member	46.5	350	4841
Fire-Lite Alarms, Inc.	672	Northford, CT	Public Family Member	30.7	350	3669
GTE Intelligent Network Svcs Inc.	673	Irving, TX	Public Family Member	44.3	350	4813
Incomnet, Inc.	674	Irvine, CA	Public	125.1	350	4813
Infinity Wireless Products	675	Chicago, IL	Private	37.0	350	3661
Koss Corporation	676	Milwaukee, WI	Public	40.6	350	3651
Lifeline Systems Inc.	677	Cambridge, MA	Public	57.0	350	3669
Mac America Communications Inc.	678	Phoenix, AZ	Private	70.0	350	4833
Mc Cain Traffic Supply Inc.	679	Vista, CA	Private	35.0	350	3669
Mitek Corporation	680	Phoenix, AZ	Private	38.3	350	3651
Network Operator Services	681	Longview, TX	Private	75.0	350	4813
North American Long Distance Corp	682	Pittsburgh, PA	Private	44.3	350	4813
Operator Service Company	683	Lubbock, TX	Private	30.2	350	4813
Peek Corporation	684	Tallahassee, FL	Public Family Member	80.0	350	3669
Prestige Cable TV Inc.	685	Cartersville, GA	Private	70.0	350	4841
R S L Communications Inc.	686	New York, NY	Private	300.8	350	4813
Senior Systems Technology Inc.	687	Palmdale, CA	Private	50.0	350	3679
TCI Cablevision Of Missouri	688	Saint Peters, MO	Public Family Member	91.0	350	4841
Unidial Incorporated	689	Louisville, KY	Private	112.3	350	4813
Wheelock Inc.	690	Long Branch, NJ	Private	37.8	350	3669
California Amplifier Inc.	691	Camarillo, CA	Public	46.9	348	3663
Exodus Communications, Inc.	692	Santa Clara, CA	Public	35.0	345	4813
Outlet Communications Inc.	693	Cranston, RI	Public Family Member	37.4	345	4833
Amnex Inc.	694	New Rochelle, NY	Public	116.5	344	4813
Zoom Telephonics Canadian Corp	695	Boston, MA	Public	61.4	342	3661
Communications Telesystems Intl	696	San Diego, CA	Private	43.0	340	4813
Multi-Tech Systems Inc.	697	Saint Paul, MN	Private	109.8	340	3661
Uniphase Telecom Products	698	Bloomfield, CT	Public Family Member	80.0	340	3661
Evercom, Inc.	699	Irving, TX	Private	42.9	339	4813
S. Carolina Educational TV Comm	700	Columbia, SC	Private	41.0	337	4833

D&B COMPANY RANKINGS BY EMPLOYMENT

Company	Rank	Location	Type	Sales ($ mil.)	Employ-ment	Primary SIC
Teletouch Communications, Inc.	701	Tyler, TX	Public	35.8	337	4812
Active Voice Corporation	702	Seattle, WA	Public	53.2	336	3661
M P D Technologies, Inc.	703	Hauppauge, NY	Public Family Member	52.0	335	3663
Tulsa Cable Television, Inc.	704	Tulsa, OK	Public Family Member	44.1	332	4841
Premisys Communications Inc.	705	Fremont, CA	Public	102.3	331	3661
Dobson Communication Corp	706	Oklahoma City, OK	Private	85.2	330	4812
Jones International LTD	707	Englewood, CO	Private	43.8	330	4841
Post-Newsweek Stations FLA Inc.	708	Hartford, CT	Private	35.7	330	4833
At Home Corp	709	Redwood City, CA	Public	48.0	329	4813
Caprock Communications Corp	710	Dallas, TX	Private	48.5	327	4813
Americom Group	711	Luthrvil Timnium, MD	Private	44.0	325	4812
Augat Communication Products	712	Kent, WA	Public Family Member	64.5	325	3663
AVT Corporation	713	Kirkland, WA	Public	81.1	325	3661
Celeritek Inc.	714	Santa Clara, CA	Public	56.3	325	3663
Centigram Communications Corp	715	San Jose, CA	Public	77.6	325	3661
Microcom Inc.	716	Norwood, MA	Public Family Member	31.1	325	3661
Netselect, Inc.	717	Westlake Village, CA	Private	41.1	325	4813
Superior Modular Products Inc.	718	Swannanoa, NC	Private	32.0	325	3663
TCI TKR Cable I Inc.	719	Miami, FL	Public Family Member	43.1	325	4841
Value Tel	720	San Francisco, CA	Private	41.1	325	4813
Pinnacle Systems Inc.	721	Mountain View, CA	Public	105.3	323	3663
Matsushita Kotobuki Electronic	722	Vancouver, WA	Private	160.9	320	3651
Microelectronic Modules Corp	723	New Berlin, WI	Private	35.0	320	3679
Cincinnati Electronics Corp	724	Mason, OH	Private	46.8	317	3663
Planar Standish	725	Lake Mills, WI	Public Family Member	33.8	316	3679
Standard Telephone Company	726	Cornelia, GA	Public Family Member	39.2	310	4813
Uunet Worldcom, Inc.	727	Fairfax, VA	Public Family Member	38.7	306	4813
Gr. Wash. Educational Telecom Assn	728	Arlington, VA	Private	58.4	305	4833
Mediaone Of Fresno	729	Fresno, CA	Public Family Member	70.0	305	4841
Boca Research Inc.	730	Boca Raton, FL	Public	70.2	304	3661
Rock Hill Telephone Company	731	Rock Hill, SC	Private	33.7	302	4813
Comm South Companies, Inc.	732	Dallas, TX	Private	130.0	301	4813
Access Communications Inc.	733	Salt Lake City, UT	Private	85.9	300	4813
American Mobile Satellite Corp	734	Reston, VA	Public	44.2	300	4899
Arkansas Democrat Gazette	735	Little Rock, AR	Private	39.8	300	4841
Chambers Communications Corp	736	Eugene, OR	Private	39.8	300	4841
Cincinnati Bell Long Distance	737	Cincinnati, OH	Public Family Member	37.9	300	4813
Cohesive Technology Solutions	738	Palo Alto, CA	Private	37.9	300	4813
Community TV Of S. California	739	Los Angeles, CA	Private	48.5	300	4833
Continental Electronics Corp	740	Dallas, TX	Public Family Member	34.1	300	3663
Courtroom TV Network LLC	741	New York, NY	Private	32.3	300	4833
Fox Broadcasting Company	742	Los Angeles, CA	Public Family Member	1,456.5	300	4833
Gabriel Inc.	743	Elgin, IL	Private	70.1	300	3663
Garden State Cable Vision, LP	744	Cherry Hill, NJ	Private	109.1	300	4841
Hitachi Telecom USA Inc.	745	Norcross, GA	Private	200.0	300	3661
Intelidata Technologies Corp	746	Herndon, VA	Public	60.3	300	3661
Interoute Telecommunications	747	New York, NY	Private	100.0	300	4813
Matanuska Telephone Assn.	748	Palmer, AK	Private	49.9	300	4813
Mediaone Of Virginia, Inc.	749	Richmond, VA	Public Family Member	39.8	300	4841
Orbital Imaging Corporation	750	Sterling, VA	Public Family Member	39.8	300	4841
Pacific Bell Video Services	751	San Ramon, CA	Private	39.8	300	4841
Recoton Audio Corporation	752	Lake Mary, FL	Public Family Member	32.7	300	3651
Solectron Massachusetts Corp	753	Westborough, MA	Public Family Member	75.0	300	3679
Sugar Land Telephone Company	754	Sugar Land, TX	Public Family Member	37.9	300	4813
Transcall America Inc.	755	Jackson, MS	Public Family Member	37.9	300	4813
Triton Cellular Partners LP	756	Malvern, PA	Private	118.0	300	4812
WHDH, TV, Inc.	757	Boston, MA	Private	32.3	300	4833
Window To The World Comm.	758	Chicago, IL	Private	43.0	300	4833
Worldcom Inc.	759	Montgomery, AL	Public Family Member	37.9	300	4813
Alltel New York Inc.	760	Jamestown, NY	Public Family Member	49.9	297	4813
Conquest Telecom Svcs	761	Dublin, OH	Public Family Member	37.4	296	4813
Mod-Tap Corp	762	Harvard, MA	Public Family Member	69.0	296	3669
Highwaymaster Corporation	763	Richardson, TX	Public	54.6	295	4812
Nassau Broadcasting Partners LP	764	Princeton, NJ	Private	33.0	295	4832
Larscom Incorporated	765	Milpitas, CA	Public	76.0	291	3661
Honolulu Cellular Telephone Co.	766	Mililani, HI	Private	57.4	290	4812
Viatel, Inc (De Corp)	767	New York, NY	Public	73.0	290	4813
Triathlon Broadcasting Company	768	San Diego, CA	Public	40.0	289	4832
Convergent Media Systems Corp	769	Atlanta, GA	Private	30.9	288	4833
Anaren Microwave Inc.	770	East Syracuse, NY	Public	37.4	285	3679

D&B COMPANY RANKINGS BY EMPLOYMENT

Company	Rank	Location	Type	Sales ($ mil.)	Employ- ment	Primary SIC
Sa Telecommunications, Inc.	771	Richardson, TX	Public	39.8	285	4813
Techsonic Industries Inc.	772	Eufaula, AL	Public Family Member	52.0	285	3679
WFAA-TV Inc.	773	Dallas, TX	Public Family Member	30.3	283	4833
Digital Link Corporation	774	Sunnyvale, CA	Public	54.6	281	3661
Cambridge Soundworks Inc.	775	Newton, MA	Private	30.4	280	3651
Seachange International, Inc.	776	Maynard, MA	Public	67.9	280	3663
Distance Long International	777	Fort Lauderdale, FL	Private	40.1	279	4813
Heritage Cablevision Of Cal	778	San Jose, CA	Public Family Member	82.2	276	4841
Insight Communications Co LP	779	New York, NY	Private	68.5	276	4841
North Pittsburgh Systems, Inc.	780	Gibsonia, PA	Public	66.2	276	4813
Display Technologies Inc.	781	Downey, CA	Private	55.0	275	3669
KBL Portland Cablesystems LP	782	Portland, OR	Private	36.4	275	4841
Raltron Electronics Corp	783	Miami, FL	Private	75.0	275	3679
Thermo Voltek Corp	784	Woburn, MA	Public	44.6	275	3679
WPIX, Inc.	785	New York, NY	Public Family Member	173.0	275	4833
Conestoga Enterprises Inc.	786	Birdsboro, PA	Public	56.2	272	4813
Microflect Co Inc.	787	Salem, OR	Public Family Member	56.0	272	3663
Advanced Circuit Technology	788	Nashua, NH	Public Family Member	30.0	270	3679
Discount Long Distance Inc.	789	Santa Ana, CA	Private	34.0	270	4813
Farmers Telephone Cooperative	790	Kingstree, SC	Private	37.6	270	4813
Positive Communications Inc.	791	Pleasanton, CA	Private	41.4	270	4812
Total-Tel USA Communications Inc.	792	Little Falls, NJ	Public	123.3	270	4813
Prime Sports Channel Network LP	793	Woodbury, NY	Private	36.3	266	4841
Encore Media Corporation	794	Englewood, CO	Public Family Member	35.0	265	4841
Prodelin Corporation	795	Conover, NC	Private	50.0	265	3663
Light Technologies LLC	796	Spokane, WA	Private	46.0	264	4813
Universal Electronics Inc.	797	Cypress, CA	Public	114.3	264	3651
Ben M Jacoby	798	Houston, TX	Private	32.8	260	4813
Boston Acoustics Inc.	799	Peabody, MA	Public	82.4	260	3651
National Cable Satellite Corp	800	Washington, DC	Private	40.8	260	4841
RSL Com U.S.A., Inc.	801	Woodland Hills, CA	Private	300.0	260	4813
TCI TKR Of South Florida, Inc.	802	Miami, FL	Private	34.4	260	4841
Krautkramer Branson Inc.	803	Lewistown, PA	Public Family Member	40.0	252	3679
ACC Long Distance Corp	804	Rochester, NY	Public Family Member	308.8	250	4813
American Communications Network	805	Troy, MI	Private	98.1	250	4813
Calltask, Incorporated	806	Atlanta, GA	Public Family Member	31.5	250	4813
Cnet Technology Corp	807	Milpitas, CA	Private	47.0	250	3661
Cumulus Broadcasting Inc.	808	Chicago, IL	Private	54.7	250	4832
Globalstar, L. P.	809	San Jose, CA	Private	31.5	250	4813
Globecast North America Inc.	810	Miami, FL	Private	120.0	250	4841
Graphnet Inc.	811	Teaneck, NJ	Private	50.0	250	4822
Kcal TV, Inc.	812	Los Angeles, CA	Public Family Member	120.0	250	4833
Kelly Broadcasting Co A LTD Partnr	813	Sacramento, CA	Private	50.0	250	4833
KTLA Inc.	814	Los Angeles, CA	Public Family Member	190.0	250	4833
National Tele & Communications	815	Irvine, CA	Public Family Member	125.0	250	4813
Netrix Corporation	816	Herndon, VA	Public	43.6	250	3679
Pacific Bell Information Services	817	San Ramon, CA	Public Family Member	200.0	250	4813
Plant Equipment Inc.	818	Temecula, CA	Private	30.0	250	3661
Radio One Inc.	819	Lanham, MD	Private	37.0	250	4832
Sprint Telecenters Inc.	820	Maitland, FL	Public Family Member	31.5	250	4813
TCI Cablevision Of Wisconsin	821	Madison, WI	Public Family Member	38.0	250	4841
Teleglobe International Corp	822	Reston, VA	Private	278.7	250	4813
TGC Inc	823	Orlando, FL	Private	33.0	250	4841
TIW Systems, Inc.	824	Santa Clara, CA	Public Family Member	45.0	250	3669
Trescom International, Inc.	825	Fort Lauderdale, FL	Public	157.6	250	4813
United Cable Television	826	Baltimore, MD	Private	33.0	250	4841
Verilink Corporation	827	San Jose, CA	Public	50.9	250	3661
Worldcom Wireless, Inc.	828	Hayward, CA	Public Family Member	31.5	250	4813
Best Internet Inc.	829	Boca Raton, FL	Public Family Member	31.2	248	4813
Omnes	830	Houston, TX	Private	30.8	245	4813
Spectronics Corp	831	Atlanta, GA	Private	30.7	244	4813
ACT Networks Inc.	832	Camarillo, CA	Public	55.0	242	3661
Auto Club Cellular Corporation	833	Newtown, PA	Private	43.1	242	4812
Applied Innovation Inc.	834	Dublin, OH	Public	46.7	240	3661
Chorus Communications Group	835	Middleton, WI	Private	36.3	240	4813
Facilicom International LLC	836	Washington, DC	Private	117.1	240	4813
Talla-Com Tallahassee Comm Ind	837	Tallahassee, FL	Private	68.4	235	3669
Alesis Studio Electronics	838	Santa Monica, CA	Private	84.7	230	3651
Colorado Springs Cablevision	839	Colorado Springs, CO	Public Family Member	30.3	230	4841
TWC Cable Partners LP	840	Staten Island, NY	Private	30.3	230	4841

D&B COMPANY RANKINGS BY EMPLOYMENT

Company	Rank	Location	Type	Sales ($ mil.)	Employ- ment	Primary SIC
Relm Communications Inc.	841	Melbourne, FL	Public Family Member	45.4	229	3663
Clarion Manufacturing Corp America	842	Walton, KY	Private	82.9	228	3651
Davel Communications Group	843	Tampa, FL	Public	48.2	226	4813
Affiliated Regional Comm	844	Los Angeles, CA	Private	115.0	225	4841
Eminence Speaker Corporation	845	Eminence, KY	Private	37.0	225	3651
Vectron Technologies Inc.	846	Hudson, NH	Public Family Member	60.0	225	3679
American Network Exchange Inc.	847	Orlando, FL	Public Family Member	75.9	224	4813
G S Communications Inc.	848	Frederick, MD	Private	45.0	221	4841
E N M R Telephone Coop	849	Clovis, NM	Private	60.0	220	4813
ITCdeltacom, Inc.	850	West Point, GA	Public	114.6	220	4813
KHOU-TV, Inc.	851	Houston, TX	Public Family Member	60.0	220	4833
Multimedia KSDK Inc.	852	Saint Louis, MO	Public Family Member	40.0	220	4833
VXI Electronics, Inc.	853	Milwaukie, OR	Private	50.0	220	3679
Vicon Industries Inc.	854	Hauppauge, NY	Public	63.3	217	3663
Harmonic Lightwaves Inc.	855	Sunnyvale, CA	Public	83.9	215	3663
Eastern Acoustic Works, Inc.	856	Whitinsville, MA	Private	35.3	212	3651
GTE Airfone Incorporated (Del)	857	Oak Brook, IL	Public Family Member	100.0	210	4812
International Telcom LTD	858	Seattle, WA	Private	68.0	210	4813
Teltronics Inc.	859	Sarasota, FL	Public	34.7	210	3661
KOIN-TV Inc.	860	Portland, OR	Public Family Member	32.0	205	4833
Tollgrade Communications, Inc.	861	Cheswick, PA	Public	45.4	205	3661
National Mobile Television Inc.	862	Seattle, WA	Private	50.0	203	4833
Comstream Corporation	863	San Diego, CA	Private	55.9	200	3663
Copley Controls Corp	864	Westwood, MA	Private	45.0	200	3679
Datron/Transco, Inc.	865	Simi Valley, CA	Public Family Member	45.0	200	3663
Diversified Data Process. Consult.	866	Ferndale, MI	Private	45.0	200	4822
Econolite Control Products	867	Anaheim, CA	Private	42.0	200	3669
G E Capital Comm Svcs Corp	868	Atlanta, GA	Public Family Member	49.1	200	4813
Gardiner Communications Corp	869	Garland, TX	Private	35.0	200	3663
GN Netcom Inc.	870	Nashua, NH	Private	45.0	200	3661
John Mezzalingua Associates	871	East Syracuse, NY	Private	70.0	200	3663
Low Country Telephone Company	872	Hilton Head Island, SC	Private	60.0	200	4813
Q Net Inc.	873	Teaneck, NJ	Private	42.0	200	4822
Robin Media Group Inc.	874	San Francisco, CA	Private	34.1	200	4841
Snap LLC	875	San Francisco, CA	Private	35.0	200	4813
Souris River Telecom Coop	876	Minot, ND	Private	31.6	200	4813
TCI Cablevision Of California	877	Redlands, CA	Public Family Member	32.0	200	4841
Telenoticias LLC	878	Hialeah, FL	Private	30.4	200	4841
Universal Logic Technologies	879	Mansfield, OH	Private	43.0	200	4813
T-Netix, Inc.	880	Englewood, CO	Public	38.2	198	4813
SMS Technologies Inc.	881	San Diego, CA	Private	41.0	197	3679
Axiom Inc.	882	Mount Laurel, NJ	Public	33.0	196	3669
Bogen Communications Intl	883	Ramsey, NJ	Private	49.8	196	3661
American Movie Classics Co.	884	Woodbury, NY	Private	139.2	195	4841
Time Warner Cable Programming	885	Stamford, CT	Public Family Member	33.4	192	4841
Asante Technologies, Inc.	886	San Jose, CA	Public	51.4	190	3661
Excel Switching Corporation	887	Hyannis, MA	Public	88.7	190	3661
Nextlink Pennsylvania LP	888	Reading, PA	Private	30.0	190	4813
Wells-Gardner Electronics Corp	889	Chicago, IL	Public	43.0	190	3663
Paramunt Stns Group Of Detroit	890	Southfield, MI	Public Family Member	60.0	185	4833
Cablevision Of Monmouth Inc.	891	Belmar, NJ	Private	123.1	180	4841
Century Telephone Of Wisconsin	892	La Crosse, WI	Public Family Member	33.8	180	4813
Helicon Group, L.P.	893	Englewood Cliffs, NJ	Private	42.9	180	4841
Infoseek Corporation	894	Sunnyvale, CA	Public	34.6	180	4813
Norlight Telecommunications	895	Brookfield, WI	Private	60.8	180	4813
TCI Of Overland Park, Inc.	896	Shawnee Mission, KS	Public Family Member	35.0	179	4841
Proxim Inc.	897	Mountain View, CA	Public	43.0	176	3663
Casio Phonemate Inc.	898	Torrance, CA	Private	100.0	175	3661
GTE Mobilnet Hawaii Inc.	899	Honolulu, HI	Public Family Member	56.0	175	4812
Polycom, Inc.	900	San Jose, CA	Public	111.7	175	3661
The Chillicothe Telephone Co.	901	Chillicothe, OH	Private	35.1	175	4813
Vodavi Technology, Inc.	902	Scottsdale, AZ	Public	47.7	173	3661
KQED Inc.	903	San Francisco, CA	Private	36.0	170	4833
Price Communications Corp	904	New York, NY	Public	43.7	169	4832
Eglobe Inc.	905	Denver, CO	Public	33.1	166	4813
Intellicall Inc.	906	Carrollton, TX	Public	117.0	166	4813
Aliant Systems Inc.	907	Lincoln, NE	Public Family Member	34.0	165	4813
M C L, Inc.	908	Bolingbrook, IL	Private	36.0	165	3663
Atlantic Cellular Company L P	909	Providence, RI	Private	45.1	160	4812
ETO Inc.	910	Colorado Springs, CO	Public Family Member	30.0	160	3663

D&B COMPANY RANKINGS BY EMPLOYMENT

Company	Rank	Location	Type	Sales ($ mil.)	Employ- ment	Primary SIC
Huber + Suhner Inc.	911	Essex Junction, VT	Private	60.0	160	3679
R F Power Products, Inc.	912	Voorhees, NJ	Public	33.8	160	3679
TCI Of Lexington, Inc.	913	Lexington, KY	Public Family Member	31.0	160	4841
Transamerica Bus Tech Corporations	914	Los Angeles, CA	Public Family Member	50.0	160	4813
Shared Communications Services	915	Salem, OR	Private	42.1	155	4813
Yahoo Inc.	916	Santa Clara, CA	Public	203.3	155	4813
MacDermid Inc.	917	Wilmington, DE	Public Family Member	80.5	152	3679
Adventist Media Center, Inc.	918	Simi Valley, CA	Private	42.6	150	4833
American Holdings LP	919	Spokane, WA	Private	38.0	150	4841
Brittan Communications Intl	920	Houston, TX	Private	48.0	150	4813
Dish, LTD	921	Englewood, CO	Public Family Member	475.9	150	4841
East Ascension Telephone Co.	922	Gonzales, LA	Private	30.0	150	4813
Echelon Corporation	923	Palo Alto, CA	Public	32.2	150	3663
Gemstar Intl Group LTD	924	Pasadena, CA	Public	126.6	150	4841
International Telecom Group LTD	925	Woodland Hills, CA	Private	300.0	150	4813
Netcom Systems Inc.	926	Chatsworth, CA	Private	56.0	150	3663
Polk Audio Inc.	927	Baltimore, MD	Public	54.2	150	3651
Prime/Matrix Inc.	928	Calabasas, CA	Private	47.7	150	4812
Telemedia International USA	929	Jersey City, NJ	Private	36.4	150	4813
Trans National Communications	930	Boston, MA	Private	63.1	150	4813
Central Kentucky Cellular	931	Richmond, KY	Public Family Member	44.0	145	4812
Georgia Public Telecom Comm	932	Atlanta, GA	Private	31.5	145	4832
Minnesota Equal Access	933	Minneapolis, MN	Private	34.7	145	4813
Pulsar Data Systems, Inc.	934	Lanham, MD	Private	160.0	145	4813
Nuera Communications, Inc.	935	San Diego, CA	Private	30.8	144	3661
United States Satellite Broadcasting	936	Saint Paul, MN	Public	456.6	142	4899
Datron World Communications	937	Escondido, CA	Public Family Member	54.6	140	3663
Krone Inc.	938	Englewood, CO	Private	34.7	140	3661
Liberty Cellular, Inc.	939	Salina, KS	Private	70.4	140	4812
STM Wireless Inc.	940	Irvine, CA	Public	52.1	140	3663
Innova Corporation	941	Seattle, WA	Public	36.1	138	3679
SDI Technologies Inc.	942	Rahway, NJ	Private	50.0	138	3651
Sigcom Inc.	943	Greensboro, NC	Private	41.8	135	4813
LIN Television Corporation	944	Providence, RI	Public	300.0	134	4833
Corsair Communications Inc.	945	Palo Alto, CA	Public	47.8	132	3663
WGNX Inc.	946	Atlanta, GA	Public Family Member	39.0	132	4833
Com21 Inc.	947	Milpitas, CA	Public	48.1	131	3663
Gannett Tennessee LTD Partnr	948	Knoxville, TN	Public Family Member	30.0	130	4833
Midwest Wireless Comm. LLC	949	Mankato, MN	Private	48.0	130	4812
Snet Mobility Inc.	950	Rocky Hill, CT	Private	227.0	130	4812
United International Holding	951	Denver, CO	Public	98.6	130	4841
1-800-Reconex, Inc.	952	Hubbard, OR	Private	48.1	125	4813
Alteon Networks Inc.	953	San Jose, CA	Private	30.0	125	3663
Justice Technology Corporation	954	Culver City, CA	Private	59.0	125	4813
WLVI, Inc.	955	Boston, MA	Public Family Member	40.0	125	4833
Netsource Communications Inc.	956	Petaluma, CA	Private	100.0	120	4813
Pacific Gateway Exchange, Inc.	957	Burlingame, CA	Public	298.6	120	4813
Primo Microphones Inc.	958	Mc Kinney, TX	Private	48.0	120	3651
Roscor Corporation	959	Mount Prospect, IL	Private	45.0	120	3663
Working Assets Funding Service	960	San Francisco, CA	Private	104.4	120	4813
Star Telecommunications, Inc.	961	Santa Barbara, CA	Public	376.2	116	4813
Communigroup Of KC, Inc.	962	Shawnee Mission, KS	Private	40.0	115	4813
Iowa Network Services Inc.	963	West Des Moines, IA	Private	38.8	114	4813
Transaction Network Services	964	Reston, VA	Public	63.3	112	4813
Cuming Corp	965	Avon, MA	Private	30.0	110	3679
E C I Telecom Inc.	966	Altamonte Springs, FL	Private	176.0	110	3661
Hartford Television, Inc.	967	Hartford, CT	Public Family Member	40.0	110	4833
Splitrock Services Inc.	968	The Woodlands, TX	Private	70.0	110	4899
Eurotherm Drives Inc.	969	Charlotte, NC	Private	37.0	106	3679
Cablevision Lightpath Inc.	970	Hicksville, NY	Public Family Member	38.0	100	4841
Choctaw Communications, Inc.	971	Houston, TX	Private	36.0	100	4813
Cooperative Communications	972	Belleville, NJ	Private	50.0	100	4813
Gemini Sound Products Corp	973	Carteret, NJ	Private	44.0	100	3651
Goldenline Network Service	974	Santa Monica, CA	Private	50.0	100	4813
Koplar Communications Inc.	975	Saint Louis, MO	Private	30.0	100	4833
KTNQ/KLVE, Inc (Not Inc)	976	Los Angeles, CA	Public Family Member	35.0	100	4832
Prominet Corporation	977	Concord, MA	Public Family Member	125.0	100	3663
RRV Enterprises Inc.	978	Houston, TX	Private	42.5	100	4813
Shared Tech Communications LLC	979	Hartford, CT	Private	30.0	100	4813
Trans World Radio	980	Cary, NC	Private	33.7	100	4832

D&B COMPANY RANKINGS BY EMPLOYMENT

Company	Rank	Location	Type	Sales ($ mil.)	Employ-ment	Primary SIC
WPGH, Inc.	981	Pittsburgh, PA	Public Family Member	35.0	100	4833
DBT Online, Inc.	982	Las Vegas, NV	Public	37.5	98	4813
Spanish Broadcasting System	983	New York, NY	Private	76.1	96	4832
TCI Central, Inc.	984	Denver, CO	Public Family Member	469.5	96	4841
Directed Electronics Inc.	985	Vista, CA	Private	74.2	95	3669
NTX, Inc.	986	Napa, CA	Public Family Member	35.0	90	4813
VAI Corporation	987	San Jose, CA	Private	53.0	90	3661
U S Media Holdings, Inc.	988	New York, NY	Private	45.0	85	4833
Texas Television Inc.	989	Corpus Christi, TX	Private	40.0	84	4833
Independent Television Network	990	New York, NY	Private	150.0	80	4833
Infinity Broadcasting Corp Cal Del	991	Los Angeles, CA	Public Family Member	40.0	80	4832
Technology Control Services	992	Fort Lauderdale, FL	Private	50.0	80	4813
Ebay, Inc.	993	San Jose, CA	Public	47.4	76	4813
Go-Video, Inc.	994	Scottsdale, AZ	Public	48.9	76	3651
Abracon Corporation	995	Aliso Viejo, CA	Private	50.0	75	3679
Arvig Telcom Inc.	996	Madison, WI	Public Family Member	40.0	75	4813
Cellnet Communications Inc.	997	Madison Heights, MI	Private	55.2	75	4812
Digitec 2000 Inc.	998	New York, NY	Private	35.0	75	4813
Sinclair Communications, Inc.	999	Baltimore, MD	Public Family Member	378.0	75	4833
Sportschannel Chicago Assoc	1000	Chicago, IL	Private	55.0	74	4841
Oneworld Systems Inc.	1001	Sunnyvale, CA	Public	61.5	70	3661
US Wats Inc.	1002	Bensalem, PA	Public	56.5	69	4813
Intelnet International Corp	1003	West Berlin, NJ	Private	58.4	60	4813
Stratos Mobile Networks USA LLC	1004	Bethesda, MD	Private	50.0	59	4899
Satellink Communications Inc.	1005	Roswell, GA	Private	39.7	57	4813
Blackstone Calling Card, Inc.	1006	Miami, FL	Private	61.0	51	4813
Chauncey Communications Corp	1007	Coudersport, PA	Public Family Member	112.0	50	4841
N I C E Systems Inc (De Corp)	1008	Secaucus, NJ	Private	69.3	50	4813
Telecard Dispensing Corp	1009	Hollywood, FL	Private	79.5	50	4813
Husko Inc.	1010	Milpitas, CA	Private	219.2	49	3679
Sportschannel Associates	1011	Woodbury, NY	Private	62.0	47	4841
Plateau Cellular Network Inc.	1012	Clovis, NM	Private	60.0	45	4812
Unity Motion, Inc.	1013	Maryland Heights, MO	Private	350.0	45	4841
Com Tech International Corp	1014	Boca Raton, FL	Private	110.0	42	4813
Harman Pro North America, Inc.	1015	Nashville, TN	Public Family Member	40.0	42	3651
American Long Lines Inc.	1016	Horsham, PA	Private	40.0	40	4813
Starpower Communications LLC	1017	Washington, DC	Private	65.0	40	4813
Teledata International Inc.	1018	Atlanta, GA	Private	80.0	40	4813
ABC Money Transactions, Inc.	1019	Garland, TX	Private	40.0	30	4822
Anaba Audio International Inc.	1020	Compton, CA	Private	42.0	30	3651
Sport South Network, LTD	1021	Atlanta, GA	Private	51.8	26	4841
Global Commerce & Media Network	1022	New York, NY	Private	100.0	25	4813
Orix Global Communications	1023	Las Vegas, NV	Private	120.0	25	4813
Satellite Services, Inc.	1024	Englewood, CO	Public Family Member	1,177.2	25	4841
Taylor University Broadcasting	1025	Fort Wayne, IN	Private	53.4	25	4832
Lloyd Daniels Dev Group	1026	Cincinnati, OH	Private	90.0	22	4822
Meridian Telecom Corp	1027	Hartsdale, NY	Private	50.0	22	4813
Phone Exchange Inc.	1028	Newport Beach, CA	Private	62.0	22	4813
Primetime 24 Joint Venture	1029	New York, NY	Private	50.7	22	4899
Communications Concepts Invest.	1030	Pompano Beach, FL	Private	50.0	21	4813
Cominex LLC	1031	Mays Landing, NJ	Private	100.0	20	4813
Cyberfone	1032	Wayne, PA	Private	70.0	20	3661
Paxson Communication Of New Lnd	1033	New London, CT	Public Family Member	88.4	20	4833
EDCO LLC	1034	Norwalk, CT	Private	93.0	18	4813
ATG International Inc.	1035	Anaheim, CA	Private	60.0	15	4813
Fnet Corp	1036	Thousand Oaks, CA	Public Family Member	210.0	15	4813
TMR Sales, Inc.	1037	Sunnyvale, CA	Private	40.0	14	3679
Emkay Communications Inc.	1038	New York, NY	Private	40.0	12	4813
R & E Associates, LLC	1039	Natick, MA	Private	45.0	12	3663
Cellular Communications Intl	1040	New York, NY	Public	105.0	10	4812
Zekko Corporation	1041	Ponte Vedra Beach, FL	Private	100.0	10	4899
Musicbox Network	1042	Oakland, CA	Private	60.0	9	4833
Amerix Electronic Inc.	1043	El Segundo, CA	Private	38.4	8	3679
Alert Marketing Inc.	1044	Lake Mary, FL	Private	108.0	7	4813
Group Long Distance Inc.	1045	Fort Lauderdale, FL	Public	54.3	7	4813
Paylexx Utilities & Telecommun	1046	Long Island City, NY	Private	40.0	7	4813
U S Digitel Inc.	1047	Hollywood, FL	Private	40.0	5	4813
Apunet	1048	Richardson, TX	Private	51.0	4	4813
G.I.K Technology, Inc.	1049	Oakland, CA	Private	50.0	4	4813
American Gateway Telecom	1050	Houston, TX	Private	50.0	3	4813

D&B COMPANY RANKINGS BY EMPLOYMENT

Company	Rank	Location	Type	Sales ($ mil.)	Employ- ment	Primary SIC
JMR Communication Corporation	1051	Dallas, TX	Private	75.0	3	4812
IXC, Inc.	1052	Boca Raton, FL	Private	40.0	2	4813

CHAPTER 6 - PART II

MERGERS & ACQUISITIONS

The following essay presents a look at merger and acquisition activity in the Broadcasting & Telecommunications sector. A general overview of M&A activity is followed by a listing of actual merger and acquisition events. Purchasing companies are listed in alphabetical order, with a paragraph set aside for each acquisition.

This essay discusses recent merger and acquisition activity in the industry and its effect on the industry. The essay is followed by a list of significant acquisitions and mergers.

The current intense pace of merger and acquisition activity in the broadcasting and telecommunications industry has at its root the passing of the Telecommunications Act of 1996. The bill deregulated the U.S. telecommunications industry, allowing phone companies, both regional and long-distance, and cable companies to begin competing in each other's markets. Almost immediately, U.S.-based telecommunications services companies, particularly phone companies and cable operators, began announcing billion dollar mergers, and an industry-wide consolidation trend was launched. While this type of convergence was already taking place on a limited basis prior to February of 1996, the act opened up cross-market penetration opportunities on both a national and an international scale.

The act helped telecommunication companies expand the services they could offer to their customers. A good example of this is WorldCom Inc. In the fall of 1998, WorldCom Inc. and MCI Communications Corp. came together for an unprecedented $37 billion. The deal reflected the quest of industry giants to provide a range of services, including Internet access and related online services. After the merger, WorldCom Inc. was the first telecommunications company able to offer local, long-distance, and international telephone service, Internet access, and data services on a single international fiber network. This grouping of services, known as *bundling,* is at the core of the industry-wide consolidation trend, and WorldCom has been at the forefront of bundling in the industry.

To become an industry leader, WorldCom made several major purchases from 1997 through 1999 aimed at increasing its Internet-related holdings. Purchases includes: OzMail; H & R Block's CompuServe; America Online's network subsidiary, ANS Communications Inc.; and Brooks Fiber, a U.S.-based Internet service provider. These acquisitions, along with the MCI Communications merger, have left MCI-WorldCom in control of more than one-half of worldwide Internet traffic and a leader in the worldwide telecommunications services market.

But MCI-WorldCom is not the only company to achieve growth through consolidation. In 1999, when AT&T bought IBM's Global Network, C. Michael Armstrong, chairman and CEO, said in a company press release that the purpose of such agreements was "growth in revenue, growth in technology, and, most importantly, growth in what AT&T can do for customers." AT&T took a step into the broadband communications arena in 1999, when it merged with number three cable operator MediaOne Group for a stock transaction valued at $58 billion. Growth was also the reason why in 1998, AT&T Corp. and cable television giant Tele-Communications Inc. agreed to an historic $48 billion merger. In August of 1998, AT&T agreed to join its international assets with those of British Telecommunications PLC to form WorldPartners; the deal, valued at $10 billion, reflects the globalization that is inherent in the industry's bundling trend.

Perhaps the impact of the merger and acquisition activity in the telecommunications market is nowhere better reflected than in the strength of the leading companies in the communications equipment sector. Revenues for the top ten companies, including Lucent Technologies Inc., Motorola Inc., and Northern Telecom Ltd., accounted for roughly 75 percent, or $162 billion, of the market's total revenue of $220 billion in 1997. The consolidation trend will only intensify according to securities analyst Alex Ciena of Bear Stearns & Co., who believes that "pretty soon there will be . . . only five or so major players" in the worldwide communications equipment sector.

In this sector, the leading U.S. telecommunications equipment company, Lucent Technologies, also holds a worldwide market share in excess of 10 percent. Between 1997 and 1999, the company made several significant transactions, including Internal Network Services, a data-networking company; Lannet Inc., a LAN equipment provider; Mass Media Communications, a developer of interworking data and voice protocol technology; Yurie Systems Inc., an ATM access technology manufacturer; Prominet Corp., an ethernet networking technology vendor; Livingston Enterprises Inc., a data networking software and services provider; and Octel Communications Corp., a messaging technology vendor.

Lucent isn't alone with acquisition fever. Canada-based communications equipment giant Northern Telecom paid $6.4 billion for Bay Networks Inc. in August of 1998. The deal was the largest to date between a telecommunications vendor and a specialist network company, yet it was only one among several record setting mergers in the networking sector. In fact, the networking market saw two of its largest acquisitions to date unfold in 1997 with the $6.6 billion merger of 3COM Corp. and U.S.Robotics Corp., which joined the LAN and WAN vendors, allowing for comprehensive networking capabilities, and the $3.7 billion merger of Ascend Communications Inc. and Cascade Communications Inc., which joined a WAN core switching technology provider with a WAN access provider.

Consolidation is fueled by the need for bundling and many networking technology companies are finding it less expensive and less time consuming to acquire existing businesses than to develop their own new technology. Aggressive acquisition campaigns over the past years have established Cisco Systems, 3COM, and Ascend Communications as clear market leaders in the networking sector. In 1999, Cisco bought two optical-networking companies for $7.35 billion and a Danish Internet access provider for $65.6 million.

In the Internet Service Provider (ISP) market, growth has been unparalleled. The ability of small ISPs to service local markets both effectively and cheaply has fueled the consolidation that has taken place in the national ISP market over the past year. For example, America Online Inc. (AOL) shored up its leadership position by acquiring the consumer online service of CompuServe Corp. from WorldCom Inc. in late 1997. In return for the CompuServe service, AOL relinquished its ANS Communications network to WorldCom. The purchase hoisted AOL's subscriber base to over 10 million, leaving chief rivals such as Prodigy, Microsoft Network, and AT&T WorldNet in a distant second place.

AOL's rapid growth also enabled it to introduce to subscribers an unprecedented $20 monthly base fee for unlimited Internet access. As a result, regional ISPs were forced to seek alliances with smaller local ISPs as a means of achieving the growth necessary to remain competitive. For example, in March of 1998 TCA Communications, Inc. bought Web International

Inc., a Texas-based ISP, to gain entrance to the Texas market. Companies like TCA Communications have also begun marketing to business customers, especially small businesses, to recover profits lost to AOL and other large national ISPs.

The late 1990s saw the broadcasting and computer industries forming mergers. For instance, throughout 1998 and 1999, CBS Corporation made a series of acquisitions of Internet sites to increase its new media holdings. Most of these purchases will be paid in advertising and promotion. These acquisitions included: a 38 percent share of Jobs.Com for $62 million; 22 percent share of wrenchead.com for $33 million; 35 percent of Medscape for $150 million; 30 percent of Third Age Media for $54 million; 35 percent of Switchboard, Inc. for $135 million; 35 percent of hollywood.com for $100 million; 50 percent of storeRunner.com for $100 million; 40 percent of womensconsumernet.com for $50 million. In September of 1999, CBS and Viacom agreed to merger in a transaction valued at $80 billion, the largest media transaction ever. The new company will be known as Viacom and will be the world's premier entertainment and media company.

Within the cable television broadcasting market, consolidation is rampant, evidenced by deals like investor Paul Allen's purchase of Communications Inc., a multiple system cable operator, for $2.5 billion in cash and a debt assumption of $2 billion in July of 1998. The total price paid was the highest to date in the cable industry. Only three months prior, Allen paid $2.7 billion for Marcus Cable, the tenth largest cable operator in the U.S.

Even in the less scrutinized segments of the broadcasting and telecommunications industry, such radio broadcasting, merger and acquisition activity has been high. In fact, in early 1997 the largest merger in radio broadcasting history took place when Westinghouse Electric Corp. folded Infinity Broadcasting's 43 radio stations into its CBS Radio group, which became the world's largest radio group owner with a total of 79 radio stations. In June of 1998 CBS Radio added the 90 radio stations of American Radio Systems Inc. to its portfolio for a record $2.6 billion. In 1999, Infinity expanded its radio group with three additional acquisitions; two in Florida and one in Ohio.

No segment of the industry remains unaffected by the Telecommunications Act of 1996 or the current pace of consolidation and convergence within the industry. The future of various segments of the industry still remains to be seen in some cases, but it's clear that the size of these industry leaders will be unprecedented and the services they offer will be highly integrated.

Mergers and Acquisitions

3COM Corp. bought **U.S. Robotics Corp.,** a remote access vendor, in one of the largest merger in the networking industry, for $8.5 billion on June 12, 1998. [*PC Week,* 6/23/97, p. 129.]

Abry Partners bought **Cable Michigan Inc.,** a multiple system operator, for $435 million in June of 1998. [*Broadcasting & Cable,* 8/8/98, p. 14.]

ADC Telecommunications Inc. bought **Princeton Optics Inc.,** a privately owned optical components supplier based in Ewing, New Jersey, in June of 1998. [*Electronic Buyers' News,* 6/29/98, p. 10.]

Alcatel Alsthom bought **DSC Communications Corp.,** a switching equipment technology vendor located in Dallas, Texas, in a stock transaction valued at $4.4 billion on September 9, 1998. The acquisition doubles Alcatel Alsthom's presence in the U.S. telecommunications market. [*Electronic News,* 8/31/98, p. 34.]

Paul Allen bought **Charter Communications Inc.,** a multiple system cable operator based in St. Louis, Missouri, for $2.5 billion in cash and a debt assumption of $2 billion in July of 1998. The total price paid was the highest to date in the cable industry. [*The Wall Street Journal,* 7/31/98, p. A3.]

—bought **Marcus Cable,** the tenth largest cable operator in the United States, for $2.7 billion in April of 1998. [*MediaWeek,* 4/13/98, p. 8.]

America Online, Inc. bought **Mirabilis Ltd.,** an Internet service provider based in Tel Aviv, Israel, for $287 million in cash on June 5, 1998. [*EDGE: Work-Group Computing Report,* 6/15/98, p. 9.]

—bought **Personal Library Software Inc.,** a privately held developer of searching and information indexing technologies located in Rockville, Maryland, on January 21, 1998. [*Information Today,* 3/98, p. 7.]

—bought the consumer online service of **CompuServe** from **WorldCom** on September 9, 1997. In exchange for the CompuServe service and $175 million in cash, AOL transferred **ANS Communications Inc.,** its network subsidiary, to WorldCom. [*Online,* 3/98, p. 77.]

American Mobile Satellite Corp. bought **Ardis,** a wireless network data operator, for $100 million in cash and stock in March of 1998. [*Satellite News,* 3/9/98, p. 9.]

American Radio Systems Inc. bought **EZ Communications Inc.,** a radio station broadcast group, on April 4, 1997. [*PR Newswire,* 4/7/97.]

Arutzei Zahav bought **Edan Cable,** based in Israel, on March 15, 1998. The purchase increased Arutzei Zahav's share of Israel's cable television market to 40 percent. [*Israel Business Today,* 3/15/98, p. 11.]

Ascend Communications Inc. bought **Stratus Computer, Inc.,** a manufacturer of OSS Software and SS7 switches, in a stock swap valued at $822 million in August of 1998. [*EDGE: On & about AT&T,* 8/10/98, p. 1.]

—bought **Cascade Communications Corp.,** a manufacturer of WAN switches, in the second largest merger to date in the networking industry, for $3.6 billion on June 30, 1997. [*InfoWorld,* 12/22/97, p. 181.]

AT&T Corp. bought **MediaOne Group,** a broadband communications company, for $58 billion in stock in May of 1999. [MediaOne press release. Available from http://www.mediaonegroup.com.]

—bought **IBM's Global Network** business for $5 billion in cash on December 8, 1998. [AT&T news release. Available from http://www.att.com.]

—bought **Teleport Communications Group,** a provider of fiber optics local network services to business clients, for $11.3 billion in July of 1998. [*Telephony,* 7/27/98.]

Bell Atlantic Corp. and **Vodafone AirTouch,** agreed to form a joint venture that will create a new coast-to-coast wireless telephone company in a deal valued at more than $70 billion. [*Reuters, 9/21/99.*]

—and **Nynex Corp.** merged into the largest regional Bell company and the second largest telecommunications company in the U.S., with estimated annual operating revenues of $29.2 billion, in a deal valued at $25.6 billion in August of 1997. The company retained the Bell Atlantic name. [*Internet Week, 9/1/97, p. S7.*]

Black Box Corp. bought **The Austin Connection Inc.,** a cabling and related products installation services company based in Tampa, Florida, on September 1, 1998. [*PR Newswire, 9/1/98.*]

British Telecommunications PLC bought the remaining shares of its global networking joint venture with **MCI Communications Corp.,** called **Concert Communications Services,** for $1 billion in August of 1998. [*Computing Canada, 9/1/98, p. 32.*]

Cable and Wireless bought all of the Internet assets of **MCI Communications Corp.,**the world's second largest long distance telephone company, for $1.6 billion, in July of 1998. [*The Wall Street Journal, 7/15/98, p. B6.*]

Cabletron Systems Inc. bought **NetVantage Inc.,** an Ethernet workgroup switching technology provider, for $100 million in stock in August of 1998. [*Telecommunications, 8/98, p. 22.*]

—bought **Flow Point Networks,** a manufacturer of digital subscriber line devices, for $25 million in cash and stock in June of 1998. [*InfoWorld, 6/15/98, p. 3.*]

—bought the Communications Systems Group of **Ariel Communications Inc.,**a manufacturer of digital subscriber line concentrators, for $33.5 million in cash in June of 1998. [*InfoWorld, 6/15/98, p. 3.*]

—bought **OASys Group Inc.,** a telecommunications software developer located in Los Gatos, California, for 240,000 shares on February 7, 1997. [*Business Wire,2/7/97.*]

Cablevision Systems Corp. bought **Nobody Beats the Wiz Inc.,** a consumer electronics retail operation,

for $100 million in February of 1998. [*Communications Daily, 2/9/98, p. 5.*]

—bought the New York and New Jersey cable assets of **TCI Communications Inc.,** a subsidiary of **Tele-Communications Inc.,** in March of 1998. In exchange for the cable systems, Tele-Communications Inc. secured a 33 percent share of Cablevision Co., as well as two board seats. [*Telecommunications Reports, 3/9/98, p. 39.*]

CBS Corporation bought **King World Productions Inc.,** a distributor of syndicated shows, for $2.5 billion in stock in April of 1999. [*PR Newswire, 4/1/99.*]

—bought the 90 radio stations of **American Radio Systems Inc.** for $2.6 billion on June 5, 1998. [*Communications Daily, 6/8/98.*]

Chancellor Broadcasting Co. and **Evergreen Media Corp.** merged to form **Chancellor Media Corp.** in September of 1997. [*Broadcasting & Cable, 9/15/97, p. 128.*]

Cisco Systems, Inc. bought two optical-networking companies in August of 1999 for a combined price of $7.35 billion. Cisco purchased **Cerent,** and Richardson, Texas-based **Monterey Networks,**. [*Wired News, 8/26/99.*]

—bought Internet access provider **CoCom A/S,** located in Copenhagen, Denmark, for $65.6 million in stock in September of 1999. [*Retuers, 9/15/99.*]

—bought **Net Speed Inc.,** a Digital Subscriber Line technology manufacturer located in Austin, Texas, for roughly $236 million in stock in March of 1998. [*EDGE: On & about AT&T, 3/16/98, p. 7.*]

—bought **Light Speed Software,** a voice signaling translation technology manufacturer located in Sterling, Virginia, for roughly $160 million in stock in January of 1998. [*PC Week, 1/5/98, p. 95.*]

—bought **Ardent Communications Corp.,** a compressed voice, LAN, and data and video traffic transmission technology provider located in San Jose, California, for $156 million in stock in July of 1997.[*EDGE: On & about AT&T, 6/30/97, p. 6.*]

—bought **Global Internet Software Group**, based in Palo Alto, California, for $40.25 million in cash in July of 1997. [*EDGE: Work-Group Computing Report*, 6/30/97, p.10.]

—bought **Skystone Systems Corp.**, a privately owned Synchronous Optical Networking/Synchronous Digital Hierarchy technology provider based in Ottawa, Ontario, Canada, for $22.6 million in cash and one million shares in July of 1997. [*EDGE: On & about AT&T*, 6/16/97, p. 24.]

Clear Channel Communications Inc. bought **Dame Media Inc.**, including its 21 radio stations, for $85 million in June of 1998. [*MEDIAWEEK*, 6/22/98, p. 3.]

—bought **More Group L.L.P.**, an outdoor advertising group based in Britain, for $932 million in June of 1998. [*MEDIAWEEK*, 6/22/98, p. 3.]

—bought **Universal Outdoor Holdings**, an outdoor advertising firm, in a stock swap worth $1.7 billion on October 27, 1997. [*Communications Daily*, 10/27/97, p. 7.]

Concentric Network Corp. bought **Delta Internet Services Inc.**, a dial-up, dedicated access, and World Wide Web hosting services provider based in California, on June 5, 1998.[*Next Wave Stocks: Mergers & Acquisitions*, 6/98.]

Cox Communications Inc. bought the Tucson, Arizona, cable assets of **TCI Communications Inc.**, a subsidiary of **Tele-Communications Inc.**, in June of 1998. [*Business Wire*, 6/16/98.]

—bought **Prime Cable of Las Vegas Inc.** for $1.3 billion in May of 1998. [*Broadcasting & Cable*, 5/11/98, p. 88.]

Ericsson bought Silver Springs, Maryland-based **Torrent Network Technologies**, which develops Internet routing solutions for operators and service provider networks, for $450 million on April 13, 1999.[Ericsson press release. Availabe from http://www.ericsson.com/pressroom.]

—bought California-based **Advanced Computer Communications**, a vendor of integrated, carrier-class remote access and Internet-working products, for $285 million in cash in September of 1999. [Ericsson press release. Available from http://www.ericsson.com/pressroom.]

Ericsson Toshiba Telecommunications Systems K.K. and **Nippon Ericsson K.K.** merged on July 1, 1998. The new company retained the Nippon Ericcson K.K. name. [*EDGE: On & about AT&T*, 7/6/98.]

France Telecom bought **Casema**, the largest cable operator in The Netherlands, on December 12, 1997. [*PR Newswire*, 12/12/97.]

Frontier Vision Partners, L.P. bought the Central Ohio cable television system of **Cox Communications Corp.**, one of the largest broadband communications companies in the United States, on December 23, 1997. [*Business Wire*, 12/23/97.]

Gray Communications Systems, Inc. bought **Busse Broadcasting Corp.** for $112 million on August 3, 1998. [*PR Newswire*, 8/3/98.]

GTE Corp. bought **BBN Corp.**, an Internet service provider, in May of 1997. GTE Corp. changed the name of BBN Corp. to GTE Internetworking. [*Next Wave Stocks: Mergers & Acquisitions*, 5/97.]

Home Shopping Network Inc. bought **Universal TV** for $4 billion on February 17, 1998. Home Shopping Network Inc. then changed its name to **USA Networks Inc.**[*Communications Daily*, 2/17/98, p. 8.]

Hungarian Broadcasting Corp. bought **Global TV Networks**, an adult programming network based in Budapest, for a total of 7.25 million shares on January 7, 1998. [*Communications Daily*, 1/7/98, p. 6.]

ICG Communications Inc. bought **Netcom Online Communications Service Inc.**,the fifth largest Internet service provider in the U.S., in October of 1997. [*Next Wave Stocks: Mergers & Acquisitions*, 10/97.]

Infinity Broadcasting Corp. bought **Outdoor Systems, Inc.**, an outdoor advertising company, for $6.5 billion in stock and $1.8 million of debt assumption in May of 1999.[*PR Newswire*, 5/27/99.]

Infinity Broadcasting Inc. bought three radio stations from **Clear Channel Broadcasting Inc.,** for $122.5 million in cash in February of 1999. The stations were Tampa, Florida-based WSJT-FM and WRBQ-FM and Cleveland, Ohio-based WNCX-FM. [*PR Newswire, 2/11/99.*]

Intermedia Communications bought Monroe, Louisiana-based **LDS Communications Group,** a provider of long distance voice and data telecommunications services, including Internet and World Wide Web access, for $151 million in stock and cash on December 17, 1997. [*NextWave Stocks: Mergers & Acquisitions, 12/97.*]

Level One Communications Inc. bought **Acclaim Communications Inc.,** a layer three switching technology maker based in San Jose, California, for $122.5 million in stock in June of 1998.[*Electronic Engineering Times, 6/29/98, p. 8.*]

Lucent Technologies Inc. bought **International Network Services,** a data-networking company, for $3.7 billion in stock in August of 1999.[*Wired News, 8/10/99.*]

—bought **Lannet Inc.,** a LAN equipment vendor based in Israel, for $117 million in cash in July of 1998. [*Electronic Buyers' News, 7/13/98, p. 6.*]

—bought **Mass Media Communications,** an interworking data and voice protocol technology developer, in July of 1998. [*Info World, 8/3/98, p. 44.*]

—bought **Yurie Systems Inc.,** an ATM access technology vendor, for $1 billion on May 29, 1998. [*Communications Daily, 6/1/98.*]

—bought **Prominet Corp.,** an ethernet networking technology provider, for $200 million on January 26, 1998. [*Communications Daily, 1/26/98, p. 5.*]

—bought **Livingston Enterprises Inc.,** a remote access data networking software and services provider located in Pleasanton, California, for $650 million on December 17, 1997.[*Communications Daily, 12/17/97, p. 6.*]

—bought **Octel Communications Corp.,** a messaging technology provider based in Milpitas, California, for $1.8 billion on September 30, 1997. [*Communications Daily,9/30/97, p. 7.*]

MCI-WorldCom, pending approval from the FCCDepartment of Justice, Federal Communications Commission, and the Federal Trade Commission, acquired **Sprint** for $129 billion in October of 1999. [*Wired News, 10/5/99.*]

Mediacom Inc. bought the cable systems of **Cablevision Systems Corp.,** previously known as **U.S. Cable,** for $311 million on January 28, 1998. [*Communications Daily,1/28/98, p. 8.*]

Microsoft Corp. bought 4 percent of **Nextel Communications Inc.,** a provider of wireless communications, for $600 million in cash in May of 1999. [*The New York Times on the Web, 5/11/99.*]

—bought a 1.3 percent of **Qwest Communications,**a fiber-optic network company, for $200 million in December of 1998. [*Red Herring, 12/14/98.*]

—bought **WebTV Networks Inc.,** a Palo Alto, California-based provider of systems which allow Internet access via television, for $425 million on August 1, 1997. [*Communications Daily, 8/4/97, p. 7.*]

Motorola Inc. bought **General Instrument,** a set-top box supplier, for $11 billion in stock in September of 1999. [*Wired News, 9/15/99.*]

—bought **Starfish Software Inc.,** a mobile communication devices software developer based in Scotts Valley, California, in August of 1998. [*Computer Reseller News,8/3/98, p. 73.*]

Netscape Communications Corp. bought **Portola Communications, Inc.,** a messaging systems manufacturer, for $56 million on June 17, 1997. [*PR Newswire, 6/17/97.*]

Nippon Telegraph and Telephone (NTT) bought a 12.5 percent stake in **Teligent,**a privately owned wireless communications company, for $100 million in September of 1997. The purchase was the first noteworthy attempt by NTT, the largest telecommunications company in the world, to secure a portion of the U.S. telecommunications market. [*The New York Times, 10/1/97.*]

Nokia Corp. bought **Ipsilon Networks Inc.,** a data switching vendor located in Sunnyvale, California, for $120 million in cash and stock in December of 1997. [*Internet Week,*12/15/97, p. 12.]

Northern Telecom Ltd. bought **Bay Networks Inc.,** a data network equipment vendor based in Santa Clara, California, for $6.4 billion on August 31, 1998. The deal was the largest to date between a telecommunications vendor and a specialist network company. [*Network Briefing,* 8/25/98.]

NTL Inc. bought **Comcast UK Cable Partners Ltd.** for $997 million on February 9, 1998. The acquisition boosted NTL Inc. to the third largest cable television and telephone company in the United Kingdom with roughly 3.8 million subscribers. [*Telecommunications Report,* 2/9/98, p. 13.]

Omnipoint Communications announced a joint venture with **NPI Wireless** to create a PCS network in North Central Michigan on June 4, 1999. [*Omnipoint press release. Available from http:// www.proteus.com.]*

One Point Communications Corp. bought the multiple dwelling unit assets of **Preferred Entertainment Inc.,** a privately held cable television operator based in Chicago, Illinois, in July of 1998.[*PR Newswire,* 6/9/ 98.]

Qualcomm Inc. bought **Navtek Corp.,** a wireless data software company based in Washington, D.C., on June 15, 1998. [*PR Newswire,* 6/15/98.]

—bought **Now Software Inc.,** a manufacturer of scheduling software technology for mobile users, in November of 1997. [*InfoWorld,* 11/17/97, p. 21.]

Qwest bought **EUnet International,** a European Internet services provider based in Amsterdam, The Netherlands, for $4.5 million in cash, $135.5 million in shares, and an additional $14.4 million in cash or shares, to be determined by Qwest, on April 15, 1998. [*Next Wave Stocks: Mergers & Acquisitions,* 4/98.]

SBC Communications Inc. bought **Comcast Cellular Corp.,** the wirless subsidiary of Comcast Corp., in a transaction valued at $1.674 billion on July 8, 1999.

[SBC news release. Available from http:// www.sbc.com.]

—bought **Ameritech Corp.** for $61 billion in June of 1999. Once combined, the two regional Bell companies would have a revenue of $40 billion, operate across 13 states, and control local access lines to one-third of all U.S. households.[*Reuters,* 6/29/99.]

—and **Telefonos de Mexico** bought **Cellular Communications of Puerto Rico,** for $814, including debt, in May of 1999. [*Reuters,* 5/3/99.]

—bought **Pacific Telesis Group** for $16.5 billion on April 2, 1997. The acquisition made SBC Communications the second largest telecommunications company in the U. S.[*Communications Daily,* 4/2/97, p. 1.]

Shop at Home Inc. bought **Global Broadcasting Systems** for $75.9 million on March 27, 1998. [*Communications Daily,* 3/30/98.]

Sinclair Broadcast Group Inc. bought **Sullivan Broadcast Holding Inc.,** including nine television stations, for $1 billion on July 2, 1998. [*Communications Daily,* 7/2/98.]

Sprint bought Colorado Springs, Colorado-based **American Telecasting Inc.,** a provider of high-speed Internet access, for $170.8 million and $283 million of debt assumption in September of 1999. [*PR Newswire,* 9/23/99.]

—bought two operating subsidiaries of **WBS America, LLC,** a provider of high-speed Internet access and pay television to California and Florida markets, in July of 1999. [*PR Newswire,* 7/27/99.]

—bought two high-speed wireless providers **Videotron USA,** for $180 million, and **Transworld Telecommunications Inc.,** for $30 million, in May of 1999. [*PR Newswire,* 5/3/99.]

—bought **People's Choice TV,** a broadband wireless company, for $123.3 million in April of 1999. [*PR Newswire,* 4/12/99.]

Sun Microsystems, Inc. bought **Chorus Systems SA,** a telecommunications equipment operating systems manufacturer based in France, in September of 1997. [*Computing Canada,* 9/29/97, p. 6.]

TCA Communications, Inc. bought **Web International Inc.,** a Texas-based Internet service provider doing business as **Internet Tyler,** on March 30, 1998. [*Communications Daily,* 3/30/98.]

Tele-Communications Inc. bought Tulsa, Oklahoma-based **United Video Satellite Group Inc.,** including its broadband satellite system, for 6.3 million shares of **TCI Ventures** stock and 4.9 million shares of **Liberty Media** stock on January 19, 1997. [*Television Digest,* 1/19/98, p. 7.]

Telecom Italia S.p.A. bought **Bouygues Telecom,** a subsidiary of **Cable and Wireless PLC,** for $734 million in April of 1998. [*Telecommunications Reports,* 4/20/98, p. 17.]

Telefonaktiebolaget LM Ericsson bought **Advanced Computer Communications,** a remote access and internetworking technology vendor located in Santa Barbara, California, for $285 million in cash on September 9, 1998. [*Business Wire,* 9/9/98.]

Teleport Communications Group, Inc. bought **Kansas City Fiber Network, LP,** a local exchange carrier, on December 2, 1997. The acquisition makes Teleport Communications Group the first and largest U.S.-based local telecommunications services provider to use both fiber optic and broadband wireless technology. [*Next Wave Stocks: Mergers & Acquisitions,* 12/97.]

TeleWest Communications Group Ltd. bought **General Cable,** based in the United Kingdom, for $1.1 billion in May of 1998. Immediately following the transaction, TeleWest Communications Group boasted a membership of roughly 5.8 million homes. [*Broadcasting & Cable,* 5/4/98, p. 103.]

Tellabs Inc. bought **Coherent Communications Systems Corp.,** a supplier of echo cancellers to carriers, for $843.2 million in stock on August 4, 1998. [*Communications Daily,* 8/4/98.]

Thomas and Betts Corp. bought **Telecommunications Devices Inc.,** a privately held manufacturer of battery packs for cellular phones, laptop computers,

and other mobile communications equipment, in a stock swap on July 3, 1998. [*Electronic News,* 7/6/98, p. 55.]

Transaction Network Services, Inc. bought the transaction access services of **AT&T Corp.** for $64 million in cash on September 10, 1998. [*Business Wire,* 9/10/98.]

USA Networks bought **Ticketmaster Group Inc.,** the largest computerized ticketing operation in the world, on June 24, 1998. [*Business Wire,* 6/24/98.]

UUNET Technologies Inc. bought **Nlnet,** the largest Internet services provider in The Netherlands, in September of 1997. [*Internet Week,* 9/8/97, p. 16.]

VoiceStream Wireless and **Omnipoint Corp.** merged to become a major provider of GSM (Global System for Mobile Communications) in June of 1999. Hutchison Telecommunications PCS Limited also made a cash investment of $957 million into the combined company, making the total value of all transactions more than $9 billion. [*Business Wire,* 6/23/99.]

Westinghouse Electric Corp. bought the cable network operations of **Gaylord Entertainment Co.,** including **TNN: The Nashville Network** and **CMT: Country Music Television,** for $1.55 billion in stock on October 1, 1997. The remaining operations of Gaylord Entertainment Co. were spun off to the company's stockholders. Westinghouse Electric Corp. merged the new acquisition into its **CBS Cable** operations. [*Business Wire,* 10/1/97.]

—bought **Infinity Broadcasting Corp.** and folded Infinity Broadcasting's 43 radio stations into its **CBS Radio** group in January of 1997. The merger was the largest to date in the radio industry, and it made CBS Radio the world's largest radio group owner, with a total of 79 radio stations. [*MEDIAWEEK,* 1/6/97, p. 41.]

World Access Inc. bought a 55 percent share of **NACT Communications Inc.,** a telephony switching systems and telecommunications software developer located in Utah, for $71 million in February of 1998. [*Computergram International,* 2/2/98.]

—bought **Advanced Tech Com Inc.,** a digital microwave radio systems designer and manufacturer based in Wilmington, Massachusetts, for $10 million in stock and $5 million in debt assumption in January of 1998. [*Computergram International,* 2/2/98.]

—bought **Galaxy Personal Communications Inc.** for $7.5 million in August of 1997.[*Computergram International,* 2/2/98.]

WorldCom Inc. bought **OzMail Ltd.,** a highly successful Australian Internet service provider, for $323 million in December of 1998. [*Red Herring Online,* 12/14/98.]

—and **MCI Communications Corp.,** the second largest long distance phone company in the world, merged to form **MCI-WorldCom,** a telecommunications giant with more than $30 billion in sales, in August of 1998. The transaction was valued at roughly $37 billion. [*Computing Canada,* 9/1/98, p. 32.]

—bought **Brooks Fiber,** a nationwide Internet service provider, for $2.9 billion in January of 1998. [*Online,* 3/98, p. 77.]

—bought **CompuServe,** an online service provider, in a $1.2 billion stock swap on September 9, 1997. WorldCom then transferred the CompuServe consumer online service to **America Online, Inc.** in exchange for AOL's network subsidiary, **ANS Communications Inc.,** and $175 million in cash. [*Online,* 3/98, p. 77.]

—bought **MFS Communications Co.,** owner of fiber optic networks across North America, as well as a trans-Atlantic cable, for $13.56 billion in January of 1997. The acquisition allowed WorldCom to offer local, long distance, and international telephone service, Internet access, and data services on a single international fiber network. [*Computerworld,* 1/6/97, p. 32.]

World Satellite Network Inc. bought **Heifner Communications** in February of 1998 [*Communications Daily,* 2/3/98, p. 10.]

Bibliography

Barker, Robert. "How to Be in the Right Spot to Catch a Merger Wave." *BusinessWeek,* 6/15/98, p. 88.

Bartash, Jeffry. "MCO WorldCom Eyes Spring Takeover." *CBS MarketWatch,* 9/24/99.

Bazzy, Jared. "Lofty Goals for World Access, Telco Systems."*Telecommunications,* 8/98, p. 16.

Blinch, Russell. "Convergence Coming." *Computer Dealer News,* 6/13/98, p. 34.

Bournellis, Cynthia. "Merger Frenzy Unfolds." *Electronic News,* 6/15/98, p. 54.

Creswell, Julie. "Will Omnipoint Be Bought—or Go Broke?" *Fortune,* 5/24/99.

Gillooly, Brian. "Be Ready for the Merger Monster." *Information Week,* 6/1/98, p. 147.

Goldblatt, Henry. "AT&T's Costly Game of Catch-Up." *Fortune,*7/20/98, p. 25.

Greene, Jay. "Microsoft Will Buy 4.25% Interest in Nextel." *Seattle Times,* 5/10/99.

Grover, Ronald. "Every Cable Company is Cinderella Now." *Business Week,*7/6/98, p. 30.

Martin, Michael. "Microsoft Bets Net and TV Converge." *InfoWorld Canada,*7/97, p. 9.

Mulqueen, John T. "Two Giant Mergers Add Fuel to Public Network-s Growth."*Internet Week,* 6/8/98, p. 9.

Noll, Michael A. "The Telecom Act of 1996: Two Years Later."*Telecommunications,* 7/98, p. 44.

Scales, Ian. "Nortel Merger Shows Appetite for Convergence." *Communications Week International,* 6/29/98, p. 1.

Schnurman, Mitchell. "Merger of Texas-based Firms Will Create Nation's Largest Radio Company." *Knight-Ridder/Tribune Business News,* 8/27/98.

"The Early Bird Gets the Merger." *Wired News,* 9/9/99.

Thyfault, Mary E. "Major Mergers in Telecom Equipment." *InformationWeek,*6/8/98, p. 180.

Slabodkin, Gregory. "DOD Raises Concerns over Possible AT&T, British Telecom Deal." *Government Computer News,* 8/3/98, p. 77.

Valovic, Tom. "The AT&T/TCI Deal: A Defining Event in Telecom." *Telecommunications,* 8/98, p. 6.

—AnnaMarie L. Sheldon, updated by Katherine Wagner.

ASSOCIATIONS

This chapter presents a selection of business and professional associations active in the Broadcasting & Telecommunications sector. The information shown is adapted from Gale's *Encyclopedia of Associations* series and provides detailed and comprehensive information on nonprofit membership organizations.

Entries are arranged in alphabetical order. Categories included are e-mail address (when provided), description, founding date, number of memberships, staff; regional, state, and local group counts; national groups; budget, publications, and other information.

ACADEMY OF TELEVISION ARTS AND SCIENCES
5220 Lankershim Blvd.
North Hollywood, CA 91601
James L. Loper, Exec. Dir.
PH: (818)754-2800
FX: (818)761-2827
E-mail: info@emmys.org
URL: www.emmys.org
Founded: 1948. **Staff:** 24. **Members:** 6,500. Professionals in the television and film industry. To advance the arts and sciences of television through services to the industry in education, preservation of television programs, and information and community relations; to foster creative leadership in the television industry. Sponsors Television Academy Hall of Fame. Maintains library on television credits and historical material, the Television Academy Archives, and archives at UCLA of over 35,000 television programs. Offers internships to students. Holds luncheon and speakers series and meetings on problems of the various crafts.

ADVANCED TELEVISION SYSTEMS COMMITTEE
1750 K St. NW, Ste. 800
Washington, DC 20006
Robert K. Graves, Chmn.
PH: (202)828-3130
FX: (202)828-3131
E-mail: atsc@atsc.org
URL: www.atsc.org
Founded: 1983. **Staff:** 3. **Members:** 55. Sponsored by the Joint Committee on Intersociety Coordination Members of the television and motion picture industry united to develop voluntary international standards in the area of advanced digital television systems.

AMERICAN FACSIMILE ASSOCIATION
2200 Ben Franklin Pkwy. Ste. N-103
Philadelphia, PA 19130
Craig Hope, Exec.Dir.
PH: (215)981-0292
FX: (215)981-0295
E-mail: faxinfo@afaxa.com
URL: www.afaxa.com
Founded: 1986. **Staff:** 10. Hardware/software manufacturers, fax service providers, and others interested in messaging. Works to serve as main resource for fax information; to promote the use of fax as the primary document and message delivery system; promote communication among members; to represent members' legislative interests. Operates placement service; compiles statistics.

AMERICAN FEDERATION OF TELEVISION AND RADIO ARTISTS
260 Madison Ave.
New York, NY 10016
Bruce A. York, Exec.Dir.
PH: (212)532-0800
FX: (212)532-2242
Founded: 1937. **Members:** 75,000. AFL-CIO.

AMERICAN MOBILE TELECOMMUNICATIONS ASSOCIATION
1150 18th. NW, Ste. 250
Washington, DC 20036
Alan R. Shark, CAE, Pres., CEO
PH: (202)331-7773
FX: (202)331-9062
URL: www.amtausa.org
Founded: 1985. **Staff:** 8. **Members:** 375. **Budget:** 900,000. Corporations, partnerships, sole proprietorships, and individuals either licensed by the FCC, or engaged in the manufacture of carrier equipment. Represents members in all federal regulatory and legislative activities pertaining to private and commercial mobile radio service carriers; distributes information and data concerning technical, regulatory, and business developments affecting operators; provides a system for carrier licensees to achieve optimal use of their allocation of frequency assignments; seeks to encourage efficient use of the electromagnetic spectrum. Offers FCC Research Service for verification of licensed applications, system-loading verification, and geographic licensing reports and maps.

AMERICAN PUBLIC COMMUNICATIONS COUNCIL
10306 Eaton Pl., Ste. 520
Fairfax, VA 22030
Vincent R. Sandusky, Pres.
PH: (703)385-5300
FX: (703)385-5301
Founded: 1988. **Staff:** 12. **Members:** 1,500. Manufacturers, suppliers, distributors, and operators involved in the sale, lease, installation, and maintenance of pay telephone equipment. Goals are to protect and expand domestic and foreign markets for public communications, and to provide services that will improve business opportunities for members. Provides members with market strategies, legal assistance, networking opportunities, and guidance in international distribution. Represents the interests of members in legislative and regulatory concerns.

AMERICAN RADIO ASSOCIATION
360 W. 31st St., Frnt. 3
New York, NY 10001-2727
William R. Schuman, Pres.
PH: (212)594-3600
FX: (212)594-7422
E-mail: arany@mindspring.com
Founded: 1948. **Staff:** 7. **Members:** 250.

AMERICAN SPORTSCASTERS ASSOCIATION
5 Beekman St., Ste. 814
New York, NY 10038
Louis O. Schwartz, Exec.Dir. & Pres.Founder
PH: (212)227-8080
FX: (212)571-0556
E-mail: asassn@juno.com
Founded: 1979. **Staff:** 3. **Members:** 500. **Budget:** 200,000. Radio and television sportscasters. Sponsors seminars, clinics, and symposia for aspiring announcers and sportscasters. Compiles statistics. Operates speakers' bureau, placement service, hall of fame, and biographical archives. Maintains American Sportscaster Hall of Fame Trust. Is currently implementing Hall of Fame Museum, Community Programs.

AMERICAN TELEMEDICINE ASSOCIATION
1010 Vermont Ave. NW, Ste. 301
Washington, DC 20005-2339
Jonathan Linkous, Dir.
PH: (202)628-4700
FX: (202)628-4277
URL: www.atmeda.org
Founded: 1993. **Members:** 850. Works to promote improvement in health care delivery by applying telecommunications technology. Supports telemedical research and education; develops policy and standards; educates government leaders, public and professional organizations; serves as a clearinghouse for telemedical information and services.

AMERICAN WOMEN IN RADIO AND TELEVISION
1650 Tysons Blvd., No. 200
Mc Lean, VA 22102
Terri Dickerson, Exec.Dir.
PH: (703)506-3290
FX: (703)506-3266
E-mail: info@awrt.org
URL: www.awrt.org
Founded: 1951. **Staff:** 3. Professionals in administrative, creative, or executive positions in broadcasting and related industries (radio, television, cable, entertainment, information, networks, etc.) as well as advertising, government, and charitable agencies, corporations, and service organizations, whose work is substantially devoted to radio and television. Maintains AWRT Educational Foundation, chartered 1960. Maintains speakers' bureau and charitable program.

ARMED FORCES BROADCASTERS ASSOCIATION
PO Box 447
Sun City, CA 92586-0447
Mary Carnes, Pres.
Founded: 1982. **Members:** 600. Former and current military and commercial broadcasters. Provides an opportunity for military broadcasters and supporters to meet and socialize. Assists broadcasters returning to the U.S. from overseas. Provides job information center.

ASSOCIATED PRESS BROADCASTERS
1825 K St. NW, Ste. 710
Washington, DC 20006-1202
Jim Williams, VP & Dir.
PH: (202)736-1100
TF: (800)821-4747
FX: (202)736-1107
Founded: 1941. **Members:** 6,000. Broadcast stations in the United States that are members of the Associated Press. To advance journalism through radio and television. Cooperates with the AP in order to make available accurate and impartial news. Serves as a liaison between radio and television stations that are members of the AP and representatives of those stations.

ASSOCIATION FOR INTERACTIVE MEDIA
1301 Connecticut Ave NW, 5th Fl. 0
Washington, DC 20036-5105
Andrew L. Sernovitz, Pres.
PH: (202)408-0008
FX: (202)408-0111
Founded: 1992. **Staff:** 23. **Members:** 87. **Budget:** 1,000,000. Organizations, corporations, and individuals interested in the interactive television industry. Promotes the interests and image of the interactive television industry through political action and press releases. Provides reporters with research assistance, expert opinions, and contact information. Works to keep members updated on issues affecting the industry. Maintains speakers' bureau; conducts research and educational programs; offers placement service.

ASSOCIATION FOR MAXIMUM SERVICE TELEVISION
1776 Massachusetts Ave. NW, Ste. 310
Washington, DC 20036
Margita E. White, Pres.
PH: (202)861-0344
FX: (202)861-0342
Founded: 1956. **Staff:** 6. **Members:** 250. Purpose is to assure the maintenance and development of an effective nationwide system of free, over-the-air television, based on local broadcast stations that provide community-oriented service of maximum technical quality. Promotes protection against interference and degradation of the public's broadcast service and opportunities for local stations to use advanced television.

ASSOCIATION FOR WOMEN IN COMMUNICATIONS
Severn Commerce Center
1244 Ritchie Hwy., Ste.6
Arnold, MD 21012
Patricia H. Troy, Exec. Dir.
PH: (410)544-7442
FX: (410)544-4640
E-mail: womcom@aol.com
URL: www.womcom.org
Founded: 1909. **Staff:** 7. **Members:** 7,500. **Budget:** 500,000. Professional association promoting the interest of women in journalism and communications.

ASSOCIATION OF AMERICA'S PUBLIC TELEVISION STATIONS
1350 Connecticut Ave. NW, Ste. 200
Washington, DC 20036
David Brugger, Pres.
PH: (202)887-1700
FX: (202)293-2422
E-mail: info@apts.org
URL: www.apts.org
Founded: 1980. **Staff:** 19. **Members:** 156. **Budget:** 2,900,000. Public television licensees whose goal is to organize efforts of public television stations in areas of planning and research, and in representation before the government. Maintains current information on the public television system including such areas as licensee characteristics, financing, and industry trends; makes projections on system growth and income. Monitors social, economic, and demographic trends that have an impact on public television services. Prepares and disseminates general information about public television to policymaking agencies, the press, and the public.

ASSOCIATION OF FEDERAL COMMUNICATIONS CONSULTING ENGINEERS
PO Box 19333, 20th St. Sta.
Washington, DC 20036
Cynthia M. Jacobson, Pres.
PH: (703)569-7704
FX: (703)569-6417
Founded: 1948. **Members:** 260. Consulting radio engineers working for the Federal Communications Commission in engineering and allocation matters. To assist and advance the proper federal administration and regulation of the engineering and technical phases of radio communication.

ASSOCIATION OF LOCAL TELEVISION STATIONS
1320 19th St. NW, Ste. 300
Washington, DC 20036
James Hedlund, Pres.
PH: (202)887-1970
FX: (202)887-0950
E-mail: altv@aol.com
URL: www.altv.com
Founded: 1972. **Staff:** 18. **Members:** 302. Represents commercial, local television broadcasting stations not affiliated with NBC, ABC television networks; national sales representatives, program distributors, and other related broadcast companies and organizations. Purpose is to act and speak on behalf of local TV stations. Informs Federal Communications Commission and Congress of members' concerns; speaks for local stations in industry councils; provides a common meeting ground for program suppliers and local stations.

ASSOCIATION OF MUSIC VIDEO BROADCASTERS
330 Beacon St., Ste. C35
Boston, MA 02116
Mort L. Nasatir, Exec.Dir.
PH: (617)262-6134
Founded: 1983. **Staff:** 1. **Members:** 26. Full and low power television stations that program music video for at least half of their broadcast time; associate members are corporations, programmers, recording companies, and interested organizations and individuals. Purposes are: to establish uniform procedures and high standards for suppliers of video programming; to attract national advertisers by forming a network of stations with a large cumulative audience; to examine and solve legal, engineering, programming, and marketing issues facing the industry. Seeks to increase public awareness of music video broadcasting; encourages exchange of ideas among persons involved with music video. Develops uniform research and ratings data formats; establishes standards to encourage entry of women and minorities into the music video business. Maintains speakers bureau; conducts seminars and trade shows; compiles statistics; disseminates information and research data about music video.

ASSOCIATION OF PROFESSIONAL COMMUNICATIONS CONSULTANTS
3924 S. Troost
Tulsa, OK 74105
Sherry B. Scott, Pres.

PH: (918)743-4793
FX: (957)564-8747
E-mail: apwc@nwu.edu
URL: www.komei.com/apcc
Founded: 1982. **Staff:** 1. **Members:** 200. Encourages the growth, development, and communication of professional writing consultants by providing an information network, programs, referral services, and a code of ethics. Strives to make business and industry aware of the need for effective communication and provides companies with consultant referrals.

ASSOCIATION OF TELEPHONE ANSWERING SERVICES

c/o Monte Engler
666 5th Ave.
Phillips, Nizer, Benjamin, Krim & Ballon LLP
New York, NY 10103-0084
Monte Engler, Counsel
PH: (212)977-9700
FX: (212)262-5152
Founded: 1955. **Members:** 40. Telephone answering services. Membership concentrated in New York City area.

ASSOCIATION OF TELESERVICES INTERNATIONAL

1200 19th St. NW, Ste. 300
Washington, DC 20036-2412
Herta Tucker, Exec.VP
PH: (202)429-5151
FX: (202)223-4579
E-mail: atsi@dc.sba.com
URL: www.atsi.org
Founded: 1942. **Staff:** 8. **Members:** 800. **Budget:** 855,000. Telephone answering and voice message service providers. Seeks to foster growth and development in the industry. Represents the industry before Congress and regulatory agencies; negotiates with telephone companies. Holds seminars and workshops on the latest telecommunications technology; compiles statistics. Maintains hall of fame.

BROADCAST CABLE CREDIT ASSOCIATION

701 Lee St., Ste. 640
Des Plaines, IL 60016
Bruce Buzogany, Pres.
PH: (847)827-9330
FX: (847)827-1653
E-mail: bcca@bcfm.com
Founded: 1972. **Staff:** 7. **Members:** 405. **Budget:** 1,000,000. A subsidiary of the Broadcast Cable Financial Management Association. Television and radio stations; cable television networks; national sales representatives. Provides industry specific credit reports on individual agencies, advertisers, or buying services (local or national).

BROADCAST CABLE FINANCIAL MANAGEMENT ASSOCIATION

701 Lee St., Ste. 640
Des Plaines, IL 60016
Buz Buzogany, Pres.
PH: (847)296-0200
FX: (847)296-7510
E-mail: info@bcfm.com
URL: www.bcfm.com
Founded: 1961. **Staff:** 5. **Members:** 1,200. **Budget:** 1,000,000. Chief financial officers, controllers, chief accountants, credit managers, auditors, business and personnel managers, corporation officers, owners, and other executives who perform or supervise the function of financial management of radio, television, and cable television operations. Develops and maintains progressive concepts of controllership, treasurership, and related financial management functions in the broadcasting-telecasting industry. Has developed a standard time order. Operates Broadcast Cable Credit Association, which provides credit information on advertising agencies advertisers or buying services. Has conducted surveys on film amortization, purchase order forms, music license fees, and salary and fringe benefits. Conducts specialized education and research programs.

BROADCAST EDUCATION ASSOCIATION

1771 N St. NW
Washington, DC 20036-2891
Louisa A. Nielsen, Exec.Dir.
PH: (202)429-5354
FX: (202)775-2981
Founded: 1955. **Staff:** 3. **Members:** 1,250. **Budget:** 300,000. Universities and colleges; faculty and students; radio and television stations that belong to the National Association of Broadcasters. Promotes improvement of curriculum and teaching methods, broadcasting research, television and radio production, and programming teaching. Offers placement services.

BROADCAST FOUNDATION OF COLLEGE/UNIVERSITY STUDENTS

89 Longview Rd.
Port Washington, NY 11050
Robert S. Tarleton, Exec.Dir.
PH: (516)883-2897
FX: (516)883-7460
Founded: 1976. **Members:** 400. College students interested in broadcasting and professional broadcasters interested in encouraging practical broadcasting experience in colleges and universities. Conducts annual survey of all professional broadcasting stations for part-time and summer employment for college students. Sponsors job advisory and placement service.

BROADCASTERS' FOUNDATION

296 Old Church Rd.
Greenwich, CT 06830
Gordon H. Hastings, Pres. and CEO
PH: (203)862-8577
FX: (203)629-5739
E-mail: ghhbcast@aol.com
Founded: 1947. **Staff:** 1. **Members:** 1,400. Men and women who have served for 15 years or more in broadcasting. Sponsors Annual Golden Mike Award. Established Broadcasting Industry Reference Center. Also sponsors Broadcasters' Foundation to assist broadcast veterans needing aid.

CABLE TELECOMMUNICATIONS ASSOCIATION

3950 Chain Bridge Rd.
PO Box 1005
Fairfax, VA 22030-1005
Stephen R. Effros, Pres.
PH: (703)691-8875
FX: (703)691-8911
Founded: 1974. **Staff:** 7. Cable television operators and owners. Works with cable groups at the state, regional, and national level. Presents an independent voice before the Federal Communications Commission, Congress, and other government agencies on national issues affecting the cable television industry. Has worked to: lower copyright rates and simplify filing forms for operators of smaller systems; offer practical assistance to help members comply with FCC rules; remove undue regulations for small operators; introduce smaller, less expensive earth stations and remove licensing requirements. Advises on legal and technical matters.

CAUCUS FOR PRODUCERS, WRITERS, AND DIRECTORS

PO Box 11236
Burbank, CA 91510-1236
Jerry Isenberg, Chairman
PH: (818)843-7572
FX: (818)846-2159
Founded: 1973. **Staff:** 4. **Members:** 234. **Budget:** 80,000. Producers, writers, and directors in the television industry. Committed to improving prime time television quality by lessening network control over production, thereby increasing artistic integrity and creative control. Acts as liaison between the creative community and public groups. Maintains speakers' bureau.

CELLULAR TELECOMMUNICATIONS INDUSTRY ASSOCIATION

1250 Connecticut Ave. NW, Ste. 200
Washington, DC 20036
Thomas E. Wheeler, Pres. & CEO
PH: (202)785-0081
FX: (202)785-0721
Founded: 1984. **Staff:** 25. **Members:** 450. **Budget:** 9,000,000. Individuals and organizations actively engaged in cellular radiotelephone communications, including: telephone companies and corporations providing radio communications; lay firms; engineering firms; consultants and manufacturers. (A cellular radiotelephone is a mobile communications device. An area is geographically divided into low frequency cells monitored by a computer that switches callers from one frequency to another as they move from cell to cell.) Objectives are to: promote, educate, and facilitate the professional interests, needs, and concerns of members with respect to the development and commercial applications of cellular technology; provide an opportunity for exchanging experience and concerns; broaden the understanding and importance of cellular communication technology. Conducts discussions, studies, and courses.

CENTER FOR COMMUNICATION

271 Madison Ave., Fl. 7
New York, NY 10016-1001
Irina Posner, Exec.Dir.
PH: (212)681-5005
FX: (212)686-6393
E-mail: info@cencom.org
URL: www.cencom.org
Founded: 1980. **Staff:** 5. Organizes educational forums designed to bring leaders from the field of communications together with young media professionals, university professors and media students interested in the communication industry. Provides e-mail transcripts and videotapes of communications-related discussions with leaders in the industry. Conducts seminars and teleconferences focusing on issues such as: the relationship between the media and human rights; the problems of universal access to the information highway; and the role of minorities in the communications industry. Offers sessions on career counseling. Sponsors 40 symposia per year.

CHRISTIAN BROADCASTING ASSOCIATION

3555 Harding Ave.
Honolulu, HI 96816
John Corts, Contact
PH: (808)735-2424
FX: (808)735-2428
E-mail: kaim@radio.org
Founded: 1964. **Staff:** 8. Broadcasts Christian programs offering music, Bible study, sermonettes, and speakers.

CHRISTIAN TELEVISION MISSION

PO Box 10242
Springfield, MO 65808-0242
Don W. Vernon, Exec.Dir.
Founded: 1956. **Staff:** 6. **Budget:** 180,000. Congregations and individuals working to produce and distribute Christian-oriented programs to television, cable, and closed circuit broadcasting stations. Presents musical programs to congregations and at conventions. Organizes religious seminars on evangelism, missions, music, and fundraising. Maintains speakers' bureau.

CLASSICAL MUSIC BROADCASTERS ASSOCIATION

WCLV
26501 Renaissance Pkwy.
Cleveland, OH 44128
Rich Marschner, Contact
PH: (216)464-0900
FX: (216)464-2206
Founded: 1969. **Members:** 150. Promotes concert music broadcasting. Compiles statistics; conducts research programs.

CLEAR CHANNEL BROADCASTING SERVICE

1776 K St. NW, Ste. 1100
Washington, DC 20006
Wayne Vriesman, Exec. Officer
PH: (202)429-7020
FX: (202)429-7207
Founded: 1934. **Members:** 40. Class I Clear Channel radio stations, providing wide broadcasting-range AM radio service. Seeks to maintain and improve standard broadcast (AM) radio service throughout the country by preserving wide area nighttime groundwave and skywave service now provided by Class I stations. Maintains legal and engineering counsel.

COALITION OPPOSING SIGNAL THEFT

1724 Massachusetts Ave. NW
Washington, DC 20036
Staci M. Pittman, Liaison
PH: (202)775-3684
FX: (202)775-3696
E-mail: ocst@ncta.com
Founded: 1986. Participants are representatives from the cable television, sports, and film programming industries, including manufacturers, producers, and distributors of programs. Provides support to the National Cable T.V. Association's Office of Cable Signal Theft. Sends representatives to national and regional trade shows to offer information and advice regarding cable signal theft.

COMMUNICATIONS MANAGERS ASSOCIATION

1201 Mt. Kemble Ave.
Morristown, NJ 07960-6628
Catherine Takacs, Managing Dir.
PH: (201)425-1700
FX: (201)425-0777
E-mail: info@cma.org
Founded: 1948. Encourages excellence in telecommunications management. Provides a forum for the evaluation of emerging technologies and their business applications. Also offers insight into regulatory and tariff issues.

COMMUNICATIONS MARKETING ASSOCIATION

2824 S. Kenyon Ct.
Aurora, CO 80014
Bernie Brownson, Exec.Sec.
PH: (303)576-9475
FX: (303)371-8158
Founded: 1974. **Staff:** 1. **Members:** 400. **Budget:** 50,000. Manufacturers, independent manufacturers representatives, and distributors who deal in two-way radio and wireless communication equipment and associated products. Promotes effective marketing and ensures professional industry standards.

COMPUTER AND COMMUNICATIONS INDUSTRY ASSOCIATION

666 11th St. NW, Ste. 600
Washington, DC 20001
Edward Black, Pres. & CEO
PH: (202)783-0070
FX: (202)783-0534
E-mail: ccianet@gte.net
URL: www.ccianet.org
Founded: 1972. **Staff:** 10. **Members:** 60. **Budget:** 1,000,000. Manufacturers and providers of computer, information processing, and telecommunications-related products and services. Represents interests of members in domestic and foreign trade, capital formation and tax policy, federal procurement policy and telecommunications policy before Congress, federal agencies, and the courts. Keeps members advised of policy, political, technological, market, and economic developments and trends. Conducts workshops. Hosts policy briefings on legislative and regulatory matters.

CORPORATION FOR PUBLIC BROADCASTING

901 E St. NW
Washington, DC 20004-2037
Robert I. Coonrod, Pres.

PH: (202)879-9600
FX: (202)783-1019
Founded: 1968. **Budget:** 253,000,000. A private, nonprofit corporation authorized under Public Broadcasting Act of 1967. Funded by U.S. government. To promote and finance the growth and development of noncommercial radio and television. Makes grants to local public television and radio stations, program producers, and regional networks; studies emerging technologies; works to provide adequate long-range financing from the U.S. government and other sources for public broadcasting. Supports children's services; compiles statistics; sponsors training programs. Presents awards annually for outstanding local television and radio programs.

COUNCIL OF COMMUNICATION MANAGEMENT
333 B Route 46 W., Ste. B 201
Fairfield, NJ 07004
Susan Dankelman, Contact
PH: (973)575-1444
FX: (973)575-1445
Founded: 1955. **Staff:** 1. **Members:** 250. **Budget:** 80,000. Managers, consultants, and educators who work at the policy level in organizational communication. Serves as a network through which members can help one another advance the practice of communications in business.

COUNTRY RADIO BROADCASTERS
819 18th Ave. South
Nashville, TN 37203
Paul Allen, Exec.Dir.
PH: (615)327-4487
FX: (615)329-4492
URL: www.crb.org
Founded: 1970. **Staff:** 4. **Budget:** 1,000,000. Seeks to advance and promote the study of the science of broadcasting through the mutual exchange of ideas by conducting seminars and workshops, as well as providing scholarships to broadcasting students.

EDUCATIONAL BROADCASTING CORPORATION
356 W. 58th St.
New York, NY 10019
William F. Baker, Pres.
PH: (212)560-2000
FX: (212)582-3297
Founded: 1961. **Staff:** 482. **Members:** 315,000. **Budget:** 107,000,000. Owner and licensee of WNET/Channel 13, the principal public television station in New York City. Produces programs distributed by the Public Broadcasting Service to 350 noncommercial television stations in the U.S., Hawaii, Guam, and Puerto Rico. Conducts educational and cultural broadcasts; operates outreach programs to schools and community groups.

HOLLYWOOD RADIO AND TELEVISION SOCIETY
13701 Riverside Dr., Ste. 205
Sherman Oaks, CA 91423-2467
Gene Herd, Exec.Dir.
PH: (818)789-1182
FX: (818)789-1210
Founded: 1947. **Staff:** 4. **Members:** 1,000. Persons involved in radio, television, broadcasting, and advertising, including program and commercial producers and radio and television networks and studios seeking to promote the broadcasting industry. Sponsors monthly luncheon featuring top industry and government speakers. Sponsors seminars on the business and creative aspects of broadcasting and competitions. Maintains film and audio library of outstanding radio and television commercials.

IEEE BROADCAST TECHNOLOGY SOCIETY
c/o Institute of Electrical and Electronics Engineers
445 Hoes Lane
Piscataway, NJ 08855-1331
Garrison Cavell, Pres.

PH: (723)562-3900
TF: (800)678-IEEE
FX: (732)981-1769
E-mail: gcovell@cmpconsulting.com
Founded: 1884. **Members:** 3,023. A society of the Institute of Electrical and Electronics Engineers. Disseminates information on broadcast transmission systems engineering, including the design and utilization of broadcast equipment.

IEEE COMMUNICATIONS SOCIETY
3 Park Ave., Ste. 17A
New York, NY 10016-5902
John M. Howell, Exec.Dir.
PH: (212)705-8900
FX: (212)705-8999
E-mail: memberservices@ieee.org
URL: www.comsoc.org
Founded: 1952. **Staff:** 23. **Members:** 50,000. Industry professionals with a common interest in advancing all communications technologies. Seeks to foster original work in all aspects of communications science, engineering, and technology and encourages the development of applications that use signals to transfer voice, data, image, and/or video information between locations. Promotes the theory and use of systems involving all types of terminals, computers, and information processors; all pertinent systems and operations that facilitate transfer; all transmission media; switched and unswitched networks; and network layout, protocols, architectures, and implementations. Advances developments toward meeting new market demands in systems, products, and technologies such personal communications services, multimedia communications systems, enterprise networks, and optical communications systems.

IEEE INFORMATION THEORY GROUP
3 Park Ave., 17th Fl.
New York, NY 10016-5997
Dan Senese, Gen. Mgr.
PH: (212)419-7900
FX: (212)328-8599
Members: 4,977. **Budget:** 200,000. A society of the Institute of Electrical and Electronics Engineers. Fields of interest include processing, transmission, storage, and use of information; theoretical and certain applied aspects of coding, communications and communications networks, complexity and cryptography, detection and estimation, learning, Shannon Theory, and stochastic processes.

INDIGENOUS COMMUNICATIONS ASSOCIATION
948 Sage St.
Grants, NM 87020
Joe Orosco, Exec.Dir.
PH: (505)775-3215
FX: (505)775-3551
Founded: 1991. **Staff:** 3. **Members:** 25. **Budget:** 150,000. Radio stations in the continental U.S. and Canada, mainly located on Indian reservations. Provides development, advocacy, and technical support to member stations, including: financial resource development and management; advocacy and communications that promote station stability and growth; station staff development and training; international, national, and regional program production and dissemination; cross-cultural programming. Conducts fundraising.

INDUSTRIAL TELECOMMUNICATIONS ASSOCIATION
1110 N. Glebe Rd., Ste. 500
Arlington, VA 22201
Mark E. Crosby, Pres. & CEO
PH: (703)528-5115
FX: (703)524-1074
URL: www.ita-relay.com
Founded: 1953. **Staff:** 32. **Members:** 8,500. **Budget:** 3,000,000. Private land mobile radio licensees and independent radio sales and service organizations. Represents members before the FCC and U.S. Congress. Provides frequency coordination, licensing, education, communications engineering, license data, and FCC research.

INTERACTIVE SERVICES ASSOCIATION
PO Box 65782
Washington, DC 20035-5782
Jeff Richards, Exec.Dir.
PH: (301)495-4955
FX: (301)495-4959
E-mail: isa@isa.net
Founded: 1981. **Staff:** 10. **Members:** 340. **Budget:** 2,000,000.
Trade association serving businesses that deliver telecommunications-based interactive services. (Interactive services refers to services that use telecommunications for information exchange, communications, transactions, and entertainment through a computer, videotex terminal, enhanced telephone, or television.) Focuses on personal use of interactive services in the home, office, and public locations.

INTERAMERICAN TELECOMMUNICATION
CONFERENCE
1889 F St. NW
Washington, DC 20006
Roberto Blois, Exec.Sec.
PH: (202)458-3004
FX: (202)245-6854
Founded: 1923. **Members:** 34. Representatives of countries organized to facilitate the advancement of telecommunications industries in the Americas. Promotes the study and implementation of new regulations governing technological developments in the field. Fosters the expansion of shared services among members such as launching and maintaining communications satellites. Disseminates information to members on technological developments.

INTERCOLLEGIATE BROADCASTING SYSTEM
367 Windsor Hwy.
New Windsor, NY 12553
Fritz Kass, Chief Operating Officer
PH: (914)565-0003
FX: (914)565-7446
E-mail: ibshq@aol.com
URL: www.ibsradio.org/
Founded: 1940. **Staff:** 6. **Members:** 832. **Budget:** 352,747. Radio stations at schools, colleges, and universities. Offers educational, informational, and consulting services. Compiles statistics; conducts research and seminars.

INTERNATIONAL ASSOCIATION OF BROADCAST
MONITORS
PO Box 27
Union City, PA 16348-0027
Pro Shermon, Pres.
PH: (814)694-3718
TF: (888)236-1741
E-mail: iabm@juno.com
URL: www.iabm.com
Founded: 1981. **Members:** 60. Companies that monitor radio and/or television transmissions, newspaper clippings, and advertising checking; interested others. Provides a forum for the exchange of information in the broadcast monitoring industry; facilitates cooperative action among members.

INTERNATIONAL COMMUNICATIONS ASSOCIATION
2735 Villa Creek Dr.
Dallas, TX 75234
Robert Harper, Pres.
PH: (972)620-7020
TF: (800)ICA-INFO
FX: (972)488-9985
Founded: 1948. **Members:** 600. **Budget:** 4,000,000. Representatives who are responsible for telecommunications services and facilities of major companies, corporations, and other organizations. Seeks to: exchange ideas and experiences in the communications field. Conducts short courses, technical, educational and research programs, and operates job placement service.

INTERNATIONAL COUNCIL - NATIONAL ACADEMY OF
TELEVISION ARTS AND SCIENCES
142 W. 57th St., 16th Fl.
New York, NY 10019
George Leclere, Exec.Dir.
PH: (212)489-6969
FX: (212)489-6557
E-mail: intcouncl@aol.com
URL: www.Intlemmys.org
Founded: 1968. **Staff:** 3. **Members:** 90. Officers of organizations active in the international television community. Seeks to further the arts and sciences of international television by bestowing an Emmy Award for excellence in television programming in the categories of international drama, documentary, arts documentary, performing arts, popular arts, and children's programs. Examines and salutes television in a member country. Provides forum for discussion of issues affecting the television industry internationally.

INTERNATIONAL FACSIMILE CONSULTATIVE
COUNCIL
4019 Lakeview Dr.
Lake Havasu City, AZ 86406
Sir Jonathan Howe, Exec.Dir.
PH: (520)453-9234
FX: (520)453-9234
E-mail: petpage@ctaz.com
Founded: 1988. **Staff:** 4. **Members:** 1,500. Promotes fee-based facsimile information consultation services. Offers legal services for international governments, and major corporations and small business.

INTERNATIONAL INTERACTIVE COMMUNICATIONS
SOCIETY
39355 California St., Ste. 307
Fremont, CA 94538-1447
Debra Palm, Mng.Dir.
PH: (510)608-5930
FX: (510)608-5917
E-mail: worldhq@iics.org
URL: www.iics.org
Founded: 1983. **Staff:** 2. **Members:** 1,200. **Budget:** 315,000. Interactive media professionals. Dedicated to the advancement of interactive arts and technologies.

INTERNATIONAL MISSION RADIO ASSOCIATION
St. Johns' University
Jamaica, NY 11439
Rev. Michael Mullen, Dir.
PH: (718)990-6744
FX: (718)380-8939
Founded: 1963. **Staff:** 1. **Members:** 800. **Budget:** 9,000. Amateur radio operators and others interested in providing radio communications between missionaries in 35 countries. Operates a short wave radio network; provides equipment for persons in countries who need help in establishing short wave stations and raises funds for this purpose. Maintain speakers' bureau.

INTERNATIONAL MOBILE TELECOMMUNICATIONS
ASSOCIATION
1150 18th St., NW, Ste. 250
Washington, DC 20036
Alan R. Shark, Pres. & CEO
PH: (202)331-7773
FX: (202)331-9062
E-mail: online@imta.org
URL: www.imta.org
Founded: 1995. **Staff:** 7. **Members:** 100. **Budget:** 250,000. Represents and serves the commercial trunked radio industry worldwide. Seeks to create a positive regulatory climate for the industry, provide research and information, and to establish forums during which issues may be addressed.

INTERNATIONAL RADIO AND TELEVISION SOCIETY FOUNDATION

420 Lexington Ave., Ste. 1714
New York, NY 10170
Joyce M. Tudryn, Pres.
PH: (212)867-6650
FX: (212)867-6653
URL: www.irts.org
Founded: 1952. **Staff:** 8. **Members:** 1,900. Individuals interested in management, sales, or executive production in the radio, television, and cable industries and their allied fields. Seeks to educate members through seminars. Conducts summer internships for college students majoring in communications.

INTERNATIONAL (TELECOMMUNICATIONS) DISASTER RECOVERY ASSOCIATION

Box 4515
Shrewsbury, MA 01545
Benjamin W. Tartaglia, Exec.Dir.
PH: (508)845-6000
FX: (508)842-2585
E-mail: idra@idra.com
URL: www.idra.com
Founded: 1990. **Staff:** 5. **Members:** 300. Disaster recovery, MIS, security, contingency planning, and emergency preparedness professionals with special interest in telecommunications. Focuses on telecommunications aspects of contingency planning, business continuation, disaster recovery, and restoration of service. Conducts research and survey studies. Organizes educational events and acts as informational clearinghouse. Fosters the professionalism of individuals in the disaster recovery/telecommunications field. Operates speakers' bureau. See www.idra.com for more information.

INTERNATIONAL TELECOMMUNICATIONS SATELLITE ORGANIZATION

3400 International Dr. NW
Washington, DC 20008-3098
Conny Kullman, Dir.Gen. & CEO
PH: (202)944-6800
FX: (202)944-7898
URL: www.intelsat.int
Founded: 1964. **Members:** 143. Governments that adhere to 2 international telecommunications agreements. Each government designates a telecommunications entity, either public or private, as its signatory to the INTELSAT Operating Agreement. Seeks to unify the design, development, construction, establishment, maintenance, and operation of the space segment of the global communications satellite system. The space segment provides overseas telecommunications services and live television, enables a number of domestic communications systems, and includes communication satellites and the telemetry, control, command, monitoring, and related facilities and equipment required to support satellite operations. As of January 1998 there were 19 satellites in geosynchronous orbit.

INTERNATIONAL TELECOMMUNICATIONS SOCIETY

GTE, PO Box 152092
Irving, TX 75015-2092
Leland Schmidt, Treas.
PH: (972)718-1881
FX: (972)718-2803
E-mail: leland.schmidt@telops.gte.com
Founded: 1986. **Members:** 400. Telecommunications professionals in consultancy, telephone operating companies, government agencies, and academic institutions. Concerned with telecommunications planning, policy formation, and economic analysis. Provides a forum for industry analysis and problem solving.

INTERNATIONAL TELECONFERENCING ASSOCIATION

100 Four Falls Corporate Center, Ste. 105
West Conshohocken, PA 19428
Henry S. Grove, III, Exec.Dir.

PH: (610)941-2020
FX: (610)941-2015
E-mail: staff@itca.org
URL: www.itca.org
Founded: 1982. **Staff:** 4. **Members:** 2,000. Vendors of teleconferencing equipment or services; users, researchers, and consultants. Seeks to: educate the public about the uses and impacts of teleconferencing technology; encourage the successful use of teleconferencing; foster information exchange; serve as a liaison with international government agencies. Organizes educational programs; compiles statistics. Maintains hall of fame.

INTERNATIONAL TELEVENT

1430 Spring Hill Rd., Ste. 500
Mc Lean, VA 22102-3000
Ronald D. Coleman, Chm. & CEO
PH: (703)556-7778
FX: (703)448-6692
Founded: 1982. **Staff:** 2. **Budget:** 250,000. Sponsors interested in disseminating information worldwide on policies, regulations, technical developments, and issues involving telecommunications.

INTERNATIONAL TELEWORK ASSOCIATION COUNCIL

204 E St. NE
Washington, DC 20002
Gail Martin, Exec. Officer
PH: (202)547-6157
URL: www.telecommute.org
Founded: 1987. **Staff:** 2. **Members:** 400. **Budget:** 175,000. Individuals, corporations, government agencies, educators, consultants and vendors. Dedicated to promoting the economic, social and environmental benefits of telecommuting and telework. Disseminates information on the design and implementation of telecommuting programs, the development of the U.S. telecommuting sector, the virtual office and telecommuting research.

IOTA BETA SIGMA

367 Windsor Hwy.
New Windsor, NY 12553-7900
Fritz Kass, Exec.Dir.
PH: (914)565-0003
FX: (914)565-7446
E-mail: ibshq@aol.com
URL: www.ibsradio.org/
Founded: 1963. **Staff:** 2. **Members:** 5,276. **Budget:** 93,063. College and high school students and graduates who are or were involved in student broadcasting. Promotes radio broadcasting through fellowship.

JAPAN HOUR BROADCASTING

151-23 34th Ave.
Flushing, NY 11354-3938
Raymond Otami, Exec.Dir.
Founded: 1974. **Staff:** 5. **Members:** 60. To present: radio and television programs in Japanese for Japanese residents in the U.S.; English language radio and television programs on Japan to foster the American people's understanding of Japan and U.S.-Japanese relations; educational and cultural programs to promote mutual understanding between Japanese and Americans.

JESUITS IN COMMUNICATION IN THE U.S.

1616 P St. N.W., Ste. 400
Washington, DC 20036
Thomas Rochford, S.J., Exec.Sec.
PH: (202)462-0400
FX: (202)328-9212
E-mail: njn@guvm.georgetown.edu
Founded: 1962. Works to acquaint U.S. members of the Society of Jesus (Jesuits) with various areas of communications, including writing, editing, radio-television direction or production, and teaching communications at the university level.

LAND MOBILE COMMUNICATIONS COUNCIL
1110 N. Glebe Rd., Ste. 500
Arlington, VA 22201
Paul B. Najarian, Pres.
PH: (703)528-5115
FX: (703)524-1074
Founded: 1967. **Members:** 22. Professional communications associations. To ensure that the Land Mobile Radio Services are allocated a sufficient portion of the radio spectrum to meet their frequency needs.

MANUFACTURERS RADIO FREQUENCY ADVISORY COMMITTEE
1041 Sterling Rd., Ste. 106
Herndon, VA 20170-3841
Jim Pakla
PH: (703)318-9206
TF: (800)262-9206
FX: (703)318-9209
E-mail: mrfacfreq@aol.com
URL: www.mrfac.com
Founded: 1970. An authorized Federal Communications Commission frequency coordinator for communications and operating systems below 800 megahertz, providing radio frequency coordination to the nation's manufacturers and private interests.

MEDIA RATING COUNCIL
200 W. 57th St., Ste. 204
New York, NY 10019
Richard Weinstein, Exec.Dir.
PH: (212)765-0200
FX: (212)765-1868
Founded: 1964. **Members:** 30. Broadcast and cable trade associations, media owners, advertising agencies, cable networks, and national networks including National Association of Broadcasters, Television Bureau of Advertising, Radio Advertising Bureau, Cable Advertising Bureau. Establishes minimum standards for electronic media ratings surveys. Commissions audits by CPA firms of the collection and processing of data gathered by audience measurement services, including A.C. Nielsen, Arbitron, Statistical Research Inc., and Mediafax.

MULTIMEDIA TELECOMMUNICATIONS ASSOCIATION
2500 Wilson Blvd. Ste 300
Arlington, VA 22201-3834
Mary Bradshaw, Pres.
PH: (703)907-7472
TF: (800)799-MMTA
FX: (703)907-7478
E-mail: info@mmta.org
URL: www.mmta.org
Founded: 1970. **Staff:** 12. **Members:** 500. **Budget:** 7,500,000. Manufacturers and distributors of communications and computer equipment; suppliers, consultants, and users of voice and data technology; related service and information providers. Provides public relations, research, and membership services. Conducts specialized education and research programs. Presents annual exhibition showcase. Compiles statistics.

NATIONAL ACADEMY OF TELEVISION ARTS AND SCIENCES
111 W. 57th St., Ste. 1020
New York, NY 10019
John Cannon, Pres.
PH: (212)586-8424
FX: (212)246-8129
Founded: 1947. **Staff:** 10. **Members:** 14,000. Persons engaged in television performing, art directing, cinematography, directing, taping, tape editing, choreography, engineering, film editing, music, production, and writing. Advances the arts and sciences of television and fosters creative leadership in the television industry for artistic, cultural, educational, and technological progress; recognizes outstanding achievements in the television industry by conferring annual awards for excellence (Emmy Awards). Utilizes a television film

and tape library at UCLA, California. Sponsors workshops and seminars; maintains library.

NATIONAL ASIAN AMERICAN TELECOMMUNICATIONS ASSOCIATION
346 9th St., 2nd Fl.
San Francisco, CA 94103
Eddie Wong, Exec.Dir.
PH: (415)863-0814
FX: (415)863-7428
E-mail: naata@naatanet.org
URL: www.naatanet.org
Founded: 1980. **Staff:** 10. **Members:** 300. Seeks to advance the ideas of cultural pluralism in the U.S. and to promote better understanding of Asian-Pacific American experiences through film, radio, and new technologies. Supports Asian Pacific American filmmakers through production support, public television programming, exhibition activities, and educational distribution.

NATIONAL ASSOCIATION BROADCAST EMPLOYEES AND TECHNICIANS -COMMUNICATIONS WORKERS OF AMERICA
501 3rd St. NW, 8th Fl.
Washington, DC 20001
John S. Clark, Pres.
PH: (202)434-1254
FX: (202)434-1426
E-mail: nabetcwa@aol.com
Founded: 1933. **Staff:** 8. **Members:** 10,000. **Budget:** 5,000,000. AFL-CIO.

NATIONAL ASSOCIATION OF BLACK OWNED BROADCASTERS
1333 New Hampshire Ave., N.W., Ste. 1000
Washington, DC 20036
James L. Winston, Exec.Dir.
PH: (202)463-8970
FX: (202)429-0657
E-mail: nabob@abs.net
Founded: 1976. **Staff:** 3. **Members:** 150. Black broadcast station owners; black formatted stations not owned or controlled by blacks; organizations having an interest in the black consumer market or black broadcast industry; individuals interested in becoming owners; and communications schools, departments, and professional groups and associations. Represents the interests of existing and potential black radio and television stations. Is currently working with the Office of Federal Procurement Policy to determine which government contracting major advertisers and advertising agencies are complying with government initiatives to increase the amount of advertising dollars received by minority-owned firms. Conducts lobbying activities; provides legal representation for the protection of minority ownership policies. Sponsors annual Communications Awards Dinner each March. Conducts workshops; compiles statistics.

NATIONAL ASSOCIATION OF BROADCASTERS
1771 N. St. NW
Washington, DC 20036
Edward O. Fritts, CEO & Pres.
PH: (202)429-5300
FX: (202)429-5343
Founded: 1922. **Staff:** 165. **Members:** 7,500. **Budget:** 27,000,000. Representatives of radio and television stations and networks; associate members include producers of equipment and programs. Seeks to ensure the viability, strength, and success of free, over-the-air broadcasters; serves as an information resource to the industry. Monitors and reports on events regarding radio and television broadcasting. Maintains Broadcasting Hall of Fame. Offers minority placement service and employment clearinghouse.

NATIONAL ASSOCIATION OF COLLEGE BROADCASTERS
71 George St.
Providence, RI 02912-1824
Kelly Cunningham, Exec. Dir.

PH: (401)863-2225
FX: (401)863-2221
E-mail: nacb@brown.edu
URL: www.hofstra.edu/nacb
Founded: 1988. **Staff:** 4. **Members:** 1,000. **Budget:** 250,000. Created to fulfill perceived needs in the student broadcasting community by opening channels of communication between college and school radio and TV stations. Operates student produced satellite programming network. Maintains reference library containing books, periodicals, clippings, audio visual material, and archival holdings pertaining to student radio and TV broadcasting. Compiles statistics; maintains placement service and speakers' bureau.

NATIONAL ASSOCIATION OF FARM BROADCASTERS
26 E. Exchange St., No. 307
St. Paul, MN 55101
Steve Pearson, Exec. Dir.
PH: (612)224-0508
FX: (612)224-1956
URL: www.nafb.com
Founded: 1944. **Staff:** 4. **Members:** 701. **Budget:** 390,000. Radio and television farm directors (200) actively engaged in broadcasting or telecasting farm news and information; associate members (479) are persons with agricultural interests who are affiliated with advertising agencies, government agencies, farm organizations, and commercial firms. Works to improve quantity and quality of farm programming and serve as a clearinghouse for new ideas in farm broadcasting. Provides placement information.

NATIONAL ASSOCIATION OF MEDIA WOMEN
1185 Niskey Lake Rd. SW
Atlanta, GA 30331
Mrs. Xernona Brady, Exec.
PH: (404)827-1718
FX: (404)588-6023
Founded: 1965. **Members:** 300. Women professionally engaged in mass communications. Purposes are: to enrich the lives of members through an exchange of ideas and experiences; to sponsor studies, research, and seminars to find solutions to mutual problems; to create opportunities for women in communications.

**NATIONAL ASSOCIATION OF RADIO AND
TELECOMMUNICATIONS ENGINEERS**
PO Box 678
Medway, MA 02053
Ray D. Thrower, Pres.
PH: (508)533-8333
TF: (800)89-NARTE
FX: (508)533-3815
E-mail: narte@110.net
URL: www.narte.org
Founded: 1982. **Staff:** 4. **Members:** 7,000. **Budget:** 310,000. Provides certification in telecommunications, Electrostatic Discharge Control and Electromagnetic Compatibility engineers and technicians. Designated and accredited by the Federal Communications Commission as a Commercial Operators License Examination Manager. Objectives are to: foster professionalism; develop and implement guidelines for certification; promote telecommunications, and EMC/ESD education in colleges and universities.

NATIONAL ASSOCIATION OF STATE RADIO NETWORKS
6060 N. Central Expy., Ste. 644
Dallas, TX 75206
Stan Koenigsfeld, Pres.
PH: (214)363-0844
FX: (214)363-0892
Founded: 1973. **Members:** 26. **Budget:** 403,000. Companies that broadcast live state news, weather, sports, and farm news to affiliated swellide interconnected radio stations within a given state.

**NATIONAL ASSOCIATION OF STATE
TELECOMMUNICATIONS DIRECTORS**
2760 Research Park Dr.
PO Box 11910
Lexington, KY 40578-1910
Jack J. Gallt, Staff Dir.
PH: (606)244-8187
FX: (606)244-8001
E-mail: nastd@csg.org
URL: www.csg.org/nastd
Founded: 1978. **Staff:** 4. **Members:** 130. **Budget:** 400,000. Directors of state telecommunications agencies. Goal is to improve state telecommunications systems by allowing members to exchange information, ideas, concepts, and practices. Seeks to provide a unified voice on matters pertaining to national communications policies and regulatory issues.

**NATIONAL ASSOCIATION OF TELECOMMUNICATIONS
OFFICERS AND ADVISORS**
1650 Tysons Blvd., Ste. 200
Mc Lean, VA 22102
Eileen Hugard, Exec.Dir.
PH: (703)506-3275
FX: (703)506-3266
E-mail: natoa@sba.com
URL: www.natoa.org
Founded: 1980. **Members:** 900. **Budget:** 350,000. Elected and appointed government officials who represent cable television and telecommunications administrators; staff personnel from local governments and public interest groups. Seeks to: establish an information-sharing network among local telecommunications regulators and users in the public sector; provide education and training for local government officials to enhance their capacity to deal with cable and telecommunications issues; provide technical and policy development assistance to members. Maintains speakers' bureau.

**NATIONAL ASSOCIATION OF TELEVISION PROGRAM
EXECUTIVES**
2425 Olympic Blvd., Ste. 550E
Santa Monica, CA 90404
Bruce Johansen, Pres./CEO
PH: (310)453-4440
FX: (310)453-5258
URL: www.natpe.org
Founded: 1963. **Staff:** 26. **Members:** 5,300. Program directors of television stations, networks, and multiple station groups; persons engaged in television programming (including cable, DBS and multimedia) or production for companies holding voting membership; representatives of related businesses, such as station representatives, advertising agencies, film and package show producers and distributors, and research organizations. Seeks to contribute to the improvement of television programming by providing a forum for discussion of ideas and exchange of information concerning programming, production, and related fields. Maintains NATPE +Educational Foundation. Sponsors faculty development program, seminars, and international exchange program. Sponsors six internships.

NATIONAL BLACK PROGRAMMING CONSORTIUM
761 Oak St., Ste. A
Columbus, OH 43205
Mable J. Haddock, Exec.Dir.
PH: (614)229-4399
FX: (614)229-4398
E-mail: nbpc@supptec.com
Founded: 1979. **Staff:** 7. **Members:** 250. **Budget:** 1,200,000. Public telecommunications systems and television stations, academic institutions, and interested individuals. Objectives are to: assist the public broadcasting system in supplying programming that serves the needs of all population segments of the U.S.; serve as a collection, distribution, and archival center for black-oriented television programming; co-produce black programming; serve as a liaison between the black community and telecommunications systems with regard to black programming; provide funds for and encourage more and better black productions. Participates in the acquisition and dis-

tribution of programs for the cable and international markets. Sponsors children's programs. Operates clearinghouse.

NATIONAL BROADCASTING SOCIETY - ALPHA EPSILON RHO
Millersville University
Dept of Communications & Theatre
Millersville, PA 17551
Jamie M. Byrne, Pres.
PH: (717)872-3996
FX: (717)872-3700
E-mail: jbyrne@mu2.millersv.edu
Founded: 1943. **Members:** 35,000. **Budget:** 150,000. Professional society - men and women, radio-television.

NATIONAL CABLE TELEVISION ASSOCIATION
1724 Massachusetts Ave. NW
Washington, DC 20036
S. Decker Anstrom, Pres. and CEO
PH: (202)775-3550
FX: (202)775-3675
Founded: 1952. **Staff:** 92. **Members:** 3,073. Franchised cable operators, programmers, and cable networks; associate members are cable hardware suppliers and distributors; affiliate members are brokerage and law firms and financial institutions; state and regional cable television associations cooperate, but are not affiliated, with NCTA. Serves as national medium for exchange of experiences and opinions through research, study, discussion, and publications. Represents the cable industry before Congress, the Federal Communications Commission, and various courts on issues of primary importance. Conducts research program in conjunction with National Academy of Cable Programming. Sponsors, in conjunction with Motion Picture Association of America, the Coalition Opposing Signal Theft, an organization designed to deter cable signal theft and to develop antipiracy materials. Provides promotional aids and information on legal, legislative, and regulatory matters. Compiles statistics.

NATIONAL CABLE TELEVISION INSTITUTE
801 W. Mineral Ave.
Littleton, CO 80120-4501
Ed Cook, Dir.
PH: (303)797-9393
FX: (303)797-9394
URL: www.ncti.com
Founded: 1968. **Staff:** 30. Provides comprehensive broadband training for the cable television industry. Offers career training resources and courses in areas ranging from customer service procedures to optical fiber system design, installation, and maintenance.

NATIONAL COMMITTEE FOR UHF TELEVISION
PO Box 5714
Virginia Beach, VA 23471
Scott Hessek, Pres.
PH: (757)463-3845
FX: (757)463-3845
Founded: 1972. **Staff:** 3. **Members:** 20. Dedicated to informing the public on how to access UHF and LPTV stations and new wireless over-the-air technologies.

NATIONAL FEDERATION OF COMMUNITY BROADCASTERS
Fort Mason Center, Bldg. D
San Francisco, CA 94123
Carol Pierson, Pres. & CEO
PH: (415)771-1160
FX: (415)771-4343
E-mail: comments@nfcb.org
URL: www.nfcb.org
Founded: 1975. **Staff:** 3. **Members:** 185. **Budget:** 450,000. Independent, community-licensed radio and radio production organizations. Fosters the development of public policy at the legislative, regulatory, and administrative levels; aids the growth of community-oriented radio stations and advances the public interest in mass communications; seeks an equitable distribution of federal funds

appropriated for noncommercial broadcasting and develops support for community-oriented broadcast projects; facilitates the exchange of program materials, information, and technical expertise; assists in the organization and expansion of new and innovative broadcast stations throughout the U.S. Provides services and consultation.

NATIONAL FEDERATION OF HISPANICS IN COMMUNICATIONS
PO Box 21032, Kalorama Sta.
Washington, DC 20009
Carlos Gaivar, Co-Chair
PH: (202)332-0019
FX: (703)978-4633
Founded: 1985. **Members:** 50. **Budget:** 20,000. Professionals in Hispanic media and related fields including writers, editors, audiovisual specialists, cinematographers, photographers, and public information specialists; non-Hispanic support groups. Works to form a network to: increase public awareness of Hispanic media; improve media coverage of the Hispanic community; provide programs and materials for and about the Hispanic community; project the needs and views of the Hispanic people; interpret and disseminate various sources of information at the community level. Promotes interchange of skills and experience among Hispanic communicators for mutual professional and career development. Encourages Hispanics to enter media-related education and training programs. Fosters collaboration among members to ensure the use of Hispanic media components in all programs affecting the Hispanic-American as a consumer. Disseminates information on training, jobs, professional development, national events, and other pertinent information. Conducts seminars and presentations.

NATIONAL HISPANIC MEDIA COALITION
3550 Wilshire Blvd., Ste. 670
Los Angeles, CA 90010
Alex Nogales, Chair
PH: (213)385-8574
FX: (213)384-1505
E-mail: anogales@earthlink.net
URL: www.nhmc.com
Founded: 1986. **Staff:** 2. **Members:** 55,000. **Budget:** 75,000. Promotes the employment and image of Hispanic Americans in radio, television, and film.

NATIONAL PUBLIC RADIO
635 Massachusetts Ave. NW
Washington, DC 20001
Kevin Klose, Pres.
PH: (202)414-2000
FX: (202)414-3329
URL: www.npr.org
Founded: 1970. **Staff:** 530. **Members:** 600. **Budget:** 65,000,000. Funded principally by its member stations, with additional support from foundations and corporations. NPR is the only nationwide interconnected public radio system in the U.S. Originates and disseminates news, cultural, and programming information through live satellite distribution.

NATIONAL RELIGIOUS BROADCASTERS
7839 Ashton Ave.
Manassas, VA 22110
Dr. Brandt Gustavson, Pres.
PH: (703)330-7000
FX: (703)330-7100
URL: www.nrb.org
Founded: 1944. **Staff:** 17. **Members:** 1,100. **Budget:** 1,900,000. Religious radio and television program producers; religious radio and television station owners and operators within the U.S. and Canada; foreign broadcasters interested in religious broadcasting throughout the world. Seeks to support those providing programming for radio and television and those engaging in the operation of religious radio and television stations. Is dedicated to the communication of the gospel and complete access to broadcast media for religious broadcasting. Serves as a central source of information concerning Christian radio and television. Sponsors one national and six re-

gional conventions, international tours, and professional training courses.

NATIONAL TRANSLATOR ASSOCIATION

Box 628
Riverton, WY 82501
Darwin Hillberry, Pres.
Founded: 1967. **Staff:** 3. Operators of translator television and FM stations; manufacturers and suppliers of equipment, as well as licensure applicants. To promote and preserve the transmission of television and FM signals to all parts of the U.S., with emphasis upon service to unserved and underserved communities. Sponsors seminars conducted by professional leaders of industry and government on topics such as engineering and technical requirements, issues of channel allocation, ownership policies, legal concerns, operating procedures, and programming options.

PACIFIC TELECOMMUNICATIONS COUNCIL

2454 S. Beretania St., Ste. 302
Honolulu, HI 96826
Richard J. Barber, Exec.Dir.
PH: (808)941-3789
FX: (808)944-4874
E-mail: info@ptc.org
URL: www.ptc.org/
Founded: 1980. **Staff:** 15. **Members:** 630. **Budget:** 1,700,000. Organizations and professionals involved as providers, users, policymakers, and analysts in telecommunications development in the Americas, Oceania, and Asia. Provides a forum for discussion between governments, academia, and telecommunications users, planners, and providers of equipment and services. Organizes conferences and seminars to exchange views and information on telecommunication services and systems in the Pacific region. Addresses immediate and future-oriented telecommunications, information services/systems and broadcasting/multimedia issues. Conducts workshops on telecommunications skills; conducts research programs.

PERSONAL COMMUNICATION INDUSTRY ASSOCIATION

500 Montgomery St. Ste. 700
Alexandria, VA 22314
Emmett B. Kitchen, Jr., Pres.
PH: (703)739-0300
TF: (800)759-0300
FX: (836)683-1608
URL: www.pcia.com
Founded: 1965. **Staff:** 60. **Members:** 2,200. **Budget:** 5,000,000. Works to protect, serve, and lead members of the mobile communications industry in their endeavors to effectively provide communications support to the U.S. business community. Acts as the industry advocate in shaping telecommunications policy to protect the mobile communications industry; serves both the industry and the government as a resource for education, information, and spectrum management. Represents businesses from all facets of the mobile communications industry including private carrier paging (PCP) and specialized mobile radio (SMR) owners and operators, wireless systems integrators, communications site owners and managers, manufacturers, dealers and service professionals, and end users. Is the FCC-certified frequency coordinator for the Business Radio Service.

PERSONAL COMMUNICATIONS INDUSTRY ASSOCIATION

500 Montgomery St., No. 700
Alexandria, VA 22314
Jay Kitchen, Pres.
PH: (703)739-0300
FX: (703)836-1608
URL: www.pcia.com
Founded: 1949. **Staff:** 85. **Members:** 1,400. **Budget:** 13,000,000. Carriers licensed by the Federal Communications Commission providing Personal Communications Services, paging and cellular services to the public; companies providing products and services to the industry. Promotes development of industry standards; publishes market studies; represents members before Congress, the administra-

tion, and the FCC; sponsors an award-winning national public relations campaign on behalf of the industry. Maintains the PCIA Science and Education Foundation including the LifePage Program, which makes pagers available to patients awaiting organ transplants.

PUBLIC BROADCASTING MANAGEMENT ASSOCIATION

PO Box 50008
Columbia, SC 29250
Skip Hinton, Exec.Dir.
PH: (803)799-5517
FX: (803)771-4831
Founded: 1981. **Members:** 300. **Budget:** 130,000. Public broadcasting stations and organizations. Seeks to aid the development, adoption, and maintenance of financial management concepts and techniques in the industry. Provides a forum for members to exchange information and ideas.

PUBLIC BROADCASTING SERVICE

1320 Braddock Pl.
Alexandria, VA 22314
Ervin S. Duggan, Pres. & CEO
PH: (703)739-5000
FX: (703)739-0775
Founded: 1969. **Staff:** 369. **Members:** 345. **Budget:** 166,980,000. Private, nonprofit membership corporation providing quality programming and related services to 345 noncommercial, educational television stations throughout the United States, Puerto Rico, the Virgin Islands, Guam and American Samoa. PBS is the leader in quality children's, cultural, educational, nature, news, public affairs, science and skills programming. Among the noteworthy programs distributed by PBS are *Sesame Street, Mr. Rogers' Neighborhood, Frontline, The Newshour with Jim Lehrer, Nova, Nature, Great Performances* and *Masterpiece Theatre.* Stations are operated by community organizations, colleges and universities, state authorities, and local educational or municipal authorities and are supported by viewer donations and funding form federal, state and local governments, businesses, and other sources.

PUBLIC RADIO NEWS DIRECTORS

PO Box 3000
Binghamton, NY 13902
Peter Iglinski, Pres.
PH: (607)729-0100
FX: (607)729-7328
Founded: 1983. **Members:** 100. **Budget:** 50,000. Conducts educational programs; holds competitions.

RADIO AMATEUR SATELLITE CORPORATION

850 Sligo Ave., Ste. 600
Silver Spring, MD 20910-4703
Ms. Martha Saragovitz, Manager
PH: (301)589-6062
FX: (301)608-3410
URL: www.amsat.org
Founded: 1969. **Staff:** 1. **Members:** 7,000. Licensed amateur radio operators and others interested in communicating through AMSAT's series of satellites. Purpose is to provide satellites for amateur radio communication and experimentation by suitably equipped amateur radio stations worldwide on a nondiscriminatory basis. Participates in data collection, extensive modifications, fabrication, spacecraft design, testing, licensing, and launch arrangements for satellite projects throughout the world. Encourages the development of skills and the fostering of specialized knowledge in the art and practice of amateur radio communications and space science. Promotes international goodwill and cooperation through joint experimentation and study and through the widespread noncommercial participation of radio amateurs in these activities. Seeks to facilitate emergency communication by means of amateur satellites. Advocates more effective and extensive use of higher frequency amateur bands. Carries out communications and experimental activities and disseminates resulting operational, scientific, and technical information. Encourages publication of this information in technical and trade journals, theses, and treatises. Works to develop long-life spacecraft and instruments designed for geostationary, near-synchronous, or high-

altitude elliptical orbits, providing a new resource for emergency communication and making further experimentation possible. Assists and participates in the activities of other world groups dealing in space communications; presents papers at amateur, professional, and technical meetings. Provides schools of physical science with reviews and advice on curricula dealing with the use of amateur satellite terminals. Sponsors OSCAR (Orbiting Satellite Carrying Amateur Radio), through which a series of communications satellites have been designed, built, and launched. Maintains speakers' bureau.

RADIO AND TELEVISION RESEARCH COUNCIL
c/o Management Solutions for Associations
234 5th Ave., Ste. 403
New York, NY 10001
Rosemarie Sharpe, Contact
PH: (212)481-3038
FX: (212)481-3071
Founded: 1941. **Members:** 200. Individuals actively engaged in radio or television research who have recognized professional standing in the field. Purpose is to provide members with presentations and discussions of radio and television research problems and of techniques used to study each as an advertising medium and as a means of social communication. Seeks to improve research methods through discussion.

RADIO CLUB OF AMERICA
Gerri Hopkins
Box 68
3 Caro Court
Red Bank, NJ 07701
Gerri Hopkins, Exec.Sec.
PH: (732)842-5070
FX: (732)219-1939
Founded: 1909. **Staff:** 2. **Members:** 1,200. **Budget:** 10,000. Radio executives, engineers, and amateurs. Operates museum.

RADIO FREE EUROPE/RADIO LIBERTY
1201 Connecticut Ave. NW, Ste. 1100
Washington, DC 20036
Joseph Dimes, Pres.
PH: (202)457-6900
FX: (202)457-6997
Founded: 1976. Provides daily broadcasting service in 21 languages to regular listeners in the former USSR, Poland, the Czech Republic, Slovakia, Romania, Latvia, Lithuania, Estonia and Bulgaria in order to meet the demand for uncensored news and comment about events in both the communist area and the rest of the world. Weekly broadcasts include news, press reviews, commentary, and entertainment to Eastern Europe and the former USSR. Supported by congressional appropriations granted through presidentially-appointed Board for International Broadcasting. subscription. Operates reference library containing over 17,000 volumes, 3000 reels of microfilm, 355 periodical subscriptions, and archival materials.

RADIO TALK SHOW HOSTS ASSOCIATION
566 Commonwealth Ave., No. 601
Boston, MA 02115-4819
Carol Nashe, CEO/Pres.
PH: (617)437-9757
TF: (888)562-2874
FX: (617)437-0797
E-mail: nashe@priority1.net
URL: www.talkshowhosts.com
Founded: 1987. **Staff:** 3. **Members:** 3,000. **Budget:** 500,000. Talk show hosts, producers, and others interested in the industry. Seeks to encourage interest and promote excellence in all aspects of national, international, and community broadcast, and to promote freedom of speech. Goals are to protect the first amendment; to advance the status of talk programming; to promote and encourage the exchange of ideas, information, and experiences among professionals in the field; and to encourage and assist qualified and dedicated people to advance in talk broadcasting. Offers educational and charitable programs; maintains a speakers' bureau and hall of fame.

RADIO-TELEVISION CORRESPONDENTS ASSOCIATION
c/o Senate Radio-TV Gallery
U.S. Capitol, Rm. S-325
Washington, DC 20510
John Nolen, Chm.
PH: (202)224-6421
Founded: 1939. **Members:** 3,000. Professional organization of correspondents, reporters, and news analysts assigned to cover Congress for radio and television broadcasting stations and networks.

RADIO-TELEVISION NEWS DIRECTORS ASSOCIATION
1000 Connecticut Ave. NW, Ste. 615
Washington, DC 20036-5302
PH: (202)659-6510
TF: (800)80-RTNDA
FX: (202)223-4007
E-mail: rtnda@rtnda.org
URL: www.rtnda.org/rtnda/
Founded: 1946. **Staff:** 15. **Members:** 3,600. **Budget:** 3,250,000. Professional society of heads of news departments for broadcast and cable stations and networks; associate members are journalists engaged in the preparation and presentation of broadcast news and teachers of electronic journalism; other members represent industry services, public relations departments of business firms, public relations firms, and networks. Works to improve standards of electronic journalism; defends rights of journalists to access news; promotes journalism training to meet specific needs of the industry. Operates placement service and speakers' bureau.

SATELLITE BROADCASTING AND COMMUNICATIONS ASSOCIATION
225 Reinekers Ln., Ste. 600
Alexandria, VA 22314
Charles C. Hewitt, Pres.
PH: (703)549-6990
TF: (800)541-5981
FX: (703)549-7640
E-mail: info@sbca.org
URL: www.sbca.com
Founded: 1986. **Staff:** 26. **Members:** 2,700. **Budget:** 5,300,000. Equipment manufacturers of satellite earth stations; dealers and distributors in satellite earth station equipment; satellite service and software and program providers; other interested individuals. Purposes are to: promote the interest of the public in satellite communications; eliminate misconceptions about the use of satellite earth stations; establish the rights of satellite earth station users to view programs from satellites. According to the organization, satellite earth stations may be perceived as a threat to existing communications systems, including television networks, broadcasters, cable television systems, motion picture companies, and others. To offset this perceived threat, SBCA seeks to defend its right to coexist in the communications community. Works with the Federal Communications Commission, Congress, and the White House to ensure private earth station development. Conducts educational and research programs. Maintains speakers' bureau; compiles statistics.

SOCIETY OF BROADCAST ENGINEERS
8445 Keystone Crossing, Ste. 140
Indianapolis, IN 46240
John L. Poray, CAE, Exec.Dir.
PH: (317)253-1640
FX: (317)253-0418
E-mail: jporay@sbe.org
URL: www.sbe.org
Founded: 1963. **Staff:** 5. **Members:** 5,400. **Budget:** 500,000. Broadcast engineers, students, and broadcast professionals in closely allied fields. Promotes professional abilities of members and provides information exchange. Provides support to local chapters. Maintains certification program; represents members' interests before the Federal Communications Commission and other governmental and industrial groups. Offers educational workshops and seminars.

SOCIETY OF SATELLITE PROFESSIONALS INTERNATIONAL
225 Reinekers Ln., Ste. 600
Alexandria, VA 22314
Constance J. Beck, Exec.Dir.
PH: (703)549-8696
E-mail: sspi@sspi.org
URL: www.sspi.org
Founded: 1983. **Staff:** 2. **Members:** 1,000. **Budget:** 200,000. Individuals with experience in the satellite industry; corporations, universities, and students. Promotes professional development in the field of satellite applications; increases public awareness; provides and supports educational development; creates a global network of contacts and associations. Created an international council of advisors in the field of satellite communications. Maintains Satellite Industry Hall of Fame.

SOCIETY OF TELECOMMUNICATIONS CONSULTANTS
13766 Center St., No. 212
Carmel Valley, CA 93924-9693
Susan Kuttner, Exec.Dir.
PH: (831)659-0110
TF: (800)STC-7670
FX: (831)659-0144
E-mail: stchdq@attmail.com
Founded: 1976. **Staff:** 2. **Members:** 275. Telecommunications consultants. Purposes are to: promote telecommunications consulting as a recognized profession; uphold high ethical and professional standards; foster a better understanding of the role, function, and contribution of telecommunications consultants. Cooperates with other industrial, technical, educational, professional, and governmental bodies on matters of mutual interest and concern. Promotes high level skills and technological advances; cooperates with educational institutions in the development of telecommunications curricula. Promotes the continuing education of telecommunication consultants through semiannual conferences and electronic and print media.

TCA - THE INFORMATION TECHNOLOGY AND TELECOMMUNICATIONS ASSOCIATION
74 New Montgomery St., Ste. 230
San Francisco, CA 94105-3419
Sherilyn Clayes, Exec.Dir.
PH: (415)777-4647
FX: (415)777-5295
Founded: 1961. **Staff:** 3. **Members:** 900. **Budget:** 1,000,000. Companies, corporations, and organizations engaged in the consultation, administration, production, sale, or rental of telecommunications service or equipment. Seeks to: enhance professional standards within the communications industry; encourage and cause rapid and timely information exchange; establish and support academic and technical training programs for the benefit of members; offer the opportunity for the presentation of viewpoints on tariffs, rules, and rates; promote technological research.

TELECOMMUNICATION BENCHMARKING INTERNATIONAL GROUP
4606 FM 1960 W. Ste. 300
Houston, TX 77069
Mark Czarnecki, Pres.
PH: (281)440-5044
FX: (281)440-6677
E-mail: tbig@ebenchmarking.com
Founded: 1995. **Staff:** 14. **Members:** 190. **Budget:** 1,000,000. Works to identify the business processes to assist members in delivering excellent services to their customers. Conducts benchmarking studies; supports the use of benchmarking; collects data; provides networking opportunities. Produces and/or distributes telecommunication services.

TELECOMMUNICATIONS INDUSTRY ASSOCIATION
2500 Wilson Blvd., Ste. 300
Arlington, VA 22201-3834
Matthew J. Flanigan, Pres.

PH: (703)907-7700
FX: (703)907-7728
E-mail: mlesso@tia.eia.org
Founded: 1988. **Staff:** 50. **Members:** 650. **Budget:** 4,800,000. Companies that manufacture products for or provide services to the telecommunications industry. Promotes the industry.

TELECOMMUNICATIONS INDUSTRY FORUM
1200 G St. NW, Ste. 500
Washington, DC 20005
Don C. Werner, Dir.
PH: (202)434-8844
FX: (202)393-5453
Founded: 1987. **Members:** 64. A committee of the Alliance for Telecommunications Industry Solutions. Purchasers, manufacturers, and suppliers of telecommunications equipment, products, and services. Works to develop guidelines for use by the telecommunications industry that facilitate effective information exchange among trading partners. Reviews and analyzes standards, reports, and other materials. Develops positions on existing standards and subjects under consideration in national and international standards bodies. Advises members of industry developments.

TELECOMMUNICATIONS RESELLERS ASSOCIATION
1730 K St., NW, No. 1201
Washington, DC 20006
Ernest B. Kelly, III, Pres.
PH: (202)835-9898
FX: (202)835-9893
URL: www.tra.org
Founded: 1992. **Staff:** 7. **Members:** 780. Fosters the business and financial interests of its members and promotes competitive telecommunications. Also promotes ethical operating practices and to create awareness of the value-added telecommunications services offered by its members to the calling public.

TELEVISION OPERATORS CAUCUS
600 New Hampshire Ave., NW, 6th Fl.
Washington, DC 20037
Mary Jo Manning, Coord.
PH: (202)944-5109
FX: (202)944-1970
Founded: 1984. Participants are executive officers in charge of operating full-service television stations in the U.S. that are not owned by the national networks. Provides forum for the definition and discussion of public policy regulatory and other issues faced by members. Conducts activities on behalf of members.

UNDA - U.S.A.
901 Irving Ave.
Dayton, OH 45409-2316
Frank Morock, Pres.
PH: (937)229-2303
FX: (937)229-2300
Founded: 1972. **Staff:** 3. **Members:** 300. Serves as USA branch of the International Catholic Association for Radio and Television. Individual members include Catholic broadcasters and allied communicators and those of all faiths who support the aims and objectives of the organization; group members include dioceses, syndicated program-producing groups, individual radio and television stations, and allied agencies in the field of communications. Promotes cooperation among those involved in communications; seeks to develop a discerning audience for social communications; assesses the sources and influences of media and the impact of U.S. media upon other nations and peoples; strives to preserve freedom of expression and foster good relations between media and government; works to develop mutual understanding among people of various cultures. Presents annual Gabriel Awards to honor commercial and religious broadcasters. Conducts training workshop for members; compiles statistics. The name of the group is taken from the Latin word "unda" meaning wave, or in this case, air wave.

UNITED STATES NATIONAL COMMITTEE FOR THE INTERNATIONAL UNION OF RADIO SCIENCE

Committee on International Organizations and Programs
2101 Constitution Ave. NW
National Research Council
Washington, DC 20418
Dr. Tamae Wong, Program Officer
PH: (202)334-2807
URL: www.usnc-ursi.org
Founded: 1919. **Staff:** 3. **Members:** 30. Works under the auspices of the National Academy of Sciences, representing the U.S. at meetings of the International Union of Radio Science (URSI). Scientists working in: electromagnetic measurement methods, including radio standards; biological interactions with electromagnetic fields; electromagnetic theory, including antennas and waveguides; scientific developments in telecommunications, including radio electronics and microwave sources; information theory, signal processing, and computing; communications systems and system theory; electromagnetic noise and interference; radio astronomy; remote sensing; wave phenomena in non-ionized media, including radiometeorology and radio-oceanography; and wave phenomena in ionized media, particularly in the earth's ionosphere, including ionospheric soundings and radio communications. Purposes are: to promote the scientific study of radio communications; to participate in radio research requiring cooperation on an international scale; to facilitate agreement upon common methods of measurement and the standardization of measuring instruments; to stimulate and coordinate studies of the scientific aspects of telecommunications using electromagnetic waves.

UTC, THE TELECOMMUNICATIONS ASSOCIATION

1140 Connecticut Ave. NW, Ste. 1140
Washington, DC 20036
William R. Moroney, Pres./CEO
PH: (202)872-0030
FX: (202)872-1331
URL: www.utc.org
Founded: 1948. **Staff:** 20. **Members:** 1,500. **Budget:** 2,000,000. Electric, gas, water, steam utilities, and gas pipelines. Assists in the development and improvement of telecommunications media used in the operation of energy utilities and gas pipelines; promotes cooperation among energy utilities and gas pipelines in all matters concerning telecommunications; represents member interests before federal and state agencies. Sponsors licensing seminars.

VETERAN WIRELESS OPERATORS ASSOCIATION

46 Murdock St.
Fords, NJ 08863-1224
Edward F. Pleuler, Sec.
PH: (732)225-2539
E-mail: vwoa@interactive.net
URL: www.interactive.net/~vwoa
Founded: 1925. **Members:** 300. Individuals in the radio-telegraph and radio-telephone commercial communications field. Maintains Wireless Operators Monument.

WIRELESS COMMUNICATIONS ASSOCIATION INTERNATIONAL

1140 Connecticut Ave. NW, Ste. 810
Washington, DC 20036
Andrew Kreig, Pres.
PH: (202)452-7823
FX: (202)452-0041
E-mail: communications@wcai.com
URL: www.wcai.com
Founded: 1975. **Staff:** 6. **Members:** 230. Broadband wireless communications providers and allied services for video, voice and data, including operators, equipment manufacturers, service providers in engineering, law and operations, and content providers broadband telecommunications services in the microwave and millimeter wireless bandwidths in the United States and worldwide for systems currently serving eight million customers in 90 nations.

WIRELESS DEALERS ASSOCIATION

9746 Tappenbeck Dr.
Houston, TX 77055
Bob Hutchinson, Pres.
TF: (800)624-6918
FX: (800)820-2284
E-mail: mail@wirelessdealers.com
URL: www.wirelessindustry.com
Founded: 1987. Individuals involved in the cellular mobile telephone industry including agents, carriers, dealers, distributors, manufacturers, and consultants. Works to: foster members' financial and professional success in the cellular industry; make available skills improvement and educational materials necessary for professional growth; develop a more professional structure conducive to career success. Promotes benefits of cellular telephones and services to current and prospective cellular users. Conducts marketing and sales training seminars. Offers customized primary training materials.

WOMEN IN CABLE AND TELECOMMUNICATIONS

230 W. Monroe St., Ste. 730
Chicago, IL 60606-4702
Pamela V. Williams, Exec.Dir.
PH: (312)634-2330
FX: (312)634-2345
E-mail: information@wict.org
URL: www.wict.org
Founded: 1979. **Staff:** 12. **Members:** 3,500. **Budget:** 1,500,000. Empowers and educates women to achieve their professional goals by providing opportunities for leadership, networking and advocacy.

WORLD TELEPORT ASSOCIATION

1 World Trade Center, Ste. 8665
New York, NY 10048-8699
Robert Bell, Exec.Dir.
PH: (212)432-2028
FX: (212)432-6356
E-mail: wta@worldteleport.org
URL: www.worldteleport.org
Founded: 1985. **Staff:** 4. **Members:** 125. **Budget:** 375,000. Professionals in telecommunications, real estate, and government. Promotes growth of the teleport industry through research, consultation, and educational programs. Maintains speakers' bureau. Offers teleport consulting service.

YOUNG BLACK PROGRAMMERS COALITION

PO Box 2261
Mobile, AL 36652-2261
Robert Rosenthal, Mgr.
PH: (214)324-9595
Founded: 1976. **Members:** 2,615. **Budget:** 300,000. Black professionals in the communications, broadcasting, and music industries. Provides professional training and offers technical assistance to black entrepreneurs in the broadcast and music industries. Conducts lobbying activities pertaining to legislation affecting the music industry. Compiles statistics.

CHAPTER 8 - PART II

CONSULTANTS

Consultants and consulting organizations active in the Broadcasting & Tele-communications sector are featured in this chapter. Entries are adapted from Gale's *Consultants and Consulting Organizations Directory (CCOD)*. Each entry represents an expertise which may be of interest to business organizations, government agencies, nonprofit institutions, and individuals requiring technical and other support. The listees shown are located in the United States and Canada.

In Canada, the use of the term "consultant" is restricted. The use of the word, in this chapter, does not necessarily imply that the firm has been granted the "consultant" designation in Canada.

Entries are arranged in alphabetical order. Categories include contact information (address, phone, fax, web site, e-mail); names and titles of executive officers; description; special services offered; geographical areas served; and other information (e.g., seminars, workshops).

A.B. DATA, LTD.
8050 N. Port Washington Rd.
Milwaukee, WI 53217
Bruce Arbit, Co-Managing Director
PH: (414)352-4404
TF: (800)558-6908
FX: (414)352-3994
E-mail: barbit@abdata.com
Founded: 1977. **Staff:** 90. Activities: Provides information management and direct marketing services to nonprofit organizations, political campaigns, direct mail marketers and publishers. Emphasis is on data base management and custom data processing services for marketing purposes.

ABRA SOFTWARE INC.
888 Executive Center Dr. W., Ste. 300
St. Petersburg, FL 33702
TF: (800)847-ABRA
FX: (800)847-9467
URL: www.bestsoftware.com
Activities: Firm offers Abra 2000, an extensive and easy-to-use human resources management system including a complete training module. This application helps organize, store, and retrieve all employee information. Program also tracks salary reviews, benefits, COBRA, EEO, and OSHA.

ACCESS INNOVATIONS, INC.
PO Box 8640
Albuquerque, NM 87198-8640
Jay Ven Eman, Ph.D., CEO
PH: (505)265-3591
FX: (505)256-1080
E-mail: marketing@accessinn.com
URL: www.accessinn.com
Founded: 1978. **Staff:** 48. Activities: An information management firm providing consulting, support, and project management services in the expert areas of: (1) database design and construction; (2) editorial abstracting and indexing, specializing in sci-tech information; (3) development of customized machine-aided indexing software; (4) data capture via keying, scanning, and/or OCR (domestic or offshore services); (5) CD-ROM data preparation; (6) CD-ROM database production; (7) Internet and intranet production; (8) Web site design; (9) SGML and HTML tagging; (10) conversion of magnetic media from one system or application format to another, and (11) workflow and production methodology assessment. Serves the private and public sectors.

ACCOUNTABLE SYSTEMS COMPANY INTERNATIONAL, INC.
PO Box 59985
17236 140th Ave. SE
Renton, WA 98058-2985
Norman Philip Dorn
PH: (425)864-0182
TF: (888)607-6267
FX: (425)254-8941
E-mail: dornn@seanet.com
URL: www.askee.org
Founded: 1979. **Staff:** 4. Activities: A consulting firm dedicated to the improvement of systems engineering practices. Areas of expertise and activity include architecture, communication, facilities management and training, electric power dispatch, gas dispatch, technology, nuclear power safety, power control development, aviation, government, psychology, physical sciences, medicine, general systems, management information systems, and telephone and other communications-related businesses. Industries served: nuclear power, electrical power, manufacturing, natural gas, computer, aerospace, transportation, defense, communication, education, banking, and material handling.

ACME INFORMATION SERVICES
2925 Dean Pky., Ste. 300
Minneapolis, MN 55416
Julie Silverman, CTO

PH: (612)928-8828
TF: (800)332-0990
FX: (612)928-0868
E-mail: julie@acmeinfo.com
URL: www.acmeinfo.com
Founded: 1991. Activities: Microsoft certified solution provider. Provides consulting, hosting and design, and database services for business to business web sites, e-commerce.

AJILON
210 W. Pennsylvania Ave., Ste. 650
Towson, MD 21204-5348
Roy Haggerty, President
PH: (410)821-0435
TF: (800)626-8082
FX: (410)828-0106
Founded: 1978. **Staff:** 1200. Activities: Offers a full range of data processing professional services including application support, technical support, operations support, management/MIS consulting, productivity services and education/training. Specific consulting services cover business planning assistance, data processing organizational analysis, data processing operational analysis, data processing project and program management, and data communications planning. Clients primarily utilize large scale mainframes, integrated micro computers and networked micros in a variety of industries including banking, insurance, manufacturing, healthcare, government and services.

ALAMON TELCO, INC.
315 W. Idaho, Ste. 100
Kalispell, MT 59901
Margaret A. Gebhardt, President
PH: (800)252-8838
TF: (800)252-8838
FX: (800)468-2645
E-mail: info@alamon.com
URL: www.alamon.com
Founded: 1975. **Staff:** 200. Activities: Provides engineering, installation, construction, and general support services to the telecommunications industry. Experienced in computer mechanization systems and modern employment techniques. A woman-owned business.

AMERIGARD ALARM & SECURITY CORP.
39 W. 37th St.
New York, NY 10018
Richard H. Cantor, President
PH: (212)302-7100
FX: (212)302-3516
Founded: 1978. **Staff:** 18. Activities: Provides security analysis and consulting including risk assessment; evaluation of current security systems (hardware and installation) and procedures; design of electronic security systems including closed-circuit TV; and access control devices and alarm systems for corporate, commercial, and residential facilities.

ANTENNA TECHNOLOGY COMMUNICATIONS, INC.
1128 E. Greenway St.
Mesa, AZ 85203
Gary S. Hatch
PH: (602)264-7275
FX: (602)898-7667
URL: www.atc:.net
Founded: 1979. **Staff:** 30. Activities: Provides international consulting services to broadcast television, satellite digital audio, radio and satellite, cable television, MMDS, ITFS, microwave, private cable, teleconferencing, and hotel pay-per-view television. Serves private industries as well as government agencies.

APPLIED RESEARCH TECHNOLOGIES, INC.
165 Regent St.
Salt Lake City, UT 84111
Brad B. Buxton, President

PH: (801)364-2000
TF: (800)234-0000
FX: (801)364-2111
E-mail: 75053.1546@compuserve.com
Founded: 1986. **Staff:** 21. **Activities:** Serves end-users of telecommunications services by providing cost control and needs analyses; troubleshooting; RFPs for PBXs, Centrexes, and WANs; voice/data/video network development; and global and domestic networking. Clients include biotechnology, finance, and high-tech industries, and government agencies located on the West and East Coasts, and in the Rocky Mountain region.

ARCHWAY CONSULTANTS, INC.
353 Sacramento, Ste. 1100
San Francisco, CA 94111
Deborah Duvall, Director of Recruiting
PH: (415)392-9900
FX: (415)392-9910
E-mail: staff@archway.com
URL: www.archway.com
Founded: 1994. **Staff:** 90. **Activities:** An information technology consulting firm organized to assist clients in the management of business and information technology needs. Consulting staff consists of project managers, business analysts and technicians with backgrounds in a variety of technical environments and business applications.

AUBERGINE INFORMATION SERVICES
PO Box 116
The Sea Ranch, CA 95497
Reva Basch, President
PH: (707)785-2160
FX: (707)785-2740
E-mail: reva@well.com
URL: www.well.com/user/reva
Founded: 1986. **Staff:** 2. **Activities:** Offers counseling to the information industry—and to organizations interested in entering that industry—on marketing opportunities, product design, user interface, and usability issues, training, and documentation. Conducts information needs assessments for corporations and presentations on Internet and online database resources and search techniques. Available for talks, workshops, and writing assignments in these fields, and on computer conferencing and virtual communities.

BASE-LINE SYSTEMS CORP.
110 Marter Ave., Ste. 311
Moorestown, NJ 08057
Thomas E. Hepler
PH: (609)778-3141
Founded: 1975. **Staff:** 15. **Activities:** The firm provides a wide variety of information and information-related services including: graphics and printing, editorial services, database design and development, keyboarding, thesaurus development, data conversion, tape conversion, tape generation, library/collection development, archive organization, cataloging, system analysis and design, applications programming, conversion programming, and desktop publishing. Serves private industries as well as government agencies.

LAWRENCE BEHR ASSOCIATES, INC.
PO Box 8026
Greenville, NC 27835
Lawrence Behr, CEO
PH: (919)757-0279
TF: (800)522-4464
FX: (919)752-9155
E-mail: lbassc@lbagroup.com
URL: www.lbagroup.com
Founded: 1962. **Staff:** 25. **Activities:** Technical specialists offering services to government and private sector clients regarding telecommunications requirements and broadcast facilities. These services include needs assessment, communications planning, procurement specification, adjudication and implementation management for local and networked voice, data and video technologies. Services in RF technology include station positioning studies and frequency

studies for AM/FM/TV design of RCC/MDS/Cellular/Mobile Radio/EMS/STL and microwave systems, equipment appraisals and FCC application preparation. Specialize in control of Electromagnetic Interference (EMI) and shielding of telecommunications facilities with certified staff.

BOOTH & ASSOCIATES, INC.
1011 Schaub Dr.
Raleigh, NC 27606
Richard K. Booth, Executive Vice President
PH: (919)851-8770
FX: (919)859-5918
Founded: 1960. **Staff:** 57. **Activities:** Provides planning, design, engineering and financial services to a wide range of utilities including publicly and privately owned electric, telephone and communications utilities. Services to clients include testimony before or presentation to federal agencies. The direct services provided to utilities include system analysis and planning functions; property records review and evaluation; system engineering and design, using in-house computer-aided design facilities; generation and transmission feasibility studies; utility rate services are provided for electric, natural gas, water, and wastewater enterprises. Services include market and fully allocated cost of service, rate design, regulatory, interruption, budget and strategic forecasts, bond offering due diligence, plant valuation, tariff design; detailed management audits; contested and non-contested electric rate cases; all levels of accounting assistance; and periodic financial reporting procedures. Industries served: REA electric cooperatives, and municipal-owned electric utilities.

THE BOSLEGO CORP.
25 Burlington Mall Rd.
Burlington, MA 01803-4100
Jane Robbins, President
PH: (781)229-7788
FX: (781)229-6108
Founded: 1988. **Activities:** Assists information owners, providers, and network companies in managing the uncertainty associated with the evolving information industry structure and markets while capitalizing on the opportunities presented by the growing demand for information. The firm's approach emphasizes the importance of long-term planning and its integration with short-term needs and tactics; the customer-and business-driven design or redesign of products; the specialized sales and marketing of information; the critical role of distribution to information service profitability; and the complexity of vendor/provider relationships. Services range from evaluating new product ideas to developing products and launch plans; representing clients in finding and negotiating with venture partners; revamping and repositioning existing product lines; thinking through strategy and all associated regulatory, pricing, competitive, and operating issues; or identifying emerging market trends and end-user profiles. The company specializes in value-added information services for direct distribution to business end-users.

BROUGHTON SYSTEMS INC.
7325 Beaufont Springs Dr., Ste. 110
Richmond, VA 23225
Dan Garfi, President
PH: (804)270-5999
FX: (804)270-6555
E-mail: info@broughton-sys.com
URL: www.broughton-sys.com
Founded: 1981. **Staff:** 400. **Activities:** Computer technology and management consulting firm specializes in contract programming, client-server projects, management consulting, turnkey development, telecommunications, network solutions and training. Also provides expertise in mid-range systems consulting, PC systems development, JDEdwards and other software packages, government contracts and developmental outsourcing. Industries served: Fortune 500 companies and mid-sized companies in all industries, and local, state and federal government departments and agencies throughout the U.S.

THE BUSKE GROUP
3001 J St., Ste. 201
Sacramento, CA 95816
Sue Buske, President
PH: (916)441-6277
FX: (916)441-7670
E-mail: tbg@buskegroup.com
URL: www.buskegroup.com
Founded: 1987. **Staff:** 4. Activities: Firm offers a broad range of telecommunication consulting services. Provides a highly experienced team of media professionals to meet the needs of local government in such areas as cable television franchise renewal, cable TV regulation and policy, cable TV rate regulation, cable company franchise compliance and performance reviews, assessments of community needs and interests that are related to the use of cable communication systems by schools, universities, local government, and nonprofit organizations; management plans for public, educational and government access facilities; and seminars and retreats that are tailored to meet specific cable information needs.

BYTESMITHS
2002 Parkside Ct.
West Linn, OR 97068-2767
Jan Steinman
PH: (503)657-7703
FX: (503)657-4358
E-mail: barbara@bytesmiths.com
URL: www.bytesmiths.com
Founded: 1987. **Staff:** 6. Activities: Provides medium to long-term, on-site assistance to firms that are beginning to use object technology, by providing training, architecture, design, documentation, and implementation services. Industries served: telecommunications, financial, engineering, and scientific.

CACI INTERNATIONAL INC.
1100 N. Glebe Rd.
Arlington, VA 22201
Dr. J.P. London, Chairman
PH: (703)841-7801
TF: (800)235-5915
FX: (703)528-4196
E-mail: jbrown@hq.caci.com
URL: www.caci.com
Founded: 1962. **Staff:** 4200. Activities: Specializes in developing and integrating systems, software, and simulation prodcuts and providing information assurance services to government agencies and commercial enterprises worldwide. Delivers client solutions for systems integration, year 2000 conversion, information assurance/ security, reengineering, electronic commerce, intelligent document management, product data management, software develoment and reuse, telcommunications and network services, and market analysis.

LUIS A. CAPESTANY & ASSOCIATES
Altavista 21 Q-46
Ponce, PR 00731
Luis A. Capestany
PH: (787)844-1448
FX: (787)843-0030
Founded: 1972. **Staff:** 21. Activities: Consulting architectural and engineering firm with design capabilities in every aspect of civil, mechanical and electrical engineering. Vast experience in the water distribution, wastewater treatment, and toxic-hazardous wastes disposal fields. Also designs and constructs CATV and telephone systems as well as communication towers and facilities. Serves private industries as well as government agencies.

CB TECHNOLOGIES, INC.
Glenloch Corporate Campus
1487 Dunwoody Dr.
West Chester, PA 19380
PH: (610)889-7300
FX: (610)993-8405
E-mail: sales@cbtech.com
URL: www.cbtech.com

Staff: 130. Activities: Delivers custom software development, e-Business solutions, and consulting services to Fortune 500 and other leading companies. Our clients gain strategic advantage through our leading-edge technology solutions and our understanding of their business processes.

CC & I ENGINEERING, INC.
1351 Page Dr., Ste. 103
Fargo, ND 58103
PH: (701)280-1558
FX: (701)280-1971
E-mail: bgriffin@cci-eng.com
URL: www.cci-eng.com
Founded: 1951. Activities: A professional consulting engineering firm that provides services in the areas of telecommunications and CATV. Services include preparation of strategic business plans, implementation of schedules, technical evaluations, project management, and preparation of feasibility studies. Also evaluates bids and technical proposals and conducts contract negotiations.

CDG AND ASSOCIATES INC.
16475 Dallas Pky., Ste. 200
Dallas, TX 75248
PH: (972)250-4104
FX: (972)250-6021
E-mail: cdg@edg-inc.com
URL: www.cdg-inc.com
Activities: Firm offers expertise in human resources information systems strategic planning, software evaluation, and implementation support for payroll, time, attendance, and benefits. Also specializes in project management, audits, reengineering, education, documentation, technical services, facilities management, and requirement definition.

CENTRAL ASSOCIATED ENGINEERS INC.
446 E. High St.
Lexington, KY 40507-1930
PH: (606)231-9831
FX: (606)233-0046
E-mail: caeinc@uky.campus.mci.net
Founded: 1965. **Staff:** 63. Activities: A firm of engineering consultants, planners, and designers organized into four service groups to best match resources and capabilities to the needs of clients: electric power group provides engineering services for electric power transmission and distribution; special studies and other related electric system requirements. The civil engineering group specializes in surveying, site planning, hydraulic and hydrological studies, and stormwater and solid waste management. The mechanical and electrical group provides engineering services for new designs, analysis, and retrofit of existing systems and other special design requirements. Also offers expertise in HVAC/plumbing and performs planning studies for developers. The telecommunications group provides engineering services for planning and studies, systems design, preparing and processing bid documents, construction supervision, and resident inspection. Serves private industry as well as government agencies.

CKC LABORATORIES INC.
5473A Clouds Rest
Mariposa, CA 95338
Mrs. Chris Kendall, President/Principal Consultant
PH: (209)966-5240
TF: (800)500-4362
FX: (209)742-6133
E-mail: ckclabs@ckc.com
URL: www.ckc.com
Founded: 1972. **Staff:** 55. Activities: Electronic engineering consultants with a specialty in Electromagnetic Computability (EMC) design and compliance testing. Consultation for FCC parts 15 and 18, CE mark (EMC, Low Voltage, Machinery and Medical Directive), TCF Preparation, Austel, VCCI, New Zealand, Mil-Std. 461/2. DO-160. Electrical product safety (UL) and telecommunications (FCC Part 68) consultation and testing also available.

CNA CONSULTING & ENGINEERING
777 108th Ave. NE, Ste. 400
Bellevue, WA 98004
Larry C. Cook, Principal
PH: (425)889-3364
FX: (425)828-9116
E-mail: dbrewer@cnaco.com
URL: www.cnaco.com
Founded: 1972. **Staff:** 100. Activities: Consulting and engineering firm with headquarters in the Northwest and a regional office in the Midwest, providing clients with integrated solutions that increase productivity, reduce costs, and meet the challenges of change and competition, in the areas of management consulting, logistics, distribution, manufacturing, information technology, facility design/ delivery/architecture, and project management. Also provides site selection and planning with architectural design for firms who are planning new operations.

COMMUNICATIONS INDUSTRY RESEARCHERS, INC.
PO Box 5387
Charlottesville, VA 22905
Lawrence D. Gasman, President
PH: (804)984-0245
FX: (804)984-0247
E-mail: info@cir-inc.com
URL: www.cir-inc.com
Founded: 1979. Activities: A consulting and publishing house that provides services to the telecommunications, data communications, cable television, computer, and broadcasting industries. Publishes studies of emerging markets in the fields of communications and information technology.

COMMUNICATIONS SUPPORT CORP.
16350 Ventura Bvld., Ste. 5100
Encino, CA 91436-2116
PH: (818)344-5100
FX: (818)343-5100
E-mail: Kramer@CableTV.com
URL: www.cabletv.com
Activities: Provides local governments with technical advice and inspection services before and during cellular, broadcast, PCS tower sitting, and cable television franchise awards, transfers, and renewals. Also serves private institutions and firms.

COMMUNICATIONS TECHNOLOGY GROUP INC.
7855 Gross Point Rd., Ste. H-1
Skokie, IL 60077
Alan G. Kraus, President
PH: (847)675-7800
FX: (847)675-2635
E-mail: marketing@ctg.comcal.compuserve.com
Founded: 1983. **Staff:** 20. Activities: Established to provide in-depth engineering and integration services to the growing high performance enterprise network market. CTG has the ability to turnkey design, install, test, and maintain large scale data communications networks of fiber, coax, twisted pair, and wireless media. Experience and expertise in all aspects of multi-product local area networking integration and installation. Projects have included the complete design, installation and certification of major facility networks for large manufacturing, educational, and office facilities.

COMMUNITRONICS CORP.
1907 S. Kings Hwy.
St. Louis, MO 63110
Robert L. Anderson, President
PH: (314)771-7160
FX: (314)771-9144
Founded: 1969. **Staff:** 25. Activities: Provides consultation, engineering, and design of presentation systems including video, audio, control technology, and computer graphics. Specializes in the integration of these technologies into presentation systems such as board rooms, conference facilities, videoconferencing, training rooms, auditoriums, and video studios. Serves private industries as well as government agencies.

COMP COMM INC.
One Echelon Plaza, Ste. 100
Voorhees, NJ 08043-2331
Christine A. Malone, CEO
PH: (609)770-1234
FX: (609)770-0111
E-mail: compcomm@compcomminc.com
URL: www.compcomm.com
Founded: 1975. **Staff:** 12. Activities: Provide wireless communications engineering, information and consulting services. Specializes in 1) consulting to municipalities on antenna tower siting issues, including RF propagation analysis, 2) performing independent facilities audits for service providers, and 3) preparing FCC applications.

COMPUTER MANAGEMENT SYSTEMS
20245 W. 12 Mile Rd., Ste. 113
Southfield, MI 48076-6406
Zelda Shay
PH: (248)799-2920
FX: (248)799-2959
Activities: Firm has experience in data processing services, either online or by transmittal. Works with nursing homes, physician billing, accounts receivable, billing, and more.

COMSEARCH
2002 Edmund Halley Dr.
Reston, VA 20191-3436
Timothy P. Eckersley, Vice President, Strategy & Bus. Dev.
PH: (703)620-6300
TF: (800)318-1234
FX: (703)476-2720
URL: www.comsearch.com
Founded: 1977. **Staff:** 254. Activities: Designs, deploys and optimizes wireless networks worldwide. Provides engineering solutions to operators of PCS, Cellular, Mobile Satellite, Microwave, and Wireless Local Loop networks. IQ Line of software addresses the engineering challenges of interconnection, spectrum relocation, cell design and optimization.

COMSONICS INC.
1350 Port Republic Rd.
Harrisonburg, VA 22801
Donn Meyerhoeffer, Mgr. of Operations
PH: (540)434-5965
TF: (800)336-9681
FX: (540)434-9847
Founded: 1965. **Staff:** 152. Activities: Consultants in the field of CATV, acoustics, microwave, closed circuit and industrial television, industrial electronic control systems, and telecommunications systems. Firm serves CATV Multiple System Operators (MSO's) industry and provides electronics design, product development and electronics manufacturing in support of CATV test equipment product line.

ARTHUR L. CONN & ASSOCIATES, LTD.
1469 E. Park Pl.
Chicago, IL 60637
Arthur L. Conn, President
PH: (773)667-1828
Founded: 1978. **Staff:** 29. Activities: Provides independent technological assessments and planning assistance in the areas of new energy technologies, management of research and development, and the application of new technologies to information management. Energy-related work includes petroleum refining; biotechnology; coal production, gasification and liquefaction; fluidized combustion, flue gas scrubbing, shale oil and tar sands extraction. Information management includes technologies involved in the organization, availability and transmittal of data; and new computer technologies, word processors and telecommunications.

CONNECTICUT RESERVE TECHNOLOGIES LLC
PO Box 81361
Cleveland, OH 44181-0361

PH: (440)572-2742
URL: www.CRTechnologies.com
Activities: Provides consulting services in the areas of engineering mechanics, civil engineering, mechanical engineering, and information technology. Civil engineering services include structural analysis, geotechnical engineering, subdivision design, and underground utilities. Information technology services include graphical user interface development, spreadsheet macro customization, and web page building and Internet related services. Staff comprised of registered professional engineers and information technology specialists.

THE CONSULTING GROUPS, INC.
12444 Powerscourt Dr., Ste. 300
St. Louis, MO 63131-3660
Larry Kehler, President
PH: (314)984-6844
FX: (314)821-1591
Founded: 1980. **Staff:** 4. Activities: Offers advisory services to top management with emphasis on objective review of client companies' policies and practices. The firm consists of four divisions in four consulting practice areas: The Behavioral Group, which offers compensation systems design and administration, incentive motivational program design, personality evaluations and testing, organizational function analysis, and conflict resolution programs; The Financial Group, which provides insurance loss value determination, product and plant feasibility studies, financial information systems design, and litigation support and expert testimony; The Strategic Group, offering productivity evaluations, operational effectiveness studies, management audits, strategic planning projects, and quality awareness programs; and The Computer Group, which is responsible for computer operations audits, information systems design and development, application programming (specialized), and turnkey system projects. Active with government, manufacturers of food, apparel and textiles, and the publishing and broadcasting industry.

CORDIANT SOFTWARE
1810 Embarcadero Rd.
Palo Alto, CA 94303-3308
Carol Realini, President and CEO
PH: (415)493-3800
FX: (415)493-2215
URL: www.chordiant.com
Founded: 1985. **Staff:** 55. Activities: Assists clients in transition to enterprise-wide client/server systems by providing initial strategy, needs analysis, strategic architecture, technology assessment, infrastructure implementation, client/server development, and staff retraining. Industries served: telecommunications, finance, computer technology, and agriculture.

CTA COMMUNICATIONS
8811 Timberlake Rd., Ste. 106
Lynchburg, VA 24502
Robert T. Forrest
PH: (804)239-9200
FX: (804)239-9221
E-mail: hsmmcta@aol.com
URL: hsmm.com
Founded: 1943. **Staff:** 16. Activities: An engineering and consulting firm, providing service in the area of specification, design, installation and implementation of communication systems including mobile, cellular, fiber optics, data and telecommunications systems. Work involves system planning, system design, system implementation, requirement analysis, specification development, site management, traffic studies, proposal development, training, analog design, digital design, path loss analysis, and data communication design. Industries served: public safety, local government, utilities, and general industry.

CUTLER-WILLIAMS, INC.
4000 McEwen S, Ste. 200
Dallas, TX 75244
Ed Burns, Vice President

PH: (972)960-7053
TF: (800)282-7413
FX: (972)991-9021
Founded: 1969. **Staff:** 630. Activities: Data processing/computer technology consultants offering information and systems integration services as well as consulting contract programming. Industries served: utilities, energy, transportation, communications, finance, retail, banking, manufacturing, and government agencies.

DALLAS-FORT WORTH TELEPORT
3838 Leone Dr.
Irving, TX 75039
Dean G. Popps, President
PH: (972)869-1800
FX: (972)869-2302
Founded: 1984. **Staff:** 16. Activities: Provides consulting services regarding all aspects of teleport operation and construction, as well as microwave placement, construction, and licensing.

DARTMOUTH RESEARCH AND CONSULTING
15 Dartmouth Place
Boston, MA 02116-6106
Ron Smith, V.P., Telecommunications
PH: (617)536-8862
FX: (617)536-8875
E-mail: consulting@dartmouth-research.com
URL: www.dartmouth-research.com
Founded: 1989. **Staff:** 11. Activities: Specializes in the implementation of strategic plans, management productivity and the implementation of productivity systems. Firm works directly with managers to design and implement results-oriented programs. The firm's Results Implementation Model(sm)draws upon the established disciplines and practices of the following management methods: reengineering business processes, operations improvement and productivity enhancement, implementation of business and marketing strategies, information technology assessment and implementation, and business research and development. Industries served: Telecommunications, Banking, Financial Services, High Technology, Customer Service.

DATA CONVERSION LABORATORY
184-13 Horace Harding Expwy.
Fresh Meadows, NY 11365
Mark Gross, President
PH: (718)357-8700
FX: (718)357-8776
E-mail: convert@dclab.com
URL: www.dclab.com
Founded: 1981. **Staff:** 50. Activities: DCL specializes in information transfer and data and text conversion services. With particular emphasis on SGML/XML conversion and CD-ROM publishing, DCL provides its services to diverse industries including publishing, pharmaceuticals, financial, manufacturing, as well as libraries, universities, and governmental agencies. The company provides conversion, imaging and document retrieval services from virtually any format, along with the preparation of optical media. Custom formatting is available for most software packages and to meet specific client requirements.

DATACENTER
464 19th St.
Oakland, CA 94612
Fred Goff, President
PH: (510)835-4692
FX: (510)835-3017
E-mail: datacenter@datacenter.org
URL: www.igc.org/datacenter
Founded: 1977. **Staff:** 15. Activities: A nonprofit public interest library and research center which focuses on domestic and international political and economic issues. Users may access this information by visiting the library in person, subscribing to one of center's publications, or contracting for customized research or clipping services. The DataCenter is staffed by professional researchers skilled in labor-management, economics, social and human rights issues. Its

library contains organized and updated files on more than 15,000 private and public corporations. DataCenter staff review and clip over 300 periodicals, including 15 daily newspapers. A fee-based Search Service offers customized research and document delivery, drawing on library collection and over 500 commercial computer databases. Industries served: labor, community and human rights groups, socially responsible investors, attorneys, journalists, scholars, governmental agencies, and public policy activists.

DEBOER EDP SERVICES INC.
3994 Ortonville Rd.
Clarkston, MI 48348
PH: (248)620-0770
FX: (248)620-1253
Founded: 1980. Activities: Firm offers advice in management, data processing, and engineering. Specializes in mainframes, mid-ranges, networking, communications, and PCs.

DELOITTE CONSULTING
10 Westport Rd.
Wilton, CT 06897
James E. Copeland, Jr., CEO
PH: (203)761-3000
FX: (203)834-2200
URL: www.dc.com
Founded: 1895. Activities: Consulting services include general management consulting, information technology consulting, strategy consulting, actuarial benefits, and compensation consulting. Management consulting offers clients general business and industry knowledge along with practical implementation skills. Unique focus is on converting strategy into action for clients. ABC Group provides services in all areas of employee benefits and annual administrative compliance services for pension and welfare funds. The Valuation Group provides a complete package of valuation services, including business, stock, intangible assets, real estate, and equipment valuations for transaction-related financing, litigation, and management information purposes. Industries served: all: target industries are food and consumer products, retailing and distribution, financial services institutions, manufacturing, public utilities, travel and leisure, telecommunications, healthcare, public sector, and government agencies.

DELTA BUSINESS SYSTEMS
4201 Northview Dr., Ste. 405
Bowie, MD 20716-2604
Patrick M. Gregory, President
PH: (301)262-0550
FX: (301)262-8711
Founded: 1981. **Staff:** 3. Activities: Provides contracting and consulting support services in the programming, software development, PC applications, networking and system management technologies to clients in the Washington/Baltimore/Mid-Atlantic area.

DRA
1276 N Warson Rd.
St. Louis, MO 63132
PH: (314)432-1100
TF: (800)325-0888
FX: (314)993-8927
E-mail: sales@dra.com
URL: www.dra.com
Activities: Provides client/server library automation systems for all sizes of academic, public, school and special libraries and library consortia. Has dedicated Internet access for libraries and provides networking consultation and design.

DVI COMMUNICATIONS, INC.
170 Broadway, 11th Fl.
New York, NY 10038
Wen-Ning Hsieh, Executive Vice President
PH: (212)267-2929
FX: (212)267-2954
E-mail: info@dvicomm.com
URL: www.dvicomm.com

Founded: 1979. **Staff:** 33. Activities: Provides expertise in telecommunications and systems engineering for projects involving new construction, relocations, renovations, and system upgrades. Plans, designs, engineers, and implements voice/data communications, trading, and cabling systems. Doesn't sell or manufacture telecommunications systems or software packages. Specializes in assessing requirements, developing specifications, assisting clients in the procurement process, managing implementation, and acceptance testing.

ECONOMICS AND TECHNOLOGY, INC.
One Washington Mall
Boston, MA 02108
Lee L. Selwyn, President
PH: (617)227-0900
FX: (617)227-5535
URL: www.econtech.com
Founded: 1972. **Staff:** 25. Activities: Consults on the economics, management and regulation of the telecommunications industry worldwide. Primary activities are telecommunications rate structure research, presentation of expert testimony in telecommunications regulatory proceedings, and telecommunications information services and management. Clients include telecommunications users, service providers, and state and federal regulatory agencies.

EDWARDS AND KELCEY, INC.
299 Madison Ave. PO 1936
Morristown, NJ 07960
Ronald A. Wiss, President
PH: (201)267-0555
TF: (800)253-9527
FX: (201)267-3555
Founded: 1946. **Staff:** 381. Activities: Offers professional and technical services to public agencies, private, industrial, and commercial clients for projects in the fields of transportation and traffic engineering; highway, airport, railroad, mass transportation and structural engineering; telecommunications; environmental impact studies; recreational and natural resource planning; community and urban renewal; military, industrial and commercial facilities; and waste-water facilities in the continental U.S.

EFFECTIVE DATA SOLUTIONS
4811 Emerson Ave., Ste. 208
Palatine, IL 60067
PH: (847)397-9900
FX: (847)397-9905
E-mail: webguy@effective-data.com
Activities: An information systems consulting firm specializing in electronic commerce. Utilizes Electronic Data Interchange (EDI) the application-to-application transfer of business documents between computers. It is a fast, inexpensive, and safe method of sending purchase orders, invoices, shipping notices, and other frequently used business documents.

ELECTRONIC SPECIALISTS, INC.
PO Box 389
Natick, MA 01760
F.J. Stifter, President
PH: (508)655-1532
TF: (800)225-4876
FX: (508)653-0268
E-mail: clipprx@ix.netcom.com
URL: www.elect-spec.com
Founded: 1978. **Staff:** 12. Activities: Assists clients who have AC power line problems and telephone interference problems. Industries served: computer, satellite, alarm, and government agencies in the United States.

ELECTRONIC SYSTEMS ASSOCIATES
11 W. 42nd St., 3rd Fl.
New York, NY 10036
Jack W. Caloz, P.E., President

PH: (212)843-3600
FX: (212)843-3699
E-mail: info@esa.com
URL: www.esa.com
Founded: 1986. **Staff:** 56. Activities: Majority-owned subsidary of Syska & Hennessy Engineers provides electronic engineering and consulting for a wide array of building electronic systems. Specializes in designing and implementing voice, data and imaging communications systems, audiovisual systems, facility management and control systems, fire/life safety and security systems and programs. Industries served: financial sector, pharmaceutical, colleges and universities, research centers, research and development labs, medical centers, hospitals, commercial and industrial construction, real estate renovations, and government agencies.

ELITE TECHNICAL SERVICES, INC.
900 Wheeler Rd., Ste. 290
Hauppauge, NY 11788
PH: (516)366-2345
TF: (800)ELITE-50
FX: (516)366-2552
E-mail: resume@elitetechnical.com
URL: www.elitetechnical.com/
Activities: Contractors and Consultants providing Application Developer, Scientific Consultants, Entry Level PC Technicians, and Network Engineers, and other technical professionals. Management Information Services Division provides information systems consultants. Contract Engineering Division specializes in the staffing of scientific contract engineers and technical support. Data Division concentrates on providing clients with network engineers, CNEs, and all types of data/PC support personnel.

ENGINEERING ASSOCIATES INC.
2625 Cumberland Pky., Ste. 100
Atlanta, GA 30339
Thomas C. Harter, President
PH: (770)432-8833
TF: (800)356-5907
FX: (770)432-8908
URL: www.engineeringassociates.com
Founded: 1954. **Staff:** 200. Activities: Offers telecommunications and engineering services, wireline and wireless, including feasibility studies, design and installation supervision for voice, data and video communications and cable television (CATV). Also offers facility management, facility planning, energy conservation assistance, and operations improvement studies. Clients include telephone companies, building owners, NASA and U.S. Navy, other governmental units, and cable television services worldwide.

ENTERPRISE DEVELOPMENT INTERNATIONAL, INC.
4903 Edgemoor Ln., L-03
Bethesda, MD 20814
Oliver Dziggel, President
PH: (301)652-0179
FX: (301)652-0177
Founded: 1983. **Staff:** 23. Activities: Designs, installs, and manages information systems; and provides competitive assessments, RFP bid analyses and preparation (federal and international), site surveys, and requirements analyses. Offers fundraising, new ventures, and technology transfer. Also provides partnership brokerage, market intelligence, and strategic planning. Industries served: computers and communications, systems integrators, and government agencies worldwide.

ENVISIONEERING, INC.
3594 Byron St. NW
Silverdale, WA 98383
James S. Kuga, President
PH: (360)692-2602
FX: (360)692-5917
URL: www.ering.com
Founded: 1984. **Staff:** 60. Activities: Provides a wide range of engineering computer, communications, and information technology management and professional services to government and commer-

cial users of computer-based technology. The company has been conducting ongoing research and design studies for automating and integrating technical documentation systems with printing and publication activities. These studies include the use of computer assisted retrieval, networking, and laser disk technology. Also provides solutions for the conversion of hardcopy graphics to electronic media; this includes a wide variety of CAD and technical publishing system formats. Industries served: government, A/E firms, construction, and environmental. Also provide environmental compliance documentation to government activities.

EPIC USA, LLC
150 S. 5th St., Ste. 1450
Minneapolis, MN 55402-4214
James E. Farstad, President
PH: (612)397-3000
TF: (800)877-3742
FX: (612)397-3144
Founded: 1984. **Staff:** 50. Activities: Strategic Technology Planning, Facility Technology Planning and Relocation, Network and Communication Solutions and Information Systems Implementation.

EPSILON
50 Cambridge St.
Burlington, MA 01803
Bob Mohr, Chairman
PH: (781)221-0092
TF: (800)225-3333
FX: (781)270-5886
E-mail: lcrewe@epsilon.com
URL: www.epsilon.com
Founded: 1969. **Staff:** 800. Activities: Information-based direct marketing consultants. Services include marketing strategy development, marketing information systems consulting, database development and management, analytic consulting, creative concept development and direct marketing program implementation. Industries served: business-to-business, financial services, healthcare, media and entertainment, travel, retail, catalog and not-for-profit.

EVOLVING SYSTEMS
9777 Mt. Pyramid Ct.
Englewood, CO 80112
George Hallenbeck, CEO, President
PH: (303)802-1000
TF: (800)360-9923
FX: (303)802-1400
E-mail: webmaster@evolving.com
URL: www.evolving.com
Founded: 1985. **Staff:** 300. Activities: Telecommunications Counsulting Specialists in the area of local number portability, voiceover IP, Network and Service Provisioning and wireless data, utilizing strategic and business process modeling techniques.

EVOTECH MICROENGINEERING CONSULTANTS, INC.
875 Cowan Rd., Ste. B-203
Burlingame, CA 94010
Basilio Chen, President
PH: (650)697-3861
FX: (650)697-6598
E-mail: info@evotech.com
Founded: 1984. **Staff:** 20. Activities: Offers product development services in software, digital hardware, telecommunications, and embedded firmware from requirement specifications to design and programming. Services include analysis, development, maintenance, and enhancement in hardware, and software for ISDN (integrated services digital network), ATM, ADSL, SNMP, real-time, scientific applications, and telecommunication systems (voice & data). Serves private industries and government agencies.

FUTURE COMMUNICATIONS CORP.
342 Madison Ave., Ste. 1414
New York, NY 10016
Peter W. Adams, Chairman

PH: (212)686-2422
FX: (212)687-1520
Founded: 1989. **Staff:** 2. Activities: Management consultants providing specialized services in technology-related areas: application of technology to book and magazine publishing in all its forms; exploitation of emerging media, such as CD-ROM, in support of information industry business; delivery of advanced marketing research and counsel; quality assurance and database integrity; and operational analysis of publishing activities for non-publishing firms. Industries served: publishing; film, broadcast, and cable entertainment; pharmaceutical; insurance, banking, and other financial services companies; small businesses and free-standing departments; professional services firms; and government agencies.

GEOTECH, INC.
4900 Cascade Rd. SE
Grand Rapids, MI 49546-3788
George J. Orphan, President
PH: (616)949-3340
FX: (616)949-8238
E-mail: yorg@voyager.net
Founded: 1971. **Staff:** 25. Activities: Telecommunications specialists offer expertise in the following: telephone outside plant, telephone central office switches, PBX switches, PBX distribution plant, microwave systems, video systems, data transmission systems, standby power systems, and uninterruptable power systems. Additional expertise available in cable television systems, central office buildings, grounding systems, lightning protection systems, casualty investigations, continuing property records, expert testimony, computer mapping, and electrical/mechanical design. Industries served: telephone industry, manufacturing industry, commercial business, hospitals, healthcare, governmental, and educational.

GEOTRAIN
171 Carlos Dr.
San Rafael, CA 94903
Jim Bensman, CEO
PH: (415)491-8950
TF: (800)268-7737
FX: (415)491-8955
E-mail: register@geotrain.com
URL: www.geotrain.com
Founded: 1985. **Staff:** 150. Activities: Offers interrelated network integration, distributed systems implementation, WAN & LAN audits, skills gap & technology analysis consulting and education. Industries served: telecommunication, government agencies, consumer products, ISPs, finance, service, and defense.

GIGA INFORMATION GROUP
1 Longwater Cir.
Norwell, MA 02061
John Struck, CEO
PH: (781)982-9500
FX: (781)878-6650
Founded: 1979. **Staff:** 300. Activities: A worldwide organization of industry analysts providing research, consulting services, and strategic advice to companies that produce and use information technology. Specializes in the fields of information processing, telecommunications, and electronic imaging technology, working with business leaders to analyze new products, technologies, markets, and opportunities. Emphasis is on integrating advanced technology with business strategies for technology vendors and users. Custom research projects for primary markets focus on market analysis, market structure, vendor image and reputation, corporate strategy, and industry strategy.

GIPE ASSOCIATES, INC.
8659 Commerce Dr.
Easton, MD 21601
Albert B. Gipe, CEO
PH: (410)822-8688
FX: (410)822-6306
Founded: 1977. **Staff:** 63. Activities: Mechanical and electrical engineering consultants. Also offers expertise in security and telecom-

munications. Serves private industries as well as government agencies.

GOLD SYSTEMS, INC.
4865 Riverbend Rd.
Boulder, CO 80301
G. Terry Gold, President
PH: (303)447-2837
FX: (303)447-0814
URL: www.goldsys.com
Founded: 1991. **Staff:** 34. Activities: Offers consulting in the telecommunications field, specifically in voice-response and PBX-to-host applications. Provides feasibility studies, requirements generation, and also develops custom applications software. Industries served: communications, banking, and telemarketing.

GORDIAN
20361 Irvine Ave.
Santa Ana, CA 92707
Gregory A. Bone, President
PH: (714)850-0205
FX: (714)850-0533
E-mail: info@gordian.com
URL: www.gordian.com
Founded: 1986. **Staff:** 25. Activities: Firm specializes in contract research, design, and prototype development, applying leading edge technologies to the creation of new products. Offers expertise in computer networking and peripherals, telecommunications, operating systems, optical technology and imaging, and raster graphics processing.

GVNW CONSULTING, INC.
2270 La Montana Way
Colorado Springs, CO 80936
Robert Adkisson, President
PH: (719)594-5800
FX: (719)599-0968
URL: www.gvnw.com
Founded: 1972. **Staff:** 85. Activities: Telecommunications consultants with experience in interstate access charge tariffs, intrastate access charge tariffs, local exchange tariffs, depreciation rate studies, NECA settlement studies, traffic engineering, accounting systems, complete business plans, cellular operations, telecommunications management seminars, and mergers and acquisitions.

HATFIELD & DAWSON, CONSULTING ELECTRICAL ENGINEERS
9500 Greenwood Ave. N
Seattle, WA 98103
Benjamin F. Dawson, III, President
PH: (206)783-9151
FX: (206)789-9834
E-mail: dawson@hatdaw.com
URL: www.halcyon.com/hatdaw
Founded: 1972. **Staff:** 12. Activities: Offers technical advice in all areas of telecommunications engineering, including planning, system design and specification, cost analysis, preparation of briefs for the Federal Communications Commission, Canadian Department of Communications, and other national and state regulatory agencies. Equipped to do field work of a technical nature in telecommunications engineering of all types. Also electromagnetic compatibility analysis and testing, and power and radio frequency non-ionizing radiation analysis and measurement. Industries served: broadcasting, private and commercial land mobile users, government agencies, and industrial concerns which use radio frequency devices.

THE HELSING GROUP, INC.
11875 Dublin Blvd., Ste. D-176
Dublin, CA 94568
TF: (800)435-7464
FX: (510)833-0706
E-mail: info@helsing.com
URL: www.helsing.com
Activities: A financial, contractual, and management consultant that

provides services to community associates. Offers services in construction management, forensic analysis, investigative testing and project scheduling. Also provides services fraud investigation services, property and casualty services, management consulting, and computer consulting

HICKS & RAGLAND ENGINEERING CO., INC.
4747 S. Loop 289
Lubbock, TX 79424-2224
David E. Sharbutt, President/CEO
PH: (806)791-7600
FX: (806)793-0632
E-mail: sw@hreng.com
Founded: 1935. **Staff:** 120. Activities: Services include strategic and network planning, project management, contract administration, marketing, financial modeling, and engineering services relating to wireline, wireless (PCS and cellular), wideband, broadband, CATV, and data communications.

HTL TELEMANAGEMENT LTD.
3901 National Dr., Ste. 270
Burtonsville, MD 20866
Michael T. Hills, President
PH: (301)236-0780
TF: (800)CAL-LHTL
FX: (301)421-9513
E-mail: sales@htlt.com
URL: www.htlt.com
Founded: 1980. **Staff:** 15. Activities: Software development consulting firm specializing in voice traffic engineering software for least-cost routing. Also active in the design and management of voice and data networks for corporations and resellers. Industries served: Fortune 500 companies, interexchange (long distance) carriers, interconnect companies, national and regional operating companies, and government agencies.

E.C. HUNTER ASSOCIATES, INC.
132 Atkinson Ave.
Syracuse, NY 13207
Everest C. Hunter, President
PH: (315)476-3811
FX: (315)476-3816
Founded: 1979. **Staff:** 5. Activities: Consultants/specialists in "Information Age Communications." Services cover telecommunications, microwave, fiber optics, computer software, health and safety, public relations, advertising and marketing, and sales support programs. Serves industrial, commercial, educational, and telecommunications organizations.

IDEAMATICS INC.
1364 Beverly Rd., #101
McLean, VA 22101-3617
David L. Danner, President
PH: (703)903-4972
TF: (800)247-IDEA
FX: (703)827-9046
E-mail: ideamatics@mclean.va.us
URL: www.mclean.va.us/~ideamatics
Founded: 1975. **Staff:** 5. Activities: Computer software development consultants. Offers microprocessor firmware design and development, productivity improvement, computer modeling and analysis, software valuation, appraisals and assessments/validation. Industries served: associations, defense manpower, government agencies, telecommunications, and attorneys.

IGI CONSULTING
214 Harvard Ave., Ste. 200
Boston, MA 02134
Paul Polishuk, President/Chairman
PH: (617)232-3111
TF: (800)323-1088
FX: (617)734-8562
E-mail: igiboston@aol.com
URL: igigroup.com

Founded: 1980. **Staff:** 15. Activities: International consulting firm offering proprietary consulting, particularly market research reports, in fiber optics, local and metropolitan area networks (LANs), integrated services digital network (ISDN), wireless and telecommunications. Conduct market and technology assessment studies. Industries served: telecommunications and government agencies.

INACOM
10810 Farnam Dr.
Omaha, NE 68154-3260
Bob Hutton, V.P. Marketing
PH: (402)392-3900
TF: (800)843-2762
FX: (402)330-7244
Founded: 1987. **Staff:** 16. Activities: Offers computer consulting services, specializing in local area networks, wide area networks, gateway design, database development, project analysis, site management, disaster recovery plans, electronic mail services, and network auditing. Also offers expertise in solution research, system integration, multi vendor connectivity, integration and test laboratory, feasibility studies, solution prototyping, performance testing, compatibility testing, executive briefings, procedures development, cable plant issues and security systems. Serves private industries as well as government agencies.

INDUSTRY IN TRANSITION
24 Standish Rd.
Bellingham, MA 02019
Walter Haug, President
PH: (508)966-1691
E-mail: IITconsult@aol.com
URL: members.tripod.com/~IITconsult
Activities: An independent management consulting firm that provides marketing and management consulting services for businesses and organizations. Develops marketing strategies. Specializes in a full range of services in the telecommunications industry.

INFOACTIV, INC.
999 W. Chester Pke., No. 202
West Chester, PA 19380
Samuel Cannavo, Chairman, CEO
PH: (610)692-6292
TF: (888)230-5430
FX: (610)692-5430
E-mail: sales@infoactiv.com
URL: www.infoactiv.com
Founded: 1988. **Staff:** 20. Activities: Provides marketing and technical consulting and systems integration services in enhanced telecommunications and customer service applications, such as voice mail, IVR, CTI, Call Center integration, provisioning, billing, decision support, statistical reporting, internet/intranet and client server applications. As part of marketing services, provides churn management, product rollout, service management, and operations consulting.

INFOCORE TELECOMMUNICATIONS SERVICES
661 Moore Rd., Ste. 110
King of Prussia, PA 19406-1317
James Chukinas, Vice President
PH: (610)337-9611
TF: (800)935-4654
FX: (610)768-5238
URL: www.infocore.com
Founded: 1981. **Staff:** 45. Activities: Firm specializes in telecommunications, voice, data and video equipment, telecom facilities management, and data analysis for commercial and industrial clients.

INFORMATION BUILDERS INC.
1250 Broadway
New York, NY 10001-3701
Gerald Cohen, President
PH: (212)736-4433
FX: (212)967-6406

Founded: 1975. **Staff:** 1500. Activities: Computer technology firm offers expertise in information system design, computer software/ hardware, systems analysis, licensing and legal services to clients in the U.S., western Europe, Canada, Africa, the Middle East, and South America.

INFORMATION PLUS/INFORMATION PLUS (AMERICA) INC.

14 Lafayette Sq., Ste. 2000
Buffalo, NY 14203-1920
D.C. Sawyer, President
PH: (716)852-2220
FX: (716)852-1653
Founded: 1979. **Staff:** 7. Activities: Does value-added research to support business development, acquisitions, competitor analysis, best practices, benchmarking, and customer service. Industries served: manufacturing, food processing, finance, retail, pharmaceuticals, telecommunications, and computers/high-technology.

INFORMATION SYSTEMS & NETWORKS CORP.

10411 Motor City Dr.
Bethesda, MD 20817
Roma Malkani, President
PH: (301)469-0400
FX: (301)469-7726
Founded: 1980. **Staff:** 600. Activities: Provides consulting services in the following areas: systems integration, software design, procurement, telecommunications networks design, engineering, implementation and operations, facilities management, data base management, office automation, C3 security systems, planning and engineering for surveillance, and security.

INFORMATION SYSTEMS TECHNOLOGY

30 Corte Ellena
Walnut Creek, CA 94598
Reuven Shaffin, President
PH: (510)932-6705
FX: (510)946-9540
Founded: 1985. **Staff:** 3. Activities: Project management consulting firm offers expertise in software development, system architecture and design, database design, software development plans, and performance evaluation. Industries served: manufacturing, medical, retail, and telephony.

INFOTECH

PO Box 150
Woodstock, VT 05091
Julie B. Schwerin, Chairman/CEO
PH: (802)763-2097
FX: (802)763-2098
E-mail: info@infotechresearch.com
URL: www.infotechresearch.com
Founded: 1984. **Staff:** 5. Activities: Firm has expertise in electronic and print publishing, personal computer hardware and software, telecommunications and broadcasting, interactive media, consumer electronics, and related technologies. Services include business planning, market and technology assessment, product development and distribution strategies, and strategic business alliances.

INNOSYS INC.

3095 Richmond Pky., Ste. 207
Richmond, CA 94806-1900
Dale Sekijima, President
PH: (510)769-7717
FX: (510)222-0323
Founded: 1973. **Staff:** 13. Activities: Develops terminal and protocol conversion products for airline and travel industry communications. Industries served: transportation and travel.

INNOVA-TECH CONSULTING INC.

82 Whittington Course
St. Charles, IL 60174-1434
Harold Cash, CSM, Principal

PH: (630)584-3977
FX: (630)584-5173
E-mail: hecash@ameritech.net
URL: innova-tech.net
Founded: 1997. **Staff:** 5. Activities: Information Technology/ Business Solutions Architecture, Custom database application development, Client-Server custom software development.

INSTITUTE FOR GLOBAL COMMUNICATIONS

Presidio Bldg. 1012, 1st Fl.
PO Box 29904
Torney Ave.
San Francisco, CA 94129-0904
Marci Lockwood, Executive Director
PH: (415)561-6100
FX: (415)561-6100
E-mail: consulting@igc.org
URL: www.igc.org/igc/services/consulting.html
Founded: 1986. **Staff:** 35. Activities: Firm provides strategic, design, and technical Internet assistance, specializing in meeting the needs of non-profit and activist organizations. Services include Web site design, Web site maintenance, Web-based forums and mailing list archives, Internet-accessible databases, online fundraising, computer communication and information strategies, training on Internet basics and how to get an organization online, special advocacy projects such as online email and fax campaigns, consultation on international telecommunications such as private newsgroups, private web services, and private databases.

INTELLIANT

1777 S. Harrison St.
Denver, CO 80210
Bruce McDowell
PH: (303)759-4484
FX: (303)759-9846
E-mail: binedowell@intelliant.com
URL: www.intelliant.com
Founded: 1976. **Staff:** 26. Activities: Information management consulting firm specializing in FDA-regulated environments. We provide consulting services, quality-systems solutions, and information-management applications to the medical device, pharmaceutical, biologics, and in vitro diagnostics industries.

INTELLIGENT INFORMATION

517 Linden St.
Glen Ellyn, IL 60137-4021
Bonnie Hohhof
PH: (630)469-0732
FX: (630)469-0752
E-mail: bhohhof@mixedsignal.com
Founded: 1988. **Staff:** 2. Activities: Active in the design and implementation of competitive intelligence information systems, in addition to developing competitive intelligence analysis capabilities within companies. Also conducts seminars and training sessions for information services staff. Industries served: communications and electronics.

THE INTERFACE EXPERTS

10536 Ohio Ave.
Los Angeles, CA 90024
Ellie Rosen
PH: (310)474-3850
FX: (310)474-3850
Founded: 1984. **Staff:** 3. Activities: Provides systems analysis and applications design and development focusing on database applications, needs assessment, assistance in selection of hardware and software, training, and technical documentation. Specializes in business, financial, legal, and medical applications. Microsoft Solution Provider. Experienced in Novell and Unix. Industries served: general business, medical, legal, distribution, accounting, and film and television production in Los Angeles, Ventura, and Orange County, California.

INTERNATIONAL TECHNOLOGY CONSULTANTS, INC.
4340 East-West Hwy., Ste. 1020
Bethesda, MD 20814-4411
S. Blake Swensrud, President
PH: (301)907-0060
FX: (301)907-6555
E-mail: cole@itcresearch.com
URL: www.itcresearch.com
Founded: 1990. **Staff:** 14. Activities: Provides contract consulting services to telecom firms, investors, financial institutions and governments. The company offers market evaluation, competitive intelligence, opportunity assessment, economic and political risk assessment, strategy formulation, business planning, partner identification, due diligence review, introductions to US and foreign government officials, financing and legal assistance, and Washington, DC representation.

IRONGATE, INC.
7 Mt. Lassen Dr., Ste. C-126
San Rafael, CA 94903
Dale W. Miller
PH: (415)491-0910
FX: (415)491-9730
E-mail: dwmiller@irongateinc.com
URL: www.irongateinc.com
Founded: 1986. **Staff:** 2. Activities: Offers information security consulting services assisting clients to protect their information from accidental or unauthorized intentional disclosure, destruction, modification, or delay. Services include: developing company-wide information security programs, evaluating the security of computer and communications systems, conducting risk assessments, recommending cost-effective information security systems and controls, implementing encryption, and developing and implementing information security standards and procedures, as well as providing training. Industries served: healthcare, banking, finance, and government worldwide.

J & B DESIGN ENGINEERING
Box D
Hatboro, PA 19040
John F. Bickel
PH: (215)675-0270
FX: (215)672-1149
E-mail: hertzog170@aol.com
Founded: 1973. **Staff:** 8. Activities: Offers consulting services in traffic engineering, traffic signal control systems, lane control systems, toll collection systems, management information systems, RF and microwave systems, site plans, wetlands analysis and conceptual plans. Also serves as expert witness for highway accident investigation, reconstruction and testimony. Clients include governmental agencies, private developers and private organizations.

C.S. JONES GROUP, INC.
725 Pellissippi Pky., Ste. 110
PO Box 30193
Knoxville, TN 37930-0193
PH: (423)675-5860
FX: (423)675-4334
E-mail: jones@consultec.com
Activities: Firm specializes in training management software, enabling clients to schedule classes, instructors, equipment, and rooms; enroll participants; track student credits and CEUs; budget training costs; develop curricula; record course outlines and content; print name tags, certificates, letters, course schedules, student transcripts, and instructor schedules; and create their own reports. Also offers system services such as planning and set-up, transferring existing data, system customization, and user training.

JP SOFTWARE INC.
PO Box 1470
East Arlington, MA 02174
Thomas E. Rawson

PH: (617)646-3975
FX: (617)646-0904
URL: www.jpsoft.com
Founded: 1984. **Staff:** 7. Activities: Software development firm provides expertise covering areas ranging from general system design to component-level hardware troubleshooting. Specific areas of expertise include: system design, microcomputer software development, hardware/software systems, database design and programming, and data communications. Also offers training in computer basics, computer operation and backup, beginning and advanced programming, troubleshooting, and the use of microcomputer software. Industries served include: electronic communications, consumer products, data processing and computer, education, electronics, food and beverage, healthcare, nonprofits, politics, printing, and service organizations.

KALBA INTERNATIONAL, INC.
1601 Trapelo Rd.
Waltham, MA 02154
Dr. Yale Braunstein, Vice President
PH: (781)259-9589
FX: (781)466-8440
E-mail: mail7495@pop.net
Founded: 1973. **Staff:** 50. Activities: Provides counsel in management, international telecommunications, cellular telephone, and interactive media. Uses multidisciplinary project teams with expertise in strategic and financial plans, market and competitive research, license applications, joint ventures and financing, and technology and regulatory assessment. Specializes in multi-country assignments. Industries served: telecommunications, electronic media, government, finance, law, and research worldwide.

KOH SYSTEMS, INC.
6011 Executive Blvd., Ste. 214
Rockville, MD 20852
Yong-Soo Koh, President
PH: (301)231-0033
FX: (301)231-5466
Founded: 1980. **Staff:** 230. Activities: Provides management and technical consulting support to federal, state, local governments, and private organizations in the following areas: management services, information systems, systems technology, litigation support, engineering and systems support, ADP/computer support, MIS and telecommunication systems support. Computer services are as follows: provides installation and troubleshooting of microcomputers, and technical support in developing stand-alone and network-based systems; develops, installs, maintains, and documents interactive and data management software; develops software and hardware control plans and inventory control procedures; performs risk assessments, security audits and reviews, and system development in support of computer security programs; administers and manages operation of Local Area Networks (LAN); and develops, tests and implements software including COBOL and FORTRAN in the VAX/VMS environment.

LABAT-ANDERSON INC.
8000 Westpark Dr., Ste. 400
McLean, VA 22101
PH: (703)506-9600
FX: (703)506-4646
E-mail: erin_cannelli@labat.com
URL: www.labat.com
Founded: 1979. Activities: Offers information services including computer facility management, records management, and publication development. Provides environmental services including environmental compliance, risk assessment, and pollution prevention. Also offers private sector development services including trade, investment, and export promotion.

LAC COMMUNICATIONS, INC.
Altavista 21-Q-46
Ponce, PR 00731
Luis A. Capestany, President

PH: (787)844-1448
FX: (787)843-0030
Founded: 1986. **Staff:** 16. Activities: Engineering firm with planning, design and construction capabilities in the communications field including CATV, telephone, microwave, earth station, and tower systems. Can perform both aerial and underground work. Industries served: telecommunications, government agencies, and general construction.

LIBRARY CO-OP, INC.
3840 Park Ave., Ste. 107
Edison, NJ 08820
Gloria Dinerman, President
PH: (732)906-1777
TF: (800)654-6275
FX: (732)906-3562
E-mail: LIBRCO@compuserve.com
Founded: 1982. **Staff:** 8. Activities: Full service library and information management corporation specializing in placements, projects, and consulting. Also offers automation counseling for library and business applications, as well as expertise in LANS, WANS, IBM, and UNIX operating systems. Firm helps clients in library development, on-line searching, data entry, space planning, moves, and database development highlight the broad scope of services. Also active in public relations, marketing, and the construction and implementation of surveys. Additional fields covered include preservation/restoration, barcoding, and reference. Serves all corporations, schools, universities, government agencies, law firms, and medical affiliates in the U.S.

LIEBER AND ASSOCIATES
3740 N. Lakeshore Dr., Ste. 15 B
Evanston, IL 60202-2529
Mitchell A. Lieber, President
PH: (773)325-9400
FX: (773)325-0621
E-mail: M_lieberm@lieberandassociates.com
Founded: 1977. **Staff:** 9. Activities: Provides telephone marketing (inbound and outbound); database marketing; and telecommunications technology services for sales, customer service, and order departments. Also upgrades existing operations and start-ups. Performs strategic planning, facility design, equipment specification, network (telephone line) design, software recommendations, staff planning, database design, management systems development, program design, scripting, and project management to meet client requirements. Projects 800 number call volumes. Industries served: direct marketing, catalog order, customer service, utilities, cable television, travel and hospitality, advertising, broadcasting, general business and government in the U.S. and worldwide.

LIFETIME MEDIA INC.
17205 Vashon Highway, SW
Vashon, WA 98070
PH: (206)567-5500
URL: www.ltmedia.com
Activities: Firm offers EXPRESS, a Windows-based Microsoft access base which ensures speedy training and quick processing of data. Software is formatted to simplify all aspects of training administration, as well as coordinating data information, correspondence, and reports.

LIGHTWAVES SPECTRUM INTERNATIONAL
5180 Parkstone Dr., Ste. 260
Chantilly, VA 20151
William C. Primrose, President
PH: (703)818-9700
FX: (703)818-9804
URL: www.lsii.com
Founded: 1986. **Staff:** 22. Activities: A telecommunications engineering and management consulting firm that specializes in the development of turnkey fiber optic networks. Staff of specialists begin with market analysis and strategic planning of network architecture, topology, and service offerings. Focus then turns to systems engineering and integration, outside plant engineering, site survey and permitting, and finally as project managers, consultants oversee construction, as well as perform installation terminating, testing and maintenance of the fiber optic networks. Industries served: telephony, cable TV, data and multimedia.

LOCKARD AND WHITE
14511 Falling Creek, Ste. 507
Houston, TX 77014
Marc Lockard, President
PH: (281)586-0574
FX: (281)586-0044
URL: www.lawtelecom.com
Founded: 1984. **Staff:** 40. Activities: A professional telecommunications engineering firm that specializes in detailed engineering and project management. Also provides feasibility studies, needs analysis, and regulatory affair coordination. Extensive experience in project management, design, engineering, installation, operation and maintenance of telecommunications systems.

LOGICAL SERVICES, INC.
3235 Kifer Rd., Ste. 210
Santa Clara, CA 95051
Robert W. Ulrickson, President
PH: (408)739-2600
FX: (408)739-6364
URL: www.logicalservices.com
Founded: 1973. **Staff:** 30. Activities: Full-service contract engineering, software development, industrial design, mechanical engineering, and turnkey-manufacturing including electronic assembly, materials management, plastic tooling and molding, sheet metal fabrication, and system assembly and test. Special emphasis on medical devices and wireless telecommunications. More than 300 ideas converted to products in control systems, analytical instrumentation, computing and networking. Proprietary Product Introduction Process takes new product ideas and market requirements, adds design teams led by program managers and its development laboratory to provide prototype designs, documentation, and pilot production of new products. Logical takes responsibility for program management and product qualification projects that require FDA QSR (510K & PMA), UL, FCC, CE and other agency approvals. Through strategic alliances, fulfills client needs for synchronized, engineering-driven manufacturing.

MACRO INTERNATIONAL INC.
11785 Beltsville Dr., #300
Beltsville, MD 20705-3121
PH: (301)572-0200
FX: (301)572-0999
URL: www.macroint.com
Founded: 1966. **Staff:** 500. Activities: Consulting services include research, management consulting, training, and information systems. Research capabilities range from statistical analysis to program evaluation, primarily for the federal government, and market and survey research for both commercial and non-commercial clients. For example, population and maternal and child health surveys are conducted in developing countries worldwide. Youth health risk surveys are conducted nationally. Financial services surveys are conducted in the U.S. and Eastern Europe. A variety of management consulting services are offered in the areas of organization development, workforce training and development, and diversity training. Training and training of trainers is provided in disciplines such as substance abuse prevention, continuous quality improvement, and survey methodology. Information systems services include application development, implementation and operation; network services; software quality assurance and testing; systems analysis, design and documentation; systems integration; and wireless data communications. Industries served: federal, state, and local governments including health and human services organizations, family planning organizations, nutrition agencies, housing agencies, and special education agencies; national and international organizations such as universities, foundations, nonprofit entities, health organizations, economic, management, and productivity development institutes, and businesses including manufacturers, banks, utilities, telecommunications companies, and the media.

MANAGEMENT INFORMATION SYSTEMS
2219 S. Kings Ave.
Brandon, FL 33511
Nevere K. Mouradran, Owner
PH: (813)651-1623
FX: (813)681-9359
Founded: 1990. **Staff:** 4. Activities: Full service consulting firm, specializing in outsourcing projects, staffing specific requirements and education. Services provided for PC and mainframe platforms. Additional services include project plans, conversion operations, systems and procedures, testing and implementation, evaluating needs and equipment. Industries served: banking, education, financial services, insurance, healthcare (HMO), government, manufacturing, telecommunication, retail, textile, utilities, and wholesale.

MANAGEMENT SERVICES GROUP, INC.
129 Sierra Vista Ln.
Valley Cottage, NY 10989
Joseph C. Scordato, President
PH: (914)358-0070
FX: (914)358-9035
E-mail: jscordato@aol.com
Founded: 1977. **Staff:** 16. Activities: An information management consulting firm offering a broad spectrum of professional support, technical assistance and turnkey systems packages for business. Provides a full range of business consulting in systems analysis and design, information systems management, systems integration and telecommunications. Firm has performed systems planning and feasibility studies, established functional and technical requirements for the purchase of hardware and/or software, prepared disaster recovery and contingency plans, conducted operational and management audits, delivered and installed customized turnkey computer systems and trained client personnel. Industries served: banking, insurance, importing, government agencies, manufacturing, distribution, professional services, transportation and publishing industries.

MATHEWS & CO.
6 Landmark Sq.
Stamford, CT 06901-2792
Richard S. Mathews, President
PH: (203)325-8419
FX: (203)325-0125
E-mail: rmathews@how-rewedoing.com
URL: www.how-rewedoing.com
Founded: 1968. Activities: Specializes in customer satisfaction measurement/improvement and benchmarking for the information systems (IS) industry. Emphasis on achieving improved customer satisfaction, increased cost effectiveness, reduced cycle time, empowered employees and enchanced IS image by delivering "world-class" quality. Industries served: computer technology, telecommunications, and information services firms.

MBG ASSOCIATES LTD.
370 Lexington Ave., 23rd Fl.
New York, NY 10017
Michael Greenspan, President
PH: (212)822-4400
FX: (212)822-4499
Founded: 1977. **Staff:** 15. Activities: Telecommunications software consulting firm provides customized billing/telecommunications software, billing applications, software accommodated to the clients needs. Experience in many computer languages. Software runs on many computer environments. Offer the following software packages: T-MIS (Telecommunications Management Information Software) which allows all users to effectively utilize the call detail data for improved network management, customized billing software for call accounting, CDR, SMDR, and telemanagement systems, and SDN and most important tariff 12 VTNS billing and audit software. In addition, firm provides all these systems as a service bureau. Has developed a tariff 12 update service to provide an in-depth analysis and consulting for the entire marketplace. Industries served: brokerage, financial, interexchange carriers, hotels, autombiles, airlines, retailing, videotex, and all Fortune 100, 500 and 1000 companies.

MCGLADREY & PULLEN, LLP
1699 E. Woodfield Rd., Ste. 200
Schaumburg, IL 60173
Larry L. Dowell, Managing Partner of Consulting
PH: (847)517-7070
TF: (800)365-8353
FX: (847)517-7095
URL: www.mcgladrey.com
Founded: 1926. **Staff:** 3000. Activities: Provides a wide range of consulting services in the following broad areas: financial management consulting (including financial planning, valuations and financial feasibility analysis); business and strategic planning services (including succession planning and family business counseling); data processing and systems consulting (including all levels of systems -micro, mini and mainframe); human resources consulting (including personnel search, compensation planning, organization planning, outplacement, etc.); office automation and telecommunication consulting; operational consulting (including inventory and production control systems, operational reviews and productivity improvement); and marketing consulting. Industries served: banking, manufacturing, apparel and textiles, construction, education, government, healthcare, hospitality, insurance, legal, printing/publishing, broadcasting, retail/wholesale, and service.

MCI COMMUNICATIONS CORP.
1801 Pennsylvania Ave. NW
Washington 20006
Bert C. Roberts, Jr., CEO & Chariman of the Board
PH: (202)872-1600
FX: (202)887-2178
URL: www.mcit.com
Founded: 1968. **Staff:** 17000. Activities: Telecommunications firm offers extensive experience and consults in areas regarding communications networking. Serves private industries as well as government agencies.

WILLIAM B. MEYER INC.
PO Box 4206
Bridgeport, CT 06607
TF: (800)873-6393
FX: (203)375-9820
Activities: Provides library relocation services, including pre-bid consultation; project planning and management; and computer/ database development. Also provides comprehensive movie services with segregation, intregration, reclassification; artwork and special collections; shelving-static and compact; furniture, office contents and electronics.

MICROWAVE FILTER CO., INC.
6743 Kinne St.
East Syracuse, NY 13057
Carl Fahrenkrug, President
PH: (315)438-4700
TF: (800)448-1666
FX: (315)463-1467
E-mail: mfcsales@.microwavefilter.com
URL: www.microwavefilter.com
Founded: 1967. **Staff:** 88. Activities: Consults and provides hardware and services for the avoidance and suppression of terrestrial interference in home and commercial satellite receive systems. Similar interference services are offered to broadcast stations, cable systems and military communications. Industries served: telecommunications.

MID-SOUTH CONSULTING ENGINEERS, INC.
3901 Roselake Dr.
Charlotte, NC 28217
Joel O. Williams, President
PH: (704)357-0004
FX: (704)357-0025
Founded: 1960. **Staff:** 34. Activities: Consultants to the communications industry, offering design, lay-out, and supervision of the construction of entire communication systems or additions thereto. Clients are independent telephone systems, both privately financed

and REA financed. Also active in the CATV field, experienced in surveys, feasibility studies, strand map lay-outs, and the design and layout of the entire system. Markets computerized plant record systems. Provides consulting services in the telephone system management and plant records areas.

MOFFET, LARSON & JOHNSON, INC.
1110 North Glebe Rd., Ste. 800
Arlington, VA 22201
A. Richard Burke
PH: (703)741-3500
TF: (800)523-3117
FX: (703)741-0312
Founded: 1952. **Staff:** 100. Activities: Specializes in the design, development and operation of advanced mobile, broadcast and common carrier radio facilities. Offers full-service engineering consultation beginning with initial FCC licensing activity through system design, operation and network optimization. Industries served: cellular, paging, PCS, broadcast, AM/FM and SMR worldwide.

NATIONAL ECONOMIC RESEARCH ASSOCIATES, INC.
50 Main St.
White Plains, NY 10606
David Robinson, Director General, Madrid
PH: (914)448-4000
FX: (914)448-4040
URL: www.nera.com
Founded: 1961. **Staff:** 275. Activities: An international firm of consulting economists that provides research and analysis on a wide variety of business and public policy issues. Expertise in antitrust matters, energy, securities litigation, telecommunications, employment and discrimination, intellectual property, environment, health, transportation, international trade and sports. Full-time staff members highly qualified in economics, finance, statistics, computer science and mathematics. Clients include large corporations and law firms, federal, state and municipal agencies, and governments worldwide.

NATIONAL ELECTRIC SERVICE CORP.
317 Madison Ave., Ste. 619
New York, NY 10017
Joel Gordon, Vice President
PH: (212)986-7033
TF: (800)NES-COA1
FX: (212)986-7076
Founded: 1927. **Staff:** 82. Activities: Utility and telecommunications cost consultants serving industrial and commercial firms throughout the United States. Services include advising clients on methods of obtaining utility and telecommunication savings and refunds through changes of rates, methods of rate application, service equipment and service procedures. Also handles negotiations with suppliers and supervises the implementation of recommended and client approved changes.

NATIONAL SECURITY SYSTEMS, INC.
511 Manhasset Woods Rd.
Manhasset, NY 11030
J.W. Walter, President
PH: (516)627-2222
FX: (516)627-2212
Founded: 1958. **Staff:** 21. Activities: A comprehensive consulting company offering consultation and design in: telephone systems, networking (capability to obtain additional revenue on long-distance telephone calling), security, energy management, fire and safety systems, MATV, and paging and sound systems. Firm has assimilated these technologies into an "integrated systems package." The results are substantial savings through innovative design of multi-purpose systems and the reduction of labor, equipment, wiring, and conduit. Serves private industries as well as government agencies.

NELSON & CO. INC.
1100 Cir. 75 Pky., Ste. 800
Atlanta, GA 30339
Robert E. Nelson, Jr., President

PH: (770)951-4859
FX: (770)256-3764
Founded: 1987. **Staff:** 20. Activities: A general management consulting firm providing services in operations improvement, turnaround management, project management, Total Quality Management, and activity based costing. Firm also provides expertise to organizations in a broad range of information management planning and system development disciplines. Industries served: manufacturing, public utilities, distribution, telecommunications, cable television, and government agencies.

NOLAN, NORTON & CO.
99 High St. 33 Fl.
Boston, MA 02110-2371
Richard L. Nolan, Chairman
PH: (617)988-1200
FX: (617)988-0800
URL: www.kpmg.com
Founded: 1975. **Staff:** 200. Activities: Consulting services span a wide range of issues facing information services management including informations systems strategies and planning, applications planning development, systems architecture, telecommunications, data center operations, professional staff, user relationships, and organization relationships.

OBJECT ORIENTED DESIGN GROUP, INC.
3716 159th Dr., SE
Snohomish, WA 98290-9339
Robert P. Folline
PH: (425)334-8889
FX: (425)335-5101
E-mail: Bobf@eskimo.com
Founded: 1988. **Staff:** 31. Activities: Services include turnkey engineering, telecommunications/datacom system design, hardware design and layout from specification through product release, and software systems design from conceptual through product life. Industries served: military, datacom, telecom, and government agencies.

CHRIS OLSON & ASSOCIATES
857 Twin Harbor Dr.
Arnold, MD 21012-1027
Christine A. Olson
PH: (410)647-6708
FX: (410)647-0415
E-mail: chris@chrisolson.com
URL: www.chrisolson.com
Founded: 1984. **Staff:** 15. Activities: Offers promotion and marketing support for libraries, information service providers and producers, outreach programs, consumer information services, information brokers, data and analysis centers, clearinghouses, public awareness programs, and online computer system environments. Typical client projects include marketing plans, fee analysis, writing/editing documentation, graphics, exhibit design, and web site design-intranet and internet. Clients include businesses and government agencies. Services available nationwide and internationally.

OMNICOM, INC.
930 Thomasville Rd., Ste. 200
Tallahassee, FL 32303
Gene A. Buzzi, President
PH: (904)224-4451
TF: (800)780-0300
FX: (904)224-3059
E-mail: omnicom@polaris.net
Founded: 1982. **Staff:** 18. Activities: Offers engineering consulting services in all areas of communications including land mobile radio, electronic security, command and control, audio/video systems, communications towers, training, telephone systems, telephone systems traffic analysis and system optimization, data systems, computer-aided dispatch systems, local area networking, microwave and fiber optic transmission systems. Serves government public safety and administrative agencies as well as private clients.

OMNIMEDIA ASSOCIATES, LLC

121 Hawkins Pl., Ste. 171
Boonton, NJ 07005
Brian D. Rezach, Exec. VP, Marketing
PH: (973)335-4327
FX: (973)335-8693
E-mail: bdr@media.com
URL: www.omedia.com
Founded: 1994. **Staff:** 3. Activities: Provides marketing and business counsel for information services; and business planning for marketing and development on digital and interactive television networks and applications. Industries served: networks, information services, government agencies, and electric utilities, including municipal utilities, LEC's and IXC's.

PA CONSULTING GROUP

315 A Enterprise Dr.
Plainsboro, NJ 08536
John V. Buckley, CEO
PH: (609)936-8300
FX: (609)936-8811
URL: www.pa-consulting.com
Founded: 1943. **Staff:** 2700. Activities: Global business/technology strategy firm that works with clients in industry and commerce to manage complex change and create business advantage through technology. Services include the development of new and advanced technology products and production processes, the planning and implementation of complex computer and telecommunications systems, and the research and analysis required for business strategies in technology oriented firms. Industries served: aerospace, energy, financial services, information industries, healthcare (pharmaceuticals and insurance), food and drink, and government agencies.

PACIFIC NETCOM, INC.

4850 SW Scholls Ferry Rd., Ste. 103
Portland, OR 97225-1691
James Harry Green, President
PH: (503)205-0050
TF: (888)624-0050
FX: (503)297-6350
E-mail: information@pacificnetcom.com
Founded: 1983. **Staff:** 16. Activities: Provides telecommunications and office automation consulting service to end user clients. Services include performing feasibility studies, developing requirements and specifications, writing RFPs and evaluating responses, implementing and managing systems, and teaching classes and seminars. Expertise in automatic call distribution and benchmarking. Performs these functions on voice and data communication systems, long distance and local exchange services, local and wide area networks, small computer systems and office automation systems. Facilities Management: Provides day-to-day telecom management, move, add, change switch programming, vendor management, budget/expense tracking, bill processing, call accounting management. Industries served: all commercial, industrial, governmental organizations, including healthcare, legal, educational and financial corporations.

PALMER COMPUTER SERVICES, INC.

19 W. 36th St., 11th Fl.
New York, NY 10018-7909
Jason Palmer, President
PH: (212)714-1710
FX: (212)714-0132
E-mail: info@palmer.net
URL: www.palmer.net
Founded: 1981. **Staff:** 7. Activities: Value added reseller/ consultants specializing in information management systems, accounting and financial office automation, and financial models for asset backed products. Provides customized software solutions for music/video/film production companies. Industries served: federal government (specifically the U.S. Federal Court system), Fortune 500, financial services, legal/professional, music/video/film production, and small business.

PB FARRADYNE INC.

3200 Tower Oaks Blvd.
Rockville, MD 20852
Walter H. Kraft, Senior Vice President
PH: (301)468-5568
FX: (301)816-1884
E-mail: jobs@pbworld.com
URL: www.pbfi.com
Founded: 1984. **Staff:** 110. Activities: Provides transportation planning and engineering software development and systems integration services for intelligent transportation system applications. Also offers telecommunications systems planning and design for data and voice communications; and LAN (local area network) design and implementation. Focuses on computer systems interoperability. Serves government agencies, transportation, and defense industries in the United States.

PERSONAL FINANCE NETWORK

119 Old Saugatuck Rd.
Norwalk, CT 06855
Thomas Woodruff, President
PH: (203)838-8181
FX: (203)838-8181
URL: wwbroadcast.com/pfn
Activities: An online personal finance information service. Customized consulting to organizations, companies government, and unions on financial education, investments, and personal savings issues.

D.L. PHILLIPS & ASSOCIATES

7731 Shagbark Ct., No. 200
Brownsburg, IN 46112
Dianne L. Phillips-Flynn, President
PH: (317)852-7300
FX: (317)852-7377
Founded: 1987. **Staff:** 3. Activities: A management consulting firm specializing in telecommunications and information management with experience in voice/data/video integration. Services include telecommunications strategic planning, needs assessment and system review, equipment and network expense audits, evaluation of existing equipment, creation of request for proposals, proposal evaluation and recommendations to management, vendor-owner contract negotiation, system implementation, integration of office automation and information processors, network design, on-site telecommunications management, performance audits, and in-house training seminars. Serves private industries as well as government agencies.

PHILLIPS INFOTECH

90 East Halsey Rd.
Parsippany, NJ 07054
Alan Mendelson, President and CEO
PH: (973)884-0100
FX: (973)884-8804
Founded: 1982. **Staff:** 50. Activities: Management consultants specializing in marketing (strategic planning, market research); communications (teleconferencing, telemarketing, teletraining); and training (custom designed training packages). Serves private industries as well as government agencies. Also serves educational institutions.

PHILLIPS PERSONNEL/SEARCH; PHILLIPS TEMPS

1675 Broadway, Ste. 2410
Denver, CO 80202
Nancy Lawrence, Vice President
PH: (303)893-1850
FX: (303)893-0639
E-mail: phillipsp@worldnet.att.net
Founded: 1967. **Staff:** 11. Activities: Personnel recruiting and staffing consultants in: accounting/finance, MIS, sales/marketing, engineering, administration and general/executive management. Industries served: telecommunications, distribution, and general business.

PLS INTERNATIONAL

11325 Seven Locks Rd., Ste. 226
Potomac, MD 20854
M.D. Bass, President

PH: (301)983-8508
FX: (301)983-0163
E-mail: pls@plsint.com
Founded: 1970. **Staff:** 10. Activities: Consultants to the information services, office automation and telecommunications industries. Services include multimedia delivery, virtual reality programs, development of marketing guides, product training, human factors analysis, productivity enhancement via performance technology, program planning, and program management. Also offers feasibility analysis, facilities specifications, and turnkey training for distance learning. Serves private industry as well as government agencies.

**POTOMAC MARINE & AVIATION, INC. - ELECTRONICS
    DIVISION**
3508 Lee Hwy.
Arlington, VA 22207
R. Barnack, President
PH: (703)525-2626
FX: (703)525-2736
Founded: 1966. **Staff:** 25. Activities: Engineering and technical services are provided for the communications industry including satellite earth stations, telegraph terminals, PBX voice and data networks. Civil and architectural services as related to communications construction are also provided including project management and installation service.

PRIORITY PROCESS ASSOCIATES, INC.
1236 E. Horshoe Ct.
Rochester Hills, MI 48306
Dr. Jim I. Jones, President
PH: (248)608-8966
FX: (248)608-8966
E-mail: jimijones@aol.com
URL: members.aol.com/jimijones/PPAssoc
Founded: 1994. **Staff:** 4. Activities: A management consulting firm with expertise in computer technology, telecommunications, and information services. Provides the following specific services: business process reengineering-establishes correctly implemented, computer technologies that empower and accelerate work groups to act autonomously but in concert with corporate goals; document workflow analysis-models and simulates the flow of documents through selected organizational processes; enterprise metrics—identifies unique metrics for enterprises to evaluate their continuous improvement of business processes; cost justification—identifies value using Activity Based Costing and innovative approaches to quantify time-to-market reductions, project profitability, and reduce and manage costs; proposal development—generates Requests for Proposals to solicit competitive quotations for cost effective off-the-shelf software, computer hardware, and communication products; implementation planning—negotiates implementation plans for clients through qualified software vendors, custom software integrators; and hardware, communication, and outsource suppliers; project auditing—audits the integration, installation and use of on-time, quality enterprise multivendor software, hardware and communications systems on computer networks; training—expands clients' knowledge through PPA's information sources, and client-specific management seminars and skill building workshops. Serves manufacturing industries in the U.S. PPA consultants have presented over 100 papers, a list of which may be obtained by contacting the firm.

PRODUCTIVE METHODS, INC.
736 28th Ave.
San Mateo, CA 94403-2608
Maxine R. Schur
PH: (650)571-8880
E-mail: metabase@earthlake.net
Founded: 1982. **Staff:** 4. Activities: Offers expertise in rightsizing, reengineering, workflow, and technology evaluation. Industries served: manufacturing and distribution, finance, telecommunications, and government agencies worldwide.

PROJECT MANAGEMENT SERVICES, INC.
100 Hannover Park Rd., Ste. 250
Atlanta, GA 30350-7503
Dan R. Bradbary, CEO
PH: (770)641-1000
FX: (770)594-0005
E-mail: info@pmsinc.com
URL: www.pmsinc.com/
Founded: 1986. **Staff:** 60. Activities: A project-management consulting firm that specializes in corporate, telecommunication, aviation, information system, fiber-optic, and merger and acquisition projects.

PROSTAR
12831 Royal Dr.
Stafford, TX 77477
Alan Barlow, Director of Operations
PH: (281)240-2800
TF: (800)967-7827
FX: (281)240-1447
E-mail: prostar@ghgcorp.com
Founded: 1984. **Staff:** 20. Activities: Communications company specializing in the encryption, networking, and the compression of satellite transmitted signals. Encrypts full motion video, audio and data and applies services to special events such as boxing and concerts, corporate videoconferencing, pay-per-view cable programming, horse racing and a variety of others.

PSYMON ASSOCIATES
35875 Plumeria Wy.
Fremont, CA 94536
P.J. Lyon
PH: (510)791-6454
FX: (510)791-6454
Founded: 1982. Activities: Develops all levels of software applications and products. Also offers contract programming and writing: specifications, proposals, and product names. Experienced in electronic voting systems design; real-time process control; satellite communications; medical, prototype development; project management; and marketing support.

**PUNCH IN INTERNATIONAL TRAVEL &
    ENTERTAINMENT SYNDICATE**
400 E. 59th St., Ste. 9F
New York, NY 10022
Jerome Walman
PH: (212)755-4363
FX: (212)755-4365
E-mail: punchin@inx.net
Founded: 1960. **Staff:** 30. Activities: Provides information and contact services for media, trade, and consumers. Offers radio and television outlets and syndication to major newspapers and magazines internationally. Serves as resource for media in all areas of travel, food, entertainment and wine. Industries served: travel, restaurant, airline, cruise ship, cinema, theater, entertainment, computer, and government agencies.

PURVIS SYSTEMS INC.
7001 Brush Hollow Rd.
Westbury, NY 11590-1743
Walter E. Landauer, President
PH: (516)952-3030
TF: (800)645-7234
FX: (516)952-3466
Founded: 1973. **Staff:** 150. Activities: Specializes in custom electronic and computer-based systems, hardware and software products, and engineering support services for complex weapons systems and computer-based military and commercial systems. Also offers custom systems support tactical system development, T&E, strategic communications and other special purpose applications. Products include electronic mail and office information systems, NTDS interfaces to commercial computers, switching systems, interfaces between HP computers and IDM database machines. Engineering support includes system engineering, system and equipment mainte-

nance, training, software support, ILS, exercise planning and reconstruction for DoD. Industries served: communications, data processing and computer electronics, and goverment agencies.

QUBE RESOURCES
12 Alfred St., Ste. 300
Woburn, MA 01801
PH: (617)937-6714
FX: (508)653-0759
E-mail: qube@qualware.com
URL: www.consultme.com/qube/index.htm
Activities: An alliance of independent consultants that provide ex-
pertise in a wide variety of areas including engineering, manage-
ment, marketing, mathematical modeling, government relations, hu-
man resources, and technology. Experienced in line management.

QUINT AND ASSOCIATES
932 11th St., Ste. 9
Santa Monica, CA 90403
Barbara Quint, Owner
PH: (310)451-0252
FX: (310)393-6911
E-mail: bquint@netcom.com
Founded: 1985. **Staff:** 3. Activities: Offers consulting on product
and service design, market trends as well as new product development to information industry and major consumer organizations.
Also offers consulting on organizing, staffing, and providing resources for information and library services. Speaks of online databases and information services. Conducts online research and literature searching. Also evaluates online search operations. Industries
served: information industry and libraries.

RADIOANALYST
PO Box 684
Cambridge, MA 02142
Harold Bausemer, President
PH: (617)491-8262
FX: (617)267-3905
Founded: 1992. **Staff:** 2. Activities: Offers consulting services in
management, sales, marketing, programming, and promotion of ra-
dio stations. Serves radio broadcasting industry.

RCC CONSULTANTS, INC.
100 Woodbridge Center Dr., Ste. 201
Woodbridge, NJ 07095
Walter Lawrence, Vice President, Sales/Marketing
PH: (732)404-2400
TF: (800)247-4796
FX: (732)404-2556
E-mail: info@rcc.com
URL: www.rcc-consult.com
Founded: 1983. **Staff:** 117. Activities: Advises in mobile radio and
telecommunications systems for public safety, utilities, transportation, emergency medical services, local government, radio common
carrier industries, and private sector clients. Offers design and licensure of cellular mobile telephone systems, microwave radio systems,
paging and simulcast systems and mobile data systems. Provides
project management and supervision of communications system
construction projects. Assists in fiber optic cable right-of-way leasing. Counsels in management of public safety and emergency medical services. Also offers full GIS (geographical information system)
mapping, addressing, and MSAG development. Serves private and
government organizations.

RCG, INC.
462 Herndon Pky., Ste. 203
Herndon, VA 20170-5234
Brij Bhushan, President
PH: (703)834-1155
FX: (703)834-3086
E-mail: joer@rcg.com
URL: www.rcg.com
Founded: 1987. **Staff:** 31. Activities: Provides consulting services
for voice, data, video and integrated communication networks; de-

velops plans for networks; prepares RFPs; and does vendor selection. In addition works with vendors for product analysis, product
comparison, product pricing and product positioning to aid vendors
to position and market their products. Operates in customer premise
environment mainly for commercial applications. Performs market/
technology studies and advises clients on strategic use of technology
in their day-to-day business via communication networks. The firm
also provides network design, engineering and integration services
(LAN, MAN, WAN). Serves private industries as well as government agencies.

REED TECHNOLOGY & INFORMATION SERVICES
1 Progress Dr.
Horsham, PA 19044
Mark Beyland, President
PH: (215)641-6000
TF: (800)872-2828
FX: (215)382-5082
URL: www.ReedTech.com
Founded: 1965. **Staff:** 1000. Activities: Provides consulting services to the communications industry specializing in the printing/ pub-
lishing/telephone fields: system consultation, hardware and software
configurations and support directed toward electronic composition
production, administrative and financial systems, and directory assistance systems, all of which are derived from proper utilization of
a "Universal Data Base System."

RELATIONAL SYSTEMS CORP.
22809 Shagbark Rd.
Beverly Hills, MI 48025
Gerry Rzeppa, President
PH: (248)645-5090
FX: (248)645-6042
Founded: 1980. **Staff:** 4. Activities: Specializes in relational data-
base design classes and structured query language (SQL) classes.
Offers its training and consulting services to clients worldwide.
Classes are very practical and highly recommended known as: ERA/
SQL Workshops.

S3 LTD.
2387 Ct. Plaza Dr., Ste. 200
Virginia Beach, VA 23456
Michael Dougherty, Vice President
PH: (757)321-8000
FX: (757)321-8809
E-mail: mail@s3ltd.com
Founded: 1985. **Staff:** 300. Activities: Founded to provide work
flow efficiency solutions utilizing computer and related telecommunication systems. The firm's philosophy is to apply human direction
to cause the most efficient, economical, and profitable disposition of
computer system resources for its clients. Recent projects include
design and development of a terrorist group profile database information system for the U.S. Department of State; design and development of membership historical databases for non-profit organizations; conversions of archival data on microfilm and paper-based
media to CD-ROM; development of distance learning tools utilizing
a desktop PC-based video teleconferencing system; and design, implementation, and maintenance of inter- and intra-network systems.

KALMAN SAFFRAN ASSOCIATES, INC.
1841 Commonwealth Ave.
Newton, MA 02466
Kalman Saffran, President
PH: (617)527-2000
FX: (617)244-3879
E-mail: info@ksa1.com
URL: www.ksa1.com
Founded: 1978. **Staff:** 110. Activities: KSA rapidly develops state
of the art products for leaders in data communications and telecom-
munications. KSA decreases time to market and reduces cost and
risk. Technology available for licensing includes SONET, Compact-
PCI Hot Swap, MPEG-2, and ATM. KSA offers technical consult-
ing in information systems, electronics engineering, software engi-
neering, and mechanical engineering.

SEEK INFORMATION SERVICE, INC.
1600 Victory Blvd.
Glendale, CA 91201
Lynn M. Ecklund, President
PH: (818)242-2793
TF: (800)722-7335
FX: (818)242-2876
E-mail: seek@netcom.com
URL: www.seekinfo.com
Founded: 1976. **Staff:** 7. Activities: Offers consulting for firms or individuals requiring background, current, or forecast information. Offers the concept of an extended library or research facility to all who need information on a timely basis. Specializes in online database searching as well as traditional methods of information gathering. Can help define, organize, strategize, and refine information requirements as well as acquire needed documents. Subject coverage ranges include general categories such as business and industry to scientific and technical. Specific coverage ranges include marketing, management, product, company, financials, legal, medical, aerospace, engineering, patents and trademarks, etc. Industries served: advertising, aerospace, banking and finance, business and commercial firms, electronics, entertainment, healthcare, individuals, legal, nonprofits, pharmaceutical, publishing and broadcasting, real estate, recreation, service, retail, travel, as well as government agencies.

S.E.I., INC.
De Diego 472 OF. A-2
San Juan, PR 00923
Fernando B. Muniz, President
PH: (809)751-1045
FX: (809)751-7811
E-mail: 71102.2105@compuserve.com
Staff: 12. Activities: Firm's services focus on integrating human systems with computers hardware and software (systems engineering). Consultants advise, exercise and implement methodology on aspects that are critical to information systems as: strategic planning, information systems administration, project management, data management, translate technical information to upper management language, bilingual Spanish-English (speaking, writing, reading), and information quality procedures. Experienced on work flow analysis; task flow analysis; computerized applications analysis, design and programming; imaging systems integration; and voice reponse systems integration. Industries served: telecommunications and telephony, banking, utilities, universities, and government agencies.

SGA BUSINESS SYSTEMS, INC.
83 Haverford Ct.
Somerville, NJ 08876-5211
Wayne Scarano, Partner
PH: (908)359-4626
FX: (908)359-4861
E-mail: wscarano@sga.com
URL: www.sga.com
Founded: 1984. **Staff:** 7. Activities: Founded in 1984, a Lotus premium Business Partner dedicated to the strategic planning and effective use of Lotus Notes throughout your organization. We collaborate with clients to develop Lotus Notes and Domino solutions that improve communication, increase productivity, and create competitive advantage. In addition, we are a founding member of the Penumbra Group, a consortium of Lotus Business Partners throughout North America. Lotus has awarded the consortium Premium Partner status for the past three years. Our Lotus Notes services range from stragegic planning to full applications development, system administration and customized training. We excel in collaborating with clients to design and implement streamlined business processes that improve communication and increase productivity, ultimately to gain competitive advantage.

SIGNATRON TECHNOLOGY CORP.
29 Domino Dr.
Concord, MA 01742-2845
Edward H. Getchell, CEO

PH: (978)371-0550
FX: (978)371-7414
E-mail: sig@world.std.com
URL: www.signatron.com
Founded: 1962. **Staff:** 18. Activities: Offers consulting and hardware for communication systems, specializing in TROPO, HF/VH digital data transmission. Activities include system evaluation, prototype development, performance prediction, error rate analysis, and cost effectiveness tradeoffs.

SIMBA INFORMATION INC.
PO Box 4234
Stamford, CT 06907-0234
Megan St. John, V.P. and General Manager
PH: (203)358-9900
FX: (203)358-5824
E-mail: info@simbanet.com
URL: www.simbanet.com
Founded: 1983. **Staff:** 60. Activities: Offers information services, specializing in monitoring, analyzing, and reporting on global market for information publishing, marketing, and distribution. Publishes fifteen newsletters and more than sixty research reports, directories, and databases. Hosts online media forum, sponsors conferences, and provides consulting services. Covers electronic marketplace, online services, Internet, interactive television, yellow pages, newspaper, book, educational, multimedia, and information publishing; computer and telecom publishing; and advertising.

CARL E. SMITH CONSULTING ENGINEERS
2324 N. Cleveland-Massillon Rd.
Bath, OH 44210
Alfred T. Warmus, President
PH: (330)659-4440
FX: (330)659-9234
Founded: 1935. **Staff:** 15. Activities: Consultants for AM-FM-TV-LPTV-microwave broadcast stations. Services include field measurements, station installation, and antenna design and adjustment. Complete design, installation and certification of communications towers. Complete turn-key installation services of towers, antennas and transmission lines.

SOFTWARE DEVELOPMENT CONSULTANTS
4701 Pine St., Ste. D12
Philadelphia, PA 19143
Don Forest, President
PH: (215)474-3311
FX: (215)476-3317
Founded: 1985. Activities: Specializes in software engineering for voice/data communication and real-time systems. Expertise in the following languages and protocols: C, Pascal, PLM, PLZ, FORTRAN, BASIC PLUS2, ALGOL, COBOL, Assembly Languages for the 680x0, 80x86, and Z80, FDDI, PHY & SMT, 3270 and 5250 SNA (LU types 0,1,2,3,4,7), X.3, X.25, X.28, X.29, X.121, SDLC, HDLC, LAP B, OSI model, Tymmet X.PC, RJE 2780 and 3780, BISYNC, DECNET, NETBIOS, URP, RS-232 and IBM System 38 synchronous terminal protocol. Industries served: retail (point-of-sale), electric power utilities, telecommunications, voice/ data switch manufacturers, and vending machine manufacturers.

SOLUTION CONSULTANTS, INC.
20863 Stevens Creek Blvd., Ste. 330
Cupertino, CA 95014-2187
Jess A. Pawlak, President
PH: (408)446-5118
FX: (408)973-1046
Founded: 1984. **Staff:** 30. Activities: A systems consulting and project development company specializing in the development, implementation, testing and certification, and support of information systems, networks, and software. Services cover all phases of project and program management - analysis, development, implementation, documentation, training, and support. Industries served: biotechnology, telecommunications, computers, real estate and financial services.

SOLVERIS, INC.
19119 N. Creek Pky., Ste. 105
Bothell, WA 98011-8023
Dave Senestraro, President
PH: (425)485-4357
TF: (800)999-4829
FX: (425)481-7633
E-mail: info@solveris.com
URL: www.solveris.com
Founded: 1986. **Staff:** 15. Activities: Offers expertise in information systems design and implementation. VAX/VMS network and systems specialists. Can assist companies with all facets of information systems management. Industries served: manufacturing, telecommunications, service, banking, education, ecumenical, and government.

J.E. SPARKS & ASSOCIATES
1404 N. Floyd Rd.
Richardson, TX 75080-4138
Jim Sparks, Principal
PH: (972)238-8593
FX: (972)238-0509
Activities: Information systems consulting to healthcare providers. Services include information systems planning, requirements, evaluations, on-site implementations, management for systems benefits, projects management, and problem solving.

SPRINT INTEGRATED MARKETING SERVICES
7015 College Blvd., Ste. 400
Overland Park, KS 66211
TF: (800)829-2955
FX: (913)491-7300
Activities: Firm is a full service marketing firm offering B-to-B and consumer integrated marketing programs which are focused on customer prospecting, retention, and continuity. Offers the following services separately or as part of a strategically developed program: Market Research; Database Modeling; Profiling & Development; and Teleservices and Direct Response.

STOUT & DEINES, INC.
1 Financial Plz.
Woodbine, KS 67492
Kenneth E. Stout, Principal
PH: (913)257-3242
FX: (913)257-3242
URL: homepage.midusa.net/~sdi
Activities: A bank management firm and bank strategists specializing in strategic planning and facilitation (independent loan review, compliance review, management assessment); assuming senior management positions or providing management assistance during transition periods or for regulatory requirements; assisting with acquisitions, holding company applications, bank analysis, due diligence; maintaining compliance with regulatory agreements and orders; negotiating bank stock loans; developing policies, procedures, and board reports; custom designing systems, implementation, and training of departments; and pricing analysis of loans and deposits.

STRATEGIC NETWORKS
175 Portland St. 4th Fl.
Boston, MA 02114
Nicholas J. Lippis, III
PH: (617)912-8200
FX: (617)912-8299
URL: www.snci.com
Founded: 1991. **Staff:** 10. Activities: A consulting firm dedicated to the strategic use and management of information and communications technology. Its goal is to assist clients faced with the challenge of implementing networks and information systems and evaluating their organizational requirements and impact. Expertise extends to local area networks and their interconnect; metropolitan- and wide-area network services and economics; multimedia and broadbank networking; and distributed client-server computing. Serves private industries as well as government agencies.

STRATEGIC TECHNOLOGY RESOURCES
343 W. Erie St., Ste. 630
Chicago, IL 60610
Bruce Kannry, Principal
PH: (312)697-3800
FX: (312)697-3801
URL: www.str.com
Founded: 1991. **Staff:** 40. Activities: A consulting firm that partners with clients to deliver business solutions in fields such as telecommunications, finance, and supply chain management. Experienced in object, web, and Java technologies. Creates next-generation systems while reducing risk and preserving investments in existing resources. Provides planning, implementation, and training services.

THE STRATEGIS GROUP
1130 Connecticut Ave. NW, Ste. 325
Washington 20036
Andrew Roscoe, President/Chairman
PH: (202)530-7500
FX: (202)530-7540
E-mail: info@strategisgroup.com
URL: www.strategisgroup.com
Founded: 1966. **Staff:** 50. Activities: Offers business planning, financial management, and engineering services in the telecommunications, wireless, internet, and cable television fields. Services include due diligence, strategic planning, feasibility studies, financial, analysis and evaluation, systems valuation and appraisals, systems engineering and design, market research, management services, and refranchising.

SYMCOM, INC.
3011 W. Lafayette Blvd., Ste. 1516
Detroit, MI 48202
PH: (313)874-3500
FX: (313)874-1570
E-mail: rjburrell@aol.com
URL: www.symconinc.com
Founded: 1983. Activities: Provides consulting products and services in the areas of business process re-engineering, information systems services (evaluation, design, development, and implementation of information systems), operation and organization review and improvement, performance and profitability improvement, strategic and business planning, and multimedia and training services.

SYSTEM STUDIES INC.
2-1340 E. Cliff Dr.
Santa Cruz, CA 95062
Robert A. Simpkins, President
PH: (831)475-5777
TF: (800)247-8255
FX: (831)475-9207
E-mail: sales@airtalk.com
URL: www.airtalk.com
Founded: 1976. **Staff:** 60. Activities: Specialists in the cable pressurization who offer training programs for telephone companies in cable pressurization management, maintenance and engineering. Programs available to domestic and international audience.

SYSTEM TECHNOLOGY GROUP
21053 Devonshire St., Ste. 106
Chatsworth, CA 91311
PH: (818)718-0990
FX: (818)718-0992
URL: www.systechgrp.com
Founded: 1981. Activities: A management consulting firm that specializes in the planning, design and implementation of management information systems. By utilizing specialized products and services, the firm helps organizations maximize their investment in information system technology. Concentrates on business re-engineering, consulting and system integration projects. Specializes in designing, developing and implementing complex customized system solutions. Projects often include project management, custom software devel-

opment, multivendor software and hardware integration and complex solution design and implementation.

SYSTEMS GROUP, INC.
50 S. Beretania St., Ste. C119B
Honolulu, HI 96813
Gordon S. Young, Vice President
PH: (808)526-1551
FX: (808)599-5098
URL: sgi-hi.com
Founded: 1972. **Staff:** 15. Activities: Specialists in data communications: network design installation and performance measurement; in telecommunications: network planning and voice data integration; and in fiber optic communications systems design and installation. Serves private industries as well as government agencies.

SYSTEMS RESEARCH AND APPLICATIONS CORP.
2000 15th St. N
Arlington, VA 22201
William K. Brehm, Chairman
PH: (703)558-4700
FX: (703)558-4723
Founded: 1978. **Staff:** 730. Activities: Information processing/communications consultants active in strategic planning and requirements analysis, systems development, and systems integration with applications to computer, logistic, command and control, and telecommunications systems; defense analyses of weapon systems, operations, and personnel; resource management; and crisis management and national emergency programs. Applies expert system technology to build artificial intelligence systems that use a natural-language interface. Consultation services include computer-aided logistic support of earth-based systems, and top-level support to and evaluations of major exercises for the Joint Chiefs of Staff, the Army, and the Federal Emergency Management Agency. Services also are provided to the Air Force, the Navy, and other Department of Defense organizations, as well as civil federal government agencies and commercial firms.

THE TANNER GROUP, INC.
26 N. State St., Ste. F-1
Salt Lake City, UT 84103
Todd A. Tanner
PH: (801)538-2320
TF: (800)827-2324
FX: (801)538-2322
E-mail: todd@tannergrp.com
URL: www.tannergroup.com
Founded: 1984. **Staff:** 12. Activities: Provides independent telecommunications and call center consulting. Assists clients in growing and exceeding their customers expectations through the strategic deployment of telecommunications technology. Specializes in the following: Call Center Management, Modeling and Development; General Telecommunications and Network Engineering; Standards Based Cable Design; Toll Analysis and Tariff Negotiations.

TCS MANAGEMENT GROUP, INC.
5410 Maryland Way
Brentwood, TN 37027
James Gordon, President
PH: (615)221-6800
FX: (615)221-6810
E-mail: info@tcsmgmt.com
URL: www.tcsmgmt.com
Founded: 1975. **Staff:** 400. Activities: Specializes in providing software and consulting solutions to the problems facing telephone call centers. A Consultant Liaison Program helps other consultants best serve their call center clients. Services range from feasibility studies to design and equip a new call center to auditing existing operations to identify areas for improvement. Consulting services include workforce planning, feasibility study/needs analysis, equipment acquisition, systems integration, disaster recovery/contingency planning, network design, and consolidation studies.

TCT TECHNICAL TRAINING, INC.
599 N. Mathilda Ave.
Sunnyvale, CA 94086
Saroj Kar, President
PH: (408)735-9990
TF: (800)743-9990
FX: (408)735-9918
Founded: 1982. **Staff:** 35. Activities: Technical training experts offer expertise on development of self-paced video/workbook courses pertaining to local area networks (LANS) and telecommunications, and video tape training products.

TECH-MAR CONSULTING GROUP, LTD.
123 Pierrepont St.
Brooklyn, NY 11201
Julio Bucatinsky, Pres.
PH: (718)488-7651
E-mail: jbucati@concentric.net
Founded: 1993. Activities: Specializes in raising business productivity and implementing plans through the application of technology. Assesses hardware and software needs.

TECHNICAL CONCEPTS CORP.
8415 Datapoint Dr.
San Antonio, TX 78229
Charles Becker
PH: (210)616-0000
FX: (210)616-0001
Founded: 1979. **Staff:** 40. Activities: A consulting, systems integration, and service company that designs innovative and cost-effective solutions to data/voice/image/video communications problems. TCC integrates, installs, and services a wide range of communications equipment from a select group of leading manufacturers. Designs systems by carefully considering cost-effectiveness, compatibility, expandability, and system maintenance. Industries served: manufacturing, distribution, government, and medical.

TECHNOLOGY FUTURES INC.
13740 Research Blvd., Bldg. C
Austin, TX 78750-1859
John H. Vanston, Ph.D., Chairman of the Board
PH: (512)258-8898
TF: (800)835-3887
FX: (512)258-0087
E-mail: info@tfi.com
URL: www.tfi.com
Founded: 1978. **Staff:** 15. Activities: Works with executives, managers, and technical professionals to enhance their effectiveness in managing technology and related business areas. Specialties include forecasting emerging technological trends, evaluating the implications of those trends, and assisting organizations in developing action programs to gain maximum benefit from these evaluations. Industries served: telecommunications, Fortune 1000, Fortune 500, Fortune 100, electric power, government, and high-tech.

THE TECHNOLOGY LIBRARY
149 Commonwealth Dr.
Menlo Park, CA 94025
Cindy Hill
PH: (415)688-7171
FX: (415)328-2690
Founded: 1987. **Staff:** 5. Activities: A research and consulting firm specializing in providing technical information to the high technology industries. Services include document delivery, literature searching, patent/prior art searching, monitoring services, and corporate library development. Provides information and database management as well as library design and services. Industries served: semiconductor, computer, computer software and networking industrial automation, sensors and instrumentation, telecommunications, and data communications.

TECOMM SYSTEMS INC.
10900 NE 8th St., Ste. No. 900
Bellevue, WA 98004-4405
Peter A. Niblock, President
PH: (425)688-1612
FX: (425)688-1612
URL: www.hntelecom
Founded: 1990. **Staff:** 15. Activities: Offers technical assistance, design, project management and contractor services in telecommunications. This includes client requirement analysis, technical feasibility, procurement, supply, installation and commissioning, and maintenance of a wide range of telecommunications systems. Specialists in mobile and cellular radio, microwave, VTMS (radar), satellite, broadcast, SCADA, EMI/EMC and public and private network planning. Industries served: all levels of government, electric utilities, public safety (police, fire, ambulance), oil and mining industries, railways, port authorities and coast guard, broadcasters, and pipeline companies.

TELE-CONTROL, INC.
6264 Sunbury Rd.
Westerville, OH 43081-9350
Rod Hoskins, President
PH: (614)818-4000
FX: (614)818-4001
Founded: 1979. **Staff:** 15. Activities: Offers telecommunications consulting, P.B.X. design and R.F.P. development. Also provides network design, cable plant design including fiber optics, feasibility studies, and long range planning. Industries served: manufacturing, healthcare, financial, insurance, and education in the U.S.

TELE-MEASUREMENTS INC.
145 Main Ave.
Clifton, NJ 07014
William E. Endres, President
PH: (201)473-8822
TF: (800)223-0052
FX: (201)473-0521
E-mail: tmcorp@aol.com
Founded: 1959. **Staff:** 30. Activities: The firm is structured to meet the diverse needs of clients in support, project engineering, and technical services areas within the fields of broadcast television, industrial and educational video; local area networking and data distribution; teleconferencing and graphic presentation; distance learning classrooms; and video surveillance and access control. Serves government agencies also.

TELEPHONICS CORP.
815 Broadhollow Rd.
Farmingdale, NY 11735
PH: (516)755-7000
FX: (516)755-7046
URL: www.telephonics.com
Activities: Specialists in electronic communications and information systems. Firm has developed military and commercial intercommunications systems for aircraft, surface ships and vehicles.

TELESTRATEGIES INC.
1355 Beverly Rd., Ste. 110
McLean, VA 22101-3641
Dr. Jerome Lucas
PH: (703)734-7050
FX: (703)893-3197
E-mail: info@telestrategies.com
URL: www.telestrategies.com
Founded: 1980. **Staff:** 23. Activities: Telecommunications consultants offer numerous seminars on telecommunications technologies for non-engineers, conferences on emerging telecom technologies and the markets being created, and conferences and trade shows on telecom billing and customer care issues.

VERNON THOMPSON ASSOCIATES
189 Lorraine Ave.
Mount Vernon, NY 10553
Vernon E. Thompson, President
PH: (914)699-5359
Founded: 1986. **Staff:** 2. Activities: Information management consultant specializing in all aspects of planning, directing, analyzing, designing and/or implementing mainframe and minicomputer systems which support business operations. Extensive experience in banking and finance, broadcasting, direct marketing, brokerage, and public utility systems.

TIA
3333 Quebee St., Ste. 7300
Denver, CO 80207
Doann Houghton-Alico, President/CEO
PH: (303)321-2122
FX: (303)322-1895
E-mail: tia@tiainc.com
URL: www.tiainc.com
Founded: 1980. **Staff:** 12. Activities: TIA has a commitment to the effective communication of technical information. Specific services offered to computer system users, data processing departments, and the software industry include the following: designing effective user/system interfaces; writing and producing user materials (interactive, text, and other forms); providing analysis of software support services and recommending support systems and procedures; assisting with new applications software design; and reviewing and editing user materials. Develops procedural documentation and standards for companies interested in increasing productivity and quality. Serves private industries as well as government agencies worldwide.

TILTED WINDMILL LTD.
527 71st St.
Darien, IL 60561
Charles Grab, President
PH: (630)887-8514
FX: (413)828-6357
E-mail: cgrab@wwwa.com
Founded: 1992. Activities: Specializes in the design and implementation of relational database applications. This includes data modeling and GUI tools development. Systems developed in Oracle, Sybase, and Informing PowerBuilder, Uniface, and Visual Basic. Back end processing done in C or C++ on a Unix, MS-DOS, or Windows environment. Industries served: manufacturing, telecommunications, publishing, insurance, billing, banking, engineering, and pension fund administration.

TMC GROUP, L.L.C.
3100 S. 176th St., Ste. 203
SeaTac, WA 98188
J.R. Simmons, COO/Principal
PH: (206)246-2868
FX: (206)246-3227
E-mail: jrs@tmcgroup.com
Founded: 1973. **Staff:** 12. Activities: Independent communications consulting on all telephone and integrated voice/data/video systems, Wide Area Networks, Local Area Networks, long distance usage, paging, music, telex, and dictation/word processing. Extensive expertise in automatic call distribution systems and applications. Serves private industries as well as government agencies.

TRANSITION MANAGEMENT INSTITUTE
1514 Sunset Ridge Rd., Ste. 100
Highlands Ranch, CO 80126
J.C. Heinen
PH: (303)683-0017
FX: (303)683-0057
E-mail: transition@csn.net
Activities: Firm offers expertise in human resources information systems. Services include: Needs Analysis, Business Case preparation, Vendor evaluation, product assessment, transition management.

TRILOGY CONSULTING CORP.
850 S. Greenbay Rd.
Waukegan, IL 60085
William J. Phillips, President
PH: (708)244-9520
TF: (800)323-7528
FX: (847)244-9335
Founded: 1982. **Staff:** 250. Activities: Trilogy provides technical professionals on a time and materials basis primarily to large companies. The firm's staff supports micro, mini and mainframe environments, in the areas of systems analysis and design; programming; systems programming; software engineering; communications; micro consulting, design and programming; database; and statistics. Industries served: pharmaceutical manufacturing, healthcare, food processors, chemical manufacturing, packaged consumer goods, agriculture/animal health, manufacturing, financial, communications, distribution, transportation, and government agencies.

TROTT COMMUNICATIONS GROUP, INC.
1425 Greenway Dr., Ste. 350
Irving, TX 75038-2476
Raymond C. Trott, Chairman
PH: (972)580-1911
FX: (972)580-0641
E-mail: info@trottgroup.com
URL: www.trottgroup.com
Founded: 1978. **Staff:** 12. Activities: Provides engineering consulting services to the land mobile and telecommunications industries. Services include: RF system design, microwave path engineering, propagation analyses, interference studies, site management services, specification preparation, and equipment selection.

TUAR-GRIMBAC INC.
PO Box 354
Flint, MI 48501-0354
PH: (248)239-5553
FX: (248)239-4321
Activities: Firm has experience in customized programming, database management, data conversion, laser and impact printing, electronic media preparation, and volume data entry.

TUCKER & ASSOCIATES, INC.
616 Girod St.
New Orleans, LA 70130
Janee Tucker, President
PH: (504)522-4627
FX: (504)523-7184
Founded: 1978. **Staff:** 150. Activities: Provides a wide range of services to federal and state government agencies, as well as private sector organizations. Services include: automated data processing (ADP) systems design and implementation, facilities operations/management, data base management, applications systems and software development; project management including quality control, verification and validation services; records, construction and energy management; technical writing and clerical services; urban planning and related environmental impact studies; cost estimating; training and curriculum development; mathematical modeling and operations research; and marketing and public relations.

TUCKER NETWORK TECHNOLOGIES
PO Box 429
50 Washington St.
Norwalk, CT 06856
Mr. Tucker McDonagh, Pres.
PH: (203)857-0080
FX: (203)857-0082
E-mail: tucker@tuckernet.com
Founded: 1988. Activities: An information technology consulting team specializing in planning, technical engineering, problem solving, networking, and telecommunications systems for F2000 companies.

TURNER GOLD FRANCE ENGINEERING/RADIO CONNECT CORP.
6041 Bristol Parkway
Culver City, CA 90230
David Turner, Vice President
PH: (310)338-3388
FX: (310)338-3399
E-mail: dturner@radioconnect.com
URL: www.radioconnect.com
Founded: 1990. **Staff:** 11. Activities: System and electronic engineering company specializing in advanced system design, product engineering, prototype and volume production, and analysis. Developers of advanced wireless communications products and safety critical, high reliability control, communication, and information systems for transportation, industrial, and research applications. Special capabilities in development of advanced communications devices including spread spectrum radio, urban transit equipment, high performance electronic systems, image processing, and integrated controls.

UBIQUINET, INC.
18 Crow Canyon Ct., Ste. 250
San Ramon, CA 94583
Richard A. Johnson, President
PH: (510)820-1510
TF: (800)800UNET
FX: (510)831-4994
Founded: 1989. **Staff:** 14. Activities: Telecommunications services include planning, engineering, and consulting. Computer systems software consulting includes inventory management, vehicle route management, dispatching operations, field service operations, network management design and implementation, as well as large and small systems integration. Expertise in Supervisory Control and Data Acquisition (SCADA) systems and cellular radio systems design. Industries served: utilities, telephone companies, cable TV, telecommunications equipment vendors, interconnects, large industrial, transportation, and public safety.

UNICA TECHNOLOGIES INC.
55 OLD Bedford Rd.
Lincoln, MA 01773-1125
Indulis Pommers, President
PH: (781)259-5900
TF: (877)864-2261
FX: (781)259-5901
E-mail: unica@unica-usa.com
URL: www.unica-usa.com
Founded: 1992. **Staff:** 35. Activities: Offers data mining and database marketing consulting. Services include: problem analysis, data preparation, modeling, model deployment, market campaign planning and design, development of campaign testing and measurement metrics, campaign optimization, campaign management process development.

UNIVERSAL ELECTRONICS, INC.
4555 Groves Rd., Ste. 12
Columbus, OH 43232
Thomas P. Harrington, President
PH: (614)866-4605
FX: (614)866-1201
Founded: 1948. **Staff:** 22. Activities: Electronics consultants providing satellite communications, electronic communications, TI surveys, satellite marketing and sales, communications marketing, and C band/KU band satellite work.

THE UPTON GROUP
770 Boylston St., Apt. 12H
Boston, MA 02199
Lewis R. Moretsky, President
PH: (617)695-3555
FX: (617)695-9035
Founded: 1978. **Staff:** 12. Activities: A full service international telecommunications consulting firm specializing in feasibility studies through system selection and implementation. Serves private industries as well as government agencies.

VANGUARD COMMUNICATIONS CORP.

100 American Rd.
Morris Plains, NJ 07950
Donald H. Van Doren, President
PH: (201)605-8000
FX: (201)605-8329
URL: www.vanguard.net/
Founded: 1980. **Staff:** 20. Activities: Concentrates on the strategic deployment and management of communications technologies in call centers and enterprise-wide. Helps end users improve how businesses operate through the effective use of communications technologies, such as voice messaging, voice response, call processing, facsimile, and computer telephone integrated systems.

VILA DEL CORRAL & CO.

PO Box 10528
San Juan, PR 00922-0528
Rodrigo G. Morell
PH: (787)751-6164
FX: (787)759-7479
URL: www.vdc-pr.com
Founded: 1977. **Staff:** 78. Activities: Computer consultants providing assistance in the definition of information requirements and the implementation of systems. Primary area of service is manufacturing, distribution and healthcare. Serves private industries as well as government agencies.

W & J PARTNERSHIP

18876 Edwin Markham Dr.
Castro Valley, CA 94552
William A. Morgan, Managing Partner
PH: (510)583-7751
FX: (510)583-7645
E-mail: warmorgan@wjpartnership.com
URL: www.wjpartnership.com
Founded: 1982. **Staff:** 13. Activities: Areas of expertise include: communications and computing, fiber optics, campus wiring, local and wide area networks, wireless networks, satellite communications, command and control, data communications, microwave and video applications, PBXs and key telephone systems, artificial intelligence, cellular communications, network management, disaster recovery for corporate data centers, ATM, frame relay, SMDS, and ISDN. Services provided include: communications systems design and specification, communications vendor proposal review, usage and needs studies, computing systems consulting, software development, and management consulting.

THE WALSH COMMUNICATIONS GROUP

312 S. 24th St.
Philadelphia, PA 19103
Eileen Walsh, President
PH: (215)735-5919
FX: (215)735-5636
Founded: 1983. **Staff:** 3. Activities: Offers telecommunications and information systems consulting, telephone equipment selection studies, voice and data traffic analysis and network design studies for general business and industry. Also offers planning, feasibility studies and system evaluations in value added and local area networks, satellite communications, electronic mail, voice messaging, ACD, and microwave.

THE WALTER GROUP, INC.

120 Lakeside Ave., Ste. 310
Seattle, WA 98122-6578
Joseph N. Walter, President
PH: (206)328-0808
FX: (206)328-0815
URL: www.waltergroup.com
Founded: 1988. **Staff:** 63. Activities: Provides specialized services to the telecommunications industry. Offers expertise in cellular personal communications services; satellite; conventional telephony; cable; paging; interactive audio/visual; multimedia; voice/data integration; and foreign government and FCC licensing. Also provides strategic planning and partnering, capital project/operations management, engineering design, analysis, and construction, market/product assessment and development, regulatory assistance, vendor selection, network planning, new business development, due diligence, and turnkey operations construction. Industries served: telecommunications, cable, and interactive audio/visual; and government agencies worldwide.

WAVE TECHNOLOGIES TRAINING, INC.

10845 Olive Blvd, Ste. 250
St. Louis, MO 63141-7760
Kenneth W. Kousky, Chairman
PH: (314)995-5767
TF: (800)828-2050
FX: (314)995-3894
E-mail: info@wavetech.com
URL: www.wavetech.com
Founded: 1988. **Staff:** 150. Activities: Computer productivity specialists offering a curriculum of more than 60 courses for users and managers in networking, desktop publishing, systems technology and information management. Offers on-site training, customized training, executive briefings and vendor-sponsored seminars that focus on business solutions. Industries served: nonprofits, food, automotive, financial aviation, telecommunications and federal government.

WESTERN TELECOMMUNICATION CONSULTING, INC. (WTC)

801 S. Grand Ave., Ste. 700
Los Angeles, CA 90017
Phillip Beidelman, President
PH: (213)622-4444
FX: (213)622-0840
E-mail: wtc@ix.netcom.com
URL: www.wtc-inc.net
Founded: 1983. **Staff:** 16. Activities: Modernization of communications equipment, infrastructure design, local and wide area network design, contract negotiations, and implementation. Each of these capabilities cover the areas of voice, data, video and image technologies. In addition, WTC conducts outsourcing feasibility studies, reengineering of departmental business processes, and develops departmental information technology application alternatives. Industries serviced: education, public sector, hospitals and healthcare, utilities, and general industry, as well as government.

XTEND COMMUNICATIONS

171 Madison Ave.
New York, NY 10016
William I. Schwartz, President
PH: (212)951-7600
TF: (800)231-2556
FX: (212)951-7683
Founded: 1967. **Staff:** 75. Activities: Computer/ telecommunications consultants offering communications, automation, and microcomputer to PBX integration. Specializes in integration of facilities and services. Industries served: healthcare, financial, legal, publishing, advertising, education, and government in the U.S. and Canada.

ZIEGLER ROSS INC.

1 Bay Plaza
1350 Bayshore Highway, Ste. 690
Burlingame, CA 94010
R.W. Ziegler, Jr.
PH: (415)548-0300
FX: (415)548-0719
E-mail: zrisf@aol.com
Founded: 1979. **Staff:** 14. Activities: Management consultants for professional service organizations in the areas of office organization, long-range planning, efficiency studies, office automation and data base management, including micrographics and communication. Extensive experience in firm culture, organization, hardware selection, application software selection, data base selection, and communication system planning and selection. Industries served: professional

service industries (law, architecture, engineering, medical, franchising) and government agencies.

ZIELINSKI PRODUCTIONS INC.
7850 Slater Ave., Ste. 80
Huntington Beach, CA 92647
Richard E. Zielinski, President
PH: (714)842-5050
FX: (714)842-5050
E-mail: zpiusa@hotmail.com
URL: www.geocities.com/Hollywood/Studio/8714/
Founded: 1972. **Staff:** 81. Activities: Television production specialists offer expertise in the following areas: TV/video systems, on-camera talent, telecommunications, teleconferencing, stock footage, training, travel productions, sales and promotion, commercials/PSA's, multimedia authoring and distribution. Firm's productions include local, national and international, broadcast and cable television, industrial television and videos. Serves private industries and government agencies.

CHAPTER 9 - PART II

TRADE INFORMATION SOURCES

Adapted from Gale's *Encyclopedia of Business Information Sources* (*EBIS*), the entries featured in this chapter show trade journals and other information sources, including web sites and databases.

Entries for publications and electronic databases list the title of the work, the name of the author (where available), name of the publisher, frequency or year of publication, prices or fees, and Internet address (in many cases).

Entries for trade associations and research centers provide the organization name, address, telephone numbers, e-mail address, and web site URL. Many of these entries include brief descriptions of the organization.

*ALMANAC OF BUSINESS AND INDUSTRIAL FINANCIAL
    RATIOS*
Prentice Hall.
One Lake St.
Upper Saddle River, NJ 07458
PH: (800)223-1360
FX: (800)445-6991
URL: http://www.prenhall.com
Leo Troy. Annual. $99.95. Contains financial ratios derived from
federal tax returns. Ratios for each of about 200 industries are ar-
ranged according to company asset size.

AMERICA'S NETWORK DIRECTORY
Advanstar Communications, Inc.
7500 Old Oak Blvd.
Cleveland, OH 44130
PH: (800)346-0085
FX: (216)891-2726
URL: http://www.advanstar.com
Annual. $195.00. Independent telephone companies in the United
States, regional Bell operating companies, cellular telephone system
operators, foreign telephone companies, long distance carriers, and
interconnects. Formerly *T E and M Directory*.

ANNUAL SURVEY OF MANUFACTURES
Available from U.S. Government Printing Office.
Washington, DC 20402
PH: (202)512-1800
FX: (202)512-2250
E-mail: gpoaccess@gpo.gov
URL: http://www.access.gpo.gov
Annual. Issued by the U. S. Census Bureau as an interim update to
the *Census of Manufactures*. Includes data on number of manufac-
turing establishments in various industries, employment, labor costs,
value of shipments, capital expenditures, inventories, energy costs,
and assets. (See also Census Bureau home page, http://www.census.
gov/.)

APPLIED SCIENCE AND TECHNOLOGY INDEX
H. W. Wilson Co.
950 University Ave.
Bronx, NY 10452
PH: (800)367-6770
FX: (718)590-1617
E-mail: hwwmsg@info.hwwilson.com
URL: http://www.hwwilson.com
11 times a year. Quarterly and annual cumulations. Service basis.
Indexes a wide variety of English language technical, industrial, and
engineering periodicals.

AUDIO
Available from FIND/SVP, Inc.
625 Ave. of the Americas
New York, NY 10011
PH: (800)346-3787
FX: (212)645-7681
Published by Euromonitor Publications Ltd. Provides market data
and forecasts to 1999 for the United States, the United Kingdom,
Germany, France, and Italy. Includes all types of consumer audio
equipment: separate components, stereo systems, portable radios,
clock radios, etc.

*BETTER BUYS FOR BUSINESS: THE INDEPENDENT
    CONSUMER GUIDE TO OFFICE EQUIPMENT*
What to Buy for Business, Inc.
Post Office Box 22857
Santa Barbara, CA 93121-2857
PH: (800)247-2185
FX: (805)963-3740
E-mail: orders@betterbuys.com
URL: http://www.betterbuys.com
10 times a year. $134.00 per year. Each issue is on a particular office
product, with detailed evaluation of specific models: 1. Low-Vol-
ume Copier Guide, 2. Mid-Volume Copier Guide, 3. High-Volume

Copier Guide, 4. Plain Paper Fax and Low-Volume Multifunctional
Guide, 5. Mid/High-Volume Multifunctional Guide, 6. Laser Printer
Guide, 7. Color Printer and Color Copier Guide, 8. Scan-to-File
Guide, 9. Business Phone Systems Guide, 10. Postage Meter Guide,
with a Short Guide to Shredders.

BROADBAND NETWORKING
Datapro Information Services Group.
600 Delran Parkway
Delran, NJ 08075
PH: (800)328-2776
FX: (609)764-2814
URL: http://www.datapro.com/products
One looseleaf volume. Monthly updates. New subscriptions,
$621.00 per year; renewals, $580.00 per year. Includes information
about microwave, satellite, fiber optics, infrared, CATV, FM sub-
carrier, and other modern methods of communication. Formerly
Datapro Reports on Communications Alternatives.

*BROADCAST ENGINEERING: EQUIPMENT REFERENCE
    MANUAL*
Intertec Publishing Corp.
P.O. Box 12901
Overland Park, KS 66218-2901
PH: (800)621-9907
FX: (800)633-6219
Annual. Free to qualified personnel; others $20.00. Lists manufac-
turers and distributors of radio and TV broadcast and recording
equipment. Included in subscription to *Broadcast Engineering*.

BROADCASTING AND CABLE YEARBOOK
R. R Bowker.
121 Chanlon Rd.
New Providence, NJ 07974
PH: (800)521-8110
FX: (908)665-6688
Annual. $179.95. Two volumes. Published in conjunction with
Broadcasting magazine. Provides information on U. S. and Canadi-
an TV stations, radio stations, cable TV companies, and radio-TV
services of various kinds.

BUSINESS COMMUNICATIONS REVIEW
BCR Enterprises, Inc.
950 York Rd.
Hinsdale, IL 60521
PH: (630)986-1432
URL: http://www.bcr.com
Monthly. $45.00 per year. Edited for communications managers in
large end-user companies and institutions. Includes special feature
issues on intranets and network management.

BUSINESS SOURCE PLUS
EBSCO Information Services.
10 Estes St.
Ipswich, MA 01938
PH: (800)653-2726
FX: (508)356-6565
E-mail: ep@epnet.com
URL: http://www.epnet.com
Monthly. $1,495.00 per year. Provides CD-ROM citations and ab-
stracts to articles in about 650 business periodicals and newspapers,
including *The Wall Street Journal*. Full text is provided from 200
selected periodicals. Covers accounting, communications, econom-
ics, finance, management, marketing, and other business subjects.

*CABLE COMMUNICATIONS-PRODUCTS DIRECTORY
    AND BUYER'S GUIDE*
Ter-Sat Media Publications, Inc.
57 Peachwood Court
Kitchener, ON, Canada N2B 1S7
PH: (519)744-4411
FX: (519)744-1261
Udo Salewsky, editor. Annual. $20.00. Lists about 300 manufactur-

ers and distributors of cable television-specific equipment and services; primarily covers United States and Canada.

CABLE TELEVISION LAW: A VIDEO COMMUNICATIONS PRACTICE GUIDE
Matthew Bender & Co., Inc.
Two Park Ave.
New York, NY 10016
PH: (800)223-1940
FX: (212)244-3188
Three looseleaf volumes, Periodic supplementation. Price on application. Examines the substantive, procedural, and strategic aspects of the law affecting cable television and other video technologies.

CABLE TV FINANCIAL DATABOOK: SOURCEBOOK FOR ALL KEY FINANCIAL DATA ON CABLE TV
Paul Kagan Associates, Inc.
126 Clock Tower Place
Carmel, CA 93923
PH: (408)624-1536
FX: (408)625-3225
Annual. $325.00. Includes analysis of operating results of private and public cable television companies, historical data and projections.

CENTER FOR RESEARCH IN COMPUTING TECHNOLOGY
Harvard University, Division of Applied Sciences
29 Oxford St.
Pierce Hall
Cambridge, MA 02138
PH: (617)495-4117
FX: (617)495-9837
E-mail: cheatham@das.harvard.edu
URL: http://www.das.harvard.edu/cs.grafs.html
Conducts research in computer vision, robotics, artificial intelligence, systems programming, programming languages, operating systems, networks, graphics, database management systems, and telecommunications.

COMMUNICATION ABSTRACTS
Sage Publications, Inc.
2455 Teller Rd.
Thousand Oaks, CA 91320
PH: (805)499-0721
FX: (805)499-0871
E-mail: libraries@sagepub.com
URL: http://www.sagepub
Bimonthly. Individuals, $147.00 per year; institutions, $498.00 per year. Provides broad coverage of the literature of communications, including broadcasting and advertising.

COMMUNICATIONS DAILY: THE AUTHORITATIVE NEWS SERVICE OF ELECTRONIC COMMUNICATIONS
Warren Publishing, Inc.
2115 Ward Court, N. W.
Washington, DC 20037
PH: (202)872-9200
FX: (202)293-3435
E-mail: warrenpub@interramp.com
Daily. $2,898.00 per year. Newsletter. Covers telecommunications, including the telephone industry, broadcasting, cable TV, satellites, data communications, and electronic publishing. Features corporate and industry news.

COMMUNICATIONS NEWS: SOLUTIONS FOR TODAY'S NETWORKING DECISION MANAGERS
Nelson Publishing, Inc.
2500 Tamiami Trail North
Nokomis, FL 34275
PH: (941)966-9521
FX: (941)966-2590
URL: http://www.comnews.com
Monthly. $79.00 per year. Includes coverage of "Internetworking"

and "Intranetworking." Emphasis is on emerging telecommunications technologies.

COMMUNICATIONS OUTLOOK
Organization for Economic Cooperation and Development
2001 L St., N.W., Suite 650
OECD Washington Center
Washington, DC 20036-4922
PH: (800)456-6323
FX: (202)785-0350
E-mail: washcont@oecd.org
URL: http://www.oecd.org
Biennial. $83.00. Provides international coverage of yearly telecommunications activity. Includes charts, graphs, and maps.

CONSUMER INTERNET REPORT
Jupiter Communications Co.
627 Broadway, 2nd Floor
New York, NY 10012
PH: (800)488-4345
FX: (212)780-6075
E-mail: jupiter@jup.com
URL: http://www.jup.com
Annual. $995.00. Market research report. Provides data and forecasts relating to various hardware and software elements of the Internet, including browsers, provision of service, telephone line modems, cable modems, wireless access devices, online advertising, programming languages, and Internet chips. Includes company profiles.

CONVERGENCE
Chilton Co.
600 South Cherry St., Suite 400
Denver, CO 80222
PH: (303)393-7449
FX: (303)329-3453
Monthly. $30.00 per year. Covers the merging of communications technologies. Includes telecommunications networks, interactive TV, multimedia, wireless phone service, and electronic information services.

CORPORATE INTERNET PLANNING GUIDE: ALIGNING INTERNET STRATEGY WITH BUSINESS GOALS
Van Nostrand Reinhold
115 Fifth Ave.
New York, NY 10003
PH: (800)842-3636
FX: (212)254-9499
E-mail: info@vnr.com
URL: http://www.vnr.com
Richard J. Gascoyne and Koray Ozcubucku. 1997. $29.95. Provides administrative advice on planning, developing, and managing corporate Internet or intranet functions. Emphasis is on strategic planning.

CREDIT CONSIDERATIONS: FINANCIAL AND CREDIT CHARACTERISTICS OF SELECTED INDUSTRIES, VOLUME ONE
Robert Morris Associates
1650 Market St.
One Liberty Place, Suite 2300
Philadelphia, PA 19103
PH: (800)677-7621
FX: (215)446-4100
URL: http://www.rmahq.org
Looseleaf. $115.00. Provides financial characteristics, credit risk appraisal, and general description of 44 industries or businesses. An appendix outlines six forms of financing.

CSA ENGINEERING
Cambridge Scientific Abstracts
7200 Wisconsin Ave., Suite 601
Bethesda, MD 20814
PH: (800)843-7751
FX: (301)961-6720

Provides the online version of *Computer and Information Systems Abstracts, Electronics and Communications Abstracts, Health and Safety Science Abstracts, ISMEC: Mechanical Engineering Abstracts (Information Service in Mechanical Engineering)* and *Solid State and Superconductivity Abstracts*. Time period is 1981 to date, with monthly updates. Inquire as to online cost and availability.

DATA NETWORKING
Datapro Information Services Group
600 Delran Parkway
Delran, NJ 08075
PH: (800)328-2776
FX: (609)764-2812
Monthly. $1,400.00 per year. Four looseleaf volumes. Provides broad coverage of data communications and networks, including product evaluation (hardware and software).

DATA SMOG: SURVIVING THE INFORMATION GLUT
HarperCollins Publishers, Inc.
10 East 53rd St.
New York, NY 10022-5299
PH: (800)242-7737
FX: (212)207-7145
URL: http://www.harpercollins.com
David Shenk. 1997. $24.00. A critical view of both the electronic and print information industries. Emphasis is on information overload.

DATAPRO REPORTS ON INTERNATIONAL COMMUNICATIONS EQUIPMENT
Datapro Information Services Group
600 Delran Parkway
Delran, NJ 08075
PH: (800)328-2776
FX: (609)764-2812
URL: http://www.datapro.com/products
Monthly. Three looseleaf volumes. New subscriptions, $1,682.00 per year, renewals, $1,412 per year. Provides standards, specifications, and protocols for international voice and data communications equipment.

DATAPRO VOICE NETWORKING SYSTEMS
600 Delran Parkway
Delran, NJ 08075
PH: (800)328-2776
FX: (609)764-2812
URL: http://www.datapro.com/products
Datapro Information Services Group. Monthly. $1,210.00 per year. Three looseleaf volumes. Provides comprehensive coverage of telephone and telecommunications systems, including planning, equipment selection, and management.

DESKTOP VIDEO COMMUNICATIONS
BCR Enterprises, Inc.
950 York Rd.
Hinsdale, IL 60521
PH: (630)986-1432
FX: (630)323-5324
Bimonthly. Price on application. Covers multimedia technologies, with emphasis on video conferencing and the "virtual office." Formerly *Virtual Workgroups*.

DIRECTORY OF CONSUMER ELECTRONICS
Chain Store Guide Information Services
3922 Coconut Palm Dr.
Tampa, FL 33619
PH: (800)925-2288
FX: (813)664-6810
E-mail: valkelly@sprynet.com
URL: http://www.d-net.com/csgis
Biennial. $125.00. Includes 3,000 "leading" retailers and over 200 "top" distributors. Formerly *Directory of Consumer Electronics Retails and Distributors*.

ELECTRONIC INFORMATION REPORT: EMPOWERING INFORMATION INDUSTRY DECISION MAKERS SINCE 1979
SIMBA Information, Inc.
Post Office Box 4234
Stamford, CT 06907-0234
PH: (800)307-2529
FX: (203)358-5824
E-mail: info@simbanet.com
URL: http://www.simbanet.com
Weekly. $499.00 per year. Newsletter. Provides business and financial news and trends for online services, electronic publishing, storage media, multimedia, and voice services. Includes information on relevant IPOs (initial public offerings) and mergers. Formerly *IDP Report*.

ELECTRONIC SERVICING & TECHNOLOGY: THE HOW-TO MAGAZINE OF ELECTRONICS
C. Q. Communications, Inc.
76 N. Broadway
Hicksville, NY 11801
PH: (516)681-2922
FX: (516)681-2926
Conrad Persson. Monthly. $24.75 per year. Provides how-to technical information to technicians who service consumer electronics equipment.

ENCYCLOPEDIA OF EMERGING INDUSTRIES
Gale Group
27500 Drake Rd
Farmington Hills, MI 48331-3535
PH: (800)877-GALE
FX: (800)414-5043
E-mail: galeord@galegroup.com
URL: http://www.galegroup.com
1998. $350.00. Provides detailed information on 88 "newly flourishing" industries. Includes historical background, organizational structure, significant individuals, current conditions, major companies, work force, technology trends, research developments, and other industry facts.

FAULKNER'S ENTERPRISE NETWORKING
Faulkner Information Services, Inc.
7905 Browning Rd.
114 Cooper Center
Pennsauken, NJ 08109-4319
PH: (609)622-2070
FX: (609)662-3380
Three looseleaf volumes, with monthly supplements. $1275.00 per year. Contains product reports and management articles relating to computer communications and networking. Available on CD-ROM. Quarterly updates. Formerly *Data Communications Reports*.

FAULKNER'S TELECOMMUNICATIONS WORLD
Faulkner Information Services, Inc.
7905 Browning Rd.
114 Cooper Center
Pennsauken, NJ 08109-4319
PH: (609)662-2070
FX: (609)662-3380
Three looseleaf volumes, with monthly supplements, $1260.00 per year. Contains product reports, technology overviews and management articles relating to all aspects of voice and data communications.

FCC REPORT: COVERING TELECOM POLICY, REGULATION, AND BUSINESS WORLDWIDE
Telecom Publishing Group
2115 Ward Court, N. W.
Washington, DC 20037-1209
PH: (202)872-9200
FX: (202)293-3435
E-mail: info@telecommunications.com
URL: http://www.telecommunications.com

Warren Publishing, Inc. Semimonthly. $649.00 per year. Newsletter concerned principally with Federal Communications Commission reglations and policy.

THE FROEHLICH-KENT ENCYCLOPEDIA OF TELECOMMUNICATIONS
Marcel Dekker, Inc.
270 Madison Ave.
New York, NY 10016
PH: (800)228-1160
FX: (212)685-4540
Fritz E. Froehlich and Allen Kent, editors. Various dates, volumes, and prices (information on request). Contains scholarly articles written by telecommunications experts. Includes bibliographies.

GALE DATABASE OF PUBLICATIONS AND BROADCAST MEDIA
Gale Group
27500 Drake Rd
Farmington Hills, MI 48331-3535
PH: (800)877-GALE
FX: (800)414-5043
URL: http://www.galegroup.com
An online directory containing detailed information on over 67,000 periodicals, newspapers, broadcast stations, cable systems, directories, and newsletters. Corresponds to the following print sources: *Gale Directory of Publications and Broadcast Media; Directories in Print; City and State Directories in Print; Newsletters in Print*. Semiannual updates. Inquire as to online cost and availability.

GALE DIRECTORY OF DATABASES, CD-ROM
Gale Group
27500 Drake Rd
Farmington Hills, MI 48331-3535
PH: (800)877-GALE
FX: (800)414-5043
URL: http://www.galegroup.com
Semiannual. $600.00 per year, single user. $920 per year, network version. Consists of the CD-ROM version of the printed *Gale Directory of Databases* - Volume 1, *Online Databases*; Volume 2, *CD-ROM, Diskette, Magnetic Tape, Handheld, and Batch Access Database Products*. Also included: *Information Industry Directory* and *Telecommunications Directory*.

GALE DIRECTORY OF PUBLICATIONS AND BROADCAST MEDIA
Gale Group
27500 Drake Rd
Farmington Hills, MI 48331-3535
PH: (800)877-GALE
FX: (800)414-5043
URL: http://www.galegroup.com
Annual. $455.00. Three volumes. A guide to publications and broadcasting stations in the U. S. and Canada, including newspapers, magazines, journals, radio stations, television stations, and cable systems. Geographic arrangement. Volume three consists of statistical tables, maps, subject indexes, and title index. Formerly *Ayer Directory of Publications*.

GLOBAL OPPORTUNITIES IN THE MOBILE SATELLITE MARKET
Telecom Publishing Group
2115 Ward Court, N. W.
Washington, DC 20037-1209
PH: (202)872-9200
FX: (202)293-3435
E-mail: info@telecommunications.com
URL: http://www.telecommunications.com
Warren Publishing, Inc. 1997. $1,695.00. Provides market research information and detailed business analysis of the mobile satellite communications industry.

GLOBALBASE
Gale Group
27500 Drake Rd
Farmington Hills, MI 48331-3535
PH: (800)877-GALE
FX: (800)414-5043
Formerly published by Information Access Co. Provides more than one million online summaries of business, industrial, and economic news reports from more than 1,000 publications worldwide. Covers a wide range of material appearing in international trade journals, professional magazines, and newspapers. Time period is 1984 to date, with weekly updates. Inquire as to online cost and availability.

THE HIGHWAYMEN: WARRIORS ON THE INFORMATION SUPERHIGHWAY
201 East 50th St.
New York, NY 10022
PH: (800)726-0600
FX: (800)659-2436
URL: http://www.randomhouse.com
Ken Auletta. Random House, Inc. 1997. $27.50. Contains critical articles about Ted Turner, Rupert Murdoch, Barry Diller, Michael Eisner, and other key figures in electronic communications, entertainment, and information.

THE HOLLYWOOD REPORTER
1515 Broadway
New York, NY 10036
PH: (212)536-5199
E-mail: info@bpi.com
URL: http://www.hollywoodreporter.com
BPI Communications. Daily. $199.00 per year. Covers the latest news in film, TV, cable, multimedia, music, and theatre. Includes box office grosses and entertainment industry financial data.

HOME OFFICE ASSOCIATION OF AMERICA, INC.
909 Third Ave., Suite 990
New York, NY 10022
PH: (800)809-4622
FX: (800)315-4622
E-mail: info@hoaa.com
URL: http://www.hoaa.com
A for-profit organization providing advice and information to home office workers and business owners. Membership ($49.00 per year) includes a monthly newsletter, *Home Office Connections*.

HOOVER'S COMPANY PROFILES ON CD-ROM
1033 La Posada Dr., Suite 250
Austin, TX 78752
PH: (800)486-8666
FX: (512)374-4501
E-mail: orders@hoovers.com
URL: http://www.hoovers.com
Hoover's, Inc. Quarterly. $449.95 per year (single-user) or $549.95 per year (2 to 10 users). Provides the CD-ROM version of *Hoover's Handbook of American Business, Hoover's Handbook of Emerging Companies, Hoover's Handbook of World Business, Hoover's Guide to Computer Companies, Hoover's Guide to Media Companies, Hoover's Handbook of Private Companies,* and various regional guides. Includes more than 2,500 detailed profiles of companies.

HOOVER'S GUIDE TO MEDIA COMPANIES
1033 La Posada Drive, Suite 250
Austin, TX 78752
PH: (800)486-8666
FX: (512)374-4501
E-mail: orders@hoovers.com
URL: http://www.hoovers.com
Hoover's, Inc. Annual. $29.95. Contains profiles of about 1,000 media and communications companies. Industries include broadcasting, publishing, the Internet, electronic media, telecommunications, and filmmaking.

I'LL GET BACK TO YOU: 156 WAYS TO GET PEOPLE TO RETURN YOUR PHONE CALLS
1221 Ave. of the Americas
New York, NY 10020
PH: (800)722-4726
FX: (212)512-2821
E-mail: customer.service@mcgraw-hill.com
URL: http://www.mcgraw-hill.com
Robert L. Shook and Eric Yaverbaum. McGraw-Hill. 1996. $9.95. Presents advice from business executives, celebrities, and others on how to make telephone calls seem important.

INDUSTRY NORMS AND KEY BUSINESS RATIOS. DESK TOP EDITION
One Diamond Hill Rd.
Murray Hill, NJ 07974
PH: (800)223-0141
FX: (908)665-5418
URL: http://www.dnb.com
Dun and Bradstreet Corp., Business Information Services. Annual. Five volumes. $475.00 per volume. $1890.00 per set. Covers over 800 kinds of businesses, arranged by Standard Industrial Classification number. More detailed editions covering longer periods of time are also available.

INSIDE THE RHCS
2115 Ward Court, N. W.
Washington, DC 20037-1209
PH: (202)872-9200
FX: (202)293-3435
E-mail: info@telecommunications.com
URL: http://www.telecommunications.com
Warren Publishing, Inc., Telecom Publishing Group. 1997. $1,695.00. 10th edition. Provides market research information, financial data, and business trends relating to the regional Bell telephone companies (RHCs - regional holding companies). Individual company reports are also available.

INSPEC
Michael Faraday House
Six Hills Way
Stevenage Herts SG1 2AY, England
PH: (38-)313311
FX: (443)-742840
Institution of Electrical Engineers. Citations and abstracts to literature on physics, electronics and electrical engineering, 1969 to present. Inquire as to online cost and availability.

INSTITUTE FOR SYSTEMS RESEARCH
University of Maryland
A. V. Williams Bldg., No. 115
College Park, MD 20742-3311
PH: (301)405-6632
FX: (301)314-9220
E-mail: isr@isr.umd.edu
URL: http://www.isr.umd.edu
A National Science Foundation Engineering Research Center. Areas of research include communication systems, manufacturing systems, chemical process systems, artificial intelligence, and systems integration.

INTERACTIVE ADVERTISING SOURCE
1700 Higgins Rd.
Des Plaines, IL 60018
PH: (800)851-7737
FX: (847)375-5001
URL: http://www.srds.com
SRDS. Quarterly. $249.00 per year. Provides descriptive profiles, rates, audience, personnel, etc., for producers of various forms of interactive or multimedia advertising: online/Internet, CD-ROM, interactive TV, interactive cable, interactive telephone, interactive kiosk, and others.

INTERACTIVE AGE: CONTENT, TECHNOLOGY, AND COMMUNICATIONS FOR THE INFORMATION HIGHWAY
600 Community Drive
Manhasset, NY 11030
PH: (800)829-0421
FX: (516)562-5474
E-mail: interact@interact.cmp.com
CMP Publications, Inc. Biweekly. Free to qualified personnel; others, $79.00 per year. Provides "coverage of developments across the interactive spectrum," including computer communications, telecommunications, the cable industry, and the "entertainment/ information/media industry."

INTERACTIVE CONSUMERS
625 Ave. of the Americas
New York, NY 10011-2002
PH: (800)346-3787
FX: (212)807-2716
E-mail: catalog@findsvp.com
URL: http://www.findsvp.com
FIND/SVP, Inc. Monthly. $395.00 per year. Newsletter. Covers the emerging markets for digital content, products, and services. Includes market information on telecommuting, online services, the Internet, online investing, and other areas of electronic commerce.

INTERACTIVE HOME
627 Broadway, 2nd Floor
New York, NY 10012
PH: (800)488-4345
FX: (212)780-6075
E-mail: jupiter@jup.com
URL: http://www.jup.com
Jupiter Communications Co. Monthly. $495.00 per year. Newsletter on devices to bring the Internet into the average American home. Covers TV set-top boxes, game devices, telephones with display screens, handheld computer communication devices, the usual PCs, etc.

INTERACTIVE SOURCE BOOK
401 N. Broad St.
Philadelphia, PA 19108-9958
PH: (215)238-5300
FX: (215)238-5099
URL: http://www.napco.com
North American Publishing Co. Annual. $545.00. Lists companies providing interactive media products and services in the following areas: television, the Internet, wireless cable, and satellite systems.

INTERNATIONAL ENCYCLOPEDIA OF COMMUNICATIONS
198 Madison Ave.
New York, NY 10016
PH: (800)451-7556
FX: (212)726-6446
Oxford University Press, Inc. 1989. $450.00. Four volumes. Published in association with the Annenberg School of Communications of the University of Pennsylvania. Broad coverage of communications, including film, theatre, television, publishing, computers, and telecommunications.

INTERNATIONAL JOURNAL OF COMMUNICATION SYSTEMS
605 Third Ave.
New York, NY 10158-0012
PH: (800)225-5945
FX: (212)850-6088
Available from John Wiley & Sons, Inc., Journals Div. Bimonthly. $795.00 per year. Published in England by John Wiley & Sons Ltd. Formerly *International Journal of Digital and Analog Communication Systems*.

INTERNET TOOLS OF THE PROFESSION
PH: (202)234-4700
FX: (202)265-9317
E-mail: hope@tiac.net
URL: http://www.sla.org/pubs/itotp
Special Libraries Association. Web site is designed to update the printed *Internet Tools of the Profession*. Provides links to a wide range of useful databases in business, finance, industry, information technology, insurance, law, library management, telecommunications, and other subject areas. Fees: Free.

INTERNET TOOLS OF THE PROFESSION: A GUIDE FOR INFORMATION PROFESSIONALS
1700 18th St., N. W.
Washington, DC 20009-2514
PH: (202)234-4700
FX: (202)265-9317
URL: http://www.sla.org
Hope N. Tillman, editor. Special Libraries Association. 1997. $49.00. Second edition. Consists of 14 sections by various authors or compilers. After two introductory articles on searching the Internet, there are 12 annotated lists of useful Web sites, covering the SLA, business and finance, chemistry, education, food and agriculture, information technology, insurance and employee benefits, law, library management, metals and materials, pharmaceuticals, and telecommunications. An index is provided.

KEY ABSTRACTS: TELECOMMUNICATIONS
PO Box 1331
Piscataway, NJ 08855-1331
PH: (800)678-4333
FX: (908)562-8737
Available from INSPEC/IEEE Operations Center. Monthly. $200.00 per year. Provides international coverage of journal and proceedings literature. Published in England by the Institution of Electrical Engineers (IEE).

LAND MOBILE RADIO NEWS
1201 Seven Locks Rd., Suite 300
Potomac, MD 20854
PH: (800)777-5006
FX: (301)309-3847
E-mail: pbi@phillips.com
Phillips Business Information, Inc. Weekly. $597.00. Newsletter emphasizing the rules and regulations of the Federal Communications Commission (FCC), particularly as applied to mobile radio communication systems. Formerly *Industrial Communications*.

MAKING TELECOMMUTING HAPPEN: A GUIDE FOR TELEMANGERS AND TELECOMMUTERS
115 Fifth Ave.
New York, NY 10003
PH: (800)842-3636
FX: (212)254-9499
E-mail: info@vnr.com
URL: http://www.vnr.com
Jack M. Nilles. Van Nostrand Reinhold. 1994. $24.95. Includes tips for working productively in a home environment while maintaining good relationships with workers in the corporate office.

MANAGEMENT CONTENTS
Gale Group
27500 Drake Rd
Farmington Hills, MI 48331-3535
PH: (800)877-GALE
FX: (800)414-5043
E-mail: galeord@gale.com
URL: http://www.galegroup.com
Formerly published by Information Access Co. Covers a wide range of management, financial, marketing, personnel, and administrative topics. About 150 leading business journals are indexed and abstracted from 1974 to date, with monthly updating. Inquire as to online cost and availability.

MANAGING VOICE NETWORKS
600 Delran Parkway
Delran, NJ 08075
PH: (800)328-2776
FX: (609)764-2812
URL: http://www.datapro.com/products
Datapro Information Services Group. Two looseleaf volumes. Monthly supplementation. New subscriptions, $926.00 per year; renewals, $843.00 per year. Covers planning, installation, and maintenance of voice communications systems. Formerly *Datapro Management of Telecommunications*.

MANUAL OF REMOTE WORKING
Old Post Rd.
Brookfield, VT 05036-9704
PH: (800)535-9544
FX: (802)276-3837
E-mail: info@gowerpub.com
URL: http://www.gowerpub.com
Kevin Curran and Geoff Williams. Gower Publishing Ltd. 1997. $110.95. A British approach to telecommuting or "remote working." Among the chapters are "Planning a Remote Working Operation," "Human Resources," "Communication Systems," and "Project Management." Includes bibliographical references, glossary, and index.

MANUFACTURING PROFILES
Washington, DC 20402
PH: (202)512-1800
FX: (202)512-2250
E-mail: gpoaccess@gpo.gov
URL: http://www.access.gpo.gov
Available from U. S. Government Printing Office. Annual. $35.00. Issued by the U. S. Census Bureau. A printed consolidation of the entire *Current Industrial Report* series, presenting "all the data compiled." Contains statistics on production, shipments, inventories, consumption, exports, imports, and orders for a wide variety of manufactured products. (See also Census Bureau home page, http://www.census.gov/.)

MARCONI'S INTERNATIONAL REGISTER: LINKING BUYERS AND SELLERS WORLDWIDE THROUGH FAX AND BUSINESS LISTINGS
P.O. Box 14
Larchmont, NY 10538
PH: (914)632-8171
FX: (914)632-1804
Telegraphic Cable and Radio Registrations, Inc. Annual. $150.00. Lists 45,000 firms throughout the world in all lines of business. In four sections.

MOODY'S PUBLIC UTILITY MANUAL
99 Church St.
New York, NY 10007-0300
PH: (800)342-5647
FX: (212)553-4700
Moody's Investors Service, Inc. Annual. $1,250.00. Two volumes. Supplemented twice weekly by *Moody's Public Utility News Reports*. Contains financial and other information concerning publicly-held utility companies (electric, gas, telephone, water).

MULTICHANNEL NEWS
825 Seventh Ave.
New York, NY 10019
PH: (800)695-1214
FX: (212)887-8384
E-mail: nmartin@chilton.ai.net
URL: http://www.chilton.com
Chilton Co. Weekly. $78.00 per year. Covers the business, programming, marketing, and technology concerns of cable television operators and their suppliers.

MUTIMEDIA TELECOMMUNICATIONS SOURCEBOOK
2500 Wilson Blvd., Suite 3
Arlington, VA 22201-3834

PH: (202)296-9800
FX: (202)296-4993
E-mail: info@mmta.org
URL: http://www.mmta.org
Multimedia Telecommunications Association. Annual. $95.00. Lists manufacturers and suppliers of interconnect telephone equipment. Formerly *Telecommunications Sourcebook.*

NEW TELECOM QUARTERLY—THE FUTURE OF TELECOMMUNICATIONS
13740 Research Blvd., Ste. C-1
Austin, TX 78750-1859
PH: (800)835-3887
FX: (512)258-0087
E-mail: info@tfi.com
URL: http://www.tfi.com
Technology Futures, Inc. Quarterly. $120.00 per year. Includes articles on trends in wireless telecommunications, fiber optics technology, interactive multimedia, online information systems, telephone systems, and telecommunications in general.

NEWSPAGE: PERSONALIZED NEWS FOR TODAY'S BUSINESS
PH: (800)-766-4224
FX: (617)273-6060
URL: http://www.newspage.com
Individual, Inc. Web site allows Boolean searching of current (past five days) business news "stories" on "2,500 topics" from more than 630 magazines, newsletters, newspapers, and newswires. Fees: Headlines, "briefs," and full-text of press releases are free; other full-text is fee-based. Extensive financial market index data and price quotes are free. Full access requires registration, including personalized news service (current awareness). Daily updates.

NTIS ALERTS: COMMUNICATION
U. S. Department of Commerce
5285 Port Royal Rd.
Technology Administration
Springfield, VA 22161
PH: (800)553-6847
FX: (703)321-8547
National Technical Information Service. Semimonthly. $160.00 per year. Formerly *Abstract Newsletter*. Provides descriptions of government-sponsored research reports and software, with ordering information. Covers common carriers, satellites, radio/TV equipment, telecommunication regulations, and related subjects.

PERSONAL COMMUNICATIONS SERVICES: THE CHALLENGE TO TRADITIONAL CELLULAR PROVIDERS
2115 Ward Court, N. W.
Washington, DC 20037-1209
PH: (202)872-9200
FX: (202)293-3435
E-mail: info@telecommunications.com
URL: http://www.telecommunications.com
Warren Publishing, Inc., Telecom Publishing Group. 1997. $695.00. Sixth edition. Provides market research and business information relating to digital wireless technology.

PHILLIPS WORLD SATELLITE ALMANAC
1201 Seven Locks Rd., Suite 300
Potomac, MD 20854
PH: (800)777-5006
FX: (301)309-3847
Phillips Business Information, Inc. Annual. $257.00. All commercial satellite systems and operators (operational and planned), booking contracts, PTT decision makers, and transportation brokers. Formerly *World Satellite Almanac.*

PHONEFACTS
1401 H St., N. W., Suite 600
Washington, DC 20005

PH: (202)326-7300
FX: (202)326-7333
United States Telephone Association. Annual. Members, $5.00; non-members, $15.00. Presents basic statistics on the independent telephone industry in the U. S.

PLUNKETT'S ENTERTAINMENT & MEDIA INDUSTRY ALMANAC
1033 La Posada Drive, Suite 250
Austin, TX 78752
PH: (800)486-8666
FX: (512)374-4501
E-mail: orders@hoovers.com
URL: http://www.hoovers.com
Available from Hoover's, Inc. Annual. $149.95. Published by Plunkett Research. Provides profiles of leading firms in online information, films, radio, television, cable, multimedia, magazines, and book publishing. Includes World Wide Web sites, where available, plus information on careers and industry trends.

PLUNKETT'S INFOTECH INDUSTRY ALMANAC: COMPLETE PROFILES ON THE INFOTECH 500—THE LEADING FIRMS IN THE MOVEMENT AND MANAGEMENT OF VOICE, DATA, AND VIDEO
1033 La Posada Dr., Suite 250
Austin, TX 78752
PH: (800)486-8666
FX: (512)374-4501
E-mail: orders@hoovers.com
URL: http://www.hoovers.com
Available from Hoover's, Inc. Annual. $131.50. Published by Plunkett Research. Five hundred major information companies are profiled, with corporate culture aspects. Discusses major trends in various sectors of the computer and information industry, including data on careers and job growth. Includes several indexes.

POINTCAST NETWORK
PH: (408)253-0894
FX: (408)253-4058
URL: http://www.pointcast.com
PointCast, Inc. Web site provides current news and information on seven "channels": News, Companies, Industries, Internet, Weather, Sports, and Lifestyle. Includes *Money* magazine and a special "TechWeb channel" featuring publications from CMP Media (*CommunicationsWeek, InformationWeek*, etc.) and other items, such as CNN financial. Fees: Free, but downloading of PointCast software is required (includes personalized news feature). Updating is continuous.

PROMT: PREDICASTS OVERVIEW OF MARKETS AND TECHNOLOGY
Gale Group
27500 Drake Rd
Farmington Hills, MI 48331-3535
PH: (800)877-GALE
FX: (800)414-5043
E-mail: galeord@gale.com
URL: http://www.galegroup.com
Formerly published by IAC. Companies, products, applied technologies and markets. U.S. and international literature coverage, 1972 to date. Daily updates. Inquire as to online cost and availability. Provides abstracts from more than 1,500 publications.

R M A ANNUAL STATEMENT STUDIES, INCLUDING COMPARATIVE HISTORICAL DATA AND OTHER SOURCES OF COMPOSITE FINANCIAL DATA
One Liberty Place, Suite 2300
1650 Market St.
Philadelphia, PA 19103
PH: (800)677-7621
FX: (215)446-4100
URL: http://www.rmahq.org
Robert Morris Associates: The Association of Lending and Credit Risk Professionals. Annual. $125.00. Median and quartile financial

ratios are given for over 400 kinds of manufacturing, wholesale, retail, construction, and consumer finance establishments. Data is sorted by both asset size and sales volume. Includes a clearly written "Definition of Ratios," a bibliography of financial ratio sources, and an alphabetical industry index.

SATELLITE WEEK: THE AUTHORITATIVE NEWS SERVICE FOR SATELLITE COMMUNICATIONS AND ALLIED FIELDS
2115 Ward Court, N. W.
Washington, DC 20037
PH: (202)872-9200
FX: (202)293-3435
E-mail: warrenpub@interramp.com
Warren Publishing, Inc. Weekly. $937.00 per year. Newsletter. Covers satellite broadcasting, telecommunications, and the industrialization of space.

SCISEARCH
3501 Market St.
Philadelphia, PA 19104
PH: (800)523-1850
FX: (215)386-2911
URL: http://www.isinet.com
Institute for Scientific Information. Broad, multidisciplinary index to the literature of science and technology, 1974 to present. Inquire as to online cost and availability. Coverage of literature is worldwide, with weekly updates.

SOHO CENTRAL
PH: (800)-809-4622
FX: (800)-315-4622
E-mail: info@hoaa.com
URL: http://www.hoaa.com
Home Office Association of America, Inc. Web site provides extensive lists of "Home Office Internet Resources" (links), including Business, Government, Continuing Education, Legal, Employment, Telecommunications, and Publishing. Includes an online newsletter. Fees: Free. (Membership in the Home Office Association of America is $49.00 per year.)

SOUND AND COMMUNICATIONS
25 Willowdale Ave.
Port Washington, NY 11050
PH: (516)767-2500
FX: (516)767-9335
Testa Communications, Inc. Monthly. $15.00 per year. A business, news and technical journal for contractors, consultants, engineers and system managers who design, install and purchase sound and communications equipment.

SOUND AND COMMUNICATIONS: THE BLUE BOOK
25 Willowdale Ave.
Port Washington, NY 11050
PH: (516)767-2500
FX: (516)767-9335
Testa Communications. Annual. $15.00. Approximately 1000 suppliers of sound and communications equipment; including audio/video products in the United States and Canada.

SPACE BUSINESS NEWS
1201 Seven Locks Rd., Suite 300
Potomac, MD 20854
PH: (800)777-5006
FX: (301)309-3847
Phillips Business Information, Inc. Biweekly. $697.00 per year. Newsletter. Covers business applications in space, including remote sensing and satellites.

STANDARD & POOR'S INDUSTRY SURVEYS
25 Broadway
New York, NY 10004-1010

PH: (800)221-5277
FX: (212)208-0040
E-mail: speqwebmaster@mcgraw-hill.com
URL: http://www.stockinfo.standardpoor.com
Standard & Poor's. Semiannual. $2,250.00 per year. Two looseleaf volumes. Provides detailed, individual surveys of 52 major industry groups. Each survey is revised on a semiannual basis. Also includes "Monthly Investment Review" (industry group investment analysis) and monthly "Trends & Projections" (economic analysis).

STANDARD & POOR'S STATISTICAL SERVICE. CURRENT STATISTICS
25 Broadway
New York, NY 10004
PH: (800)221-5277
FX: (212)412-0040
Standard & Poor's. Monthly. $655.00 per year. Includes 10 Basic Statistics sections, Current Statistics Supplements and Annual Security Price Index Record.

SWITCHBOARD
PH: (508)898-1000
FX: (508)898-1755
E-mail: webmaster@switchboard.com
URL: http://www.switchboard.com
Banyan Systems, Inc. Web site provides telephone numbers and street addresses for more than 100 million business locations and residences in the U. S. Broad industry categories are available. Fees: Free.

TELCO BUSINESS REPORT: ANALYZING U. S. TELEPHONE COMPANY STRATEGIES AT HOME AND ABROAD
2115 Ward Court, N. W.
Washington, DC 20037-1209
PH: (202)872-9200
FX: (202)293-3435
E-mail: info@telecommunications.com
URL: http://www.telecommunications.com
Warren Publishing, Inc., Telecom Publishing Group. Semimonthly. $759.00 per year. Newsletter. Covers long-distance markets, emerging technologies, strategies of Bell operating companies, and other telephone business topics.

TELECOM LINGO GUIDE
2115 Ward Court, N. W.
Washington, DC 20037-1209
PH: (202)872-9200
FX: (202)293-3435
E-mail: info@telecommunications.com
URL: http://www.telecommunications.com
Warren Publishing, Inc., Telecom Publishing Group. 1996. $60.00. Eighth edition. Defines more than 1,000 words, phrases, and acronyms frequently used in the telecommunications industry.

TELECOM PERSPECTIVES
1221 Ave. of the Americas
New York, NY 10020-1001
PH: (212)512-2898
FX: (212)512-2859
Northern Business Information. Monthly. $995.00 per year. Newsletter. Emphasis is on the "market opportunities" that exist within various segments of the telecommunications industry. Provides detailed analysis of both emerging and obsolescing market segments.

TELECOMMUNICATIONS DIRECTORY
Gale Group
27500 Drake Rd
Farmington Hills, MI 48331-3535
PH: (800)877-GALE
FX: (800)414-5043
URL: http://www.galegroup.com
National and international voice, data, facsimile, and video commu-

nications services. Formerly *Telecommunications Systems and Services Directory.*

TELECOMMUTER'S HANDBOOK: HOW TO EARN A LIVING WITHOUT GOING TO THE OFFICE
1221 Ave. of the Americas
New York, NY 10020
PH: (800)722-4726
FX: (212)512-2821
E-mail: customer.service@mcgraw-hill.com
URL: http://www.mcgraw-hill.com
Debra Schepp. McGraw-Hill. 1995. $12.95. Second edition. Discusses "The Upside" and "The Downside" of telecommuting. Lists the best 50 jobs for telecommuting and 100 companies using telecommuters. An appendix includes a form: "Telecommuter's Agreement."

TELECOMMUTING: A MANAGER'S GUIDE TO FLEXIBLE WORK ARRANGEMENTS
1230 Ave. of the Americas
New York, NY 10020
PH: (800)223-2348
FX: (212)698-7007
URL: http://www.thefreepress.com
Joel Kugelmass. Free Press. 1995. $25.00. Part one is "Understanding Flexible Work" and part two is "Implementing Flexible Work." Includes bibliography and index.

TELECOMMUTING REVIEW
10 Donner Court
Monmouth Junction, NJ 08852
PH: (908)329-2266
FX: (908)329-2703
E-mail: 74375.1667@compuserve.com
URL: http://www.gilgordon.com
Gil Gordon Associates. Monthly. $197.00 per year. Newsletter. Provides news and information about telecommuting (working from home by means of computers and telecommunication technology).

TELECOMMUTING, TELEWORKING, AND ALTERNATIVE OFFICING
PH: (732)329-2266
FX: (732)329-2703
URL: http://www.gilgordon.com
Gil Gordon Associates. Web site includes "About Telecommuting" (questions and answers), "Worldwide Resources" (news groups, publications, conferences), and "Technology" (virtual office, intranets, groupware). Other features include monthly updates and an extensive list of telecommuting/telework related books. Fees: Free.

TELECONS
Post Office Box 5106
San Ramon, CA 94583
PH: (510)606-5150
FX: (510)606-9410
Applied Business Telecommunications. Bimonthly. $30.00 per year. Topics include teleconferencing, videoconferencing, distance learning, telemedicine, and telecommuting.

TELEFACTS
1221 Ave. of the Americas, 37th Floor
New York, NY 10020-1095
PH: (800)328-2776
FX: (212)512-2859
Northern Business Information/McGraw-Hill. Monthly. $460.00 per year. Newsletter. Covers telecommunications market news and trends. Edited for executives in marketing, sales, and business development.

TELEPHONE ANSWERING SERVICE
2392 Morse Ave.
Irvine, CA 92714

PH: (800)421-2300
FX: (714)851-9088
Entrepreneur, Inc. Looseleaf. $59.50. A practical guide to starting a telephone answering service. Covers profit potential, start-up costs, market size evaluation, owner's time required, pricing, accounting, advertising, promotion, etc. (Start-Up Business Guide No. E1148).

TELEPHONE INDUSTRY DIRECTORY
1201 Seven Locks Rd., Suite 300
Potomac, MD 20854
PH: (800)777-5006
FX: (301)309-3847
Phillips Business Information, Inc. Annual. $249.00. Lists telecommunications carriers, equipment manufacturers, distributors, agencies, and organizations.

TELEPROFESSIONAL: EFFECTIVE MARKETING VIA TELECOMMUNICATIONS
209 West Fifth St., Suite N
Waterloo, IA 50701-5402
PH: (888)835-3776
FX: (319)235-9850
TeleProfessional, Inc. Monthly. $39.00 per year. Emphasis is on business use of in-house call centers. Includes special features on telecommuting ("Telecommuting, It's Here to Stay").

TELESELLING: A SELF-TEACHING GUIDE
605 Third Ave.
New York, NY 10158-0012
PH: (800)225-5945
FX: (212)850-6088
E-mail: business@jwiley.com
URL: http://www.wiley.com
James D. Porterfield. John Wiley and Sons, Inc. 1996. $16.95. Second edition. Provides practical information and advice on selling by telephone, including strategy, prospecting, script development, and performance evaluation.

TELEVISION DIGEST WITH CONSUMER ELECTRONICS
2115 Ward Court, N. W.
Washington, DC 20037
PH: (202)872-9200
FX: (202)293-3435
E-mail: warrenpub@interramp.com
Warren Publishing, Inc. Weekly. $918.00 per year. Newsletter featuring new consumer entertainment products utilizing electronics. Also covers the television broadcasting and cable TV industries, with corporate and industry news.

THOMAS REGISTER OF AMERICAN MANUFACTURERS AND THOMAS REGISTER CATALOG FILE
Five Penn Plaza
250 W. 34th St.
New York, NY 10001
PH: (800)699-9822
FX: (212)290-7365
URL: http://www.thomasregister.com
Thomas Publishing Co., Inc. Annual. $240.00. 33 volumes. A three-part system offering information on a wide variety of industrial equipment and supplies.

TPG BRIEFING ON LOCAL EXCHANGE STATISTICS
2115 Ward Court, N. W.
Washington, DC 20037-1209
PH: (202)872-9200
FX: (202)293-3435
E-mail: info@telecommunications.com
URL: http://www.telecommunications.com
Warren Publishing, Inc., Telecom Publishing Group. Annual. $325.00. Contains statistics on local telephone companies: revenues, expenses, debt, income, advertising, access lines, network usage, etc. Provides "Current Information on Major Competitors."

TRADE & INDUSTRY INDEX
Gale Group
27500 Drake Rd
Farmington Hills, MI 48331-3535
PH: (800)877-GALE
FX: (800)414-5043
E-mail: galeord@gale.com
URL: http://www.galegroup.com
Formerly published by Information Access Co. Provides indexing of business periodicals, January 1981 to date. Daily updates. (Full text articles from some periodicals are available online, 1983 to date, in the companion database, *Trade & Industry ASAP*.) Inquire as to on-line cost and availability.

TRANSPORTATION AND PUBLIC UTILITIES U.S.A.
Gale Group
27500 Drake Rd
Farmington Hills, MI 48331-3535
PH: (800)877-GALE
FX: (800)414-5043
E-mail: galeord@gale.com
URL: http://www.galegroup.com
1998. $199.00. Provides comprehensive statistical data and precalculated ratios for U. S. transportation industries and utilities, including the communications sector.

TV AND CABLE SOURCE
1700 Higgins Rd.
Des Plaines, IL 60018
PH: (800)851-7737
FX: (847)375-5001
URL: http://www.srds.com
SRDS. Quarterly. $380.00 per year. Provides detailed information on U. S. television stations, cable systems, networks, and group owners, with maps and market data. Includes key personnel.

TWICE: THIS WEEK IN CONSUMER ELECTRONICS
245 West 17th St.
New York, NY 10011-5300
PH: (800)662-7776
FX: (212)337-7066
E-mail: marketaccess@cahners.com
URL: http://www.cahners.com
Cahners Publishing Co. 29 times a year. $90.00 per year. Free to qualified personnel. Contains marketing and manufacturing news relating to a wide variety of consumer electronic products, including video, audio, telephone, and home office equipment.

U. S. INDUSTRY AND TRADE OUTLOOK
1221 Ave. of the Americas
New York, NY 10020
PH: (800)722-4726
FX: (212)512-2821
E-mail: customer.service@mcgraw-hill.com
URL: http://www.mcgraw-hill.com
McGraw-Hill. Annual. $69.95. Produced by the International Trade Administration, U. S. Department of Commerce, in a "public-private" partnership with DRI/McGraw-Hill and Standard & Poor's. Provides basic data, outlook for the current year, and "Long-Term Prospects" (five-year projections) for a wide variety of products and services. Includes high technology industries. Formerly *U. S. Industrial Outlook*.

UNDERGROUND GUIDE TO TELECOMMUTING:
   SLIGHTLY ASKEW ADVICE ON LEAVING THE RAT
   RACE BEHIND
One Jacob Way
Reading, MA 01867
PH: (800)447-2226
FX: (617)944-9351
URL: http://www.aw.com
Woody Leonhard. Addison-Wesley Longman, Inc. 1995. $24.95. Provides advice on hardware, software, telecommunications, zoning, taxes, mail, and other topics for telecommuters.

VIRTUAL OFFICE SURVIVAL HANDBOOK: WHAT
   TELECOMMUTERS AND ENTREPRENEURS NEED TO
   SUCCEED IN TODAY'S NONTRADITIONAL
   WORKPLACE
605 Third Ave.
New York, NY 10158-0012
PH: (800)225-5945
FX: (212)850-6088
E-mail: business@jwiley.com
URL: http://www.wiley.com
Alice Breden. John Wiley and Sons, Inc. 1996. $34.95. Presents broad coverage of telecommuting considerations, including workplace customizing and the evaluation of electronic office equipment. Coping with distractions and psychological issues are discussed.

WARREN'S CABLE REGULATION MONITOR: THE
   AUTHORITATIVE WEEKLY NEWS SERVICE COVERING
   FEDERAL, STATE, AND LOCAL CABLE ACTIVITIES
   AND TRENDS
2115 Ward Court, N. W.
Washington, DC 20037-1209
PH: (202)872-9200
FX: (202)293-3435
E-mail: info@telecommunications.com
URL: http://www.telecommunications.com
Warren Publishing, Inc., Telecom Publishing Group. Weekly. $594.00 per year. Newsletter. Emphasis is on Federal Communications Commission regulations affecting cable television systems. Covers rate increases made by local systems and cable subscriber complaints filed with the FCC.

WEFA INDUSTRIAL MONITOR
605 Third Ave.
New York, NY 10158-0012
PH: (800)225-5945
FX: (212)850-6088
E-mail: business@jwiley.
URL: http://www.wiley.com
John Wiley and Sons, Inc. Annual. $59.95. Prepared by industry analysts at WEFA, an economic forecasting and consulting firm (originally Wharton Econometric Forecasting Associates). Contains discussions of the outlook for major U. S. industries, with many 10-year forecasts (WEFA Web site is http://www.wefa.com).

WHAT WILL BE: HOW THE NEW WORLD OF
   INFORMATION WILL CHANGE OUR LIVES
10 East 53rd St.
New York, NY 10022-5299
PH: (800)331-3761
FX: (212)207-7145
URL: http://www.harpercollins.com
Michael L. Dertouzos. HarperCollins Publishers, Inc. 1997. $25.00. A discussion of the "information market place" of the future, including telecommuting, virtual reality, and computer recognition of speech. The author is director of the MIT Laboratory for Computer Science. (Harper Edge, San Francisco.)

WIRED NEIGHBORHOOD
302 Temple St.
New Haven, CT 06511
PH: (800)987-7323
FX: (203)432-0948
E-mail: yupmkt@yalevm.cls.yale.edu
URL: http://www.yale.edu/yup
Stephen Doheny-Farina. Yale University Press. 1996. $25.00. The author examines both the hazards and the advantages of "making the computer the center of our public and private lives," as exemplified by the Internet and telecommuting.

WIRED NEWS
PH: (415)276-5000
FX: (415)276-5100
E-mail: newsfeedback@wired.com
URL: http://www.wired.com

HotWired, Inc. Provides summaries and full-text of "Top Stories" relating to the Internet, computers, multimedia, telecommunications, and the electronic information industry in general. These news stories are placed in the broad categories of Politics, Business, Culture, and Technology. Affiliated with *Wired* magazine. Fees: Free.

WIRELESS AND CABLE VOICE SERVICES: FORECASTS AND COMPETITIVE IMPACTS
13740 Research Blvd., Ste. C-1
Austin, TX 78750-1859
PH: (800)835-3887
FX: (512)258-0087
E-mail: info@tfi.com
URL: http://www.tfi.com
Lawrence K. Vanston and Curt Rogers. Technology Futures, Inc. 1995. $495.00. Sponsored by the Telecommunications Technology Forecasting Group (telephone companies). Includes forecast data for prices, demand, and competitive factors.

WIRELESS DATA NETWORKS
2115 Ward Court, N. W.
Washington, DC 20037-1209
PH: (202)872-9200
FX: (202)293-3435
E-mail: info@telecommunications.com
URL: http://www.telecommunications.com
Warren Publishing, Inc., Telecom Publishing Group. 1998. $1,995.00. Fourth edition. Presents market research information relating to cellular data networks, paging networks, packet radio networks, satellite systems, and other areas of wireless communication. Contains "summaries of recent developments and trends in wireless markets."

WIRELESS WEEK
600 South Cherry St., Suite 400
Denver, CO 80222
PH: (303)393-7449
FX: (303)399-2034
URL: http://www.chiltonco.com
Chilton Co. Weekly. $60.00 per year. Covers news of cellular telephones, mobile radios, communications satellites, microwave transmission, and the wireless industry in general.

YELLOW PAGES AND DIRECTORY REPORT: THE NEWSLETTER FOR THE DIRECTORY PUBLISHING INDUSTRY
Post Office Box 4234
Stamford, CT 06907-0234
PH: (800)307-2529
FX: (203)358-5824
E-mail: info@simbanet.com
URL: http://www.simbanet.com
SIMBA Information, Inc. Semimonthly. $549.00 per year. Newsletter. Covers the yellow pages publishing industry, including electronic directory publishing, directory advertising, and special interest directories.

Information presented in this chapter is adapted from Gale's *Trade Shows Worldwide* (*TSW*) or, where appropriate, from Gale's *Encyclopedia of Associations* (industry conferences). Entries present information needed for all those planning to visit or to participate in trade shows for the Broadcasting & Telecommunications sector. *TSW* entries include U.S. and international shows and exhibitions as well as companies, organizations, and information sources relating to the trade industry. Events, such as conferences and conventions, are included only if they feature exhibitions.

Entries are arranged in alphabetical order by the name of the event and include the exhibition management company with full contact information, frequency of the event, audience, principal exhibits, dates and locations, and former name of the show (if applicable).

AAR ANNUAL CONVENTION AND EXHIBIT
10507 Timberwood Cir., Ste. 208
Louisville, KY 40223-5313
Frequency: Annual. **Audience:** Trade professionals. **Principal Exhibits:** Railroad signal and communication equipment.

ACQUISITIONS
600 Harrison St.
San Francisco, CA 94107
PH: (415)905-2200
TF: (800)227-4675
FX: (415)905-2232
URL: http://www.mfi.com
Principal Exhibits: Electronics communications. **Held in conjunction with:** Data Acquisition Conference and Expo ; International Conference on Signal Processing Applications & Technology, DSP World Expo.

AFCEA EUROPEAN SYMPOSIUM AND EXPOSITION
4400 Fair Lakes Ct.
Fairfax, VA 22033
PH: (703)631-6200
TF: (800)336-4583
FX: (703)818-9177
E-mail: info@jspargo.com
URL: http://jspargo.com
Frequency: Annual. **Audience:** Personnel who engineer, procure, manage, operate, and maintain communications, computer, and command and control equipment. **Principal Exhibits:** Antennas, avionics equipment, communications components and systems, computers, fiber optics, graphics equipment, high-frequency radios, microwave systems, power supplies, radar systems, satellites, software, telecommunications equipment, word processing equipment, and related products.

AFCEA TECHNET ASIA PACIFIC - ARMED FORCES COMMUNICATIONS AND ELECTRONICS ASSOCIATION
4400 Fair Lakes Ct.
Fairfax, VA 22033
PH: (703)631-6200
TF: (800)336-4583
FX: (703)818-9177
E-mail: info@jspargo.com
URL: http://jspargo.com
Frequency: Annual. **Audience:** Military, government, and industry communications and electronics professionals. **Principal Exhibits:** Communications and electronics equipment, supplies, and services.

AFRICA TELECOM
Place des Nations
CH-1211 Geneva, Switzerland
PH: 41 22 730 6161
FX: 41 22 730 6444
URL: http://www.itu.int/TELECOM
Frequency: Quadrennial. **Audience:** Trade professionals. **Principal Exhibits:** Telecommunications equipment, supplies, and services, including video terminals, high definition television, receivers for direct broadcasting satellite TV, broadcast transmitters and receivers, graphic art application, and interactive television systems for educational, medical, and information service applications.

AMERICAN TRANSLATORS ASSOCIATION ANNUAL CONFERENCE
1800 Diagonal Rd., Ste. 220
Alexandria, VA 22314-2840
PH: (703)683-6100
FX: (703)683-6122
E-mail: ata@atanet.org
URL: http://www.atanet.org
Frequency: Annual. **Audience:** Translators and interpreters. **Principal Exhibits:** Publications, software and services. **Dates and Locations:** 2000 Oct; Orlando, FL.

AMERICAS TELECOM
Place des Nations
CH-1211 Geneva, Switzerland
PH: 41 22 730 6161
FX: 41 22 730 6444
URL: http://www.itu.int/TELECOM
Frequency: Quadrennial. **Audience:** Trade professionals. **Principal Exhibits:** Telecommunications equipment, supplies and services, including video terminals, high definition television, receivers for direct broadcasting satellite TV, cable TV, broadcast transmitters and receivers, graphic art application, and interactive television systems for educational, medical, and information service applications. **Formerly:** Europa Telecom.

ANTENNES ET COLLECTIVES RESEAUX - CABLE AND SATELLITE TRADE SHOW
383 Main Ave.
PO Box 6059
Norwalk, CT 06851
PH: (203)840-5358
FX: (203)840-4804
E-mail: inquiry@nepcon.reedexpo.com
Frequency: Annual. **Audience:** Manufacturers, importers, distributors and service companies. **Principal Exhibits:** Communication, broadcasting and television.

APCC - ASIA-PACIFIC CONFERENCE ON COMMUNICATIONS
118 Alfred St., Level 1
PO Box 495
Milsons Point, NSW 1565, Australia
PH: 61 2 9929 0099
FX: 61 2 9929 0587
E-mail: ireeoffice@ozemail.com.au
Frequency: Annual. **Principal Exhibits:** Communications technology, equipment, supplies, and services. **Incorporating:** ACOFT - Australian Conference on Optical Fibre Technology; ATNAC - Australian Telecommunication Networks and Applications Conference.

ASCB - ASIA CABLE, SATELLITE, AND BROADCAST EXHIBITION AND CONFERENCE
Level 21, 19A-21-2, UOA Centre
19 Jalan Pinang
50450 Kuala Lumpur, Malaysia
PH: 60 3 264 5663
FX: 60 2 264 5660
Frequency: Annual. **Principal Exhibits:** Audio equipment; broadcast systems; cable digital, audio, and recording systems and equipment; satellite and electronics communication services.

ASIA COMMUNITECH/ASIA WIRELESS - THE ASIAN TELECOMMUNICATIONS, MOBILE COMMUNICATIONS & WIRELESS TECHNOLOGY SHOW & CONFERENCE
Units 901-902, 9/F Shiu Lam Bldg.
23 Luard Rd.
Wanchai, Hong Kong
PH: 852 2804 1500
FX: 852 2528 3103
E-mail: exhibit@hkesmontnet.com.hk
Frequency: Biennial. **Principal Exhibits:** Telecommunications.

ASIA-PACIFIC BROADCASTING UNION GENERAL ASSEMBLY
Pejabat Pos Jalan Pantai Bahru
PO Box 1164
59700 Kuala Lumpur, Malaysia
PH: 60 3 2822480
FX: 60 3 2825292
E-mail: sg@abu.org.my
Frequency: Annual. **Principal Exhibits:** Exhibits for the study of problems related to broadcasting.

ASIA TELECOM
Place des Nations
CH-1211 Geneva, Switzerland
PH: 41 22 730 6161
FX: 41 22 730 6444
URL: http://www.itu.int/TELECOM
Frequency: Quadrennial. **Audience:** Trade professionals. **Principal Exhibits:** Telecommunications equipment, supplies, and services, including video terminals, high definition televisions, receivers for direct broadcasting satellite TV, broadcast transmitters and receivers, graphic art application, and interactive television systems for educational, medical, and information service applicants. **Dates and Locations:** 2001.

ASSOCIATION OF COLLEGE AND UNIVERSITY TELECOMMUNICATIONS ADMINISTRATORS CONFERENCE
152 W Zandale Dr., Ste. 200
Lexington, KY 40503
PH: (606)278-3338
FX: (606)278-3268
URL: http://www.acuta.org
Frequency: Annual. **Audience:** Senior managers of Telecom/MIS from colleges and universities in North America. **Principal Exhibits:** Educational telecommunications equipment, supplies, and services. **Dates and Locations:** Nashville, TN • 2000 Jul 30 - Aug 03; Washington, DC.

ASSOCIATION OF PUBLIC SAFETY OFFICIALS CONFERENCE AND EXPOSITION
2040 S. Ridgewood Ave.
Daytona Beach, FL 32119
PH: (904)322-2500
TF: (888)APCO-911
FX: (904)323-2501
E-mail: apco@apcointl.org
URL: http://www.apcointl.org
Frequency: Annual. **Audience:** Trade professionals. **Principal Exhibits:** Equipment, supplies, and services for public safety communications.

ATLANTIC CABLE SHOW
6900 Grove Rd.
Thorofare, NJ 08086
PH: (609)848-1000
FX: (609)848-3522
Frequency: Annual. **Audience:** Chief executives manager, engineers technicians, marketing managers, programmers, and suppliers in the cable industry. **Principal Exhibits:** Cable related services.

ATUG - AUSTRALIAN TELECOMMUNICATIONS EXHIBITION & CONFERENCE
Riddell House
137 Burnley St.
Richmond, VIC 3121, Australia
PH: 3 9429 6088
FX: 3 9427 0829
Frequency: Annual. **Audience:** Business operators and related professionals. **Principal Exhibits:** Telephone, telegraph and data switching, line transmission, radio transmission, data processing systems and networks, terminal equipment, design, planning, construction, installation, ancillary equipment and service calls, and electronic instrumentation. **Formerly:** Australian Telecommunications Exhibition & Conference.

AUVICOM - INTERNATIONAL AUDIO, VIDEO, AND COMMUNICATIONS SHOW
Rua Brasilio Machado, 60
01230-905 Sao Paulo, SP, Brazil
PH: 55 11 8269111
FX: 55 11 8256043
E-mail: amfp@alcantara.com.br
URL: http://www.alcantara.com.br
Frequency: Annual. **Audience:** Trade professionals. **Principal Ex-**

hibits: Audio and video equipment, supplies, and services; communications and telecommunications equipment, supplies, and services.

AV AND BROADCAST CHINA - INTERNATIONAL AUDIOVISUAL AND BROADCASTING EQUIPMENT EXHIBITION FOR CHINA
Unit 1223, 12/F, Hong Kong International Trade & Exhibition
1 Trademart Dr.
Kowloon Bay, Hong Kong
PH: 852 2865 2633
FX: 852 2866 1770
Frequency: Semiannual. **Audience:** Trade professionals. **Principal Exhibits:** Broadcasting, and TV equipment; lighting; cinema, theater, stage, and processing equipment. **Held in conjunction with:** CATV CHINA.

BAKU TELECOMMUNICATIONS EXHIBITION
Byron House
112A Shirland Rd.
London W9 EQ, England
PH: 44 171 286 9720
FX: 44 171 266 1126
E-mail: healthcare@ITE-Group.com
Principal Exhibits: Telecommunications exhibition.

BITE - INTERNATIONAL COMPUTER AND COMMUNICATION SHOW
Heidenkampsweg 51
D-20097 Hamburg, Germany
PH: 040 235240
FX: 040 2352 4400
URL: http://www.gima.de
Frequency: Annual. **Principal Exhibits:** Computer equipment, supplies, and services.

BKSTS - BRITISH KINEMATOGRAPH, SOUND, AND TELEVISION SOCIETY -INTERNATIONAL FILM AND TELEVISION TECHNOLOGY CONFERENCE AND EXHIBIT
547-549 Victoria House
Vernon Pl.
London WC1B 4DJ, England
PH: 71 2428400
FX: 71 4053560
Frequency: Biennial. **Principal Exhibits:** Film, television, and video industry equipment.

BROADCAST CABLE FINANCIAL MANAGEMENT ASSOCIATION CONFERENCE
701 Lee St., Ste. 640
Des Plaines, IL 60016
PH: (847)296-0200
FX: (847)296-7510
URL: http://www.bcfm.com
Frequency: Annual. **Audience:** Business managers, CFO's. **Principal Exhibits:** Exhibits relating to the financial management of radio, television, and cable television operations, including issues such as film amortization, purchase order forms, music license fees, and salary and fringe benefits.

BROADCAST - INTERNATIONAL RADIO AND TELEVISION EQUIPMENT EXHIBITION
PO Box 67067
Parque Ferial Juan Carlos I
28067 Madrid, Spain
PH: 34 1 722 5000
FX: 34 1 722 5788
URL: http://www.arco.sei.es.
Frequency: Biennial. **Audience:** Trade professionals. **Principal Exhibits:** Radio and television equipment, audio and video facilities, cable and satellite TV equipment, multimedia for broadcasting, broadcasting management applications, computer graphics, and audio and video telecommunications.

BROADCAST ISTANBUL
Mim Kemal Oke Cad, No. 10 Nisantasi
TR-80200 Istanbul, Turkey
PH: 212 2250920
FX: 212 2250933
Frequency: Annual. **Principal Exhibits:** Radio and TV equipment, professional audio-visual applications, program production, and cable and satellite technology and services.

BROADCOM/ABU DHABI - INTERNATIONAL COMMUNICATIONS, BROADCASTING, & STUDIO PRODUCTION SHOW
PO Box 2460
Germantown, MD 20875-2460
PH: (301)515-0012
FX: (301)515-0016
E-mail: glahe@glahe.com
Frequency: Biennial. **Audience:** Trade professionals. **Principal Exhibits:** Defense electronics, navigational aids, planning, construction, antenna systems, broadcasting equipment, data communications, and mobile communications.

BTV CHINA - INTERNATIONAL BROADCASTING, TELEVISION EQUIPMENT, AND TECHNOLOGY EXHIBITION FOR CHINA
Unit 1223, 12/F, Hong Kong International Trade & Exhibition
1 Trademart Dr.
Kowloon Bay, Hong Kong
PH: 852 2865 2633
FX: 852 2866 1770
Frequency: Annual. **Principal Exhibits:** Audio, Video, and RF equipment, supplies, and services for the broadcasting industry.

CABLE & SATELLITE ASIA: THE ASIAN BROADCASTING AND COMMUNICATIONS SHOW
19/F, 8 Commercial Tower
8 Sun Yip St.
Chaiwan, Hong Kong
PH: 2824 0330
FX: 2824 0246
Frequency: Annual. **Principal Exhibits:** Cable and satellite equipment, supplies, and services.

CABLE AND SATELLITE UK
Frequency: Annual. **Audience:** Cable and satellite operators, retailers, distributors, and engineers. **Principal Exhibits:** Direct to home (DTH) systems, CATV, decoders, switching, SMATV, TVRO systems, satellite uplink facilities, installation equipment, and accessories.

CABLE-TEC EXPO
140 Philips Rd.
Exton, PA 19341-1316
PH: (610)363-6888
TF: (800)542-5040
FX: (610)363-5898
Frequency: Annual. **Audience:** Cable television engineers and technicians. **Principal Exhibits:** Equipment, supplies, and services for cable television engineering.

CABLE TV ADVERTISING BUREAU - CABLE ADVERTISING CONFERENCE
830 3rd Ave., 2nd Fl.
New York, NY 10022
PH: (212)508-1200
FX: (212)832-3268
URL: http://www.cabletvadbureau.com
Frequency: Annual. **Audience:** Cable television and advertising trade. **Principal Exhibits:** Advertising-supported cable television networks; services to support local advertising sales.

CABLESATASIA - ASIAN INTERNATIONAL TRADE SHOWCASE FOR CABLE & SATELLITE TECHNOLOGY & SERVICES
2 Handy Rd.
15-09 Cathay Bldg.
Singapore 229233, Singapore
PH: 65 3384747
FX: 65 3395651
E-mail: info@sesmontnet.com
URL: http://www.sesmontnet.com
Frequency: Biennial. **Principal Exhibits:** Equipment, supplies, and services for cable & satellite technology.

CALL CENTER CONFERENCE & EXPOSITION
201 E. Sandpointe Ave., Ste. 600
Santa Ana, CA 92707-5761
PH: (714)513-8400
TF: (800)854-3112
FX: (714)513-8481
URL: http://www.advanstar-expos.com
Frequency: Annual. **Audience:** Managers of call centers, customer service and telemarketing operations, help desks, direct-marketing agencies, telcos, and other call intensive organizations. **Principal Exhibits:** Companies offering stand-alone and/or integrated products and services that improve call center productivity and profitability.

CANADIAN ASSOCIATION OF BROADCASTERS
PO Box 627 Station B
Ottawa, ON, Canada K1R 5S2
PH: (613)233-4035
FX: (613)233-6961
E-mail: sylvleb@cab-acr.ca
URL: http://www.ottawa.net./~cabl
Frequency: Annual. **Principal Exhibits:** Broadcasting equipment, supplies, and services.

CANADIAN CABLE TELEVISION ASSOCIATION CONVENTION AND CABLEXPO
360 Albert St., Ste. 1010
Ottawa, ON, Canada K1R 7X7
PH: (613)232-2631
FX: (613)232-2137
Frequency: Annual. **Audience:** Cable licensees, equipment suppliers, regulators, and federal and provincial government representatives. **Principal Exhibits:** Cable television equipment, supplies, and services, including hardware/software for cable television, and satellite head-end equipment; distribution systems, studio equipment, and converter and signal encoding and decoding equipment.

CANADIAN WIRELESS
500-275 Slater Street
Ottawa, ON, Canada K1P 5H9
PH: (613)233-4888
FX: (613)233-2032
URL: http://www.cwta.ca
Frequency: Annual. **Audience:** Buyers of wireless telecommunication products and services. **Principal Exhibits:** Cellular telephones, paging systems, mobile data systems, and personal communication services, LMCS, ESMR, Satellite Communications. **Dates and Locations:** 2000 Jun 06-08; Toronto, ON. **Formerly:** RADIOCOMM.

CATV CHINA - INTERNATIONAL CABLE TV AND EQUIPMENT EXHIBITION FOR CHINA
Unit 1223, 12/F, Hong Kong International Trade & Exhibition
1 Trademart Dr.
Kowloon Bay, Hong Kong
PH: 852 2865 2633
FX: 852 2866 1770
Frequency: Biennial. **Audience:** Trade professionals. **Principal Exhibits:** Equipment, supplies, and services for the Cable-TV industry. **Held in conjunction with:** AV Broadcast China.

CEBIT - WORLD BUSINESS CENTER FOR OFFICE, INFORMATION, AND TELECOMMUNICATIONS TECHNOLOGY
Messegelande
D-30521 Hannover, Germany
PH: 511 89 32116
FX: 511 893 3126
URL: http://www.messe.de
Frequency: Annual. **Audience:** Trade professionals; general public. **Principal Exhibits:** Computer peripherals, software, OEM products, communications equipment and services, office products, satellites, video equipment, computers, CAD/CAM, and banking equipment, supplies, and services.

CMA TELCOM
19 Mantua Rd.
Mount Royal, NJ 08061
PH: (609)423-7222
TF: (800)262-3976
FX: (609)423-3420
Frequency: Annual. **Audience:** Voice, data, and image specialists, telecommunications and information managers, industry consultants, and related communications professionals. **Principal Exhibits:** Telecommunications equipment, supplies, and services.

COM-P.A. - EXHIBITION OF PUBLIC COMMUNICATION SYSTEMS AND COMMUNITY SERVICES
Via Tagliapietre, 18/B
I-40123 Bologna, Italy
PH: 51 331466
FX: 51 333804
Frequency: Annual. **Principal Exhibits:** Citizen information equipment, supplies, and services, including audiovisual equipment, data processing centers, computer technology, research institutes, and telecommunication.

COMBRAZIL - INTERNATIONAL COMMUNICATIONS EXHIBITION
Byron House
112A Shirland Rd.
London W9 EQ, England
PH: 44 171 286 9720
FX: 44 171 266 1126
E-mail: healthcare@ITE-Group.com
Principal Exhibits: Communication exhibition.

COMDEX/EGYPT
PO Box 28943
Dubai, United Arab Emirates
PH: 9714 365161
FX: 9714 360137
E-mail: iirx@emirates.net.ae
Frequency: Biennial. **Principal Exhibits:** Computer, telecommunications, and office equipment.

COMDEX/RIO - COMPUTING AND TELECOMMUNICATIONS INFORMATION TECHNOLOGY CONFERENCE AND PROFESSIONAL EXPOSITION
Al. Rio Negro, 433
Predio I
3 andar
06454-904 Barueri, SP, Brazil
PH: 55 11 7291 0440
FX: 55 11 7291 0660
E-mail: guafair@guazzelli.com.br
URL: http://www.guazzelli.com.br
Frequency: Annual. **Principal Exhibits:** Peripherals, supplies, and services for computers and telecommunications.

COMEXPO/ARGENTINA - INTERNATIONAL TELECOMMUNICATIONS EXHIBITION OF ARGENTINA
200 N. Glebe Rd., Ste. 900
Arlington, VA 22203

PH: (703)527-8000
FX: (703)527-8006
E-mail: micexpos@aol.com
Frequency: Annual. **Audience:** Trade and general public. **Principal Exhibits:** Computer equipment and telecommunications systems.

COMEXPO/VENEZUELA - INTERNATIONAL COMMUNICATIONS EXPO/VENEZUELA
200 N. Glebe Rd., Ste. 900
Arlington, VA 22203
PH: (703)527-8000
FX: (703)527-8006
E-mail: micexpos@aol.com
Frequency: Biennial. **Principal Exhibits:** Computer and telecommunications equipment, systems, and supplies.

COMISAT EXPO
C. so palladio, 114
36100 Vicenza, Italy
PH: 0444 543133
FX: 0444 543466
URL: http://www.comisatexpo.it
Frequency: Annual. **Audience:** Installers of satellite and cable television. **Principal Exhibits:** Satellite operators, data bases, parabolic antennas, receivers, coaxial cables equipment, supplies, and services.

COMJAPAN
Sankei Bldg., Annex
Chiyoda-ku
1-7-2 Ohte-machi
Tokyo 100, Japan
PH: 3 32313002
FX: 3 32313110
URL: http://www.ciaj.or.jp
Frequency: Annual. **Audience:** Policy makers and buying agents from government and private industry in Japan and surrounding Asian nations. **Principal Exhibits:** Telecommunications equipment, systems, and services, computers equipment, systems and software. **Formerly:** Communications Tokyo.

COMMTEL CHINA - INTERNATIONAL TELECOMMUNICATIONS EQUIPMENT, TECHNOLOGIES, AND SERVICES EXHIBITION FOR CHINA
Unit 1223, 12/F, Hong Kong International Trade & Exhibition
1 Trademart Dr.
Kowloon Bay, Hong Kong
PH: 852 2865 2633
FX: 852 2866 1770
Frequency: Annual. **Principal Exhibits:** Telecommunications equipment and technologies.

COMMUNIC PHILIPPINES - INTERNATIONAL ELECTRONIC COMMUNICATIONS & INFORMATION TECHNOLOGY EXHIBITION
Room 909, 9th Floor
Sen. Gil Puyat Avenue, corner Urban Ave.
PS Bank Tower
Makati City 1200, Philippines
PH: 632 759 3263
FX: 632 759 3228
E-mail: piecinc@portalink.com
Frequency: Biennial. **Principal Exhibits:** Electronic communications & information technology.

COMMUNICASIA - ASIAN INTERNATIONAL INFORMATION AND COMMUNICATION TECHNOLOGY EXHIBITION AND CONFERENCE
2 Handy Rd.
15-09 Cathay Bldg.
Singapore 229233, Singapore

PH: 65 3384747
FX: 65 3395651
E-mail: info@sesmontnet.com
URL: http://www.sesmontnet.com
Frequency: Biennial. **Audience:** Communications trade professionals. **Principal Exhibits:** Telecommunication equipment, systems, and services for private and public networks, including intercoms, security and paging systems, and broadcasting equipment. **Held in conjunction with:** Mobile CommAsia; Networking Asia.

**COMMUNICATION DESIGN ENGINEERING
  CONFERENCE**
600 Harrison St.
San Francisco, CA 94107
PH: (415)905-2200
TF: (800)227-4675
FX: (415)905-2232
URL: http://www.mfi.com
Frequency: Annual. **Principal Exhibits:** Hardware designs of communication equipment.

**COMMUNICATIONS - ISTANBUL INTERNATIONAL
  TELECOMMUNICATIONS, MOBILE
  COMMUNICATIONS, AND NETWORK TECHNOLOGY
  FAIR**
Mim Kemal Oke Cad, No. 10 Nisantasi
TR-80200 Istanbul, Turkey
PH: 212 2250920
FX: 212 2250933
Frequency: Annual. **Audience:** Trade professionals. **Principal Exhibits:** Electronic communications equipment, supplies, and services.

**COMMUNICATIONS TECHNOLOGY INDONESIA -
  INTERNATIONAL TELECOMMUNICATIONS AND
  BUSINESS COMMUNICATIONS SYSTEMS EXHIBITION**
Deutsche Bank Bldg.
Jl. Imam Bonjol 80
13th Fl
10310 Jakarta, Indonesia
PH: 62 0 21 3162001
FX: 62 0 21 3161981
E-mail: pamindo@rad.net.id
Frequency: Biennial. **Principal Exhibits:** Antennas, broadcasting equipment, business computing equipment, cellular mobile telephone systems, and optical fiber transmission. **Held in conjunction with:** Broadcast Technology Indonesia.

COMNET PRAGUE
111 Speen St., Ste. 415
PO Box 9107
Framingham, MA 01701-9107
PH: (508)879-6700
TF: (800)545-EXPO
FX: (508)872-8237
Frequency: Annual. **Audience:** Buyers of WAN services & products, network computing and LAN communications, and government, manufacturing, corporate and usually communities. **Principal Exhibits:** Communications equipment, supplies, publications, and services. **Dates and Locations:** 2000 Jan; Washington, DC • 2001 Jan; Washington, DC • 2002 Jan; Washington, DC • 2003 Jan; Washington, DC • 2004 Jan; Washington, DC • 2005 Jan; Washington, DC.

COMPUTER, TELECOM EXPO
1 Maritime Sq., No. 09-43
World Trade Centre, Lobby B
Singapore 099253, Singapore
PH: 65 2788666
FX: 65 2784077
E-mail: cemssvs@singnet.com.sg
URL: http://www.cems-sg.com
Frequency: Annual. **Principal Exhibits:** Computers and telecommunication systems.

CONNECT
PO Box 318
450080 Ufa, Russia
PH: 3472 525386
FX: 3472 525593
Frequency: Annual. **Principal Exhibits:** Communication and telecommunication equipment, supplies, and services.

**DIGITAL MEDIA WORLD BERLIN - INTERNATIONAL
  TRADE FAIR FOR DIGITAL INFORMATION,
  COMMUNICATION, AND INTERACTION**
Messedamm 22
D-14055 Berlin, Germany
PH: 49 30 3038 0
FX: 49 30 3038 2325
E-mail: marketing@messe-berlin.de
URL: http://www.messe-berlin.de
Frequency: Biennial. **Principal Exhibits:** Equipment, supplies, and services for digital information and communication.

**DSP WORLD EXPOSITION AND THE DATA ACQUISITION
  CONFERENCE & EXPO**
600 Harrison St.
San Francisco, CA 94107
PH: (415)905-2200
TF: (800)227-4675
FX: (415)905-2232
URL: http://www.mfi.com
Frequency: Annual. **Principal Exhibits:** Hardware and software tools.

DSP WORLD SPRING DESIGN CONFERENCE
600 Harrison St.
San Francisco, CA 94107
PH: (415)905-2200
TF: (800)227-4675
FX: (415)905-2232
URL: http://www.mfi.com
Frequency: Annual. **Principal Exhibits:** Digital signal processing and communication.

**EASTERN CABLE TELEVISION TRADE SHOW AND
  CONVENTION**
6175 Barfield Rd., Ste. 220
Atlanta, GA 30328
PH: (404)252-2454
FX: (404)252-0215
Frequency: Annual. **Audience:** Cable system operators and investors. **Principal Exhibits:** Cable television industry equipment, supplies, and services.

**ECTB - THE INTERNATIONAL ELECTRONICS,
  COMPUTERS, TELECOMMUNICATIONS AND
  BROADCASTING TECHNOLOGY EXPO FOR CHINA**
Unit 1223, 12/F, Hong Kong International Trade & Exhibition
1 Trademart Dr.
Kowloon Bay, Hong Kong
PH: 852 2865 2633
FX: 852 2866 1770
Principal Exhibits: Electronical equipment.

**ELECTRICAL ENGINEERING AND
  TELECOMMUNICATIONS IN BUILDING**
PO Box 127
FIN-40101 Jyvaskyla, Finland
PH: 3340000
FX: 610 272
Frequency: Annual. **Principal Exhibits:** Construction equipment, supplies, and services.

ELECTRONICS: INDUSTRIAL ELECTRONICS TRADE FAIR

Europaplein 8
PO Box 77777
1070 MS Amsterdam, Netherlands
PH: 20 5491212
FX: 20 6464469
E-mail: mail@rai.nl
Frequency: Biennial. **Principal Exhibits:** Parts, semi-conductors, integrated circuits and electron tubes, custom made IC's, components (standard and to measure); electronic measuring and test equipment; electro-acoustic equipment for industrial and scientific use; materials for telecommunication installations and electronic audio-visual equipment for professional purposes; computer hardware and software for the development of electronics; mechanical aids; supplies and tools for service and production purposes.

ELEKTRO EXPO

ul. Sniadeckich 10
00-656 Warsaw, Poland
PH: 022 621 17 55
FX: 022 29 96 71
Frequency: Annual. **Principal Exhibits:** Telecommunication, security systems, automatic systems, control, signaling, lighting technology and equipment, and electrical fittings and fixtures.

EMOTION

Europaplein 8
PO Box 77777
1070 MS Amsterdam, Netherlands
PH: 20 5491212
FX: 20 6464469
E-mail: mail@rai.nl
Frequency: Biennial. **Principal Exhibits:** Multimedia, video, audio, computer, and telecommunication equipment, supplies, and services.

ENER-NET

PO Box 163
FIN-33201 Tampere, Finland
PH: 358 3 2516 111
FX: 358 3 2123 888
E-mail: helpdesk@tampereenmessut.fi
URL: http://www.tampereenmessut.fi
Principal Exhibits: Electricity and telecommunications equipment, supplies, and services.

ENTELEC - ENERGY TELECOMMUNICATIONS AND ELECTRICAL ASSOCIATION

1001 W. Euless Blvd., Ste. 320
PO Box 279
Euless, TX 76039
PH: (817)255-8030
FX: (817)255-8066
Frequency: Annual. **Audience:** Telecommunications, technicians, management, and related personnel. **Principal Exhibits:** Telecommunications equipment, supplies, and services for the energy industry and related fields.

EUROPEAN TELEVISION AND FILM FORUM

Kaistrasse 13
40221 Dusseldorf, Germany
PH: 49 211 901040
FX: 49 211 9010456
E-mail: info@eim.org
URL: http://www.eim.org
Frequency: Annual. **Principal Exhibits:** Media equipment, supplies, and services.

EXPO COM - COMMUNICATION AND CORPORATE EVENTS.

97 rue du cherche midi
F-75006 Paris, France
PH: 01 44 39 85 00
FX: 01 45 44 30 40
E-mail: info@infopromotions.fr
URL: http://www.infopromotions.fr
Frequency: Annual. **Principal Exhibits:** Communication equipment.

EXPO COMM BRAZIL

6550 Rock Spring Dr., Ste. 500
Bethesda, MD 20817-1126
PH: (301)493-5500
FX: (301)493-5705
E-mail: ejkinfo@ejkrause.com
URL: http://www.ejkrause.com
Frequency: Annual. **Principal Exhibits:** Wireless technology.

EXPO COMM CHINA SOUTH

6550 Rock Spring Dr., Ste. 500
Bethesda, MD 20817-1126
PH: (301)493-5500
FX: (301)493-5705
E-mail: ejkinfo@ejkrause.com
URL: http://www.ejkrause.com
Frequency: Annual. **Principal Exhibits:** Telecommunications, wireless, networking and broadband communications technology.

EXPO COMM TELECOMMUNICACIONES MEXICO

Av. Homero 109-101
C.P. 11570
Col. Polanco
Mexico City, Mexico
PH: 525 531 3363
FX: 525 254 0077
Frequency: Annual. **Audience:** Trade professionals. **Principal Exhibits:** Telecommunications, computer, and office automation technology.

EXPO COMM TELECOMUNICACIONES ARGENTINA

6550 Rock Spring Dr., Ste. 500
Bethesda, MD 20817-1126
PH: (301)493-5500
FX: (301)493-5705
E-mail: ejkinfo@ejkrause.com
URL: http://www.ejkrause.com
Frequency: Annual. **Principal Exhibits:** Telecommunications, wireless and broadband technology.

EXPO COMM/WIRELESS HONG KONG

6550 Rock Spring Dr., Ste. 500
Bethesda, MD 20817-1126
PH: (301)493-5500
FX: (301)493-5705
E-mail: ejkinfo@ejkrause.com
URL: http://www.ejkrause.com
Frequency: Annual. **Principal Exhibits:** Telecommunications, computers, computer networking, and wireless technologies.

EXPO COMM AND WIRELESS JAPAN

6550 Rock Spring Dr., Ste. 500
Bethesda, MD 20817-1126
PH: (301)493-5500
FX: (301)493-5705
E-mail: ejkinfo@ejkrause.com
URL: http://www.ejkrause.com
Frequency: Annual. **Principal Exhibits:** Wireless technology.

EXPONET

Stockumer Kirchstrasse 61
PO Box 101006
D-40474 Dusseldorf, Germany
PH: 211 4560 01
FX: 211 4560 668
URL: http://messe.dus.tradefair.de
Principal Exhibits: Networking, telecommunications & computing.

FALL INTERNET WORLD
20 Ketchum St.
Westport, CT 06880
PH: (203)226-6967
FX: (203)454-5840
E-mail: international@mecklermedia.com
URL: http://events.iworld.com
Principal Exhibits: Internet, intranet and Web applications.

FASTENER, CABLE, AND WIRE KOREA -
INTERNATIONAL FASTENER, CABLE, AND WIRE
FINISHED PRODUCTS, PRODUCTION MACHINERY,
AND TECHNOLOGY
Unit 1223, 12/F, Hong Kong International Trade & Exhibition
1 Trademart Dr.
Kowloon Bay, Hong Kong
PH: 852 2865 2633
FX: 852 2866 1770
Frequency: Biennial. **Audience:** Trade professionals. **Principal Exhibits:** Fastener, cable, and wire, production machinery; fasteners and precision formed parts, and fastening and assembly systems.

FED NET
383 Main Ave.
PO Box 6059
Norwalk, CT 06851
PH: (203)840-5358
FX: (203)840-4804
E-mail: inquiry@nepcon.reedexpo.com
Frequency: Annual. **Audience:** Government professionals. **Principal Exhibits:** Internet/Intranet and EC Products equipment, supplies, and services.

FERA - THE WORLD OF ELECTRONICS
Wallisellenstrasse 49
CH-8050 Zurich, Switzerland
PH: 41 1 16 50 00
FX: 41 1 316 50 50
E-mail: messe-zuerich@messe-zuerich.com
URL: http://www.messe-zuerich.com
Frequency: Biennial. **Audience:** Trade and general public. **Principal Exhibits:** Consumer electronics and small computers.

FINANCIAL INFORMATION TECHNOLOGY
383 Main Ave.
PO Box 6059
Norwalk, CT 06851
PH: (203)840-5358
FX: (203)840-4804
E-mail: inquiry@nepcon.reedexpo.com
Frequency: Annual. **Audience:** Trade professionals. **Principal Exhibits:** Communications, EDI, safety, smartcards for the financial industry.

FORUM DES MEDIA ELECTRONIQUES - ELECTRONIC
AND MULTIMEDIA
97 rue du cherche midi
F-75006 Paris, France
PH: 01 44 39 85 00
FX: 01 45 44 30 40
E-mail: info@infopromotions.fr
URL: http://www.infopromotions.fr
Frequency: Annual. **Principal Exhibits:** Electronic and multimedia.

GREAT LAKES CABLE EXPO
6910 N. Shadeland Ave., Ste. 206
Indianapolis, IN 46220
PH: (317)845-8100
FX: (317)578-0621
Frequency: Annual. **Audience:** Trade professionals. **Principal Exhibits:** Cable industry-related equipment, supplies, and services.

GULF INTERNATIONAL EXHIBITION - INTERNATIONAL
TRADE FAIR FOR BUILDING, CONSTRUCTION, PUBLIC
WORKS, ELECTRONIC ENGINEERING, AND CON
PO Box 2460
Germantown, MD 20875-2460
PH: (301)515-0012
FX: (301)515-0016
E-mail: glahe@glahe.com
Frequency: Biennial. **Principal Exhibits:** Building, construction, public works, electrical equipment, electronic engineering, communication, office systems, education, production technology, material transport and consumer goods.

HYPER & RF
17 avenue ledru rollin
75012 Paris, France
PH: 33 1 53 17 11 40
FX: 33 1 53 17 11 45
URL: http://www.birp.com
Frequency: Annual. **Principal Exhibits:** Radio frequencies and microwave for civil and military applications.

IBC - INTERNATIONAL BROADCASTING CONVENTION
IEE, Savoy Pl.
London WC2R OBL, England
PH: 71 2403839
FX: 71 4973633
Frequency: Biennial. **Audience:** Broadcasting engineers, technicians, and managers. **Principal Exhibits:** Broadcasting equipment and services.

IBTS - INTERNATIONAL AUDIO, VIDEO, BROADCASING,
AND TELECOMMUNICATIONS SHOW
Via Domenichino 11
20149 Milan, Italy
PH: 02 4813204
FX: 02 4694313
E-mail: assoexpo@assoexpo.com
Frequency: Biennial. **Audience:** Technicians, radio and television owners, and engineers. **Principal Exhibits:** Broadcasting equipment, professional audio and video equipment, postproduction, radio and television network information, public address systems, local radio and television information, audio and video services, recording studio information, and telecommunications equipment.

ICA ANNUAL CONFERENCE
PO Box 9589
Austin, TX 78766
PH: (512)454-8299
FX: (512)454-4221
E-mail: icahdq@uts.cc.utexas.edu
Frequency: Annual. **Audience:** Teachers in colleges and universities, businessmen, government workers, military personnel. **Principal Exhibits:** Communications study equipment, supplies, and services.

ICE - INTERNET COMMERCE EXPO
1400 Providence Hwy.
PO Box 9127
Norwood, MA 02062-9127
PH: (617)551-9800
FX: (617)440-0351
Principal Exhibits: Commercial application of electronic mail.

IFABO PRAGUE - INTERNATIONAL TRADE FAIR FOR
OFFICE ORGANIZATION AND COMMUNICATION
TECHNOLOGY
Messeplatz 1
Postfach 124, 284
1071 Vienna, Austria
PH: 1 521 200
FX: 1 521 20290
Frequency: Annual. **Audience:** General public. **Principal Exhibits:** Office communication equipment, supplies, and services. **For-**

merly: IFABO PRAGUE - International Trade Fair for Office and Communications Engineering, with the Software Fair PROGRAM-MA.

IFCOM - USER FAIR FOR INFORMATION AND COMMUNICATION
Messeplatz 1
D-50679 Cologne, Germany
PH: 221 821 0
FX: 221 821 2574
URL: http://www.koelnmesse.de
Frequency: Biennial. **Held in conjunction with:** ORGATEC.

IMAGINATION - TRADE EVENT ON DIGITAL, TEXTUAL, VISUAL AND AUDIO CREATION AND COMMUNICATION
Jaarbeursplein-Utrecht
PO Box 8500
NL-3503 RM Utrecht, Netherlands
PH: 30 295 5911
FX: 30 294 0379
E-mail: info@jaarbeursutrecht.nl
URL: http://www.jaarbeursutrecht.nl
Frequency: Annual. **Audience:** Technology suppliers and creative users. **Principal Exhibits:** Digital text; screen and sound engineering techniques and solutions. **Formerly:** Multimedia.

INDIA COMM
1 Temasek Ave.
17-01 Millenia Tower
Singapore 039192, Singapore
PH: 65 338 2002
FX: 65 338 2112
Frequency: Biennial. **Audience:** Trade and business professionals. **Principal Exhibits:** Telecommunications and computer technology, equipment, supplies, and services.

INFO-GRYF - INTERNATIONAL FAIR OF ELECTRONIC, TELECOMMUNICATION AND COMPUTER TECHNOLOGY
ul. Struga 6-8
70-777 Szczecin, Poland
PH: 091 64 44 01
FX: 091 64 44 02
Frequency: Annual. **Principal Exhibits:** Computers, peripherals, system and application software, telecommunication in administration, data bases text processing, and cellular phones.

INFOCOMM INTERNATIONAL
11242 Waples Mill Rd., Ste. 200
Fairfax, VA 22030-6070
PH: (703)273-7200
FX: (703)278-8082
E-mail: icia@icia.org
URL: http://www.usa.net/icia
Frequency: Annual. **Audience:** Dealers; educational and corporate end-users. **Principal Exhibits:** Video, audiovisual, computer hardware and qualifier software, and multimedia.

INFORMATEX ASIA/PHIL TELECOM
191 Findon Rd.
Findon 5023, Australia
PH: 61 8 268 8202
Frequency: Biennial. **Principal Exhibits:** Telecommunications and information systems equipment and technology.

INFORMATIKA - INTERNATIONAL EXHIBITION OF COMPUTERS AND INFORMATION SCIENCE
Krasnopresnenskaya nab. 14
123100 Moscow, Russia
PH: 095 268 1340
FX: 095 205 60 55
Frequency: Annual. **Audience:** Trade professionals and general public. **Principal Exhibits:** Automated communication systems in-

cluding digital networks, automated control systems, space and satellite communication facilities.

INFOSEC ASIA
383 Main Ave.
PO Box 6059
Norwalk, CT 06851
PH: (203)840-5358
FX: (203)840-4804
E-mail: inquiry@nepcon.reedexpo.com
Frequency: Annual. **Principal Exhibits:** Equipment, supplies, and services for communication.

INFOSYSTEM - INTERNATIONAL FAIR OF ELECTRONICS, TELECOMMUNICATION, AND COMPUTER ENGINEERING
Glogowska 14
PL-60-734 Poznan, Poland
PH: 61 692592
FX: 61 665827
E-mail: MTP@POL.PL
URL: http://www.mtp.pol.pl
Frequency: Annual. **Audience:** Trade and general public. **Principal Exhibits:** Installations, equipment, systems, and technologies for the electronic industry, including software, electronic subunits, teletransmission and telecommunications equipment, and computer hardware. **Held in conjunction with:** POLYGRAFIA - International Exhibition of Printing Machines.

INTEGRATED COMMUNICATIONS EXHIBITION
P.O. Box 277
Peterborough PE2 6UN, England
PH: 44 1733 394304
FX: 44 1733 390042
Frequency: Annual. **Principal Exhibits:** Integrated services digital networks, modems, video conferencing, and latest communication technology.

INTER COMM
2500-1177 W. Hastings
Vancouver, BC, Canada V6E 3W1
PH: (604)669-1090
FX: (604)682-5703
Frequency: Biennial. **Principal Exhibits:** Telecommunication equipment, supplies, and services.

INTERNATIONAL EXHIBITION OF TV, CINE-AND RADIO ENGINEERING
Krasnopresnenskaya nab. 14
123100 Moscow, Russia
PH: 095 268 1340
FX: 095 205 60 55
Frequency: Quadrennial. **Audience:** Trade professionals and general public. **Principal Exhibits:** Industry related equipment, supplies, and services, including TV equipment, AV equipment, film projection.

INTERNATIONAL TELEVISION BROADCAST SHANGHAI
383 Main Ave.
PO Box 6059
Norwalk, CT 06851
PH: (203)840-5358
FX: (203)840-4804
E-mail: inquiry@nepcon.reedexpo.com
Principal Exhibits: Broadcasting and television.

INTERNATIONALE FUNKAUSSTELLUNG BERLIN - WORLD OF CONSUMER ELECTRONICS
Messedamm 22
D-14055 Berlin, Germany
PH: 49 30 3038 0
FX: 49 30 3038 2325
E-mail: marketing@messe-berlin.de
URL: http://www.messe-berlin.de

Frequency: Biennial. **Audience:** Trade professionals from the communications electronics sector and consumers. **Principal Exhibits:** Audio, hi-fi, television, video, camcorders, components and accessories, terrestrial and satellite receiving systems, broadcasting and studio systems, mobile communications, equipment and the media.

INTERWIRE
1570 Boston Post Rd.
PO Box 578
Guilford, CT 06437
PH: (203)453-2777
FX: (203)453-8384
Frequency: Biennial. **Audience:** Trade. **Principal Exhibits:** Machinery, engineering services, fiber optic machinery, chemicals, coatings, lubricants, dies, compounds, spools, reels, wire, rod, cable, extruders, measuring, testing, inspecting, fastener machinery, spring machinery, metal forming and fabricating, and other fabricated wire products.

IOWA POWER FARMING SHOW
2215 Sanders Rd.
Northbrook, IL 60062
PH: (847)509-9700
Frequency: Annual. **Audience:** Farmers and farm equipment dealers.

ISAAC BIENNIAL CONFERENCE
PO Box 1762, Sta. R
Toronto, ON, Canada M4G 4A3
PH: (905)737-9308
FX: (905)737-0624
Frequency: Biennial. **Principal Exhibits:** Exhibits in the field of alternative and augumentative communication.

KOMTEL-INTERBANK - TELECOMMUNICATION, BANKING EQUIPMENT AND SERVICES FAIR
ul. Flory 9
PL-00-586 Warsaw, Poland
PH: 22 49 60 06
FX: 22 49 35 84
Frequency: Annual. **Principal Exhibits:** Professional equipment for public and private networks, modern telecomputer networks, software and hardware, bank equipment, and security systems.

LATIN DIGITAL IMAGING & DOCUMENT MANAGEMENT SHOW
8000 Victor Pittsford Rd.
Victor, NY 14564-1050
PH: (716)383-8330
FX: (716)383-8442
Frequency: 3/yr. **Principal Exhibits:** PC digital imaging electronic document managemetn, groupware & workflow systems, micrographics, electronic print-on-demand, WWW publishing, all imaging systems & solutions.

LUDIMAT EXPO
97 rue du cherche midi
F-75006 Paris, France
PH: 01 44 39 85 00
FX: 01 45 44 30 40
E-mail: info@infopromotions.fr
URL: http://www.infopromotions.fr
Frequency: Annual. **Principal Exhibits:** Communication equipment.

MECOM - MIDDLE EAST INTERNATIONAL ELECTRONIC COMMUNICATIONS SHOW AND CONFERENCE
PO Box 20200
Exhibition House
Manama, Bahrain
PH: 973 550033
FX: 973 553288
E-mail: aeminfo@batelco.com.bh
URL: http://www.batelco.com.bh/aeminfo/

Frequency: Biennial. **Audience:** Engineers and engineering management personnel from Arabian Gulf markets. **Principal Exhibits:** Communications equipment, including antennas, broadcasting equipment, data communications and data processing equipment, fiber optics, integrated services digital networks, mobile communications, networks, public telephones, office systems, power supplies, solar power systems, satellite communications, security equipment, transmission equipment, and test and measurement equipment.

MIDDLE EAST BROADCAST - MIDDLE EAST INTERNATIONAL EXHIBITION AND CONFERENCE FOR BROADCASTING EQUIPMENT AND PROGRAMMING
PO Box 20200
Exhibition House
Manama, Bahrain
PH: 973 550033
FX: 973 553288
E-mail: aeminfo@batelco.com.bh
URL: http://www.batelco.com.bh/aeminfo/
Frequency: Biennial. **Principal Exhibits:** Radio and TV broadcasting and program production equipment.

MIFED - CINEMA AND TELEVISION INTERNATIONAL MULTIMEDIA MARKET
Largo Domodossola, 1
I-20145 Milan, Italy
PH: 39 2 48550 1
FX: 39 2 4800545 0
E-mail: mce@planet.it
URL: http://www.fmi.it
Frequency: Annual. **Principal Exhibits:** Television and Cinema Markets.

MILIA - THE INTERNATIONAL CONTENT MARKET FOR INTERACTIVE MEDIA
BP 572
11 rue du Colonel Pierre Avia
F-75726 Paris, France
PH: 33 1 41 90 4480
FX: 33 1 41 44 70
E-mail: 100321.1310@compuserve.com
Frequency: Annual. **Audience:** Publishers, producers and developers, on-line service providers. **Principal Exhibits:** Art, books and publishing, computers, communication equipment, supplies, and services.

MIP ASIA - INTERNATIONAL FIRM AND PROGRAMME MARKET FOR TV, VIDEO, CABLE AND SATELLITE
383 Main Ave.
PO Box 6059
Norwalk, CT 06851
PH: (203)840-5358
FX: (203)840-4804
E-mail: inquiry@nepcon.reedexpo.com
Frequency: Annual. **Audience:** Producers, distributors and broadcasters. **Principal Exhibits:** International TV programme market for the Asian and Pacific region.

MIP TV - THE INTERNATIONAL TELEVISION PROGRAM MARKET
BP 572
11 rue du Colonel Pierre Avia
F-75726 Paris, France
PH: 33 1 41 90 4480
FX: 33 1 41 44 70
E-mail: 100321.1310@compuserve.com
Frequency: Annual. **Audience:** Television industry professionals, including program buyers and sellers. **Principal Exhibits:** Supplies and services for television networks, production, and distribution; related service companies, publishers, and media.

MIPCOM - INTERNATIONAL FILM AND PROGRAMME MARKET FOR TV, VIDEO, CABLE, AND SATELLITE
BP 572
11 rue du Colonel Pierre Avia
F-75726 Paris, France
PH: 33 1 41 90 4480
FX: 33 1 41 44 70
E-mail: 100321.1310@compuserve.com
Frequency: Annual. **Audience:** Television industry professionals, including buyers and sellers. **Principal Exhibits:** Equipment and services for television networks, production, and distribution, publishers, and media.

MIPCOM JUNIOR - YOUTH PROGRAMMING SCREENINGS
383 Main Ave.
PO Box 6059
Norwalk, CT 06851
PH: (203)840-5358
FX: (203)840-4804
E-mail: inquiry@nepcon.reedexpo.com
Frequency: Annual. **Audience:** Broadcasters, producers and distributors. **Principal Exhibits:** Specialist market for youth programming.

MOBILECOMM PHILIPPINES - INTERNATIONAL CELLULAR, RADIO & SATELLITE COMMUNICATIONS EXHIBITION
Room 909, 9th Floor
Sen. Gil Puyat Avenue, corner Urban Ave.
PS Bank Tower
Makati City 1200, Philippines
PH: 632 759 3263
FX: 632 759 3228
E-mail: piecinc@portalink.com
Frequency: Biennial. **Principal Exhibits:** Equipment, supplies, and services for cellular, radio & satellite communications.

MOBILECOMMASIA - ASIAN INTERNATIONAL CELLULAR, RADIO & SATELLITE COMMUNICATIONS EXHIBITION & CONFERENCE
2 Handy Rd.
15-09 Cathay Bldg.
Singapore 229233, Singapore
PH: 65 3384747
FX: 65 3395651
E-mail: info@sesmontnet.com
URL: http://www.sesmontnet.com
Frequency: Biennial. **Principal Exhibits:** Cellular, radio & satellite communications equipment, supplies, and services.

NAB RADIO SHOW AND WORLD MEDIA EXPO
1771 N. St. NW
Washington, DC 20036-2891
PH: (202)429-5300
TF: (800)342-2460
FX: (202)429-5343
URL: http://www.nab.org
Frequency: Annual. **Audience:** Radio and television broadcasters and related broadcasting industry professionals. **Principal Exhibits:** Radio and television broadcasting equipment, supplies, and services; supplies and services for production, post-production, computing, multimedia, telecommunications and corporate communications. **Dates and Locations:** 2000 Apr 10-13; Las Vegas, NV.

NATIONAL ASSOCIATION OF STATE TELECOMMUNICATIONS DIRECTORS CONFERENCE
Iron Works Pike
PO Box 11910
Lexington, KY 40578-1910
PH: (606)244-8187
FX: (606)244-8001
Frequency: Annual. **Principal Exhibits:** Exhibits for state telecommunications systems.

NATIONAL CABLE TELEVISION ASSOCIATION CONVENTION AND EXPOSITION
1225 19th St. SW, Ste. 310
Washington, DC 20036
PH: (202)463-7905
FX: (202)467-6944
Frequency: Annual. **Audience:** Persons involved in the cable television industry. **Principal Exhibits:** Cable television system equipment, supplies, and services; programmers, financial services, computers, and collection services.

NATIONAL TELEPHONE COOPERATIVE ASSOCIATION ANNUAL MEETING & EXPO
2626 Pennsylvania Ave., NW
Washington, DC 20037
PH: (202)298-2385
FX: (202)298-2390
Frequency: Annual. **Principal Exhibits:** Equipment, supplies, and services for the telephone industry.

NATPE ANNUAL PROGRAM CONFERENCE
2425 W. Olympic Blvd., Ste. 550 East
Santa Monica, CA 90404
PH: (310)453-4440
FX: (310)453-5258
URL: http://www.natpe.org
Frequency: Annual. **Audience:** Television executives. **Principal Exhibits:** Equipment, supplies, and services for syndicated television programs. **Dates and Locations:** 2000 Jan 24-27; New Orleans, LA • 2001 Jan 22-25; Los Angeles, CA.

NEPCON AUSTRALIA
383 Main Ave.
PO Box 6059
Norwalk, CT 06851
PH: (203)840-5358
FX: (203)840-4804
E-mail: inquiry@nepcon.reedexpo.com
Principal Exhibits: Equipment, supplies, and services for communication.

NEPCON INDIA
383 Main Ave.
PO Box 6059
Norwalk, CT 06851
PH: (203)840-5358
FX: (203)840-4804
E-mail: inquiry@nepcon.reedexpo.com
Principal Exhibits: Equipment, supplies, and services for communication.

NEPCON SHANGHAI
383 Main Ave.
PO Box 6059
Norwalk, CT 06851
PH: (203)840-5358
FX: (203)840-4804
E-mail: inquiry@nepcon.reedexpo.com
Frequency: Biennial. **Principal Exhibits:** Equipment, supplies, and services for communication.

NETVAERK
International House
Central Blvd. 5
DK-2300 Copenhagen, Denmark
PH: 45 32 47 33 22
FX: 45 32 52 35 66
Frequency: Annual. **Principal Exhibits:** Tele- and data-communication products and technology.

NETWORKS TELECOM
Box 468 (V. Varvsgatan 10)
201 24 Malmo, Sweden

PH: 46 40 690 85 00
FX: 46 40 690 85 01
E-mail: info@millerfreeman.se
URL: http://www.millerfreeman.se
Frequency: Annual. Principal Exhibits: Equipment, supplies, and services relating to network and communication, business telecommunications, Internet and World Wide Web, electronic document processing, computer security, and databases.

NETWORKS - THE EUROPEAN COMPUTER
  COMMUNICATIONS CONFERENCE AND EXHIBITION
630 Chiswick High Rd.
London W4 5BG, England
PH: 44 181 742 2828
FX: 44 181 747 3856
URL: http://www.mf-exhibitions.co.uk
Frequency: Annual. Audience: Network and telecommunications managers; data processing, and computer managers; technical specialists, and related professionals. Principal Exhibits: Computer communications equipment, including LANs, WANs, value-added network services, packet switching systems, electronic mail equipment and services, security systems, PABXs, and work stations.

NETWORLD INTEROP
14 Pl. Marie-Jeanne-Bassot
92593 Levallois-Perret, France
PH: 33 1 46 39 5656
Frequency: Annual. Principal Exhibits: Telecommunications equipment, supplies, and services.

NETWORLD INTEROP CONFERENCE AND EXPOSITION
334 Chiswick High Rd.
London W45 TA, England
PH: 44 181 849 6200
Principal Exhibits: Digital communications.

PRO A/V - THE PROFESSIONAL AUDIO VIDEO
  EXHIBITION AND CONFERENCE
383 Main Ave.
PO Box 6059
Norwalk, CT 06851
PH: (203)840-5358
FX: (203)840-4804
E-mail: inquiry@nepcon.reedexpo.com
Frequency: Annual. Audience: Engineers and marketeers. Principal Exhibits: Digital audio and video equipment, broadcasting equipment, microwave equipment and satellite technology.

PROMIT INTERNATIONAL EXPO
Gardens Plaza Bldg.
3300 PGA Blvd., Ste. 520
Palm Beach Gardens, FL 33410
PH: (407)624-1139
FX: (407)625-4042
E-mail: npbc@disasters-hazardmit.org
URL: http://www.disasters-hazardmit.org
Principal Exhibits: Equipment, supplies, and services for the protection of buildings against natural and human-made disasters such as hurricanes, earthquakes, floods, fires, explosions, slides, terrorism, and environmental problems.

PROMOTION - INTERNATIONAL MARKETING
  COMMUNICATION TRADE FAIR
PO Box 44
H-1441 Budapest, Hungary
PH: 36 1 263 6000
FX: 36 1 263 6098
E-mail: hungexpo@hungexpo.hu
URL: http://www.hungexpo.hu
Frequency: Biennial. Principal Exhibits: Advertising agencies and contractors, giftware makers and distributors, exhibition, and program organizers.

PT/EXPO COMM CHINA
6550 Rock Spring Dr., Ste. 500
Bethesda, MD 20817-1126
PH: (301)493-5500
FX: (301)493-5705
E-mail: ejkinfo@ejkrause.com
URL: http://www.ejkrause.com
Frequency: Biennial. Audience: Nationwide audience of Chinese policy makers and technical experts. Principal Exhibits: Equipment, supplies, and services for the telecommunications, computer, and information industries.

PT/WIRELESS COMM BEIJING - BEIJING
  INTERNATIONAL WIRELESS COMMUNICATIONS
  EXHIBITION
4/F Stanhope House
734 King's Rd.
North Point, Hong Kong
PH: 852 2811 8897
FX: 852 2516 5024
E-mail: aes@adsaleexh.com
URL: http://www.adsaleexh.com
Frequency: Biennial. Principal Exhibits: Wireless communication.

PTC
2454 S. Beretania St., Ste. 302
Honolulu, HI 96826-1596
PH: (808)941-3789
FX: (808)944-4874
URL: http://www.ptc.org
Frequency: Annual. Audience: Telecommunications industry, government officials, top management from telecommunication companies, consultants, policy analysts, educators, trade press reps. Principal Exhibits: Telecommunication products, services, and publications.

RADIO ADVERTISING BUREAU ANNUAL MANAGING
  SALES CONFERENCE
261 Madison Ave., 23rd Fl.
New York, NY 10016-2303
PH: (212)254-4800
FX: (212)254-8713
Frequency: Annual. Audience: Radio station, network, and group operator sales executives. Principal Exhibits: Computer software for radio and television productions; radio networks; specialty advertising; program syndication; sales consulting and market research; related products and services.

RADIO-TELEVISION NEWS DIRECTORS ASSOCIATION
  INTERNATIONAL CONFERENCE AND EXHIBITION
1000 Connecticut Ave., NW, Ste. 615
Washington, DC 20036-5302
PH: (202)659-6510
TF: (800)80-RTNDA
FX: (202)223-4007
E-mail: rtnda@rtnda.org
URL: http://www.rtnda.org/
Frequency: Annual. Audience: News directors, producers, technicians, management, educators and other professionals involved in electronic journalism. Principal Exhibits: Equipment, supplies, and services for the radio and television news industries, including cameras, recorders, weather equipment, computers, and software.

SAUDICOMMUNICATIONS - ELECTRONIC
  COMMUNICATIONS SHOW
PO Box 56010
Riyadh 11554, Saudi Arabia
PH: 966 1 454 1448
FX: 966 1 454 4846
E-mail: recsa@midleast.net
Frequency: Biennial. Principal Exhibits: Communication equipment, supplies, and services, including antenna systems, broadcasting equipment, data communications, data processing equipment, integrated services digital network (ISDN), mobile communications,

networks, public telephones, office systems, power supplies, satellite communications, security equipment, transmission equipment, and test and measurement equipment.

SCEC - SATELLITE COMMUNICATIONS EXPO AND CONFERENCE
6300 South Syracuse Way, Ste. 650
Englewood, CO 80111
PH: (303)220-0600
FX: (303)770-0253
URL: http://www.intertec.com
Frequency: Annual. **Audience:** Technical, engineering, operations, purchasing, and executive management from corporate and commercial satellite users, broadcasters, and service providers. **Principal Exhibits:** Satellite communications services, systems, and products.

SEYBOLD SEMINAR CONFERENCE AND EXPOSITION/ TOKYO
303 Vintage Park Dr.
Foster City, CA 94404-1138
PH: (650)578-6897
TF: (800)488-2883
FX: (650)525-0193
E-mail: mtrask@zdcf.com
Principal Exhibits: Internet publishing, multimedia design tools, workflow automation and color management.

SIBTELECOM - THE INTERNATIONAL TELECOMMUNICATIONS, BROADCASTING, AND PROGRAMMING EXHIBITION
16 Gorky St.
6300099 Novosibirsk, Russia
PH: 7 3832 102674
FX: 7 3832 236335
E-mail: siberian.fair@sovcust.sprint.com
Frequency: Annual. **Principal Exhibits:** Telecommunications and business communications systems, professional sound, film, video, and audio.

SIRCOM PARIS - CELLULAR, MOBILES, AND TELECOM EQUIPMENT
1 rue du Parc
F-92593 Levallois Perret, France
PH: 331 49685100
FX: 331 47377438
E-mail: simd@cepexposium.fr
URL: http://www.simd.fr
Frequency: Annual. **Principal Exhibits:** Cellular, Mobiles and Telecommunications.

SOCIETY OF BROADCAST ENGINEERS ENGINEERING CONFERENCE
8445 Keystone Crossing, Ste. 140
Indianapolis, IN 46240
PH: (317)253-1640
FX: (317)253-0418
Frequency: Annual. **Principal Exhibits:** Equipment, supplies, and services for the broadcast industry.

SODOBNA ELEKTRONICA
Dunajska 10
P.P. 3558
SL-1001 Ljubljana, Slovenia
PH: 386 61 173 53 31
FX: 386 61 1735 232
E-mail: lsejem@eunet-si
URL: http://www.isa.tp-lj-si/lsejem
Frequency: Annual. **Principal Exhibits:** Electronics, telecommunication, and RTV diffusion equipment, supplies, and services.

SOUTHERN STATES COMMUNICATION ASSOCIATION CONVENTION
College of Communication and Fine Arts
University of Memphis
Campus Box 526546
Memphis, TN 38152
PH: (901)678-2350
FX: (901)678-5118
E-mail: director@sca.net
URL: http://www.ssca.net/
Frequency: Annual. **Audience:** Communications professionals. **Principal Exhibits:** Communications equipment; textbooks. **Dates and Locations:** 2000 Mar 29 - Apr 03; New Orleans, LA.

SPECIALIZED EXHIBITION FOR ELECTRICAL INDUSTRY, TELECOMMUNICATIONS, LIGHT
PO Box 127
FIN-40101 Jyvaskyla, Finland
PH: 3340000
FX: 610 272
Frequency: Biennial. **Principal Exhibits:** Electrical, lighting, and telecommunications equipment, supplies, and services.

SPRING INTERNET WORLD
20 Ketchum St.
Westport, CT 06880
PH: (203)226-6967
FX: (203)454-5840
E-mail: international@mecklermedia.com
URL: http://events.iworld.com
Principal Exhibits: Internet, intranet and Web applications.

SUPERCOMM
National Bureau of Standards
Bldg. 245-C-333
Washington, DC 20034
PH: (202)921-2518
Frequency: Annual. **Principal Exhibits:** Telecommunications equipment, supplies, and services.

SVIAZ/EXPO COMM MOSCOW
11 Novinsky Blvd.
121099 Moscow, Russia
PH: 095 255 4792
FX: 095 252 5475
Frequency: Annual. **Principal Exhibits:** Telecommunications, networking, and wireless/broadband technology.

TAIPEI ELEC INTERNATIONAL ELECTRONICS SPRING SHOW
CETRA Exhibition Dept.
5 Hsinyi Rd., Sec. 5
Taipei World Trade Center Exhibition Hall
Taipei 110, Taiwan
PH: 886 2 2725 1111
FX: 886 2 2725 1314
E-mail: cetra@cetra.org.tw
URL: http://www.taipeitradeshows.org.tw
Frequency: Annual. **Audience:** Trade professionals and general public. **Principal Exhibits:** Electronic manufacturing equipment, electronic components and parts, cable TV equipment, instruments and meters, consumer electronics, telecommunication equipment, computers and peripherals, and illumination devices.

TAIPEI TELECOM - INTERNATIONAL TELECOMMUNICATIONS, MOBILE COMMUNICATIONS, AND NETWORKING SHOW
5 Hsinyi Rd.
Section 5
Taipei 110, Taiwan
Frequency: Biennial. **Principal Exhibits:** Antenna systems, data communications and processing equipment, ISDN, networks, mobile communications, security equipment, telephones, transmission equipment, and test and measurement equipment.

TAREL FAIR OF ELECTRONICS, TELECOMMUNICATION AND ELECTRICAL ENGINEERING
ul. Wystawowa 1
51-618 Wroclaw, Poland
PH: 071 72 81 41
FX: 071 48 36 78
Frequency: Annual. **Principal Exhibits:** Computer systems and equipment, telecommunication, automatic control mechanisms, and office and communication systems.

TECHNOLOGY MYANMAR - TECHNOLOGY EXHIBITION WITH CONFERENCE
Postfach 120709
80033 Munich, Germany
PH: 89 500610
FX: 89 5028497
Frequency: Annual. **Principal Exhibits:** Products and services for the energy sector, telecommunications, agricultural technology, light industries, forestry, construction industry and mining.

TECNOTRON - INTERNATIONAL FAIR FOR TELECOMMUNICATIONS, INFORMATICS, AND OFFICE EQUIPMENT
Av. la Marina 2355
Apartado postal 4900
San Miguel
Lima 100, Peru
PH: 51 1 5660775
FX: 51 1 5660320
E-mail: fip@feria.com.pe
URL: http://www.feria.com.pe
Frequency: Annual. **Audience:** Trade and general public. **Principal Exhibits:** Equipment, supplies, and services for informatics, telecommunications, and office automation.

TELECOM, OA & COMPUTER/PAKISTAN
Tung Wai Commercial Bldg., Rm. 1703
109 Gloucester Rd.
Wanchai, Hong Kong
PH: 852 2 511 7427
FX: 852 2 511 9692
E-mail: cpexhbit@hk.super.net
URL: http://www.hk.super.net/~cpexhbit
Principal Exhibits: Telecommunications and computers.

TELECOM - WORLD TELECOMMUNICATION EXHIBITION, FORUM, AND BOOK FAIR
6550 Rock Spring Dr., Ste. 500
Bethesda, MD 20817-1126
PH: (301)493-5500
FX: (301)493-5705
E-mail: ejkinfo@ejkrause.com
URL: http://www.ejkrause.com
Frequency: Quadrennial. **Audience:** Worldwide trade professionals, including decision makers, engineers, financiers, and users of telecommunication. **Principal Exhibits:** Developments in telecommunications technology, ranging from basic services to integrated telecommunications systems.

TELECOMLATINA
6300 South Syracuse Way, Ste. 650
Englewood, CO 80111
PH: (303)220-0600
FX: (303)770-0253
URL: http://www.intertec.com
Principal Exhibits: Telecommunications equipment and information.

TELECOMMUNICATIONS - INTERNATIONAL DATA AND TELECOMMUNICATIONS TRADE FAIR AND CONFERENCE FOR BUSINESS COMMUNICATIONS SOLUTIONS AND
Jaarbeursplein-Utrecht
PO Box 8500
NL-3503 RM Utrecht, Netherlands
PH: 30 295 5911
FX: 30 294 0379
E-mail: info@jaarbeursutrecht.nl
URL: http://www.jaarbeursutrecht.nl
Frequency: Annual. **Principal Exhibits:** Consultants, management, services, applications, processing platforms, communications, transmission, and cabling.

TELECOMMUTING & HOME OFFICE EXPOSITION & CONFERENCE
1400 Providence Hwy.
PO Box 9127
Norwood, MA 02062-9127
PH: (617)551-9800
FX: (617)440-0351
Principal Exhibits: Equipment, supplies, and services for virtual offices, remote business locations and work-at-home employees.

TELECON - CANADIAN BUSINESS TELECOMMUNICATIONS ALLIANCE NATIONAL CONFERENCE AND EXPOSITION
20 Butterick Rd.
Toronto, ON, Canada M8W 3Z8
PH: (416)252-7791
FX: (416)252-9848
Frequency: Annual. **Audience:** CBTA members, telecommunicators, and users of telecommunications systems and services. **Principal Exhibits:** Communications products, including voice, data, and image communications; radio paging; facsimiles; local area networks (LANS); electronic mail; satellite systems; telephone systems and services. **Dates and Locations:** 1999 Aug 31 - Sep 02; Toronto, ON • 2000 Oct 03-05; Toronto, ON.

THE TEXAS SHOW
506 W. 16th St.
Austin, TX 78701
PH: (512)474-2082
TF: (800)666-2082
FX: (512)474-0966
E-mail: wda@txcable.com
Frequency: Annual. **Principal Exhibits:** Computer software and hardware for the cable television industry.

TMA - CONVENTION OF THE TELECOMMUNICATIONS MANAGERS ASSOCIATION
Ranmore Hse, The Crescent
Leatherhead KT22 8DY, England
PH: 01372361000
FX: 01372818888
Frequency: Annual. **Audience:** Providers, installers and users of telecommunications equipment. **Principal Exhibits:** Telecommunications equipment and services for industrial and commercial uses.

TNC - TELENETCOM: THE SWISS EXHIBITION FOR TELEMATICS
Bruggacherstrasse 26
PO Box 185
CH-8117 Fallenden-Zurich, Switzerland
PH: 411 806 33 77
FX: 411 806 3343
E-mail: reed@active.ch
URL: http://www.reed.ch
Frequency: Annual. **Principal Exhibits:** Mobile communications, data communications, telecommunications, and building wiring systems.

TV LINK
383 Main Ave.
PO Box 6059
Norwalk, CT 06851
PH: (203)840-5358
FX: (203)840-4804
E-mail: inquiry@nepcon.reedexpo.com
Frequency: Annual. **Audience:** Trade professionals. **Principal Exhibits:** Broadcasting and television, communication, computers and entertainment.

UNICOM - INTERNATIONAL TELECOMMUNICATIONS EXHIBITION
Rm. 3808
26 Harbour Rd.
China Resources Bldg.
Wanchai, Hong Kong
PH: 852 2827 6766
FX: 852 2827 6870
E-mail: general@coastal.com.hk
URL: http://www.coastal.com.hk
Principal Exhibits: Equipment, supplies, and services for telecommunication.

URALLNFOCOM
PO Box 318
450080 Ufa, Russia
PH: 3472 525386
FX: 3472 525593
Frequency: Annual. **Principal Exhibits:** Information technology equipment, supplies, and services.

UTILITIES TELECOMMUNICATIONS COUNCIL ANNUAL CONFERENCE AND EXHIBITION
1140 Connecticut Ave., NW, Ste. 1140
Washington, DC 20036
PH: (202)872-0030
FX: (202)872-1331
Frequency: Annual. **Audience:** Telecommunications managers and engineers. **Principal Exhibits:** Telecommunications equipment and services.

VARIETY PRESENTS SHOWBIZ EXPO CANADA
383 Main Ave.
PO Box 6059
Norwalk, CT 06851
PH: (203)840-5358
FX: (203)840-4804
E-mail: inquiry@nepcon.reedexpo.com
Frequency: Annual. **Audience:** Trade professionals. **Principal Exhibits:** Products, services and technology for the motion picture, television and commercial production and post-production industry.

VIETNAM BROADCASTING - VIETNAM INTERNATIONAL EXHIBITION ON BROADCASTING TECHNOLOGY
4/F Stanhope House
734 King's Rd.
North Point, Hong Kong
PH: 852 2811 8897
FX: 852 2516 5024
E-mail: aes@adsaleexh.com
URL: http://www.adsaleexh.com
Frequency: Annual. **Principal Exhibits:** Broadcasting technology.

VIETNAM TELECOMP - VIETNAM INTERNATIONAL EXHIBITION ON COMMUNICATION, COMPUTER, AND OFFICE SYSTEMS
4/F Stanhope House
734 King's Rd.
North Point, Hong Kong

PH: 852 2811 8897
FX: 852 2516 5024
E-mail: aes@adsaleexh.com
URL: http://www.adsaleexh.com
Frequency: Annual. **Audience:** Trade professionals. **Principal Exhibits:** Telecommunication and information technology; office equipment and computers.

WEB DEVELOPER
20 Ketchum St.
Westport, CT 06880
PH: (203)226-6967
FX: (203)454-5840
E-mail: international@mecklermedia.com
URL: http://events.iworld.com
Principal Exhibits: Tools and techniques for maintaining and growing business web sites and intranets.

WEB INTERACTIVE
20 Ketchum St.
Westport, CT 06880
PH: (203)226-6967
FX: (203)454-5840
E-mail: international@mecklermedia.com
URL: http://events.iworld.com
Principal Exhibits: Interactive tools and techniques.

WINDOWS NT INTRANET SOLUTIONS CONFERENCE AND EXHIBITION, JAPAN
303 Vintage Park Dr.
Foster City, CA 94404-1138
PH: (650)578-6897
TF: (800)488-2883
FX: (650)525-0193
E-mail: mtrask@zdcf.com
Principal Exhibits: Premier technology and tools.

WINDOWS NT INTRANET SOLUTIONS CONFERENCE AND EXHIBITION, U.S.
303 Vintage Park Dr.
Foster City, CA 94404-1138
PH: (650)578-6897
TF: (800)488-2883
FX: (650)525-0193
E-mail: mtrask@zdcf.com
Principal Exhibits: Premier technology and tools.

WIRE - INTERNATIONAL WIRE AND CABLE TRADE FAIR
Stockumer Kirchstrasse 61
PO Box 101006
D-40474 Dusseldorf, Germany
PH: 211 4560 01
FX: 211 4560 668
URL: http://messe.dus.tradefair.de
Frequency: Biennial. **Audience:** Wire and cable industry professionals; general public. **Principal Exhibits:** Equipment, supplies, and services for the wire and cable industry. **Held in conjunction with:** TUBE - International Tube and Pipe Trade Fair.

WIRE SINGAPORE - ALL ASIA WIRE AND CABLE TRADE FAIR
Stockumer Kirchstrasse 61
PO Box 101006
D-40474 Dusseldorf, Germany
PH: 211 4560 01
FX: 211 4560 668
URL: http://messe.dus.tradefair.de
Frequency: Biennial. **Principal Exhibits:** Wire manufacturing and finishing machinery, process technology tools, auxiliary process technology materials, special wires and cables, measuring and control technology, and test engineering. **Held in conjunction with:** TUBE Singapore.

**WIREASIA - INTERNATIONAL EXHIBITION AND
  CONFERENCE FOR PRODUCTION OF WIRE,
  FASTENERS, SPRINGS, CABLE, AND WIRE PRODUCTS**
110 Station Rd. E.
Surrey RH8 0QA, England
PH: 883 717755
FX: 883 714554
Frequency: Biennial. **Audience:** Trade professionals. **Principal
Exhibits:** Equipment and machines for the production of cable and
wire. **Formerly:** Cablewire China.

WIRELESS WORLD EXPO AND CONFERENCE
6550 Rock Spring Dr., Ste. 500
Bethesda, MD 20817-1126
PH: (301)493-5500
FX: (301)493-5705
E-mail: ejkinfo@ejkrause.com
URL: http://www.ejkrause.com
Frequency: Annual. **Audience:** Wireless service providers, paging
service providers, mobile data network operators, dealers, resellers,
agents, and large-volume end users. **Principal Exhibits:** Wireless
technology and related equipment, supplies, and services.

**WORKPLACE - INNOVATIONS IN OFFICE FURNITURE
  WITH TECHNOLOGY**
Oriel House
26 The Quadrant
Richmond, Surrey TW9 1DL, England
PH: 181 910 7825
FX: 181 910 7926
E-mail: info@reedexpo.co.uk
URL: http://www.reedexpo.com
Frequency: Biennial. **Audience:** Trade professonals. **Principal Ex-
hibits:** Office furniture, technology and communications systems.

WUHAN TELECOM & COMPUTER EXPO
Tung Wai Commercial Bldg., Rm. 1703
109 Gloucester Rd.
Wanchai, Hong Kong
PH: 852 2 511 7427
FX: 852 2 511 9692
E-mail: cpexhbit@hk.super.net
URL: http://www.hk.super.net/~cpexhbit
Audience: Trade professionals. **Principal Exhibits:** Telecommunication equipment, including automatic dialers, cable and ancillary
technology, Earth stations, electronic communication, fibre optics,
instrumentation, mobile telecommunication, paging systems, radio
communications, satellite communications, switching equipment,
test equipment, and wire systems; Computer and Office Automation
equipment, including data communications and networks, end-user
applications and software, hardware, peripherals, and add-ons, imaging and multi-media, copiers, fax and telex machines, office furniture, stationery, calculators, filing systems, and supplies.

MASTER INDEX

The Master Index presents company and organization names, names of individuals, SIC industry names, and terms. Each entry in the index is followed by one or more page numbers.

Master Index

GEOGRAPHICAL COMPANY INDEX

The Geographical Company Index presents company names by state. Page references are to the company's listing in Chapter 4, Company Directory, in both Part I and Part II.

Michigan

American Communications Network, p. 408
Barden Companies, Inc., p. 102
Booth American Company, p. 414
Cellnet Communications Inc., p. 416
Clover Technologies Inc., p. 109
Code-Alarm Inc., p. 109
Complete Business Solutions, p. 110
Compuware Corporation, p. 111
Comshare Incorporated, p. 111
Data Systems Network Corp., p. 114
Decision Consultants Inc., p. 115
Diversified Data Processing Consulting, p. 425
Gale Group, p. 122
Interface Systems Inc., pp. 129-130
Lason, Inc., pp. 134-135
MC Liquidating Corporation, p. 446
MCE Companies, Inc., pp. 138, 446
Medstat Holdings Inc., p. 139
Michigan Bell Telephone Co., p. 448
Par Computer-Leasing, p. 147
Paramunt Stns Group of Detroit, p. 456
Prestolite Wire Corporation, p. 149
Rofin-Sinar Technologies Inc., p. 153
Rowe International Inc., p. 463
Saga Communications Inc., p. 463
Saturn Electronics & Engrg, p. 154
Superior Conslt Holdings Corp., p. 160
Syntel, Inc., p. 161
U M I & Company, p. 165
UACC Midwest, Inc., p. 476

Minnesota

ADC Telecommunications, Inc., p. 405
Analysts International Corp., p. 98
Artesyn North America Inc., pp. 100, 410
Born Information Services, p. 104
Bureau Engraving Incorporated, p. 105
Centron Dpl Company, Inc., p. 107
Communications Systems, Inc., p. 420
Computer Network Tech Corp., p. 110
Control Data Systems, Inc., pp. 111-112
Cray Research, Inc., p. 112
Digi International Inc., p. 116
Diversified Phrm Services, p. 116
Fourth Shift Corporation, p. 122
Hickory Tech Corporation, p. 436
Hutchinson Technology Inc., pp. 127, 437
Imation Corp., p. 127
Innovex Precision Components, pp. 128, 438
ITI Technologies, Inc., p. 131
Johnson Matthey Advanced Circuits, p. 132
Lawson Associates, Inc., p. 135
Magnetic Data, Inc., p. 137
Micro Voice Applications Inc., p. 140
Midcontinent Media, Inc., p. 448
Midwest Wireless Communications LLC, p. 448
Minnesota Equal Access, p. 449
Multi-Tech Systems Inc., p. 450
National Computer Systems, p. 143
Nortech Systems Incorporated, pp. 452-453
Norwest Services, Inc., p. 145
Pemstar Inc., p. 147

Rural Cellular Corporation, p. 463
Safetran Systems Corporation, p. 463
Sheldahl, Inc., p. 155
Telex Communications Inc., p. 472
United States Satellite Broadcasting, p. 476
US Bancorp Info Services Corp., p. 166
Virtualfund.Com, Inc., p. 167
VTC Inc., p. 168

Mississippi

Communigroup Inc., pp. 420-421
Durant Electric Company, p. 117
Hood Cable Company, p. 126
Hughes Aircraft Mississippi, p. 126
MCI Worldcom Inc., pp. 446-447
Mississippi Band Choctaw Indians, pp. 141-142, 449
Multicraft International Ltd., p. 143
Peavey Electronics Corporation, p. 457
Skytel Communications Inc., p. 465
Tele-Fibernet Corporation, p. 471
Telephone Electronics Corp., p. 472
Transcall America Inc., p. 474
Wireless One, Inc., p. 481

Missouri

Advanced Communications Group, p. 405
American Century Services Corp., p. 97
Berg Electronics Corp., pp. 103-104
Cerner Corporation, p. 107
Charter Communications, Inc., p. 417
Computer Sales International, p. 111
DST Systems, Inc., p. 117
Galaxy Telecom, L P, p. 430
GenAmerica Corporation, p. 123
Golden Sky Systems, Inc., p. 432
GTE Midwest Incorporated, p. 433
H C Crown Corp., p. 434
Harmon Industries Inc., p. 435
Kansas City Cable Partners, LP, p. 441
Koplar Communications Inc., p. 442
MEMC Electronic Materials, p. 139
Multimedia KSDK Inc., p. 450
NPG Holdings, Inc., p. 453
Pulitzer Broadcasting Company, p. 461
St. Louis Music Inc., p. 464
Southwestern Bell Telephone Co., p. 466
Sprint Communications Co. LP, p. 467
TCI Cablevision of Missouri, p. 469
Unigraphics Solutions Inc., p. 165
Unity Motion, Inc., p. 477
Viasystems Group Inc., p. 167
Viasystems Inc., p. 167
Wirekraft Industries, Inc., p. 169

Montana

Confederated Slish Ktnai Tribes, pp. 111, 421
Powerhouse Technologies Inc., p. 149

Nebraska

A C I Worldwide Inc., p. 94
Aliant Communications Co., p. 406

New York - continued

Prime Sports Channel Network LP, p. 460

Primetime 24 Joint Venture, p. 460

Princeton Information Ltd., p. 149

Prodigy Communications Inc., p. 460

PSC Automation, Inc., p. 150

PSC Inc., p. 150

R S L Communications Inc., p. 461

Schlumberger Technologies Inc., p. 154

Spanish Broadcasting System, p. 466

Sportschannel Associates, p. 467

Standard Microsystems Corp., p. 158

Staveley Inc., pp. 158, 468

Sutherland Group Ltd. Inc., p. 160

Symbol Technologies Inc., p. 161

Telephonics Corporation, p. 472

Todd Products Corp, p. 473

Toshiba America Inc., pp. 473-474

Triad Data Inc., p. 164

TSR Consulting Services Inc., p. 164

TSR, Inc., pp. 164-165

Tullett & Tokyo Forex Inc., p. 165

TWC Cable Partners LP, p. 475

TWI Cable Inc., p. 475

U S Media Holdings, Inc., p. 475

United Industrial Corporation, p. 165

USA Networks, p. 478

Veba Corporation, p. 166

Viacom Inc., p. 479

Viatel, Inc (De Corp), p. 479

Vicon Industries Inc., p. 479

Video Monitoring Svcs Amer LP, p. 167

Volt Delta Resources, Inc., p. 168

Winstar Communications Inc., p. 481

WPIX, Inc., p. 482

Young Broadcasting Inc., p. 482

North Carolina

Bahakel Communications LTD, p. 411

Broadway & Seymour, Inc., p. 105

BTI Telecom Corp., p. 414

Channel Master LLC, pp. 107, 417

Communications Instruments, pp. 109, 420

CT Communications Inc., p. 423

Eurotherm Drives Inc., p. 428

Glenayre Technologies Inc., p. 432

International Resistive Co., p. 130

Jefferson-Plot Communications Co., p. 440

Medic Computer Systems Inc., p. 138

MJD Communications, Inc., p. 449

North State Telecommunications, p. 453

Polygram Manufacturing & Dist Centers, p. 149

Prodelin Corporation, p. 460

Prodelin Holding Corporation, p. 460

Radio Frequency Systems Inc., pp. 461-462

SAS Institute Inc., p. 154

Seer Technologies Inc., p. 155

Sigcom Inc., p. 465

Solectron Technology, Inc., p. 157

Superior Modular Products Inc., p. 468

Trans World Radio, p. 474

United Telephone-Southeast, p. 477

Vanguard Cellular Systems Inc., p. 478

Verbatim Corporation, p. 166

North Dakota

Great Plains Software Inc., p. 124

Souris River Telecom Coop, p. 466

Ohio

Allen Telecom Inc., p. 407

Applied Innovation Inc., p. 409

Buckeye Cable Vision Inc., p. 414

Central Telephone Co of Illinois, pp. 416-417

Champion Spark Plug Company, p. 107

Cincinnati Bell Inc., p. 418

Cincinnati Bell Info Systems, p. 108

Cincinnati Bell Long Distance, p. 418

Cincinnati Bell Telephone Co., p. 418

Cincinnati Electronics Corp, p. 418

Cincom Systems Inc., p. 108

Compuserve Corporation, p. 110

Conquest Telecom Svcs, p. 421

Diebold Incorporated, p. 116

GTE Wireless of Midwest Inc., p. 434

Horizon Telecom Inc., p. 436

Huntington Service Company, p. 126

Key Services Corporation, p. 133

Lloyd Daniels Dev Group, p. 444

Malrite Communications Group, p. 445

MediaOne of Ohio Inc., p. 447

Metatec Corp, p. 448

Midwest Payment Systems, Inc., p. 141

Mitsubishi Electric Auto Amer, p. 142

Mosler Inc., p. 142

NCR Corporation, p. 144

New Par, p. 451

OCLC Online Cmpt Lib Ctr Inc., p. 145

Peco Ii Inc., p. 457

Phonetel Technologies Inc., p. 458

Reltec Communications Inc., p. 462

Scripps Howard Broadcasting Co., p. 464

Smartalk Teleservices, Inc., p. 465

Spectra Precision Inc., p. 158

Stoneridge, Inc., pp. 159, 468

Structural Dynamics Res Corp., p. 159

Sygnet Wireless Inc., p. 469

Telxon Corporation, pp. 162-163

The Chillicothe Telephone Co., p. 418

The Ohio Bell Telephone Co., p. 454

United Telephone Co of Indiana, p. 476

United Telephone Co of Ohio, p. 477

Universal Logic Technologies, p. 477

Western Reserve Tele Co Inc., p. 480

Worldcom Advanced Networks Inc., p. 170

Oklahoma

Amerivision Communications, p. 409

Applied Automation Inc., p. 99

Cherokee Nation, pp. 417-418

Dobson Communication Corp., p. 425

Pioneer Telephone Coop Inc., p. 458

Prevue Networks, Inc., p. 460

Tulsa Cable Television, Inc., p. 475

Unit Parts Company, p. 165

United Video Satellite Group, p. 477

VYVX, Inc., p. 479

Geographical Index

COMPANY INDEX BY SIC

The Company Index by SIC presents company names arranged by Standard Industrial Classification codes. Page references are to the company's listing in Chapter 4, Company Directory, in both Part I and Part II.

3661 - continued
Boca Research Inc., p. 413
Bogen Communications Intl, p. 413
Brite Voice Systems Inc., p. 414
Cable Systems Intl Inc., p. 415
Casio Phonemate Inc., p. 416
Centigram Communications Corp, p. 416
Cidco Incorporated, p. 418
Ciena Corporation, p. 418
CMC Industries Inc., p. 419
Cnet Technology Corp, p. 419
Comdial Corporation, p. 420
Communications Systems, Inc., p. 420
Comverse Network Systems Inc., p. 421
Conexant Systems, Inc., p. 421
Contel Federal Systems Inc., p. 422
Cyberfone, p. 423
Dialogic Corporation, p. 424
Digital Link Corporation, p. 424
E C I Telecom Inc., p. 426
EIS International Inc., p. 427
Elcotel Inc., p. 427
Excel Switching Corporation, p. 428
Executone Information Systems, p. 428
Fujitsu Network Communications, p. 430
Gai-Tronics Corporation, p. 430
General Datacomm Inc., p. 431
GN Netcom Inc., p. 432
GTE Government Systems Corp, p. 433
Hayes Corporation, p. 435
Hitachi Telecom USA Inc., p. 436
Hub Fabricating Company, p. 436
Infinity Wireless Products, p. 438
Intecom Inc., p. 438
Intelidata Technologies Corp, p. 438
Inter-Tel Incorporated, p. 439
Intervoice Inc., p. 439
IPC Information Systems Inc., p. 439
Kentrox Industries Inc., p. 442
Keptel Inc., p. 442
Krone Inc., p. 443
Larscom Incorporated, p. 443
Lucent Technologies Inc., p. 445
Matra Communication USA Inc., p. 446
Microcom Inc., p. 448
Milgo Solutions, pp. 448-449
Mitel Inc., p. 449
Mosaix Inc., p. 449
Multi-Tech Systems Inc., p. 450
NEC America Inc., pp. 450-451
Network Equipment Technologies, p. 451
Newbridge Networks Inc., p. 451
Northern Telecom Inc Del, p. 453
Nuera Communications, Inc., p. 453
Octel Communications Corp, pp. 453-454
Oneworld Systems Inc., p. 454
Osicom Technologies Inc., p. 455
P-Com Inc., p. 455
Pairgain Technologies, Inc., p. 456
Paradyne Corporation, p. 456
Peco Ii Inc., p. 457
Periphonics Corporation, p. 457
Plant Equipment Inc., p. 458
Plantronics Inc., p. 458
Polycom, Inc., p. 459

Premisys Communications Inc., p. 459
Qualcomm Per Electric A Cal Partnr, p. 461
Racal Corporation, p. 461
Reltec Communications Inc., p. 462
Siemens Info & Comm Network Inc., p. 465
Symmetricom Inc., p. 469
Tekelec, p. 471
Telect, Inc., p. 471
Tellabs Inc., p. 472
Teltrend Inc., p. 472
Teltronics Inc., p. 472
Timeplex Inc., p. 473
Tollgrade Communications, Inc., p. 473
Uniphase Telecom Products, p. 476
UTstarcom, Inc., p. 478
VAI Corporation, p. 478
Verilink Corporation, p. 478
Vodavi Technology, Inc., p. 479
Westell, Inc., p. 480
Westell Technologies Inc., p. 480
World Access Inc., p. 481
Zoom Telephonics Canadian Corp, p. 482

3663 - Radio & TV Communications Equipment

Alcatel Data Networks, Inc., p. 406
Allen Telecom Inc., p. 407
Alteon Networks Inc., p. 407
Andrew Corporation, p. 409
Antec Corporation (Del), p. 409
Antronix Inc., p. 409
Applied Signal Technology Inc., p. 410
Augat Communication Products, p. 411
Aydin Corporation, p. 411
Bee Tronics Inc., p. 411
Blonder-Tongue Laboratories, p. 413
C-Cor Electronics Inc., p. 414
California Amplifier Inc., p. 415
California Microwave Inc., p. 415
Celeritek Inc., p. 416
Chyron Corporation, p. 418
Cincinnati Electronics Corp, p. 418
Clark David Company Inc., p. 419
Com21 Inc., p. 420
Comstream Corporation, p. 421
Continental Electronics Corp, p. 422
Corsair Communications Inc., p. 422
Customtracks Corporation, p. 423
Cylink Corporation, p. 423
Datron/Transco, Inc., p. 423
Datron World Communications, p. 423
Digital Microwave Corporation, p. 424
Dolby Laboratories Inc., p. 425
Dukane Corporation, p. 426
Eagle Comtronics Inc., p. 426
Echelon Corporation, p. 426
Efdata Corp., pp. 426-427
Electromagnetic Sciences, Inc., p. 427
Ericsson Inc., p. 428
ETO Inc., p. 428
F E L Corporation, p. 428
Gabriel Inc., p. 430
Gardiner Communications Corp, p. 431
Gemini Industries Inc., p. 431
General Instrument Corporation, p. 431

4813 - continued
Central Telephone Co of Illinois, pp. 416-417
Century Telephone Enterprises, p. 417
Century Telephone of Washington, p. 417
Century Telephone of Wisconsin, p. 417
CFW Communications Company, p. 417
Choctaw Communications, Inc., p. 418
Chorus Communications Group, p. 418
Cincinnati Bell Inc., p. 418
Cincinnati Bell Long Distance, p. 418
Cincinnati Bell Telephone Co., p. 418
Citizens Communications, p. 418
Citizens Telecom Co of NY, p. 419
Citizens Utilities Company, p. 419
Cohesive Technology Solutions, p. 419
Com Tech International Corp, p. 420
Cominex LLC, p. 420
Comm South Companies, Inc., p. 420
Commonwealth Telephone Co., p. 420
Communications Concepts Investments, p. 420
Communications Telesystems Intl, p. 420
Communigroup Inc., pp. 420-421
Communigroup of KC, Inc., p. 421
Concentric Network Corporation, p. 421
Conestoga Enterprises Inc., p. 421
Conquest Telecom Svcs, p. 421
Consolidated Communication, p. 421
Contel of California Inc., p. 422
Contel of New York, Inc., p. 422
Convergent Communications Svcs, p. 422
Cooperative Communications, p. 422
CT Communications Inc., p. 423
Datek Online Holding Company, p. 423
Davel Communications Group, p. 424
DBT Online, Inc., p. 424
Destia Communications, Inc., p. 424
Digex, Incorporated, p. 424
Digitec 2000 Inc., p. 424
Discount Long Distance Inc., p. 425
Distance Long International, p. 425
E N M R Telephone Coop, p. 426
East Ascension Telephone Co., p. 426
Ebay, Inc., p. 426
EDCO LLC, p. 426
Eglobe Inc., p. 427
Electric Lightwave Inc., p. 427
Emkay Communications Inc., p. 427
E.Spire Communications Inc., p. 428
Evercom, Inc., p. 428
Excel Communications, Inc., p. 428
Excite Inc., p. 428
Exodus Communications, Inc., p. 428
Facilicom International LLC, p. 429
Farmers Telephone Cooperative, p. 429
Fnet Corp, p. 429
Frontier Corporation, p. 430
G E Capital Comm Svcs Corp, p. 430
G S T Telecom, Inc., p. 430
General Communication, Inc., p. 431
Georgia Alltel Inc., p. 431
G.I.K Technology, Inc., p. 432
Global Commerce & Media Network, p. 432
Global Telesystems Group Inc., p. 432
Globalstar, L. P., p. 432
Goldenline Network Service, p. 432

Group Long Distance Inc., p. 433
GST Telecommunications Inc., p. 433
GTE Corporation, p. 433
GTE Cybertrust Solutions Inc., p. 433
GTE Intelligent Network Svcs Inc., p. 433
GTE Midwest Incorporated, p. 433
GTE Service Corporation, p. 434
GTE West Coast Incorporated, p. 434
G.T.E. World Headquarters, p. 434
Gulf Coast Services Inc., p. 434
Gulf Telephone Company, Inc., p. 434
Hickory Tech Corporation, p. 436
Horizon Telecom Inc., p. 436
Horry Telephone Cooperative, p. 436
ICG Communications Inc., p. 437
ICG Holdings, Inc., p. 437
ICG Telecom Group Inc., p. 437
IDT Corporation, p. 437
ILD Telecommunications Inc., p. 437
Illinois Bell Telephone Co., p. 437
Incomnet, Inc., p. 437
Indiana Bell Telephone Co Inc., p. 438
Infoseek Corporation, p. 438
Intellicall Inc., p. 438
Intelnet International Corp, p. 439
Intermedia Communications Inc., p. 439
International Telcom LTD, p. 439
International Telecom Group LTD, p. 439
Interoute Telecommunications, p. 439
Iowa Network Services Inc., p. 439
Islandlife LLC, pp. 439-440
ITC Holding Company, Inc., p. 440
ITCdeltacom, Inc., p. 440
IXC Communications, Inc., p. 440
IXC, Inc., p. 440
Justice Technology Corporation, p. 441
LCI International Inc., p. 443
Level 3 Communications, Inc., p. 443
Level 3 Telecom Holdings, Inc., p. 443
Light Technologies LLC, p. 444
Long Distance Savers Inc., p. 444
Los Angeles Cellular Tele Co., pp. 444-445
Low Country Telephone Company, p. 445
Lufkin-Conroe Communications Co., p. 445
Matanuska Telephone Assn., p. 446
MC Liquidating Corporation, p. 446
MCI Communications Corporation, p. 446
MCI International Inc., p. 446
MCI Worldcom Inc., pp. 446-447
McLeod USA Incorporated, p. 447
McLeod USA Telecommunications, p. 447
Meridian Telecom Corp, p. 448
MFS Telecom, Inc. (Del), p. 448
Michigan Bell Telephone Co., p. 448
Minnesota Equal Access, p. 449
MJD Communications, Inc., p. 449
N I C E Systems Inc (De Corp), p. 450
National Dispatch Center Inc., p. 450
National Tele & Communications, p. 450
Netselect, Inc., p. 451
Netsource Communications Inc., p. 451
Network Operator Services, p. 451
Network Plus Inc., p. 451
Nevada Bell, p. 451
New England Tele & Telegraph Co., p. 451

4822 - Telegraph and Other Communications

4832 - Radio Broadcasting Stations

Allsup Enterprises, Inc., p. 407
Bonneville International Corp, pp. 413-414
Booth American Company, p. 414
Capstar Broadcasting Corp, p. 416
Chancellor Media Corporation, p. 417
Citadel Broadcasting Company, p. 418
Clear Channel Communications, p. 419
Cumulus Broadcasting Inc., p. 423
Deseret Management Corporation, p. 424
Emmis Communications Corp, p. 427
Entercom Communications Corp, p. 427
Georgia Public Telecom Comm, p. 431
Heftel Broadcasting Corp, p. 435
Infinity Broadcasting Corp Cal Del, p. 438
Infinity Broadcasting Corp Del, p. 438
Jacor Broadcasting of Tampa Bay, p. 440
Jacor Communications Inc., p. 440
KTNQ/KLVE, Inc (Not Inc), p. 443
Nassau Broadcasting Partners LP, p. 450
Osborn Communications Corp, p. 455
Price Communications Corp, p. 460
Radio One Inc., p. 462
Raycom America, Inc., p. 462
Saga Communications Inc., p. 463
Salem Communication Corp, p. 464
Spanish Broadcasting System, p. 466
Taylor University Broadcasting, p. 469
Trans World Radio, p. 474
Triathlon Broadcasting Company, p. 474
Wisconsin Educational Communications Bd, p. 481

4833 - Television Broadcasting Stations

ABC Inc, p. 404
Adventist Media Center, Inc., p. 405
Allbritton Communications Co., p. 407
American Broadcasting Companies, pp. 407-408
Bahakel Communications LTD, p. 411
Benedek Broadcasting Corp., p. 413
BHC Communications, Inc., p. 413
CBS Broadcasting Inc., p. 416
CBS Corporation, p. 416
Chris-Craft Industries Inc., p. 418
CNBC, Inc., p. 419
Community TV of Southern California, p. 421
Convergent Media Systems Corp, p. 422
Cordillera Communications Inc., p. 422
Cosmos Broadcasting Corp, p. 422
Courtroom TV Network LLC, p. 422
Diversified Communications, p. 425
Educational Broadcasting Corp, p. 426
Evening Telegram Co Inc., p. 428
Federal Broadcasting Company, p. 429
Fisher Broadcasting Inc., p. 429
Fox Broadcasting Company, p. 430
Fox Television Stations Inc., p. 430
Gannett Tennessee LTD Partnr, p. 431
Granite Broadcasting Corp, p. 432
Gray Communications Systems, p. 433
Greater Washington Educational Telecom Assn., p. 433
H C Crown Corp, p. 434
Hartford Television, Inc., p. 435

Hearst-Argyle Television Inc., p. 435
Independent Television Network, p. 437
Jefferson-Plot Communications Co., p. 440
Journal Broadcast Group Inc., p. 441
Kcal TV, Inc., p. 441
Kelly Broadcasting Co A LTD Partnr, p. 442
KHOU-TV, Inc., p. 442
KOIN-TV Inc., p. 442
Koplar Communications Inc., p. 442
KQED Inc., p. 442
KTLA Inc., p. 443
Liberty Corporation, pp. 443-444
LIN Television Corporation, p. 444
LIN Television of Texas, L P, p. 444
Mac America Communications Inc., p. 445
Malrite Communications Group, p. 445
McGraw-Hill Broadcasting Co., p. 446
Meredith Corporation, p. 448
Multimedia KSDK Inc., p. 450
Musicbox Network, p. 450
National Broadcasting Co Inc., p. 450
National Mobile Television Inc., p. 450
Outlet Communications Inc., p. 455
Paramount Stations Group, Inc., p. 456
Paramunt Stns Group of Detroit, p. 456
Paxson Communication of New Lnd, p. 457
Paxson Communications Corp, p. 457
Pegasus Communications Corp, p. 457
Pegasus Media & Communications, p. 457
Perpetual Corporation, p. 457
Post-Newsweek Stations FLA Inc., p. 459
Post-Newsweek Stations Inc., p. 459
Prevue Networks, Inc., p. 460
Public Broadcasting Service, p. 461
Pulitzer Broadcasting Company, p. 461
Quincy Newspapers Inc., p. 461
Raycom Media Inc., p. 462
Renaissance Communications, p. 463
Retlaw Enterprises Inc., p. 463
Scripps Howard Broadcasting Co., p. 464
Sinclair Communications, Inc., p. 465
Sinclair Properties L.L.C., p. 465
South Carolina Educational TV Comm, p. 466
Sullivan Broadcasting Company, p. 468
Sunbeam Television Corp, p. 468
Sunbelt Communications Company, p. 468
Superstation Inc., pp. 468-469
Telemundo Group Inc., p. 472
Texas Television Inc., p. 472
Tribune Broadcasting Company, p. 474
Turner Broadcasting System, p. 475
Turner Original Productions Inc., p. 475
Twentieth Century-Fox TV Intl, p. 475
U S Media Holdings, Inc., p. 475
United Television Inc., p. 477
Univision Communications, Inc., p. 477
Univision Television Group, p. 477
WFAA-TV Inc., p. 480
WGNX Inc., p. 480
WHDH, TV, Inc., p. 480
Window to the World Communications, p. 481
WLVI, Inc., p. 481
WPGH, Inc., pp. 481-482
WPIX, Inc., p. 482
Young Broadcasting Inc., p. 482

4841 - Cable and Other Pay TV

A & E Television Networks, p. 404
A-R Cable Services Inc., p. 404
Adelphia Communications Corp, p. 405
Affiliated Regional Comm, p. 406
American CableSystems of Mass, p. 408
American Holdings LP, p. 408
American Movie Classics Co., p. 408
American Telecasting, Inc., p. 408
Arkansas Democrat Gazette, p. 410
Ascent Entertainment Group, p. 410
BET Holdings Inc., p. 413
Black Entertainment Television, p. 413
Bresnan Communications LP, p. 414
Buckeye Cable Vision Inc., p. 414
Buford Television Inc., p. 414
C-Net, Inc., pp. 414-415
Cable Network Services LLC, p. 415
Cable News Network Inc., p. 415
Cable One, Inc., p. 415
Cablevision Connecticut Corp, p. 415
Cablevision Lightpath Inc., p. 415
Cablevision of Monmouth Inc., p. 415
Cablevision Systems Corp, p. 415
Century Communications Corp, p. 417
Chambers Communications Corp, p. 417
Charter Communications, Inc., p. 417
Chauncey Communications Corp, p. 417
Classic Cable Inc., p. 419
Colony Communications, Inc., p. 419
Colorado Springs Cablevision, p. 419
Comcast Cablevision of Mercer County, p. 420
Comcast Cablevision of NJ, p. 420
Cox Communications Inc., p. 422
Cox Communications New Orleans, pp. 422-423
Cox Communications San Diego Inc., p. 423
CSC Holdings, Inc., p. 423
DirecTV, Inc., p. 425
Discovery Communications Inc., p. 425
Dish, LTD, p. 425
Disney Channel Inc., p. 425
Echostar Communications Corp, p. 426
Encore Media Corporation, p. 427
Entertainment Inc., p. 427
ESPN Inc., p. 428
Falcon Holding Group LP, p. 429
FPL Group Capital Inc., p. 430
G S Communications Inc., p. 430
Galaxy Telecom, L P, p. 430
Garden State Cable Vision, LP, p. 431
Gemstar Intl Group LTD, p. 431
Globecast North America Inc., p. 432
Golden Sky Systems, Inc., p. 432
Harron Communications Corp, p. 435
Hauser Communications Inc., p. 435
Heartland Wireless Communications, p. 435
Helicon Group, L.P., p. 435
Heritage Cablevision, (Ia), p. 436
Heritage Cablevision of Cal, p. 436
Heritage Communications Inc., p. 436
Insight Communications Co LP, p. 438
Intermedia Management Inc., p. 439
Intermedia Partners, p. 439
International Family Entertainment, p. 439

Jones Communications, p. 441
Jones Global Group, Inc., p. 441
Jones Intercable Inc., p. 441
Jones International LTD, p. 441
Kansas City Cable Partners, LP, p. 441
KBL Portland Cablesystems LP, p. 441
Lenfest Communications Inc., p. 443
Liberty Media Corporation, p. 444
Lifetime Entertainment Svcs, p. 444
Lodgenet Entertainment Corp, p. 444
Marcus Cable Company LLC, p. 445
Media Gen Cable of Fairfax Cnty, p. 447
Mediacom Southeast LLC, p. 447
Mediaone Group, Inc., p. 447
Mediaone Northern Illinois Inc., p. 447
Mediaone of Fresno, p. 447
Mediaone of Greater Florida, p. 447
Mediaone of Los Angeles, Inc., p. 447
Mediaone of New England Inc., p. 447
MediaOne of Ohio Inc., p. 447
Mediaone of Sierra Valleys, p. 447
Mediaone of Virginia, Inc., pp. 447-448
Metromedia Intl Group Inc., p. 448
Midcontinent Cable Co., p. 448
Midcontinent Media, Inc., p. 448
Ml Media Partners, L.P., p. 449
Multimedia Cablevision, Inc., p. 450
National Cable Satellite Corp, p. 450
Northland Telecom Corp, p. 453
NPG Holdings, Inc., p. 453
NTL Incorporated, p. 453
Olympus Communications, L P, p. 454
On Command Corporation, p. 454
Optel, Inc., p. 455
Orbital Imaging Corporation, p. 455
Pacific Bell Video Services, p. 455
Prestige Cable TV Inc., p. 459
Prime Sports Channel Network LP, p. 460
RCN Cable Systems Inc., p. 462
RCN Telecom Services of Pa, p. 462
Robin Media Group Inc., p. 463
Satellite Services, Inc., p. 464
SBC Media Ventures Inc., p. 464
Service Electric Television, p. 464
Sport South Network, LTD, p. 467
Sportschannel Associates, p. 467
Sportschannel Chicago Assoc, p. 467
Suburban Cable TV Co Inc., p. 468
TAL Financial Corporation, p. 469
TCA Cable TV Inc., p. 469
TCI Cable Investments Inc., p. 469
TCI Cablevision of Alabama, p. 469
TCI Cablevision of California, p. 469
TCI Cablevision of Missouri, p. 469
TCI Cablevision of Wisconsin, p. 469
TCI Central, Inc., p. 469
TCI Communications, Inc., p. 470
TCI Great Lakes, Inc., p. 470
TCI Holdings, Inc., p. 470
TCI of Lexington, Inc., p. 470
TCI of Overland Park, Inc., p. 470
TCI of Pennsylvania, Inc., p. 470
TCI Southeast Inc., p. 470
TCI TKR Cable I Inc., p. 470
TCI TKR of South Florida, Inc., p. 470

4841 - continued
TCI West, Inc., p. 470
Tele-Communications, Inc., p. 471
Telenoticias LLC, p. 472
TGC Inc, pp. 472-473
Time Warner Cable Programming, p. 473
Time Warner Entertainment, p. 473
Triax USA Associates, LP, p. 474
Tulalip Tribes Inc., p. 475
Tulsa Cable Television, Inc., p. 475
Turner-Vision, Inc., p. 475
TWC Cable Partners LP, p. 475
TWI Cable Inc., p. 475
UACC Midwest, Inc., p. 476
United Artists Entertainment Co., p. 476
United Artists Holdings, Inc., p. 476
United Cable Television, p. 476
United International Holding, p. 476
United Video Satellite Group, p. 477
Unity Motion, Inc., p. 477
USA Networks, p. 478
Viacom Inc., p. 479
Warner Cable Communication, p. 479
Weather Channel Inc., p. 479
Wireless One, Inc., p. 481

4899 - Communications Services, nec

Advanced Communications Systems, p. 405
AlliedSignal Technical Svcs, p. 407
American Mobile Satellite Corp, p. 408
American Tower Corp, p. 408
Computer Science Raytheon, p. 421
Comsat Corporation, p. 421
Concert Management Services, p. 421
G E American Communications, p. 430
Global One Communications LLC, p. 432
Hughes Communications Inc., p. 437
International Telecomm Satellite Org, p. 439
ITT Federal Services Corp, p. 440
Lockheed Martin Tech Oper, p. 444
Loral Orion Network Systems, p. 444
Pamplin Communications Corp, p. 456
Panamsat Corporation, p. 456
Primetime 24 Joint Venture, p. 460
Roseville Communications Co., p. 463
Splitrock Services Inc., p. 467
Stratos Mobile Networks USA LLC, p. 468
United States Satellite Broadcasting, p. 476
VYVX, Inc., p. 479
Zekko Corporation, p. 482

7371 - Computer programming services

4Front Software International, p. 94
Aardvark, Inc., p. 94
ABR Benefits Services, Inc., p. 94
ACS Technology Solutions, Inc., p. 95
Agena Corporation, p. 96
Allied Business Systems Inc., pp. 96-97
Alltel Financial Services Inc., p. 97
AMS Management Systems Group Inc., p. 98
Analysts International Corp., p. 98
Anstec, Inc., pp. 98-99
Applied Systems Inc., p. 99

Ardent Software Inc., p. 99
Avant Corporation, p. 101
Axent Technologies Inc., p. 102
Barden Companies, Inc., p. 102
Bea Systems, Inc., p. 103
Born Information Services, p. 104
Brooktrout Technology Inc., p. 105
BTG, Inc., p. 105
Cambridge Technology Partners, p. 106
Camelot Corporation, p. 106
CCC Information Serices Group, p. 107
Cheyenne Software Inc., p. 108
Citrix Systems Inc., p. 109
Cognizant Tech Solutions Corp., p. 109
Complete Business Solutions, p. 110
Computer Aid Inc., p. 110
Computer Horizons Corp., p. 110
Computer Task Group Inc., p. 111
Compuware Corporation, p. 111
Consist International, Inc., p. 111
Cooperative Computing Inc., p. 112
Cotelligent, Inc., p. 112
Covenant Computer Laboratory, p. 112
CSX Technology Inc., p. 112
CVSI Inc., p. 113
Cybernetics & Systems Inc., p. 113
DBC Holding Corp., p. 114
Decision Consultants Inc., p. 115
Dendrite International Inc., p. 115
Digicon Corporation, p. 116
DMR Consulting Group Inc., p. 116
Eclipsys Corporation, p. 118
Foxconn Corporation, p. 122
GEAC Computer Systems, Inc., p. 123
Genesys Telecom Labs, p. 123
Geoscience Corp., p. 123
Gerber Garment Technology, p. 123
Goldleaf Technologies, Inc., p. 124
H T E Inc., p. 125
HNC Software Inc., p. 126
Howard Systems Intl Inc., p. 126
Hyperion Solutions Corp., p. 127
IDX Systems Corporation, p. 127
Industri-Matematik International, p. 128
Informix Corporation, p. 128
Inspire Insurance Solutions, p. 128
Intelligroup Inc., p. 129
Inter-National Research Inst, p. 129
Interim Technology Inc., p. 130
Kanbay LLC, p. 133
Kenan Systems Corporation, p. 133
Kenda Systems Inc., p. 133
Kirchman Corporation, p. 134
L H S Group Inc., p. 134
Lacerte Software Corporation, p. 134
Landmark Graphics Corporation, p. 134
Logicon Space & Information, p. 135
Logicon Syscon Inc., p. 136
Manugistics Group Inc., p. 137
Manugistics, Inc., p. 137
Martin Collier, p. 137
Mastech Corporation, pp. 137-138
Medical Information Technology, p. 138
Melita International Corp., p. 139
Metamor Information Tech Services, p. 139

7371 - continued
Metamor Worldwide Inc., p. 139
Metro Information Services, p. 139
Micro Voice Applications Inc., p. 140
Mobius Management Systems Inc., p. 142
NCI Information Systems Inc., pp. 143-144
Netmanage, Inc., p. 144
Netscout Systems Inc., p. 144
Network Associates Inc., p. 144
OAO Corporation, p. 145
Objective Systems Integrators, p. 145
Onix Systems Inc., p. 146
P S I Holding Group Inc., p. 146
Pegasus Consulting Group Inc., p. 147
Peregrine Systems Inc., p. 148
Phoenix Technologies Ltd., p. 148
Platinum Technology Solutions, p. 149
PRC Inc., p. 149
Printrak International Inc., p. 150
Progress Software Corporation, p. 150
Qad Inc., pp. 150-151
Remedy Corporation, p. 152
Sabre Group, Inc., p. 153
Santa Cruz Operation Inc., p. 153
SAP America Inc., p. 153
SAP America Pubic Sector, Inc., p. 153
Sapient Corporation, p. 154
SCB Computer Technology Inc., p. 154
SCT Software & Resources Mgt, p. 154
Seagate Sftwr Stor Mgt Group, p. 154
Seer Technologies Inc., p. 155
Smith Wall Associates LLC, p. 157
Stargate Systems, Inc., p. 158
Stealthsoft Corporation, p. 158
Sunsoft, Inc., p. 160
Sykes Enterprises Incorporated, pp. 160-161
Synopsys, Inc., p. 161
Syntel, Inc., p. 161
Telcordia Technologies Inc., p. 162
Tivoli Systems Inc., p. 163
Transquest Holdings Inc., p. 164
TSR, Inc., pp. 164-165
Tullett & Tokyo Forex Inc., p. 165
USCS International, Inc., p. 166
Versyss Incorporated, p. 167
Viasoft, Inc., p. 167
Walker Interactive Systems, p. 168
Whittman-Hart Inc., p. 169

7372 - Prepackaged software

A C I Worldwide Inc., p. 94
Acclaim Entertainment, p. 94
Adobe Systems Incorporated, p. 95
Advent Software Inc., p. 96
American Software, Inc., p. 98
AMS Services Inc., p. 98
Aspect Telecommunications Corp., p. 100
Aspen Technology Inc., p. 100
Astea International Inc., p. 100
Autodesk Inc., p. 101
B M C Software Inc., p. 102
Barra, Inc., pp. 102-103
Boole & Babbage Inc., p. 104
Broderbund Software Inc., p. 105

Cadence Design Systems Inc., p. 106
Caere Corporation, p. 106
Candle Corporation, p. 106
Cendant Software, p. 107
Cerner Corporation, p. 107
Clarify Inc., p. 109
Computer Associates International, p. 110
Computron Software Inc., p. 111
Comshare Incorporated, p. 111
Cyborg Systems Inc., p. 113
Datastream Systems Inc., p. 114
Davidson & Associates Inc., p. 114
Documentum, Inc., p. 117
Eastman Software, Inc., p. 118
Edify Corporation, p. 118
Electronic Arts, p. 118
Ericsson Hewlett-Packard, p. 120
Filemaker, Inc., p. 120
Filenet Corporation, p. 121
Forte Software, Inc., p. 122
Fourth Shift Corporation, p. 122
Getty Images Inc., p. 123
Gores Technology Group, p. 124
Great Plains Software Inc., p. 124
GT Interactive Software Corp., p. 124
Harbinger Corporation, p. 125
HBO & Company, p. 125
Holland America Inv Corp., p. 126
Hyperion Software Corporation, p. 127
I2 Technologies Inc., p. 127
Indus International Inc., p. 127
Infinium Software Inc., p. 128
Inprise Corporation, p. 128
Interleaf Inc., p. 130
Intersolv, Inc., p. 130
Intuit Inc., p. 131
Isaac Fair and Company Inc., p. 131
J.D. Edwards & Company, p. 132
J.D. Edwards World Solutions Co., p. 132
Kronos Incorporated, p. 134
Lawson Associates, Inc., p. 135
Learning Company Inc., p. 135
Legato Systems, Inc., p. 135
Lotus Development Corporation, p. 136
Macromedia Inc., p. 137
Mapics, Inc., p. 137
Mapinfo Corporation, p. 137
Marcam Solutions Inc., p. 137
MDL Information Systems, Inc., p. 138
Medical Manager Corporation, pp. 138-139
Medstat Holdings Inc., p. 139
Micrografx, Inc., p. 140
Microsoft Corporation, p. 141
Microsoft Puerto Rico Inc., p. 141
Microstrategy Incorporated, p. 141
Mindscape, Inc., p. 141
Netscape Communications Corp., p. 144
Oracle Corporation, p. 146
Parametric Technology Corp., p. 147
Peachtree Software Inc., p. 147
Peoplesoft, Inc., p. 148
Platinum Software Corporation, p. 148
Platinum Technology International, p. 149
Policy Management Systems Corp., p. 149
Print Northwest Co LP, pp. 149-150

SIC Index

671

SIC Index

7376 - Computer facilities management

GenAmerica Corporation, p. 123
New Resources Corporation, p. 144
Perot Systems Corporation, p. 148
Raytheon Service Company, p. 152

7377 - Computer rental & leasing

Amplicon Inc., p. 98
Comdisco Inc., p. 109
Computer Sales International, p. 111
CRA Inc., p. 112
El Camino Resources International, p. 118
Forsythe Technology, Inc., p. 122
General Electric Capital, p. 123
Jacom Computer Services, Inc., p. 131
JLC Holding Inc., p. 132
Jostens Learning Corporation, p. 132
MFP Technology Services Inc., p. 140
MLC Holdings Inc., p. 142
Par Computer-Leasing, p. 147
U S Capital Equipment Lessors, p. 165
Universal Computer Network, p. 166

7378 - Computer maintenance & repair

Amdahl Corporation, p. 97
Cerplex, Inc., p. 107
DecisionOne Corporation, p. 115
Fanuc America Corporation, p. 120
Sequel Inc., p. 155
Technology Service Solutions, p. 162
Telos Field Engineering Inc., p. 162
Wang Laboratories, Inc., p. 169

7379 - Computer related services, nec

ACS Government Solutions Group Inc., p. 95
Ajilon Services Inc., p. 96
Amdahl Finance Corporation, p. 97
Amdahl International Corp., p. 97
American Mgt Systems Inc., p. 98
Anteon Corp., p. 99
Applied Cellular Technology, p. 99
Aris Corporation, p. 99
Automated Concepts Inc., p. 101
Berger & Co., p. 104
Bindco Corporation, p. 104
Ciber, Inc., p. 108
Claremont Technology Group, p. 109
Comp-Sys Designs, p. 109
Computer Management Sciences, p. 110
Computer Merchant Ltd., p. 110
Computer Sciences Corporation, p. 111
ESG Consulting Inc., p. 120
Impact Innovations Holdings, p. 127
Information Mgt Resources, p. 128
Instinet Corporation, p. 128
Inteliant Corporation, p. 129
Interactive Business Systems, p. 129
International Network Svcs, p. 130
Micro Modeling Associates Inc., p. 140
Micros-To-Mainframes, Inc., p. 141
Modus Media International Inc., p. 142

N B S G III, p. 143
Paragon Computer Professionals, p. 147
Pinkerton Computer Consultants, p. 148
PKS Information Services LLC, p. 148
Princeton Information Ltd., p. 149
R C G Information Technology, p. 151
Sears Home Services Group, p. 155
Signal Corporation, p. 156
Spectrum Technology Group Inc., p. 158
Summit Group Inc., p. 160
Superior Conslt Holdings Corp., p. 160
Tekmark Global Solutions LLC, p. 162
Triad Data Inc., p. 164
Trident Data Systems Inc., p. 164
TSR Consulting Services Inc., p. 164
Xlconnect Systems, Inc., p. 170

SIC TO NAICS AND NAICS TO SIC
CONVERSION GUIDE

This appendix presents complete conversion tables from SIC codes to NAICS codes. SIC stands for *Standard Industrial Classification*, the "old" system of classifying economic activities. NAICS stands for *North American Industry Classification System*, the new classification for classifying economic activities in the United States, Canada, and Mexico.

The first part of the appendix presents the SIC to NAICS Conversion Guide. Four-digit SIC codes and names are shown in bold type. NAICS codes and names are shown beneath, indented, each item labelled "NAICS". An SIC industry may convert to one or more NAICS industries.

The second part, starting on page 703, shows the same information but in the reverse format: the NAICS to SIC Conversion Guide. NAICS codes and names are shown in bold type; the equivalent SIC codes, beneath, are shown indented. A NAICS-coded industry may have one, more than one, or no SIC equivalent (two instances).

SIC TO NAICS CONVERSION GUIDE

AGRICULTURE, FORESTRY, & FISHING

0111 Wheat
NAICS 11114   Wheat Farming
0112 Rice
NAICS 11116   Rice Farming
0115 Corn
NAICS 11115   Corn Farming
0116 Soybeans
NAICS 11111   Soybean Farming
0119 Cash Grains, nec
NAICS 11113   Dry Pea & Bean Farming
NAICS 11112   Oilseed Farming
NAICS 11115   Corn Farming
NAICS 111191 Oilseed & Grain Combination Farming
NAICS 111199 All Other Grain Farming
0131 Cotton
NAICS 11192   Cotton Farming
0132 Tobacco
NAICS 11191   Tobacco Farming
0133 Sugarcane & Sugar Beets
NAICS 111991 Sugar Beet Farming
NAICS 11193   Sugarcane Farming
0134 Irish Potatoes
NAICS 111211 Potato Farming
0139 Field Crops, Except Cash Grains, nec
NAICS 11194   Hay Farming
NAICS 111992 Peanut Farming
NAICS 111219 Other Vegetable & Melon Farming
NAICS 111998 All Other Miscellaneous Crop Farming
0161 Vegetables & Melons
NAICS 111219 Other Vegetable & Melon Farming
0171 Berry Crops
NAICS 111333 Strawberry Farming
NAICS 111334 Berry Farming
0172 Grapes
NAICS 111332 Grape Vineyards
0173 Tree Nuts
NAICS 111335 Tree Nut Farming
0174 Citrus Fruits
NAICS 11131   Orange Groves
NAICS 11132   Citrus Groves
0175 Deciduous Tree Fruits
NAICS 111331 Apple Orchards
NAICS 111339 Other Noncitrus Fruit Farming
0179 Fruits & Tree Nuts, nec
NAICS 111336 Fruit & Tree Nut Combination Farming
NAICS 111339 Other Noncitrus Fruit Farming
0181 Ornamental Floriculture & Nursery Products
NAICS 111422 Floriculture Production
NAICS 111421 Nursery & Tree Production
0182 Food Crops Grown under Cover
NAICS 111411 Mushroom Production
NAICS 111419 Other Food Crops Grown under Cover
0191 General Farms, Primarily Crop
NAICS 111998 All Other Miscellaneous Crop Farming
0211 Beef Cattle Feedlots
NAICS 112112 Cattle Feedlots
0212 Beef Cattle, Except Feedlots
NAICS 112111 Beef Cattle Ranching & Farming

0213 Hogs
NAICS 11221   Hog & Pig Farming
0214 Sheep & Goats
NAICS 11241   Sheep Farming
NAICS 11242   Goat Farming
0219 General Livestock, Except Dairy & Poultry
NAICS 11299   All Other Animal Production
0241 Dairy Farms
NAICS 112111 Beef Cattle Ranching & Farming
NAICS 11212   Dairy Cattle & Milk Production
0251 Broiler, Fryers, & Roaster Chickens
NAICS 11232   Broilers & Other Meat-type Chicken
           Production
0252 Chicken Eggs
NAICS 11231   Chicken Egg Production
0253 Turkey & Turkey Eggs
NAICS 11233   Turkey Production
0254 Poultry Hatcheries
NAICS 11234   Poultry Hatcheries
0259 Poultry & Eggs, nec
NAICS 11239   Other Poultry Production
0271 Fur-bearing Animals & Rabbits
NAICS 11293   Fur-bearing Animal & Rabbit Production
0272 Horses & Other Equines
NAICS 11292   Horse & Other Equine Production
0273 Animal Aquaculture
NAICS 112511 Finfish Farming & Fish Hatcheries
NAICS 112512 Shellfish Farming
NAICS 112519 Other Animal Aquaculture
0279 Animal Specialties, nec
NAICS 11291   Apiculture
NAICS 11299   All Other Animal Production
0291 General Farms, Primarily Livestock & Animal Specialties
NAICS 11299   All Other Animal Production
0711 Soil Preparation Services
NAICS 115112 Soil Preparation, Planting & Cultivating
0721 Crop Planting, Cultivating & Protecting
NAICS 48122   Nonscheduled Speciality Air Transportation
NAICS 115112 Soil Preparation, Planting & Cultivating
0722 Crop Harvesting, Primarily by Machine
NAICS 115113 Crop Harvesting, Primarily by Machine
**0723 Crop Preparation Services for Market, Except Cotton
   Ginning**
NAICS 115114 Postharvest Crop Activities
0724 Cotton Ginning
NAICS 115111 Cotton Ginning
0741 Veterinary Service for Livestock
NAICS 54194   Veterinary Services
0742 Veterinary Services for Animal Specialties
NAICS 54194   Veterinary Services
0751 Livestock Services, Except Veterinary
NAICS 311611 Animal Slaughtering
NAICS 11521   Support Activities for Animal Production
0752 Animal Specialty Services, Except Veterinary
NAICS 11521   Support Activities for Animal Production
NAICS 81291   Pet Care Services
0761 Farm Labor Contractors & Crew Leaders
NAICS 115115 Farm Labor Contractors & Crew Leaders
0762 Farm Management Services
NAICS 115116 Farm Management Services
0781 Landscape Counseling & Planning
NAICS 54169   Other Scientific & Technical Consulting
           Services
NAICS 54132   Landscape Architectural Services

0782 Lawn & Garden Services
NAICS 56173 Landscaping Services
0783 Ornamental Shrub & Tree Services
NAICS 56173 Landscaping Services
0811 Timber Tracts
NAICS 111421 Nursery & Tree Production
NAICS 11311 Timber Tract Operations
0831 Forest Nurseries & Gathering of Forest Products
NAICS 111998 All Other Miscellaneous Crop
NAICS 11321 Forest Nurseries & Gathering of Forest Products
0851 Forestry Services
NAICS 11531 Support Activities for Forestry
0912 Finfish
NAICS 114111 Finfish Fishing
0913 Shellfish
NAICS 114112 Shellfish Fishing
0919 Miscellaneous Marine Products
NAICS 114119 Other Marine Fishing
NAICS 111998 All Other Miscellaneous Crop Farming
0921 Fish Hatcheries & Preserves
NAICS 112511 Finfish Farming & Fish Hatcheries
NAICS 112512 Shellfish Farming
0971 Hunting, Trapping, & Game Propagation
NAICS 11421 Hunting & Trapping

MINING INDUSTRIES

1011 Iron Ores
NAICS 21221 Iron Ore Mining
1021 Copper Ores
NAICS 212234 Copper Ore & Nickel Ore Mining
1031 Lead & Zinc Ores
NAICS 212231 Lead Ore & Zinc Ore Mining
1041 Gold Ores
NAICS 212221 Gold Ore Mining
1044 Silver Ores
NAICS 212222 Silver Ore Mining
1061 Ferroalloy Ores, Except Vanadium
NAICS 212234 Copper Ore & Nickel Ore Mining
NAICS 212299 Other Metal Ore Mining
1081 Metal Mining Services
NAICS 213115 Support Activities for Metal Mining
NAICS 54136 Geophysical Surveying & Mapping Services
1094 Uranium-radium-vanadium Ores
NAICS 212291 Uranium-radium-vanadium Ore Mining
1099 Miscellaneous Metal Ores, nec
NAICS 212299 Other Metal Ore Mining
1221 Bituminous Coal & Lignite Surface Mining
NAICS 212111 Bituminous Coal & Lignite Surface Mining
1222 Bituminous Coal Underground Mining
NAICS 212112 Bituminous Coal Underground Mining
1231 Anthracite Mining
NAICS 212113 Anthracite Mining
1241 Coal Mining Services
NAICS 213114 Support Activities for Coal Mining
1311 Crude Petroleum & Natural Gas
NAICS 211111 Crude Petroleum & Natural Gas Extraction
1321 Natural Gas Liquids
NAICS 211112 Natural Gas Liquid Extraction
1381 Drilling Oil & Gas Wells
NAICS 213111 Drilling Oil & Gas Wells

1382 Oil & Gas Field Exploration Services
NAICS 48122 Nonscheduled Speciality Air Transportation
NAICS 54136 Geophysical Surveying & Mapping Services
NAICS 213112 Support Activities for Oil & Gas Field Operations
1389 Oil & Gas Field Services, nec
NAICS 213113 Other Oil & Gas Field Support Activities
1411 Dimension Stone
NAICS 212311 Dimension Stone Mining & Quarry
1422 Crushed & Broken Limestone
NAICS 212312 Crushed & Broken Limestone Mining & Quarrying
1423 Crushed & Broken Granite
NAICS 212313 Crushed & Broken Granite Mining & Quarrying
1429 Crushed & Broken Stone, nec
NAICS 212319 Other Crushed & Broken Stone Mining & Quarrying
1442 Construction Sand & Gravel
NAICS 212321 Construction Sand & Gravel Mining
1446 Industrial Sand
NAICS 212322 Industrial Sand Mining
1455 Kaolin & Ball Clay
NAICS 212324 Kaolin & Ball Clay Mining
1459 Clay, Ceramic, & Refractory Minerals, nec
NAICS 212325 Clay & Ceramic & Refractory Minerals Mining
1474 Potash, Soda, & Borate Minerals
NAICS 212391 Potash, Soda, & Borate Mineral Mining
1475 Phosphate Rock
NAICS 212392 Phosphate Rock Mining
1479 Chemical & Fertilizer Mineral Mining, nec
NAICS 212393 Other Chemical & Fertilizer Mineral Mining
1481 Nonmetallic Minerals Services Except Fuels
NAICS 213116 Support Activities for Non-metallic Minerals
NAICS 54136 Geophysical Surveying & Mapping Services
1499 Miscellaneous Nonmetallic Minerals, Except Fuels
NAICS 212319 Other Crushed & Broken Stone Mining or Quarrying
NAICS 212399 All Other Non-metallic Mineral Mining

CONSTRUCTION INDUSTRIES

1521 General Contractors-single-family Houses
NAICS 23321 Single Family Housing Construction
1522 General Contractors-residential Buildings, Other than Single-family
NAICS 23332 Commercial & Institutional Building Construction
NAICS 23322 Multifamily Housing Construction
1531 Operative Builders
NAICS 23321 Single Family Housing Construction
NAICS 23322 Multifamily Housing Construction
NAICS 23331 Manufacturing & Industrial Building Construction
NAICS 23332 Commercial & Institutional Building Construction
1541 General Contractors-industrial Buildings & Warehouses
NAICS 23332 Commercial & Institutional Building Construction
NAICS 23331 Manufacturing & Industrial Building Construction

1542 **General Contractors-nonresidential Buildings, Other than Industrial Buildings & Warehouses**
NAICS 23332 Commercial & Institutional Building Construction

1611 **Highway & Street Construction, Except Elevated Highways**
NAICS 23411 Highway & Street Construction

1622 **Bridge, Tunnel, & Elevated Highway Construction**
NAICS 23412 Bridge & Tunnel Construction

1623 **Water, Sewer, Pipeline, & Communications & Power Line Construction**
NAICS 23491 Water, Sewer & Pipeline Construction
NAICS 23492 Power & Communication Transmission Line Construction

1629 **Heavy Construction, nec**
NAICS 23493 Industrial Nonbuilding Structure Construction
NAICS 23499 All Other Heavy Construction

1711 **Plumbing, Heating, & Air-conditioning**
NAICS 23511 Plumbing, Heating & Air-conditioning Contractors

1721 **Painting & Paper Hanging**
NAICS 23521 Painting & Wall Covering Contractors

1731 **Electrical Work**
NAICS 561621 Security Systems Services
NAICS 23531 Electrical Contractors

1741 **Masonry, Stone Setting & Other Stone Work**
NAICS 23541 Masonry & Stone Contractors

1742 **Plastering, Drywall, Acoustical & Insulation Work**
NAICS 23542 Drywall, Plastering, Acoustical & Insulation Contractors

1743 **Terrazzo, Tile, Marble, & Mosaic Work**
NAICS 23542 Drywall, Plastering, Acoustical & Insulation Contractors
NAICS 23543 Tile, Marble, Terrazzo & Mosaic Contractors

1751 **Carpentry Work**
NAICS 23551 Carpentry Contractors

1752 **Floor Laying & Other Floor Work, nec**
NAICS 23552 Floor Laying & Other Floor Contractors

1761 **Roofing, Siding, & Sheet Metal Work**
NAICS 23561 Roofing, Siding, & Sheet Metal Contractors

1771 **Concrete Work**
NAICS 23542 Drywall, Plastering, Acoustical & Insulation Contractors
NAICS 23571 Concrete Contractors

1781 **Water Well Drilling**
NAICS 23581 Water Well Drilling Contractors

1791 **Structural Steel Erection**
NAICS 23591 Structural Steel Erection Contractors

1793 **Glass & Glazing Work**
NAICS 23592 Glass & Glazing Contractors

1794 **Excavation Work**
NAICS 23593 Excavation Contractors

1795 **Wrecking & Demolition Work**
NAICS 23594 Wrecking & Demolition Contractors

1796 **Installation or Erection of Building Equipment, nec**
NAICS 23595 Building Equipment & Other Machinery Installation Contractors

1799 **Special Trade Contractors, nec**
NAICS 23521 Painting & Wall Covering Contractors
NAICS 23592 Glass & Glazing Contractors
NAICS 56291 Remediation Services
NAICS 23599 All Other Special Trade Contractors

FOOD & KINDRED PRODUCTS

2011 **Meat Packing Plants**
NAICS 311611 Animal Slaughtering

2013 **Sausages & Other Prepared Meats**
NAICS 311612 Meat Processed from Carcasses

2015 **Poultry Slaughtering & Processing**
NAICS 311615 Poultry Processing
NAICS 311999 All Other Miscellaneous Food Manufacturing

2021 **Creamery Butter**
NAICS 311512 Creamery Butter Manufacturing

2022 **Natural, Processed, & Imitation Cheese**
NAICS 311513 Cheese Manufacturing

2023 **Dry, Condensed, & Evaporated Dairy Products**
NAICS 311514 Dry, Condensed, & Evaporated Milk Manufacturing

2024 **Ice Cream & Frozen Desserts**
NAICS 31152 Ice Cream & Frozen Dessert Manufacturing

2026 **Fluid Milk**
NAICS 311511 Fluid Milk Manufacturing

2032 **Canned Specialties**
NAICS 311422 Specialty Canning
NAICS 311999 All Other Miscellaneous Food Manufacturing

2033 **Canned Fruits, Vegetables, Preserves, Jams, & Jellies**
NAICS 311421 Fruit & Vegetable Canning

2034 **Dried & Dehydrated Fruits, Vegetables, & Soup Mixes**
NAICS 311423 Dried & Dehydrated Food Manufacturing
NAICS 311211 Flour Milling

2035 **Pickled Fruits & Vegetables, Vegetables Sauces & Seasonings, & Salad Dressings**
NAICS 311421 Fruit & Vegetable Canning
NAICS 311941 Mayonnaise, Dressing, & Other Prepared Sauce Manufacturing

2037 **Frozen Fruits, Fruit Juices, & Vegetables**
NAICS 311411 Frozen Fruit, Juice, & Vegetable Processing

2038 **Frozen Specialties, nec**
NAICS 311412 Frozen Specialty Food Manufacturing

2041 **Flour & Other Grain Mill Products**
NAICS 311211 Flour Milling

2043 **Cereal Breakfast Foods**
NAICS 31192 Coffee & Tea Manufacturing
NAICS 31123 Breakfast Cereal Manufacturing

2044 **Rice Milling**
NAICS 311212 Rice Milling

2045 **Prepared Flour Mixes & Doughs**
NAICS 311822 Flour Mixes & Dough Manufacturing from Purchased Flour

2046 **Wet Corn Milling**
NAICS 311221 Wet Corn Milling

2047 **Dog & Cat Food**
NAICS 311111 Dog & Cat Food Manufacturing

2048 **Prepared Feed & Feed Ingredients for Animals & Fowls, Except Dogs & Cats**
NAICS 311611 Animal Slaughtering
NAICS 311119 Other Animal Food Manufacturing

2051 **Bread & Other Bakery Products, Except Cookies & Crackers**
NAICS 311812 Commercial Bakeries

2052 **Cookies & Crackers**
NAICS 311821 Cookie & Cracker Manufacturing
NAICS 311919 Other Snack Food Manufacturing
NAICS 311812 Commercial Bakeries

2053 Frozen Bakery Products, Except Bread
NAICS 311813 Frozen Bakery Product Manufacturing
2061 Cane Sugar, Except Refining
NAICS 311311 Sugarcane Mills
2062 Cane Sugar Refining
NAICS 311312 Cane Sugar Refining
2063 Beet Sugar
NAICS 311313 Beet Sugar Manufacturing
2064 Candy & Other Confectionery Products
NAICS 31133 Confectionery Manufacturing from Purchased Chocolate
NAICS 31134 Non-chocolate Confectionery Manufacturing
2066 Chocolate & Cocoa Products
NAICS 31132 Chocolate & Confectionery Manufacturing from Cacao Beans
2067 Chewing Gum
NAICS 31134 Non-chocolate Confectionery Manufacturing
2068 Salted & Roasted Nuts & Seeds
NAICS 311911 Roasted Nuts & Peanut Butter Manufacturing
2074 Cottonseed Oil Mills
NAICS 311223 Other Oilseed Processing
NAICS 311225 Fats & Oils Refining & Blending
2075 Soybean Oil Mills
NAICS 311222 Soybean Processing
NAICS 311225 Fats & Oils Refining & Blending
2076 Vegetable Oil Mills, Except Corn, Cottonseed, & Soybeans
NAICS 311223 Other Oilseed Processing
NAICS 311225 Fats & Oils Refining & Blending
2077 Animal & Marine Fats & Oils
NAICS 311613 Rendering & Meat By-product Processing
NAICS 311711 Seafood Canning
NAICS 311712 Fresh & Frozen Seafood Processing
NAICS 311225 Edible Fats & Oils Manufacturing
2079 Shortening, Table Oils, Margarine, & Other Edible Fats & Oils, nec
NAICS 311225 Edible Fats & Oils Manufacturing
NAICS 311222 Soybean Processing
NAICS 311223 Other Oilseed Processing
2082 Malt Beverages
NAICS 31212 Breweries
2083 Malt
NAICS 311213 Malt Manufacturing
2084 Wines, Brandy, & Brandy Spirits
NAICS 31213 Wineries
2085 Distilled & Blended Liquors
NAICS 31214 Distilleries
2086 Bottled & Canned Soft Drinks & Carbonated Waters
NAICS 312111 Soft Drink Manufacturing
NAICS 312112 Bottled Water Manufacturing
2087 Flavoring Extracts & Flavoring Syrups nec
NAICS 31193 Flavoring Syrup & Concentrate Manufacturing
NAICS 311942 Spice & Extract Manufacturing
NAICS 311999 All Other Miscellaneous Food Manufacturing
2091 Canned & Cured Fish & Seafood
NAICS 311711 Seafood Canning
2092 Prepared Fresh or Frozen Fish & Seafoods
NAICS 311712 Fresh & Frozen Seafood Processing
2095 Roasted Coffee
NAICS 31192 Coffee & Tea Manufacturing
NAICS 311942 Spice & Extract Manufacturing
2096 Potato Chips, Corn Chips, & Similar Snacks
NAICS 311919 Other Snack Food Manufacturing

2097 Manufactured Ice
NAICS 312113 Ice Manufacturing
2098 Macaroni, Spaghetti, Vermicelli, & Noodles
NAICS 311823 Pasta Manufacturing
2099 Food Preparations, nec
NAICS 311423 Dried & Dehydrated Food Manufacturing
NAICS 111998 All Other Miscellaneous Crop Farming
NAICS 31134 Non-chocolate Confectionery Manufacturing
NAICS 311911 Roasted Nuts & Peanut Butter Manufacturing
NAICS 311991 Perishable Prepared Food Manufacturing
NAICS 31183 Tortilla Manufacturing
NAICS 31192 Coffee & Tea Manufacturing
NAICS 311941 Mayonnaise, Dressing, & Other Prepared Sauce Manufacturing
NAICS 311942 Spice & Extract Manufacturing
NAICS 311999 All Other Miscellaneous Food Manufacturing

TOBACCO PRODUCTS

2111 Cigarettes
NAICS 312221 Cigarette Manufacturing
2121 Cigars
NAICS 312229 Other Tobacco Product Manufacturing
2131 Chewing & Smoking Tobacco & Snuff
NAICS 312229 Other Tobacco Product Manufacturing
2141 Tobacco Stemming & Redrying
NAICS 312229 Other Tobacco Product Manufacturing
NAICS 31221 Tobacco Stemming & Redrying

TEXTILE MILL PRODUCTS

2211 Broadwoven Fabric Mills, Cotton
NAICS 31321 Broadwoven Fabric Mills
2221 Broadwoven Fabric Mills, Manmade Fiber & Silk
NAICS 31321 Broadwoven Fabric Mills
2231 Broadwoven Fabric Mills, Wool
NAICS 31321 Broadwoven Fabric Mills
NAICS 313311 Broadwoven Fabric Finishing Mills
NAICS 313312 Textile & Fabric Finishing Mills
2241 Narrow Fabric & Other Smallware Mills: Cotton, Wool, Silk, & Manmade Fiber
NAICS 313221 Narrow Fabric Mills
2251 Women's Full-length & Knee-length Hosiery, Except Socks
NAICS 315111 Sheer Hosiery Mills
2252 Hosiery, nec
NAICS 315111 Sheer Hosiery Mills
NAICS 315119 Other Hosiery & Sock Mills
2253 Knit Outerwear Mills
NAICS 315191 Outerwear Knitting Mills
2254 Knit Underwear & Nightwear Mills
NAICS 315192 Underwear & Nightwear Knitting Mills
2257 Weft Knit Fabric Mills
NAICS 313241 Weft Knit Fabric Mills
NAICS 313312 Textile & Fabric Finishing Mills
2258 Lace & Warp Knit Fabric Mills
NAICS 313249 Other Knit Fabric & Lace Mills
NAICS 313312 Textile & Fabric Finishing Mills
2259 Knitting Mills, nec
NAICS 315191 Outerwear Knitting Mills
NAICS 315192 Underwear & Nightwear Knitting Mills
NAICS 313241 Weft Knit Fabric Mills
NAICS 313249 Other Knit Fabric & Lace Mills

2261 Finishers of Broadwoven Fabrics of Cotton
NAICS 313311 Broadwoven Fabric Finishing Mills
2262 Finishers of Broadwoven Fabrics of Manmade Fiber & Silk
NAICS 313311 Broadwoven Fabric Finishing Mills
2269 Finishers of Textiles, nec
NAICS 313311 Broadwoven Fabric Finishing Mills
NAICS 313312 Textile & Fabric Finishing Mills
2273 Carpets & Rugs
NAICS 31411 Carpet & Rug Mills
2281 Yarn Spinning Mills
NAICS 313111 Yarn Spinning Mills
2282 Yarn Texturizing, Throwing, Twisting, & Winding Mills
NAICS 313112 Yarn Texturing, Throwing & Twisting Mills
NAICS 313312 Textile & Fabric Finishing Mills
2284 Thread Mills
NAICS 313113 Thread Mills
NAICS 313312 Textile & Fabric Finishing Mills
2295 Coated Fabrics, Not Rubberized
NAICS 31332 Fabric Coating Mills
2296 Tire Cord & Fabrics
NAICS 314992 Tire Cord & Tire Fabric Mills
2297 Nonwoven Fabrics
NAICS 31323 Nonwoven Fabric Mills
2298 Cordage & Twine
NAICS 314991 Rope, Cordage & Twine Mills
2299 Textile Goods, nec
NAICS 31321 Broadwoven Fabric Mills
NAICS 31323 Nonwoven Fabric Mills
NAICS 313312 Textile & Fabric Finishing Mills
NAICS 313221 Narrow Fabric Mills
NAICS 313113 Thread Mills
NAICS 313111 Yarn Spinning Mills
NAICS 314999 All Other Miscellaneous Textile Product Mills

APPAREL & OTHER FINISHED PRODUCTS MADE FROM FABRICS & SIMILAR MATERIALS

2311 Men's & Boys' Suits, Coats & Overcoats
NAICS 315211 Men's & Boys' Cut & Sew Apparel Contractors
NAICS 315222 Men's & Boys' Cut & Sew Suit, Coat, & Overcoat Manufacturing
2321 Men's & Boys' Shirts, Except Work Shirts
NAICS 315211 Men's & Boys' Cut & Sew Apparel Contractors
NAICS 315223 Men's & Boys' Cut & Sew Shirt, Manufacturing
2322 Men's & Boys' Underwear & Nightwear
NAICS 315211 Men's & Boys' Cut & Sew Apparel Contractors
NAICS 315221 Men's & Boys' Cut & Sew Underwear & Nightwear Manufacturing
2323 Men's & Boys' Neckwear
NAICS 315993 Men's & Boys' Neckwear Manufacturing
2325 Men's & Boys' Trousers & Slacks
NAICS 315211 Men's & Boys' Cut & Sew Apparel Contractors
NAICS 315224 Men's & Boys' Cut & Sew Trouser, Slack, & Jean Manufacturing
2326 Men's & Boys' Work Clothing
NAICS 315211 Men's & Boys' Cut & Sew Apparel Contractors
NAICS 315225 Men's & Boys' Cut & Sew Work Clothing Manufacturing
2329 Men's & Boys' Clothing, nec
NAICS 315211 Men's & Boys' Cut & Sew Apparel Contractors

NAICS 315228 Men's & Boys' Cut & Sew Other Outerwear Manufacturing
NAICS 315299 All Other Cut & Sew Apparel Manufacturing
2331 Women's, Misses', & Juniors' Blouses & Shirts
NAICS 315212 Women's & Girls' Cut & Sew Apparel Contractors
NAICS 315232 Women's & Girls' Cut & Sew Blouse & Shirt Manufacturing
2335 Women's, Misses' & Junior's Dresses
NAICS 315212 Women's & Girls' Cut & Sew Apparel Contractors
NAICS 315233 Women's & Girls' Cut & Sew Dress Manufacturing
2337 Women's, Misses' & Juniors' Suits, Skirts & Coats
NAICS 315212 Women's & Girls' Cut & Sew Apparel Contractors
NAICS 315234 Women's & Girls' Cut & Sew Suit, Coat, Tailored Jacket, & Skirt Manufacturing
2339 Women's, Misses' & Juniors' Outerwear, nec
NAICS 315999 Other Apparel Accessories & Other Apparel Manufacturing
NAICS 315212 Women's & Girls' Cut & Sew Apparel Contractors
NAICS 315299 All Other Cut & Sew Apparel Manufacturing
NAICS 315238 Women's & Girls' Cut & Sew Other Outerwear Manufacturing
2341 Women's, Misses, Children's, & Infants' Underwear & Nightwear
NAICS 315212 Women's & Girls' Cut & Sew Apparel Contractors
NAICS 315211 Men's & Boys' Cut & Sew Apparel Contractors
NAICS 315231 Women's & Girls' Cut & Sew Lingerie, Loungewear, & Nightwear Manufacturing
NAICS 315221 Men's & Boys' Cut & Sew Underwear & Nightwear Manufacturing
NAICS 315291 Infants' Cut & Sew Apparel Manufacturing
2342 Brassieres, Girdles, & Allied Garments
NAICS 315212 Women's & Girls' Cut & Sew Apparel Contractors
NAICS 315231 Women's & Girls' Cut & Sew Lingerie, Loungewear, & Nightwear Manufacturing
2353 Hats, Caps, & Millinery
NAICS 315991 Hat, Cap, & Millinery Manufacturing
2361 Girls', Children's & Infants' Dresses, Blouses & Shirts
NAICS 315291 Infants' Cut & Sew Apparel Manufacturing
NAICS 315223 Men's & Boys' Cut & Sew Shirt, Manufacturing
NAICS 315211 Men's & Boys' Cut & Sew Apparel Contractors
NAICS 315232 Women's & Girls' Cut & Sew Blouse & Shirt Manufacturing
NAICS 315233 Women's & Girls' Cut & Sew Dress Manufacturing
NAICS 315212 Women's & Girls' Cut & Sew Apparel Contractors
2369 Girls', Children's & Infants' Outerwear, nec
NAICS 315291 Infants' Cut & Sew Apparel Manufacturing
NAICS 315222 Men's & Boys' Cut & Sew Suit, Coat, & Overcoat Manufacturing
NAICS 315224 Men's & Boys' Cut & Sew Trouser, Slack, & Jean Manufacturing
NAICS 315228 Men's & Boys' Cut & Sew Other Outerwear Manufacturing
NAICS 315221 Men's & Boys' Cut & Sew Underwear & Nightwear Manufacturing
NAICS 315211 Men's & Boys' Cut & Sew Apparel Contractors

NAICS 315234 Women's & Girls' Cut & Sew Suit, Coat, Tailored Jacket, & Skirt Manufacturing

NAICS 315238 Women's & Girls' Cut & Sew Other Outerwear Manufacturing

NAICS 315231 Women's & Girls' Cut & Sew Lingerie, Loungewear, & Nightwear Manufacturing

NAICS 315212 Women's & Girls' Cut & Sew Apparel Contractors

2371 Fur Goods

NAICS 315292 Fur & Leather Apparel Manufacturing

2381 Dress & Work Gloves, Except Knit & All-leather

NAICS 315992 Glove & Mitten Manufacturing

2384 Robes & Dressing Gowns

NAICS 315231 Women's & Girls' Cut & Sew Lingerie, Loungewear, & Nightwear Manufacturing

NAICS 315221 Men's & Boys' Cut & Sew Underwear & Nightwear Manufacturing

NAICS 315211 Men's & Boys' Cut & Sew Apparel Contractors

NAICS 315212 Women's & Girls' Cut & Sew Apparel Contractors

2385 Waterproof Outerwear

NAICS 315222 Men's & Boys' Cut & Sew Suit, Coat, & Overcoat Manufacturing

NAICS 315234 Women's & Girls' Cut & Sew Suit, Coat, Tailored Jacket, & Skirt Manufacturing

NAICS 315228 Men's & Boys' Cut & Sew Other Outerwear Manufacturing

NAICS 315238 Women's & Girls' Cut & Sew Other Outerwear Manufacturing

NAICS 315291 Infants' Cut & Sew Apparel Manufacturing

NAICS 315999 Other Apparel Accessories & Other Apparel Manufacturing

NAICS 315211 Men's & Boys' Cut & Sew Apparel Contractors

NAICS 315212 Women's & Girls' Cut & Sew Apparel Contractors

2386 Leather & Sheep-lined Clothing

NAICS 315292 Fur & Leather Apparel Manufacturing

2387 Apparel Belts

NAICS 315999 Other Apparel Accessories & Other Apparel Manufacturing

2389 Apparel & Accessories, nec

NAICS 315999 Other Apparel Accessories & Other Apparel Manufacturing

NAICS 315299 All Other Cut & Sew Apparel Manufacturing

NAICS 315231 Women's & Girls' Cut & Sew Lingerie, Loungewear, & Nightwear Manufacturing

NAICS 315212 Women's & Girls' Cut & Sew Apparel Contractors

NAICS 315211 Mens' & Boys' Cut & Sew Apparel Contractors

2391 Curtains & Draperies

NAICS 314121 Curtain & Drapery Mills

2392 Housefurnishings, Except Curtains & Draperies

NAICS 314911 Textile Bag Mills

NAICS 339994 Broom, Brush & Mop Manufacturing

NAICS 314129 Other Household Textile Product Mills

2393 Textile Bags

NAICS 314911 Textile Bag Mills

2394 Canvas & Related Products

NAICS 314912 Canvas & Related Product Mills

2395 Pleating, Decorative & Novelty Stitching, & Tucking for the Trade

NAICS 314999 All Other Miscellaneous Textile Product Mills

NAICS 315211 Mens' & Boys' Cut & Sew Apparel Contractors

NAICS 315212 Women's & Girls' Cut & Sew Apparel Contractors

2396 Automotive Trimmings, Apparel Findings, & Related Products

NAICS 33636 Motor Vehicle Fabric Accessories & Seat Manufacturing

NAICS 315999 Other Apparel Accessories, & Other Apparel Manufacturing

NAICS 323113 Commercial Screen Printing

NAICS 314999 All Other Miscellaneous Textile Product Mills

2397 Schiffli Machine Embroideries

NAICS 313222 Schiffli Machine Embroidery

2399 Fabricated Textile Products, nec

NAICS 33636 Motor Vehicle Fabric Accessories & Seat Manufacturing

NAICS 315999 Other Apparel Accessories & Other Apparel Manufacturing

NAICS 314999 All Other Miscellaneous Textile Product Mills

LUMBER & WOOD PRODUCTS, EXCEPT FURNITURE

2411 Logging

NAICS 11331 Logging

2421 Sawmills & Planing Mills, General

NAICS 321913 Softwood Cut Stock, Resawing Lumber, & Planing

NAICS 321113 Sawmills

NAICS 321914 Other Millwork

NAICS 321999 All Other Miscellaneous Wood Product Manufacturing

2426 Hardwood Dimension & Flooring Mills

NAICS 321914 Other Millwork

NAICS 321999 All Other Miscellaneous Wood Product Manufacturing

NAICS 337139 Other Wood Furniture Manufacturing

NAICS 321912 Hardwood Dimension Mills

2429 Special Product Sawmills, nec

NAICS 321113 Sawmills

NAICS 321913 Softwood Cut Stock, Resawing Lumber, & Planing

NAICS 321999 All Other Miscellaneous Wood Product Manufacturing

2431 Millwork

NAICS 321911 Wood Window & Door Manufacturing

NAICS 321914 Other Millwork

2434 Wood Kitchen Cabinets

NAICS 337131 Wood Kitchen Cabinet & Counter Top Manufacturing

2435 Hardwood Veneer & Plywood

NAICS 321211 Hardwood Veneer & Plywood Manufacturing

2436 Softwood Veneer & Plywood

NAICS 321212 Softwood Veneer & Plywood Manufacturing

2439 Structural Wood Members, nec

NAICS 321913 Softwood Cut Stock, Resawing Lumber, & Planing

NAICS 321214 Truss Manufacturing

NAICS 321213 Engineered Wood Member Manufacturing

2441 Nailed & Lock Corner Wood Boxes & Shook

NAICS 32192 Wood Container & Pallet Manufacturing

2448 Wood Pallets & Skids

NAICS 32192 Wood Container & Pallet Manufacturing

2449 Wood Containers, nec
NAICS 32192   Wood Container & Pallet Manufacturing
2451 Mobile Homes
NAICS 321991 Manufactured Home Manufacturing
2452 Prefabricated Wood Buildings & Components
NAICS 321992 Prefabricated Wood Building Manufacturing
2491 Wood Preserving
NAICS 321114 Wood Preservation
2493 Reconstituted Wood Products
NAICS 321219 Reconstituted Wood Product Manufacturing
2499 Wood Products, nec
NAICS 339999 All Other Miscellaneous Manufacturing
NAICS 337139 Other Wood Furniture Manufacturing
NAICS 337148 Other Nonwood Furniture Manufacturing
NAICS 32192   Wood Container & Pallet Manufacturing
NAICS 321999 All Other Miscellaneous Wood Product
    Manufacturing

FURNITURE & FIXTURES

2511 Wood Household Furniture, Except Upholstered
NAICS 337122 Wood Household Furniture Manufacturing
2512 Wood Household Furniture, Upholstered
NAICS 337121 Upholstered Household Furniture
    Manufacturing
2514 Metal Household Furniture
NAICS 337124 Metal Household Furniture Manufacturing
2515 Mattresses, Foundations, & Convertible Beds
NAICS 33791   Mattress Manufacturing
NAICS 337132 Upholstered Wood Household Furniture
    Manufacturing
**2517 Wood Television, Radio, Phonograph & Sewing Machine
Cabinets**
NAICS 337139 Other Wood Furniture Manufacturing
2519 Household Furniture, nec
NAICS 337143 Household Furniture (except Wood & Metal)
    Manufacturing
2521 Wood Office Furniture
NAICS 337134 Wood Office Furniture Manufacturing
2522 Office Furniture, Except Wood
NAICS 337141 Nonwood Office Furniture Manufacturing
2531 Public Building & Related Furniture
NAICS 33636   Motor Vehicle Fabric Accessories & Seat
    Manufacturing
NAICS 337139 Other Wood Furniture Manufacturing
NAICS 337148 Other Nonwood Furniture Manufacturing
NAICS 339942 Lead Pencil & Art Good Manufacturing
**2541 Wood Office & Store Fixtures, Partitions, Shelving, &
Lockers**
NAICS 337131 Wood Kitchen Cabinet & Counter Top
    Manufacturing
NAICS 337135 Custom Architectural Woodwork, Millwork, &
    Fixtures
NAICS 337139 Other Wood Furniture Manufacturing
**2542 Office & Store Fixtures, Partitions Shelving, & Lockers,
Except Wood**
NAICS 337145 Nonwood Showcase, Partition, Shelving, &
    Locker Manufacturing
2591 Drapery Hardware & Window Blinds & Shades
NAICS 33792   Blind & Shade Manufacturing
2599 Furniture & Fixtures, nec
NAICS 339113 Surgical Appliance & Supplies Manufacturing
NAICS 337139 Other Wood Furniture Manufacturing

NAICS 337148 Other Nonwood Furniture Manufacturing

PAPER & ALLIED PRODUCTS

2611 Pulp Mills
NAICS 32211   Pulp Mills
NAICS 322121 Paper Mills
NAICS 32213   Paperboard Mills
2621 Paper Mills
NAICS 322121 Paper Mills
NAICS 322122 Newsprint Mills
2631 Paperboard Mills
NAICS 32213   Paperboard Mills
2652 Setup Paperboard Boxes
NAICS 322213 Setup Paperboard Box Manufacturing
2653 Corrugated & Solid Fiber Boxes
NAICS 322211 Corrugated & Solid Fiber Box Manufacturing
2655 Fiber Cans, Tubes, Drums, & Similar Products
NAICS 322214 Fiber Can, Tube, Drum, & Similar Products
    Manufacturing
2656 Sanitary Food Containers, Except Folding
NAICS 322215 Non-folding Sanitary Food Container
    Manufacturing
2657 Folding Paperboard Boxes, Including Sanitary
NAICS 322212 Folding Paperboard Box Manufacturing
2671 Packaging Paper & Plastics Film, Coated & Laminated
NAICS 322221 Coated & Laminated Packaging Paper &
    Plastics Film Manufacturing
NAICS 326112 Unsupported Plastics Packaging Film & Sheet
    Manufacturing
2672 Coated & Laminated Paper, nec
NAICS 322222 Coated & Laminated Paper Manufacturing
2673 Plastics, Foil, & Coated Paper Bags
NAICS 322223 Plastics, Foil, & Coated Paper Bag
    Manufacturing
NAICS 326111 Unsupported Plastics Bag Manufacturing
2674 Uncoated Paper & Multiwall Bags
NAICS 322224 Uncoated Paper & Multiwall Bag
    Manufacturing
2675 Die-cut Paper & Paperboard & Cardboard
NAICS 322231 Die-cut Paper & Paperboard Office Supplies
    Manufacturing
NAICS 322292 Surface-coated Paperboard Manufacturing
NAICS 322298 All Other Converted Paper Product
    Manufacturing
2676 Sanitary Paper Products
NAICS 322291 Sanitary Paper Product Manufacturing
2677 Envelopes
NAICS 322232 Envelope Manufacturing
2678 Stationery, Tablets, & Related Products
NAICS 322233 Stationery, Tablet, & Related Product
    Manufacturing
2679 Converted Paper & Paperboard Products, nec
NAICS 322215 Non-folding Sanitary Food Container
    Manufacturing
NAICS 322222 Coated & Laminated Paper Manufacturing
NAICS 322231 Die-cut Paper & Paperboard Office Supplies
    Manufacturing
NAICS 322298 All Other Converted Paper Product
    Manufacturing

PRINTING, PUBLISHING, & ALLIED INDUSTRIES

2711 Newspapers: Publishing, or Publishing & Printing
NAICS 51111 Newspaper Publishers
2721 Periodicals: Publishing, or Publishing & Printing
NAICS 51112 Periodical Publishers
2731 Books: Publishing, or Publishing & Printing
NAICS 51223 Music Publishers
NAICS 51113 Book Publishers
2732 Book Printing
NAICS 323117 Book Printing
2741 Miscellaneous Publishing
NAICS 51114 Database & Directory Publishers
NAICS 51223 Music Publishers
NAICS 511199 All Other Publishers
2752 Commercial Printing, Lithographic
NAICS 323114 Quick Printing
NAICS 323110 Commercial Lithographic Printing
2754 Commercial Printing, Gravure
NAICS 323111 Commercial Gravure Printing
2759 Commercial Printing, nec
NAICS 323113 Commercial Screen Printing
NAICS 323112 Commercial Flexographic Printing
NAICS 323114 Quick Printing
NAICS 323115 Digital Printing
NAICS 323119 Other Commercial Printing
2761 Manifold Business Forms
NAICS 323116 Manifold Business Form Printing
2771 Greeting Cards
NAICS 323110 Commercial Lithographic Printing
NAICS 323111 Commercial Gravure Printing
NAICS 323112 Commercial Flexographic Printing
NAICS 323113 Commercial Screen Printing
NAICS 323119 Other Commercial Printing
NAICS 511191 Greeting Card Publishers
2782 Blankbooks, Loose-leaf Binders & Devices
NAICS 323110 Commercial Lithographic Printing
NAICS 323111 Commercial Gravure Printing
NAICS 323112 Commercial Flexographic Printing
NAICS 323113 Commercial Screen Printing
NAICS 323119 Other Commercial Printing
NAICS 323118 Blankbook, Loose-leaf Binder & Device Manufacturing
2789 Bookbinding & Related Work
NAICS 323121 Tradebinding & Related Work
2791 Typesetting
NAICS 323122 Prepress Services
2796 Platemaking & Related Services
NAICS 323122 Prepress Services

CHEMICALS & ALLIED PRODUCTS

2812 Alkalies & Chlorine
NAICS 325181 Alkalies & Chlorine Manufacturing
2813 Industrial Gases
NAICS 32512 Industrial Gas Manufacturing
2816 Inorganic Pigments
NAICS 325131 Inorganic Dye & Pigment Manufacturing
NAICS 325182 Carbon Black Manufacturing
2819 Industrial Inorganic Chemicals, nec
NAICS 325998 All Other Miscellaneous Chemical Product Manufacturing

NAICS 331311 Alumina Refining
NAICS 325131 Inorganic Dye & Pigment Manufacturing
NAICS 325188 All Other Basic Inorganic Chemical Manufacturing
2821 Plastics Material Synthetic Resins, & Nonvulcanizable Elastomers
NAICS 325211 Plastics Material & Resin Manufacturing
2822 Synthetic Rubber
NAICS 325212 Synthetic Rubber Manufacturing
2823 Cellulosic Manmade Fibers
NAICS 325221 Cellulosic Manmade Fiber Manufacturing
2824 Manmade Organic Fibers, Except Cellulosic
NAICS 325222 Noncellulosic Organic Fiber Manufacturing
2833 Medicinal Chemicals & Botanical Products
NAICS 325411 Medicinal & Botanical Manufacturing
2834 Pharmaceutical Preparations
NAICS 325412 Pharmaceutical Preparation Manufacturing
2835 In Vitro & in Vivo Diagnostic Substances
NAICS 325412 Pharmaceutical Preparation Manufacturing
NAICS 325413 In-vitro Diagnostic Substance Manufacturing
2836 Biological Products, Except Diagnostic Substances
NAICS 325414 Biological Product Manufacturing
2841 Soaps & Other Detergents, Except Speciality Cleaners
NAICS 325611 Soap & Other Detergent Manufacturing
2842 Speciality Cleaning, Polishing, & Sanitary Preparations
NAICS 325612 Polish & Other Sanitation Good Manufacturing
2843 Surface Active Agents, Finishing Agents, Sulfonated Oils, & Assistants
NAICS 325613 Surface Active Agent Manufacturing
2844 Perfumes, Cosmetics, & Other Toilet Preparations
NAICS 32562 Toilet Preparation Manufacturing
NAICS 325611 Soap & Other Detergent Manufacturing
2851 Paints, Varnishes, Lacquers, Enamels, & Allied Products
NAICS 32551 Paint & Coating Manufacturing
2861 Gum & Wood Chemicals
NAICS 325191 Gum & Wood Chemical Manufacturing
2865 Cyclic Organic Crudes & Intermediates, & Organic Dyes & Pigments
NAICS 32511 Petrochemical Manufacturing
NAICS 325132 Organic Dye & Pigment Manufacturing
NAICS 325192 Cyclic Crude & Intermediate Manufacturing
2869 Industrial Organic Chemicals, nec
NAICS 32511 Petrochemical Manufacturing
NAICS 325188 All Other Inorganic Chemical Manufacturing
NAICS 325193 Ethyl Alcohol Manufacturing
NAICS 32512 Industrial Gas Manufacturing
NAICS 325199 All Other Basic Organic Chemical Manufacturing
2873 Nitrogenous Fertilizers
NAICS 325311 Nitrogenous Fertilizer Manufacturing
2874 Phosphatic Fertilizers
NAICS 325312 Phosphatic Fertilizer Manufacturing
2875 Fertilizers, Mixing Only
NAICS 325314 Fertilizer Manufacturing
2879 Pesticides & Agricultural Chemicals, nec
NAICS 32532 Pesticide & Other Agricultural Chemical Manufacturing
2891 Adhesives & Sealants
NAICS 32552 Adhesive & Sealant Manufacturing
2892 Explosives
NAICS 32592 Explosives Manufacturing
2893 Printing Ink
NAICS 32591 Printing Ink Manufacturing

2895 Carbon Black
NAICS 325182 Carbon Black Manufacturing
2899 Chemicals & Chemical Preparations, nec
NAICS 32551 Paint & Coating Manufacturing
NAICS 311942 Spice & Extract Manufacturing
NAICS 325199 All Other Basic Organic Chemical
                Manufacturing
NAICS 325998 All Other Miscellaneous Chemical Product
                Manufacturing

PETROLEUM REFINING & RELATED INDUSTRIES

2911 Petroleum Refining
NAICS 32411 Petroleum Refineries
2951 Asphalt Paving Mixtures & Blocks
NAICS 324121 Asphalt Paving Mixture & Block Manufacturing
2952 Asphalt Felts & Coatings
NAICS 324122 Asphalt Shingle & Coating Materials
                Manufacturing
2992 Lubricating Oils & Greases
NAICS 324191 Petroleum Lubricating Oil & Grease
                Manufacturing 2999

RUBBER & MISCELLANEOUS PLASTICS PRODUCTS

3011 Tires & Inner Tubes
NAICS 326211 Tire Manufacturing
3021 Rubber & Plastics Footwear
NAICS 316211 Rubber & Plastics Footwear Manufacturing
3052 Rubber & Plastics Hose & Belting
NAICS 32622 Rubber & Plastics Hoses & Belting
                Manufacturing
3053 Gaskets, Packing, & Sealing Devices
NAICS 339991 Gasket, Packing, & Sealing Device
                Manufacturing
**3061 Molded, Extruded, & Lathe-cut Mechanical Rubber
     Products**
NAICS 326291 Rubber Product Manufacturing for Mechanical
                Use
3069 Fabricated Rubber Products, nec
NAICS 31332 Fabric Coating Mills
NAICS 326192 Resilient Floor Covering Manufacturing
NAICS 326299 All Other Rubber Product Manufacturing
3081 Unsupported Plastics Film & Sheet
NAICS 326113 Unsupported Plastics Film & Sheet
                Manufacturing
3082 Unsupported Plastics Profile Shapes
NAICS 326121 Unsupported Plastics Profile Shape
                Manufacturing
3083 Laminated Plastics Plate, Sheet, & Profile Shapes
NAICS 32613 Laminated Plastics Plate, Sheet, & Shape
                Manufacturing
3084 Plastic Pipe
NAICS 326122 Plastic Pipe & Pipe Fitting Manufacturing
3085 Plastics Bottles
NAICS 32616 Plastics Bottle Manufacturing
3086 Plastics Foam Products
NAICS 32615 Urethane & Other Foam Product
                Manufacturing
NAICS 32614 Polystyrene Foam Product Manufacturing

3087 Custom Compounding of Purchased Plastics Resins
NAICS 325991 Custom Compounding of Purchased Resin
3088 Plastics Plumbing Fixtures
NAICS 326191 Plastics Plumbing Fixtures Manufacturing
3089 Plastics Products, nec
NAICS 326122 Plastics Pipe & Pipe Fitting Manufacturing
NAICS 326121 Unsupported Plastics Profile Shape
                Manufacturing
NAICS 326199 All Other Plastics Product Manufacturing

LEATHER & LEATHER PRODUCTS

3111 Leather Tanning & Finishing
NAICS 31611 Leather & Hide Tanning & Finishing
3131 Boot & Shoe Cut Stock & Findings
NAICS 321999 All Other Miscellaneous Wood Product
                Manufacturing
NAICS 339993 Fastener, Button, Needle, & Pin Manufacturing
NAICS 316999 All Other Leather Good Manufacturing
3142 House Slippers
NAICS 316212 House Slipper Manufacturing
3143 Men's Footwear, Except Athletic
NAICS 316213 Men's Footwear Manufacturing
3144 Women's Footwear, Except Athletic
NAICS 316214 Women's Footwear Manufacturing
3149 Footwear, Except Rubber, nec
NAICS 316219 Other Footwear Manufacturing
3151 Leather Gloves & Mittens
NAICS 315992 Glove & Mitten Manufacturing
3161 Luggage
NAICS 316991 Luggage Manufacturing
3171 Women's Handbags & Purses
NAICS 316992 Women's Handbag & Purse Manufacturing
**3172 Personal Leather Goods, Except Women's Handbags &
     Purses**
NAICS 316993 Personal Leather Good Manufacturing
3199 Leather Goods, nec
NAICS 316999 All Other Leather Good Manufacturing

STONE, CLAY, GLASS, & CONCRETE PRODUCTS

3211 Flat Glass
NAICS 327211 Flat Glass Manufacturing
3221 Glass Containers
NAICS 327213 Glass Container Manufacturing
3229 Pressed & Blown Glass & Glassware, nec
NAICS 327212 Other Pressed & Blown Glass & Glassware
                Manufacturing
3231 Glass Products, Made of Purchased Glass
NAICS 327215 Glass Product Manufacturing Made of
                Purchased Glass
3241 Cement, Hydraulic
NAICS 32731 Hydraulic Cement Manufacturing
3251 Brick & Structural Clay Tile
NAICS 327121 Brick & Structural Clay Tile Manufacturing
3253 Ceramic Wall & Floor Tile
NAICS 327122 Ceramic Wall & Floor Tile Manufacturing
3255 Clay Refractories
NAICS 327124 Clay Refractory Manufacturing

3259 Structural Clay Products, nec
NAICS 327123 Other Structural Clay Product Manufacturing
**3261 Vitreous China Plumbing Fixtures & China &
Earthenware Fittings & Bathroom Accessories**
NAICS 327111 Vitreous China Plumbing Fixture & China &
Earthenware Fittings & Bathroom Accessories
Manufacturing
3262 Vitreous China Table & Kitchen Articles
NAICS 327112 Vitreous China, Fine Earthenware & Other
Pottery Product Manufacturing
3263 Fine Earthenware Table & Kitchen Articles
NAICS 327112 Vitreous China, Fine Earthenware & Other
Pottery Product Manufacturing
3264 Porcelain Electrical Supplies
NAICS 327113 Porcelain Electrical Supply Manufacturing
3269 Pottery Products, nec
NAICS 327112 Vitreous China, Fine Earthenware, & Other
Pottery Product Manufacturing
3271 Concrete Block & Brick
NAICS 327331 Concrete Block & Brick Manufacturing
3272 Concrete Products, Except Block & Brick
NAICS 327999 All Other Miscellaneous Nonmetallic Mineral
Product Manufacturing
NAICS 327332 Concrete Pipe Manufacturing
NAICS 32739 Other Concrete Product Manufacturing
3273 Ready-mixed Concrete
NAICS 32732 Ready-mix Concrete Manufacturing
3274 Lime
NAICS 32741 Lime Manufacturing
3275 Gypsum Products
NAICS 32742 Gypsum & Gypsum Product Manufacturing
3281 Cut Stone & Stone Products
NAICS 327991 Cut Stone & Stone Product Manufacturing
3291 Abrasive Products
NAICS 332999 All Other Miscellaneous Fabricated Metal
Product Manufacturing
NAICS 32791 Abrasive Product Manufacturing
3292 Asbestos Products
NAICS 33634 Motor Vehicle Brake System Manufacturing
NAICS 327999 All Other Miscellaneous Nonmetallic Mineral
Product Manufacturing
3295 Minerals & Earths, Ground or Otherwise Treated
NAICS 327992 Ground or Treated Mineral & Earth
Manufacturing
3296 Mineral Wool
NAICS 327993 Mineral Wool Manufacturing
3297 Nonclay Refractories
NAICS 327125 Nonclay Refractory Manufacturing
3299 Nonmetallic Mineral Products, nec
NAICS 32742 Gypsum & Gypsum Product Manufacturing
NAICS 327999 All Other Miscellaneous Nonmetallic Mineral
Product Manufacturing

PRIMARY METALS INDUSTRIES

3312 Steel Works, Blast Furnaces , & Rolling Mills
NAICS 324199 All Other Petroleum & Coal Products
Manufacturing
NAICS 331111 Iron & Steel Mills
3313 Electrometallurgical Products, Except Steel
NAICS 331112 Electrometallurgical Ferroalloy Product
Manufacturing

NAICS 331492 Secondary Smelting, Refining, & Alloying of
Nonferrous Metals
3315 Steel Wiredrawing & Steel Nails & Spikes
NAICS 331222 Steel Wire Drawing
NAICS 332618 Other Fabricated Wire Product Manufacturing
3316 Cold-rolled Steel Sheet, Strip, & Bars
NAICS 331221 Cold-rolled Steel Shape Manufacturing
3317 Steel Pipe & Tubes
NAICS 33121 Iron & Steel Pipes & Tubes Manufacturing
from Purchased Steel
3321 Gray & Ductile Iron Foundries
NAICS 331511 Iron Foundries
3322 Malleable Iron Foundries
NAICS 331511 Iron Foundries
3324 Steel Investment Foundries
NAICS 331512 Steel Investment Foundries
3325 Steel Foundries, nec
NAICS 331513 Steel Foundries
3331 Primary Smelting & Refining of Copper
NAICS 331411 Primary Smelting & Refining of Copper
3334 Primary Production of Aluminum
NAICS 331312 Primary Aluminum Production
**3339 Primary Smelting & Refining of Nonferrous Metals,
Except Copper & Aluminum**
NAICS 331419 Primary Smelting & Refining of Nonferrous
Metals
3341 Secondary Smelting & Refining of Nonferrous Metals
NAICS 331314 Secondary Smelting & Alloying of Aluminum
NAICS 331423 Secondary Smelting, Refining, & Alloying of
Copper
NAICS 331492 Secondary Smelting, Refining, & Alloying of
Nonferrous Metals
3351 Rolling, Drawing, & Extruding of Copper
NAICS 331421 Copper Rolling, Drawing, & Extruding
3353 Aluminum Sheet, Plate, & Foil
NAICS 331315 Aluminum Sheet, Plate, & Foil Manufacturing
3354 Aluminum Extruded Products
NAICS 331316 Aluminum Extruded Product Manufacturing
3355 Aluminum Rolling & Drawing, nec
NAICS 331319 Other Aluminum Rolling & Drawing,
**3356 Rolling, Drawing, & Extruding of Nonferrous Metals,
Except Copper & Aluminum**
NAICS 331491 Nonferrous Metal Rolling. Drawing, &
Extruding
3357 Drawing & Insulating of Nonferrous Wire
NAICS 331319 Other Aluminum Rolling & Drawing
NAICS 331422 Copper Wire Drawing
NAICS 331491 Nonferrous Metal Rolling, Drawing, &
Extruding
NAICS 335921 Fiber Optic Cable Manufacturing
NAICS 335929 Other Communication & Energy Wire
Manufacturing
3363 Aluminum Die-castings
NAICS 331521 Aluminum Die-castings
3364 Nonferrous Die-castings, Except Aluminum
NAICS 331522 Nonferrous Die-castings
3365 Aluminum Foundries
NAICS 331524 Aluminum Foundries
3366 Copper Foundries
NAICS 331525 Copper Foundries
3369 Nonferrous Foundries, Except Aluminum & Copper
NAICS 331528 Other Nonferrous Foundries

3398 Metal Heat Treating
NAICS 332811 Metal Heat Treating
3399 Primary Metal Products, nec
NAICS 331111 Iron & Steel Mills
NAICS 331314 Secondary Smelting & Alloying of Aluminum
NAICS 331423 Secondary Smelting, Refining & Alloying of
Copper
NAICS 331492 Secondary Smelting, Refining, & Alloying of
Nonferrous Metals
NAICS 332618 Other Fabricated Wire Product Manufacturing
NAICS 332813 Electroplating, Plating, Polishing, Anodizing, &
Coloring

FABRICATED METAL PRODUCTS, EXCEPT MACHINERY & TRANSPORTATION EQUIPMENT

3411 Metal Cans
NAICS 332431 Metal Can Manufacturing
3412 Metal Shipping Barrels, Drums, Kegs & Pails
NAICS 332439 Other Metal Container Manufacturing
3421 Cutlery
NAICS 332211 Cutlery & Flatware Manufacturing
3423 Hand & Edge Tools, Except Machine Tools & Handsaws
NAICS 332212 Hand & Edge Tool Manufacturing
3425 Saw Blades & Handsaws
NAICS 332213 Saw Blade & Handsaw Manufacturing
3429 Hardware, nec
NAICS 332439 Other Metal Container Manufacturing
NAICS 332919 Other Metal Valve & Pipe Fitting
Manufacturing
NAICS 33251 Hardware Manufacturing
3431 Enameled Iron & Metal Sanitary Ware
NAICS 332998 Enameled Iron & Metal Sanitary Ware
Manufacturing
3432 Plumbing Fixture Fittings & Trim
NAICS 332913 Plumbing Fixture Fitting & Trim Manufacturing
NAICS 332999 All Other Miscellaneous Fabricated Metal
Product Manufacturing
3433 Heating Equipment, Except Electric & Warm Air Furnaces
NAICS 333414 Heating Equipment Manufacturing
3441 Fabricated Structural Metal
NAICS 332312 Fabricated Structural Metal Manufacturing
3442 Metal Doors, Sash, Frames, Molding, & Trim Manufacturing
NAICS 332321 Metal Window & Door Manufacturing
3443 Fabricated Plate Work
NAICS 332313 Plate Work Manufacturing
NAICS 33241 Power Boiler & Heat Exchanger Manufacturing
NAICS 33242 Metal Tank Manufacturing
NAICS 333415 Air-conditioning & Warm Air Heating
Equipment & Commercial & Industrial
Refrigeration Equipment Manufacturing
3444 Sheet Metal Work
NAICS 332322 Sheet Metal Work Manufacturing
NAICS 332439 Other Metal Container Manufacturing
3446 Architectural & Ornamental Metal Work
NAICS 332323 Ornamental & Architectural Metal Work
Manufacturing
3448 Prefabricated Metal Buildings & Components
NAICS 332311 Prefabricated Metal Building & Component
Manufacturing

3449 Miscellaneous Structural Metal Work
NAICS 332114 Custom Roll Forming
NAICS 332312 Fabricated Structural Metal Manufacturing
NAICS 332321 Metal Window & Door Manufacturing
NAICS 332323 Ornamental & Architectural Metal Work
Manufacturing
3451 Screw Machine Products
NAICS 332721 Precision Turned Product Manufacturing
3452 Bolts, Nuts, Screws, Rivets, & Washers
NAICS 332722 Bolt, Nut, Screw, Rivet, & Washer
Manufacturing
3462 Iron & Steel Forgings
NAICS 332111 Iron & Steel Forging
3463 Nonferrous Forgings
NAICS 332112 Nonferrous Forging
3465 Automotive Stamping
NAICS 33637 Motor Vehicle Metal Stamping
3466 Crowns & Closures
NAICS 332115 Crown & Closure Manufacturing
3469 Metal Stamping, nec
NAICS 339911 Jewelry Manufacturing
NAICS 332116 Metal Stamping
NAICS 332214 Kitchen Utensil, Pot & Pan Manufacturing
3471 Electroplating, Plating, Polishing, Anodizing, & Coloring
NAICS 332813 Electroplating, Plating, Polishing, Anodizing, &
Coloring
3479 Coating, Engraving, & Allied Services, nec
NAICS 339914 Costume Jewelry & Novelty Manufacturing
NAICS 339911 Jewelry Manufacturing
NAICS 339912 Silverware & Plated Ware Manufacturing
NAICS 332812 Metal Coating, Engraving , & Allied Services to
Manufacturers
3482 Small Arms Ammunition
NAICS 332992 Small Arms Ammunition Manufacturing
3483 Ammunition, Except for Small Arms
NAICS 332993 Ammunition Manufacturing
3484 Small Arms
NAICS 332994 Small Arms Manufacturing
3489 Ordnance & Accessories, nec
NAICS 332995 Other Ordnance & Accessories Manufacturing
3491
3492 Fluid Power Valves & Hose Fittings
NAICS 332912 Fluid Power Valve & Hose Fitting
Manufacturing
3493 Steel Springs, Except Wire
NAICS 332611 Steel Spring Manufacturing
3494 Valves & Pipe Fittings, nec
NAICS 332919 Other Metal Valve & Pipe Fitting
Manufacturing
NAICS 332999 All Other Miscellaneous Fabricated Metal
Product Manufacturing
3495 Wire Springs
NAICS 332612 Wire Spring Manufacturing
NAICS 334518 Watch, Clock, & Part Manufacturing
3496 Miscellaneous Fabricated Wire Products
NAICS 332618 Other Fabricated Wire Product Manufacturing
3497 Metal Foil & Leaf
NAICS 322225 Laminated Aluminum Foil Manufacturing for
Flexible Packaging Uses
NAICS 332999 All Other Miscellaneous Fabricated Metal
Product Manufacturing
3498 Fabricated Pipe & Pipe Fittings
NAICS 332996 Fabricated Pipe & Pipe Fitting Manufacturing

3499 Fabricated Metal Products, nec
NAICS 337148 Other Nonwood Furniture Manufacturing
NAICS 332117 Powder Metallurgy Part Manufacturing
NAICS 332439 Other Metal Container Manufacturing
NAICS 33251 Hardware Manufacturing
NAICS 332919 Other Metal Valve & Pipe Fitting Manufacturing
NAICS 339914 Costume Jewelry & Novelty Manufacturing
NAICS 332999 All Other Miscellaneous Fabricated Metal Product Manufacturing

INDUSTRIAL & COMMERCIAL MACHINERY & COMPUTER EQUIPMENT

3511 Steam, Gas, & Hydraulic Turbines, & Turbine Generator Set Units
NAICS 333611 Turbine & Turbine Generator Set Unit Manufacturing
3519 Internal Combustion Engines, nec
NAICS 336399 All Other Motor Vehicle Parts Manufacturing
NAICS 333618 Other Engine Equipment Manufacturing
3523 Farm Machinery & Equipment
NAICS 333111 Farm Machinery & Equipment Manufacturing
NAICS 332323 Ornamental & Architectural Metal Work Manufacturing
NAICS 332212 Hand & Edge Tool Manufacturing
NAICS 333922 Conveyor & Conveying Equipment Manufacturing
3524 Lawn & Garden Tractors & Home Lawn & Garden Equipment
NAICS 333112 Lawn & Garden Tractor & Home Lawn & Garden Equipment Manufacturing
NAICS 332212 Hand & Edge Tool Manufacturing
3531 Construction Machinery & Equipment
NAICS 33651 Railroad Rolling Stock Manufacturing
NAICS 333923 Overhead Traveling Crane, Hoist, & Monorail System Manufacturing
NAICS 33312 Construction Machinery Manufacturing
3532 Mining Machinery & Equipment, Except Oil & Gas Field Machinery & Equipment
NAICS 333131 Mining Machinery & Equipment Manufacturing
3533 Oil & Gas Field Machinery & Equipment
NAICS 333132 Oil & Gas Field Machinery & Equipment Manufacturing
3534 Elevators & Moving Stairways
NAICS 333921 Elevator & Moving Stairway Manufacturing
3535 Conveyors & Conveying Equipment
NAICS 333922 Conveyor & Conveying Equipment Manufacturing
3536 Overhead Traveling Cranes, Hoists & Monorail Systems
NAICS 333923 Overhead Traveling Crane, Hoist & Monorail System Manufacturing
3537 Industrial Trucks, Tractors, Trailers, & Stackers
NAICS 333924 Industrial Truck, Tractor, Trailer, & Stacker Machinery Manufacturing
NAICS 332999 All Other Miscellaneous Fabricated Metal Product Manufacturing
NAICS 332439 Other Metal Container Manufacturing
3541 Machine Tools, Metal Cutting Type
NAICS 333512 Machine Tool Manufacturing
3542 Machine Tools, Metal Forming Type
NAICS 333513 Machine Tool Manufacturing

3543 Industrial Patterns
NAICS 332997 Industrial Pattern Manufacturing
3544 Special Dies & Tools, Die Sets, Jigs & Fixtures, & Industrial Molds
NAICS 333514 Special Die & Tool, Die Set, Jig, & Fixture Manufacturing
NAICS 333511 Industrial Mold Manufacturing
3545 Cutting Tools, Machine Tool Accessories, & Machinists' Precision Measuring Devices
NAICS 333515 Cutting Tool & Machine Tool Accessory Manufacturing
NAICS 332212 Hand & Edge Tool Manufacturing
3546 Power-driven Handtools
NAICS 333991 Power-driven Hand Tool Manufacturing
3547 Rolling Mill Machinery & Equipment
NAICS 333516 Rolling Mill Machinery & Equipment Manufacturing
3548 Electric & Gas Welding & Soldering Equipment
NAICS 333992 Welding & Soldering Equipment Manufacturing
NAICS 335311 Power, Distribution, & Specialty Transformer Manufacturing
3549 Metalworking Machinery, nec
NAICS 333518 Other Metalworking Machinery Manufacturing
3552
3553 Woodworking Machinery
NAICS 33321 Sawmill & Woodworking Machinery Manufacturing
3554 Paper Industries Machinery
NAICS 333291 Paper Industry Machinery Manufacturing
3555 Printing Trades Machinery & Equipment
NAICS 333293 Printing Machinery & Equipment Manufacturing
3556 Food Products Machinery
NAICS 333294 Food Product Machinery Manufacturing
3559 Special Industry Machinery, nec
NAICS 33322 Rubber & Plastics Industry Machinery Manufacturing
NAICS 333319 Other Commercial & Service Industry Machinery Manufacturing
NAICS 333295 Semiconductor Manufacturing Machinery
NAICS 333298 All Other Industrial Machinery Manufacturing
3561 Pumps & Pumping Equipment
NAICS 333911 Pump & Pumping Equipment Manufacturing
3562 Ball & Roller Bearings
NAICS 332991 Ball & Roller Bearing Manufacturing
3563 Air & Gas Compressors
NAICS 333912 Air & Gas Compressor Manufacturing
3564 Industrial & Commercial Fans & Blowers & Air Purification Equipment
NAICS 333411 Air Purification Equipment Manufacturing
NAICS 333412 Industrial & Commercial Fan & Blower Manufacturing
3565 Packaging Machinery
NAICS 333993 Packaging Machinery Manufacturing
3566 Speed Changers, Industrial High-speed Drives, & Gears
NAICS 333612 Speed Changer, Industrial High-speed Drive, & Gear Manufacturing
3567 Industrial Process Furnaces & Ovens
NAICS 333994 Industrial Process Furnace & Oven Manufacturing
3568 Mechanical Power Transmission Equipment, nec
NAICS 333613 Mechanical Power Transmission Equipment Manufacturing

3569 General Industrial Machinery & Equipment, nec
NAICS 333999 All Other General Purpose Machinery
Manufacturing
3571 Electronic Computers
NAICS 334111 Electronic Computer Manufacturing
3572 Computer Storage Devices
NAICS 334112 Computer Storage Device Manufacturing
3575 Computer Terminals
NAICS 334113 Computer Terminal Manufacturing
3577 Computer Peripheral Equipment, nec
NAICS 334119 Other Computer Peripheral Equipment
Manufacturing
**3578 Calculating & Accounting Machines, Except Electronic
Computers**
NAICS 334119 Other Computer Peripheral Equipment
Manufacturing
NAICS 333313 Office Machinery Manufacturing
3579 Office Machines, nec
NAICS 339942 Lead Pencil & Art Good Manufacturing
NAICS 334518 Watch, Clock, & Part Manufacturing
NAICS 333313 Office Machinery Manufacturing
3581 Automatic Vending Machines
NAICS 333311 Automatic Vending Machine Manufacturing
3582 Commercial Laundry, Drycleaning, & Pressing Machines
NAICS 333312 Commercial Laundry, Drycleaning, & Pressing
Machine Manufacturing
**3585 Air-conditioning & Warm Air Heating Equipment &
Commercial & Industrial Refrigeration Equipment**
NAICS 336391 Motor Vehicle Air Conditioning Manufacturing
NAICS 333415 Air Conditioning & Warm Air Heating
Equipment & Commercial & Industrial
Refrigeration Equipment Manufacturing
3586 Measuring & Dispensing Pumps
NAICS 333913 Measuring & Dispensing Pump Manufacturing
3589 Service Industry Machinery, nec
NAICS 333319 Other Commercial and Service Industry
Machinery Manufacturing
3592 Carburetors, Pistons, Piston Rings & Valves
NAICS 336311 Carburetor, Piston, Piston Ring & Valve
Manufacturing
3593 Fluid Power Cylinders & Actuators
NAICS 333995 Fluid Power Cylinder & Actuator
Manufacturing
3594 Fluid Power Pumps & Motors
NAICS 333996 Fluid Power Pump & Motor Manufacturing
3596 Scales & Balances, Except Laboratory
NAICS 333997 Scale & Balance Manufacturing
3599 Industrial & Commercial Machinery & Equipment, nec
NAICS 336399 All Other Motor Vehicle Part Manufacturing
NAICS 332999 All Other Miscellaneous Fabricated Metal
Product Manufacturing
NAICS 333319 Other Commercial & Service Industry
Machinery Manufacturing
NAICS 33271 Machine Shops
NAICS 333999 All Other General Purpose Machinery
Manufacturing

ELECTRONIC & OTHER ELECTRICAL EQUIPMENT & COMPONENTS, EXCEPT COMPUTER EQUIPMENT

3612 Power, Distribution, & Specialty Transformers
NAICS 335311 Power, Distribution, & Specialty Transformer
Manufacturing
3613 Switchgear & Switchboard Apparatus
NAICS 335313 Switchgear & Switchboard Apparatus
Manufacturing
3621 Motors & Generators
NAICS 335312 Motor & Generator Manufacturing
3624 Carbon & Graphite Products
NAICS 335991 Carbon & Graphite Product Manufacturing
3625 Relays & Industrial Controls
NAICS 335314 Relay & Industrial Control Manufacturing
3629 Electrical Industrial Apparatus, nec
NAICS 335999 All Other Miscellaneous Electrical Equipment
& Component Manufacturing
3631 Household Cooking Equipment
NAICS 335221 Household Cooking Appliance Manufacturing
3632 Household Refrigerators & Home & Farm Freezers
NAICS 335222 Household Refrigerator & Home Freezer
Manufacturing
3633 Household Laundry Equipment
NAICS 335224 Household Laundry Equipment Manufacturing
3634 Electric Housewares & Fans
NAICS 335211 Electric Housewares & Fan Manufacturing
3635 Household Vacuum Cleaners
NAICS 335212 Household Vacuum Cleaner Manufacturing
3639 Household Appliances, nec
NAICS 335212 Household Vacuum Cleaner Manufacturing
NAICS 333298 All Other Industrial Machinery Manufacturing
NAICS 335228 Other Household Appliance Manufacturing
3641 Electric Lamp Bulbs & Tubes
NAICS 33511 Electric Lamp Bulb & Part Manufacturing
3643 Current-carrying Wiring Devices
NAICS 335931 Current-carrying Wiring Device Manufacturing
3644 Noncurrent-carrying Wiring Devices
NAICS 335932 Noncurrent-carrying Wiring Device
Manufacturing
3645 Residential Electric Lighting Fixtures
NAICS 335121 Residential Electric Lighting Fixture
Manufacturing
**3646 Commercial, Industrial, & Institutional Electric Lighting
Fixtures**
NAICS 335122 Commercial, Industrial, & Institutional Electric
Lighting Fixture Manufacturing
3647 Vehicular Lighting Equipment
NAICS 336321 Vehicular Lighting Equipment Manufacturing
3648 Lighting Equipment, nec
NAICS 335129 Other Lighting Equipment Manufacturing
3651 Household Audio & Video Equipment
NAICS 33431 Audio & Video Equipment Manufacturing 3652
NAICS 51222 Integrated Record Production/distribution
3661 Telephone & Telegraph Apparatus
NAICS 33421 Telephone Apparatus Manufacturing
NAICS 334416 Electronic Coil, Transformer, & Other Inductor
Manufacturing
NAICS 334418 Printed Circuit/electronics Assembly
Manufacturing

3663 Radio & Television Broadcasting & Communication Equipment
NAICS 33422　Radio & Television Broadcasting & Wireless Communications Equipment Manufacturing
3669 Communications Equipment, nec
NAICS 33429　Other Communication Equipment Manufacturing
3671 Electron Tubes
NAICS 334411 Electron Tube Manufacturing
3672 Printed Circuit Boards
NAICS 334412 Printed Circuit Board Manufacturing
3674 Semiconductors & Related Devices
NAICS 334413 Semiconductor & Related Device Manufacturing
3675 Electronic Capacitors
NAICS 334414 Electronic Capacitor Manufacturing
3676 Electronic Resistors
NAICS 334415 Electronic Resistor Manufacturing
3677 Electronic Coils, Transformers, & Other Inductors
NAICS 334416 Electronic Coil, Transformer, & Other Inductor Manufacturing
3678 Electronic ConNECtors
NAICS 334417 Electronic ConNECtor Manufacturing
3679 Electronic Components, nec
NAICS 33422　Radio & Television Broadcasting & Wireless Communications Equipment Manufacturing
NAICS 334418 Printed Circuit/electronics Assembly Manufacturing
NAICS 336322 Other Motor Vehicle Electrical & Electronic Equipment Manufacturing
NAICS 334419 Other Electronic Component Manufacturing
3691 Storage Batteries
NAICS 335911 Storage Battery Manufacturing
3692 Primary Batteries, Dry & Wet
NAICS 335912 Dry & Wet Primary Battery Manufacturing
3694 Electrical Equipment for Internal Combustion Engines
NAICS 336322 Other Motor Vehicle Electrical & Electronic Equipment Manufacturing
3695 Magnetic & Optical Recording Media
NAICS 334613 Magnetic & Optical Recording Media Manufacturing
3699 Electrical Machinery, Equipment, & Supplies, nec
NAICS 333319 Other Commercial & Service Industry Machinery Manufacturing
NAICS 333618 Other Engine Equipment Manufacturing
NAICS 334119 Other Computer Peripheral Equipment Manufacturing Classify According to Function
NAICS 335129 Other Lighting Equipment Manufacturing
NAICS 335999 All Other Miscellaneous Electrical Equipment & Component Manufacturing

TRANSPORTATION EQUIPMENT

3711 Motor Vehicles & Passenger Car Bodies
NAICS 336111 Automobile Manufacturing
NAICS 336112 Light Truck & Utility Vehicle Manufacturing
NAICS 33612　Heavy Duty Truck Manufacturing
NAICS 336211 Motor Vehicle Body Manufacturing
NAICS 336992 Military Armored Vehicle, Tank, & Tank Component Manufacturing
3713 Truck & Bus Bodies
NAICS 336211 Motor Vehicle Body Manufacturing

3714 Motor Vehicle Parts & Accessories
NAICS 336211 Motor Vehicle Body Manufacturing
NAICS 336312 Gasoline Engine & Engine Parts Manufacturing
NAICS 336322 Other Motor Vehicle Electrical & Electronic Equipment Manufacturing
NAICS 33633　Motor Vehicle Steering & Suspension Components Manufacturing
NAICS 33634　Motor Vehicle Brake System Manufacturing
NAICS 33635　Motor Vehicle Transmission & Power Train Parts Manufacturing
NAICS 336399 All Other Motor Vehicle Parts Manufacturing
3715 Truck Trailers
NAICS 336212 Truck Trailer Manufacturing
3716 Motor Homes
NAICS 336213 Motor Home Manufacturing
3721 Aircraft
NAICS 336411 Aircraft Manufacturing
3724 Aircraft Engines & Engine Parts
NAICS 336412 Aircraft Engine & Engine Parts Manufacturing 3728
NAICS 336413 Other Aircraft Part & Auxiliary Equipment Manufacturing
3731 Ship Building & Repairing
NAICS 336611 Ship Building & Repairing
3732 Boat Building & Repairing
NAICS 81149　Other Personal & Household Goods Repair & Maintenance
NAICS 336612 Boat Building
3743 Railroad Equipment
NAICS 333911 Pump & Pumping Equipment Manufacturing
NAICS 33651　Railroad Rolling Stock Manufacturing
3751 Motorcycles, Bicycles, & Parts
NAICS 336991 Motorcycle, Bicycle, & Parts Manufacturing
3761 Guided Missiles & Space Vehicles
NAICS 336414 Guided Missile & Space Vehicle Manufacturing 3764
3769 Guided Missile Space Vehicle Parts & Auxiliary Equipment, nec
NAICS 336419 Other Guided Missile & Space Vehicle Parts & Auxiliary Equipment Manufacturing
3792 Travel Trailers & Campers
NAICS 336214 Travel Trailer & Camper Manufacturing
3795 Tanks & Tank Components
NAICS 336992 Military Armored Vehicle, Tank, & Tank Component Manufacturing
3799 Transportation Equipment, nec
NAICS 336214 Travel Trailer & Camper Manufacturing
NAICS 332212 Hand & Edge Tool Manufacturing
NAICS 336999 All Other Transportation Equipment Manufacturing

MEASURING, ANALYZING, & CONTROLLING INSTRUMENTS

3812 Search, Detection, Navigation, Guidance, Aeronautical, & Nautical Systems & Instruments
NAICS 334511 Search, Detection, Navigation, Guidance, Aeronautical, & Nautical System & Instrument Manufacturing
3821 Laboratory Apparatus & Furniture
NAICS 339111 Laboratory Apparatus & Furniture Manufacturing

3822 Automatic Controls for Regulating Residential & Commercial Environments & Appliances
NAICS 334512 Automatic Environmental Control Manufacturing for Regulating Residential, Commercial, & Appliance Use

3823 Industrial Instruments for Measurement, Display, & Control of Process Variables & Related Products
NAICS 334513 Instruments & Related Product Manufacturing for Measuring Displaying, & Controlling Industrial Process Variables

3824 Totalizing Fluid Meters & Counting Devices
NAICS 334514 Totalizing Fluid Meter & Counting Device Manufacturing

3825 Instruments for Measuring & Testing of Electricity & Electrical Signals
NAICS 334416 Electronic Coil, Transformer, & Other Inductor Manufacturing
NAICS 334515 Instrument Manufacturing for Measuring & Testing Electricity & Electrical Signals

3826 Laboratory Analytical Instruments
NAICS 334516 Analytical Laboratory Instrument Manufacturing

3827 Optical Instruments & Lenses
NAICS 333314 Optical Instrument & Lens Manufacturing

3829 Measuring & Controlling Devices, nec
NAICS 339112 Surgical & Medical Instrument Manufacturing
NAICS 334519 Other Measuring & Controlling Device Manufacturing

3841 Surgical & Medical Instruments & Apparatus
NAICS 339112 Surgical & Medical Instrument Manufacturing

3842 Orthopedic, Prosthetic, & Surgical Appliances & Supplies
NAICS 339113 Surgical Appliance & Supplies Manufacturing
NAICS 334510 Electromedical & Electrotherapeutic Apparatus Manufacturing

3843 Dental Equipment & Supplies
NAICS 339114 Dental Equipment & Supplies Manufacturing

3844 X-ray Apparatus & Tubes & Related Irradiation Apparatus
NAICS 334517 Irradiation Apparatus Manufacturing

3845 Electromedical & Electrotherapeutic Apparatus
NAICS 334517 Irradiation Apparatus Manufacturing
NAICS 334510 Electromedical & Electrotherapeutic Apparatus Manufacturing

3851 Ophthalmic Goods
NAICS 339115 Ophthalmic Goods Manufacturing

3861 Photographic Equipment & Supplies
NAICS 333315 Photographic & Photocopying Equipment Manufacturing
NAICS 325992 Photographic Film, Paper, Plate & Chemical Manufacturing

3873 Watches, Clocks, Clockwork Operated Devices & Parts
NAICS 334518 Watch, Clock, & Part Manufacturing

MISCELLANEOUS MANUFACTURING INDUSTRIES

3911 Jewelry, Precious Metal
NAICS 339911 Jewelry Manufacturing

3914 Silverware, Plated Ware, & Stainless Steel Ware
NAICS 332211 Cutlery & Flatware Manufacturing
NAICS 339912 Silverware & Plated Ware Manufacturing

3915 Jewelers' Findings & Materials, & Lapidary Work
NAICS 339913 Jewelers' Material & Lapidary Work Manufacturing

3931 Musical Instruments
NAICS 339992 Musical Instrument Manufacturing

3942 Dolls & Stuffed Toys
NAICS 339931 Doll & Stuffed Toy Manufacturing

3944 Games, Toys, & Children's Vehicles, Except Dolls & Bicycles
NAICS 336991 Motorcycle, Bicycle & Parts Manufacturing
NAICS 339932 Game, Toy, & Children's Vehicle Manufacturing

3949 Sporting & Athletic Goods, nec
NAICS 33992 Sporting & Athletic Good Manufacturing

3951 Pens, Mechanical Pencils & Parts
NAICS 339941 Pen & Mechanical Pencil Manufacturing

3952 Lead Pencils, Crayons, & Artist's Materials
NAICS 337139 Other Wood Furniture Manufacturing
NAICS 337139 Other Wood Furniture Manufacturing
NAICS 325998 All Other Miscellaneous Chemical Manufacturing
NAICS 339942 Lead Pencil & Art Good Manufacturing

3953 Marking Devices
NAICS 339943 Marking Device Manufacturing

3955 Carbon Paper & Inked Ribbons
NAICS 339944 Carbon Paper & Inked Ribbon Manufacturing

3961 Costume Jewelry & Costume Novelties, Except Precious Metals
NAICS 339914 Costume Jewelry & Novelty Manufacturing

3965 Fasteners, Buttons, Needles, & Pins
NAICS 339993 Fastener, Button, Needle & Pin Manufacturing

3991 Brooms & Brushes
NAICS 339994 Broom, Brush & Mop Manufacturing

3993 Signs & Advertising Specialties
NAICS 33995 Sign Manufacturing

3995 Burial Caskets
NAICS 339995 Burial Casket Manufacturing

3996 Linoleum, Asphalted-felt-base, & Other Hard Surface Floor Coverings, nec
NAICS 326192 Resilient Floor Covering Manufacturing

3999 Manufacturing Industries, nec
NAICS 337148 Other Nonwood Furniture Manufacturing
NAICS 321999 All Other Miscellaneous Wood Product Manufacturing
NAICS 31611 Leather & Hide Tanning & Finishing
NAICS 335121 Residential Electric Lighting Fixture Manufacturing
NAICS 325998 All Other Miscellaneous Chemical Product Manufacturing
NAICS 332999 All Other Miscellaneous Fabricated Metal Product Manufacturing
NAICS 326199 All Other Plastics Product Manufacturing
NAICS 323112 Commercial Flexographic Printing
NAICS 323111 Commercial Gravure Printing
NAICS 323110 Commercial Lithographic Printing
NAICS 323113 Commercial Screen Printing
NAICS 323119 Other Commercial Printing
NAICS 332212 Hand & Edge Tool Manufacturing
NAICS 339999 All Other Miscellaneous Manufacturing

TRANSPORTATION, COMMUNICATIONS, ELECTRIC, GAS, & SANITARY SERVICES

4011 Railroads, Line-haul Operating
NAICS 482111 Line-haul Railroads
4013 Railroad Switching & Terminal Establishments
NAICS 482112 Short Line Railroads
NAICS 48821   Support Activities for Rail Transportation
4111 Local & Suburban Transit
NAICS 485111 Mixed Mode Transit Systems
NAICS 485112 Commuter Rail Systems
NAICS 485113 Bus & Motor Vehicle Transit Systems
NAICS 485119 Other Urban Transit Systems
NAICS 485999 All Other Transit & Ground Passenger
Transportation
4119 Local Passenger Transportation, nec
NAICS 62191   Ambulance Service
NAICS 48541   School & Employee Bus Transportation
NAICS 48711   Scenic & Sightseeing Transportation , Land
NAICS 485991 Special Needs Transportation
NAICS 485999 All Other Transit & Ground Passenger
Transportation
NAICS 48532   Limousine Service
4121 Taxicabs
NAICS 48531   Taxi Service
4131 Intercity & Rural Bus Transportation
NAICS 48521   Interurban & Rural Bus Transportation
4141 Local Bus Charter Service
NAICS 48551   Charter Bus Industry
4142 Bus Charter Service, Except Local
NAICS 48551   Charter Bus Industry
4151 School Buses
NAICS 48541   School & Employee Bus Transportation
4173 Terminal & Service Facilities for Motor Vehicle Passenger Transportation
NAICS 48849   Other Support Activities for Road
Transportation
4212 Local Trucking Without Storage
NAICS 562111 Solid Waste Collection
NAICS 562112 Hazardous Waste Collection
NAICS 562119 Other Waste Collection
NAICS 48411   General Freight Trucking, Local
NAICS 48421   Used Household & Office Goods Moving
NAICS 48422   Specialized Freight Trucking, Local
4213 Trucking, Except Local
NAICS 484121 General Freight Trucking, Long-distance,
Truckload
NAICS 484122 General Freight Trucking, Long-distance, less
than Truckload
NAICS 48421   Used Household & Office Goods Moving
NAICS 48423   Specialized Freight Trucking, Long-distance
4214 Local Trucking with Storage
NAICS 48411   General Freight Trucking, Local
NAICS 48421   Used Household & Office Goods Moving
NAICS 48422   Specialized Freight Trucking, Local
4215 Couriers Services Except by Air
NAICS 49211   Couriers
NAICS 49221   Local Messengers & Local Delivery
4221 Farm Product Warehousing & Storage
NAICS 49313   Farm Product Storage Facilities
4222 Refrigerated Warehousing & Storage
NAICS 49312   Refrigerated Storage Facilities

4225 General Warehousing & Storage
NAICS 49311   General Warehousing & Storage Facilities
NAICS 53113   Lessors of Miniwarehouses & Self Storage
Units
4226 Special Warehousing & Storage, nec
NAICS 49312   Refrigerated Warehousing & Storage Facilities
NAICS 49311   General Warehousing & Storage Facilities
NAICS 49319   Other Warehousing & Storage Facilities
4231 Terminal & Joint Terminal Maintenance Facilities for Motor Freight Transportation
NAICS 48849   Other Support Activities for Road
Transportation
4311 United States Postal Service
NAICS 49111   Postal Service
4412 Deep Sea Foreign Transportation of Freight
NAICS 483111 Deep Sea Freight Transportation
4424 Deep Sea Domestic Transportation of Freight
NAICS 483113 Coastal & Great Lakes Freight Transportation
4432 Freight Transportation on the Great Lakes - St. Lawrence Seaway
NAICS 483113 Coastal & Great Lakes Freight Transportation
4449 Water Transportation of Freight, nec
NAICS 483211 Inland Water Freight Transportation
4481 Deep Sea Transportation of Passengers, Except by Ferry
NAICS 483112 Deep Sea Passenger Transportation
NAICS 483114 Coastal & Great Lakes Passenger
Transportation
4482 Ferries
NAICS 483114 Coastal & Great Lakes Passenger
Transportation
NAICS 483212 Inland Water Passenger Transportation
4489 Water Transportation of Passengers, nec
NAICS 483212 Inland Water Passenger Transportation
NAICS 48721   Scenic & Sightseeing Transportation, Water
4491 Marine Cargo Handling
NAICS 48831   Port & Harbor Operations
NAICS 48832   Marine Cargo Handling
4492 Towing & Tugboat Services
NAICS 483113 Coastal & Great Lakes Freight Transportation
NAICS 483211 Inland Water Freight Transportation
NAICS 48833   Navigational Services to Shipping
4493 Marinas
NAICS 71393   Marinas
4499 Water Transportation Services, nec
NAICS 532411 Commercial Air, Rail, & Water Transportation
Equipment Rental & Leasing
NAICS 48831   Port & Harbor Operations
NAICS 48833   Navigational Services to Shipping
NAICS 48839   Other Support Activities for Water
Transportation
4512 Air Transportation, Scheduled
NAICS 481111 Scheduled Passenger Air Transportation
NAICS 481112 Scheduled Freight Air Transportation
4513 Air Courier Services
NAICS 49211   Couriers
4522 Air Transportation, Nonscheduled
NAICS 62191   Ambulance Services
NAICS 481212 Nonscheduled Chartered Freight Air
Transportation
NAICS 481211 Nonscheduled Chartered Passenger Air
Transportation
NAICS 48122   Nonscheduled Speciality Air Transportation
NAICS 48799   Scenic & Sightseeing Transportation , Other

4581 Airports, Flying Fields, & Airport Terminal Services
NAICS 488111 Air Traffic Control
NAICS 488112 Airport Operations, Except Air Traffic Control
NAICS 56172 Janitorial Services
NAICS 48819 Other Support Activities for Air Transportation
4612 Crude Petroleum Pipelines
NAICS 48611 Pipeline Transportation of Crude Oil
4613 Refined Petroleum Pipelines
NAICS 48691 Pipeline Transportation of Refined Petroleum
Products
4619 Pipelines, nec
NAICS 48699 All Other Pipeline Transportation
4724 Travel Agencies
NAICS 56151 Travel Agencies
4725 Tour Operators
NAICS 56152 Tour Operators
4729 Arrangement of Passenger Transportation, nec
NAICS 488999 All Other Support Activities for Transportation
NAICS 561599 All Other Travel Arrangement & Reservation
Services
4731 Arrangement of Transportation of Freight & Cargo
NAICS 541618 Other Management Consulting Services
NAICS 48851 Freight Transportation Arrangement
4741 Rental of Railroad Cars
NAICS 532411 Commercial Air, Rail, & Water Transportation
Equipment Rental & Leasing
NAICS 48821 Support Activities for Rail Transportation
4783 Packing & Crating
NAICS 488991 Packing & Crating
**4785 Fixed Facilities & Inspection & Weighing Services for
Motor Vehicle Transportation**
NAICS 48839 Other Support Activities for Water
Transportation
NAICS 48849 Other Support Activities for Road
Transportation
4789 Transportation Services, nec
NAICS 488999 All Other Support Activities for Transportation
NAICS 48711 Scenic & Sightseeing Transportation, Land
NAICS 48821 Support Activities for Rail Transportation
4812 Radiotelephone Communications
NAICS 513321 Paging
NAICS 513322 Cellular & Other Wireless Telecommunications
NAICS 51333 Telecommunications Resellers
4813 Telephone Communications, Except Radiotelephone
NAICS 51331 Wired Telecommunications Carriers
NAICS 51333 Telecommunications Resellers
4822 Telegraph & Other Message Communications
NAICS 51331 Wired Telecommunications Carriers
4832 Radio Broadcasting Stations
NAICS 513111 Radio Networks
NAICS 513112 Radio Stations
4833 Television Broadcasting Stations
NAICS 51312 Television Broadcasting
4841 Cable & Other Pay Television Services
NAICS 51321 Cable Networks
NAICS 51322 Cable & Other Program Distribution
4899 Communications Services, nec
NAICS 513322 Cellular & Other Wireless Telecommunications
NAICS 51334 Satellite Telecommunications
NAICS 51339 Other Telecommunications
4911 Electric Services
NAICS 221111 Hydroelectric Power Generation
NAICS 221112 Fossil Fuel Electric Power Generation
NAICS 221113 Nuclear Electric Power Generation

NAICS 221119 Other Electric Power Generation
NAICS 221121 Electric Bulk Power Transmission & Control
NAICS 221122 Electric Power Distribution
4922 Natural Gas Transmission
NAICS 48621 Pipeline Transportation of Natural Gas
4923 Natural Gas Transmission & Distribution
NAICS 22121 Natural Gas Distribution
NAICS 48621 Pipeline Transportation of Natural Gas
4924 Natural Gas Distribution
NAICS 22121 Natural Gas Distribution
**4925 Mixed, Manufactured, or Liquefied Petroleum Gas
Production And/or Distribution**
NAICS 22121 Natural Gas Distribution
4931 Electric & Other Services Combined
NAICS 221111 Hydroelectric Power Generation
NAICS 221112 Fossil Fuel Electric Power Generation
NAICS 221113 Nuclear Electric Power Generation
NAICS 221119 Other Electric Power Generation
NAICS 221121 Electric Bulk Power Transmission & Control
NAICS 221122 Electric Power Distribution
NAICS 22121 Natural Gas Distribution
4932 Gas & Other Services Combined
NAICS 22121 Natural Gas Distribution
4939 Combination Utilities, nec
NAICS 221111 Hydroelectric Power Generation
NAICS 221112 Fossil Fuel Electric Power Generation
NAICS 221113 Nuclear Electric Power Generation
NAICS 221119 Other Electric Power Generation
NAICS 221121 Electric Bulk Power Transmission & Control
NAICS 221122 Electric Power Distribution
NAICS 22121 Natural Gas Distribution
4941 Water Supply
NAICS 22131 Water Supply & Irrigation Systems
4952 Sewerage Systems
NAICS 22132 Sewage Treatment Facilities
4953 Refuse Systems
NAICS 562111 Solid Waste Collection
NAICS 562112 Hazardous Waste Collection
NAICS 56292 Materials Recovery Facilities
NAICS 562119 Other Waste Collection
NAICS 562211 Hazardous Waste Treatment & Disposal
NAICS 562212 Solid Waste Landfills
NAICS 562213 Solid Waste Combustors & Incinerators
NAICS 562219 Other Nonhazardous Waste Treatment &
Disposal
4959 Sanitary Services, nec
NAICS 488112 Airport Operations, Except Air Traffic Control
NAICS 56291 Remediation Services
NAICS 56171 Exterminating & Pest Control Services
NAICS 562998 All Other Miscellaneous Waste Management
Services
4961 Steam & Air-conditioning Supply
NAICS 22133 Steam & Air-conditioning Supply
4971 Irrigation Systems
NAICS 22131 Water Supply & Irrigation Systems

WHOLESALE TRADE

5012 Automobiles & Other Motor Vehicles
NAICS 42111 Automobile & Other Motor Vehicle
Wholesalers

5013 Motor Vehicle Supplies & New Parts
NAICS 44131 Automotive Parts & Accessories Stores - Retail
NAICS 42112 Motor Vehicle Supplies & New Part Wholesalers
5014 Tires & Tubes
NAICS 44132 Tire Dealers - Retail
NAICS 42113 Tire & Tube Wholesalers
5015 Motor Vehicle Parts, Used
NAICS 42114 Motor Vehicle Part Wholesalers
5021 Furniture
NAICS 44211 Furniture Stores
NAICS 42121 Furniture Wholesalers
5023 Home Furnishings
NAICS 44221 Floor Covering Stores
NAICS 42122 Home Furnishing Wholesalers
5031 Lumber, Plywood, Millwork, & Wood Panels
NAICS 44419 Other Building Material Dealers
NAICS 42131 Lumber, Plywood, Millwork, & Wood Panel Wholesalers
5032 Brick, Stone & Related Construction Materials
NAICS 44419 Other Building Material Dealers
NAICS 42132 Brick, Stone & Related Construction Material Wholesalers
5033 Roofing, Siding, & Insulation Materials
NAICS 42133 Roofing, Siding, & Insulation Material Wholesalers
5039 Construction Materials, nec
NAICS 44419 Other Building Material Dealers
NAICS 42139 Other Construction Material Wholesalers
5043 Photographic Equipment & Supplies
NAICS 42141 Photographic Equipment & Supplies Wholesalers
5044 Office Equipment
NAICS 42142 Office Equipment Wholesalers
5045 Computers & Computer Peripheral Equipment & Software
NAICS 42143 Computer & Computer Peripheral Equipment & Software Wholesalers
NAICS 44312 Computer & Software Stores - Retail
5046 Commercial Equipment, nec
NAICS 42144 Other Commercial Equipment Wholesalers
5047 Medical, Dental, & Hospital Equipment & Supplies
NAICS 42145 Medical, Dental & Hospital Equipment & Supplies Wholesalers
NAICS 446199 All Other Health & Personal Care Stores - Retail
5048 Ophthalmic Goods
NAICS 42146 Ophthalmic Goods Wholesalers
5049 Professional Equipment & Supplies, nec
NAICS 42149 Other Professional Equipment & Supplies Wholesalers
NAICS 45321 Office Supplies & Stationery Stores - Retail
5051 Metals Service Centers & Offices
NAICS 42151 Metals Service Centers & Offices
5052 Coal & Other Minerals & Ores
NAICS 42152 Coal & Other Mineral & Ore Wholesalers
5063 Electrical Apparatus & Equipment Wiring Supplies, & Construction Materials
NAICS 44419 Other Building Material Dealers
NAICS 42161 Electrical Apparatus & Equipment, Wiring Supplies & Construction Material Wholesalers
5064 Electrical Appliances, Television & Radio Sets
NAICS 42162 Electrical Appliance, Television & Radio Set Wholesalers

5065 Electronic Parts & Equipment, Not Elsewhere Classified
NAICS 42169 Other Electronic Parts & Equipment Wholesalers
5072 Hardware
NAICS 42171 Hardware Wholesalers
5074 Plumbing & Heating Equipment & Supplies
NAICS 44419 Other Building Material Dealers
NAICS 42172 Plumbing & Heating Equipment & Supplies Wholesalers
5075 Warm Air Heating & Air-conditioning Equipment & Supplies
NAICS 42173 Warm Air Heating & Air-conditioning Equipment & Supplies Wholesalers
5078 Refrigeration Equipment & Supplies
NAICS 42174 Refrigeration Equipment & Supplies Wholesalers
5082 Construction & Mining Machinery & Equipment
NAICS 42181 Construction & Mining Machinery & Equipment Wholesalers
5083 Farm & Garden Machinery & Equipment
NAICS 42182 Farm & Garden Machinery & Equipment Wholesalers
NAICS 44421 Outdoor Power Equipment Stores - Retail
5084 Industrial Machinery & Equipment
NAICS 42183 Industrial Machinery & Equipment Wholesalers
5085 Industrial Supplies
NAICS 42183 Industrial Machinery & Equipment Wholesalers
NAICS 42184 Industrial Supplies Wholesalers
NAICS 81131 Commercial & Industrial Machinery & Equipment Repair & Maintenence
5087 Service Establishment Equipment & Supplies
NAICS 42185 Service Establishment Equipment & Supplies Wholesalers
NAICS 44612 Cosmetics, Beauty Supplies, & Perfume Stores
5088 Transportation Equipment & Supplies, Except Motor Vehicles
NAICS 42186 Transportation Equipment & Supplies Wholesalers
5091 Sporting & Recreational Goods & Supplies
NAICS 42191 Sporting & Recreational Goods & Supplies Wholesalers
5092 Toys & Hobby Goods & Supplies
NAICS 42192 Toy & Hobby Goods & Supplies Wholesalers
5093 Scrap & Waste Materials
NAICS 42193 Recyclable Material Wholesalers
5094 Jewelry, Watches, Precious Stones, & Precious Metals
NAICS 42194 Jewelry, Watch , Precious Stone, & Precious Metal Wholesalers
5099 Durable Goods, nec
NAICS 42199 Other Miscellaneous Durable Goods Wholesalers
5111 Printing & Writing Paper
NAICS 42211 Printing & Writing Paper Wholesalers
5112 Stationery & Office Supplies
NAICS 45321 Office Supplies & Stationery Stores
NAICS 42212 Stationery & Office Supplies Wholesalers
5113 Industrial & Personal Service Paper
NAICS 42213 Industrial & Personal Service Paper Wholesalers
5122 Drugs, Drug Proprietaries, & Druggists' Sundries
NAICS 42221 Drugs, Drug Proprietaries, & Druggists' Sundries Wholesalers

5131 Piece Goods, Notions, & Other Dry Goods
NAICS 313311 Broadwoven Fabric Finishing Mills
NAICS 313312 Textile & Fabric Finishing Mills
NAICS 42231 Piece Goods, Notions, & Other Dry Goods
Wholesalers
5136 Men's & Boys' Clothing & Furnishings
NAICS 42232 Men's & Boys' Clothing & Furnishings
Wholesalers
5137 Women's Children's & Infants' Clothing & Accessories
NAICS 42233 Women's, Children's, & Infants' Clothing &
Accessories Wholesalers
5139 Footwear
NAICS 42234 Footwear Wholesalers
5141 Groceries, General Line
NAICS 42241 General Line Grocery Wholesalers
5142 Packaged Frozen Foods
NAICS 42242 Packaged Frozen Food Wholesalers
5143 Dairy Products, Except Dried or Canned
NAICS 42243 Dairy Products Wholesalers
5144 Poultry & Poultry Products
NAICS 42244 Poultry & Poultry Product Wholesalers
5145 Confectionery
NAICS 42245 Confectionery Wholesalers
5146 Fish & Seafoods
NAICS 42246 Fish & Seafood Wholesalers
5147 Meats & Meat Products
NAICS 311612 Meat Processed from Carcasses
NAICS 42247 Meat & Meat Product Wholesalers
5148 Fresh Fruits & Vegetables
NAICS 42248 Fresh Fruit & Vegetable Wholesalers
5149 Groceries & Related Products, nec
NAICS 42249 Other Grocery & Related Product Wholesalers
5153 Grain & Field Beans
NAICS 42251 Grain & Field Bean Wholesalers
5154 Livestock
NAICS 42252 Livestock Wholesalers
5159 Farm-product Raw Materials, nec
NAICS 42259 Other Farm Product Raw Material Wholesalers
5162 Plastics Materials & Basic Forms & Shapes
NAICS 42261 Plastics Materials & Basic Forms & Shapes
Wholesalers
5169 Chemicals & Allied Products, nec
NAICS 42269 Other Chemical & Allied Products Wholesalers
5171 Petroleum Bulk Stations & Terminals
NAICS 454311 Heating Oil Dealers
NAICS 454312 Liquefied Petroleum Gas Dealers
NAICS 42271 Petroleum Bulk Stations & Terminals
5172 Petroleum & Petroleum Products Wholesalers, Except Bulk Stations & Terminals
NAICS 42272 Petroleum & Petroleum Products Wholesalers
5181 Beer & Ale
NAICS 42281 Beer & Ale Wholesalers
5182 Wine & Distilled Alcoholic Beverages
NAICS 42282 Wine & Distilled Alcoholic Beverage
Wholesalers
5191 Farm Supplies
NAICS 44422 Nursery & Garden Centers - Retail
NAICS 42291 Farm Supplies Wholesalers
5192 Books, Periodicals, & Newspapers
NAICS 42292 Book, Periodical & Newspaper Wholesalers
5193 Flowers, Nursery Stock, & Florists' Supplies
NAICS 42293 Flower, Nursery Stock & Florists' Supplies
Wholesalers
NAICS 44422 Nursery & Garden Centers - Retail

5194 Tobacco & Tobacco Products
NAICS 42294 Tobacco & Tobacco Product Wholesalers
5198 Paint, Varnishes, & Supplies
NAICS 42295 Paint, Varnish & Supplies Wholesalers
NAICS 44412 Paint & Wallpaper Stores
5199 Nondurable Goods, nec
NAICS 54189 Other Services Related to Advertising
NAICS 42299 Other Miscellaneous Nondurable Goods
Wholesalers

RETAIL TRADE

5211 Lumber & Other Building Materials Dealers
NAICS 44411 Home Centers
NAICS 42131 Lumber, Plywood, Millwork & Wood Panel
Wholesalers
NAICS 44419 Other Building Material Dealers
5231 Paint, Glass, & Wallpaper Stores
NAICS 42295 Paint, Varnish & Supplies Wholesalers
NAICS 44419 Other Building Material Dealers
NAICS 44412 Paint & Wallpaper Stores
5251 Hardware Stores
NAICS 44413 Hardware Stores
5261 Retail Nurseries, Lawn & Garden Supply Stores
NAICS 44422 Nursery & Garden Centers
NAICS 453998 All Other Miscellaneous Store Retailers
NAICS 44421 Outdoor Power Equipment Stores
5271 Mobile Home Dealers
NAICS 45393 Manufactured Home Dealers
5311 Department Stores
NAICS 45211 Department Stores
5331 Variety Stores
NAICS 45299 All Other General Merchandise Stores
5399 Miscellaneous General Merchandise Stores
NAICS 45291 Warehouse Clubs & Superstores
NAICS 45299 All Other General Merchandise Stores
5411 Grocery Stores
NAICS 44711 Gasoline Stations with Convenience Stores
NAICS 44511 Supermarkets & Other Grocery Stores
NAICS 45291 Warehouse Clubs & Superstores
NAICS 44512 Convenience Stores
5421 Meat & Fish Markets, Including Freezer Provisioners
NAICS 45439 Other Direct Selling Establishments
NAICS 44521 Meat Markets
NAICS 44522 Fish & Seafood Markets
5431 Fruit & Vegetable Markets
NAICS 44523 Fruit & Vegetable Markets
5441 Candy, Nut, & Confectionery Stores
NAICS 445292 Confectionary & Nut Stores
5451 Dairy Products Stores
NAICS 445299 All Other Specialty Food Stores
5461 Retail Bakeries
NAICS 722213 Snack & Nonalcoholic Beverage Bars
NAICS 311811 Retail Bakeries
NAICS 445291 Baked Goods Stores
5499 Miscellaneous Food Stores
NAICS 44521 Meat Markets
NAICS 722211 Limited-service Restaurants
NAICS 446191 Food Supplement Stores
NAICS 445299 All Other Specialty Food Stores
5511 Motor Vehicle Dealers
NAICS 44111 New Car Dealers

5521 Motor Vehicle Dealers
NAICS 44112 Used Car Dealers
5531 Auto & Home Supply Stores
NAICS 44132 Tire Dealers
NAICS 44131 Automotive Parts & Accessories Stores
5541 Gasoline Service Stations
NAICS 44711 Gasoline Stations with Convenience Store
NAICS 44719 Other Gasoline Stations
5551 Boat Dealers
NAICS 441222 Boat Dealers
5561 Recreational Vehicle Dealers
NAICS 44121 Recreational Vehicle Dealers
5571 Motorcycle Dealers
NAICS 441221 Motorcycle Dealers
5599 Automotive Dealers, nec
NAICS 441229 All Other Motor Vehicle Dealers
5611 Men's & Boys' Clothing & Accessory Stores
NAICS 44811 Men's Clothing Stores
NAICS 44815 Clothing Accessories Stores
5621 Women's Clothing Stores
NAICS 44812 Women's Clothing Stores
5632 Women's Accessory & Specialty Stores
NAICS 44819 Other Clothing Stores
NAICS 44815 Clothing Accessories Stores
5641 Children's & Infants' Wear Stores
NAICS 44813 Children's & Infants' Clothing Stores
5651 Family Clothing Stores
NAICS 44814 Family Clothing Stores
5661 Shoe Stores
NAICS 44821 Shoe Stores
5699 Miscellaneous Apparel & Accessory Stores
NAICS 315 Included in Apparel Manufacturing Subsector Based on Type of Garment Produced
NAICS 44819 Other Clothing Stores
NAICS 44815 Clothing Accessories Stores
5712 Furniture Stores
NAICS 337133 Wood Household Furniture, Except Upholstered, Manufacturing
NAICS 337131 Wood Kitchen Cabinet & Counter Top Manufacturing
NAICS 337132 Upholstered Household Furniture Manufacturing
NAICS 44211 Furniture Stores
5713 Floor Covering Stores
NAICS 44221 Floor Covering Stores
5714 Drapery, Curtain, & Upholstery Stores
NAICS 442291 Window Treatment Stores
NAICS 45113 Sewing, Needlework & Piece Goods Stores
NAICS 314121 Curtain & Drapery Mills
5719 Miscellaneous Homefurnishings Stores
NAICS 442291 Window Treatment Stores
NAICS 442299 All Other Home Furnishings Stores
5722 Household Appliance Stores
NAICS 443111 Household Appliance Stores
5731 Radio, Television, & Consumer Electronics Stores
NAICS 443112 Radio, Television, & Other Electronics Stores
NAICS 44131 Automotive Parts & Accessories Stores
5734 Computer & Computer Software Stores
NAICS 44312 Computer & Software Stores
5735 Record & Prerecorded Tape Stores
NAICS 45122 Prerecorded Tape, Compact Disc & Record Stores

5736 Musical Instrument Stores
NAICS 45114 Musical Instrument & Supplies Stores
5812 Eating & Drinking Places
NAICS 72211 Full-service Restaurants
NAICS 722211 Limited-service Restaurants
NAICS 722212 Cafeterias
NAICS 722213 Snack & Nonalcoholic Beverage Bars
NAICS 72231 Foodservice Contractors
NAICS 72232 Caterers
NAICS 71111 Theater Companies & Dinner Theaters
5813 Drinking Places
NAICS 72241 Drinking Places
5912 Drug Stores & Proprietary Stores
NAICS 44611 Pharmacies & Drug Stores
5921 Liquor Stores
NAICS 44531 Beer, Wine & Liquor Stores
5932 Used Merchandise Stores
NAICS 522298 All Other Non-depository Credit Intermediation
NAICS 45331 Used Merchandise Stores
5941 Sporting Goods Stores & Bicycle Shops
NAICS 45111 Sporting Goods Stores
5942 Book Stores
NAICS 451211 Book Stores
5943 Stationery Stores
NAICS 45321 Office Supplies & Stationery Stores
5944 Jewelry Stores
NAICS 44831 Jewelry Stores
5945 Hobby, Toy, & Game Shops
NAICS 45112 Hobby, Toy & Game Stores
5946 Camera & Photographic Supply Stores
NAICS 44313 Camera & Photographic Supplies Stores
5947 Gift, Novelty, & Souvenir Shops
NAICS 45322 Gift, Novelty & Souvenir Stores
5948 Luggage & Leather Goods Stores
NAICS 44832 Luggage & Leather Goods Stores
5949 Sewing, Needlework, & Piece Goods Stores
NAICS 45113 Sewing, Needlework & Piece Goods Stores
5961 Catalog & Mail-order Houses
NAICS 45411 Electronic Shopping & Mail-order Houses
5962 Automatic Merchandising Machine Operator
NAICS 45421 Vending Machine Operators
5963 Direct Selling Establishments
NAICS 72233 Mobile Caterers
NAICS 45439 Other Direct Selling Establishments
5983 Fuel Oil Dealers
NAICS 454311 Heating Oil Dealers
5984 Liquefied Petroleum Gas Dealers
NAICS 454312 Liquefied Petroleum Gas Dealers
5989 Fuel Dealers, nec
NAICS 454319 Other Fuel Dealers
5992 Florists
NAICS 45311 Florists
5993 Tobacco Stores & Stands
NAICS 453991 Tobacco Stores
5994 News Dealers & Newsstands
NAICS 451212 News Dealers & Newsstands
5995 Optical Goods Stores
NAICS 339117 Eyeglass & Contact Lens Manufacturing
NAICS 44613 Optical Goods Stores
5999 Miscellaneous Retail Stores, nec
NAICS 44612 Cosmetics, Beauty Supplies & Perfume Stores
NAICS 446199 All Other Health & Personal Care Stores
NAICS 45391 Pet & Pet Supplies Stores

NAICS 45392   Art Dealers
NAICS 443111 Household Appliance Stores
NAICS 443112 Radio, Television & Other Electronics Stores
NAICS 44831   Jewelry Stores
NAICS 453999 All Other Miscellaneous Store Retailers

FINANCE, INSURANCE, & REAL ESTATE

6011 Federal Reserve Banks
NAICS 52111   Monetary Authorities-central Banks
6019 Central Reserve Depository Institutions, nec
NAICS 52232   Financial Transactions Processing, Reserve, &
              Clearing House Activities
6021 National Commercial Banks
NAICS 52211   Commercial Banking
NAICS 52221   Credit Card Issuing
NAICS 523991 Trust, Fiduciary & Custody Activities
6022 State Commercial Banks
NAICS 52211   Commercial Banking
NAICS 52221   Credit Card Issuing
NAICS 52219   Other Depository Intermediation
NAICS 523991 Trust, Fiduciary & Custody Activities
6029 Commercial Banks, nec
NAICS 52211   Commercial Banking
6035 Savings Institutions, Federally Chartered
NAICS 52212   Savings Institutions
6036 Savings Institutions, Not Federally Chartered
NAICS 52212   Savings Institutions
6061 Credit Unions, Federally Chartered
NAICS 52213   Credit Unions
6062 Credit Unions, Not Federally Chartered
NAICS 52213   Credit Unions
6081 Branches & Agencies of Foreign Banks
NAICS 522293 International Trade Financing
NAICS 52211   Commercial Banking
NAICS 522298 All Other Non-depository Credit
              Intermediation
6082 Foreign Trade & International Banking Institutions
NAICS 522293 International Trade Financing
6091 Nondeposit Trust Facilities
NAICS 523991 Trust, Fiduciary, & Custody Activities
6099 Functions Related to Deposit Banking, nec
NAICS 52232   Financial Transactions Processing, Reserve, &
              Clearing House Activities
NAICS 52313   Commodity Contracts Dealing
NAICS 523991 Trust, Fiduciary, & Custody Activities
NAICS 523999 Miscellaneous Financial Investment Activities
NAICS 52239   Other Activities Related to Credit
              Intermediation
6111 Federal & Federally Sponsored Credit Agencies
NAICS 522293 International Trade Financing
NAICS 522294 Secondary Market Financing
NAICS 522298 All Other Non-depository Credit
              Intermediation
6141 Personal Credit Institutions
NAICS 52221   Credit Card Issuing
NAICS 52222   Sales Financing
NAICS 522291 Consumer Lending
**6153 Short-term Business Credit Institutions, Except
       Agricultural**
NAICS 52222   Sales Financing
NAICS 52232   Financial Transactions Processing, Reserve, &
              Clearing House Activities

NAICS 522298 All Other Non-depository Credit
              Intermediation
6159 Miscellaneous Business Credit Institutions
NAICS 52222   Sales Financing
NAICS 532   Included in Rental & Leasing Services
              Subsector by Type of Equipment & Method of
              Operation
NAICS 522293 International Trade Financing
NAICS 522298 All Other Non-depository Credit
              Intermediation
6162 Mortgage Bankers & Loan Correspondents
NAICS 522292 Real Estate Credit
NAICS 52239   Other Activities Related to Credit
              Intermediation
6163 Loan Brokers
NAICS 52231   Mortgage & Other Loan Brokers
6211 Security Brokers, Dealers, & Flotation Companies
NAICS 52311   Investment Banking & Securities Dealing
NAICS 52312   Securities Brokerage
NAICS 52391   Miscellaneous Intermediation
NAICS 523999 Miscellaneous Financial Investment Activities
6221 Commodity Contracts Brokers & Dealers
NAICS 52313   Commodity Contracts Dealing
NAICS 52314   Commodity Brokerage
6231 Security & Commodity Exchanges
NAICS 52321   Securities & Commodity Exchanges
6282 Investment Advice
NAICS 52392   Portfolio Management
NAICS 52393   Investment Advice
**6289 Services Allied with the Exchange of Securities or
       Commodities, nec**
NAICS 523991 Trust, Fiduciary, & Custody Activities
NAICS 523999 Miscellaneous Financial Investment Activities
6311 Life Insurance
NAICS 524113 Direct Life Insurance Carriers
NAICS 52413   Reinsurance Carriers
6321 Accident & Health Insurance
NAICS 524114 Direct Health & Medical Insurance Carriers
NAICS 52519   Other Insurance Funds
NAICS 52413   Reinsurance Carriers
6324 Hospital & Medical Service Plans
NAICS 524114 Direct Health & Medical Insurance Carriers
NAICS 52519   Other Insurance Funds
NAICS 52413   Reinsurance Carriers
6331 Fire, Marine, & Casualty Insurance
NAICS 524126 Direct Property & Casualty Insurance Carriers
NAICS 52519   Other Insurance Funds
NAICS 52413   Reinsurance Carriers
6351 Surety Insurance
NAICS 524126 Direct Property & Casualty Insurance Carriers
NAICS 52413   Reinsurance Carriers
6361 Title Insurance
NAICS 524127 Direct Title Insurance Carriers
NAICS 52413   Reinsurance Carriers
6371 Pension, Health, & Welfare Funds
NAICS 52392   Portfolio Management
NAICS 524292 Third Party Administration for Insurance &
              Pension Funds
NAICS 52511   Pension Funds
NAICS 52512   Health & Welfare Funds
6399 Insurance Carriers, nec
NAICS 524128 Other Direct Insurance Carriers

6411 Insurance Agents, Brokers, & Service
NAICS 52421   Insurance Agencies & Brokerages
NAICS 524291 Claims Adjusters
NAICS 524292 Third Party Administrators for Insurance &
　　　　　　　Pension Funds
NAICS 524298 All Other Insurance Related Activities
6512 Operators of Nonresidential Buildings
NAICS 71131   Promoters of Performing Arts, Sports & Similar
　　　　　　　Events with Facilities
NAICS 53112   Lessors of Nonresidential Buildings
6513 Operators of Apartment Buildings
NAICS 53111   Lessors of Residential Buildings & Dwellings
6514 Operators of Dwellings Other than Apartment Buildings
NAICS 53111   Lessors of Residential Buildings & Dwellings
6515 Operators of Residential Mobile Home Sites
NAICS 53119   Lessors of Other Real Estate Property
6517 Lessors of Railroad Property
NAICS 53119   Lessors of Other Real Estate Property
6519 Lessors of Real Property, nec
NAICS 53119   Lessors of Other Real Estate Property
6531 Real Estate Agents & Managers
NAICS 53121   Offices of Real Estate Agents & Brokers
NAICS 81399   Other Similar Organizations
NAICS 531311 Residential Property Managers
NAICS 531312 Nonresidential Property Managers
NAICS 53132   Offices of Real Estate Appraisers
NAICS 81222   Cemeteries & Crematories
NAICS 531399 All Other Activities Related to Real Estate
6541 Title Abstract Offices
NAICS 541191 Title Abstract & Settlement Offices
6552 Land Subdividers & Developers, Except Cemeteries
NAICS 23311   Land Subdivision & Land Development
6553 Cemetery Subdividers & Developers
NAICS 81222   Cemeteries & Crematories
6712 Offices of Bank Holding Companies
NAICS 551111 Offices of Bank Holding Companies
6719 Offices of Holding Companies, nec
NAICS 551112 Offices of Other Holding Companies
6722 Management Investment Offices, Open-end
NAICS 52591   Open-end Investment Funds
6726 Unit Investment Trusts, Face-amount Certificate Offices, &
**　　　Closed-end Management Investment Offices**
NAICS 52599   Other Financial Vehicles
6732 Education, Religious, & Charitable Trusts
NAICS 813211 Grantmaking Foundations
6733 Trusts, Except Educational, Religious, & Charitable
NAICS 52392   Portfolio Management
NAICS 523991 Trust, Fiduciary, & Custody Services
NAICS 52519   Other Insurance Funds
NAICS 52592   Trusts, Estates, & Agency Accounts
6792 Oil Royalty Traders
NAICS 523999 Miscellaneous Financial Investment Activities
NAICS 53311   Owners & Lessors of Other Non-financial
　　　　　　　Assets
6794 Patent Owners & Lessors
NAICS 53311   Owners & Lessors of Other Non-financial
　　　　　　　Assets
6798 Real Estate Investment Trusts
NAICS 52593   Real Estate Investment Trusts
6799 Investors, nec
NAICS 52391   Miscellaneous Intermediation
NAICS 52392   Portfolio Management
NAICS 52313   Commodity Contracts Dealing
NAICS 523999 Miscellaneous Financial Investment Activities

SERVICE INDUSTRIES

7011 Hotels & Motels
NAICS 72111   Hotels & Motels
NAICS 72112   Casino Hotels
NAICS 721191 Bed & Breakfast Inns
NAICS 721199 All Other Traveler Accommodation
7021 Rooming & Boarding Houses
NAICS 72131   Rooming & Boarding Houses
7032 Sporting & Recreational Camps
NAICS 721214 Recreational & Vacation Camps
7033 Recreational Vehicle Parks & Campsites
NAICS 721211 Rv & Campgrounds
7041 Organization Hotels & Lodging Houses, on Membership
**　　　Basis**
NAICS 72111   Hotels & Motels
NAICS 72131   Rooming & Boarding Houses
7211 Power Laundries, Family & Commercial
NAICS 812321 Laundries, Family & Commercial
7212 Garment Pressing, & Agents for Laundries
NAICS 812391 Garment Pressing & Agents for Laundries
7213 Linen Supply
NAICS 812331 Linen Supply
7215 Coin-operated Laundry & Drycleaning
NAICS 81231   Coin-operated Laundries & Drycleaners
7216 Drycleaning Plants, Except Rug Cleaning
NAICS 812322 Drycleaning Plants
7217 Carpet & Upholstery Cleaning
NAICS 56174   Carpet & Upholstery Cleaning Services
7218 Industrial Launderers
NAICS 812332 Industrial Launderers
7219 Laundry & Garment Services, nec
NAICS 812331 Linen Supply
NAICS 81149   Other Personal & Household Goods Repair &
　　　　　　　Maintenance
NAICS 812399 All Other Laundry Services
7221 Photographic Studios, Portrait
NAICS 541921 Photographic Studios, Portrait
7231 Beauty Shops
NAICS 812112 Beauty Salons
NAICS 812113 Nail Salons
NAICS 611511 Cosmetology & Barber Schools
7241 Barber Shops
NAICS 812111 Barber Shops
NAICS 611511 Cosmetology & Barber Schools
7251 Shoe Repair Shops & Shoeshine Parlors
NAICS 81143   Footwear & Leather Goods Repair
7261 Funeral Services & Crematories
NAICS 81221   Funeral Homes
NAICS 81222   Cemeteries & Crematories
7291 Tax Return Preparation Services
NAICS 541213 Tax Preparation Services
7299 Miscellaneous Personal Services, nec
NAICS 62441   Child Day Care Services
NAICS 812191 Diet & Weight Reducing Centers
NAICS 53222   Formal Wear & Costume Rental
NAICS 812199 Other Personal Care Services
NAICS 81299   All Other Personal Services
7311 Advertising Agencies
NAICS 54181   Advertising Agencies
7312 Outdoor Advertising Services
NAICS 54185   Display Advertising

7313 Radio, Television, & Publishers' Advertising Representatives
NAICS 54184   Media Representatives
7319 Advertising, nec
NAICS 481219 Other Nonscheduled Air Transportation
NAICS 54183   Media Buying Agencies
NAICS 54185   Display Advertising
NAICS 54187   Advertising Material Distribution Services
NAICS 54189   Other Services Related to Advertising
7322 Adjustment & Collection Services
NAICS 56144   Collection Agencies
NAICS 561491 Repossession Services
7323 Credit Reporting Services
NAICS 56145   Credit Bureaus
7331 Direct Mail Advertising Services
NAICS 54186   Direct Mail Advertising
7334 Photocopying & Duplicating Services
NAICS 561431 Photocopying & Duplicating Services
7335 Commercial Photography
NAICS 48122   Nonscheduled Speciality Air Transportation
NAICS 541922 Commercial Photography
7336 Commercial Art & Graphic Design
NAICS 54143   Commercial Art & Graphic Design Services
7338 Secretarial & Court Reporting Services
NAICS 56141   Document Preparation Services
NAICS 561492 Court Reporting & Stenotype Services
7342 Disinfecting & Pest Control Services
NAICS 56172   Janitorial Services
NAICS 56171   Exterminating & Pest Control Services
7349 Building Cleaning & Maintenance Services, nec
NAICS 56172   Janitorial Services
7352 Medical Equipment Rental & Leasing
NAICS 532291 Home Health Equipment Rental
NAICS 53249   Other Commercial & Industrial Machinery & Equipment Rental & Leasing
7353 Heavy Construction Equipment Rental & Leasing
NAICS 23499   All Other Heavy Construction
NAICS 532412 Construction, Mining & Forestry Machinery & Equipment Rental & Leasing
7359 Equipment Rental & Leasing, nec
NAICS 53221   Consumer Electronics & Appliances Rental
NAICS 53231   General Rental Centers
NAICS 532299 All Other Consumer Goods Rental
NAICS 532412 Construction, Mining & Forestry Machinery & Equipment Rental & Leasing
NAICS 532411 Commercial Air, Rail, & Water Transportation Equipment Rental & Leasing
NAICS 562991 Septic Tank & Related Services
NAICS 53242   Office Machinery & Equipment Rental & Leasing
NAICS 53249   Other Commercial & Industrial Machinery & Equipment Rental & Leasing
7361 Employment Agencies
NAICS 541612 Human Resources & Executive Search Consulting Services
NAICS 56131   Employment Placement Agencies
7363 Help Supply Services
NAICS 56132   Temporary Help Services
NAICS 56133   Employee Leasing Services
7371 Computer Programming Services
NAICS 541511 Custom Computer Programming Services
7372 Prepackaged Software
NAICS 51121   Software Publishers
NAICS 334611 Software Reproducing

7373 Computer Integrated Systems Design
NAICS 541512 Computer Systems Design Services
7374 Computer Processing & Data Preparation & Processing Services
NAICS 51421   Data Processing Services
7375 Information Retrieval Services
NAICS 514191 On-line Information Services
7376 Computer Facilities Management Services
NAICS 541513 Computer Facilities Management Services
7377 Computer Rental & Leasing
NAICS 53242   Office Machinery & Equipment Rental & Leasing
7378 Computer Maintenance & Repair
NAICS 44312   Computer & Software Stores
NAICS 811212 Computer & Office Machine Repair & Maintenance
7379 Computer Related Services, nec
NAICS 541512 Computer Systems Design Services
NAICS 541519 Other Computer Related Services
7381 Detective, Guard, & Armored Car Services
NAICS 561611 Investigation Services
NAICS 561612 Security Guards & Patrol Services
NAICS 561613 Armored Car Services
7382 Security Systems Services
NAICS 561621 Security Systems Services
7383 News Syndicates
NAICS 51411   New Syndicates
7384 Photofinishing Laboratories
NAICS 812921 Photo Finishing Laboratories
NAICS 812922 One-hour Photo Finishing
7389 Business Services, nec
NAICS 51224   Sound Recording Studios
NAICS 51229   Other Sound Recording Industries
NAICS 541199 All Other Legal Services
NAICS 81299   All Other Personal Services
NAICS 54137   Surveying & Mapping Services
NAICS 54141   Interior Design Services
NAICS 54142   Industrial Design Services
NAICS 54134   Drafting Services
NAICS 54149   Other Specialized Design Services
NAICS 54189   Other Services Related to Advertising
NAICS 54193   Translation & Interpretation Services
NAICS 54135   Building Inspection Services
NAICS 54199   All Other Professional, Scientific & Technical Services
NAICS 71141   Agents & Managers for Artists, Athletes, Entertainers & Other Public Figures
NAICS 561422 Telemarketing Bureaus
NAICS 561432 Private Mail Centers
NAICS 561439 Other Business Service Centers
NAICS 561491 Repossession Services
NAICS 56191   Packaging & Labeling Services
NAICS 56179   Other Services to Buildings & Dwellings
NAICS 561599 All Other Travel Arrangement & Reservation Services
NAICS 56192   Convention & Trade Show Organizers
NAICS 561591 Convention & Visitors Bureaus
NAICS 52232   Financial Transactions, Processing, Reserve & Clearing House Activities
NAICS 561499 All Other Business Support Services
NAICS 56199   All Other Support Services
7513 Truck Rental & Leasing, Without Drivers
NAICS 53212   Truck, Utility Trailer & Rv Rental & Leasing

7514 Passenger Car Rental
NAICS 532111 Passenger Cars Rental
7515 Passenger Car Leasing
NAICS 532112 Passenger Cars Leasing
7519 Utility Trailer & Recreational Vehicle Rental
NAICS 53212 Truck, Utility Trailer & Rv Rental & Leasing
7521 Automobile Parking
NAICS 81293 Parking Lots & Garages
7532 Top, Body, & Upholstery Repair Shops & Paint Shops
NAICS 811121 Automotive Body, Paint, & Upholstery Repair & Maintenance
7533 Automotive Exhaust System Repair Shops
NAICS 811112 Automotive Exhaust System Repair
7534 Tire Retreading & Repair Shops
NAICS 326212 Tire Retreading
NAICS 811198 All Other Automotive Repair & Maintenance
7536 Automotive Glass Replacement Shops
NAICS 811122 Automotive Glass Replacement Shops
7537 Automotive Transmission Repair Shops
NAICS 811113 Automotive Transmission Repair
7538 General Automotive Repair Shops
NAICS 811111 General Automotive Repair
7539 Automotive Repair Shops, nec
NAICS 811118 Other Automotive Mechanical & Electrical Repair & Maintenance
7542 Carwashes
NAICS 811192 Car Washes
7549 Automotive Services, Except Repair & Carwashes
NAICS 811191 Automotive Oil Change & Lubrication Shops
NAICS 48841 Motor Vehicle Towing
NAICS 811198 All Other Automotive Repair & Maintenance
7622 Radio & Television Repair Shops
NAICS 811211 Consumer Electronics Repair & Maintenance
NAICS 443112 Radio, Television & Other Electronics Stores
7623 Refrigeration & Air-conditioning Services & Repair Shops
NAICS 443111 Household Appliance Stores
NAICS 81131 Commercial & Industrial Machinery & Equipment Repair & Maintenance
NAICS 811412 Appliance Repair & Maintenance
7629 Electrical & Electronic Repair Shops, nec
NAICS 443111 Household Appliance Stores
NAICS 811212 Computer & Office Machine Repair & Maintenance
NAICS 811213 Communication Equipment Repair & Maintenance
NAICS 811219 Other Electronic & Precision Equipment Repair & Maintenance
NAICS 811412 Appliance Repair & Maintenance
NAICS 811211 Consumer Electronics Repair & Maintenance
7631 Watch, Clock, & Jewelry Repair
NAICS 81149 Other Personal & Household Goods Repair & Maintenance
7641 Reupholster & Furniture Repair
NAICS 81142 Reupholstery & Furniture Repair
7692 Welding Repair
NAICS 81149 Other Personal & Household Goods Repair & Maintenance
7694 Armature Rewinding Shops
NAICS 81131 Commercial & Industrial Machinery & Equipment Repair & Maintenance
NAICS 335312 Motor & Generator Manufacturing
7699 Repair Shops & Related Services, nec
NAICS 561622 Locksmiths
NAICS 562991 Septic Tank & Related Services

NAICS 56179 Other Services to Buildings & Dwellings
NAICS 48839 Other Supporting Activities for Water Transportation
NAICS 45111 Sporting Goods Stores
NAICS 81131 Commercial & Industrial Machinery & Equipment Repair & Maintenance
NAICS 11521 Support Activities for Animal Production
NAICS 811212 Computer & Office Machine Repair & Maintenance
NAICS 811219 Other Electronic & Precision Equipment Repair & Maintenance
NAICS 811411 Home & Garden Equipment Repair & Maintenance
NAICS 811412 Appliance Repair & Maintenance
NAICS 81143 Footwear & Leather Goods Repair
NAICS 81149 Other Personal & Household Goods Repair & Maintenance
7812 Motion Picture & Video Tape Production
NAICS 51211 Motion Picture & Video Production
7819 Services Allied to Motion Picture Production
NAICS 512191 Teleproduction & Other Post-production Services
NAICS 56131 Employment Placement Agencies
NAICS 53222 Formal Wear & Costumes Rental
NAICS 53249 Other Commercial & Industrial Machinery & Equipment Rental & Leasing
NAICS 541214 Payroll Services
NAICS 71151 Independent Artists, Writers, & Performers
NAICS 334612 Prerecorded Compact Disc , Tape, & Record Manufacturing
NAICS 512199 Other Motion Picture & Video Industries
7822 Motion Picture & Video Tape Distribution
NAICS 42199 Other Miscellaneous Durable Goods Wholesalers
NAICS 51212 Motion Picture & Video Distribution
7829 Services Allied to Motion Picture Distribution
NAICS 512199 Other Motion Picture & Video Industries
NAICS 51212 Motion Picture & Video Distribution
7832 Motion Picture Theaters, Except Drive-ins.
NAICS 512131 Motion Picture Theaters, Except Drive-in
7833 Drive-in Motion Picture Theaters
NAICS 512132 Drive-in Motion Picture Theaters
7841 Video Tape Rental
NAICS 53223 Video Tapes & Disc Rental
7911 Dance Studios, Schools, & Halls
NAICS 71399 All Other Amusement & Recreation Industries
NAICS 61161 Fine Arts Schools
7922 Theatrical Producers & Miscellaneous Theatrical Services
NAICS 56131 Employment Placement Agencies
NAICS 71111 Theater Companies & Dinner Theaters
NAICS 71141 Agents & Managers for Artists, Athletes, Entertainers & Other Public Figures
NAICS 71112 Dance Companies
NAICS 71131 Promoters of Performing Arts, Sports, & Similar Events with Facilities
NAICS 71132 Promoters of Performing Arts, Sports, & Similar Events Without Facilities
NAICS 51229 Other Sound Recording Industries
NAICS 53249 Other Commercial & Industrial Machinery & Equipment Rental & Leasing
7929 Bands, Orchestras, Actors, & Other Entertainers & Entertainment Groups
NAICS 71113 Musical Groups & Artists
NAICS 71151 Independent Artists, Writers, & Performers

NAICS 71119   Other Performing Arts Companies
7933 Bowling Centers
NAICS 71395   Bowling Centers
7941 Professional Sports Clubs & Promoters
NAICS 711211 Sports Teams & Clubs
NAICS 71141   Agents & Managers for Artists, Athletes, Entertainers , & Other Public Figures
NAICS 71132   Promoters of Arts, Sports & Similar Events Without Facilities
NAICS 71131   Promoters of Arts, Sports, & Similar Events with Facilities
NAICS 711219 Other Spectator Sports
7948 Racing, Including Track Operations
NAICS 711212 Race Tracks
NAICS 711219 Other Spectator Sports
7991 Physical Fitness Facilities
NAICS 71394   Fitness & Recreational Sports Centers
7992 Public Golf Courses
NAICS 71391   Golf Courses & Country Clubs
7993 Coin Operated Amusement Devices
NAICS 71312   Amusement Arcades
NAICS 71329   Other Gambling Industries
NAICS 71399   All Other Amusement & Recreation Industries
7996 Amusement Parks
NAICS 71311   Amusement & Theme Parks
7997 Membership Sports & Recreation Clubs
NAICS 48122   Nonscheduled Speciality Air Transportation
NAICS 71391   Golf Courses & Country Clubs
NAICS 71394   Fitness & Recreational Sports Centers
NAICS 71399   All Other Amusement & Recreatior Industries
7999 Amusement & Recreation Services, nec
NAICS 561599 All Other Travel Arrangement & Reservation Services
NAICS 48799   Scenic & Sightseeing Transportation, Other
NAICS 71119   Other Performing Arts Companies
NAICS 711219 Other Spectator Sports
NAICS 71392   Skiing Facilities
NAICS 71394   Fitness & Recreational Sports Centers
NAICS 71321   Casinos
NAICS 71329   Other Gambling Industries
NAICS 71219   Nature Parks & Other Similar Institutions
NAICS 61162   Sports & Recreation Instruction
NAICS 532292 Recreational Goods Rental
NAICS 48711   Scenic & Sightseeing Transportation, Land
NAICS 48721   Scenic & Sightseeing Transportation, Water
NAICS 71399   All Other Amusement & Recreation Industries
8011 Offices & Clinics of Doctors of Medicine
NAICS 621493 Freestanding Ambulatory Surgical & Emergency Centers
NAICS 621491 Hmo Medical Centers
NAICS 621112 Offices of Physicians, Mental Health Specialists
NAICS 621111 Offices of Physicians
8021 Offices & Clinics of Dentists
NAICS 62121   Offices of Dentists
8031 Offices & Clinics of Doctors of Osteopathy
NAICS 621111 Offices of Physicians
NAICS 621112 Offices of Physicians, Mental Health Specialists
8041 Offices & Clinics of Chiropractors
NAICS 62131   Offices of Chiropractors
8042 Offices & Clinics of Optometrists
NAICS 62132   Offices of Optometrists
8043 Offices & Clinics of Podiatrists
NAICS 621391 Offices of Podiatrists

8049 Offices & Clinics of Health Practitioners, nec
NAICS 62133   Offices of Mental Health Practitioners
NAICS 62134   Offices of Physical, Occupational, & Speech Therapists & Audiologists
NAICS 621399 Offices of All Other Miscellaneous Health Practitioners
8051 Skilled Nursing Care Facilities
NAICS 623311 Continuing Care Retirement Communities
NAICS 62311   Nursing Care Facilities
8052 Intermediate Care Facilities
NAICS 623311 Continuing Care Retirement Communities
NAICS 62321   Residential Mental Retardation Facilities
NAICS 62311   Nursing Care Facilities
8059 Nursing & Personal Care Facilities, nec
NAICS 623311 Continuing Care Retirement Communities
NAICS 62311   Nursing Care Facilities
8062 General Medical & Surgical Hospitals
NAICS 62211   General Medical & Surgical Hospitals
8063 Psychiatric Hospitals
NAICS 62221   Psychiatric & Substance Abuse Hospitals
8069 Specialty Hospitals, Except Psychiatric
NAICS 62211   General Medical & Surgical Hospitals
NAICS 62221   Psychiatric & Substance Abuse Hospitals
NAICS 62231   Specialty Hospitals
8071 Medical Laboratories
NAICS 621512 Diagnostic Imaging Centers
NAICS 621511 Medical Laboratories
8072 Dental Laboratories
NAICS 339116 Dental Laboratories
8082 Home Health Care Services
NAICS 62161   Home Health Care Services
8092 Kidney Dialysis Centers
NAICS 621492 Kidney Dialysis Centers
8093 Specialty Outpatient Facilities, nec
NAICS 62141   Family Planning Centers
NAICS 62142   Outpatient Mental Health & Substance Abuse Centers
NAICS 621498 All Other Outpatient Care Facilities
8099 Health & Allied Services, nec
NAICS 621991 Blood & Organ Banks
NAICS 54143   Graphic Design Services
NAICS 541922 Commercial Photography
NAICS 62141   Family Planning Centers
NAICS 621999 All Other Miscellaneous Ambulatory Health Care Services
8111 Legal Services
NAICS 54111   Offices of Lawyers
8211 Elementary & Secondary Schools
NAICS 61111   Elementary & Secondary Schools
8221 Colleges, Universities, & Professional Schools
NAICS 61131   Colleges, Universities & Professional Schools
8222 Junior Colleges & Technical Institutes
NAICS 61121   Junior Colleges
8231 Libraries
NAICS 51412   Libraries & Archives
8243 Data Processing Schools
NAICS 611519 Other Technical & Trade Schools
NAICS 61142   Computer Training
8244 Business & Secretarial Schools
NAICS 61141   Business & Secretarial Schools
8249 Vocational Schools, nec
NAICS 611513 Apprenticeship Training
NAICS 611512 Flight Training
NAICS 611519 Other Technical & Trade Schools

8299 Schools & Educational Services, nec
NAICS 48122   Nonscheduled speciality Air Transportation
NAICS 611512 Flight Training
NAICS 611692 Automobile Driving Schools
NAICS 61171   Educational Support Services
NAICS 611691 Exam Preparation & Tutoring
NAICS 61161   Fine Arts Schools
NAICS 61163   Language Schools
NAICS 61143   Professional & Management Development
   Training Schools
NAICS 611699 All Other Miscellaneous Schools & Instruction
8322 Individual & Family Social Services
NAICS 62411   Child & Youth Services
NAICS 62421   Community Food Services
NAICS 624229 Other Community Housing Services
NAICS 62423   Emergency & Other Relief Services
NAICS 62412   Services for the Elderly & Persons with
   Disabilities
NAICS 624221 Temporary Shelters
NAICS 92215   Parole Offices & Probation Offices
NAICS 62419   Other Individual & Family Services
8331 Job Training & Vocational Rehabilitation Services
NAICS 62431   Vocational Rehabilitation Services
8351 Child Day Care Services
NAICS 62441   Child Day Care Services
8361 Residential Care
NAICS 623312 Homes for the Elderly
NAICS 62322   Residential Mental Health & Substance Abuse
   Facilities
NAICS 62399   Other Residential Care Facilities
8399 Social Services, nec
NAICS 813212 Voluntary Health Organizations
NAICS 813219 Other Grantmaking & Giving Services
NAICS 813311 Human Rights Organizations
NAICS 813312 Environment, Conservation & Wildlife
   Organizations
NAICS 813319 Other Social Advocacy Organizations
8412 Museums & Art Galleries
NAICS 71211   Museums
NAICS 71212   Historical Sites
8422 Arboreta & Botanical or Zoological Gardens
NAICS 71213   Zoos & Botanical Gardens
NAICS 71219   Nature Parks & Other Similar Institutions
8611 Business Associations
NAICS 81391   Business Associations
8621 Professional Membership Organizations
NAICS 81392   Professional Organizations
8631 Labor Unions & Similar Labor Organizations
NAICS 81393   Labor Unions & Similar Labor Organizations
8641 Civic, Social, & Fraternal Associations
NAICS 81341   Civic & Social Organizations
NAICS 81399   Other Similar Organizations
NAICS 92115   American Indian & Alaska Native Tribal
   Governments
NAICS 62411   Child & Youth Services
8651 Political Organizations
NAICS 81394   Political Organizations
8661 Religious Organizations
NAICS 81311   Religious Organizations
8699 Membership Organizations, nec
NAICS 81341   Civic & Social Organizations
NAICS 81391   Business Associations
NAICS 813312 Environment, Conservation, & Wildlife
   Organizations

NAICS 561599 All Other Travel Arrangement & Reservation
   Services
NAICS 81399   Other Similar Organizations
8711 Engineering Services
NAICS 54133   Engineering Services
8712 Architectural Services
NAICS 54131   Architectural Services
8713 Surveying Services
NAICS 48122   Nonscheduled Air Speciality Transportation
NAICS 54136   Geophysical Surveying & Mapping Services
NAICS 54137   Surveying & Mapping Services
8721 Accounting, Auditing, & Bookkeeping Services
NAICS 541211 Offices of Certified Public Accountants
NAICS 541214 Payroll Services
NAICS 541219 Other Accounting Services
8731 Commercial Physical & Biological Research
NAICS 54171   Research & Development in the Physical
   Sciences & Engineering Sciences
NAICS 54172   Research & Development in the Life Sciences
**8732 Commercial Economic, Sociological, & Educational
   Research**
NAICS 54173   Research & Development in the Social Sciences
   & Humanities
NAICS 54191   Marketing Research & Public Opinion Polling
8733 Noncommercial Research Organizations
NAICS 54171   Research & Development in the Physical
   Sciences & Engineering Sciences
NAICS 54172   Research & Development in the Life Sciences
NAICS 54173   Research & Development in the Social Sciences
   & Humanities
8734 Testing Laboratories
NAICS 54194   Veterinary Services
NAICS 54138   Testing Laboratories
8741 Management Services
NAICS 56111   Office Administrative Services
NAICS 23   Included in Construction Sector by Type of
   Construction
8742 Management Consulting Services
NAICS 541611 Administrative Management & General
   Management Consulting Services
NAICS 541612 Human Resources & Executive Search Services
NAICS 541613 Marketing Consulting Services
NAICS 541614 Process, Physical, Distribution & Logistics
   Consulting Services
8743 Public Relations Services
NAICS 54182   Public Relations Agencies
8744 Facilities Support Management Services
NAICS 56121   Facilities Support Services
8748 Business Consulting Services, nec
NAICS 61171   Educational Support Services
NAICS 541618 Other Management Consulting Services
NAICS 54169   Other Scientific & Technical Consulting
   Services
8811 Private Households
NAICS 81411   Private Households
8999 Services, nec
NAICS 71151   Independent Artists, Writers, & Performers
NAICS 51221   Record Production
NAICS 54169   Other Scientific & Technical Consulting
   Services
NAICS 51223   Music Publishers
NAICS 541612 Human Resources & Executive Search
   Consulting Services
NAICS 514199 All Other Information Services

NAICS 54162   Environmental Consulting Services

PUBLIC ADMINISTRATION

9111 Executive Offices
NAICS 92111   Executive Offices
9121 Legislative Bodies
NAICS 92112   Legislative Bodies
9131 Executive & Legislative Offices, Combined
NAICS 92114   Executive & Legislative Offices, Combined
9199 General Government, nec
NAICS 92119   All Other General Government
9211 Courts
NAICS 92211   Courts
9221 Police Protection
NAICS 92212   Police Protection
9222 Legal Counsel & Prosecution
NAICS 92213   Legal Counsel & Prosecution
9223 Correctional Institutions
NAICS 92214   Correctional Institutions
9224 Fire Protection
NAICS 92216   Fire Protection
9229 Public Order & Safety, nec
NAICS 92219   All Other Justice, Public Order, & Safety
9311 Public Finance, Taxation, & Monetary Policy
NAICS 92113   Public Finance
9411 Administration of Educational Programs
NAICS 92311   Administration of Education Programs
9431 Administration of Public Health Programs
NAICS 92312   Administration of Public Health Programs
9441 Administration of Social, Human Resource & Income Maintenance Programs
NAICS 92313   Administration of Social, Human Resource & Income Maintenance Programs
9451 Administration of Veteran's Affairs, Except Health Insurance
NAICS 92314   Administration of Veteran's Affairs
9511 Air & Water Resource & Solid Waste Management
NAICS 92411   Air & Water Resource & Solid Waste Management
9512 Land, Mineral, Wildlife, & Forest Conservation
NAICS 92412   Land, Mineral, Wildlife, & Forest Conservation
9531 Administration of Housing Programs
NAICS 92511   Administration of Housing Programs
9532 Administration of Urban Planning & Community & Rural Development
NAICS 92512   Administration of Urban Planning & Community & Rural Development
9611 Administration of General Economic Programs
NAICS 92611   Administration of General Economic Programs
9621 Regulations & Administration of Transportation Programs
NAICS 488111 Air Traffic Control
NAICS 92612   Regulation & Administration of Transportation Programs
9631 Regulation & Administration of Communications, Electric, Gas, & Other Utilities
NAICS 92613   Regulation & Administration of Communications, Electric, Gas, & Other Utilities
9641 Regulation of Agricultural Marketing & Commodity
NAICS 92614   Regulation of Agricultural Marketing & Commodity

9651 Regulation, Licensing, & Inspection of Miscellaneous Commercial Sectors
NAICS 92615   Regulation, Licensing, & Inspection of Miscellaneous Commercial Sectors
9661 Space Research & Technology
NAICS 92711   Space Research & Technology
9711 National Security
NAICS 92811   National Security
9721 International Affairs
NAICS 92812   International Affairs
9999 Nonclassifiable Establishments
NAICS 99999   Unclassified Establishments

NAICS TO SIC CONVERSION GUIDE

AGRICULTURE, FORESTRY, FISHING, & HUNTING

11111 Soybean Farming
SIC 0116 Soybeans
11112 Oilseed Farming
SIC 0119 Cash Grains, nec
11113 Dry Pea & Bean Farming
SIC 0119 Cash Grains, nec
11114 Wheat Farming
SIC 0111 Wheat
11115 Corn Farming
SIC 0115 Corn
SIC 0119 Cash Grains, nec
11116 Rice Farming
SIC 0112 Rice
111191 Oilseed & Grain Combination Farming
SIC 0119 Cash Grains, nec
111199 All Other Grain Farming
SIC 0119 Cash Grains, nec
111211 Potato Farming
SIC 0134 Irish Potatoes
111219 Other Vegetable & Melon Farming
SIC 0161 Vegetables & Melons
SIC 0139 Field Crops Except Cash Grains
11131 Orange Groves
SIC 0174 Citrus Fruits
11132 Citrus Groves
SIC 0174 Citrus Fruits
111331 Apple Orchards
SIC 0175 Deciduous Tree Fruits
111332 Grape Vineyards
SIC 0172 Grapes
111333 Strawberry Farming
SIC 0171 Berry Crops
111334 Berry Farming
SIC 0171 Berry Crops
111335 Tree Nut Farming
SIC 0173 Tree Nuts
111336 Fruit & Tree Nut Combination Farming
SIC 0179 Fruits & Tree Nuts, nec
111339 Other Noncitrus Fruit Farming
SIC 0175 Deciduous Tree Fruits
SIC 0179 Fruit & Tree Nuts, nec
111411 Mushroom Production
SIC 0182 Food Crops Grown Under Cover
111419 Other Food Crops Grown Under Cover
SIC 0182 Food Crops Grown Under Cover
111421 Nursery & Tree Production
SIC 0181 Ornamental Floriculture & Nursery Products
SIC 0811 Timber Tracts
111422 Floriculture Production
SIC 0181 Ornamental Floriculture & Nursery Products
11191 Tobacco Farming
SIC 0132 Tobacco
11192 Cotton Farming
SIC 0131 Cotton
11193 Sugarcane Farming
SIC 0133 Sugarcane & Sugar Beets

11194 Hay Farming
SIC 0139 Field Crops, Except Cash Grains, nec
111991 Sugar Beet Farming
SIC 0133 Sugarcane & Sugar Beets
111992 Peanut Farming
SIC 0139 Field Crops, Except Cash Grains, nec
111998 All Other Miscellaneous Crop Farming
SIC 0139 Field Crops, Except Cash Grains, nec
SIC 0191 General Farms, Primarily Crop
SIC 0831 Forest Products
SIC 0919 Miscellaneous Marine Products
SIC 2099 Food Preparations, nec
112111 Beef Cattle Ranching & Farming
SIC 0212 Beef Cattle, Except Feedlots
SIC 0241 Dairy Farms
112112 Cattle Feedlots
SIC 0211 Beef Cattle Feedlots
11212 Dairy Cattle & Milk Production
SIC 0241 Dairy Farms
11213 Dual Purpose Cattle Ranching & Farming
No SIC equivalent
11221 Hog & Pig Farming
SIC 0213 Hogs
11231 Chicken Egg Production
SIC 0252 Chicken Eggs
11232 Broilers & Other Meat Type Chicken Production
SIC 0251 Broiler, Fryers, & Roaster Chickens
11233 Turkey Production
SIC 0253 Turkey & Turkey Eggs
11234 Poultry Hatcheries
SIC 0254 Poultry Hatcheries
11239 Other Poultry Production
SIC 0259 Poultry & Eggs, nec
11241 Sheep Farming
SIC 0214 Sheep & Goats
11242 Goat Farming
SIC 0214 Sheep & Goats
112511 Finfish Farming & Fish Hatcheries
SIC 0273 Animal Aquaculture
SIC 0921 Fish Hatcheries & Preserves
112512 Shellfish Farming
SIC 0273 Animal Aquaculture
SIC 0921 Fish Hatcheries & Preserves
112519 Other Animal Aquaculture
SIC 0273 Animal Aquaculture
11291 Apiculture
SIC 0279 Animal Specialties, nec
11292 Horse & Other Equine Production
SIC 0272 Horses & Other Equines
11293 Fur-Bearing Animal & Rabbit Production
SIC 0271 Fur-Bearing Animals & Rabbits
11299 All Other Animal Production
SIC 0219 General Livestock, Except Dairy & Poultry
SIC 0279 Animal Specialties, nec
SIC 0291 General Farms, Primarily Livestock & Animal
    Specialties;
11311 Timber Tract Operations
SIC 0811 Timber Tracts
11321 Forest Nurseries & Gathering of Forest Products
SIC 0831 Forest Nurseries & Gathering of Forest Products
11331 Logging
SIC 2411 Logging

114111 Finfish Fishing
SIC 0912 Finfish
114112 Shellfish Fishing
SIC 0913 Shellfish
114119 Other Marine Fishing
SIC 0919 Miscellaneous Marine Products
11421 Hunting & Trapping
SIC 0971 Hunting & Trapping, & Game Propagation;
115111 Cotton Ginning
SIC 0724 Cotton Ginning
115112 Soil Preparation, Planting, & Cultivating
SIC 0711 Soil Preparation Services
SIC 0721 Crop Planting, Cultivating, & Protecting
115113 Crop Harvesting, Primarily by Machine
SIC 0722 Crop Harvesting, Primarily by Machine
115114 Other Postharvest Crop Activities
SIC 0723 Crop Preparation Services For Market, Except Cotton Ginning
115115 Farm Labor Contractors & Crew Leaders
SIC 0761 Farm Labor Contractors & Crew Leaders
115116 Farm Management Services
SIC 0762 Farm Management Services
11521 Support Activities for Animal Production
SIC 0751 Livestock Services, Except Veterinary
SIC 0752 Animal Specialty Services, Except Veterinary
SIC 7699 Repair Services, nec
11531 Support Activities for Forestry
SIC 0851 Forestry Services

MINING

211111 Crude Petroleum & Natural Gas Extraction
SIC 1311 Crude Petroleum & Natural Gas
211112 Natural Gas Liquid Extraction
SIC 1321 Natural Gas Liquids
212111 Bituminous Coal & Lignite Surface Mining
SIC 1221 Bituminous Coal & Lignite Surface Mining
212112 Bituminous Coal Underground Mining
SIC 1222 Bituminous Coal Underground Mining
212113 Anthracite Mining
SIC 1231 Anthracite Mining
21221 Iron Ore Mining
SIC 1011 Iron Ores
212221 Gold Ore Mining
SIC 1041 Gold Ores
212222 Silver Ore Mining
SIC 1044 Silver Ores
212231 Lead Ore & Zinc Ore Mining
SIC 1031 Lead & Zinc Ores
212234 Copper Ore & Nickel Ore Mining
SIC 1021 Copper Ores
212291 Uranium-Radium-Vanadium Ore Mining
SIC 1094 Uranium-Radium-Vanadium Ores
212299 All Other Metal Ore Mining
SIC 1061 Ferroalloy Ores, Except Vanadium
SIC 1099 Miscellaneous Metal Ores, nec
212311 Dimension Stone Mining & Quarrying
SIC 1411 Dimension Stone
212312 Crushed & Broken Limestone Mining & Quarrying
SIC 1422 Crushed & Broken Limestone
212313 Crushed & Broken Granite Mining & Quarrying
SIC 1423 Crushed & Broken Granite

212319 Other Crushed & Broken Stone Mining & Quarrying
SIC 1429 Crushed & Broken Stone, nec
SIC 1499 Miscellaneous Nonmetallic Minerals, Except Fuels
212321 Construction Sand & Gravel Mining
SIC 1442 Construction Sand & Gravel
212322 Industrial Sand Mining
SIC 1446 Industrial Sand
212324 Kaolin & Ball Clay Mining
SIC 1455 Kaolin & Ball Clay
212325 Clay & Ceramic & Refractory Minerals Mining
SIC 1459 Clay, Ceramic, & Refractory Minerals, nec
212391 Potash, Soda, & Borate Mineral Mining
SIC 1474 Potash, Soda, & Borate Minerals
212392 Phosphate Rock Mining
SIC 1475 Phosphate Rock
212393 Other Chemical & Fertilizer Mineral Mining
SIC 1479 Chemical & Fertilizer Mineral Mining, nec
212399 All Other Nonmetallic Mineral Mining
SIC 1499 Miscellaneous Nonmetallic Minerals, Except Fuels
213111 Drilling Oil & Gas Wells
SIC 1381 Drilling Oil & Gas Wells
213112 Support Activities for Oil & Gas Operations
SIC 1382 Oil & Gas Field Exploration Services
SIC 1389 Oil & Gas Field Services, nec
213113 Other Gas & Field Support Activities
SIC 1389 Oil & Gas Field Services, nec
213114 Support Activities for Coal Mining
SIC 1241 Coal Mining Services
213115 Support Activities for Metal Mining
SIC 1081 Metal Mining Services
213116 Support Activities for Nonmetallic Minerals, Except Fuels
SIC 1481 Nonmetallic Minerals Services, Except Fuels

UTILITIES

221111 Hydroelectric Power Generation
SIC 4911 Electric Services
SIC 4931 Electric & Other Services Combined
SIC 4939 Combination Utilities, nec
221112 Fossil Fuel Electric Power Generation
SIC 4911 Electric Services
SIC 4931 Electric & Other Services Combined
SIC 4939 Combination Utilities, nec
221113 Nuclear Electric Power Generation
SIC 4911 Electric Services
SIC 4931 Electric & Other Services Combined
SIC 4939 Combination Utilities, nec
221119 Other Electric Power Generation
SIC 4911 Electric Services
SIC 4931 Electric & Other Services Combined
SIC 4939 Combination Utilities, nec
221121 Electric Bulk Power Transmission & Control
SIC 4911 Electric Services
SIC 4931 Electric & Other Services Combined
SIC 4939 Combination Utilities, NEC
221122 Electric Power Distribution
SIC 4911 Electric Services
SIC 4931 Electric & Other Services Combined
SIC 4939 Combination Utilities, nec
22121 Natural Gas Distribution
SIC 4923 Natural Gas Transmission & Distribution
SIC 4924 Natural Gas Distribution

SIC 4925 Mixed, Manufactured, or Liquefied Petroleum Gas Production and/or Distribution
SIC 4931 Electronic & Other Services Combined
SIC 4932 Gas & Other Services Combined
SIC 4939 Combination Utilities, nec

22131 Water Supply & Irrigation Systems
SIC 4941 Water Supply
SIC 4971 Irrigation Systems

22132 Sewage Treatment Facilities
SIC 4952 Sewerage Systems

22133 Steam & Air-Conditioning Supply
SIC 4961 Steam & Air-Conditioning Supply

CONSTRUCTION

23311 Land Subdivision & Land Development
SIC 6552 Land Subdividers & Developers, Except Cemeteries

23321 Single Family Housing Construction
SIC 1521 General contractors-Single-Family Houses
SIC 1531 Operative Builders

23322 Multifamily Housing Construction
SIC 1522 General Contractors-Residential Building, Other Than Single-Family
SIC 1531 Operative Builders

23331 Manufacturing & Industrial Building Construction
SIC 1531 Operative Builders
SIC 1541 General Contractors-Industrial Buildings & Warehouses

23332 Commercial & Institutional Building Construction
SIC 1522 General Contractors-Residential Building Other than Single-Family
SIC 1531 Operative Builders
SIC 1541 General Contractors-Industrial Buildings & Warehouses
SIC 1542 General Contractor-Nonresidential Buildings, Other than Industrial Buildings & Warehouses

23411 Highway & Street Construction
SIC 1611 Highway & Street Construction, Except Elevated Highways

23412 Bridge & Tunnel Construction
SIC 1622 Bridge, Tunnel, & Elevated Highway Construction

2349 Other Heavy Construction

23491 Water, Sewer, & Pipeline Construction
SIC 1623 Water, Sewer, Pipeline, & Communications & Power Line Construction

23492 Power & Communication Transmission Line Construction
SIC 1623 Water, Sewer, Pipelines, & Communications & Power Line Construction

23493 Industrial Nonbuilding Structure Construction
SIC 1629 Heavy Construction, nec

23499 All Other Heavy Construction
SIC 1629 Heavy Construction, nec
SIC 7353 Construction Equipment Rental & Leasing

23511 Plumbing, Heating & Air-Conditioning Contractors
SIC 1711 Plumbing, Heating & Air-Conditioning

23521 Painting & Wall Covering Contractors
SIC 1721 Painting & Paper Hanging
SIC 1799 Special Trade Contractors, nec

23531 Electrical Contractors
SIC 1731 Electrical Work

23541 Masonry & Stone Contractors
SIC 1741 Masonry, Stone Setting & Other Stone Work

23542 Drywall, Plastering, Acoustical & Insulation Contractors
SIC 1742 Plastering, Drywall, Acoustical, & Insulation Work
SIC 1743 Terrazzo, Tile, Marble & Mosaic work
SIC 1771 Concrete Work

23543 Tile, Marble, Terrazzo & Mosaic Contractors
SIC 1743 Terrazzo, Tile, Marble, & Mosaic Work

23551 Carpentry Contractors
SIC 1751 Carpentry Work

23552 Floor Laying & Other Floor Contractors
SIC 1752 Floor Laying & Other Floor Work, nec

23561 Roofing, Siding & Sheet Metal Contractors
SIC 1761 Roofing, Siding, & Sheet Metal Work

23571 Concrete Contractors
SIC 1771 Concrete Work

23581 Water Well Drilling Contractors
SIC 1781 Water Well Drilling

23591 Structural Steel Erection Contractors
SIC 1791 Structural Steel Erection

23592 Glass & Glazing Contractors
SIC 1793 Glass & Glazing Work
SIC 1799 Specialty Trade Contractors, nec

23593 Excavation Contractors
SIC 1794 Excavation Work

23594 Wrecking & Demolition Contractors
SIC 1795 Wrecking & Demolition Work

23595 Building Equipment & Other Machinery Installation Contractors
SIC 1796 Installation of Erection of Building Equipment, nec

23599 All Other Special Trade Contractors
SIC 1799 Special Trade Contractors, nec

FOOD MANUFACTURING

311111 Dog & Cat Food Manufacturing
SIC 2047 Dog & Cat Food

311119 Other Animal Food Manufacturing
SIC 2048 Prepared Feeds & Feed Ingredients for Animals & Fowls, Except Dogs & Cats

311211 Flour Milling
SIC 2034 Dehydrated Fruits, Vegetables & Soup Mixes
SIC 2041 Flour & Other Grain Mill Products

311212 Rice Milling
SIC 2044 Rice Milling

311213 Malt Manufacturing
SIC 2083 Malt

311221 Wet Corn Milling
SIC 2046 Wet Corn Milling

311222 Soybean Processing
SIC 2075 Soybean Oil Mills
SIC 2079 Shortening, Table Oils, Margarine, & Other Edible Fats & Oils, nec

311223 Other Oilseed Processing
SIC 2074 Cottonseed Oil Mills
SIC 2079 Shortening, Table Oils, Margarine & Other Edible Fats & Oils, nec
SIC 2076 Vegetable Oil Mills, Except Corn, Cottonseed, & Soybean

311225 Edible Fats & Oils Manufacturing
SIC 2077 Animal & Marine Fats & Oil, nec
SIC 2074 Cottonseed Oil Mills
SIC 2075 Soybean Oil Mills

SIC 2076 Vegetable Oil Mills, Except Corn, Cottonseed, &
Soybean
SIC 2079 Shortening, Table Oils, Margarine, & Other Edible
Fats & Oils, nec
31123 Breakfast Cereal Manufacturing
SIC 2043 Cereal Breakfast Foods
311311 Sugarcane Mills
SIC 2061 Cane Sugar, Except Refining
311312 Cane Sugar Refining
SIC 2062 Cane Sugar Refining
311313 Beet Sugar Manufacturing
SIC 2063 Beet Sugar
**31132 Chocolate & Confectionery Manufacturing from Cacao
Beans**
SIC 2066 Chocolate & Cocoa Products
31133 Confectionery Manufacturing from Purchased Chocolate
SIC 2064 Candy & Other Confectionery Products
31134 Non-Chocolate Confectionery Manufacturing
SIC 2064 Candy & Other Confectionery Products
SIC 2067 Chewing Gum
SIC 2099 Food Preparations, nec
311411 Frozen Fruit, Juice & Vegetable Processing
SIC 2037 Frozen Fruits, Fruit Juices, & Vegetables
311412 Frozen Specialty Food Manufacturing
SIC 2038 Frozen Specialties, NEC
311421 Fruit & Vegetable Canning
SIC 2033 Canned Fruits, Vegetables, Preserves, Jams, & Jellies
SIC 2035 Pickled Fruits & Vegetables, Vegetable Sauces, &
Seasonings & Salad Dressings
311422 Specialty Canning
SIC 2032 Canned Specialties
311423 Dried & Dehydrated Food Manufacturing
SIC 2034 Dried & Dehydrated Fruits, Vegetables & Soup
Mixes
SIC 2099 Food Preparation, nec
311511 Fluid Milk Manufacturing
SIC 2026 Fluid Milk
311512 Creamery Butter Manufacturing
SIC 2021 Creamery Butter
311513 Cheese Manufacturing
SIC 2022 Natural, Processed, & Imitation Cheese
311514 Dry, Condensed, & Evaporated Milk Manufacturing
SIC 2023 Dry, Condensed & Evaporated Dairy Products
31152 Ice Cream & Frozen Dessert Manufacturing
SIC 2024 Ice Cream & Frozen Desserts
311611 Animal Slaughtering
SIC 0751 Livestock Services, Except Veterinary
SIC 2011 Meat Packing Plants
SIC 2048 Prepared Feeds & Feed Ingredients for Animals &
Fowls, Except Dogs & Cats
311612 Meat Processed from Carcasses
SIC 2013 Sausages & Other Prepared Meats
SIC 5147 Meat & Meat Products
311613 Rendering & Meat By-product Processing
SIC 2077 Animal & Marine Fats & Oils
311615 Poultry Processing
SIC 2015 Poultry Slaughtering & Processing
311711 Seafood Canning
SIC 2077 Animal & Marine Fats & Oils
SIC 2091 Canned & Cured Fish & Seafood
311712 Fresh & Frozen Seafood Processing
SIC 2077 Animal & Marine Fats & Oils
SIC 2092 Prepared Fresh or Frozen Fish & Seafood

311811 Retail Bakeries
SIC 5461 Retail Bakeries
311812 Commercial Bakeries
SIC 2051 Bread & Other Bakery Products, Except Cookies &
Crackers
SIC 2052 Cookies & Crackers
311813 Frozen Bakery Product Manufacturing
SIC 2053 Frozen Bakery Products, Except Bread
311821 Cookie & Cracker Manufacturing
SIC 2052 Cookies & Crackers
**311822 Flour Mixes & Dough Manufacturing from Purchased
Flour**
SIC 2045 Prepared Flour Mixes & Doughs
311823 Pasta Manufacturing
SIC 2098 Macaroni, Spaghetti, Vermicelli & Noodles
31183 Tortilla Manufacturing
SIC 2099 Food Preparations, nec
311911 Roasted Nuts & Peanut Butter Manufacturing
SIC 2068 Salted & Roasted Nuts & Seeds
SIC 2099 Food Preparations, nec
311919 Other Snack Food Manufacturing
SIC 2052 Cookies & Crackers
SIC 2096 Potato Chips, Corn Chips, & Similar Snacks
31192 Coffee & Tea Manufacturing
SIC 2043 Cereal Breakfast Foods
SIC 2095 Roasted Coffee
SIC 2099 Food Preparations, nec
31193 Flavoring Syrup & Concentrate Manufacturing
SIC 2087 Flavoring Extracts & Flavoring Syrups
**311941 Mayonnaise, Dressing & Other Prepared Sauce
Manufacturing**
SIC 2035 Pickled Fruits & Vegetables, Vegetable Seasonings, &
Sauces & Salad Dressings
SIC 2099 Food Preparations, nec
311942 Spice & Extract Manufacturing
SIC 2087 Flavoring Extracts & Flavoring Syrups
SIC 2095 Roasted Coffee
SIC 2099 Food Preparations, nec
SIC 2899 Chemical Preparations, nec
311991 Perishable Prepared Food Manufacturing
SIC 2099 Food Preparations, nec
311999 All Other Miscellaneous Food Manufacturing
SIC 2015 Poultry Slaughtering & Processing
SIC 2032 Canned Specialties
SIC 2087 Flavoring Extracts & Flavoring Syrups
SIC 2099 Food Preparations, nec

BEVERAGE & TOBACCO PRODUCT MANUFACTURING

312111 Soft Drink Manufacturing
SIC 2086 Bottled & Canned Soft Drinks & Carbonated Water
312112 Bottled Water Manufacturing
SIC 2086 Bottled & Canned Soft Drinks & Carbonated Water
312113 Ice Manufacturing
SIC 2097 Manufactured Ice
31212 Breweries
SIC 2082 Malt Beverages
31213 Wineries
SIC 2084 Wines, Brandy, & Brandy Spirits
31214 Distilleries
SIC 2085 Distilled & Blended Liquors

31221 Tobacco Stemming & Redrying
SIC 2141 Tobacco Stemming & Redrying
312221 Cigarette Manufacturing
SIC 2111 Cigarettes
312229 Other Tobacco Product Manufacturing
SIC 2121 Cigars
SIC 2131 Chewing & Smoking Tobacco & Snuff
SIC 2141 Tobacco Stemming & Redrying

TEXTILE MILLS

313111 Yarn Spinning Mills
SIC 2281 Yarn Spinning Mills
SIC 2299 Textile Goods, nec
313112 Yarn Texturing, Throwing & Twisting Mills
SIC 2282 Yarn Texturing, Throwing, Winding Mills
313113 Thread Mills
SIC 2284 Thread Mills
SIC 2299 Textile Goods, NEC
31321 Broadwoven Fabric Mills
SIC 2211 Broadwoven Fabric Mills, Cotton
SIC 2221 Broadwoven Fabric Mills, Manmade Fiber & Silk
SIC 2231 Broadwoven Fabric Mills, Wool
SIC 2299 Textile Goods, nec
313221 Narrow Fabric Mills
SIC 2241 Narrow Fabric & Other Smallware Mills: Cotton,
      Wool, Silk & Manmade Fiber
SIC 2299 Textile Goods, nec
313222 Schiffli Machine Embroidery
SIC 2397 Schiffli Machine Embroideries
31323 Nonwoven Fabric Mills
SIC 2297 Nonwoven Fabrics
SIC 2299 Textile Goods, nec
313241 Weft Knit Fabric Mills
SIC 2257 Weft Knit Fabric Mills
SIC 2259 Knitting Mills nec
313249 Other Knit Fabric & Lace Mills
SIC 2258 Lace & Warp Knit Fabric Mills
SIC 2259 Knitting Mills nec
313311 Broadwoven Fabric Finishing Mills
SIC 2231 Broadwoven Fabric Mills, Wool
SIC 2261 Finishers of Broadwoven Fabrics of Cotton
SIC 2262 Finishers of Broadwoven Fabrics of Manmade Fiber
      & Silk
SIC 2269 Finishers of Textiles, nec
SIC 5131 Piece Goods & Notions
313312 Textile & Fabric Finishing Mills
SIC 2231 Broadwoven Fabric Mills, Wool
SIC 2257 Weft Knit Fabric Mills
SIC 2258 Lace & Warp Knit Fabric Mills
SIC 2269 Finishers of Textiles, nec
SIC 2282 Yarn Texturizing, Throwing, Twisting, & Winding
      Mills
SIC 2284 Thread Mills
SIC 2299 Textile Goods, nec
SIC 5131 Piece Goods & Notions
31332 Fabric Coating Mills
SIC 2295 Coated Fabrics, Not Rubberized
SIC 3069 Fabricated Rubber Products, nec

TEXTILE PRODUCT MILLS

31411 Carpet & Rug Mills
SIC 2273 Carpets & Rugs
314121 Curtain & Drapery Mills
SIC 2391 Curtains & Draperies
SIC 5714 Drapery, Curtain, & Upholstery Stores
314129 Other Household Textile Product Mills
SIC 2392 Housefurnishings, Except Curtains & Draperies
314911 Textile Bag Mills
SIC 2392 Housefurnishings, Except Curtains & Draperies
SIC 2393 Textile Bags
314912 Canvas & Related Product Mills
SIC 2394 Canvas & Related Products
314991 Rope, Cordage & Twine Mills
SIC 2298 Cordage & Twine
314992 Tire Cord & Tire Fabric Mills
SIC 2296 Tire Cord & Fabrics
314999 All Other Miscellaneous Textile Product Mills
SIC 2299 Textile Goods, nec
SIC 2395 Pleating, Decorative & Novelty Stitching, & Tucking
      for the Trade
SIC 2396 Automotive Trimmings, Apparel Findings, & Related
      Products
SIC 2399 Fabricated Textile Products, nec

APPAREL MANUFACTURING

315111 Sheer Hosiery Mills
SIC 2251 Women's Full-Length & Knee-Length Hosiery,
      Except socks
SIC 2252 Hosiery, nec
315119 Other Hosiery & Sock Mills
SIC 2252 Hosiery, nec
315191 Outerwear Knitting Mills
SIC 2253 Knit Outerwear Mills
SIC 2259 Knitting Mills, nec
315192 Underwear & Nightwear Knitting Mills
SIC 2254 Knit Underwear & Nightwear Mills
SIC 2259 Knitting Mills, nec
315211 Men's & Boys' Cut & Sew Apparel Contractors
SIC 2311 Men's & Boys' Suits, Coats, & Overcoats
SIC 2321 Men's & Boys' Shirts, Except Work Shirts
SIC 2322 Men's & Boys' Underwear & Nightwear
SIC 2325 Men's & Boys' Trousers & Slacks
SIC 2326 Men's & Boys' Work Clothing
SIC 2329 Men's & Boys' Clothing, nec
SIC 2341 Women's, Misses', Children's, & Infants' Underwear
      & Nightwear
SIC 2361 Girls', Children's, & Infants' Dresses, Blouses &
      Shirts
SIC 2369 Girls', Children's, & Infants' Outerwear, nec
SIC 2384 Robes & Dressing Gowns
SIC 2385 Waterproof Outerwear
SIC 2389 Apparel & Accessories, nec
SIC 2395 Pleating, Decorative & Novelty Stitching, & Tucking
      for the Trade
315212 Women's & Girls' Cut & Sew Apparel Contractors
SIC 2331 Women's, Misses', & Juniors' Blouses & Shirts
SIC 2335 Women's, Misses' & Juniors' Dresses
SIC 2337 Women's, Misses', & Juniors' Suits, Skirts, & Coats
SIC 2339 Women's, Misses', & Juniors' Outerwear, nec

SIC 2341 Women's, Misses', Children's, & Infants' Underwear
& Nightwear
SIC 2342 Brassieres, Girdles, & Allied Garments
SIC 2361 Girls', Children's, & Infants' Dresses, Blouses, &
Shirts
SIC 2369 Girls', Children's, & Infants' Outerwear, nec
SIC 2384 Robes & Dressing Gowns
SIC 2385 Waterproof Outerwear
SIC 2389 Apparel & Accessories, nec
SIC 2395 Pleating, Decorative & Novelty Stitching, & Tucking
for the Trade
**315221 Men's & Boys' Cut & Sew Underwear & Nightwear
Manufacturing**
SIC 2322 Men's & Boys' Underwear & Nightwear
SIC 2341 Women's, Misses', Children's, & Infants' Underwear
& Nightwear
SIC 2369 Girls', Children's, & Infants' Outerwear, nec
SIC 2384 Robes & Dressing Gowns
**315222 Men's & Boys' Cut & Sew Suit, Coat & Overcoat
Manufacturing**
SIC 2311 Men's & Boys' Suits, Coats, & Overcoats
SIC 2369 Girls', Children's, & Infants' Outerwear, nec
SIC 2385 Waterproof Outerwear
315223 Men's & Boys' Cut & Sew Shirt Manufacturing
SIC 2321 Men's & Boys' Shirts, Except Work Shirts
SIC 2361 Girls', Children's, & Infants' Dresses, Blouses, &
Shirts
**315224 Men's & Boys' Cut & Sew Trouser, Slack & Jean
Manufacturing**
SIC 2325 Men's & Boys' Trousers & Slacks
SIC 2369 Girls', Children's, & Infants' Outerwear, NEC
315225 Men's & Boys' Cut & Sew Work Clothing Manufacturing
SIC 2326 Men's & Boys' Work Clothing
**315228 Men's & Boys' Cut & Sew Other Outerwear
Manufacturing**
SIC 2329 Men's & Boys' Clothing, nec
SIC 2369 Girls', Children's, & Infants' Outerwear, nec
SIC 2385 Waterproof Outerwear
**315231 Women's & Girls' Cut & Sew Lingerie, Loungewear &
Nightwear Manufacturing**
SIC 2341 Women's, Misses', Children's, & Infants' Underwear
& Nightwear
SIC 2342 Brassieres, Girdles, & Allied Garments
SIC 2369 Girls', Children's, & Infants' Outerwear, nec
SIC 2384 Robes & Dressing Gowns
SIC 2389 Apparel & Accessories, NEC
**315232 Women's & Girls' Cut & Sew Blouse & Shirt
Manufacturing**
SIC 2331 Women's, Misses', & Juniors' Blouses & Shirts
SIC 2361 Girls', Children's, & Infants' Dresses, Blouses, &
Shirts
315233 Women's & Girls' Cut & Sew Dress Manufacturing
SIC 2335 Women's, Misses', & Juniors' Dresses
SIC 2361 Girls', Children's, & Infants' Dresses, Blouses, &
Shirts
**315234 Women's & Girls' Cut & Sew Suit, Coat, Tailored Jacket
& Skirt Manufacturing**
SIC 2337 Women's, Misses', & Juniors' Suits, Skirts, & Coats
SIC 2369 Girls', Children's, & Infants' Outerwear, nec
SIC 2385 Waterproof Outerwear
**315238 Women's & Girls' Cut & Sew Other Outerwear
Manufacturing**
SIC 2339 Women's, Misses', & Juniors' Outerwear, nec
SIC 2369 Girls', Children's, & Infants' Outerwear, nec

SIC 2385 Waterproof Outerwear
315291 Infants' Cut & Sew Apparel Manufacturing
SIC 2341 Women's, Misses', Children's, & Infants' Underwear
& Nightwear
SIC 2361 Girls', Children's, & Infants' Dresses, Blouses, &
Shirts
SIC 2369 Girls', Children's, & Infants' Outerwear, nec
SIC 2385 Waterproof Outerwear
315292 Fur & Leather Apparel Manufacturing
SIC 2371 Fur Goods
SIC 2386 Leather & Sheep-lined Clothing
315299 All Other Cut & Sew Apparel Manufacturing
SIC 2329 Men's & Boys' Outerwear, nec
SIC 2339 Women's, Misses', & Juniors' Outerwear, nec
SIC 2389 Apparel & Accessories, nec
315991 Hat, Cap & Millinery Manufacturing
SIC 2353 Hats, Caps, & Millinery
315992 Glove & Mitten Manufacturing
SIC 2381 Dress & Work Gloves, Except Knit & All-Leather
SIC 3151 Leather Gloves & Mittens
315993 Men's & Boys' Neckwear Manufacturing
SIC 2323 Men's & Boys' Neckwear
**315999 Other Apparel Accessories & Other Apparel
Manufacturing**
SIC 2339 Women's, Misses', & Juniors' Outerwear, nec
SIC 2385 Waterproof Outerwear
SIC 2387 Apparel Belts
SIC 2389 Apparel & Accessories, nec
SIC 2396 Automotive Trimmings, Apparel Findings, & Related
Products
SIC 2399 Fabricated Textile Products, nec

LEATHER & ALLIED PRODUCT MANUFACTURING

31611   Leather & Hide Tanning & Finishing
SIC 3111 Leather Tanning & Finishing
SIC 3999 Manufacturing Industries, nec
316211 Rubber & Plastics Footwear Manufacturing
SIC 3021 Rubber & Plastics Footwear
316212 House Slipper Manufacturing
SIC 3142 House Slippers
316213 Men's Footwear Manufacturing
SIC 3143 Men's Footwear, Except Athletic
316214 Women's Footwear Manufacturing
SIC 3144 Women's Footwear, Except Athletic
316219 Other Footwear Manufacturing
SIC 3149 Footwear Except Rubber, NEC
316991 Luggage Manufacturing
SIC 3161 Luggage
316992 Women's Handbag & Purse Manufacturing
SIC 3171 Women's Handbags & Purses
316993 Personal Leather Good Manufacturing
SIC 3172 Personal Leather Goods, Except Women's Handbags
& Purses
316999 All Other Leather Good Manufacturing
SIC 3131 Boot & Shoe Cut Stock & Findings
SIC 3199 Leather Goods, nec

WOOD PRODUCT MANUFACTURING

321113 Sawmills
SIC 2421 Sawmills & Planing Mills, General
SIC 2429 Special Product Sawmills, nec
321114 Wood Preservation
SIC 2491 Wood Preserving
321211 Hardwood Veneer & Plywood Manufacturing
SIC 2435 Hardwood Veneer & Plywood
321212 Softwood Veneer & Plywood Manufacturing
SIC 2436 Softwood Veneer & Plywood
321213 Engineered Wood Member Manufacturing
SIC 2439 Structural Wood Members, nec
321214 Truss Manufacturing
SIC 2439 Structural Wood Members, nec
321219 Reconstituted Wood Product Manufacturing
SIC 2493 Reconstituted Wood Products
321911 Wood Window & Door Manufacturing
SIC 2431 Millwork
321912 Hardwood Dimension Mills
SIC 2426 Hardwood Dimension & Flooring Mills
321913 Softwood Cut Stock, Resawing Lumber, & Planing
SIC 2421 Sawmills & Planing Mills, General
SIC 2429 Special Product Sawmills, nec
SIC 2439 Structural Wood Members, nec
321914 Other Millwork
SIC 2421 Sawmills & Planing Mills, General
SIC 2426 Hardwood Dimension & Flooring Mills
SIC 2431 Millwork
32192   Wood Container & Pallet Manufacturing
SIC 2441 Nailed & Lock Corner Wood Boxes & Shook
SIC 2448 Wood Pallets & Skids
SIC 2449 Wood Containers, NEC
SIC 2499 Wood Products, nec
321991 Manufactured Home Manufacturing
SIC 2451 Mobile Homes
321992 Prefabricated Wood Building Manufacturing
SIC 2452 Prefabricated Wood Buildings & Components
321999 All Other Miscellaneous Wood Product Manufacturing
SIC 2426 Hardwood Dimension & Flooring Mills
SIC 2499 Wood Products, nec
SIC 3131 Boot & Shoe Cut Stock & Findings
SIC 3999 Manufacturing Industries, nec
SIC 2421 Sawmills & Planing Mills, General
SIC 2429 Special Product Sawmills, nec

PAPER MANUFACTURING

32211   Pulp Mills
SIC 2611 Pulp Mills
322121 Paper Mills
SIC 2611 Pulp Mills
SIC 2621 Paper Mills
322122 Newsprint Mills
SIC 2621 Paper Mills
32213   Paperboard Mills
SIC 2611 Pulp Mills
SIC 2631 Paperboard Mills
322211 Corrugated & Solid Fiber Box Manufacturing
SIC 2653 Corrugated & Solid Fiber Boxes
322212 Folding Paperboard Box Manufacturing
SIC 2657 Folding Paperboard Boxes, Including Sanitary

322213 Setup Paperboard Box Manufacturing
SIC 2652 Setup Paperboard Boxes
322214 Fiber Can, Tube, Drum, & Similar Products Manufacturing
SIC 2655 Fiber Cans, Tubes, Drums, & Similar Products
322215 Non-Folding Sanitary Food Container Manufacturing
SIC 2656 Sanitary Food Containers, Except Folding
SIC 2679 Converted Paper & Paperboard Products, NEC
322221 Coated & Laminated Packaging Paper & Plastics Film Manufacturing
SIC 2671 Packaging Paper & Plastics Film, Coated & Laminated
322222 Coated & Laminated Paper Manufacturing
SIC 2672 Coated & Laminated Paper, nec
SIC 2679 Converted Paper & Paperboard Products, nec
322223 Plastics, Foil, & Coated Paper Bag Manufacturing
SIC 2673 Plastics, Foil, & Coated Paper Bags
322224 Uncoated Paper & Multiwall Bag Manufacturing
SIC 2674 Uncoated Paper & Multiwall Bags
322225 Laminated Aluminum Foil Manufacturing for Flexible Packaging Uses
SIC 3497 Metal Foil & Leaf
322231 Die-Cut Paper & Paperboard Office Supplies Manufacturing
SIC 2675 Die-Cut Paper & Paperboard & Cardboard
SIC 2679 Converted Paper & Paperboard Products, nec
322232 Envelope Manufacturing
SIC 2677 Envelopes
322233 Stationery, Tablet, & Related Product Manufacturing
SIC 2678 Stationery, Tablets, & Related Products
322291 Sanitary Paper Product Manufacturing
SIC 2676 Sanitary Paper Products
322292 Surface-Coated Paperboard Manufacturing
SIC 2675 Die-Cut Paper & Paperboard & Cardboard
322298 All Other Converted Paper Product Manufacturing
SIC 2675 Die-Cut Paper & Paperboard & Cardboard
SIC 2679 Converted Paper & Paperboard Products, NEC

PRINTING & RELATED SUPPORT ACTIVITIES

323110 Commercial Lithographic Printing
SIC 2752 Commercial Printing, Lithographic
SIC 2771 Greeting Cards
SIC 2782 Blankbooks, Loose-leaf Binders & Devices
SIC 3999 Manufacturing Industries, nec
323111 Commercial Gravure Printing
SIC 2754 Commercial Printing, Gravure
SIC 2771 Greeting Cards
SIC 2782 Blankbooks, Loose-leaf Binders & Devices
SIC 3999 Manufacturing Industries, nec
323112 Commercial Flexographic Printing
SIC 2759 Commercial Printing, NEC
SIC 2771 Greeting Cards
SIC 2782 Blankbooks, Loose-leaf Binders & Devices
SIC 3999 Manufacturing Industries, nec
323113 Commercial Screen Printing
SIC 2396 Automotive Trimmings, Apparel Findings, & Related Products
SIC 2759 Commercial Printing, nec
SIC 2771 Greeting Cards
SIC 2782 Blankbooks, Loose-leaf Binders & Devices
SIC 3999 Manufacturing Industries, nec

323114 Quick Printing
SIC 2752 Commercial Printing, Lithographic
SIC 2759 Commercial Printing, nec
323115 Digital Printing
SIC 2759 Commercial Printing, nec
323116 Manifold Business Form Printing
SIC 2761 Manifold Business Forms
323117 Book Printing
SIC 2732 Book Printing
323118 Blankbook, Loose-leaf Binder & Device Manufacturing
SIC 2782 Blankbooks, Loose-leaf Binders & Devices
323119 Other Commercial Printing
SIC 2759 Commercial Printing, nec
SIC 2771 Greeting Cards
SIC 2782 Blankbooks, Loose-leaf Binders & Devices
SIC 3999 Manufacturing Industries, nec
323121 Tradebinding & Related Work
SIC 2789 Bookbinding & Related Work
323122 Prepress Services
SIC 2791 Typesetting
SIC 2796 Platemaking & Related Services

PETROLEUM & COAL PRODUCTS MANUFACTURING

32411 Petroleum Refineries
SIC 2911 Petroleum Refining
324121 Asphalt Paving Mixture & Block Manufacturing
SIC 2951 Asphalt Paving Mixtures & Blocks
324122 Asphalt Shingle & Coating Materials Manufacturing
SIC 2952 Asphalt Felts & Coatings
324191 Petroleum Lubricating Oil & Grease Manufacturing
SIC 2992 Lubricating Oils & Greases
324199 All Other Petroleum & Coal Products Manufacturing
SIC 2999 Products of Petroleum & Coal, nec
SIC 3312 Blast Furnaces & Steel Mills

CHEMICAL MANUFACTURING

32511 Petrochemical Manufacturing
SIC 2865 Cyclic Organic Crudes & Intermediates, & Organic
          Dyes & Pigments
SIC 2869 Industrial Organic Chemicals, nec
32512 Industrial Gas Manufacturing
SIC 2813 Industrial Gases
SIC 2869 Industrial Organic Chemicals, nec
325131 Inorganic Dye & Pigment Manufacturing
SIC 2816 Inorganic Pigments
SIC 2819 Industrial Inorganic Chemicals, nec
325132 Organic Dye & Pigment Manufacturing
SIC 2865 Cyclic Organic Crudes & Intermediates, & Organic
          Dyes & Pigments
325181 Alkalies & Chlorine Manufacturing
SIC 2812 Alkalies & Chlorine
325182 Carbon Black Manufacturing
SIC 2816 Inorganic pigments
SIC 2895 Carbon Black
325188 All Other Basic Inorganic Chemical Manufacturing
SIC 2819 Industrial Inorganic Chemicals, nec
SIC 2869 Industrial Organic Chemicals, nec

325191 Gum & Wood Chemical Manufacturing
SIC 2861 Gum & Wood Chemicals
325192 Cyclic Crude & Intermediate Manufacturing
SIC 2865 Cyclic Organic Crudes & Intermediates & Organic
          Dyes & Pigments
325193 Ethyl Alcohol Manufacturing
SIC 2869 Industrial Organic Chemicals
325199 All Other Basic Organic Chemical Manufacturing
SIC 2869 Industrial Organic Chemicals, nec
SIC 2899 Chemical & Chemical Preparations, nec
325211 Plastics Material & Resin Manufacturing
SIC 2821 Plastics Materials, Synthetic & Resins, &
          Nonvulcanizable Elastomers
325212 Synthetic Rubber Manufacturing
SIC 2822 Synthetic Rubber
325221 Cellulosic Manmade Fiber Manufacturing
SIC 2823 Cellulosic Manmade Fibers
325222 Noncellulosic Organic Fiber Manufacturing
SIC 2824 Manmade Organic Fibers, Except Cellulosic
325311 Nitrogenous Fertilizer Manufacturing
SIC 2873 Nitrogenous Fertilizers
325312 Phosphatic Fertilizer Manufacturing
SIC 2874 Phosphatic Fertilizers
325314 Fertilizer Manufacturing
SIC 2875 Fertilizers, Mixing Only
32532 Pesticide & Other Agricultural Chemical Manufacturing
SIC 2879 Pesticides & Agricultural Chemicals, nec
325411 Medicinal & Botanical Manufacturing
SIC 2833 Medicinal Chemicals & Botanical Products
325412 Pharmaceutical Preparation Manufacturing
SIC 2834 Pharmaceutical Preparations
SIC 2835 In-Vitro & In-Vivo Diagnostic Substances
325413 In-Vitro Diagnostic Substance Manufacturing
SIC 2835 In-Vitro & In-Vivo Diagnostic Substances
325414 Biological Product Manufacturing
SIC 2836 Biological Products, Except Diagnostic Substance
32551 Paint & Coating Manufacturing
SIC 2851 Paints, Varnishes, Lacquers, Enamels & Allied
          Products
SIC 2899 Chemicals & Chemical Preparations, nec
32552 Adhesive & Sealant Manufacturing
SIC 2891 Adhesives & Sealants
325611 Soap & Other Detergent Manufacturing
SIC 2841 Soaps & Other Detergents, Except Specialty Cleaners
SIC 2844 Toilet Preparations
325612 Polish & Other Sanitation Good Manufacturing
SIC 2842 Specialty Cleaning, Polishing, & Sanitary Preparations
325613 Surface Active Agent Manufacturing
SIC 2843 Surface Active Agents, Finishing Agents, Sulfonated
          Oils, & Assistants
32562 Toilet Preparation Manufacturing
SIC 2844 Perfumes, Cosmetics, & Other Toilet Preparations
32591 Printing Ink Manufacturing
SIC 2893 Printing Ink
32592 Explosives Manufacturing
SIC 2892 Explosives
325991 Custom Compounding of Purchased Resin
SIC 3087 Custom Compounding of Purchased Plastics Resin
**325992 Photographic Film, Paper, Plate & Chemical
          Manufacturing**
SIC 3861 Photographic Equipment & Supplies

325998 All Other Miscellaneous Chemical Product Manufacturing
SIC 2819 Industrial Inorganic Chemicals, nec
SIC 2899 Chemicals & Chemical Preparations, nec
SIC 3952 Lead Pencils & Art Goods
SIC 3999 Manufacturing Industries, nec

PLASTICS & RUBBER PRODUCTS MANUFACTURING

326111 Unsupported Plastics Bag Manufacturing
SIC 2673 Plastics, Foil, & Coated Paper Bags
326112 Unsupported Plastics Packaging Film & Sheet Manufacturing
SIC 2671 Packaging Paper & Plastics Film, Coated, & Laminated
326113 Unsupported Plastics Film & Sheet Manufacturing
SIC 3081 Unsupported Plastics Film & Sheets
326121 Unsupported Plastics Profile Shape Manufacturing
SIC 3082 Unsupported Plastics Profile Shapes
SIC 3089 Plastics Product, nec
326122 Plastics Pipe & Pipe Fitting Manufacturing
SIC 3084 Plastics Pipe
SIC 3089 Plastics Products, nec
32613 Laminated Plastics Plate, Sheet & Shape Manufacturing
SIC 3083 Laminated Plastics Plate, Sheet & Profile Shapes
32614 Polystyrene Foam Product Manufacturing
SIC 3086 Plastics Foam Products
32615 Urethane & Other Foam Product Manufacturing
SIC 3086 Plastics Foam Products
32616 Plastics Bottle Manufacturing
SIC 3085 Plastics Bottles
326191 Plastics Plumbing Fixture Manufacturing
SIC 3088 Plastics Plumbing Fixtures
326192 Resilient Floor Covering Manufacturing
SIC 3069 Fabricated Rubber Products, nec
SIC 3996 Linoleum, Asphalted-Felt-Base, & Other Hard Surface Floor Coverings, nec
326199 All Other Plastics Product Manufacturing
SIC 3089 Plastics Products, nec
SIC 3999 Manufacturing Industries, nec
326211 Tire Manufacturing
SIC 3011 Tires & Inner Tubes
326212 Tire Retreading
SIC 7534 Tire Retreading & Repair Shops
32622 Rubber & Plastics Hoses & Belting Manufacturing
SIC 3052 Rubber & Plastics Hose & Belting
326291 Rubber Product Manufacturing for Mechanical Use
SIC 3061 Molded, Extruded, & Lathe-Cut Mechanical Rubber Goods
326299 All Other Rubber Product Manufacturing
SIC 3069 Fabricated Rubber Products, nec

NONMETALLIC MINERAL PRODUCT MANUFACTURING

327111 Vitreous China Plumbing Fixture & China & Earthenware Fittings & Bathroom Accessories Manufacturing
SIC 3261 Vitreous China Plumbing Fixtures & China & Earthenware Fittings & Bathroom Accessories

327112 Vitreous China, Fine Earthenware & Other Pottery Product Manufacturing
SIC 3262 Vitreous China Table & Kitchen Articles
SIC 3263 Fine Earthenware Table & Kitchen Articles
SIC 3269 Pottery Products, nec
327113 Porcelain Electrical Supply Manufacturing
SIC 3264 Porcelain Electrical Supplies
327121 Brick & Structural Clay Tile Manufacturing
SIC 3251 Brick & Structural Clay Tile
327122 Ceramic Wall & Floor Tile Manufacturing
SIC 3253 Ceramic Wall & Floor Tile
327123 Other Structural Clay Product Manufacturing
SIC 3259 Structural Clay Products, nec
327124 Clay Refractory Manufacturing
SIC 3255 Clay Refractories
327125 Nonclay Refractory Manufacturing
SIC 3297 Nonclay Refractories
327211 Flat Glass Manufacturing
SIC 3211 Flat Glass
327212 Other Pressed & Blown Glass & Glassware Manufacturing
SIC 3229 Pressed & Blown Glass & Glassware, nec
327213 Glass Container Manufacturing
SIC 3221 Glass Containers
327215 Glass Product Manufacturing Made of Purchased Glass
SIC 3231 Glass Products Made of Purchased Glass
32731 Hydraulic Cement Manufacturing
SIC 3241 Cement, Hydraulic
32732 Ready-Mix Concrete Manufacturing
SIC 3273 Ready-Mixed Concrete
327331 Concrete Block & Brick Manufacturing
SIC 3271 Concrete Block & Brick
327332 Concrete Pipe Manufacturing
SIC 3272 Concrete Products, Except Block & Brick
32739 Other Concrete Product Manufacturing
SIC 3272 Concrete Products, Except Block & Brick
32741 Lime Manufacturing
SIC 3274 Lime
32742 Gypsum & Gypsum Product Manufacturing
SIC 3275 Gypsum Products
SIC 3299 Nonmetallic Mineral Products, nec
32791 Abrasive Product Manufacturing
SIC 3291 Abrasive Products
327991 Cut Stone & Stone Product Manufacturing
SIC 3281 Cut Stone & Stone Products
327992 Ground or Treated Mineral & Earth Manufacturing
SIC 3295 Minerals & Earths, Ground or Otherwise Treated
327993 Mineral Wool Manufacturing
SIC 3296 Mineral Wool
327999 All Other Miscellaneous Nonmetallic Mineral Product Manufacturing
SIC 3272 Concrete Products, Except Block & Brick
SIC 3292 Asbestos Products
SIC 3299 Nonmetallic Mineral Products, nec

PRIMARY METAL MANUFACTURING

331111 Iron & Steel Mills
SIC 3312 Steel Works, Blast Furnaces , & Rolling Mills
SIC 3399 Primary Metal Products, nec
331112 Electrometallurgical Ferroalloy Product Manufacturing
SIC 3313 Electrometallurgical Products, Except Steel

33121 Iron & Steel Pipes & Tubes Manufacturing from Purchased Steel
SIC 3317 Steel Pipe & Tubes
331221 Cold-Rolled Steel Shape Manufacturing
SIC 3316 Cold-Rolled Steel Sheet, Strip & Bars
331222 Steel Wire Drawing
SIC 3315 Steel Wiredrawing & Steel Nails & Spikes
331311 Alumina Refining
SIC 2819 Industrial Inorganic Chemicals, nec
331312 Primary Aluminum Production
SIC 3334 Primary Production of Aluminum
331314 Secondary Smelting & Alloying of Aluminum
SIC 3341 Secondary Smelting & Refining of Nonferrous Metals
SIC 3399 Primary Metal Products, nec
331315 Aluminum Sheet, Plate & Foil Manufacturing
SIC 3353 Aluminum Sheet, Plate, & Foil
331316 Aluminum Extruded Product Manufacturing
SIC 3354 Aluminum Extruded Products
331319 Other Aluminum Rolling & Drawing
SIC 3355 Aluminum Rolling & Drawing, nec
SIC 3357 Drawing & Insulating of Nonferrous Wire
331411 Primary Smelting & Refining of Copper
SIC 3331 Primary Smelting & Refining of Copper
331419 Primary Smelting & Refining of Nonferrous Metal
SIC 3339 Primary Smelting & Refining of Nonferrous Metals, Except Copper & Aluminum
331421 Copper Rolling, Drawing & Extruding
SIC 3351 Rolling, Drawing, & Extruding of Copper
331422 Copper Wire Drawing
SIC 3357 Drawing & Insulating of Nonferrous Wire
331423 Secondary Smelting, Refining, & Alloying of Copper
SIC 3341 Secondary Smelting & Refining of Nonferrous Metals
SIC 3399 Primary Metal Products, nec
331491 Nonferrous Metal Rolling, Drawing & Extruding
SIC 3356 Rolling, Drawing & Extruding of Nonferrous Metals, Except Copper & Aluminum
SIC 3357 Drawing & Insulating of Nonferrous Wire
331492 Secondary Smelting, Refining, & Alloying of Nonferrous Metal
SIC 3313 Electrometallurgical Products, Except Steel
SIC 3341 Secondary Smelting & Reining of Nonferrous Metals
SIC 3399 Primary Metal Products, nec
331511 Iron Foundries
SIC 3321 Gray & Ductile Iron Foundries
SIC 3322 Malleable Iron Foundries
331512 Steel Investment Foundries
SIC 3324 Steel Investment Foundries
331513 Steel Foundries,
SIC 3325 Steel Foundries, nec
331521 Aluminum Die-Castings
SIC 3363 Aluminum Die-Castings
331522 Nonferrous Die-Castings
SIC 3364 Nonferrous Die-Castings, Except Aluminum
331524 Aluminum Foundries
SIC 3365 Aluminum Foundries
331525 Copper Foundries
SIC 3366 Copper Foundries
331528 Other Nonferrous Foundries
SIC 3369 Nonferrous Foundries, Except Aluminum & Copper

FABRICATED METAL PRODUCT MANUFACTURING

332111 Iron & Steel Forging
SIC 3462 Iron & Steel Forgings
332112 Nonferrous Forging
SIC 3463 Nonferrous Forgings
332114 Custom Roll Forming
SIC 3449 Miscellaneous Structural Metal Work
332115 Crown & Closure Manufacturing
SIC 3466 Crowns & Closures
332116 Metal Stamping
SIC 3469 Metal Stampings, nec
332117 Powder Metallurgy Part Manufacturing
SIC 3499 Fabricated Metal Products, nec
332211 Cutlery & Flatware Manufacturing
SIC 3421 Cutlery
SIC 3914 Silverware, Plated Ware, & Stainless Steel Ware
332212 Hand & Edge Tool Manufacturing
SIC 3423 Hand & Edge Tools, Except Machine Tools & Handsaws
SIC 3523 Farm Machinery & Equipment
SIC 3524 Lawn & Garden Tractors & Home Lawn & Garden Equipment
SIC 3545 Cutting Tools, Machine Tools Accessories, & Machinist Precision Measuring Devices
SIC 3799 Transportation Equipment, nec
SIC 3999 Manufacturing Industries, nec
332213 Saw Blade & Handsaw Manufacturing
SIC 3425 Saw Blades & Handsaws
332214 Kitchen Utensil, Pot & Pan Manufacturing
SIC 3469 Metal Stampings, nec
332311 Prefabricated Metal Building & Component Manufacturing
SIC 3448 Prefabricated Metal Buildings & Components
332312 Fabricated Structural Metal Manufacturing
SIC 3441 Fabricated Structural Metal
SIC 3449 Miscellaneous Structural Metal Work
332313 Plate Work Manufacturing
SIC 3443 Fabricated Plate Work
332321 Metal Window & Door Manufacturing
SIC 3442 Metal Doors, Sash, Frames, Molding & Trim
SIC 3449 Miscellaneous Structural Metal Work
332322 Sheet Metal Work Manufacturing
SIC 3444 Sheet Metal Work
332323 Ornamental & Architectural Metal Work Manufacturing
SIC 3446 Architectural & Ornamental Metal Work
SIC 3449 Miscellaneous Structural Metal Work
SIC 3523 Farm Machinery & Equipment
33241 Power Boiler & Heat Exchanger Manufacturing
SIC 3443 Fabricated Plate Work
33242 Metal Tank Manufacturing
SIC 3443 Fabricated Plate Work
332431 Metal Can Manufacturing
SIC 3411 Metal Cans
332439 Other Metal Container Manufacturing
SIC 3412 Metal Shipping Barrels, Drums, Kegs, & Pails
SIC 3429 Hardware, nec
SIC 3444 Sheet Metal Work
SIC 3499 Fabricated Metal Products, nec
SIC 3537 Industrial Trucks, Tractors, Trailers, & Stackers
33251 Hardware Manufacturing
SIC 3429 Hardware, nec
SIC 3499 Fabricated Metal Products, nec

332611 Steel Spring Manufacturing
SIC 3493 Steel Springs, Except Wire
332612 Wire Spring Manufacturing
SIC 3495 Wire Springs
332618 Other Fabricated Wire Product Manufacturing
SIC 3315 Steel Wiredrawing & Steel Nails & Spikes
SIC 3399 Primary Metal Products, nec
SIC 3496 Miscellaneous Fabricated Wire Products
33271 Machine Shops
SIC 3599 Industrial & Commercial Machinery & Equipment,
nec
332721 Precision Turned Product Manufacturing
SIC 3451 Screw Machine Products
332722 Bolt, Nut, Screw, Rivet & Washer Manufacturing
SIC 3452 Bolts, Nuts, Screws, Rivets, & Washers
332811 Metal Heat Treating
SIC 3398 Metal Heat Treating
**332812 Metal Coating, Engraving , & Allied Services to
Manufacturers**
SIC 3479 Coating, Engraving, & Allied Services, nec
332813 Electroplating, Plating, Polishing, Anodizing & Coloring
SIC 3399 Primary Metal Products, nec
SIC 3471 Electroplating, Plating, Polishing, Anodizing, &
Coloring
332911 Industrial Valve Manufacturing
SIC 3491 Industrial Valves
332912 Fluid Power Valve & Hose Fitting Manufacturing
SIC 3492 Fluid Power Valves & Hose Fittings
SIC 3728 Aircraft Parts & Auxiliary Equipment, nec
332913 Plumbing Fixture Fitting & Trim Manufacturing
SIC 3432 Plumbing Fixture Fittings & Trim
332919 Other Metal Valve & Pipe Fitting Manufacturing
SIC 3429 Hardware, nec
SIC 3494 Valves & Pipe Fittings, nec
SIC 3499 Fabricated Metal Products, nec
332991 Ball & Roller Bearing Manufacturing
SIC 3562 Ball & Roller Bearings
332992 Small Arms Ammunition Manufacturing
SIC 3482 Small Arms Ammunition
332993 Ammunition Manufacturing
SIC 3483 Ammunition, Except for Small Arms
332994 Small Arms Manufacturing
SIC 3484 Small Arms
332995 Other Ordnance & Accessories Manufacturing
SIC 3489 Ordnance & Accessories, nec
332996 Fabricated Pipe & Pipe Fitting Manufacturing
SIC 3498 Fabricated Pipe & Pipe Fittings
332997 Industrial Pattern Manufacturing
SIC 3543 Industrial Patterns
332998 Enameled Iron & Metal Sanitary Ware Manufacturing
SIC 3431 Enameled Iron & Metal Sanitary Ware
**332999 All Other Miscellaneous Fabricated Metal Product
Manufacturing**
SIC 3291 Abrasive Products
SIC 3432 Plumbing Fixture Fittings & Trim
SIC 3494 Valves & Pipe Fittings, nec
SIC 3497 Metal Foil & Leaf
SIC 3499 Fabricated Metal Products, NEC
SIC 3537 Industrial Trucks, Tractors, Trailers, & Stackers
SIC 3599 Industrial & Commercial Machinery & Equipment,
nec
SIC 3999 Manufacturing Industries, nec

MACHINERY MANUFACTURING

333111 Farm Machinery & Equipment Manufacturing
SIC 3523 Farm Machinery & Equipment
**333112 Lawn & Garden Tractor & Home Lawn & Garden
Equipment Manufacturing**
SIC 3524 Lawn & Garden Tractors & Home Lawn & Garden
Equipment
33312 Construction Machinery Manufacturing
SIC 3531 Construction Machinery & Equipment
333131 Mining Machinery & Equipment Manufacturing
SIC 3532 Mining Machinery & Equipment, Except Oil & Gas
Field Machinery & Equipment
**333132 Oil & Gas Field Machinery & Equipment
Manufacturing**
SIC 3533 Oil & Gas Field Machinery & Equipment
33321 Sawmill & Woodworking Machinery Manufacturing
SIC 3553 Woodworking Machinery
33322 Rubber & Plastics Industry Machinery Manufacturing
SIC 3559 Special Industry Machinery, nec
333291 Paper Industry Machinery Manufacturing
SIC 3554 Paper Industries Machinery
333292 Textile Machinery Manufacturing
SIC 3552 Textile Machinery
333293 Printing Machinery & Equipment Manufacturing
SIC 3555 Printing Trades Machinery & Equipment
333294 Food Product Machinery Manufacturing
SIC 3556 Food Products Machinery
333295 Semiconductor Machinery Manufacturing
SIC 3559 Special Industry Machinery, nec
333298 All Other Industrial Machinery Manufacturing
SIC 3559 Special Industry Machinery, nec
SIC 3639 Household Appliances, nec
333311 Automatic Vending Machine Manufacturing
SIC 3581 Automatic Vending Machines
**333312 Commercial Laundry, Drycleaning & Pressing Machine
Manufacturing**
SIC 3582 Commercial Laundry, Drycleaning & Pressing
Machines
333313 Office Machinery Manufacturing
SIC 3578 Calculating & Accounting Machinery, Except
Electronic Computers
SIC 3579 Office Machines, nec
333314 Optical Instrument & Lens Manufacturing
SIC 3827 Optical Instruments & Lenses
**333315 Photographic & Photocopying Equipment
Manufacturing**
SIC 3861 Photographic Equipment & Supplies
**333319 Other Commercial & Service Industry Machinery
Manufacturing**
SIC 3559 Special Industry Machinery, nec
SIC 3589 Service Industry Machinery, nec
SIC 3599 Industrial & Commercial Machinery & Equipment,
nec
SIC 3699 Electrical Machinery, Equipment & Supplies, nec
333411 Air Purification Equipment Manufacturing
SIC 3564 Industrial & Commercial Fans & Blowers & Air
Purification Equipment
333412 Industrial & Commercial Fan & Blower Manufacturing
SIC 3564 Industrial & Commercial Fans & Blowers & Air
Purification Equipment
333414 Heating Equipment Manufacturing
SIC 3433 Heating Equipment, Except Electric & Warm Air
Furnaces

SIC 3634 Electric Housewares & Fans

333415 Air-Conditioning & Warm Air Heating Equipment & Commercial & Industrial Refrigeration Equipment Manufacturing

SIC 3443 Fabricated Plate Work

SIC 3585 Air-Conditioning & Warm Air Heating Equipment & Commercial & Industrial Refrigeration Equipment

333511 Industrial Mold Manufacturing

SIC 3544 Special Dies & Tools, Die Sets, Jigs & Fixtures, & Industrial Molds

333512 Machine Tool Manufacturing

SIC 3541 Machine Tools, Metal Cutting Type

333513 Machine Tool Manufacturing

SIC 3542 Machine Tools, Metal Forming Type

333514 Special Die & Tool, Die Set, Jig & Fixture Manufacturing

SIC 3544 Special Dies & Tools, Die Sets, Jigs & Fixtures, & Industrial Molds

333515 Cutting Tool & Machine Tool Accessory Manufacturing

SIC 3545 Cutting Tools, Machine Tool Accessories, & Machinists' Precision Measuring Devices

333516 Rolling Mill Machinery & Equipment Manufacturing

SIC 3547 Rolling Mill Machinery & Equipment

333518 Other Metalworking Machinery Manufacturing

SIC 3549 Metalworking Machinery, nec

333611 Turbine & Turbine Generator Set Unit Manufacturing

SIC 3511 Steam, Gas, & Hydraulic Turbines, & Turbine Generator Set Units

333612 Speed Changer, Industrial High-Speed Drive & Gear Manufacturing

SIC 3566 Speed Changers, Industrial High-Speed Drives, & Gears

333613 Mechanical Power Transmission Equipment Manufacturing

SIC 3568 Mechanical Power Transmission Equipment, nec

333618 Other Engine Equipment Manufacturing

SIC 3519 Internal Combustion Engines, nec

SIC 3699 Electrical Machinery, Equipment & Supplies, nec

333911 Pump & Pumping Equipment Manufacturing

SIC 3561 Pumps & Pumping Equipment

SIC 3743 Railroad Equipment

333912 Air & Gas Compressor Manufacturing

SIC 3563 Air & Gas Compressors

333913 Measuring & Dispensing Pump Manufacturing

SIC 3586 Measuring & Dispensing Pumps

333921 Elevator & Moving Stairway Manufacturing

SIC 3534 Elevators & Moving Stairways

333922 Conveyor & Conveying Equipment Manufacturing

SIC 3523 Farm Machinery & Equipment

SIC 3535 Conveyors & Conveying Equipment

333923 Overhead Traveling Crane, Hoist & Monorail System Manufacturing

SIC 3536 Overhead Traveling Cranes, Hoists, & Monorail Systems

SIC 3531 Construction Machinery & Equipment

333924 Industrial Truck, Tractor, Trailer & Stacker Machinery Manufacturing

SIC 3537 Industrial Trucks, Tractors, Trailers, & Stackers

333991 Power-Driven Hand Tool Manufacturing

SIC 3546 Power-Driven Handtools

333992 Welding & Soldering Equipment Manufacturing

SIC 3548 Electric & Gas Welding & Soldering Equipment

333993 Packaging Machinery Manufacturing

SIC 3565 Packaging Machinery

333994 Industrial Process Furnace & Oven Manufacturing

SIC 3567 Industrial Process Furnaces & Ovens

333995 Fluid Power Cylinder & Actuator Manufacturing

SIC 3593 Fluid Power Cylinders & Actuators

333996 Fluid Power Pump & Motor Manufacturing

SIC 3594 Fluid Power Pumps & Motors

333997 Scale & Balance Manufacturing

SIC 3596 Scales & Balances, Except Laboratory

333999 All Other General Purpose Machinery Manufacturing

SIC 3599 Industrial & Commercial Machinery & Equipment, nec

SIC 3569 General Industrial Machinery & Equipment, nec

COMPUTER & ELECTRONIC PRODUCT MANUFACTURING

334111 Electronic Computer Manufacturing

SIC 3571 Electronic Computers

334112 Computer Storage Device Manufacturing

SIC 3572 Computer Storage Devices

334113 Computer Terminal Manufacturing

SIC 3575 Computer Terminals

334119 Other Computer Peripheral Equipment Manufacturing

SIC 3577 Computer Peripheral Equipment, nec

SIC 3578 Calculating & Accounting Machines, Except Electronic Computers

SIC 3699 Electrical Machinery, Equipment & Supplies, nec

33421 Telephone Apparatus Manufacturing

SIC 3661 Telephone & Telegraph Apparatus

33422 Radio & Television Broadcasting & Wireless Communications Equipment Manufacturing

SIC 3663 Radio & Television Broadcasting & Communication Equipment

SIC 3679 Electronic Components, nec

33429 Other Communications Equipment Manufacturing

SIC 3669 Communications Equipment, nec

33431 Audio & Video Equipment Manufacturing

SIC 3651 Household Audio & Video Equipment

334411 Electron Tube Manufacturing

SIC 3671 Electron Tubes

334412 Printed Circuit Board Manufacturing

SIC 3672 Printed Circuit Boards

334413 Semiconductor & Related Device Manufacturing

SIC 3674 Semiconductors & Related Devices

334414 Electronic Capacitor Manufacturing

SIC 3675 Electronic Capacitors

334415 Electronic Resistor Manufacturing

SIC 3676 Electronic Resistors

334416 Electronic Coil, Transformer, & Other Inductor Manufacturing

SIC 3661 Telephone & Telegraph Apparatus

SIC 3677 Electronic Coils, Transformers, & Other Inductors

SIC 3825 Instruments for Measuring & Testing of Electricity & Electrical Signals

334417 Electronic Connector Manufacturing

SIC 3678 Electronic Connectors

334418 Printed Circuit/Electronics Assembly Manufacturing

SIC 3679 Electronic Components, nec

SIC 3661 Telephone & Telegraph Apparatus

334419 Other Electronic Component Manufacturing
SIC 3679 Electronic Components, nec
334510 Electromedical & Electrotherapeutic Apparatus Manufacturing
SIC 3842 Orthopedic, Prosthetic & Surgical Appliances & Supplies
SIC 3845 Electromedical & Electrotherapeutic Apparatus
334511 Search, Detection, Navigation, Guidance, Aeronautical, & Nautical System & Instrument Manufacturing
SIC 3812 Search, Detection, Navigation, Guidance, Aeronautical, & Nautical Systems & Instruments
334512 Automatic Environmental Control Manufacturing for Residential, Commercial & Appliance Use
SIC 3822 Automatic Controls for Regulating Residential & Commercial Environments & Appliances
334513 Instruments & Related Products Manufacturing for Measuring, Displaying, & Controlling Industrial Process Variables
SIC 3823 Industrial Instruments for Measurement, Display, & Control of Process Variables; & Related Products
334514 Totalizing Fluid Meter & Counting Device Manufacturing
SIC 3824 Totalizing Fluid Meters & Counting Devices
334515 Instrument Manufacturing for Measuring & Testing Electricity & Electrical Signals
SIC 3825 Instruments for Measuring & Testing of Electricity & Electrical Signals
334516 Analytical Laboratory Instrument Manufacturing
SIC 3826 Laboratory Analytical Instruments
334517 Irradiation Apparatus Manufacturing
SIC 3844 X-Ray Apparatus & Tubes & Related Irradiation Apparatus
SIC 3845 Electromedical & Electrotherapeutic Apparatus
334518 Watch, Clock, & Part Manufacturing
SIC 3495 Wire Springs
SIC 3579 Office Machines, nec
SIC 3873 Watches, Clocks, Clockwork Operated Devices, & Parts
334519 Other Measuring & Controlling Device Manufacturing
SIC 3829 Measuring & Controlling Devices, nec
334611 Software Reproducing
SIC 7372 Prepackaged Software
334612 Prerecorded Compact Disc , Tape, & Record Reproducing
SIC 3652 Phonograph Records & Prerecorded Audio Tapes & Disks
SIC 7819 Services Allied to Motion Picture Production
334613 Magnetic & Optical Recording Media Manufacturing
SIC 3695 Magnetic & Optical Recording Media

ELECTRICAL EQUIPMENT, APPLIANCE, & COMPONENT MANUFACTURING

33511 Electric Lamp Bulb & Part Manufacturing
SIC 3641 Electric Lamp Bulbs & Tubes
335121 Residential Electric Lighting Fixture Manufacturing
SIC 3645 Residential Electric Lighting Fixtures
SIC 3999 Manufacturing Industries, nec
335122 Commercial, Industrial & Institutional Electric Lighting Fixture Manufacturing
SIC 3646 Commercial, Industrial, & Institutional Electric Lighting Fixtures

335129 Other Lighting Equipment Manufacturing
SIC 3648 Lighting Equipment, nec
SIC 3699 Electrical Machinery, Equipment, & Supplies, nec
335211 Electric Housewares & Fan Manufacturing
SIC 3634 Electric Housewares & Fans
335212 Household Vacuum Cleaner Manufacturing
SIC 3635 Household Vacuum Cleaners
SIC 3639 Household Appliances, nec
335221 Household Cooking Appliance Manufacturing
SIC 3631 Household Cooking Equipment
335222 Household Refrigerator & Home Freezer Manufacturing
SIC 3632 Household Refrigerators & Home & Farm Freezers
335224 Household Laundry Equipment Manufacturing
SIC 3633 Household Laundry Equipment
335228 Other Household Appliance Manufacturing
SIC 3639 Household Appliances, nec
335311 Power, Distribution & Specialty Transformer Manufacturing
SIC 3548 Electric & Gas Welding & Soldering Equipment
SIC 3612 Power, Distribution, & Speciality Transformers
335312 Motor & Generator Manufacturing
SIC 3621 Motors & Generators
SIC 7694 Armature Rewinding Shops
335313 Switchgear & Switchboard Apparatus Manufacturing
SIC 3613 Switchgear & Switchboard Apparatus
335314 Relay & Industrial Control Manufacturing
SIC 3625 Relays & Industrial Controls
335911 Storage Battery Manufacturing
SIC 3691 Storage Batteries
335912 Dry & Wet Primary Battery Manufacturing
SIC 3692 Primary Batteries, Dry & Wet
335921 Fiber-Optic Cable Manufacturing
SIC 3357 Drawing & Insulating of Nonferrous Wire
335929 Other Communication & Energy Wire Manufacturing
SIC 3357 Drawing & Insulating of Nonferrous Wire
335931 Current-Carrying Wiring Device Manufacturing
SIC 3643 Current-Carrying Wiring Devices
335932 Noncurrent-Carrying Wiring Device Manufacturing
SIC 3644 Noncurrent-Carrying Wiring Devices
335991 Carbon & Graphite Product Manufacturing
SIC 3624 Carbon & Graphite Products
335999 All Other Miscellaneous Electrical Equipment & Component Manufacturing
SIC 3629 Electrical Industrial Apparatus, nec
SIC 3699 Electrical Machinery, Equipment, & Supplies, nec

TRANSPORTATION EQUIPMENT MANUFACTURING

336111 Automobile Manufacturing
SIC 3711 Motor Vehicles & Passenger Car Bodies
336112 Light Truck & Utility Vehicle Manufacturing
SIC 3711 Motor Vehicles & Passenger Car Bodies
33612 Heavy Duty Truck Manufacturing
SIC 3711 Motor Vehicles & Passenger Car Bodies
336211 Motor Vehicle Body Manufacturing
SIC 3711 Motor Vehicles & Passenger Car Bodies
SIC 3713 Truck & Bus Bodies
SIC 3714 Motor Vehicle Parts & Accessories
336212 Truck Trailer Manufacturing
SIC 3715 Truck Trailers

336213 Motor Home Manufacturing
SIC 3716 Motor Homes

336214 Travel Trailer & Camper Manufacturing
SIC 3792 Travel Trailers & Campers
SIC 3799 Transportation Equipment, nec

336311 Carburetor, Piston, Piston Ring & Valve Manufacturing
SIC 3592 Carburetors, Pistons, Piston Rings, & Valves

336312 Gasoline Engine & Engine Parts Manufacturing
SIC 3714 Motor Vehicle Parts & Accessories

336321 Vehicular Lighting Equipment Manufacturing
SIC 3647 Vehicular Lighting Equipment

336322 Other Motor Vehicle Electrical & Electronic Equipment Manufacturing
SIC 3679 Electronic Components, nec
SIC 3694 Electrical Equipment for Internal Combustion Engines
SIC 3714 Motor Vehicle Parts & Accessories

33633 Motor Vehicle Steering & Suspension Components Manufacturing
SIC 3714 Motor Vehicle Parts & Accessories

33634 Motor Vehicle Brake System Manufacturing
SIC 3292 Asbestos Products
SIC 3714 Motor Vehicle Parts & Accessories

33635 Motor Vehicle Transmission & Power Train Parts Manufacturing
SIC 3714 Motor Vehicle Parts & Accessories

33636 Motor Vehicle Fabric Accessories & Seat Manufacturing
SIC 2396 Automotive Trimmings, Apparel Findings, & Related Products
SIC 2399 Fabricated Textile Products, nec
SIC 2531 Public Building & Related Furniture

33637 Motor Vehicle Metal Stamping
SIC 3465 Automotive Stampings

336391 Motor Vehicle Air-Conditioning Manufacturing
SIC 3585 Air-Conditioning & Warm Air Heating Equipment & Commercial & Industrial Refrigeration Equipment

336399 All Other Motor Vehicle Parts Manufacturing
SIC 3519 Internal Combustion Engines, nec
SIC 3599 Industrial & Commercial Machinery & Equipment, NEC
SIC 3714 Motor Vehicle Parts & Accessories

336411 Aircraft Manufacturing
SIC 3721 Aircraft

336412 Aircraft Engine & Engine Parts Manufacturing
SIC 3724 Aircraft Engines & Engine Parts

336413 Other Aircraft Part & Auxiliary Equipment Manufacturing
SIC 3728 Aircraft Parts & Auxiliary Equipment, nec

336414 Guided Missile & Space Vehicle Manufacturing
SIC 3761 Guided Missiles & Space Vehicles

336415 Guided Missile & Space Vehicle Propulsion Unit & Propulsion Unit Parts Manufacturing
SIC 3764 Guided Missile & Space Vehicle Propulsion Units & Propulsion Unit Parts

336419 Other Guided Missile & Space Vehicle Parts & Auxiliary Equipment Manufacturing
SIC 3769 Guided Missile & Space Vehicle Parts & Auxiliary Equipment

33651 Railroad Rolling Stock Manufacturing
SIC 3531 Construction Machinery & Equipment
SIC 3743 Railroad Equipment

336611 Ship Building & Repairing
SIC 3731 Ship Building & Repairing

336612 Boat Building
SIC 3732 Boat Building & Repairing

336991 Motorcycle, Bicycle, & Parts Manufacturing
SIC 3944 Games, Toys, & Children's Vehicles, Except Dolls & Bicycles
SIC 3751 Motorcycles, Bicycles & Parts

336992 Military Armored Vehicle, Tank & Tank Component Manufacturing
SIC 3711 Motor Vehicles & Passenger Car Bodies
SIC 3795 Tanks & Tank Components

336999 All Other Transportation Equipment Manufacturing
SIC 3799 Transportation Equipment, nec

FURNITURE & RELATED PRODUCT MANUFACTURING

337121 Upholstered Household Furniture Manufacturing
SIC 2512 Wood Household Furniture, Upholstered
SIC 2515 Mattress, Foundations, & Convertible Beds
SIC 5712 Furniture

337122 Nonupholstered Wood Household Furniture Manufacturing
SIC 2511 Wood Household Furniture, Except Upholstered
SIC 5712 Furniture Stores

337124 Metal Household Furniture Manufacturing
SIC 2514 Metal Household Furniture

337125 Household Furniture Manufacturing
SIC 2519 Household Furniture, NEC

337127 Institutional Furniture Manufacturing
SIC 2531 Public Building & Related Furniture
SIC 2599 Furniture & Fixtures, nec
SIC 3952 Lead Pencils, Crayons, & Artist's Materials
SIC 3999 Manufacturing Industries, nec

337129 Wood Television, Radio, & Sewing Machine Cabinet Manufacturing
SIC 2517 Wood Television, Radio, Phonograph, & Sewing Machine Cabinets

337131 Wood Kitchen & Counter Top Manufacturing
SIC 2434 Wood Kitchen Cabinets
SIC 2541 Wood Office & Store Fixtures, Partitions, Shelving, & Lockers
SIC 5712 Furniture Stores

337132 Upholstered Wood Household Furniture Manufacturing
SIC 2515 Mattresses, Foundations, & Convertible Beds
SIC 5712 Furniture Stores

337133 Wood Household Furniture
SIC 5712 Furniture Stores

337134 Wood Office Furniture Manufacturing
SIC 2521 Wood Office Furniture

337135 Custom Architectural Woodwork, Millwork, & Fixtures
SIC 2541 Wood Office & Store Fixtures, Partitions, Shelving, and Lockers

337139 Other Wood Furniture Manufacturing
SIC 2426 Hardwood Dimension & Flooring Mills
SIC 2499 Wood Products, nec
SIC 2517 Wood Television, Radio, Phonograph, & Sewing Machine Cabinets
SIC 2531 Public Building & Related Furniture
SIC 2541 Wood Office & Store Fixtures, Partitions., Shelving, & Lockers
SIC 2599 Furniture & Fixtures, nec
SIC 3952 Lead Pencils, Crayons, & Artist's Materials

337141 Nonwood Office Furniture Manufacturing
SIC 2522 Office Furniture, Except Wood
337143 Household Furniture Manufacturing
SIC 2519 Household Furniture, NEC
337145 Nonwood Showcase, Partition, Shelving, & Locker Manufacturing
SIC 2542 Office & Store Fixtures, Partitions, Shelving, & Lockers, Except Wood
337148 Other Nonwood Furniture Manufacturing
SIC 2499 Wood Products, NEC
SIC 2531 Public Building & Related Furniture
SIC 2599 Furniture & Fixtures, nec
SIC 3499 Fabricated Metal Products, nec
SIC 3952 Lead Pencils, Crayons, & Artist's Materials
SIC 3999 Manufacturing Industries, nec
337212 Custom Architectural Woodwork & Millwork Manufacturing
SIC 2541 Wood Office & Store Fixtures, Partitions, Shelving, & Lockers
337214 Nonwood Office Furniture Manufacturing
SIC 2522 Office Furniture, Except Wood
337215 Showcase, Partition, Shelving, & Locker Manufacturing
SIC 2542 Office & Store Fixtures, Partitions, Shelving & Lockers, Except Wood
SIC 2541 Wood Office & Store Fixtures, Partitions, Shelving, & Lockers
SIC 2426 Hardwood Dimension & Flooring Mills
SIC 3499 Fabricated Metal Products, nec
33791 Mattress Manufacturing
SIC 2515 Mattresses, Foundations & Convertible Beds
33792 Blind & Shade Manufacturing
SIC 2591 Drapery Hardware & Window Blinds & Shades

MISCELLANEOUS MANUFACTURING

339111 Laboratory Apparatus & Furniture Manufacturing
SIC 3829 Measuring & Controlling Devices, nec
339112 Surgical & Medical Instrument Manufacturing
SIC 3841 Surgical & Medical Instruments & Apparatus
SIC 3829 Measuring & Controlling Devices, nec
339113 Surgical Appliance & Supplies Manufacturing
SIC 2599 Furniture & Fixtures, nec
SIC 3842 Orthopedic, Prosthetic, & Surgical Appliances & Supplies
339114 Dental Equipment & Supplies Manufacturing
SIC 3843 Dental Equipment & Supplies
339115 Ophthalmic Goods Manufacturing
SIC 3851 Opthalmic Goods
SIC 5995 Optical Goods Stores
339116 Dental Laboratories
SIC 8072 Dental Laboratories 339117 Eyeglass & Contact Lens Manufacturing
SIC 5995 Optical Goods Stores
339911 Jewelry Manufacturing
SIC 3469 Metal Stamping, nec
SIC 3479 Coating, Engraving, & Allied Services, nec
SIC 3911 Jewelry, Precious Metal
339912 Silverware & Plated Ware Manufacturing
SIC 3479 Coating, Engraving, & Allied Services, nec
SIC 3914 Silverware, Plated Ware, & Stainless Steel Ware
339913 Jewelers' Material & Lapidary Work Manufacturing
SIC 3915 Jewelers' Findings & Materials, & Lapidary Work

339914 Costume Jewelry & Novelty Manufacturing
SIC 3479 Coating, Engraving, & Allied Services, nec
SIC 3499 Fabricated Metal Products, nec
SIC 3961 Costume Jewelry & Costume Novelties, Except Precious Metal
33992 Sporting & Athletic Goods Manufacturing
SIC 3949 Sporting & Athletic Goods, nec
339931 Doll & Stuffed Toy Manufacturing
SIC 3942 Dolls & Stuffed Toys
339932 Game, Toy, & Children's Vehicle Manufacturing
SIC 3944 Games, Toys, & Children's Vehicles, Except Dolls & Bicycles
339941 Pen & Mechanical Pencil Manufacturing
SIC 3951 Pens, Mechanical Pencils, & Parts
339942 Lead Pencil & Art Good Manufacturing
SIC 2531 Public Buildings & Related Furniture
SIC 3579 Office Machines, nec
SIC 3952 Lead Pencils, Crayons, & Artists' Materials
339943 Marking Device Manufacturing
SIC 3953 Marking Devices
339944 Carbon Paper & Inked Ribbon Manufacturing
SIC 3955 Carbon Paper & Inked Ribbons
33995 Sign Manufacturing
SIC 3993 Signs & Advertising Specialties
339991 Gasket, Packing, & Sealing Device Manufacturing
SIC 3053 Gaskets, Packing, & Sealing Devices
339992 Musical Instrument Manufacturing
SIC 3931 Musical Instruments
339993 Fastener, Button, Needle & Pin Manufacturing
SIC 3965 Fasteners, Buttons, Needles, & Pins
SIC 3131 Boat & Shoe Cut Stock & Findings
339994 Broom, Brush & Mop Manufacturing
SIC 3991 Brooms & Brushes
SIC 2392 Housefurnishings, Except Curtains & Draperies
339995 Burial Casket Manufacturing
SIC 3995 Burial Caskets
339999 All Other Miscellaneous Manufacturing
SIC 2499 Wood Products, NEC
SIC 3999 Manufacturing Industries, nec

WHOLESALE TRADE

42111 Automobile & Other Motor Vehicle Wholesalers
SIC 5012 Automobiles & Other Motor Vehicles
42112 Motor Vehicle Supplies & New Part Wholesalers
SIC 5013 Motor Vehicle Supplies & New Parts
42113 Tire & Tube Wholesalers
SIC 5014 Tires & Tubes
42114 Motor Vehicle Part Wholesalers
SIC 5015 Motor Vehicle Parts, Used
42121 Furniture Wholesalers
SIC 5021 Furniture
42122 Home Furnishing Wholesalers
SIC 5023 Homefurnishings
42131 Lumber, Plywood, Millwork & Wood Panel Wholesalers
SIC 5031 Lumber, Plywood, Millwork, & Wood Panels
SIC 5211 Lumber & Other Building Materials Dealers - Retail
42132 Brick, Stone & Related Construction Material Wholesalers
SIC 5032 Brick, Stone, & Related Construction Materials
42133 Roofing, Siding & Insulation Material Wholesalers
SIC 5033 Roofing, Siding, & Insulation Materials

42139 Other Construction Material Wholesalers
SIC 5039 Construction Materials, nec
42141 Photographic Equipment & Supplies Wholesalers
SIC 5043 Photographic Equipment & Supplies
42142 Office Equipment Wholesalers
SIC 5044 Office Equipment
42143 Computer & Computer Peripheral Equipment & Software Wholesalers
SIC 5045 Computers & Computer Peripherals Equipment & Software
42144 Other Commercial Equipment Wholesalers
SIC 5046 Commercial Equipment, nec
42145 Medical, Dental & Hospital Equipment & Supplies Wholesalers
SIC 5047 Medical, Dental & Hospital Equipment & Supplies
42146 Ophthalmic Goods Wholesalers
SIC 5048 Ophthalmic Goods
42149 Other Professional Equipment & Supplies Wholesalers
SIC 5049 Professional Equipment & Supplies, nec
42151 Metal Service Centers & Offices
SIC 5051 Metals Service Centers & Offices
42152 Coal & Other Mineral & Ore Wholesalers
SIC 5052 Coal & Other Mineral & Ores
42161 Electrical Apparatus & Equipment, Wiring Supplies & Construction Material Wholesalers
SIC 5063 Electrical Apparatus & Equipment, Wiring Supplies & Construction Materials
42162 Electrical Appliance, Television & Radio Set Wholesalers
SIC 5064 Electrical Appliances, Television & Radio Sets
42169 Other Electronic Parts & Equipment Wholesalers
SIC 5065 Electronic Parts & Equipment, nec
42171 Hardware Wholesalers
SIC 5072 Hardware
42172 Plumbing & Heating Equipment & Supplies Wholesalers
SIC 5074 Plumbing & Heating Equipment & Supplies
42173 Warm Air Heating & Air-Conditioning Equipment & Supplies Wholesalers
SIC 5075 Warm Air Heating & Air-Conditioning Equipment & Supplies
42174 Refrigeration Equipment & Supplies Wholesalers
SIC 5078 Refrigeration Equipment & Supplies
42181 Construction & Mining Machinery & Equipment Wholesalers
SIC 5082 Construction & Mining Machinery & Equipment
42182 Farm & Garden Machinery & Equipment Wholesalers
SIC 5083 Farm & Garden Machinery & Equipment
42183 Industrial Machinery & Equipment Wholesalers
SIC 5084 Industrial Machinery & Equipment
SIC 5085 Industrial Supplies
42184 Industrial Supplies Wholesalers
SIC 5085 Industrial Supplies
42185 Service Establishment Equipment & Supplies Wholesalers
SIC 5087 Service Establishment Equipment & Supplies Wholesalers
42186 Transportation Equipment & Supplies Wholesalers
SIC 5088 Transportation Equipment and Supplies, Except Motor Vehicles
42191 Sporting & Recreational Goods & Supplies Wholesalers
SIC 5091 Sporting & Recreational Goods & Supplies
42192 Toy & Hobby Goods & Supplies Wholesalers
SIC 5092 Toys & Hobby Goods & Supplies

42193 Recyclable Material Wholesalers
SIC 5093 Scrap & Waste Materials
42194 Jewelry, Watch, Precious Stone & Precious Metal Wholesalers
SIC 5094 Jewelry, Watches, Precious Stones, & Precious Metals
42199 Other Miscellaneous Durable Goods Wholesalers
SIC 5099 Durable Goods, nec
SIC 7822 Motion Picture & Video Tape Distribution
42211 Printing & Writing Paper Wholesalers
SIC 5111 Printing & Writing Paper
42212 Stationary & Office Supplies Wholesalers
SIC 5112 Stationery & Office Supplies
42213 Industrial & Personal Service Paper Wholesalers
SIC 5113 Industrial & Personal Service Paper
42221 Drug, Drug Proprietaries & Druggists' Sundries Wholesalers
SIC 5122 Drugs, Drug Proprietaries, & Druggists' Sundries
42231 Piece Goods, Notions & Other Dry Goods Wholesalers
SIC 5131 Piece Goods, Notions, & Other Dry Goods
42232 Men's & Boys' Clothing & Furnishings Wholesalers
SIC 5136 Men's & Boys' Clothing & Furnishings
42233 Women's, Children's, & Infants' & Accessories Wholesalers
SIC 5137 Women's, Children's, & Infants' Clothing & Accessories
42234 Footwear Wholesalers
SIC 5139 Footwear
42241 General Line Grocery Wholesalers
SIC 5141 Groceries, General Line
42242 Packaged Frozen Food Wholesalers
SIC 5142 Packaged Frozen Foods
42243 Dairy Product Wholesalers
SIC 5143 Dairy Products, Except Dried or Canned
42244 Poultry & Poultry Product Wholesalers
SIC 5144 Poultry & Poultry Products
42245 Confectionery Wholesalers
SIC 5145 Confectionery
42246 Fish & Seafood Wholesalers
SIC 5146 Fish & Seafoods
42247 Meat & Meat Product Wholesalers
SIC 5147 Meats & Meat Products
42248 Fresh Fruit & Vegetable Wholesalers
SIC 5148 Fresh Fruits & Vegetables
42249 Other Grocery & Related Products Wholesalers
SIC 5149 Groceries & Related Products, nec
42251 Grain & Field Bean Wholesalers
SIC 5153 Grain & Field Beans
42252 Livestock Wholesalers
SIC 5154 Livestock
42259 Other Farm Product Raw Material Wholesalers
SIC 5159 Farm-Product Raw Materials, nec
42261 Plastics Materials & Basic Forms & Shapes Wholesalers
SIC 5162 Plastics Materials & Basic Forms & Shapes
42269 Other Chemical & Allied Products Wholesalers
SIC 5169 Chemicals & Allied Products, nec
42271 Petroleum Bulk Stations & Terminals
SIC 5171 Petroleum Bulk Stations & Terminals
42272 Petroleum & Petroleum Products Wholesalers
SIC 5172 Petroleum & Petroleum Products Wholesalers, Except Bulk Stations & Terminals
42281 Beer & Ale Wholesalers
SIC 5181 Beer & Ale

42282 Wine & Distilled Alcoholic Beverage Wholesalers
SIC 5182 Wine & Distilled Alcoholic Beverages
42291 Farm Supplies Wholesalers
SIC 5191 Farm Supplies
42292 Book, Periodical & Newspaper Wholesalers
SIC 5192 Books, Periodicals, & Newspapers
42293 Flower, Nursery Stock & Florists' Supplies Wholesalers
SIC 5193 Flowers, Nursery Stock, & Florists' Supplies
42294 Tobacco & Tobacco Product Wholesalers
SIC 5194 Tobacco & Tobacco Products
42295 Paint, Varnish & Supplies Wholesalers
SIC 5198 Paints, Varnishes, & Supplies
SIC 5231 Paint, Glass & Wallpaper Stores
42299 Other Miscellaneous Nondurable Goods Wholesalers
SIC 5199 Nondurable Goods, nec

RETAIL TRADE

44111 New Car Dealers
SIC 5511 Motor Vehicle Dealers, New and Used
44112 Used Car Dealers
SIC 5521 Motor Vehicle Dealers, Used Only
44121 Recreational Vehicle Dealers
SIC 5561 Recreational Vehicle Dealers
441221 Motorcycle Dealers
SIC 5571 Motorcycle Dealers
441222 Boat Dealers
SIC 5551 Boat Dealers
441229 All Other Motor Vehicle Dealers
SIC 5599 Automotive Dealers, NEC
44131 Automotive Parts & Accessories Stores
SIC 5013 Motor Vehicle Supplies & New Parts
SIC 5731 Radio, Television, & Consumer Electronics Stores
SIC 5531 Auto & Home Supply Stores
44132 Tire Dealers
SIC 5014 Tires & Tubes
SIC 5531 Auto & Home Supply Stores
44211 Furniture Stores
SIC 5021 Furniture
SIC 5712 Furniture Stores
44221 Floor Covering Stores
SIC 5023 Homefurnishings
SIC 5713 Floor Coverings Stores
442291 Window Treatment Stores
SIC 5714 Drapery, Curtain, & Upholstery Stores
SIC 5719 Miscellaneous Homefurnishings Stores
442299 All Other Home Furnishings Stores
SIC 5719 Miscellaneous Homefurnishings Stores
443111 Household Appliance Stores
SIC 5722 Household Appliance Stores
SIC 5999 Miscellaneous Retail Stores, nec
SIC 7623 Refrigeration & Air-Conditioning Service & Repair Shops
SIC 7629 Electrical & Electronic Repair Shops, nec
443112 Radio, Television & Other Electronics Stores
SIC 5731 Radio, Television, & Consumer Electronics Stores
SIC 5999 Miscellaneous Retail Stores, nec
SIC 7622 Radio & Television Repair Shops
44312 Computer & Software Stores
SIC 5045 Computers & Computer Peripheral Equipment & Software
SIC 7378 Computer Maintenance & Repair '
SIC 5734 Computer & Computer Software Stores

44313 Camera & Photographic Supplies Stores
SIC 5946 Camera & Photographic Supply Stores
44411 Home Centers
SIC 5211 Lumber & Other Building Materials Dealers
44412 Paint & Wallpaper Stores
SIC 5198 Paints, Varnishes, & Supplies
SIC 5231 Paint, Glass, & Wallpaper Stores
44413 Hardware Stores
SIC 5251 Hardware Stores
44419 Other Building Material Dealers
SIC 5031 Lumber, Plywood, Millwork, & Wood Panels
SIC 5032 Brick, Stone, & Related Construction Materials
SIC 5039 Construction Materials, nec
SIC 5063 Electrical Apparatus & Equipment, Wiring Supplies, & Construction Materials
SIC 5074 Plumbing & Heating Equipment & Supplies
SIC 5211 Lumber & Other Building Materials Dealers
SIC 5231 Paint, Glass, & Wallpaper Stores
44421 Outdoor Power Equipment Stores
SIC 5083 Farm & Garden Machinery & Equipment
SIC 5261 Retail Nurseries, Lawn & Garden Supply Stores
44422 Nursery & Garden Centers
SIC 5191 Farm Supplies
SIC 5193 Flowers, Nursery Stock, & Florists' Supplies
SIC 5261 Retail Nurseries, Lawn & Garden Supply Stores
44511 Supermarkets & Other Grocery Stores
SIC 5411 Grocery Stores
44512 Convenience Stores
SIC 5411 Grocery Stores
44521 Meat Markets
SIC 5421 Meat & Fish Markets, Including Freezer Provisioners
SIC 5499 Miscellaneous Food Stores
44522 Fish & Seafood Markets
SIC 5421 Meat & Fish Markets, Including Freezer Provisioners
44523 Fruit & Vegetable Markets
SIC 5431 Fruit & Vegetable Markets
445291 Baked Goods Stores
SIC 5461 Retail Bakeries
445292 Confectionery & Nut Stores
SIC 5441 Candy, Nut & Confectionery Stores
445299 All Other Specialty Food Stores
SIC 5499 Miscellaneous Food Stores
SIC 5451 Dairy Products Stores
44531 Beer, Wine & Liquor Stores
SIC 5921 Liquor Stores
44611 Pharmacies & Drug Stores
SIC 5912 Drug Stores & Proprietary Stores
44612 Cosmetics, Beauty Supplies & Perfume Stores
SIC 5087 Service Establishment Equipment & Supplies
SIC 5999 Miscellaneous Retail Stores, nec
44613 Optical Goods Stores
SIC 5995 Optical Goods Stores
446191 Food Supplement Stores
SIC 5499 Miscellaneous Food Stores
446199 All Other Health & Personal Care Stores
SIC 5047 Medical, Dental, & Hospital Equipment & Supplies
SIC 5999 Miscellaneous Retail Stores, nec
44711 Gasoline Stations with Convenience Stores
SIC 5541 Gasoline Service Station
SIC 5411 Grocery Stores
44719 Other Gasoline Stations
SIC 5541 Gasoline Service Station

44811 Men's Clothing Stores
SIC 5611 Men's & Boys' Clothing & Accessory Stores
44812 Women's Clothing Stores
SIC 5621 Women's Clothing Stores
44813 Children's & Infants' Clothing Stores
SIC 5641 Children's & Infants' Wear Stores
44814 Family Clothing Stores
SIC 5651 Family Clothing Stores
44815 Clothing Accessories Stores
SIC 5611 Men's & Boys' Clothing & Accessory Stores
SIC 5632 Women's Accessory & Specialty Stores
SIC 5699 Miscellaneous Apparel & Accessory Stores
44819 Other Clothing Stores
SIC 5699 Miscellaneous Apparel & Accessory Stores
SIC 5632 Women's Accessory & Specialty Stores
44821 Shoe Stores
SIC 5661 Shoe Stores
44831 Jewelry Stores
SIC 5999 Miscellaneous Retailer, nec
SIC 5944 Jewelry Stores
44832 Luggage & Leather Goods Stores
SIC 5948 Luggage & Leather Goods Stores
45111 Sporting Goods Stores
SIC 7699 Repair Shops & Related Services, NEC
SIC 5941 Sporting Goods Stores & Bicycle Shops
45112 Hobby, Toy & Game Stores
SIC 5945 Hobby, Toy, & Game Stores
45113 Sewing, Needlework & Piece Goods Stores
SIC 5714 Drapery, Curtain, & Upholstery Stores
SIC 5949 Sewing, Needlework, & Piece Goods Stores
45114 Musical Instrument & Supplies Stores
SIC 5736 Musical Instruments Stores
451211 Book Stores
SIC 5942 Book Stores
451212 News Dealers & Newsstands
SIC 5994 News Dealers & Newsstands
45122 Prerecorded Tape, Compact Disc & Record Stores
SIC 5735 Record & Prerecorded Tape Stores
45211 Department Stores
SIC 5311 Department Stores
45291 Warehouse Clubs & Superstores
SIC 5399 Miscellaneous General Merchandise Stores
SIC 5411 Grocery Stores
45299 All Other General Merchandise Stores
SIC 5399 Miscellaneous General Merchandise Stores
SIC 5331 Variety Stores
45311 Florists
SIC 5992 Florists
45321 Office Supplies & Stationery Stores
SIC 5049 Professional Equipment & Supplies, nec
SIC 5112 Stationery & Office Supplies
SIC 5943 Stationery Stores
45322 Gift, Novelty & Souvenir Stores
SIC 5947 Gift, Novelty, & Souvenir Shops
45331 Used Merchandise Stores
SIC 5932 Used Merchandise Stores
45391 Pet & Pet Supplies Stores
SIC 5999 Miscellaneous Retail Stores, NEC
45392 Art Dealers
SIC 5999 Miscellaneous Retail Stores, nec
45393 Manufactured Home Dealers
SIC 5271 Mobile Home Dealers

453991 Tobacco Stores
SIC 5993 Tobacco Stores & Stands
453999 All Other Miscellaneous Store Retailers
SIC 5999 Miscellaneous Retail Stores, nec
SIC 5261 Retail Nurseries, Lawn & Garden Supply Stores
45411 Electronic Shopping & Mail-Order Houses
SIC 5961 Catalog & Mail-Order Houses
45421 Vending Machine Operators
SIC 5962 Automatic Merchandise Machine Operators
454311 Heating Oil Dealers
SIC 5171 Petroleum Bulk Stations & Terminals
SIC 5983 Fuel Oil Dealers
454312 Liquefied Petroleum Gas Dealers
SIC 5171 Petroleum Bulk Stations & Terminals
SIC 5984 Liquefied Petroleum Gas Dealers
454319 Other Fuel Dealers
SIC 5989 Fuel Dealers, nec
45439 Other Direct Selling Establishments
SIC 5421 Meat & Fish Markets, Including Freezer Provisioners
SIC 5963 Direct Selling Establishments

TRANSPORTATION & WAREHOUSING

481111 Scheduled Passenger Air Transportation
SIC 4512 Air Transportation, Scheduled
481112 Scheduled Freight Air Transportation
SIC 4512 Air Transportation, Scheduled
481211 Nonscheduled Chartered Passenger Air Transportation
SIC 4522 Air Transportation, Nonscheduled
481212 Nonscheduled Chartered Freight Air Transportation
SIC 4522 Air Transportation, Nonscheduled
481219 Other Nonscheduled Air Transportation
SIC 7319 Advertising, nec
48122 Nonscheduled Speciality Air Transportation
SIC 0721 Crop Planting, Cultivating, & Protecting
SIC 1382 Oil & Gas Field Exploration Services
SIC 4522 Air Transportation, Nonscheduled
SIC 7335 Commercial Photography
SIC 7997 Membership Sports & Recreation Clubs
SIC 8299 Schools & Educational Services, nec
SIC 8713 Surveying Services
482111 Line-Haul Railroads
SIC 4011 Railroads, Line-Haul Operating
482112 Short Line Railroads
SIC 4013 Railroad Switching & Terminal Establishments
483111 Deep Sea Freight Transportation
SIC 4412 Deep Sea Foreign Transportation of Freight
483112 Deep Sea Passenger Transportation
SIC 4481 Deep Sea Transportation of Passengers, Except by Ferry
483113 Coastal & Great Lakes Freight Transportation
SIC 4424 Deep Sea Domestic Transportation of Freight
SIC 4432 Freight Transportation on the Great Lakes - St. Lawrence Seaway
SIC 4492 Towing & Tugboat Services
483114 Coastal & Great Lakes Passenger Transportation
SIC 4481 Deep Sea Transportation of Passengers, Except by Ferry
SIC 4482 Ferries
483211 Inland Water Freight Transportation
SIC 4449 Water Transportation of Freight, nec
SIC 4492 Towing & Tugboat Services

483212 Inland Water Passenger Transportation
SIC 4482 Ferries
SIC 4489 Water Transportation of Passengers, nec
48411　General Freight Trucking, Local
SIC 4212 Local Trucking without Storage
SIC 4214 Local Trucking with Storage
484121 General Freight Trucking, Long-Distance, Truckload
SIC 4213 Trucking, Except Local
484122 General Freight Trucking, Long-Distance, Less Than Truckload
SIC 4213 Trucking, Except Local
48421　Used Household & Office Goods Moving
SIC 4212 Local Trucking Without Storage
SIC 4213 Trucking, Except Local
SIC 4214 Local Trucking With Storage
48422　Specialized Freight Trucking, Local
SIC 4212 Local Trucking without Storage
SIC 4214 Local Trucking with Storage
48423　Specialized Freight Trucking, Long-Distance
SIC 4213 Trucking, Except Local
485111 Mixed Mode Transit Systems
SIC 4111 Local & Suburban Transit
485112 Commuter Rail Systems
SIC 4111 Local & Suburban Transit
485113 Bus & Motor Vehicle Transit Systems
SIC 4111 Local & Suburban Transit
485119 Other Urban Transit Systems
SIC 4111 Local & Suburban Transit
48521　Interurban & Rural Bus Transportation
SIC 4131 Intercity & Rural Bus Transportation
48531　Taxi Service
SIC 4121 Taxicabs
48532　Limousine Service
SIC 4119 Local Passenger Transportation, nec
48541　School & Employee Bus Transportation
SIC 4151 School Buses
SIC 4119 Local Passenger Transportation, nec
48551　Charter Bus Industry
SIC 4141 Local Charter Bus Service
SIC 4142 Bus Charter Services, Except Local
485991 Special Needs Transportation
SIC 4119 Local Passenger Transportation, nec
485999 All Other Transit & Ground Passenger Transportation
SIC 4111 Local & Suburban Transit
SIC 4119 Local Passenger Transportation, nec
48611　Pipeline Transportation of Crude Oil
SIC 4612 Crude Petroleum Pipelines
48621　Pipeline Transportation of Natural Gas
SIC 4922 Natural Gas Transmission
SIC 4923 Natural Gas Transmission & Distribution
48691　Pipeline Transportation of Refined Petroleum Products
SIC 4613 Refined Petroleum Pipelines
48699　All Other Pipeline Transportation
SIC 4619 Pipelines, nec
48711　Scenic & Sightseeing Transportation, Land
SIC 4119 Local Passenger Transportation, nec
SIC 4789 Transportation Services, nec
SIC 7999 Amusement & Recreation Services, nec
48721　Scenic & Sightseeing Transportation, Water
SIC 4489 Water Transportation of Passengers, nec
SIC 7999 Amusement & Recreation Services, nec
48799　Scenic & Sightseeing Transportation, Other
SIC 4522 Air Transportation, Nonscheduled
SIC 7999 Amusement & Recreation Services, nec

488111 Air Traffic Control
SIC 4581 Airports, Flying Fields, & Airport Terminal Services
SIC 9621 Regulation & Administration of Transportation Programs
488112 Airport Operations, except Air Traffic Control
SIC 4581 Airports, Flying Fields, & Airport Terminal Services
SIC 4959 Sanitary Services, nec
488119 Other Airport Operations
SIC 4581 Airports, Flying Fields, & Airport Terminal Services
SIC 4959 Sanitary Services, nec
48819　Other Support Activities for Air Transportation
SIC 4581 Airports, Flying Fields, & Airport Terminal Services
48821　Support Activities for Rail Transportation
SIC 4013 Railroad Switching & Terminal Establishments
SIC 4741 Rental of Railroad Cars
SIC 4789 Transportation Services, nec
48831　Port & Harbor Operations
SIC 4491 Marine Cargo Handling
SIC 4499 Water Transportation Services, nec
48832　Marine Cargo Handling
SIC 4491 Marine Cargo Handling
48833　Navigational Services to Shipping
SIC 4492 Towing & Tugboat Services
SIC 4499 Water Transportation Services, nec
48839　Other Support Activities for Water Transportation
SIC 4499 Water Transportation Services, nec
SIC 4785 Fixed Facilities & Inspection & Weighing Services for Motor Vehicle Transportation
SIC 7699 Repair Shops & Related Services, nec
48841　Motor Vehicle Towing
SIC 7549 Automotive Services, Except Repair & Carwashes
48849　Other Support Activities for Road Transportation
SIC 4173 Terminal & Service Facilities for Motor Vehicle Passenger Transportation
SIC 4231 Terminal & Joint Terminal Maintenance Facilities for Motor Freight Transportation
SIC 4785 Fixed Facilities & Inspection & Weighing Services for Motor Vehicle Transportation
48851　Freight Transportation Arrangement
SIC 4731 Arrangement of Transportation of Freight & Cargo
488991 Packing & Crating
SIC 4783 Packing & Crating
488999 All Other Support Activities for Transportation
SIC 4729 Arrangement of Passenger Transportation, nec
SIC 4789 Transportation Services, nec
49111　Postal Service
SIC 4311 United States Postal Service
49211　Couriers
SIC 4215 Courier Services, Except by Air
SIC 4513 Air Courier Services
49221　Local Messengers & Local Delivery
SIC 4215 Courier Services, Except by Air
49311　General Warehousing & Storage Facilities
SIC 4225 General Warehousing & Storage
SIC 4226 Special Warehousing & Storage, nec
49312　Refrigerated Storage Facilities
SIC 4222 Refrigerated Warehousing & Storage
SIC 4226 Special Warehousing & Storage, nec
49313　Farm Product Storage Facilities
SIC 4221 Farm Product Warehousing & Storage
49319　Other Warehousing & Storage Facilities
SIC 4226 Special Warehousing & Storage, nec

INFORMATION

51111 Newspaper Publishers
SIC 2711 Newspapers: Publishing or Publishing & Printing
51112 Periodical Publishers
SIC 2721 Periodicals: Publishing or Publishing & Printing
51113 Book Publishers
SIC 2731 Books: Publishing or Publishing & Printing
51114 Database & Directory Publishers
SIC 2741 Miscellaneous Publishing
511191 Greeting Card Publishers
SIC 2771 Greeting Cards
511199 All Other Publishers
SIC 2741 Miscellaneous Publishing
51121 Software Publishers
SIC 7372 Prepackaged Software
51211 Motion Picture & Video Production
SIC 7812 Motion Picture & Video Tape Production
51212 Motion Picture & Video Distribution
SIC 7822 Motion Picture & Video Tape Distribution
SIC 7829 Services Allied to Motion Picture Distribution
512131 Motion Picture Theaters, Except Drive-Ins.
SIC 7832 Motion Picture Theaters, Except Drive-In
512132 Drive-In Motion Picture Theaters
SIC 7833 Drive-In Motion Picture Theaters
512191 Teleproduction & Other Post-Production Services
SIC 7819 Services Allied to Motion Picture Production
512199 Other Motion Picture & Video Industries
SIC 7819 Services Allied to Motion Picture Production
SIC 7829 Services Allied to Motion Picture Distribution
51221 Record Production
SIC 8999 Services, nec
51222 Integrated Record Production/Distribution
SIC 3652 Phonograph Records & Prerecorded Audio Tapes & Disks
51223 Music Publishers
SIC 2731 Books: Publishing or Publishing & Printing
SIC 2741 Miscellaneous Publishing
SIC 8999 Services, nec
51224 Sound Recording Studios
SIC 7389 Business Services, nec
51229 Other Sound Recording Industries
SIC 7389 Business Services, nec
SIC 7922 Theatrical Producers & Miscellaneous Theatrical Services
513111 Radio Networks
SIC 4832 Radio Broadcasting Stations
513112 Radio Stations
SIC 4832 Radio Broadcasting Stations
51312 Television Broadcasting
SIC 4833 Television Broadcasting Stations
51321 Cable Networks
SIC 4841 Cable & Other Pay Television Services
51322 Cable & Other Program Distribution
SIC 4841 Cable & Other Pay Television Services
51331 Wired Telecommunications Carriers
SIC 4813 Telephone Communications, Except Radiotelephone
SIC 4822 Telegraph & Other Message Communications
513321 Paging
SIC 4812 Radiotelephone Communications
513322 Cellular & Other Wireless Telecommunications
SIC 4812 Radiotelephone Communications
SIC 4899 Communications Services, nec

51333 Telecommunications Resellers
SIC 4812 Radio Communications
SIC 4813 Telephone Communications, Except Radiotelephone
51334 Satellite Telecommunications
SIC 4899 Communications Services, NEC
51339 Other Telecommunications
SIC 4899 Communications Services, NEC
51411 News Syndicates
SIC 7383 News Syndicates
51412 Libraries & Archives
SIC 8231 Libraries
514191 On-Line Information Services
SIC 7375 Information Retrieval Services
514199 All Other Information Services
SIC 8999 Services, nec
51421 Data Processing Services
SIC 7374 Computer Processing & Data Preparation & Processing Services

FINANCE & INSURANCE

52111 Monetary Authorities - Central Bank
SIC 6011 Federal Reserve Banks
52211 Commercial Banking
SIC 6021 National Commercial Banks
SIC 6022 State Commercial Banks
SIC 6029 Commercial Banks, nec
SIC 6081 Branches & Agencies of Foreign Banks
52212 Savings Institutions
SIC 6035 Savings Institutions, Federally Chartered
SIC 6036 Savings Institutions, Not Federally Chartered
52213 Credit Unions
SIC 6061 Credit Unions, Federally Chartered
SIC 6062 Credit Unions, Not Federally Chartered
52219 Other Depository Credit Intermediation
SIC 6022 State Commercial Banks
52221 Credit Card Issuing
SIC 6021 National Commercial Banks
SIC 6022 State Commercial Banks
SIC 6141 Personal Credit Institutions
52222 Sales Financing
SIC 6141 Personal Credit Institutions
SIC 6153 Short-Term Business Credit Institutions, Except Agricultural .
SIC 6159 Miscellaneous Business Credit Institutions
522291 Consumer Lending
SIC 6141 Personal Credit Institutions
522292 Real Estate Credit
SIC 6162 Mortgage Bankers & Loan Correspondents
522293 International Trade Financing
SIC 6081 Branches & Agencies of Foreign Banks
SIC 6082 Foreign Trade & International Banking Institutions
SIC 6111 Federal & Federally-Sponsored Credit Agencies
SIC 6159 Miscellaneous Business Credit Institutions
522294 Secondary Market Financing
SIC 6111 Federal & Federally Sponsored Credit Agencies
522298 All Other Nondepository Credit Intermediation
SIC 5932 Used Merchandise Stores
SIC 6081 Branches & Agencies of Foreign Banks
SIC 6111 Federal & Federally-Sponsored Credit Agencies
SIC 6153 Short-Term Business Credit Institutions, Except Agricultural
SIC 6159 Miscellaneous Business Credit Institutions

52231 Mortgage & Other Loan Brokers
SIC 6163 Loan Brokers
52232 Financial Transactions Processing, Reserve, & Clearing House Activities
SIC 6019 Central Reserve Depository Institutions, nec
SIC 6099 Functions Related to Depository Banking, nec
SIC 6153 Short-Term Business Credit Institutions, Except Agricultural
SIC 7389 Business Services, nec
52239 Other Activities Related to Credit Intermediation
SIC 6099 Functions Related to Depository Banking, nec
SIC 6162 Mortgage Bankers & Loan Correspondents
52311 Investment Banking & Securities Dealing
SIC 6211 Security Brokers, Dealers, & Flotation Companies
52312 Securities Brokerage
SIC 6211 Security Brokers, Dealers, & Flotation Companies
52313 Commodity Contracts Dealing
SIC 6099 Functions Related to depository Banking, nec
SIC 6799 Investors, nec
SIC 6221 Commodity Contracts Brokers & Dealers
52314 Commodity Brokerage
SIC 6221 Commodity Contracts Brokers & Dealers
52321 Securities & Commodity Exchanges
SIC 6231 Security & Commodity Exchanges
52391 Miscellaneous Intermediation
SIC 6211 Securities Brokers, Dealers & Flotation Companies
SIC 6799 Investors, nec
52392 Portfolio Management
SIC 6282 Investment Advice
SIC 6371 Pension, Health, & Welfare Funds
SIC 6733 Trust, Except Educational, Religious, & Charitable
SIC 6799 Investors, nec
52393 Investment Advice
SIC 6282 Investment Advice
523991 Trust, Fiduciary & Custody Activities
SIC 6021 National Commercial Banks
SIC 6022 State Commercial Banks
SIC 6091 Nondepository Trust Facilities
SIC 6099 Functions Related to Depository Banking, nec
SIC 6289 Services Allied With the Exchange of Securities or Commodities, nec
SIC 6733 Trusts, Except Educational, Religious, & Charitable
523999 Miscellaneous Financial Investment Activities
SIC 6099 Functions Related to Depository Banking, nec
SIC 6211 Security Brokers, Dealers, & Flotation Companies
SIC 6289 Services Allied With the Exchange of Securities or Commodities, nec
SIC 6799 Investors, nec
SIC 6792 Oil Royalty Traders
524113 Direct Life Insurance Carriers
SIC 6311 Life Insurance
524114 Direct Health & Medical Insurance Carriers
SIC 6324 Hospital & Medical Service Plans
SIC 6321 Accident & Health Insurance
524126 Direct Property & Casualty Insurance Carriers
SIC 6331 Fire, Marine, & Casualty Insurance
SIC 6351 Surety Insurance
524127 Direct Title Insurance Carriers
SIC 6361 Title Insurance
524128 Other Direct Insurance Carriers
SIC 6399 Insurance Carriers, nec
52413 Reinsurance Carriers
SIC 6311 Life Insurance
SIC 6321 Accident & Health Insurance

SIC 6324 Hospital & Medical Service Plans
SIC 6331 Fire, Marine, & Casualty Insurance
SIC 6351 Surety Insurance
SIC 6361 Title Insurance
52421 Insurance Agencies & Brokerages
SIC 6411 Insurance Agents, Brokers & Service
524291 Claims Adjusters
SIC 6411 Insurance Agents, Brokers & Service
524292 Third Party Administration for Insurance & Pension Funds
SIC 6371 Pension, Health, & Welfare Funds
SIC 6411 Insurance Agents, Brokers & Service
524298 All Other Insurance Related Activities
SIC 6411 Insurance Agents, Brokers & Service
52511 Pension Funds
SIC 6371 Pension, Health, & Welfare Funds
52512 Health & Welfare Funds
SIC 6371 Pension, Health, & Welfare Funds
52519 Other Insurance Funds
SIC 6321 Accident & Health Insurance
SIC 6324 Hospital & Medical Service Plans
SIC 6331 Fire, Marine, & Casualty Insurance
SIC 6733 Trusts, Except Educational, Religious, & Charitable
52591 Open-End Investment Funds
SIC 6722 Management Investment Offices, Open-End
52592 Trusts, Estates, & Agency Accounts
SIC 6733 Trusts, Except Educational, Religious, & Charitable
52593 Real Estate Investment Trusts
SIC 6798 Real Estate Investment Trusts
52599 Other Financial Vehicles
SIC 6726 Unit Investment Trusts, Face-Amount Certificate Offices, & Closed-End Management Investment Offices

REAL ESTATE & RENTAL & LEASING

53111 Lessors of Residential Buildings & Dwellings
SIC 6513 Operators of Apartment Buildings
SIC 6514 Operators of Dwellings Other Than Apartment Buildings
53112 Lessors of Nonresidential Buildings
SIC 6512 Operators of Nonresidential Buildings
53113 Lessors of Miniwarehouses & Self Storage Units
SIC 4225 General Warehousing & Storage
53119 Lessors of Other Real Estate Property
SIC 6515 Operators of Residential Mobile Home Sites
SIC 6517 Lessors of Railroad Property
SIC 6519 Lessors of Real Property, nec
53121 Offices of Real Estate Agents & Brokers
SIC 6531 Real Estate Agents Managers
531311 Residential Property Managers
SIC 6531 Real Estate Agents & Managers
531312 Nonresidential Property Managers
SIC 6531 Real Estate Agents & Managers
53132 Offices of Real Estate Appraisers
SIC 6531 Real Estate Agents & Managers
531399 All Other Activities Related to Real Estate
SIC 6531 Real Estate Agents & Managers
532111 Passenger Car Rental
SIC 7514 Passenger Car Rental
532112 Passenger Car Leasing
SIC 7515 Passenger Car Leasing

53212 Truck, Utility Trailer, & RV Rental & Leasing
SIC 7513 Truck Rental & Leasing Without Drivers
SIC 7519 Utility Trailers & Recreational Vehicle Rental

53221 Consumer Electronics & Appliances Rental
SIC 7359 Equipment Rental & Leasing, nec

53222 Formal Wear & Costume Rental
SIC 7299 Miscellaneous Personal Services, nec
SIC 7819 Services Allied to Motion Picture Production

53223 Video Tape & Disc Rental
SIC 7841 Video Tape Rental

532291 Home Health Equipment Rental
SIC 7352 Medical Equipment Rental & Leasing

532292 Recreational Goods Rental
SIC 7999 Amusement & Recreation Services, nec

532299 All Other Consumer Goods Rental
SIC 7359 Equipment Rental & Leasing, nec

53231 General Rental Centers
SIC 7359 Equipment Rental & Leasing, nec

532411 Commercial Air, Rail, & Water Transportation Equipment Rental & Leasing
SIC 4499 Water Transportation Services, nec
SIC 4741 Rental of Railroad Cars
SIC 7359 Equipment Rental & Leasing, nec

532412 Construction, Mining & Forestry Machinery & Equipment Rental & Leasing
SIC 7353 Heavy Construction Equipment Rental & Leasing
SIC 7359 Equipment Rental & Leasing, nec

53242 Office Machinery & Equipment Rental & Leasing
SIC 7359 Equipment Rental & Leasing
SIC 7377 Computer Rental & Leasing

53249 Other Commercial & Industrial Machinery & Equipment Rental & Leasing
SIC 7352 Medical Equipment Rental & Leasing
SIC 7359 Equipment Rental & Leasing, nec
SIC 7819 Services Allied to Motion Picture Production
SIC 7922 Theatrical Producers & Miscellaneous Theatrical Services

53311 Owners & Lessors of Other Nonfinancial Assets
SIC 6792 Oil Royalty Traders
SIC 6794 Patent Owners & Lessors

PROFESSIONAL, SCIENTIFIC, & TECHNICAL SERVICES

54111 Offices of Lawyers
SIC 8111 Legal Services

541191 Title Abstract & Settlement Offices
SIC 6541 Title Abstract Offices

541199 All Other Legal Services
SIC 7389 Business Services, nec

541211 Offices of Certified Public Accountants
SIC 8721 Accounting, Auditing, & Bookkeeping Services

541213 Tax Preparation Services
SIC 7291 Tax Return Preparation Services

541214 Payroll Services
SIC 7819 Services Allied to Motion Picture Production
SIC 8721 Accounting, Auditing, & Bookkeeping Services

541219 Other Accounting Services
SIC 8721 Accounting, Auditing, & Bookkeeping Services

54131 Architectural Services
SIC 8712 Architectural Services

54132 Landscape Architectural Services
SIC 0781 Landscape Counseling & Planning

54133 Engineering Services
SIC 8711 Engineering Services

54134 Drafting Services
SIC 7389 Business Services, nec

54135 Building Inspection Services
SIC 7389 Business Services, nec

54136 Geophysical Surveying & Mapping Services
SIC 8713 Surveying Services
SIC 1081 Metal Mining Services
SIC 1382 Oil & Gas Field Exploration Services
SIC 1481 Nonmetallic Minerals Services, Except Fuels

54137 Surveying & Mapping Services
SIC 7389 Business Services, nec
SIC 8713 Surveying Services

54138 Testing Laboratories
SIC 8734 Testing Laboratories

54141 Interior Design Services
SIC 7389 Business Services, nec

54142 Industrial Design Services
SIC 7389 Business Services, nec

54143 Commercial Art & Graphic Design Services
SIC 7336 Commercial Art & Graphic Design
SIC 8099 Health & Allied Services, nec

54149 Other Specialized Design Services
SIC 7389 Business Services, nec

541511 Custom Computer Programming Services
SIC 7371 Computer Programming Services

541512 Computer Systems Design Services
SIC 7373 Computer Integrated Systems Design
SIC 7379 Computer Related Services, nec

541513 Computer Facilities Management Services
SIC 7376 Computer Facilities Management Services

541519 Other Computer Related Services
SIC 7379 Computer Related Services, nec

541611 Administrative Management & General Management Consulting Services
SIC 8742 Management Consulting Services

541612 Human Resources & Executive Search Consulting Services
SIC 8742 Management Consulting Services
SIC 7361 Employment Agencies
SIC 8999 Services, nec

541613 Marketing Consulting Services
SIC 8742 Management Consulting Services

541614 Process, Physical, Distribution & Logistics Consulting Services
SIC 8742 Management Consulting Services

541618 Other Management Consulting Services
SIC 4731 Arrangement of Transportation of Freight & Cargo
SIC 8748 Business Consulting Services, nec

54162 Environmental Consulting Services
SIC 8999 Services, nec

54169 Other Scientific & Technical Consulting Services
SIC 0781 Landscape Counseling & Planning
SIC 8748 Business Consulting Services, nec
SIC 8999 Services, nec

54171 Research & Development in the Physical Sciences & Engineering Sciences
SIC 8731 Commercial Physical & Biological Research
SIC 8733 Noncommercial Research Organizations

54172 Research & Development in the Life Sciences
SIC 8731 Commercial Physical & Biological Research
SIC 8733 Noncommercial Research Organizations
54173 Research & Development in the Social Sciences & Humanities
SIC 8732 Commercial Economic, Sociological, & Educational Research
SIC 8733 Noncommercial Research Organizations
54181 Advertising Agencies
SIC 7311 Advertising Agencies
54182 Public Relations Agencies
SIC 8743 Public Relations Services
54183 Media Buying Agencies
SIC 7319 Advertising, nec
54184 Media Representatives
SIC 7313 Radio, Television, & Publishers' Advertising Representatives
54185 Display Advertising
SIC 7312 Outdoor Advertising Services
SIC 7319 Advertising, nec
54186 Direct Mail Advertising
SIC 7331 Direct Mail Advertising Services
54187 Advertising Material Distribution Services
SIC 7319 Advertising, NEC
54189 Other Services Related to Advertising
SIC 7319 Advertising, nec
SIC 5199 Nondurable Goods, nec
SIC 7389 Business Services, nec
54191 Marketing Research & Public Opinion Polling
SIC 8732 Commercial Economic, Sociological, & Educational Research
541921 Photography Studios, Portrait
SIC 7221 Photographic Studios, Portrait
541922 Commercial Photography
SIC 7335 Commercial Photography
SIC 8099 Health & Allied Services, nec
54193 Translation & Interpretation Services
SIC 7389 Business Services, NEC
54194 Veterinary Services
SIC 0741 Veterinary Services for Livestock
SIC 0742 Veterinary Services for Animal Specialties
SIC 8734 Testing Laboratories
54199 All Other Professional, Scientific & Technical Services
SIC 7389 Business Services

MANAGEMENT OF COMPANIES & ENTERPRISES

551111 Offices of Bank Holding Companies
SIC 6712 Offices of Bank Holding Companies
551112 Offices of Other Holding Companies
SIC 6719 Offices of Holding Companies, nec
551114 Corporate, Subsidiary, & Regional Managing Offices
No SIC equivalent

ADMINISTRATIVE & SUPPORT, WASTE MANAGEMENT & REMEDIATION SERVICES

56111 Office Administrative Services
SIC 8741 Management Services

56121 Facilities Support Services
SIC 8744 Facilities Support Management Services
56131 Employment Placement Agencies
SIC 7361 Employment Agencies
SIC 7819 Services Allied to Motion Pictures Production
SIC 7922 Theatrical Producers & Miscellaneous Theatrical Services
56132 Temporary Help Services
SIC 7363 Help Supply Services
56133 Employee Leasing Services
SIC 7363 Help Supply Services
56141 Document Preparation Services
SIC 7338 Secretarial & Court Reporting
561421 Telephone Answering Services
SIC 7389 Business Services, nec
561422 Telemarketing Bureaus
SIC 7389 Business Services, nec
561431 Photocopying & Duplicating Services
SIC 7334 Photocopying & Duplicating Services
561432 Private Mail Centers
SIC 7389 Business Services, nec
561439 Other Business Service Centers
SIC 7334 Photocopying & Duplicating Services
SIC 7389 Business Services, nec
56144 Collection Agencies
SIC 7322 Adjustment & Collection Services
56145 Credit Bureaus
SIC 7323 Credit Reporting Services
561491 Repossession Services
SIC 7322 Adjustment & Collection
SIC 7389 Business Services, nec
561492 Court Reporting & Stenotype Services
SIC 7338 Secretarial & Court Reporting
561499 All Other Business Support Services
SIC 7389 Business Services, NEC
56151 Travel Agencies
SIC 4724 Travel Agencies
56152 Tour Operators
SIC 4725 Tour Operators
561591 Convention & Visitors Bureaus
SIC 7389 Business Services, nec
561599 All Other Travel Arrangement & Reservation Services
SIC 4729 Arrangement of Passenger Transportation, nec
SIC 7389 Business Services, nec
SIC 7999 Amusement & Recreation Services, nec
SIC 8699 Membership Organizations, nec
561611 Investigation Services
SIC 7381 Detective, Guard, & Armored Car Services
561612 Security Guards & Patrol Services
SIC 7381 Detective, Guard, & Armored Car Services
561613 Armored Car Services
SIC 7381 Detective, Guard, & Armored Car Services
561621 Security Systems Services
SIC 7382 Security Systems Services
SIC 1731 Electrical Work
561622 Locksmiths
SIC 7699 Repair Shops & Related Services, nec
56171 Exterminating & Pest Control Services
SIC 4959 Sanitary Services, NEC
SIC 7342 Disinfecting & Pest Control Services
56172 Janitorial Services
SIC 7342 Disinfecting & Pest Control Services
SIC 7349 Building Cleaning & Maintenance Services, nec
SIC 4581 Airports, Flying Fields, & Airport Terminal Services

56173 Landscaping Services
SIC 0782 Lawn & Garden Services
SIC 0783 Ornamental Shrub & Tree Services
56174 Carpet & Upholstery Cleaning Services
SIC 7217 Carpet & Upholstery Cleaning
56179 Other Services to Buildings & Dwellings
SIC 7389 Business Services, nec
SIC 7699 Repair Shops & Related Services, nec
56191 Packaging & Labeling Services
SIC 7389 Business Services, nec
56192 Convention & Trade Show Organizers
SIC 7389 Business Services, NEC
56199 All Other Support Services
SIC 7389 Business Services, nec
562111 Solid Waste Collection
SIC 4212 Local Trucking Without Storage
SIC 4953 Refuse Systems
562112 Hazardous Waste Collection
SIC 4212 Local Trucking Without Storage
SIC 4953 Refuse Systems
562119 Other Waste Collection
SIC 4212 Local Trucking Without Storage
SIC 4953 Refuse Systems
562211 Hazardous Waste Treatment & Disposal
SIC 4953 Refuse Systems
562212 Solid Waste Landfill
SIC 4953 Refuse Systems
562213 Solid Waste Combustors & Incinerators
SIC 4953 Refuse Systems
562219 Other Nonhazardous Waste Treatment & Disposal
SIC 4953 Refuse Systems
56291 Remediation Services
SIC 1799 Special Trade Contractors, nec
SIC 4959 Sanitary Services, nec
56292 Materials Recovery Facilities
SIC 4953 Refuse Systems
562991 Septic Tank & Related Services
SIC 7359 Equipment Rental & Leasing, nec
SIC 7699 Repair Shops & Related Services, nec
562998 All Other Miscellaneous Waste Management Services
SIC 4959 Sanitary Services, nec

EDUCATIONAL SERVICES

61111 Elementary & Secondary Schools
SIC 8211 Elementary & Secondary Schools
61121 Junior Colleges
SIC 8222 Junior Colleges & Technical Institutes
61131 Colleges, Universities & Professional Schools
SIC 8221 Colleges, Universities, & Professional Schools
61141 Business & Secretarial Schools
SIC 8244 Business & Secretarial Schools
61142 Computer Training
SIC 8243 Data Processing Schools
61143 Professional & Management Development Training Schools
SIC 8299 Schools & Educational Services, nec
611511 Cosmetology & Barber Schools
SIC 7231 Beauty Shops
SIC 7241 Barber Shops
611512 Flight Training
SIC 8249 Vocational Schools, nec
SIC 8299 Schools & Educational Services, nec

611513 Apprenticeship Training
SIC 8249 Vocational Schools, nec
611519 Other Technical & Trade Schools
SIC 8249 Vocational Schools, NEC
SIC 8243 Data Processing Schools
61161 Fine Arts Schools
SIC 8299 Schools & Educational Services, nec
SIC 7911 Dance Studios, Schools, & Halls
61162 Sports & Recreation Instruction
SIC 7999 Amusement & Recreation Services, nec
61163 Language Schools
SIC 8299 Schools & Educational Services, nec
611691 Exam Preparation & Tutoring
SIC 8299 Schools & Educational Services, nec
611692 Automobile Driving Schools
SIC 8299 Schools & Educational Services, nec
611699 All Other Miscellaneous Schools & Instruction
SIC 8299 Schools & Educational Services, nec
61171 Educational Support Services
SIC 8299 Schools & Educational Services nec
SIC 8748 Business Consulting Services, nec

HEALTH CARE & SOCIAL ASSISTANCE

621111 Offices of Physicians
SIC 8011 Offices & Clinics of Doctors of Medicine
SIC 8031 Offices & Clinics of Doctors of Osteopathy
621112 Offices of Physicians, Mental Health Specialists
SIC 8011 Offices & Clinics of Doctors of Medicine
SIC 8031 Offices & Clinics of Doctors of Osteopathy
62121 Offices of Dentists
SIC 8021 Offices & Clinics of Dentists
62131 Offices of Chiropractors
SIC 8041 Offices & Clinics of Chiropractors
62132 Offices of Optometrists
SIC 8042 Offices & Clinics of Optometrists
62133 Offices of Mental Health Practitioners
SIC 8049 Offices & Clinics of Health Practitioners, nec
62134 Offices of Physical, Occupational & Speech Therapists & Audiologists
SIC 8049 Offices & Clinics of Health Practitioners, nec
621391 Offices of Podiatrists
SIC 8043 Offices & Clinics of Podiatrists
621399 Offices of All Other Miscellaneous Health Practitioners
SIC 8049 Offices & Clinics of Health Practitioners, nec
62141 Family Planning Centers
SIC 8093 Speciality Outpatient Facilities, NEC
SIC 8099 Health & Allied Services, nec
62142 Outpatient Mental Health & Substance Abuse Centers
SIC 8093 Specialty Outpatient Facilities, nec
621491 HMO Medical Centers
SIC 8011 Offices & Clinics of Doctors of Medicine
621492 Kidney Dialysis Centers
SIC 8092 Kidney Dialysis Centers
621493 Freestanding Ambulatory Surgical & Emergency Centers
SIC 8011 Offices & Clinics of Doctors of Medicine
621498 All Other Outpatient Care Centers
SIC 8093 Specialty Outpatient Facilities, nec
621511 Medical Laboratories
SIC 8071 Medical Laboratories
621512 Diagnostic Imaging Centers
SIC 8071 Medical Laboratories

62161 Home Health Care Services
SIC 8082 Home Health Care Services
62191 Ambulance Services
SIC 4119 Local Passenger Transportation, nec
SIC 4522 Air Transportation, Nonscheduled
621991 Blood & Organ Banks
SIC 8099 Health & Allied Services, nec
621999 All Other Miscellaneous Ambulatory Health Care Services
SIC 8099 Health & Allied Services, nec
62211 General Medical & Surgical Hospitals
SIC 8062 General Medical & Surgical Hospitals
SIC 8069 Specialty Hospitals, Except Psychiatric
62221 Psychiatric & Substance Abuse Hospitals
SIC 8063 Psychiatric Hospitals
SIC 8069 Specialty Hospitals, Except Psychiatric
62231 Specialty Hospitals
SIC 8069 Specialty Hospitals, Except Psychiatric
62311 Nursing Care Facilities
SIC 8051 Skilled Nursing Care Facilities
SIC 8052 Intermediate Care Facilities
SIC 8059 Nursing & Personal Care Facilities, nec
62321 Residential Mental Retardation Facilities
SIC 8052 Intermediate Care Facilities
62322 Residential Mental Health & Substance Abuse Facilities
SIC 8361 Residential Care
623311 Continuing Care Retirement Communities
SIC 8051 Skilled Nursing Care Facilities
SIC 8052 Intermediate Care Facilities
SIC 8059 Nursing & Personal Care Facilities, nec
623312 Homes for the Elderly
SIC 8361 Residential Care
62399 Other Residential Care Facilities
SIC 8361 Residential Care
62411 Child & Youth Services
SIC 8322 Individual & Family Social Services
SIC 8641 Civic, Social, & Fraternal Organizations
62412 Services for the Elderly & Persons with Disabilities
SIC 8322 Individual & Family Social Services
62419 Other Individual & Family Services
SIC 8322 Individual & Family Social Services
62421 Community Food Services
SIC 8322 Individual & Family Social Services
624221 Temporary Shelters
SIC 8322 Individual & Family Social Services
624229 Other Community Housing Services
SIC 8322 Individual & Family Social Services
62423 Emergency & Other Relief Services
SIC 8322 Individual & Family Social Services
62431 Vocational Rehabilitation Services
SIC 8331 Job Training & Vocational Rehabilitation Services
62441 Child Day Care Services
SIC 8351 Child Day Care Services
SIC 7299 Miscellaneous Personal Services, nec

ARTS, ENTERTAINMENT, & RECREATION

71111 Theater Companies & Dinner Theaters
SIC 5812 Eating Places
SIC 7922 Theatrical Producers & Miscellaneous Theatrical Services

71112 Dance Companies
SIC 7922 Theatrical Producers & Miscellaneous Theatrical Services
71113 Musical Groups & Artists
SIC 7929 Bands, Orchestras, Actors, & Entertainment Groups
71119 Other Performing Arts Companies
SIC 7929 Bands, Orchestras, Actors, & Entertainment Groups
SIC 7999 Amusement & Recreation Services, nec
711211 Sports Teams & Clubs
SIC 7941 Professional Sports Clubs & Promoters
711212 Race Tracks
SIC 7948 Racing, Including Track Operations
711219 Other Spectator Sports
SIC 7941 Professional Sports Clubs & Promoters
SIC 7948 Racing, Including Track Operations
SIC 7999 Amusement & Recreation Services, nec
71131 Promoters of Performing Arts, Sports & Similar Events with Facilities
SIC 6512 Operators of Nonresidential Buildings
SIC 7922 Theatrical Procedures & Miscellaneous Theatrical Services
SIC 7941 Professional Sports Clubs & Promoters
71132 Promoters of Performing Arts, Sports & Similar Events without Facilities
SIC 7922 Theatrical Producers & Miscellaneous Theatrical Services
SIC 7941 Professional Sports Clubs & Promoters
71141 Agents & Managers for Artists, Athletes, Entertainers & Other Public Figures
SIC 7389 Business Services, nec
SIC 7922 Theatrical Producers & Miscellaneous Theatrical Services
SIC 7941 Professional Sports Clubs & Promoters
71151 Independent Artists, Writers, & Performers
SIC 7819 Services Allied to Motion Picture Production
SIC 7929 Bands, Orchestras, Actors, & Other Entertainers & Entertainment Services
SIC 8999 Services, nec
71211 Museums
SIC 8412 Museums & Art Galleries
71212 Historical Sites
SIC 8412 Museums & Art Galleries
71213 Zoos & Botanical Gardens
SIC 8422 Arboreta & Botanical & Zoological Gardens
71219 Nature Parks & Other Similar Institutions
SIC 7999 Amusement & Recreation Services, nec
SIC 8422 Arboreta & Botanical & Zoological Gardens
71311 Amusement & Theme Parks
SIC 7996 Amusement Parks
71312 Amusement Arcades
SIC 7993 Coin-Operated Amusement Devices
71321 Casinos
SIC 7999 Amusement & Recreation Services, nec
71329 Other Gambling Industries
SIC 7993 Coin-Operated Amusement Devices
SIC 7999 Amusement & Recreation Services, nec
71391 Golf Courses & Country Clubs
SIC 7992 Public Golf Courses
SIC 7997 Membership Sports & Recreation Clubs
71392 Skiing Facilities
SIC 7999 Amusement & Recreation Services, nec
71393 Marinas
SIC 4493 Marinas

71394 Fitness & Recreational Sports Centers
SIC 7991 Physical Fitness Facilities
SIC 7997 Membership Sports & Recreation Clubs
SIC 7999 Amusement & Recreation Services, nec
71395 Bowling Centers
SIC 7933 Bowling Centers
71399 All Other Amusement & Recreation Industries
SIC 7911 Dance Studios, Schools, & Halls
SIC 7993 Amusement & Recreation Services, nec
SIC 7997 Membership Sports & Recreation Clubs
SIC 7999 Amusement & Recreation Services, nec

ACCOMMODATION & FOODSERVICES

72111 Hotels & Motels
SIC 7011 Hotels & Motels
SIC 7041 Organization Hotels & Lodging Houses, on
Membership Basis
72112 Casino Hotels
SIC 7011 Hotels & Motels
721191 Bed & Breakfast Inns
SIC 7011 Hotels & Motels
721199 All Other Traveler Accommodation
SIC 7011 Hotels & Motels
721211 RV Parks & Campgrounds
SIC 7033 Recreational Vehicle Parks & Campgrounds
721214 Recreational & Vacation Camps
SIC 7032 Sporting & Recreational Camps
72131 Rooming & Boarding Houses
SIC 7021 Rooming & Boarding Houses
SIC 7041 Organization Hotels & Lodging Houses, on
Membership Basis
72211 Full-Service Restaurants
SIC 5812 Eating Places
722211 Limited-Service Restaurants
SIC 5812 Eating Places
SIC 5499 Miscellaneous Food Stores
722212 Cafeterias
SIC 5812 Eating Places
722213 Snack & Nonalcoholic Beverage Bars
SIC 5812 Eating Places
SIC 5461 Retail Bakeries
72231 Foodservice Contractors
SIC 5812 Eating Places
72232 Caterers
SIC 5812 Eating Places
72233 Mobile Caterers
SIC 5963 Direct Selling Establishments
72241 Drinking Places
SIC 5813 Drinking Places

OTHER SERVICES

811111 General Automotive Repair
SIC 7538 General Automotive Repair Shops
811112 Automotive Exhaust System Repair
SIC 7533 Automotive Exhaust System Repair Shops
811113 Automotive Transmission Repair
SIC 7537 Automotive Transmission Repair Shops

811118 Other Automotive Mechanical & Electrical Repair & Maintenance
SIC 7539 Automotive Repair Shops, nec
811121 Automotive Body, Paint & Upholstery Repair & Maintenance
SIC 7532 Top, Body, & Upholstery Repair Shops & Paint Shops
811122 Automotive Glass Replacement Shops
SIC 7536 Automotive Glass Replacement Shops
811191 Automotive Oil Change & Lubrication Shops
SIC 7549 Automotive Services, Except Repair & Carwashes
811192 Car Washes
SIC 7542 Carwashes
811198 All Other Automotive Repair & Maintenance
SIC 7534 Tire Retreading & Repair Shops
SIC 7549 Automotive Services, Except Repair & Carwashes
811211 Consumer Electronics Repair & Maintenance
SIC 7622 Radio & Television Repair Shops
SIC 7629 Electrical & Electronic Repair Shops, nec
811212 Computer & Office Machine Repair & Maintenance
SIC 7378 Computer Maintenance & Repair
SIC 7629 Electrical & Electronic Repair Shops, nec
SIC 7699 Repair Shops & Related Services, nec
811213 Communication Equipment Repair & Maintenance
SIC 7622 Radio & Television Repair Shops
SIC 7629 Electrical & Electronic Repair Shops, nec
811219 Other Electronic & Precision Equipment Repair & Maintenance
SIC 7629 Electrical & Electronic Repair Shops, nec
SIC 7699 Repair Shops & Related Services, NEC
81131 Commercial & Industrial Machinery & Equipment Repair & Maintenance
SIC 7699 Repair Shops & Related Services, nec
SIC 7623 Refrigerator & Air-Conditioning Service & Repair Shops
SIC 7694 Armature Rewinding Shops
811411 Home & Garden Equipment Repair & Maintenance
SIC 7699 Repair Shops & Related Services, nec
811412 Appliance Repair & Maintenance
SIC 7623 Refrigeration & Air-Conditioning Service & Repair Shops
SIC 7629 Electrical & Electronic Repair Shops, NEC
SIC 7699 Repairs Shops & Related Services, nec
81142 Reupholstery & Furniture Repair
SIC 7641 Reupholstery & Furniture Repair
81143 Footwear & Leather Goods Repair
SIC 7251 Shoe Repair & Shoeshine Parlors
SIC 7699 Repair Shops & Related Services
81149 Other Personal & Household Goods Repair & Maintenance
SIC 3732 Boat Building & Repairing
SIC 7219 Laundry & Garment Services, nec
SIC 7631 Watch, Clock, & Jewelry Repair
SIC 7692 Welding Repair
SIC 7699 Repair Shops & Related Services, nec
812111 Barber Shops
SIC 7241 Barber Shops
812112 Beauty Salons
SIC 7231 Beauty Shops
812113 Nail Salons
SIC 7231 Beauty Shops
812191 Diet & Weight Reducing Centers
SIC 7299 Miscellaneous Personal Services, nec

812199 Other Personal Care Services
SIC 7299 Miscellaneous Personal Services, nec,
81221   Funeral Homes
SIC 7261 Funeral Services & Crematories
81222   Cemeteries & Crematories
SIC 6531 Real Estate Agents & Managers
SIC 6553 Cemetery Subdividers & Developers
SIC 7261 Funeral Services & Crematories
81231   Coin-Operated Laundries & Drycleaners
SIC 7215 Coin-Operated Laundry & Drycleaning
812321 Laundries, Family & Commercial
SIC 7211 Power Laundries, Family & Commercial
812322 Drycleaning Plants
SIC 7216 Drycleaning Plants, Except Rug Cleaning
812331 Linen Supply
SIC 7213 Linen Supply
SIC 7219 Laundry & Garment Services, nec,
812332 Industrial Launderers
SIC 7218 Industrial Launderers
812391 Garment Pressing, & Agents for Laundries
SIC 7212 Garment Pressing & Agents for Laundries
812399 All Other Laundry Services
SIC 7219 Laundry & Garment Services, NEC
81291   Pet Care Services
SIC 0752 Animal Speciality Services, Except Veterinary
812921 Photo Finishing Laboratories
SIC 7384 Photofinishing Laboratories
812922 One-Hour Photo Finishing
SIC 7384 Photofinishing Laboratories
81293   Parking Lots & Garages
SIC 7521 Automobile Parking
81299   All Other Personal Services
SIC 7299 Miscellaneous Personal Services, nec
SIC 7389 Miscellaneous Business Services
81311   Religious Organizations
SIC 8661 Religious Organizations
813211 Grantmaking Foundations
SIC 6732 Educational, Religious, & Charitable Trust
813212 Voluntary Health Organizations
SIC 8399 Social Services, nec
813219 Other Grantmaking & Giving Services
SIC 8399 Social Services, NEC
813311 Human Rights Organizations
SIC 8399 Social Services, nec
813312 Environment, Conservation & Wildlife Organizations
SIC 8399 Social Services, nec
SIC 8699 Membership Organizations, nec
813319 Other Social Advocacy Organizations
SIC 8399 Social Services, NEC
81341   Civic & Social Organizations
SIC 8641 Civic, Social, & Fraternal Organizations
SIC 8699 Membership Organizations, nec
81391   Business Associations
SIC 8611 Business Associations
SIC 8699 Membership Organizations, nec
81392   Professional Organizations
SIC 8621 Professional Membership Organizations
81393   Labor Unions & Similar Labor Organizations
SIC 8631 Labor Unions & Similar Labor Organizations
81394   Political Organizations
SIC 8651 Political Organizations
81399   Other Similar Organizations
SIC 6531 Real Estate Agents & Managers
SIC 8641 Civic, Social, & Fraternal Organizations

SIC 8699 Membership Organizations, nec
81411   Private Households
SIC 8811 Private Households

PUBLIC ADMINISTRATION

92111   Executive Offices
SIC 9111 Executive Offices
92112   Legislative Bodies
SIC 9121 Legislative Bodies
92113   Public Finance
SIC 9311 Public Finance, Taxation, & Monetary Policy
92114   Executive & Legislative Offices, Combined
SIC 9131 Executive & Legislative Offices, Combined
92115   American Indian & Alaska Native Tribal Governments
SIC 8641 Civic, Social, & Fraternal Organizations
92119   All Other General Government
SIC 9199 General Government, nec
92211   Courts
SIC 9211 Courts
92212   Police Protection
SIC 9221 Police Protection
92213   Legal Counsel & Prosecution
SIC 9222 Legal Counsel & Prosecution
92214   Correctional Institutions
SIC 9223 Correctional Institutions
92215   Parole Offices & Probation Offices
SIC 8322 Individual & Family Social Services
92216   Fire Protection
SIC 9224 Fire Protection
92219   All Other Justice, Public Order, & Safety
SIC 9229 Public Order & Safety, nec
92311   Administration of Education Programs
SIC 9411 Administration of Educational Programs
92312   Administration of Public Health Programs
SIC 9431 Administration of Public Health Programs
**92313   Administration of Social, Human Resource & Income
     Maintenance Programs**
SIC 9441 Administration of Social, Human Resource & Income
     Maintenance Programs
92314   Administration of Veteran's Affairs
SIC 9451 Administration of Veteran's Affairs, Except Health
     Insurance
92411   Air & Water Resource & Solid Waste Management
SIC 9511 Air & Water Resource & Solid Waste Management
92412   Land, Mineral, Wildlife, & Forest Conservation
SIC 9512 Land, Mineral, Wildlife, & Forest Conservation
92511   Administration of Housing Programs
SIC 9531 Administration of Housing Programs
**92512   Administration of Urban Planning & Community &
     Rural Development**
SIC 9532 Administration of Urban Planning & Community &
     Rural Development
92611   Administration of General Economic Programs
SIC 9611 Administration of General Economic Programs
**92612   Regulation & Administration of Transportation
     Programs**
SIC 9621 Regulations & Administration of Transportation
     Programs
**92613   Regulation & Administration of Communications,
     Electric, Gas, & Other Utilities**
SIC 9631 Regulation & Administration of Communications,
     Electric, Gas, & Other Utilities

92614   Regulation of Agricultural Marketing & Commodities
SIC 9641 Regulation of Agricultural Marketing & Commodities
**92615   Regulation, Licensing, & Inspection of Miscellaneous
            Commercial Sectors**
SIC 9651 Regulation, Licensing, & Inspection of Miscellaneous
            Commercial Sectors
92711   Space Research & Technology
SIC 9661 Space Research & Technology
92811   National Security
SIC 9711 National Security
92812   International Affairs
SIC 9721 International Affairs
99999   Unclassified Establishments
SIC 9999 Nonclassifiable Establishments